Best Practices in
Quantitative Methods

Best Practices in Quantitative Methods

Edited by **Jason W. Osborne**

North Carolina State University

SAGE Publications

Los Angeles • London • New Delhi • Singapore

For information:

Sage Publications, Inc.
2455 Teller Road
Thousand Oaks, California 91320
E-mail: order@sagepub.com

Sage Publications Ltd.
1 Oliver's Yard
55 City Road
London EC1Y 1SP
United Kingdom

Sage Publications India Pvt. Ltd.
B 1/I 1 Mohan Cooperative Industrial Area
Mathura Road, New Delhi 110 044
India

Sage Publications Asia-Pacific Pte. Ltd.
33 Pekin Street #02-01
Far East Square
Singapore 048763

Printed in the United States of America.

Library of Congress Cataloging-in-Publication Data

Best practices in quantitative methods / edited by Jason Osborne.
    p. cm.
Includes bibliographical references and index.
ISBN 978-1-4129-4065-8 (cloth)
    1. Social sciences—Research—Methodology. 2. Social sciences—Mathematical models. I. Osborne, Jason.

H62.B467 2008
001.4′2—dc22   2007020488

This book is printed on acid-free paper.

07 08 09 10 11 10 9 8 7 6 5 4 3 2 1

Acquisitions Editor:	Lisa Cuevas Shaw/Vicki Knight
Associate Editor:	Sean Connelly
Editorial Assistant:	Lauren Habib
Production Editor:	Karen Wiley
Copy Editor:	Gillian Dickens
Typesetter:	C&M Digitals (P) Ltd.
Proofreader:	Scott Oney
Indexer:	Sheila Bodell
Cover Designer:	Candice Harman
Marketing Manager:	Stephanie Adams

CONTENTS

USING BEST PRACTICES IS A MORAL AND ETHICAL OBLIGATION

JASON W. OSBORNE

I magine you're a doctor, and your patient is dying. You have three choices: no treatment, standard practice, and an experimental treatment. Standard practice and the new procedure put the patient through a great deal of pain and trauma and, if unsuccessful, dramatically reduce that patient's quality of life and financial situation in his or her remaining days. Standard practice is effective 33% of the time. The experimental treatment is expected to be more effective but is still experimental.

What do you do? Do you let the patient quietly ease into death, or do you make heroic efforts to save that patient, gambling on a positive outcome being worth the expense, hassle, and pain and suffering?

Now imagine you're the superintendent of a school district and you have (severely) limited resources and students not achieving the level you desire. You are mulling three potential options for helping your struggling students. One is to give teachers a large raise, theoretically encouraging talented individuals to enter the teaching profession and retaining valuable master teachers. Another is to purchase an expensive new reading program that is getting rave reviews. And your teachers and school board members are telling you that if you just give every student a laptop (or PDA, or iPod),[1] everyone will meet expected yearly growth.

Where do you put your resources? Do you spend your resources on flashy gimmicks that may be the Next Great Thing in education, or do you go with the mundane (but solidly effective) pay raise for teachers?

RESEARCHERS ARE ROMANTIC FOOLS. RESEARCH IS MAGICAL.

Some of you may be scratching your heads, cleaning your glasses, wondering if you read that right. Yes, you did. Research *is* magical, research *is* romantic.

The word *research* (especially the word *statistics*) and the words *romantic* and *magical* seem antithetical, yet if you distill the research process to the most basic process, you find people who believe in miracles, who believe in the magic of research. Researchers are not (always) cardigan-wearing, ivory-tower recluses interested in only their esoteric, irrelevant theories, or myopic clipboard-toting socially inept nerds in lab coats.[2] Researchers are the intrepid explorers and adventurers and trailblazers of the 21st century, striving to explore phenomena, understand processes, and, most of all, go where no other human has gone before. The goal? Most researchers I know want to create knowledge that might one day change the world, reduce misery, and improve quality of life. We are the Knights of the New Round Table, on a Quest.[3]

Research is magical. The creation of knowledge is a uniquely human endeavor, and those of you who have participated in this compelling process know its charms. To perform quantitative analysis is to be present at the creation of new knowledge, and that is a magical thing, a romantic endeavor. We researchers create knowledge. What an amazing, powerful, exciting, maddening, profound process that can be!

This book is dedicated to you, the researcher, who labors (often in obscurity) attempting to change the world, or at least your small corner of it. But why do we need yet another research methods book when there are already approximately a billion research methods books already on the market?[4] There are two answers to that question. The first, and most direct, is because I couldn't find a book that gave me and my students the answers we sought to some very basic questions. Most of the chapters and other articles I have written over the years are in direct response to wondering how to do something, not finding it clearly laid out in any text I had, and writing it down so my next semester's students could use it.

More important, I think we can do better. I know how difficult it is to do high-quality research, to spend months, sometimes years, gathering data, and then what? Do a median split on a continuous variable and perform a t test to see if something worked?[5] Plod through a repeated-measures ANOVA despite violating all assumptions that were never checked, losing half your data due to missing values? No, my fellow Knights, we can do better. We owe it to ourselves to do better. We owe it to the decision makers of the world to do better—and better does *not* mean maximizing the probability of getting $p <$ .05. It means getting the most accurate picture of *what is really happening out there in the world*. It means getting the most generalizable, replicable result so that others (like our hypothetical doctor and superintendent introduced above) may be most likely to profit from all your long hours of toil. In my opinion, this is not just good common sense but a moral imperative.

DOES RESEARCH HAVE ETHICAL IMPLICATIONS? IS QUANTITATIVE ANALYSIS OF DATA A MORAL PROCESS?

You bet!

Think about the two scenarios at the beginning of this introduction. What if you, as superintendent, decide to bet your resources (and your students' education) on laptops because some research showed that path to be of more benefit to the student. And what if, in reality, those results are the unintentional outcome of poor research practice and do not really reflect the true benefit of giving all students laptops? You just wasted millions of taxpayer dollars, and worse, the students get no benefit from that money, whereas if you had spent the money another way that is effective, they might have received significant benefit. Is that a moral or ethical issue? I think so.

And now what if you are agonizing over how to treat your sick patient? What if the experimental therapy is really 95% effective in saving lives, but research failed to note such an impressive effect because the analyses were not the best they could be. Imagine that because of this Type II error, the patient is directed toward palliative care rather than aggressive treatment. Or what if the experimental therapy is the worst possible choice, eliminating chances for successful treatment when initial (faulty) research indicated it might be highly effective? Doing nothing might have been better, and you have just harmed your patient. And now imagine that patient is your child, and that child's death is now, in hindsight, needless. Is that an ethical or moral issue? Most definitely.

Most of us don't research life-and-death issues, but that doesn't mean our research successes and failures do not have consequences. Best practices in quantitative methods is not intellectual snobbery, not a bunch of curmudgeons sitting around griping about how everybody but them is wrong. It is critical that we constantly improve the state of the art so that we maximize the benefit of our labors—so that policy makers and practitioners and the public at large can make the best decisions possible.

Evidence-based decisions are only as good as the evidence they are based on. It seems every year we are hearing about new, expensive "miracle drugs" that initially looked quite promising from the available evidence but then were found to either cause serious, sometimes deadly, side effects or turned out to be no more effective than simple, cheap, commonly available medicines. Sometimes it is better to do nothing for a patient. Sometimes standard practice or even archaic practice (e.g., using leeches) is more effective than snazzy new drugs or procedures. And sometimes the newest is best.

Every year we read about newer, better, and necessarily more expensive educational interventions for our students. How many billions of dollars have we spent on instructional technology in public schools in the United States, with precious little high-quality evidence that these billions have been the *best* way to spend those scarce resources? How often do we hear about the absolute best reading or math program, the last one we will ever need, if only your school district has X millions of dollars to pay for it? And how often is it true that a highly qualified, motivated, and happy teacher with a blackboard and piece of chalk could be considered "best practice" in education?

Does research have ethical and moral consequences? How can it not? Is research a magical, wonderful, intoxicating process? Often, yes! If you are a researcher and you use best practices, not only are you maximizing the probability of experiencing the magic and romance of positive research outcomes, but you are also maximizing the probability that your research will actually be of use to someone else. The world depends on research to give accurate, unbiased evidence for decision making and sometimes to speak truth to power.

I am biased in this argument, obviously. I believe science exists to answer questions, to create real knowledge (not just further partisan argumentation). If you believe this as well, then you cannot engage in quantitative research without attempting to do it in the best way possible. There is almost never a (good) reason not to use best practices.

And so, we come back to the real reason for this book. While many texts grind over the same hallowed ground that researchers have trodden for decades or more, my challenge to the research community was this: Show me the best way to do *everything*. And put your money where your mouth is. Show me it really is the best way; demonstrate the advantages to me. Motivate the reader to change behavior by showing the true benefit of doing something differently than how we were taught.

In the course of the past 2 years, I and the noble Knights of this Round Table who contributed chapters to this volume have attempted to leave behind the baggage of the 20th century.[6] I have recruited the most forward-thinking methodologists, challenging them to wipe the canvas clean and paint for us a new era of research methods. These authors represent some of the most revered methodologists working today and some of the brightest new talents coming on the scene. They come from several different continents and from an amazing array of backgrounds, and all worked long hours to share their wisdom with you, so that you, laboring to create knowledge, will have the best chance at doing so. We want you to succeed, so that you may make our world, and our children's world, a better place.

In this volume, you will probably find concepts foreign to you and probably some things you don't agree with. That's exactly my goal. The world doesn't need another textbook reviewing how to calculate correlation coefficients, treating ANOVA and regression like two different worlds, and genuflecting at the altar of $p < .05$. This book is a challenge to you, fellow researcher. Shrug off the shackles of 20th-century methodology, and the next time you sit down to examine your hard-won data, challenge yourself to implement *one new idea or method* discussed in this book (or elsewhere). Use Rasch measurement rather than averaging items to form scale scores. Calculate $p_{(rep)}$ instead of power or p. Use hierarchical linear modeling (HLM) to study change over time, or use propensity scores to create more sound comparison groups. Choose just one best practice, and use it. And next time, add another new tool to your toolbox.

There it is. The gauntlet has been cast down. Do you pick it up, accepting my challenge? To help you in your quest, many authors have provided data sets to allow you to explore or practice the concepts discussed in their chapters. I encourage you to explore those at this book's Web site: http://best-practices-online.com

One final request: If you disagree with something one of the chapters posits, write me and demonstrate why the argument that author makes is wrong. If you know of a new methodology that could legitimately be called a "best practice" that is not included in this version of the book, tell me about it (and if you know of someone, including yourself, who would be great at writing a chapter on it, please share that with me as well!). If it truly is a best practice, I will do my best to get it into the next version of this book. My email is jason_osborne@ncsu.edu or jason@jwosborne.com. I look forward to hearing from you.

NOTES

1. Sadly, there really are schools, school districts, and even highly prestigious universities that are doing this, despite an almost complete lack of evidence or even theory to support these expensive practices.

2. Thank you, Gary Larson!

3. Before you ask, the air-speed velocity of an unladen swallow is pretty darn fast.

4. There may be a bit of a confidence interval around that estimate.

5. Believe it or not, I still have colleagues who do this, despite my haranguing. You know who you are! Shame! SHAME!!!

6. No disrespect to the 20th century—it tried its best.

1

THE NEW STATS

Attitudes for the 21st Century

FIONA FIDLER

GEOFF CUMMING

How should a researcher decide what statistical analysis to use? Across medicine and many other disciplines, *best practice* is now defined as being *evidence based*. As a professional, you must be able to justify your choice of diagnosis or therapies in terms of evidence that they are appropriate to the situation and effective. No less a standard should apply to researchers choosing how to analyze their data. Alas, statistical practices in psychology, in education, and across the social sciences too often fail to meet this standard: The journals in these fields publish studies full of outdated techniques, inappropriate analyses, errors, wrong conclusions, and opportunities missed.

Several questions are addressed in this introductory chapter. First, what do we mean by evidence-based statistical practice? Second, what are the problems with the dominant approach to quantitative analysis in the social sciences, null hypothesis significance testing (NHST)? How can evidence guide adoption of better practices? What lessons are there from attempts in other disciplines to do better? Finally, what attitudes should researchers adopt to statistical practices in the 21st century?

BEST PRACTICE IS EVIDENCE-BASED PRACTICE

The most widely cited medical definition of evidence-based practice is "the integration of best research evidence with clinical expertise" (Institute of Medicine, 2001, p. 147). Following this, we need to consider what kinds of research evidence should guide statistical practice and what corresponds to "clinical expertise." Statistics textbooks typically give the impression that they are just setting out instructions: Learn and apply these rules and you will analyze your data correctly. If instead we accept that there are at least the following three main stages to statistical practice, then we can consider how evidence and judgment are needed to guide statistical best practice at each stage.

The first stage is choosing an experimental design that is best for the research setting and the questions we wish to ask. The second is choosing one or more statistical analyses to apply to the data, and third is presenting and interpreting the results. Before discussing approaches to best practice at each stage, we consider the role of judgment.

The Role of Judgment

Medical practitioners are justified in believing that their professional and clinical judgment and their insights into the situations of individual patients are essential elements of best practice. Many worry that evidence-based practice may be a blunt and mechanistic weapon that devalues clinical insight, to the detriment of patients. The definition we quoted above, however, makes clear that evidence-based practice requires the integration of clinical judgment with relevant research evidence.

Indeed, it is often a matter of expert medical judgment just which evidence is relevant in a particular case and whether particular circumstances make this case an exception, requiring a different approach. Best practice is guided by evidence, but the evidence is not chosen or applied mindlessly. So it is also with statistics: Evidence informs us about characteristics—strengths and weaknesses—of particular techniques, but judgment is required to assess the suitability of a design, or an analysis technique, for our specific research setting and questions.

Stage 1: Selecting an Experimental Design and Statistical Model

A statistical analysis assumes a statistical model, which must fit the setting, design of the experiment, and research questions sufficiently well; otherwise, the outcome of the analysis is likely to be misleading. Many common statistical models assume that populations have a normal distribution, observations are independent, and sampling is random. Does our research setting comply with these assumptions? Do our independent and dependent variables fit any requirements of the statistical model? Are our manipulations likely to be effective? Do our measures have desirable properties, considering especially reliability and validity? Relevant evidence may be available on some of these issues, such as the properties of measures, but the core issue at this first stage concerns the fit between our research setting and our chosen model. That is largely a matter for judgment, based on our expert understanding of the research and experimental context, as well as our knowledge of the statistical model. We may need to revise our choice of statistical approach, or we may need to refine our procedure or measures so our experimental work will fit sufficiently well with our chosen model.

Evidence About Statistical Techniques and Their Application

The other side of the same coin is to ask how robust the statistical technique is to departures from strict compliance with the assumptions of the statistical model. Modern methods of Monte Carlo and other types of simulation have in many cases been applied to investigate how widely it is reasonable to apply a statistical technique. Such evidence guides our judgment on how anxious to be about such departures and may suggest alternative analyses that are more robust to likely departures in our situation.

Evidence About the Communication of Results

As is known from common experience, and confirmed by research findings from psychology, presenting information in a different format may change the message that is received (e.g., Gigerenzer & Hoffrage, 1995). When presenting research results, one makes many choices: numbers or words, tables or figures, broad overview or precise details, and so on. Evidence as well as judgment should guide our choice of reporting format, so readers are most likely to gain an accurate appreciation of our results and take away correct and justified conclusions.

In his book on graph design, Kosslyn (1994) draws on evidence from classic studies in visual perception and from contemporary studies of graph interpretation. Many recommendations for better graphical displays of data are derived from well-known perceptual principles such as proximity ("important for associating labels with scales," p. 6), similarity ("used to help readers to pair corresponding bars, lines or regions," p. 7), and good continuation ("bars that are arranged in order of increasing or decreasing size will be more easily apprehended," p. 7). His other recommendations are also evidence based—for example, "use a line graph to display interactions over two levels on the X axis" (p. 33). Here Kosslyn's claim is that interpreting interactions from bar graphs requires more time and effort, and he cites two studies as evidence. One study provides evidence that we judge bars by their height and lines by their slope; to judge slope from bars then requires the extra step of imaging a line connecting the top of each bar. A second study found that trends were more easily detected when participants were given line graphs rather than bar graphs (Simcox, 1983, and Schutz, 1961, respectively, cited in Kosslyn, 1994).

Coulson, Healey, Fidler, and Cumming (2006) investigated how researchers interpret a simple graph (see Figure 1.1) showing two means with 95% confidence intervals (CIs) by comparison with conventional statements of statistical significance. They found that researchers who chose to simply interpret the CIs in terms of NHST—one result is statistically significant because the CI misses zero, the other is not—usually thought the two studies gave conflicting evidence. Researchers, on the other hand, who considered the extent and overlap of the two intervals usually thought the two studies gave consistent findings—a much more justifiable conclusion. Coulson et al. thus presented evidence that a figure can prompt a better understanding than conventional statements in words of statistical significance, but only if readers can break from their habit of seeing everything in terms of NHST and read Figure 1.1 in terms of intervals—as CIs typically should be read.

Statistical Judgment as Well as Evidence

Best practice in statistics brings together evidence about statistical techniques and their performance, as well as researcher judgment—about statistics as well as in the substantive research area. It is the job of researchers to develop their judgment expertise as well as to draw on evidence relevant to statistical analyses used in their research program. Statistics education researchers and specialists now talk of teaching *statistical thinking* or *statistical reasoning*, rather than merely rules for specific techniques. This is an excellent development and needs to extend explicitly to developing statistical judgment. Statistics and research methods textbooks should more frequently cite evidence about statistical models—well, common experimental paradigms,

anyway—and their fit with the world and also more deliberately provide practice and encouragement for students to build their confidence and judgment.

We now turn to a discussion of NHST. We devote so much space to this for several reasons: (a) NHST is used in almost all (97% according to the survey by Cumming et al., 2007) empirical journal articles in psychology and a large majority in most empirically oriented social science disciplines; (b) there is strong and diverse evidence of its misuse and dangers; (c) for decades, it has been repeatedly and cogently criticized; (d) other disciplines have grappled with statistical reform, meaning progress beyond total reliance on NHST, and may have lessons for the social sciences; and (e) we find it an astonishing and intriguing story. However, the main reason is that it is the best case study of the need for evidence-based statistical practice and may have some general lessons about how this can be achieved. We start with a review of criticisms of NHST.

WHAT IS WRONG WITH THE OLD WAY? CRITICISMS OF NHST

Here we describe four main categories of criticisms: first, those that relate to the *logic* of NHST within the frequentist philosophy of probability; second, those scrutinizing the *relevance* of NHST in science; third, problems of *misinterpretation;* and fourth, problems of *misuse.*[1]

Logic

What we, as scientists, often need is not the probability of the data, given a hypothesis, $P(D|H)$, but the probability of our hypothesis, given the data, $P(H|D)$. However, it is the former that is the basis of NHST, and this apparent

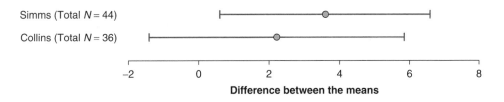

Figure 1.1   The figure presented via e-mail to researchers by Coulson et al. (2006). Researchers were asked to briefly state in their own words what they felt to be the main message of the results presented in the figure.

disjunction between the basis of NHST and what scientists seek is the most fundamental logical issue with NHST. In case this seems a pedantic distinction, suppose D refers to death and H to being hanged. Then, $P(D|H)$ is the probability of being dead, given that you have been hanged—fairly close to certain. In stark contrast, $P(H|D)$ is the chance that, given that you are dead, the method was hanging—a tiny probability. The distinction between these two conditional probabilities is fundamental to the nature of NHST and also to its problems.

Finding $P(H|D)$ requires a Bayesian approach and specification of prior probabilities—which are anathema to most frequentists. It is not surprising, therefore, that Bayesians are among the most passionate critics of NHST. Most Bayesians would agree with all the criticisms below of NHST. They would, in addition, argue that even when NHST is correctly used and interpreted, it can offer little to the progress of science because of its fundamentally irrelevant outcome. We note later that Bayesian statistical techniques are becoming more widespread in other disciplines—notably ecology and conservation biology—and may have much to offer the social sciences.

Relevance

The basis of NHST is a dichotomous decision to reject the null hypothesis H_0 or not to reject it. NHST leads a researcher to conclude simply that A is different from B (or, at best, that A is greater than B) or that no evidence has been found of a difference. Many critics argue, however, that such mere binary decisions provide an impoverished view of what science seeks or can achieve.

What would be better than the dichotomous decisions of NHST? Along with many other critics of NHST in various disciplines, we believe that estimation of effect sizes by using CIs should be the primary outcome of research and that science would have progressed further had this been the case. As Kirk (1996) argued,

> How far would physics have progressed if their researchers had focused on discovering ordinal relationships? What we want to know is the size of the difference between A and B and the error associated with our estimate; knowing A is greater than B is not enough. (p. 754)

Kirk's comments reflected those made earlier by Tukey (1991): "The effects of A and B are always different—in some decimal place—for any A and B. Thus asking 'Are the effects different?' is foolish" (p. 100).

Cohen (1994) claimed that even when NHST is used and interpreted correctly, "it is not the way any science is done" (p. 999). In fact, it is the way much science is done, but not the way it ought to be done. Rozeboom (1960) made the same point more than 30 years earlier: NHST is "seldom if ever appropriate to the aims of scientific research" (p. 417). Carver (1978) too expressed this sentiment: "Even if properly used in the scientific method . . . research would still be better off without statistical significance testing" (p. 398). To become more quantitative, precise, and theoretically rich, the social sciences need to move beyond dichotomous decision making.

Misinterpretations

We offer here a taxonomy of major misconceptions of NHST and the p values on which it is based—and evidence that these misconceptions are widespread and damaging. All sentences in italics are statements of misconceptions; they are wrong!

> (i). (a) The p value is the probability the null hypothesis is true, given the data; (b) the p value is the probability the null is true.

The first, (a), is a simple confusion of two conditional probabilities, $P(D|H_0)$ and $P(H_0|D)$, as we discussed above. The second, (b), may be just a loose abbreviation of (a) but, taken literally, is a failure to recognize that the probability used by NHST is a conditional probability, $P(D|H_0)$, and this is erroneously converted to $P(H_0)$, probably via $P(H_0|D)$.

In fact, p values provide no *direct* information about the truth or falsity of the null hypothesis, conditional or otherwise. The underlying misconception here has variously been called the *inverse probability fallacy,* the *permanent illusion, confusion of the inverse,* and the *illusion of probabilistic proof by contradiction.* Cohen (1994) provided this explanation for the origin of these misconceptions: "[NHST] doesn't tell us what we want to know [$P(H_0|D)$], but we so much want to know what it is we want to know that, out of desperation, we nevertheless believe that is does!" (p. 997).

Oakes (1986) reported that more than one third (36%) of 70 academic psychologists agreed with a direct statement of inverse probability: "The probability of the null hypothesis has been found" (p. 80). Not only did many researchers agree with this statement as a plausible interpretation of *p*, but almost half (46%) described it as typical of their usual interpretation of NHST results. When statements of the fallacy were slightly less explicit, even more researchers slipped. For example, 66% agreed that "the probability of the experimental hypothesis can be deduced," and 86% agreed that "the probability that the decision taken is wrong is known" (p. 80).

Haller and Krauss (2002), repeating Oakes's (1986) survey in six German universities, found that almost 20 years on, the misconception had diminished only slightly among psychologists (26%, of 39) and was common among students (32%, of 44)—perhaps not surprising! What is surprising, however, is that 17% (5 of 30) of the methodology instructors surveyed also demonstrated the misconception, and even more methodology instructors (33%, 10 of 30) agreed that "you can deduce the probability of the experimental hypothesis being true" (p. 5).

How serious is this fallacy for the progress of science? Oakes (1986) used widespread endorsement of the inverse fallacy to explain the neglect of statistical power in the psychology research literature. His argument can be paraphrased: Why would researchers bother about calculating the probability of detecting an effect of a given size (statistical power) when they (believe they) already know the probability of the null hypothesis being true? (Oakes, 1986, pp. 82–83). Unfortunately, statistical power is reported in only approximately 5% of articles in psychology journals (Fidler et al., 2005; Finch, Cumming, & Thomason, 2001).

(ii). 1 – p is the probability of the alternative hypothesis being true.

This misconception is closely related to (i); in fact, it is entailed by it. A *p* value does not provide direct information about the truth or falsity of the alternative hypothesis for reasons already given—although many students, researchers, and even methodology instructors believe it does (Haller & Krauss, 2002; Oakes, 1986).

(iii). The p value is the probability that the results are due to chance.

Carver (1978) called this the "odds-against-chance fantasy." Kline (2004) explained it as the false belief that $p = .05$ means there is 5% likelihood the results are the product of chance alone. It also manifests in interpretations of the *p* value as a measure of sampling error (Finch et al., 2001).

In fact, the 5% Type I error rate has a much more specific interpretation. It is the probability of rejecting the null when the null is in fact true. The odds-against-chance fallacy may lead to ignoring the usually much higher chance of making a Type II error because one believes 5% is the overall error rate. Furthermore, this misconception could contribute to the common failure to control for spurious statistically significant results in studies where multiple hypotheses are tested. In a study testing 20 null hypotheses (which is not uncommon in many disciplines), we should expect on average about one test to lead to rejection of the null when all nulls are true. The problem of inflated Type I error rates is well-known, so one consequence, at least, of this *p* value misconception is recognized.

(iv). The p value is an inverse indicator of effect size.

Because *p* values are a function of both sample size and effect size, neither can be read directly from a *p* value. Kline (2004) called the belief that *p* values provide direct information about effect size the "magnitude fallacy" (p. 66). Nickerson (2000) provided a typical example: "I recently reviewed a manuscript that described a response time that was about 16% slower than another as being 'marginally slower' than the latter, because $.05 < p < .06$" (p. 257). Effects of practical importance that fail to reach statistical significance are often dismissed. Similarly, very small or unimportant effects that do reach $p < .05$ are often taken to be meaningful on that basis alone.

(v). The p value is an inverse indicator of the probability of replication.

Sometimes called the *replicability fallacy*, this is the false belief that a *p* value of .05 means that 95 times out of 100, the observed statistically significant difference will hold up in future investigations. In Oakes's (1986) survey, 60% of researchers agreed with this statement of the replicability fallacy, referring to a *p* value of .01:

> You have a reliable experimental
> finding in the sense that if, hypothetically,
> the experiment were repeated a great number
> of times, you would obtain a significant result
> on 99% of occasions. (p. 79)

In Haller and Krauss's (2002) update of Oakes's (1986) study, 37% of methodology instructors, 49% of academic psychologists, and 41% of psychology students agreed with the statement. If there is any true decrease in the hold of this fallacy since Oakes, it is disappointingly slight, and the misconception's pervasiveness among methodology teachers is alarming.

Carver (1978) claimed that replication largely remains an empirical question, to be answered only by future studies. That was perhaps the case in 1978. However, computer-intensive resampling strategies have made replication a question that can also be addressed by simulation, for example, bootstrapping, jackknifing, and Monte Carlo Markov chain (MCMC) methods. A recent development is Killeen's (2005) measure of replicability, p_{rep}, which offers a replication-based approach to interpreting data.[2] Cumming (2005) discussed an equivalent estimation-based approach.

(vi). Statistical nonsignificance means "no effect."

Researchers frequently report statistically nonsignificant results and interpret them as evidence of no effect or no impact, usually without any reference to statistical power. Without statistical power and effect size reports, statistically nonsignificant results are virtually uninterpretable. The misconception that statistical nonsignificance is direct evidence of "no effect" has the potential to cause damage of various kinds in all disciplines.

(vii). Statistically significant results are necessarily theoretically important.

A statistically significant result is not necessarily theoretically important. An effect of even trivial size will be statistically significant in a very high-powered experiment. Similarly, important effects can fail to reach statistical significance in poorly designed, low-powered experiments. For

this reason, authors must report not merely statistical significance but also the clinical, practical, or theoretical importance of effects (Kendall, 1997; Kendall, Marrs-Garcia, Nath, & Sheldrick, 1999; Kirk, 1996). Kline (2004) referred to the confusion of statistical and practical significance as the "meaningfulness fallacy" (p. 66). This fallacy also entails the false belief that rejecting the null proves not only the statistical alternative hypothesis but also the research and theory behind the statistical hypothesis (Meehl, 1978).

Misuse

The overuse of, or overreliance on, NHST is also often cited as a serious problem; it has become ubiquitous, to the exclusion of other forms of analysis. The neglect of Type II errors and statistical power may be the most widespread offense.

Low and Unknown Statistical Power. In 1962, Jacob Cohen published the first survey of statistical power in the psychological literature. He calculated the average power for small, medium, and large effect sizes of 70 articles published in 1960 issues of the *Journal of Abnormal and Social Psychology*. For medium effect sizes, thought to be typical of psychological effect sizes in that subdiscipline, the average power was .48 (median = .46). Sedlmeier and Gigerenzer (1989) surveyed the same journal and found that the average power for medium effect sizes was .5 (median = .37)—certainly no great improvement since Cohen's 1962 survey. Little wonder, then, that Hunter (1997) compared the average psychology experiment to flipping a coin![3]

The problem is not limited to a single journal. Rossi (1990) summarized 25 studies of statistical power in published articles, covering 40 journals in diverse areas of psychology and other disciplines. In only 2 journals did the average power for detecting a medium effect reach .8 or higher.

Occasionally, there is no way to avoid a low-power experiment. When working with natural groups, one cannot infect extra patients with a rare disease or increase the population of an endangered species. Conducting a large-scale study may simply be too costly or time-consuming. These problems are understandable and hard to avoid.[4] However, even low-powered studies can make valuable contributions to a meta-analysis that combines the findings of a large number of studies on related issues. Serious problems arise only when statistical power is both low *and* unknown, and this leads to misinterpretation of the low-powered study considered in isolation.

Low and unreported statistical power has made research literature in many disciplines difficult to interpret. For example, given that in psychology, the average power (for effect sizes considered typical of the discipline) is roughly 50%, it should not be surprising that one study would find a statistically significant result and the following study not. However, this often leads research programs astray with the search for illusory moderating factors, as researchers seek substantive explanations for apparent inconsistencies between studies caused by mere sampling variability (Hunter & Schmidt, 1990). The inability to draw conclusions from inconsistent results can lead to researchers giving up on important theories: As Meehl (1978) famously said, many theories in psychology "suffer the fate that General MacArthur ascribed to old generals—they never die, they just slowly fade away" (p. 807).

Implausible Nil Nulls. NHST is often upheld as the operationalism of the Popperian philosophy of science. However, Popper specified that conjectures must be bold, and there is nothing bold about a nil null conjecture (Meehl, 1978). Nil nulls—hypotheses of no difference, zero correlation, etc.—are virtually always implausible and therefore guaranteed to be falsified with sufficient power. For example, "This therapy or intervention has no effect." Of course it will have *some* effect. The more relevant questions are, "To what extent does it have an effect?" and "Does it matter?"

STATISTICAL REFORM: BEYOND NHST

The criticisms reviewed above present a strong case against NHST, raising challenges on many levels. The case against NHST is based on evidence, which includes surveys of NHST misconceptions occurring in journals (e.g., Dar, Serlin, & Omer, 1994; Finch et al., 2001; Kieffer, Reese, & Thompson, 2001), as well as studies of researchers' (mis)understanding (e.g., Haller & Krauss, 2002; Oakes, 1986; Tversky & Kahneman, 1971). Even if one is not convinced by arguments that the logic of NHST is fatally flawed, it

is harder to argue against claims that NHST is largely irrelevant to the enterprise of scientific research. On top of that, NHST is demonstrably widely misinterpreted and misused—and half a century of criticisms has done little to change these practices in disciplines where it remains the dominant technique. This alone is reason enough for some critics to call for its abandonment. The availability and advantages of alternative techniques only serve to make the case for statistical reform stronger.

Why, despite the decades of strong evidence and cogent argument, does NHST still overwhelmingly dominate? How can researchers be persuaded to change? These are vital and fascinating questions in the sociology—as well as the history and politics—of the social sciences.

Reform Attempts by Journal Editors

Journal editors and their manuscript reviewers are the gatekeepers to the published literature and therefore should, if they wished, be able to determine what statistical practices are used in published articles. In medicine, the convinced and energetic statistical reformer Kenneth Rothman worked to eliminate NHST and *p* values and replace them with CIs, first at the *American Journal of Public Health* and then at *Epidemiology.* Fidler, Thomason, Cumming, Finch, and Leeman (2004) surveyed those journals and found that Rothman's strong and persistent editorial requirements were very largely successful in achieving a switch to CIs.

In psychology, Geoff Loftus (1993) stated that as editor of *Memory & Cognition,* he wanted authors to use figures with error bars (CIs or standard error [SE] bars) as the primary way to analyze, present, and interpret their data, preferably without using NHST at all. Despite extraordinary efforts (in approximately 100 cases, doing the would-be author's calculations himself), his reform had a limited and short-lived impact (Finch et al., 2004). A similar attempt by then-editor Philip Kendall (1997) to introduce reporting of effect sizes and clinical significance in the *Journal of Consulting and Clinical Psychology* was also largely unsuccessful (Fidler et al., 2005). These pioneering editors should be saluted for their enterprise, but NHST is so deeply entrenched in psychology's culture that even determined editorial efforts have been unable to achieve major and lasting change.

Statistical Reform in Medicine

We have mentioned Rothman's pioneering and relatively successful attempts as a journal editor to replace NHST with CIs. Rothman had earlier been one of a number of reformers who published articles and editorials criticizing NHST, advocating CIs, and explaining how CIs can be used in various situations common in medical research. Rothman also published a leading statistics text (Rothman & Greenland, 1998) and provided CI software for some designs used in epidemiology.

The efforts of Rothman and other reformers led to policy intervention from the International Committee of Medical Journal Editors (ICMJE; 1988) and the adoption of strong and consistent editorial policies in more than 300 medical journals, including leading journals (e.g., *New England Journal of Medicine, British Medical Journal*).

It is a notable success of medicine that CIs have now, for more than 20 years, been routinely reported in medical research. Important factors in achieving this were the efforts of reformers not only to make their case in strong and highly visible journal articles but also to provide helpful resources, including tutorial articles, software, and textbooks—for example, the very useful *Statistics With Confidence* (Altman, Machin, Bryant, & Gardner, 2000; the first edition was published in 1989!). These efforts led to the crucial step by editors, acting as a united international body, to institute editorial requirements across medical research.

The medical reform story is notable but cannot be regarded as complete: For example, *p* values are still common (even if routinely accompanied by effect sizes and CIs), and interpretation of results is often not based on the reported CIs (Fidler, Thomason, et al., 2004).

Statistical Reform in Psychology

Despite having limited impact, reform advocates in psychology have been at least as distinguished, just as determined, and vocal for more decades than those in medicine. Their efforts prompted the American Psychological Association (APA) to set up a Task Force on Statistical Inference, whose report (Wilkinson & the Task Force on Statistical Inference, 1999) is a fine statement of good practice in the design of research, as well as statistical analysis and reporting of results. Fidler (2002) explained that it did not, however, lead to strong, reformed statistical

recommendations in the subsequent edition of the highly influential APA *Publication Manual* (APA, 2001). Nor did it lead to any notable moves by journal editors to reform statistical practice, except perhaps by encouraging reporting of effect sizes.

A number of differences between medicine and psychology may underlie the different reform experiences. Medical reformers were more active than their psychology counterparts in providing textbooks, tutorial articles, and software to assist researchers who wished to adopt recommended reform practices. Perhaps the life-or-death consequences of much medical research played a role.

A further important factor may be that medical researchers more often work with a consultant statistician and so may be more open to taking statistical advice, including from journal editors. By contrast, social scientists have a tradition of teaching their own statistics and researchers often doing their own statistical analysis. At worst, this tradition may lead researchers to feel insufficiently confident about their statistical expertise to critically assess their statistical options, yet not have expert statistical advice readily available. So researchers cling to cookbook approaches from textbooks and the methods used by other researchers in the same research area. The inevitable result is uncritical statistical inertia and stagnation. One sign of this is that the reform "debate" in psychology is hardly a debate at all, in that very few detailed arguments in defense of NHST have been published (Siu Chow's prolific defenses are an obvious exception, e.g., Chow, 1996, 1998). Reformers have largely encountered silence rather than opposition, and entrenched practices have to a large extent simply persisted.

Statistical Reform in Ecology

Fidler, Cumming, Burgman, and Thomason (2004) discussed the statistical reform stories in medicine, psychology, and ecology. That article appeared in an economics journal, as part of statistical reform discussions in that discipline. Every discipline has its own traditions and particular research challenges, but many statistical reform issues are common across many disciplines, and it is encouraging that the reform discussion is active now in more disciplines than ever—for example, in economics.

In ecology, criticism of NHST and debate about desirable statistical reforms came later than in medicine or psychology but have been active since the 1980s. Notable in ecology has been increased use of a variety of approaches to building and testing quantitative models. Such modeling is an important step beyond estimation of effect sizes and thus two large steps beyond the impoverished dichotomous decision making of NHST. One prominent approach to model selection is the information-theoretic approach of Akaike (1992), which is a likelihood-based technique in which the Akaike information criterion (AIC) is used to assess model fit and guide the development and combination of models. Bayesian methods are also becoming more popular for model selection and estimation, especially with the widespread availability of software, notably WinBUGS (e.g., McCarthy, 2007). NHST still dominates in ecology, but changes in reporting practice in leading journals, including *Conservation Biology* and *Biological Conservation,* can now be detected (Fidler, Burgman, Cumming, Buttrose, & Thomason, 2006).

EVIDENCE-BASED STATISTICAL REFORM

One conclusion from our preceding review is that there is overwhelming evidence of severe and diverse problems with NHST. Another is that case studies provide evidence that statistical reform is hard to achieve and is most likely if a broad approach is taken, including provision of advice and resources, reform of statistics education, and concerted strong policy action by journal editors and other influential players in a particular discipline.

Statistical reform must not be seen as a narrow crusade against the *p* value but as a striving for a more quantitative, sophisticated, and diverse way to design research, develop theory, and learn from data. CIs and estimation of effect size is one step, quantitative modeling another, and wider use of meta-analysis to integrate bodies of research a further crucial development. Reform also embraces more generic practices, including use of graphical representations; consideration of clinical, biological, or practical importance of results (as opposed to merely statistical significance); consideration of sample size issues; and thoughtful treatments of trends and patterns of effects. Most generally, statistical best practice requires consideration of the full range of possible statistical techniques and researchers' informed judgment to choose the most appropriate design, measures, and analyses to serve particular research goals.

As we have argued above, there is evidence to justify severe doubt about NHST and to guide efforts toward reform. There is, however, a glaring and serious lack of evidence to support the effectiveness of many techniques advocated by reformers. For example, while there is ample evidence of misconceptions held about NHST, there is virtually no corresponding evidence that CIs are better understood by researchers and are thus likely to yield in practice the advantages claimed by reformers. In fact, Cumming, Williams, and Fidler (2004) and Belia, Fidler, Williams, and Cumming (2005) identified a number of misconceptions about CIs that are widespread among researchers in psychology, behavioral neuroscience, and medicine. We take those findings, however, as a guide to the developments needed in CI techniques and advice rather than an excuse to retreat from reform.

Throughout this book, there are examples of evidence being presented to justify particular statistical recommendations and to assist readers in developing their own statistical judgment skills. There are also pointers to substantial further research needed to support recommendations that are currently opinion, as well as to provide more complete information about robustness and other properties of particular statistical techniques. This research is partly statistical but also cognitive—for example, the study of how researchers and research consumers understand various ways of presenting data and conclusions from data—and thus presents psychologists in particular with challenging and important research opportunities.

ATTITUDES FOR THE 21ST CENTURY

Based on our discussion above, here we mention some basic attitudes we recommend to researchers and students—attitudes this book seeks to exemplify and encourage.

Best Statistical Practice Is a Moving Target

Peruse this book's reference lists: The recency of many items demonstrates that new statistical techniques continue to be developed and further knowledge gained about classical techniques. This book will be gradually superseded over coming years,[5] and that's a good thing. In their substantive research areas, researchers read the journals, participate in conferences, and build a worldwide network of colleagues. They should do similarly for experimental techniques and statistical methods best for their field of research.

Too many modern statistics textbooks look too similar to those of the 1970s. There is great inertia in statistics teaching, and too many teachers go along with student anxiety just to grasp the basics of a fixed canon of statistical doctrine rather than to appreciate that statistical possibilities keep changing, and that's to be celebrated and exploited. Best practice in statistics is a moving target, and researchers and students need to keep striving to achieve it. Research progress across the whole discipline depends on this!

Researcher Expertise and Judgment

NHST has been seen as a tool for all situations. Reformers such as Cohen (1994) and Wilkinson and the Task Force on Statistical Inference (1999) made it clear that there is no single tool that can replace NHST, but researchers must select from a range of more specialized and appropriate statistical tools. Judgment is required, and a major part of developing research expertise is the development of well-informed statistical judgment. Statistical expertise is to be nurtured and celebrated. From even the introductory statistics course, students need to be taught and encouraged to practice and build their statistical judgment skills and the self-confidence to apply and enjoy those skills.

When selecting and using statistical techniques, critical appraisal must always be in play. Apply reality tests at every stage and to the results. Try another analysis, expect findings to make sense, and enjoy being in control.

Colleagues and Statistical Experts

Exhortation to develop statistical expertise may ring hollow for researchers who already feel overstretched. There is constant pressure, and strong tradition, urging knee-jerk use of ANOVA rather than thought and experimenting to find a possibly more suitable statistical model. The practical solution may be to consult colleagues, locally or anywhere around the world, or a statistics specialist. Development of statistical

insight can be a collaborative venture in which all can gain.[6]

Research to Build the Evidence Base

Researchers are best placed to identify problems with current statistical tools and gaps in the knowledge needed to guide statistical judgment in particular settings. Taking the time, perhaps with a statistics collaborator, to build the evidence base of statistical understanding can be rewarding and a highly valuable research contribution. A good applied statistics article may gain more citations than just another report of a couple of experiments. Psychologists can make important contributions by studying statistical cognition—for example, how effectively various statistical presentations communicate research information and help readers avoid misconception.

Statistical judgment must be based on relevant evidence. Use evidence wherever you can to guide decisions about research design, experimental procedures and measures, choice of analyses, and ways to present results. Then cite this evidence as justification for methodology in your research article. If evidence is lacking, consider carrying out the research to find it!

Specialist Doctoral Training in Statistics

Norcross, Kohourt, and Wicherski (2005) reported data on the numbers of students commencing specialist PhD programs in quantitative psychology within U.S. university psychology departments. In 1992, there were 76 programs enrolling an average of 3.9 students each, but in 2003, there were only 17 programs enrolling an average of 1.9 students—that's a drop from approximately 296 enrollments to just 32 in 10 years (Norcross et al., 2005, Table 5, p. 967)! This is a troublesome collapse of vital specialist research training within a decade and requires investigation and remedial action. For researchers, however, it may offer an opportunity: Developing strong secondary expertise in statistics may be a valuable career move, as well as a valuable component of expertise in one's primary research area. It is yet one more reason for students and researchers to seek, celebrate, and enjoy evidence-based best practice in statistics, as this book presents.

NOTES

1. Wilkinson and the Task Force on Statistical Inference (1999). These criticisms have all been made before; they have also been reviewed before (e.g., Kline, 2004; Nickerson, 2000).

2. Interested readers can refer to Chapter 7 for more information on p_{rep}.

3. Editor's note: Osborne, Christensen, and Gunter (2001) reported that in the late 1990s, power for educational psychology studies in top-tier journals was in excess of .70 and had increased dramatically from 1969, implying there may be hope for change in other fields.

4. Interested readers can refer to Chapter 9 on best practices in small-N studies.

5. Editor's note: Egads, they're already writing this book's epitaph and it's not published yet! My hope is that you, the reader, will help me keep this book continually updated through revision in the coming years as new ideas and best practices emerge! See my introduction for my contact information if you have ideas on new and emerging best practices you'd like to see in revisions of this volume.

6. Editor's note: In many physical sciences, it is common for papers to have 6 to 10 authors or more, each representing expertise in different aspects of the research process, and single-author papers are almost extinct. Perhaps we in the social sciences should move toward that model.

REFERENCES

Akaike, H. (1992). Information theory and an extension of the maximum likelihood principle. In S. Kotz & N. Johnson (Eds.), *Breakthroughs in statistics* (pp. 610–624). New York: Springer Verlag.

Altman, D. G., Machin, D., Bryant, T. N., & Gardner, M. J. (2000). *Statistics with confidence: Confidence intervals and statistical guidelines* (2nd ed.). London: British Medical Journal Books.

American Psychological Association. (2001). *Publication manual of the American Psychological Association* (5th ed.). Washington, DC: Author.

Belia, S., Fidler, F., Williams, J., & Cumming, G. (2005). Researchers misunderstand confidence intervals and standard error bars. *Psychological Methods, 10*, 389–396.

Carver, R. P. (1978). The case against statistical significance testing. *Harvard Educational Review, 48*, 378–399.

Chow, S. (1996). *Statistical significance: Rationale, validity and utility.* Thousand Oaks, CA: Sage.

Chow, S. (1998). A précis of "Statistical significance: Rationale, validity and utility." *Behavioral and Brain Sciences, 21*, 169–194.

Cohen, J. (1962). The statistical power of abnormal–social psychological research: A review. *Journal of Abnormal and Social Psychology, 65*, 145–153.

Cohen, J. (1994). The earth is round ($p < .05$). *American Psychologist, 49*, 997–1003.

Coulson, M., Healey, M., Fidler, F., & Cumming, G. (2006). *Understanding of confidence intervals by researchers in psychology, behavioural neuroscience, and medicine.* Manuscript in preparation.

Cumming, G. (2005). Understanding the average probability of replication: Comment on Killeen (2005). *Psychological Science, 16*, 1002–1004.

Cumming, G., Fidler, F., Leonard, M., Kalinowski, P., Christiansen, A., Kleinig, A., et al. (2007). Statistical reform in psychology: Is anything changing? *Psychological Science, 18*, 230–232.

Cumming, G., Williams, J., & Fidler, F. (2004). Replication, and researchers' understanding of confidence intervals and standard error bars. *Understanding Statistics, 3*, 299–311.

Dar, R., Serlin, R. C., & Omer, H. (1994). Misuse of statistical tests in three decades of psychotherapy research. *Journal of Consulting and Clinical Psychology, 62*, 75–82.

Fidler, F. (2002). The 5th edition of the APA publication manual: Why its statistics recommendations are so controversial. *Educational and Psychological Measurement, 62*, 749–770.

Fidler, F., Burgman, M., Cumming, G., Buttrose, R., & Thomason, N. (2006). Impact of criticism of null hypothesis significance testing on statistical reporting practices in conservation biology. *Conservation Biology, 20*, 1539–1544.

Fidler, F., Cumming, G., Burgman, M., & Thomason, N. (2004). Statistical reform in medicine, psychology and ecology. *Journal of Socio-Economics, 33*, 615–630.

Fidler, F., Cumming, G., Thomason, N., Pannuzzo, D., Smith, J., Fyffe, P., et al. (2005). Toward improved statistical reporting in the *Journal of Consulting and Clinical Psychology. Journal of Consulting and Clinical Psychology, 73*, 136–143.

Fidler, F., Thomason, N., Cumming, G., Finch, S., & Leeman, J. (2004). Editors can lead researchers to confidence intervals but they can't make them think: Statistical reform lessons from medicine. *Psychological Science, 15*, 119–126.

Finch, S., Cumming, G., & Thomason, N. (2001). Reporting of statistical inference in the *Journal of Applied Psychology:* Little evidence of reform. *Educational and Psychological Measurement, 61*, 181–210.

Finch, S., Cumming, G., Williams, J., Palmer, L., Griffith, E., Alders, C., et al. (2004). Reform of statistical inference in psychology: The case of memory and cognition. *Behavior Research Methods, Instruments, & Computers, 36,* 312–324.

Gigerenzer, G., & Hoffrage, U. (1995). How to improve Bayesian reasoning without instruction: Frequency formats. *Psychological Review, 102,* 684–704.

Haller, H., & Krauss, S. (2002). Misinterpretations of significance: A problem students share with their teachers? *Methods of Psychological Research, 7,* 1–20.

Hunter, J. E. (1997). Needed: A ban on the significance test. *Psychological Science, 8,* 3–7.

Hunter, J. E., & Schmidt, F. L. (1990). *Methods of meta-analysis: Correcting error and bias in research findings.* Newbury Park, CA: Sage.

Institute of Medicine. (2001). *Crossing the quality chasm: A new health system for the 21st century.* Washington, DC: National Academy Press.

International Committee of Medical Journal Editors. (1988). Uniform requirements for manuscripts submitted to biomedical journals. *Annals of Internal Medicine, 108,* 258–265.

Kendall, P. C. (1997). Editorial. *Journal of Consulting and Clinical Psychology, 65,* 3–5.

Kendall, P. C., Marrs-Garcia, A., Nath, S. R., & Sheldrick, R. C. (1999). Normative comparisons for the evaluation of clinical significance. *Journal of Consulting and Clinical Psychology, 67,* 285–299.

Kieffer, K. M., Reese, R. J., & Thompson, B. (2001). Statistical techniques employed in *AERA* and *JCP* articles from 1988 to 1997: A methodological review. *Journal of Experimental Education, 69,* 280–309.

Killeen, P. (2005). An alternative to null hypothesis significance tests. *Psychological Science, 16,* 345–353.

Kirk, R. E. (1996). Practical significance: A concept whose time has come. *Educational and Psychological Measurement, 56,* 746–759.

Kline, R. B. (2004). *Beyond significance testing: Reforming data analysis methods in behavioral research.* Washington, DC: American Psychological Association.

Kosslyn, S. M. (1994). *Elements of graph design.* New York: W. H. Freeman.

Loftus, G. R. (1993). Editorial comment. *Memory & Cognition, 21,* 1–3.

McCarthy, M. (2007). *Bayesian methods for ecologists.* Cambridge, UK: Cambridge University Press.

Meehl, P. E. (1978). Theoretical risks and tabular asterisks: Sir Karl, Sir Ronald, and the slow progress of soft psychology. *Journal of Consulting and Clinical Psychology, 46,* 806–834.

Nickerson, R. S. (2000). Null hypothesis significance testing: A review of an old and continuing controversy. *Psychological Methods, 5,* 241–301.

Norcross, J. C., Kohout, J. L., & Wicherski, M. (2005). Graduate study in psychology 1971 to 2004. *American Psychologist, 60,* 959–975.

Oakes, M. W. (1986). *Statistical inference: A commentary for the social and behavioural sciences.* Chichester, UK: John Wiley.

Osborne, J. W., Christensen, W. R., & Gunter, J. (2001, April). *Educational psychology from a statistician's perspective: A review of the power and goodness of educational psychology research.* Paper presented at the national meeting of the American Education Research Association (AERA), Seattle, WA.

Rossi, J. (1990). Statistical power of psychological research: What have we gained in 20 years? *Journal of Consulting and Clinical Psychology, 58,* 646–656.

Rothman, K. J., & Greenland, S. (Eds.). (1998). *Modern epidemiology* (2nd ed.). Philadelphia: Lippincott-Raven.

Rozeboom, W. W. (1960). The fallacy of the null-hypothesis significance test. *Psychological Bulletin, 57,* 416–428. [Reprinted in Morrison, D. E., & Henkel, R. E. (Eds.). (1970). *The significance testing controversy* (pp. 216–231). Chicago: Aldine.]

Schutz, H. G. (1961). An evaluation of methods for presentation of graphic multiple trends—Experiment III. *Human Factors, 3,* 99–107.

Sedlmeier, P., & Gigerenzer, G. (1989). Do studies of statistical power have an effect on the power of studies? *Psychological Bulletin, 105,* 309–315.

Simcox, W. A. (1983). *A perceptual analysis of graphic information processing.* Unpublished doctoral dissertation, Tufts University.

Tukey, J. W. (1991). The philosophy of multiple comparisons. *Statistical Science, 6,* 100–116.

Tversky, A., & Kahneman, D. (1971). Belief in the law of small numbers. *Psychological Bulletin, 76,* 105–110.

Wilkinson, L., & the Task Force on Statistical Inference. (1999). Statistical methods in psychology journals: Guidelines and explanations. *American Psychologist, 54,* 594–604.

PART I

BEST PRACTICES IN MEASUREMENT

2

SETTING STANDARDS AND ESTABLISHING CUT SCORES ON CRITERION-REFERENCED ASSESSMENTS

Some Technical and Practical Considerations

J. THOMAS KELLOW

VICTOR L. WILLSON

The first author recently was privileged to be included in a conversation with a prominent politician regarding the legitimacy of a high school exit examination that all students (in that state) must pass to obtain a high school diploma. Indeed, this person was the principal architect of the mandated exit-level test policy. Ironically, when asked if he could pass the exam, he commented that "it really didn't make a difference, since so many other factors contributed to success in life after high school"! Our hope is that readers take mind of these issues and think about them in applied settings.

Cut scores are widely used by educators and psychologists in a variety of contexts. Technically, a cut score is a prescribed value on a continuum of values (given the instrument employed) that is seen to be a "threshold" that demarcates the presence or absence of a particular state or condition (e.g., proficient or nonproficient; depressed or not depressed). Cut scores are usually associated with criterion-referenced tests (CRTs) when used to indicate a minimal level of proficiency or mastery; however, in some instances, cut scores are invoked when using norm-referenced tests (NRTs). An example of this might be when a psychologist uses a normative threshold on the Minnesota Multiphasic Personality Inventory (MMPI) scales to infer potential psychopathology or when a school diagnostician uses IQ and achievement measures to determine the presence of a learning disability based on a 1–standard deviation discrepancy (Anastasi, 1988). Similarly, one of the criteria for determining the presence of mental retardation is a full-scale IQ below 70 (American Association on Mental Retardation,

2005). Universities often employ cut scores on NRTs as a partial determinant of who is accepted into their schools (e.g., SAT; Graduate Record Examination [GRE]). Undoubtedly, however, the greatest use of cut scores lies in determining mastery or proficiency in a content domain by virtue of CRT performance.

After determining appropriate behavioral learning outcomes in a given content area (content standards), a CRT is constructed of items that link directly back to the content criteria—hence the term *criterion referenced* (Crocker & Algina, 1986). Expectations for performance standards are then set demarcating levels of performance based on what a proficient examinee should be able to do. As an example, the No Child Left Behind (NCLB) legislation of 2002 demands performance expectations based on cut scores—students, schools, and school districts that fail to make the cut are "left behind" and are subject to considerable punitive actions with respect to federal school funding. The cut score on the examination represents the operationalization of performance standards based on the content standards. Sometimes, the cut score indicates a dichotomous performance level (e.g., pass-fail), while at other times there may be multiple performance levels (e.g., below proficient–proficient–advanced). In certain professions, such as medicine, cut scores are used to decide who is eligible for licensure in the field. In K–12 settings, student CRT performance is used not only to gauge mastery of learning outcomes but also for determining whether a student should be retained in grade or denied a high school diploma. What is often overlooked by both educators and public stakeholders is that the validity of decisions made based on CRT performance is dependent on the quality of the method used for establishing performance standards and the technical adequacy of the tests themselves.

Our purpose in this chapter is to outline some of the technical and practical concerns with CRTs related to establishing performance standards and cut scores. We start with the premise that a meaningful, legitimate, and well-defined set of learning goals and objectives has been established. Moreover, we assume that a comprehensive and technically sound pool of items has been constructed to measure these outcomes. Having taken this leap of faith (see Glass, 1978), we focus on two central issues:

(a) the relative merit of methods for establishing cut scores to define performance levels and (b) methods of compensating for errors in the standard-setting process and errors in tests. These methods are briefly elaborated, potential disadvantages of each are discussed, and suggestions for proper practice are provided.

ESTABLISHING PERFORMANCE STANDARDS

Crocker and Algina (1986) outlined three major approaches to setting performance standards: (a) holistic, (b) content based, and (c) performance based. All of these methods typically invoke the judgment of *experts* in the content area of interest. These individuals possess substantive content knowledge as well as intimate familiarity with the target population. In addition, each method involves establishing clear descriptors for the respective levels of examinee competence (e.g., pass-fail; below proficient–proficient–advanced), as well as training on their interpretation. Descriptors may be provided to judges from an external source, or they may be developed by the judges themselves before proceeding to standard-setting activities.

The selection of judges is itself a sampling problem. That is, what is the sampling adequacy of the judges selected in relation to the population of such experts? This aspect is, to our knowledge, never considered or even acknowledged, nor has a multilevel model including between-judge variance been developed in standard-setting models to date. This technical aspect, however, is beyond the scope of this chapter.

Holistic Standard Setting

In this approach, a panel of judges is convened to examine a test and estimate the percentage of items that should be answered correctly by a person with minimally proficient knowledge of the content domain of interest. These judges examine the test *holistically* rather than focusing on individual item content. After each judge provides a passing standard estimate, the results are averaged to obtain the final cut score.

The main advantage of the holistic method is its simplicity. Compared with other standard-setting methods, the holistic approach has a relatively light cognitive load. There are several disadvantages to the holistic standard-setting procedure. First, the reliability of the judges' estimates may be highly variable. It is likely that different sets of expert panelists with similar backgrounds would arrive at a different perception of minimal competence when evaluating the same test content. As Crocker and Algina (1986) note, a logical procedure to overcome this problem would be to use multiple, independent panels. This is in itself, however, an inadequate mechanism to address the population sampling problem referenced above and will at best merely estimate sample-to-sample variance. If, however, the number of experts available is finite, or financial resources are limited, conducting replication studies would reduce the size of each panel. This, in turn, would likely lead to more fluctuation within the respective groups. A second problematic aspect of this method is that, because it lacks any systematic rationale for setting the standard other than an overall impression of the test, it is the least defensible of standard-setting methods available. This is of particular concern in high-stakes testing programs, where decisions based on cut scores that are perceived as unfair are often challenged in court.

There are no published contemporary examples of holistic standard-setting procedures used with selected-response items in formal practice (i.e., large-scale assessment systems). We feel that, despite its simplicity, use of the holistic procedure for setting standards in a high-stakes testing context does not represent a best practice. Our principal concern is that the lack of a formal, systematic process leaves this method vulnerable to legal challenges. This is of particular concern given the rampant use of high-stakes testing in K–12 settings, where schools, school districts, and state education agencies are under increasing demands to defend decisions they make regarding student outcomes. Moreover, there is the persistent issue of choosing which important skills students need to master to make them "competent" in a given area. Rather, current literature focuses on content-based and performance-based strategies, which are discussed below.

Content-Based Standard Setting

A number of different content-based methods have been developed, but all share a common focus on determining expectations for performance by evaluating tests at the *item level*.

The most popular content-based approaches by far are the Angoff and modified Angoff procedures (Zieky, 2001). Space precludes an elaboration of lesser known methods such as those developed by Nedelsky (1954) and Ebel (1972), but the interested reader is referred to Berk (1986) for more on these alternatives.

Basic Angoff Procedure

The basic Angoff procedure involves assembling a panel of judges (ideally 15–20 [Brandon, 2004; Jaeger, 1991]) who are presented with a series of test items. The judges, working independently, are asked to think of a reference group of 100 "minimally acceptable," "borderline," or "barely proficient" examinees and estimate the number of these examinees that should answer each item correctly. This is conceptually equivalent to estimating a probability of success on the target item for the referent student. For each judge, the proportions across items are totaled, and the average for all judges is computed. This average then becomes the estimated cut score for the test in a number-correct metric. As Ricker (2004) notes,

> This method does not just apply to minimally competent candidates, but could also be used to create a cut score for any grouping within the population. For example, Angoff methods could be used to set a cut score for a standard of excellence on a test. In this case, judges would be required to conceptualize a group of "minimally excellent" examinees. (p. 6)

The basic Angoff procedure represents a conceptual improvement over the holistic method given the systematic method judges employ to assess expected student performance at the item level. Indeed, this method has held up well when challenged in the courts (Hibshmann, 2004).

Since Angoff proposed his method of standard setting, there have been a number of modifications suggested. Some of these modifications are presented below.

Modified (Yes-No) Angoff Procedure

The original Angoff method has been criticized on the grounds of being too cognitively complex for judges (Shepard, Glaser, Linn, & Bohrnstedt, 1993). The argument is that keeping in mind characteristics of a borderline examinee while simultaneously trying to estimate a probability of success is onerous. A modification proposed to lessen this cognitive demand is the yes-no procedure. It is identical to the original Angoff method, with the exception that, rather than estimate the probability of success on an item, judges are simply asked to indicate whether a borderline proficient student would be able to answer the item correctly (Impara & Plake, 1997). The number of items recommended by each judge is then averaged across judges to provide a cut score indicating minimal proficiency.

Several studies have empirically compared results from the traditional and modified yes-no approaches. Impara and Plake (1997) concluded that both methods resulted in nearly identical cut scores and recommended the yes-no approach based on its simplicity. Chin and Hertz (2002) examined both methods and found that the same judges, over repeated iterations of the process, produced less stable estimates using the yes-no procedure as opposed to the traditional proportion-correct method. Moreover, these authors concluded that judges using the yes-no procedure, when presented with normative data on the test and the opportunity to change their initial ratings, were more influenced by these data than judges using the traditional approach. Berk (1986) questioned this approach based on the all-or-none probability of the yes-no format and suggested that "a continuum of probabilities is more appropriate for most types of items" (p. 148).

The modified Angoff procedures in either form have also been criticized as being inadequate for constructed-response items (Cizek, 2001; Hambleton & Plake, 1997). Such items typically require rubrics for scoring that have many parts and typically produce multiple part scores; what constitutes "minimally acceptable" performance becomes too complex for these methods.

Successive Iterations

According to Ricker (2004), using an iterative process is the most common of the modified Angoff procedures. In this approach, judges use either a traditional or yes-no method to initially arrive (independently) at a cut score for the test. A second and sometimes third round, using the same judges, is then conducted (Busch & Jaeger, 1990). During these rounds, the judges discuss their original estimates at the item and total score level. This is facilitated by providing distributions of the item probabilities and total cut scores for all panelists. After reviewing this information and discussing the results, the original estimates may be modified by participants.

Hambleton (2001) has stated that, when evaluating the appropriateness of standard-setting procedures, the use of iterative standard-setting sessions with the same panel is desirable. Research documenting the effects of iterative standard-setting sessions is mixed. Hambleton suggested that changes from the original standard set by judges as a result of successive iterations were minimal, with no noteworthy differences between ratings over sessions. Busch and Jaeger (1990) found that using successive iterations tended to produce slight modifications of panelists' original ratings and that the variability of final estimates was reduced as a result. While the reduction of variance in initial ratings vis-à-vis repeated standard-setting sessions is appealing, the extent to which this convergence of estimates is due to influence from other judges and not a representation of the judges' "true" conceptualization of a passing score is somewhat problematic. Social psychologists (e.g., Asch, 1956; Ross, Bierbauer, & Hoffman, 1976) have repeatedly demonstrated that group pressure, either explicit or implicit, tends to produce acquiescence to group norms that are not indicative of a person's true perceptions.

Presentation of Normative Data

At times, judges may be presented with empirical test data from the target population after making their initial cut score estimates. After a discussion of these data, the panelists may adjust their original estimates. As Brandon (2004) explains,

> Between standard-setting rounds, modified Angoff judges typically review empirical information about tests and items . . . and discuss this information and their item estimates from the previous round. This is an iterative form of standard setting. Having judges review empirical information was first proposed by Shepard (1976) and endorsed later by others (e.g., Hambleton & Eignor, 1980; Jaeger, 1982; Livingston & Zieky, 1982). The information that judges review and discuss can include empirical item p values,

the distributions of scores on a test, [and] the estimated percentages of examinees above cut scores . . . (Reckase, 2001). Item p values are the most commonly provided information. Judges are given p values to help ensure that cut scores are realistic and that interjudge and intrajudge consistency are enhanced (Plake, Melican, & Mills, 1991). Reviewing and discussing p values is particularly helpful for judges who are insufficiently familiar with the examinee group. (p. 76)

Although the presentation of normative data during the standard-setting process may seem antithetical to the purpose of criterion-referenced assessment, several authors have stated advantages of this practice (e.g., Linn, 2003; Zieky, 2001).

Linn (2003) suggests that,

in addition to knowing the percentile rank corresponding to particular cut scores, it would also be desirable to have some means of providing judges with comparative information about the relative stringency of their standards in comparison to standards set in other states before judgments are finalized. Normative information would be one way of making comparisons to standards in other states.

Recommendations for Using Content-Based Methods

The Angoff and modified Angoff procedures offer a more comprehensive approach to standard setting than holistic methods. Although the use of a yes-no modification may be less taxing on judges, the few empirical studies that address this method leave us unconvinced that important information is not lost in the process (Berk, 1986). Until more information becomes available regarding the technical merit of this modification, we recommend the traditional Angoff instructions.

The use of multiple standard-setting sessions has a certain appeal (Hambleton, 2001). The intent of reducing the variance of judges by virtue of an iterative process fits well with the democratic nature of informed discourse that results in, at least, partial closure on agreeable cut scores based on expert judgment. Weighing against this approach is the possibility that judges will be unduly influenced by others in modifying their original estimates. Our position is that the use of successive iterations may

ultimately facilitate reasoned judgment, particularly if the process is moderated by an independent panel referee (Ricker, 2004).

While the presentation of normative data in the context of content-based procedures has been challenged, we agree with Linn (2003) and Brandon (2002) that this additional information may assist judges in making more reasonable cut score estimates. Not considering actual score distributions of target examinees and item difficulty levels in setting performance standards could be construed as a lack of concern for the potentially arbitrary judgments that are made by panelists. In addition to consulting item difficulty (p) values, we recommend considering the overall impact of the cut score decision on passing rates. This can be extended to examining the potential for disparate impact of the cut score on minority students (Haney, 2000).

Much of the research and most of the conclusions about content-based procedures have been predicated on getting groups of judges together physically. Over the past decade, new interactive procedures based on Internet-oriented real-time activities (e.g., focus groups, Delphi techniques) have emerged in marketing and other fields that might be employed. These techniques open up new alternatives for standard setting that have not yet been explored. The American National Standards Institute published a recent work advocating such methods (Suett, n.d.).

Performance-Based Standard Setting

Standard-setting methods based on *examinee performance* involve the use of empirical data as the foundation for determining cut scores. Two methods are discussed here: (a) contrasting groups and (b) the bookmark procedure.

Contrasting-Groups Method

This method invokes the judgment of individuals (e.g., teachers) who are intimately familiar with a specific group of candidates who are representative of the target population (e.g., their own students). The judges are provided with the behavioral criteria, the test, and a description of "proficient" and "nonproficient" candidates. Judges then identify individuals who, based on previous classroom assessments, clearly fall into one of the two categories (borderline candidates are excluded). According to

Cizek (2001), at least 100 candidates should represent each classification group. These individuals are then tested, and separate frequency distributions are generated for each group. The intersection between the two distributions is then used as the cut score that differentiates nonproficient from proficient examinees (see Figure 2.1).

The contrasting-groups method has an advantage over Angoff-related procedures in that it asks judges to consider all achievement-related information they possess about student candidates to answer the following question: "Given the specifications for nonproficient and proficient students described in the standards, which of your students fit clearly into one category?" This would include numerous sources of evidence, including both selected and open-ended response-formatted tests. There are, however, several limitations of the approach. One obvious limitation of this method is its practicality. Judges must not only be familiar with the content domain and knowledge of the general target population but also have sufficient knowledge of the previous performance of their own students. An additional limitation is the potential for judges to evaluate their own students in an overly favorable manner, a form of self-serving bias; or personal characteristics of students that are extraneous to achievement (e.g., physical attractiveness; disruptive behavior patterns) may contaminate judges' perceptions (Brandon, 2002).

Clauser and Clyman (1994) describe an alternative to the traditional contrasting-groups approach that involves examination of actual performance of members of the target population rather than the individuals themselves. Brandon (2002) has termed this a *response-focused* method as opposed to the original *person-focused* approach. In their response-focused contrasting-groups study, Clauser and Clyman presented experienced physician judges with previously scored performance examinations detailing the diagnostic findings of third-year medical students based on their evaluation of standardized patients (judges were unaware of the results of previous scoring). Judges then classified students as either "passing" or "not passing" based on their performance expectations for the target students. In addition, the judges were allowed to confer and discuss their respective ratings; however, no consensus between judges was required, presumably reducing the influence of strongly opinionated panelists. The previous results on the examinations were then used to plot the scores for each group and set a cut score, much as in the original contrasting-groups method. The authors reported relatively high interjudge and intrajudge agreement using this approach.

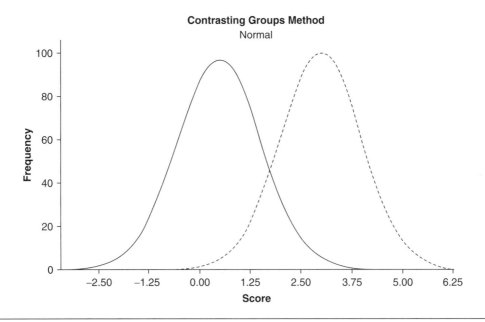

Figure 2.1   Demarcation of nonproficient (solid line) and proficient (dotted line) examinees.

The response-centered method would seem to overcome several problems related to the person-centered approach. First, judges need only to have experience with the content domain and knowledge of the general target population: No experience with specific respondents is necessary. Second, since judges are not rating their own students, the potential for a self-serving bias or other criterion contamination should largely be eliminated. While the response-centered approach is appealing, it is considered appropriate only within the context of constructed-response items (Brandon, 2002; Kane, 1998).

Bookmark Method

This approach is a relatively new addition to the standard-setting literature (Mitzel, Lewis, Patz, & Green, 2001). The bookmark method (sometimes referred to as an item-mapping strategy) involves first testing examinees in the target domain. Using item response theory (IRT), test items (which may be selected-response or open-ended) are mapped onto a common scale. Item difficulties are then computed, and a booklet is developed with items arranged vertically based on empirically derived difficulty levels (easiest to hardest). Judges are allowed to examine—and sometimes take—the test and are provided with item content specifications, content standards, scoring rubrics for open-ended items, and other relevant materials, such as initial descriptors for performance levels. Typically, panels of 15 to 21 judges are selected for each subject area and grade level (Kiplinger, 1997). Judges then separate into smaller groups and examine the ordered item booklet. Starting with the easiest items, each judge examines each item and determines whether a student meeting a particular performance level would be expected to answer the item correctly. This procedure continues until the judge reaches the first item that is perceived as unlikely to be answered correctly by a student at the prescribed level. A "bookmark" is then placed next to this item.

Kiplinger's (1997) explanation of the process used by the Colorado Department of Education illustrates the bookmarking process. Colorado developed a polytomous classification system (unsatisfactory–partially proficient–proficient–advanced). The expectations for performance levels are described here:

- The items prior to the first bookmark (partially proficient) are items that all partially proficient students, with a high probability, should know and be able to do. Students who are not likely to respond correctly to these items are probably performing at the "unsatisfactory" level. Mastery of these items separates the "partially proficient" student from one who is performing unsatisfactorily.
- The items between the first bookmark and the second bookmark (proficient) are items that all proficient students, with a high probability, should know and be able to do. Students who are not likely to respond correctly to these items are probably "partially proficient" or "unsatisfactory." Mastery of these items separates the "proficient" student from the "partially proficient" student.
- The items between the second bookmark and the third bookmark (advanced) are items that all advanced students, with a high probability, should know and be able to do. Students who are not likely to respond correctly to these items are probably performing at the "proficient," "partially proficient," or "unsatisfactory" level. Mastery of these items separates the "advanced" student from the "proficient" student.
- The items after the last bookmark (advanced) are items that some, but not all, advanced students are likely to know and be able to do.

After the first round, participants in the small group are allowed to discuss their bookmark ratings for each group and may modify initial ratings based on group discussion. In a final round, the small group findings are discussed by all judges, and additional information, such as the impact of the various cut scores on the percentage of students who would be classified in each category, is considered. A final determination is reached either through consensus or by taking the median ratings between groups. The last step involves revising the initial performance descriptors based on information provided by panelists (and the impact data) during the iterative rounds.

One advantage of this method is the wealth of information provided to judges, including the use of empirical data at two different stages (item difficulty ordering and student impact). Although performance-based methods have been criticized by some authors (e.g., Glass, 1978), Crocker and Algina (1986) noted that

> since judges' standards are inevitably influenced by their perceptions of how examinees they know would perform on the test, it may be more appropriate to use actual data from a well-chosen sample of examinees than to rely on arbitrary judgments based on more limited (idiosyncratic) perceptions of examinees' ability to perform on a given test. (p. 414)

The use of successive iterations in the process may also be desirable provided that a concerted effort is made to ensure a truly egalitarian standard-setting process.

One persistent concern with the bookmark method relates to the presentation of items in order of difficulty. It is typical for judges to disagree as to the ordering of items, a phenomenon called "item disordinality" (Skaggs & Tessema, 2001). This is often a function of differential exposure to test content or local curricular emphases that may be idiosyncratic to a school district. Clearly, this phenomenon has the potential to affect variability among judges. Concerns over item disordinality can be addressed by a careful presentation and discussion of the content standards, as well as the individual items (Lewis & Green, 1997).

As noted with content-based methods, new technology has the potential to greatly alter performance-based methods through online sources of information from students, teachers, and experts. There is more to learn than is now known about how these innovations will affect standard setting.

While there is an almost religious belief that IRT-based methods produce the best information available, IRT itself has significant problems with unidimensionality and local independence assumptions about the items that are almost never met. It is not clear how the ubiquitous violation of these assumptions affects estimates of item parameters and the consequent interpretation by judges.

Recommendations for Using Performance-Based Methods

Of the performance-based standard-setting procedures, the traditional contrasting-groups method has received the most attention in the literature (Brandon, 2002). Mills (1983) reported fairly consistent results when comparing the contrasting-groups and Angoff procedures. The disadvantages of this method, however, such as difficulties in assembling qualified judges and the lack of an interjudge agreement process, seem to preclude its routine use in practice. The response-focused method proposed by Clauser and Clyman (1994) seems to be a tractable alternative, although it appears most suitable for constructed-response items.

The appeal of the bookmark procedure is evident given its adoption by at least 31 state education departments for K–12 high-stakes standard setting (Lin, n.d.). Although we do not necessarily endorse this method (i.e., popularity does not imply quality), it combines a number of attractive features found in other approaches, such as the use of (a) normative and impact data, (b) successive iterations, and (c) open (typically) moderated panel discussions (Ricker, 2004).

General Discussion of Standard-Setting Methods

Each of the standard-setting methods previously discussed has certain merits. There also are corresponding disadvantages, and the informed practitioner must consider these issues when designing CRTs. Below, we elaborate two concerns regarding the use of CRTs in establishing standards that have been repeatedly addressed in the literature.

First, numerous studies have provided evidence that different standard-setting methods often yield markedly different results. Moreover, using the same method, different panels of judges arrive at very different conclusions regarding the appropriate cut score (Crocker & Algina, 1986; Jaeger, 1991). Ideally, multiple methods would be used to determine the stability of scores generated by different methods and different judges. Unfortunately, this is not typically an economic or logistic reality. Rudner (2001) and Glass (1978) have noted the "arbitrary" nature of the standard-setting process. Glass, in particular, has condemned the notion of cut scores as "a common expression of wishful thinking" (p. 237). When decisions based on cut scores have both substantive legal consequences and personal consequences for the examinee, it would seem prudent to have multiple, defensible sources of evidence for the validity of the cut points. For instance, scores from standardized examinations such as the SAT have been predictive of future performance, as evidenced by first-year college grade point average (GPA). And, indeed, many colleges use SAT cut scores as *one* source of information regarding an applicant's potential (e.g., SAT at or above 1,000). They also, however, use other indicators such as cumulative high school GPA and writing samples, providing additional support to defend their decisions.

A second concern related to standard setting involves the concept of a minimally proficient, competent, acceptable, or master examinee. Glass (1978) has noted that valid external criteria for assessing the legitimacy of such distinctions in the context of subject matter areas are virtually nonexistent. They may hold only in rare instances, such as when a person who types zero words per minute with zero accuracy (a complete absence of skill) may be deemed incapable of working as a typist. But would one dare suggest that a minimal amount of reading skill is necessary to be a competent parent—and if so, what would this level be? Glass concludes that "the attempt to base criterion scores on a concept of minimal competence fails for two reasons: (1) it has virtually no foundation in psychology; (2) when its arbitrariness is granted but judges attempt nonetheless to specify minimal competence, they disagree wildly" (p. 251).

Compensating for Error in the Standard-Setting and Cut Score Process

Psychometricians have long recognized that measurements of any kind (including physical and observational measures) depend on instruments that are inherently, to some degree, unreliable, therefore containing error (Anastasi, 1988). With regard to standard setting, two sources of error at two levels have been considered: (a) errors associated with judges and methods and (b) errors associated with responses to the test itself. We briefly comment on the first source of error and elaborate more fully on the second source—which is, in our opinion, the more salient aspect of standard setting for researchers and practitioners.

Errors Associated With Judges and Methods

One persistent criticism of the standard-setting process is that different judges using different methods often arrive at discrepant conclusions about the "true" score of a passing, or competent, examinee.

Since the vast majority of standard-setting endeavors employ a single method, one might invoke the principles of classical test theory (CTT) to estimate error due to inconsistency among judges. Under this model, the independent ratings of judges regarding a true cut score are treated as fallible indicators of the true status of an examinee. The mean of these ratings is considered the true score of the proficient examinee, and the standard deviation of these ratings serves as the standard error of measurement for the observed ratings, which is located around the true score.

Alternatively, some have advocated using the standard error of the mean (SE_x) as a measure of error in rater judgments (MacCann & Stanley, 2004). This approach has been used empirically to estimate differences in cut score judgments across years using the same method but different judges. The outcome is presumably an indicator of the significance of longitudinal shifts in ratings as a function of rater characteristics.

An even more current approach would be to embed judges' scores within a multilevel model that estimates properly variances at the between-judge level and within-judge level using mixed model methods. Such analyses will point out the relative variance components for each score estimated. Modern advanced statistical programs permit estimation with logistic outcomes under IRT or other multinomial models. To date, we know of no case where such methods have been incorporated into standard setting.

Recommendations for Judge and Method Errors

Our treatment of this approach is brief based on our judgment that such methods are sufficiently fraught with difficulties that both are, to some degree, intractable from a statistical standpoint.

With respect to invoking CTT to make an argument regarding the error associated with judges using the same method, we would assert that, since the vast majority of standard-setting panels use an iterative process, the subsequent judgments are no longer independent. Rather, these judgments are influenced to some degree by other ratings, which clearly violates the CTT assumption of independence of observations. The entire purpose of the iterative method is to gain convergence of judges on an appropriate true cut score. If this purpose is accomplished, the corresponding standard deviation of the ratings is reduced. This would make the resulting standard error a biased underestimate of the original estimate.

The second method mentioned relies on the (SE_X) as a measure of rater variability. Several limitations of this approach are apparent. Since the (SE_X) is defined as

$$SE_X = S\sqrt{(n-1)},$$

this measure obviously depends on the number of raters used in the standard-setting process. If one desires a greater measure of precision, it is simply a matter of acquiring more raters. Moreover, if the attempt is to compare ratings over time, even with the same number of judges, it is likely that the same judges may be represented more that once over successive standard-setting sessions because a conceptually infinite pool of qualified judges to be sampled is hard to conceive. This, again, would violate the notion of independent observations and thus render the associated standard error a biased estimate. While it is theoretically possible to construct clusters of judges under multilevel models, the number required per cluster and number of clusters necessary for stable estimation typically are too large for the resources allocated for standard setting.

For the reasons articulated above, we believe that attempts to address measurement error in the standard-setting process are misguided and ill-conceived in general. In addition, while these methods may conceivably be implemented correctly, in our opinion, the real focus of addressing measurement error should be directed toward scores on the examination of interest— standard errors associated with the test itself. In this context, we examine two methods to estimate the impact of imprecision of test score responses on the misclassification of examinees.

Estimation of Classification Errors for Groups of Examinees

CTT Estimation of Misclassification

Estimates of test score reliability may be used to determine the expected rates of misclassification of examinees due to measurement error. To reiterate, *all* tests yield observed scores that are contaminated to a certain extent by error. Two types of error may occur: (a) *False positives* happen when an examinee who has not mastered the material is designated as *passing* (i.e., having mastered the material), and (b) *false negatives* happen when an examinee who has mastered the material is designated as *nonpassing* (i.e., having not mastered the material).

Procedures for using CTT estimates to develop misclassification rates have been developed by a number of authors (e.g., Huynh & Saunders, 1980). This approach is presented below, based on a paper (Kellow & Willson, 2001) examining misclassification rates associated with the Texas Assessment of Academic Skills (TAAS). The metric of interest was the Texas Learning Index (TLI). The TLI was developed for the purpose of, among other things, providing a consistent passing standard across test forms.

The TLI is a linear standardized scoring transformation with a standard deviation of 15 and an anchor (rather than mean) of 70, which represents the passing standard for a given subtest at a given grade. The TLI is calculated in *z* score form as

$$TLI = [(z_{observed} - z_{passing}) \cdot 15] + 70.$$

Using a statistical procedure developed by Huynh and Saunders (1980), we focused on the estimated true score of examinees when transformed to a TLI score metric. Put simply, what is the passing TLI adjusted for measurement error for a given subtest in a given grade for a given student, and what percentage and number of students met this adjusted criterion but not the standard cut score of 70?

On the basis of this analysis, we estimated that false-negative rates averaged about 3% across grades and content areas. An error rate of 3% may, at first blush, be satisfactory, but it so happens that approximately 80,000 students in the state of Texas were potentially misclassified as nonmasters in one year when in fact their true score would indicate mastery status based on this statistic. Through extrapolation, this would translate to approximately *1.1 million students* nationwide who would fail a high-stakes test despite having a true score indicating mastery in a given year. Haney (2000) notes that another probability exists, that of false positives: A student may pass an exit-level examination when in fact the boundary of error suggests the possibility of a true score below the passing threshold. Haney's survey of 500 randomly selected teachers in the state of Texas indicated that the cost, or risk, of denying a high school diploma to a qualified candidate was rated below only granting (a) a pilot license to an unqualified pilot, (b) a medical license to an unqualified doctor, or (c) a teaching certificate to an unqualified teacher. This evidence suggests that, while erring on the side of caution, respondents clearly regarded false negatives as the greater evil when compared with false positives with respect to awarding a high school diploma. Possession of a high school diploma does not entitle one to any "special" privileges, but it does provide an entry-level qualification for any number of preferred jobs. Since possessing the high school diploma has potentially profound consequences for students who lack such a degree, we agree with both Haney and his survey respondents that, when in doubt, granting a degree to students "on the bubble" may be prudent policy.

IRT Estimation of Misclassification

Rudner (2001) has presented a method for estimating misclassification errors based on an IRT formulation. The IRT approach has an advantage over classical methods in that, in addition to yielding an overall reliability estimate, standard errors of measurement (SEMs) can be estimated for each score in the distribution. Scores that deviate more from the mean typically have more associated error, and thus the associated SEM is larger than the error associated with scores closer to the mean (Price, Raju, Lurie, Wilkins, & Zhu, 2004). Rudner reasoned that, since IRT reliability estimates can be obtained at each value of theta (θ), which corresponds to a true score for a group of examinees at a given level, this estimate could be used to determine misclassification rates at each level of examinee performance. This would represent a conceptual improvement over traditional CTT methods. Clearly, the relationship between the SEM and the observed score becomes less relevant to the extent that the observed score deviates from the prescribed passing cut point; however, observed scores that abut or are close to the cut deserve special consideration in light of the SEM.

An excellent program, available at http://pareonline.net/misclass/class.asp, is provided by Rudner (2001) that illustrates the impact of changing cut scores in relation to observed scores and the mean of the distribution. As one might expect, when cut scores are lowered based on the standard error, the rate of false negatives decreases, while the rate of false-positive results increases. Of course, an upward shift in the cut point would result in the opposite effect: More examinees would be erroneously classified as nonmasters while the number of examinees misclassified as masters would decrease. These results would apply to any cut score adjustment used whether based on CTT or IRT methods and would be violated only when scores were distributed in an unusual fashion.

A full explication of the mathematical logic of the IRT approach is beyond the scope of this chapter. Interested readers are strongly encouraged to explore both the paper and the program developed by Rudner (2001).

Recommendations for the Estimation of Classification Errors for Groups of Examinees

The principal disadvantage of CTT methods for estimating misclassification rates is the use of a single estimate of reliability for the observed scores. IRT methods offer a better alternative in that standard error around a determined cut score can be uniquely determined. The IRT method, however, is generally considered a large sample technique. While modern methods such as IRT have a number of desirable features, they are generally considered inappropriate for small samples. In addition, there is a conceptual simplicity with CTT that avoids a number of assumptions associated with IRT. While most large testing companies routinely report conditional SEM estimates for a given score, it may be that CTT methods are more tractable for small-scale efforts. The definition of what constitutes a small-scale versus large-scale testing process is not easily made. Since, in our experience, most high-stakes test development efforts involve thousands of examinees, IRT seems to be a best solution. In addition, IRT methods may be used to map both selected-response and constructed-response items onto the same scale, which is a decided advantage over the CTT method. Nevertheless, it is important that simulation studies based on empirical parameter estimates be conducted with IRT models when multidimensional structures are present, such as in most reading and math tests to evaluate the problems involved in standard-setting methods.

"Authentic" Methods of Student Classification

Increasingly, efforts to gauge student learning have emphasized "authentic" assessments, such as portfolio, product, and performance evidence of content mastery (Popham, 2002). These methods are appealing to many because of the focus on truly "learned skills" as opposed to pencil-and-paper mastery. We are sanguine about such approaches, particularly with respect to informal evaluations of student progress. But, notwithstanding the potential "richness" of such assessment methods, there are evident complications when relying on human observers to rate or rank such data. The problems associated with using scoring rubrics, including the inherent vagaries associated with using a rubric approach, and the subsequent potential for both random and systematic error variance are substantial. Interested readers are referred to Popham (2002) and Carey (2001) for contemporary thinking on this issue.

We hope the reader has noted the reservations we have expressed throughout this chapter about using tests to classify persons, particularly the use of CRT methods in educational settings. We conclude with a few comments related to this issue.

Concluding Remarks

The purpose of classifying people has a long history in psychology, with roots in the Army Alpha test of World War I, if not earlier (e.g., classifying gifted students based on Stanford-Binet scores of three standard deviations above the mean). Since standard setting is intended to scale persons, placing them into two or more groups, it formally fits into the theory of scaling, which is the measurement process of assigning a number or label to an observed behavior. When the criterion condition is a state (e.g., possessing bipolar disorder or not), methods using contrasted groups are used with statistical methods such as discriminant analysis. These require longitudinal studies in which a sample of the targeted population is assessed and then followed over a period of time, at the end of which the criterion state is determined. In areas such as career

interest, such studies have lasted for decades, compiling evidence for the validity of the assessment process using multiple indicators in criterion outcomes, which include performance appraisal, satisfaction, career changing, longevity in career, and many other considerations. In standard setting for state-mandated testing, most criteria focus on performance at the next grade level, and only for exit-type tests is there a less well-defined criterion of "life competency" related to computation, literacy, or citizenship. Thus, the time frame is no more than a year, not an onerous period in which to study outcomes.

In standard setting, there has been little effort to develop sampling-based trials with longitudinal follow-ups. It is not clear why such trials are avoided since in situations such as state-mandated assessments, it is relatively easy to construct designs in which multiple-matrix sampling of items is embedded into existing assessments (as is done with assessments such as the SAT). While longitudinal follow-ups are expensive to conduct in most applications, in state assessments, the sampled groups can be tracked over the next year and various criteria measured more easily. Since the intent of standard setting in state assessments is, for most grades, to predict success in the following grade, and since states collect much of the data relevant to that success, correlating the item measurement in one year with the item, subtest, and total test scores for the following year is feasible. The data from such predictive analyses would then be available for standard-setting judging panels as discussed above. Even retention in grade can be examined as an outcome, as long as the test itself has not contaminated the decision. Since, in most states, the test scores are not made available before retention decisions have been made, this has up to now been a potentially useful criterion as well.

The interesting limitation on longitudinal validity methods applied to standard-setting evidence is that CRTs do not necessarily lend themselves well to predictive validity analysis. This is ironic in that the standard-setting method is intended to produce a cut score for a CRT at one grade that is predictive of performance at the next. While the correlation between total test score performance at one grade and the next in an area such as reading may be high, it tends to be due to different growth trajectories for students that result in increasing variance on the tests. Individual items on CRT tests may exhibit little predictive validity themselves by the very nature of CRT item development and selection, which is content and domain specific to the grade level. In social studies, for example, studying American history in one grade and state history in the next grade has little construct validity for the standard-setting process. In areas such as reading, the procedures and focus change over the course of the curriculum across grades. What is measured then is a global construct that itself changes, particularly from the early elementary grades to the later ones. In mathematics, the curriculum is generally hierarchically organized, but in upper elementary grades, specific topics are added that do not necessarily provide any prediction about different topics in later grades beyond the general "mathematics ability" construct that seems to be the target of standard setting. Learning about geometry properties in Grade 7 may do little to assist or prepare students for statistical data analysis in Grade 8. Even expert teachers will have little experience beyond assuming good students will succeed and poor ones fail in rating individual items for future success. The lack of conceptual focus on what is assessed in CRT approaches to testing with respect to later performance limits any standard-setting process to a sort of "here is what a minimally proficient student is expected to do on this test, but it really does not relate much to what they do next year."

The issues related to predictive validity above are of paramount concern, but we are not sanguine that appropriate predictive methods will be considered. Although such methods are commonplace in other testing arenas, stakeholders in the educational process have yet to include them in contemporary practice. We believe strongly that such evidence is vital not only as a source of evidence in standard-setting procedures but also in determining the utility of these tests overall.

REFERENCES

American Association on Mental Retardation. (2005, March). *Definition of mental retardation.* Retrieved February 11, 2006, from http://www.aamr.org/Policies/faq_mental_retardation.shtml

Anastasi, A. (1988). *Psychological testing* (6th ed.). New York: Macmillan.

Asch, S. (1956). Studies of independence and conformity: A minority of one against a unanimous majority. *Psychological Monographs, 70*(9), 111–119.

Berk, R. (1986). A consumer's guide to setting performance standards of criterion-referenced tests. *Review of Educational Research, 56,* 137–172.

Brandon, P. R. (2002). Two versions of the contrasting-groups standard-setting method: A review. *Measurement and Evaluation in Counseling and Development, 35,* 161–181.

Brandon, P. R. (2004). Conclusions about frequently studied modified Angoff standard-setting topics. *Applied Measurement in Education, 17,* 59–88.

Busch, J. C., & Jaeger, R. M. (1990). Influence of type of judge, normative information, and discussion on standards recommended for the National Teacher Examinations. *Journal of Educational Measurement, 27,* 145–163.

Carey, L. M. (2001). *Measuring and evaluating school learning.* Needham Heights, MA: Allyn & Bacon.

Chin, R. N., & Hertz, N. R. (2002). Alternative approaches to standard setting for licensing and certification examinations. *Applied Measurement in Education, 15,* 1–14.

Cizek, G. (2001). Conjectures on the rise and call of standard setting: An introduction to context and practice. In G. Cizek (Ed.), *Setting performance standards: Concepts, methods, and perspectives* (pp. 3–17). Mahwah, NJ: Lawrence Erlbaum.

Clauser, B. E., & Clyman, S. G. (1994). A contrasting groups approach to standard setting for performance assessments of clinical skills. *Academic Medicine, 69,* 542–544.

Crocker, L., & Algina, J. (1986). *Introduction to classical and modern test theory.* New York: Harcourt Brace.

Ebel, R. L. (1972). *Essentials of educational measurement* (2nd ed.). Englewood Cliffs, NJ: Prentice Hall.

Glass, G. V. (1978). Standards and criteria. *Journal of Educational Measurement, 15,* 237–261.

Hambleton, R. K. (2001). Setting performance standards on educational assessments and criteria for evaluating the process. In G. Cizek (Ed.), *Setting performance standards: Concepts, methods and perspectives* (pp. 89–116). Mahwah, NJ: Lawrence Erlbaum.

Hambleton, R. K., & Plake, B. (1997, April). *An anchor-based procedure for setting standards on performance assessments.* Paper presented at the annual meeting of the American Educational Research Association, Chicago.

Haney, W. (2000). The myth of the Texas miracle in education. *Education Policy Analysis Archives, 8*(41). Retrieved October 11, 2005, from http://epaa.asu.edu/epaa/v8n41/

Hibshmann, T. (2004). *Considerations related to setting cut scores for teacher tests.* Kentucky Education Standards Board. Retrieved January 19, 2006, from http://www.kyepsb.net/documents/Stats/Journals/cut_score_analysis.pdf

Hunyh, H., & Saunders, J. C. (1980). Accuracy of two procedures for estimating reliability of mastery tests. *Journal of Educational Measurement, 17,* 351–358.

Impara, J. C., & Plake, B. S. (1997). Standard setting: An alternative approach. *Journal of Educational Measurement, 34,* 353–366.

Jaeger, R. M. (1991). Selection of judges for standard-setting. *Educational Measurement: Issues and Practice, 10*(2), 3–10.

Kane, M. (1998). Choosing between examinee-centered and test-centered standard-setting methods. *Educational Assessment, 5,* 129–145.

Kellow, J. T., & Willson, V. L. (2001). Consequences of (mis)use of the Texas Assessment of Academic Skills (TAAS) for high-stakes decisions: A comment on Haney and the Texas miracle in education. *Practical Assessment, Research, and Evaluation, 7*(24). Retrieved December 14, 2005, from http://ericae.net/pare/getvn.asp?v=7&n=24

Kiplinger, V. L. (1997). *The bookmark procedure: Specification of performance levels for the Colorado student assessment program.* Colorado Department of Education. Retrieved June 22, 2006, from www.cde.state.co.us/cdeassess/csap/asbookmk.htm

Lewis, D. M., & Green, D. R. (1997, April). *The validity of performance level descriptors.* Paper presented at the Council of Chief State School Officers National Conference on Large Scale Assessment, Phoenix, AZ.

Lin, J. (n.d.). *The bookmark standard setting procedure: Strengths and weaknesses.* Alberta, Canada: Centre for Research in Applied Measurement and Evaluation. Retrieved June 12, 2006, from www.education.ualberta.ca/educ/psych/crame/files/standard_setting.pdf

Linn, R. L. (2003). Performance standards: Utility for different uses of assessments. *Education Policy Analysis Archives, 11*(31). Retrieved December 1, 2005, from http://epaa.asu.edu/epaa/v11n31/

MacCann, R. G., & Stanley, G. (2004). Estimating the standard error of the judging in a modified-Angoff standard setting procedure. *Practical Assessment, Research, and Evaluation, 9*(5). Retrieved December 3, 2005, from http://PAREonline.net/getvn.asp?v=9&n=5

Mills, C. N. (1983). A comparison of three methods of establishing cutoff scores on criterion-referenced tests. *Journal of Educational Measurement, 20,* 283–292.

Mitzel, H., Lewis, D., Patz, R., & Green, D. (2001). The bookmark procedure: Psychological perspectives. In G. Cizek (Ed.), *Setting performance standards: Concepts, methods, and perspectives* (pp. 249–281). Mahwah, NJ: Lawrence Erlbaum.

Nedelsky, L. (1954). Absolute grading standards for objective tests. *Educational and Psychological Measurement, 14,* 3–19.

Popham, W. J. (2002). *Classroom assessment: What teachers need to know.* Boston: Allyn & Bacon.

Price, L. R., Raju, N., Lurie, N., Wilkins, C., & Zhu, J. (2004, July). *Conditional standard errors of measurement for composite scores on the WPPSI-III.* Paper presented at the annual meeting of the American Psychological Association, Honolulu, HI.

Ricker, K. L. (2004). *Setting cutscores: Critical review of Angoff and modified-Angoff methods.* Alberta: Centre for Research in Applied Measurement and Evaluation, University of Edmonton, Alberta.

Ross, L., Bierbrauer, G., & Hoffman, S. (1976). The role of attribution processes in conformity and dissent: Revisiting the Asch situation. *American Psychologist, 31,* 148–157.

Rudner, L. M. (2001). Computing the expected proportions of misclassified examinees. *Practical Assessment, Research & Evaluation, 7*(14). Retrieved December 3, 2005, from http://PAREonline.net/getvn.asp?v=7&n=14

Shepard, L., Glaser, R., Linn, R., & Bohrnstedt, G. (1993). *Setting performance standards for student achievement tests.* Stanford, CA: National Academy of Education.

Skaggs, G., & Tessema, A. (2001, April). *Item disordinality with the bookmark standard setting procedure.* Paper presented at the annual meeting of the National Council for Measurement in Education, Seattle, WA.

Suett, P. (n.d.). *The changing options for delivering standards education.* Retrieved June 19, 2006, from http://www.ansi.org/news_publications/other_documents/standards_education.aspx?menuid=7

Zieky, M. J. (2001). So much has changed: How the setting of cut scores has evolved since the 1980s. In G. Cizek (Ed.), *Setting performance standards: Concepts, methods and perspectives* (pp. 19–51). Mahwah, NJ: Lawrence Erlbaum.

3

Best Practices in Interrater Reliability

Three Common Approaches

Steven E. Stemler

Jessica Tsai

The concept of interrater reliability[1] permeates many facets of modern society. For example, court cases based on a trial by jury require unanimous agreement from jurors regarding the verdict, life-threatening medical diagnoses often require a second or third opinion from health care professionals, student essays written in the context of high-stakes standardized testing receive points based on the judgment of multiple readers, and Olympic competitions, such as figure skating, award medals to participants based on quantitative ratings of performance provided by an international panel of judges.

Any time multiple judges are used to determine important outcomes, certain technical and procedural questions emerge. Some of the more common questions are as follows: How many raters do we need to be confident in our results? What is the minimum level of agreement that my raters should achieve? And is it necessary for raters to agree exactly, or is it acceptable for them to differ from each other so long as their difference is systematic and can therefore be corrected?

Key Questions to Ask Before Conducting an Interrater Reliability Study

If you are at the point in your research where you are considering conducting an interrater reliability study, then there are three important questions worth considering:

1. What is the purpose of conducting your interrater reliability study?

2. What is the nature of your data?

3. What resources do you have at your disposal (e.g., technical expertise, time, money)?

The answers to these questions will help determine the best statistical approach to use for your study.

What Is the Purpose of Conducting Your Interrater Reliability Study?

There are three main reasons why people may wish to conduct an interrater reliability study. Perhaps the most popular reason is that the researcher is interested in getting a single final score on a variable (such as an essay grade) for use in subsequent data analysis and statistical modeling but first must prove that the scoring is not "subjective" or "biased." For example, this is often the goal in the context of educational testing where large-scale state testing programs might use multiple raters to grade student essays for the ultimate purpose of providing an overall appraisal of each student's current level of academic achievement. In such cases, the documentation of interrater reliability is usually just a means to an end—the end of creating a single summary score for use in subsequent data analyses—and the researcher may have little inherent interest in the details of the interrater reliability analysis per se. This is a perfectly acceptable reason for wanting to conduct an interrater reliability study; however, researchers must be particularly cautious about the assumptions they are making when summarizing the data from multiple raters to generate a single summary score for each student. For example, simply taking the mean of the ratings of two independent raters may, in some circumstances, actually lead to biased estimates of student ability, even when the scoring by independent raters is highly correlated (we return to this point later in the chapter).

A second common reason for conducting an interrater reliability study is to evaluate a newly developed scoring rubric to see if it is "working" or if it needs to be modified. For example, one may wish to evaluate the accuracy of multiple ratings in the absence of a "gold standard." Consider a situation in which independent judges must rate the creativity of a piece of artwork. Because there is no objective rule to indicate the "true" creativity of a piece of art, a minimum first step in establishing that there is such a thing as creativity is to demonstrate that independent raters can at least reliably classify objects according to how well they meet the assumptions of the construct. Thus, independent observers must subjectively interpret the work of art and rate the degree to which an underlying construct (e.g., creativity) is present. In situations such as these, the establishment of interrater reliability becomes

a goal in and of itself. If a researcher is able to demonstrate that independent parties can reliably rate objects along the continuum of the construct, this provides some good objective evidence for the existence of the construct. A natural subsequent step is to analyze individual scores according to the criteria.

Finally, a third reason for conducting an interrater reliability study is to validate how well ratings reflect a known "true" state of affairs (e.g., a validation study). For example, suppose that a researcher believes that he or she has developed a new colon cancer screening technique that should be highly predictive. The first thing the researcher might do is train another provider to use the technique and compare the extent to which the independent rater agrees with him or her on the classification of people who have cancer and those who do not. Next, the researcher might attempt to predict the prevalence of cancer using a formal diagnosis via more traditional methods (e.g., biopsy) to compare the extent to which the new technique is accurately predicting the diagnosis generated by the known technique. In other words, the reason for conducting an interrater reliability study in this circumstance is because it is not enough that independent raters have high levels of interrater reliability; what really matters is the level of reliability in predicting the actual occurrence of cancer as compared with a "gold standard"—in this case, the rate of classification based on an established technique.

Once you have determined the primary purpose for conducting an interrater reliability study, the next step is to consider the nature of the data that you have or will collect.

What Is the Nature of Your Data?

There are four important points to consider with regard to the nature of your data. First, it is important to know whether your data are considered nominal, ordinal, interval, or ratio (Stevens, 1946). Certain statistical techniques are better suited to certain types of data. For example, if the data you are evaluating are nominal (i.e., the differences between the categories you are rating are qualitative), then there are relatively few statistical methods for you to choose from (e.g., percent agreement, Cohen's kappa). If, on the other hand, the data are measured at the ratio level, then the data meet the criteria for use by most of the techniques discussed in this chapter.

Once you have determined the type of data used for the rating scale, you should then examine the distribution of your data using a histogram or bar chart. Are the ratings of each rater normally distributed, uniformly distributed, or skewed? If the rating data exhibit restricted variability, this can severely affect consistency estimates as well as consensus-based estimates, threatening the validity of the interpretations made from the interrater reliability estimates. Thus, it is important to have some idea of the distribution of ratings in order to select the best statistical technique for analyzing the data.

The third important thing to investigate is whether the judges who rated the data agreed on the underlying trait definition. For example, if two raters are judging the creativity of a piece of artwork, one rater may believe that creativity is 50% novelty and 50% task appropriateness. By contrast, another rater may judge creativity to consist of 50% novelty, 35% task appropriateness, and 15% elaboration. These differences in perception will introduce extraneous error into the ratings. The extent to which your raters are defining the construct in a similar way can be empirically evaluated using measurement approaches to interrater reliability (e.g., factor analysis, a procedure that is further described later in this chapter).

Finally, even if the raters agree as to the structure, do they assign people into the same category along the continuum, or does one judge assign a person "poor" in mathematics while another judge classifies that same person as "good"? In other words, are they using the rating categories the same way? This can be evaluated using consensus estimates (e.g., via tests of marginal homogeneity).

After specifying the purpose of the study and thinking about the nature of the data that will be used in the analysis, the final question to ask is the pragmatic question of what resources you have at your disposal.

What Resources Do You Have at Your Disposal?

As most people know from their life experience, "best" does not always mean most expensive or most resource intensive. Similarly, within

the context of interrater reliability, it is not always necessary to choose a technique that yields the maximum amount of information or that requires sophisticated statistical analyses in order to gain useful information. There are times when a crude estimate may yield sufficient information—for example, within the context of a low-stakes, exploratory research study. There are other times when the estimates must be as precise as possible—for example, within the context of situations that have direct, important stakes for the participants in the study.

The question of resources often has an influence on the way that interrater reliability studies are conducted. For example, if you are a newcomer who is running a pilot study to determine whether to continue on a particular line of research, and time and money are limited, then a simpler technique such as the percent agreement, kappa, or even correlational estimates may be the best match. On the other hand, if you are in a situation where you have a high-stakes test that needs to be graded relatively quickly, and money is not a major issue, then a more advanced measurement approach (e.g., the many-facets Rasch model) is most likely the best selection.

As an additional example, if the goal of your study is to understand the underlying nature of a construct that to date has no objective, agreed-on definition (e.g., wisdom), then achieving consensus among raters in applying a scoring criterion will be of paramount importance. By contrast, if the goal of the study is to generate summary scores for individuals that will be used in later analyses, and it is not critical that raters come to exact agreement on how to use a rating scale, then consistency or measurement estimates of interrater reliability will be sufficient.

Summary

Once you have answered the three main questions discussed in this section, you will be in a much better position to choose a suitable technique for your project. In the next section of this chapter, we will discuss (a) the most popular statistics used to compute interrater reliability, (b) the computation and interpretation of the results of statistics using worked examples, (c) the implications for summarizing data that follow from each technique, and (d) the advantages and disadvantages of each technique.

CHOOSING THE BEST
APPROACH FOR THE JOB

Many textbooks in the field of educational and psychological measurement and statistics (e.g., Anastasi & Urbina, 1997; Cohen, Cohen, West, & Aiken, 2003; Crocker & Algina, 1986; Hopkins, 1998; von Eye & Mun, 2004) describe interrater reliability as if it were a unitary concept lending itself to a single, "best" approach across all situations. Yet, the methodological literature related to interrater reliability constitutes a hodgepodge of statistical techniques, each of which provides a particular kind of solution to the problem of establishing interrater reliability.

Building on the work of Uebersax (2002) and J. R. Hayes and Hatch (1999), Stemler (2004) has argued that the wide variety of statistical techniques used for computing interrater reliability coefficients may be theoretically classified into one of three broad categories: (a) consensus estimates, (b) consistency estimates, and (c) measurement estimates. Statistics associated with these three categories differ in their assumptions about the purpose of the interrater reliability study, the nature of the data, and the implications for summarizing scores from various raters.

Consensus Estimates of Interrater Reliability

Consensus estimates are often used when one is attempting to demonstrate that a construct that traditionally has been considered highly subjective (e.g., creativity, wisdom, hate) can be reliably captured by independent raters. The assumption is that if independent raters are able to come to exact agreement about how to apply the various levels of a scoring rubric (which operationally defines behaviors associated with the construct), then this provides some defensible evidence for the existence of the construct. Furthermore, if two independent judges demonstrate high levels of agreement in their application of a scoring rubric to rate behaviors, then the two judges may be said to share a common interpretation of the construct.

Consensus estimates tend to be the most useful when data are nominal in nature and different levels of the rating scale represent qualitatively different ideas. Consensus estimates also can be useful when different levels of the rating scale are assumed to represent a linear continuum of the construct but are ordinal in nature (e.g., a Likert-type scale). In such cases, the judges must come to exact agreement about each of the quantitative levels of the construct under investigation.

The three most popular types of consensus estimates of interrater reliability found in the literature include (a) percent agreement and its variants, (b) Cohen's kappa and its variants (Agresti, 1996; Cohen, 1960, 1968; Krippendorff, 2004), and (c) odds ratios. Other less frequently used statistics that fall under this category include Jaccard's J and the G-Index (see Barrett, 2001).

Percent Agreement. Perhaps the most popular method for computing a consensus estimate of interrater reliability is through the use of the simple percent agreement statistic. For example, in a study examining creativity, Sternberg and Lubart (1995) asked sets of judges to rate the level of creativity associated with each of a number of products generated by study participants (e.g., draw a picture illustrating Earth from an insect's point of view, write an essay based on the title "2983"). The goal of their study was to demonstrate that creativity could be detected and objectively scored with high levels of agreement across independent judges. The authors reported percent agreement levels across raters of .92 (Sternberg & Lubart, 1995, p. 31).

The percent agreement statistic has several advantages. For example, it has a strong intuitive appeal, it is easy to calculate, and it is easy to explain. The statistic also has some distinct disadvantages, however. If the behavior of interest has a low or high incidence of occurrence in the population, then it is possible to get artificially inflated percent agreement figures simply because most of the values fall under one category of the rating scale (J. R. Hayes & Hatch, 1999). Another disadvantage to using the simple percent agreement figure is that it is often time-consuming and labor-intensive to train judges to the point of exact agreement.

One popular modification of the percent agreement figure found in the testing literature involves broadening the definition of agreement by including the adjacent scoring categories on the rating scale. For example, some testing programs include writing sections that are scored by judges using a rating scale with levels ranging from 1 (*low*) to 6 (*high*) (College Board, 2006). If a percent adjacent agreement approach were used to score this section of the exam, this would mean that the judges would not need to come to exact agreement about the ratings they assign to each participant; rather, so long as the ratings did not differ by more than one point above or below the other judge, then the two judges would be said to have reached consensus. Thus, if Rater A assigns an essay a score of 3 and Rater B assigns the same essay a score of 4, the two raters are close enough together to say that they "agree," even though their agreement is not exact.

The rationale for the adjacent percent agreement approach is often a pragmatic one. It is extremely difficult to train independent raters to come to exact agreement, no matter how good one's scoring rubric. Yet, raters often give scores that are "pretty close" to the same, and we do not want to discard this information. Thus, the thinking is that if we have a situation in which two raters never differ by more than one score point in assigning their ratings, then we have a justification for taking the average score across all ratings. This logic holds under two conditions. First, the difference between raters must be randomly distributed across items. In other words, Rater A should not give systematically lower scores than Rater B. Second, the scores assigned by raters must be evenly distributed across all possible score categories. In other words, both raters should give equal numbers of 1s, 2s, 3s, 4s, 5s, and 6s across the population of essays that they have read. If both of these assumptions are met, then the adjacent percent agreement approach is defensible. If, however, either of these assumptions is violated, this could lead to a situation in which the validity of the resultant summary scores is dubious (see the box below).

Consider a situation in which Rater A systematically assigns scores that are one power lower than Rater B. Assume that they have each rated a common set of 100 essays. If we average the scores of the two raters across all essays to arrive at individual student scores, this seems, on the surface, to be defensible because it really does not matter whether Rater A or Rater B is assigning the high or low score because even if Rater A and Rater B had no systematic difference in severity of ratings, the average score would be the same. However, suppose that dozens of raters are used to score the essays. Imagine that Rater C is also called in to rate the same essay for a different sample of students. Rater C is paired up with Rater B within the context of an overlapping design to maximize rater efficiency (e.g., McArdle, 1994). Suppose that we find a situation in which Rater B is systematically lower than Rater C in assigning grades. In other words, Rater A is systematically one point lower than Rater B, and Rater B is systematically one point lower than Rater C.

On the surface, again, it seems logical to average the scores assigned by Rater B and Rater C. Yet, we now find ourselves in a situation in which the students rated by the Rater B/C pair score systematically one point higher than the students rated by the Rater A/B pair, even though neither combination of raters differed by more than one score point in their ratings, thereby demonstrating "interrater reliability." Which student would you rather be? The one who was lucky enough to draw the B/C rater combination or the one who unfortunately was scored by the A/B combination?

Thus, in order to make a validity argument for summarizing the results of multiple raters, it is not enough to demonstrate adjacent percent agreement between rater pairs; it must also be demonstrated that there is no systematic difference in rater severity between the rater set pairs.

This can be demonstrated (and corrected for in the final score) through the use of the many-facet Rasch model.

Now let us examine what happens if the second assumption of the adjacent percent agreement approach is violated. If you are a rater for a large testing company, and you are told that you will be retained only if you are able to demonstrate interrater reliability with everyone else, you would naturally look for your best strategy to maximize interrater reliability. If you are then told that your scores can differ by no more than one point from the other raters, you would quickly discover that your best bet then is to avoid giving any ratings at the extreme ends of the scale (i.e., a rating of 1 or a rating of 6). Why? Because a rating at the extreme end of the scale (e.g., 6) has two potential scores with which it can overlap (i.e., 5 or 6), whereas a rating of 5 would allow you to potentially "agree" with three scores

(Continued)

(Continued)

(i.e., 4, 5, or 6), thereby maximizing your chances of agreeing with the second rater. Thus, it is entirely likely that the scale will go from being a 6-point scale to a 4-point scale, reducing the overall variability in scores given across the spectrum of participants. If only four categories are used, then the percent agreement statistics will be artificially inflated due to chance factors. For example, when a scale is 1 to 6, two participants are expected to agree on ratings by chance alone only 17% of the time. When the scale is reduced to 1 to 4, the percent agreement expected by chance jumps to 25%. If three categories, a 33% chance agreement is expected; if two categories, a 50% chance agreement is expected. In other words, a 6-point scale that uses adjacent percent agreement scoring is most likely functionally equivalent to a 4-point scale that uses exact agreement scoring.

This approach is advantageous in that it relaxes the strict criterion that the judges agree exactly. On the other hand, percent agreement using adjacent categories can lead to inflated estimates of interrater reliability if there are only a limited number of categories to choose from (e.g., a 1–4 scale). If the rating scale has a limited number of points, then nearly all points will be adjacent, and it would be surprising to find agreement lower than 90%.

Cohen's Kappa. Another popular consensus estimate of interrater reliability is Cohen's kappa statistic (Cohen, 1960, 1968). Cohen's kappa was designed to estimate the degree of consensus between two judges and determine whether the level of agreement is greater than would be expected to be observed by chance alone (see Stemler, 2001, for a practical example with calculation). The interpretation of the kappa statistic is slightly different from the interpretation of the percent agreement figure (Agresti, 1996). A value of zero on kappa does not indicate that the two judges did not agree at all; rather, it indicates that the two judges did not agree with each other any more than would be predicted by chance alone. Consequently, it is possible to have negative values of kappa if judges agree less often than chance would predict. Kappa is a highly useful statistic when one is concerned that the percent agreement statistic may be artificially inflated due to the fact that most observations fall into a single category.

Kappa is often useful within the context of exploratory research. For example, Stemler and Bebell (1999) conducted a study aimed at detecting the various purposes of schooling articulated in school mission statements. Judges were given a scoring rubric that listed 10 possible thematic categories under which the main idea of each mission statement could be classified (e.g., social development, cognitive development, civic development). Judges then read a series of mission statements and attempted to classify each sampling unit according to the major purpose of schooling articulated. If both judges consistently rated the dominant theme of the mission statement as representing elements of citizenship, then they were said to have communicated with each other in a meaningful way because they had both classified the statement in the same way. If one judge classified the major theme as social development, and the other judge classified the major theme as citizenship, then a breakdown in shared understanding occurred. In that case, the judges were not coming to a consensus on how to apply the levels of the scoring rubric. The authors chose to use the kappa statistic to evaluate the degree of consensus because they did not expect the frequency of the major themes of the mission statements to be evenly distributed across the 10 categories of their scoring rubric.

Although some authors (Landis & Koch, 1977) have offered guidelines for interpreting kappa values, other authors (Krippendorff, 2004; Uebersax, 2002) have argued that the kappa values for different items or from different studies cannot be meaningfully compared unless the base rates are identical. Consequently, these authors suggest that although the statistic gives some indication as to whether the agreement is better than that predicted by chance alone, it is difficult to apply rules of thumb for interpreting kappa across different circumstances. Instead, Uebersax (2002) suggests that researchers using the kappa coefficient look at it for up or down evaluation of whether ratings are different from chance, but they should not get too invested in its interpretation.

Krippendorff (2004) has introduced a new coefficient alpha into the literature that claims to be superior to kappa because alpha is capable of incorporating the information from multiple raters, dealing with missing data, and yielding a chance-corrected estimate of interrater reliability. The major disadvantage of Krippendorff's alpha is that it is computationally complex; however, statistical macros that compute Krippendorff's alpha have been created and are freely available (K. Hayes, 2006). In addition, however, some research suggests that in practice, alpha values tend to be nearly identical to kappa values (Dooley, 2006).

Odds Ratios. A third consensus estimate of interrater reliability is the odds ratio. The odds ratio is most often used in circumstances where raters are making dichotomous ratings (e.g., presence/ absence of a phenomenon), although it can be extended to ordered category ratings. In a 2 × 2 contingency table, the odds ratio indicates how much the odds of one rater making a given rating (e.g., positive/negative) increase for cases when the other rater has made the same rating. For example, suppose that in a music competition with 100 contestants, Rater 1 gives 90 of them a positive score for vocal ability, while in the same sample of 100 contestants, Rater 2 only gives 20 of them a positive score for vocal ability. The odds of Rater 1 giving a positive vocal ability score are 90 to 10, or 9:1, while the odds of Rater 2 giving a positive vocal ability score are only 20 to 80, or 1:4 = 0.25:1. Now, 9/0.25 = 36, so the odds ratio is 36. Within the context of interrater reliability, the important idea captured by the odds ratio is whether it deviates substantially from 1.0. From the perspective of interrater reliability, it would be most desirable to have an odds ratio that is close to 1.0, which would indicate that Rater 1 and Rater 2 rated the same proportion of contestants as having high vocal ability. The larger the odds ratio value, the larger the discrepancy there is between raters in terms of their level of consensus.

The odds ratio has the advantage of being easy to compute and is familiar from other statistical applications (e.g., logistic regression). The disadvantage to the odds ratio is that it is most intuitive within the context of a 2 × 2 contingency table with dichotomous rating categories. Although the technique can be generalized to ordered category ratings, it involves extra computational complexity that undermines its intuitive advantage. Furthermore, as Osborne (2006) has pointed out, although the odds ratio is straightforward to compute, the interpretation of the statistic is not always easy to convey, particularly to a lay audience.

Computing Common Consensus Estimates of Interrater Reliability

Let us now turn to a practical example of how to calculate each of these coefficients. As an example data set, we will draw from Stemler, Grigorenko, Jarvin, and Sternberg's (2006) study in which they developed augmented versions of the Advanced Placement Psychology Examination. Participants were required to complete a number of essay items that were subsequently scored by different sets of raters. Essay Question 1, Part d was a question that asked participants to give advice to a friend who is having trouble sleeping, based on what they know about various theories of sleep. The item was scored using a 5-point scoring rubric. For this particular item, 75 participants received scores from two independent raters.

Percent Agreement. Percent agreement is calculated by adding up the number of cases that received the same rating by both judges and dividing that number by the total number of cases rated by the two judges. Using SPSS, one can run the crosstabs procedure and generate a table to facilitate the calculation (see Table 3.1). The percent agreement on this item is 42%; however, the percent adjacent agreement is 87%.

Cohen's Kappa. The formula for computing Cohen's kappa is listed in Formula 1.

$$ \kappa = \frac{P_A - P_C}{1 - P_C}, \tag{1} $$

where P_A = proportion of units on which the raters agree, and P_C = the proportion of units for which agreement is expected by chance.

It is possible to compute Cohen's kappa in SPSS by simply specifying in the crosstabs procedure the desire to produce Cohen's kappa (see Table 3.1). For this data set, the kappa value

Table 3.1   SPSS Code and Output for Percent Agreement and Percent Adjacent Agreement and Cohen's Kappa

SPSS CODE

CROSSTABS

/TABLES = Rater_1 BY Rater_2

/FORMAT = AVALUE TABLES

/STATISTIC = KAPPA

/CELLS = COUNT

/COUNT ROUND CELL

SPSS OUTPUT

		Rater_2					
		0	1	2	3	4	Total
Rater_1	0	1	0	0	0	0	1
	1	1	4	0	0	0	5
	2	1	8	3	1	0	13
	3	0	3	12	10	1	26
	4	0	0	6	11	13	30
Total		3	15	21	22	14	75

RESULTS

Percent agreement = 31/75 = 42%

Percent adjacent agreement = 65/75 = 87%

Cohen's kappa = .23

is .23, which indicates that the two raters agreed on the scoring only slightly more often than we would predict based on chance alone.

Odds Ratios. The formula for computing an odds ratio is shown in Formula 2.

	Rater_2		
Rater_1	+	−	
+	a	b	a + b
−	c	d	c + d
	a + c	b + d	Total

$$OR = \frac{[a/(a + b)]/[b/(a + b)]}{[c/(c + d)]/[d/(c + d)]}$$
$$= \frac{a/b}{c/d} = \frac{ad}{bc}. \tag{2}$$

The SPSS code for computing the odds ratio is shown in Table 3.2. In order to compute the odds ratio using the crosstabs procedure in SPSS, it was necessary to recode the data so that the ratings were dichotomous. Consequently, ratings of 0, 1, and 2 were assigned a value of 0 (failing) while ratings of 3 and 4 were assigned a value of 1 (passing). The odds ratio for the current data set is 30, indicating that there was a substantial difference between the raters in terms of the proportion of students classified as passing versus failing.

Implications for Summarizing Scores From Various Raters

If raters can be trained to the point where they agree on how to assign scores from a rubric, then scores given by the two raters may be treated as equivalent. This fact has practical implications for determining the number of raters needed to complete a study. Thus, the remaining work of rating subsequent items can be split between the raters without both raters having to score all items. Furthermore, the

Table 3.2   SPSS Code and Output for Odds Ratios

SPSS CODE

CROSSTABS

/TABLES = Rater_1 BY Rater_2

/FORMAT = AVALUE TABLES

/STATISTIC = RISK

/CELLS = COUNT

/COUNT ROUND CELL

SPSS OUTPUT

		Rater_2		Total
		.00	1.00	
Rater_1	.00	18	1	19
	1.00	21	35	56
Total		39	36	75

	Value	95% Confidence Interval	
		Lower	Upper
Odds Ratio for Rater_1r (.00 / 1.00)	30.000	3.729	241.357
For cohort Rater_2r = .00	2.526	1.773	3.601
For cohort Rater_2r = 1.00	.084	.012	.574
N of Valid Cases	75		

RESULTS

Odds ratio for Rater 1 (0/1) = 30

summary scores may be calculated by simply taking the score from one of the judges or by averaging the scores given by all of the judges, since high interrater reliability indicates that the judges agree about how to apply the rating scale. A typical guideline found in the literature for evaluating the quality of interrater reliability based on consensus estimates is that they should be 70% or greater. If raters are shown to reach high levels of consensus, then adding more raters adds little extra information from a statistical perspective and is probably not justified from the perspective of resources.

Advantages of Consensus Estimates

One particular advantage of the consensus approach to estimating interrater reliability is that the calculations are easily done by hand.

A second advantage is that the techniques falling within this general category are well suited to dealing with nominal variables whose levels on the rating scale represent qualitatively different categories. A third advantage is that consensus estimates can be useful in diagnosing problems with judges' interpretations of how to apply the rating scale. For example, inspection of the information from a crosstab table may allow the researcher to realize that the judges may be unclear about the rules for when they are supposed to score an item as zero as opposed to when they are supposed to score the item as missing. A visual analysis of the output allows the researcher to go back to the data and clarify the discrepancy or retrain the judges.

When judges exhibit a high level of consensus, it implies that both judges are essentially providing the same information. One implication of a high consensus estimate of interrater reliability is that both judges need not score all remaining items. For example, if there were 100 tests to be scored after the interrater reliability study was finished, it would be most efficient to ask Judge A to rate exams 1 to 50 and Judge B to rate exams 51 to 100 because the two judges have empirically demonstrated that they share a similar meaning for the scoring rubric. In practice, however, it is usually a good idea to build in a 30% overlap between judges even after they have been trained, in order to provide evidence that the judges are not drifting from their consensus as they read more items.

Disadvantages of Consensus Estimates

One disadvantage of consensus estimates is that interrater reliability statistics must be computed separately for each item and for each pair of judges. Consequently, when reporting consensus-based interrater reliability estimates, one should report the minimum, maximum, and median estimates for all items and for all pairs of judges.

A second disadvantage is that the amount of time and energy it takes to train judges to come to exact agreement is often substantial, particularly in applications where exact agreement is unnecessary (e.g., if the exact application of the levels of the scoring rubric is not important, but rather a means to the end of getting a summary score for each respondent).

Third, as Linacre (2002) has noted, training judges to a point of forced consensus may actually reduce the statistical independence of the ratings and threaten the validity of the resulting scores.

Finally, consensus estimates can be overly conservative if two judges exhibit systematic differences in the way that they use the scoring rubric but simply cannot be trained to come to a consensus. As we will see in the next section, it is possible to have a low consensus estimate of interrater reliability while having a high consistency estimate and vice versa. Consequently, sole reliance on consensus estimates of interrater reliability might lead researchers to conclude that "interrater reliability is low" when it may be more precisely stated that the *consensus estimate* of interrater reliability is low.

Consistency Estimates of Interrater Reliability

Consistency estimates of interrater reliability are based on the assumption that it is not really necessary for raters to share a common interpretation of the rating scale, so long as each judge is consistent in classifying the phenomenon according to his or her own definition of the scale. For example, if Rater A assigns a score of 3 to a certain group of essays, and Rater B assigns a score of 1 to that same group of essays, the two raters have not come to a consensus about how to apply the rating scale categories, but the difference in how they apply the rating scale categories is predictable.

Consistency approaches to estimating interrater reliability are most useful when the data are continuous in nature, although the technique can be applied to categorical data if the rating scale categories are thought to represent an underlying continuum along a unidimensional construct. Values greater than .70 are typically acceptable for consistency estimates of interrater reliability (Barrett, 2001).

The three most popular types of consistency estimates are (a) correlation coefficients (e.g., Pearson, Spearman), (b) Cronbach's alpha (Cronbach, 1951), and (c) intraclass correlation. For information regarding additional consistency estimates of interrater reliability, see Bock, Brennan, and Muraki (2002); Burke and Dunlap (2002); LeBreton, Burgess, Kaiser, Atchley, and James (2003); and Uebersax (2002).

Correlation Coefficients. Perhaps the most popular statistic for calculating the degree of consistency between raters is the Pearson correlation coefficient. Correlation coefficients measure the association between independent raters. Values approaching +1 or −1 indicate that the two raters are following a systematic pattern in their ratings, while values approaching zero indicate that it is nearly impossible to predict the score one rater would give by knowing the score the other rater gave. It is important to note that even though the correlation between scores assigned by two judges may be nearly perfect, there may be substantial mean differences between the raters. In other words, two raters may differ in the absolute values they assign to each rating by two points; however, so long as there is a 2-point difference for each rating they assign, the raters will have achieved high consistency estimates of interrater reliability. Thus, a large value for a measure of association does not imply that the raters are agreeing on the actual application of the rating scale, only that they are consistent in applying the ratings according to their own unique understanding of the scoring rubric.

The Pearson correlation coefficient can be computed by hand (Glass & Hopkins, 1996) or can easily be computed using most statistical packages. One beneficial feature of the Pearson correlation coefficient is that the scores on the rating scale can be continuous in nature (e.g., they can take on partial values such as 1.5). Like the percent agreement statistic, the Pearson correlation coefficients can be calculated only for one pair of judges at a time and for one item at a time.

A potential limitation of the Pearson correlation coefficient is that it assumes that the data underlying the rating scale are normally distributed. Consequently, if the data from the rating scale tend to be skewed toward one end of the distribution, this will attenuate the upper limit of the correlation coefficient that can be observed. The Spearman rank coefficient provides an approximation of the Pearson correlation coefficient but may be used in circumstances where the data under investigation are not normally distributed. For example, rather than using a continuous rating scale, each judge may rank order the essays that he or she has scored from best to worst. In this case, then, since both ratings being correlated are in the form of rankings, a correlation coefficient can be computed that is governed by the number of pairs of ratings (Glass & Hopkins, 1996). The major disadvantage to Spearman's rank coefficient is that it requires both judges to rate all cases.

Cronbach's Alpha. In situations where more than two raters are used, another approach to computing a consistency estimate of interrater reliability would be to compute Cronbach's alpha coefficient (Crocker & Algina, 1986). Cronbach's alpha coefficient is a measure of internal consistency reliability and is useful for understanding the extent to which the ratings from a group of judges hold together to measure a common dimension. If the Cronbach's alpha estimate among the judges is low, then this implies that the majority of the variance in the total composite score is really due to error variance and not true score variance (Crocker & Algina, 1986).

The major advantage of using Cronbach's alpha comes from its capacity to yield a single consistency estimate of interrater reliability across multiple judges. The major disadvantage of the method is that each judge must give a rating on every case, or else the alpha will only be computed on a subset of the data. In other words, if just one rater fails to score a particular individual, that individual will be left out of the analysis. In addition, as Barrett (2001) has noted, "because of this 'averaging' of ratings, we reduce the variability of the judges' ratings such that when we average all judges' ratings, we effectively remove all the error variance for judges" (p. 7).

Intraclass Correlation. A third popular approach to estimating interrater reliability is through the use of the intraclass correlation coefficient. An interesting feature of the intraclass correlation coefficient is that it confounds two ways in which raters differ: (a) consensus (or bias—i.e., mean differences) and (b) consistency (or association). As a result, the value of the intraclass correlation coefficient will be decreased in situations where there is a low correlation between raters *and* in situations where there are large mean differences between raters. For this reason, the intraclass correlation may be considered a conservative estimate of interrater reliability. If the intraclass correlation coefficient is close to 1, then chances are good that this implies that excellent interrater reliability has been achieved.

The major advantage of the intraclass correlation is its capacity to incorporate information from different types of rater reliability data. On the other hand, as Uebersax (2002) has noted, "If the goal is to give feedback to raters to improve future ratings, one should distinguish between these two sources of disagreement" (p. 5). In addition, because the intraclass correlation represents the ratio of within-subject variance to between-subject variance on a rating scale, the results may not look the same if raters are rating a homogeneous subpopulation as opposed to the general population. Simply by restricting the between-subject variance, the intraclass correlation will be lowered. Therefore, it is important to pay special attention to the population being assessed and to understand that this can influence the value of the intraclass correlation coefficient (ICC). For this reason, ICCs are not directly comparable across populations. Finally, it is important to note that, like the Pearson correlation coefficient, the intraclass correlation coefficient will be attenuated if assumptions of normality in rating data are violated.

Computing Common Consistency Estimates of Interrater Reliability

Let us now turn to a practical example of how to calculate each of these coefficients. We will use the same data set and compute each estimate on the data.

Correlation Coefficients. The formula for computing the Pearson correlation coefficient is listed in Formula 3.

$$r = \frac{\sum XY - \frac{\sum X \sum Y}{N}}{\sqrt{\left(\sum X^2 - \frac{(\sum X)^2}{N}\right)\left(\sum Y^2 - \frac{(\sum Y)^2}{N}\right)}}. \quad (3)$$

Using SPSS, one can run the correlate procedure and generate a table similar to Table 3.3. One may request both Pearson and Spearman correlation coefficients. The Pearson correlation coefficient on this data set is .76; the Spearman correlation coefficient is .74.

Cronbach's Alpha. The Cronbach's alpha value is calculated using Formula 4,

$$\alpha = \frac{N}{N-1}\left(\frac{\sigma_x^2 - \sum_{i=1}^{N}\sigma^2 Y_i}{\sigma_x^2}\right), \quad (4)$$

where

N is the number of components (raters),

σ_x^2 is the variance of the observed total scores, and

$\sigma^2 Y_i$ is the variance of component i.

In order to compute Cronbach's alpha using SPSS, one may simply specify in the crosstabs procedure the desire to produce Cronbach's alpha (see Table 3.4). For this example, the alpha value is .86.

Table 3.3   SPSS Code and Output for Pearson and Spearman Correlations

SPSS CODE

CROSSTABS

/TABLES = Rater_1 BY Rater_2

/FORMAT = AVALUE TABLES

/STATISTIC = CORR KAPPA

/CELLS = COUNT

/COUNT ROUND CELL

SPSS OUTPUT

		Value	Asymp. Std. Error[a]	Approx. T[b]	Asymp. Sig.
Interval by Interval	Pearson's R	.761	.044	10.027	.000[c]
Ordinal by Ordinal	Spearman Correlation	.744	.057	9.504	.000[c]
Measure of Agreement	Kappa	.229	.071	3.765	.000
N of Valid Cases		75			

a. Not assuming the null hypothesis.

b. Using the asymptotic standard error assuming the null hypothesis.

c. Based on normal approximation.

RESULTS

Pearson correlation r = .76

Spearman correlation rho = .74

Table 3.4   SPSS Code and Output for Cronbach's Alpha

SPSS CODE

RELIABILITY

/VARIABLES = Rater_1 Rater_2

/SCALE('ALL VARIABLES') ALL/MODEL = ALPHA

SPSS OUTPUT

Cronbach's Alpha	N of Items
.860	2

RESULTS

Cronbach's alpha = .86

Intraclass Correlation. Formula 5 presents the equation used to compute the intraclass correlation value.

$$ICC = \frac{\sigma^2(b)}{\sigma^2(b) + \sigma^2(w)}, \qquad (5)$$

where

$\sigma^2(b)$ is the variance of the ratings between judges, and

$\sigma^2(w)$ is the pooled variance within raters.

In order to compute intraclass correlation, one may specify the procedure in SPSS using the code listed in Table 3.5. The intraclass correlation coefficient for this data set is .75.

IMPLICATIONS FOR SUMMARIZING SCORES FROM VARIOUS RATERS

It is important to recognize that although consistency estimates may be high, the means and medians of the different judges may be very different. Thus, if one judge consistently gives scores that are 2 points lower on the rating scale than does a second judge, the scores will ultimately need to be corrected for this difference in judge severity if the final scores are to be summarized or subjected to further analyses.

Table 3.5   SPSS Code and Output for Intraclass Correlation

SPSS CODE

RELIABILITY

/VARIABLES = Rater_1 Rater_2

/SCALE('ALL VARIABLES') ALL/MODEL = ALPHA

/ICC = MODEL(MIXED) TYPE(CONSISTENCY) CIN = 95 TESTVAL = 0

SPSS OUTPUT

	Intraclass Correlation[a]	95% Confidence Interval		F Test With True Value 0			
		Lower Bound	Upper Bound	Value	df1	df2	Sig.
Single Measures	.754[b]	.637	.837	7.143	74.0	74	.000
Average Measures	.860[c]	.778	.912	7.143	74.0	74	.000

Two-way mixed effects model where people effects are random and measures effects are fixed.

a. Type C intraclass correlation coefficients using a consistency definition; the between-measure variance is excluded from the denominator variance.

b. The estimator is the same, whether the interaction effect is present or not.

c. This estimate is computed assuming the interaction effect is absent because it is not estimable otherwise.

RESULTS

Intraclass correlation = .75

Advantages of Consistency Estimates

There are three major advantages to using consistency estimates of interrater reliability. First, the approach places less stringent demands on the judges in that they need not be trained to come to exact agreement with one another so long as each judge is consistent within his or her own definition of the rating scale (i.e., exhibits high intrarater reliability). It is sometimes the case that the exact application of the levels of the scoring rubric is not important in itself. Instead, the scoring rubric is a means to the end of creating scores for each participant that can be summarized in a meaningful way. If summarization is the goal, then what is most important is that each judge apply the rating scale consistently within his or her own definition of the rating scale, regardless of whether the two judges exhibit exact agreement. Consistency estimates allow for the detection of systematic differences between judges, which may then be adjusted statistically. For example, if Judge A consistently gives scores that are 2 points lower than Judge B does, then adding 2 extra points to the exams of all students who were scored by Judge A would provide an equitable adjustment to the raw scores.

A second advantage of consistency estimates is that certain methods within this category (e.g., Cronbach's alpha) allow for an overall estimate of consistency among multiple judges. The third advantage is that consistency estimates readily handle continuous data.

Disadvantage of Consistency Estimates

One disadvantage of consistency estimates is that if the construct under investigation has some objective meaning, then it may not be desirable for the two judges to "agree to disagree." Instead, it may be important for the judges to come to an exact agreement on the scores that they are generating.

A second disadvantage of consistency estimates is that judges may differ not only systematically in the raw scores they apply but also in the number of rating scale categories they use. In that case, a mean adjustment for a severe judge may provide a partial solution, but the two judges may also differ on the variability in scores they give. Thus, a mean adjustment alone will not effectively correct for this difference.

A third disadvantage of consistency estimates is that they are highly sensitive to the distribution of the observed data. In other words, if most of the ratings fall into one or two categories, the correlation coefficient will necessarily be deflated due to restricted variability. Consequently, a reliance on the consistency estimate alone may lead the researcher to falsely conclude that interrater reliability was poor without specifying more precisely that the *consistency estimate* of interrater reliability was poor and providing an appropriate rationale.

Measurement Estimates of Interrater Reliability

Measurement estimates are based on the assumption that one should use all of the information available from all judges (including discrepant ratings) when attempting to create a summary score for each respondent. In other words, each judge is seen as providing some unique information that is useful in generating a summary score for a person. As Linacre (2002) has noted, "It is the accumulation of information, not the ratings themselves, that is decisive" (p. 858). Consequently, under the measurement approach, it is not necessary for two judges to come to a consensus on how to apply a scoring rubric because differences in judge severity can be estimated and accounted for in the creation of each participant's final score.

Measurement estimates are also useful in circumstances where multiple judges are providing ratings, and it is impossible for all judges to rate all items. They are best used when different levels of the rating scale are intended to represent different levels of an underlying unidimensional construct (e.g., mathematical competence).

The two most popular types of measurement estimates are (a) factor analysis and (b) the many-facets Rasch model (Linacre, 1994; Linacre, Englehard, Tatem, & Myford, 1994; Myford & Cline, 2002) or log-linear models (von Eye & Mun, 2004).

Factor Analysis. One popular measurement estimate of interrater reliability is computed using factor analysis (Harman, 1967). Using this method, multiple judges may rate a set of participants. The judges' scores are then subjected to a common factor analysis in order to determine the amount of shared variance in the ratings that could be accounted for by a single factor. The percentage of variance that is explainable by the first factor gives some indication of the extent to which the multiple judges are reaching agreement. If the shared variance is high (e.g., greater than 60%), then this gives some indication that the judges are rating a common construct. The technique can also be used to check the extent to which judges agree on the number of underlying dimensions in the data set.

Once interrater reliability has been established in this way, each participant may then receive a single summary score corresponding to his or her loading on the first principal component underlying the set of ratings. This score can be computed automatically by most statistical packages.

The advantage of this approach is that it assigns a summary score for each participant that is based only on the relevance of the strongest dimension underlying the data. The disadvantage to the approach is that it assumes that ratings are assigned without error by the judges.

Many-Facets Rasch Measurement and Log-Linear Models. A second measurement approach to estimating interrater reliability is through the use of the many-facets Rasch model (Linacre, 1994).[2] Recent advances in the field of measurement have led to an extension of the standard Rasch measurement model (Rasch, 1960/1980; Wright & Stone, 1979). This new, extended model, known as the many-facets Rasch model, allows judge severity to be derived using the same scale (i.e., the logit scale) as person ability and item difficulty. In other words, rather than simply assuming that a score of 3 from Judge A is equally difficult for a participant to achieve as a score of 3 from Judge B, the equivalence of the ratings between judges can be empirically determined. Thus, it could be the case that a score of 3 from Judge A is really closer to a score of 5 from Judge B (i.e., Judge A is a more severe rater). Using a many-facets analysis, each essay item or behavior that was rated can be directly compared.

In addition, the difficulty of each item, as well as the severity of all judges who rated the items, can also be directly compared. For example, if a history exam included five essay questions and each of the essay questions was rated by 3 judges (2 unique judges per item and 1 judge who scored all items), the facets approach would allow the researcher to directly compare the severity of a judge who rated only Item 1 with

the severity of a judge who rated only Item 4. Each of the 11 judges (2 unique judges per item + 1 judge who rated all items = 5*2 + 1 = 11) could be directly compared. The mathematical representation of the many-facets Rasch model is fully described in Linacre (1994).

Finally, in addition to providing information that allows for the evaluation of the severity of each judge in relation to all other judges, the facets approach also allows one to evaluate the extent to which each of the individual judges is using the scoring rubric in a manner that is internally consistent (i.e., an estimate of intrarater reliability). In other words, even if judges differ in their interpretation of the rating scale, the fit statistics will indicate the extent to which a given judge is faithful to his or her own definition of the scale categories across items and people.

The many-facets Rasch approach has several advantages. First, the technique puts rater severity on the same scale as item difficulty and person ability (i.e., the logit scale). Consequently, this feature allows for the computation of a single final summary score that is already corrected for rater severity. As Linacre (1994) has noted, this provides a distinct advantage over generalizability studies since the goal of a generalizability study is to determine

> the error variance associated with each judge's ratings, so that correction can be made to ratings awarded by a judge when he is the only one to rate an examinee. For this to be useful, examinees must be regarded as randomly sampled from some population of examinees which means that there is no way to correct an individual examinee's score for judge behavior, in a way which would be helpful to an examining board. This approach, however, was developed for use in contexts in which only estimates of population parameters are of interest to researchers. (p. 29)

Second, the item fit statistics provide some estimate of the degree to which each individual rater was applying the scoring rubric in an internally consistent manner. In other words, high-fit statistic values are an indication of rater drift over time.

Third, the technique works with multiple raters and does not require all raters to evaluate all objects. In other words, the technique is well suited to overlapping research designs, which allows the researcher to use resources more efficiently. So long as there is sufficient connectedness in the data set (Engelhard, 1997), the severity of all raters can be evaluated relative to each other.

The major disadvantage to the many-facets Rasch approach is that it is computationally intensive and therefore is best implemented using specialized statistical software (Linacre, 1988). In addition, this technique is best suited to data that are ordinal in nature.

Computing Common Measurement Estimates of Interrater Reliability

Measurement estimates of interrater reliability tend to be much more computationally complex than consensus or consistency estimates. Consequently, rather than present the detailed formulas for each technique in this section, we instead refer to some excellent sources that are devoted to fully expounding the detailed computations involved. This will allow us to focus on the interpretation of the results of each of these techniques.

Factor Analysis. The mathematical formulas for computing factor-analytic solutions are expounded in several excellent texts (e.g., Harman, 1967; Kline, 1998). When using factor analysis to estimate interrater reliability, the data set should be structured in such a way that each column in the data set corresponds to the score given by Rater X on Item Y to each object in the data set (objects each receive their own row). Thus, if five raters were to score three essays from 100 students, the data set should contain 15 columns (e.g., Rater1_Item1, Rater2_Item1, Rater1_Item2) and 100 rows. In this example, we would run a separate factor analysis for each essay item (e.g., a 5×100 data matrix). Table 3.6 shows the SPSS code and output for running the factor analysis procedure.

There are two important pieces of information generated by the factor analysis. The first important piece of information is the value of the explained variance in the first factor. In the example output, the shared variance of the first factor is 76%, indicating that independent raters agree on the underlying nature of the construct being rated, which is also evidence of interrater reliability. In some cases, it may turn out that the variance in ratings is distributed over more than one factor. If that is the case, then this provides some evidence to suggest that the raters are not interpreting the underlying construct in the same manner (e.g., recall the example about creativity mentioned earlier in this chapter).

The second important piece of information comes from the factor loadings. Each object that has been rated will have a loading on each underlying factor. Assuming that the first factor explains most of the variance, the score to be used in subsequent analyses should be the loading on the primary factor.

Many-Facets Rasch Measurement. The mathematical formulas for computing results using the many-facets Rasch model may be found in Linacre (1994). In practice, the many-facets Rasch model is best implemented through the use of specialized software (Linacre, 1988). An example output of a many-facets Rasch analysis is listed in Table 3.7. The example output presented here is derived from the larger Stemler et al. (2006) data set.

The key values to interpret within the context of the many-facets Rasch approach are rater severity measures and fit statistics. Rater severity indices are useful for estimating the extent to which systematic differences exist between raters with regard to their level of severity. For example, rater CL was the most severe rater, with an estimated severity measure of +0.89 logits. Consequently, students whose test items were scored by CL would be more likely to receive lower raw scores than students who had the same test item scored by any of the other raters used in this project. At the other extreme, rater AP was the most lenient rater, with a rater severity measure of −0.91 logits. Consequently, simply using raw scores would lead to biased estimates of student proficiency since student estimates would depend, to an important degree, on which rater scored their essay. The facets program corrects for these differences and incorporates them into student ability estimates. If these differences were not taken into account when calculating student ability, students who had their exams scored by AP would be more likely to receive substantially higher raw scores than if the same item were rated by any of the other raters.

The results presented in Table 3.7 show that there is about a 1.5-logit spread in systematic

Table 3.6   SPSS Code and Output for Factor Analysis

SPSS CODE

FACTOR

/VARIABLES Rater_1 Rater_2 /MISSING LISTWISE /ANALYSIS Rater_1 Rater_2

/PRINT INITIAL EXTRACTION

/CRITERIA FACTORS(1) ITERATE(25)

/EXTRACTION PAF

/ROTATION NOROTATE

/SAVE REG(ALL)

/METHOD = CORRELATION

SPSS OUTPUT

	Initial	Extraction
Rater_1	.579	.760
Rater_2	.579	.760

Extraction Method: Principal Axis Factoring.

Total Variance Explained

Factor	Initial Eigenvalues			Extraction Sums of Squared Loadings		
	Total	% of Variance	Cumulative %	Total	% of Variance	Cumulative %
1	1.761	88.057	88.057	1.521	76.043	76.043
2	.239	11.943	100.000			

Extraction Method: Principal Axis Factoring.

RESULTS

Shared variance between raters = 76%

---

differences in rater severity (from −0.91 to +0.89). Consequently, assuming that all raters are defining the rating scales they are using in the same way is not a tenable assumption, and differences in rater severity must be taken into account in order to come up with precise estimates of student ability.

In addition to providing information that allows us to evaluate the severity of each rater in relation to all other raters, the facets approach also allows us to evaluate the extent to which each of the individual raters is using the scoring rubric in a manner that is internally consistent (i.e., intrarater reliability). In other words, even if raters differ in their own definition of how

they use the scale, the fit statistics will indicate the extent to which a given rater is faithful to his or her own definition of the scale categories across items and people. Rater fit statistics are presented in columns 5 and 6 of Table 3.7.

Fit statistics provide an empirical estimate of the extent to which the expected response patterns for each individual match the observed response patterns. These fit statistics are interpreted much the same way as item or person infit statistics are interpreted (Bond & Fox, 2001; Wright & Stone, 1979). An infit value greater than 1.4 indicates that there is 40% more variation in the data than predicted by the Rasch model. Conversely, an infit value of 0.5 indicates that there is 50% less

Table 3.7   Output for a Many-Facets Rasch Analysis

Rater	N of ratings	Measure	SE	InfitMS	OutfitMS
CL	258	0.89	0.04	3.4	3.3
SK	1,896	0.38	0.01	1.4	1.6
AM	1,491	0.14	0.02	2.2	2.1
JJ	756	0.11	0.02	1.3	1.4
LM	758	0.09	0.02	1.2	1.3
CK	956	0.03	0.02	1.0	1.0
SG	815	0.02	0.02	1.9	2.0
KV	2,685	0.01	0.01	1.6	1.6
ER	3,369	−0.02	0.01	1.0	1.1
JW	940	−0.17	0.02	2.4	2.5
KA	1,662	−0.57	0.02	1.1	1.0
AP	869	−0.91	0.03	1.0	0.9

variation in the data than predicted by the Rasch model. Infit mean squares that are greater than 1.3 indicate that there is more unpredictable variation in the raters' responses than we would expect based on the model. Infit mean square values that are less than 0.7 indicate that there is less variation in the raters' responses than we would predict based on the model. Myford and Cline (2002) note that high infit values may suggest that ratings are noisy as a result of the raters' overuse of the extreme scale categories (i.e., the lowest and highest values on the rating scale), while low infit mean square indices may be a consequence of overuse of the middle scale categories (e.g., moderate response bias).

The infit and outfit mean-square indices are unstandardized, information-weighted indices; by constrast the infit and outfit standardized indices are unweighted indices that are standardized toward a unit-normal distribution. These standardized indices are sensitive to sample size and, consequently, the accuracy of the standardization is data dependent. The expectation for the mean square index is 1.0; the range is 0 to infinity (Myford & Cline, 2002, p. 14).

The results in Table 3.7 reveal that 6 of the 12 raters had infit mean-square indices that exceeded 1.3. Raters CL (infit of 3.4), JW (infit

of 2.4), and AM (infit of 2.2) appear particularly problematic. Their high infit values suggest that these raters are not using the scoring rubrics in a consistent way. The table of misfitting ratings provided by the facets computer program output allowed for an investigation of the exact nature of the highly unexpected response patterns associated with each of these raters. The table of misfitting ratings provides information on discrepant ratings based on two criteria: (a) how the other raters scored the item and (b) the particular raters' typical level of severity in scoring items of similar difficulty.

Implications for Summarizing Scores From Various Raters

Measurement estimates allow for the creation of a summary score for each participant that represents that participant's score on the underlying factor of interest, taking into account the extent to which each judge influences the score.

Advantages of Measurement Estimates

There are several advantages to estimating interrater reliability using the measurement approach. First, measurement estimates can take into account errors at the level of each judge or for groups of judges. Consequently, the summary scores generated from measurement estimates of interrater reliability tend to more accurately represent the underlying construct of interest than do the simple raw score ratings from the judges.

Second, measurement estimates effectively handle ratings from multiple judges by simultaneously computing estimates across all of the items that were rated, as opposed to calculating estimates separately for each item and each pair of judges.

Third, measurement estimates have the distinct advantage of not requiring all judges to rate all items in order to arrive at an estimate of interrater reliability. Rather, judges may rate a particular subset of items, and as long as there is sufficient connectedness (Linacre, 1994; Linacre et al., 1994) across the judges and ratings, it will be possible to directly compare judges.

Disadvantages of Measurement Estimates

The major disadvantage of measurement estimates is that they are unwieldy to compute by hand. Unlike the percent agreement figure or correlation coefficient, measurement approaches typically require the use of specialized software to compute.

A second disadvantage is that certain methods for computing measurement estimates (e.g., facets) can handle only ordinal-level data. Furthermore, the file structure required to use facets is somewhat counterintuitive.

SUMMARY AND CONCLUSION

In this chapter, we have attempted to outline a framework for thinking about interrater reliability as a multifaceted concept. Consequently, we believe that there is no silver bullet "best" approach for its computation. There are multiple techniques for computing interrater reliability, each with its own assumptions and implications. As Snow, Cook, Lin, Morgan, and Magaziner (2005) have noted, "Percent/proportion agreement is affected by chance; kappa and weighted kappa are affected by low prevalence of condition of interest; and correlations are affected by low variability, distribution shape, and mean shifts" (p. 1682). Yet each technique (and class of techniques) has its own strengths and weaknesses.

Consensus estimates of interrater reliability (e.g., percent agreement, Cohen's kappa, odds ratios) are generally easy to compute and useful for diagnosing rater disparities; however, training raters to exact consensus requires substantial time and energy and may not be entirely necessary, depending on the goals of the study.

Consistency estimates of interrater reliability (e.g., Pearson and Spearman correlations, Cronbach's alpha, and intraclass correlations) are familiar and fairly easy to compute. They have the additional advantage of not requiring raters to perfectly agree with each other but only require consistent application of a scoring rubric within raters—systematic variance between raters is easily tolerated. The disadvantage to consistency estimates, however, is that they are sensitive to the distribution of the data (the more it departs from normality, the more attenuated the results). Furthermore, even if one achieves high consistency estimates, further adjustment to an individual's raw scores may be required in order to arrive at an unbiased final score that may be used in subsequent data analyses.

Measurement estimates of interrater reliability (e.g., factor analysis, many-facets Rasch measurement) can deal effectively with multiple raters, easily derive adjusted summary scores that are corrected for rater severity, and allow for highly efficient designs (e.g., not all raters need to rate all objects); however, this comes at the expense of added computational complexity and increased demands on resources (e.g., time and expertise).

In the end, the best technique will always depend on (a) the goals of the analysis (e.g., the stakes associated with the study outcomes), (b) the nature of the data, and (c) the desired level of information based on the resources available. The answers to these three questions will help to determine how many raters one needs, whether the raters need to be in perfect agreement with each other, and how to approach creating summary scores across raters.

We conclude this chapter with a brief table that is intended to provide rough interpretive guidance with regard to acceptable interrater reliability values (see Table 3.8). These values simply represent conventions the authors have encountered in the literature and via discussions with colleagues and reviewers; however, keep in mind that these guidelines are just rough estimates and will vary depending on the purpose of the study and the stakes associated with the outcomes. The conventions articulated here assume that the interrater reliability study is part of a low-stakes, exploratory research study.

Table 3.8   General Guidelines for Interpreting Various Interrater Reliability Coefficients

Consensus Estimates	Acceptable
Percent agreement	70%
Cohen's kappa	0.50
Odds ratio	Close to 1.0
Consistency Estimates	Acceptable
Pearson correlation	0.70
Cronbach's alpha	0.70
Intraclass correlation	0.60
Measurement Estimates	Acceptable
Factor analysis	70% explained variance
Many-facets Rasch	.70 < rater infit values < 1.3

NOTE: The odds ratio should always be computed so that the outcome is greater than 1.0.

NOTES

1. Also known as interobserver or interjudge reliability or agreement.
2. Readers interested in this model can refer to Chapters 4 and 5 on Rasch measurement for more information.

REFERENCES

Agresti, A. (1996). *An introduction to categorical data analysis* (2nd ed.). New York: John Wiley.

Anastasi, A., & Urbina, S. (1997). *Psychological testing* (7th ed.). Upper Saddle River, NJ: Prentice Hall.

Barrett, P. (2001, March). *Assessing the reliability of rating data.* Retrieved June 16, 2003, from http://www.liv.ac.uk/~pbarrett/rater.pdf

Bock, R., Brennan, R. L., & Muraki, E. (2002). The information in multiple ratings. *Applied Psychological Measurement, 26*(4), 364–375.

Bond, T., & Fox, C. (2001). *Applying the Rasch model.* Mahwah, NJ: Lawrence Erlbaum.

Burke, M. J., & Dunlap, W. P. (2002). Estimating interrater agreement with the average deviation

index: A user's guide. *Organizational Research Methods, 5*(2), 159–172.

Cohen, J. (1960). A coefficient for agreement for nominal scales. *Educational and Psychological Measurement, 20,* 37–46.

Cohen, J. (1968). Weighted kappa: Nominal scale agreement with provision for scale disagreement or partial credit. *Psychological Bulletin, 70,* 213–220.

Cohen, J., Cohen, P., West, S. G., & Aiken, L. S. (2003). *Applied multiple regression/correlation analysis for the behavioral sciences* (3rd ed.). Mahwah, NJ: Lawrence Erlbaum.

College Board. (2006). *How the essay is scored.* Retrieved November 4, 2006, from http://www.collegeboard.com/student/testing/sat/about/sat/essay_scoring.html

Crocker, L., & Algina, J. (1986). *Introduction to classical and modern test theory.* Orlando, FL: Harcourt Brace Jovanovich.

Cronbach, L. J. (1951). Coefficient alpha and the internal structure of tests. *Psychometrika, 16,* 297–334.

Dooley, K. (2006). *Questionnaire Programming Language—Interrater reliability report.* Retrieved November 4, 2006, from http://qpl.gao.gov/ca050404.htm

Engelhard, G. (1997). Constructing rater and task banks for performance assessment. *Journal of Outcome Measurement, 1*(1), 19–33.

Glass, G. V., & Hopkins, K. H. (1996). *Statistical methods in education and psychology.* Boston: Allyn & Bacon.

Harman, H. H. (1967). *Modern factor analysis.* Chicago: University of Chicago Press.

Hayes, J. R., & Hatch, J. A. (1999). Issues in measuring reliability: Correlation versus percentage of agreement. *Written Communication, 16*(3), 354–367.

Hayes, K. (2006). *SPSS Macro for computing Krippendorff's alpha.* Retrieved from http://www.comm.ohio-state.edu/ahayes/SPSS%20programs/kalpha.htm

Hopkins, K. H. (1998). *Educational and psychological measurement and evaluation* (8th ed.). Boston: Allyn & Bacon.

Kline, R. (1998). *Principles and practice of structural equation modeling.* New York: Guilford.

Krippendorff, K. (2004). Reliability in content analysis: Some common misconceptions and recommendations. *Human Communication Research, 30*(3), 411–433.

Landis, J. R., & Koch, G. G. (1977). The measurement of observer agreement for categorical data. *Biometrics, 33,* 159–174.

LeBreton, J. M., Burgess, J. R., Kaiser, R. B., Atchley, E., & James, L. R. (2003). The restriction of variance hypothesis and interrater reliability and agreement: Are ratings from multiple sources really dissimilar? *Organizational Research Methods, 6*(1), 80–128.

Linacre, J. M. (1988). FACETS: A computer program for many-facet Rasch measurement (Version 3.3.0). Chicago: MESA Press.

Linacre, J. M. (1994). *Many-facet Rasch measurement.* Chicago: MESA Press.

Linacre, J. M. (2002). Judge ratings with forced agreement. *Rasch Measurement Transactions, 16*(1), 857–858.

Linacre, J. M., Englehard, G., Tatem, D. S., & Myford, C. M. (1994). Measurement with judges: Many-faceted conjoint measurement. *International Journal of Educational Research, 21*(4), 569–577.

McArdle, J. J. (1994). Structural factor analysis experiments with incomplete data. *Multivariate Behavioral Research, 29*(4), 409–454.

Myford, C. M., & Cline, F. (2002, April 1–5). *Looking for patterns in disagreements: A facets analysis of human raters' and e-raters' scores on essays written for the Graduate Management Admission Test (GMAT).* Paper presented at the annual meeting of the American Educational Research Association, New Orleans, LA.

Osborne, J. W. (2006). Bringing balance and technical accuracy to reporting odds ratios and the results of logistic regression analyses. *Practical Assessment, Research & Evaluation, 11*(7). Retrieved from http://pareonline.net/getvn.asp?v=11&n=17

Rasch, G. (1980). *Probabilistic models for some intelligence and attainment tests* (Expanded ed.). Chicago: University of Chicago Press. (Original work published 1960)

Snow, A. L., Cook, K. F., Lin, P.-S., Morgan, R. O., & Magaziner, J. (2005). Proxies and other external raters: Methodological considerations. *Health Services Research, 40*(5), 1676–1693.

Stemler, S. E. (2001). An overview of content analysis. *Practical Assessment, Research and Evaluation, 7*(17). Retrieved from http://ericae.net/pare/getvn.asp?v=7&n=17

Stemler, S. E. (2004). A comparison of consensus, consistency, and measurement approaches to estimating interrater reliability. *Practical Assessment, Research & Evaluation, 9*(4). Retrieved from http://pareonline.net/getvn.asp?v=9&n=4

Stemler, S. E., & Bebell, D. (1999, April). *An empirical approach to understanding and analyzing the mission statements of selected educational institutions.* Paper presented at the New England Educational Research Organization (NEERO), Portsmouth, NH.

Stemler, S. E., Grigorenko, E. L., Jarvin, L., & Sternberg, R. J. (2006). Using the theory of successful intelligence as a basis for augmenting AP exams in psychology and statistics. *Contemporary Educational Psychology, 31*(2), 75–108.

Sternberg, R. J., & Lubart, T. I. (1995). *Defying the crowd: Cultivating creativity in a culture of conformity.* New York: Free Press.

Stevens, S. S. (1946). On the theory of scales of measurement. *Science, 103,* 677–680.

Uebersax, J. (2002). *Statistical methods for rater agreement.* Retrieved August 9, 2002, from http://ourworld.compuserve.com/homepages/jsuebersax/agree.htm

von Eye, A., & Mun, E. Y. (2004). *Analyzing rater agreement: Manifest variable methods.* Mahwah, NJ: Lawrence Erlbaum.

Wright, B. D., & Stone, M. H. (1979). *Best test design.* Chicago: MESA Press.

4

AN INTRODUCTION TO RASCH MEASUREMENT

CHERDSAK IRAMANEERAT

EVERETT V. SMITH JR.

RICHARD M. SMITH

Rasch measurement is a model-based approach in measurement that has become increasingly popular for scale construction in the social (and other) sciences. Rasch measurement provides a way to convert ordinal observations (raw scores) into linear measures (logits) (Fischer, 1995a; Rasch, 1960; Wright & Mok, 2004), thus making it an important tool in scientific research where phenomena are observed on an ordinal scale and parametric statistics, which assume an interval/ratio scale, are employed for analysis (Wright & Linacre, 1989). This chapter introduces basic concepts of Rasch measurement models and their applications.

WHAT IS MEASUREMENT?

A common definition of measurement is the assignment of numerals to objects or events according to rules (Stevens, 1946). Stevens (1946) classified measurement scales into four categories:

1. nominal (assigning numerals as labels or names of objects),

2. ordinal (assigning numerals to represent rank order of objects),

3. interval (assigning numbers in a way that the same amount of numerical difference represents equivalent differences in the amount of objects being measured, thereby allowing mathematical operations such as addition and subtraction), and

4. ratio (assigning numbers in the same way as an interval scale but with an absolute zero point on the scale, thereby allowing meaningful operations using multiplication and division).

Authors' Note: The authors dedicate this chapter to the memory of Scott Acton from the Rochester Institute of Technology, the initial intended author of this chapter. Correspondence should be addressed to Cherdsak Iramaneerat, MD, Department of Surgery Siriraj Hospital Siamindra Building, 13th Floor, 2 Prannok Rd., Bangkoknoi, Bangkok 10700, Thailand; e-mail: Cherdsak@sbcglobal.net.

Researchers who conduct scientific studies using various statistical techniques must keep in mind the nature of scale of measurement for their observations. Many observations in the physical sciences (e.g., weight, height, speed) are made on a ratio scale, allowing researchers to apply various parametric statistical techniques to their data. However, observations in the social sciences (e.g., attitude, intelligence, performance) are commonly made on an ordinal scale, making them unsuitable for parametric statistics (Merbitz, Morris, & Grip, 1989; E. V. Smith, Conrad, Chang, & Piazza, 2002; Wright & Mok, 2004). Thus, social science researchers need a tool to help transform raw ordinal observations into measures on an interval scale. This is particularly true if parametric statistical techniques are to be used for further analysis of the data, as it has been demonstrated that the analysis of ordinal data using, for example, factorial ANOVA can lead to spurious interactions and underestimation of effect sizes (Embretson, 1996; Romanoski & Douglas, 2002). Rasch models are the tools that serve this need (Bond & Fox, 2001; Wright & Masters, 1982; Wright & Mok, 2004; Wright & Stone, 1979).

What Measurement Approaches Have Been Used to Analyze Ordinal Data?

The act of measurement generally involves at least two facets: the objects that are being measured and the measuring instrument. For example, in educational testing, the objects are the students who are being tested, and the measuring instrument is a set of items used in the test. Measurement is the process of making sense of these two facets. Researchers in the social sciences have used predominantly two measurement approaches to analyze ordinal data: (a) true-score theory and (b) latent trait theory.

True-Score Theory

Methods based in true-score theory (aka classical test theory) represent a traditional approach to data analysis in the social sciences that has been used widely for most of the 20th century. Some of its techniques have been around since the beginning of the 20th century (Gulliksen, 1950; Spearman, 1907, 1913). Its

basic concept is that observed scores can be decomposed into true scores and error, which can be expressed mathematically as

$$X = T + E, \qquad (1)$$

where X is an observed score, T is a true score, and E is an error. This measurement model has many shortcomings, including the following:

1. Measures of persons and items are test and sample dependent, respectively (E. V. Smith et al., 2002). In a context of educational testing, if a student encounters a difficult test, his or her ability measure will be lower. But if that same student encounters an easy test, his or her ability measure will be higher. On the other hand, if items are used with a group of above-average students, they will appear to be easier than when they are used with a group of below-average students. Thus, person ability and item difficulty cannot be generalized to other samples of items and persons, respectively, with different distributions (E. V. Smith, 2004b).

2. Researchers require complete responses from every person to make score comparisons within the sample. Measures of person ability or item difficulty in true-score theory cannot be compared fairly if there are missing data, unless some type of missing data imputation/estimation method is employed (E. V. Smith et al., 2002). This can become problematic in settings that have missing data due to various reasons (e.g., noncompliance, incidental interference, physical limitation of a person) (Wright & Mok, 2004).

3. Typically, only one standard error of measurement is calculated and applied to all scores in a particular population (Embretson & Reise, 2000). Despite knowing that extreme scores are less precise, there are few procedures in true-score theory to determine how measurement error varies across the measurement scale (E. V. Smith, 2004b; E. V. Smith et al., 2002). This may lead to inaccurate estimation of internal consistency reliability of the test scores.

4. Measures of persons and items are on different metrics. This makes it difficult to predict the outcome of the interaction between a given person and a given item, despite having an estimate of that person's ability and that item's difficulty (E. V. Smith et al., 2002).

5. Mathematical operations and parametric statistical analyses performed on ordinal scale values often violate basic parametric statistical analysis assumptions and sometimes lead to invalid inferences made from the analysis. For example, Embretson (1996) found spurious interactions in a two-way ANOVA using raw scores and demonstrated underestimation of effect sizes while Romanoski and Douglas (2002) confirmed these results and demonstrated that raw scores may, depending on fit, targeting, and the distribution of item difficulties, underestimate main effects and may lead to spurious interaction effects.

6. There are few techniques for validating response patterns. Often, all observations are considered as valid responses with no anomalies (E. V. Smith et al., 2002). However, anomalies in response patterns do happen in real-world observations. For example, in educational testing, a highly able student might answer an easy item wrong because he or she runs out of time at the end of the test, while a less able student might answer a difficult item correctly because of guessing. The significant role of measurement in scientific discovery lies in its ability to display serious anomalies to direct scientists where to look for new qualitative phenomena (Kuhn, 1961). Thus, the lack of methods to detect abnormal response patterns not only leads to a distorted measurement system but may also prohibit some important scientific discoveries.

Latent Trait Theory

Latent trait theory (LTT) is a model-based measurement approach in which trait-level estimates depend both on persons' responses and on the properties of the items that were used to elicit those responses (Embretson & Reise, 2000). Two independent developments in test theory appeared in the 1960s that led to LTT. The first is the work by Georg Rasch (1960), a Danish mathematician who developed a measurement model that can fully separate the estimation of person and item parameters from each other. This property is called *specific objectivity* (Stenner, 1994). The second development is the concept of latent trait models as elaborated by Birnbaum (1968). LTT models can address several shortcomings found in true-score theory. LTT models have been widely used in educational, psychological, and medical and health care assessment (Embretson & Reise, 2000; Hambleton, 2000; Hays, Morales, & Reise, 2000; Way, 1994). They are considered very useful in assessing performance and achievement across groups in ways that different persons can respond to different sets of items (Andrich, 2004a; Embretson & Reise, 2000).

Although the work of both Rasch (1960) and Birnbaum (1968) attempted to solve the measurement problems using probabilistic models that have very similar mathematical forms, their work diverged into two unique measurement paradigms: (a) the mathematical (or LTT) paradigm and (b) the Rasch paradigm. In the mathematical (LTT) paradigm, the goal of measurement is to choose the model that accounts for the most variance in the data. Generally, the model with a greater number of parameters can explain more variance in the data. However, if two models with different numbers of parameters can explain the data equally well, the model with fewer parameters is chosen. On the other hand, the Rasch paradigm considers a measurement model as a tool for making sense of a particular theoretical framework. The measurement model is not chosen because it describes the observations the best but because it provides measures of the amount of latent trait of persons and items that are *invariant,* allowing comparison between persons that are independent of item characteristics and vice versa (Andrich, 2004a; M. Wilson, 2004a).

Another point on which the two paradigms diverge is the concept of *invariance* (Engelhard, 1994). In the LTT paradigm, the measurement system is modeled in a way that, when comparing two people, the person who has the higher probability of getting an item correct (or endorsing, for example, a clinical symptom) depends on which items they encounter; when comparing two items, determining which item is more difficult (to get correct or endorse) depends on which persons encounter the items. On the other hand, in the Rasch paradigm, the measurement system is modeled in a way that the order of persons according to their level on the trait being measured and the order of items according to their difficulties are invariant. In other words, a person with more of the trait should always have a higher probability of getting an item correct (or endorsing, for example, a clinical symptom) than a person with less of the trait, no matter which items they encounter, and a more difficult item should always have a lower probability of being answered correctly or endorsed than an easier item, regardless of the trait level of the persons who answer those items (Rasch, 1960; E. V. Smith, 2004b; E. V. Smith & Andrich, 2005).

How Can the Rasch Models Establish the Property of Invariance?

To demonstrate the property of invariance in the Rasch models, we begin by discussing basic characteristics of logistic LTT models. We focus here on the Rasch model for dichotomous responses (items with only two possible responses, such as correct-incorrect, yes-no, present-absent) to first build a basic understanding of this Rasch model, which we later generalize to polytomous Rasch models (for items that have more than two response categories, such as agree-neutral-disagree, always-often-seldom-never).

The basic characteristic of LTT models is that they all use a probabilistic function to describe the interaction between persons and items. Such probabilistic functions are called *item response functions* (IRFs) and are generally represented by

a line graph showing the amount of the latent trait on the horizontal axis and the probability of a response on the vertical axis. The most commonly used form of the IRF is the logistic function, $\exp(\theta)/[1 + \exp(\theta)]$, where θ represents the amount of latent trait (e.g., ability of a person). This function increases monotonically as the amount of latent trait (θ) increases in an S-shaped curve (Sijtsma & Molenaar, 2002) (Figure 4.1).

The Rasch model for dichotomous data defines the IRF as a function of person ability (β_n) and item difficulty (δ_i) in the following mathematical expression:

$$P_{ni} = \frac{\exp(\beta_n - \delta_i)}{1 + \exp(\beta_n - \delta_i)}. \qquad (2)$$

(Note that we have switched from θ to β to represent ability as β is commonly used in the Rasch literature.) According to this model, the probability that person n will answer item i correctly (P_{ni}) is determined by the ability of that person (β_n) and the difficulty of the item (δ_i). If a person has ability equal to the difficulty of an item, he or she will have a .50 probability of answering it correctly. If his or her ability is higher than the difficulty of an item, he or she will have

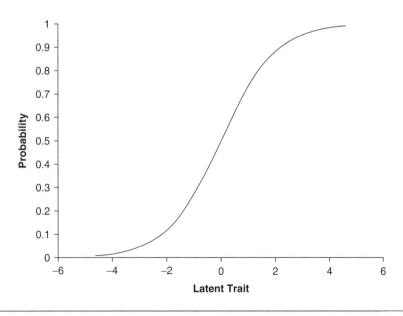

Figure 4.1   A logistic item response function curve, $P = \exp(\beta)/[1 + \exp(\beta)]$, where P is the probability of getting an item correct and β is the latent trait.

greater than a .50 probability of answering it correctly. On the other hand, if his or her ability is lower than the difficulty of an item, he or she will have less than a .50 probability of answering it correctly (simply insert values for β_n and δ_i to get the probability of a person of given ability β_n getting correct an item of difficulty δ_i). IRF curves of the Rasch model are illustrated in Figure 4.2.

Other classes of LTT models use more than one parameter to specify the properties of each item. This reflects the attempt to account for more variance in observations of the LTT paradigm. To demonstrate this, the two-parameter logistic (2PL) model is used as an example. The 2PL model adds a *discrimination parameter* (α_i) (aka, slope parameter) to the Rasch model in the following form:

$$P_{ni} = \frac{\exp[\alpha_i(\beta_n - \delta_i)]}{1 + [\exp \alpha_i(\beta_n - \delta_i)]}. \quad (3)$$

According to this model, in addition to person ability (β_n) and item difficulty (δ_i), the probability of getting a correct response is also determined by the discrimination power of that item (α_i). Figure 4.3 shows how the discrimination parameter influences the IRF curves.

As can be seen from Figure 4.3, by adding the slope parameter into the model, IRF curves are no longer parallel to one another, allowing IRFs to intersect. With this type of model, the orders of items according to their probability of a correct answer are different from one ability level to another. Thus, the property of invariant item ordering does not hold for this type of model (Sijtsma & Molenaar, 2002).

It can be seen that the Rasch model establishes the property of invariance by requiring all items to have a common slope. Having parallel IRF curves results in the ordering of items by their difficulties to be the same for all ability levels (as can be seen in Figure 4.2, in which item *a* is easier than item *b*, which is easier than item *c* for all levels of ability). Identical interpretations can be made when these IRFs are drawn as person response functions (PRFs; the ordering of persons by their abilities stays the same regardless of which item is attempted).

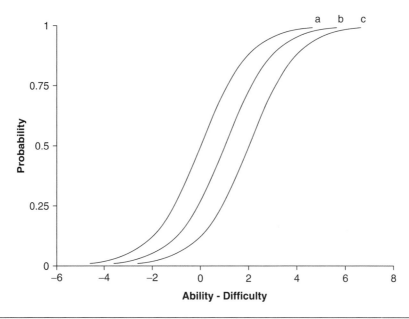

Figure 4.2   Item response function curves of the Rasch model for dichotomous data. Each curve represents one item. Item *a* is the easiest item, requiring the least amount of the latent trait to be answered correctly. Item *c* is the most difficult item, requiring more of the latent trait to be answered correctly. Difficulty is defined as the point on the latent trait where the probability of a correct answer is .50.

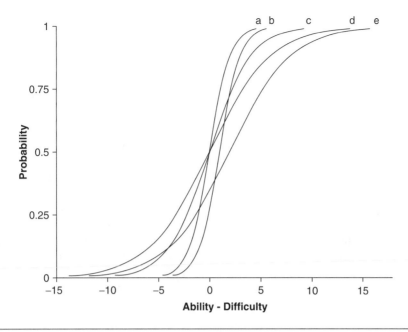

Figure 4.3   Item response function (IRF) curves for the two-parameter logistic (2PL) model for dichotomous data. Each curve represents one item. Item *a* is the "easiest" item for persons with high ability (above where the IRFs for *a* and *d* intersect), but item *d* is the "easiest" item for persons with low ability (below where the IRFs for *a* and *d* intersect). Item *e* is the most "difficult" item for persons with high ability (above where the IRFs for *b* and *e* intersect), but item *b* is the most "difficult" item for persons with low ability (below where the IRFs for *b* and *e* intersect).

WHAT KIND OF DATA CAN BE ANALYZED WITH THE RASCH MODEL?

Not all types of data are suitable for analysis with the Rasch model. As with all other types of model-based approaches in data analysis, to make valid inferences from the analysis, the data have to meet certain requirements of the model. The most commonly used Rasch models require that the data conform to four requirements: (a) unidimensionality (see Briggs & Wilson, 2004, for an introduction to multidimensional Rasch models), (b) local independence, (c) monotonicity of the latent trait, and (d) nonintersecting IRFs (Sijtsma & Molenaar, 2002).

Unidimensionality means that all items on the instrument measure the same trait (Sijtsma & Molenaar, 2002; E. V. Smith, 2004a, 2004b). However, this does not mean that performance on the items strictly has to be caused by a single psychological process. The unidimensionality assumption will hold even if multiple psychological processes are involved in the act of responding to items as long as they are affected by the same underlying process (Bejar, 1983).

Local independence means that a response of a person on one item is not influenced by his or her responses to other items on the same test. Technically, this means that after accounting for the latent trait (β), there will be no significant covariance between any pairs of items (Embretson & Reise, 2000; Sijtsma & Molenaar, 2002; Yen, 1993). Item dependence can lead to inaccurate estimation of item difficulties and person abilities, as well as overestimation of reliability and information functions (Sireci, Thissen, & Wainer, 1991; E. V. Smith, 2005; Thissen, Steinberg, & Mooney, 1989; Zenisky, Hambleton, & Sireci, 2003).

Monotonicity of the latent trait implies that the probability that a person will answer an item correctly (P_{ni}) is monotonically nondecreasing over the range of the latent trait (Sijtsma & Molenaar, 2002). In other words, the model does not allow the probability of getting a correct response to fluctuate up and down.

Nonintersecting IRFs are an important requirement to attain the property of invariance as described earlier. This requirement is what differentiates the Rasch models from other LTT models.

WHAT ARE THE CONSEQUENCES OF ANALYZING DATA WITH THE RASCH MODEL?

If the data fit the Rasch model, measurement construction using the Rasch model provides measures of the amount of latent trait for both persons and items that have many desirable measurement properties:

1. The measures of persons and items are put on the same scale. This allows the direct comparison of the two facets of measurement. Unlike raw scores, where one cannot tell whether a person should answer a given item correctly because raw scores reflecting person ability and item difficulty are on different metrics, the Rasch model puts all the measures on a common logit scale. The logit scale is the logarithm of odds of the probability of getting a correct response over an incorrect response (E. V. Smith, 2004b). One logit is the distance along the measurement scale that increases the odds of getting a correct response by a factor of 2.718, the value of e, the base of natural logarithms (Linacre & Wright, 1989; O'Neill, 2005).

2. Measures are on an interval scale when the data fit the model. Perline, Wright, and Wainer (1979) demonstrated that when data fit the Rasch model, and since the model is a form of additive conjoint measurement (Luce & Tukey, 1964), the model is able to transform ordinal data into interval measures (also see Brogden, 1977; Fischer, 1995a; Karabatsos, 2001; Mislevy, 1987). Wright (1985) demonstrated that the 2PL and three-parameter logistic (3PL) models cannot maintain units or enable the construction of additivity (i.e., interval scales). This is a direct result of the interaction between the person and item parameters caused by the inclusion of the multiplicative item discrimination parameters (see Equation 3).

3. Measures have the property of invariance. This property allows us to place persons and

items on a *construct or variable map*. The idea of mapping out where a person is relative to items and where an item is relative to persons to represent the concept of a measurement construct requires that the relative ordering of items and persons be invariant (M. Wilson, 2004a, 2005).

4. Rasch analysis results in the separability of parameter estimates (Hambleton, Swaminathan, & Rogers, 1991). Measures of person ability are freed from the distributional properties of items used. At the same time, measures of item difficulty are freed from the distributional properties of people who attempt those items (Stone, 2004). In other words, measures of person ability are the same (within measurement error), no matter which subset of items is used for calibration when the data fit model expectations. These are basic requirements for objective measurement.

5. Each individual person measure and item difficulty has a unique standard error associated with its estimate (Wright, 1999; Wright & Stone, 1979). Persons with extreme measures have higher standard errors than those around the center of the item distribution. This reflects the fact that there is less information to estimate the ability of these persons. Having individual standard errors for persons and items also leads to a more accurate calculation of the internal consistency reliability coefficient (see E. V. Smith, 2004b).

6. The Rasch analysis produces expected responses of each person-item interaction. Comparing these expected responses with the observed responses can reveal whether the responses fit the model expectations. The ability to identify anomalies provides an opportunity to scrutinize these abnormal response patterns to diagnose certain response behaviors (e.g., guessing, miscodes, response sets, judge rating errors, cheating, speededness at the end of the test) (Andrich, 2004a; Linacre & Wright, 1994; Mead, 1980; Myford & Wolfe, 2004a, 2004b; R. M. Smith, 2004).

HOW CAN WE USE THE RASCH MODELS TO ANALYZE POLYTOMOUS DATA?

Rasch models are applicable not only to dichotomous data but also to polytomous data.

This can be accomplished by adding parameters describing the rating scale functioning to the basic Rasch model for dichotomous data. The two most widely used Rasch models for polytomous data are the rating scale model (RSM) and the partial credit model (PCM).

To accommodate multiple response categories in each item, the RSM (Andrich, 1978a, 1978b; Embretson & Reise, 2000; Wright & Masters, 1982) adds a threshold parameter (τ_j) to the model to represent the relative difficulty of transitioning between rating categories. These threshold parameters are located at the intersections of the probability curve of one rating category with the probability curve of the next rating category. The RSM can be described mathematically as

$$p_{nix} = \frac{\exp \sum_{j=0}^{x} \left(\beta_n - (\delta_i + \tau_j)\right)}{\sum_{k=0}^{m} \exp \sum_{j=0}^{k} \left(\beta_n - (\delta_i + \tau_j)\right)}, \quad (4)$$

where p_{nix} is the probability that a person n will respond x to item i, $x_{ni} \in \{0, \dots, m\}$; k is the response category on a rating scale that has $(m+1)$ rating categories; β_n is the latent trait ability measure of a person n; δ_i is the difficulty level of an item i; τ_j are the thresholds (locations of the latent trait where adjacent categories are equally probable); and $\tau_0 = 0$ so that $\exp \sum_{j=0}^{0} (\beta n - (\delta_i + \tau j)) = 1$. Unlike the model for dichotomous data, where each item has one IRF curve, the RSM generates a probability curve for each response category of the item. These probability curves are called category characteristic curves (CCCs; aka, category probability curves or category response curves) (Embretson & Reise, 2000; Wright & Masters, 1982) (Figure 4.4).

Because the RSM employs only one set of threshold parameters (τ_j) across all items on the scale, it can only be used with data collected with a common rating scale structure (the number of rating categories and relative difficulty between categories) for all items. In certain situations, that assumption should not be made (e.g., for

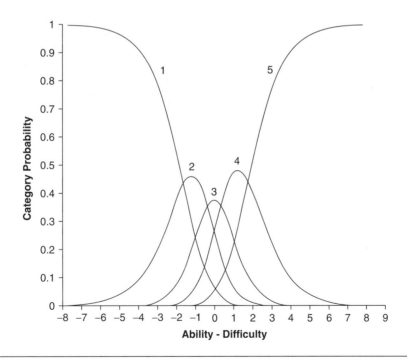

Figure 4.4   Category characteristic curves of a polytomous item with five categories. Each curve represents a response category. Category 1 is the response category that is easiest to endorse or observe in a person low on the latent trait. As the amount of the latent trait increases, the probability to endorse this response category gradually decreases, while the probability to endorse a more difficult category increases.

a set of rating scale items that have different numbers of rating categories or when the relative difficulty between categories may be expected to vary from item to item). In these cases, the PCM (Embretson & Reise, 2000; Masters, 1982; Masters & Wright, 1996) should be used. The PCM defines threshold parameters for each item (δ_{ij}), allowing each item to have a unique scale structure. The PCM can be described mathematically as

$$P_{nix} = \frac{\exp \sum\limits_{j=0}^{x}(\beta_n - \delta_{ij})}{\sum\limits_{k=0}^{m_i} \exp \sum\limits_{j=0}^{k}(\beta_n - \delta_{ij})}, \qquad (5)$$

where $x_{ni} \in \{0, \ldots, m\}$; and $\delta_{i0} = 0$, so that $\exp \sum\limits_{j=0}^{0}(\beta_n - \delta_j) = 1$.

How Can We Know That the Data Set Is Suitable for the Rasch Analysis?

Because the Rasch model is a model that is based on strong requirements, it is pertinent to ensure that the data fit the model before making inferences from the Rasch analysis. A commonly used method in determining whether the data fit the model is the fit statistics using the Pearsonian chi-square approach (Wright & Panchapakesan, 1969). Two types of fit statistics are commonly used: infit and outfit. Both statistics can be reported in two forms: mean square statistics (MNSQ) and standardized statistics (ZSTD).

Outfit is based on a sum of squared standardized residuals. Dividing this sum of squared standardized residuals by its degree of freedom yields an outfit mean square statistic, which has an expectation of 1.0 and can range from 0 to infinity. Values larger than 1.0 indicate more variability than expected. Values less than 1.0 indicate less variability than expected in the data (Linacre & Wright, 1994; R. M. Smith, 2004; Wright & Masters, 1982).

Outfit statistics are unweighted and thus more sensitive to anomalous responses by very high-ability or very low-ability persons, particularly on tests that have a wide range of item difficulties and person abilities (Mead, 1980). Infit weighs each squared standardized residual by the information function ($p_{ni}(1 - p_{ni})$) before it is summed

to reduce the influence of less informative, off-target responses and overweights the completely unexpected responses by persons near the center of the item distribution. Similar to the outfit mean square statistic, the infit mean square statistic has an expectation of 1.0 and can range from 0 to infinity (Linacre & Wright, 1994; R. M. Smith, 2004; Wright & Masters, 1982).

Because the distribution of mean square statistics is not symmetrical around the mean and their distributions vary from item to item (and person to person), the use of a single criterion to detect misfit may result in different Type I error rates being applied (R. M. Smith, 2004). To assist with the distribution-based interpretation of fit statistics, mean square fit statistics can be transformed into standardized fit statistics using a Wilson-Hilferty cube root transformation (R. M. Smith, 1982; E. B. Wilson & Hilferty, 1931). Standardized fit statistics have an approximate unit normal distribution (0, 1). Standardized fit statistics less than 0 may indicate dependency in the data. Standardized fit statistics larger than 0 indicate unexpected variability in the data (Linacre, 2002). Because standardized fit statistics have an approximate unit normal distribution when the data fit the model, interpreting the fit of the observations to the model is similar to interpreting how likely the observations would be to happen in a z–score distribution. For a conventional Type I error rate of .05, the acceptable range of standardized fit statistics is -2.0 to 2.0 (Linacre, 2002), although for large samples, a -3.0 to 3.0 may be warranted.

How Can We Do the Rasch Analysis Practically?

There are a variety of computer programs for conducting Rasch analysis. WINSTEPS (Linacre, 2006), which is a Windows-based application that can handle analyses using the basic Rasch model, RSM, and PCM will be employed in our examples. An evaluation version, Ministeps, can be downloaded from www.WINSTEPS.com. A list of other Rasch calibration programs can be found at www.WINSTEPS.com/rasch.htm. Many of these offer free evaluation versions, and each varies in the models estimated and the depth and breadth of diagnostic information provided.

What Are the General Steps in Interpreting the Results of Rasch Analysis?

There are no rigorous rules on the order in which one has to proceed in reviewing the results of a Rasch analysis. They depend on the research questions and the findings from the analysis. What is found at one step may necessarily require revisiting prior steps. Therefore, the following is a general recommendation for standard analyses and may not fit all data sets or analyses. The steps for the simple case of dichotomous data analysis are outlined first, and then additional aspects to consider in polytomous data analysis are discussed.

Dichotomous Data

The first thing to check is the internal consistency reliability. Because there are two facets of measurement interest (persons and items), the analyst examines the internal consistency reliability of both facets. Person separation reliability is the index of reliability that corresponds to the traditional KR-20 or Cronbach's alpha commonly reported in the true-score theory (Stone, 2004; Wright & Masters, 1982). Person separation reliability (R_p) is calculated using the following formula:

$$R_p = \frac{SD_p^2 - MSE_p}{SD_p^2},\qquad(6)$$

where SD_p^2 is the observed variance of the persons, and MSE_p is the mean square measurement error for person ability. This separation reliability is on a nonlinear scale and suffers from ceiling effects in the same manner as KR-20 and coefficient alpha (E. V. Smith, 2004b). To avoid this ceiling effect, a person separation index (G_p) can be used. The person separation index is calculated using the following formula:

$$G_p = \sqrt{\frac{R_p}{1 - R_p}}.\qquad(7)$$

G_p is on a ratio scale and can range from 0 to infinity (Schumacker, 2004; Wright & Masters, 1982). It indicates the spread of person (or item) measures in standard error units (Fisher, 1992; Wright & Masters, 1982). The higher the G_p value,

the more dispersed persons on the scale (as a frame of reference, a value of G_p of 2 is equivalent to an R_p of .80). Another useful indicator of internal consistency is strata, which can be calculated using the following formula:

$$Strata = \frac{(4G_p + 1)}{3}.\qquad(8)$$

Strata indicates the number of statistically distinct levels (separated by at least 3 SEM) of person ability that the items distinguished (Fisher, 1992; Wright & Masters, 1982). If the interest is in how well persons separate the items, it is possible to calculate item separation reliability, item separation index, and item strata in the same way, using the item SD and the mean square measurement error of item difficulty.

The next thing to examine is a variable map (Figure 4.5). This map shows the distribution of persons and items on a common logit scale. Unless anchoring or rescaling is used, the mean item difficulty is usually set to 0 logits (R. M. Smith, 1999). The mean person ability is compared with the mean item difficulty to see if items, on average, are difficult or easy for this group of persons. The distribution of person ability should be matched with the distribution of item difficulty when norm reference interpretations are desired (Linacre, 2005). For criterion reference interpretations, the bulk of the items should be distributed around the cut score(s).

An item analysis report (Table 4.1) provides detailed information of each item (raw score, logit measure, standard error, fit statistics, and point-biserial correlations). It is possible to check which items are the easiest (Items 3 and 19; see values under MEASURE to determine this) and which are the most difficult (Items 11 and 12) and evaluate the fit of the items to the Rasch model using infit and/or outfit statistics. As a follow-up for misfitting items, response residuals (not shown) can be examined to try to understand why certain items misfit the model (e.g., differential item functioning, poorly worded items, differential curriculum exposure). This can lead to discussions among the instrument developers on how to improve the items. Depending on the fit criteria defined by the researcher, misfitting items should be considered for deletion to eliminate noise or data redundancy from the analysis. Nevertheless, statistical decisions to remove certain items from

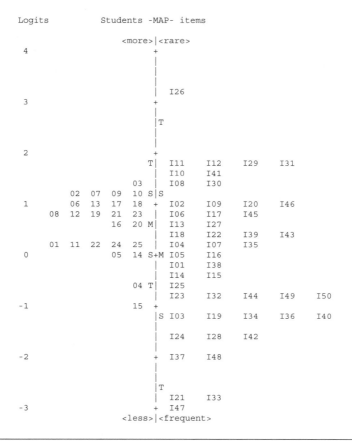

```
Logits           Students -MAP- items
                      <more>|<rare>
    4                      +
                           |
                           |
                           |  I26
    3                      +
                           |
                           |T
                           |
                           |
    2                      +
                         T| I11    I12    I29    I31
                           | I10    I41
                     03    | I08    I30
           02 07 09 10 S|S
    1         06 13 17 18  + I02    I09    I20    I46
        08 12 19 21 23    | I06    I17    I45
              16 20 M| I13    I27
                           | I18    I22    I39    I43
        01 11 22 24 25    | I04    I07    I35
                 05 14 S+M I05    I16
    0                      | I01    I38
                           | I14    I15
                 04 T| I25
                           | I23    I32    I44    I49    I50
   -1            15  +
                          |S I03    I19    I34    I36    I40
                           |
                           | I24    I28    I42
                           |
   -2                      + I37    I48
                           |
                           |
                           |T
                           | I21    I33
   -3                      + I47
                      <less>|<frequent>
```

Figure 4.5   A variable map of student ability and item difficulty obtained from an analysis of a 50-item multiple-choice examination of 25 students. Students are listed on the left side of the scale (01–25). Items are listed on the right side of the scale (I01–I50). On the far-left side of the map is the logit metric. Higher logits indicate students with higher ability and items with higher difficulty. M = mean, S = 1 SD, T = 2 SD.

the analysis are no substitute for consideration of content coverage of the construct being measured (Schumacker, 2004). Eliminating items based on fit criteria alone without the consideration of content coverage might lead to failure of the instrument to capture important aspects of the construct, causing construct underrepresentation (American Educational Research Association, American Psychological Association, & National Council on Measurement in Education, 1999).

A person analysis report provides information on each person included in the calibration in a similar manner as the item analysis report. It is possible to determine which person has the highest level of ability and which person has the lowest. It is also possible to evaluate the fit of persons to the Rasch model. In some instances

where the focus of the analysis is on the items and no decision is required for individual persons, misfitting persons should also be considered for removal from the analysis to eliminate noise or data redundancy. If individual differences are of interest, measures between any pair of persons can be compared to see if they are statistically different in their ability measures, using the following formula:

$$z = \frac{\beta_1 - \beta_2}{\sqrt{SE_1^2 + SE_2^2}}, \quad (9)$$

where β_1 and β_2 are ability measures of Persons 1 and 2, and SE_1 and SE_2 are the standard errors of the measures of Persons 1 and 2 (Wright & Stone, 1979). If z is equal to or greater than 1.96,

Table 4.1   An Item Analysis of a 20-Item Multiple-Choice Examination

```
+------------------------------------------------------------------------+
|ENTRY   RAW                       MODEL|  INFIT  |  OUTFIT |PTBIS|       |
|NUMBER  SCORE  COUNT  MEASURE  S.E. |MNSQ  ZSTD|MNSQ  ZSTD|CORR.|item    |
|------------------------------------+----------+----------+-----+-----|
|    1     17     25    -.71    .46|1.41   1.8|1.44   1.6| -.21|I01 |
|    2     10     25     .62    .43|1.22   1.5|1.14    .7| -.04|I02 |
|    3     21     25   -1.74    .58| .74   -.7| .59   -.7|  .51|I03 |
|    4     15     25    -.31    .44| .99    .0| .92   -.3|  .26|I04 |
|    5     16     25    -.50    .45|1.08    .5|1.08    .4|  .12|I05 |
|    6     12     25     .25    .43| .85  -1.1| .80  -1.1|  .41|I06 |
|    7     15     25    -.31    .44|1.16   1.0|1.19   1.0|  .04|I07 |
|    8      8     25    1.01    .45| .97   -.1| .90   -.3|  .23|I08 |
|    9     10     25     .62    .43|1.01    .1| .95   -.1|  .20|I09 |
|   10      7     25    1.22    .47| .74  -1.3| .62  -1.2|  .52|I10 |
|   11      6     25    1.45    .49| .92   -.2|1.26    .7|  .15|I11 |
|   12      6     25    1.45    .49|1.07    .4|1.21    .6|  .03|I12 |
|   13     13     25     .07    .43|1.08    .6|1.07    .4|  .12|I13 |
|   14     18     25    -.93    .48| .86   -.5| .83   -.5|  .38|I14 |
|   15     18     25    -.93    .48| .76  -1.0| .72   -.9|  .51|I15 |
|   16     16     25    -.50    .45|1.09    .5|1.17    .8|  .12|I16 |
|   17     11     25     .44    .43| .88   -.9| .83   -.8|  .37|I17 |
|   18     14     25    -.12    .43|1.23   1.5|1.32   1.6| -.08|I18 |
|   19     21     25   -1.74    .58| .74   -.6| .51  -1.0|  .55|I19 |
|   20     10     25     .62    .43| .97   -.1| .97    .0|  .23|I20 |
|------------------------------------+----------+----------+-----+-----|
| MEAN   13.2   25.0     .00    .46| .99    .1| .98    .0|     |    |
| S.D.    4.5     .0     .92    .04| .18    .9| .25    .8|     |    |
+------------------------------------------------------------------------+
```

NOTE: Raw score is the number of students who answered the item correctly. Count is the number of students who answered that item. Measures are the item difficulty estimates in logits for each item. Model SEs are the standard errors associated with the difficulty estimates. Infit and outfit statistics are given in mean square and standardized form. PTBIS CORR. is the traditional point-biserial correlation. Summary statistics (mean and *SD*) are provided at the bottom of the table.

Person 1 has a significantly higher measure than Person 2, under the assumption of a Type I error rate of .05. If *z* is equal to or less than −1.96, Person 1 has a significantly lower measure than Person 2, under the assumption of a Type I error rate of .05 (Luppescu, 1995). For more on interpreting a Rasch analysis with dichotomous data, see R. M. Smith (1992, 1999) and Schumacker (2004).

Example 1

In this example, a Rasch analysis of data obtained from a test of short-term memory of 35 children using 18 items, each of which are scored as correct (1) or incorrect (0), is presented. The WINSTEPS control file for this data set is provided with the installation of the WIN-STEPS program. To run a Rasch analysis of this dichotomous data set, open up the WINSTEPS program. At the prompt asking for a control file

name, press [Enter]. A control file window will show a list of files from an examples folder. Open a file named "kct.txt." Then press [Enter] to request a temporary output file. Finally, press [Enter] again to skip providing extra specification. The WINSTEPS program will then start running the analysis, using a Rasch model for dichotomous data.

1. Checking internal consistency reliability

From the menu, select "Output Tables" and choose "3.1 Summary statistics." A new window showing four tables of summary statistics will appear. The first two tables focus on measures of children's short-term memory. The last two tables focus on item difficulty estimates. Generally, results only from nonextreme measures are interpretable because extreme measures (those who get all items right or all items wrong) contain little statistical information regarding their level on the construct of interest. The person separation reliability is in the right lower corner of the first table (real reliability = .64). If the interest is in the separation of items, the item separation reliability is found in the third table (real item reliability = .95).

2. Checking a variable map

From the menu, select "Output Tables" and choose "1. Variable maps." A new window will show various variable maps. The map that is used most often is the first one. From this map, it is possible to compare the locations of children (on the left side of the map) with the locations of items (on the right side of the map) to see, for example, whether there is a gap in the item distribution that does not have items targeted to children who are at that level of ability (e.g., a gap of 2.36 logits between Items 11 [0.79 logits] and 10 [−1.57 logits]).

3. Checking an item analysis report

From the menu, select "Output Tables" and choose "14. TAP: entry." A new window will show measures of the items (which are labeled *tap* in this data set), sorted by their entry numbers. This makes it possible to determine which items are the easiest (Items 1, 2, and 3 at −6.59 logits), which item is the most difficult (Item 18 at 6.13 logits), which items had the highest standardized fit statistics (Item 14 with an infit ZSTD of 1.2 and Items 15, 16, and 17 with an outfit ZSTD of 1.4), and which items had the lowest standardized fit statistic (Item 8 with an infit ZSTD of −1.3 and Item 13 with an outfit ZSTD of −0.3).

4. Checking a person analysis report

From the menu, select "Output Tables" and choose "17. KID: measure." A new window will show measures of all children who took this test (which are labeled *kid* in this data set), sorted by their measures of ability from the highest to the lowest. It is possible to determine which kids earned the highest measure (Kids 7 and 24 at 3.73 logits), which kid earned the lowest measure (Kid 35 at −6.62 logits), which kids had the highest standardized infit statistic (Kids 13 and 29 with an infit ZSTD of 2.5), which kid had the highest standardized outfit statistic (Kid 25 with

an outfit ZSTD of 4.1), which kid had the lowest standardized infit statistic (Kid 15 with an infit ZSTD of −1.5), and which kids had the lowest standardized outfit statistic (Kids 2, 5, 6, 8, 9, 26, and 31 with an outfit ZSTD of −0.3).

For more examples of dichotomous data analysis, see R. M. Smith (1992, 1999) and Schumacker (2004).

Polytomous Data

In addition to all the considerations in the analysis of dichotomous data, employing the RSM or PCM to analyze polytomous data requires additional attention to the rating scale structure. It is pertinent to ensure the proper functioning of rating scale structure before making inferences from these ratings. There are eight basic guidelines to evaluate the functioning of a rating scale in the RSM or PCM analyses (Linacre, 2004).

1. All items are oriented with the latent trait variable.

Some survey questionnaires are designed to have the polarity of some items reversed so that persons with high levels on the latent trait will provide low ratings on these items. The items with reversed polarity can be detected from an item analysis report (Table 4.1), as those with negative point biserial correlation coefficient (PTBIS CORR. in the table). To have the rating scale structure function properly, those items whose polarities contradict the general item consensus must be rescored to have their polarities conform to other items.

2. There are at least 10 observations in each rating category.

In order to get accurate threshold calibrations, at least 10 observations per rating category are needed. For the RSM, the number of observations per rating category is obtained by aggregating the observations for each category across all items. For the PCM, the number of observations for each rating category is assessed on an item-by-item basis. If the recommended minimum of 10 observations is not met, options may include gathering more data, collapsing adjacent categories if they are conceptually similar, switching from a PCM to an RSM (assuming the data are amenable to both models), or forcing estimation of thresholds involving categories that contain no data (see Linacre, 2005). Check this criterion from the rating scale functioning report (Table 4.2). The numbers in the observed count column should be at least 10 for all categories.

3. The observations are regularly distributed across all rating categories.

Irregularity in the observed frequency across categories may signal aberrant category usage. To ensure a properly functioning rating scale, one should check that the numbers of observed counts in the rating scale functioning report (Table 4.2) are approximately evenly distributed. If one category is rarely used while its adjacent category has numerous observations, one could consider combining the two categories together. See Linacre (2004) and Zhu, Updyke, and Lewandowski (1997) for more information on combining adjacent categories to optimize the rating scale.

4. Average measures advance monotonically with category.

A properly functioning rating scale should have observations in higher rating categories producing higher logit measures. This can be determined by checking the OBSVD AVRGE column in the rating scale functioning report (Table 4.2). These observed average logit measures should increase with increasing rating scale categories. When a higher rating category has a lower average measure than a lower rating category, uncertainty in the meaning of the rating scale is suggested as this disordering suggests, for example, that category 4 does not represent more of the latent variable than category 3. This often occurs with the use of "neutral" as a middle category or when many categories are unlabeled, which allows each respondent to create his or her own definitions of the unlabeled categories.

5. Outfit mean square values are less than 2.0.

A high outfit mean square value of a rating scale category (reported under the OUTFIT MNSQ column in Table 4.2) is an indicator of unexpected usage of that rating category, causing a threat to the measurement system. When a high outfit mean square value is observed for a particular rating category, one should consider

omitting the observations, combining the observations with another rating category, or dropping that rating category entirely. Note that while Linacre (2004) uses the MNSQ to evaluate rating scale functioning, it might be appropriate to use the standardized versions of these fit statistics for their approximate unit normal distributions when the data fit the model.

6. Thresholds (τ_j in RSM or δ_{ij} in PCM) advance with categories.

The use of rating scales assumes that it should take increasing levels of the trait to be observed in higher categories. This is a similar check as was made with the average measures. The difference lies in that average measures are calculated one category at a time, while thresholds are all estimated simultaneously. This can be checked from the rating scale functioning report under the column structure measure (i.e., thresholds). These thresholds correspond to the intersecting points between the CCCs shown in the probability plot at the bottom of the rating scale functioning report (Table 4.2). Failure of these thresholds to advance is called *threshold disordering*, which can degrade the interpretability of resulting measures (Andrich, 2004b). When this threshold disordering is observed, one might consider combining the disordered category with its lower category and investigating why the sample did not use the rating scale as intended.

7. Thresholds advance by at least 1.4 logits (for a three-category rating scale) or by at least 1.0 logits (for a five-category rating scale) (Linacre, 2004).

Having thresholds that advance too little suggests that the two categories are practically inseparable. When two thresholds are noted to be too close together from the rating scale functioning report, combining the two categories together might be indicated and further qualitative work on the meanings of the selected categories with respect to the construct being measured undertaken.

8. Thresholds advance no more than 5.0 logits (Linacre, 2004).

Having thresholds that are too far apart is an indication of a *dead zone* in the middle of the category where the measurement loses its precision. Such wide distances between thresholds suggest a need to put in an additional rating category between these categories to obtain more precise calibrations (lower standard errors for a portion of the ability continuum).

When using rating scales, the analysis of polytomous data is also a bit more complicated in terms of determining the matching of the item difficulty distribution with person ability distribution. Unlike dichotomous items, which have only one intersecting point of response transition (from 0 to 1) per item, polytomous items have many points where successive category probability curves cross (i.e., thresholds), which allows one item to target a wider range on the latent trait scale. Thus, assessing item targeting to person ability from the variable map (Figure 4.5) does not give a complete picture. One should evaluate

an expected score map (Figure 4.6) or other variations of variable maps that incorporate the thresholds to assess targeting. An expected score map shows the expected response to each item for a person with a specified ability measure. One can evaluate the targeting of the items to the person ability distribution by comparing the coverage of the thresholds of all items (the "colons" in Figure 4.6 represent the thresholds) with the distribution of person ability measures at the bottom of the map.

Example 2

In this example, an analysis of a "liking for science" questionnaire using the Rasch rating scale model is presented. This questionnaire asked for ratings of various activities from a

Table 4.2   Rating Scale Functioning Report Obtained From the Analysis of a Performance Assessment of 47 Students Using an 11-Item Instrument, Which Employed a 4-Point Rating Scale

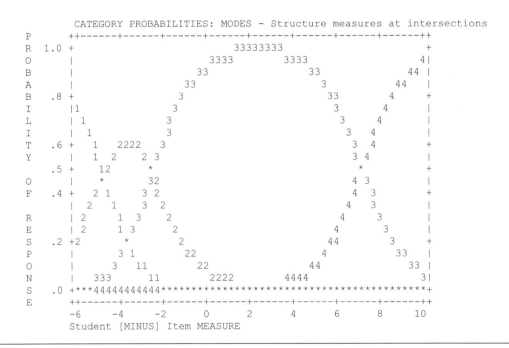

```
+--------------------------------------------------------
|CATEGORY    OBSERVED|OBSVD |INFIT OUTFIT||STRUCTURE|
|LABEL SCORE COUNT %|AVRGE |  MNSQ  MNSQ||CALIBRATN|
|-------------------+------+------------++---------+
|  1   1      17    4| -5.38|  .90   .99||  NONE   | 1 Poor
|  2   2      37    9| -3.17|  .58   .23|| -4.76   | 2 Fair
|  3   3     272   64|  3.19|  .91   .78|| -2.49   | 3 Acceptable
|  4   4      97   23|  8.78| 1.14  1.93||  7.24   | 4 Good
+--------------------------------------------------------
```

```
            CATEGORY PROBABILITIES: MODES - Structure measures at intersections
P      ++------+------+------+------+------+------+------+------++
R  1.0 +                        33333333                         +
O      |                   3333          3333                  4 |
B      |               33                   33              44   |
A      |             33                      3             44    |
B   .8 +            3                         33          4       +
I      |1          3                          3          4        |
L      | 1        3                           3        4          |
I      | 1        3                          3       4            |
T   .6 +  1    2222   3                       3     4             +
Y      |  1   2     2 3                       3    4              |
    .5 +    12      *                         *                   +
O      |    *       32                       4 3                  |
F   .4 +   2 1     3 2                       4   3                 +
       |   2   1     3 2                     4    3                |
R      | 2      1  3     2                  4      3               |
E      | 2       1 3       2               4        3             |
S   .2 +2        *          2             44         3            +
P      |       3 1          22           4           33           |
O      |      3   11          22        44              33        |
N      |    333       11        2222    4444                 3    |
S   .0 +***44444444444*****************************************+
E      ++------+------+------+------+------+------+------+------++
       -6     -4     -2      0      2      4      6      8     10
       Student [MINUS] Item MEASURE
```

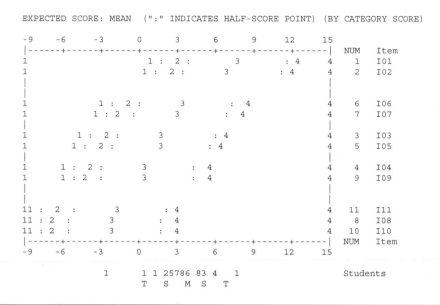

```
EXPECTED SCORE: MEAN  (":" INDICATES HALF-SCORE POINT) (BY CATEGORY SCORE)

 -9     -6     -3      0      3      6      9     12     15
|------+------+------+------+------+------+------+------|  NUM    Item
1                          1 :   2 :          3      : 4      4    1    I01
1                          1 :   2 :          3      : 4      4    2    I02
|                                                              |
|                                                              |
1                     1 :   2 :        3        : 4           4    6    I06
1                    1 : 2   :         3         : 4          4    7    I07
|                                                              |
1                 1 :   2 :        3           : 4           4    3    I03
1                 1 :   2 :        3          : 4            4    5    I05
|                                                              |
1             1 :   2 :        3            : 4             4    4    I04
1             1 : 2   :        3            : 4             4    9    I09
|                                                              |
|                                                              |
11 :   2   :        3              : 4                      4    11   I11
11 : 2   :         3          : 4                           4    8    I08
11 : 2   :         3          : 4                           4    10   I10
|------+------+------+------+------+------+------+------|  NUM    Item
 -9     -6     -3      0      3      6      9     12     15

            1        1 1 25786 83 4    1                    Students
                     T  S  M  S  T
```

Figure 4.6   An expected score map obtained from an analysis of a performance assessment of 47 students using an 11-item instrument, which employed a 4-point rating scale. Because the rating scale model (RSM) is used, the distance between rating categories is assumed constant across all items, having only a horizontal shift of the scale according to the difficulty of each item. The items are listed from the easiest (I10) at the bottom of the map to the most difficult at the top (I01). The distribution of student ability measures is shown at the bottom of the map as a number of students at each logit. To find expected ratings of a student with a given logit measure, one can draw a vertical line up from the specified logit measure and check what rating region the line passes through for each item. For example, a student with 3 logits ability is expected to get ratings of 2 on Items 1 and 2; ratings of 3 on Items 6, 7, 3, 5, 4, and 9; and ratings of 4 on Items 11, 8, and 10.

group of 75 students using a three-category rating scale ranging from 0 to 2, where 0 represents *dislike*, 1 represents *neutral* (note that we do not advocate the use of a "neutral" option in rating scales due to the potential misuse of the neutral category), and 2 represents *like*. The WINSTEPS control file for this data set is available in the WINSTEPS folder after installation of the program. To run the analysis of this data set using the Rasch rating scale model, press [Enter] at the control file prompt after opening the WINSTEPS program. Open the file named "sf.txt." Then press [Enter] twice. The WINSTEPS program will then run the analysis using the rating scale model.

To interpret the results of the analysis, the following steps are recommended:

1. Checking internal consistency reliability

Check the separation reliability of students (pupils) and items (acts) from Table 3.1 (student separation reliability = .88, item separation reliability = .97). The high student separation

reliability (analogous to Cronbach's alpha) indicates that the items have spread the students out on the "liking for science" variable, and individual difference can be reliably examined. The high item separation reliability indicates that students spread out the items in terms of difficulty to endorse, which is useful for construct validation efforts (see Wolfe & Smith, 2007b).

2. Checking an expected score map

Check the distribution of students' measures of liking scientific activities and the distribution of the item thresholds from an expected score map (Table 2.2).

3. Checking an item analysis report

Check which items misfit the measurement model in Table 10.1 (ACT: fit order). Employing a conventional fit criterion for standardized fit statistics of −2.0 to 2.0, there are three underfitting items (Item 23 with an infit ZSTD of 6.3

and an outfit ZSTD of 9.0, Item 5 with an infit ZSTD of 5.6 and an outfit ZSTD of 7.3, and Item 20 with an infit ZSTD of 2.0 and an outfit ZSTD of 3.7) and four overfitting items (Items 1, 3, 17, and 11 with infit ZSTDs of −3.5, −3.5, −2.7, and −2.4 and outfit ZSTDs of −2.5, −3.0, −2.4, and −1.9, respectively). It is also possible to check the item difficulty estimates from Table 13.1 (ACT: measure) where the items are sorted from the easiest (Item 18 at −3.15 logits) to the most difficult (Item 5 at 2.42 logits).

4. Checking a person analysis report

To sort the students according to their degree of liking for scientific activities, open Table 17.1 (PUPIL: measure). The student with the highest level of "liking of science" is LF Rossner (entry number 2 at 6.07 logits). The student with the lowest level of "liking of science" is A Sabol (entry number 53 at −1.61 logits).

5. Checking the rating scale functioning

To determine how well the rating scale functions, first check the item analysis report (Table 13.1) in the column PTMEA CORR. to see if there is any item that should have its polarity reversed. Because no negative point measure correlations are observed, proceed to checking out the rating scale functioning from Table 3.2 (Rating (partial credit) scale). This rating scale satisfies the second and third criteria of rating scale functioning, as shown in the observed count column in the top table. The progression of observed averages (in the OBSVD AVRGE column) satisfied the fourth criterion. Next, check the outfit mean square value of each rating category to see that none of these three categories have their outfit values above 2.0. Finally, check the thresholds (structure measures) from the table in the middle of the report as well as the CCCs at the bottom of the report. The advancement of these thresholds conforms to the sixth, seventh, and eighth criteria. Thus, the rating scale for the "liking for science" questionnaire functioned properly.

ARE THERE ANY OTHER TYPES OF RASCH MODELS?

The Rasch model for dichotomous responses, RSM, and PCM are basic Rasch models that can handle many types of data in the social sciences. However, there are some circumstances when the response types can be better analyzed using other types of Rasch models. Listed below are brief descriptions of other commonly employed Rasch models that may be useful (note that there are even more Rasch models available for less frequently encountered types of data).

1. The binomial trials model (Wright & Masters, 1982) is a model suitable for data obtained from a study where persons are given multiple independent attempts at an item and the number of successes in those attempts is counted. An example is a shooting competition where each person is allowed to shoot several times at a target and the number of hits is counted (Wright & Mok, 2004).

2. The Poisson model (Rasch, 1960) is a model applied for the count of the occurrences of an event that can happen an infinite number of times. An example is a count of the number of reading errors a person makes while reading aloud a passage. The count can range from 0 to the number of words in the passage (Stone, 2004; Wolfe & Smith, 2007a).

3. The Saltus model (M. Wilson, 1989, 2004b) is a model developed for scaling of developmental data where the latent trait ability progresses in stages, and the leap from one stage to the next changes the way in which the measurement instrument functions. One example would be the Piagetian theory of development where the progression of students' understandings from one stage to the next can result in changes in the hierarchy of item difficulty estimates (M. Wilson & Draney, 1997).

4. Rank-ordered data can be analyzed using the technique proposed by Linacre (1989b). This form of a Rasch model is applicable to the analysis of data where respondents are asked to rank order a group of objects (or persons) based on the amount of latent trait that the objects (or persons) possess. An example is a judge ordering pianists from the most to least proficient (Wright & Mok, 2004).

5. The many-faceted Rasch measurement (MFRM) model (Linacre, 1989a) is an extension of the basic Rasch model to analyze data that have more than two facets. For example, using judges to assess the performance of students on a complicated task generally involves three

measurement facets: the ability of students, the difficulty of tasks, and the severity of judges (Linacre & Wright, 2004). The MFRM model allows researchers to calibrate many interacting measurement facets onto a common scale.

6. The linear logistic test model (LLTM) (Fischer, 1973) is an extension of the Rasch model, allowing item difficulty parameters to be decomposed into specified linear combinations of predictors of item difficulty. An example of its application is in testing the hypothesis that item difficulty is a function of multiple cognitive operations involved in the solution process, each of which has a unique difficulty parameter (Fischer, 1995b).

7. The mixed Rasch model (Rost, 1990, 1991) is a combination of Rasch models and latent class models in a way that a Rasch model holds within each latent class, but model parameters are allowed to vary across classes. The main purpose of using it is to classify a possible inhomogeneous sample into Rasch-homogeneous subsamples. An example is the analysis of neurological deficits in a group of stroke patients, which is composed of two possible subpopulations of patients: those with right hemispheric stroke and those with left hemispheric stroke whose patterns of neurological deficits may be different (Wolfe & Smith, 2007a). Another example, by Wagner-Menghin (2007), demonstrates using the mixed Rasch model to identify subsamples that exhibited different types of response sets.

8. The multidimensional random coefficient multinomial logit model (MRCMLM) (Adams, Wilson, & Wang, 1997; Briggs & Wilson, 2004) is a flexible multidimensional extension of the various unidimensional Rasch models described in this section (except the mixed Rasch model). The MRCMLM models multiple dimensions for each of these models in a confirmatory mode (i.e., item mappings onto the various latent dimensions must be specified by the analyst). Such a model is appropriate when multiple latent traits are measured simultaneously and those latent traits are likely to be correlated.

Summary

Rasch measurement is an important tool for quality control (item and person fit, rating scale functioning), construct validation (see Wolfe & Smith, 2007a, 2007b), theory development (variable and expected score maps), and the creation of interval measures from ordinal observations in the social sciences (see E. V. Smith & Smith, 2004, 2007, for many more applications). This chapter introduced basic measurement concepts and described how Rasch models may resolve many perceived shortcomings found in true-score theory and other classes of LTT models. The underlying psychometric requirements of the Rasch models were discussed. Three commonly used Rasch models—the basic Rasch model for dichotomous data, the RSM, and the PCM—were described. General guidelines on how to evaluate the fit of the data to the Rasch model using various types of fit statistics were described, and general steps in interpreting results from Rasch analysis, both for dichotomous and polytomous data, were provided. Finally, many other types of Rasch models that researchers may find useful to apply with other types of data were described. It is hoped that this short introduction helps interested researchers to see how Rasch models can help improve measurement systems in social science research.

References

Adams, R. J., Wilson, M. R., & Wang, W. C. (1997). The multidimensional random coefficients multinomial logit. *Applied Psychological Measurement, 21,* 1–23.

American Educational Research Association, American Psychological Association, & National Council on Measurement in Education. (1999). *Standards for educational and psychological testing.* Washington, DC: American Educational Research Association.

Andrich, D. (1978a). Application of a psychometric model to ordered categories which are scored with successive integers. *Applied Psychological Measurement, 2,* 581–594.

Andrich, D. (1978b). A rating formulation for ordered response categories. *Psychometrika, 43,* 561–573.

Andrich, D. (2004a). Controversy and the Rasch model: A characteristic of incompatible paradigms? In E. V. Smith Jr. & R. M. Smith (Eds.), *Introduction to Rasch measurement* (pp. 143–166). Maple Grove, MN: JAM Press.

Andrich, D. (2004b). Understanding resistance to the data-model relationship in Rasch's paradigm: A reflection for the next generation. In E. V. Smith Jr. & R. M. Smith (Eds.), *Introduction to*

Rasch measurement (pp. 167–200). Maple Grove, MN: JAM Press.

Bejar, I. I. (1983). *Achievement testing: Recent advances.* Beverly Hills, CA: Sage.

Birnbaum, A. (1968). Some latent trait models and their use in inferring an examinee's ability. In F. M. Lord & M. R. Novick (Eds.), *Statistical theories of mental test scores* (pp. 397–545). Reading, MA: Addison-Wesley.

Bond, T. G., & Fox, C. M. (2001). *Applying the Rasch model: Fundamental measurement in the human sciences.* Mahwah, NJ: Lawrence Erlbaum.

Briggs, D. C., & Wilson, M. (2004). An introduction to multidimensional measurement using Rasch models. In E. V. Smith Jr. & R. M. Smith (Eds.), *Introduction to Rasch measurement* (pp. 322–341). Maple Grove, MN: JAM Press.

Brogden, H. E. (1977). The Rasch model, the law of comparative judgment and additive conjoint measurement. *Psychometrika, 42,* 631–634.

Embretson, S. E. (1996). Item response theory models and spurious interaction effects in factorial ANOVA designs. *Applied Psychological Measurement, 20,* 201–212.

Embretson, S. E., & Reise, S. P. (2000). *Item response theory for psychologists.* Mahwah, NJ: Lawrence Erlbaum.

Engelhard, G., Jr. (1994). Historical views of the concept of invariance in measurement theory. In M. Wilson (Ed.), *Objective measurement: Theory into practice* (Vol. 2, pp. 73–99). Norwood, NJ: Ablex.

Fischer, G. H. (1973). The linear logistic test model as an instrument in educational research. *Acta Psychologica, 37,* 359–374.

Fischer, G. H. (1995a). Derivations of the Rasch model. In G. H. Fischer & I. W. Molenaar (Eds.), *Rasch models: Foundations, recent developments, and applications* (pp. 15–38). New York: Springer Verlag.

Fischer, G. H. (1995b). The linear logistic test model. In G. H. Fischer & I. W. Molenaar (Eds.), *Rasch models: Foundations, recent developments, and applications* (pp. 131–155). New York: Springer Verlag.

Fisher, W. P., Jr. (1992). Reliability statistics. *Rasch Measurement Transactions, 6*(3), 238.

Gulliksen, H. (1950). *Theory of mental tests.* New York: John Wiley.

Hambleton, R. K. (2000). Emergence of item response modeling in instrument development and data analysis. *Medical Care, 38*(9, Suppl. II), II60–II65.

Hambleton, R. K., Swaminathan, H., & Rogers, H. J. (1991). *Fundamentals of item response theory.* Newbury Park, CA: Sage.

Hays, R. D., Morales, L. S., & Reise, S. P. (2000). Item response theory and health outcomes measurement in the 21st century. *Medical Care, 38*(9, Suppl. II), II28–II42.

Karabatsos, G. (2001). The Rasch model, additive conjoint measurement, and new models of probabilistic measurement theory. *Journal of Applied Measurement, 2,* 389–423.

Kuhn, T. S. (1961). The function of measurement in modern physical science. *Isis, 52,* 161–190.

Linacre, J. M. (1989a). *Many-faceted Rasch measurement.* Chicago: MESA Press.

Linacre, J. M. (1989b). Rank ordering and Rasch measurement. *Rasch Measurement Transactions, 2*(4), 41–42.

Linacre, J. M. (2002). What do infit and outfit mean-square and standardized mean? *Rasch Measurement Transactions, 16*(2), 878.

Linacre, J. M. (2004). Optimizing rating scale category effectiveness. In E. V. Smith Jr. & R. M. Smith (Eds.), *Introduction to Rasch measurement* (pp. 258–278). Maple Grove, MN: JAM Press.

Linacre, J. M. (2005). *A user's guide to WINSTEPS Rasch-model computer programs.* Chicago: WINSTEPS.com.

Linacre, J. M. (2006). WINSTEPS: Rasch measurement computer program (Version 3.60). Chicago: WINSTEPS.com.

Linacre, J. M., & Wright, B. D. (1989). The "length" of a logit. *Rasch Measurement Transactions, 3*(2), 54–55.

Linacre, J. M., & Wright, B. D. (1994). Chi-square fit statistics. *Rasch Measurement Transactions, 8*(2), 350.

Linacre, J. M., & Wright, B. D. (2004). Construction of measures from many-facet data. In E. V. Smith Jr. & R. M. Smith (Eds.), *Introduction to Rasch measurement* (pp. 296–321). Maple Grove, MN: JAM Press.

Luce, R. D., & Tukey, J. W. (1964). Simultaneous conjoint measurement: A new type of fundamental measurement. *Journal of Mathematical Psychology, 1,* 1–27.

Luppescu, S. (1995). Comparing measures. *Rasch Measurement Transactions, 9*(1), 410–411.

Masters, G. N. (1982). A Rasch model for partial credit scoring. *Psychometrika, 47*(2), 149–174.

Masters, G. N., & Wright, B. D. (1996). The partial credit model. In W. J. van der Linden & R. K. Hambleton (Eds.), *Handbook of modern item response theory* (pp. 101–122). New York: Springer.

Mead, R. J. (1980). Using the Rasch model to identify person-based measurement disturbances. In *Proceedings of the 1979 Computer Adaptive Testing Conference.* Minneapolis: University of Minnesota.

Merbitz, C., Morris, J., & Grip, J. C. (1989). Ordinal scales and foundations of misinference. *Archives of Physical Medicine and Rehabilitation, 70,* 308–312.

Mislevy, R. (1987). Recent developments in item response theory with implications for teacher certification. In E. Rothkopf (Ed.), *Review of research in education* (Vol. 14, pp. 239–275). Washington, DC: American Educational Research Association.

Myford, C. M., & Wolfe, E. W. (2004a). Detecting and measuring rater effects using many-facet Rasch measurement: Part I. In E. V. Smith Jr. & R. M. Smith (Eds.), *Introduction to Rasch measurement* (pp. 460–517). Maple Grove, MN: JAM Press.

Myford, C. M., & Wolfe, E. W. (2004b). Detecting and measuring rater effects using many-facet Rasch measurement: Part II. In E. V. Smith Jr. & R. M. Smith (Eds.), *Introduction to Rasch measurement* (pp. 518–574). Maple Grove, MN: JAM Press.

O'Neill, T. (2005). *NCLEX psychometric technical brief: Definition of a logit.* Retrieved May 2006 from www.ncsbn.org/pdfs/02_18_05_brief.pdf

Perline, R., Wright, B. D., & Wainer, H. (1979). The Rasch model as additive conjoint measurement. *Applied Psychological Measurement, 3,* 237–255.

Rasch, G. (1960). *Probabilistic models for some intelligence and achievement tests.* Copenhagen, Denmark: Danish Institute for Educational Research.

Romanoski, J., & Douglas, G. (2002). Rasch-transformed raw scores and two-way ANOVA: A simulation analysis. *Journal of Applied Measurement, 3,* 421–430.

Rost, J. (1990). Rasch models in latent classes: An integration of two approaches to item analysis. *Applied Psychological Measurement, 14,* 271–282.

Rost, J. (1991). A logistic mixture distribution model for polytomous item responses. *British Journal of Mathematical and Statistical Psychology, 44,* 75–92.

Schumacker, R. E. (2004). Rasch measurement: The dichotomous model. In E. V. Smith Jr. & R. M. Smith (Eds.), *Introduction to Rasch measurement* (pp. 226–257). Maple Grove, MN: JAM Press.

Sijtsma, K., & Molenaar, I. W. (2002). *Introduction to nonparametric item response theory.* Thousand Oaks, CA: Sage.

Sireci, S. G., Thissen, D., & Wainer, H. (1991). On the reliability of testlet-based tests. *Journal of Educational Measurement, 28*(3), 237–247.

Smith, E. V., Jr. (2004a). Detecting and evaluating the impact of multidimensionality using item fit statistics and principal component analysis of residuals. In E. V. Smith Jr. & R. M. Smith (Eds.), *Introduction to Rasch measurement* (pp. 575–600). Maple Grove, MN: JAM Press.

Smith, E. V., Jr. (2004b). Evidence for the reliability of measures and validity of measure interpretation: A Rasch measurement perspective. In E. V. Smith Jr. & R. M. Smith (Eds.), *Introduction to Rasch measurement* (pp. 93–122). Maple Grove, MN: JAM Press.

Smith, E. V., Jr. (2005). Effect of item redundancy on Rasch item and person estimates. *Journal of Applied Measurement, 6,* 147–163.

Smith, E. V., Jr., & Andrich, D. (2005, April). *Why Rasch measurement or why don't (some) psychometricians get along?* Paper presented at the annual meeting of the American Educational Research Association, Montreal, Canada.

Smith, E. V., Jr., Conrad, K. M., Chang, K., & Piazza, J. (2002). An introduction to Rasch measurement for scale development and person assessment. *Journal of Nursing Measurement, 10*(3), 189–206.

Smith, E. V., Jr., & Smith, R. M. (Eds.). (2004). *Introduction to Rasch measurement: Theory, models, and applications.* Maple Grove, MN: JAM Press.

Smith, E. V., Jr., & Smith, R. M. (Eds.). (2007). *Rasch measurement: Advanced and specialized applications.* Maple Grove, MN: JAM Press.

Smith, R. M. (1982). *Detecting measurement disturbances with the Rasch model.* Unpublished doctoral dissertation, University of Chicago.

Smith, R. M. (1992). *Applications of Rasch measurement.* Chicago: MESA Press.

Smith, R. M. (1999). *Rasch measurement models: Interpreting WINSTEPS/Bigsteps and Facets output.* Morgan Hill, CA: JAM Press.

Smith, R. M. (2004). Fit analysis in latent trait measurement models. In E. V. Smith Jr. & R. M. Smith (Eds.), *Introduction to Rasch measurement* (pp. 73–92). Maple Grove, MN: JAM Press.

Spearman, C. (1907). Demonstration of formulae for true measurement of correlation. *American Journal of Psychology, 18,* 161–169.

Spearman, C. (1913). Correlations of sums and differences. *British Journal of Psychology, 5,* 417–426.

Stenner, A. J. (1994). Specific objectivity. *Rasch Measurement Transactions, 8*(3), 374.

Stevens, S. S. (1946). On the theory of scales of measurement. *Science, 103,* 677–680.

Stone, M. H. (2004). Substantive scale construction. In E. V. Smith Jr. & R. M. Smith (Eds.), *Introduction to Rasch measurement* (pp. 201–225). Maple Grove, MN: JAM Press.

Thissen, D., Steinberg, L., & Mooney, J. (1989). Trace lines for testlets: A use of multiple-categorical response models. *Journal of Educational Measurement, 26*(3), 247–260.

Wagner-Menghin, M. M. (2007). The mixed-Rasch model: An example for analyzing the meaning of response latencies in a personality questionnaire. In E. V. Smith Jr. & R. M. Smith (Eds.), *Rasch measurement: Advanced and specialized applications* (pp. 103–120). Maple Grove, MN: JAM Press.

Way, W. D. (1994, September). *Psychometric models for computer-based licensure testing.* Paper presented at the annual meeting of CLEAR, Boston.

Wilson, E. B., & Hilferty, M. M. (1931). The distribution of chi-square. *Proceedings of the National Academy of Sciences of the United States of America, 17,* 684–688.

Wilson, M. (1989). Saltus: A psychometric model for discontinuity in cognitive development. *Psychological Bulletin, 105,* 276–289.

Wilson, M. (2004a). On choosing a model for measuring. In E. V. Smith Jr. & R. M. Smith (Eds.), *Introduction to Rasch measurement* (pp. 123–142). Maple Grove, MN: JAM Press.

Wilson, M. (2004b). The Saltus model. *Rasch Measurement Transactions, 17*(4), 953.

Wilson, M. (2005). *Constructing measures: An item response modeling approach.* Mahwah, NJ: Lawrence Erlbaum.

Wilson, M., & Draney, K. (1997, March). *Beyond Rasch in the measurement of stage-like development.* Paper presented at the annual meeting of the American Educational Research Association, Chicago.

Wolfe, E., & Smith, E. V., Jr. (2007a). Instrument development tools and activities for measure validation using Rasch models: Part I—Instrument development tools. In E. V. Smith Jr. & R. M. Smith (Eds.), *Rasch measurement: Advanced and specialized applications* (pp. 202–242). Maple Grove, MN: JAM Press.

Wolfe, E., & Smith, E. V., Jr. (2007b). Instrument development tools and activities for measure validation using Rasch models: Part II—Validation activities. In E. V. Smith Jr. & R. M. Smith (Eds.), *Rasch measurement: Advanced and specialized applications* (pp. 243–290). Maple Grove, MN: JAM Press.

Wright, B. D. (1985). Additivity in psychological measurement. In E. E. Roskam (Ed.), *Measurement and personality assessment* (pp. 101–111). Amsterdam: Elsevier.

Wright, B. D. (1999). Rasch measurement models. In G. N. Masters & J. P. Keeves (Eds.), *Advances in measurement in educational research and assessment* (pp. 85–97). New York: Pergamon.

Wright, B. D., & Linacre, J. M. (1989). Observations are always ordinal; measurement, however, must be interval. *Archives of Physical Medicine and Rehabilitation, 70,* 857–860.

Wright, B. D., & Masters, G. N. (1982). *Rating scale analysis.* Chicago: MESA Press.

Wright, B. D., & Mok, M. M. C. (2004). An overview of the family of Rasch measurement models. In E. V. Smith Jr. & R. M. Smith (Eds.), *Introduction to Rasch measurement* (pp. 1–24). Maple Grove, MN: JAM Press.

Wright, B. D., & Panchapakesan, N. (1969). A procedure for sample-free item analysis. *Educational and Psychological Measurement, 29,* 23–48.

Wright, B. D., & Stone, M. H. (1979). *Best test design.* Chicago: MESA Press.

Yen, W. M. (1993). Scaling performance assessments: Strategies for managing local item dependence. *Journal of Educational Measurement, 30*(3), 187–213.

Zenisky, A. L., Hambleton, R. K., & Sireci, S. G. (2003). *Effects of local item dependence on the validity of IRT item, test, and ability statistics.* Washington, DC: Association of American Medical Colleges.

Zhu, W., Updyke, W. F., & Lewandowski, C. (1997). Post-hoc Rasch analysis of optimal categorization of an ordered-response scale. *Journal of Outcome Measurement, 1,* 286–304.

5

APPLICATIONS OF THE MULTIFACETED RASCH MODEL

EDWARD W. WOLFE

LIDIA DOBRIA

This chapter describes the multifaceted extension to the family of Rasch models, identifies the advantages of using these models for scaling data in the behavioral sciences, identifies software that implements multifaceted Rasch models (MFRMs), and presents three examples that apply the MFRM. The MFRM extends the family of Rasch models to include multiple facets of the measurement context. We use the term *facets* to refer to any component of the measurement context that is assumed to contribute systematic measurement error or create a main effect that is of substantive interest. In this sense, the family of models that has been traditionally called Rasch models contains single-faceted models that include items as the only facet of measurement. In many contexts, however, multiple facets are of interest. For example, items may represent different domains of performance, raters may rate responses to multiple items, or groups may respond to a variety of items. In each case, the MFRM allows one to estimate person measures while correcting for variation across subsets of these measurement facets.

MULTIFACETED RASCH MODEL SPECIFICATIONS

The MFRM specifies a parameter for each of the facets of the measurement context, where the responses may be dichotomous, polytomous, binomial trials, or Poisson counts, and partial credit versus rating scale structures can be applied to each facet of polytomous models (Linacre, 1994). For example, in a context in which raters (with bias represented by β_r) rate person (with latent trait represented by θ_n) responses to several items (with difficulty represented by δ_i) on a multipoint rating scale (with threshold difficulties represented by τ), one could choose any of the following configurations of the MFRM: (a) Raters apply a common rating scale across all items, $LN(\pi_{nirk}/\pi_{nirk-1}) = \theta_n - \delta_i - \beta_r - \tau_k$—a multifaceted rating scale model; (b) each rater uses a unique rating scale but applies that rating scale consistently across items, $LN(\pi_{nirk}/\pi_{nirk-1}) = \theta_n - \delta_i - \beta_r - \tau_{rk}$—a rater partial credit model; or (c) raters assign a common rating scale but that rating scale varies across items, $LN(\pi_{nirk}/\pi_{nirk-1}) = \theta_n - \delta_i - \beta_r - \tau_{ik}$—an item

71

partial credit model. As with other members of the family of Rasch models, the MFRM that is depicted here measures a single latent trait (i.e., is a unidimensional model), although it can be extended to measure multiple latent traits (i.e., a multidimensional model).

The general equation for the MFRM in its rating scale form, $LN(\pi_{nk}/\pi_{nk-1}) = \theta_n - \sum_{facets} \varepsilon - \tau_k$, indicates that the log-odds (logit) of a person being assigned an item score in category k rather than category $k - 1$ is a linear equation in which θ_n represents the latent trait being measured, $\sum_{facets} \varepsilon$ represents a linear combination of the various documented facets of the measurement context that contribute systematic error (e.g., items, raters, item types, domains, person groups), and τ_k represents the relative difficulty of rating scale category k. As is true for other models in the family of Rasch models, the estimate of θ_n, the measure for person n, is the parameter estimate of primary interest. The parameters assumed under $\sum_{facets} \varepsilon$, on the other hand, represent sources of systematic error variance for which the MFRM controls in the estimation of θ_n. One alternative to allowing the components of $\sum_{facets} \varepsilon$ to influence the θ_n estimates would be to obtain a score for every combination of persons with every element of every facet of the measurement context (e.g., every person responds to every item, and all responses are rated by every rater—a fully crossed design for data collection) so that the cumulative systematic error is the same for all persons. However, this approach is not efficient. The MFRM removes the influence of small samplings of the elements represented by $\sum_{facets} \varepsilon$ from the estimation of θ_n.

The parameter estimates assumed under $\sum_{facets} \varepsilon$ may be of substantive interest. For example, in the rating scale version of the MFRM that controls for rater bias and item difficulty, $LN(\pi_{nirk}/\pi_{nirk-1}) = \theta_n - \delta_i - \beta_r - \tau_k$, item difficulty estimates may provide insights into the internal structure of the domain in question. In fact, agreement between these empirical estimates of item difficulty and the expected rank ordering of item difficulties based on expert judgment or theory-based predictions may provide important evidence relating to the substantive aspect of validity (Wolfe & Smith, in press-a, in press-b). Similarly, and as we will demonstrate in an example application that follows, rater bias estimates may be useful for identifying differences in standards being used by raters and, therefore, raters who may need additional training.

Parameter estimates for the MFRMs are obtained by applying numerical methods, such as maximum likelihood or Bayesian approaches, to observed data, and commercial software that implements the MFRMs is readily available. Parameter estimation results in a parameter estimate for each case (i.e., person) and for each element of each facet depicted by the MFRM, and these parameter estimates are placed on a common scale so that descriptive comparisons can be made between persons, items, raters, or other components of the MFRM. In addition, the parameter estimation process allows for the depiction of the precision of each parameter estimate by a standard error that is associated with each estimated parameter. A common problem with the standard errors that are produced by commercial software is the fact that implementation of the MFRM typically ignores dependence among the multiple ratings assigned to a particular person so that the standard errors are overly optimistic in terms of their depiction of the precision of the parameter estimates.

Four useful indices can be computed when estimating parameters for the MFRM. First and second, the *parameter estimates* for each person and for each element of each facet in the MFRM and the *fair average* transformations of these values to the original raw score metric indicate the degree to which missing data and sparse sampling may result in invalid raw score comparisons between persons across elements of a particular facet. Both of these indices indicate the degree to which the person or element in question differs from the remaining persons or elements, taking into account discrepancies that arise due to sampling among the other facets contained in the MFRM. For example, person measures indicate, on a log-odds unit (*logit*) scale, the degree to which a person differs on the target construct, adjusting for differences between the levels of rater bias and/or item difficulty encountered by that person, from other persons. The person fair average simply transforms this logit value to the raw score scale. These indices are particularly useful when persons do not respond to all items or are not rated by all raters in an MFRM, but they are also helpful when one desires to make comparisons between elements of a particular facet (e.g., comparing levels of rater bias) when each element of that facet is not coupled with all persons (e.g., raters only rate a subset of persons).[1]

Third, *data-to-model fit indices* can be computed for each person and for each element of each facet of the MFRM. Although there are numerous fit indices used in the field of item response modeling (Karabatsos, 2003), we focus on the standardized version of the mean squared residuals (z_{msq}) because of its ready availability in commercial software (Linacre, 2006; Wu, Adams, & Wilson, 1998) and because of the accuracy of its asymptotically expected Type I error rates (Smith, Schumacker, & Bush, 1998). This index has a range from $-\infty$ to $+\infty$, with negative values indicating vectors of scores that are overly consistent with the expected values based on the MFRM, positive values indicating vectors of scores that are overly inconsistent with the expected values, and values near zero indicating that the vectors of scores exhibit a reasonable amount of variation around expected values. As we will demonstrate in the examples that follow, these fit indices may be useful for identifying a wide variety of potentially problematic issues relating to the measurement context. The long list of issues includes poor item quality, differential item dimensionality or differential item functioning, differential use of tools or differential implementation of instruction relating to achievement tests, cheating, examinee carelessness or deception, guessing or aberrant rating behaviors, idiosyncratic use of rating scale categories (overuse, underuse), rater drift, and non-reverse-scored negatively worded items (Linacre, 1995; Smith, 1996; Wolfe, 2004; Wolfe, Chiu, & Myford, 2000; Wolfe, Moulder, & Myford, 2001; Wright, 1991, 1995).

Fourth, parameters may be estimated for interactions between persons and the facets contained in the model or between two facets in the MFRM. Specifically, the general form of the MFRM can be extended to include *interaction terms* that depict the deviation of pairings of between-facet elements from their average parameter estimates. The model for that extension, $LN(\pi_{nk}/\pi_{nk-1}) = \theta_n - \sum_{facets} \varepsilon - \tau_k - \iota_{ab}$, includes a parameter ($\iota_{ab}$) that can be estimated and that indicates how far each element of two facets or persons and a single facet (indexed as *a* and *b*) deviate from the average parameter estimate of their respective distributions of parameter estimates. As an example, consider the issue of differential item functioning (DIF). When DIF exists, the difficulty of a particular item changes across groups of persons. That is, there is a group-by-item interaction. The appropriate MFRM for DIF would take the following form: $LN(\pi_k/\pi_{k-1}) = \theta_{person} - \delta_{item} - \gamma_{group} - \tau_{category} - \iota_{Item \times Group}$, where γ_{group} indicates the degree to which person groups differ from one another on the construct of interest, and $\iota_{Item \times Group}$ indicates the degree to which groups differ from one another on a particular item beyond the amount captured by an item's overall difficulty across groups and a group's overall performance across items. If the value of $\iota_{Item \times Group}$ differs from a null value of zero beyond what is considered a chance level for a particular item-by-group combination, then the item exhibits DIF.

ADVANTAGES OF THE MULTIFACETED RASCH MODEL

Historically, measurement data have been scaled within the true-score test theory (TSTT) framework (Lord & Novick, 1968), in which an observed score is decomposed into a true-score and an error score component. In TSTT, measurement error is assumed to be random, and sources of error are not differentiated from one another. Because of this, different measures of the impact of error on observed measures are created, each depicting the impact of a different kind of measurement error. For example, test-retest reliability indices indicate the stability of measures across measurement occasions, parallel-test form reliability indices indicate the stability of measures across test forms, and interrater reliability indices indicate the stability of measures across raters (Smith & Kulikowich, 2004).

This interpretation of error ignores the possibility that the data may contain multiple sources of error, preventing them from being isolated, identified, or differentiated among (Gilmore, 1983). Generalizability theory (G-theory) provides an alternative conceptual framework that permits the investigation of multiple sources of error simultaneously (Cronbach, Gleser, Nanda, & Rajaratnam, 1972). In G-theory, a universe score, defined as the average score for the object of measurement (usually persons) over all identified measurement conditions, replaces the notion of true score, and error is viewed as being systematic and as originating from multiple sources. A generalizability study identifies and estimates the variances associated with each error source, as well as with interactions between error sources. These variance components are subsequently used in a decision study to obtain measurements for a particular purpose and optimize future data collections.

While G-theory provides an effective tool for identifying multiple sources of error and estimating the error variance associated with raw scores, it does so by depicting group-level effects rather than effects exhibited by individuals. More important, G-theory does not attempt to correct individual raw scores for the impact of the measurement conditions that produced them. When the raw score is reported as the measure of a person's ability, without taking into consideration the impact that other measurement facets (e.g., item difficulty, rater severity) might have had on the estimate of ability, luck of the draw rules the day. The particular raw score a person receives could be a reflection of great unfairness, depending on the difficulty of the item he or she responded to and/or the severity of the rater(s) that scored the performance.

One advantage of the MFRM is that it corrects each observed score for the presence of systematic measurement error it models. The MFRM transforms each raw score into a linear measure corrected for the impact that sampling across measurement facets has on person measures. For example, suppose we want to take into account the impact of rater severity on examinee ability estimates. Under the MFRM, ability estimates are expressed as a function of the facet elements that produced them. A person rated on a task by two lenient raters will have an ability estimate adjusted to reflect the raters' leniency. Another person, hypothetically of the same ability, rated on the same task by two severe raters, will have, under the MFRM, an ability estimate approximately equal to that of the first person. The ability estimates of both persons are thus freed from the potentially unfair influence of rater bias. The approach adopted by G-theory, on the other hand, would only estimate the magnitude of the systematic variance contributed by raters without making any corrections to individual raw scores, while the approach adopted by TSTT would treat all raters as displaying the same level of bias.

Another advantage of the MFRM is that it can depict and correct for the systematic error associated with interactions between measurement facets. As mentioned previously, interaction terms can be included in the MRFM, and these interaction terms can provide information beyond what

is available from the single-facet Rasch models. For example, if we are interested in determining the degree to which a rater rates particular groups of persons differentially, we can introduce a rater-by-group interaction term in the model. In addition to estimating the size of the interaction between each rater and the group in question, the MFRM will correct person ability measures to account for this interaction. G-theory also estimates variances associated with interactions between multiple sources of error, but it does so at the group level and does not adjust individual ability estimates for the presence of the interactions. TSTT treats all such interactions as random error and assumes that they have no systematic impact on observed scores.

As another advantage of the MFRM, we mention its capability to overcome the sample dependency of both persons and facets of the measurement context. When the data meet the model's dimensionality and parameter invariance requirements, the resulting measures are disentangled from the distributional details of the various persons, items, or raters included in the analysis and can be generalized to other samples (Andrich, 1988). Yet another advantage of the MFRM is that, when data fit model expectations, the measures produced by the model meet additivity requirements. That is—unlike raw scores, which do not necessarily increase in equal increments across the construct being measured—the measurement units produced when measurement data are scaled using a Rasch model express equal intervals over their range.

Because of its probabilistic approach to constructing measures, the MFRM is also capable of routinely handling missing data. In contrast with G-theory and TSTT, both of which require complete data sets, the MFRM relaxes this requirement and makes it possible to estimate measures from surprisingly sparse data matrices. As Linacre (1996) notes, the only constraints the MFRM imposes on data collection designs are that "the measures be estimable unambiguously in one frame of reference or that the relationship between disjointed subsets of observations be specifiable" (p. 95).

MULTIFACETED RASCH MODEL SOFTWARE

Two commonly available pieces of commercial software can implement the MFRM: Facets

(Linacre, 2006) and ACER ConQuest (Wu et al., 1998).

Facets (currently Version 3.62). available from www.winsteps.com/facets.htm, is a user-friendly, Windows-native program, specifically developed for the analysis of Rasch models that encompass multiple facets of measurement. The program uses a joint maximum likelihood estimation procedure to calculate parameter estimates as well as the corresponding standard errors and fit statistics for each element of every facet included in the analysis. Facets also provides calibrations of response format structures such as rating scales, rank orders, and letter grades. Once parameter estimates are calculated, the Facets program has the capability of investigating interactions between elements of various facets of measurement (differential facet functioning). The bias/interaction reports produced by the program identify the size and statistical significance of each interaction in detailed format. The Facets program automatically produces a results output file at the end of the estimation process. Users can also request specific output tables and result files (in both tabular and graphical formats) via pull-down menus.

ACER ConQuest is another popular program that can implement the MFRM. ConQuest (currently Version 2.2.0), available from http://www.assess.com/Software/ConQuest.htm, is a computer program that can scale unidimensional and multidimensional versions of both item response and latent regression models. The item response model fitted by ConQuest is the generalized multidimensional random coefficients multinomial logit model (MRCMLM; Adams, Wilson, & Wang, 1997), and level of generality in the specification of this model allows the program to analyze a wide variety of Rasch models, including the MFRM. ConQuest uses marginal maximum likelihood methods to estimate model parameters. The estimation process uses a two-level formulation of the model, which treats person parameters as random variables. This is different from the Facets program implementation of the MFRM, which considers all parameters, including person parameters, as fixed. As a result, parameter estimates obtained in ConQuest will differ slightly from those produced by Facets for the same data. ConQuest fit statistics are also slightly different from the ones used by the Facets program, in that they constitute an extension for use with marginal maximum likelihood estimates in the context of a more generalized model (Wu, 1987).

When calculating parameter estimates, ConQuest constrains one element of each facet (usually the last), so that the average of the parameters for that facet equals zero. The program calculates standard errors and fit statistics for all nonconstrained parameters. In addition, ConQuest produces deviance statistics and a test of parameter equality. This allows researchers to use hierarchical model-fitting techniques to compare the fit of competing models and select the model that provides the most parsimonious fit to the given data set. ConQuest analysis results appear automatically in the output window or in a separate file when requested in the command file. ConQuest produces a total of six different tables and figures similar to, but less elaborate than, those available in the Facets computer program.

MULTIFACETED RASCH MODEL APPLICATIONS

Analysis of Cognitive Tasks Example

Our first example application of the MFRM investigates the scores obtained by 31 calculus students on a unit examination designed to determine student competency on differentiation techniques. The 20 items included in this examination were clustered into four groups of 5 items each, based on the type of function to be differentiated. The four types of functions present in the examination—polynomial/rational, exponential/logarithmic, trigonometric, and composite functions—required the use of increasingly more complex differentiation formulas and techniques. Student responses were scored by a single instructor on a 4-point rating scale ranging from 0 = *incorrect solution* to 3 = *correct solution,* with intermediary scores representing two successive stages of a partially correct response. Presentation of this example focuses on the interpretation of indices generated in an MFRM analysis. Specialized applications of the MFRM, to differential item functioning and to the evaluation of ratings, will be presented in the second and third examples.

To analyze the data in this example, we employ a three-facet rating scale version of the MFRM, $\text{LN}(\pi_{nijk}/\pi_{nijk-1}) = \theta_n - \lambda_i - \delta_{ij} - \tau_k$, as implemented in the Facets computer program. In addition to student proficiency, θ_n, this model accounts for the relative difficulties of different function types, λ_i, and items associated with each type, δ_{ij}. Since all responses were scored with the same 0-to-3 rating scale, we will assume a common scale across all items and employ the rating scale form of the MFRM for this analysis.

A variable map, shown in Figure 5.1, provides a graphic summary of the results of scaling these data to the MFRM. The logit scale displayed in the first column represents the metric within which the elements of every facet are measured. The single frame of reference provided by the logit scale allows for comparisons within and between facets, thus facilitating the interpretation of the results. The second column of the map displays the distribution of student proficiency measures (θ_n). Students appear in order of their proficiency measure from highest scoring, at the top of the column, to lowest scoring, at the bottom of the column. Student proficiencies group to form a relatively symmetrical, somewhat platykurtic distribution, with three outliers located at the high scoring end. The third column

lists the four function types in order of their difficulty (λ_i). Polynomial/rational and exponential/logarithmic functions types, the easiest to differentiate of the four, appear below the more difficult ones, trigonometric and composite function types. The fourth column compares the 20 items that appeared on this examination in terms of their difficulties (δ_{ij}). Items appearing higher in the column were more difficult for students to answer correctly than items appearing lower in the column. The rightmost column of the variable map displays the 4-point rating scaled used to score student responses. The horizontal lines across the column correspond to the thresholds between categories (τ_k). These indicate the point at which the probability of obtaining one rating begins to exceed the probability of obtaining the next highest rating.

Interpretation of these indicators follows a logical sequence. First, we evaluate the degree to which the rating scale functions as intended. Second, once that interpretive framework has

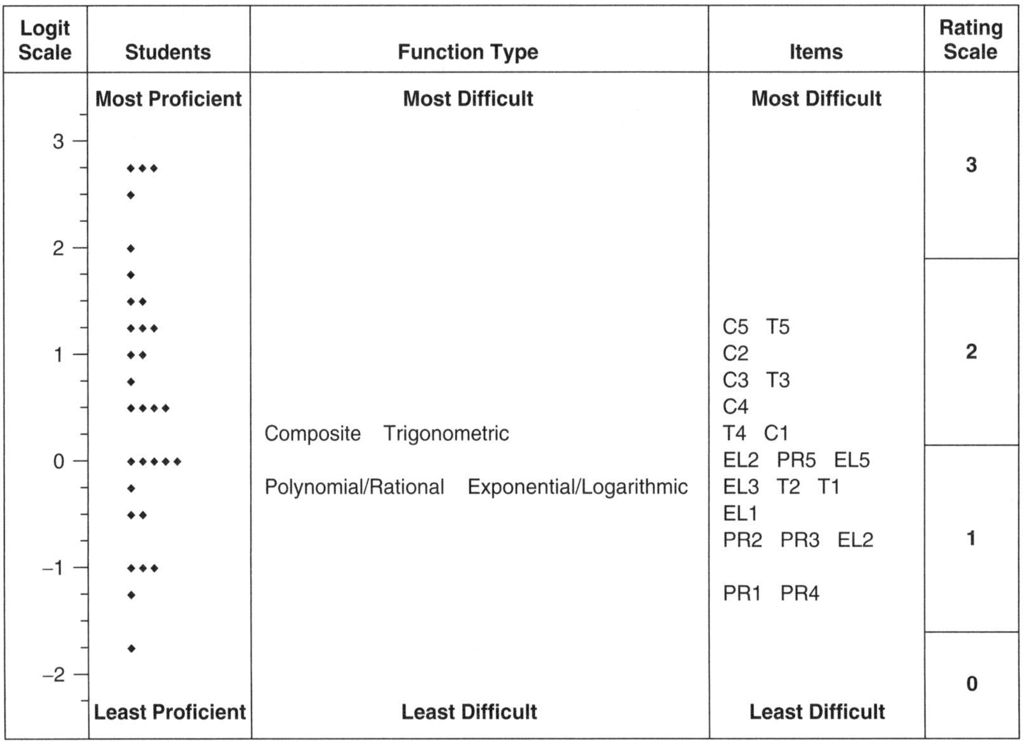

Logit Scale	Students	Function Type	Items	Rating Scale
	Most Proficient	Most Difficult	Most Difficult	
3 —				
	♦♦♦			3
	♦			
2 —	♦			
	♦			
	♦♦			
	♦♦♦		C5 T5	
1 —	♦♦		C2	2
	♦		C3 T3	
	♦♦♦♦		C4	
		Composite Trigonometric	T4 C1	
0 —	♦♦♦♦♦		EL2 PR5 EL5	
	♦	Polynomial/Rational Exponential/Logarithmic	EL3 T2 T1	
	♦♦		EL1	
			PR2 PR3 EL2	1
−1 —	♦♦♦		PR1 PR4	
	♦			
	♦			
−2 —				0
	Least Proficient	Least Difficult	Least Difficult	

♦ = 1 student; C = Composite Function Item; EL = Exponential/Logarithmic Function Item; PR = Polynomial/Rational Function Item; T = Trigonometric Function Item.

Figure 5.1   Variable map.

been established, we evaluate the degree to which the indicators through which we have elicited our observations—in this case, the function types and items—are suitable for making those observations. Third, when we are satisfied that the interpretive framework and the vehicles for making observations are functioning adequately, we interpret student performance. Table 5.1 presents indices relevant for evaluating functioning of the four-category rating scale (Linacre, 2004). First, we note that a sizable percentage of ratings were assigned to each rating category, meaning that the instructor made appropriate use of the rating scale by using all categories when scoring student answers. As a result, we can have confidence that the threshold parameter estimates are sufficiently precise. Second, the average student proficiency measures increase in parallel with the rating scale categories, indicating that, on average, students who obtained higher scores tended to receive high ratings across the test items—a prerequisite for using the rating scale to establish a frame of reference for the measures. Third, for each category, the unweighted mean square fit statistic values are equal or very close to the expected value of 1.0, indicating that the data exhibit a reasonable amount of unmodeled variability. Finally, category thresholds increase in a strictly monotonic

fashion. The clearly spaced threshold calibrations ($\tau_1 = -1.45 < \tau_2 = .07 < \tau_3 = 1.38$) imply that the variability in student performance can be adequately captured by the rating scale used.

Table 5.2 summarizes the four function types included in the model. Function-type difficulties span the length of about half of a logit (0.52). The mean difficulty was set at zero, and the standard deviation is 0.26. The ordering of the four function types matches the theory-based expectations of their difficulties, supporting the notion that these indicators function as intended. Unweighted mean square fit statistics associated with each function type are fairly close to the expected value of 1.0, indicating that student responses across items for each function type exhibit a reasonable amount of unmodeled variability.

Item difficulty calibrations provide additional insight into the difference between the difficulties of the four domains and the quality of the observations provided by the test. The fourth column of Figure 5.1 displays the location of each item's calibration, and the item labels indicate the function type each item represents. It is immediately apparent that composite function items are the most difficult and polynomial/rational items are the easiest—an outcome that is consistent with instructional practice and pedagogical theory. Students must

Table 5.1   Rating Scale Category Statistics

Category	Count %	Average Measure	Unweighted Mean Square	Threshold
0	13	−0.30	1.0	—
1	26	−0.23	1.1	−1.45
2	31	0.78	1.0	0.07
3	30	1.88	1.1	1.38

Table 5.2   Function-Type Summary Statistics

Function Type	Calibration	SE	Unweighted Mean Square
Polynomial/rational	−0.28	0.12	1.07
Exponential/logarithmic	−0.17	0.12	1.23
Trigonometric	0.20	0.12	0.85
Composite	0.24	0.11	0.95
Mean	0.00	0.12	1.02
SD	0.26	0.00	0.16

master the differentiation of simple polynomial/rational functions before differentiation of the more complex composite functions is introduced.

Table 5.3 presents the values of the calibrations for each of the 20 items. The item difficulties range from a low of −1.19 logits to a high of 1.36 logits, a range of 2.55 logits that evenly covers the middle and lower portions of the variable continuum. However, the items do not adequately cover the upper end of the performance continuum. The proficiency of 25% of the students is greater than the most difficult item, indicating that the measures of high-ability students may be insufficiently precise. Unweighted mean square fit statistics are adequate for the majority of the items, but two items (PR5 and C1) exhibit misfit. Examination of responses to both items indicates that some

low-performing students received higher than expected scores, and some high-performing students received lower than expected scores—the opposite of what would be expected, given the calibrations of these items.

The distribution of student proficiency measures spans the length of 4.64 logits, with the least proficient student located at −1.88 logits and the most proficient student at 2.69 logits ($M = 0.58$, $SD = 1.23$). The average standard error of the measures is 0.33. The reliability with which the test separates the sample of students is high ($r_{separation} = .92$), indicating that the variance attributable to individual differences between students far exceeds the error variance in the student proficiency measures. The student unweighted mean squared fit indices ($M = 1.02$, $SD = 0.38$) indicate good fit of the data to the MFRM. The response pattern of most students

Table 5.3   Item Summary Statistics

Item	Calibration	SE	Unweighted Mean Square
PR1	−1.18	0.28	0.73
PR2	−0.78	0.26	0.78
PR3	−0.85	0.28	1.48
PR4	−1.19	0.30	1.08
PR5	−0.30	0.26	1.60
EL1	−0.51	0.27	1.32
EL2	−0.88	0.27	1.29
EL3	−0.17	0.26	1.30
EL4	−0.26	0.25	0.99
EL5	−0.13	0.26	0.83
T1	0.65	0.25	0.52
T2	0.02	0.25	1.13
T3	−0.10	0.26	0.81
T4	0.32	0.25	1.31
T5	1.20	0.26	0.84
C1	0.29	0.25	1.54
C2	1.14	0.26	0.77
C3	0.81	0.25	0.63
C4	0.57	0.25	0.63
C5	1.36	0.26	0.89
Mean	0.00	0.26	1.02
SD	0.74	0.01	0.32

(87%) shows adequate fit, with unweighted mean squared fit values ranging within acceptable limits—0.6 to 1.4 (Wright & Linacre, 1994). The fit statistics of two students exceed the upper limit. In both cases, students received a higher than expected score on items of difficulty greater than their proficiency, suggesting that these students may have specialized knowledge relating to these items.

Differential Item Functioning Example

Our second example application of the MFRM is to an analysis of differential item functioning[2] between items on two versions of a literacy test developed for English- and Chinese-speaking preschool children. The two versions of the 51-item instrument were created by translating the English-language version into Chinese. The English and Chinese versions were administered to 557 children in the United States and 871 children in China, respectively. Responses of each child to each item were scored as correct or incorrect, and these data were scaled to the dichotomous DIF MFRM, $LN(\pi_k/\pi_{k-1}) = \theta_{person} - \delta_{item} - \gamma_{group} - \iota_{Item \times Group}$, using ConQuest (Wu et al., 1998). In this model, we are interested in determining whether the logits for a particular item differ for two groups when overall group differences are controlled. That is, we want to focus on the $\iota_{Item \times Group}$ component of the DIF MFRM while including the γ_{group} component in the model for the sake of removing overall group differences at the instrument level. Specifically, we want to determine whether the estimates of

$\iota_{Item \times Group}$ differ from a null value of zero, which can be evaluated in a hypothesis-testing framework by constructing a Wald t statistic,

$$t_{Wald} = \frac{\iota_{Item \times Group}}{SE}.$$

The box on this page contains an abbreviated version of the ConQuest command file that estimates the DIF MFRM.

Table 5.4 presents the $\iota_{Item \times Group}$ parameter estimates for two items and summarizes the distribution of these statistics across the 50 items for which parameters were estimated.[3] The parameter estimates for the item-by-group interaction on Item 47 indicate that the conditional probabilities of the two groups answering this item correctly only differed by a small amount—the absolute difference in the logit values of the parameter estimates equals 0.03. When this value is divided by the standard error of the difference, it is clear that the difference is within what would be expected due to chance variation (i.e., $|t_{Wald}| = 0.36$). Item 46, on the other hand, is an item for which these two groups did differ. Specifically, the groups exhibited a logit difference of answering this item correctly of 1.43. This difference is 15.32 times greater than the expected chance variation in these parameter estimates, meaning that we would reject the null hypothesis that the values of the parameters describing the performance of the two groups on this item are equal. As a result, we would conclude that there is evidence of DIF on this item and would investigate

---

Excerpt From Conquest Command File for DIF Analysis Example

```
datafile conquest.dat;
format group 1 id 2-7 responses 8-58 ! tasks(51);
set constraints=cases,update=yes,warnings=no;
score (0,1) (0,1) ! tasks(1-51);
model group+tasks+group*tasks;
estimate ! method=montecarlo,nodes=1000;
title CHINESE-US DIF;
itanal >> conquest.ita;
show !tables=1:2:3:4:5:6 >> conquest.out;
show cases ! estimates=latent >> conquest.prs;
quit;
```

substantive explanations for potential item bias relating to these groups on this item.

The bottom row of Table 5.4 presents summary statistics for the difference between the group-by-item parameter estimates across items, the standard error of these differences, the absolute values of the DIF estimates, and the Wald t statistic associated with these differences. From the means of the group-by-item interaction differences and the Wald t statistics, it is clear that there is a prevalence of DIF for these groups in this pool of items. In fact, if criteria were applied that are comparable to those used in similar Rasch analyses (Draba, 1977) (specifically, if all items exhibiting statistically significant DIF and absolute logit differences for the two groups greater than 0.50 were flagged for DIF[4]), then 28 (56%) of the items would have been flagged for review by a sensitivity panel.

Finally, for the sake of comparison, Figure 5.2 displays the scatterplot of the relationship between the values of $|t_{i \times G=1} - t_{i \times G=2}|$ produced by these MFRM DIF analyses and the standardized difference of the item parameter estimates (Wright & Masters, 1982) between separate scalings of the data for the two groups using the Rasch rating scale model conducted with the WINSTEPS software (Linacre, 2005).[5] This plot indicates that the values of the person-by-item interaction in the MFRM are nearly identical ($r = .99$) to those produced using the more "standard" and burdensome approach that focuses on standardized differences from separate analyses of the data.

Analysis of Ratings Example

Our third example application of the MFRM is to the scores assigned to 5,026 examinees who responded to five multiple-choice items and a single essay question, which was rated by a single randomly selected rater from a pool of 100 raters using a 10-point rating scale. In this example, our focus will be on evaluating the ratings assigned by the raters rather than the performance of the examinees or the difficulties of the items. These particular raters were extensively trained as part of a large-scale, high-stakes writing assessment designed for high school students as an end-of-course examination. It should be noted that the five multiple-choice items were only a few selected from a larger test, and they were included in this example to create a link between the raters. Because each examinee was rated by only a single rater, disconnected subsets of ratings (examinees nested within raters) would have been created, making it impossible to place all raters onto a common scale. This points out a considerable advantage of the MFRM for data such as these—because raters rated no examinees in common, it would have been impossible to make direct comparisons between raters in a true-score test theory framework without making fairly strong distributional assumptions. The statistics reported in this example are simple descriptive statistics or were generated using the Facets computer program (Linacre, 2006). An abbreviated version of the Facets code is presented in the box on page 81.

Table 5.4   DIF MFRM Parameter Estimates Summary

Item × Group	$t_{Item \times Group}$	SE	$|DIF|$	$|t_{Wald}|$
Item 47, Group 1	−0.11	0.07	0.03	0.36
Item 47, Group 2	−0.08	0.06		
Item 46, Group 1	−0.93	0.08	1.43	15.32
Item 46, Group 2	0.50	0.05		
All items, $|t_{i \times G=1}| - |t_{i \times G=2}|$				
Mean	0.69	0.09	0.69	7.44
SD	0.59	0.008	0.59	6.42
Minimum	0.001	0.08	0.001	0.01
Maximum	2.58	0.11	2.58	29.59

Excerpt From Facets Command File for Analysis of Ratings Example

```
Title = ANALYSIS OF RATINGS EXAMPLE
Output = AP.out
Facets = 3
Models =?,?,#,R
*
Labels =
1,EXAMINEE
10000441=
.

.

.
9977228 =
*
2,RATER
10209 =
.

.

.
10978 =
*
3,ITEM
1-20=
100=
*
data =
391051 ,10388,100,5
.

.

.
13401357,0,1-5,0,1,1,1,1
```

Table 5.5 summarizes the distribution of ratings assigned by the raters to the examinees' essays for all raters and three individual raters (labeled *Typical, Misfit,* and *Overfit*—these cases will be discussed in upcoming paragraphs). The *All Raters* column of this table indicates that the distribution approximates a normal curve in shape, being slightly positively skewed and slightly platykurtic, with the majority of ratings assigned to categories 3 through 7. It is worth noting that, in practice, rating scales that contain a large number of rating categories often do not perform optimally according to indices relating to the Rasch rating scale or partial credit models (Linacre, 1995, 1999, 2004; Zhu, 2002; Zhu, Updyke, & Lewandowski, 1997). With rating scales such as these, it is likely that raters will not be able to reliably differentiate between the large number of rating categories and may allow idiosyncratic patterns to appear in the scores that they assign.

Table 5.6 summarizes the distribution of the differences between the ratings assigned by the raters and the fair averages (i.e., transformed values of the rater logits to the original raw score metric). This index indicates the degree to which a particular rater's ratings deviate from the average rating across all raters. That is, this is the degree to which we can expect an examinee's rating by a particular rater to deviate from what would be a fair average of the ratings that all raters would assign to that examinee. This summary indicates that 20% of the raters assigned average scores across all examinees that were at least 0.50 raw score points from the average of all raters. Assuming that raters rated examinee

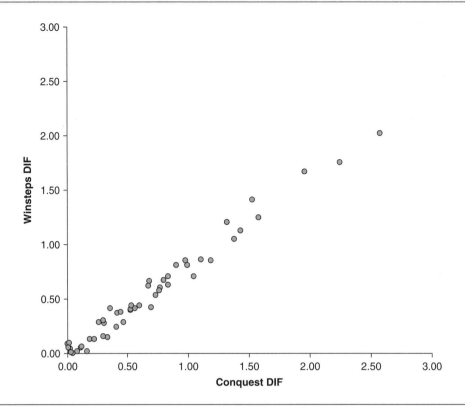

Figure 5.2   Scatterplot of MFRM and Rasch rating scale model DIF indices.

Table 5.5   Rating Category Use Distribution

	% Ratings Assigned			
Category	All Raters	Typical	Misfit	Overfit
0	0.06	0.00	0.00	0.00
1	1.19	6.45	3.03	0.00
2	4.58	12.90	9.09	0.00
3	13.49	20.97	16.67	11.03
4	26.26	14.52	24.24	27.21
5	23.74	25.81	9.09	36.76
6	16.87	12.90	10.61	13.97
7	9.39	6.45	15.15	10.29
8	3.58	0.00	10.61	0.74
9	0.84	0.00	1.52	0.00
Statistic				
N	5,026	62	66	136
Mean	4.78	4.05	4.82	4.88
SD	1.54	1.64	2.04	1.15
Skew	0.17	−0.08	0.18	0.34
Kurtosis	−0.13	−0.84	−0.99	−0.34

Table 5.6   Deviations of Raters' Observed and Fair Average Ratings ($N = 100$)

Deviation	% Raters
−1.00	2
−0.75	1
−0.50	4
−0.25	28
0.00	34
0.25	18
0.50	10
0.75	2
1.00	1

essays at uniform rates, this means that about 20% of the examinees were assigned ratings that were more than one half of a raw score from the average that would be assigned by all raters. This provides fairly strong support for the notion that the use of a single rater, as was the case in this program, has the potential to influence decisions that are made about examinees based on the essay scores.

To this point, the demonstration has highlighted only one strength of the MFRM analysis of ratings—that missing data and linking are routinely handled by the scaling process. The comparisons shown in Table 5.6 could not have been produced in a straightforward manner within a raw score framework because each rater rated a subset of examinees, and the MFRM allowed us to link the performance of those raters using five multiple-choice items. The real strengths of the MFRM lie in the diagnostic power of various data-to-model fit statistics. As demonstrated elsewhere (Wolfe, 2004, 2005; Wolfe et al., 2000; Wolfe et al., 2001), various fit statistics behave in predictable ways when rater effects are introduced into simulated data, so a variety of rater effects may be detected by examining these statistics. The Facets computer program computes the weighted and unweighted versions of the mean squared and standardized mean squared fit statistics.

The three rightmost columns in Table 5.5 indicate the distribution of ratings assigned by three raters. The column labeled *Typical* summarizes the ratings for a rater with typical values of the standardized weighted mean squared fit index. From the statistics at the bottom of this column, it is clear that this rater uses a standard

that is slightly more demanding than that of most other raters—this rater's average score was about three quarters of a point less than the average of all raters. In addition, this rater assigned ratings with variability consistent with that of other raters, on average. The *Typical* rater's ratings were not skewed, but they were slightly more platykurtic than all ratings were, on average. This is evident from the distribution of ratings for this rater—the shoulders of the distribution (rating categories 3 and 5) are thicker, and the tails are thinner.

The column labeled *Misfit* summarizes the ratings for a rater with somewhat elevated values of the standardized weighted mean squared fit index. The statistics at the bottom of this column indicate that the rater's ratings were consistent with those of other raters, on average, but they were slightly more widely distributed—a possible indicator of elevated levels of randomness within the rater's ratings or overuse of the extreme rating categories. The ratings are not skewed, but they are slightly more platykurtic than the population of ratings—in this case, rating category 5 was used fairly infrequently. Finally, the column labeled *Overfit* summarizes the ratings for a rater with a fairly low (negative) value of the standardized weighted mean squared fit index. This rater assigned ratings that were also consistent, on average, with the ratings assigned by other raters, but this rater's distribution was more tightly clustered around that central value—a possible indicator of overuse of the central rating categories. This conjecture is supported by the distribution of ratings across categories—almost 64% of the *Overfit* rater's ratings fall into categories 4 and 5. The ratings are slightly positively skewed, but the distribution is only slightly platykurtic.

SUMMARY

In this chapter, we have illustrated the usefulness of the MFRM, which has the general rating scale form of $LN(\pi_{nk}/\pi_{nk-1}) = \theta_n - \sum_{facets} \varepsilon - \tau_k$. Because of the flexibility of the MFRM, it can be applied to many contexts that are commonly encountered in measuring psychological and behavioral constructs, especially when there is a need on the part of the researcher to identify and correct for systematic error that may be contributed to the measures by the various indicators used to elicit performance relating to the construct (e.g., items, raters, etc.). The MFRM is particularly useful in situations in which data are missing at random across these measurement indicators. Two pieces of commercially available software, ConQuest and Facets, estimate parameters for the wide range of models within the family of Rasch models that can be implemented within this general MFRM, and our examples demonstrated how parameter estimates can provide substantively informative information, fit indices can provide diagnostically useful feedback, and parameter estimation procedures can provide useful corrections to what would otherwise be biased depictions of objects of measurement.

Notes

1. Readers should be aware that mutually exclusive subsets, referred to in the MFRM literature as "disconnected subsets," preclude comparison of elements within a facet. That is, when raters rate nonoverlapping subsets of examinees, there is no way to make direct comparisons between those raters with respect to their levels of bias.

2. A detailed explanation of differential item functioning is beyond the scope of this chapter. Briefly, differential item functioning analyses seek to determine whether the probabilities that individuals in different groups will provide a particular response to an item, when those individuals are matched on measures of the construct in question, are equal. When they are not equal, it is possible that item bias or construct-irrelevant variance (such as multidimensionality) exist. Readers seeking a more detailed introduction to differential item functioning should consult Clauser and Mazor (1998) or R. M. Smith (2004).

3. More recently, Wilson (2005) suggests that differences greater than 0.43 logits are consistent with what is defined elsewhere in the literature relating to DIF as a moderate effect (e.g., the Mantel-Haenszel criteria described by Zieky, 1993), and differences greater than 0.64 logits are consistent with what has been defined as a substantial difference.

4. ConQuest estimates constrain the value of one parameter in each distribution to equal the negative of the sum of the remaining parameter estimates, so the value of $\iota_{Item \times Group}$ and the associated standard error was not estimated for one item.

5. Specifically, this index compares absolute values of the item parameter estimates for Group 1 with the comparable values for Group 2, an index that is also referred to as the unsigned area index (UAI; Raju, 1988, 1990).

References

Adams, R. J., Wilson, M., & Wang, W. C. (1997). The multidimensional random coefficients multinomial logit model. *Applied Psychological Measurement, 21*, 1–23.

Andrich, D. (1988). *Rasch models for measurement.* Beverly Hills, CA: Sage.

Clauser, B. E., & Mazor, K. M. (1998). Using statistical procedures to identify differentially functioning test items. *Educational Measurement: Issues and Practice, 17*, 31–44.

Cronbach, L. J., Gleser, F. C., Nanda, H., & Rajaratnam, N. (1972). *The dependability of behavioral measurements: Theory of generalizability for scores and profiles.* New York: John Wiley.

Draba, R. E. (1977). *The identification and interpretation of item bias* (Research Memorandum No. 26). Chicago: University of Chicago Press.

Gilmore, G. M. (1983). Generalizability theory: Applications to program evaluation. In L. J. Fyans Jr. (Ed.), *Generalizability theory: Inferences and practical applications* (pp. 3–16). San Francisco: Jossey-Bass.

Karabatsos, G. (2003). Comparing the aberrant response detection performance of thirty-six person fit statistics. *Applied Measurement in Education, 16*, 277–298.

Linacre, J. M. (1994). *Many-facet Rasch measurement.* Chicago: MESA Press.

Linacre, J. M. (1995). Categorical misfit statistics. *Rasch Measurement Transactions, 9*, 450–451.

Linacre, J. M. (1996). Generalizability theory and Rasch measurement. In G. Engelhard & M. Wilson (Eds.), *Objective measurement: Theory into practice* (Vol. 3, pp. 85–98). Stamford, CT: Ablex.

Linacre, J. M. (1999). Category disordering vs. step disordering. *Rasch Measurement Transactions, 13*, 675–679.

Linacre, J. M. (2004). Optimal rating scale category effectiveness. In E. V. Smith Jr. & R. M. Smith (Eds.), *Introduction to Rasch measurement* (pp. 258–278). Maple Grove, MN: JAM Press.

Linacre, J. M. (2005). *A user's guide to WINSTEPS/MINISTEP Rasch-model computer programs* (Version 3.55). Chicago: MESA Press.

Linacre, J. M. (2006). Facets—Rasch measurement computer program (Version 3.61.1) [Computer program]. Chicago: MESA Press.

Lord, F. M., & Novick, M. R. (1968). *Statistical theories of mental test scores.* Reading, MA: Addison-Wesley.

Raju, N. S. (1988). The area between two item characteristic curves. *Psychometrika, 53*, 495–502.

Raju, N. S. (1990). Determining the significance of estimated signed and unsigned areas between two item response functions. *Applied Psychological Measurement, 14,* 197–207.

Smith, E. V., Jr., & Kulikowich, J. M. (2004). An application of generalizability theory and many-facet Rasch measurement using a complex problem solving skills assessment. *Educational and Psychological Measurement, 64,* 617–639.

Smith, R. M. (1996). Polytomous mean-square fit statistics. *Rasch Measurement Transactions, 10,* 516–517.

Smith, R. M. (2004). Detecting item bias with the Rasch model. In E. V. Smith Jr. & R. M. Smith (Eds.), *Introduction to Rasch measurement* (pp. 391–418). Maple Grove, MN: JAM Press.

Smith, R. M., Schumacker, R. E., & Bush, M. J. (1998). Using item mean squares to evaluate fit to the Rasch model. *Journal of Outcome Measurement, 2*(1), 66–78.

Wilson, M. (2005). *Constructing measure: An item response modeling approach.* Mahwah, NJ: Lawrence Erlbaum.

Wolfe, E. W. (2004). Identifying rater effects using latent trait models. *Psychology Science, 46,* 35–51.

Wolfe, E. W. (2005). Identifying rater effects in performance ratings. In S. Reddy (Ed.), *Performance appraisals: A critical view* (pp. 91–103). Hyderabad, India: ICFAI University Press.

Wolfe, E. W., Chiu, C. W. T., & Myford, C. M. (2000). Detecting rater effects with a multi-faceted Rasch rating scale model. In M. Wilson & G. Engelhard (Eds.), *Objective measurement: Theory into practice* (Vol. 5, pp. 147–164). Stamford, CT: Ablex.

Wolfe, E. W., Moulder, B. C., & Myford, C. M. (2001). Detecting differential rater functioning over time (DRIFT) using a Rasch multi-faceted rating scale model. *Journal of Applied Measurement, 2,* 256–280.

Wolfe, E. W., & Smith, E. V., Jr. (in press-a). Instrument development tools and activities for measure validation using Rasch models: Part I. Instrument development tools. In E. V. Smith Jr. & R. M. Smith (Eds.), *Rasch measurement: Advanced and specialized applications.* Maple Grove, MN: JAM Press.

Wolfe, E. W., & Smith, E. V., Jr. (in press-b). Instrument development tools and activities for measure validation using Rasch models: Part II. Validation activities. In E. V. Smith Jr. & R. M. Smith (Eds.), *Rasch measurement: Advanced and specialized applications.* Maple Grove, MN: JAM Press.

Wright, B. D. (1991). Diagnosing misfit. *Rasch Measurement Transactions, 5,* 156.

Wright, B. D. (1995). Diagnosing person misfit. *Rasch Measurement Transactions, 9,* 430–431.

Wright, B. D., & Linacre, M. (1994). Reasonable mean-square fit values. *Rasch Measurement Transactions, 8,* 370.

Wright, B. D., & Masters, G. N. (1982). *Rating scale analysis: Rasch measurement.* Chicago: MESA Press.

Wu, M. L. (1987). *The development and application of a fit test for use with marginal maximum likelihood estimation and generalized item response models.* Unpublished master's thesis, University of Melbourne.

Wu, M. L., Adams, R. J., & Wilson, M. R. (1998). ACER ConQuest: Generalized item response modeling software (Version 1.0) [Computer program]. Melbourne, Victoria: Australian Council for Educational Research.

Zhu, W. (2002). A confirmatory study of Rasch-based optimal categorization of a rating scale. *Journal of Applied Measurement, 3,* 1–15.

Zhu, W., Updyke, W. F., & Lewandowski, C. (1997). Post-hoc Rasch analysis of optimal categorization of an ordered-response scale. *Journal of Outcome Measurement, 1,* 286–304.

Zieky, M. (1993). Practical questions in the use of DIF statistics in test development. In P. W. Holland & H. Wainer (Eds.), *Differential item functioning.* Hillsdale, NJ: Lawrence Erlbaum.

6

BEST PRACTICES IN
EXPLORATORY FACTOR ANALYSIS

JASON W. OSBORNE

ANNA B. COSTELLO

J. THOMAS KELLOW

Exploratory factor analysis (EFA) is rightly described as both an art and a science, where researchers follow a series of analytic steps involving judgments more reminiscent of qualitative inquiry, an interesting irony given the mathematical sophistication underlying EFA models.

EFA is a widely used and broadly applied statistical technique in the social sciences. When we surveyed a recent 2-year period in PsycINFO, we found more than 1,700 studies that used some form of EFA. The widespread nature of EFA is both gratifying and problematic. On one hand, it is a powerful tool that can help researchers explore complex data efficiently. On the other

hand, EFA is a complex procedure with few absolute guidelines, no inferential statistics for hypothesis testing,[1] and many (often ill-defined) options. To make matters worse, terminology can vary significantly across software packages.

EFA is open to abuse by researchers ill-informed as to the limitations of the procedure. For example, using EFA to "confirm" or "validate" a measure is most likely a misapplication of the procedure since EFA does not have inferential statistics available to test goodness of fit (as confirmatory factor analysis [CFA] does), yet one sees studies that claim to do just that.

Even when EFA is the correct choice, researchers must deal with issues such as (a) factor extraction

Authors' Note: Portions of this chapter are based on previously published articles:

Costello, A. B., & Osborne, J. W. (2005). Exploratory factor analysis: Four recommendations for getting the most from your analysis. *Practical Assessment, Research, and Evaluation, 10*(7), 1–9. Available at http://pareonline.net/pdf/v10n7.pdf

Kellow, J. T. (2005). Exploratory factor analysis in two prominent measurement journals: Hegemony by default. *Journal of Modern Applied Statistical Methods, 4*(1), 283–287.

Osborne, J. W., & Costello, A. B. (2004). Sample size and subject to item ratio in principal components analysis. *Practical Assessment, Research, and Evaluation, 9*. Available at http://pareonline.net/getvn.asp?v=9&n=11

Correspondence relating to this chapter should be addressed to jason_osborne@ncsu.edu.

methods, (b) rules for retaining factors, (c) factor rotation strategies, and (d) sample size issues. Perusing the EFA literature, one will quickly discover that most researchers use principal components analysis (PCA) with varimax rotation, using the Kaiser (1970) criterion (retaining factors with eigenvalues greater than 1.0) as the decision rule for deciding how many factors to interpret. Readers will also find analyses reported where the sample size is woefully inadequate to ensure even marginal generalizability.

So, while this state of affairs represents the norm in the literature (and often the defaults in popular statistical software packages), it will not always yield the best results for a particular data set. This chapter will review standard practice in the social sciences, review and propose best practices for researchers wishing to use EFA, and examine how sample size affects the "goodness" of EFA results in detail. Aside from sample size, we will discuss (a) component versus factor extraction, (b) number of factors to retain for rotation, and (c) orthogonal versus oblique rotation. Finally, we will briefly discuss FACTOR, freely available software that implements EFA options nicely.

STANDARD PRACTICE IN SOCIAL SCIENCE

One of the challenges to using best practices is that for three of the important EFA analytic decisions (extraction, rotation, and number of factors to retain), the defaults in common statistical packages (e.g., SPSS, SAS) are suboptimal. When conducting EFA, one is usually guided to (a) use principal components as the *extraction method* of choice (note that PCA is not a *factor analysis* methodology at all), (b) use the Kaiser (1970) criterion (retaining factors with eigenvalues greater than 1.0), and (c) use varimax for rotation of factors (which requires factors to be orthogonal or completely uncorrelated with each other, a generally untenable constraint).

Although many have written on different aspects of EFA, it is our experience that software defaults tend to drive analysis decision making (and furthermore, as Lorenzo-Seva and Ferrando [2006] point out, many best practices are not available in popular software such as SPSS and SAS).

In order to examine the prevalence of EFA practices, we surveyed two prominent measurement journals: *Educational and Psychological Measurement* (*EPM*) and *Personality and Individual*

Differences (*PID*) over a 6-year period. These journals were chosen because of their prominence in the field of measurement and the prolific presence of EFA articles within their pages.

An electronic search was conducted using the PsycINFO database for *EPM* and *PID* studies published from January 1998 to October 2003 that contained the keyword *factor analysis*. After screening out studies that employed only CFA or examined the statistical properties of EFA or CFA approaches using simulated data sets, a total of 184 articles were identified, reporting on 212 distinct EFA analyses. Variables extracted from the EFA articles were factor extraction methods, factor retention rules, factor rotation strategies, and saliency criteria for including variables.

Factor Extraction Methods. Almost two thirds of all researchers (64%) used PCA. The next most popular choice was principal axis factoring (PAF) (27%). Techniques such as maximum likelihood were infrequently invoked (6%). A modest percentage of authors (8%) conducted both principal components and principal axis methods on their data and compared the results for similar structure.

Factor Extraction Rules. The most popular method used for deciding the number of factors to retain was the Kaiser (1970) criterion of eigenvalues greater than 1.0 (45%). An almost equal proportion used the scree test (42%). Use of other methods, such as percent of variance explained logics and parallel analysis, was comparatively infrequent (about 8% each). Many authors (41%) explored multiple criteria for factor retention. Among these authors, the most popular choice was a combination of the Kaiser criterion and scree methods (67%).

Factor Rotation Strategies. As expected, varimax rotation was most often employed (47%), with oblimin being the next most common (38%). Promax (another oblique rotation) also was used in 11% of analyses. A number of authors (18%) employed both varimax and oblimin solutions to examine the influence of correlated factors on the resulting factor pattern/structure matrices.

Saliency Criteria for Including Variables. Thirty-one percent of EFA authors did not articulate a specific criterion for interpreting salient pattern/structure coefficients, preferring instead to examine the matrix in a logical fashion, considering not only the size of the pattern/structure coefficient but also the discrepancy between coefficients for the same variable across different factors (components) and the logical "fit" of the variable with a particular factor.

Of the 69% of authors who identified an a priori criterion as an absolute cutoff, 27% opted to interpret coefficients with an absolute value of 0.30 or higher, while 24% chose a 0.40 cutoff. Other criteria chosen with modest frequency (both about 6%) included 0.35 and 0.50 as absolute cutoff values, with the rest ranging from the marginally defensible 0.25 to the almost indefensible 0.80.

Summary. Not surprisingly, the hegemony of default settings in major statistical packages continues to dominate the pages of *EPM* and *PID*. The "Little Jiffy" model espoused by Kaiser (1970; espoused PCA with varimax rotation and retention of all factors with an eigenvalue greater than 1.0) is alive and well. It should be noted that this situation is almost certainly not unique to *EPM* or *PID* authors. A survey of a recent 2-year period in PsycINFO (reported in Costello & Osborne, 2005) yielded more than 1,700 studies that showed similar results. An informal perusal of social science journals easily confirms the prevalence of this situation as current practice.

So What's Wrong With Standard Practice?

In short, there are good reasons why these defaults make little sense from a conceptual and empirical point of view. Yes, the "Little Jiffy" method will often yield acceptable results that will generalize, but a significant body of research points to the fallibility of this methodology. But how do you know when your results are erroneous because the methodology you are using is suboptimal? You don't. Following best practices will increase the odds of achieving a generalizable, defensible solution.

Choosing an Extraction Technique

Principal Components Versus Factor Analysis. As mentioned above, PCA is the default method of extraction in many popular statistical software

packages, including SPSS and SAS, which probably contributes to its prevalence. PCA became common decades ago when computers were slow and expensive to use; it was a quicker, cheaper alternative to factor analysis and was designed to be only a data reduction method (Gorsuch, 1990). It is computed without regard to any underlying structure caused by latent variables; components are calculated using all of the variance of the manifest variables, and all of that variance appears in the solution (Ford, MacCallum, & Tait, 1986). However, researchers rarely collect and analyze data without an a priori idea about how the variables are related (Floyd & Widaman, 1995).

During factor extraction, the shared variance of a variable is partitioned from its unique variance and error variance to reveal the underlying factor structure; only shared variance appears in the solution. Principal components analysis does not discriminate between shared and unique variance. When the factors are uncorrelated and communalities are moderate, it can produce inflated values of variance accounted for by the components (Gorsuch, 1997; McArdle, 1990). Since factor analysis only analyzes shared variance, factor analysis should yield the same general solution (all other things being equal) while also avoiding the illegitimate inflation of variance estimates.

Most authors agree that there is little compelling reason to choose PCA over other extraction methods (Bentler & Kano, 1990; Floyd & Widaman, 1995; Ford et al., 1986; Gorsuch, 1990; Loehlin, 1990; MacCallum & Tucker, 1991; Mulaik, 1990; Snook & Gorsuch, 1989; Widaman, 1990, 1993), while others note that there is almost no difference between principal components and factor analysis or that PCA is preferable (Arrindell & van der Ende, 1985; Guadagnoli & Velicer, 1988; Schonemann, 1990; Steiger, 1990; Velicer & Jackson, 1990). They are, however, in the minority, and if one is to seek best practices, one is hard-pressed to conclude PCA is ever a best practice.

Alternatives to PCA. Depending on the statistical software available, you may have six or more extraction methods to choose from. They often include unweighted least squares, generalized least squares, maximum likelihood, principal axis factoring, alpha factoring, and image factoring. Information on the relative strengths and weaknesses of these techniques is scarce, often only available in obscure references. To complicate matters further, the same extraction technique may be called by different names in different texts or software packages. This probably explains the popularity of PCA—not only is it the default, but it is also familiar.

Fabrigar, Wegener, MacCallum, and Strahan (1999) argued that if data are relatively normally distributed, maximum likelihood is the best extraction technique. If the assumption of multivariate normality is severely violated, they recommend one of the principal factor methods; in SPSS, this procedure is called *principal axis factors*. Other authors have argued that in specialized cases, or for particular applications, other extraction techniques (e.g., alpha extraction) are most appropriate, but the evidence of advantage is slim. In general, maximum likelihood (ML) or PAF will give you the best results, depending on whether your data are generally normally distributed or significantly nonnormal, respectively.

How Many Factors Do I Have?

After extraction, the researcher must decide how many factors to retain for rotation. Both overextraction and underextraction of factors retained for rotation can have deleterious effects on the results. The default in most statistical software packages is the Kaiser criterion, despite the consensus in the literature that this is probably the least accurate method for selecting the number of factors to retain (e.g., Velicer & Jackson, 1990). In Monte Carlo analyses, we tested this assertion (via methodology described below); 36% of our samples retained too many factors using this criterion. Alternate tests for factor retention include the scree test, Velicer's minimum average partial (MAP) criteria, and parallel analysis (e.g., Velicer & Jackson, 1990). The latter two methods are accurate and easy to use and can be calculated by hand or via specialty software (particularly appealing is the relatively recent FACTOR software, available from http://psico.fcep.urv.es/utilitats/factor/ and described in Lorenzo-Seva & Ferrando, 2006). The scree test is also generally considered superior to the Kaiser criterion.

The scree test involves examining the graph of the eigenvalues (available via every software package) and looking for the natural bend or "elbow" in the data where the slope of the curve changes. The number of data points above the

"break" (i.e., not including the point at which the break occurs) is usually the number of factors to retain, although it can be unclear if there are data points clustered together near the bend. This can be tested simply by running multiple factor analyses and setting the number of factors to retain manually—once at the projected number based on the a priori factor structure, again at the number of factors suggested by the scree test if it is different from the predicted number, and then at numbers above and below those numbers. For example, if the predicted number of factors is six and the scree test suggests five, then run the data four times, setting the number of factors extracted at four, five, six, and seven. After rotation (see below for rotation criteria), compare the item loading tables; the one with the factor structure that is conceptually and empirically most sensible—item loadings above .30, no or few item crossloadings, no factors with fewer than three items—has the best fit to the data. If all loading tables look messy or uninterpretable, then there may be a problem with the data that cannot be resolved by manipulating the number of factors retained. Sometimes dropping problematic items (ones that are low loading, crossloading, or freestanding) and rerunning the analysis can solve the problem, but the researcher has to consider if doing so compromises the integrity of the data.

What Is Rotation and How Do I Decide What Method to Use?

The goal of rotation is to simplify and clarify the data structure. Rotation cannot improve the basic aspects of the analysis, such as the amount of variance extracted from the items (specifically, every rotation will work with the same variance).

As with extraction, there are many choices. As noted above, varimax is the most common choice. Varimax, quartimax, and equamax are commonly available orthogonal methods of rotation; direct oblimin, quartimin, and promax are oblique. Orthogonal rotations produce factors that are uncorrelated (i.e., factor intercorrelations are constrained to be exactly $r = .00$); oblique methods allow the factors to correlate. Conventional wisdom advises researchers to use orthogonal rotation because it produces more easily interpretable results, but this is a flawed argument. In the social sciences, we generally expect some correlation among factors, particularly scales that reside within the same instrument or questionnaire, regardless of the intentions of the researcher to produce uncorrelated scales (i.e., shared method variance will generally produce nonzero correlations). Therefore, using orthogonal rotation results in a loss of valuable information (and reduced generalizability) if the factors are really correlated, and oblique rotation should theoretically render a more accurate and perhaps more reproducible solution. Furthermore, in the unlikely event that researchers manage to produce truly uncorrelated factors, orthogonal and oblique rotation produce nearly identical results, leaving oblique rotation a very low-risk, potentially high-benefit choice.

Oblique rotation output is only slightly more complex than orthogonal rotation output. In SPSS output, the rotated factor matrix is interpreted after orthogonal rotation; when using oblique rotation, the pattern matrix is examined for factor/item loadings, and the factor correlation matrix reveals any correlation between the factors. The substantive interpretations are essentially the same.

There is no widely preferred method of oblique rotation; all tend to produce similar results (Fabrigar et al., 1999), and it is fine to use the default delta (0) or kappa (4) values in the software packages. Manipulating delta or kappa changes the amount the rotation procedure "allows" the factors to correlate, and this appears to introduce unnecessary complexity for interpretation of results.

Why Size Matters

Larger samples are better than smaller samples (all other things being equal) because larger samples tend to minimize the probability of errors, maximize the accuracy of population estimates, and increase the generalizability of the results. Unfortunately, there are few sample size guidelines for researchers using EFA or PCA, and many of these have minimal empirical evidence (e.g., Guadagnoli & Velicer, 1988).

This is problematic because statistical procedures that create optimized linear combinations of variables (e.g., multiple regression, canonical correlation, and EFA) tend to "overfit" the data. This means that these procedures optimize the fit of the model to the given data, yet no sample is perfectly reflective of the population. Thus, this overfitting can result in erroneous conclusions if models fit to one data set are applied to

others. In multiple regression, this manifests itself as inflated R^2 (shrinkage) and misestimated variable regression coefficients (Cohen & Cohen, 1983, p. 106). In EFA, this "overfitting" can result in erroneous conclusions in several ways, including the extraction of erroneous factors or misassignment of items to factors (e.g., Tabachnick & Fidell, 2001, p. 588; this is also discussed in Chapter 20).

The ultimate concern is error. At the end of the analysis, if one has too small a sample, errors of inference can easily occur, particularly with techniques such as EFA.

Published Sample Size Guidelines. In multiple regression texts, some authors (e.g., Pedhazur, 1997, p. 207) suggest subject-to-variable ratios of 15:1 or 30:1 when generalization is critical. But there are few explicit guidelines such as this for EFA (e.g., Baggaley, 1983). Two different approaches have been taken: suggesting a minimum total sample size or examining the ratio of subjects to variables, as in multiple regression.

Comfrey and Lee (1992) suggest that "the adequacy of sample size might be evaluated very roughly on the following scale: 50—very poor; 100—poor; 200—fair; 300—good; 500—very good; 1000 or more—excellent" (p. 217). Guadagnoli and Velicer (1988) review several studies that conclude that absolute minimum sample sizes, rather than subject to item ratios, are more relevant. These studies range in their recommendations from an *N* of 50 (Barrett & Kline, 1981) to 400 (Aleamoni, 1976). We should note that some of these recommendations are clearly ridiculous, as they could result in analyses estimating far more parameters than available subjects.

The Case for Ratios. There are few in the multiple regression camp who would argue that total *N* is a better guideline than the ratio of subjects to variables, yet individuals focusing on EFA occasionally vehemently defend this position. It is interesting precisely because the general goal for both analyses is the same: to take individual variables and create optimally weighted linear composites that will generalize to other samples or to the population. While the mathematics and procedures differ in their details, the essence and the pitfalls are the same. Both EFA and multiple regression experience shrinkage and the overfitting of the estimates to the data (Bobko & Schemmer, 1984), and both suffer from lack of generalizability and inflated error rates when sample size is too small.

We find absolute sample sizes simplistic given the range of complexity that scales can exhibit—each scale differs in the number of factors or components, the number of items on each factor, the magnitude of the item-factor correlations, and the correlation between factors, for example. This has led some authors to focus on the ratio of subjects to items or, more recently, the ratio of subjects to parameters (as each item will have a loading for each factor or component extracted), as authors do with regression, rather than absolute sample size when discussing guidelines concerning EFA.

Gorsuch (1983, p. 332) and Hatcher (1994, p. 73) recommend a *minimum* subject-to-item ratio of at least 5:1 in EFA, but they also have stringent guidelines for when this ratio is acceptable, and they both note that higher ratios are generally better. There is a widely cited rule of thumb from Nunnally (1978, p. 421) that the subject-to-item ratio for exploratory factor analysis should be at least 10:1, but that recommendation was not supported by empirical research. There is no one ratio that will work in all cases; the number of items per factor and communalities and item loading magnitudes can make any particular ratio overkill or hopelessly insufficient (MacCallum, Widaman, Preacher, & Hong, 2001).

Previous Research on Ratios. Unfortunately, much of the literature that has attempted to address this issue, particularly the studies attempting to dismiss subject-to-item ratios, use flawed data. We will purposely not cite studies here to protect the guilty, but consider it sufficient to say that many of these studies either tend to use highly restricted ranges of subject-to-item ratios or fail to adequately control for or vary other confounding variables (e.g., factor loadings, number of items per scale or per factor/component) or restricted range of *N*. Some of these studies purporting to address the subject-to-item ratio fail to actually test the subject-to-item ratio in their analyses.

Thus, researchers seeking guidance concerning sufficient sample size in EFA are left between two entrenched camps—those arguing for looking at total sample size and those looking at ratios. This is unfortunate because both probably matter in some sense, and ignoring either one can have the

same result: errors of inference. Failure to have a representative sample of sufficient size results in unstable loadings (Cliff, 1970); random, non-replicable factors (Aleamoni, 1976; Humphreys, Ilgen, McGrath, & Montanelli, 1969); and lack of generalizability to the population (MacCallum, Widaman, Zhang, & Hong, 1999).

Sample Size in Practice. If one were to take either set of guidelines (e.g., 10:1 ratio or a minimum *N* of 400–500) as reasonable, a casual perusal of the published literature shows that a large portion of studies come up short. One can easily find articles using EFA or (more commonly) PCA based on samples with fewer subjects than items or parameters estimated that nevertheless draw substantive conclusions based on these questionable analyses. Many more have hopelessly insufficient samples by either guideline.

For example, Ford et al. (1986) examined common practice in factor analysis in industrial and organizational psychology during the 10-year period from 1974 to 1984. They found that out of 152 studies using EFA or PCA, 27.3% had a subject-to-item ratio of less than 5:1, and 56% had a ratio of less than 10:1. This matches the perception that readers of social science journals get, which is that often samples are too small for the analyses to be stable or generalizable.

To summarize current practices in the social sciences literature, we sampled from 2 years' (2002, 2003) worth of articles archived in PsycINFO that both reported some form of EFA and listed both the number of subjects and the number of items analyzed (*N* = 303). We decided that the best method for standardizing our sample size data was via the subject-to-item ratio since we needed a criterion for a reasonably direct comparison to our own data analysis. The results of this survey are summarized in Table 6.1. A large percentage of researchers report factor analyses using relatively small samples. In a majority of the studies (62.9%), researchers performed analyses with subject-to-item ratios of 10:1 or less. A surprisingly high proportion (almost one sixth) reported factor analyses based on subject-to-item ratios of only 2:1 or less (note that in this case, there would be more parameters estimated than subjects if more than one factor is extracted). Given the stakes and the empirical evidence on the consequences of insufficient sample size, this is not exactly a desirable state of affairs.

Table 6.1   Subject-to-Item Ratios in the
Psychology Literature, 2002–2003

Subject-to-Item Ratio	% of Studies	Cumulative %
2:1 or less	14.7	14.7
> 2:1, ≤ 5:1	25.8	40.5
> 5:1, ≤ 10:1	22.7	63.2
> 10:1, ≤ 20:1	15.4	78.6
> 20:1, ≤ 100:1	18.4	97.0
> 100:1	3.0	100.0

A Reanalysis of Guadagnoli and Velicer (1988): Compelling Evidence That Size Matters Two Different Ways

This section focuses on one particularly interesting and relatively well-executed study on this issue—that of Guadagnoli and Velicer (1988). In this study, the authors used Monte Carlo methods to examine the effects of number of factors (3, 6, 9, 18), the number of variables (36, 72, 108, and 144), average item loadings (.40, .60, or .80), and number of subjects (Ns of 50, 100, 150, 200, 300, 500, and 1,000) on the stability of factor patterns in EFA. In these data, each item loaded on only one factor, all items had identical factor loadings, and each factor contained an equal number of variables. This study represents one of the few studies to manipulate all of these important aspects across the range of variation seen in the literature (with two possible exceptions: First, people often have fewer than 36 items in a scale, and second, the factor loading patterns are rarely as clear and homogeneous as in these data).

Guadagnoli and Velicer's (1988) study was also interesting in that they used several different high-quality fit/agreement indices. Equally interesting is the authors' strong assertion that total sample size is critical, although they never actually operationalize the subject-to-item ratio or test whether total N is a better predictor of important outcomes than the subject-to-item ratio, although given their data, it was possible to do so. The following analyses directly examine competing claims regarding sample size: whether overall sample size or the subject-to-item ratio uniquely contributes to the "goodness" of outcomes in PCA, beyond the contributions of other important variables, such as the number of variables or components and average

item loading that have been identified as important in the literature. To do this, we will examine the following variables, included by the authors in the original article:

Number of factors. The number of factors examined included 3, 6, 9, and 18.

Loadings. The authors used loadings of .40, .60, and .80. It should be noted that in these data sets, items not intended to load on a component were assigned a loading of 0.00, making these pattern matrices artificially clear.

Number of items. The number of items in the analyses included 36, 72, 108, and 144.

Number of subjects. The number of subjects in the analyses included 50, 100, 150, 200, 300, 500, and 1,000. Note, however, that certain cases were omitted or altered by the authors, such as when N was less than the number of items in the analysis.

Pattern comparison (g^2). In order to compare sample factor patterns with population factor patterns, the average of the squared differences between the two matrices was computed. Furthermore, the authors identified $g^2 = .01$ as the maximum value that indicates acceptable fit.

Pattern agreement (kappa). Salient variables (loadings > .40) and nonsalient variables (loadings < .40) were identified and noted in decision tables. These decision tables were then compared with the population decision table via the kappa statistic. As kappa approaches 1.0, the two matrices become more in agreement with each other. A zero indicates random chance level of agreement, and negative kappas indicate poorer than chance agreement.

Type I errors. The authors calculated the percentage of variables that should not have been considered salient but were in a particular data set, indicating Type I error classifications.

Type II errors. The authors also calculated the percentage of variables that should have been considered salient but were not found to be so, indicating Type II error classifications.

For our purposes, we calculated the following variables based on the information obtained from the data set:

Subject-to-item ratio. The ratio of the number of subjects per item in a particular analysis was calculated from the information given.

Variable-to-factor ratio. As some authors have argued that the number of variables per factor is important (see Guadagnoli & Velicer, 1988), we included this variable in analyses.

Extra matrices. In describing their data generation procedures, Guadagnoli and Velicer (1988) indicated that under certain conditions, certain data sets produced errors of inference regarding the number of factors extracted from the data. The authors discarded these data matrices and replaced them until 5 good matrices for a particular set of criteria were obtained. They noted cases where up to 10 additional matrices were required before 5 good matrices were obtained and cases where 10 or more matrices were required (a phenomenally high error rate). From an applied research point of view, this could be viewed as an important outcome, where a researcher would find results that differ radically from the population, and thus should be examined as a variable of interest. Thus, this variable was coded into the data set for the current analyses as 0 (no extra matrices), 1 (up to 10 extra matrices required), or 2 (more than 10 extra matrices required), as that is how this information was reported.

Correct factor structure. What many people are looking for when they do an EFA is the pattern—what variables "load" on what factors. Researchers are generally less interested in the absolute magnitude of the loading (above a certain "salient" level—that is a source of debate in and of itself) than in which variable goes with which factor. Thus, we included information in our data set that indicated when this had or had not occurred, based on the number of Type I and Type II errors. Matrices that had no errors were considered "correct," while matrices with errors were considered not correct. Some might think this a strict criterion, and they are correct. However, the presence of these errors can significantly alter the interpretation of an EFA. In this study, 34.3% of the cases failed to faithfully replicate the pattern found in the population, which is a much higher error rate than social scientists generally are willing to accept.

Note: The authors generated five samples for each of the 205 valid conditions described. The average g^2, kappa, Type I error, and Type II error for the five samples in each condition were reported in tables. Thus, these results represent analyses of the data aggregated across five samples in each condition.

Main Effects. With the exception of the newly calculated variables described above, we attempted to faithfully reproduce the authors' analyses.

We performed multiple regression analyses on the dependent variables (g^2, kappa, Type I error, and Type II error), a binomial logistic multiple regression predicting correct factor structure, and a multinomial logistic regression predicting the presence of extra matrices. As in the original article, we examined all possible two-way interactions. The difference is that we now simultaneously can examine total N and the subject-to-item ratio for their unique and joint contributions to the goodness of EFA outcomes.

The results of these analyses are presented in Tables 6.2 to 6.4. As Table 6.2 indicates, the number of factors was not a significant predictor of any dependent variable once other variables were controlled for. As previous research has reported, item loading magnitude accounted for significant unique variance in the expected direction in all but one case and, in most cases, was the strongest unique predictor of congruence between sample and population. Specifically, as item loadings increased, average squared discrepancy between population and sample results (g^2) decreased, agreement (kappa) increased, Type II errors decreased, and the odds of getting the correct component pattern increased dramatically. Unfortunately, the magnitude of item loadings is not realistically within the control of the researcher.

Contrary to other studies, neither the absolute number of variables nor the overall N had a significant unique effect when all other variables were held constant (except for the relationship between N and the odds of a Type II error). The lack of findings for these two variables might be directly attributable to the presence of the ratios of subject to item and variable to component, which are likely collinear. To test this hypothesis, a blockwise multiple regression was performed entering number of components, loadings, number of variables, and N in Block 1, as well as the subject-to-item ratio and variable-to-factor ratio in Block 2. Number of variables was a significant predictor in two of the five analyses where the two ratio variables were not in the equation. Total N was significant in all five analyses until the ratio variables were entered into the equation.

The ratio of subjects to items had a significant and substantial influence on three outcomes in the expected direction. As the subject-to-item ratio increased, the squared discrepancy between population and sample matrices decreased, the

Table 6.2   Predictors of Component Pattern Stability: Main Effects

Dependent Variable	Number of Components	Loadings	Number of Variables	Number of Subjects	Subject-to-Item Ratio	Variable: Component Ratio
g^2	−.08	−.41***	−.26	−.11	−.37***	−.25
	(.15**)	(−.45***)	(−.30***)	(−.41***)		
Kappa	−.09	.62***	.16	.20	.14	−.08
	(−.01)	(.62***)	(.03)	(.31***)		
Type I error	−.12	−.22	−.23	.12	−.36***	−.20
	(−.12)	(−.22***)	(−.23***)	(−.17***)		
Type II error	.09	−.67***	−.03	−.29***	−.03	.10
	(−.01)	(−.67***)	(.07)	(−.31***)		
Correct pattern	1.14	.58***	1.01	1.00	1.44**	1.15
	(1.10)	(.99)	(.99)	(1.01***)		
	.76***					
	(.99)					

NOTE: Statistics reported represent betas (standardized regression coefficients) when all predictors are in the equation. Betas in parentheses are from regression equations with two ratio variables removed. Odds ratio reported. For loadings, as there was only .40, .60, and .80 for values, this was considered a categorical variable. Thus, the first odds ratio represents the relative odds of getting correct pattern structures with a .40 versus a .80 average loading, while the second odds ratio represents the relative odds of getting correct pattern structures with a .60 versus a .80 average loading.

**p < .01. ***p < .001.

odds of a Type I error decreased, and the odds of getting a correct factor pattern matrix increased. Finally, the ratio of variables to factors had no unique effect.

The multinomial logistic regression predicting the need for extra matrices did not identify any significant predictors, nor did a binomial logistic regression analysis predicting the need for any extra matrices or none. Whatever the reason for this lack of results, it is clear that this outcome is related to the subject-to-item ratio, the number of subjects, and the ratio of variables to factors (all $p < .001$ when analyzed individually), as Table 6.3 shows. Note that this event only occurred when loadings were relatively weak (.40), and thus loading magnitude was held constant.

Interactions

To test for interaction effects, a blockwise multiple regression analysis was performed entering all main effects in Block 1 and all interactions in Block 2. In all cases, when Block 2 was entered, there was a significant change in R and R^2 (all $p < .0001$).

As the results in Table 6.4 show, there were several interesting interactions present in these

Table 6.3   Relationship Between the Number of Extra Matrices Drawn and Subject-to-Item Ratio

	10+ Extra	1–9 Extra	No Extra
S:I ratio			
< 5:1	8	7	30
5:1–10:1		1	14
> 10:1			9
Number of subjects			
50	2		1
100	2	1	3
150	2	4	6
200	2		10
300		2	10
500		1	11
1,000			12
V:F ratio			
< 10:1	8	7	15
10:1–19:1		1	27
> 19:1			11

Table 6.4   Predictors of Factor Pattern Stability: Interactions

Interaction	g^2	Kappa	Type I Error	Type II Error
# Factors × Loadings	.003	—	—	—
# Factors × # Variables	—	—	—	—
# Factors × # Subjects	—	—	—	—
# Factors × S:I Ratio	—	—	—	—
Loading × # Variables	.0001	—	.0001	—
Loading × # Subjects	—	.004	—	.0001
Loading × S:I Ratio	.007	—	.003	—
# Variables × # Subjects	.0001	.03	.003	—
# Variables × S:I Ratio	—	—	—	—
# Subjects × S:I Ratio	.0001	.0001	.0001	.0001

Table 6.5   The Effects of the Subject-to-Item Ratio on Exploratory Factor Analysis

Variable	2:1	5:1	10:1	20:1	$F_{(3,76)}$
% samples with correct factor structure	10	40	60	70	13.64*** (.21)
Average number of items misclassified on wrong factor	1.93	1.20	0.70	0.60	9.25*** (.16)
Average error in eigenvalues	.41	.33	.20	.16	25.36*** (.33)
Average error in factor loadings	.15	.12	.09	.07	36.38*** (.43)
% analyses failing to converge after 250 iterations	30	0	0	0	8.14*** (.24)
% with Heywood cases	15	20	0	0	2.81* (.10)

NOTE: η^2 reported in parentheses for significant effects.

$^*p < .05.$ $^{***}p < .0001.$

data. There were no significant interactions involving the ratio of variables to factors.

Number of factors and factor loadings. There was a significant interaction between the number of factors extracted and the magnitude of factor loadings. The nature of the interaction indicated that more factors tended to inflate g^2 when loadings were relatively weak but had less of an effect when the loadings were very strong.

Factor loadings and the number of variables. This interaction indicated that, while stronger factor loadings are related to lower g^2 and Type I error rates, loadings had less of an effect as the number of variables increased.

Factor loadings and the number of subjects. This interaction indicated that, while stronger factor loadings are related to higher kappas and lower Type II error rates, loadings had less of an effect as the number of subjects increased.

Factor loadings and the ratio of subjects to variables. This interaction indicated that, while stronger factor loadings were generally related to lower g^2 and Type I error rates, loadings had less of an effect as the ratio of subjects to variables increased.

Number of variables and the number of subjects. While increasing the number of variables was generally related to more favorable outcomes (lower g^2, higher kappa, and lower Type I error rates), as the number of subjects increased, the effect of the number of variables decreased.

Number of subjects and the ratio of subjects to variables. While increasing ratios of subjects to variables was generally related to more favorable outcomes (lower g^2, higher kappa, and lower Type I and Type II error rates), as N increased, this effect became less important.

DISCUSSION

While the original authors of this study concluded that the only two important factors in determining the correspondence between an EFA and the population were the raw number of subjects and the magnitude of the factor loadings, the examination of the ratio of subjects to variables and variables to factors and their various interactions tell a slightly more subtle story.

First, while the magnitude of factor loadings has a large influence on goodness of the analyses, the raw number of subjects had a significant influence on the average percentage of Type II errors. The ratio of subjects to variables had a significant unique effect on g^2, Type I error rates, and obtaining the correct loading pattern. In looking at Table 6.2, it is difficult to dismiss factor loadings and the ratio of subjects to variables as the most consistent predictors of these variables. Equally notable was the relative lack of the unique impact of N once the ratio of subject to variables was accounted for.

These main effects were in some ways qualified by interactions. For example, the ratio of subjects to variables appeared to have a larger effect when the raw number of subjects was lower, the number of subjects appeared to have less of an effect when there were fewer variables in the analysis, and the number of variables, the number of subjects, and the subject-to-variable ratio had larger effects when the factor loadings were smaller.

The interaction of N and the subject-to-variable ratio was particularly interesting. Although the ratio of subject to variable is an important predictor of the goodness of EFA, it appears that as total N increases, this ratio becomes less important (the converse is also true—as the subject-to-item ratio increases, total N becomes less important). In some sense, then, authors from both sides of this debate are correct—total N matters (but more so when the subject-to-item ratio is low), and the ratio of subjects to items matters (but more so when N is relatively low), and if you have a large N or large ratio, your results will be more reliable. It should be clear from both the main effect and interaction analyses that it is difficult to dismiss any of these

factors in discussing the reproducibility of population values and patterns in sample analyses.

WHY SIZE MATTERS, PART II

While the data from Guadagnoli and Velicer (1988) are illuminating, one frustration is the unrealistically clean nature of the data. Real data are messier than that, and we wanted to replicate and extend the findings from these artificial data with real data. Using data from the National Education Longitudinal Survey defining the "population" as the entire sample of almost 25,000 students, we drew samples (with replacement between samplings), extracting 20 samples of sizes ranging from 2:1, 5:1, 10:1, and 20:1 subject-to-item ratios (creating sample sizes of $N = 26, 65, 130$, and 260, respectively). The samples drawn from the population data were analyzed using maximum likelihood extraction with direct oblimin rotation, as best practices would indicate. For each sample, the magnitude of the eigenvalues, the number of eigenvalues greater than 1.0, the factor loadings of the individual items, and the number of items incorrectly loading on a factor were recorded. In order to assess accuracy as a function of sample size, we computed average error in eigenvalues and average error in factor loadings. We also recorded aberrations such as Heywood cases (occasions when a loading exceeds 1.0) and instances of failure for ML to converge on a solution after 250 iterations.

Finally, a global assessment of the correctness or incorrectness of the factor structure was made. If a factor analysis for a particular sample produced three factors, and the items loaded on the correct factors (all five parent items loaded together on a single factor, all language items loaded together on a single factor, all math items loaded together on a single factor), that analysis was considered to have produced the correct factor structure (i.e., a researcher drawing that sample and performing that analysis would draw the correct conclusions regarding the underlying factor structure for those items). If a factor analysis produced an incorrect number of factors with eigenvalues greater than 1.0 (some produced up to 5), or if one or more items failed to load on the appropriate factor, that analysis was considered to have produced an incorrect factor structure (i.e., a researcher drawing that sample and performing that analysis would *not* draw the correct conclusions regarding the underlying factor structure).

Sample Size. In order to examine how sample size affected the likelihood of errors of inference regarding factor structure of this scale, an analysis of variance was performed, examining the number of samples producing correct factor structures as a function of the sample size. The results of this analysis are presented in Table 6.5. As expected, larger samples tended to produce solutions that were more accurate. Only 10% of samples in the smallest (2:1) sample produced correct solutions (identical to the population parameters), while 70% in the largest (20:1) produced correct solutions. Furthermore, the number of misclassified items was also significantly affected by sample size. Almost 2 of 13 items on average were misclassified on the wrong factor in the smallest samples, whereas just over 1 item in every two analyses was misclassified in the largest samples. Finally, two indicators of extreme trouble—the presence of Heywood cases (factor loadings greater than 1.0, an impossible outcome) or failure to converge—were both exclusively observed in the smaller samples, with almost one third of analyses in the smallest sample size category failing to produce a solution.

What is particularly illuminating is to go back to Table 6.1, noting that while the majority of recent papers have subject-to-item ratios in the lower ranges, the error rates for these ranges are extraordinarily high—much higher than the $\alpha = .05$ criterion we are used to as a Type I error rate. Specifically, approximately two thirds of published EFA studies have subject-to-item ratios of less than 10:1, while at the same time this ratio is associated with an error rate of approximately 40%.

CONCLUSION

Conventional wisdom states that even though there are many options for executing the steps of EFA, the actual differences between them are small, so it does not really matter which methods the practitioner chooses. We disagree and hope the evidence presented herein is persuasive. Exploratory factor analysis is a complex procedure, apparently a highly error-prone procedure as well, and this situation is exacerbated

by the lack of inferential statistics and the imperfections of "real-world" data we all face.

While principal components with varimax rotation and the Kaiser criterion are the norm, they are not optimal either conceptually or empirically, particularly when data do not meet assumptions, as is often the case in the social sciences. We believe that the data and literature support the argument that optimal results (i.e., results that will generalize to other samples and that reflect the nature of the population) are more likely achieved via use of a true-factor analysis extraction method (we prefer maximum likelihood), oblique rotation (such as direct oblimin), and scree plots plus multiple test runs for information on how many meaningful factors might be in a data set. As for sample size, even at relatively large sample sizes, EFA is an error-prone procedure. Our analyses demonstrate that at a 20:1 subject-to-item ratio, there are error rates well above the field standard $\alpha = .05$ level. The most replicable results are obtained by using large samples (unless you have unusually strong data as discussed above).

This raises another point that bears discussion: By nature and design, EFA is *exploratory*. There are usually no inferential statistics available to help with decision making. As implemented in popular statistical packages, it should be used *only* for exploring data, not hypothesis or theory testing, nor is it suited to "validation" of instruments. It is, as our analyses show, an error-prone procedure even with very large samples and optimal data. We have seen many cases where researchers used EFA when they should have used CFA. Once an instrument has been developed using EFA and other techniques, it is time to move to CFA to answer questions such as, "Does an instrument have the same structure across certain population subgroups?" We would strongly caution researchers against drawing substantive conclusions based on exploratory analyses. CFA, as well as other latent variable modeling techniques, can allow researchers to test hypotheses via inferential techniques and can provide more informative analytic options.

The exception to the above rule is the freely available FACTOR software (presented in Lorenzo-Seva & Ferrando, 2006) that implements many progressive elements of EFA such as fit indices and hypothesis testing, interesting extraction and rotation options, and progressive methodologies for determining the number of factors, including a high-quality parallel analysis option. It is an interesting paradox that the more one improves EFA, the more it begins to resemble CFA. That is not necessarily a bad thing, as CFA is a powerful and useful procedure. But as lines blur between exploratory and confirmatory procedures, we will have to discuss and debate whether EFA can be considered a best practice and, if so, under what conditions.

In conclusion, researchers using large samples and making informed choices from the options available for data analysis are the ones most likely to accomplish their goal: to come to conclusions that will generalize beyond a particular sample either to another sample or to the population (or *a* population) of interest. To do less is to arrive at conclusions that are unlikely to be of any use or interest beyond that sample and that analysis.

NOTE

1. Although some procedures provide inferential statistics (e.g., maximum likelihood extraction), they are unevenly implemented and are heavily influenced by sample size, limiting their effectiveness substantially.

REFERENCES

Aleamoni, L. M. (1976). The relation of sample size to the number of variables in using factor analysis techniques. *Educational and Psychological Measurement, 36,* 879–883.

Arrindell, W. A., & van der Ende, J. (1985). An empirical-test of the utility of the observations-to-variables ratio in factor and components-analysis. *Applied Psychological Measurement, 9*(2), 165–178.

Baggaley, A. R. (1983). Deciding on the ratio of number of subjects to number of variables in factor analysis. *Multivariate Experimental Clinical Research, 6*(2), 81–85.

Barrett, P. T., & Kline, P. (1981). The observation to variable ratio in factor analysis. *Personality Study and Group Behavior, 1,* 23–33.

Bentler, P. M., & Kano, Y. (1990). On the equivalence of factors and components. *Multivariate Behavioral Research, 25*(1), 67–74.

Bobko, P., & Schemmer, F. M. (1984). Eigenvalue shrinkage in principal component based factor analysis. *Applied Psychological Measurement, 8,* 439–451.

Cliff, N. (1970). The relation between sample and population characteristic vectors. *Psychometrika, 35,* 163–178.

Cohen, J., & Cohen, P. (1983). *Applied multiple regression/correlation analysis for the behavioral sciences.* Hillsdale, NJ: Lawrence Erlbaum.

Comfrey, A. L., & Lee, H. B. (1992). *A first course in factor analysis.* Hillsdale, NJ: Lawrence Erlbaum.

Costello, A. B., & Osborne, J. W. (2005). Exploratory factor analysis: Four recommendations for getting the most from your analysis. *Practical Assessment, Research, and Evaluation, 10*(7), 1–9. Available at http://pareonline.net/pdf/v10n7.pdf

Fabrigar, L. R., Wegener, D. T., MacCallum, R. C., & Strahan, E. J. (1999). Evaluating the use of exploratory factor analysis in psychological research. *Psychological Methods, 4*(3), 272–299.

Floyd, F. J., & Widaman, K. F. (1995). Factor analysis in the development and refinement of clinical assessment instruments. *Psychological Assessment, 7*(3), 286–299.

Ford, J. K., MacCallum, R. C., & Tait, M. (1986). The application of exploratory factor analysis in applied psychology: A critical review and analysis. *Personnel Psychology, 39,* 291–314.

Gorsuch, R. L. (1983). *Factor analysis* (2nd ed.). Hillsdale, NJ: Lawrence Erlbaum.

Gorsuch, R. L. (1990). Common factor-analysis versus component analysis: Some well and little known facts. *Multivariate Behavioral Research, 25*(1), 33–39.

Gorsuch, R. L. (1997). Exploratory factor analysis: Its role in item analysis. *Journal of Personality Assessment, 68*(3), 532–560.

Guadagnoli, E., & Velicer, W. F. (1988). Relation of sample size to the stability of component patterns. *Psychological Bulletin, 103,* 265–275.

Hatcher, L. (1994). *A step-by-step approach to using the SAS® system for factor analysis and structural equation modeling.* Cary, NC: SAS Institute.

Humphreys, L. G., Ilgen, D., McGrath, D., & Montanelli, R. (1969). Capitalization on chance in rotation of factors. *Educational and Psychological Measurement, 29*(2), 259–271.

Kaiser, H. F. (1970). A second generation Little Jiffy. *Psychometrika, 35,* 401–415.

Loehlin, J. C. (1990). Component analysis versus common factor-analysis: A case of disputed authorship. *Multivariate Behavioral Research, 25*(1), 29–31.

Lorenzo-Seva, U., & Ferrando, P. J. (2006). FACTOR: A computer program to fit the exploratory factor analysis model. *Behavior Research Methods, 38*(1), 88–91.

MacCallum, R. C., & Tucker, L. R. (1991). Representing sources of error in the common-factor model:

Implications for theory and practice. *Psychological Bulletin, 109*(3), 502–511.

MacCallum, R. C., Widaman, K. F., Preacher, K. J., & Hong, S. (2001). Sample size in factor analysis: The role of model error. *Multivariate Behavioral Research, 36,* 611–637.

MacCallum, R. C., Widaman, K. F., Zhang, S., & Hong, S. (1999). Sample size in factor analysis. *Psychological Methods, 4,* 84–99.

Mulaik, S. A. (1990). Blurring the distinctions between component analysis and common factor-analysis. *Multivariate Behavioral Research, 25*(1), 53–59.

Nunnally, J. C. (1978). *Psychometric theory* (2nd ed.). New York: McGraw-Hill.

Pedhazur, E. J. (1997). *Multiple regression in behavioral research: Explanation and prediction.* Fort Worth, TX: Harcourt Brace.

Schonemann, P. H. (1990). Facts, fictions, and common-sense about factors and components. *Multivariate Behavioral Research, 25*(1), 47–51.

Snook, S. C., & Gorsuch, R. L. (1989). Component analysis versus common factor-analysis: A Monte-Carlo study. *Psychological Bulletin, 106*(1), 148–154.

Steiger, J. H. (1990). Some additional thoughts on components, factors, and factor- indeterminacy. *Multivariate Behavioral Research, 25*(1), 41–45.

Tabachnick, B. G., & Fidell, L. S. (2001). *Using multivariate statistics.* Boston: Allyn & Bacon.

Velicer, W. F., & Jackson, D. N. (1990). Component analysis versus common factor-analysis: Some further observations. *Multivariate Behavioral Research, 25*(1), 97–114.

Widaman, K. F. (1990). Bias in pattern loadings represented by common factor-analysis and component analysis. *Multivariate Behavioral Research, 25*(1), 89–95.

Widaman, K. F. (1993). Common factor-analysis versus principal component analysis: Differential bias in representing model parameters. *Multivariate Behavioral Research, 28*(3), 263–311.

PART II

SELECTED BEST PRACTICES IN RESEARCH DESIGN

7

REPLICATION STATISTICS

PETER R. KILLEEN

We come finally, however, to the relation of the ideal theory to real world, or "real" probability. . . . To someone who wants [applications, a consistent mathematician] would say that the ideal system runs parallel to the usual theory: "If this is what you want, try it: it is not my business to justify application of the system; that can only be done by philosophizing; I am a mathematician." In practice he is apt to say: "try this; if it works that will justify it." But now he is not merely philosophizing; he is committing the characteristic fallacy. Inductive experience that the system works is not evidence.

Littlewood (1953, p. 73)

PROBABILITY AS A MODEL SYSTEM

For millennia, Euclidean geometry was a statement of fact about the world order. Only in the 19th century did it come to be recognized instead as a model system—an "ideal theory"—that worked exceedingly well when applied to many parts of the real world. It then stepped down from a truth about the world to its current place as first among equals as models of the world—the most useful of a cohort of geometries, each of differential service in particular cases, on spherical surfaces and relativistic universes and fractal percolates. In like manner, probability theory was born as an explanation of the contingent world—"'real' probability"—and, with the work of Kolmogorov among many

others, it matured as a coherent model system, inheriting most features of the earlier versions of the probability calculus.

The abstraction of model systems from the world permits their development as coherent, clear, and concise logics. But the abstraction has another legacy: the eventual need for scientists to reconnect the model system to the empirical world. That such rapprochement is even possible is amazing; it stimulated Wigner's well-known allusion to "the unreasonable effectiveness of mathematics in describing the world." Realizing such "unreasonably effective" descriptions, however, can present reasonably formidable difficulties—difficulties that are sometimes overcome only by fiat, as noted by Littlewood, a mathematician of no mean ability,

Author's Note: The research was supported by National Science Foundation Grant IBN 0236821 and National Institute of Mental Health Grant 1R01MH066860.

and M. Kline (1980), a scholar of comparable acuity. The toolbox that helps us apply the "ideal theory" of probability to scientific questions is called inferential statistics. These tools are being continually sharpened, with new designs replacing old.

Intellectual ontogeny recapitulates its cultural phylogeny. Just as we must outgrow naive physics, we must outgrow naive statistics. The former is an easier transition than the latter. Not only must we as students of contingency deal with the gamblers' fallacies and exchange paradoxes; we must also cope with the academics' fallacies and statistical paradoxes that are visited upon us as idols of our theater, the university classroom. The first step, one already taken by most readers of this volume, is to recognize that we deal with model systems, some more useful than others, not with truths about real things. The second step is to understand the character of the most relevant tools for their application, their strengths and weaknesses, and attempt to determine in which cases their marriage to data is one of mere convenience and in which it is blessed with a deeper, Wignerian resonance. That step requires us to remain appreciative but critical craftsmen. It requires us to look through the halo of mathematics that surrounds all statistical inference to assess the goodness of fit between tool and task, to ask of each statistical technique whether it gives us leverage or just adds decoration.

This chapter briefly reviews—briefly, because there are so many good alternative sources (e.g., Harlow, Mulaik, & Steiger, 1997; R. B. Kline, 2004)—the most basic statistical technique we use, null hypothesis statistical testing (NHST) and its limits. It then describes an alternative statistic, p_{rep}, that predicts replicability. We remain mindful of Littlewood's (1953) observation that "inductive experience that the system works is not evidence [that it is true]." But then Littlewood was a mathematician, not a scientist. The search for truth about parameters has often befuddled the progress of science, which recognizes simpler goals as well: to understand and predict. If we "try [a tool, and] it works," that can be very good news and may constitute a significant advance over what has been. So, try this new tool, and see if it works for your inferential problems.

Connecting Probability to Data

You are faced with two columns of numbers, data collected from two groups of subjects. What do you want to know? Not, of course, "whether there's a significant difference between them." If they are identical, you would have looked for the clerical error. If they are different, they are different. You can review them 100 times, and they will continue to be different, hopefully 100 times; $p = 1.0$. "*Significantly* different," you might emphasize, irritated. But what does that mean? "That the probability that they would be so different by chance is less than 5%," you recite. OK. Progress. Now we just need clarification of *probability, so,* and *chance.*

Probability. Probability theory is a deductive calculus. One starts with probability generators, such as coins or cards or dice, and makes deductions about their behavior. The premises are precise: coins with a probability of heads of .50, perfectly balanced dice, perfectly shuffled cards. Then elegant theorems solve problems such as "Given an unbiased coin, what is the probability of flipping 6 heads in a row?" But scientists are never given such ideal objects. Their modal inferences are inductions, not deductions: An informant gives them a series of outcomes from flipping a coin that landed heads six times in a row, and they must determine what probability of heads should be assigned to the coin. They can solve this mystery either as Dr. Watson or as Mr. Holmes in the cherished tale, "The Case of the Hypothesis That Had No Teeth." As you well remember, Dr. Watson studiously purged his mind of all prior biases and opined that the probability of the coin being fair was manifestly $(\frac{1}{2})^6$, < .025 and, further, that the best estimate of the probability of a heads was $1 - 2^{-6}$. Mr. Holmes stuffed his pipe; examined the coin; spun it; asked about its origin, how the coin was released and caught, and how many sequences were required to get that run of six; and then inquired about the bank account of the informant and his recent associates. Dr. Watson objected that that was going beyond the information given; in any case, how could one ever combine all those diverse clues into a probability statement that was not intrinsically subjective? "Elementary," Mr. Holmes observed, "probability theory this is not, my dear Watson; nor is it deduction. When I infer a state of nature from evidence, the more evidence the better I infer. My colleague shall explain how to concatenate evidence in a later chapter of this sage book I saw you nodding over."

How do we infer probability from a situation in which there is no uncertainty—the six heads in a row, last week's soccer cup, your two columns of experimental data? There are two root metaphors for probability: For frequentists, probability is the long-run relative frequency of an outcome; it does not apply to novel events (no long run) or to accomplished events (*faits accomplis* support no probability other than unity). For Bayesians, probability is the relative odds that an individual gives to an outcome.

You do not have resources or interest to reconduct your experiment thousands of times, to estimate the relative frequency of two means being so different. And even if you did, you'd just be left with a much larger sample of accomplished data. This seems to eliminate the frequentist solution. On the other hand, the odds that you give to your outcome will be different from the odds your reviewers or editor or your significant other gives to your outcome. This eliminates any unique Bayesian probability. What next? Just imagine.

Instead of conducting the experiment thousands of times, just *imagine* that it has been conducted thousands of times. This is Fisher's brilliant solution to the problem of connecting data to the "ideal theory" of probability. Well then, just how big an effect should we imagine that your experiment yielded? Here we must temper imagination with discipline: We must imagine that the experiment never worked— that there was never a real effect in all those imaginary trials but that the outcomes were distributed by that rogue called Chance. Next, graph the proportion of outcomes at various effect sizes to give a sampling distribution. If your measured outcome happens only rarely among this cohort of no real effects, you may conclude that it really is not of their type—it does not belong on the group null bench. It is so deviant, you infer, because more than Chance was at work—the experimental manipulation was at work! This last inference is, as we shall see, as common, and commonly sanctioned, as it is unjustified.

If the thousands-of-hypothetical-trials scenario taxes the computational resources of your imagination, then imagine instead that the data were drawn from a large, normally distributed population of data similar to those of the control group. Increase the power of the test by estimating the population variance from the variances of both the experimental and control groups. Then a theoretical sampling distribution, such as the t distribution, can be directly used to infer how often so deviant an outcome as what you measured would have happened by chance under repeated sampling. This set of tactics is the paradigmatic modus operandi for statistical inference. In modern applications, the theoretical sampling distribution may be replaced with an empirical one, obtained by Monte Carlo elaboration of the original empirical distribution function (e.g., Davison & Hinkley, 1997; Mooney & Duval, 1993).

So in this standard scenario, *probability* means the long-run relative frequency that you *stipulate* in your test of the behavior of an ideal object. It is against this that you will test your data. Unlike a Bayesian probability, the parameters tested (e.g., the null hypothesis that the means of the two populations are equal) are not inferred from data. Indeed, authorities such as Kyburg (1987) argue that use of Bayesian inverse inference, leading up from statistics to parameters, undermines all direct inference thereafter, including NHST.

So. Let us assume your experiment recorded a standardized difference between the responses of 30 control subjects and 30 experimental subjects of $d = 0.50$, from which you calculated a p value of $< .05$. What does that mean? Does it mean that the probability of getting a d of 0.50 under the null is less than 5%? No, because we know a priori that the probability of getting exactly that value is always very close to zero; in fact, the more decimal places in your measurements, the closer to zero. That's true for any real number you might have recorded, even $d = 0.00$, which Chance favors.

Again an impasse, but again one that can be solved through imagination (providing inductive evidence supporting Einstein's chestnut "Imagination is more important than knowledge"). To get a probability requires an interval on the x-axis. We could take one around the observed value: say, $d \pm 0.05$. This would work; as we let the interval shrink toward zero, comparison with a similar extent around 0 would give us a likelihood analysis of the null versus the observed (Royall, 1997). Fisher was a pioneer of likelihood analyses but could not get likelihoods to behave like probabilities, and so he suggested a different interval on the evidence axis: He gave the investigator credit for everything more extreme than the observed statistic (a benefice that amazed and pleased many generations of young researchers, who might have been told instead, "The null will give effects *up to* that size 95% of the time"). So, what *so* means here is "more extreme than" what you found, including *d* scores of 1, 2, . . . 100. . . . Don't ask why those extents of the *x*-axis never visited by data should play a role in the decision; take the *p* < .05 and run.

Chance. "The probability [relative frequency under random sampling] that your data would be so [at least that] extreme by chance." Here *chance* means your manipulation did not work and only the null did. How does the null work? Typically, thanks to the central limit theorem, in ways that result in a Gaussian distribution of effects (although for other test statistics or inferences, related distributions such as the *t* or *F* are the correct asymptotic distributions). Two parameters completely determine the Gaussian: its mean and variance. Under the null, the mean is zero. Its variance? Since we have no other way to determine it, we use the data you brought with you, the variance of your control group. Well . . . the experimental group could also provide information. Hoping that the experimental operations have not perturbed that too much, we will pool the information from both sources. Then *chance* means that "with no help from my experimental manipulation, the impotent null could have given rise to the observed difference by the luck of the draw [of a sample from our hypothetical population]." If it would happen in less than 5% of the samples we hypothetically take, we call the data *significantly* different from that expected under the null.

You knew all that from Stat 101, but it is worth the review. What do you conclude with a gratifying *p* < .05? Also as learned in Stat 101, you conclude that those are improbably extreme data. But what many of us *thought* we heard was that we could then reject the null. That, of course, is simplistic at best, false at worst.

FOUNDATIONAL PROBLEMS WITH STATISTICAL INFERENCE

The Inverse Inference Problem. Assume the probability of the statistic S given the null (N) is less than a prespecified critical number, $p(S|N) < \alpha$, where the null may be a hypothesis such as $\mu_E - \mu_C = 0$. It does not then follow that the probability of the null given the statistic, $p(N|S)$, is less than α. We can get from one to the other, however, via Bayes theorem:

$$p(N|S) = p(S|N)p(N)/p(S).$$

By the (prior) probability of the null, $p(N)$, we mean the probability of the mathematical implication of the null (for instance, that two population means are equal, $\mu_E - \mu_C = 0$). That prior must be assigned a value before looking at the new data (S). By the probability of the statistic, $p(S)$, we mean its probability under relevant states of the world—in this case, the probability of the data given that the null is true, plus the probability of the data given that the null is false: $p(S) = p(S|N)p(N) + p(S|{\sim}N)(1 - p(N))$. By normalizing the right-hand side of Bayes's equation, $p(S)$ makes the posterior probabilities sum to 1. Only in the unlikely case that the prior probability of the null equals the probability of the statistic, $p(N) = p(S)$, does $p(N|S) = p(S|N)$. Otherwise, to have any sense of the probability of the null (and, by implication, of the alternative we favor, that our manipulation was effective: $\mu_E - \mu_C > 0$), we must be able to estimate $p(N)/p(S)$. This is not easy. Even if we could agree on assigning a prior probability to the null, Bayes would not give us the probability of our favored hypothesis (unless we defined it broadly as "anything but the null"). In light of these difficulties, Fisher (1959) made it crystal clear that we generally cannot get from our *p* value to *any* statement about the probability of the hypotheses. But it was to make exactly such statements about our hypotheses, with the blessings of statistical rigor, that we attended all those statistics courses. We were misled, but it was not, we suspect, the first or last time that happened, which goes some distance to explaining the conflation of *statistics* with *lies* in the public's mind.

"It is important to remember that [relative frequency] is but one interpretation that can be given to the formal notion of probability" (Hays,

1963, p. 63); given our inferential imbroglio, we may well wonder if that interpreter ever spoke the language of science. Neyman and Pearson solved the problem of inverse inference by emphasizing comparison with an alternate hypothesis, setting criterial regions into which our statistic would either fall, or not, and noting that, whereas we have no license to change our beliefs about the null even if our statistic falls into such a critical ($p < \alpha$) region, it would nonetheless be prudent to change our behavior, absent a change in belief. Like Augustine's *credo quia impossibile,* this tergiversation does solve the problem—but only for those whose faith is stronger than their reason.

What did we ever do that got us into this mess? We wanted to know if our manipulation (or someone else's, perhaps Nature's, if this was an observational study) really worked. We wanted to know how much of the difference between groups was caused by the factor that we used to sort the numbers into two or more columns. We wanted to know if our results will replicate or if we are likely to be embarrassed by that most odious of situations, publication of unreplicable results. Null hypothesis statistical tests cannot get us from here to there. Let us go back to basics and see if we cannot find a viable alternate route to some of our valid goals.

DEFINING REPLICATION

Curious, isn't it, that we have license to use the measured variance (s^2) in estimating a parameter of the population under the null hypothesis (σ^2), but we do not use the measured mean to estimate a parameter? Why evaluate data with one hand tied behind our back? Assay the following hypothesis instead: H_A: $\delta = d$, where δ is the value of the population effect size, and d is the effect size you measured in your experiment. But to ask the probability that this alternative to the null is true seems to be creating a new logical fallacy: *post hoc, ergo hoc.* (Gigerenzer [2004] called a similar solecism "The Feynman Fallacy" because Feynman was so exasperated when a young colleague asked him to calculate the probability of an accomplished event.) But we can ask a different, noncircular question, one that takes advantage of the first two moments of the observed data. What is the probability that, using the same experimental operations and population of subjects, another investigator can replicate those results? This can be computed once we agree on the meaning of *replicate.* Consider this definition:

To *replicate* means to repeat the empirical operations and to record data that support the original claim.

- If the claim is as modest as "This operation works [generates a positive effect]," then any replication attempt that finds a positive effect could be deemed a successful replication. Although this may seem a too-modest threshold for replication, put it in the context of what traditional significance tests test: In a one-tailed test, $1 - p$ gives us the probability that our statistic d has the same sign as the population parameter (Jones & Tukey, 2000).
- If the claim is "This operation generates an effect size of at least d_L," then only replication attempts that return $d \geq d_L$ count as successful replications.
- If the claim is "This operation generates a significant effect," then only replication attempts that return a $p < .05$ are successful replications.
- If the claim is "This operation is essentially worthless, generating effect sizes less than d_U," then any replication attempt that returned a $d < d_U$ could be deemed a successful replication. One would have to decide beforehand if a d less than, say, −0.5 was as consistent with the claim or constituted evidence for a stronger alternative claim, such as "This operation could backfire."

In the following, we shall show how to compute such probabilities.

PREDICTING REPLICABILITY
RATHER THAN INFERRING PARAMETERS

How. How to estimate these probabilities? The sampling distribution of effect sizes in replication, $p(d_2|d_1)$, is required.

Effect size is calculated as

$$d = \frac{M_E - M_C}{s_p}, \tag{1}$$

with M_E the mean of the experimental group, M_C the mean of the control group, and s_p the estimate of the population standard deviation based on the pooled standard deviations of both groups (see the appendix for more information). Consider an effect size $d = d_1$ based on a total of n observations randomly sampled from a population with unknown mean δ and variance σ^2. The effect size d_2 for the next m observations constitutes the datum that we wish to predict based on the original observations: $f(d_2|d_1)$. Because d_1 provides information about d_2, these statistics are not independent. They are only independent when considered as samples from a large population whose parameter is δ. Solution proceeds by considering the joint density of d_2 and δ conditional on the primary observations. This is developed in the appendix, leading to the distribution shown as the flatter curve in Figure 7.1. In evaluating a claim concerning experimental results, calculate replicability by integrating that density between the appropriate limits:

$$p_{\text{rep}} = \int_{d_L}^{d_U} n(d_1, s_{d_R}^2) = \Phi\frac{d_U - d_1}{s_{d_R}} - \Phi\frac{d_L - d_1}{s_{d_R}}, \quad (2)$$

In cases where a positive effect has been claimed, and we stipulate that the hypothetical replication would have the same power as the accomplished experiment—everything is done exactly as in the original experiment—then $d_L = 0$, $d_U = \infty$, and $S_{d_R}^2 = 2S_d^2$. This is shown as the gray

area of the predictive distribution on the right in Figure 7.1. If the claim is that the effect size is greater than d^*, the probability of getting supportive evidence is predicted by p_{rep} with $d_L = d^*$ and $d_U = \infty$. The probability of finding a significant effect size in replication is given by p_{rep} with $d_L = S_{d_R}^2 z_\alpha$. Other claims take other limits.

For convenience in calculation of the standard case, Equation 2 may be rewritten as

$$p_{\text{rep}} = \int_{-\infty}^{d_1/\sigma_{dR}} n(0, 1) = \Phi\left(d_1/s_{d_R}\right), \quad (3)$$

with σ_{d_R} estimated by S_{d_R}.

The variance of d is

$$s_d^2 \approx \frac{n^2}{n_E n_C (n - 4)},$$

with $n = n_E + n_C$. When experimental and control groups are of equal size, $n_E = n_C$, then

$$s_d^2 \approx \frac{4}{n - 4},$$

and $s_{d_R}^2 = 2s_d^2$. Predicting the effects in a different-size prospective sample requires adjusting the variance. These considerations are reviewed in Killeen (2005a), whose derivation was corrected along the lines of the appendix by Doros and Geier (2005).

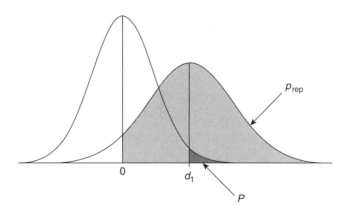

Figure 7.1   The dark area to the right of the observed effect size d_1 gives the probability of finding data more extreme than d_1, given the null. The gray area to the right of 0 gives the probability of finding a positive effect in replication (Equation 2). The figure is reproduced from Killeen (2005a), with permission.

Relation to p. How does the probability of replication compare to traditional indices of replicability such as *p*? The *p* value is the probability of rejecting the null hypothesis given that the datum, d_1, is sampled from a world in which the null is true. It is shown as the area to the right of d_1 in Figure 7.1, under a normal density centered at 0 and having a variance of σ_{d}^2, estimated from s_d^2. The value of p_{rep} for the same data—the probability of finding a positive effect in replication—is the shaded area to the right of 0 in the normal curve centered on d_1 and having a variance of σ_{dR}^2, estimated from $s_{d_R}^2 = 2s_d^2$. As d_1 moves to the right, or as the variance of d_1, s_d^2, decreases, p_{rep} will increase and *p* decrease in complement. For use in spreadsheets such as Excel, Cumming (2005) suggested the notation p_{rep} = NORMSDIST([NORMSINV($1 - p$)]/√2), where NORMSDIST is the standardized normal distribution function, and NORMSINV is the normal *p*-to-*z* transformation. Drawn in probability coordinates, the relation between these two probabilities is transparent: The *z* scores for p_{rep} decrease linearly with the *z*-scores for *p*, $z_{Prep} = -kz_p$, with $k = 1/√2$.

Advantages of p_{rep} *over* p. Given the affinity between *p* and p_{rep}, why switch? Indeed, a first reading may give the impression that *p* is preferable: Sentences that contain it also contain *hypotheses,* and those are what scientists are interested in. Conversely, p_{rep} does not give the probability that your hypothesis is true, or that the null is true, or that one or the other or both are false. It gives the long-run probability that an exact replication will support a claim. Both the original and the replicate may work for the wrong reasons—widdershins sampling errors in both cases. Rational scientists would prefer to know whether their hypotheses are true or false, not just whether their data are likely to replicate.

But that knowledge is not granted by statistical inference. Null hypothesis statistical tests never let us assign probabilities to hypotheses (Fisher, 1959). This is a manifestation of the unsolved problem of inverse statistical inference (Cohen, 1994; Killeen, 2005c). Students are admonished, "Never use the unfortunate expression 'accept the null hypothesis'" (Wilkinson & the Task Force on Statistical Inference, 1999, p. 599); without priors on the null, they should also be admonished, "Never use the equally unfortunate expression 'reject the null hypothesis.'" One can make no

claims more interesting than "My data are absurdly improbable under the null," leaving the implication unsaid. Stipulating the null keeps its truth value off the table as a conclusion.

A researcher *can* say, "My hypothesis led me to predict a positive effect from this manipulation. I found one, and if you repeat my manipulation, you have a probability of approximately p_{rep} of also finding one." As ever, the investigator can assert that the manipulation caused the effect, and the hypothesis that birthed the manipulation was correct, only to the extent all confounds were eliminated, as other causes may have been more operative than the ones manipulated; those alternative causes may have been systematic, or possibly discernable only as "error [sampling] variance." In the long run (as *n* increases), nonetheless, exact replications should succeed with probability p_{rep}. Whereas *failure to reject the null* is not easily interpreted, a p_{rep} = .85 is just as interpretable as a p_{rep} = .95. Other advantages are discussed in Killeen (2005a), who did not adequately emphasize that p_{rep}, based on a single experiment, is only an estimate of replication probability (Cumming, 2005; Iverson, Myung, & Karabatsos, 2006). Like confidence intervals and *p* values, its accuracy depends on just how representative of the population the original sample happened to be. Any one estimate of replicability may be off, but in the long run, p_{rep} provides a reliable estimate of replicability. Evidence of this is seen in p_{rep}'s ability to predict the proportion of replications in meta-analyses (Killeen, 2005a).

THE DISTRIBUTION OF *P*, P_{REP}, AND LOG-LIKELIHOOD RATIOS

In order to compare p_{rep} with its cousins, *p* and the log-likelihood ratio (LLR), a simulation was conducted to generate an empirical sampling distribution of effect sizes d_i. Twenty thousand samples of size *n* = 60 were taken from a normal distribution with mean 0.5 and variance $\sigma_d^2 = 4/(60 - 4)$. This corresponds to the sampling distribution of differences between the means of experimental and control groups of 30 observations each, when the true difference between them is half a standard deviation ($\delta = 0.5$). This should yield a typical p_{rep} = .907 and *p* = .029. Values of p_{rep}, *p*, and LLR were calculated, along with the *z* score transformation of

p_{rep}, NORMSINV(p_{rep}). As expected, the distribution of p_{rep} is negatively skewed (coefficient of skewness [CS] = −1.60; mean = .859; median = .906; see Figure 7.2 and Cumming, 2005). This skew has been cited as a fault of p_{rep} (Iverson et al., 2006). However, the distribution of p is even *more* strongly skewed (CS = 2.41; mean = .093; median = .031). Even though the means are biased, however, both cases the median values of the test statistics are very close to their predicted values. The sampling distribution for the z scores of p_{rep} closely approximated a normal density, having a CS of 0.02. To aggregate values of p_{rep} over studies, it is therefore the z transform of p_{rep} that should be averaged (inversely weighted by the number of observations in each sample, if those differ).

For comparison, consider the likelihood of the data (d_i) given that the parameter equals zero, divided by the likelihood given that the parameter equals that observed, here 0.5. In the present scenario, its expected value is the ratio of the ordinate of the normal density at $d = 0.5$ under the null (with mean at 0) to that of the density under the alternate (with mean at 0.5). The natural logarithm of this ratio is the LLR, which is simply computed as $-z^2/2$. For the present

exercise, this is $-(.5)^2/(4/(60 − 4))/2 = −1.75$. The distribution of LLRs is shown in the right panel of Figure 7.2. The likelihood ratio is positively skewed (CS = 0.93) and, as visible in Figure 7.2, the LLR is negatively skewed, to about the same degree as p_{rep} (CS = −1.46; mean = −2.25, median = −1.75, just as predicted). Readers may experiment with these and related distributions at the excellent site maintained by Cumming (2006).

The Bayes factor is an analogous statistic favored by Bayesians such as Iverson et al. (2006) and M. D. Lee and Wagenmakers (2005). If the hypotheses are simple and their prior plausibilities equal, than the Bayes factor is the likelihood ratio (P. M. Lee, 2004). If these conditions are not met, then a prior distribution for the parameters must be chosen and then integrated out (see, e.g., Wagenmakers & Grünwald, 2006). The distribution of the Bayes factor will depend on the nature of that prior distribution.

REFUTATION AND VINDICATION

Predicting a positive effect of any size in replication may seem too weak a prediction to merit

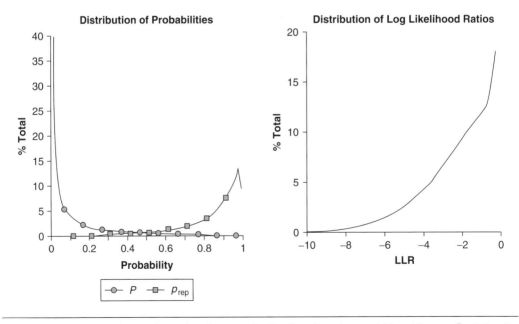

Figure 7.2   Twenty thousand samples of a normally distributed random variable, with mean $\delta = 0.5$ and variance $\sigma^2 = 4/(60 − 4)$, yielded these distributions of three test statistics.

attention. It is therefore useful to identify two kindred indices of replicability, the probability of strong support, p_{sup}, and the probability of strong contradictory results, p_{con}. Let us measure the degree of support that a real replication gives as its own value of p_{rep}. Set some threshold for calling a result *strong*, say, $p^* = .8$. Then a replication that returns a $p_{rep} > p^*$ is called "strong support," and one that returns a p_{rep} greater than p^* *in the wrong direction* (i.e., the replication's $p_{rep} < 1 - p^*$) is called "strong contradiction." The middling outcomes between these are called weak support or contradiction depending on their sign. The criteria for just what constitutes strong support and strong refutation are arbitrary; we could use p^*s of .75 or .8 or .9 or any other percentile. It is easy to calculate the resulting probabilities of support and refutation:

$$p_{sup} = 1 - \text{normsdist}[\text{normsinv}(p^*) - \text{normsinv}(p_{rep})];$$

$$p_{con} = 1 - \text{normsdist}[\text{normsinv}(p^*) + \text{normsinv}(p_{rep})].$$

Selected values of these expectations are found in Table 7.1. The first criterion in that table is $p^* = .5$. This returns the probability that a replication will have an effect of the same sign. This is obviously just p_{rep}. The probability of a contradiction—an effect of an opposite sign—is the complement of p_{rep}. Consider next the row indexed by $p_{rep} = .95$. This corresponds to the threshold LLR that Bayesians consider strong

evidence, as well as to a one-tailed critical region for p of .01. The probability of strong support at a $p^* = .8$ is .789. The probability of a replication retuning an effect that is significant at $p < .05$ is given by $p^* = .88$, close to $p^* = .9$. For $p_{rep} = .95$, this happens about 2/3 of the time.

The probability of bad news—strong contradiction—is also found in Table 7.1. For $p_{rep} = .95$, $p^* = .8$, it is .006: Fewer than one attempted replication out of a hundred will go that far in the opposite direction from the original data. Experiments that yield a p_{rep} in excess of .9 are unlikely to be refuted (on statistical grounds, at least!). Variations in the execution of replication attempts (e.g., those deriving from changes in the measurement instruments and experimental or observational context) will inevitably add realization variance and, to the extent that they do so, will make these estimates optimistic.

Readers familiar with signal detection theory will immediately see that effect size d is nothing other than their familiar index of discriminability d'. The criterion p^* is analogous to bias: Changes in p^* do not move the criterion from left to right but move two criteria in and out. The data in Table 7.1 can be represented as points along receiver operating characteristics (ROCs), with p_{sup} corresponding to hits and p_{con} to false alarms. The resulting isosensitivity functions for the first few columns of Table 7.1 are shown in Figure 7.3, with the criterion p^* increasing from .5 to .98 in smaller steps than shown in that table to draw the curves. These

Table 7.1   The Probability That a Result Will Be Replicated or Refuted at Different Levels of Confidence Given the Strength of the Original Results

Criteria for strong support or contradiction		0.5		0.75		0.8		0.85		0.9	
p	P_{rep}	P_{sup}	P_{con}	P_{sup}	P_{con}	P_{sup}	P_{con}	P_{sup}	P_{con}	P_{sup}	P_{con}
0.1000	0.818	0.818	0.182	0.592	0.057	0.526	0.040	0.448	0.026	0.354	0.014
0.0500	0.878	0.878	0.122	0.687	0.033	0.626	0.022	0.550	0.014	0.453	0.007
0.0250	0.917	0.917	0.083	0.762	0.020	0.707	0.013	0.637	0.008	0.542	0.004
0.0100	0.950	0.950	0.050	0.834	0.010	0.789	0.006	0.729	0.004	0.642	0.002
0.0050	0.966	0.966	0.034	0.874	0.006	0.836	0.004	0.784	0.002	0.705	0.001
0.0025	0.976	0.976	0.024	0.905	0.004	0.874	0.002	0.829	0.001	0.759	0.001
0.0010	0.986	0.986	0.014	0.935	0.002	0.910	0.001	0.875	0.001	0.817	0.000

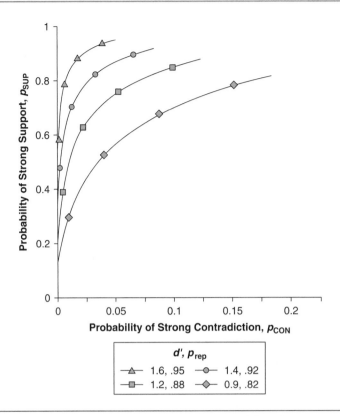

Figure 7.3   The probability of strong support (ordinates) and probability of strong contradiction (abcissae) both increase as the criterion for *strong* (p^*) is reduced from an austere .98 (lower left origin of curves) to a magnanimous .50. The parameter is p_{rep} and its corresponding z score, d'.

are not the traditional *yes/no* ROCs, but *yes/no/uncertain,* with the last category corresponding to replications that will fall between p_{sup} and p_{con} in strength.

One may also calculate the probability of a nil effect in replication. This is analogous to the probability of the null. If one takes a nil effect to be one that falls within, say, 10% of chance (.4 < p_{rep} < .6), the probability of a nil effect in replication when p_{rep} = .95 is 5%. This probability may easily be calculated as $p_{nil} = P^{L}_{sup} - P^{U}_{sup}$, where P^{L}_{sup} corresponds to the probability of support returned by the lower limit ($p^* = .4$ in the example), and P^{U}_{sup} corresponds to the probability of support returned by the upper limit ($p^* = .6$ in the example). For further discussion, see Sanabria and Killeen (2007).

Credible Confidence Intervals. A small but increasing number of editors are encouraging researchers to report measures of effect size (Cumming & Finch, 2005). A convenient way to

specify the margin of error in effect size is by bounding it with confidence intervals (CI; see Chapter 17). Unfortunately, most investigators do not really understand what confidence intervals mean (Fidler, Thomason, Cumming, Finch, & Leeman, 2004). This confusion can be remedied by study of Cumming and Finch (2001), Loftus and Masson (1994), and Thompson (1999), along with the handy chapters of this volume. An alternate approach provides a more intuitive measure of the margin of error in data. One such measure is the range over which a replication will fall with some stipulated probability. A convenient interval to use is the standard error of the statistic. Approximately half the replication attempts will fall within ± 1 standard error, centered on the measured statistic (Cumming, Williams, & Fidler, 2004). I call this kind of CI a *replication interval* (RI). Its interpretation is direct, its calculation routine, and its presentation as error bars hedging the datum unchallenged (Estes, 1997).

EVIDENCE, BELIEF, AND ACTION

What prior information should be incorporated in the evaluation of a research claim? If there is a substantial literature in relevant areas, then the replicability of a new claim can be predicted more accurately by incorporating that information. For some uses, this is an optimal tactic and constitutes a running meta-analysis of the relevant literature. The evaluation of the evidence at hand would then, however, be confounded with the particular prior information that was engaged to optimize predictions. Other consumers, with other background information, would then have to deconvolute the experimental results from those priors. For most audiences, it seems best to bypass this step, letting the data speak for themselves and letting the consumers of the results add their own qualification based on their own sense of the prior results in the area (Killeen, 2005b). This decision is equivalent to assuming that the prior distribution of the population effect size is flat and is consistent with some analysts' advice to use only likelihood ratios (e.g., Glover & Dixon, 2004; Royall, 1997), not Bayesian posteriors, thereby eschewing the difficulties in the choice of priors. Royall (2004) is perhaps the most cogent, noting three questions that our statistical toolbox can help us address:

1. How should I evaluate this evidence?

2. What should I believe?

3. What should I do?

1. The first question confronts us when data are first assembled. Here, considerations of the past (priors) and the future (different prospective populations) confound analysis of the data on the table. Such externals "can obfuscate formal tests by including information not specifically contained within the experiment itself" (Maurer, 2004, p. 17). Royall (2004) and Maurer (2004) argue for an evidential approach using the likelihood ratios. They eschew the use of priors to convert these into the probability of the null because this ties the analysis to a reference set that may not be shared by other interested consumers of the evidence.

2. *Belief*, however, should take into account prior information, even information that may be particular to the individual. Each of us carries

a unique reference set with which we update our beliefs in light of evidence. This is why serious crimes are evaluated by large juries of peers: large, to accommodate a range of reference sets; peers, to relate those priors to ones most relevant to the defendant. The transformation of evidence into belief (concerning a hypothesis or proposition) transforms a public datum into a personal probability. Shared evaluation of strong evidence will bring those personal probabilities toward convergence, but they will be identical only for those with identical reference sets. Savage (1972) took such personal probabilities to be "the only probability concept essential to science" (p. 56). Royall (2004) and Maurer (2004) disagree. Belief is indeed best constructed with Bayesian updating and motivates the acceptance or rejection of scientific theories, but evidence evaluation must be kept insulated from priors. Once that evaluation is executed, belief adjustment is natural. But beliefs should concern claims and hypotheses; they should not contaminate evidence.

3. What we should *do* depends both on what we believe and what we value. Decision theory tells us how to combine these factors to determine the course of action yielding the greatest expected benefit. In particular, the posterior predictive distribution shown in Figures 7.1 and 7.3 estimate the probability of different effect sizes in replication. If we can assign utility to outcomes as a function of their expected effect size, we can determine what values of d_1 fall above a threshold of action. The sigmoid function in Figure 7.4 represents such a utility function. Multiplying the probability of each effect size in replication by the utility function and summing gives the expected utility of replicating the original results.

Given a posterior predictive distribution, it is straightforward to construct a decision theory to guide our action. Winkler (2003) teaches the basics, and Killeen (2006) applies them to recover traditional practices and extends them in nontraditional ways. The execution may employ flat priors and identical prospective populations; it then will guide disposition of the evidence: whether it be admitted to a corpus or rejected, whether the paper be published or not. Or the execution may employ informative priors and may take into consideration the realization variance involved in generalizing to new

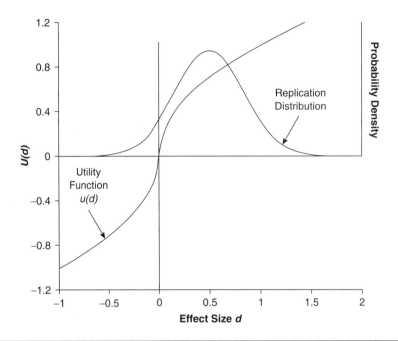

Figure 7.4   The Gaussian density is the posterior predictive distribution for a result with an effect size of $d_1 = 0.5$. The sigmoid is an example of a utility function on effect size that expresses decreasing marginal utility as a function of effect size and treats positive and negative effects symmetrically.

prospective populations. It then becomes a pragmatic guide for action, an optimal tool to guide medical, industrial, and civic programs.

REALIZATION VARIANCE

Whenever an attempt is made to replicate, it is inevitable that details of the procedure and subject population will vary. Successful replication with different instruments, instructions, and kinds of subjects lends generality to the results—but it also increases the risk of different results. This risk may be represented as *realization variance*, σ_{δ_j}, the uncertainty added by deviations from exact replication (Raudenbush, 1994; Rubin, 1981; van den Noortgate & Onghena, 2003). The subscript j indicates that this variance is indexed to a particular field of research. The estimated variance of effect size in replication becomes

$$s_{d_R}^2 = (s_{d_1}^2 + s_{\delta_j}^2) + (s_{d_2}^2 + s_{\delta_j}^2). \tag{4}$$

If the replication involves the same number of subjects, then $s_{d_2}^2 = s_{d_1}^2$, and the estimated standard error of replication is

$$s_{d_r} = \sqrt{2(s_{d_1}^2 + s_{\delta_j}^2)}. \tag{5}$$

In a meta-analysis of studies involving 8 million participants, Richard, Bond, and Stokes-Zoota (2003) reported a mean *within-literature* variance of $\sigma_\delta^2 = 0.092$ (median = 0.08; $\sigma_\delta = 0.30$), after correction for sampling variance (Hedges & Vevea, 1998). This substantial realization variance puts an upper limit on the probability of replicating results, even with n approaching infinity. The limit is given by Equation 3 with $d_L = -\infty$ and

$$d_U = d_1 / \sqrt{2} s_{\delta_j}.$$

This limit on replicability is felt most severely when d_1 is small: For the typical realization variance within a field (0.08), the asymptotic p_{rep} for $d_1 = 0.1$, 0.2, and 0.3 is .60, .69, and .77. It requires an effect size of $d_1 = 0.5$ to raise replicability into the respectable range ($p_{\text{rep}} = .9$). Alas, that is substantially larger than the effect size typical of the social psychological literature, found by Richard and associates to be $d_1 \approx 0.3$. It appears that we can expect a typical ($d_1 = 0.3$)

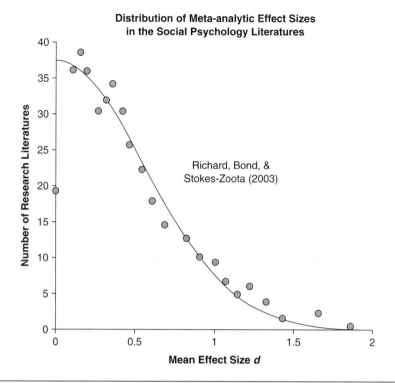

**Distribution of Meta-analytic Effect Sizes
in the Social Psychology Literatures**

Richard, Bond, &
Stokes-Zoota (2003)

Number of Research Literatures (y-axis)

Mean Effect Size d (x-axis)

Figure 7.5   The distribution of effect sizes measured in 474 research literatures in social psychology. The data were extracted from Richard et al. (2003, Figure 1). The curve is Gaussian with mean 0 and overall variance 0.3.

research finding to receive positive support at any level in replication only about 75% of the time.

Validation. Simulations were conducted to validate the logic of p_{rep} and the accuracy of normal approximation for the noncentral t sampling distribution of d for small n. The analysis of Richard et al. (2003) provided a representative set of parameters. These investigators displayed the distribution of effect sizes for social psychological research involving 457 literatures, comprising 25,000 studies. Their measure of effect size, r, was converted into d by the relation $d = 2r(1 - r^2)^{-1/2}$ (Rosenthal, 1994). The authors reported absolute values of effect sizes because the direction of effect often reflects an arbitrary coding of dependent variables; however, it also may inflate the impression of replicability. The smooth curve through the data in Figure 7.5 provides another perspective on their report. (The nonpublication of small or conflicting effects—the "file drawer effect"—might be responsible for the outlier near $d = 0$.) The data in Figure 7.5 are used to create a population from which the simulation will sample effect sizes. The within-literature standard deviation σ_δ was set to 0.30, consistent with Richard and associates' estimate. Given these fingerposts, the simulation is described in Figure 7.6.

The relative frequency of successful replication was gauged for values of $n = n_C + n_E$ ranging from 6 to 200, for nine ranges of $|d|$ starting at 0 with upper limits of 0.08, 0.16, 0.24, 0.33, 0.43, 0.53, 0.65, 0.81, and 1.10. These frequencies, expressed as probabilities of replication (p_{rep}), are the ordinates of Figure 7.7. The abscissae are from Equation 2, with d_1 taken as the midpoints of the nine ranges. s_d^2 was calculated from the simulata (see the appendix). The only parametric information used in the predictions was the realization variance σ_δ^2, set to 0.09. The predictions held good down through very small ns, with average absolute deviations of 1.2 percentage points, on the order of binomial variability around exact predictions.

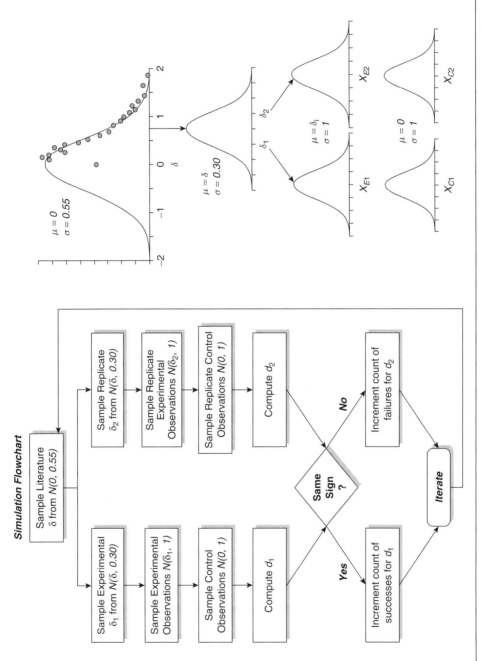

Figure 7.6 The simulation: A representative effect size of δ was first sampled from the distribution shown in Figure 7.5. Then two instances of δ_j from the literature it represents were selected, one for the original study and one for the replicate. The data were normally distributed random variables for the control and experimental groups, with the latter sampled from a population shifted by δ_1 (original study) or δ_2 (replicate). The difference between these parameters arises from the realization variance of 0.09 ($\sigma_\delta = 0.3$). The proportion of times an effect size from the original study predicted the sign of the replicate was retained. The process was iterated 20,000 times for each n studied.

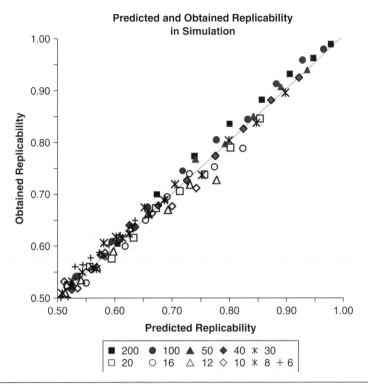

Figure 7.7   Results of the simulation. The obtained proportions of successful replications are plotted against the area over the positive axis of $N(d_1, s^2_{d_R})$. Symbols indicate the total number of observations in the experimental and control groups combined.

META-ANALYSIS

Despite the width of the distributions of p_{rep} shown in Figure 7.2, p_{rep} proves generally accurate in predicting replicability, both in simulations such as those above and in meta-analytic compendia. For any one study, conclusions should always be tempered by the image of Figure 7.2 and the recognition that our test statistics were sampled from one like it. This is why real replications are crucial for science. These replications are best aggregated using meta-analyses. Consider, for example, the recent meta-analysis of body satisfaction among women of different ethnic groups (Grabe & Hyde, 2006). Ninety-three studies contributed data, whose median effect size was 0.30, indicating that Black women were more satisfied with their body image than were White women. The authors of the meta-analysis reported a random effects variance of 0.09, which is the average value Richard et al. (2003) reported for social-psychological literatures in general. Using that realization variance, the median p_{rep}

for these studies was 0.78, and the proportion predicted by the 20% trimmed mean (Wilcox, 1998) of the $z_{p_{rep}}$ was $p_{rep} = .80$. The percentage of published studies showing a positive effect was close to these predictions, .85. These are unweighted predictions because the point is to demonstrate predictive validity of single estimates of p_{rep}, not to combine studies in an optimal fashion. Note that with realization variance set to zero, p_{rep} would seriously overestimate replicability ($p_{rep} = .93$), as expected.

Based on comparison of published and unpublished studies, as well as of studies that focused on ethnicity and those not so focused, the authors concluded that there was little evidence of publication bias—the inflation of effect sizes due to nonpublication of nonsignificant effects. Another way of estimating the influence of studies left in the "file drawer" because they did not yield a significant p value is to use the posterior predictive distribution to estimate the number of studies that should have reported nonsignificant effects. For the median number of observations in each group of the meta-analysis, the effect size would have to exceed 0.36 for significance ($\alpha = .05$, assuming a fixed effect model with zero realization variance, as is typical in conducting tests of significance, and a one-tailed critical region). Integration of the posterior predictive distribution (Equation 3) from $d_L = -\infty$ up to $d_U = 0.36$ gives an expected number of studies with non-significant effects equal to 56; 53 were found in the literature. This corroborates the authors' inference of little publication bias. Assuming instead that authors of the original studies used two-tailed tests requires us to compare the expected and observed number of studies with effect sizes falling between ± 0.43. Integration between these limits predicts 66 such results, 10 greater than the 56 observed. If 10 additional studies are inferred to reside only in file drawers because their effect sizes averaged around 0, when these are added to the 93 analyzed, the median effect size decreases from 0.30 to 0.27, leaving all conclusions intact. The same would be the case if this process were iterated, assuming the same proportion were filed for the larger hypostatized population. This further corroborates the authors' inference of little effect from publication bias.

A serious attempt to generalize—to predict replicability—must incorporate realization variance, just as traditional random and mixed effects models and hierarchical Bayesian models internalize it. But few original studies attempt to incorporate such estimates, resulting in discomfiture when results do not replicate (Ioannidis, 2005a, 2005b). This is compounded by the prevalent notion that "to replicate" means getting a significant effect in replication, rather than increasing our confidence in the original claim or narrowing our confidence intervals around an estimate. The posterior predictive distribution of Figure 7.1 and its integration over relevant domains by Equation 2 provide useful tools in the meta-analysis of results.

Deployment

This development of p_{rep} concerns only the simplest scenario, corresponding to a t test. Most inferential questions are more complicated. How does one calculate and interpret p_{rep} values in more interesting scenarios, such as analyses of variance (ANOVAs) with multiple levels, multivariate ANOVAs (MANOVAs), and multiple regression analysis? The provisional answer,

given users' familiarity with traditional analyses, is to calculate a p value and transform it to p_{rep} using the standard conversion, $z(p_{rep}) = -z(p)/\sqrt{2}$. The p values returned from ANOVA stat-packs are analogous to t^2 and thus allow deviation among scores in either direction (even though they employ just the right tail of the F distribution). They should therefore be halved before converting to p_{rep}. In the case of multiple independent comparisons, the probability of replicating each of the observed effects equals the product of the constituent p_{rep}s. This may be contrasted with the probability of finding positive effects if the null was true in all k cases, 2^{-k}. Cortina and Nouri (2000) show how to adjust d for correlated measures, and Bakeman (2005) provides detailed recommendations for the use of generalized eta squared as the preferred effect size statistic for repeated-measure designs. Manly (1997) and Westfall and Young (1993) describe resampling techniques for multiple testing. It is trivial to adjust such resampling to calculate p_{rep} directly: (a) Resample from within the control data and independently from within the experimental data, (b) calculate the resampled statistics (e.g., mean difference, trimmed mean difference, etc.) over half the resampled numbers to double the variance for the predictive distribution, (c) count the number of statistics of the same sign as the measured test, and (d) divide by the total number of resamples to estimate p_{rep}.

Realization variance (σ_δ^2) inflates the sampling variance of the effect size. This is awkward to introduce into the resampling process, but an adjustment can be easily made after the fact. The variance of d in replication is approximately $8/(n-4) + 2\sigma_\delta^2$. The resampling operation is essentially a compound Bernoulli process that can, for these purposes, be approximated by the normal distribution. Compute the z score corresponding to the p_{rep} resampled as above with no allowance for realization variance, and divide it by

$$\sqrt{1 + \sigma_\delta^2(n-4)/4}\,.$$

The normal transform of this adjusted z score gives the p_{rep} that can be expected in realistic attempts to replicate.[1]

Conversion of the voluminous statistical literature into p_{rep}-native applications remains a task for the future—one that will be most expeditiously and accurately accomplished with randomization techniques, discussed below.

PROBLEMS WITH p_{rep}

Frequentists will object to the introduction of distributions of parameters needed for the present derivation of p_{rep}. Parameters are by their definition fixed, if unknown, quantities. Frequentists will also be concerned that the choice of any particular informative prior can introduce an element of subjectivity into the calculation of probability. The introduction of uninformative priors, on the other hand, will expose the arbitrariness of choosing the particular version of them: Should an ignorance prior for the mass of a box be uniform on the length of its side or uniform on the cube of that length (Seidenfeld, 1979)? This debate has a long and nuanced history.

Bayesians (e.g., Wagenmakers & Grünwald, 2006) object that p_{rep} distracts us from an opportunity to compare alternative hypotheses. If credible alternate hypotheses are available, both the Neyman-Pearson framework and Bayesian analyses are to be preferred to the present one. But if those are not available, postulating them reintroduces the very sources of subjectivity and dependence on context-sensitive perspectives that p_{rep} permits us to sidestep.

An inelegance in the above analyses is that they invoked the unknown population parameter δ, only to marginalize it. Why not go directly from d_1 to d_2? As noted by O'Hagan and Forster (2004), "If we take the view that all inference is directly or indirectly motivated by decision problems, then it can be argued that all inference should be predictive, since inference about unobservable parameters has no direct relevance to decisions. . . . An extreme version of the predictivist approach is to regard parameters as neither meaningful nor necessary" (p. 90). Alas, as these authors, as well as Cumming (2005) and Doros and Geier (2005), note, unless d_1 and d_2 are treated as random samples from a population, they are not independent of one another, and the requisite evaluation of joint distributions of nonindependent variables is difficult. Fisher spent many of his latter years attempting to accomplish such direct inference with his fiducial probability theory, but his work was judged unsuccessful (Macdonald, 2005; Seidenfeld, 1979). We must resort to the introduction and marginalization of parameters described in the appendix.

More important than the above objections is the invalidity of a fundamental assumption in all of the above analyses. Traditional statistical tests, as well as p_{rep} as developed to this point, assume that the data are randomly sampled from the population to which generalization is desired—from the population whose parameter under the null (e.g., δ_0) is typically assumed to be zero. But this is a feat that is rarely attempted in science. Ludbrook and Dudley (1998; cited in Lunneborg, 2000, p. 551) surveyed 252 studies from biomedical journals and found that experimental groups were constructed by random sampling in only 4% of the cases. Of the 96% that were randomly assigned (rather than randomly sampled), 84% of the analyses employed inappropriate t or F tests—inappropriate because those tests assume random samples, not convenience samples. The situation is unlikely to be different in the fields known to the readers of this book. One can speculate why analyses are so misaligned with data. The potential causes are multivariate and include bad education, limitations to otherwise convenient stat-packs, the desire for statistics that permit generalization to a population (even though the data collection technique a fortiori prohibits such generalization), and the ubiquity of reviewers who recognize that, even though statistical tests are merely arbitrary conventional filters that cannot legitimately be used to reject null hypotheses, they retain pragmatic value for rejecting dull hypotheses (Nickerson, 2000).

PERMUTATION STATISTICS

There is another way. It was introduced by Fisher, developed for general cases by Pitman (Pitman, 1937a, 1937b), and realized in a practical manner by modern randomization techniques. Randomization, or rerandomization, or permutation tests are ways of comparing distributions of scores. They do not, like their computerized siblings the bootstrap tests, attempt to estimate or conditionalize on population parameters. Instead, they ask how frequently a random reassignment of the observed scores would generate differences at least as large as those observed. In executing such tests, the observed scores are randomly reassigned (without replacement) to ad hoc groups, the relevant statistics (mean, trimmed mean, median, variance, t score, etc.) computed, another random reassignment executed, and so on, thousands of times to create a distribution of the sampling error expected under chance. Calculate the percentile of the observed statistic in that distribution. One minus that percentile gives an analog to the *p* value. If the observed statistic is in the 95th percentile, only 5% of the time would random assignments give deviations that large or larger.

What the Permutation Distribution Means. In a deterministic world, no effects are uncaused, although the causes may be varied and complex and different for each observation (Hacking, 1990). *Chance* is the name for these otherwise unnamed, and generally unnamable, causes; it appears as the error variance that is added to our regression equations to permit them to balance. In resampling, we give the error variance free rein. The resulting randomization distributions may be viewed as random samples from thousands of these unnamed "hypotheses"— each corresponding to a different pattern in the data—that might account for the observations with more or less accuracy. The empirical distribution function generated by the random shuffles of data among groups gives the final rankings of hypotheses. All hypotheses except the investigator's are vague ("chance") and post hoc, so the investigator's are typically preferred, unless there are too many alternate reshuffles that sort the data into more extreme configurations—that is, unless they constitute more than, say, 5% of the distribution.

Another way of thinking about the partitioning is as the result of the random motion of particles (data) in space. This is a problem in thermodynamics, for analysis of which Boltzman created the measure of randomness called *entropy*. Using similar logic and mathematics, we may calculate the amount by which entropy is reduced by learning to which group—experimental or control—each observation belongs. If there is no real effect, the information transmitted by the group designation will be approximately 0. The information transmitted by knowledge of the group grows with effect size and with the logarithm of the number of observations. Information-theoretic measures such as Kullback-Leibler (K-L) distance, as well as its unbiased realization in the Akaike information criterion, are modern extensions of Boltzman's approach. The K-L distance is the average information that each observation adds toward discriminating the experimental and control groups. There is a natural affinity between permutation techniques and information-theoretic analyses: As the information gained from distinguishing groups increases, there will be a corresponding decrease in the number of alternate hypotheses that will provide more information than the investigator's. Replicability may be measured in terms of the probability of finding effects in replication that continue to make the distinction between groups worthwhile.

Although these considerations can give deeper meaning to the analysis, most consumers of statistics will be content to understand the results of permutation analyses as an analog of the *p* value, the proportion of randomizations that provide a more informative sorting of the observations than the experimenter's labels "experimental" and "control." There are many good programs available to carry out this analysis; see Cai (2006) and the references in Good (2000), Higgins (2004), and Manly (1997).

Permutation tests ask, "How often would this happen by chance?" not "How likely is this to happen again by design?" The short answer to "How can I generalize this result?" is the same as that given to users of traditional statistical design who have not sampled randomly from the populations to which they would generalize: "At your own hazard." To predict replicability in an attempt with an *n* of the same size, follow the same steps as given for bootstrap techniques above, including within-group shuffling, half-sizing, and correction for realization variance. For permutation techniques, however, the randomization is without replacement (whereas in bootstrapping, it is with replacement). The half-sizing makes this analysis a hybrid of permutation and bootstrap techniques—the bootstrap is constructed not out of the unlimited population of the bootstrap but out of populations twice the size of the original investigation. It permits extrapolation to a replication that samples from a small population derived from individuals identical to those in the original experiment, one from which the original was also ostensibly sampled. Because permutation techniques are generally more powerful than bootstrap techniques (see Mielke & Berry, 2001, and Chapter 19, this volume), predictions of replicability will be higher than for bootstrap techniques, making inclusion of nonzero realization variance even more important for realistic projections. The same post hoc correction described above may be used: Divide the z score of replicability by

$$\sqrt{1 + \sigma_\delta^2(n-4)/4}\,.$$

As noted by Higgins (2004), Lunneborg (2000), and others, computer-implemented permutation tests are the gold standard to which modern techniques such as ANOVA are an approximation; they are worth learning to use.

THE THREE PATHS OF STATISTICAL INFERENCE

Traditional Fisher/Neyman-Pearson statistics have been the primary mode of inference in the field for half a century, despite the fact that "frequentist theory is logically inadequate for the task of uncertain estimation (it provides right answers to wrong questions), . . . the bridge from statistical technologies to actual working science remains sketchy" (Dempster, 1987, p. 2). Twenty years have not greatly changed that assessment. Littlewood, if you remember from the epigraph, did not see it as his "business to justify application of the system"—an Olympian view shared by some modern statisticians. Because NHST in particular cannot provide mathematical estimates of the probabilities of hypotheses, it is constitutionally unfit for deciding between null and alternate hypotheses. Introductory statistics texts should carry warning labels: "The Statistician General warns that use of the algorithms contained herein justifies no inferences about hypotheses and no generalization to populations unsampled. Their assumptions seldom match their applications. Their critical regions can displace critical judgments. Their peremptory authority can damage unborn hypotheses. Their punctilio shifts authority from scientists to stat-packs. Addictive."

Bayesian analysis (Chapter 33, this volume) is a step forward. It provides the machinery for deriving the posterior predictive distribution on which p_{rep} is based and on which a decision theory for science may be erected. It has a vigorous literature (e.g., Howson & Urbach, 1996; Jaynes & Bretthorst, 2003). As currently deployed, it is sometimes hobbled by continuing to maintain the frequentists' focus on parameters. It has been blamed for making probabilities

subjective, but as long as reference sets are unique, probabilities must always be conditional on those priors.

Permutation techniques are another step forward, in that they more closely model the scientific process. Modern computer packages make them easy to implement and easier to teach than traditional statistical pedagogy based on Fisher/Neyman-Pearson inference.

What this chapter hopes to convey is that by setting our sights a bit lower—down from the heavens of Platonic parameters to the earthier Aristotelian enterprise of predicting replicability—our inferences will be simpler and more useful. Much work needs yet to be accomplished: generalizing replicability statistics to cases with multiple degrees of freedom in the numerator, securing their implementation with permutation tests, and utilizing those tests for predicting replicability in contexts involving substantial realization variance. But accomplishing these tasks should be straightforward, and their execution will bring us closer to the fundamental task of scientists: to validate observations through prediction and replication.

APPENDIX

The Statistics of Effect Size

Pooled variance is

$$s_p^2 = \frac{s_C^2(n_C - 1) + s_E^2(n_E - 1)}{n - 2}. \quad (A1)$$

The Route to Posterior Predictive Distributions

Bayesian statistics provides a standard way to calculate $f(d_2|d_1)$ (see, e.g., Bolstad, 2004; Winkler, 2003): Predicate the unknown parameter, such as the population mean effect size δ; update that predication with the observed data; and then calculate the posterior predictions over all possible values of the parameter, weighted by the probability of the parameter given the observed data. The predication is a nuisance, and eliminating the nuisance parameter by integrating it out in the last step is called marginalization.

$$f(d_2|d_1) = \int f(d_2, \delta|d_1)\ d\delta$$
$$= \int f(d_2|\delta,d_1)\ f(\delta|d_1)\ d\delta$$
$$= \int f(d_2|\delta,d_1)\ f(d_1|\delta)\ f(\delta)d\delta$$

where $f(\delta|d_1)$ is the posterior distribution of the parameter in light of the observations, and $f(\delta)$ is the prior distribution of the parameter. Integration of the last line over all population parameters δ delivers the posterior predictive distribution. If $f(\delta)$ is assumed to have a very large variance (*flat* or *ignorance* priors), then the observed data dominate the result. If a credible prior distribution is available (it is generally sought by "empirical Bayesians"), then the final predictions of replicability will be more accurate.

Consider the case in which the prior on the population mean δ is normally distributed. Then its posterior $f(\delta|d_1)$ is $n(d_1', s_1'^2)$, where the primed variables are weighted averages of the priors and the observed statistics, with the weights proportional to the precisions (reciprocal variances) of the means (s_{prior}^{-2} and s_1^{-2}). If we are relatively ignorant a priori of the value of the parameter, its distribution is flat relative to that of the observed statistic ($s_{prior}^2 \gg s_1^2$), and then $d_1' \approx d_1$ and $s_1' \approx s_1$. This is the case developed here. When the sampling distribution of the statistic is also approximately normal—a reasonable assumption for measures of effect size even when n is relatively small (Hedges & Olkin, 1985)—then factoring, completing the square, and removing constants leads eventually (Bolstad, 2004; Winkler, 2003) to a normal density with mean d_1 and variance $s_{dR}^2 = s_1^2 + s_2^2 = 2s_1^2$:

$$f(d_2|d_1) \propto e^{-\frac{1}{2(s_2^2+s_1^2)}(d_2-d_1)^2}.$$

Integration of this between appropriate limits, as in Equations 2 and 3, leads to the central results of this chapter.

The Simulations

In the simulations for Figures 7.6 and 7.7, d' was calculated using Equations 1 and A1. Variance was calculated using Equation 5 and

$$s_d^2 \approx \frac{4}{n-4}.$$

All simulations in this chapter used Resampling Stats© software (Bruce, 2003), which creates random numbers with Park and Miller's (1988) "Real Version 1" multiplicative linear congruential algorithm.

NOTE

1. The half-sizing recommended in Step b can be bypassed by replacing the 1 in this radical with 2, which allows for the increased variance inherent in the posterior predictive distribution.

REFERENCES

Bakeman, R. (2005). Recommended effect size statistics for repeated measures designs. *Behavior Research Methods, 37*, 379–384.

Bolstad, W. M. (2004). *Introduction to Bayesian statistics.* Hoboken, NJ: John Wiley.

Bruce, P. (2003). Resampling Stats [Excel Add-in]. Arlington, VA: Resampling Stats, Inc.

Cai, L. (2006). Multi-response permutation procedure as an alternative to the analysis of variance: An SPSS implementation. *Behavior Research Methods, 38*, 51–59.

Cohen, J. (1994). The earth is round ($p < .05$). *American Psychologist, 49*, 997–1003.

Cortina, J. M., & Nouri, H. (2000). *Effect size for ANOVA designs.* Thousand Oaks, CA: Sage.

Cumming, G. (2005). Understanding the average probability of replication: Comment on Killeen (2005). *Psychological Science, 16*, 1002–1004.

Cumming, G. (2006). *ESCI.* Retrieved from http://www.latrobe.edu.au/psy/esci/

Cumming, G., & Finch, S. (2001). A primer on the understanding, use and calculation of confidence intervals based on central and noncentral distributions. *Educational and Psychological Measurement, 61*, 532–575.

Cumming, G., & Finch, S. (2005). Inference by eye: Confidence intervals, and how to read pictures of data. *American Psychologist, 60*, 170–180.

Cumming, G., Williams, J., & Fidler, F. (2004). Replication and researchers' understanding of confidence intervals and standard error bars. *Understanding Statistics, 3*, 299–311.

Davison, A. C., & Hinkley, D. V. (1997). *Bootstrap methods and their application.* New York: Cambridge University Press.

Dempster, A. P. (1987). Probability and the future of statistics. In I. B. MacNeill & G. J. Umphrey (Eds.), *Foundations of statistical inference* (Vol. 2, pp. 1–7). Dordrecht, Holland: D. Reidel.

Doros, G., & Geier, A. B. (2005). Comment on "An alternative to null-hypothesis significance tests." *Psychological Science, 16,* 1005–1006.

Estes, W. K. (1997). On the communication of information by displays of standard errors and confidence intervals. *Psychonomic Bulletin & Review, 4,* 330–341.

Fidler, F., Thomason, N., Cumming, G., Finch, S., & Leeman, J. (2004). Editors can lead researchers to confidence intervals, but can't make them think: Statistical reform lessons from medicine. *Psychological Science, 15,* 119–126.

Fisher, R. A. (1959). *Statistical methods and scientific inference* (2nd ed.). New York: Hafner.

Gigerenzer, G. (2004). Mindless statistics. *Journal of Socio-economics, 33*(5), 587–606.

Glover, S., & Dixon, P. (2004). Likelihood ratios: A simple and flexible statistic for empirical psychologists. *Psychonomic Bulletin & Review, 11,* 791–806.

Good, P. (2000). *Permutation tests: A practical guide to resampling methods for testing hypotheses* (2nd ed.). New York: Springer-Verlag.

Grabe, S., & Hyde, J. S. (2006). Ethnicity and body satisfaction among women in the United States: A meta-analysis. *Psychological Bulletin, 132,* 622–640.

Hacking, I. (1990). *The taming of chance.* New York: Cambridge University Press.

Harlow, L. L., Mulaik, S. A., & Steiger, J. H. (Eds.). (1997). *What if there were no significance tests?* Mahwah, NJ: Lawrence Erlbaum.

Hays, W. L. (1963). *Statistics for psychologists.* New York: Holt, Rinehart and Winston.

Hedges, L. V., & Olkin, I. (1985). *Statistical methods for meta-analysis.* New York: Academic Press.

Hedges, L. V., & Vevea, J. L. (1998). Fixed- and random-effects models in meta-analysis. *Psychological Methods, 3,* 486–504.

Higgins, J. J. (2004). *An introduction to modern nonparameteric statistics.* Pacific Grove, CA: Brooks/Cole.

Howson, C., & Urbach, P. (1996). *Scientific reasoning: The Bayesian approach* (2nd ed.). Chicago: Open Court.

Ioannidis, J. P. A. (2005a). Contradicted and initially stronger effects in highly cited clinical research. *Journal of the American Medical Association, 294*(2), 218–228.

Ioannidis, J. P. A. (2005b). Why most published research findings are false. *PLoS Medicine, 2*(8), e124.

Iverson, G., Myung, I. J., & Karabatsos, G. (2006, August). *P-rep, p-values and Bayesian inference.* Paper presented at the Society for Mathematical Psychology, Vancouver, BC.

Jaynes, E. T., & Bretthorst, G. L. (2003). *Probability theory: The logic of science.* Cambridge, UK: Cambridge University Press.

Jones, L. V., & Tukey, J. W. (2000). A sensible formulation of the significance test. *Psychological Methods, 5,* 411–414.

Killeen, P. R. (2005a). An alternative to null hypothesis significance tests. *Psychological Science, 16,* 345–353.

Killeen, P. R. (2005b). Replicability, confidence, and priors. *Psychological Science, 16,* 1009–1012.

Killeen, P. R. (2005c). Tea-tests. *The General Psychologist, 40*(2), 16–19.

Killeen, P. R. (2006). Beyond statistical inference: A decision theory for science. *Psychonomic Bulletin & Review, 13,* 549–562.

Kline, M. (1980). *Mathematics, the loss of certainty.* New York: Oxford University Press.

Kline, R. B. (2004). *Beyond significance testing: Reforming data analysis methods in behavioral research.* Washington, DC: American Psychological Association.

Kyburg, H. E., Jr. (1987). The basic Bayesian blunder. In I. B. MacNeill & G. J. Umphrey (Eds.), *Foundations of statistical inference: Vol. 2. Biostatistics* (pp. 219–232). Boston: D. Reidel.

Lee, M. D., & Wagenmakers, E.-J. (2005). Bayesian statistical inference in psychology: Comment on Trafimow (2003). *Psychological Review, 112,* 662–668.

Lee, P. M. (2004). *Bayesian statistics: An introduction* (3rd ed.). New York: Hodder/Oxford University Press.

Littlewood, J. E. (1953). *A mathematician's miscellany.* London: Methuen.

Loftus, G. R., & Masson, M. E. J. (1994). Using confidence intervals in within-subject designs. *Psychonomic Bulletin & Review, 1,* 476–490.

Ludbrook, J., & Dudley, H. (1998). Why permutation tests are superior to *t* and *F* tests in medical research. *American Statistician, 52,* 127–132.

Lunneborg, C. E. (2000). *Data analysis by resampling: Concepts and applications.* Pacific Grove, CA: Brooks/Cole/Duxbury.

Macdonald, R. R. (2005). Why replication probabilities depend on prior probability distributions: A rejoinder to Killeen (2005). *Psychological Science, 16*(12), 1007–1008.

Manly, B. F. J. (1997). *Randomization, bootstrap and Monte Carlo methods in biology.* New York: Chapman & Hall/CRC.

Maurer, B. A. (2004). Models of scientific inquiry and statistical practice: Implications for the structure of scientific knowledge. In M. L. Taper & S. R. Lele (Eds.), *The nature of scientific evidence: Statistical, philosophical, and empirical considerations* (pp. 17–50). Chicago: University of Chicago Press.

Mielke, P. W., & Berry, K. J. (2001). *Permutation methods: A distance function approach.* New York: Springer.

Mooney, C. Z., & Duval, R. D. (1993). *Bootstrapping: A nonparametric approach to statistical inference* (Vol. 95). Newbury Park, CA: Sage.

Nickerson, R. S. (2000). Null hypothesis significance testing: A review of an old and continuing controversy. *Psychological Methods, 5,* 241–301.

O'Hagan, A., & Forster, J. (2004). *Kendall's advanced theory of statistics: Vol. 2B. Bayesian inference* (2nd ed.). New York: Oxford University Press.

Park, S. K., & Miller, K. W. (1988). Random number generators: Good ones are hard to find. *Communications of the ACM, 31*(10), 1192–1201.

Pitman, E. J. G. (1937a). Significance tests which may be applied to samples from any populations. *Supplement to the Journal of the Royal Statistical Society, 4*(1), 119–130.

Pitman, E. J. G. (1937b). Significance tests which may be applied to samples from any populations: II. The correlation coefficient test. *Supplement to the Journal of the Royal Statistical Society, 4*(2), 225–232.

Raudenbush, S. W. (1994). Random effects models. In H. Cooper & L. V. Hedges (Eds.), *The handbook of research synthesis* (pp. 301–321). New York: Russell Sage Foundation.

Richard, F. D., Bond, C. F. J., & Stokes-Zoota, J. J. (2003). One hundred years of social psychology quantitatively described. *Review of General Psychology, 7,* 331–363.

Rosenthal, R. (1994). Parametric measures of effect size. In H. Cooper & L. V. Hedges (Eds.), *The handbook of research synthesis* (pp. 231–244). New York: Russell Sage Foundation.

Royall, R. (1997). *Statistical evidence: A likelihood paradigm.* London: Chapman & Hall.

Royall, R. (2004). The likelihood paradigm for statistical evidence. In M. L. Taper & S. R. Lele (Eds.), *The nature of scientific evidence: Statistical, philosophical, and empirical considerations* (pp. 119–152). Chicago: University of Chicago Press.

Rubin, D. B. (1981). Estimation in parallel randomized experiments. *Journal of Educational Statistics, 6,* 377–400.

Sanabria, F., & Killeen, P. R. (2007). Better statistics for better decisions: Rejecting null hypotheses statistical tests in favor of replication statistics. *Psychology in Schools, 44,* 471–481.

Savage, L. J. (1972). *The foundations of statistics* (2nd ed.). New York: Dover.

Seidenfeld, T. (1979). *Philosophical problems of statistical inference: Learning from R. A. Fisher.* London: D. Reidel.

Thompson, B. (1999). If statistical significance tests are broken/misused, what practices should supplement or replace them? *Theory Psychology, 9*(2), 165–181.

van den Noortgate, W., & Onghena, P. (2003). Estimating the mean effect size in meta-analysis: Bias, precision, and mean squared error of different weighting methods. *Behavior Research Methods, Instruments, & Computers, 35,* 504–511.

Wagenmakers, E.-J., & Grünwald, P. (2006). A Bayesian perspective on hypothesis testing: A comment on Killeen (2005). *Psychological Science, 17,* 641–642.

Westfall, P. H., & Young, S. S. (1993). *Resampling-based multiple testing: Examples and methods for p-value adjustments.* New York: John Wiley.

Wilcox, R. R. (1998). How many discoveries have been lost by ignoring modern statistical methods? *American Psychologist, 53,* 300–314.

Wilkinson, L., & the Task Force on Statistical Inference. (1999). Statistical methods in psychology: Guidelines and explanations. *American Psychologist, 54,* 594–604.

Winkler, R. L. (2003). *An introduction to Bayesian inference and decision* (2nd ed.). Gainesville, FL: Probabilistic Publishing.

8

MIXED METHODS RESEARCH IN THE SOCIAL SCIENCES

JESSICA T. DECUIR-GUNBY

Within the social sciences, the paradigm wars between qualitative and quantitative research have received considerable attention (Lincoln & Guba, 2000; Sale, Lohfeld, & Brazil, 2002). Purist camps on both sides question the opposing viewpoints' usefulness in social science research. Some qualitative researchers argue that quantitative research does not capture participants' experience and voice, while some quantitative researchers argue that qualitative research is not scientific because it lacks the rigidity of the scientific method (Sechrest & Sidani, 1995). There has not been an adequate resolution to the issue; largely, zealots from both camps have agreed to disagree. However, there is an alternative to the qualitative/quantitative dilemma: Quantitative and qualitative research can be viewed as complementary (rather than mutually exclusive) and as a continuum rather than polar opposites (e.g., Ercikan & Roth, 2006). Such a perspective is best illustrated through combining the best aspects of both methods, creating what is called mixed methods or multimethods research.

DEFINING MIXED METHODS

Mixed methods research is grounded in Campbell and Fiske's (1959) discussion of multitrait-multimethods, which exclaimed that "in order to estimate the relative contributions of trait and method variance, more than one trait as well as more than one method must be employed" (p. 81). This suggests that a phenomenon is best understood if it is viewed from various perspectives. Although Campbell and Fiske's discussion focused on multiple quantitative methods, there are implications for combining multiple qualitative methods as well as both qualitative and quantitative methods or mixed methods research. Mixed methods can occur in a single study, sequentially within a program of research, or in an area of research (Rocco, Bliss, Gallagher, & Perez-Prado, 2003; Schutz, Chambless, & DeCuir, 2003). This suggests that any research involving multiple methods (quantitative and/or qualitative) can be considered mixed methods.

In combining methods, it is imperative that methods be chosen that will enhance each other, balancing strengths and weaknesses. To that end, the fundamental principle of mixed methods research is to combine methods in a manner that considers the strengths and weaknesses of each individual method (Johnson & Turner, 2003). There are numerous strengths and weaknesses of mixed methods research. These include both the strengths of qualitative research (e.g., it reflects participants' understanding, it is useful in exploring in-depth cases, etc.) and quantitative research (e.g., its generalizability, usefulness for studying a large number of people, etc.), as well as the weaknesses of both qualitative research (e.g., its findings are not necessarily generalizable, it is data intensive, etc.) and quantitative research (e.g., researchers' conceptualizations may not reflect participants' understanding or experience of the constructs). However, there are strengths and weaknesses that are unique to mixed methods research. Such strengths include the ability to generate and test theory, the capability to answer complex research questions, and the possibility of corroborating findings. Weaknesses include needing the knowledge of multiple methods; engaging in time-consuming research design, data collection, and analysis; and the criticizing of both quantitative and qualitative purists (Johnson & Onwuegbuzie, 2004).

Despite the limitations of mixed methods research, the ability to combine the strengths of both quantitative and qualitative methods is appealing to many researchers. In essence, it can be considered the best of both worlds. Mixed methods approaches have been widely used in a variety of research disciplines, including health sciences (e.g., Schillaci et al., 2004) and nursing (e.g., Burr, 1998). In addition, mixed methods research is growing in popularity in disciplines such as business (e.g., Bansal & Roth, 2000), sociology (e.g., Green, 2003), psychology (e.g., Eggleston, Jackson, & Hardee, 1999), and education (e.g., Igo, Bruning, & McCrudden, 2005).

As such, the purpose of this chapter is to explicate how the use of mixed methods research can be further expanded in social science research. I will demonstrate how mixed methods research can be effectively implemented in social science research through the discussion of the development of the African American Adolescent Racial Identity Scale (AAARIS). Proper scale development involves both qualitative and quantitative elements (Benson, 1998; Benson & Clark, 1982). A scale development example is being used because scale development is a common process in social science research. It is also being used because few researchers realize that they are engaging in mixed methods research when creating a scale, while others neglect to include a qualitative component. Thus, a secondary purpose of this chapter is to illustrate best practices in instrument design.

Designing Mixed Methods Research

In designing a mixed methods study in social science research, it is imperative to address several methodological concerns. Maxwell and Loomis (2003) have created an interactive model of design in order to organize the various stages of mixed methods research. This model involves five interrelated aspects: (1) purpose, (2) conceptual framework, (3) research questions, (4) methods, and (5) validity. This chapter will discuss the design of mixed methods research according to these stages. Each stage of the interactive model will be discussed in detail as well as illustrated by examples that highlight the qualitative and quantitative components that are involved in the scale development process.

Purpose

The first component of designing a mixed methods study is to understand the purpose of the study. The research purpose is considered an explanation of why the research is being conducted (Newman, Ridenour, Newman, & DeMarco, 2003). Understanding the research purpose is essential because it allows for the making of proper methodological decisions, which includes the designing of research questions. There are several reasons to conduct a research study. Such reasons include prediction, adding to knowledge, measuring change, understanding phenomena, testing new ideas, generating new ideas, informing constituencies, and examining the past (Newman et al., 2003). However, for mixed methods research, there are specific purposes.

According to Greene, Caracelli, and Graham (1989), there are five purposes for conducting mixed methods research: triangulation, complementarity, development, initiation, and expansion. Triangulation refers to using both quantitative and qualitative methods to demonstrate convergence. Complementarity studies use qualitative and quantitative methods to examine intersecting but different aspects of a phenomenon. Development involves using quantitative and qualitative methods sequentially, with one method informing the development of the other. Initiation, most often an after-the-fact purpose, is used to discover as well as explore contradictions found when using quantitative and qualitative methods to explore the same phenomenon. Expansion involves a multiple approach to "extend the breadth and range of the study" (Greene et al., 1989, p. 259). The reason chosen for conducting mixed methods research plays a significant role in the design of the research study.

Purpose Example

The purpose of this study is to develop the AAARIS. This will occur in three stages. The first stage is to explore themes that affect the racial identity development of African American adolescents within the school context. The second stage is to use the themes discovered in the first stage in order to develop an instrument concerning the African American racial identity development of adolescents in the school context. The third stage is to begin the process of construct validation, including examining the structure of the AAARIS and exploring the AAARIS's relationship with similar constructs.

Conceptual Framework/ Theoretical Perspective

After the research purpose is determined, it is essential that the researcher examine his or her theoretical perspective. The theoretical perspective "reflects researchers' personal stances toward the topics they are studying, a stance based on personal history, experience, culture, gender, and class perspectives" (Creswell, Clark, Gutmann, & Hanson, 2003, p. 222). One's theoretical perspective influences the types of research questions that are asked, the way data are collected, and the manner in which data are interpreted. Exploring one's theoretical perspective includes examining one's worldview or paradigm.

One's theoretical paradigm helps to determine how one sees, understands, and interprets the world. Because of the brevity of this chapter, the descriptions of the paradigms are oversimplified. For more detailed explanations, see Mertens (2003) and Lincoln and Guba (2000). According to Mertens, three major families of paradigms guide current research practices: positivist/ postpositivist, interpretive/constructivist, and transformative/emancipatory. Qualitative methods stem from the interpretivist/constructivist paradigm. This perspective examines the multiplicity of realities or truths that are based on one's construction of reality (Sale & Brazil, 2004). The transformative/emancipatory paradigm is an extension of the interpretivist/constructivist paradigm; it includes critical, cultural, and feminist perspectives, among others. However, in addition to understanding multiple realities, the goal of the transformative/emancipatory paradigm is to critique inequitable practices and promote change. Alternatively, quantitative methods stem from the positivist paradigm. The positivist perspective suggests "that all phenomena can be reduced to empirical indicators which represent the truth" (Sale & Brazil, 2004, p. 353). Postpositivism, a modification of positivism, contends that empirical indicators can be used to approximate the truth; there is no method to obtain the absolute truth. However, it must be added that there is a philosophical movement that views empiricism, the belief of neutrality and objectivity that is based on observation and experimentation, as the basis of quantitative methods rather than positivism. This reassertion has emerged because of the emphasis on scientifically based research in the social sciences (Slavin, 2002; Smith & Hodkinson, 2005; Yu, 2006).

Although exploring one's theoretical perspective involves examining one's theoretical paradigm, it also involves understanding the specific theories that may be used to guide inquiry. A theory is a statement that describes the phenomena the researcher wants to explore (Maxwell, 1996). Theories are helpful in that they help expand the understanding of a specific phenomenon. However, few research studies are influenced by a single theory. Most research studies are indeed guided by multiple theories. Because of the use of multiple theories, it is necessary to explore the relationships between theories and their impact on specific phenomena through the use of theoretical models. Theoretical models should explain the major concepts, factors, constructs, or variables under study in addition to their proposed relationships (Miles & Huberman, 1994, p. 18). Theoretical models can be visually depicted or textually described. Regardless of the representative medium, theoretical models are essential to the research process because they provide the foundation that guides the creation of research questions and the collection and analysis of data.

Theoretical Framework Example

The theoretical framework for the proposed study involves a constructivist perspective for the qualitative approach and a postpositivist perspective for the quantitative aspect. (It must be noted that quantitative researchers do not explicitly label their work as positivist or post-positivist. I am choosing to make this label explicit because I want to highlight the differing approaches within a mixed methods framework.) Constructivism examines how one constructs meaning from life experiences (Crotty, 1998; Vygotsky, 1978). Using such a perspective will allow the understanding of how African American students develop their identities as students in that people have different perspectives regarding race and racial identity that are based on their own life experiences. Next, a postpositive approach will be used for the development of the AAARIS as well as its implementation. Racial identity theory (e.g., Duncan, 2005; Helms, 1990) will be used in the scale's development.

In the school context, creating a climate where all students belong is important (Osterman, 2000; Zirkel, 2004). However, not all students feel as though they are valued members of the school context. Within some schools, particularly pre-dominately White schools, many African American students feel as though they do not belong in the school community. The feelings of not belonging occur because the educational context has a history of racial discrimination that has contributed to the lack of African American teachers and administrators, the limited exposure to African Americans in the curricula, the underrepresentation of African Americans in advanced and gifted classes, and the overrepre-sentation of African Americans in special educa-tion (DeCuir & Dixson, 2004; Farkas, 2003; Ladson-Billings & Tate, 1995). These race-related issues have greatly affected African American students' sense of self, including their sense of racial identity. As such, developing a positive sense of racial identity is important within the context of education.

Racial identity is the collection of attitudes and beliefs that a person has regarding being a part of his or her racial group and about his or her racial group as a whole, and his or her feel-ings toward other racial groups (DeCuir-Gunby, 2007; Duncan, 2005; Helms, 1990; Sellers, Rowley, Chavous, Shelton, & Smith, 1997; Tatum, 1997). For African American adolescents, racial identity largely concerns feelings regarding being African American within the school con-text. In developing a racial identity, it is impor-tant to establish a relationship between being African American and school (Akom, 2003;

O'Connor, 1997; Oyserman & Harrison, 1998). Developing a healthy racial identity in the school context not only includes feelings toward one's racial group but also establishing a positive rela-tionship between the self and school.

Research Questions

In any research study, the keys to designing the appropriate methods are research questions. Research questions are the interrogative ques-tions that a researcher would like to investigate (Creswell, 2002). Research questions help guide the choice of methods. In mixed methods stud-ies, both qualitative and quantitative questions are created. Qualitative research questions are broad questions that most often begin with "what" or "how." Such questions concern process. They usually involve central questions and subquestions. Hypothesis statements tend not to be used for the qualitative portion of mixed methods research (or qualitative research). Quantitative research questions, on the other hand, are specific questions that compare, relate, or describe. Their aim is to examine variance. For a mixed methods study (or any quantitative study), research questions or hypotheses are needed. Including both is gen-erally redundant, although there are exceptions.

Research Question Examples

Qualitative Questions:

1. How do African American adolescents develop their identities in the school context?
   A. What role does race play in the development of African American adolescents' identities?
   B. What role do academics play in the development of African American adolescents' identities?

Quantitative Questions:

1. Does the African American Adolescent Racial Identity Scale define the construct of African American racial identity in the school context?

2. Are the scores from the African American Adolescent Racial Identity Scale consistent for African American adolescents in the school context?

3. Is there a relationship between the African American Adolescent Racial Identity Scale and similar constructs?

Methodology/Methods

After the research questions are chosen, the methodology of the study should be planned. Methodology can be described as "the best means for acquiring knowledge about the world" (Denzin & Lincoln, 2005, p. 183). Various qualitative and quantitative practices can be used to acquire knowledge about the world. Qualitative methods include interviews (individual/personal and focus groups), observations, and archival/documents. With quantitative methods, on the other hand, there are experiments and questionnaires/surveys. As previously stated, mixed methods research involves combining both qualitative and quantitative research practices. This is accomplished by what is referred to as intramethod and intermethod mixing. Intramethod mixing involves using a single method that has both qualitative and quantitative components (Johnson & Turner, 2003, p. 298). For example, this could be the use of a survey that includes both Likert and open-ended responses. On the other hand, intermethod mixing involves the mixing of two or more methods (Johnson & Turner, 2003). For example, this could include using both a Likert-type survey and an interview.

According to Morse (1991, 2003), there are two basic manners of collecting mixed methods data—simultaneously and sequentially. In simultaneous data collection, both the quantitative and qualitative aspects are collected at the same time. There are three options: QUAN + qual (emphasis on quantitative aspect), QUAL + quan (emphasis on qualitative aspect), and QUAN + QUAL (equal emphasis on both methods). On the other hand, in sequential data collection, both the quantitative and qualitative aspects are collected in stages. There are four options: QUAN → qual (emphasis on quantitative aspect, with quantitative leading to qualitative), QUAL → quan (emphasis on qualitative aspect, with qualitative leading to quantitative), QUAN → QUAL (equal emphasis on both methods, with quantitative leading to qualitative), and QUAL → QUAN (equal emphasis on both methods, with qualitative leading to quantitative). It must be noted that it is possible to combine the aforementioned data collection strategies.

Methodology Example

In the African American racial identity example, a QUAL → quan approach will be taken. It must be added that despite the quantitative aspect's appearance of receiving more emphasis, the design is still considered to be QUAL → quan because the quantitative process stems from the qualitative process. This is the most commonly used design, one that involves a qualitative aspect, most likely a pilot study, followed by a quantitative aspect (Morgan, 1998). This approach is often used in model or theory development, theory verification, and scale development.

In scale development, it is important to engage in proper theoretical planning, scale construction, scale evaluation, and scale validation (see Benson & Clark, 1982). Planning involves reviewing the literature, defining the construct, and questioning the target group. For the qualitative aspect, needless to say, the appropriate literature will be reviewed and the construct will be defined. Next, semistructured interviews (personal and focus group) will be used to better understand the various aspects that contribute to African American students' sense of racial identity within the school context (see Kreuger & Casey, 2000; Kvale, 1996). The information received from the interviews will provide the foundations for the creation of the scale's preliminary items. During the construction phase, a Likert-type scale will be developed to assess the categories that emerged during the qualitative analysis (see Table 8.1 for sample items). These items will then be evaluated by experts in the area of African American identity; revisions will be made if needed. Next, in the third phase, the instrument will be pilot tested using various statistical methods, revised, and readministered. Last, in the validation phase, a continuous phase, the AAARIS's nomological network will be explored. The AAARIS will be compared with instruments measuring racial identity and related constructs (e.g., self-efficacy, academic attitudes, etc.). It is imperative to add that these stages will occur in multiple research studies.

Sampling. Determining issues regarding sampling is also important in designing a mixed methods study. Sampling involves the manner in which participants are accessed as well as the number of participants needed. Qualitative methods often involve purposeful sampling. This is done because researchers are often specific regarding their research choices. There are generally 16 types of sampling within qualitative

Table 8.1   African American Adolescent Racial Identity Scale Sample Items

Item Subscale	Sample Item
Student Attitudes	School is important to me.
	I am a good student.
	Being a good student is important to my future.
Racial Identity Attitudes	I like being African American.
	I am proud of my African American heritage.
	Learning is important to African American culture.

research (for detailed descriptions, see Miles & Huberman, 1994). Sampling decisions must be theoretically driven. In other words, the means of sampling is contingent on one's research purpose and theoretical perspective. Sampling procedures for quantitative research differ from those of qualitative research. Within quantitative research, there are generally two types of sampling designs: probability or random sampling and nonprobability or nonrandom sampling. Random sampling consists of four types: simple random sampling (everyone in the population has an equal opportunity for participation), stratified random sampling (separating the population into groups and randomly sampling within the groups), cluster random sampling (random sample of groups that naturally occur in a setting), and systematic random sampling (selecting every nth person from a randomly selected sample of the population) (Kemper, Stringfield, & Teddlie, 2003; Onwuegbuzie & Leech, 2005). Nonrandom sampling includes two types: convenience and purposive (Trochim, 2001). Convenience sampling is the most commonly used sampling procedure. It involves using easily accessible samples that are not always representative of the population. Purposive sampling, on the other hand, involves sampling of predefined groups. This involves sampling of specific groups that may not be representative of the population.

Sampling Example

For the qualitative aspect, purposeful sampling will be used; the focus will be on African American adolescents (high school). It is necessary to find participants who are knowledgeable, are able to provide balanced perspectives, and will contribute to the proposed theory regarding African American racial identity (Rubin & Rubin, 2005). In locating participants, snowball or chain sampling will be used. Snowball or chain sampling involves locating an informant to identify initial participants. The initial participants will be used to recommend other participants who may have a similar or dissimilar perspective (see Patton, 1990). Both personal and focus group interviews will be conducted until "saturation" is reached or when the same information is heard repeatedly or when no new information is found (Glaser & Strauss, 1967). However, personal interviews will be conducted with an equal number of boys and girls, ranging from 6 to 10 students (see Kvale, 1996); the focus group interviews will consist of both boys and girls in groups of 5 to 7 (Kreuger & Casey, 2000).

The quantitative portion will involve cluster random sampling. African American adolescents will be targeted. In order to conduct specific statistical analyses used in scale development (e.g., confirmatory factor analysis), a minimum of 7 to 10 participants per item of the AAARIS will be needed (see Benson & Nasser, 1998). This means that if the AAARIS has 30 items, the sample size needed will minimally range from 210 to 300 participants. In short, the goal is to obtain at least 210 participants, although this number could significantly increase depending on the number of items created in the development of the AAARIS.

Data Analysis. There are several ways in which mixed methods data can be analyzed. But before mixed methods data can be analyzed, the relationship between the quantitative and qualitative methods must be determined. Also, the analyses should follow the known procedures for whatever method is being used. In other words, in conducting analyses, the researcher must take into consideration the manner in which the data were collected and use the appropriate data analysis procedures. Mixed methods data analysis includes parallel mixed analysis, concurrent mixed analysis, and sequential mixed analysis (Onwuegbuzie & Leech, 2004). Parallel mixed analysis involves analyzing the quantitative and qualitative data separately. The results are compared only after data analysis for each approach is completed. Concurrent mixed analysis, on the other hand, involves analyzing simultaneously collected quantitative and qualitative data at the same time. This means that both the quantitative and qualitative aspects are integrated. One aspect influences the analysis of the other aspect. Sequential mixed analysis involves analyzing quantitative and qualitative data that have been collected sequentially. However, in sequential mixed analyses, data analysis is an ongoing process that occurs as the data are collected (Onwuegbuzie & Leech, 2004).

Data Analysis Example

For this study, sequential mixed analysis will be used. The data from the interviews will be analyzed using thematic content analysis or inductive analysis (see Coffey & Atkinson, 1996; Strauss & Corbin, 1990; Wolcott, 1994). Thematic content analysis involves examining interviews and finding common as well as uncommon themes through the process of coding, the opening up of text, and exposing the "thoughts, ideas, and meanings contained therein" (Strauss & Corbin, 1990, p. 102). The analysis of the interviews will consist of three processes of coding: identifying, organizing, and interrelating themes (Coffey & Atkinson, 1996). First, the process of coding will allow the data to be broken into small pieces of information called concepts. Next, similar concepts will be grouped into categories and further developed according to their properties or characteristics. The significant themes that appear across most or all interviews will be identified, a process Wolcott (1994) refers to as the identification of patterned regularities in the data. In addition, the significant themes that are unique to particular individuals will be identified; patterned irregularities may be as valuable as or more valuable than patterned regularities. Next, the various themes will be interrelated, as suggested by Wolcott, by contextualizing them in a broader analytical framework by making connections to the research literature. The coding process will focus on the areas of racial identity attitudes and academics. The information collected from this section will be essential to informing the quantitative aspect.

The quantitative aspect will be analyzed in an ongoing process and will consist of multiple studies. After the scale is created and data have been collected using the preliminary items that were created from the interviews, the item reduction process will begin. Reliability analyses will be conducted, eliminating items with low reliability coefficients (below .80). Confirmatory factor analysis will then be used to determine how factor structures fit the data. Items with low loadings (less than .30) or items with double loadings (loading on multiple factors) will be eliminated (see Ebel, 1972). Later, after the items have been reduced, additional data will be collected with the refined scale as well as other scales (e.g., other racial identity scales, academic attitudes, etc.). This will be done in order to explore the nomological network (see Cronbach & Meehl, 1955) of the AAARIS. Reliability and confirmatory factor analyses will again be conducted on the data. However, correlation analyses and structural equation modeling (SEM) will be used in order to further explore the AAARIS's nomological network.

Validity and Trustworthiness

The last concept to address is validity and trustworthiness. Addressing issues of validity and trustworthiness is essential to conducting mixed methods research. In fact, validity and trustworthiness should be considered throughout all aspects of a study. However, addressing issues of validity and trustworthiness in mixed methods research suggests addressing such issues in both the quantitative and qualitative components. This means that validity should be addressed in both qualitative and quantitative terms. Validity and trustworthiness in mixed methods research concerns examining aspects of truth value, applicability, consistency, and neutrality (Sale & Brazil, 2004).

The issue of validity is important to qualitative research. In qualitative research, validity is often referred to as trustworthiness, credibility, dependability, confirmability, and understanding (Kvale, 1996; Maxwell, 1996). In this respect, validity can be defined as "the trustworthiness of inferences drawn from data" (Eisenhart & Howe, 1992, p. 644). Examining validity often involves exploring aspects of invalidity. A proposition is considered trustworthy once falsification attempts have survived (Kvale, 1996).

In quantitative research, truth value, applicability, consistency, and neutrality are addressed in terms of construct validity. According to Messick (1995a), validity is "the meaning of the test scores" as well as "a summary of both the evidence for and the actual as well as potential consequences of score interpretation and use" (p. 5). The integration of test score meaning, interpretation, and use creates a construct framework known as construct validity. As stated by Messick (1995b), construct validity addresses six areas: content (content relevance), substantive (theoretical and empirical evidence), structural (relationship between the structures of the scoring instruments and the construct domain), generalizability (how scores generalize to population), external (comparisons to multiple sources), and consequential (value implications of the scores). In creating a program of construct validation, Benson (1998) suggests collapsing these six aspects into three stages: the substantive stage (e.g., exploring theory regarding the construct), the structural stage (e.g., exploring the observed variables), and the external stage (e.g., exploring the scales' nomological network). The exploration of these various areas encompasses Campbell and Fisk's (1959) notion of multitrait-multimethods in that multiple methods are needed to adequately examine a phenomenon.

Validity and Trustworthiness Example

In the qualitative aspect, there are several ways to address trustworthiness, including reflexivity, triangulation, and member checks. First, the process of reflexivity will be used. Reflexivity involves the examination of one's beliefs, subjectivities, and biases concerning the various aspects of the study (Finlay, 1998; Parker, 1994; Sword, 1999). This will be accomplished by acknowledging beliefs, subjectivities, and biases toward the research area and participants. Being reflexive allows the researcher to be less subjective when analyzing the data. Next, the data will be triangulated. Triangulation involves using various methods to collect information from a wide range of individuals and settings (Mathison, 1988). This strategy helps to reduce risk of bias and allow for

a better assessment of the phenomena. Triangulation will be accomplished by comparing the consistency in responses from the data collected from both the personal and focus group interviews. Last, member checks will be used. Member checks are a process that allows the researcher to obtain feedback from the participants of the study regarding the data and the conclusions made from data (Merriam, 1998). Participants will be shown interpretations of their interviews and asked to examine the interpretations for accuracy. The use of member checks helps to clear up any misinterpretations that may be made by the researcher.

In order to address validity in the quantitative perspective, Benson's (1998) stages of construct validation will be followed. First, the substantive stage will be explored by using theory found in the research literature and empirical evidence (qualitative interviews) to define the construct of African American racial identity. Next, the structural stage will be examined by exploring the relationships between the variables and constructs that compose the AAARIS. This will constitute using both univariate and multivariate statistical procedures, including descriptive statistics, item analysis, reliability analysis, and confirmatory factor analyses. Last, the external stage will be examined by exploring the nomological network of the AAARIS (see Cronbach & Meehl, 1955) or how it relates to constructs that are theoretically similar and dissimilar. The procedures that will be used include correlating the AAARIS with other instruments as well as SEM (see Bollen, 1989; Loehlin, 1998).

DISCUSSION: WRITING UP THE FINDINGS AND PUBLISHING

As demonstrated through the proposed development of the AAARIS, a mixed methods approach is a useful way to engage in scale development. By using the interactive model of design by Maxwell and Loomis (2003), the stages of mixed methods research were examined. This included the purpose of the research, conceptual framework, research questions, methods, and validity. All of these stages are interrelated and necessary components for conducting a quality research study, particularly a study involved in scale design. Although the interactive model of design provides a useful framework to discuss mixed methods and is a helpful tool to organize mixed methods research, the interactive model of design fails to discuss the writing of mixed methods research. Learning how to write mixed methods research is imperative.

After data collection and analysis have occurred, the researcher will need to determine how the data are to be written. The manner in which the data are written is influenced by the initial research design (e.g., QUAN → qual, QUAN + qual, etc.). Thus, mixed methods findings can be represented in three ways. First, quantitative and qualitative findings can be written up separately within one study, presenting quantitative and then qualitative findings (or vice versa). This is the most used manner to present mixed methods findings (see Sandelowski, 2003). Second, the findings can be written jointly within one study through the intertwining of quantitative and qualitative findings. Intertwined findings are the most time-consuming and difficult to write; this approach requires a skilled writer (see Sandelowski, 2003). Last, findings can be presented individually in different studies as a series of research studies in a program of research. In this approach, the individual studies are all related to each other; later studies build on earlier studies. This approach is useful if the researcher is conducting a series of quantitative and qualitative projects. Although the type of mixed methods designs often influences how findings are written, it must be added that this is not always the case. The decision of how the data are presented is often influenced by publication outlets.

Writing/Publishing Example

The development of the AAARIS will be written up as individual studies that contribute to a program of research. This approach is being chosen because scale development, as previously described, is a lengthy process that consists of numerous stages. As such, at least three publications are proposed: (1) a qualitative article, (2) a scale development article featuring the preliminary items, and (3) an article examining the AAARIS's nomological network.

While writing up the findings, it is essential to consider the possible publication outlets for mixed methods research. If attempting to publish research findings separately within one study or individually across studies, a researcher will have an easier time finding a publication outlet. After all, most of the mixed methods research that has been published in mainstream journals features findings that are presented separately within one study. However, if the researcher decides to publish the two components jointly within one study, it is important to consider the possibility of limited publication outlets. Within the social sciences, mixed methods articles periodically appear in journals such as *American Educational Research Journal, Journal of Counseling Psychology, Academy of Management Journal,* and a few others. Although acceptance of mixed methods research is growing, many research journals are not receptive to mixed methods articles. As such, the *Journal of Mixed Methods Research* has recently been created in order to fill this research outlet need. This journal is dedicated to advancing mixed methods methodology and research across disciplines.

The Future of Mixed Methods Research

Although use of mixed methods is not a new methodology, the recognition of mixed methods as a distinct methodology is a recent research trend. As previously stated, the popularity of mixed methods research continues to grow in numerous disciplines, including health sciences, nursing, business, sociology, psychology, and education. Although the outlook is positive within these disciplines, several issues still need to be addressed. First, there still exists a considerable amount of bias against mixed methods. Purists from both sides of the quantitative/qualitative debate are often unreceptive to the combining of methods. As such, the belief systems of such purists need to be challenged. In order to do so, the research community needs to start viewing quantitative and qualitative methods as a continuum rather than polar opposites. Such an approach will help mixed methods research to be seen in a more positive light. This will also increase the receptiveness of research journals to mixed methods research. In addition to challenging beliefs, there needs to be an increase in mixed methods research training. Very few doctoral research programs offer mixed methods research classes. This is problematic because graduate students are not being exposed to possibilities other than quantitative and qualitative research methods. This greatly limits their abilities to address complex questions.

Despite the challenges, the future of mixed methods research is promising in various disciplines. Very few researchers encounter noncomplex problems; in fact, all disciplines encounter research problems that are multilayered. As such, using a single method to effectively address multilayered problems is difficult and nearly impossible. Complicated problems require research approaches that are equipped to handle complexity. Mixed methods research provides the various lenses needed to address such problems.

REFERENCES

Akom, A. A. (2003). Reexamining resistance as oppositional behavior: The Nation of Islam and the creation of a Black achievement ideology. *Sociology of Education, 76,* 305–325.

Bansal, P., & Roth, K. (2000). Why companies go green: A model of ecological responsiveness. *Academy of Management Journal, 43,* 717–736.

Benson, J. (1998). Developing a strong program of construct validation: A test anxiety example. *Educational Measurement: Issues and Practices, 17*(1), 10–17.

Benson, J., & Clark, F. (1982). A guide for instrument development and validation. *American Journal of Occupational Therapy, 36*(12), 789–800.

Benson, J., & Nasser, F. (1998). On the use of factor analysis as a research tool. *Journal of Vocational Education Research, 23*(1), 13–33.

Bollen, K. A. (1989). *Structural equations with latent variables.* New York: John Wiley.

Burr, G. (1998). Contextualizing critical care family need through triangulation: An Australian study. *Intensive and Critical Care Nursing, 14,* 161–169.

Campbell, D. T., & Fiske, D. W. (1959). Convergent and discriminant validation by the multitrait-multimethod matrix. *Psychological Bulletin, 56*(2), 81–105.

Coffey, A., & Atkinson, P. (1996). *Making sense of qualitative data: Complementary research strategies.* Thousand Oaks, CA: Sage.

Creswell, J. (2002). *Research design: Qualitative, quantitative, and mixed methods approaches.* Thousand Oaks, CA: Sage.

Creswell, J., Clark, V. L., Gutmann, M. L., & Hanson, W. E. (2003). Advanced mixed methods research designs. In A. Tashakkori & C. Teddlie (Eds.), *Handbook of mixed methods in social and behavioral research* (pp. 209–240). Thousand Oaks, CA: Sage.

Cronbach, L. J., & Meehl, P. E. (1955). Construct validity in psychological tests. *Psychological Bulletin, 52*(4), 281–302.

Crotty, M. J. (1998). *The foundations of social research: Meaning and perspective in the research process.* London: Sage.

DeCuir, J. T., & Dixson, A. (2004). "So when it comes out, they aren't that surprised that it is there": Using critical race theory as a tool of analysis of race and racism in education. *Educational Researcher, 33*(5), 26–31.

DeCuir-Gunby, J. T. (2007). Negotiating identity in a bubble: The experiences of African American high school students at Wells Academy. *Equity & Excellence in Education, 40*(1), 26–35.

Denzin, N., & Lincoln, Y. (2005). Paradigms and perspectives in contention. In N. Denzin & Y. Lincoln (Eds.), *Handbook of qualitative research* (3rd ed., pp. 183–190). Thousand Oaks, CA: Sage.

Duncan, G. A. (2005). Black youth, identity, and ethics. *Educational Theory, 55*(1), 3–22.

Ebel, R. L. (1972). *Essentials of educational measurement* (2nd ed.). Englewood Cliffs, NJ: Prentice Hall.

Eggleston, E., Jackson, J., & Hardee, K. (1999). Sexual attitudes and behavior among young adolescents in Jamaica. *International Family Planning Perspectives, 25,* 78–84, 91.

Eisenhart, M. A., & Howe, K. R. (1992). Validity in educational research. In M. D. LeCompte, W. L. Millroy, & J. Preissle (Eds.), *The handbook of qualitative research in education* (pp. 643–680). New York: Academic Press.

Ercikan, K., & Roth, W. (2006). What good is polarizing research into qualitative and quantitative? *Educational Researcher, 35*(5), 14–23.

Farkas, G. (2003). Racial disparities and discrimination in education: What do we know, how do we know it, and what do we need to know? *Teachers College Record, 105*(6), 1119–1146.

Finlay, L. (1998). Reflexivity: An essential component for all research? *British Journal of Occupational Therapy, 61*(10), 453–456.

Glaser, B. G., & Strauss, A. L. (1967). *The discovery of grounded theory: Strategies for qualitative research.* Hawthorne, NY: Aldine de Gruyter.

Green, S. E. (2003). "What do you mean 'what's wrong with her?'" Stigma and the lives of families of children with disabilities. *Social Science & Medicine, 57*(8), 1361–1374.

Greene, J. C., Caracelli, V. J., & Graham, W. D. (1989). Toward a conceptual framework for mixed-method evaluation designs. *Educational Evaluation and Policy Analysis, 11*(3), 255–274.

Helms, J. E. (1990). *Black and White racial identity: Theory, research, and practice.* Westport, CT: Praeger.

Igo, L. B., Bruning, R., & McCrudden, M. T. (2005). Exploring differences in students' copy-and-paste decision making and processing: A mixed-methods study. *Journal of Educational Psychology, 97*(1), 103–116.

Johnson, R. B., & Onwuegbuzie, A. J. (2004). Mixed methods research: A research paradigm whose time has come. *Educational Researcher, 33*(7), 14–26.

Johnson, R. B., & Turner, L. A. (2003). Data collection strategies in mixed methods research. In A. Tashakkori & C. Teddlie (Eds.), *Handbook of mixed methods in social and behavioral research* (pp. 297–320). Thousand Oaks, CA: Sage.

Kemper, E. A., Stringfield, S., & Teddlie, C. (2003). Mixed methods sampling strategies in social science research. In A. Tashakkori & C. Teddlie (Eds.), *Handbook of mixed methods in social and behavioral research* (pp. 273–296). Thousand Oaks, CA: Sage.

Kreuger, R. A., & Casey, M. A. (2000). *Focus groups: A practical guide for applied research* (3rd ed.). Thousand Oaks, CA: Sage.

Kvale, S. (1996). *Interviews: An introduction to qualitative research interviewing.* Thousand Oaks, CA: Sage.

Ladson-Billings, G., & Tate, W. F. (1995). Towards a critical race theory of education. *Teachers College Record, 97*(1), 47–68.

Lincoln, Y., & Guba, E. (2000). Paradigmatic controversies, contradictions, and emerging confluences. In N. Denzin & Y. Lincoln (Eds.), *Handbook of qualitative research* (2nd ed., pp. 163–188). Thousand Oaks, CA: Sage.

Loehlin, J. C. (1998). *Latent variable models: An introduction to factor, path, and structural analysis* (3rd ed.). Mahwah, NJ: Lawrence Erlbaum.

Mathison, S. (1988). Why triangulate? *Educational Researcher, 17*(2), 13–17.

Maxwell, J. A. (1996). *Qualitative research design: An interactive approach.* Thousand Oaks, CA: Sage.

Maxwell, J. A., & Loomis, D. M. (2003). Mixed methods design: An alternative approach. In A. Tashakkori & C. Teddlie (Eds.), *Handbook of mixed methods in social and behavioral research* (pp. 241–271). Thousand Oaks, CA: Sage.

Merriam, S. (1998). *Qualitative research and case study applications in education.* San Francisco: Jossey-Bass.

Mertens, D. M. (2003). Mixed methods and the politics of human research: The transformative-emancipatory perspective. In A. Tashakkori &

C. Teddlie (Eds.), *Handbook of mixed methods in social and behavioral research* (pp. 135–164). Thousand Oaks, CA: Sage.

Messick, S. (1995a). Standards of validity and the validity of standards in performance assessment. *Educational Measurement: Issues and Practice, 14*(4), 5–8.

Messick, S. (1995b). Validity of psychological assessment: Validation of inferences from persons' responses and performances as scientific inquiry into score meaning. *American Psychologist, 50*(9), 741–749.

Miles, M., & Huberman, A. M. (1994). *Qualitative data analysis* (2nd ed.). Thousand Oaks, CA: Sage.

Morgan, D. L. (1998). Practical strategies for combining qualitative and quantitative methods: Applications to health research. *Qualitative Health Research, 8,* 362–376.

Morse, J. M. (2003). Principles of mixed methods and multimethods research design. In A. Tashakkori & C. Teddlie (Eds.), *Handbook of mixed methods in social and behavioral research* (pp. 189–208). Thousand Oaks, CA: Sage.

Morse, J. M. (1991). Approaches to qualitative-quantitative methodological triangulation. *Nursing Research, 40,* 120–123.

Newman, I., Ridenour, C. S., Newman, C., & DeMarco, G. M. (2003). A typology of research purposes and its relationship to mixed methods. In A. Tashakkori & C. Teddlie (Eds.), *Handbook of mixed methods in social and behavioral research* (pp. 167–188). Thousand Oaks, CA: Sage.

O'Connor, C. (1997). Dispositions toward (collective) struggle and educational resilience in the inner city: A case analysis of six African-American high school students. *American Educational Research Journal, 34*(4), 593–629.

Onwuegbuzie, A. J., & Leech, N. L. (2004). Enhancing the interpretation of "significant" findings: The role of mixed methods research. *Qualitative Report, 9*(4), 770–792.

Onwuegbuzie, A. J., & Leech, N. L. (2005). Taking the "Q" out of research: Teaching research methodology courses without the divide between quantitative paradigms. *Quality & Quantity, 39,* 267–296.

Osterman, K. F. (2000). Students' need for belonging in the school community. *Review of Educational Research, 70*(3), 323–367.

Oyserman, D., & Harrison, K. (1998). Implications of cultural context: African American identity and possible selves. In J. K. Swim & C. Stangor (Eds.), *Prejudice: The target's perspective* (pp. 281–300). San Diego: Academic Press.

Parker, I. (1994). Reflexive research and the grounding of analysis: Social psychology and the psy-complex. *Journal of Community and Applied Social Psychology, 4,* 239–252.

Patton, M. Q. (1990). *Qualitative research and evaluation methods* (2nd ed.). Newbury Park, CA: Sage.

Rocco, T. S., Bliss, L. A., Gallagher, S., & Perez-Prado, A. (2003).Taking the next step: Mixed methods research in organizational systems. *Information Technology, Learning, and Performance Journal, 21*(1), 19–29.

Rubin, H. J., & Rubin, I. S. (2005). *Qualitative interviewing: The art of hearing data* (2nd ed.). Thousand Oaks, CA: Sage.

Sale, J. E., & Brazil, K. (2004). A strategy to identify critical appraisal criteria for primary mixed-method studies. *Quality & Quantity, 38,* 351–365.

Sale, J. M., Lohfeld, L. H., & Brazil, K. (2002). Revisiting the quantitative-qualitative debate: Implications for mixed-methods research. *Quality & Quantity, 36,* 43–53.

Sandelowski, M. (2003). Tables or tableaux? The challenges of writing and reading mixed methods studies. In A. Tashakkori & C. Teddlie (Eds.), *Handbook of mixed methods in social and behavioral research* (pp. 321–350). Thousand Oaks, CA: Sage.

Schillaci, M. A., Waitzkin, H., Carson, E. A., Lopez, C. M., Boehm, D. A., Lopez, L. A., et al. (2004). Immunization coverage and Medicaid managed care in New Mexico: A multimethod assessment. *Annals of Family Medicine, 2,* 13–21.

Schutz, P. A., Chambless, C. B., & DeCuir, J. T. (2003). Multimethods research. In K. B. deMarrais & S. D. Lapan (Eds.), *Foundations for research: Methods of inquiry in education and the social sciences* (pp. 267–282). Hillsdale, NJ: Lawrence Erlbaum.

Sechrest, L., & Sidani, S. (1995). Quantitative and qualitative methods: Is there an alternative? *Evaluation and Program Planning, 18*(1), 77–87.

Sellers, R. M., Rowley, S. A. J., Chavous, T. M., Shelton, J. N., & Smith, M. A. (1997). Multidimensional Inventory of Black Identity: A preliminary investigation of reliability and construct validity. *Journal of Personality and Social Psychology, 73*(4), 805–815.

Slavin, R. E. (2002). Evidence-based education policies: Transforming educational practice and research. *Educational Researcher, 31*(7), 15–21.

Smith, J., & Hodkinson, P. (2005). Relativism, criteria, and politics. In N. Denzin & Y. Lincoln (Eds.), *Handbook of qualitative research* (3rd ed., pp. 915–932). Thousand Oaks, CA: Sage.

Strauss, A., & Corbin, J. (1990). *Basics of qualitative research: Grounded theory procedures and techniques* (2nd ed.). Newbury Park, CA: Sage.

Sword, W. (1999). Accounting for presence of self: Reflections on doing qualitative research. *Qualitative Health Research, 9*(2), 270–278.

Tatum, B. D. (1997). *"Why are all the Black kids sitting together in the cafeteria?" And other conversations about race.* New York: Basic Books.

Trochim, W. (2001). *The research methods knowledge base* (2nd ed.). Cincinnati, OH: Atomic Dog Publishing.

Vygotsky, L. S. (1978). *Mind in society: The development of higher psychological processes.* Cambridge, MA: Harvard University Press.

Wolcott, H. (1994). *Transforming qualitative data.* Thousand Oaks, CA: Sage.

Yu, C. H. (2006). *Philosophical foundations of quantitative research methodology.* Lanham, MD: University Press of America.

Zirkel, S. (2004). What will you think of me? Racial integration, peer relationships and achievement among White students and students of color. *Journal of Social Issues, 60*(1), 57–74.

9

Designing a Rigorous Small Sample Study

Naomi Jeffery Petersen

This chapter is an effort to summarize a few best practices for using esoteric samples. As we shall see, standard principles of quality research design apply to samples of any size, but smaller samples are more vulnerable to bias. In order to address the common problems of bias that will weaken the quality of the findings, we consider the crucial importance of providing a well-developed rationale for using a small sample. In this way, your decisions are transparent and well grounded.

Many of the current conventions for sample size may be credited to Jacob Cohen's (1988, 1992) tireless efforts to improve the quality of social science research. His voice is joined by a large group of methodologists deploring the failure of researchers to fully report the details needed to put the findings in context with the rest of the field. Therefore, an empirical study based on a limited sample is further weakened by superficial reporting that will not allow fellow scientists to replicate the complete study or even duplicate the calculations. This is a pointed cautionary note for novice researchers who have not yet grasped the nuances of the decisions to be made.

There are myriad ways in which your data set may be compromised, and each of these influences the quality of the study. The first point of

best practice is therefore to provide a compelling rationale for using a small sample instead of a large sample. This means that throughout the report, you must justify the method and analysis, connecting every decision to the professional literature. A rigorous literature review provides theoretical justification for the particular population. It should clearly extend the existing body of knowledge by replicating or improving sample or the method of study. Note that a rigorous reading of the literature does not mean a lengthy report of it.

Thus, the conceptual rationale, the statistical rationale, and the voice of cautious parsimony all help mediate the reception of a design that at first blush appears insufficient. Addressed here is the broad discussion of first "why" and then "how" the research design uses relatively few participants. These broad topics are followed by some discussion of the many ways in which a study may be considered small, each of which will need to be addressed in the rationale.

Articulating a Compelling Conceptual Rationale

For ethical and practical reasons, a small sample size may be the most responsible design, and its use can be conducted rigorously to establish validity. For studies with human subjects, there are ethical concerns for any invasions of privacy or long-term effects, so the smaller the number of people at risk of inconvenience or worse, the better. For experimental designs, a small sample provides a pilot study that may suggest a larger replication. As Antliffe (1993) argued, a small sample size may be a false economy because its reduced statistical power means it is more likely to make a "costly" Type II error, yet large samples do not guarantee sufficient power if the data are not normally distributed or are non-representative. This means there is no simple answer because the research question will define the type of data to be collected, which in turn will define the statistical procedures necessary to use the data in order to answer the question.

Yet another compelling reason to use a small sample is that the population of interest is small. People suffering from rare diseases or conditions will of course be a small group from which to get a sample, but they are nonetheless important to study. Research conducted on a small scale is valuable for local evaluation and practitioner feedback (i.e., classroom-level action research). Given that there is some justification possible for using a small sample, let's consider four components of the rationale that require special attention when using them: (a) defining the research design, (b) defining the population, (c) defining the context, and (d) using cautious language.

Define the Research Design. The research question is crucial for determining the adequacy of the sample. The research question frames the hypothesis, and the rationale merely justifies the question first and then your procedure to answer it. Ultimately, all empirical studies are concerned with measures that can then be compared or correlated in order to test hypotheses. An educational researcher might ask, "How does fourth-grade writing proficiency change throughout the year?" This requires a thoughtful description of the participants in order to provide some context for interpreting the measures of writing proficiency. Another sort of question requires data to be collected at regular intervals (e.g., "Does the pace of developing writing proficiency vary among fourth graders?"). The scores are then dependent, meaning that they must be linked to each participant at every point in the sequence. However, if a research question focuses on differences within the group (e.g., "Do boys and girls develop writing proficiency at the same rate?" "Do immigrant children develop writing proficiency at the same pace as the rest of the class?" "Do children who qualify for free or reduced-price lunch develop writing proficiency at the same rate as those who do not qualify for poverty assistance?"), the scores are independent. The independence of the data will influence the choice of statistical procedure, whether the data are used to answer a question of comparison or correlation and whether the scale is ratio, interval, ordinal, or nominal. This is no different than a research design using any size sample, but it may be more crucial to recognize the vulnerability of its validity because of the sample size and to address rival hypotheses and rigorous investigation at the outset.

Define the Population. For experimental designs that compare groups, the greater the control of similar characteristics, the greater the tolerance of smaller sample sizes. One tactic for improving the validity of a small sample study is to take a cue from our qualitative colleagues: Carefully document a range of characteristics that may be of interest. Part of the rationale for the demographic questions that may be challenged by the institutional review board (IRB) is therefore the research design necessitated by the small sample. Because educational and social research is rarely conducted in laboratory settings with as much control of factors as is research in the physical sciences, the circumstances surrounding the data collection as well as the participants' lives in general are important to mention. This means that if the only qualitative differences between groups are in the variables mentioned in the research hypothesis, if all possible explanations of the rival hypothesis are negligible, and also if the samples are quantitatively similar (i.e., of equivalent size [N] and distribution [skewness and kurtosis]), the assumptions of inferential statistics will not be violated and the findings will be less likely to be spurious.

It goes without saying that the participants must be carefully described in order to help define the population that the sample, however small, might represent. Human subject research typically includes gender, ethnicity, and socioeconomic status at a minimum; educational studies always include developmental level. A study of a small sample that is well described is that much more useful to other researchers conducting meta-analyses of many studies. This is the reason for the conventions of reporting adopted by different disciplines—for example, the *Publication Manual of the American Psychological Association* (American Psychological Association, 2001).

Fortunately, there are now very comprehensive and easily accessible databases that make it possible for you to establish what is already known about the population. For human subjects, the U.S. Bureau of the Census provides not only data about Americans (http://www.census.gov/) but international information as well (http://www.census.gov/ipc/www/idbnew.html). The U.S. Bureau of Labor and Statistics describes nearly every occupation, including different educator and medical roles (http://www.bls.gov/home.htm). The National Center for Education Statistics (NCES) is an invaluable mine of school-related statistics, including specific school district profiles (http://nces.ed.gov/). The Kaiser Family Foundation provides reliable health parameters (http://www.statehealthfacts.kff.org/cgi-bin/healthfacts.cgi). The Centers for Disease Control and Prevention maintain the *Mortality and Morbidity Weekly Report* at http://www.cdc.gov/mmwr/—particularly useful for epidemiology studies. The National Center for Health Statistics provides extensive data from the National Health Interview Survey (NHIS) at http://www.cdc.gov/nchs/nhis.htm. So there are no excuses for merely describing the subjects of your study without a larger context. For nonhuman subjects, the U.S. Environmental Protection Agency (http://www.epa.gov/) and others share information.

Define the Context. Even if your study is purely descriptive, intended to be used for evaluating some local condition, your interest in sharing your results must acknowledge others' interest in connecting those results to their own contexts. Therefore, the first step is to describe your sample in the most specific terms relative to the largest population it might represent. Without sacrificing the parsimony prized by empiricists, you can still include enough narrative to picture the sampling strategy and participants.

The careful researcher will therefore also describe any recent changes in the instructional experience as well as the historical context (i.e., Hurricane Katrina). A small sample may highlight a trend in a changing population. For instance, educators are tasked with accountability for all students, of any minority status, achieving "adequate yearly progress," or AYP. Currently, school databases make it possible to track the students' classroom experiences (i.e., teachers and curricula) in order to determine "value added." This is the crux of the accountability reforms and an important influence on educational settings. Therefore, most educational research includes some mention of the No Child Left Behind Act of 2001 or other legislation influencing curriculum, either to measure the achievement of mandates or the effects of the mandate.

Other social science research will mention policies, legislation, cultural norms, and community dynamics that may affect human subjects' behavior. As pointed out in a *Wall Street Journal* editorial ("Tales From the Crypt," 2006), the World Economic Forum considers Algeria a "star performer" in terms of budget surplus, national savings, public debt, inflation, interest rate spread, and real effective exchange rate, although some 200,000 people perished in the civil war and millions are "struggling to build better lives in Europe" (p. A16). A similar concern emerges regarding the *U.S. News's* ranking of institutions of higher education that focuses on important but not comprehensive criteria. Both systems of ranking are flawed in part because the methodology is not adequately justified.

Use Cautious, Tentative Language. By using qualifying language, you avoid appearing to promote your finding as a universal truth. This is especially important as you make transitions from the introduction to the methods section to the results section of your report. Each transition requires at least a nodding reference to the narrow nature of your sample, or its circumstances. Your readers may have skipped all the technicalities to find the nuggets of concise conclusion they are interested in, so your summary must allude to the limitations. As is expected, your closing discussion will return to ideas in your rationale to show that your small study is aligned with the knowledge base for future meta-analyses.

After a clear presentation of your rationale for the research design, you will explain the method of collection and the strategy of interpretation. As mentioned above, a small sample size will complicate choices of statistical procedure, and therefore you must not only acknowledge its influence but also propose a comprehensive strategy for making sense of the data in response to the guiding questions of the design.

ARTICULATING A COMPELLING STATISTICAL RATIONALE

The implications of small sample size are actually better known than the absolute definition of how much is enough. It is fair to say the definition has changed with advancing technology, for at one time, statistical calculations were done by hand, and therefore a sample size of 30 was considered reasonable for doctoral dissertations. Equally complex is the task of determining the minimum sample size needed, for it depends on the acceptable significance criteria (alpha), the anticipated effect size, and the desired level of statistical power.[1] A thorough explanation of the importance of each of these four elements of any quantitative research design is beyond the scope of this chapter. Consult Cohen—for example, "A Power Primer," his 1992 article that includes not only very clear definitions of these terms but also the common statistical procedures used to analyze data. A few standard components of empirical design are worth mentioning because of their importance to determining acceptable sample size: operational definitions, strategic sampling, valid instruments, and specific scaling.

Frame the Hypothesis in Quantitative Terms. This means using numbers and will be quite familiar to educators who have crafted measurable behavioral objectives. Just as a teacher should determine the criteria for success before giving the test, the researcher should determine the criteria for significance before analyzing the data.

Explain the Sampling Strategy. A true random sample is a key assumption for interpreting data as representative, so any other method must be explained and also justified. You must defend not only who was included but why others who would have made the sample more representative were excluded. One reason to use a stratified sampling frame is in order to compare relatively scarce groups that may be missed in a true random sampling of a population. You would be justified in targeting particular, smaller populations and therefore samples if your research

design intends to compare them. Later we will discuss the difficulty of ad hoc subgrouping.

Once you determine the rationale for your sampling strategy, all else must be aligned with that logic, and all decisions that rest on the size and quality of the sample must be transparent. Therefore, you must clearly indicate the steps you have taken to improve the quality if not the quantity of the sample. A typical problem for all researchers is nonresponse and subject mortality (i.e., participants who do not provide a complete set of data points or participants who do not complete the study). They are of course within their protected rights as informed human subjects to discontinue participation at any time, but you may be left with a somewhat smaller sample than you had originally hoped. Therefore, you must also discuss how you treated any missing data.

The researcher who must settle for a small sample may also have to sacrifice the ideal of randomness. If the sample is one of convenience, then the investigator may also share an organizational relationship (i.e., a nurse employed by the co-op or a teacher employed by the school district). Best practice would therefore include mention of such story elements as the time during the school year, the phase of reform affecting the faculty, historical circumstances such as a hurricane, or the researcher's personal connection. We take a page from qualitative research when we choose small one-samples, often equivalent to case studies. Of course, one of the charms of quantitative research is its focus on neatly proscribed objectives, unlike the comparatively nonlinear experience of its qualitative cousin more interested in developing than testing hypotheses.

Explain the Data to Be Collected. This means that the instrument you use must be appropriate to the research question. Note that unless the instrument is reliable, validated (a separate study, or conducted during a pilot study), and developed for use with your particular population, the data set is of very little value. Therefore, you must report the psychometric properties published about the instrument or explain how the instrument was developed.

Define the Scale. Directly address the issue of scale, which will limit the options of the statistical procedure. For instance, a mean cannot be

Table 9.1   Sample Size Plateaus

Scale	Sample Size Range With Noticeable Change in Variance and Standard Deviation	Threshold at Which Changes Plateau
Nominal	8–24	64
Interval	8–32	64
Ordinal	8–40	40

NOTE: Minimum sample size = 8, with all others as multiples of 8.

computed if the data are categorical (mutually exclusive categories, i.e., gender) or ordinal (ranks). In those cases, the appropriate central tendency would be the mode (value occurring most often) or median (centralmost value in the middle of the range of participants), and the choice of statistical procedure would be restricted to the nonparametric. Wangcharoen, Ngarmsak, and Wilkinson (2005) compared the variances (R^2) of a large ($N = 522$) sample to those of different, smaller size random samples. Their study included different scales (i.e., nominal, interval, and ordinal data), which is of particular importance because the scale determines the statistical method appropriate for analysis. Their findings, summarized in Table 9.1, suggest minimums based on the point at which the changes in effect do not improve with increasing the size of the sample.

THE SHRINKING N

Apart from the characteristics and the circumstances of the sample, the simple number must also be justified. Note that this is not in order to explain why you used the particular sample (for external validity of generalizing the findings) but to warrant the use of the particular statistical procedure (internal validity of analyzing and interpreting data).

The Simple N. The smallest possible sample size ($N = 1$) is appropriate for case study—that is, qualitative research—which is outside the parameters of this volume. However, it is important to note this difference between the two research paradigms: Case studies are convenience samples, that is, selected in order to target the population of interest or because they are the complete population of interest. For instance, a school district's self-study may employ some

quantitative methods for descriptive purposes and internal assessment, but the findings will not necessarily be generalized to other districts. The unit of analysis is the one district, and any comparisons within it are probably spurious because so few characteristics will be controlled.

Although it is easiest to determine the size by simple counting, or frequency, the overall sample size is an unsatisfactory measure because the nature of the population, the data collection, and the data analysis all influence the quality of the sample size. Aspects of smallness must be addressed in the rationale for the methodology (i.e., inadequate number of cases in the data set, misidentified units of analysis, unequal subgroups, unrepresentative proportions of the population, poorly defined participants, and low response rates).

Unit of Analysis. The research design is crucial to determine the unit of analysis. For instance, a small sample of individuals may be tested over time, meaning each contributes to a much larger whole that analyzes the variance among all the trials with slight variations (Ahn & Jung, 2005). To the empirical researcher, the highest quality sample of any size is randomly selected. It is tedious to supersede the convenience of a convenient sample, but random assignment within a classroom can occur with subjects (or participants) sorted into subgroups from which they are randomly assigned. This is a stratified model that still requires a minimum pool for each characteristic. In order to establish these minimums, it is a good idea to create a frequency distribution chart to illustrate the proportions within the sample. Each cell of intersecting paths must have a minimum number, and the cells should have similar sizes. Best practice for developing a small sample study, then, is to construct the frequency distribution table before collecting the data.

The complexity of this table will perhaps provide counsel against too many research questions of comparison that overreach the data. Regarding contingency tables, each additional cell increases the degrees of freedom (*df*), which in turn influences the size of the minimum sample necessary to detect the target effect size of the chi-square, with greater samples suggested for more degrees of freedom for each case to occur in different, mutually exclusive combinations. Multiple regression techniques require increasingly large sample sizes as the number of independent variables, or population characteristics, increases.

Another example of the unit of analysis problem can be seen in a typical action research scenario conducted by a teacher using a classroom of students. Although each student might be considered a case in the data set, it is likely that all the students are in the same classroom and share the same intervention and context. This may mean the unit of analysis is only 1 because it is one classroom (i.e., students within this classroom are not independent observations, violating a critical tenet of many statistical procedures).[2] Action research is a form of self-study, used for making local decisions. Its value outside the immediate context is enhanced by the quality of the description that allows for others to recognize similar combinations of characteristics. By definition, it will not be experimental nor the statistics inferential.

Define Subgroups. A large sample may be subdivided according to traits that are not evenly distributed. For instance, ethnicity is often reported, but minorities will, by definition, be unequal. When reporting differences among ethnicities, researchers may choose to aggregate minorities to have a critical mass for comparison or may include small minority groups in the large sample but not report them separately (e.g., http://nces.ed.gov/pubs2002/2002114.pdf). This is even more problematic when ad hoc subgroups are not homogeneous—for example, the "latino" subgroup label may contain people from different countries as well as different sociocultural and educational backgrounds. The differences within the subgroup may be greater than between subgroups. If the integrity of the subgroup can be established, it is then important to (a) recognize when a subgroup becomes too small to analyze and (b) report its relation to the larger study. Unequal subgroup proportions will reduce the statistical power.

A simple frequency chart will reveal whether the subsamples are similar enough to be compared. It is therefore best practice on the part of the classroom educator to collect data in order to demonstrate the influence of factors the researcher thinks might skew the results (i.e., rival hypotheses). This helpful information can be presented simply in a table that places the sample for a survey of educators into the context of the state and/or national demographics. If the sample's subgroup proportions are not greatly different from the population's—for example, Washington State public school teachers in Table 9.2—the sample may be adequately proportioned.

Once the subgroups are used for comparison rather than description, though, their size is problematic. According to Krejcie and Morgan (1970), a sample size of 448 far exceeds the

Table 9.2   Gender and Ethnicity of Washington State Educators for School Year 2001–2002 and of the Study Sample

Educator Population	Total	Gender		Ethnicity	
		Female	Male	Majority	Minority
Washington State	54,641	32,070	13,227	51,029	3,512
	100%	70.8%	29.2%	93.4%	6.6%
Study sample	448	331	110	362	56
		74%	25%	81%	13%

NOTE: Washington data from Office of the Superintendent of Public Instruction, 1/10/02. Note that the contingency table is 2 × 2: two categories of gender (male and female) and two categories of career status (pre- and in-service). This means 3 degrees of freedom, and so the minimum sample will range from 44 to 1,090 depending on the required effect size (large or small) and Cohen's alpha.

minimum required for the population of 54,000. However, notice the very uneven quantities in each variable: There are far fewer men than women, and minorities are by definition not of the same proportion. A sample of 375 is recommended for a population of 32,000 female teachers, while the population of 13,000 males would need 373—almost as many—in order to adequately represent their populations. A comparison study would therefore require approximately 750 participants. Therefore, carefully and quantitatively describing the participants and the population is crucial for justifying the sample size. Advanced methods (i.e., repeated measures analysis of variance [ANOVA]) may tolerate smaller sizes, but this is again dependent on the research design. Beyond the scope of this chapter is a discussion of the value of aggregating multiple small samples via meta-analysis; suffice it to say that such a method adds more understanding of the data if appropriate for the design.

Predict and Report the Response Rate. The actual data collected must be analyzed for not only their proportion to the larger population but also their proportion to the sampling frame. The sampling frame is the scope of people who were invited to participate, and while the frame may be of adequate size to generalize to a larger population, the actual data set will be the responses from within the frame. For example, a small response rate for survey research is anything less than 80%. Although Nguyen (2005) demonstrated (with the clever use of different-size pots of soup) that the absolute, not the relative, size of the sample is of importance for accuracy with opinion polls, most methodologists agree that a percentage of the total sampling frame is a quality indicator. Even if the sample includes thousands of data points, if the response is less than 80% of the total sampling frame, it is considered statistically weak, even though social science research is often reported with a much lower percentage.

Barry (2005) noted that many articles reporting longitudinal studies do not even acknowledge the rate of attrition. He expressed concern "when those who drop out of the intervention have unique characteristics, such that the remaining sample ceases to be representative of the original sample" (p. 268). Best practice, therefore, requires the total sample to be accurately described, and the demographic features of the dropouts described as well in order to determine new limits of external validity. When attrition does occur, you must decide how to analyze the data and explain your logic. The same is true for incomplete responses. Will you delete all cases with any missing data (listwise) or use the items that are there for all cases (pairwise)?

In education research, there is a heightened concern for accountability given federal funding policies. Federal agencies have long been directed by the Office of Federal Statistical Policy and Standards that a 75% response rate is the minimum to consider data adequate. Because of the importance of federal funding, this became an unquestioned rule of thumb among educational researchers. This is not new with the No Child Left Behind Act of 2001, which, along with its implementation policies, further recognized only empirical studies as credible. More recently, the U.S. government's NCES (at http://nces.ed.gov/statprog/2002/std2_2.asp) published standards for different aspects of survey research (e.g., rate of response for the screeners, for respondents who are individuals, for respondents that are institutions, for longitudinal studies, for random samples), and no guideline is less than 70%, while any below 90% will prompt a special analysis of bias in the sample. This is echoed by McMillan and Schumacher (2006) in the sixth edition of their text widely used to teach research methods to graduate students in the field of education. They commented that "if the researchers can obtain a total return rate of 70 percent or better, they are doing very well" (p. 236) but further cautioned that "for most surveys with a large sample (e.g., 200 or more), the nonrespondents will probably not affect the results in an appreciable way if the return rate is at least 70 percent," and "special attention should be focused on a study with a relatively low rate of return (lower than 70 percent) and without an analysis of the way in which nonrespondents may have changed the results" (p. 238).

The low response rate is a chronic problem with human subjects research because ethically, subjects must be informed and must give their consent after understanding the study. The pattern of people willing to respond is problematic, for people who have something they feel has not been heard will be motivated to express it until they do feel heard, and consequently, people with complaints are more likely to take the time and complete a survey. Another difficulty concerns the complexity of the items and the interest in understanding them. Therefore, the design of the study must include instruments and communication that will not impede participation, and the method of gathering cases must be scrupulously followed. There is no graver offense than tampering with data, unless it is to cause undue harm to the subjects. J. W. Osborne (personal communication, 2006) recommends comparing respondents and nonrespondents where any data at all are known about the nonrespondents to help establish the representativeness of the sample or understand the differences between retained and withdrawn participants.

Describe the Distribution. This is different from the distribution of participant or subject characteristics. This is the distribution of data generated by the study that will need to be analyzed in order to answer the research questions. A normal distribution is a key assumption for using (parametric) inferential statistics. As Kline (1994) pointed out, a large sample would mitigate substantial deviations from normality, so in small samples, it is especially important to describe the range and frequency of data points. The size of the standard deviation relative to the volume of the central tendency (i.e., kurtosis) is another concern because the sampling error increases as the standard deviation increases. Note that the larger the standard deviation, the larger the sampling error.

Calculate the Statistical Power. The researcher should not wait until entering data into a program to know whether the sample is likely to reject a false hypothesis. A priori power analyses are for the purpose of providing a rationale for the choice of sample size. Post hoc analyses are to confirm the actual power once the effect size is known rather than merely posited. A quality research proposal includes the a priori power analysis; the final report is of course post hoc. (Readers interested in power analysis can refer to Chapter 7, this volume, on the probability of replication.)

As with all formulas, if you isolate the missing variable (i.e., know the value of the other variables), you can calculate it. There are many applets available on free Web sites (i.e., http://www.dssresearch.com/toolkit/sscalc/size_a1.asp) by which you can calculate the sample size, but they will ask for that information. By playing with any of these programs, you will notice some trends, for alpha changes as N changes. This means with smaller samples, you are more likely to see large effect sizes. This does not mean that the effect size changes. It means if the effect size is large, you can see it with a smaller sample. Therefore, if you hypothesize a large effect, you can use a smaller sample. If you are not interested in medium or small effects, you need not bother with a large sample.

Use Current References and Tools. Thanks to a continuing agenda of investigating the effects of sample size, researchers have ever more helpful guidelines for minimum sample size for different research designs. Statistics scholars do continually test old assumptions and seek empirical evidence for recommendations (Mundfrom, Shaw, & Tian, 2005). For instance, Bonett (2006) insisted that an increase in sample size did not improve the accuracy of confidence intervals and introduced a new formula for planning sample size. Blair (1980) challenged the conventional wisdom when she concluded that Wilcoxon's ranked sums test was more powerful than the *t* test, a parametric measure. Rutherford (2001) commented that "while formulae . . . reveal the nature of variance quite well, they do not lend themselves to easy calculation" (p. 19). Fair enough, but you must know how to ask one of the statistical programs to calculate them for you.

Van Belle (2002) dismissed differences in statistical programs (as well as statistics textbooks) as inconsequential, due to the near-universal consensus regarding the formulas and their strengths. That said, it is best practice to use the most recent version of whatever statistical program you choose (e.g., at the time of this writing, SPSS had recently issued Version 15.0); the upgrades appear with increasing frequency as with all publications, and there are differences in the formulas, so it is also best to mention which program you use in your bibliography. The savvy statistician will then know at a glance what actually happened to your data between the spreadsheet and the summary.

A Handful of Thumbs

Most rules of thumb have been established based not on precedent or intuition but on careful empirical research that discovers a plateau after which a change in sample size has little bearing on the results. That said, many such rules have been discredited, such as the Kaiser criterion[3] (eigenvalue > 1 rule for deciding how many factors or components to analyze), and the conventional wisdom of ANOVA cells having at least 10 members is not scientifically established.

The reality is that minimum sample sizes differ for various statistical procedures and are at least partially dependent on the research design. For instance, having a greater number of groups to analyze for variance (ANOVA) has the opposite influence on sample size: More group means require lower sizes, but each group must be that size. For a large effect size to be detected among six groups at $\alpha = .05$, for example, each group need only have 13 members. Cohen (2005) recommended samples for different effect sizes (small, medium, or large) at different levels of confidence ($\alpha = .01$, .05, or .10) and further identified minimums for different numbers of groups (k), or variables. For a simple comparison (i.e., a Student's t test) of differences between two independent means, a small effect size can be found at $\alpha = .05$ in $n = 393$; a large effect size will be detectable in only 26 randomly selected participants. Pretz (2003) noted that as tolerance levels increase (i.e., p value decreases), the sample size can be smaller; indeed, a small correlation can be detected at the commonly accepted 95% confidence, with a sample of 1,362, but a large correlation can be detected with only 30. This means that if you have a small sample size of 30, and you detect not large but small correlations, you cannot in good faith report the findings without great caution.

The need to provide a more detailed rationale is now a standard requirement of journals in all fields of empirical study, for the same statistical procedures will be used (e.g., Livingston & Cassidy, 2005). In the intriguingly titled "Dietary Analysis From Fecal Samples: How Many Scats Are Enough?" Trites, Joy, and Weckerly (2005) reported that statistical power was adequate with $N = 59$ for one level of analysis, but $N = 95$ for more advanced analyses. Hogarty et al. (2006) studied the influence of sample size on factor analysis and found that there is less influence when communalities are high. Your rationale should include reference to the particular statistical procedure, for example, the relationship

of sample size structural equation modeling studied by Kim (2005).

There are now elaborate programs that allow researchers to simulate data sets in order to test procedures (Wang, Rasch, & Verdooren, 2005). Two methods to compensate for small sample size use the statistical creation of many more randomly defined sample sets, based either on random-number generators (i.e., Monte Carlo) or existing data banks (i.e., bootstrap).[4] The Monte Carlo method (Fan & Fan, 2005) will generate thousands of samples from a random-number generator in order to provide a large number of samples. This accommodates the need for a greater number of samples, as does the bootstrap method that selects (with replacement) smaller samples from a large existing database (Thompson, 2005). These artificial sampling techniques are helpful because the central tendency of each sample is paramount for ANOVA. However, they will likely be pursued only after the study of the original sample yields promising results and the researcher is interested in establishing the generalizability requiring the large sample size.

In summary, there are many times when the use of small samples is not only justifiable but necessary. Before using small samples, simply be aware of limitations and implications in their use, and follow the same concerns of rigor that all quantitative studies require. Best practice for using less-than-ideal sample sizes begins with appreciating that there are no absolute minimums, but power analyses can inform the research design to maximize the validity of findings. Like all empirical studies using any size data set, the context and nature of the data related to the hypothesis must be explained, and decisions must be grounded in respected literature: The rationale for the sample size, the consequent limitations of the method, and the modest interpretation of findings will improve the quality of the report.

Finally, interest in small data sets should be encouraged because different statistical procedures are so sensitive to sample size. There is considerable need for further studies and innovations to help more researchers achieve accuracy with more accessible formulas (e.g., Kim, 2005), so any rigorous study employing a small sample could contribute by focusing on that aspect of the methodology as well as the actual findings.

NOTES

1. Editor's note: Readers will note that Peter Killeen (Chapter 7, this volume) argues that the probability of replication might be more important to attend to.

2. Researchers encountering nested data may refer to Chapter 29 on HLM (hierarchical linear modeling), which can easily handle this type of data, although larger *N*s are generally required for this type of analysis.

3. Interested readers can refer to Chapter 6 on exploratory factor analysis for more information on best practices relating to these procedures.

4. The interested reader will refer to Chapter 19, which covers these intriguing topics and their applications.

REFERENCES

Ahn, C., & Jung, S. (2005, February). Effects of dropouts on sample size estimates for test on trends across repeated measurements. *Journal of Biopharmaceutical Statistics, 15*, 33–41.

American Psychological Association. (2001). *Publication manual of the American Psychological Association* (5th ed.). Washington, DC: Author.

Antliffe, B. (1993). *Impact assessment and environmental monitoring: The role of statistical power and decision analysis.* Unpublished thesis, Simon Fraser University.

Barry, A. (2005). How attrition impacts the internal and external validity of longitudinal research. *Journal of School Health, 75*, 267–270.

Blair, R. (1980). *A comparison of the power of the two independent means* t-*test with that of Wilcoxson's rank sum test for samples of various sizes that have been drawn from non-normal populations.* Unpublished doctoral dissertation, University of South Florida.

Bonett, D. (2006, February). Approximate confidence interval for standard deviation of nonnormal distributions. *Computational Statistics & Data Analysis, 50*, 775–782.

Cohen, J. (1988). *Statistical power analysis for the behavioral sciences* (2nd ed.). Hillsdale, NJ: Lawrence Erlbaum.

Cohen, J. (1992). A power primer. *Psychological Bulletin, 112*, 155–159.

Fan, X., & Fan, X. (2005). Using SAS for Monte Carlo simulation research in SEM. *Structural Equation Modeling, 12*, 299–333.

Hogarty, K., Hines, C., Kromrey, J., Ferron, J. & Mumford, K. (2005). The quality of factor solutions in exploratory factor analysis: The influence of sample size, communality, and overdetermination. *Educational and Psychological Measurement, 65*, 202–226.

Kim, K. (2005). The relation among fit indexes, power, and sample size in structural equation modeling. *Structural Equation Modeling, 12*, 368–390.

Kline, P. (1994). *An easy guide to factor analysis.* London: Routledge.

Krejcie, R., & Morgan, D. (1970). Determining sample size for research activities. *Educational and Psychological Measurements, 36*, 607–610.

Livingston, E., & Cassidy, L. (2005, June). Statistical power and estimation of the number of required subjects for a study based on the *t*-test: A surgeon's primer. *Journal of Surgical Research, 126*, 149–159.

McMillan, J., & Schumacher, S. (2006). *Research in education: Evidence-based inquiry* (6th ed.). New York: Pearson.

Mundfrom, D., Shaw, D., & Tian, L. K. (2005). Minimum sample size recommendations for conducting factor analyses. *International Journal of Testing, 5*, 159–168.

Nguyen, P. (2005). Public opinion polls, chicken soup and sample size. *Teaching Statistics, 27*(3), 89–92.

Pretz, C. (2003). *Minimum sample sizes for conducting two-group discriminant analysis.* Unpublished doctoral dissertation, University of Northern Colorado.

Rutherford, A. (2001). *Introducing ANOVA and ANCOVA: A GLM approach.* London: Sage.

Tales from the crypt. (2006, September 29). *Wall Street Journal,* p. A16.

Thompson, B. (2005). *Exploratory and confirmatory factor analysis.* Washington, DC: American Psychological Association.

Trites, A., Joy, R., & Weckerly, F. (2005, August). Dietary analysis from fecal samples: How many scats are enough? *Journal of Mammalogy, 86*, 704–712.

Van Belle, G. (2002). *Statistical rules of thumb.* New York: John Wiley.

Wang, M., Rasch, D., & Verdooren, R. (2005, June). Determination of the size of a balanced experiment in mixed ANOVA models using the modified approximate-test. *Journal of Statistical Planning & Inference, 132*, 183–201.

Wangcharoen, W., Ngarmsak, T., & Wilkinson, B. (2005). Snack product consumer surveys: Large versus small samples. *Food Quality and Preference, 16*, 511–516.

10

REPLICATED FIELD STUDY DESIGN

WILLIAM D. SCHAFER

This chapter discusses the use of replications in order to enhance the ability of a researcher to make causal inferences from data gathered in field (nonexperimental) settings. Replications are common in experimental research and are used both to study interactions between treatments and other variables (e.g., gender or aptitude in two-way designs) and to increase the power of the design. In many of these designs, each condition of a blocking variable often constitutes a self-contained true experiment (Campbell & Stanley, 1963), with internal randomization. In such research, the data are processed statistically to study generalizability of treatment effects across replications.

I argue that replicating even weak research designs can greatly expand the usefulness of research in settings, such as field research, where experimental control is difficult or even impossible to achieve. Some examples of this approach, called *replicated field study design*, are given, as well as some suggestions for data collection and analysis.

CONTROL AND CAUSAL INFERENCES

The principle of control is fundamental to making an inference that variability on a dependent variable is caused by differences on an independent variable. In experimental settings, a researcher determines which of the research participants under study receives which level of the independent variable(s) and observes the effect of their states on the dependent variable(s). But if there are systematic differences between the participants on any other variable(s), those differences may be the causes of the differences on the dependent variable(s). In order to resist variation on these extraneous or irrelevant variables, researchers use the principle of control. In general, then, control of extraneous variables is a basic condition for causal interpretations of research (Johnson, 2001).

Control over a variable is achieved when the variable is not correlated with the independent variable(s). For example, if one group of research participants were to receive their experimental experience in a room different from the other group, differences between rooms (e.g., instructive wall art) might be plausible as a rival explanation for any difference between the groups on the dependent variable. But if the two groups of participants were in the same room (as opposed to different rooms) or were equally represented in each of multiple rooms, then there would be no correlation between room (an extraneous

Author's Note: This project was funded by the Maryland State Department of Education (MSDE) under a contract to the Maryland Assessment Research Center for Education Success (MARCES). The opinions expressed do not necessarily reflect those of MSDE or MARCES.

variable) and group membership (an independent variable) since the distribution of rooms would be the same in each group. Then, if a relationship between group membership and the dependent variable were to be observed, location would not be plausible as a competing (rival) explanation of the relationship.

One important class of extraneous variables that requires control is those that are descriptive of the participants, such as gender, age, genetic makeup, or experiential background. A plausible rival explanation that relies on a member of this class is an example of what has been called a selection threat to the internal validity of the research (Campbell & Stanley, 1963).

Randomization of research participants to treatment groups is a powerful means of control over selection threats. This aspect of control is so important that Campbell and Stanley (1963) use it to distinguish true experimental from other types of research designs. When randomization is used, it is clear that the basis for which participants receive which treatment condition is unrelated (uncorrelated) except by chance with any variable descriptive of participants that could be confounded with the treatments.

In education, many research studies are carried out in field settings. District-based or state-level researchers, for example, commonly are interested in practical interventions that could occur naturally in schools. Yet randomization is usually unavailable to researchers who are working in field settings because they are not able to assign treatment conditions to individual participants since agencies such as schools resist moving participants (e.g., students) among groups (e.g., classes or schools) or otherwise assigning them to groups according to a researcher's needs. Moreover, it is often not possible even to assign randomly which group is to receive which treatment condition, such as when teachers choose which instructional methods they want to use.

One approach often used in the field when randomization is impossible is to measure extraneous variables and then to match or to use some means of statistical control (e.g., analysis of covariance). Three common purposes for statistical control when using intact groups are described by Pedhazur (1997): equating the participants on the outcome variable(s) prior to the study using one or more pretest(s), controlling for other variable(s) when looking at mean differences, and controlling for other variable(s)

when looking at differences in regression surfaces. He notes that these are commonly invalid uses of analysis of covariance. Matching is only as effective as the ability of the matching variables to exhaust all relevant correlates of group membership.

Since statistical procedures are viewed as less effective than experimental control, causal inferences observed in field settings are susceptible to many reasonable internal validity threats. Indeed, in many cases, it may not even be possible to measure extraneous variables, perhaps because limited time is available, the number of participants in the research is too limited, or the measurement would be too intrusive. In the face of considerations such as these, Johnson (2001) has concluded that there is not much that can be learned from a single, nonexperimental research study. Clearly, it would be advantageous to have a feasible alternative for researchers in field settings to use in order to draw causal inferences from their work.

REPLICATED FIELD STUDY DESIGN

While there are clearly important limitations, in field contexts, there often are many opportunities available to the researcher that are not available in more controlled (e.g., laboratory) settings. Laboratory researchers typically have only small potential participant pools to select from and might need to expend significant resources to obtain their cooperation. In applied settings such as classrooms and schools, however, and especially for employees of these institutions, potential participants such as students are often generously available, especially when the intrusion of the research is minimal. Thus, field researchers often have broad research opportunities available to them that laboratory researchers do not. It is therefore possible in typical applied research settings to be able to replicate (i.e., repeat) a study design more than once.

Schafer (2001) has proposed that carefully planned replications can enhance the internal validity of applied research. There is a stronger basis for the validity of observed relationship(s) when results are consistent across several studies than there is for each study separately since results that have been replicated are considered more likely to generalize (continue to be observed) to further replications. Furthermore, it is possible to compare the replicate studies with each other to study whether there are constructs that interact with (i.e., moderate) observed relationships. While these are possible advantages whether or not research includes experimental control, the opportunity to replicate a basic study design is more likely to be available to the applied researcher working in multiple field contexts. It is recommended, therefore, that persons who work in field research settings try to include replication as a fundamental feature in their work. Hence the name of this approach: replicated field study design.

Once the data are collected, they can be viewed as multiple studies, each with the same basic design. Whether or not studies have identical designs, meta-analysis is an attractive vehicle for synthesizing, or combining, a series of replications. While meta-analysis is usually thought of as a way to study an existing research literature quantitatively, it also can be used for a series of related studies generated as replications within a single project.

In the remainder of this chapter, pertinent features of meta-analysis are discussed briefly, and then four examples of actual replicated field studies are described. In each of these, meta-analysis was used to study multiple replications of a basic design in order to strengthen the inferences that could be made. The basic designs that were replicated differ markedly in the examples. Finally, some design approaches for replication in field settings are discussed.

META-ANALYSIS

Meta-analysis is commonly used to synthesize the results of multiple, related research studies. Those who are not familiar with meta-analysis can find a brief overview and a completely worked example in Schafer (1999). Extensive discussions on a wide array of meta-analysis topics can be found in Hedges and Olkin (1985), Cooper and Hedges (1994), and Chapters 12 and 31 in this volume.

An effect size measure calculated within a study is fundamental to meta-analysis. The effect size measure might be used to compare two groups or to relate two variables. For example, Hedges and Olkin's (1985) d index is the bias-adjusted difference between the means of two groups divided by the pooled standard deviation. The correlation between two variables

in a study is another example of an effect size index. To be used in meta-analysis, the effect size measure must have a transformation to a normally distributed statistic with a known (or very stably estimable) variance.

Ways for a researcher to relate the size of the effect (i.e., the effect size index) with study characteristics are described in the references above. Equations such as those in multiple regression may be written using study characteristics as predictors of the effect size index as the criterion. The study characteristics may be descriptive of settings, participants, treatment implementations, or outcome variables. Virtually anything that might differentiate studies from each other could be analyzed as study characteristics. Indeed, one way to extend the use of replicated field study (or other) designs is to plan for the study of effect sizes in replicates that differ from each other systematically.

EXAMPLES OF REPLICATED FIELD STUDY DESIGNS

Example 1: Replicates of a One-Group Pre-Post Design

Our first example used a one-group, pre-post study, which is a descriptive (nonexperimental) design, as the basic building block. The research problem studied by Guthrie, Schafer, Von Secker, and Alban (2000) was the relationship between reading instruction in schools and gains or losses (growth) in student achievement in these schools over a year's time. Each school provided one replicate of the basic design.

All teachers in each school were surveyed using a questionnaire with six subscales, each of which gauged the degree of emphasis devoted to an approach to reading instruction. The questionnaire had been developed using factor analysis on data from a fourth district in an earlier study. These provided the independent variables in the meta-analysis, which were the school means across teachers on the six subscales.

The pretest and posttest data came from two consecutive yearly administrations of a statewide achievement test that reported school means and standard deviations in six content areas for two grade levels (third and fifth) in each school. The effect size index used was the bias-corrected, pretest-posttest difference between school means at a given grade level in a content area, divided by the pooled standard deviation across the two years. The order of subtraction was such that a positive difference showed improvement. The study was replicated in the six content areas at both grade levels in each of the 33 schools in three volunteer districts, so there was a total of 396 effect sizes to serve as dependent variables in the meta-analysis.

The meta-analysis was used to evaluate the relationships between the six instructional variables and the achievement growth effect sizes at the school level. Each instructional variable was studied as it related individually to growth and as a unique correlate of growth in a six-predictor model. Each of the six content areas at each of the grade levels was analyzed separately. The results of the meta-analysis were interpretable and were generally consistent with expectations based on an extensive literature review for these variables.

A comparison of 2 years of achievement test data for one school would not have been very interesting. Although the school might develop hypotheses to help it explain the observed direction and degree of growth, there are far too many plausible competing explanations for the difference for the results to have broader interest for insights about instruction. Effects of noninstructional events such as teacher turnover, test form calibrations, and student aptitude could also produce change over a 1-year time interval, for example. However, at least some of these and other rival explanations become less plausible if instruction-achievement relationships are observed across replicates, as they were in this study. Indeed, only through the availability of replications of the fundamental growth study design was it possible to relate instructional characteristics of the schools with school-level differences among gains.

Example 2: Replicates of a Static Groups Comparison Design

The building block in this study was a static groups comparison design, in which intact groups are randomly assigned to treatments (Campbell & Stanley, 1963). Schafer, Swanson, Bené, and Newberry (2001) studied the effects of a treatment for high school teachers on achievement of their students. The treatment consisted of receiving (vs. not receiving) a workshop centering on an element of an instructional method (use of rubrics).

Within each of four content areas, districts nominated teacher pairs, also nominating a class for each member of each pair with comparable abilities. The researchers had 46 teacher pairs who completed the study, evenly divided among the four content areas (i.e., 92 teachers and 3,191 of their students supplied data that were analyzed in the study).

The teachers in each pair were randomly assigned to treatment or control conditions. The respective workshops on ways to use rubrics instructionally (there were four workshops, one for each content area) were received by the teachers in the treatment group; the other 46 teachers were excused. All 92 teachers then returned to their regular classrooms. At the end of the study's duration, each student completed a test in the appropriate content area. Each test had two sections, a selected-response part and a constructed-response part. It was hypothesized that there might be a greater effect on the constructed-response sections since they were scored using the rubrics that were discussed in the workshops, so effect sizes were defined separately for the two item formats. Each effect size was the difference between the means of the teacher pair's two classes divided by the pooled standard deviation and was scaled such that a positive effect size favored the treatment.

This study was included within a larger study that necessitated more than one form of the test, so there were three forms in each content area. They were distributed randomly within each classroom, which yielded 276 effect sizes in all, across the four content areas: six effect sizes (three forms for each of the two formats) for each of the 46 teacher pairs.

Using meta-analysis, it was possible to synthesize the results of these disparate conditions (six nonequated test scores in each of four distinct content areas) and to differentiate the findings by contents and by item types. The pattern of outcomes was interpretable and related to prior literature and the research context.

There are too many plausible explanations other than the workshops for observed achievement differences between the two intact groups for any one of this study's single-replicate designs, in isolation, to be interesting as evidence that the independent variable caused differences between the groups. Using meta-analysis, however, it was possible to synthesize findings from these multiple parallel replications in order to enhance the ability to draw inferences from the overall results.

Example 3: Replicates of a Correlated-Groups Design

The building block in the third example was a correlated-groups design, in which there are paired observations, one member from one condition and the other from another condition. Schafer, Gagné, and Lissitz (2005) were interested in studying whether trained scorers could be resistant to variation in quality of expression when grading essays, where quality of expression was irrelevant to the response characteristics being scored. Working with a statewide test that measured two writing content areas and four nonwriting content areas using single student answer booklets with exclusively constructed-response formats, they selected 130 already scored booklets, half (65) of which were scored high and half (65) low in all six content areas, and used trained professionals to improve the quality of expression (but not scored response characteristics) in the booklets that were scored low and deteriorate the quality of expression in the booklets that were scored high. The new booklets were rated by trained scorers, interspersed among a larger sample of booklets that came from the next year's state administration.

The basic replicate in their study was the item. There were 81 items in each booklet that were studied, ranging from 3 in the writing content area to 30 in mathematics. Each item was responded to by 130 students, and each student had two scores, one for the original response and one for the altered response. The two scores that were of interest in the research were the score from the poorer expression condition and the score from the better expression condition.

The effect size index was defined for each item as the mean from the better expression condition minus the mean from the poorer expression condition, divided by the square root of the average of the item variances from the two conditions. The standard error of the effect size took the correlation between the two conditions across students into account. The independent variable in the meta-analysis was the content areas.

The effectiveness of the manipulation was supported by the sizable effect sizes found for the two writing content areas. The negligible effect sizes found in the other four content areas supported the ability of the raters to resist characteristics of expression when grading other aspects of student responses.

The basic replicate design in this example is stronger than in the other examples since it is fundamentally a repeated-measures design. For any one replicate (item), however, the information is too sparse to reach interesting conclusions; only one content would be studied, the item may have characteristics that limit the degree to which its finding could be generalized, and the effectiveness of the manipulation could not have been evaluated, for example. But by using multiple replications of the basic design, it was possible to overcome all the limitations cited and to compare findings across the content areas.

Example 4: Replicates of a Correlational Design

The fourth example used a correlational design, in which two variables are correlated, as its building block. Effects of test administrator characteristics on test scores were investigated by Schafer, Papapolydorou, Rahman, and Parker (2005). They studied a statewide test that included multiple preassessment activities such as discussions, demonstrations, and projects and was administered by teachers who, within schools, were randomly assigned to randomly formed groups of students. Within each school, the researchers found correlations between test scores on six content areas and teacher characteristics such as gender, teaching experience, and familiarity with the test.

Both the third and fifth grades completed the test, and both were studied in the research. Thus, the basic replicate in this study was the school–grade level combination. Only schools that showed variation among the teacher administrators were included for the analysis of any given characteristic.

The effect size measure in this study was the correlation coefficient. There were five teacher-administrator characteristics, six tested content areas, and two grade levels, so there were as many as 60 correlations possible at each school. These were treated as unrelated correlation sources and analyzed separately in 60 meta-analyses. To enhance the ability to generalize to other contexts, the researchers used mixed model analyses as recommended by Hedges and Vevea (1998).

The findings were interpreted to support the assignment of examiners to test groups without regard for their effects on scores. Had the study been restricted to one grade at one school, the sample size would have been too small, there would have been too few test groups, and the breadth of possible variables that could be confounded with examiner characteristics for a small number of teachers would have meant that the results would not have been very interesting. The large number of school-grade combinations alone enhanced the significance of the research, as well as the ability to evaluate consistency between the results for different grades and different content areas.

Discussion

This chapter advocated the use of replicated field studies by planning replications when doing research in field settings, thus capitalizing on the availability of multiple study venues usually found in the field. Four examples of replicated field studies were presented. The examples illustrate not only different basic designs but also ways in which replicated field studies have been synthesized through meta-analysis, thus enhancing the inferences that they can yield. Furthermore, when replicated field studies are used, it is possible to plan for the measurement and analysis of variables that could prove useful to model effect sizes in a meta-analysis (such as the instructional variables in Example 1). Fortunately, meta-analysis for a replicated field study is far easier to implement than a traditional meta-analysis of a disparate literature because there are fewer challenges such as differences in design, incompleteness of information, and inconsistencies in reporting results across studies.

Best Practices in Replication

A researcher who is planning to use a replicated field study design must make several decisions. Some of these are discussed here.

Choice of Basic Design

The strongest design that can be used should be chosen. When the basic design is stronger, so are the inferences that can be derived from each replicate and thus from the meta-analysis across replicates. Cook and Campbell (1979) provide a useful overview of designs that are appropriate

for applied research and discuss their comparable strengths and weaknesses.

It is important to be clear what variables are independent and dependent in the basic design. If the independent variable can be assigned to groups, the researcher should capitalize on that, which was done in two of the examples. It was possible to manipulate the workshop in the second example and to assign teachers randomly to groups in the fourth.

The Effect Size Measure

The size of the effect for each replicate must be represented in terms of both direction and strength of relationship between independent and dependent variables. It must result in a normally distributed index that has a known (or estimable) variance. Rosenthal (1994) provides several possibilities. Three common examples that depend on how the independent and dependent variables are scaled are the correlation coefficient, r (both variables are continuous); the log-odds ratio, L (both variables are dichotomous); or bias-corrected d (the independent variable is a dichotomy, and the dependent variable is continuous).

Maintaining Effect Size Independence

Effect sizes are assumed independent in a meta-analysis. That is generally true across studies but not always within studies. There were differences in the degrees of dependence among effect sizes in our examples. Some dependencies were created by measuring the six content areas in each school in the first study. These were ignored in the analysis because each grade level and content area was analyzed separately. In the second study, the six tests were analyzed together. However, a Bonferroni-like correction was applied in the analyses to correct for effect size dependencies, as discussed by Gleser and Olkin (1994). The items were independent in the third example, except that they appeared in the same positions across the booklets; this was not reflected in the analysis. The fourth example was much like the first in that each school produced several effect sizes, but they were analyzed separately.

Care should be taken in replicated field studies to maintain separation among the sites at which the replications occur. Sharing of information among participants can threaten effect size independence across replications. This could have been a problem in the third example, for instance.

The Variables to Be Measured

It is an advantage in any meta-analysis to measure variables that might be related to the effect size across studies (these are usually called study characteristics). In replicated field studies, these would be replicate characteristics. To develop a list of possible replicate characteristics that would be useful to measure, a researcher could think about how he or she might explain why differences might appear in effect sizes across the replicates (i.e., when might effects be larger, smaller, or even in reversed directions, from replicate to replicate). These explanations will virtually always be based on variables that could be measured or isolated, such as the different content areas in all of our examples. Other such variables might be descriptive of persons, such as their demographics or aptitudes, or of settings such as physical characteristics of schools or classrooms. Replicate characteristics are data that can be analyzed by correlating them, as independent variables, to the effect sizes, as dependent variables, in the meta-analysis, similar to what is done in multiple regression. The possibility of assessing replicate characteristics that could be related to effect sizes is an opportunity for creatively designing robust multistudy research through replication.

Finally, the principle of replication can be used sequentially to study whether effects generalize to groups, areas, or variables beyond those that have already been studied in a research program. This may require the researcher to involve populations beyond those available in the original field setting.

Meta-Analysis Model

Meta-analysis is a relatively new method of data analysis. A recent advance has been development of methods for random effects model analyses. Hedges and Vevea (1998) describe a straightforward and relatively simple modification that was used in the fourth example. They provide a worked example for researchers who are interested in using random or mixed models. Recent work has shown how hierarchical linear modeling can be used to implement random

and mixed model analyses (Chapter 31, this volume); see Kalaian (2003) for applications that are specifically designed for replicated field study designs. An advantage of using a random model is that the results generalize to a population of studies not included in the present analysis, whereas in fixed analyses, the conclusions are restricted to the specific replications themselves. Hedges and Vevea discuss the conditions under which each type of analysis, fixed or random, is more appropriate.

REFERENCES

Campbell, D. T., & Stanley, J. C. (1963). Experimental and quasi-experimental designs for research on teaching. In N. L. Gage (Ed.), *Handbook of research on teaching* (pp. 171–246). Chicago: Rand McNally.

Cook, T. D., & Campbell, D. T. (1979). *Quasi-experimentation: Design & analysis issues for field settings.* Chicago: Rand McNally.

Cooper, H., & Hedges, L. V. (1994). *The handbook of research synthesis.* New York: Russell Sage Foundation.

Gleser, L. J., & Olkin, I. (1994). Stochastically dependent effect sizes. In H. Cooper & L. V. Hedges (Eds.), *The handbook of research synthesis* (pp. 339–355). New York: Russell Sage Foundation.

Guthrie, J. T., Schafer, W. D., Von Secker, C., & Alban, T. (2000). Contributions of instructional practices to reading achievement in a statewide improvement program. *Journal of Educational Research, 93,* 211–225.

Hedges, L. V., & Olkin, I. (1985). *Statistical methods for meta-analysis.* Orlando, FL: Academic Press.

Hedges, L. V., & Vevea, J. (1998). Fixed- and random-effects models in meta-analysis. *Psychological Methods, 3,* 486–504.

Johnson, B. (2001). Toward a new classification of nonexperimental quantitative research. *Educational Researcher, 30*(2), 3–13.

Kalaian, S. A. (2003). Meta-analysis methods for synthesizing treatment effects in multisite studies: Hierarchical linear modeling (HLM) perspective. *Practical Assessment, Research & Evaluation, 8*(15). Retrieved June 5, 2006, from http://PAREonline.net/getvn.asp?v=8&n=15

Pedhazur, E. J. (1997). *Multiple regression in behavioral research: Explanation and prediction* (3rd ed.). Orlando, FL: Harcourt Brace.

Rosenthal, R. (1994). Parametric measures of effect size. In H. Cooper & L. V. Hedges (Eds.), *The handbook of research synthesis* (pp. 231–244). New York: Russell Sage Foundation.

Schafer, W. D. (1999). An overview of meta-analysis. *Measurement and Evaluation in Counseling and Development, 32,* 43–61.

Schafer, W. D. (2001). Replication: A design principle for field research. *Practical Assessment, Research & Evaluation, 7*(15). Retrieved June 5, 2006, from http://PAREonline.net/getvn.asp?v=7&n=15

Schafer, W. D., Gagné, P., & Lissitz, R. W. (2005). Resistance to confounding style and content in scoring constructed response items. *Educational Measurement: Issues and Practice, 24*(2), 22–28.

Schafer, W. D., Papapolydorou, M., Rahman, T., & Parker, L. (2005). *Effects of test administrator characteristics on achievement test scores.* Montreal, Canada: National Council on Measurement in Education Convention. Retrieved October 9, 2007 from http://marces.org/files/NCME SchaferPaperFNL3%5B1%5D%5B1%5D.8.05.doc

Schafer, W. D., Swanson, G., Bené, N., & Newberry, G. (2001). Effects of teacher knowledge of rubrics on student achievement in four content areas. *Applied Measurement in Education, 14,* 151–170.

11

BEST PRACTICES IN QUASI-EXPERIMENTAL DESIGNS

Matching Methods for Causal Inference

Elizabeth A. Stuart

Donald B. Rubin

Many studies in social science that aim to estimate the effect of an intervention suffer from treatment selection bias, where the units who receive the treatment may have different characteristics from those in the control condition. These preexisting differences between the groups must be controlled to obtain approximately unbiased estimates of the effects of interest. For example, in a study estimating the effect of bullying on high school graduation, students who were bullied are likely to be very different from students who were not bullied on a wide range of characteristics, such as socioeconomic status and academic performance, even before the bullying began. It is crucial to try to separate out the causal effect of the bullying from the effect of these preexisting differences between the "treated" and "control" groups. Matching methods provide a way to attempt to do so.

Random assignment of units to receive (or not receive) the treatment of interest ensures that there are no systematic differences between the treatment and control groups before treatment assignment. However, random assignment is often infeasible in social science research, due to either ethical or practical concerns. Matching methods constitute a growing collection of techniques that attempt to replicate, as closely as possible, the ideal of randomized experiments when using observational data.

There are two key ways in which the matching methods we discuss replicate a randomized experiment. First, matching aims to select subsamples of the treated and control groups that are, at worst, only randomly different from one another on all observed covariates. In other words, matching seeks to identify subsamples of treated and control units that are "balanced" with respect to observed covariates: The observed covariate distributions are essentially the same in the treatment and control groups. The methods described in this chapter examine how best to choose subsamples from the original treated and control groups such that the distributions of covariates in the matched groups are substantially more similar than in the original groups, when this is possible. A second crucial similarity between a randomized experiment and a matched observational study is that each study has two clear stages. The first stage is design, in which the units to be compared are selected, without use of the values of the outcome variables. Like the design of a randomized experiment, the matches are chosen without access to any of the outcome data, thereby preventing intentional or unintentional bias when selecting a particular matched sample to achieve a desired result. Only after the design is set does the second stage begin, which involves the analyses of the outcome, estimating treatment effects using the matched sample. We only discuss propensity score methods that are applicable at the design stage in the sense that they do not involve any outcome data. Some methods that use propensity scores, including some weighting techniques, can involve outcome data, and such methods are not discussed here.

This chapter reviews the diverse literature on matching methods, with particular attention paid to providing practical guidance based on applied and simulation results that indicate the potential of matching methods for bias reduction in observational studies. We first provide an introduction to the goal of matching and a very brief history of these methods; the second section presents the theory and motivation behind propensity scores, discussing how they are a crucial component when using matching methods. We then discuss other methods of controlling for covariates in observational studies, such as regression analysis, and explain why matching methods (particularly when combined with regression in the analysis stage) are more effective. The implementation of matching methods, including challenges and evaluations of their performance, is then discussed. We conclude with recommendations for researchers and a discussion of software currently available. Throughout the chapter, we motivate the methods using data from the National Supported Work Demonstration (Dehejia & Wahba, 1999; LaLonde, 1986).

Designing Observational Studies

The methods described here are relevant for two types of situations. The first, which is arguably more common in social science research, is a situation where all covariate and outcome data are already available on a large set of units, but a subset of those units will be chosen for use in the analysis. This subsetting (or "matching") is done with the aim of selecting subsets of the treated and control groups with similar observed covariate distributions, thereby increasing robustness in observational studies by reducing reliance on modeling assumptions. The main objective of the matching is to reduce bias. But what about variance? Although discarding units in the matching process will result in smaller sample sizes and thus might appear to lead to increases in sampling variance, this is not always the case because improved balance in the covariate distributions will decrease the variance of estimators (Snedecor & Cochran, 1980). H. Smith (1997) gives an empirical example where estimates from one-to-one matching have lower estimated standard deviations than estimates from a linear regression, even though thousands of observations were discarded in the one-to-one matching, and all were used in the regression.

The second situation is one in which outcome data are not yet collected on the units, and cost constraints prohibit measuring the outcome variables on all units. In that situation, matching methods can help choose for follow-up the control units most similar to those in the treated group. The matching identifies those control units who are most similar to the treated units so that rather than random samples of units being discarded, the units discarded are those most irrelevant as points of comparison with the treated units. This second situation motivated much of the early work in matching methods (Althauser & Rubin, 1970; Rubin, 1973a, 1973b), which compared the benefits of choosing matched versus random samples for follow-up.

Matching methods can be considered as one method for designing an observational study, in the sense of selecting the most appropriate data for reliable estimation of causal effects, as discussed in Cochran and Rubin (1973), Rubin (1977, 1997, 2004), Rosenbaum (1999, 2002), and Heckman, Hidehiko, and Todd (1997). These papers stress the importance of carefully designing an observational study by making appropriate choices when it is impossible to have full control (e.g., randomization). The careful design of an observational study must involve making careful choices about the data used in making comparisons of outcomes in treatment and control conditions.

Other approaches that attempt to control for covariate differences between treated and control units include regression analysis or selection models, which estimate parameters of a model for the outcome of interest conditional on the covariates (and a treatment/control indicator). Matching methods are preferable to these model-based adjustments for two key reasons. First, matching methods do not use the outcome values in the design of the study and thus preclude the selection of a particular design to yield a desired result. As stated by Rubin (2001),

> Arguably, the most important feature of experiments is that we must decide on the way data will be collected before observing the outcome data. If we could try hundreds of designs and for each see the resultant answer, we could capitalize on random variation in answers and choose the design that generated the answer we wanted! The lack of availability of outcome data when designing experiments is a tremendous stimulus for "honesty" in experiments and can be in well-designed observational studies as well. (p. 169)

Second, when there are large differences in the covariate distributions between the groups, standard model-based adjustments rely heavily on extrapolation and model-based assumptions. Matching methods highlight these differences and also provide a way to limit reliance on the inherently untestable modelling assumptions and the consequential sensitivity to those assumptions.

Matching methods and regression-based model adjustments should also not be seen as competing methods but rather as complementary, which is a decades-old message. In fact, as discussed earlier, much research over a period of decades (Cochran & Rubin, 1973; Ho, Imai, King, & Stuart, 2007; Rubin, 1973b, 1979; Rubin & Thomas, 2000) has shown that the best approach is to combine the two methods by, for example, doing regression adjustment on matched samples. Selecting matched samples reduces bias due to covariate differences, and regression analysis on those matched samples can adjust for small remaining differences and increase efficiency of estimates. These approaches are similar in spirit to the recent "doubly robust" procedures of Robins and Rotnitzky (2001), which provide consistent estimation of causal effects if either the model of treatment assignment (e.g., the propensity scores) or the model of the outcome is correct, although these later methods are more sensitive to a correctly specified model used for weighting and generally do not have the clear

separation of stages of design and analysis that we advocate here.

The National Supported Work Demonstration

The National Supported Work (NSW) Demonstration was a federally and privately funded randomized experiment done in the 1970s to estimate the effects of a job training program for disadvantaged workers. Since a series of analyses beginning in the 1980s (Dehejia & Wahba, 1999, 2002; LaLonde, 1986; J. Smith & Todd, 2005), the data set from this study has become a canonical example in the literature on matching methods.

In the NSW Demonstration, eligible individuals were randomly selected to participate in the training program. Treatment group members and control group members (those not selected to participate) were followed up to estimate the effect of the program on later earnings. Because the NSW program was a randomized experiment, the difference in means in the outcomes between the randomized treated and control groups is an unbiased estimate of the average treatment effect for the subjects in the randomized experiment, and indicated that, on average, among all male participants, the program raised annual earnings by approximately $800.

To investigate whether certain nonexperimental methods yielded a result similar to that from the randomized experiment, LaLonde (1986) attempted to use certain nonexperimental methods to estimate the treatment effect, with the experimental estimate of the treatment effect as a benchmark. LaLonde used, in analogy with then current econometric practice, two sources of comparison units, both large national databases: the Panel Survey of Income Dynamics (PSID) and the Current Population Survey (CPS). LaLonde found that the nonexperimental methods gave a wide range of impact estimates, ranging from approximately −$16,000 to $700, and concluded that it was difficult to replicate the experimental results with any of the nonexperimental methods available at that time.

In the 1990s, Dehejia and Wahba (1999) used propensity score matching methods to estimate the effect of the NSW program, using comparison groups similar to those used by LaLonde. They found that most of the comparison group members used by LaLonde were in fact very dissimilar to the treated group members and that by restricting the analysis to the comparison group members who looked most similar to the treated group, they were able to replicate results found in the NSW experimental data. Using the CPS, which had a larger pool of individuals comparable to those in the treated group, for the sample of men with 2 years of pretreatment earnings data available, Dehejia and Wahba (1999) obtained a range of treatment effect estimates of $1,559 to $1,681, quite close to the experimental estimate of approximately $1,800 for the same sample. Although there is still debate regarding the use of nonexperimental data to estimate the effects of the NSW program (see, e.g., Dehejia, 2005; J. Smith & Todd, 2005), this example has nonetheless remained an important illustration of the use of matching methods in practice.

We will use a subset of these data as an illustrative example throughout this chapter. The "full" data set that we use has 185 treated males who had 2 years of preprogram earnings data (1974 and 1975) as well as 429 comparison males from the CPS who were younger than age 55, unemployed in 1976, and had income below the poverty line in 1975. The goal of matching will be to select the comparison males who look most similar to the treated group on other covariates. The covariates available in this data set include age, education level, high school degree, marital status, race, ethnicity, and earnings in 1974 and 1975. In this chapter, we do not attempt to obtain a reliable estimate of the effect of the NSW program but rather use the data only to illustrate matching methods.[1]

Notation and Background

As first formalized by Rubin (1974), the estimation of causal effects, whether from data in a randomized experiment or from information obtained from an observational study, is inherently a comparison of potential outcomes on individual units, where a unit is a physical object (e.g., a person or a school) at a particular point in time. In particular, the causal effect for unit i is the comparison of unit i's outcome if unit i receives the treatment (unit i's potential outcome under treatment), $Y_i(1)$, and unit i's outcome if unit i receives the control (unit i's potential outcome under control), $Y_i(0)$. The "fundamental problem of causal inference"

(Holland, 1986; Rubin, 1978) is that, for each unit, we can observe only one of these potential outcomes because each unit will receive either treatment or control, not both. The estimation of causal effects can thus be thought of as a missing data problem, where at least half of the values of interest (the unobserved potential outcomes) are missing (Rubin, 1976a). We are interested in predicting the unobserved potential outcomes, thus enabling the comparison of the potential outcomes under treatment and control.

For efficient causal inference and good estimation of the unobserved potential outcomes, we would like to compare groups of treated and control units that are as similar as possible. If the groups are very different, the prediction of the $Y_i(1)$ for the control group will be made using information from treated units, who look very different from those in the control group, and likewise, the prediction of the $Y_i(0)$ for the treated units will be made using information from control units, who look very different from the treated units.

Randomized experiments use a known randomized assignment mechanism to ensure "balance" of the covariates between the treated and control groups: The groups will be only randomly different from one another on all background covariates, observed and unobserved. In observational studies, we must posit an assignment mechanism, which stochastically determines which units receive treatment and which receive control. A key initial assumption in observational studies is that of strongly ignorable treatment assignment (Rosenbaum & Rubin, 1983b), which implies that (a) treatment assignment (W) is unconfounded (Rubin, 1990); that is, it is independent of the potential outcomes ($Y(0), Y(1)$) given the covariates (X): $W \perp (Y(0), Y(1)) | X$, and (b) there is a positive probability of receiving each treatment for all values of X: $0 < P(W = 1 | X) < 1$ for all X. Part (b) essentially states that there is overlap in the propensity scores. However, since below we discuss methods to impose this by discarding units outside the region of overlap, in the rest of the chapter, we focus on the first part of the strong ignorability assumption: unconfounded treatment assignment, sometimes called "selection on observables" or "no hidden bias." Imbens (2004) discusses the plausibility of this assumption in economics, and this issue is discussed further later in this chapter, including tests for sensitivity to the assumption of unconfounded treatment assignment.

A second assumption that is made in nearly all studies estimating causal effects (including randomized experiments) is the stable unit treatment value assumption (SUTVA; Rubin, 1980). There are two components to this assumption. The first is that there is only one version of each treatment possible for each unit. The second component is that of no interference: The treatment assignment of one unit does not affect the potential outcomes of any other units. This is also sometimes referred to as the assumption of "no spillover." Some recent work has discussed relaxing this SUTVA assumption, in the context of school effects (Hong & Raudenbush, 2006) or neighborhood effects (Sobel, 2006).

History of Matching Methods

Matching methods have been in use since the first half of the 20th century, with much of the early work in sociology (Althauser & Rubin, 1970; Chapin, 1947; Greenwood, 1945). However, a theoretical basis for these methods was not developed until the late 1960s and early 1970s. This development began with a paper by Cochran (1968), which particularly examined subclassification but had clear connections with matching, including Cochran's occasional use of the term *stratified matching* to refer to subclassification. Cochran and Rubin (1973) and Rubin (1973a, 1973b) continued this development for situations with one covariate, and Cochran and Rubin (1973) and Rubin (1976b, 1976c) extended the results to multivariate settings.

Dealing with multiple covariates was a challenge due to both computational and data problems. With more than just a few covariates, it becomes very difficult to find matches with close or exact values of all covariates. An important advance was made in 1983 with the introduction of the propensity score by Rosenbaum and Rubin (1983b), a generalization of discriminant matching (Cochran & Rubin, 1973; Rubin, 1976b, 1976c). Rather than requiring close or exact matches on all covariates, matching on the scalar propensity score enables the construction of matched sets with similar distributions of covariates.

Developments were also made regarding the theory behind matching methods, particularly in the context of affinely invariant matching methods (such as most implementations of propensity score matching) with ellipsoidally symmetric covariate distributions (Rubin & Stuart, 2006; Rubin & Thomas, 1992a, 1992b, 1996). Affinely invariant matching methods are those that yield the same matches following an affine (e.g., linear) transformation of the data (Rubin & Thomas, 1992a). This theoretical development grew out of initial work on equal percent bias-reducing (EPBR) matching methods in Rubin (1976a, 1976c). EPBR methods reduce bias in all covariate directions by the same percentage, thus ensuring that if close matches are obtained in some direction (such as the discriminant), then the matching is also reducing bias in all other directions and so cannot be increasing bias in an outcome that is a linear combination of the covariates. Methods that are not EPBR will infinitely increase bias for some linear combinations of the covariates.

Since the initial work on matching methods, which was primarily in sociology and statistics, matching methods have been growing in popularity, with developments and applications in a variety of fields, including economics (Imbens, 2004), medicine (D'Agostino, 1998), public health (Christakis & Iwashyna, 2003), political science (Ho et al., 2007), and sociology (Morgan & Harding, 2006; Winship & Morgan, 1999). A review of the older work and more recent applications can also be found in Rubin (2006).

PROPENSITY SCORES

In applications, it is often very difficult to find close matches on each covariate. Rather than attempting to match on all of the covariates individually, propensity score matching matches on the scalar propensity score, which is the most important scalar summary of the covariates. Propensity scores, first introduced in Rosenbaum and Rubin (1983b), provided a key step in the continual development of matching methods by enabling the formation of matched sets that have balance on a large number of covariates.

The propensity score for unit i is defined as the probability of receiving the treatment given the observed covariates: $e_i(X) = P(W_i = 1|X)$. There are two key theorems relating to their use (Rosenbaum & Rubin, 1983b). The first is that propensity scores are balancing scores: At each value of the propensity score, the distribution of the covariates, X, that define the propensity score is the same in the treated and control groups. In other words, within a small range of propensity score values, the treated and control groups' observed covariate distributions are only randomly different from each other, thus replicating a mini-randomized experiment, at least with respect to these covariates. Second, if treatment assignment is unconfounded given the observed covariates (i.e., does not depend on the potential outcomes), then treatment assignment is also unconfounded given only the propensity score. This justifies matching or forming subclasses based on the propensity score rather than on the full set of multivariate covariates. Thus, when treatment assignment is unconfounded, for a specific value of the propensity score, the difference in means in the outcome between the treated and control units with that propensity score value is an unbiased estimate of the mean treatment effect at that propensity score value.

Abadie and Imbens (2006) present theoretical results that provide additional justification for matching on the propensity score, showing that creating estimates based on matching on one continuous covariate (such as the propensity score) is $N^{\frac{1}{2}}$ consistent, but attempting to match on more than one covariate without discarding any units is not. Thus, in this particular case, using the propensity score enables consistent estimation of treatment effects.

Propensity Score Estimation

In practice, the true propensity scores are rarely known outside of randomized experiments and thus must be estimated. Propensity scores are often estimated using logistic regression, although other methods such as classification and regression trees (CART; Breiman, Friedman, Olshen, & Stone, 1984), discriminant analysis, or generalized boosted models (McCaffrey, Ridgeway, & Morral, 2004) can also be used. Matching or subclassification is then done using the estimated propensity score (e.g., the fitted values from the logistic regression).

In the matching literature, there has been some discussion of the effects of matching using estimated rather than true propensity scores, especially regarding the variance of estimates. Theoretical and analytic work has shown that, although more bias reduction can be obtained using true propensity scores, matching on estimated

propensity scores can control variance orthogonal to the discriminant and thus can lead to more precise estimates of the treatment effect (Rubin & Thomas, 1992b, 1996). Analytic expressions for the bias and variance reduction possible for these situations are given in Rubin and Thomas (1992b). Specifically, Rubin and Thomas (1992b) state that "with large pools of controls, matching using estimated linear propensity scores results in approximately half the variance for the difference in the matched sample means as in corresponding random samples for all covariates uncorrelated with the population discriminant" (p. 802). This finding is confirmed in simulation work in Rubin and Thomas (1996) and in an empirical example in Hill, Rubin, and Thomas (1999). Hence, in situations where nearly all bias can be eliminated relatively easily, matching on the estimated propensity scores is superior to matching on the true propensity score because it will result in more precise estimates of the average treatment effect.

Model Specification

The model specification and diagnostics when estimating propensity scores are not the standard model diagnostics for logistic regression or CART, as discussed by Rubin (2004). With propensity score estimation, concern is not with the parameter estimates of the model but rather with the quality of the matches and sometimes in the accuracy of the predictions of treatment assignment (the propensity scores themselves). When the propensity scores will be used for matching or subclassification, the key diagnostic is covariate balance in the resulting matched samples or subclasses. When propensity scores are used directly in weighting adjustments, more attention should be paid to the accuracy of the model predictions since the estimates of the treatment effect may be very sensitive to the accuracy of the propensity score values themselves.

Rosenbaum and Rubin (1984); Perkins, Tu, Underhill, Zhou, and Murray (2000); Dehejia and Wahba (2002); and Michalopoulos, Bloom, and Hill (2004) described propensity score model-fitting strategies that involve examining the resulting covariate balance in subclasses defined by the propensity score. If covariates (or their squares or cross-products) are found to be unbalanced, those terms are then included in the propensity score specification, which should improve balance, subject to sample size limitations.

Drake (1993) stated that treatment effect estimates are more sensitive to misspecification of the model of the outcome than to misspecification of the propensity score model. Dehejia and Wahba (1999, 2002) and Zhao (2004) also provided evidence that treatment effect estimates may not be too sensitive to the propensity score specification. However, these evaluations are fairly limited; for example, Drake considered only two covariates.

WHEN IS REGRESSION ANALYSIS TRUSTWORTHY?

It has been known for many years that regression analysis can lead to misleading results when the covariate distributions in the groups are very different (e.g., Cochran, 1957; Cochran & Rubin, 1973; Rubin, 1973b). Rubin (2001, p. 174) stated the three basic conditions that must generally be met for regression analyses to be trustworthy, in the case of approximately normally distributed covariates:[2]

1. The difference in the means of the propensity scores in the two groups being compared must be small (e.g., the means must be less than half a standard deviation apart), unless the situation is benign in the sense that:
   a. the distributions of the covariates in both groups are nearly symmetric,
   b. the distributions of the covariates in both groups have nearly the same variances, and
   c. the sample sizes are approximately the same.

2. The ratio of the variances of the propensity score in the two groups must be close to 1 (e.g., 1/2 or 2 are far too extreme).

3. The ratio of the variances of the residuals of the covariates after adjusting for the propensity score must be close to 1 (e.g., 1/2 or 2 are far too extreme).

These guidelines arise from results on the bias resulting from regression analysis in samples with large initial covariate bias that show that linear regression adjustment can grossly overcorrect or undercorrect for bias when these conditions are not met (Cochran & Rubin, 1973; Rubin, 1973b, 1979, 2001). For example, when the propensity score means are one quarter of a standard deviation apart in the two groups, the ratio of the treated to control group variance is 1/2, and the model of the outcome is moderately nonlinear ($y = e^{x/2}$), linear regression adjustment can lead to 300% reduction in bias. In other words, an increase in the original bias, but 200% in the opposite direction! Results are even more striking for larger initial bias between the groups, where the amount of bias remaining can be substantial even if most (in percentage) of the initial bias has been removed (see Rubin, 2001, Table 1).

Despite these striking results, regression adjustment on unmatched data is still a common method for attempting to estimate causal effects. Matching methods provide a way to avoid extrapolation and reliance on the modeling assumptions, by ensuring the comparison of treated and control units with similar covariate distributions, when this is possible, and warning of the inherent extrapolation in regression models when there is little overlap in distributions.

IMPLEMENTATION OF MATCHING METHODS

We now turn to the implementation of matching methods. There are five key steps when using matching methods to estimate causal effects. These are (1) choosing the covariates to be used in the matching process; (2) defining a distance measure, used to assess whether units are "similar"; (3) choosing a specific matching algorithm to form matched sets; (4) diagnosing the matches obtained (and iterating between [2] and [3]); and finally, (5) estimating the effect of the treatment on the outcome, using the matched sets found in (4) and possibly other adjustments. The following sections provide further information on each of these steps.

Choosing the Covariates

The first step is to choose the covariates on which close matches are desired. As discussed earlier, an underlying assumption when estimating causal effects using nonexperimental data is that treatment assignment is unconfounded (Rosenbaum & Rubin, 1983b) given the covariates used in the matching process. To make this assumption plausible, it is important to include in the matching procedure any covariates that may be related to treatment assignment and the outcome; the most important covariates to include are those that are related to treatment assignment because the matching will typically be done for many outcomes. Theoretical and empirical research has shown the importance of including a large set of covariates in the matching procedure (Hill, Reiter, & Zanutto, 2004; Lunceford & Davidian, 2004; Rubin & Thomas, 1996). Greevy, Lu, Silber, and Rosenbaum (2004) provide an example where the power of the subsequent analysis in a randomized experiment is increased by matching on 14 covariates, even though only 2 of those covariates are directly related to the outcome (the other 12 are related to the outcome only through their correlation with the 2 on which the outcome explicitly depends).

A second consideration is that the covariates included in the matching must be "proper" covariates in the sense of not being affected by treatment assignment. It is well-known that matching or subclassifying on a variable affected by treatment assignment can lead to substantial bias in the estimated treatment effect (Frangakis & Rubin, 2002; Greenland, 2003; Imbens, 2004). All variables should thus be carefully considered as to whether they are "proper" covariates. This is especially important in fields such as epidemiology and political science, where the treatment assignment date is often somewhat undefined. If it is deemed to be critical to control for a variable potentially affected by treatment assignment, it is better to exclude that variable in the matching procedure and include it in the analysis model for the outcome (Reinisch, Sanders, Mortensen, & Rubin, 1995) and hope for balance on it, or use principal stratification methods (Frangakis & Rubin, 2002) to deal with it.

Selecting a Distance Measure

The next step when using matching methods is to define the "distance" measure that will be used to decide whether units are "similar" in terms of their covariate values. "Distance" is in quotes because the measure will not necessarily be a proper "full-rank" distance in the mathematical sense. One extreme distance measure is that of exact matching, which groups units only if they have the same values of all the covariates. Because limited sample sizes (and large numbers of covariates) make it very difficult to obtain exact matches, distance measures that are not full rank and that combine distances on

individual covariates, such as propensity scores, are commonly used in practice.

Two measures of the distance between units on multiple covariates are the Mahalanobis distance, which is full rank, and the propensity score distance, which is not. The Mahalanobis distance on covariates X between units i and j is $(X_i - X_j)\Sigma^{-1}(X_i - X_j)$, where Σ can be the true or estimated variance-covariance matrix in the treated group, the control group, or a pooled sample; the control group variance-covariance matrix is usually used. The propensity score distance is defined as the absolute difference in (true or estimated) propensity scores between two units. See the "Propensity Score Estimation" section for more details on estimating propensity scores. Gu and Rosenbaum (1993) and Rubin and Thomas (2000) compare the performance of matching methods based on Mahalanobis metric matching and propensity score matching and find that the two distance measures perform similarly when there are a relatively small number of covariates, but propensity score matching works better than Mahalanobis metric matching with large numbers of covariates (greater than 5). One reason for this is that the Mahalanobis metric is attempting to obtain balance on all possible interactions of the covariates (which is very difficult in multivariate space), effectively considering all of the interactions as equally important. In contrast, propensity score matching allows the exclusion of terms from the propensity score model and thereby the inclusion of only the important terms (e.g., main effects, two-way interactions) on which to obtain balance.

As discussed below, these distance measures can be combined or used in conjunction with exact matching on certain covariates. Combining these distance measures with exact matching on certain covariates sets the distance between two units equal to infinity if the units are not exactly matched on those covariates.

Selecting Matches

Once the distance measure is defined, the next step is to choose the matched samples. This section provides a summary of some of the most common types of matching methods, given a particular distance measure. These methods include nearest neighbor matching and its variations (such as caliper matching) and subclassification methods (such as full matching). We provide an overview of each, as well as references for further information and examples.

Nearest Neighbor Matching

Nearest neighbor matching (Rubin, 1973a) generally selects k matched controls for each treated unit (often, $k = 1$). The simplest nearest neighbor matching uses a "greedy" algorithm, which cycles through the treated units one at a time, selecting for each the available control unit with the smallest distance to the treated unit. A more sophisticated algorithm, "optimal" matching, minimizes a global measure of balance (Rosenbaum, 2002). Rosenbaum (2002) argues that the collection of matches found using optimal matching can have substantially better balance than matches found using greedy matching, without much loss in computational speed. Generally, greedy matching performs poorly with respect to average pair differences when there is intense competition for controls and performs well when there is little competition. In practical situations, when assessing the matched groups' covariate balance, Gu and Rosenbaum (1993) find that optimal matching does not in general perform any better than greedy matching in terms of creating groups with good balance but does do better at reducing the distance between pairs. As summarized

by Gu and Rosenbaum (1993), "Optimal matching picks about the same controls [as greedy matching] but does a better job of assigning them to treated units" (p. 413).

Figure 11.1 illustrates the result of a one-to-one greedy nearest neighbor matching algorithm implemented using the NSW data described in "The National Supported Work Demonstration" section. The propensity score was estimated using all covariates available in the data set. Of the 429 available control individuals, the 185 with propensity scores closest to those of the 185 treated individuals were selected as matches. We see that there is fairly good overlap throughout most of the range of propensity scores and that most of the control individuals not used as matches had very low propensity scores and so were inapposite for use as points of comparison.

When there are large numbers of control units, it is sometimes possible to get multiple good matches for each treated unit, which can reduce sampling variance in the treatment effect estimates. Although one-to-one matching is the most common, a larger number of matches for each treated unit are often possible. Unless there are many units with the same covariate values, using multiple controls for each treated unit is expected to increase bias because the second, third, and fourth closest matches are, by definition,

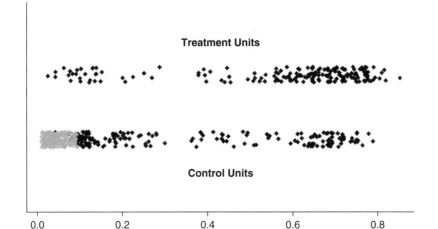

Figure 11.1   Matches chosen using 1:1 nearest neighbor matching on the propensity score. Black units were matched; gray units were unmatched. A total of 185 treated units were matched to 185 control units; 244 control units were discarded.

further away from the treated unit than is the first closest match, but using multiple matches can decrease sampling variance due to the larger matched sample size. Of course, in settings where the outcome data have yet to be collected and there are cost constraints, researchers must balance the benefit of obtaining multiple matches for each unit with the increased costs. Examples using more than one control match for each treated unit include H. Smith (1997) and Rubin and Thomas (2000).

Another key issue is whether controls can be used as matches for more than one treated unit, that is, whether the matching should be done "with replacement" or "without replacement." Matching with replacement can often yield better matches because controls that look similar to many treated units can be used multiple times. In addition, like optimal matching, when matching with replacement, the order in which the treated units are matched does not matter. However, a drawback of matching with replacement is that it may be that only a few unique control units will be selected as matches; the number of times each control is matched should be monitored and reflected in the estimated precision of estimated causal effects.

Using the NSW data, Dehejia and Wahba (2002) match with replacement from the PSID sample because there are few control individuals comparable to those in the treated group, making matching with replacement appealing. When one-to-one matching is done without replacement, nearly half of the treated group members end up with matches that are quite far away. They conclude that matching with replacement can be useful when there are a limited number of control units with values similar to those in the treated group.

Limited Exact Matching

Rosenbaum and Rubin (1985a) illustrate the futility in attempting to find matching treated and control units with the same values of all the covariates and thus not being able to find matches for most units. However, it is often desirable (and possible) to obtain exact matches on a few key covariates, such as race or sex. Combining exact matching on key covariates with propensity score matching can lead to large reductions in bias and can result in a design analogous to blocking in a randomized experiment.

For example, in Rubin (2001), the analyses are done separately for males and females, with male smokers matched to male nonsmokers and female smokers matched to female nonsmokers. Similarly, in Dehejia and Wahba (1999), the analysis is done separately for males and females.

Mahalanobis Metric Matching on Key Covariates Within Propensity Score Calipers

Caliper matching (Althauser & Rubin, 1970) selects matches within a specified range (caliper c) of a one-dimensional covariate X (which may actually be a combination of multiple covariates, such as the propensity score): $| X_{tj} - X_{cj} | \le c$ for all treatment/control matched pairs, indexed by j. Cochran and Rubin (1973) investigate various caliper sizes and show that with a normally distributed covariate, a caliper of 0.2 standard deviations can remove 98% of the bias due to that covariate, assuming all treated units are matched. Althauser and Rubin (1970) find that even a looser matching (1.0 standard deviations of X) can still remove approximately 75% of the initial bias due to X. Rosenbaum and Rubin (1985b) show that if the caliper matching is done using the propensity score, the bias reduction is obtained on all of the covariates that went into the propensity score. They suggest that a caliper of 0.25 standard deviations of the logit transformation of the propensity score can work well in general.

For situations where there are some key continuous covariates on which particularly close matches are desired, Mahalanobis matching on the key covariates can be combined with propensity score matching, resulting in particularly good balance (Rosenbaum & Rubin, 1985b; Rubin & Thomas, 2000). The Mahalanobis distance is usually calculated on covariates that are believed to be particularly predictive of the outcome of interest or of treatment assignment. For example, in the NSW Demonstration data, Mahalanobis metric matching on the 2 years of preprogram earnings could be done within propensity score calipers.

Subclassification

Rosenbaum and Rubin (1984) discuss reducing bias due to multiple covariates in observational studies through subclassification on estimated propensity scores, which forms groups of units with similar propensity scores and thus similar covariate distributions. For example, subclasses may be defined by splitting the treated and control groups at the quintiles of the propensity score in the treated group, leading to five subclasses with approximately the same number of treated units in each. That work builds on the work by Cochran (1968) on subclassification using a single covariate; when the conditional expectation of the outcome variable is a monotone function of the propensity score, creating just five propensity score subclasses removes at least 90% of the bias in the estimated treatment effect due to each of the observed covariates. Thus, five subclasses are often used, although with large sample sizes, more subclasses, or even variable-sized subclasses, are often desirable. This method is clearly related to making an ordinal version of a continuous underlying covariate.

Lunceford and Davidian (2004) assess subclassification on the propensity score and find that subclassification without subsequent within-strata model adjustment (as discussed earlier) can lead to biased answers due to residual imbalance within the strata. They suggest a need for further research on the optimal number of subclasses, a topic also discussed in Du (1998).

Subclassification is illustrated using the NSW data in Figure 11.2, where six propensity score subclasses were formed to have approximately equal numbers of treated units. All units are placed into one of the six subclasses. The control units within each subclass are given equal weight, proportional to the number of treated units in the subclass; thus the treated and control units in each subclass receive the same total weight.

If the balance achieved in matched samples selected using nearest neighbor matching is not adequate, subclassification of the matches chosen using nearest neighbor matching can be done to yield improved balance. This is illustrated in Figure 11.3, where, after one-to-one nearest neighbor matching, six subclasses have been formed with approximately the same number of treated units in each subclass. This process is illustrated in Rubin (2001) and Rubin (2007).

Full Matching

An extension of subclassification is "full matching" (Rosenbaum, 1991a, 2002), in which the matched sample is composed of matched sets (subclasses), where each matched set contains either (a) one treated unit and one or more controls or (b) one control unit and one or more treated units. Full matching is optimal in terms of minimizing a weighted average of the distances between each treated subject and each control subject within each matched set. Hansen (2004) gives a practical evaluation of the

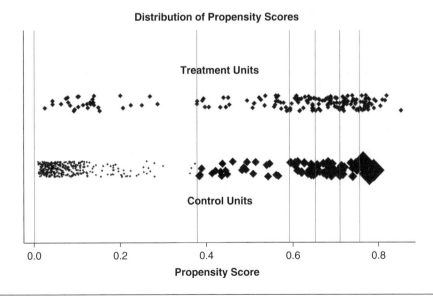

Distribution of Propensity Scores

Treatment Units

Control Units

Propensity Score

0.0   0.2   0.4   0.6   0.8

Figure 11.2   Results from subclassification on the propensity score. Subclasses are indicated by vertical lines. The weight given to each unit is represented by its symbol size; larger symbols correspond to larger weight.

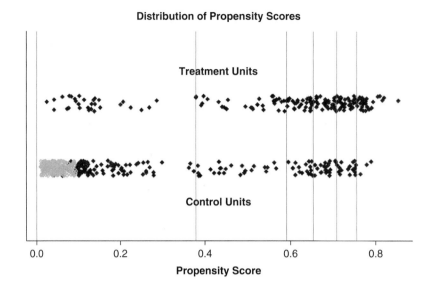

Figure 11.3   One-to-one nearest neighbor matching on the propensity score followed by subclassification. Black units were matched; gray units were unmatched. Subclasses indicated by vertical lines.

method, estimating the effect of SAT coaching, illustrating that, although the original treated and control groups had propensity score differences of 1.1 standard deviations, the matched sets from full matching differed by less than 2% of a standard deviation. To achieve efficiency gains, Hansen (2004) also describes a variation of full matching that restricts the ratio of the number of treated units to the number of control units in each matched set, a method also applied in Stuart and Green (in press).

The output from full matching is illustrated using the NSW data in Figure 11.4. Because it is not feasible to show the individual matched sets (in these data, 103 matched sets were created), the units are represented by their relative weights. All treated units receive a weight of 1 (and thus the symbols are all the same size). Control units in matched sets with many control units and few treated units receive small weight (e.g., the units with propensity scores close to 0), whereas control units in matched sets with few control units and many treated units (e.g., the units with propensity scores close to 0.8) receive large weight. The weighted treated and control group covariate distributions look very similar. As in simple subclassification, all control units within a matched set receive equal weight. However, because there are many more matched sets than with simple subclassification, the variation in the weights is much larger across matched sets.

Because subclassification and full matching place all available units into one of the subclasses, these methods may have particular appeal for researchers who are reluctant to discard some of the control units. However, these methods are not relevant for situations where the matching is being used to select units for follow-up or for situations where some units have essentially zero probability of receiving the other treatment.

Weighting Adjustments

Another method that uses all units is weighting, where observations are weighted by their inverse propensity score (Czajka, Hirabayashi, Little, & Rubin, 1992; Lunceford & Davidian, 2004; McCaffrey et al., 2004). Weighting can also be thought of as the limit of subclassification as the number of observations and the number of subclasses go to infinity. Weighting methods are based on Horvitz-Thompson estimation (Horvitz & Thompson, 1952), used frequently in sample surveys. A drawback of weighting adjustments is that, as with Horvitz-Thompson estimation, the sampling variance of resulting weighted estimators can be very large if the weights are extreme (if the propensity scores are close to 0 or 1). Thus, the subclassification or full matching approaches, which also use all units, may be more appealing because the resulting weights are less variable.

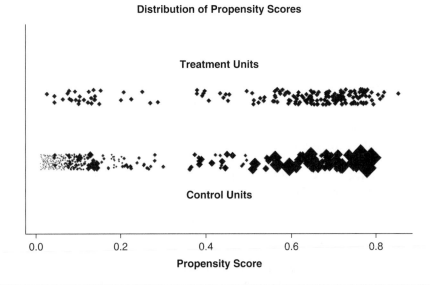

Figure 11.4   Results from full matching on the propensity score. The weight given to each unit is represented by its size; larger symbols correspond to higher weight.

Another type of weighting procedure is that of kernel weighting adjustments, which average over multiple persons in the control group for each treated unit, with weights defined by their distance from the treated unit. Heckman, Ichimura, Smith, and Todd (1998) and Heckman, Ichimura, and Todd (1998) describe a local linear matching estimator that requires specifying a bandwidth parameter. Generally, larger bandwidths increase bias but reduce variance by putting weight on units that are further away from the treated unit of interest. A complication with these methods is this need to define a bandwidth or smoothing parameter, which does not generally have an intuitive meaning; Imbens (2004) provides some guidance on that choice.

With all of these weighting approaches, it is still important to separate clearly the design and analysis stages. The propensity score should be carefully estimated, using approaches such as those described earlier, and the weights set before any use of those weights in models relating the outcomes to covariates.

Diagnostics for Matching Methods

Diagnosing the quality of the matches obtained from a matching method is of primary importance. Extensive diagnostics and propensity score model specification checks are required for each data set, as discussed by

Dehejia (2005). Matching methods have a variety of simple diagnostic procedures that can be used, most based on the idea of assessing balance between the treated and control groups. Although we would ideally compare the multivariate covariate distributions in the two groups, that is difficult when there are many covariates, and so generally comparisons are done for each univariate covariate separately, for two-way interactions of covariates, and for the propensity score, as the most important univariate summary of the covariates.

At a minimum, the balance diagnostics should involve comparing the mean covariate values in the groups, sometimes standardized by the standard deviation in the full sample; ideally, other characteristics of the distributions, such as variances, correlations, and interactions between covariates, should also be compared. Common diagnostics include t tests of the covariates, Kolmogorov-Smirnov tests, and other comparisons of distributions (e.g., Austin & Mamdani, 2006). Ho et al. (2007) provide a summary of numerical and graphical summaries of balance, including empirical quantile-quantile plots to examine the empirical distribution of each covariate in the matched samples. Rosenbaum and Rubin (1984) examine F ratios from a two-way analysis of variance performed for each covariate, where the factors are treatment/ control and propensity score subclasses. Rubin

(2001) presents diagnostics related to the conditions given in the previous section that indicate when regression analyses are trustworthy. These diagnostics include assessing the standardized difference in means of the propensity scores between the two treatment groups, the ratio of the variances of the propensity scores in the two groups, and, for each covariate, the ratio of the variance of the residuals orthogonal to the propensity score in the two groups. The standardized differences in means should generally be less than 0.25, and the variance ratios should be close to 1, certainly between 0.5 and 2, as discussed earlier.

Analysis of Outcome Data After Matching

The analysis of outcome(s) should proceed only after the observational study design has been set in the sense that the matched samples have been chosen, and it has been determined that the matched samples have adequate balance. In keeping with the idea of replicating a randomized experiment, the same methods that would be used in an experiment can be used in the matched data. In particular, matching methods are not designed to "compete" with modeling adjustments such as linear regression, and in fact, the two methods have been shown to work best in combination. Many authors have discussed for decades the benefits of combining matching or propensity score weighting and regression adjustment (Abadie & Imbens, 2006; Heckman et al., 1997; Robins & Rotnitzky, 1995; Rubin, 1973b, 1979; Rubin & Thomas, 2000).

The intuition for using both is the same as that behind regression adjustment in randomized experiments, where the regression adjustment is used to "clean up" small residual covariate imbalance between the treatment and control groups. The matching method reduces large covariate bias between the treated and control groups, and the regression is used to adjust for any small residual biases and to increase efficiency. These "bias-corrected" matching methods have been found by Abadie and Imbens (2006) and Glazerman, Levy, and Myers (2003) to work well in practice, using simulated and actual data. Rubin (1973b, 1979), Rubin and Thomas (2000), and Ho et al. (2007) show that models based on matched data are much less sensitive to model misspecification and more robust than are models fit in the full data sets.

Some slight adjustments to the analysis methods are required with some particular matching methods. With procedures such as full matching, subclassification, or matching with replacement, where there may be different numbers of treated and control units at each value of the covariates, the analysis should incorporate weights to account for these varying weights. Examples of this can be found in Dehejia and Wahba (1999), Hill et al. (2004), and Michalopoulos et al. (2004). When subclassification has been used, estimates should be obtained separately within each subclass and then aggregated across subclasses to obtain an overall effect (Rosenbaum & Rubin, 1984). Estimates within each subclass are sometimes calculated using simple differences in means, although empirical (Lunceford & Davidian, 2004) and theoretical (Abadie & Imbens, 2006) work has shown that better results are obtained if regression adjustment is used in conjunction with the subclassification. When aggregating across subclasses, weighting the subclass estimates by the number of treated units in each subclass estimates the average treatment effect for the units in the treated group; if there was no matching done before subclassification, weighting by the overall number of units in each subclass estimates the overall average treatment effect for the population of treated and control units.

COMPLICATIONS IN USING MATCHING METHODS

Overlap in Distributions

In some analyses, some of the control units may be very dissimilar from all treated units, or some of the treated units may be very dissimilar from all control units, potentially exhibited by propensity scores outside the range of the other treatment group. Thus, it is sometimes desirable to explicitly discard units with "extreme" values of the propensity score—for example, treated units for whom there are no control units with propensity score values as large. Doing the analysis only in the areas where there is distributional overlap—that is, with "common support" (regions of the covariate space that have both treated and control units)—will lead to more robust inference. This, in essence, is what matching is usually attempting to do; defining the area of common support is a way to discard units that are unlike all units in the other treatment group.

However, it is often difficult to determine whether there is common support in multidimensional space. One way of doing so is to examine the overlap of the propensity score distributions. This is illustrated in Dehejia and Wahba (1999), where control units with propensity scores lower than the minimum propensity score for the treated units are discarded. A second method of examining the multivariate overlap involves examining the "convex hull" of the covariates, essentially identifying the multidimensional space that allows interpolation rather than extrapolation (King & Zeng, 2007). Imbens (2004) also discusses these issues in an economic context.

Missing Covariate Values

Most of the literature on matching and propensity scores assumes fully observed covariates, so that models such as logistic regression can be used to estimate the propensity scores. However, there are often missing values in the covariates, which complicates matching and propensity score estimation. Two complex statistical models used to estimate propensity scores in this case are pattern mixture models (Rosenbaum & Rubin, 1984) and general location models (D'Agostino & Rubin, 2000). A key consideration when thinking about missing covariate values is that the pattern of missing covariates can be prognostically important, and in such cases, the methods should condition on the observed values of the covariates and on the observed missing data indicators.

There has not been much theoretical work done on the appropriate procedures for dealing with missing covariate values. Multiple researchers have done empirical comparisons of methods, but this is clearly an area for further research. D'Agostino, Lang, Walkup, and Morgan (2001) compare three simpler methods of dealing with missing covariate values: The first uses only units with complete data and discards all units with any missing data, the second does a simple imputation for missing values and includes indicators for missing values in the propensity score model, and the third fits separate propensity score models for each pattern of missing data (a pattern mixture approach, as in

Rosenbaum & Rubin, 1984). All three methods perform well in terms of creating well-matched samples. They find that the third method performs the best, evaluated by treating the original complete-case data set (i.e., all individuals with no missing values) as the "truth," imposing additional nonignorable missing data values on that complete-case data set and examining which method best reproduces the estimate observed in the original complete-case data, given the imposed missingness. Song, Berlin, Lee, Gao, and Rotheram-Borus (2001) compare two methods of using propensity scores with missing covariate data. The first uses mean imputation for the missing values and then estimates the propensity scores. The second multiply imputes the covariates (Rubin, 1987) and estimates propensity scores in each "complete" data set. A mixed effects model is used to analyze the longitudinal outcome data in each data set, and the multiple imputation combining rules are used to obtain one estimate of the treatment effect. Results are similar using the two methods. Both methods show that the covariates are very poorly balanced between the treated and control groups, and that good matches are hard to find (a finding that standard modeling approaches would not necessarily have discovered). Hill (2004) finds that methods using multiple imputation work better than complete data or complete variable methods (which use only units with complete data or only variables with complete data).

Unobserved Variables

A critique of any observational study is that there may be unobserved covariates that affect both treatment assignment and the outcome, thus violating the assumption of unconfounded treatment assignment. The approach behind matching is that of dealing as well as possible with the observed covariates; close matching on the observed covariates will also lessen the bias due to unobserved covariates that are correlated with the observed covariates. However, there may still be concern regarding unobserved differences between the treated and control groups.

The assumption of unconfounded treatment assignment can never be directly tested. However, some researchers have proposed tests in which an estimate is obtained for an effect that is "known" to be zero, such as the difference in a pretreatment measure of the outcome variable

(Imbens, 2004) or the difference in outcomes between multiple control groups (Rosenbaum, 1987b). If the test indicates that the effect is not equal to zero, then the assumption of unconfounded treatment assignment is deemed to be less plausible.

Analyses can also be performed to assess sensitivity to an unobserved variable. Rosenbaum and Rubin (1983a) extend the ideas of Cornfield et al. (1959), who examined how strong the correlations would have to be between a hypothetical unobserved covariate and both treatment assignment and the outcome to make the observed estimate of the treatment effect be zero. This approach is also discussed and applied to an economic application in Imbens (2003). Rosenbaum (1991b) describes a sensitivity analysis for case control studies and discusses how sensitivity could also be assessed in situations where there are multiple sources of control units available—some closer on some (potentially unobserved) dimensions and others closer on other (potentially unobserved) dimensions. See Stuart and Rubin (in press) for another example of using multiple sources of control units.

Multiple Treatment Doses

Throughout this discussion of matching, it has been assumed that there are just two groups: treated and control. However, in many studies, there are actually multiple levels of the treatment (e.g., doses of a drug). Rosenbaum (2002) summarizes two methods for dealing with multiple treatment levels. In the first method, the propensity score is still a scalar function of the covariates (Joffe & Rosenbaum, 1999). This method uses a model such as an ordinal logit model to match on a linear combination of the covariates. This is illustrated in Lu, Zanutto, Hornik, and Rosenbaum (2001), where matching is used to form pairs that balance covariates but differ markedly in dose of treatment received. This differs from the standard matching setting in that there are not clear "treatment" and "control" groups, and thus any two subjects could conceivably be paired. An optimal matching algorithm for this setting is described and applied to the evaluation of a media campaign against drug abuse. In the second method, each of the levels of treatment has its own propensity score (e.g., Imbens, 2000; Rosenbaum, 1987a), and each propensity score is used one at a time

to estimate the distribution of responses that would have been observed if all units had received that treatment level. These distributions are then compared.

Encompassing these two methods, Imai and van Dyk (2004) generalize the propensity score to arbitrary treatment regimes (including ordinal, categorical, and multidimensional). They provide theorems for the properties of this generalized propensity score (the propensity function), showing that it has properties similar to that of the propensity score for binary treatments in that adjusting for the low-dimensional (not always scalar, but always low-dimensional) propensity function balances the covariates. They advocate subclassification rather than matching and provide two examples as well as simulations showing the performance of adjustment based on the propensity function.

Diagnostics are especially crucial in this setting because it becomes more difficult to assess the balance of the resulting samples when there are multiple treatment levels. It is even unclear what balance precisely means in this setting; does there need to be balance among all of the levels or only among pairwise comparisons of dose levels? Future work is needed to examine these issues.

EVALUATION OF MATCHING METHODS

Two major types of evaluations of matching methods have been done, one using simulated data and another trying to replicate results from randomized experiments using observational data. Simulations that compare the performance of matching methods in terms of bias reduction include Cochran and Rubin (1973), Rubin (1973a, 1973b, 1979), Rubin and Thomas (2000), Gu and Rosenbaum (1993), Frolich (2004), and Zhao (2004). These generally include relatively small numbers of covariates drawn from known distributions. Many of the results from these simulations have been included in the discussions of methods provided in this chapter.

A second type of evaluation has attempted to replicate the results of randomized experiments using observational data. Glazerman et al. (2003) summarize the results from 12 case studies that attempted to replicate experimental estimates using nonexperimental data, all in the context of job training, welfare, and employment programs with earnings as the outcome of interest. The nonexperimental methods include matching and covariance adjustment. From the 12 studies, they extract 1,150 estimates of the bias (approximately 96 per study), where bias is defined as the difference between the result from the randomized experiment and the result using observational data. They determine that it is in general difficult to replicate experimental results consistently and that nonexperimental estimates are often dramatically different from experimental results. However, some general guidance can be obtained.

Glazerman et al. (2003) find that one-to-one propensity score matching performs better than other propensity score matching methods or non–propensity score matching and that standard econometric selection correction procedures, such as instrumental variables or the Heckman selection correction, tend to perform poorly. As discussed earlier, their results also show that combining methods, such as matching and covariance adjustment, is better than using those methods individually. They also stress the importance of high-quality data and a rich set of covariates, and they discuss the difficulties in trying to use large publicly available data sets for this purpose. However, there are counterexamples to this general guidance. For example, using the NSW data, Dehejia and Wahba (1999) found that propensity score matching methods using a large, publicly available national data set replicated experimental results very well.

A number of authors, particularly Heckman and colleagues, use data from the U.S. National Job Training Partnership Act (JTPA) study to evaluate matching methods (Heckman et al., 1997; Heckman, Ichimura, Smith, & Todd, 1998; Heckman, Ichimura, & Todd, 1998). Some of their results are similar to those of Glazerman et al. (2003), particularly stressing the importance of high-quality data. Matching is best able to replicate the JTPA experimental results when (a) the same data sources are used for the participants and nonparticipants, thereby ensuring similar covariate meaning and measurement; (b) participants and nonparticipants reside in the same local labor markets; and (c) the data set contains a rich set of covariates to model the probability of receiving the treatment. Reaching somewhat similar conclusions, Michalopoulos

et al. (2004) use data on welfare-to-work programs that had random assignment and again find that within-state comparisons have less bias than out-of-state comparisons. They compare estimates from propensity score matching, ordinary least squares, a fixed-effects model, and a random-growth model and find that no method is consistently better than the others but that the matching method was more useful for diagnosing situations in which the data set was insufficient for the comparison. Hill et al. (2004) also stress the importance of matching on geography as well as other covariates; using data from a randomized experiment of a child care program for low-birth-weight children and comparison data from the National Longitudinal Study of Youth, they were able to replicate well the experimental results using matching with a large set of covariates, including individual-level and geographic area–level covariates. Ordinary least squares with the full set of covariates or matching with a smaller set of covariates did not perform as well as the propensity score matching with the full set of covariates. Agodini and Dynarski (2004) describe an example where matching methods highlighted the fact that the data were insufficient to estimate causal effects without heroic assumptions.

ADVICE TO AN INVESTIGATOR

To conclude, this section provides advice to investigators interested in implementing matching methods.

Control Group and Covariate Selection

As discussed in Cochran (1965), Cochran and Rubin (1973), and Rosenbaum (1999), a key to estimating causal effects with observational data is to identify an appropriate control group, ideally with good overlap with the treated group. Care should be taken to find data sets that have units similar to those in the treated group, with comparable covariate meaning and availability. Approximations for the maximum percent bias reduction possible can be used to determine which of a set of control groups are likely to provide the best matches or to help guide sample sizes and matching ratios (Rubin, 1976c; Rubin & Thomas, 1992b, 1996). Large pools of potential controls are beneficial, as many articles show that much better balance is achieved when there are many controls available for the matching (Rubin, 1976c; Rubin & Thomas, 1996). As discussed earlier, researchers should include all available covariates in the propensity score specification; excluding potentially relevant covariates can create bias in the estimation of treatment effects, but including potentially irrelevant covariates will typically not reduce the quality of the matches much (Rubin & Thomas, 1996).

Distance Measure

Once the control pool is selected, propensity score matching is the most effective method for reducing bias due to many covariates (Gu & Rosenbaum, 1993; Rosenbaum & Rubin, 1985b). As discussed earlier, propensity scores can be estimated using logistic regression, and the propensity score specification should be assessed using a method such as that in the "Model Specification" subsection. This generally involves examining the balance of covariates in subclasses defined by the propensity score. If there are a few covariates designated as particularly related to the outcome, and thus it is considered desirable to obtain especially close matches on those covariates, Mahalanobis matching on those key covariates can be done within propensity score calipers (Rosenbaum & Rubin, 1985b; Rubin & Thomas, 2000).

Recommended Matching Methods

Our advice for the matching method itself is very general: Try a variety of methods and use the diagnostics discussed earlier to determine which approach yields the most closely matched samples. Since the design and analysis stages are clearly separated and the outcome is not used in the matching process, trying a variety of methods and selecting the one that leads to the best covariate balance cannot bias the results. Although the best method will depend on the individual data set, below we highlight some methods that are likely to produce good results for the two general situations considered in this chapter.

To Select Units for Follow-Up

For the special case of doing matching for the purpose of selecting well-matched controls for follow-up (i.e., when the outcome values are not yet available), optimal matching is generally best

for producing well-matched pairs (Gu & Rosenbaum, 1993). Optimal matching aims to reduce a global distance measure, rather than just considering each match one at a time, and thus reconsiders earlier matches if better overall balance could be obtained by breaking that earlier match. Further details are given in the "Nearest Neighbor Matching" subsection. However, if overall balanced samples are all that is desired (rather than specifically matched pairs), then an easier and more straightforward nearest neighbor greedy matching algorithm can be used to select the controls.

Researchers should also consider whether it is feasible (or desirable) to obtain more than one matched control for each treated unit (or even some treated units), as discussed earlier. With relatively small control pools, it may be difficult to obtain more than one match for each treated unit and still obtain large reductions in bias. However, with larger control pools, it may be possible to obtain more than one match for each treated unit without sacrificing bias reduction. This decision is also likely to involve cost considerations.

If Outcome Data Are Already Available

When the outcome values are already available, first put the outcome values away when matching! Then, a variety of good methods exist and should be considered and tried. In particular, one-to-one propensity score matching is often a good place to start (or *k*-to-one if there are many controls relative to the number of treated units). If there is still substantial bias between the groups in the matched samples (e.g., imbalance in the propensity score of more than 0.5 standard deviations), the nearest neighbor matching can be combined with subclassification on the matched samples, as discussed earlier. Full matching and subclassification on the full data sets also often work well in practice, where full matching can be thought of as in between the two extremes of one-to-one matching and weighting.

Outcome Analysis

After matched samples are selected, the outcome analysis can proceed: linear regression, logistic regression, hierarchical modeling, and so on. As discussed earlier, results should be less sensitive to the modeling assumptions and thus should be fairly insensitive to the model specification, as compared with the same analysis on the original unmatched samples. With procedures such as full matching, subclassification, or matching with replacement, where there may be different numbers of treated and control units at each value of the covariates, the analysis should incorporate weights to account for these varying distributions.

SOFTWARE

A variety of software packages are currently available to implement matching methods. These include multiple R packages (MatchIt, Ho, Imai, King, & Stuart, 2006; twang, Ridgeway, McCaffrey, & Morral, 2006; Matching, Sekhon, 2006), multiple Stata packages (Abadie, Drukker, Herr, & Imbens, 2004; Becker & Ichino, 2002; Leuven & Sianesi, 2003), and SAS code for propensity score matching (D'Agostino, 1998; Parsons, 2001). A major benefit of the R packages (particularly MatchIt and twang) is that they clearly separate the design and analysis stages and have extensive propensity score diagnostics. The Stata and SAS packages and procedures do not explicitly separate these two stages.

NOTES

1. The data for this example are available at http://www.nber.org/%7Erdehejia/nswdata.html and in the MatchIt matching package for R, available at http://gking.harvard.edu/matchit.

2. With nonnormally distributed covariates, the conditions are even more complex.

REFERENCES

Abadie, A., Drukker, D., Herr, J. L., & Imbens, G. W. (2004). Implementing matching estimators for average treatment effects in Stata. *The Stata Journal, 4*(3), 290–311.

Abadie, A., & Imbens, G. W. (2006). Large sample properties of matching estimators for average treatment effects. *Econometrica, 74*(1), 235–267.

Agodini, R., & Dynarski, M. (2004). Are experiments the only option? A look at dropout prevention programs. *Review of Economics and Statistics, 86*(1), 180–194.

Althauser, R., & Rubin, D. (1970). The computerized construction of a matched sample. *American Journal of Sociology, 76,* 325–346.

Austin, P. C., & Mamdani, M. M. (2006). A comparison of propensity score methods: A case-study illustrating the effectiveness of post-ami statin use. *Statistics in Medicine, 25,* 2084–2106.

Becker, S. O., & Ichino, A. (2002). Estimation of average treatment effects based on propensity scores. *The Stata Journal, 2*(4), 358–377.

Breiman, L. J., Friedman, J., Olshen, R., & Stone, C. (1984). *Classification and regression trees.* Belmont, CA: Wadsworth.

Chapin, F. (1947). *Experimental designs in sociological research.* New York: Harper.

Christakis, N. A., & Iwashyna, T. I. (2003). The health impact of health care on families: A matched cohort study of hospice use by decedents and mortality outcomes in surviving, widowed spouses. *Social Science & Medicine, 57,* 465–475.

Cochran, W. G. (1957). Analysis of covariance: Its nature and uses. *Biometrics, 13,* 261–281.

Cochran, W. G. (1965). The planning of observational studies of human populations (with discussion). *Journal of the Royal Statistical Society, Series A, 128,* 234–255.

Cochran, W. G. (1968). The effectiveness of adjustment by subclassification in removing bias in observational studies. *Biometrics, 24,* 295–313.

Cochran, W. G., & Rubin, D. B. (1973). Controlling bias in observational studies: A review. *Sankhya: The Indian Journal of Statistics, Series A, 35,* 417–446.

Cornfield, J., Haenszel, W., Hammond, E. C., Lilienfeld, A. M., Shimkin, M. B., & Wynder, E. L. (1959). Smoking and lung cancer: Recent evidence and a discussion of some questions. *Journal of the National Cancer Institute, 22,* 173–203.

Czajka, J. C., Hirabayashi, S., Little, R., & Rubin, D. B. (1992). Projecting from advance data using propensity modeling. *Journal of Business and Economic Statistics, 10,* 117–131.

D'Agostino, R. B., Jr. (1998). Propensity score methods for bias reduction in the comparison of a treatment to a non-randomized control group. *Statistics in Medicine, 17,* 2265–2281.

D'Agostino, R. B., Jr., Lang, W., Walkup, M., & Morgan, T. (2001). Examining the impact of missing data on propensity score estimation in determining the effectiveness of self-monitoring of blood glucose (SMBG). *Health Services & Outcomes Research Methodology, 2,* 291–315.

D'Agostino, R. B., Jr., & Rubin, D. B. (2000). Estimating and using propensity scores with partially missing data. *Journal of the American Statistical Association, 95,* 749–759.

Dehejia, R. H. (2005). Practical propensity score matching: A reply to Smith and Todd. *Journal of Econometrics, 125*, 355–364.

Dehejia, R. H., & Wahba, S. (1999). Causal effects in nonexperimental studies: Re-evaluating the evaluation of training programs. *Journal of the American Statistical Association, 94*, 1053–1062.

Dehejia, R. H., & Wahba, S. (2002). Propensity score matching methods for non-experimental causal studies. *Review of Economics and Statistics, 84*, 151–161.

Drake, C. (1993). Effects of misspecification of the propensity score on estimators of treatment effects. *Biometrics, 49*, 1231–1236.

Du, J. (1998). *Valid inferences after propensity score subclassification using maximum number of subclasses as building blocks.* Unpublished doctoral dissertation, Harvard University, Department of Statistics.

Frangakis, C. E., & Rubin, D. B. (2002). Principal stratification in causal inference. *Biometrics, 58*, 21–29.

Frolich, M. (2004). Finite-sample properties of propensity-score matching and weighting estimators. *Review of Economics and Statistics, 86*(1), 77–90.

Glazerman, S., Levy, D. M., & Myers, D. (2003). Nonexperimental versus experimental estimates of earnings impacts. *The Annals of the American Academy of Political and Social Science, 589*, 63–93.

Greenland, S. (2003). Quantifying biases in causal models: classical confounding vs collider-stratification bias. *Epidemiology, 14*(3), 300–306.

Greenwood, E. (1945). *Experimental sociology: A study in method.* New York: King's Crown Press.

Greevy, R., Lu, B., Silber, J. H., & Rosenbaum, P. (2004). Optimal multivariate matching before randomization. *Biostatistics, 5*, 263–275.

Gu, X., & Rosenbaum, P. R. (1993). Comparison of multivariate matching methods: Structures, distances, and algorithms. *Journal of Computational and Graphical Statistics, 2*, 405–420.

Hansen, B. B. (2004). Full matching in an observational study of coaching for the SAT. *Journal of the American Statistical Association, 99*(467), 609–618.

Heckman, J. J., Hidehiko, H., & Todd, P. (1997). Matching as an econometric evaluation estimator: Evidence from evaluating a job training programme. *Review of Economic Studies, 64*, 605–654.

Heckman, J. J., Ichimura, H., Smith, J., & Todd, P. (1998). Characterizing selection bias using experimental data. *Econometrika, 66*(5), 1017–1098.

Heckman, J. J., Ichimura, H., & Todd, P. (1998). Matching as an econometric evaluation estimator. *Review of Economic Studies, 65*, 261–294.

Hill, J. (2004). *Reducing bias in treatment effect estimation in observational studies suffering from missing data.* Working Paper 04-01, Columbia University Institute for Social and Economic Research and Policy (ISERP).

Hill, J., Reiter, J., & Zanutto, E. (2004). A comparison of experimental and observational data analyses. In A. Gelman & X.-L. Meng (Eds.), *Applied Bayesian modeling and causal inference from an incomplete-data perspective* (pp. 44–56). New York: John Wiley.

Hill, J., Rubin, D. B., & Thomas, N. (1999). The design of the New York School Choice Scholarship Program evaluation. In L. Bickman (Ed.), *Research designs: Inspired by the work of Donald Campbell* (pp. 155–180). Thousand Oaks, CA: Sage.

Ho, D. E., Imai, K., King, G., & Stuart, E. A. (2006). *MatchIt: Nonparametric preprocessing for parametric causal inference.* Software for using matching methods in R. Available at http://gking.harvard.edu/matchit/

Ho, D. E., Imai, K., King, G., & Stuart, E. A. (2007). Matching as nonparametric preprocessing for reducing model dependence in parametric causal inference. *Political Analysis, 15*(3), 199–236. Available at http://pan.oxfordjournals.org/cgi/reprint/mpl013?ijkey=K17Pjban3gH2zs0&keytype=ref.

Holland, P. W. (1986). Statistics and causal inference. *Journal of the American Statistical Association, 81*, 945–960.

Hong, G., & Raudenbush, S. W. (2006). Evaluating kindergarten retention policy: A case study of causal inference for multilevel observational data. *Journal of the American Statistical Association, 101*(475), 901–910.

Horvitz, D., & Thompson, D. (1952). A generalization of sampling without replacement from a finite universe. *Journal of the American Statistical Association, 47*, 663–685.

Imai, K., & van Dyk, D. A. (2004). Causal inference with general treatment regimes: Generalizing the propensity score. *Journal of the American Statistical Association, 99*(467), 854–866.

Imbens, G. W. (2000). The role of the propensity score in estimating dose-response functions. *Biometrika, 87*, 706–710.

Imbens, G. W. (2003). Sensitivity to exogeneity assumptions in program evaluation. *American Economic Review, 96*(2), 126–132.

Imbens, G. W. (2004). Nonparametric estimation of average treatment effects under exogeneity: A review. *Review of Economics and Statistics, 86*(1), 4–29.

Joffe, M. M., & Rosenbaum, P. R. (1999). Propensity scores. *American Journal of Epidemiology, 150*, 327–333.

King, G., & Zeng, L. (2007). When can history be our guide? The pitfalls of counterfactual inference. *International Studies Quarterly, 51,* 183–210.

LaLonde, R. (1986). Evaluating the econometric evaluations of training programs with experimental data. *American Economic Review, 76*(4), 604–620.

Leuven, E., & Sianesi, B. (2003). *psmatch2. Stata module to perform full Mahalanobis and propensity score matching, common support graphing, and covariate imbalance testing.* Available at http://www1.fee.uva.nl/scholar/mdw/leuven/stata

Lu, B., Zanutto, E., Hornik, R., & Rosenbaum, P. R. (2001). Matching with doses in an observational study of a media campaign against drug abuse. *Journal of the American Statistical Association, 96,* 1245–1253.

Lunceford, J. K., & Davidian, M. (2004). Stratification and weighting via the propensity score in estimation of causal treatment effects: A comparative study. *Statistics in Medicine, 23,* 2937–2960.

McCaffrey, D. F., Ridgeway, G., & Morral, A. R. (2004). Propensity score estimation with boosted regression for evaluating causal effects in observational studies. *Psychological Methods, 9*(4), 403–425.

Michalopoulos, C., Bloom, H. S., & Hill, C. J. (2004). Can propensity-score methods match the findings from a random assignment evaluation of mandatory welfare-to-work programs? *Review of Economics and Statistics, 56*(1), 156–179.

Morgan, S. L., & Harding, D. J. (2006). Matching estimators of causal effects: Prospects and pitfalls in theory and practice. *Sociological Methods & Research, 35*(1), 3–60.

Parsons, L. S. (2001, April). *Reducing bias in a propensity score matched-pair sample using greedy matching techniques.* Paper presented at SAS SUGI 26, Long Beach, CA.

Perkins, S. M., Tu, W., Underhill, M. G., Zhou, X.-H., & Murray, M. D. (2000). The use of propensity scores in pharmacoepidemiological research. *Pharmacoepidemiology and Drug Safety, 9,* 93–101.

Reinisch, J., Sanders, S., Mortensen, E., & Rubin, D. B. (1995). In utero exposure to phenobarbital and intelligence deficits in adult men. *Journal of the American Medical Association, 274,* 1518–1525.

Ridgeway, G., McCaffrey, D., & Morral, A. (2006). *twang: Toolkit for weighting and analysis of nonequivalent groups.* Software for using matching methods in R. Available at http://cran.r-project.org/src/contrib/Descriptions/twang.html

Robins, J., & Rotnitzky, A. (1995). Semiparametric efficiency in multivariate regression models with missing data. *Journal of the American Statistical Association, 90,* 122–129.

Robins, J., & Rotnitzky, A. (2001). Comment on P. J. Bickel and J. Kwon, "Inference for semiparametric models: Some questions and an answer." *Statistica Sinica, 11*(4), 920–936.

Rosenbaum, P. R. (1987a). Model-based direct adjustment. *Journal of the American Statistical Association, 82,* 387–394.

Rosenbaum, P. R. (1987b). The role of a second control group in an observational study (with discussion). *Statistical Science, 2*(3), 292–316.

Rosenbaum, P. R. (1991a). A characterization of optimal designs for observational studies. *Journal of the Royal Statistical Society, Series B (Methodological), 53*(3), 597–610.

Rosenbaum, P. R. (1991b). Sensitivity analysis for matched case-control studies. *Biometrics, 47*(1), 87–100.

Rosenbaum, P. R. (1999). Choice as an alternative to control in observational studies (with discussion and rejoinder). *Statistical Science, 14*(3), 259–304.

Rosenbaum, P. R. (2002). *Observational studies* (2nd ed.). New York: Springer-Verlag.

Rosenbaum, P. R., & Rubin, D. B. (1983a). Assessing sensitivity to an unobserved binary covariate in an observational study with binary outcome. *Journal of the Royal Statistical Society, Series B, 45*(2), 212–218.

Rosenbaum, P. R., & Rubin, D. B. (1983b). The central role of the propensity score in observational studies for causal effects. *Biometrika, 70,* 41–55.

Rosenbaum, P. R., & Rubin, D. B. (1984). Reducing bias in observational studies using subclassification on the propensity score. *Journal of the American Statistical Association, 79,* 516–524.

Rosenbaum, P. R., & Rubin, D. B. (1985a). The bias due to incomplete matching. *Biometrics, 41,* 103–116.

Rosenbaum, P. R., & Rubin, D. B. (1985b). Constructing a control group using multivariate matched sampling methods that incorporate the propensity score. *The American Statistician, 39,* 33–38.

Rubin, D. B. (1973a). Matching to remove bias in observational studies. *Biometrics, 29,* 159–184.

Rubin, D. B. (1973b). The use of matched sampling and regression adjustment to remove bias in observational studies. *Biometrics, 29,* 185–203.

Rubin, D. B. (1974). Estimating causal effects of treatments in randomized and nonrandomized studies. *Journal of Educational Psychology, 66,* 688–701.

Rubin, D. B. (1976a). Inference and missing data (with discussion). *Biometrika, 63,* 581–592.

Rubin, D. B. (1976b). Multivariate matching methods that are equal percent bias reducing: I. Some examples. *Biometrics, 32,* 109–120.

Rubin, D. B. (1976c). Multivariate matching methods that are equal percent bias reducing: II. Maximums on bias reduction. *Biometrics, 32,* 121–132.

Rubin, D. B. (1977). Assignment to treatment group on the basis of a covariate. *Journal of Educational Statistics, 2,* 1–26.

Rubin, D. B. (1978). Bayesian inference for causal effects: The role of randomization. *The Annals of Statistics, 6,* 34–58.

Rubin, D. B. (1979). Using multivariate matched sampling and regression adjustment to control bias in observational studies. *Journal of the American Statistical Association, 74,* 318–328.

Rubin, D. B. (1980). Discussion of "Randomization analysis of experimental data in the Fisher randomization test" by D. Basu. *Journal of the American Statistical Association, 75,* 591–593.

Rubin, D. B. (1987). *Multiple imputation for nonresponse in surveys.* New York: John Wiley.

Rubin, D. B. (1990). Formal modes of statistical inference for causal effects. *Journal of Statistical Planning and Inference, 25,* 279–292.

Rubin, D. B. (1997). Estimating causal effects from large data sets using propensity scores. *Annals of Internal Medicine, 127,* 757–763.

Rubin, D. B. (2001). Using propensity scores to help design observational studies: Application to the tobacco litigation. *Health Services & Outcomes Research Methodology, 2,* 169–188.

Rubin, D. B. (2004). On principles for modeling propensity scores in medical research. *Pharmacoepidemiology and Drug Safety, 13,* 855–857.

Rubin, D. B. (2006). *Matched sampling for causal inference.* Cambridge, UK: Cambridge University Press.

Rubin, D. B. (2007). The design versus the analysis of observational studies for causal effects: Parallels with the design of randomized trials. *Statistics in Medicine, 26*(1), 20–30.

Rubin, D. B., & Stuart, E. A. (2006). Affinely invariant matching methods with discriminant mixtures of proportional ellipsoidally symmetric distributions. *The Annals of Statistics, 34*(4), 1814–1826.

Rubin, D. B., & Thomas, N. (1992a). Affinely invariant matching methods with ellipsoidal distributions. *The Annals of Statistics, 20,* 1079–1093.

Rubin, D. B., & Thomas, N. (1992b). Characterizing the effect of matching using linear propensity score methods with normal distributions. *Biometrika, 79,* 797–809.

Rubin, D. B., & Thomas, N. (1996). Matching using estimated propensity scores, relating theory to practice. *Biometrics, 52,* 249–264.

Rubin, D. B., & Thomas, N. (2000). Combining propensity score matching with additional adjustments for prognostic covariates. *Journal of the American Statistical Association, 95,* 573–585.

Sekhon, J. S. (2006). *Matching: Multivariate and propensity score matching with balance optimization.* Software for using matching methods in R. Available at http://sekhon.berkeley.edu/matching

Smith, H. (1997). Matching with multiple controls to estimate treatment effects in observational studies. *Sociological Methodology, 27,* 325–353.

Smith, J., & Todd, P. (2005). Does matching overcome LaLonde's critique of nonexperimental estimators? *Journal of Econometrics, 125,* 305–353.

Snedecor, G. W., & Cochran, W. G. (1980). *Statistical methods* (7th ed.). Ames: Iowa State University Press.

Sobel, M. E. (2006). What do randomized studies of housing mobility demonstrate? Causal inference in the face of interference. *Journal of the American Statistical Association, 101*(476), 1398–1407.

Song, J., Belin, T. R., Lee, M. B., Gao, X., & Rotheram-Borus, M. J. (2001). Handling baseline differences and missing items in a longitudinal study of HIV risk among runaway youths. *Health Services & Outcomes Research Methodology, 2,* 317–329.

Stuart, E. A., & Green, K. M. (in press). Using full matching to estimate causal effects in non-experimental studies: Examining the relationship between adolescent marijuana use and adult outcomes. *Developmental Psychology.*

Stuart, E. A., & Rubin, D. B. (in press). Matching with multiple control groups with adjustment for group differences. *Journal of Educational and Behavioral Statistics.*

Winship, C., & Morgan, S. L. (1999). The estimation of causal effects from observational data. *Annual Review of Sociology, 25,* 659–706.

Zhao, Z. (2004). Using matching to estimate treatment effects: Data requirements, matching metrics, and Monte Carlo evidence. *Review of Economics and Statistics, 86*(1), 91–107.

12

AN INTRODUCTION TO META-ANALYSIS

SPYROS KONSTANTOPOULOS

Researchers in the social sciences often already have access to completed studies in the literature that relate to or address their hypotheses. How best, then, to organize and summarize findings from these studies in order to identify and exploit what is known and focus research on promising areas? While narrative summaries and analyses of the literature are important (and the norm), quantitative research synthesis or meta-analysis is currently considered a best practice across many disciplines (see Cooper & Hedges, 1994; Hedges & Olkin, 1985).

Meta-analysis refers to quantitative methods of synthesizing empirical research evidence from a sample of studies that examine a certain topic and test comparable hypotheses (Hedges & Olkin, 1985). The first step in meta-analysis involves describing the results of each study via numerical indicators (e.g., estimates of effect sizes such as a standardized mean difference, a correlation coefficient, or an odds ratio). These effect size estimates reflect the magnitude of the association of interest in each study. The second step involves combining the effect size estimates from each study to produce a single indicator that summarizes the relationship of interest across the sample of studies. Hence, meta-analytic procedures produce summary statistics, which are then tested to determine their statistical significance and importance.

The specific analytic techniques involved will depend on the question the meta-analytic summary is intended to address. Sometimes the question of interest concerns the typical or average study result, such as the effect of some treatment or intervention, where the average effect of the treatment is often of interest (see, e.g., Smith & Glass, 1977). In other cases, the degree of variation in results across studies will be of primary interest, where meta-analysis can be used to study the generalizability of employment test validities across situations (see, e.g., Schmidt & Hunter, 1977). Meta-analysis is also frequently used to identify the contexts in which a treatment or intervention is most successful or has the largest effect (see, e.g., Cooper, 1989).

Meta-analytic reviews are designed to integrate empirical research with the objective to create research generalizations; hence, one substantial advantage of meta-analysis is the generality of the summary estimates (Cooper & Hedges, 1994). This constitutes a unique aspect of meta-analysis that is crucial for the external validation of the estimates (see Shadish, Cook, & Campbell, 2002). Generally, the estimates that are produced from meta-analyses have higher external validity than estimates reported in single studies. Other advantages of meta-analytic reviews include the fact that the summary estimates that are generated from such reviews can support or refute theories (and hence facilitate the improvement of substantive theory) and can guide future research by identifying important issues (Cooper, 1989). In addition, from a statistical point of view, the results of meta-analytic procedures have higher statistical power than do indicators obtained from individual studies, which increases the probability of detecting associations of interest (Cohn & Becker, 2003).

The term *meta-analysis* is sometimes used to describe the entire process of research synthesis or integrative research review. However, more recently, it has been used specifically for the statistical component of research synthesis (Cooper, 1989; Cooper & Hedges, 1994). Other components of research synthesis that take place prior to meta-analysis include the formulation of the question of interest (or problem), the search of the literature or data collection, and the evaluation and coding of the data that involve the evaluation of the quality of the data and the creation of variables and quantitative indexes (see Cooper, 1989). It is crucial to understand that in research synthesis, as in any research, statistical methods are only one part of the enterprise. Statistical methods cannot remedy the problem of poor-quality data. Excellent treatments of the nonstatistical aspects of research synthesis are available in Cooper (1989), Cooper and Hedges (1994), and Lipsey and Wilson (2001).

Early Stages of Research Synthesis

In the very early stages of meta-analytic reviews, the reviewers need to clearly formulate a question of interest and familiarize themselves with what theorists and empirical researchers have discussed on that specific topic. The next step involves constructing a coding sheet to record important information from the sample of studies collected. The coding sheet can include general information about the authors of the study, the year of publication of the study, the source of the study (e.g., journal title), the research design used in the study (e.g., correlational or experimental), the characteristics of the individuals who participated in the study (e.g., age, gender,

numbers of participants), and the outcome measures of the study. Most important for meta-analysis, however, the coding sheet should include information about the summary statistics of the study. In the social sciences, these statistical outcomes typically include means, standard deviations, and sample sizes (for groups of individuals); correlation coefficients; odds ratios; and the value of the test (e.g., t test) and the sample or the p value of the test and the sample size. Cooper (1989) provides a thorough discussion about coding sheets. Recently, software packages such as Comprehensive Meta-Analysis (CMA), which are designed especially to conduct meta-analysis, have offered multiple formats for entering meta-analytic data.[1]

The next stage involves the literature review in order to locate the relevant studies. In this stage, it is important that the meta-analyst use multiple sources of literature retrieval in order to ensure that useful studies that are related directly to the question of interest are included in the sample (see White, 1994). Common ways of conducting literature searches include tracing references in previous relevant review studies, references in relevant books, references in nonreview relevant studies from journals that researchers subscribe to, references through computer searches of relevant databases (e.g., web of science, ERIC, PsycINFO, Econ Lit, Sociological Abstracts, Dissertation Abstracts, etc.), and references through a manual search of journals that typically publish work on the specific topic. In addition, informal channels of locating studies include communication with researchers who work or have worked on the specific topic and informal conversations with other researchers or students in conferences (see Cooper, 1989; White, 1994).

It is important at this stage that the sample of studies includes published and unpublished work so that the sample represents accurately the number of studies that were actually undertaken. This indicates that the inclusion of a study in the sample should not depend on the statistical significance of the results but on the relevance of the study. Specifically, if the sample of studies includes only published work, it is possible that the largest or more significant effect size estimates are overrepresented in the sample since significant results (or larger estimates) are more likely to be published. Hence, the estimates derived from published work form a selected subsample, and this can lead to selection or publication bias. There are several ways to examine publication bias. A common way to examine publication bias is the funnel plot that plots the sample size versus the effect size for each study (see Light & Pillemer, 1984). When the graph resembles a funnel, publication bias seems unlikely. Another way to examine publication bias is through a z test (see Begg, 1994). In this case, when the z test is statistically significant, there is evidence of publication bias. Rosenthal's (1979) fail-safe (or file drawer) method is another well-known technique that computes the number of missing studies (with a mean effect of zero) that would need to be added to the analysis to yield a statistically insignificant overall effect. Large numbers of missing studies would indicate that publication bias is rather unlikely. A recent method, called trim and fill, also accounts for publication bias by imputing the missing studies, adding them to the analysis, and recomputing an overall effect size (Duval & Tweedie, 2000). A thorough discussion about publication bias in meta-analysis is provided by Rothstein, Sutton, and Borenstein (2005). Software packages such as CMA provide multiple methods that examine publication bias and assess its impact on the summary estimates.

Finally, at the evaluation stage, the reviewer needs to make critical judgments about the quality of the data and create consistent and objective criteria for including studies in the sample (Cooper, 1989; Wortman, 1994). According to Cooper (1989), the validity of the study's methods is a crucial criterion for discarding or including data. That is, the reviewer needs to evaluate whether the study was conducted in a way that secures the validity of its estimates. Sometimes, reviewers decide to include a study in the sample (or exclude it). Other times, the quality of the study can be represented in a continuous scale and can be used to weight studies according to their quality (i.e., higher quality studies are assigned higher weights). Notice that a weight of zero is equivalent to excluding a study. Shadish and Haddock (1994) demonstrate how weights that indicate the quality of the study can be incorporated in the computation of meta-analytic summary estimates. Of course, the inclusion of the study also depends on whether the study provides the required information for computing estimates related to the question of interest of the review. A thorough discussion about data evaluation is provided by Cooper (1989) and Wortman (1994).

Meta-Analysis

Effect Size Estimates

Effect sizes are quantitative indexes that are used to summarize the results of a study in meta-analysis. That is, effect sizes reflect the magnitude of the association between variables of interest in each study. There are many different effect sizes, and the effect size used in a meta-analysis should be chosen so that it represents the results of a study in a way that is easily interpretable and is comparable across studies. In a sense, effect sizes should put the results of all studies "on a common scale" so that they can be readily interpreted, compared, and combined. It is important to distinguish the effect size estimate in a study from the effect size parameter (the true effect size) in that study. In principle, the effect size estimates will vary somewhat from study to study (sampling variation), while the effect size parameter is in principle fixed (fixed effects models). One might think of the effect size parameter as the estimate that would be obtained if the study had a very large (essentially infinite) sample, so that the sampling variation is negligible.

The choice of an effect size index will depend on the design of the studies, the way in which the outcome is measured, the statistical analysis used in each study, and the information provided in each study. Most of the effect size indexes used in the social sciences will fall into one of three families of effect sizes: the standardized mean difference family, the odds ratio family, and the correlation coefficient family.

The Standardized Mean Difference

In many studies of the effects of a treatment or intervention that measure the outcome on a continuous scale, a natural effect size is the standardized mean difference. The standardized mean difference is the difference between the mean outcome in the treatment group and the mean outcome in the control group divided by the within-group standard deviation. That is, the standardized mean difference is

$$d = \frac{\overline{Y}^T - \overline{Y}^C}{S}, \qquad (1)$$

where $\overline{Y}^T$ is the sample mean of the outcome in the treatment group, $\overline{Y}^C$ is the sample mean of the outcome in the control group, and S is the within-group standard deviation of the outcome. The corresponding standardized mean difference parameter is

$$\delta = \frac{\mu^T - \mu^C}{\sigma}, \qquad (2)$$

where μ^T is the population mean in the treatment group, μ^C is the population mean outcome in the control group, and σ is the population within-group standard deviation of the outcome. This effect size is easy to interpret since it is just the treatment effect in standard deviation units. It can also be interpreted as having the same meaning across studies (see Hedges & Olkin, 1985). The sampling uncertainty of the standardized mean difference is characterized by its variance, which is

$$v = \frac{n^T + n^C}{n^T n^C} + \frac{d^2}{2(n^T + n^C)}, \qquad (3)$$

where n^T and n^C are the treatment and control group sample sizes, respectively. Note that this variance can be computed from a single observation of the effect size if the sample sizes of the two groups within a study are known. Because the standardized mean difference is approximately normally distributed, the square root of the variance (the standard error) can be used to compute confidence intervals for the true effect size or effect size parameter δ. Specifically, a 95% confidence interval for the effect size is given by

$$d - 2\sqrt{v} \leq \delta \leq d + 2\sqrt{v}. \qquad (4)$$

Several variations of the standardized mean difference are also sometimes used as effect sizes (see Rosenthal, 1994). A standardized mean difference can easily be computed so long as a study reports sufficient information for its computation (e.g., means, standard deviation, sample sizes, the value and p value of the test, etc.).

The Log-Odds Ratio

In many studies of the effects of a treatment or intervention that measures the outcome on a dichotomous scale, a natural effect size is the log-odds ratio. The log-odds ratio is just the log of the ratio of the odds of a particular one of the two outcomes (the target outcome) in the treatment group to the odds of that particular outcome in the control group. That is, the log-odds ratio is

$$\log(OR) = \log\left(\frac{p^T/(1 - p^T)}{p^C/(1 - p^C)}\right)$$
$$= \log\left(\frac{p^T(1 - p^C)}{p^C(1 - p^T)}\right), \qquad (5)$$

where p^T and p^C are the proportion of the treatment and control groups, respectively, that have the target outcome. The corresponding odds ratio parameter is

$$\omega = \log\left(\frac{\pi^T/(1 - \pi^T)}{\pi^C/(1 - \pi^C)}\right)$$
$$= \log\left(\frac{\pi^T(1 - \pi^C)}{\pi^C(1 - \pi^T)}\right), \qquad (6)$$

where π^T and π^C are the population proportions in the treatment and control groups, respectively, that have the target outcome. The log-odds ratio is widely used in the analysis of data that have dichotomous outcomes and is readily interpretable by researchers who frequently encounter this kind of data. It also has the same meaning across studies, so it is suitable for combining (see Fleiss, 1994).

The sampling uncertainty of the log-odds ratio is characterized by its variance, which is

$$v = \frac{1}{n^T p^T} + \frac{1}{n^T(1 - p^T)}$$
$$+ \frac{1}{n^C p^C} + \frac{1}{n^C(1 - p^C)}, \qquad (7)$$

where n^T and n^C are the treatment and control group sample sizes, respectively. As in the case of the standardized mean difference, the log-odds ratio is approximately normally distributed, and the square root of the variance (the standard error) can be used to compute confidence intervals for the true effect size or effect size parameter ω. Specifically, a 95% confidence interval for the effect size is given by

$$d - 2\sqrt{v} \le \omega \le d + 2\sqrt{v}. \quad (8)$$

There are several other indexes in the odds ratio family, including the risk ratio (the ratio of proportion having the target outcome in the treatment group to that in the control group, or p^T/p^C) and the risk difference (the difference between the proportion having a particular one of the two outcomes in the treatment group, and that in the control group, or $p^T - p^C$). For a discussion of effect size measures for studies with dichotomous outcomes, including the odds ratio family of effect sizes, see Fleiss (1994). Odds ratios are often reported in studies in medicine and the health sciences.

The Correlation Coefficient

In many studies of the relation between two continuous variables, the correlation coefficient is a natural measure of effect size. Often, this correlation is transformed via the Fisher z transform,

$$z = \tfrac{1}{2} \log\left(\frac{1+r}{1-r}\right), \quad (9)$$

in carrying out statistical analyses. The corresponding correlation parameter is ρ, the population correlation, and the parameter that corresponds to the estimate z is ξ, the z transform of ρ. The advantage of this transformation is that the variance of the Fisher z transform is independent of the correlation coefficient and is simply a function of the sample size of the study. Specifically, the sampling uncertainty of the z-transformed correlation is characterized by its variance,

$$v = \frac{1}{n-3}, \quad (10)$$

where n is the sample size of the study, and it is used in the same way as are the variances of the standardized mean difference and log-odds ratio to obtain confidence intervals. Bivariate correlations are often reported in studies in the social sciences.

The statistical methods for meta-analysis are quite similar, regardless of the effect size measure used. Therefore, in the rest of this chapter, we do not describe statistical methods that are specific to

a particular effect size index but describe them in terms of a generic effect size measure T_i. We assume that the T_i are normally distributed about the corresponding θ_i with known variance v_i. That is, assuming k studies and one estimate per study,

$$T_i \sim N(\theta_i, v_i), i = 1, \ldots, k. \quad (11)$$

This assumption is very nearly true for effect sizes such as the Fisher z-transformed correlation coefficient and standardized mean differences. However, for effect sizes such as the untransformed correlation coefficient, or the log-odds ratio, the results are not exact but remain true as large sample approximations. For a discussion of effect size measures for studies with continuous outcomes, see Rosenthal (1994), and for a treatment of effect size measures for studies with categorical outcomes, see Fleiss (1994). A nice feature of software packages such as CMA is that the allow for transformations from one effect size estimate to another. For example, a reviewer can enter data in CMA that initially allow the computation of a standardized mean difference. However, once the standardized effect size estimate is computed, CMA can transform this estimate to a correlation coefficient, or an odds ratio, and so on (and hence the summary estimates can be expressed in various forms).

UNIVARIATE FIXED EFFECTS MODELS

Two somewhat different statistical models have been developed for inference about effect size data from a collection of studies, called the fixed effects and the mixed (or random) effects models (see, e.g., Hedges & Vevea, 1998). Fixed effects models treat the effect size parameters as fixed but unknown constants to be estimated and usually (but not necessarily) are used in conjunction with assumptions about the homogeneity of effect size parameters (see, e.g., Hedges, 1982, 1994; Rosenthal & Rubin, 1982). The logic of fixed effects models is that inferences are not about any hypothesized population of studies but about the particular collection of studies that is observed. The simplest fixed effects model involves the estimation of an average effect size by combining the effect size estimates across all studies in the sample.

Let θ_i be the (unobserved) effect size parameter (the true effect size) in the ith study, let T_i be the corresponding observed effect size estimate from the ith study, and let v_i be its variance. Thus, the data from a set of k studies are the effect size estimates $T_1, \ldots, T_k$ and their variances $v_1, \ldots, v_k$. The effect size estimate T_i is modeled as the effect size parameter plus a sampling error ε_i. That is,

$$T_i = \theta_i + \varepsilon_i, \ \varepsilon_i \sim N(0, v_i). \quad (12)$$

The parameter θ is the mean effect size parameter for all of the studies. It has the interpretation that θ is the mean of the distribution from which the study-specific effect size parameters $(\theta_1, \theta_2, \ldots, \theta_k)$ were sampled. Note that this is not conceptually the same as the mean of $\theta_1, \theta_2, \ldots, \theta_k$, the effect size parameters of the k studies that were observed. The effect size parameters are in turn determined by a mean effect size β_0—that is, $\theta_i = \beta_0$—which indicates that the θ_is are fixed and thus

$$T_i = \beta_0 + \varepsilon_i. \quad (13)$$

Note that in meta-analysis, the variances (the v_is) are different for each of the studies. That is, each study has a *different* sampling error variance. In addition, in meta-analysis, these variances are known. Since the amount of sampling uncertainty is not identical in every study, it seems reasonable that, if an average effect size is to be computed across studies, it would be desirable to give more weight in that average to studies that have more precise estimates (or smaller variances) than those with less precise estimates.

The weighted least squares (and maximum likelihood) estimate of β_0 under the model is

$$\hat{\beta}_0 = \frac{\sum_{i=1}^{k} w_i T_i}{\sum_{i=1}^{k} w_i}, \quad (14)$$

where $w_i = 1/v_i$. Note that this estimator corresponds to a weighted mean of the T_i, giving more weight to the studies whose estimates have smaller unconditional variance (are more precise) when pooling. This is actually a weighted regression including only the constant term (intercept).

The sampling variance $v_\bullet$ of $\hat{\beta}_0$ is simply the reciprocal of the sum of the weights,

$$v_\bullet = \left(\sum_{i=1}^{k} w_i \right)^{-1}, \quad (15)$$

and the standard error $SE(\hat{\beta}_0)$ of $\hat{\beta}_0$ is just the square root of $v_\bullet$. Under this model, $\hat{\beta}_0$ is normally distributed, so a $100(1 - ?)$ percent confidence interval for β_0 is given by

$$\hat{\beta}_0 - t_{\alpha/2}\sqrt{v_\bullet} \leq \beta_0 \leq \hat{\beta}_0 + t_{\alpha/2}\sqrt{v_\bullet}, \quad (16)$$

where t_α is the 100α percent point of the t distribution with $(k-1)$ degrees of freedom. Similarly, a two-sided test of the hypothesis that $\beta_0 = 0$ at significance level α uses the test statistic

$$Z = \hat{\beta}_0^* / \sqrt{v_\bullet}$$

and rejects if $|Z|$ exceeds $t_{\alpha/2}$. Note that the same test and confidence intervals can be computed for any individual coefficient (when multiple predictors are included in the regression model).

A more general fixed effects model includes predictors in the regression equation. Suppose that there are k studies and that in each study there are p predictors. Then the effect size parameter θ_i for the ith study is modeled as

$$\theta_i = \beta_1 x_{i1} + \cdots + \beta_p x_{ip}, \ i = 1, \ldots, k, \quad (17)$$

where $\beta_1, \ldots, \beta_p$ are unknown regression coefficients that need to be estimated, and $x_{i1}, \ldots, x_{ip}$ represent values of the p predictors for study i. Thus, the model for T_i is written as

$$T_i = \beta_1 x_{i1} + \cdots + \beta_p x_{ip} + \varepsilon_i. \quad (18)$$

To compute the regression coefficients, we use the method of generalized least squares (see appendix).

Tests for Blocks of Regression Coefficients

In the fixed effects model, researchers sometimes want to test whether a subset $\beta_1, \ldots, \beta_m$ of the regression coefficients are simultaneously zero, that is,

$$H_0: \beta_1 = \ldots = \beta_m = 0. \quad (19)$$

This test arises, for example, in stepwise analyses, where it is desired to determine whether a set of m of the p predictor variables ($m \leq p$) are related to the outcome after controlling for the effects of the other predictor variables. For example, suppose one is interested in testing the importance of a conceptual variable such as research design, which is coded as a set of predictors. Specifically, such a variable can be coded as multiple dummies for randomized experiment, matched samples, nonequivalent comparison group samples, and other quasi-experimental designs, but it is treated as one conceptual variable, and its importance is tested simultaneously. To test this hypothesis, we compute the statistic

$$Q = (\hat{\beta}_1, \ldots, \hat{\beta}_m) (\mathbf{\Sigma}_{11})^{-1} (\hat{\beta}_1, \ldots, \hat{\beta}_m)', \quad (20)$$

where $\mathbf{\Sigma}_{11}$ is the variance-covariance matrix of the m regression coefficients. The test that $\beta_1 = \ldots = \beta_m = 0$ at the 100α percent significance level consists of rejecting the null hypothesis if Q exceeds the $100(1 - \alpha)$ percentage point of the chi-square distribution with m degrees of freedom. If $m = p$, then the procedure above yields a test that all the β_j are simultaneously zero. In this case, the test statistic Q given in (20) becomes the weighted sum of squares due to regression (see appendix).

Example

Gender differences in field articulation ability (sometimes called visual-analytic spatial ability) were studied by Hyde (1981). She reported standardized mean differences from 14 studies that examined gender differences in spatial ability tasks that call for the joint application of visual and analytic processes (see Maccoby & Jacklin, 1974). All estimates are positive and indicate that, on average, males scored higher than females in field articulation. The effect size estimates are reported in column 2 of Table 12.1. The variances of the effect size estimates are reported in column 3. The year the study was conducted is in column 4.

First, we compute the weighted mean of the effect size estimates. This yields an overall mean estimate of $\hat{\beta}_0$ with a variance of v. = 0.005. The 95% confidence interval for β_0 is given by $0.40 \leq \beta_0 \leq 0.69$. This confidence interval does not include zero, so the data are incompatible with the hypothesis that $\beta_0 = 0$. Alternatively, the ratio

$$\hat{\beta}_0 / \sqrt{v_\bullet} = 7.78,$$

which indicates that the overall mean is significantly different from zero since the observed value is larger than the two-tailed critical t value at the .05 significance level with 13 degrees of freedom (2.16).

Table 12.1	Field Articulation Data From Hyde (1981)		
ID	Effect Size	Variance	Year
1	0.76	0.071	1955
2	1.15	0.033	1959
3	0.48	0.137	1967
4	0.29	0.135	1967
5	0.65	0.140	1967
6	0.84	0.095	1967
7	0.70	0.106	1967
8	0.50	0.121	1967
9	0.18	0.053	1967
10	0.17	0.025	1968
11	0.77	0.044	1970
12	0.27	0.092	1970
13	0.40	0.052	1971
14	0.45	0.095	1972

NOTE: ID = study ID; Year = year of study.

Second, we compute the effect of the year of the study. This yields an estimate of $\hat{\beta}_1 = -0.04$, with a variance var$(\hat{\beta}_1) = 0.0002$. The 95% confidence interval for β_1 is given by $-0.07 \leq \beta_1 \leq -0.01$. This confidence interval does not include 0, so the data are incompatible with the hypothesis that $\beta_1 = 0$. Alternatively, the ratio

$$\hat{\beta}_1 / \sqrt{\text{var}(\hat{\beta}_1)} = -2.83,$$

which indicates that the year of the study effect is significantly different from zero since the absolute observed value is larger than the two-tailed critical t value at the .05 significance level with 12 degrees of freedom (2.18). This indicates that the effect size estimates get slightly smaller over time. The above results are easily obtained from the second version of CMA, developed by Hedges, Borenstein, Higgings, and Rothstein (2005).

UNIVARIATE MIXED EFFECTS MODELS

Mixed effects models treat the effect size parameters as if they were a random sample from a population of effect parameters and estimate hyperparameters (usually the mean and variance) describing this population of effect parameters (see, e.g., DerSimonian & Laird, 1986; Hedges, 1983; Schmidt & Hunter, 1977). The term *mixed effects model* is appropriate since the parameter structure of these models is identical to those of the general linear mixed model (and their important application in social sciences, hierarchical linear models).

In this case, there is nonnegligible variation among effect size parameters even after controlling for the factors that are of interest in the analysis. That is, there is greater residual variation than would be expected from sampling error alone after controlling for all of the study-level covariates. If the researcher believes that this variation should be included in computations of the uncertainty of the regression coefficient estimates, fixed effects models are *not* appropriate because such excess residual variation has no effect on the computation of estimates or their uncertainty in fixed effects models. The mixed effects model is a generalization of the fixed effects model that incorporates a component of between-study variation into the uncertainty of the effect size parameters and their estimates.

As in fixed effects models, the simplest mixed effects model involves the estimation of an average effect size by combining the effect size estimates across all studies in the sample. In the mixed effects model, the effect size parameter is modeled by a mean effect size β_0^* plus a study-specific random effect η_i, that is,

$$\theta_i = \beta_0^* + \eta_i \; \eta_i \sim N(0, \tau^2). \qquad (21)$$

In this model, the η_i represent differences between the effect size parameters from study to study. The parameter τ^2, often called the between-study variance component, describes the amount of variation across studies in the random effects (the η_is) and therefore effect parameters (the θ_is). It follows that the effect size estimate T_i is modeled as

$$T_i = \beta_0^* + \eta_i + \varepsilon_i = \beta_0^* + \xi_i, \qquad (22)$$

where ξ_i is a composite error defined by $\xi_i = \eta_i + \varepsilon_i$. Equation 22 indicates that each effect size is an estimate of β_0^* with a variance that depends on both v_i and τ^2. Hence, it is necessary to distinguish between the variance of the effect size estimate T_i, assuming a fixed

parameter θ_i and the variance of T_i incorporating the variance of the parameter θ_i as well. The latter is the *unconditional sampling variance* of T_i (denoted v_i^*). Since the sampling error ε_i and the random effect η_i are assumed to be independent, and the sample variance of η_i is $\hat\tau^2$, it follows that the unconditional sampling variance of T_i is $v_i^* = v_i + \hat\tau^2$.

The least squares (and maximum likelihood) estimate of the mean β_0 under the model is

$$\hat\beta_0^* = \frac{\sum\limits_{i=1}^{k} w_i^* T_i}{\sum\limits_{i=1}^{k} w_i^*}, \qquad (23)$$

where $w_i^* = 1/(v_i + \hat\tau^2) = 1/v_i^*$, and $\hat\tau^2$ is the between-study variance component estimate. Note that this estimator corresponds to a weighted mean of the T_i, giving more weight to the studies whose estimates have smaller variance (are more precise) when pooling. Also, note that the estimate of the between-study variance is close to zero or very small, so the estimates of the mixed effects model will be similar to those obtain from a fixed effects model.

The sampling variance $v_\bullet^*$ of $\hat\beta_0^*$ is simply the reciprocal of the sum of the weights,

$$v_\bullet^* = \left(\sum\limits_{i=1}^{k} w_i^* \right)^{-1}, \qquad (24)$$

and the standard error $SE(\hat\beta_0^*)$ of $\hat\beta_0^*$ is just the square root of $v_\bullet^*$. Under this model, $\hat\beta_0^*$ is normally distributed, so a $100(1 - \alpha)$ percent confidence interval for β_0 is given by

$$\hat\beta_0^* - t_{\alpha/2}\sqrt{v_\bullet^*} \le \beta_0^* \le \hat\beta_0^* + t_{\alpha/2}\sqrt{v_\bullet^*}, \qquad (25)$$

where t_α is the 100α percent point of the t distribution with $(k-1)$ degrees of freedom. Similarly, a two-sided test of the hypothesis that $\beta_0^* = 0$ at significance level α uses the test statistic

$$Z = = \hat\beta_0^*/\sqrt{}$$

and rejects if $|Z|$ exceeds $t_{\alpha/2}$. Note that the same test and confidence intervals can be computed for any individual coefficient (when multiple predictors are included in the regression).

A more general mixed effects model includes predictors in the regression equation. Suppose that there are k studies and that in each study, there are p predictors. Then the effect size parameter θ_i for the ith study is modeled as

$$\theta_i = \beta_1^* x_{i1} + \cdots + \beta_p^* x_{ip} + \eta_i, \; \eta_i \sim N(0, \tau^2), \quad (26)$$

where η_i is a study-specific random effect with zero expectation and variance τ^2 (and all other terms have been defined previously).

Then, the T_i is modeled as

$$\begin{aligned} T_i &= \beta_1^* x_{i1} + \cdots + \beta_p^* x_{ip} + \eta_i + \varepsilon_i \\ &= \beta_1^* x_{i1} + \cdots + \beta_p^* x_{ip} + \xi_i, \end{aligned} \quad (27)$$

where $\xi_i = \eta_i + \varepsilon_i$ is a composite residual incorporating both study-specific random effect and sampling error. Because we assume that η_i and ε_i are independent, it follows that the variance of ξ_i is $\tau^2 + v_i$. If τ^2 were known, we could estimate the regression coefficients via weighted least squares (which would also yield the maximum likelihood estimates of the β_i^*s). The description of the weighted least squares estimation is facilitated by describing the model in matrix notation, and as in fixed effects models to compute the regression coefficients, we use the method of generalized least squares (see appendix).

Tests for Blocks of Regression Coefficients

As in the fixed effects model, we sometimes want to test whether a subset $\beta_1^*, \ldots, \beta_m^*$ of the regression coefficients is simultaneously zero, that is,

$$H_0: \beta_1^* = \ldots = \beta_m^* = 0. \quad (28)$$

This test arises, for example, in stepwise analyses, where it is desired to determine whether a set of m of the p predictor variables $(m \leq p)$ is related to the outcome after controlling for the effects of the other predictor variables. To test this hypothesis, we compute the statistic

$$Q^* = (\hat{\beta}_1^*, \ldots, \hat{\beta}_m^*), (\boldsymbol{\Sigma}_{11}^*)^{-1} (\hat{\beta}_1^*, \ldots, \hat{\beta}_m^*)', \quad (29)$$

where $(\boldsymbol{\Sigma}_{11}^*)$ is the variance-covariance matrix of the m regression coefficients. The test that

$\beta_1^*, \ldots, \beta_m^* = 0$ at the 100α percent significance level consists of rejecting the null hypothesis if Q^* exceeds the $100(1 - \alpha)$ percentage point of the chi-square distribution with m degrees of freedom.

If $m = p$, then the procedure above yields a test that all the β_j^* are simultaneously zero. In this case, the test statistic Q^* given in Equation 29 becomes the weighted sum of squares due to regression (see appendix).

Testing Whether the Between-Studies Variance Component $\tau^2 = 0$

It seems reasonable that the greater the variation in the observed effect size estimates, the stronger the evidence that $\tau^2 > 0$. A simple test (the likelihood ratio test) of the hypothesis that $\tau^2 = 0$ uses the weighted sum of squares about the weighted mean that would be obtained if $\tau^2 = 0$. Specifically, it uses the statistic

$$Q = \sum_{i=1}^{k} (T_i - \hat{\beta}_0)^2 / v_i, \quad (30)$$

where $\hat{\beta}_0$ is the estimate of β_0 that would be obtained under the hypothesis that $\tau^2 = 0$. The statistic Q has the chi-squared distribution with $(k-1)$ degrees of freedom if $\tau^2 = 0$. Therefore, a test of the null hypothesis that $\tau^2 = 0$ at significance level α rejects the hypothesis if Q exceeds the $100(1 - \alpha)$ percent point of the chi-square distribution with $(k-1)$ degrees of freedom.

This (or any other statistical hypothesis test) should not be interpreted too literally. The test is not very powerful if the number of studies is small or if the conditional variances (the v_i) are large (see Hedges & Pigott, 2001). Consequently, even if the test does not reject the hypothesis that $\tau^2 = 0$, the actual variation in effects across studies may be consistent with a substantial range of nonzero values of τ^2, some of them rather large. That is, it is unlikely that the between-study variance is *exactly* zero. This suggests that it is important to consider estimation of τ^2 and use these estimates in constructing estimates of the mean.

Estimating the Between-Studies Variance Component τ^2

Estimation of τ^2 can be accomplished without making assumptions about the distribution of the random effects or under various assumptions about the distribution of the random effects using other methods such as maximum likelihood estimation. Maximum likelihood estimation is more efficient if the distributional assumptions about the study-specific random effects are correct, but these assumptions are often difficult to justify theoretically and difficult to verify empirically. Thus, distribution-free estimates of the between-studies variance component are often attractive.

A simple, distribution-free estimate of τ^2 is given by

$$\hat{\tau}^2 = \left[\begin{array}{ll} \dfrac{Q - (k-1)}{a} & if \ Q \geq (k-1) \\ 0 & if \ Q < (k-1) \end{array} \right], (31)$$

where a is given by

$$a = \sum_{j=1}^{k} w_i - \frac{\sum_{j=1}^{k} w_i^2}{\sum_{j=1}^{k} w_i}, \qquad (32)$$

and $w_i = 1/v$. Estimates of τ^2 are set to 0 when $Q - (k-1)$ yields a negative value since τ^2, by definition, cannot be negative.

Testing the Significance of the Residual Variance Component

It is sometimes useful to test the statistical significance of the residual variance component τ^2 in addition to estimating it. The test statistic used is Q_E (see appendix).

If the null hypothesis

$$H_0: \tau^2 = 0 \qquad (33)$$

is true, then the weighted residual sum of squares Q_E has a chi-square distribution with $k - p$ degrees of freedom (where p is the total number of predictors, including the intercept). Therefore, the test of H_0 at level α is to reject if Q_E exceeds the $100(1 - \alpha)$ percent point of the chi-square distribution with $(k - p)$ degrees of freedom.

Example

We return to our example of the studies of gender differences in field articulation ability (data presented in Table 12.1). First we turn to the question of whether the effect sizes have more sampling variation than would be expected from the size of their conditional variances. Computing the test statistic Q, we obtain $Q = 24.10$, which is slightly larger than 22.36, which is the $100(1 - .05) = 95\%$ point of the chi-square distribution with $14 - 1 = 13$ degrees of freedom. Actually, a Q value of 24.10 would occur only about 3% of the time if $\tau^2 = 0$. Thus, there is some evidence that the variation in effects across studies is not simply due to chance sampling variation.

The next step is to investigate how much variation there might be across studies. Hence, we compute the estimate of τ^2 (the variation of effect size estimates across studies) using the distribution-free method described above and $\hat{\tau}^2 = (24.10 - (14 - 1)/195.38 = 0.06$. Notice that this value of $\hat{\tau}^2$ is about 65% of the average sampling error variance. This indicates that the between-study variation is not negligible in this sample.

Now, we compute the weighted mean of the effect size estimates. In this case, the weights include the estimate of $\hat{\tau}^2$. This yields an overall mean estimate of $\hat{\beta}_0^* = 0.55$ with a variance of $\upsilon_\bullet^* = 0.01$. Notice that the variance of the weighted mean is now two times as large as in the fixed effects case. The 95% confidence interval for β_0^* is given by $0.34 \leq \beta_0^* \leq 0.76$. This confidence interval does not include 0, so the data are incompatible with the hypothesis that $\beta_0^* = 0$. Alternatively, the ratio

$$\hat{\beta}_0^* / \sqrt{v_\bullet^*} = 5.5,$$

which indicates that the overall mean is significantly different from zero since the observed value is larger than the two-tailed critical t value with 13 degrees of freedom at the $\alpha = .05$ significance level (2.16).

Now consider the case where the year of study is entered in the regression equation. Since the year of study will explain between-study variation, we need to compute the residual estimate of $\hat{\tau}^2$. The distribution-free method of the estimation involves computing an estimate of the residual variance component and then computing a weighted least squares analysis conditional on this variance component estimate. Whereas the estimates are "distribution free" in the sense that they do not depend on the form of the distribution of the random effects, the tests and confidence statements associated with these methods are only strictly true if the random effects are normally distributed. The usual estimator is based on the statistic used to test the significance of the residual variance component. It is the natural generalization of the estimate of the between-study variance component given, for example, by DerSimonian and Laird (1986). Specifically, the usual estimator of the residual variance component is given by

$$\hat{\tau}^2 = (Q_E - k + p)/c, \tag{34}$$

where Q_E is the test statistic used to test whether the residual variance component is zero (the residual sum of squares from the weighted regression using weights $w_i = 1/v_i$ for each study), and c is defined in the appendix.

First we compute the constant c as $c = 174.54$ and the Q_E as $Q_E = 15.11$. Hence, $\hat{\tau}^2 = (15.11 - 12)/174.54 = 0.018$, which is nearly three times smaller now. This value of $\hat{\tau}^2$ is now incorporated in the weights and the computation of the regression coefficients. The estimated regression coefficients are $\hat{\beta}_0^* = 3.22$ for the intercept term and $\hat{\beta}_1^* = -0.04$ for the effect of year. The variances of the regression estimates are 1.26 for the intercept term and 0.0003 for the year of study effect. The 95% confidence interval for $\hat{\beta}_1^*$ is given by $-0.08 \leq \beta_1^* \leq -0.004$. This confidence interval does not include 0, so the data are incompatible with the hypothesis that $\beta_1^* = 0$. Alternatively, the ratio

$$\hat{\beta}_1^*/\sqrt{\text{var}(\hat{\beta}_1^*)} = -2.3,$$

which indicates that the year effect is significantly different from zero since the absolute observed value is larger than the two-tailed critical t value at the $\alpha = .05$ significance level with 12 degrees of freedom (2.18). This indicates that the effect size estimates get smaller over time (as in the fixed effects analyses). Again, the above results are easily obtained using the second version of CMA by Hedges et al. (2005).

Multivariate Meta-Analysis

In the previous sections, we portrayed methods for fitting general linear models to the effect sizes from a series of studies when the effect size estimates are independent. This assumption is reasonable when each study provides only one effect size estimate (e.g., a correlation coefficient). However, there are cases where studies

provide information on two or more effect size estimates. In such cases, the effect size estimates are correlated, and hence the sampling errors are not independent. Appropriate analyses should take this correlation between the effect size estimates into account. In this section, we sketch analogues to the methods portrayed in previous sections when the sampling errors are not independent. These methods are essentially multivariate generalizations of the fixed and mixed effects models given above for univariate meta-analysis. To use these methods, the joint distribution of the nonindependent effect size estimates must be known, which typically involves knowing both the variances and the covariance structure of the effect size estimates. The sampling distribution of correlated effect size estimates is discussed by Gleser and Olkin (1994).

Fixed Effects Models for Correlated Effect Size Estimates

A researcher may be interested in fixed effects models for the analysis of the relation between study characteristics (study-level covariates) and effect sizes. In fixed effects models, the effect size parameter is assumed to be fixed at a certain value. The only source of variation in such models is the sampling variation due to different samples of individuals. As in the univariate case, natural tests of goodness of fit are provided for the fixed effects analysis. They test the hypothesis that the variability among studies is no greater than would be expected if all of the variation among effect size parameters is explained by the linear model. These tests are generalizations of the test of homogeneity of effect size and the tests of goodness of fit for linear models given previously.

In the multivariate case, assuming there are q effect size estimates in each study, the effect size parameter θ_{ij} for the ith study and the jth estimate is modeled as

$$\theta_{ij} = \beta_{1j}x_{i1} + \cdots + \beta_{pj}x_{ip}, \; i = 1, \ldots, k; j = 1, \ldots, q, \tag{35}$$

where $\beta_{1j}, \ldots, \beta_{pj}$ are unknown regression coefficients that need to be estimated. Hence, the T_{ij} in each study is modeled as

$$T_{ij} = \beta_{1j}x_{i1} + \cdots + \beta_{pj}x_{ip} + \varepsilon_{ij}. \tag{36}$$

To compute the regression coefficients, we use the generalized least squares, which is also the maximum likelihood estimator (see appendix). Once the regression estimates and their standard errors are computed, one can construct tests and confidence intervals for individual regression coefficients or tests for blocks of regression coefficients that are similar to those used in the univariate fixed effects models. Tests of goodness of fit of regression models are straightforward generalizations of those used in the univariate general linear model.

Example: Studies of the Effects of Coaching on the SAT

A collection of 19 studies of the effects of coaching on SAT verbal and mathematics scores was assembled by Kalaian and Raudenbush (1996). The authors examined the question of whether the effects of coaching were greater if the length of coaching was greater. The study-level covariate was the log of the number of hours spent in coaching classes. The effect size estimates are standardized mean differences expressing the difference in SAT mathematics or verbal scores between students who received coaching and students who did not receive any coaching. These data are summarized in Table 12.2. Positive estimates indicate the benefits of coaching, while negative estimates indicate higher performance for students who did not receive coaching. Using the formulas illustrated in the appendix, we first compute the estimates of the regression coefficients as $\hat{\beta}_1 = -0.13$ (the intercept for SAT verbal standardized mean differences), $\hat{\beta}_2 = 0.08$ (the association between hours of coaching and SAT verbal standardized mean differences), $\hat{\beta}_3 = -0.29$ (the intercept for SAT mathematics standardized mean differences), and $\hat{\beta}_4 = 0.13$ (the association between hours of coaching and SAT verbal standardized mean differences). Then, we compute the standard errors of the coefficients as $SE(\hat{\beta}_1) = \sqrt{\sigma_{11}} = 0.22$, $SE(\hat{\beta}_2) = \sqrt{\sigma_{22}} = 0.07$, $SE(\hat{\beta}_3) = \sqrt{\sigma_{33}} = 0.22$, and $SE(\hat{\beta}_4) = \sqrt{\sigma_{44}} = 0.07$. Finally, we compute the individual test statistics for the four regression coefficients and obtain $t_1 = -0.59$, $t_2 = 1.12$, $t_3 = -1.34$, and $t_4 = 1.91$. Notice that none of the two-tailed tests is statistically significant at the .05 significance level, except t_4 if we assume a one-tailed test. Hence, it looks like hours of coaching is not significantly associated with SAT mathematics or verbal effect size estimates.

Mixed Models for Correlated Effect Size Estimates

When there is nonnegligible covariation among effect size parameters, even after controlling for the factors that are of interest in the analysis, a general linear model analysis of effect size data is more appropriate. In this case, there is greater residual covariation than would be expected from sampling variability alone, which indicates systematic variation between studies. The mixed model incorporates a component of between-study covariation into the uncertainty of effect size parameters and their estimates, which has the effect of increasing residual variation. The multivariate version of mixed effects models is a straightforward extension of the univariate case.

Let's assume that there are q effect size estimates in each study. Then, the effect size parameter θ_{ij} for the ith study is modeled as

$$\theta_{ij} = \beta_{1j}^* x_{i1} + \cdots + \beta_{pj}^* x_{ip} + \xi_{ij},$$
$$i = 1, \ldots, k; j = 1, \ldots, q, \qquad (37)$$

where $\beta_{1j}^*, \ldots, \beta_{pj}^*$ are unknown regression coefficients that need to be estimated, and ξ_{ij} are study- and effect size–specific random effects. Hence, the T_{ij} in each study is modeled as

$$T_{ij} = \beta_{1j}^* x_{i1} + \cdots + \beta_{pj}^* x_{ip} + \xi_{ij} + \varepsilon_{ij}. \qquad (38)$$

Estimation of the Regression Coefficients and the Covariance Components

The regression coefficients and the covariance components can be estimated by weighted least squares as in the case of the univariate mixed model. The usual procedure is to first estimate the covariance components and then reweight to estimate the regression coefficients and their standard errors. There are usually advantages (among them software availability) in considering the problem as a special case of the hierarchical linear model considered in the previous section in conjunction with univariate mixed model analyses. The multivariate mixed model analyses can be carried out as instances of the multivariate hierarchical linear model (HLM; see Thum, 1997), estimating parameters by the method of maximum likelihood. However, a simpler alternative is available since

Table 12.2   SAT Coaching Data From Kalaian and Raudenbush (1996): Selected Sample

ID	SAT (V)	SAT (M)	VAR (V)	COV (V,M)	VAR (M)	Log (Hours)	Year
9	0.13	0.12	0.01468	0.00968	0.01467	3.044522438	73
10	0.25	0.06	0.02180	0.01430	0.02165	3.044522438	73
11	0.31	0.09	0.02208	0.01444	0.02186	3.044522438	73
12	0.00	0.07	0.14835	0.09791	0.14844	2.186051277	86
26	0.13	0.48	0.12158	0.08049	0.12481	3.178053830	88
29	−0.23	0.33	0.25165	0.16397	0.25340	2.890371758	87
30	0.13	0.13	0.09327	0.06151	0.09327	2.708050201	85
31	0.13	0.34	0.04454	0.02944	0.04509	3.401197382	60
33	0.09	0.11	0.03850	0.02536	0.03852	2.302585093	62
34	−0.10	0.08	0.10657	0.07030	0.10653	1.791759469	88
35	−0.14	−0.29	0.10073	0.06654	0.10152	1.791759469	88
36	−0.16	−0.34	0.10917	0.07214	0.11039	1.791759469	88
37	−0.07	−0.06	0.10889	0.07185	0.10887	1.791759469	88
38	−0.02	0.21	0.01857	0.01225	0.01861	2.708050201	58
39	0.06	0.17	0.00963	0.00636	0.00966	2.708050201	53
42	0.15	0.03	0.00668	0.00440	0.00667	3.688879454	78
43	0.17	0.19	0.10285	0.06748	0.10294	2.639057330	76
45	−0.04	0.60	0.03203	0.02110	0.03331	4.143134726	87
47	0.54	0.57	0.07968	0.05206	0.07998	3.295836866	88

NOTE: ID = study ID; SAT = Scholastic Assessment Test; V = verbal; M = math; VAR = variance; COV = covariance.

the sampling error covariance matrix is known (Kalaian & Raudenbush, 1996). In particular, it is possible to transform the within-study model so that the sampling errors are independent (see appendix). Eventually, the model that results from this procedure resembles a conventional two-level linear model with independent sampling errors at the first level. Therefore, conventional software can be used to estimate the regression coefficients and the variance components (such as HLM).

Multivariate Meta-Analysis Using HLM

HLM is a software package designed especially for fitting multilevel models, and it can be used to fit mixed effects models to effect size data with study-level covariates (Raudenbush, Bryk, Cheong, & Congdon, 2005; readers can refer to Chapter 31 for more information on this application of HLM). It can also be used to fit multivariate mixed models to effect size data in meta-analysis. Table 12.3 describes the input file for a mixed model multivariate meta-analysis of the SAT coaching data reported by Kalaian and Raudenbush (1996). The data for the analysis are read from a separate file and consist of 19 pairs of effect sizes from 19 studies of the effects of coaching on the SAT verbal and SAT math tests. The first two lines set the maximum number of iterations the program will run (NUMIT:1000) and the criterion for stopping iteration (STOP-VAL:0.0000010000), and the third line specifies that a linear model will be used (NONLIN: n). Lines 4 to 6 indicate the Level 1 model (LEVEL 1: MATH = VERBAL + MATH + RANDOM) and the Level 2 models (LEVEL 2: VERBAL = INTR-CPT2 + HOURS + RANDOM/ and LEVEL 2: MATH = INTRCPT2 + HOURS + RANDOM/). Lines 7 and 8 indicate that no weights are used in the computations (LEVELWEIGHT:NONE). Line 9 indicates that the variance is not known (VARIANCEKNOWN:NONE), line 10 that no output file of residuals is requested (RESFIL:N), and line 11 that the Level 1 variances are not heterogeneous (HETEROL1VAR:n). Line 12 indicates that the default value of the accelerator should be used in estimation (ACCEL:5), line 13 that a latent variable regression is not used (LVR:N), and line 14 that the OL equations should be printed to 19 units (LEV1OLS:10). Line 15 indicates that restricted maximum likelihood is used (MLF:N), line 16 that no optional hypothesis testing will be done (HYPOTH:N), and line 17 that unacceptable starting values of τ will be automatically corrected (FIXTAU:3). Line 18 indicates that none of the fixed effects is constrained to be equal to one another (CONSTRAIN:N). Line 19 specifies that the output file is named "COACHING.OUT," line 20 specifies that the full output will be given (FULLOUTPUT:Y), and line 21 specifies the title of the output.

The results are reported in Table 12.4. The top panel of Table 12.4 shows the regression coefficient estimates. The estimates are only slightly different from those in the fixed effects analyses. Overall, as in the fixed effects analyses, most of the regression estimates are not significantly different from zero (except for hours of coaching). The predictor, hours of coaching, is significant in verbal, indicating that hours of coaching matters in verbal. The bottom panel of Table 12.4 shows the variance component estimates for the residuals about the SAT verbal and SAT math regressions, respectively, along with the chi-square test of the hypothesis that the variance component is zero and the p value for that test. Variance components for both math and verbal are not significantly different from zero, indicating that there is negligible between-study variation. This indicates that a fixed effects model is appropriate.

CONCLUSION

This study presented univariate and multivariate models for meta-analysis. The use of fixed and mixed effects models in univariate and multivariate cases was also demonstrated. Specialized statistical software packages such as CMA can be

Table 12.3 HLM Input for Mixed Model Multivariate Analyses of SAT Coaching Data From Kalaian and Raudenbush (1996)

Input File

NUMIT:1000
STOPVAL:0.0000010000
NONLIN:n
LEVEL1:MATH=VERBAL+MATH+RANDOM
LEVEL2:VERBAL=INTRCPT2+HOURS+RANDOM/
LEVEL2:MATH=INTRCPT2+HOURS+RANDOM/
LEVEL1WEIGHT:NONE
LEVEL2WEIGHT:NONE
VARIANCEKNOWN:NONE
RESFIL2:N
HETEROL1VAR:n
ACCEL:5
LVR:N
LEV1OLS:10
MLF:n
HYPOTH:n
FIXTAU:3
CONSTRAIN:N
OUTPUT:COACHING.OUT
FULLOUTPUT:Y
TITLE:MULTIVARIATE META ANALYSIS USING HLM

easily used to conduct univariate weighted least squares analyses in meta-analysis (for both fixed and mixed effects analyses). Other specialized software packages, such as HLM, can carry out multivariate mixed models analyses for meta-analytic data with nested structure. Mixed effects models analyses can also be performed with specialized software such as MLwin and the SAS procedure proc mixed. The mixed effects models presented here can be extended to three or more levels of hierarchy capturing random variation at higher levels. For example, a three-level meta-analysis can model and compute variation between investigators or laboratories at the third level (Konstantopoulos, 2005).

Table 12.4   HLM Output for Mixed Model Multivariate Analyses of SAT Coaching Data From Kalaian and Raudenbush (1996)

Output File

Final estimation of fixed effects:

Fixed Effect	Standard Coefficient	Error	Approximate T Ratio	df	p Value
For VERBAL, B1					
INTRCPT2, G10	−0.051329	0.227003	−0.226	17	0.824
HOURS, G11	0.049071	0.073447	0.668	17	0.513
For MATH, B2					
INTRCPT2, G20	−0.496924	0.264238	−1.881	17	0.077
HOURS, G21	0.212755	0.087375	2.435	17	0.026

Final estimation of variance components:

Random Effect	Standard Deviation	Variance Component	df	Chi-Square	p Value
VERBAL, U1	0.05144	0.00265	17	8.80514	> .500
MATH, U2	0.12414	0.01541	17	18.40913	0.363

APPENDIX

Univariate Meta-Analysis

Fixed Effects Models

The model in Equation 18 can be written in matrix notation as

$$T = \theta + \varepsilon = X\beta + \varepsilon, \quad (A1)$$

where $\theta = (\theta_1, \ldots, \theta_k)'$ and $T = (T_1, \ldots, T_k)'$ denote the k-dimensional vectors of population and sample effect sizes, respectively; $\beta = (\beta_1, \ldots, \beta_p)'$ is the p-dimensional vector of regression coefficients; $\varepsilon = (\varepsilon_1, \ldots, \varepsilon_k)' = T - \theta$ is a k-dimensional vector of residuals; and X is a $k \times p$ matrix

$$X = \begin{bmatrix} 1 & x_{12} & \ldots & x_{1p} \\ 1 & x_{22} & \ldots & x_{2p} \\ \cdot & \cdot & \ldots & \cdot \\ \cdot & \cdot & \ldots & \cdot \\ 1 & x_{k2} & \ldots & x_{kp} \end{bmatrix} \quad (A2)$$

called the *design matrix*, which is assumed to have no linearly dependent columns. The generalized least squares estimator $\hat{\beta}$, which is also the maximum likelihood estimator of β, is given by

$$\hat{\beta} = (X'V^{-1}X)^{-1} XV^{-1}T, \quad (A3)$$

which has a normal distribution, with mean β and covariance matrix Σ given by

$$\Sigma = (X'V^{-1}X)^{-1}, \quad (A4)$$

where V is a diagonal covariance matrix,

$$V = \text{Diag}(v_1, v_2, \ldots, v_k). \quad (A5)$$

Testing the Significance of All Regression Coefficients

When a meta-analyst is interested in testing whether all the β_js are simultaneously zero, the test statistic becomes the weighted sum of squares due to regression, namely,

$$Q_R = \hat{\beta}'\Sigma^{-1}\hat{\beta}. \quad (A6)$$

The test that $\beta = 0$ is simply a test of whether the weighted sum of squares due to the regression is larger than would be expected if $\beta = 0$, and the test consists of rejecting the hypothesis that $\beta = 0$

if Q_R exceeds the $100(1 - \alpha)$ percentage point of a chi-square with p degrees of freedom.

Mixed Effects Models

The model in Equation 27 can be written in matrix notation as

$$T = \theta + \varepsilon = X\beta^* + \eta + \varepsilon = X\beta^* + \xi, \quad (A7)$$

where $\eta = (\eta_1, \ldots, \eta_k)'$ is the k-dimensional vector of random effects, and $\xi = (\xi_1, \ldots, \xi_k)'$ is a k-dimensional vector of residuals of T about $X\beta^*$, and all other terms have been defined previously. The covariance matrix of ξ is a diagonal matrix where the ith diagonal element is $v_i + \hat{\tau}^2$. If the residual variance component τ^2 were known, we could use the method of generalized least squares to obtain an estimate of β^*. Although we do not know the residual variance component τ^2, we can compute an estimate of τ^2 and use this estimate to compute the generalized least squares estimate of β^* —namely, $\hat{\beta}^*$—as

$$\hat{\beta}^* = [X'(V^*)^{-1}X]^{-1} X(V^*)^{-1}T, \quad (A8)$$

which is normally distributed with mean β^* and covariance matrix Σ^* given by

$$\Sigma^* = [X'(V^*)^{-1}X]^{-1}, \quad (A9)$$

where V^* is defined as

$$V^* = \text{Diag}(v_1 + \hat{\tau}^2, v_2 + \hat{\tau}^2, \ldots, v_k + \hat{\tau}^2 \quad (A10)$$

That is, the estimate of the between-study variance component $\hat{\tau}^2$ is incorporated as a constant term in the computation of the regression coefficients and their dispersion via the variance covariance matrix of the effect size estimates.

Testing the Significance of All Regression Coefficients

When a meta-analyst is interested in testing whether all the β_js are simultaneously zero, the test statistic becomes the weighted sum of squares due to regression, namely,

$$Q_R^* = (\hat{\beta}^*)' (\Sigma^*)^{-1} \hat{\beta}^*. \quad (A11)$$

The test that $\beta^* = 0$ is simply a test of whether the weighted sum of squares due to the regression is larger than would be expected if $\beta^* = 0$, and the test consists of rejecting the hypothesis that $\beta^* = 0$ if Q_R^* exceeds the $100(1 - \alpha)$ percentage point of a chi-square with p degrees of freedom.

Testing the Significance of the Residual Variance Component

It is sometimes useful to test the statistical significance of the residual variance component τ^2 in addition to estimating it. The test statistic used is

$$Q_E = T'[V^{-1} - V^{-1}X (X'V^{-1}X)^{-1}X'V^{-1}]T, \quad (A12)$$

where $V = \text{Diag}(v_1, \ldots, v_k)$. This statistics is also used to compute the residual variance component

$$\hat{\tau}^2 = (Q_E - k + p)/c,$$

where c is given by

$$c = \text{tr}(V^{-1}) - \text{tr}[(X'V^{-1}X)^{-1}X'V^{-2}X], \quad (A13)$$

where $\text{tr}(A)$ is the trace of the matrix A.

Multivariate Meta-Analysis

Fixed Effects

Equation 36 can be expressed in matrix notation as

$$T = \theta + \varepsilon = X\beta + \varepsilon, \quad (A14)$$

where we denote the kq-dimensional column vectors of population and sample effect sizes by $\theta = (\theta_1', \ldots, \theta_k')'$ and $T = (T_1', \ldots, T_k')'$, respectively, where $\theta_i = (\theta_{i1}, \ldots, \theta_{iq})'$ and $T_i = (T_{i1}, \ldots, T_{iq})'$; $X = (I_q \otimes x_1, I_q \otimes x_2, \ldots, I_q \otimes x_k)'$ is a $kq \times pq$ design matrix, where $x_i = (x_{i1}, \ldots, x_{ip})'$; I_q is a $q \times q$ identity matrix; $\otimes$ is the Kronecker product operator; $\beta = (\beta_{11}, \ldots, \beta_{p1}, \beta_{21}, \ldots, \beta_{pq})'$ is a pq column vector of regression coefficients that need to be estimated; and $\varepsilon = (\varepsilon_1, \ldots, \varepsilon_{kq})' = T - \theta$ is a kq-dimensional column vector of residuals. Each T_i is assumed to have a q-variate normal distribution (since there are q effect size estimates in each study) about the corresponding θ_i with known $q \times q$ covariance matrix Σ_i. Although there is no need for all studies to have the same number of effect sizes, we make that assumption here to simplify notation.

The vector of residuals $\boldsymbol{\varepsilon} = \mathbf{T} - \boldsymbol{\theta}$ follows a kq-variate normal with mean zero and known $kq \times kq$ block-diagonal covariance matrix $\mathbf{V}$ given by

$$\begin{aligned} \mathbf{V} &= \mathrm{Diag}\,(\boldsymbol{\Sigma}_1, \boldsymbol{\Sigma}_2, \ldots, \boldsymbol{\Sigma}_k) \\ &= \mathbf{I}_k \otimes \boldsymbol{\Sigma}_i,\, i = 1, \ldots, k \end{aligned} \quad (A15)$$

where $\boldsymbol{\Sigma}_i$ is a known $q \times q$ covariance matrix for study i. We can hence use the method of generalized least squares to obtain an estimate of the regression coefficients vector $\boldsymbol{\beta}$. This is essentially the approach employed by Raudenbush, Becker, and Kalaian (1988); Gleser and Olkin (1994); and Berkey, Anderson, and Hoaglin (1996). Specifically, the generalized least squares estimator $\hat{\boldsymbol{\beta}}$, which is also the maximum likelihood estimator of $\hat{\boldsymbol{\beta}}$, with covariance matrix $\mathbf{V}$, is given by

$$\hat{\boldsymbol{\beta}} = (\mathbf{X}'\mathbf{V}^{-1}\mathbf{X})^{-1}\mathbf{X}'\mathbf{V}^{-1}\mathbf{T}, \quad (A16)$$

which has a pq-variate normal distribution with mean $\boldsymbol{\beta}$ and covariance matrix $\boldsymbol{\Sigma}$ given by

$$\boldsymbol{\Sigma} = (\mathbf{X}'\mathbf{V}^{-1}\mathbf{X})^{-1}. \quad (A17)$$

Mixed Effects

Equation 38 can be expressed in matrix notation as

$$\mathbf{T} = \boldsymbol{\theta} + \boldsymbol{\varepsilon} = \mathbf{X}\boldsymbol{\beta}^* + \mathbf{I}\boldsymbol{\Xi} + \boldsymbol{\varepsilon}, \quad (A18)$$

where $\mathbf{I}$ is a kq-dimensional identity matrix, $\boldsymbol{\Xi}$ is a kq-dimensional vector of the between-study random effects, and all other terms have been defined previously. The vector $\boldsymbol{\beta}^*$ of the between-study random effects follows a q-variate normal with mean zero and $q \times q$ covariance matrix $\boldsymbol{\Omega}$.

The regression coefficient vector $\boldsymbol{\beta}^*$ and the covariance component matrix $\boldsymbol{\Omega}$ can be estimated by weighted least squares as in the case of the univariate mixed model. The usual procedure is to first estimate the covariance component matrix $\boldsymbol{\Omega}$ and then reweight to estimate the regression coefficient vector $\boldsymbol{\beta}^*$ and its covariance matrix $\boldsymbol{\Sigma}^*$. Alternatively, one could orthogonalize the error terms. To achieve this, one can perform the Cholesky factorization on each sampling error covariance matrix $\boldsymbol{\Sigma}_i^*$ in each study so that

$$\boldsymbol{\Sigma}_i^* = \mathbf{F}_i\mathbf{F}_i', \quad (A19)$$

where $\mathbf{F}_i$ is a known matrix (since $\boldsymbol{\Sigma}_i^*$ is a known matrix) and is the lower triangular (square root) matrix of the Cholesky decomposition. The within-study model is then transformed to

$$\mathbf{F}_i^{-1}\,\mathbf{T}_i = \mathbf{F}_i^{-1}\,\boldsymbol{\theta}_i + \mathbf{F}_i^{-1}\,\boldsymbol{\varepsilon}_i, \quad (A20)$$

where the transformed effect size vector $\mathbf{Z}_i$ is given by

$$\mathbf{Z}_i = \mathbf{F}_i^{-1}\,\mathbf{T}_i \quad (A21)$$

and has a sampling error vector

$$\tilde{\boldsymbol{\varepsilon}}_i = \mathbf{F}_i^{-1}\,\boldsymbol{\varepsilon}_i, \quad (A22)$$

which has covariance matrix $\mathbf{I}$, a $q_i \times q_i$ identity matrix. Thus, one might write the model as

$$\mathbf{Z}_i = \mathbf{F}_i^{-1}\,\boldsymbol{\theta}_i + \tilde{\boldsymbol{\varepsilon}}_i, \quad (A23)$$

where the transformed effect size estimates $\mathbf{Z}_i$ are now independent with a constant variance, and the effect size parameter vector $\boldsymbol{\theta}_i$ is the same as in the original model. Thus, the within-study model along with the between-study model is now a conventional two-level linear model with independent sampling errors at the first level. Therefore, conventional software can be used to estimate $\boldsymbol{\beta}^*$ and $\boldsymbol{\Omega}$ by the method of maximum likelihood such as HLM (Raudenbush et al., 2005).

Note

1. Comprehensive Meta-Analysis offers about 100 different formats for entering data and is especially designed to cover various methods for meta-analytic data (see www.meta-analysis.com).

References

Begg, C. B. (1994). Publication bias. In H. Cooper & L. V. Hedges (Eds.), *The handbook of research synthesis* (pp. 399–410). New York: Russell Sage Foundation.

Berkey, C. S., Anderson, J. J., & Hoaglin, D. C. (1996). Multiple-outcome meta-analysis of clinical trials. *Statistics in Medicine, 15,* 537–557.

Cohn, L. D., & Becker, B. J. (2003). Title: How meta-analysis increases statistical power. *Psychological Methods, 8,* 243–253.

Cooper, H. (1989). *Integrating research* (2nd ed.). Newbury Park, CA: Sage.

Cooper, H., & Hedges, L. V. (1994). *The handbook of research synthesis*. New York: Russell Sage Foundation.

DerSimonian, R., & Laird, N. (1986). Meta-analysis in clinical trials. *Controlled Clinical Trials, 7,* 177–188.

Duval, S., & Tweedie, R. (2000). A nonparametric trim and fill method of accounting for publication bias in meta-analysis. *Journal of the American Statistical Association, 95,* 89–98.

Fleiss, J. L. (1994). Measures of effect size for categorical data. In H. Cooper & L. V. Hedges (Eds.), *The handbook of research synthesis* (pp. 245–260). New York: Russell Sage Foundation.

Gleser, L. J., & Olkin, I. (1994). Stochastically dependent effect sizes. In H. Cooper & L. V. Hedges (Eds.), *The handbook of research synthesis* (pp. 339–356). New York: Russell Sage Foundation.

Hedges, L. V. (1982). Estimation of effect size from a series of independent experiments. *Psychological Bulletin, 92,* 490–499.

Hedges, L. V. (1983). A random effects model for effect sizes. *Psychological Bulletin, 93,* 388–395.

Hedges, L. V. (1994). Fixed effects models. In H. Cooper & L. V. Hedges (Eds.), *The handbook of research synthesis* (pp. 285–299). New York: Russell Sage Foundation.

Hedges, L. V., Borenstein, M., Higgings, J., & Rothstein, H. (2005). *Comprehensive meta-analysis*. Englewood, NJ: Biostat.

Hedges, L. V., & Olkin, I. (1985). *Statistical methods for meta-analysis*. New York: Academic Press.

Hedges, L. V., & Pigott, T. D. (2001). The power of statistical test in meta-analysis. *Psychological Methods, 6,* 203–217.

Hedges, L. V., & Vevea, J. L. (1998). Fixed and random effects models in meta analysis. *Psychological Methods, 3,* 486–504.

Hyde, J. S. (1981). How large are cognitive gender differences: A meta-analysis using omega and d. *American Psychologist, 36,* 892–901.

Kalaian, H., & Raudenbush, S. W. (1996). A multivariate mixed linear model for meta-analysis. *Psychological Methods, 1,* 227–235.

Konstantopoulos, S. (2005, April). *Three-level models in meta-analysis*. Paper presented at the annual conference of the American Educational Association, Montreal, Canada.

Light, R. J., & Pillemer, D. B. (1984). *Summing up: The science of reviewing research*. Cambridge, MA: Harvard University Press.

Lipsey, M. W., & Wilson, D. B. (2001). *Practical meta-analysis*. Thousand Oaks, CA: Sage.

Maccoby, E. E., & Jacklin, C. N. (1974). *The psychology of sex differences*. Stanford, CA: Stanford University Press.

Raudenbush, S. W., Becker, B. J., & Kalaian, S. (1988). Modeling multivariate effect sizes. *Psychological Bulletin, 103,* 111–120.

Raudenbush, S. W., Bryk, A., Cheong, Y. F., & Congdon, R. (2005). *HLM 6: Hierarchical linear and onlinear modeling*. Lincolnwood, IL: Scientific Software International.

Rosenthal, R. (1979). The "file-drawer problem" and tolerance for null results. *Psychological Bulletin, 86,* 638–641.

Rosenthal, R. (1994). Parametric measures of effect size. In H. Cooper & L. V. Hedges (Eds.), *The handbook of research synthesis* (pp. 231–244). New York: Russell Sage Foundation.

Rosenthal, R., & Rubin, D. B. (1982). Comparing effect sizes of independent studies. *Psychological Bulletin, 92,* 500–504.

Rothstein, H., Sutton, A. J., & Borenstein, M. (2005). *Publication bias in meta-analysis: Prevention, assessment, and adjustments*. Hoboken, NJ: John Wiley.

Schmidt, F. L., & Hunter, J. (1977). Development of a general solution to the problem of validity generalization. *Journal of Applied Psychology, 62,* 529–540.

Shadish, W. R., Cook, T. D., & Campbell, D. T. (2002). *Experimental and quasi-experimental designs for generalized causal inference*. Boston: Houghton Mifflin.

Shadish, W. R., & Haddock, C. K. (1994). Combining estimates of effect size. In H. Cooper & L. V. Hedges (Eds.), *The handbook of research synthesis* (pp. 261–281). New York: Russell Sage Foundation.

Smith, M. I., & Glass, G. V. (1977). Meta-analysis of psychotherapy outcome studies. *American Psychologist, 32,* 752–760.

Thum, Y. M. (1997). Hierarchical linear models for multivariate outcomes. *Journal of Educational and Behavioral Statistics, 22,* 77–108.

White, H. D. (1994). Scientific communication and literature retrieval. In H. Cooper & L. V. Hedges (Eds.), *The handbook of research synthesis* (pp. 41–55). New York: Russell Sage Foundation.

Wortman, P. M. (1994). Judging research quality. In H. Cooper & L. V. Hedges (Eds.), *The handbook of research synthesis* (pp. 97–110). New York: Russell Sage Foundation.

PART III

BEST PRACTICES IN DATA CLEANING AND THE BASICS OF DATA ANALYSIS

13

Best Practices in Data Transformation

The Overlooked Effect of Minimum Values

Jason W. Osborne

D
ata transformations are commonly used tools that can serve many functions in quantitative analysis of data, including meeting assumptions and improving effect sizes, thus constituting important aspects of best practice.

A transformation is a mathematical modification of the variable to achieve a particular goal (e.g., normality, enhanced interpretability). There are an almost infinite variety of possible data transformations, from adding constants to multiplying, squaring, or raising to a power; converting to logarithmic scales; inverting and reflecting; taking the square root of the values; and even applying trigonometric transformations such as sine wave transformations.

While these are important options for analysts, they do fundamentally transform the nature of the variable, making the interpretation of the results somewhat more complex. Furthermore, few (if any) statistical texts discuss the tremendous influence a distribution's minimum value has on the efficacy of a transformation.

Specifically, the lowest value (anchor) in your variable's distribution can influence the efficacy of a particular transformation. The goal of this chapter is to promote thoughtful and informed use of data transformations, focusing on three data transformations most commonly discussed in social sciences texts (square root, log, and inverse) for improving the normality of variables.

Data Transformation and Normality

Many statistical procedures assume that the variables (or their error terms, more technically) are normally distributed. Significant violation of this assumption of normality can increase the chances of the researcher committing either a Type I or a Type II error (depending on the nature of the analysis and the nonnormality). Yet few of us have truly normally distributed data (Micceri, 1989), while at the same time, few authors in peer-reviewed

Author's Note: This chapter is based on Osborne, J. W. (2002). Notes on the use of data transformations. *Practical Assessment, Research & Evaluation, 8*(6). Available at http://pareonline.net/getvn.asp?v=8&n=6

journals note the use of data transformations to correct for this issue.

Even when one is using nonparametric tests (that do not explicitly assume normally distributed error terms), authors such as Zimmerman (e.g., 1995, 1998) have pointed out that violations of this assumption can adversely harm nonparametric tests as much as, or more than, parametric tests, confirming the importance of normality in all statistical analysis.

There are multiple options for dealing with nonnormal data. First, the researcher must make certain that the nonnormality is due to a valid reason (real observed data points). Invalid reasons for nonnormality include things such as mistakes in data entry and missing data values not declared missing. Researchers using National Center for Education Statistics databases such as the National Education Longitudinal Survey of 1988 will often find extreme values that are intended to be missing. In Figure 13.1, we see that the Composite Achievement Test scores variable (BY2XCOMP) ranges from about 30 to about 75 but also has a group of missing values assigned a value of 99. If the researcher fails to remove these, the skew for this variable is 1.46, but with the missing values appropriately removed, skew drops to 0.35 (where 0.00 is the skew for the standard normal distribution), and thus no further

action is needed. Issues such as these are simple to remedy through correction of the value or declaration of missing values (readers interested in handling missing data can refer to Chapter 15, this volume).

However, not all nonnormality is due to data entry error or nondeclared missing values. Two other reasons for nonnormality are the presence of outliers (scores that are extreme relative to the rest of the sample) and the nature of the variable itself. There is a long-running debate in the literature about whether outliers should be removed. I am sympathetic to Judd and McClelland's (1989) argument that outlier removal is desirable, honest, and important. However, not all researchers feel that way (cf. Orr, Sackett, & DuBois, 1991; more detailed discussion of handling outliers is presented in Chapter 14, this volume). Should a researcher remove outliers and find substantial nonnormality or choose not to remove outliers, data transformation is a viable option for improving normality of a variable.

How Does One Tell When a Variable is Violating the Assumption of Normality?

There are several ways to tell whether a variable is substantially nonnormal. While researchers tend to report favoring "eyeballing

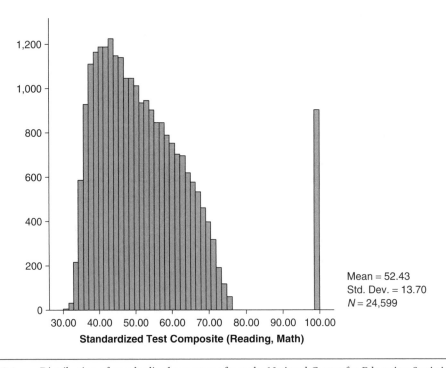

Figure 13.1   Distribution of standardized test scores from the National Center for Education Statistics.

the data," or visual inspection (Orr et al., 1991), researchers and reviewers often are more comfortable with a more objective assessment of normality, which can range from simple examination of skew and kurtosis to examination of P-P plots (available through most statistical software packages) and inferential tests of normality, such as the Kolmorogov-Smirnov (K-S) test (and adaptations of this test—researchers wanting more information on the K-S test and other similar tests should consult the manual for their software as well as Goodman [1954], Lilliefors [1967], Rosenthal [1968], and Wilcox [1997], probably in that order). These can be useful to a researcher needing to know whether a variable's distribution is significantly different from a normal (or other) distribution.

As stated above, skew of 0 is the ideal, and increasing deviation from 0 should be met with increasing concern on the part of the researcher. A rule of thumb often used is that skew should be less than 1.0, although closer to 0 is always better for a variety of reasons.

Notes on the Mathematics of These Data Transformations

While many researchers in the social sciences are well trained in statistical methods, not many of us have had significant mathematical training, or if we have, it has often been long forgotten. This section is intended to give a brief refresher on what really happens when one applies a data transformation.

Square Root Transformation. Most readers will be familiar with this procedure—when one applies a square root transformation, the square root of every value is taken. However, as one cannot take the square root of a negative number, if there are negative values for a variable, a constant must be added to move the minimum value of the distribution above 0, preferably to 1.00, primarily because numbers above 0.00 and below 1.0 behave differently than numbers 0.00, 1.00, and those larger than 1.00. The square root of 1.00 and 0.00 remains 1.00 and 0.00, respectively, and remains constant, while numbers above 1.00 always become smaller, and numbers between 0.00 and 1.00 become *larger* (the square root of 4 is 2, but the square root of 0.40 is 0.63). Thus, if you apply a square root to a continuous variable that contains values between 0 and 1 as well as above 1,

you are treating some numbers differently than others, which is probably not desirable in most cases. The constancy of 1.0 is important to remember as we make recommendations below.

Log Transformation(s). Logarithmic transformations are actually a class of transformations, rather than a single transformation. In brief, a logarithm is the power (exponent) a base number must be raised to in order to get the original number. Any given number can be expressed as y to the x power in an infinite number of ways. For example, if we were talking about base 10, 1 is 10^0, 100 is 10^2, 16 is $10^{1.2}$, and so on. Thus, $\log_{10}(100) = 2$ and $\log_{10}(16) = 1.2$. However, base 10 is not the only option for log transformations. Another common option is the natural logarithm, where the constant e (2.7182818 . . .) is the base. In this case, the natural log of 100 is 4.605. As the logarithm of any negative number or number less than 1 is undefined, if a variable contains values less than 1.0, a constant must be added to move the minimum value of the distribution, preferably to 1.00.

There are good reasons to consider a range of bases (Cleveland, 1984, argues that base 10, 2, and e should always be considered at a minimum). For example, in cases where there are extremes of range, base 10 is desirable, as this draws the extreme values in closer to the center of the distribution. But when there are ranges that are less extreme, using base 10 will result in a loss of resolution in your data (i.e., will make all values overly compact, limiting variance), and using a lower base (e or 2) will serve. Thus, in general, higher bases tend to pull extreme values in more drastically than lower bases when using this transformation. Figure 13.2 graphically presents the different effects of using different log bases. Readers are encouraged to consult Cleveland (1984) for further discussion of this issue.

Inverse Transformation. To take the inverse of a number (x) is to compute $1/x$. What this does is essentially make very small numbers very large and very large numbers very small, thus reversing the order of your scores. Therefore, one must be careful to reflect, or reverse, the distribution prior to applying an inverse transformation. To reflect, one multiplies a variable by -1 and then adds a constant to the distribution to bring the minimum value back above 1.0. Then, once the inverse transformation is complete, the ordering of the values will be identical to the original data.

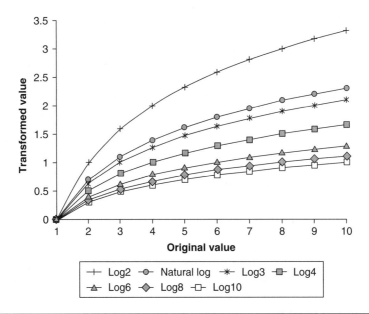

Figure 13.2   The effect of log base on the efficacy of transformations.

In general, these three transformations have been presented in the relative order of power (from weakest to most powerful). It is my preference to use the minimum amount of transformation necessary to improve normality.

Positive vs. Negative Skew. There are, of course, two types of skew: positive and negative. All of the above-mentioned transformations work by compressing the right side of the distribution toward the center, making them effective on positively skewed distributions. Should a researcher have a negatively skewed distribution, the researcher must reflect the distribution (multiply by −1 and add a constant to bring the minimum value to 1.0, apply the transformation, and then reflect again to restore the original order of the variable).

Best Practices in the Use of Data Transformations

Data transformations are valuable tools, with many benefits, but only if used in an informed manner. Too many statistical texts gloss over this issue, leaving researchers ill-prepared to use these tools appropriately. All of the transformations examined here reduce nonnormality by reducing the relative spacing of scores on the

right side of the distribution more than the scores on the left side.

The very act of altering the relative distances between data points, which is how these transformations improve normality, raises issues in the interpretation of the data. If done correctly, all data points remain in the same relative order as prior to transformation. This allows researchers to continue to interpret results in terms of increasing scores. However, this might be undesirable if the original variables were meant to be substantively interpretable (e.g., annual income, years of age, grade, grade point average [GPA]), as the variables become more complex to interpret due to the curvilinear nature of the transformations. Researchers must therefore be careful when interpreting results based on transformed data. This issue is illustrated in Figure 13.3 and Table 13.1.

In Figure 13.3, you can see that while the original variable has equal spacing between values, the other transformed variables show the curvilinear nature of the transformations. The quality of the transformed variable is different from the original variable. If a variable with those qualities were subjected to a square root transformation, where the variable's old values were {0, 1, 2, 3, 4}, the new values are now {0.00, 1.00, 1.41, 1.73, 2.00}—the intervals are no

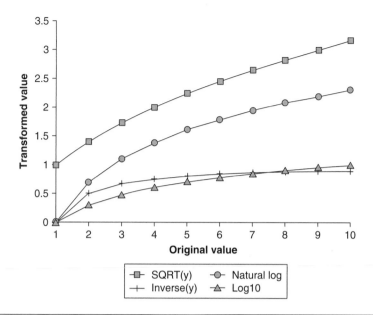

Figure 13.3   Different transformations have more powerful effects on variables.

longer equal between successive values. The examples presented in Table 13.1 elaborate on this point. It quickly becomes evident that these transformations change the relative distance between adjacent values that were previously equidistant (assuming interval or ratio measurement). In the nontransformed variable, the distance between values would be an equal 1.0 distance between each increment (1, 2, 3, etc.). However, the action of the transformations dramatically alters this equal spacing. For example, where the original distance between 1 and 2 had been 1.0 in the untransformed data, now it is 0.41, 0.30, or 0.50, depending on the transformation. Furthermore, while the original distance between 19 and 20 had been 1.0 in the original data, it is now 0.11, 0.02, or 0.00, depending on the transformation. Thus, while the order of the variable has been retained, order is all that has been maintained. The equal spacing of the original variable has been eliminated. If a variable had been measured on interval or ratio scales, it has now been reduced to ordinal (rank) data.

Does the Minimum Value of a Distribution Influence the Efficacy of a Transformation?

For researchers with a strong mathematical or statistical background, the points made in this section are self-evident. However, over the years, many of my students and colleagues have helped me to realize that this point is not always self-evident to all researchers; furthermore, it is explicitly discussed in few (if any) statistical texts.

First, note that adding a constant to a variable changes only the mean, not the standard deviation or variance, skew, or kurtosis. In other words, adding a constant to a variable does not change the shape of the distribution at all. However, the size of the constant and the place on the number line that the constant moves the distribution to can influence the effect of any subsequent data transformations. As hinted at above, it is my opinion that researchers seeking to use any of the above-mentioned data transformations should first move the distribution so its leftmost point (minimum value) is anchored at 1.0.

This is due to the differential effects of the transformations across the number line. All three transformations will have the greatest effect if the distribution is anchored at 1.0, and as the minimum value of the distribution moves away from 1.0, the effectiveness of the transformation diminishes dramatically.

Recalling that these transformations improve normality by compressing one part of a distribution more than another, the data presented in Table 13.1 illustrate this point. For all three transformations, the gap between 1 and 2 is

Table 13.1   Effects of Various Transformations on Variables

Original Y	1.00	2.00	3.00	4.00	5.00	6.00	7.00	8.00	9.00	10.00
SquareRoot(Y)	1.00	1.41	1.73	2.00	2.24	2.45	2.65	2.83	3.00	3.16
gap		0.41	0.32	0.27	0.24	0.21	0.20	0.18	0.17	0.16
% reduction	0.00	29.29	42.26	50.00	55.28	59.18	62.20	64.64	66.67	68.38
Log10(Y)	0.00	0.30	0.48	0.60	0.70	0.78	0.85	0.90	0.95	1.00
gap		0.30	0.18	0.12	0.10	0.08	0.07	0.06	0.05	0.05
% reduction	100.00	84.95	84.10	84.95	86.02	87.03	87.93	88.71	89.40	90.00
Reflected Inverse(Y)	0.00	0.50	0.67	0.75	0.80	0.83	0.86	0.88	0.89	0.90
gap		0.50	0.17	0.08	0.05	0.03	0.02	0.02	0.01	0.01
% reduction	100.00	75.00	77.78	81.25	84.00	86.11	87.76	89.06	90.12	91.00

Original Y	11.00	12.00	13.00	14.00	15.00	16.00	17.00	18.00	19.00	20.00
SquareRoot(Y)	3.32	3.46	3.61	3.74	3.87	4.00	4.12	4.24	4.36	4.47
gap		0.15	0.14	0.14	0.13	0.13	0.12	0.12	0.12	0.11
% reduction	69.85	71.13	72.26	73.27	74.18	75.00	75.75	76.43	77.06	77.64
Log10(Y)	1.04	1.08	1.11	1.15	1.18	1.20	1.23	1.26	1.28	1.30
gap		0.04	0.03	0.03	0.03	0.03	0.03	0.02	0.02	0.02
% reduction	90.53	91.01	91.43	91.81	92.16	92.47	92.76	93.03	93.27	93.49
Reflected Inverse(Y)	0.91	0.92	0.92	0.93	0.93	0.94	0.94	0.94	0.95	0.95
gap		0.01	0.01	0.01	0.00	0.00	0.00	0.00	0.00	0.00
% reduction	91.74	92.36	92.90	93.37	93.78	94.14	94.46	94.75	95.01	95.25

Original Y	100.00	101.00	102.00	103.00	104.00	105.00	106.00	107.00	108.00	109.00
SquareRoot(Y)	10.00	10.05	10.10	10.15	10.20	10.25	10.30	10.34	10.39	10.44
gap		0.05	0.05	0.05	0.05	0.05	0.05	0.05	0.05	0.05
% reduction	90.00	90.05	90.10	90.15	90.19	90.24	90.29	90.33	90.38	90.42
Log10(Y)	2.00	2.00	2.01	2.01	2.02	2.02	2.03	2.03	2.03	2.04
gap		0.00	0.00	0.00	0.00	0.00	0.00	0.00	0.00	0.00
% reduction	98.00	98.02	98.03	98.05	98.06	98.08	98.09	98.10	98.12	98.13
Reflected Inverse(Y)	0.99	0.99	0.99	0.99	0.99	0.99	0.99	0.99	0.99	0.99
gap		0.00	0.00	0.00	0.00	0.00	0.00	0.00	0.00	0.00
% reduction	99.01	99.02	99.03	99.04	99.05	99.06	99.07	99.07	99.08	99.09

much larger than between 9 and 10 (0.41, 0.30, and 0.50 vs. 0.16, 0.05, and 0.01). Across this range, the transformations are having an effect by compressing the higher numbers much more than the lower numbers. This does not hold once one moves the anchor point from 1.0, however. If one had a distribution anchored at 10 and ranging to 20, the gap between 10 and 11

(0.15, 0.04, 0.01) is not that much different from the gaps between 19 and 20 (0.11, 0.02, 0.00). In a more extreme example, the difference between 100 and 101 is almost the same as between 108 and 109. In other words, over the same 10-point span, all three of these transformations are more efficacious if anchored at 1.0.

In order to demonstrate the effects of minimum values on the efficacy of transformations, data were drawn from the National Education Longitudinal Survey of 1988. The variable used, which had been created by the author for another project, represented the number of undesirable things (offered drugs, had something stolen, threatened with violence, etc.) that had happened to a student. This variable ranged from 0 to 6 and was highly skewed, with 40.4% reporting none of the events occurring, 34.9% reporting only one event, and less than 10% reporting more than two of the events occurring. The initial skew was 1.58, a substantial deviation from normality, making this variable a good candidate for transformation. The relative effects of transformations on the skew of this variable are presented in Table 13.2.

As the results indicate, all three types of transformations worked very well on the original distribution, anchored at a minimum of 1. However, the efficacy of the transformation quickly diminished as constants were added to the distribution. Even moving the distribution anchor from 1.0 to 2.0 diminished the effectiveness of the transformation. Once the minimum reached 10, the skew was over 1.0 for all three transformations, and at a minimum of 100, the skew was approaching the original, nontransformed skew in all three cases. These results highlight the importance of the minimum value of a distribution should a researcher intend to employ data transformations on that variable.

These results should also be considered when a variable has a range of, say, 200 to 800, as with

SAT or Graduate Record Examination (GRE) scores, where nonnormality might be an issue. In cases where variables do not naturally have 1.0 as their minimum, it might be useful to subtract a constant to move the distribution to a minimum value of 1.0 prior to applying the data transformation.

Conclusions and Other Directions

Unfortunately, many statistical texts provide minimal instruction on the utilization of simple data transformations for the purpose of improving the normality of variables, and coverage of the use of other transformations or of using transformations for purposes other than improving normality is almost nonexistent. While seasoned statisticians or mathematicians might intuitively understand what is discussed in this chapter, many social scientists might not be aware of some of these issues.

The first recommendation from this chapter is that researchers always examine and understand their data *prior to* performing those long-awaited analyses. To do less is to slight your data and potentially draw incorrect conclusions.

The second recommendation is to know the requirements of the data analysis technique to be used. As Zimmerman (e.g., 1995, 1998) and others have pointed out, even nonparametric analyses, which are generally thought to be relatively "assumption free," can benefit from examination of the data.

The third recommendation is to use data transformations with care—and never without a clear reason. Data transformations can alter the fundamental nature of the data, such as by changing the measurement scale from interval or ratio to ordinal, creating curvilinear relationships, and reversing the order of your values, all of which can confound and complicate interpretation. As discussed above, there are many

Table 13.2   Variable Skew as a Function of the Minimum Score of a Distribution at Transformation

	Original Variable	Transformed Data With Anchor at					
		1	2	3	5	10	100
Square Root	1.58	0.93	1.11	1.21	1.31	1.42	1.56
Log$_{10}$	1.58	0.44	0.72	0.88	1.07	1.27	1.54
Inverse	1.58	0.12	0.18	0.39	0.67	1.00	1.50

valid reasons for using data transformations, including improvement of normality, variance stabilization, and conversion of scales to interval measurement (for more on this, see the introductory chapters of Bond and Fox [2001], particularly pages 17–19).

The fourth recommendation is that, if transformations are to be used, researchers should ensure that they anchor the variable at a place where the transformation will have the optimal effect (in the case of these three, I argue that the anchor point should be 1.0).

Beyond that, there are many other issues that researchers need to familiarize themselves with. In particular, there are several peculiar types of variables that benefit from attention. For example, proportion and percentage variables (e.g., percentage of students in a school passing end-of-grade tests) and count variables of the type I presented above (number of events happening) tend to violate several assumptions of analyses and produce highly skewed distributions. While beyond the scope of this chapter, these types of variables are becoming increasingly common in education and the social sciences and need to be dealt with appropriately. The reader interested in these issues should refer to sources such as Zubin (1935), Bartlett (1947), or other, more modern sources that deal with these issues (Hopkins, 2002; Chapters 21 and 26, this volume).

References

Bartlett, M. S. (1947). The use of transformation. *Biometric Bulletin, 3*, 39–52.

Bond, T. G., & Fox, C. M. (2001). *Applying the Rasch model: Fundamental measurement in the human sciences.* Mahwah, NJ: Lawrence Erlbaum.

Cleveland, W. S. (1984). Graphical methods for data presentation: Full scale breaks, dot charts, and multibased logging. *The American Statistician, 38*(4), 270–280.

Goodman, L. A. (1954). Kolmogorov-Smirnov tests for psychological research. *Psychological Bulletin, 51*, 160–168.

Hopkins, W. G. (2002). *A new view of statistics.* Available at http://www.sportsci.org/resource/stats/index.html

Judd, C. M., & McClelland, G. H. (1989). *Data analysis: A model-comparison approach.* San Diego: Harcourt Brace Jovanovich.

Lilliefors, H. W. (1967). On the Kolmogorov-Smirnov test for normality with mean and variance unknown. *Journal of the American Statistical Association, 62*, 399–402.

Micceri, T. (1989). The unicorn, the normal curve, and other improbable creatures. *Psychological Bulletin, 105*, 156–166.

Orr, J. M., Sackett, P. R., & DuBois, C. L. Z. (1991). Outlier detection and treatment in I/O psychology: A survey of researcher beliefs and an empirical illustration. *Personnel Psychology, 44*, 473–486.

Rosenthal, R. (1968). An application of the Kolmogorov-Smirnov test for normality with estimated mean and variance. *Psychological-Reports, 22*, 570.

Wilcox, R. R. (1997). Some practical reasons for reconsidering the Kolmogorov-Smirnov test. *British Journal of Mathematical and Statistical Psychology, 50*(1), 9–20.

Zimmerman, D. W. (1995). Increasing the power of nonparametric tests by detecting and downweighting outliers. *Journal of Experimental Education, 64*, 71–78.

Zimmerman, D. W. (1998). Invalidation of parametric and nonparametric statistical tests by concurrent violation of two assumptions. *Journal of Experimental Education, 67*, 55–68.

Zubin, J. (1935). Note on a transformation function for proportions and percentages. *Journal of Applied Psychology, 19*, 213–220.

14

BEST PRACTICES IN DATA CLEANING

How Outliers and "Fringeliers" Can Increase Error Rates and Decrease the Quality and Precision of Your Results

JASON W. OSBORNE

AMY OVERBAY

The presence of outliers can lead to inflated error rates and substantial distortions of parameter and statistic estimates when using either parametric or nonparametric tests (e.g., Zimmerman, 1994, 1995, 1998). Casual observation of the literature suggests that researchers rarely report checking for outliers of any sort. This inference is supported empirically by Osborne (in press), who found that authors of articles in top-tier educational psychology journals reported testing assumptions of the statistical procedure(s) used in their studies—including checking for the presence of outliers—only 8% of the time. Given what we know of the importance of assumptions to the accuracy of estimates and error rates, this in itself is troubling. There is no reason to believe that the situation is different in other social science disciplines.

WHAT ARE OUTLIERS AND FRINGELIERS AND WHY DO WE CARE ABOUT THEM?

Although definitions vary, an outlier is generally considered to be a data point that is far outside the norm for a variable or population (e.g., Jarrell, 1994; Rasmussen, 1988; Stevens, 1984). Hawkins (1980) described an outlier as an observation that "deviates so much from other observations as to arouse suspicions that it was generated by a different mechanism" (p. 1). Outliers have also been defined as values that are "dubious in the eyes of the researcher" (Dixon, 1950, p. 488) and contaminants (Wainer, 1976).

Wainer (1976) also introduced the concept of the "fringelier," referring to "unusual events which occur more often than seldom" (p. 286).

Authors' Note: This chapter was originally published as Osborne, J. W., & Overbay, A. (2004). The power of outliers (and why researchers should ALWAYS check for them). *Practical Assessment, Research, and Evaluation, 9*(6). Available at http://pareonline.net/getvn.asp?v=9&n=6

These points lie near three standard deviations from the mean and hence may have a disproportionately strong influence on parameter estimates, yet are not as obvious or easily identified as ordinary outliers due to their relative proximity to the distribution center. As fringeliers are a special case of outlier, for much of the rest of the chapter, we will use the generic term *outlier* to refer to any single data point of dubious origin or disproportionate influence.

Outliers can have deleterious effects on statistical analyses. First, they generally serve to increase error variance and reduce the power of statistical tests. Second, if nonrandomly distributed, they can decrease normality (and, in multivariate analyses, violate assumptions of sphericity and multivariate normality), altering the odds of making both Type I and Type II errors. Third, they can seriously bias or influence estimates that may be of substantive interest (for more information on these points, see Rasmussen, 1988; Schwager & Margolin, 1982; Zimmerman, 1994).

Screening data for univariate, bivariate, and multivariate outliers is simple in these days of high-powered personal computing. The consequences of not doing so can be substantial.

What Causes Outliers and What Should We Do About Them?

Outliers can arise from several different mechanisms or causes. Anscombe (1960) sorts outliers into two major categories: those arising from errors in the data and those arising from the inherent variability of the data. We elaborate on this to summarize six possible reasons for data points that may be suspect.

Let us first be careful to note that not all outliers are illegitimate contaminants, and not all illegitimate scores show up as outliers (Barnett & Lewis, 1994). It is therefore important to consider the range of causes that may be responsible for outliers in a given data set. What should be done about an outlying data point is at least partly a function of the inferred cause.

Outliers From Data Errors. Outliers are often caused by human error, such as errors in data collection, recording, or entry. Data from an interview can be recorded incorrectly or miskeyed upon data entry. One survey the first author was involved with (reported in Brewer, Nauenberg, &

Osborne, 1998) gathered data on nurses' hourly wages, which at that time averaged about $12.00 per hour with a standard deviation of about $2.00. In our data set, one nurse had reported an hourly wage of $42,000.00. This figure represented a data collection error (specifically, a failure for the respondent to read the question carefully). Errors of this nature can often be corrected by returning to the original documents—or even the subjects if necessary and possible—and entering the correct value. In cases such as that of the nurse who made $42,000.00 per hour, another option is available—recalculation or reestimation of the correct answer. We had used anonymous surveys, but because the nature of the error was obvious, we were able to convert this nurse's salary to an estimated hourly wage because we knew how many hours per week she worked and how many weeks per year she worked. Thus, if sufficient information is available, recalculation is a method of saving important data and eliminating an obvious outlier.

Another common source of outliers is data entry. For example, on a Likert-type scale of 1 to 7, the first author recently found some *0* and *57* values in the data. This obviously arose from human entry error, and returning to the original documents can solve this problem. If outliers of this nature cannot be corrected, they should be eliminated as they do not represent valid population data points.

Outliers From Intentional or Motivated Misreporting. There are times when participants purposefully report incorrect data to experimenters or surveyors. A participant may make a conscious effort to sabotage the research (Huck, 2000) or may be acting from other motives. Social desirability and self-presentation motives can be powerful. This can also happen for obvious reasons when data are sensitive (e.g., teenagers misreporting drug or alcohol use, misreporting of sexual behavior). If all but a few teens underreport a behavior (e.g., cheating on a test, driving under the influence of alcohol, etc.), the few honest responses might appear to be outliers when in fact they are legitimate and valid scores. Motivated overreporting can occur when the variable in question is socially desirable (e.g., income, educational attainment, grades, study time, church attendance, sexual experience) and can work in the same manner.

Environmental conditions can motivate overreporting or misreporting, such as if an attractive female researcher is interviewing male undergraduates about attitudes on gender equality in marriage. Depending on the details of the research, one of two things can happen: inflation of all estimates or production of outliers. If all subjects respond the same way, the distribution will shift upward, not generally causing outliers. However, if only a small subsample of the group responds this way to the experimenter, or if multiple researchers conduct interviews, then outliers can be created.

Identifying and reducing this issue is difficult unless researchers take care to triangulate or validate data in some manner.

Outliers From Sampling Error. Another cause of outliers is sampling. It is possible that a few members of a sample were inadvertently drawn from a different population than the rest of the sample. For example, in the previously described survey of nurse salaries, RNs who had moved into hospital administration were included in the database we sampled from, as they had maintained their nursing license, despite our being primarily interested in floor nurses. In education, inadvertently sampling academically gifted or mentally retarded students is a possibility and (depending on the goal of the study) might provide undesirable outliers. These cases should be removed as they do not reflect the target population.

Outliers From Standardization Failure. Outliers can be caused by research methodology, particularly if something anomalous happened during a particular subject's experience. One might argue that a study of stress levels in schoolchildren around the country might have found some significant outliers if the sample had included schoolchildren in New York City schools during the fall of 2001 (or in New Orleans following Hurricane Katrina in 2005). Researchers experience such challenges all the time. Unusual phenomena such as construction noise outside a research lab, or an experimenter feeling particularly grouchy, or even events outside the context of the research lab, such as a student protest, a rape or murder on campus, observations in a classroom the day before a big holiday recess, and so on can produce outliers. Faulty or noncalibrated equipment is another common cause of outliers. These data can be legitimately discarded if the researchers are not interested in studying the particular phenomenon in question (e.g., if one were

not interested in studying subjects' reactions to construction noise outside the lab).

Outliers From Faulty Distributional Assumptions. Incorrect assumptions about the distribution of the data can also lead to the presence of suspected outliers (e.g., Iglewicz & Hoaglin, 1993). Blood sugar levels, disciplinary referrals, scores on classroom tests where students are well prepared, and self-reports of low-frequency behaviors (e.g., number of times a student has been suspended or held back a grade) may give rise to bimodal, skewed, asymptotic, or flat distributions, depending on the sampling design and variable of interest. Similarly, the data may have a different structure than the researcher originally assumed, and long- or short-term trends may affect the data in unanticipated ways. For example, a study of college library usage rates during the month of September in the United States may find outlying values at the beginning and end of the month, with exceptionally low rates at the beginning of the month when students have just returned to campus or are on break for Labor Day weekend, and exceptionally high rates at the end of the month, when midterm exams have begun. Depending on the goal of the research, these extreme values may or may not represent an aspect of the inherent variability of the data and may or may not have a legitimate place in the data set.

Outliers as Legitimate Cases Sampled From the Correct Population. Finally, it is possible that an outlier can come from the population being sampled legitimately through random chance. It is important to note that sample size plays a role in the probability of outlying values. Within a normally distributed population, it is more probable that a given data point will be drawn from the most densely concentrated area of the distribution, rather than one of the tails (Evans, 1999; Sachs, 1982). As a researcher casts a wider net and the data set becomes larger, the more the sample resembles the population from which it was drawn, and thus the likelihood of outlying values becomes greater.

Specifically, if you sample in a truly random fashion from a population that is distributed in an exact standard normal distribution, there is about a 1% chance you will get a data point at or beyond three standard deviations from the mean. This means that, on average, *about 1% of your subjects should be three standard deviations from the mean.* There is also a nontrivial probability of getting individuals far beyond the three standard deviation threshold.

When outliers occur as a function of the inherent variability of the data, opinions differ widely on what to do. Due to the deleterious effects on power, accuracy, and error rates that outliers and fringeliers can have, it might be desirable to use a transformation or recoding/truncation strategy to both keep the individual in the data set and at the same time minimize the harm to statistical inference (for more on this point, see Chapter 13, this volume).

Outliers as a Potential Focus of Inquiry

We all know that interesting research is often as much a matter of serendipity as planning and inspiration. Outliers can represent a nuisance, error, or legitimate data. They can also be inspiration for inquiry. When researchers in Africa discovered that some women were living with HIV just fine for many years longer than expected despite being untreated, those rare cases were outliers compared with most untreated women, who were dying fairly rapidly. They could have been discarded as noise or error, but instead they serve as inspiration for inquiry: What makes these women different or unique, and what can we learn from them? In a study the first author was involved with many years ago on social support, a teenager reported 100 *close* friends. Is it possible? Yes. Is it likely? Not generally, given any reasonable definition of "close friends." So this data point could represent motivated misreporting, an error of data recording or entry (it wasn't), a protocol error reflecting a misunderstanding of the question, or something more interesting. This extreme score might shed light on an important principle or issue. Before discarding outliers, researchers need to consider whether those data contain valuable information that may not necessarily relate to the intended study but has importance in a more global sense.

How to Deal With Outliers

There is a great deal of debate as to what to do with identified outliers. A thorough review of

the various arguments is not possible here. We argue that what to do depends in large part on why an outlier is in the data in the first place. Where outliers are *illegitimately* included in the data, it is only common sense that those data points should be removed (see also Barnett & Lewis, 1994).

When the outlier is either a legitimate part of the data or the cause is unclear, the issue becomes murkier. Judd and McClelland (1989) make several strong points for removal even in these cases in order to get the most honest estimate of population parameters possible. However, not all researchers feel that way (e.g., Orr, Sackett, & DuBois, 1991). This is a case where researchers must use their training, intuition, reasoned argument, and thoughtful consideration in making decisions.

Keeping Legitimate Outliers and Still Not Violating Your Assumptions. One means of accommodating outliers is the use of transformations or truncation. By using transformations, extreme scores can be kept in the data set, and the relative ranking of scores remains, yet the skew and error variance present in the variable(s) can be reduced (Hamilton, 1992).

Transformations may not be appropriate for the model being tested or may affect its interpretation in undesirable ways (see Newton & Rudestam, 1999; Osborne, 2002; Chapter 13, this volume). One alternative to transformation is truncation, wherein extreme scores are recoded to the highest (or lowest) reasonable score. For example, a researcher might decide that in reality, it is impossible for a teenager to have more than 15 close friends. Thus, all teens reporting more than this value (even 100) would be recoded to 15. Through truncation, the relative ordering of the data is maintained, and the highest or lowest scores remain the highest or lowest scores, yet the distributional problems are reduced. However, this may not be ideal if those cases really represent bad data or sampling error.

Robust Methods.[1] Instead of transformations or truncation, researchers sometimes use various "robust" procedures to protect their data from being distorted by the presence of outliers. These techniques "accommodate the outliers at no serious inconvenience—or are *robust* against the presence of outliers" (Barnett & Lewis, 1994, p. 35). Certain parameter estimates, especially the mean and least squares estimations, are particularly vulnerable to outliers or have "low breakdown" values. For this reason, researchers turn to robust or "high breakdown" methods to provide alternative estimates for these important aspects of the data.

A common robust estimation method for univariate distributions involves the use of a trimmed mean, which is calculated by temporarily eliminating extreme observations at both ends of the sample (Anscombe, 1960). Alternatively, researchers may choose to compute a Windsorized mean, for which the highest and lowest observations are temporarily censored and replaced with adjacent values from the remaining data (Barnett & Lewis, 1994).

Assuming that the distribution of prediction errors is close to normal, several common robust regression techniques can help reduce the influence of outlying data points. The least trimmed squares (LTS) and the least median of squares (LMS) estimators are conceptually similar to the trimmed mean, helping to minimize the scatter of the prediction errors by eliminating a specific percentage of the largest positive and negative outliers (Rousseeuw & Leroy, 1987), while Windsorized regression smoothes the Y-data by replacing extreme residuals with the next closest value in the data set (Lane, 2002).

Many options exist for analysis of nonideal variables. In addition to the above-mentioned options, analysts can choose from nonparametric analyses, as these types of analyses have few if any distributional assumptions, although research by Zimmerman and others (e.g., Zimmerman, 1995) does point out that even nonparametric analyses suffer from outlier cases.

Identification of Outliers

There is as much controversy over what constitutes an outlier as there is over whether to remove them or not. Simple rules of thumb (e.g., data points three or more standard deviations from the mean) are good starting points. Some researchers prefer visual inspection of the data. Others (e.g., Lornez, 1987) argue that outlier detection is merely a special case of the examination of data for influential data points.

Rules such as $z = 3$ are simple and relatively effective, although Miller (1991) and Van Selst and Jolicoeur (1994) demonstrated that this procedure (nonrecursive elimination of extreme scores) can produce problems with certain distributions (e.g., highly skewed distributions

characteristic of response latency variables), particularly when the sample is relatively small. To help researchers deal with this issue, Van Selst and Jolicoeur (1994) present a table of suggested cutoff scores for researchers to use with varying sample sizes that will minimize these issues with extremely nonnormal distributions. In univariate data cleaning, we tend to use a $z = 3$ guideline as an initial screening tool and, depending on the results of that screening, examine the data more closely and modify the outlier detection strategy accordingly.

Bivariate and multivariate outliers are typically measured using either an index of influence or leverage, or distance. Popular indices, including Mahalanobis's distance and Cook's D, are both frequently used to calculate the leverage that specific cases may exert on the predicted value of the regression line (Newton & Rudestam, 1999). Standardized or studentized residuals in regression can also be useful, and often the $z = 3$ rule works well for residuals as well.

For analysis of variance (ANOVA)–type paradigms, most modern statistical software will produce a range of statistics, including standardized residuals. In ANOVA, the biggest issue after screening for univariate outliers is the issue of within-cell outliers, or the distance of an individual from the subgroup. Standardized residuals represent the distance from the subgroup and thus are effective in assisting analysts in examining data for multivariate outliers. Tabachnick and Fidell (2000) discuss data cleaning in the context of other analyses.

The Effects of Outlier Removal

The rest of this chapter is devoted to a demonstration of the effects of outliers and fringeliers on the accuracy of parameter estimates, as well as Type I and Type II error rates.

In order to simulate a real study where a researcher samples from a particular population, we defined our population as the 23,396 subjects in the data file from the National Education Longitudinal Study (NELS) of 1988, produced by the National Center for Education Statistics with complete data on all variables of interest. For the purposes of the analyses reported below, this population was sorted into two groups: "normal" individuals, whose scores on relevant variables were between $z = -3$ and $z = 3$, and "outliers," who scored at least $z = 3$ on one of the relevant variables.

In order to simulate the normal process of sampling from a population but standardize the proportion of outliers in each sample, one hundred samples of $N = 50$, $N = 100$, and $N = 400$ each were randomly sampled (with replacement between each sample but not during the creation of a single sample) from the population of "normal" subjects. Then, an additional 4% were randomly selected from the separate pool of outliers, bringing each sample to $N = 52$, $N = 104$, or $N = 416$, respectively. This procedure produced samples that could easily have been drawn at random from the full population.

The following variables were calculated for each of the analyses below:

Accuracy was assessed by checking whether the original or cleaned correlation was closer to the population correlation. In these calculations, the absolute difference was examined.

Error rates were calculated by comparing the outcome from a sample to the outcome from the population. If a particular sample yielded a different conclusion than was warranted by the population, that was considered an error of inference.

The Effect of Outliers on Correlations

The first example looks at simple zero-order correlations. The goal was to demonstrate the effect of outliers on two different types of correlations: correlations close to zero (to demonstrate the effects of outliers on Type I error rates) and

correlations that were moderately strong (to demonstrate the effects of outliers on Type II error rates). Toward this end, two different correlations were identified for study in the NELS data set: the correlation between locus of control and family size ("population" $r = -.06$) and the correlation between composite achievement test scores and socioeconomic status ("population" $r = .46$). Variable distributions were examined and found to be reasonably normal.

Correlations were then calculated in each sample, both before removal of outliers and after. For our purposes, $r = -.06$ was not significant at any of the sample sizes, and $r = .46$ was significant at all sample sizes. Thus, if a sample correlation led to a decision that deviated from the "correct" state of affairs, it was considered an error of inference.

As Table 14.1 demonstrates, outliers had adverse effects on correlations. In all cases, removal of the outliers had significant effects on the magnitude of the correlations, and the cleaned correlations were more accurate (i.e., closer to the known "population" correlation) 70% to 100% of the time. Furthermore, in most cases, errors of inference were significantly less common with cleaned than with uncleaned data.

The Effect of Outliers on *t* Tests and ANOVAs

The second example deals with analyses that look at group mean differences, such as *t* tests

Table 14.1   The Effects of Outliers on Correlations

Population r	N	Average Initial r	Average Cleaned r	t	% More Accurate	% Errors Before Cleaning	% Errors After Cleaning	t
$r = -.06$	52	.01	−.08	2.5**	95	78	8	13.40***
	104	−.54	−.06	75.44***	100	100	6	39.38***
	416	0	−.06	16.09***	70	0	21	5.13***
$r = .46$	52	.27	.52	8.1***	89	53	0	10.57***
	104	.15	.50	26.78***	90	73	0	16.36***
	416	.30	.50	54.77***	95	0	0	—

NOTE: One hundred samples were drawn for each row. Outliers were actual members of the population who scored at least $z = 3$ on the relevant variable. With $N = 52$, a correlation of .274 is significant at $p < .05$. With $N = 104$, a correlation of .196 is significant at $p < .05$. With $N = 416$, a correlation of .098 is significant at $p < .05$, two-tailed.
**$p < .01$. ***$p < .001$.

and ANOVA. For the purpose of simplicity, these analyses are simple *t* tests, but these results should generalize to ANOVA. For these analyses, two different conditions were examined: when there were no significant differences between the groups in the population (sex differences in socioeconomic status [SES] produced a mean group difference of 0.0007 with an *SD* of 0.80 and, with 24,501 *df*, produced a *t* of 0.29) and when there were significant group differences in the population (sex differences in mathematics achievement test scores produced a mean difference of 4.06 and an *SD* of 9.75, and 24,501 *df* produced a *t* of 10.69, *p* < .0001). For both variables, the effects of having outliers in only one cell as compared with both cells were examined. Distributions for both dependent variables were examined and found to be reasonably normal.

For these analyses, *t* tests were calculated in each sample, both before removal of outliers and after. For our purposes, *t* tests looking at SES should not produce significant group differences, whereas *t* tests looking at mathematics achievement test scores should. Two different issues were examined: mean group differences and the magnitude of the *t*. If an analysis from a sample led to a different conclusion, it was considered an error.

The results in Table 14.2 illustrate the effects of outliers on *t* tests and ANOVAs. Removal of outliers produced a significant change in the mean differences between the two groups when the groups were equal in the population but tended not to when there were strong group differences. Removal of outliers produced significant change in the *t* statistics primarily when there were strong group differences. In both cases, the tendency was for both group differences and *t* statistics to become more accurate in a majority of the samples. Interestingly, there was little evidence that outliers produced Type I errors when group means were equal, and thus removal had little discernable effect. But when there were strong group differences, outlier removal tended to have a significant beneficial effect on error rates, although not as substantial an effect as seen in the correlation analyses.

The presence of outliers in one or both cells, surprisingly, failed to produce any differential effects. The expectation had been that the presence of outliers in a single cell would increase the incidence of Type I errors.

To Remove or Not to Remove?

Although some authors argue that removal of extreme scores produces undesirable outcomes, they are in the minority, particularly when the outliers are illegitimate. When the data points are suspected of being legitimate, some authors (e.g., Orr et al., 1991) argue that data are more likely to be representative of the population as a whole if outliers are not removed.

Conceptually, there are strong arguments for removal or alteration of outliers. The analyses reported in this chapter also empirically demonstrate the benefits of outlier removal. Both correlations and *t* tests tend to show significant changes in statistics as a function of removal of outliers, and in the overwhelming majority of analyses, accuracy of estimates was enhanced. In most cases, errors of inference were significantly reduced, a prime argument for screening and removal of outliers.

Although these were two fairly simple statistical procedures, it is straightforward to argue that the benefits of data cleaning extend to simple and multiple regression, as well as to different types of ANOVA procedures. There are other procedures outside these, but the majority of social science research uses one of these procedures (which are of course related directly to each other as special cases of the general linear model). Other research (e.g., Zimmerman, 1995) has shown the importance of dealing with the effects of extreme scores in less commonly used procedures, such as nonparametric analyses.

NOTE

1. Readers interested in a more thorough discussion of robust methods are referred to Rand Wilcox's chapter in this volume (Chapter 18).

REFERENCES

Anscombe, F. J. (1960). Rejection of outliers. *Technometrics, 2*, 123–147.

Barnett, V., & Lewis, T. (1994). *Outliers in statistical data* (3rd ed.). New York: John Wiley.

Brewer, C. S., Nauenberg, E., & Osborne, J. W. (1998, June). *Differences among hospital and non-hospital RNs participation, satisfaction, and organizational commitment in western New York.* Paper presented at the National Meeting of the

Table 14.2 The Effects of Outliers on *t* Tests

	N	Initial Mean Difference	Cleaned Mean Difference	t	% More Accurate Mean Difference	Average Initial t	Average Cleaned t	t	% Type I or II Errors Before Cleaning	% Type I or II Errors After Cleaning	t
Equal group means, outliers in one cell	52	0.34	0.18	3.70***	66.0	−0.20	−0.12	1.02	2.0	1.0	<1
	104	0.22	0.14	5.36***	67.0	0.05	−0.08	1.27	3.0	3.0	<1
	416	0.09	0.06	4.15***	61.0	0.14	0.05	0.98	2.0	3.0	<1
Equal group means, outliers in both cells	52	0.27	0.19	3.21***	53.0	0.08	−0.02	1.15	2.0	4.0	<1
	104	0.20	0.14	3.98***	54.0	0.02	−0.07	0.93	3.0	3.0	<1
	416	0.15	0.11	2.28*	68.0	0.26	0.09	2.14*	3.0	2.0	<1
Unequal group means, outliers in one cell	52	4.72	4.25	1.64	52.0	0.99	1.44	−4.70***	82.0	72.0	2.41**
	104	4.11	4.03	0.42	57.0	1.61	2.06	−2.78**	68.0	45.0	4.70***
	416	4.11	4.21	−0.30	62.0	2.98	3.91	−12.97***	16.0	0.0	4.34***
Unequal group means, outliers in both cells	52	4.51	4.09	1.67	56.0	1.01	1.36	−4.57***	81.0	75.0	1.37
	104	4.15	4.08	0.36	51.0	1.43	2.01	−7.44***	71.0	47.0	5.06***
	416	4.17	4.07	1.16	61.0	3.06	4.12	−17.55***	10.0	0.0	3.13***

NOTE: One hundred samples were drawn for each row. Outliers were actual members of the population who scored at least $z = 3$ on the relevant variable.

$*p < .05.$ $**p < .01.$ $***p < .001.$

Association for Health Service Research, Washington, DC.

Dixon, W. J. (1950). Analysis of extreme values. *Annals of Mathematical Statistics, 21,* 488–506.

Evans, V. P. (1999). Strategies for detecting outliers in regression analysis: An introductory primer. In B. Thompson (Ed.), *Advances in social science methodology* (Vol. 5, pp. 213–233). Stamford, CT: JAI.

Hamilton, L. C. (1992). *Regressions with graphics: A second course in applied statistics.* Monterey, CA: Brooks/Cole.

Hawkins, D. M. (1980). *Identification of outliers.* London: Chapman & Hall.

Huck, S. W. (2000). *Reading statistics and research* (3rd ed.). New York: Longman.

Iglewicz, B., & Hoaglin, D. C. (1993). *How to detect and handle outliers.* Milwaukee, WI: ASQC Quality Press.

Jarrell, M. G. (1994). A comparison of two procedures, the Mahalanobis distance and the Andrews-Pregibon statistic, for identifying multivariate outliers. *Research in the Schools, 1,* 49–58.

Judd, C. M., & McClelland, G. H. (1989). *Data analysis: A model comparison approach.* San Diego: Harcourt Brace Jovanovich.

Lane, K. (2002, February). *What is robust regression and how do you do it?* Paper presented at the annual meeting of the Southwest Educational Research Association, Austin, TX.

Lornez, F. O. (1987). Teaching about influence in simple regression. *Teaching Sociology, 15*(2), 173–177.

Miller, J. (1991). Reaction time analysis with outlier exclusion: Bias varies with sample size. *Quarterly Journal of Experimental Psychology, 43*(4), 907–912.

Newton, R. R., & Rudestam, K. E. (1999). *Your statistical consultant: Answers to your data analysis questions.* Thousand Oaks, CA: Sage.

Orr, J. M., Sackett, P. R., & DuBois, C. L. Z. (1991). Outlier detection and treatment in I/O psychology: A survey of researcher beliefs and an empirical illustration. *Personnel Psychology, 44,* 473–486.

Osborne, J. W. (2002). Notes on the use of data transformations. *Practical Assessment, Research, and Evaluation, 8.* Available at http://ericae .net/pare/getvn.asp?v=8&n=6

Osborne, J. W. (in press). Sweating the small stuff in educational psychology: How trends in effect size and power reporting failed to change from 1969 to 1999, and what that means for the future of changing practices. *Educational Psychology.*

Rasmussen, J. L. (1988). Evaluating outlier identification tests: Mahalanobis D squared and Comrey D. *Multivariate Behavioral Research, 23*(2), 189–202.

Rousseeuw, P., & Leroy, A. (1987). *Robust regression and outlier detection.* New York: John Wiley.

Sachs, L. (1982). *Applied statistics: A handbook of techniques* (2nd ed.). New York: Springer-Verlag.

Schwager, S. J., & Margolin, B. H. (1982). Detection of multivariate outliers. *The Annals of Statistics, 10,* 943–954.

Stevens, J. P. (1984). Outliers and influential data points in regression analysis. *Psychological Bulletin, 95,* 334–344.

Tabachnick, B. G., & Fidell, L. S. (2000). *Using multivariate statistics* (4th ed.). Boston: Pearson Allyn & Bacon.

Van Selst, M., & Jolicoeur, P. (1994). A solution to the effect of sample size on outlier elimination. *Quarterly Journal of Experimental Psychology, 47*(3), 631–650.

Wainer, H. (1976). Robust statistics: A survey and some prescriptions. *Journal of Educational Statistics, 1*(4), 285–312.

Zimmerman, D. W. (1994). A note on the influence of outliers on parametric and nonparametric tests. *Journal of General Psychology, 121*(4), 391–401.

Zimmerman, D. W. (1995). Increasing the power of nonparametric tests by detecting and downweighting outliers. *Journal of Experimental Education, 64*(1), 71–78.

Zimmerman, D. W. (1998). Invalidation of parametric and nonparametric statistical tests by concurrent violation of two assumptions. *Journal of Experimental Education, 67*(1), 55–68.

15

HOW TO DEAL WITH MISSING DATA

Conceptual Overview and Details for Implementing Two Modern Methods

JASON C. COLE

In the past, when data were missing from our sets, any number of reactions were common. Positive emotions, such as happiness and contentment, never occurred. Rather, the emotions we felt (often in this order) were frustration, anger, guilt, fear, and sadness.

Graham, Cumsille, and Elek-Fisk (2003, p. 87)

We stand at the beginning of an era in which useful and accessible missing data procedures are an integral part of mainstream statistical packages.

Graham et al. (2003, p. 88)

The days when journals tolerate the absence of analysis of the missing values and the use of traditional approaches to missing values should be numbered.

Acock (2005, p. 1026)

UNDERSTANDING MISSINGNESS: WHY IS IT IMPORTANT TO ADDRESS MISSINGNESS

Missing data is a prevalent issue in many fields, yet only about half of published studies mention dropouts, and less than 20% of those studies incorporated dropouts into their analyses (Ladouceur, Gosselin, Laberge, & Blaszcynski, 2001). Nearly all common statistical analyses assume complete data, yet many statistics books do not deal with missingness. Proper missing data techniques have therefore gone mostly ignored by researchers until recently (Rubin, 1996).

Three major problems with incomplete data are (1) loss of information or power due to loss of data; (2) complication during data management and analysis, partially because of limitations with standard statistical software; and (3) potential marked bias because of systematic differences between observed and missing values (Barnard & Meng, 1999).

Recent advancements in software have made missing data analyses easier and more prolific. This is critical because gatekeepers in research, such as grant reviews, regulatory agencies, and journal reviewers, are becoming more critical of the treatment of missing data.

But when are data truly missing? Many surveys incorporate "skip patterns," for example, where a respondent may be instructed to skip a subsequent question based on a certain response to a key beginning question in the section. Overall, missing data fall into a similar category of latent variables—true values exist, but we cannot always accurately determine the exact value (D. F. Heitjan & Rubin, 1991; Schafer & Graham, 2002).

INTRODUCTION TO THE CONCEPTS OF MISSING DATA

In this section, I introduce three key concepts to the discussion of missing data: the models (missingness augmentation and analytic), auxiliary variables, and the missingness mechanism. Effective missing data techniques will provide unbiased parameter estimates (the expected value of an estimate from the missing technique is equal to the population value) and efficient standard errors (the standard error around the estimate is small and accurate to that with known values) (Graham et al., 2003).

The Models

Many of the modern techniques for addressing missing data require a synergy between the way we augment our database to address missingness and the way we analyze our data to test our hypotheses, labeled the missingness augmentation (MA)[1] model and analytic model, respectively. Simply stated, a model description is a list of the analyzed observed variables (dependent and independent variables), their interactions, and any auxiliary variables (variables that attempt to explain why data are missing though they are superfluous to the analytic model).[2]

The analytic model drives the creation of the MA model. For example, the researcher may intend to analyze the influence of age and income (and their interaction) on the health-related quality-of-life measure (physical component summary [PCS]). With the analytic model set, we can now determine the MA model, which would include PCS, age, income, a variable to represent the interaction of Age × Income, and any necessary auxiliary variables.

It is important that combinatorial relationships (e.g., interactions) included in the analytic model must be included in the MA model. Other nonlinear relationships, such as quadratic trends over time, must be anticipated before imputation and created as part of the model because nonlinear relationships are washed out of the imputed values with standard multivariate normal multiple imputation (MI). Of course, with smaller amounts of missingness, the washout of nonlinear trends is negligible and thus may still be appropriate.

The issues of interactions highlight a more general issue: The MA model and the analytic model should be compatible. Including combinatorial information in the MA model that will not be analyzed will lead to spurious underfitting of the data, leading to poor predictive power (Barnard & Meng, 1999) and increasing the odds of a Type II error (Meng, 1994; Rubin, 1996). Meng (1994) has noted that even if an interaction may not be readily planned in the current analytic model, it should be included in the MA model if it is commonly examined within the field of research, especially if the imputer and analyst are not the same person.

Auxiliary Variables

Collins, Schafer, and Kam (2001) introduced the term *auxiliary variables* to describe variables added to an MA model solely for the purpose of improving the accuracy of the missing data method. Auxiliary variables are included in the MA model when they are potential causes or correlates of the missingness or if they are strongly correlated with the variables that have missing data, as they improve estimation of the missing data, particularly if the auxiliary variables have high correlations with the variables that have higher rates of missingness.

The Missingness Mechanism

Data may be missing for three general reasons (referred to as the missingness mechanism). In Table 15.1, we have six columns of data. The first four columns are subject ID, Health Assessment Questionnaire (HAQ) score, physical quality of life (PCS), and a mental quality-of-life composite score (MCS). We create two other variables—PCS-M and MCS-M, coded 0 for observed data and 1 for missing data—and these variables are measures of the missingness mechanism. Because not all potential causes of missingness can be known in most studies, these variables are best conceived as a mathematical procedure to describe rates and patterns of missingness as well as to capture relationships between missingness and the likely values of the missing data (Schafer & Graham, 2002). Rather than obscuring the issue as a cause of missingness, Schafer and Graham (2002) recommended the use of the term *probabilities of missingness.* These probabilities of missingness help describe the types of missingness: missing completely at random (MCAR; the probability of missingness has no correlation with our variables of interest), missing at random (MAR; the missing data process is related to the variables of interest, but that relationship is fully captured with other observed variables), and missing not at random (MNAR; the missingness mechanism is correlated with our variable of interest and cannot be fully explained by other observed variables; see Rubin, 1976).

MCAR: Missing Completely at Random. The missingness mechanism is MCAR if the probability of missingness is unrelated to all observed and all unobserved variables (Abraham & Russell, 2004). When this assumption holds for all variables in the data set, the set of individuals with complete data is considered a random subsample of all participants in the database. The problem with the MCAR assumption is that understanding the relationship of missingness to all unobserved variables is untenable. There are times, however, when we have some certainty that specific missingness is MCAR (e.g., when missingness is part of the research design; Graham, Taylor, Olchowski, & Cumsille, 2006), wherein certain outcomes are randomly omitted for each participant to both reduce participant burden and still collect many outcomes.

Despite the theoretical rarity of unplanned MCAR data, MCAR allows for a major empirical benefit over the other missingness mechanism. MCAR is the only missingness mechanism that can be objectively tested (Enders, 2006a). Little's (1988) MCAR test has been adapted into SAS code and is available in the SPSS missing value analysis module. The curious reader can examine Little's description of the MCAR test for more information.

MAR: Missing at Random. MAR is present if the probability of missingness on a given variable is not related to the participant's score on that variable, after controlling for other variables in the study (Acock, 2005). Essentially, the other variables serve as an explanatory mechanism for the missingness (Collins et al., 2001) on the

Table 15.1   Missing Data Mechanisms

ID	HAQ	PCS	MCS	PCS-M	MCS-M
101	4	38	40	0	0
102	5	45	40	0	0
103	4		48	1	0
104	5	42	46	0	0
105	6		44	1	0
106	6	48	50	0	0
107	8	50	52	0	0
108	10	55		0	1
109	11	55		0	1
110	10	52		0	1

given variable. Using Table 15.1 again, this would mean that PCS-M and PCS are unrelated, once we partial out the relationship of MCS and HAQ. Thus, even if those who scored in the lower range of PCS were somewhat more likely to have missing data on PCS, the increased likelihood was fully omitted when controlling for the relationship between PCS and HAQ, PCS and MCS, or some combination thereof. It is, of course, impossible to test if the MAR assumption is satisfied because we do not know the values of the missingness on PCS (Allison, 2002). Although we can often expect deviations from MAR in many data sets (Schafer & Graham, 2002), an erroneous assumption of MAR for all data may often have only a very minor impact on estimates and standard errors according to results from simulation work (Collins et al., 2001). Indeed, when data may be classified as MAR (or MCAR), then there are marked benefits for the statistician in that one does not need to model the mechanism by which data became missing. This is why many researchers label MAR and MCAR data as ignorable. Data are said to be ignorable if they are (a) MAR or MCAR and (b) the parameters that govern the missingness mechanism are unrelated to the processes to be estimated.

Longitudinal studies are particularly susceptible to missingness. Missing data on an outcome assessed repeatedly throughout a longitudinal study often are ignorable missingness (Abraham & Russell, 2004). In fact, ignorable missingness is still valid when the likelihood of missingness depends on the actual missing values, as long as the outcome with missingness has zero residual correlations with other variables once the outcome is controlled (Schafer & Graham, 2002). This does not hold, however, when one time point does not predict missingness on the same outcome at another time point, such as in dementia studies (Harezlak, Gao, & Hui, 2003).

MNAR: Missing Not at Random. MNAR missingness occurs when the likelihood of missingness depends on the actual value of the missing datum and not other variables. MNAR missing data are also referred to as *nonignorable* missing data. Modeling the missingness mechanism for nonignorable missingness typically requires highly specialized techniques that vary with each scenario (Allison, 2002). Therefore,

I have not covered MNAR techniques in detail in this chapter but instead provide references for the curious reader.

BRIEF HISTORY OF TRADITIONAL TECHNIQUES USED TO ADDRESS MISSINGNESS

A recent small survey I conducted among users of SEMNET and the APA Division 5 listserv (Cole, 2007) showed that even skilled applied statisticians use antiquated procedures for handling missing data: 55% noted using casewise deletion, 36% noted using mean imputation, and 31% used regression-based imputation. Moreover, only 35% of the sample of sophisticated users noted using missing data techniques (of any sort) "most of the time" or "all of the time." Although many cogent reviews of the problems associated with these procedures are available (Allison, 2002; Graham et al., 2003; Schafer & Graham, 2002), I discuss them briefly below in order to stress their problematic nature in addressing missingness.

Casewise and Pairwise Deletion

Casewise deletion represents the default technique for addressing missingness in most statistical software and is therefore the most common method for addressing missing data (Abraham & Russell, 2004; Acock, 2005; Cole, 2007). This mostly comes from historical apathy for missingness. As Schafer and Olsen (1998) noted, missingness was viewed as something "to be gotten rid of" (p. 546) rather than understood.

Casewise deletion refers to a system whereby all participants with any missingness in an analysis are removed from the analysis. A related technique, pairwise deletion (otherwise known as available-case analysis), refers to a technique whereby all available participants for a specific part of an analysis are used. Detailed reviews of the serious limitations for casewise and pairwise deletion are abundant in the literature (Little & Rubin, 2002; Schafer & Graham, 2002). Primarily, disadvantages to these techniques center on assumption problems, power issues, and generalizability.

Casewise and pairwise deletion require missing data to be MCAR, an often untenable assumption when removing all of the partici-pants with any missingness. Yet even if the data meet the MCAR assumption, the smaller sample size will increase Type II error rates (Abraham & Russell, 2004). If the assumption of MCAR is not met, then standard errors will be inefficient, pro-viding either conservative or liberal results with-out knowledge as to which has been obtained (Acock, 1989). Furthermore, removal of partici-pants can reduce generalizability of the findings. Pairwise deletion brings other issues, particularly in advanced procedures such as structural equa-tion modeling (Acock, 2005; Wothke, 1993).

There are a few very specific instances where the use of casewise deletion may be desired, such as when the amount of missingness is less than 5% (Fairclough, 2002; Graham & Hofer, 2000; Graham, Taylor, & Cumsille, 2001). However, overall, there are few instances when casewise deletion is desirable. Nevertheless, it is prefer-able to nearly all other antiquated techniques (Allison, 2002).

Mean Substitution

Mean substitution (imputation) involves imputing any missing value for a variable with the mean of all observed values on the given variable. The process is simple to implement in many statistical packages, thereby making mean imputation one of the most commonly used missing data techniques. However, mean impu-tation has been known to produce biased estimates of the variances and covariances for nearly 40 years (Haitovsky, 1968).

Simulation studies have consistently demon-strated the biased results from mean imputation (Wothke, 2000). First, people who answer in the middle of a distribution are more likely to answer questions (Acock, 2005); therefore, we are typically trying to impute for people who have a lower likelihood of having the values that we have ascribed to them. Second, mean impu-tation increasingly warps the distribution of the imputed variable as missingness increases because the imputed variable becomes increas-ingly leptokurtic and decreasingly variable. The decreasing variability leads to spuriously smaller correlations with other variables. Moreover, in a multivariate analysis, when one or more vari-ables have been mean imputed, their relation-ships will be biased downward, but other variables with no imputation will have their

relationships biased upward because of the improper attenuation of the mean-imputed variables (Acock, 1989).

The marked inefficiency and bias created by mean imputation because of distribution distor-tion have precluded me from recommending it under any circumstance.

Regression Imputation

In a regression model, we can regress all other independent variables on our variable with miss-ingness to obtain a predicted value for each miss-ing datum (Allison, 2002). For example, if we know that observed data predict depression scores on the Center for Epidemiologic Studies–Depression scale (CES-D; Radloff, 1977) based at 1.67^*age + -2.8^*education + -0.34^*SES for observed data, then we can use these values to estimate a missing CES-D score based on the regression formula.

Regression-based imputation offers the abil-ity to incorporate multiple indicators in the imputation of missing values, thereby enhanc-ing the robustness of the process. Moreover, the bias involved in the point estimates from regres-sion imputation is consistent (Enders, 2006a), thereby potentially allowing for control of the bias. These benefits, however, rarely supersede the significant problems associated with regres-sion imputation.

Model complexity, monotone data, and a lack of efficiency and bias control are all found in regression imputation. When more than one variable contains missingness, if the data are not MCAR, or if the dependent variable is involved in the missingness mechanism, regression mod-els more complex than standard ordinary least squares must be used (Gourieroux & Monfort, 1981). Regression imputation also demands that the data have an unusual format to the missing-ness, called *monotone missingness.* Imagine 10 cases on the three aforementioned predictor variables (age, education, and socioeconomic status [SES]), wherein age had the least amount of missingness, education the second least miss-ingness, and SES the most missingness. For the missingness to be monotone, no SES data could be present when either of the variables with a lower percentage of missingness had missing data. Likewise, educational data could not be present for any instance in which age was missing (though SES could be missing). Little and Rubin

(2002) provide an excellent description on monotone missingness, including the algorithmic benefits and impractical demands. Thus, regression imputation can be very time-consuming given that each pattern of missingness requires a different predictive equation (Enders, 2006a) when nonmonotone missingness is present. Finally, as with all imputation methods that allow the analyses to treat the data as though they were complete, regression imputation contributes to underestimated standard errors and overestimated test statistics (Allison, 2002) because it reduces the variation around the regression line, leaving the imputed values with an artificially inflated correlation compared with cases with complete data.

Last Observation Carried Forward

Last observation carried forward (LOCF) is a popular technique used in randomized clinical trials when there is a need to account for the intent to treat for participants who drop out before study completion (Peto et al., 1977). The purpose of intent to treat is to include some logical value for all outcome variables after a participant has dropped out of a study in order to ensure that every patient randomized to a clinical trial will be analyzed. The alternative to some sort of intent to treat has long been casewise deletion, something problematic for randomized clinical trials. LOCF and worst-case scenario are two options (which we treat similarly here). In LOCF, the last observed value for an outcome variable is imputed for all later times the outcome would have been collected but was missing because of dropout. In worst-case scenario imputation, a similar process is conducted by imputing a logical value for all outcome variables after dropout. Rather than carry the last value forward, worst-case scenario imputes the lowest possible value on a scale to participants who dropped out for any reason other than death and assigns a zero to all participants who died during the trial (though this particular value could be readjusted depending on the particular outcome).

LOCF imputation has the advantage of providing a particular method to address intent to treat in randomized clinical trials. Moreover, the method has long been recognized as acceptable by important regulatory agencies, such as the Food and Drug Administration. If the researchers can argue that (a) drop-out rates are similar between the randomized groups and (b) either LOCF or worst-case imputation reflects a viable imputed value for dropouts based on prior empirical work, then the process may provide an effective control for intent to treat (Fairclough, 2002).

Unfortunately, LOCF imputation has been critiqued by most missing data statisticians as inappropriate on theoretical and practical grounds. Abraham and Russell (2004) noted that, despite LOCF being touted as a conservative approach in the past, recent simulations suggest it is not as conservative as was once believed (Mallinckrodt, Clark, Carroll, & Molenberghs, 2003). LOCF overestimates treatment effects and underestimates standard errors, thereby resulting in greater Type I error (Liu & Gould, 2002; Mallinckrodt, Sanger, et al., 2003). Fairclough (2002) has also noted serious concerns about the use of LOCF in that authors who use this technique rarely justify the appropriateness of LOCF for their data or examine the pattern of change in conjunction with the pattern of dropout (Rabound, Singer, Thorne, Schechter, & Shafran, 1998). She has further noted that the assumption that an outcome variable does not change after dropout is untenable in most studies, and LOCF has such limited utility (Gould, 1980; Heyting, Tolbomm, & Essers, 1992; Little & Yau, 1996) that it should be employed only with great caution.

Imputing Items on a Scale

Rather than imputing an entire scale for someone, there may be instances when we are only interested in imputing values for specific items on a scale in order to create a new total score for the outcome. Although taking the mean (or sum) of observed items appears to be akin to mean imputation, it is different on one key aspect: Variables are being imputed rather than cases (Graham et al., 2003). It is somewhat akin to a single regression-based imputation, but rather than having too little variability (as regression-based imputation can have), it has more error because scores are based on fewer items. Despite theoretical problems, Schafer and Graham (2002) have suggested that if MI is not feasible for item-level imputation (e.g., if there are fewer subjects than variables at the item level), then averaging of the available items works reasonably well, especially if the reliability is moderately high ($\alpha > .70$) and the items to be averaged form a single unified construct (for applied and theoretical discussion on a single unified scale, respectively, see Cole et al., 2006; Messick, 1995).

MODERN METHODS

The problem with antiquated techniques is that imputed values must be treated as estimates and not real data. An analysis with imputed data that ignores this uncertainty in the imputed values will lead to artificially small standard errors and *p* values, as well as inflated Type I error rates (Schafer & Olsen, 1998). Two techniques that overcome the uncertainty issue are discussed in detail: maximum likelihood (ML) and MI (Schafer & Graham, 2002).

In 1987, four publications came out that changed how we handle missing data (Graham et al., 2003). First, ML was introduced using structural equation modeling (SEM) by Allison (1987) and Muthén, Kaplan, and Hollis (1987). Second, Little and Rubin's (1987) seminal book on analysis with missing data was released, which included discussion of handling missingness with the expectation-maximization (EM) algorithm (Dempster, Laird, & Rubin, 1977). Last, but not least, Rubin (1987) introduced MI. Empirical evidence of modern methods has consistently shown the comparative value of modern methods for handling missing data (Arbuckle, 1996; Enders, 2001; Enders & Bandalos, 2001; Graham & Schafer, 1999; Muthén et al., 1987).

Graham and Schafer (1999) suggested being ready to use any of these techniques based on the appropriateness and ease of use for each situation. There are many similarities between these methods. Both ML and MI are based on sound theory, reproduce the data structure accurately, and incorporate a necessary measure of uncertainty given the estimation of missing data (Collins et al., 2001). Both MI and ML regard missingness as a source of random variation to be averaged over rather than simply editing an incomplete data set until it approximates a complete data set. In addition, when ML and MI are conducted properly, the results are fully parametric, using joint probability of manifest and latent data.

Prior to detailing ML and MI, I believe it is important to explain one of their key building blocks: the EM algorithm, once a popular missing data technique unto itself (Graham et al., 2003).

A Brief Overview of the EM Process

EM is a maximum likelihood approach that can be used to create a new data set in which all missing values are imputed with maximum likelihood values. The EM algorithm (Dempster et al., 1977) is easy to use and has lots of software to produce it (freeware and commercial). Estimates obtained from EM are often unbiased, and the EM algorithm provides a data set with imputed values from which additional analyses can be conducted or used as an initial step in more advanced missing data techniques (Abraham & Russell, 2004). In addition, EM avoids one of the difficulties with standard regression imputation in that there is no decision about which variables should be used as the predictors, as EM uses all available data as predictors for the imputed values. However, EM is problematic to use by itself, as the standard errors and test statistics with EM are not correct.

There are two steps to the EM algorithm: expectation and maximization. These processes work iteratively to impute missing values and to estimate the covariance matrix and mean vector. Before the E and M steps begin, an initial estimate of the covariance matrix and mean vector is calculated from the observed data (Little & Rubin, 2002). For the first E step, a series of regressions are derived from the observed covariance matrix and mean vector in order to determine the contribution of each missing value (for each missing cell) to the sufficient statistics (i.e., variable sums and sums of products) necessary for calculating the covariance matrix and mean vector (Enders, 2006a). A random residual term is added because otherwise, all predicted values would fall directly on the predicted regression line. Based on the predicted regressions and residuals, estimates of the sufficient statistics necessary to calculate a missing-data augmented covariance matrix and mean vector during the M step are estimated. During the M step, new estimates of the covariance matrix and mean vector are derived from the sufficient statistics calculated during the E step. No special techniques are used for missingness during this step, and the subsequent matrix and vector are passed along to the next iteration of the E step. The EM algorithm concludes once the difference between the covariance matrices from two adjacent M steps is trivial. Figure 15.1 describes the EM sequence of events.

Running the EM algorithm before MI is highly recommended for two reasons. First, the resulting parameter estimates make great starting values for the data augmentation process used in MI. Second, the convergence behavior witnessed during EM is predictive of the convergence behavior of data augmentation, which, as will be discussed, is far more esoteric (Schafer & Olsen, 1998). EM may even provide better estimates under nonnormality than a nonparametric MI estimation when the missingness mechanism is MCAR or ignorable, as long as the sample size is 500 or more (Gold, Bentler, & Kim, 2003).

As has been noted, EM parameter estimates are excellent, but the standard errors are problematic. Thus, some specific uses of EM work quite well, including data checks that do not involve hypothesis tests such as coefficient alpha and exploratory factor analysis (Graham et al., 2003; Graham & Hofer, 2000). Nevertheless, with the growing software availability of ML and MI, the use of EM as its own missing data technique is nearly all but outdated.

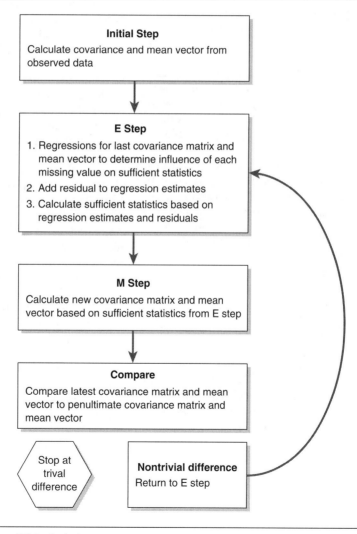

Figure 15.1   Progression of EM calculations.

Maximum Likelihood

The ML process for handling missing data was introduced by Allison (1987) and Muthén et al. (1987). It was when Arbuckle (1996) included ML in the user-friendly SEM program AMOS in the mid-1990s that the popularity of this technique increased such that now all of the major SEM programs (and many other packages) include ML to address missing data.

ML is particularly well suited for handling missing data because ML estimation is a tool to select estimates that, if correct, would maximize the probability of observing the data that have been collected (Allison, 2002). ML estimates are consistent, in that they are essentially unbiased. ML estimates are efficient, in that standard errors are close to the true standard errors (especially as sample sizes increase). Finally, ML estimates are normally distributed in repeated sampling (again, improving with larger sample sizes), thereby justifying normal probability testing (Agresti & Finlay, 1997). Simulations have shown that ML is virtually always superior to traditional missingness techniques (Wothke, 2000), though the quality of ML does depend on the missing data rate, the covariance structure of the data, and size of the sample (as with all advanced missing data techniques). ML is a step beyond EM in that rather than maximizing for the entire correlation (or covariance) matrix, we maximize just for the model to be analyzed. This process provides more accurate standard errors (Allison, 2002).

Despite the advantages of ML, one major limitation exists: It requires specialized software to use it, usually software in the latent variable modeling realm. ML is available in SEM programs such as AMOS (Arbuckle, 2006), EQS (Bentler, 2006), LISREL (Jöreskog & Sörbom, 2001), Mplus (Muthén & Muthén, 2006), and Mx (Neale, Boker, Xie, & Maes, 1999). Nevertheless, ML provides one very important advantage over MI in that the goodness-of-fit values in SEM are based on the final ML covariance matrix (Wothke, 2000), whereas MI cannot use Rubin's rules to combine fit indices determined for each database.

The ML Process. The calculation details of ML are quite rigorous (Schafer & Graham, 2002) and beyond the scope of this chapter (for more formulaic details, see Allison, 1987, 2002, 2003).

With missing data, ML uses observed data in order to calculate a log likelihood from the observed data points for each case (using information from both the covariance matrix and the mean vector). The sum of the individual case likelihoods is used for the total sample log-likelihood function. It should be noted that missing values are not imputed in this process. Instead, the full observed information is used to estimate parameter estimates and standard errors (*SE*s) by iteratively fitting the sample log likelihood (Enders, 2006a). Also, *SE*s should not be calculated using estimated data given that such *SE*s would require the missingness to be MCAR (Kenward & Molenberghs, 1998). Instead, the imputer should opt to use observed data only for the calculation of *SE*s in ML (Enders, 2006a). When the missingness is ignorable, the likelihood function is simply the marginal likelihood for all remaining predictors (Allison, 2002).

One major aspect of using ML for controlling missing data is that the MA model and analysis model are conducted concurrently. Indeed, this is also a limitation of ML: The missingness augmentation cannot be conducted outside of the statistical analysis. This means that any auxiliary variable included in the MA model must also be included in the analysis model, thereby limiting how many auxiliary variables can realistically be used in ML.

Assumptions of ML. As with all statistical techniques, understanding the assumptions behind the modern missing data techniques is critical to the unfettered interpretation of results. First, ML assumes that the missingness mechanism is ignorable. Enders (2001) found that most of the other assumptions for ML for missing data are similar to the assumptions for ML extraction in SEM: ML estimates should come from a sample of sufficient size, and the covariance matrix should be multivariate normal. When the data are multivariate nonnormal, three data issues are standard: (1) Parameter estimates were relatively unbiased, (2) *SE*s estimated were biased downward, and (3) chi-square-based model fit statistics had excessive rejection rates. This was true for both MCAR and MAR missingness. ML also assumes that the analysis model is correct for the data (i.e., fit statistics meet appropriate criteria).

There are a few considerations to these assumptions. Regarding multivariate normality, there are a number of ways to ensure that the covariance matrix is multivariate normal.[3] Regarding the assumption that the analysis model is correct, it is important to evaluate one's model from multiple perspectives using various model fit statistics. When a model is misfit, the amount of missingness corrected by ML will increasingly affect the efficacy of techniques used to improve model fit, such as modification indices (Steiger, 1990).

Finally, although ML is designed for ignorable missingness, it may be even more generalizable. ML estimates are both consistent and efficient under MAR (Wothke, 2000), and some have shown that the estimates remain favorable even when the missingness deviates from MAR (Little & Rubin, 2002; Muthén et al., 1987).

Limitations. ML provides an excellent modern tool for addressing missingness and does so with much simplicity, especially given that few variants to the ML process exist. However, when some of the assumptions are violated, they can be difficult to overcome. For example, small sample sizes simply obviate the use of ML for addressing missingness (there are no studies to determine what a sufficient sample is for ML). Currently, it may be best to rely on the same standards used in determining a sufficient sample size for latent models using ML (e.g., Hancock, 2006). Another limitation of ML for addressing missing data is the inclusion of auxiliary variables. As discussed above, auxiliary variables can be beneficial in dealing with missing data, but in ML, that means adding auxiliary variables to the analysis, which may complicate the analysis (Enders, 2006a).

Multiple Imputation

When the simplicity of ML does not work for a particular situation, the multiple imputation approach may work. MI is a three-step process to handling missing data. In the first step, missing data are imputed through a Bayesian procedure. The key for MI is that more than one data set is generated during the imputation stage, providing a means of determining the bias associated from imputing. The second step involves analyzing each of the imputed databases with standard statistics, such as multiple linear regression. In the third step, the results of the analyses from each data set are combined and estimates are adjusted to account for the

level of bias within and between data sets introduced from the use of imputed values as real data during Step 2.

As noted by Abraham and Russell (2004), the appeal of MI comes from its adaptability, as shown in many simulation studies (Weinfurt et al., 2003). MI has been shown to result in efficient and unbiased parameter estimates and standard errors (Enders, 2006a; Graham et al., 2003), as well as flexibility in handling numerous data scenarios (Schafer & Olsen, 1998). MI can be used for data with a higher percentage of missingness (Sinhary, Stern, & Russell, 2001, found that MI was appropriate for up to 40% missingness), is appropriate with nested and clustered data (Allison, 2002; Badzioch, Thomas, & Jarvik, 2003), and is appropriate for categorical data (Schafer & Graham, 2002; Schafer & Olsen, 1998). Although standard MI is based on normal modeling theory (Abraham & Russell, 2004), MI performs well with small sample sizes and nonnormal data (Graham & Schafer, 1999). Finally, MI splits the imputation and analysis stages into different steps. Such separation allows for the easy use of numerous auxiliary variables during the MA stage without affecting the analyses, imputation that can be conducted on many variables from different analyses at once to allow for more stable variable interrelationships across analyses, and incorporation of higher-order data into the imputation stage such as interactions or hierarchically organized data.

There are many variants to the MI process, and I will focus on the multivariate normal random MI model, one of the best performing and most widely available (Allison, 2002, p. 56).[4]

Processes. Multiple data set imputation, single data set analysis, and parameter combination are the three steps of MI (for more information on the process and calculations, see Little & Rubin, 2002; Rubin, 1987, 1996; Rubin & Schenker, 1991).

Step 1—Imputation. The first task to undertake when conducting MI is to consider how many data sets of imputations are needed. A small number of imputations ($m = 10$) will be adequate for most situations. In fact, when assumptions are met, 10 imputations will produce standard errors just 2% larger than an infinite number of imputations (von Hippel, 2005). Rubin (1987) provided a formula for determining the efficiency of m imputations with a given fraction of missingness,

$$\left(1 + \frac{\gamma}{m}\right)^{-1},$$

where γ is the fraction of missing data. With this formula, one can see that with 30% missingness, 91% efficiency is obtained with just three imputed databases, 94% with $m = 5$, and 97% with $m = 10$: More than three times the imputations are necessary to increase efficiency just 6%. Thus, researchers should consider what level of efficiency is necessary (I would recommend no less than 90%) and then determine how many imputations will be necessary given the level of missingness in their database.

Next, one calculates the imputed values. It is important to note that we do not impute in order to divine what an individual would have said if he or she had given us data but rather to preserve important characteristics of parameters (e.g., variances, covariances, means, regression coefficients, etc.) and distributions (Graham et al., 2003, p. 88). The imputed values in MI only have purpose in creating an efficient and unbiased manner by which to properly evaluate all of the observed data in the data set.

Akin to the two-step process of EM, the data imputation in Step 1 of MI also has a two-step process. During the estimation of values for missing data, called data augmentation, two steps, called imputation and posterior distribution, are iteratively conducted. Data augmentation is a type of an increasingly popular method for determining a posterior distribution in Bayesian statistics, the Markov chain Monte Carlo (MCMC) algorithm (Schafer & Olsen, 1998). The starting values for the data augmentation process are based on an initial estimate of the covariance matrix, usually garnered from the EM algorithm (Schafer & Olsen, 1998). At this point, the two-step process begins with the first imputation step, wherein regressions are conducted from the basal covariance matrix replacing missing values with the predicted scores from the regressions. Random draws from the normal residual distribution are added to the missing values in order to adjust for all estimates being perfectly on the prediction line of the regressions, thereby adding in a measure of uncertainty for our understanding of the missing value. After the missingness is replaced, the covariance matrix and mean vectors are recalculated with the imputed values, and the imputation step

ends. The posterior step then commences by introducing the Bayesian aspect to the data augmentation calculations. Randomly sampling elements from a posterior distribution derived from the covariance matrix and mean vector in the imputation step allows for refinement of the covariance and mean elements. Values during the random draws in MI should be based on the Bayesian posterior distribution of the parameter values in order to fully enmesh the uncertainty of our parameter estimates. However, if the sample size is large enough, then random sampling from the Bayesian posterior may not be required (Allison, 2002). This process continues updating the mean and covariance elements and random selections of the posterior distribution until indiscriminant differences are obtained between two consecutive data augmentation steps. There are several ways of calculating the posterior distribution, but Schaefer's (1997) noninformative prior is considered a standard (Enders, 2006a).

Step 2—Single Data Set Analysis. Once m data sets have been created with imputed values from Step 1, hypothesis testing is conducted with one's predefined statistical analysis. The statistical analyses are conducted once for each of the m data sets. For example, if a researcher planned for multiple regression with three predictor variables and one indicator, then after extracting her five data sets from Step 1, she would analyze the first data set with her multiple regression model, then the second data set, and so forth. These results would then be used to guide calculations in Step 3.

Step 3—Combination. The true benefit of MI comes in the third step, as we enact controls for our uncertainty in using imputed data as observed data during Step 2. Step 3 involves three tasks: Calculate means for all pertinent parameter values, calculate *SEs* for all pertinent parameters, and then calculate p values for the parameters based on a modified *df* formula. The first task is the easiest: Create a mean for each important parameter by summing each variable's parameter values across the m data sets and dividing that sum by m, as in Equation 1,

$$\bar{Q} = \frac{1}{m} \sum_{i=1}^{m} \hat{Q}_i, \qquad (1)$$

where $\hat{Q}_i$ is the parameter estimate for the ith data set from the m imputed data sets.

Next, we determine the SE of the parameter by calculating within and between data set error from the imputations. To do this, (a) calculate the within-imputation variance with Equation 2, (b) calculate the between-imputation variance with Equation 3, and (c) determine the total variance by combining within- and between-imputation variances per Equation 4:

$$\bar{U} = \frac{1}{m} \sum_{i=1}^{m} \hat{U}_i, \quad (2)$$

where $\hat{U}_i$ is the variance estimate from the ith imputed data set, and m remains the number of imputation, and

$$B = \frac{1}{m} \sum_{i=1}^{m} (\hat{Q} - \bar{Q})^2, \quad (3)$$

which is the mean of the variances for a parameter across all databases, and

$$T = \bar{U} + \left(1 + \frac{1}{m}\right) B. \quad (4)$$

To get the standard error for multiple imputation for a specific parameter, just take the square root of T for that parameter (Rubin, 1987).

Finally, we are ready to determine the probability level for each parameter. Begin by calculating the degrees of freedom via Equation 5. The df may vary from $m-1$ to infinity depending on the rate of missingness. The following formula is used to get the df:

$$df = (m-1) \left[1 + \frac{\bar{U}}{\left(1 + \frac{1}{m}\right) B} \right]^2, \quad (5)$$

where $\bar{U}$ is Equation 2 and B is Equation 3. If the computed value of the df is less than about 10, then one should consider increasing the number of imputations (Schafer & Olsen, 1998).

From here, use a Student's t approximation of

$$t \approx \frac{\bar{Q}}{\sqrt{T}}$$

and base the p value off of this t test with the above df. As an example, let's examine results from a simple regression where scores from the Beck Depression Inventory (BDI; Beck, Ward, Mendelson, Mock, & Erbaugh, 1961) were used to predict scores on the 10-item short form of the CES-D that I previously developed (Cole, Rabin, Smith, & Kaufman, 2004). Ten data sets were imputed, and the resultant regression coefficients and related standard errors are now provided in Table 15.2. It should be evident that the overall standard error, $\sqrt{T}$, should be low, and the results of the t test will be high, as all of the coefficients are markedly higher than their respective standard errors with little deviation between data sets. Indeed, using the above formulas, we get the following results: $\bar{Q} = 0.593$, $\bar{U} = 0.001362$, $B = 0.0002229$, $\sqrt{T} = .037227$, $df = 23{,}413$, and $t = 15.91$ (with a resulting p value that is off the charts given the df).

There are other methods for combining more complex estimates, such as likelihood ratios and chi-square statistics (see Schafer, 1997).

Assumptions

Four general assumptions exist for MI: (1) The missingness mechanism is MAR (or better), (2) the model used to generate imputed values must be valid, (3) the analysis and MA models must align, and (4) MI assumes that the data are both univariate and multivariate normally distributed.

Table 15.2   CES-D Short Form Regressed on the Beck Depression Inventory

Data Set	Unstandardized Regression Coefficient	Standard Error
1	0.597	0.037
2	0.593	0.038
3	0.602	0.038
4	0.590	0.036
5	0.586	0.036
6	0.593	0.037
7	0.592	0.038
8	0.596	0.036
9	0.586	0.037
10	0.596	0.036

Missing at Random. The theory behind MI does not preclude using MI models for nonignorable missingness, and some studies have been published using MI with nonignorable missingness (Glynn, Laird, & Rubin, 1993; Verbeke & Molenberghs, 2000). However, without special techniques applied to the MI process, MI conducted without MAR or MCAR missingness can result in biased parameter estimates.

Valid Imputation Model. Using the Bayesian sampling from the posterior distribution to treat parameters as random rather than fixed is a major benefit of MI. However, a few aspects of Bayesian inference should be understood when conducting MI. First, all of the data's evidence about parameter estimates is summarized in a likelihood function with an assumed distribution. If the assumption is incorrect, than the prior distribution from which the likelihood function is derived may be wrong. Second, Bayesian analysis requires the use of a prior distribution, which is not always accepted as purely scientific. Nevertheless, with the increase in sample size comes a decrease of the influence the prior distribution has on the MI results. Indeed, Schafer and Graham (2002) have noted that the prior rarely exerts a marked influence on the results in MI. For example, an alterative to data augmentation can be conducted with an unrestricted multinomial model or a log-linear model (allowing for restrictions of the multinomial parameters) (Little & Rubin, 2002; Schafer, 1997). Given the scope of the current chapter, I will not cover these methods but encourage the interested reader to review the aforementioned references. If one has reason to suspect that the MA model may be invalid for a particular use, it would be beneficial to run a sensitivity analysis examining different priors or even different Bayesian techniques (such as from different MI software programs). Sensitivity analyses are discussed in the last section of this chapter.

Fit Between Analysis and Imputation Model. It is critical to ensure that the MA model has at least as much information as needed to calculate the analysis model correctly. For example, if interactions between two variables will be analyzed, then the interaction term itself must also be in the MI model. The same is true for multilevel data: Appropriate representation of the multilevel structure must be present in the MA model

if the data are to be analyzed with multilevel techniques. It is also important to consider which variables will be used in the imputation phase to help enable the missingness mechanism to be at least MAR. If auxiliary variables are not appropriately considered in the MA model, or if they are inserted in during MA but ultimately inserted into the analysis model as well, the missingness mechanism could be compromised to become MNAR.

Normality. The typical MI model assumes multivariate normality, thereby requiring all variables to be normally distributed, as well as that each variable can be expressed as a linear function of all other variables with a normal homoscedastic residual (Allison, 2002). However, the MI model works well even when some of the distributions of the present data are not normal (Schafer, 1997). Still, normalizing variables with missing data can have a marked impact on the quality of the imputations (Allison, 2002).

Schafer (1997) argued that the multivariate normal model of MI can be used for nominal and ordinal variables. When nonnormal data are imputed with the multivariate normal MI, the imputed values are more normal than the rest of the data. Given that the imputed values typically make up only a smaller part of the overall data set, the influence of imputed normality among nonnormal data has relatively little impact on the results (Graham & Hofer, 2000; Graham & Schafer, 1999). Moreover, as nonnormality has little impact on parameter estimates compared with standard errors, it is important to note that MI has little effect on the computation of *SEs*. Indeed, it is one's software and statistical analysis that has the greatest impact on the accuracy of *SEs* under nonnormality (Graham & Hofer, 2000).

Nonnormal, ordinal, and even nominal data have been shown to work quite well with the multivariate MI model, even with relatively small sample sizes (Schafer, 1997).

Advanced Issues With MI

Partially Parametric and Nonparametric MI. When the aforementioned assumptions for MI are known to be violated and irreconcilable, it may be necessary to invoke a partially parametric or nonparametric MI process. Many of these exist, and they are detailed well elsewhere.

Limitations of MI

MI provides a process that can be used with almost any software and nearly any kind of data. Nevertheless, the downside to MI is that it (a) is time-consuming, (b) can be quite technical, and (c) provides different estimates with every execution (unless the random start value is fixed). In addition, whereas ML works sufficiently with only one sampling, critics of MI have argued that prior simulation studies have failed to control for random sampling theory issues, and therefore MI may require more than 500 imputations (Hershberger & Fisher, 2003). This issue, however, requires more investigation (Abraham & Russell, 2004), and most studies in MI have suggested otherwise (Rubin, 1987; Schafer, 1997).

ML VERSUS MI: WHEN TO USE ONE OR THE OTHER

ML and MI are really not dissimilar techniques. Collins et al. (2001) have discouraged considering ML and MI as competitors, noting that the two approaches produce similar results, even indistinguishably different under certain conditions. Because MI is a Monte Carlo–based method, when $m < \infty$, estimates from MI will contain random error not found in the ML estimates and thus will have larger standard errors, although this is usually minimal. Rubin (1987) provides a formula for comparing the relative efficiency of MI compared with an appropriate ML model, given specific levels of missingness of a number of imputations.

Alas, there are times when selecting one model over the other makes sense. I have summarized in Table 15.3 the major scenarios when one technique may provide benefits over the other techniques.

When ML May Be Best. According to Allison (2002), if the analysis involves any linear model that can be estimated with SEM software, then ML is probably the preferred method for conducting MI. This is because ML in such circumstances is quite easy to implement (literally requiring only the click of a button or the addition of one to two lines of code, depending on the software) and, if the model is correct, will produce estimates that are quite accurate.

There are a few more considerations, however, in order to feel comfortable with using ML. First, one should have reason to believe that only a few auxiliary variables will provide sufficient control for the missingness mechanism to be at least MAR (such as Little's MCAR test or previous research on similar data examining the missingness mechanism). Adding a few auxiliary variables into an ML analysis is not too cumbersome but quickly becomes difficult when (a) there are a large number of variables to be analyzed in the analysis model, (b) there are more than two or three auxiliary variables to be added to the model, or (a) and (b) are both true. In addition, when one has a large sample size (and other issues are appropriately attended), ML should work well. Smaller samples will work best in MI. As noted previously, determining the size of a sufficiently large sample is not straightforward. Finally, if only one analysis is needed, or the relationship between the same variable in different analyses is not critical, then ML may be sufficient. Otherwise, MI may be more appropriate.

In sum, ML is likely to be the preferred option when the MA model is simple, only

Table 15.3   ML Versus MI: When to Favor One Process Over the Other

Use ML When	Use MI When
Software is available, and the analysis model is a simple linear function	Control of MNAR requires many auxiliary variables
There is a need to obtain model fit indices after adjusting for missingness	A polychoric covariance matrix does not make sense for your data, but you have multivariate normality violations
There is a sufficient *n* with only a few auxiliary variables and few normality issues	There are small sample sizes or a large percentage of missing data
Only one analysis is required or the relationship between analyses is not critical	It is easier to impute many variables at once and do separate analyses based on the same MA model

a single analysis is required, and the sample size is moderate to large. ML's accuracy in this case is equal to an infinite number of imputations in MI. Indeed, ML can even handle mixtures of continuous and categorical data now (Song & Lee, 2003). Nevertheless, ML does not offer the flexibility that can be found with MI when the data or MA models are more problematic.

When MI May Be Best. Whereas ML is easy to implement but has limited flexibility to handle diverse data and MA scenarios, MI is more technically difficult but has much flexibility and appropriateness with many different data and imputation scenarios. The three most commonly experienced benefits for MI are the control of MNAR with auxiliary variables, appropriateness with small sample sizes, and ability to have consistent data (or sets of data) for any one variable across different analyses.

Because of the simplicity of adding dozens (even hundreds!) of auxiliary variables into the MA model, MI can provide far greater protection against MNAR missingness compared with ML. Not only is it easy to add many auxiliary variables into the MA model, but it is even easier to make sure the effect of the auxiliary variables is incorporated in the analysis model. As long as one does not include the intended auxiliary variables in the analysis model, their protection remains.

Some simulation work suggests that MI may work better with smaller sample sizes than ML (Graham & Schafer, 1999; Schafer & Graham, 2002). MI will still require more participants than variables during calculation of the MA model, and at least a ratio of 10 participants to one variable would be advisable. However, little work has been conducted to provide empirically guided instructions on the minimum number of participants needed for a sufficiently stable MA model. Finally, imputation of an entire data set can be conducted during a single, carefully considered MA model calculation. The benefit of such an MA model over ML is that ML will have differing covariances with the same variable in another model, assuming that some of the other variables in the model have changed. If stability of the variable information is important, then MI can provide better protection. Of course, the analyst will still need to heed caution in that imputation results will change if the MA model is recalculated and the random starting seed is not the same.

MISSINGNESS IMPUTATION SEQUENTIAL SYSTEM (MISS): DISCUSSION AND EXAMPLE

Now that we have discussed basic language and issues related to missing data, detailed critiques of classic techniques, and provided discussion on the processes of ML and MI, we are ready to discuss details on how to implement a full process for handling missing data in one's database. This section of the chapter introduces a step-by-step process, the missingness imputation sequential system (MISS), which is designed to walk a researcher through each of the pertinent steps necessary to properly rectify missing data. MISS is presented in the context of a full example using data and related files, all of which may be downloaded from www.webcmg.com/ missing-example.htm.

Discussion of the Missingness Imputation Sequential System

MISS is an 11-step approach that can be used to ensure that all pertinent aspects of conquering your missing data are addressed. I have labeled it a sequential system because most of the steps must be conducted in a sequential order for later steps to be appropriately conducted. MISS is intended to encourage its users to consider many of the relevant issues necessary in addressing missing data, provide instruction on how to implement ML and MI techniques, and help understand the flow and relationship of the different steps involved in addressing missing data. Of course, use MISS with forethought: It is not a panacea, nor can it be used without knowledge of the issues already discussed in this chapter.

Step 1: Create the Missingness Augmentation Model

Implementation of MISS begins with creation of the MA model. As noted previously, the MA model must capture at least as much information as will be analyzed in the analysis model. This means that the MA model should contain (a) all of the variables in the analysis model (auxiliary variables will be added in a later step); (b) any advanced relationships in the analysis model, such as interactions and multilevel data; and (c) the same level of data that will be analyzed in the analysis. The first aspect is self-explanatory. For interactions, the type of interaction must be considered. If one of the variables in an interaction is categorical, the more appropriate manner for imputation is to conduct a data augmentation run for m data sets for each group on the categorical variable. After imputation, merge the data sets and create the interaction term (or evaluate with an interaction-friendly analysis). However, when both variables are continuous (or have multiple points on an ordinal scale), then the separate imputations are either impossible or very laborious. In this instance, one can create an interaction term before imputation based on centered first-order data (for detailed information on centering, see Tabachnick & Fidell, 2007) and impute with this term in the model. This will almost always lead to nonnormal data, but the results will frequently be appropriate (Allison, 2002). Moreover, if just group differences are going to be examined, group membership should be included in the MA model (Schafer & Graham, 2002). To include multilevel or clustering information, the categorical variables detailing levels or clusters should be included in the MA model. Consider if interactions between different levels or clusters will be analyzed. If so, the interaction terms will also be added to the MA model.

In addition, consider if the level of analysis will take place on summary scores or item-level data. If your statistical analyses are on scale-level data, then there may not be much advantage to imputing the item-level data. I tend to favor keeping the MA and analysis models consistent by imputing the scale-level data when analyzing scale-level data.

Depression Example. For our example that we will use throughout these steps, our database once again involves 189 general-population participants (Cole et al., 2004). Among other collected data, our analysis model examines the influence of BDI and age in predicting scores on the 10-item CES-D short form. Moreover, we have added in an interaction term between age and BDI score. These data are contained in the online Excel database called depression database. Currently, our MA model now contains age, BDI, the centered interaction between age and BDI, and CESD_10.

Step 2: Examine the Data for Missingness

The second step is where we start digging into the observed data set in order to determine how missing data may be missing and prepare

them for ML or MI. Before anything else, determine which empty cells are truly missing. Hopefully, the creator of the database has created several codes for missing data, including a differentiation between missing and not applicable. Defining the participants who met inclusion criteria, eliminating those who do not meet inclusion criteria, and imputing true missingness must be done with great care.

Next, see if you can determine the type of missingness mechanism (MCAR, MAR, or MNAR, as discussed above; if the data are not MCAR, conduct a sensitivity analysis between MAR and MNAR techniques). Afterward, determine whether your data preclude use of particular missing data techniques (e.g., discrete data may require MI rather than ML).

Finally, determine the normality of the continuous variables. Although MI has shown robustness to nonnormal continuous data, adjustment of the distributions can only help ensure that appropriate standard errors are obtained. Finally, assessment of multivariate normality can be beneficial, such as the Mahalanobis test (Tabachnick & Fidell, 2007) or Mardia's coefficient (Mardia, 1970). Large violations of these statistics may suggest that a multivariate normality model could be inappropriate, although MI has been shown to be relatively robust to such violations.

Depression Example. No inclusion or exclusion criteria were necessary to control in the current data set. Moreover, all missing cells were intended to be collected and analyzed; therefore, I did not have applicable missingness here. Data have been coded so that a "–9" defines a missing value.

Using SAS code from Enders (2006c), Little's MCAR test obtained a nonsignificant chi-square = 17.56 (df = 14, p = .227), indicating that the missing mechanism for the MA model was MCAR. However, there is evidence that, at least for some depression items, gender leads to differential bias (Santor, Ramsay, & Zuroff, 1994). Thus, although we achieved MCAR missingness, it may be prudent to add gender as an auxiliary variable during Step 5.

We have four variables in the analysis and MA models currently, and all of these variables are continuous. Standardized skewness and kurtosis scores (respectively) for the four variables were 4.16 and –0.04 for age, 6.75 and 5.65 for BDI, 5.49 and 5.03 for Age × BDI, and 5.94 and 3.35 for CES-D. Mardia's coefficient was a standardized score of 8.81. Overall, it is clear that these data have moderate normality violations, which should be appropriately corrected with a square root transformation (Tabachnick & Fidell, 2007).[5] These transformations will be conducted in the imputation software.

Step 3: Select Which Software to Use

There are too many software programs out there to provide a thorough review in this chapter, though some reviews do exist (e.g., Acock, 2005). A few particular programs are worthy of specific mention. Mplus provides for the use of ML for missing data with data that are continuous, censored, binary, ordered categorical, nominal (multinomial), counts, or combinations of all of these. Moreover, it will do so with or without latent variables, allowing for simple regression, correlation, or other manifest-only analyses (Muthén & Muthén, 2006). Indeed, Acock (2005) noted that Mplus has a warehouse of options for handling missing values, including approaches for data that are MCAR, ignorable, and even nonignorable, as well as the integration of robust or bootstrapped standard errors. The release of AMOS 7 (Arbuckle, 2006) provides us with the first commercial package that will conduct MA for both ML and MI. Moreover, Version 7 also allows for proper calculation of censored, dichotomous, order-categorical, and similar ordinal-level data with either ML or MI.

A growing number of programs will conduct MI, including multivariate normal random MI. One example is NORM, freeware from Schafer (2000)[6] that performed quite well in a simulation study (Allison, 2000) using data augmentation. NORM performs well with nonnormal data and with small sample sizes (Graham & Schafer, 1999). Moreover, the graphical interface is more user-friendly than some. Finally, the SAS PROC MI and MIANALYZE set of commands work quite nicely. The ability to conduct the imputation step, analysis step, and combination of results steps all in one program without much additional coding is a major benefit. Moreover, PROC MI has a very useful command for restricting the upper and lower limits of acceptable random draws for imputed values.

Depression Example. Given the markedly easy interface for NORM and that it is freeware, I have provided the remainder of the MI

examples with this software. Nevertheless, in order to conserve space, many of the example figures have been reserved for the supplementary Web site for this chapter at www.webcmg .com/missing-example.htm.

Step 4: Determine the Number of Imputations Needed

Rubin (1987) provided Equation 6 for determining the efficiency of an estimate based on m imputations with a given fraction of missingness:

$$\left(1 + \frac{\gamma}{m}\right)^{-1}, \qquad (6)$$

where γ is the fraction of missing data. Until research determines a minimum amount of efficiency necessary, I recommend using 90% to 95%.

Depression Example. I began by looking at the variable with the highest percentage of missingness because if I could achieve acceptable efficiency without too many imputations for this variable, all other variables should also be sufficient. For the current data, the interaction term has the largest amount of missingness (18.52%). With three imputations, we get 94.19% efficiency; five imputations give us 96.3% efficiency, which is acceptable.

Step 5: Select the Auxiliary Variables

Unless Little's MCAR test affirms that the data are MCAR, I strongly encourage the use of auxiliary variables in every missing data problem; even then, auxiliary variables can help with the estimation accuracy. The major decision in this step is to determine how many auxiliary variables should be included. If there is reason to believe that more than three or four auxiliary variables will be necessary, then MI should be used.

Depression Example. As noted in Step 1, I have included gender as a covariate in the MA model, mostly for pedagogical purposes, given the MCAR finding. Gender is a dichotomous variable, with females coded as a 1 and males coded as 2. This variable has no missingness, though Enders (2006b) has noted that missingness in auxiliary variables does not affect the quality of MI estimates.

Step 6: Configure the Data in the MI Software

Begin by ensuring that all missing value points have been set to a specific value, such as −9 (as long as the value is sufficiently out of the range of possible values for all variables with missingness). The details of processing the data will vary from program to program, and readers should consult the documentation for help in this step. I have included some details on NORM on the supporting Web site.

Depression Example. The supporting Web site shows the final set of options I have marked in the Data—Variables tab. All five variables are marked to be in the MA model and in the final imputed databases. All of the variables except gender are to be transformed during imputation calculations with a square root transformation, including shifts for CES-D, BDI, and the interaction. I used integer rounding for all but gender and the interaction. Gender gets no rounding, which is because it has no missing data. The interaction term is allowed to go to the ninth decimal place, reflecting the number of decimal places used by Excel to create the interaction (although two decimal places is generally sufficient). The output file (summary.out) for the data summary is provided online.

Step 7: EM Algorithm

Once all of the options have been set on the Data tab, we are ready to move to the first set of calculations. As you may recall, we begin MI by calculating the EM algorithm to get an initial covariance matrix and mean vector for the data augmentation (DA) calculations of MI. One should take note of the number of iterations necessary to calculate the EM covariance matrix. This is a good indicator of how many iterations will be necessary for the DA step. NORM examples are on the supporting Web site.

Depression Example. Using the default settings for the EM algorithm, convergence occurred in just 12 iterations. The output report (em.out) is located online.

Step 8: Data Augmentation Step[7]

This is the first true step of MI. Starting parameters can be calculated either from the data (skipping the EM algorithm) or from EM results. The EM results are almost always

best here. Make sure your software will have enough iterations to work with (more is always better). In other words, if we determine that 40 iterations are required and five databases will be imputed, then the number of iterations should be no less than $40 \times 5 = 200$. Using more iterations will not create less stability, but having too few will create problems with the data sets. You also need a random number seed. It is important to note this number, as the ability to re-create the same imputed results demands the use of the same random seed. Finally, options are given for the type of prior to use in the Bayesian estimation. For almost all circumstances, the noninformative prior will work quite well. If problems persist, one can consider the ridge prior, but review critiques first. Upon completion of this step, it is important to review the diagnostics before moving on to Step 9. Upon verifying that the DA model has converged, you can open and examine the data sets.

Depression Example. All options from the main DA screen were left as their defaults. Under computing options, I selected 500 iterations. First, recall that I selected to impute five data sets during Step 5. Next, although I only needed twice the amount of iterations than was necessary for the EM algorithm convergence ($12 \times 2 = 24$), I opted to use 100 iterations per data set. Given the small sample size and number of variables, I was not worried about extra computational time. I noted my random seed of 55,028 for any future need (and saved it in my report for NORM). Finally, I opted to keep the default standard noninformative prior. For imputation options, I selected to impute at the end of every kth iteration, and $k = 100$. Finally, under the series options, I opted to save on the worst linear function at every one cycle. The worst linear function and autocorrelations plots (Figure 15.2) looked excellent, demonstrating clear convergence for the DA step.

Step 9: Calculate the Analysis Model

I will begin by discussing the calculation of the analysis model for MI first, as it is far easier than for ML, mostly because of auxiliary variables.

MI. There are two general ways to proceed in calculating the analysis model for multiply imputed data sets, differing by one's comfort level with SAS. For those who do not wish to use

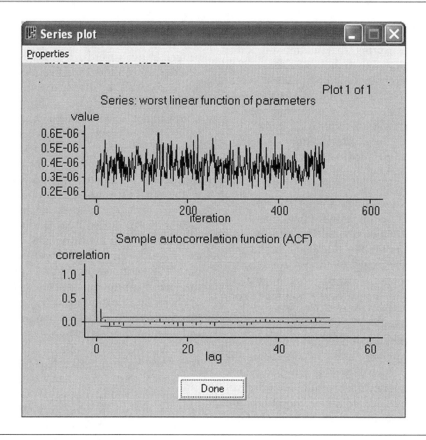

Figure 15.2   NORM series plot of worst linear trend.

SAS, one simply needs to conduct the analyses for each of the *m* imputed databases, recording the parameter estimates and standard errors. These are entered into a database for combination in NORM or are used to calculate on one's own summary statistics (see Step 10). Indeed, one could even get creative by combining the different databases in a single database, adding a dummy code for the database, and using a process such as SPSS's *organize output by group* command.

However, if one is comfortable conducting statistical analyses in SAS, then Step 9 and Step 10 can be concatenated into a single step (even if the imputation was conducted with NORM) using the SAS Inference command available in Version 8.2 and later (see Allison, 2002).

ML. To calculate the analysis model for ML, the model must be created within the desired modeling software. For the current discussion, I have used AMOS, given that the graphical interface is

quite intuitive and easily translates into other software coding. The basal MA model without auxiliary variables is simple and is presented in Figure 15.3. In order to incorporate auxiliary variables into the model, Graham (2003) outlined three rules that must be applied. An auxiliary variable must be modeled so it (a) correlates with all other auxiliary variables, (b) correlates with all exogenous manifest variables, and (c) correlates with the residual of all endogenous manifest variables. Figure 15.4 displays the MA model, with the auxiliary variable of gender added in using Graham rules. As you can see, adding in additional auxiliary variables can be quite cumbersome with even a small model.

Once the model is created, complete the rest of the model specifications and add in the specification for using ML to account for missing data (often called full-information maximum likelihood in latent modeling programs). When this option is selected, other options, such as modification indices, normality estimates, and

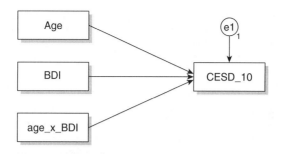

Figure 15.3   ML analysis model without auxiliary variable.

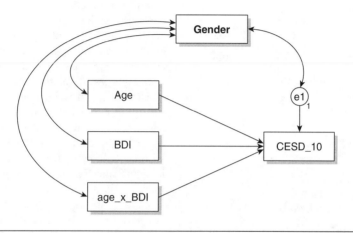

Figure 15.4   ML analysis model with one auxiliary variable.

other features, may, depending on the program, no longer be available. You will want to consult your software manual for specific details.

Depression Example. For the MI results, I calculated the regression coefficients and standard errors for each of the five databases, and these results are provided in Table 15.4. A cursory review suggests that age and BDI are significant predictors of CES-D short-form scores, but the interaction between age and BDI is not. Steps 10 and 11 will formalize these observations. For the ML results, estimates for the single calculation are also presented in Table 15.4. The results from ML tell a story similar to the cursory review of the MI parameters. However, an important finding from the ML results is that the model was not appropriate for the data: Fit statistics were all well off from necessary levels. Modification to the model was limited because of its small number of variables and many paths necessary

for the auxiliary variable. No appropriate modifications made the model fit sufficiently. Given that the ML augments to control for missing data depend on the model being correct, we cannot have much faith in the ML results at this point.

Step 10: Analyze Combined Results

One could undertake the calculation of Rubin's rules for combining multiple parameters and *SE*s with Excel or a calculator, although NORM and other MI programs often undertake this task for you.

Depression Example. Based on the integration of results from NORM (see the Web site for detailed examples), the output report (mi.out) conveyed the combined parameter estimates and *SE* results: age = −0.07 with *SE* = 0.02, BDI = 0.54 with *SE* = 0.04, and interaction = −0.21 with *SE* = 0.36.

Table 15.4   Parameter Estimates (*SEs*) for Step 9 Analysis Model Results From Five Imputed Databases

m	Age	BDI	Age × BDI
1	−0.064	0.547	−0.129
	(0.019)	(0.042)	(0.304)
2	−0.053	0.545	0.070
	(.018)	(0.043)	(0.292)
3	−0.068	0.535	−0.281
	(.018)	(0.040)	(0.288)
4	−0.079	0.536	−0.267
	(0.018)	(0.039)	(0.284)
5	−0.089	0.513	−0.429
	(0.018)	(0.042)	(0.300)
ML	−0.065	0.555	−0.059
	(0.018)	(0.037)	(0.300)

Step 11: Calculate p *Values for Estimates Using Modified* df *Calculations*

Using the MI Inference: Scalar option in MI automatically provides the *df*, *t*, and *p* values for each of the estimates. Recall that if the recalculated *df* is below 10, then more imputed databases should be calculated (using the same random number seed will allow you to generate the same original databases, with all additional databases being subsequent independent data sets).

Depression Example. Two significant findings were found: age, *t* = −2.98, *df* = 23, *p* = .0067; BDI, *t* = 12.22, *df* = 307, *p* < .0001. The *t* value for the interaction was not above 1 and thus was far from significant. Nevertheless, it did have more *df* than age (36 vs. 23), indicating greater stability of the MI results compared with age. BDI had 307 *df*, indicating marked stability. The percent missing information for age, BDI, and interaction was 45.5, 12.0, and 36.3, respectively.

Sensitivity Analyses

Sensitivity analyses are a systematic comparison of the effects of different missing data techniques. For example, sensitivity analyses can be

used to compare MI with simpler, less accurate data replacement techniques (Cook, 1997; Crawford, Tennstedt, & McKinlay, 1995; Lavori, Dawson, & Shera, 1995) or to explore the impact of various assumptions made during the imputation process (Allison, 2002; D. A. Heitjan & Landis, 1994; Little & Yau, 1996; Van Burren, Boshuizen, & Knoock, 1999). Moreover, the impact of assuming different missingness mechanisms can be explored (i.e., MAR vs. MNAR). Although the impact of nonignorable missingness typically results in only slight differences when examined with through sensitivity analyses (Graham, Donaldson, MacKinnon, & Schafer, 1997), it is still recommended that some kind of sensitivity analysis be conducted in every research situation to determine the impact of missingness (Graham & Hofer, 2000).

Despite much writing on the topic, there is very little consistent guidance on how to best conduct a sensitivity analysis. Some researchers (Fairclough, 2002; Fairclough, Fetting, Cella, Wonson, & Moinpour, 1999) will compare changes in significance (significant vs. nonsignificant) as well as various descriptive statistics, such as medians and quartiles. Others examine mean differences (Little & Rubin, 2002) between various missing data techniques. It is my belief that the outcome is critical to the sensitivity analysis. Therefore, I posit that two tests should be undertaken in a sensitivity analysis. First, a comparison between the various missing data techniques should compare which analyses result in significant results and which do not. However, just reviewing the significant versus nonsignificant results can lead to fallacious interpretation of significant differences when none exist for effects that are right around one's alpha level. Is it proper to declare the following results as leading to important differences: MNAR technique with a result of *p* = .049 and MAR technique with a result of *p* = .052? This is why I also advocate examining significant differences in the test statistic or parameter estimate.

As an example, with the depression data examined throughout this chapter, the result for the CES-D short form regressed on BDI for ML was 0.555 (84% CI:[8] 0.503–0.607), whereas the same parameter under MI was 0.535 (84% CI: 0.474–0.597). Both of these results are markedly significant, so they pass the first test. Moreover, they are not significantly different from each other, so they pass the second test. Therefore, the sensitivity test comparing ML and MI for CES-D regressed on BDI showed no important differences.

SUMMARY

The pervasive, nearly omnipresent, nature of missing data will evermore demand the attention of the applied researcher. More and more grant reviewers, journal editors, regulatory agencies, and other gatekeepers are demanding more attention to missing data from applied researchers. Traditional techniques for addressing missing data are nearly all antiquated, having been shown to perform poorly in creating efficient parameter estimates and unbiased standard errors. However, the readily available software for techniques such as ML and MI provides a new era of opportunity for the applied researcher to address missing data with techniques that are appropriate for a wide array of missing data problems. Some missing data problems may require more advanced techniques, such as pattern mixture models. Whereas ML and MI are now within the grasp of many applied researchers, some more advanced techniques will require far greater sophistication. Ideally, as with ML and MI, more advanced models will be made easier to implement with carefully designed software as demand for their use increases.

NOTES

1. Others use the term *imputation model,* but I prefer the term *missingness augmentation* because maximum likelihood does not technically impute anything. Instead, it adjusts the covariance matrix and mean vector to incorporate the influence of the missingness. Thus, missingness augmentation is meant to describe a process for handling missing data in some particular manner.

2. For example, in family research, men tend to have more missing data than women regardless of the content (Acock, 2005). Therefore, even though the analytic model may not examine gender differences, including gender in the MA model can help make sure the missing data technique is appropriate.

3. For example, the use of polychoric correlations (Song & Lee, 2003) for ordinal data or corrections to the standard errors and chi-square statistics. In SEM, for example, nonnormal data are quite frequent among psychological measures (Cole et al., 2004), despite the typical use of ML extraction in SEM. This will lead to unbiased estimates, but *SEs* may be quite misleading (Satorra & Bentler, 1994), thus mandating that the missingness be MCAR (Yuan & Bentler, 2000). Robust standard errors are used in complete data analysis to correct for nonnormality (Finney & DiStefano, 2006), and these techniques can be conducted for ML analyses with missing data as well. Although the robust *SEs* assume MCAR missingness, Enders (2001) found the *SEs* to be relatively accurate under MAR missingness as well. In addition, the Bollen-Stine bootstrap can be used for nonnormal data with missingness, as shown in Enders (2002).

4. The multivariate normal random MI model is available in several software packages, including an excellent freeware program by Schafer (2000).

5. See Chapter 13 (this volume) on transformations for specific detail on how best to do this.

6. Downloadable at http://www.stat.psu.edu/~jls/misoftwa.html.

7. Of course, there is no data augmentation step for ML.

8. The 84% confidence interval is ideal for comparing two different effects, as no overlap between the confidence intervals equates to a significance level of .05 (Belia, Fiona, Williams, & Cumming, 2005; Goldstein & Healey, 1995; Tyron, 2001).

REFERENCES

Abraham, W. T., & Russell, D. W. (2004). Missing data: A review of current methods and applications in epidemiological research. *Current Opinions in Psychiatry, 17,* 315–321.

Acock, A. C. (1989). Measurement error in secondary data analysis. In K. Namboodiri & R. Corwin (Eds.), *Research in sociology of education and socialization* (Vol. 8, pp. 201–230). Greenwich, CT: JAI.

Acock, A. C. (2005). Working with missing values. *Journal of Marriage and the Family, 67,* 1012–1028.

Agresti, A., & Finlay, B. (1997). *Statistical methods for the social sciences.* Englewood Cliffs, NJ: Prentice Hall.

Allison, P. D. (1987). Estimation of linear models with incomplete data. In C. C. Clogg (Ed.), *Sociological methodology 1987* (pp. 71–103). San Francisco: Jossey-Bass.

Allison, P. D. (2000). Multiple imputation for missing data. *Sociological Methods & Research, 28,* 301–309.

Allison, P. D. (2002). *Missing data* (Vol. 136). Thousand Oaks, CA: Sage.

Allison, P. D. (2003). Missing data techniques for structural equation modeling. *Journal of Abnormal Psychology, 112,* 545–557.

Arbuckle, J. L. (1996). Full information estimation in the presence of incomplete data. In G. A. Marcoulides & R. E. Schumacker (Eds.), *Advanced structural equation modeling: Issues and techniques* (pp. 243–278). Mahwah, NJ: Lawrence Erlbaum.

Arbuckle, J. L. (2006). Amos (Version 7.0) [Computer software]. Chicago: Small Waters.

Badzioch, M. D., Thomas, D. C., & Jarvik, G. P. (2003). Summary report: Missing data and pedigree and genotyping errors. *Genetic Epidemiology, 25*(Suppl. 1), S36–S42.

Barnard, J., & Meng, X.-L. (1999). Applications of multiple imputation in medical studies: From AIDS to NHANES. *Statistical Methods in Medical Research, 8,* 17–36.

Beck, A. T., Ward, C. H., Mendelson, M., Mock, J., & Erbaugh, J. (1961). An inventory for measuring depression. *Archives of General Psychiatry, 4,* 561–571.

Belia, S., Fiona, F., Williams, J., & Cumming, G. (2005). Researchers misunderstand confidence intervals and standard error bars. *Psychological Methods, 10,* 389–396.

Bentler, P. M. (2006). *EQS structural equation program manual* (Version 6.1). Encino, CA: Multivariate Software.

Cole, J. C. (2007). *Current trends in missing data for latent models.* Manuscript submitted for publication.

Cole, J. C., Khanna, D., Clements, P. J., Seibold, J. R., Tashkin, D. P., Paulus, H. E., et al. (2006). Single-factor scoring validation for the Health Assessment Questionnaire–Disability Index (HAQ-DI) in patients with systemic sclerosis and comparison with early rheumatoid arthritis patients. *Quality of Life Research, 15,* 1383–1394.

Cole, J. C., Rabin, A. S., Smith, T. L., & Kaufman, A. S. (2004). Development and validation of a Rasch-derived CES-D short form. *Psychological Assessment, 16,* 360–372.

Collins, L. M., Schafer, J. L., & Kam, C.-H. (2001). A comparison of inclusive and restrictive strategies in modern missing data procedures. *Psychological Methods, 6,* 330–351.

Cook, N. R. (1997). An imputation method for nonignorable missing data in studies of blood pressure. *Statistical Medicine, 16,* 2713–2728.

Crawford, S. L., Tennstedt, S. L., & McKinlay, J. B. (1995). A comparison of analytic methods for non-random missingness of outcome data. *Journal of Clinical Epidemiology, 48,* 209–219.

Dempster, A., Laird, N., & Rubin, D. B. (1977). Maximum likelihood from incomplete data via the EM algorithm (with discussion). *Journal of the Royal Statistical Society, 39,* 1–18.

Enders, C. K. (2001). The impact of nonnormality on full information maximum likelihood estimation for structural equation models with missing data. *Psychological Methods, 6,* 352–370.

Enders, C. K. (2002). Applying the Bollen-Stine bootstrap for goodness-of-fit measures to structural equation models with missing data. *Multivariate Behavioral Research, 37,* 359–377.

Enders, C. K. (2006a). Analyzing structural equation models with missing data. In G. R. Hancock & R. O. Mueller (Eds.), *Structural equation modeling: A second course* (pp. 313–344). Greenwich, CT: Information Age Publishing.

Enders, C. K. (2006b, April). *Analyzing structural equation models with missing data.* Paper presented at the 2006 annual meeting of the American Education Research Association, San Francisco.

Enders, C. K. (2006c). *Little's (1998) test of missing completely at random (MCAR) missing data.* Phoenix, AZ: Author.

Enders, C. K., & Bandalos, D. L. (2001). The relative performance of full information maximum likelihood estimation for missing data in structural equation models. *Structural Equation Modeling, 8,* 430–457.

Fairclough, D. L. (2002). *Design and analysis of quality of life studies in clinical trials.* Boca Raton, FL: Chapman & Hall/CRC.

Fairclough, D. L., Fetting, J. H., Cella, D., Wonson, W., & Moinpour, C. M. (1999). Quality of life and quality adjusted survival for breast cancer patients receiving adjuvant therapy. Eastern Cooperative Oncology Group (ECOG). *Quality of Life Research, 8,* 723–731.

Finney, S. J., & DiStefano, C. (2006). Nonnormal and categorical data in structural equation modeling. In G. R. Hancock & R. O. Mueller (Eds.), *Structural equation modeling: A second course* (pp. 269–314). Greenwich, CT: Information Age Publishing.

Glynn, R. J., Laird, N. M., & Rubin, D. B. (1993). Multiple imputation in mixture models for nonignorable nonresponse with followups. *Journal of the American Statistical Association, 88,* 984–993.

Gold, M. S., Bentler, P. M., & Kim, K. H. (2003). A comparison of maximum-likelihood and asymptotically distribution-free method of treating incomplete nonnormal data. *Structural Equation Modeling, 10,* 47–79.

Goldstein, H., & Healey, M. J. R. (1995). The graphical presentation of a collection of means. *Journal of the Royal Statistical Society, 158A,* 175–177.

Gould, A. L. (1980). A new approach to the analysis of clinical drug trials with withdrawals. *Biometrics, 36,* 721–727.

Gourieroux, C., & Monfort, A. (1981). On the problem of missing data in linear models. *Review of Economic Studies, 48,* 579–586.

Graham, J. W. (2003). Adding missing-data relevant variables to FIML-based structural equation models. *Structural Equation Modeling, 10,* 80–100.

Graham, J. W., Cumsille, P. E., & Elek-Fisk, E. (2003). Methods for handling missing data. In J. A. Schinka & W. F. Velicer (Eds.), *Handbook of psychology* (Vol. 2, pp. 87–114). New York: John Wiley.

Graham, J. W., Donaldson, S. I., MacKinnon, D. P., & Schafer, J. L. (1997). Analysis with missing data in prevention research. In K. Bryant, M. Windle, & S. West (Eds.), *The science of prevention: Methodological advances from alcohol and substance abuse research* (pp. 325–366). Washington, DC: American Psychological Association.

Graham, J. W., & Hofer, S. M. (2000). Multiple imputation in multivariate research. In T. D. Little, K. U. Schnabel, & J. Baumert (Eds.), *Modeling longitudinal and multilevel data* (pp. 201–218). Mahwah, NJ: Lawrence Erlbaum.

Graham, J. W., & Schafer, J. L. (1999). On the performance of multiple imputation for multivariate data with small sample size. In R. H. Hoyle (Ed.), *Statistical strategies for small sample size* (pp. 1–29). Thousand Oaks, CA: Sage.

Graham, J. W., Taylor, B. J., & Cumsille, P. E. (2001). Planned missing data designs in analysis of change. In L. M. Collins & A. G. Sayer (Eds.), *New methods for the analysis of change* (pp. 335–353). Washington, DC: American Psychological Association.

Graham, J. W., Taylor, B. J., Olchowski, A. E., & Cumsille, P. E. (2006). Planned missing data designs in psychological research. *Psychological Methods, 11,* 323–343.

Haitovsky, Y. (1968). Missing data in regression analysis. *Journal of the Royal Statistical Society, 30B,* 67–82.

Hancock, G. R. (2006). Power analysis in covariance structure modeling. In G. R. Hancock & R. O. Mueller (Eds.), *Structural equation modeling: A second course* (pp. 69–118). Greenwich, CT: Information Age Publishing.

Harezlak, J., Gao, S., & Hui, S. L. (2003). An illness-death stochastic model in the analysis of longitudinal dementia data. *Statistics in Medicine, 22,* 1465–1475.

Heitjan, D. A., & Landis, J. R. (1994). Assessing secular trends in blood pressure: A multiple imputation approach. *Journal of the American Statistical Association, 89,* 750–759.

Heitjan, D. F., & Rubin, D. B. (1991). Ignorability and coarse data. *Annals of Statistics, 19,* 2244–2253.

Hershberger, S. L., & Fisher, D. G. (2003). A note on determining the number of imputations for missing data. *Structural Equation Modeling, 10,* 648–650.

Heyting, D. A., Tolbomm, T. B. M., & Essers, J. G. A. (1992). Statistical handling of dropouts in longitudinal clinical trials. *Statistical Medicine, 11,* 2043–2061.

Jöreskog, K. G., & Sörbom, D. (2001). *LISREL 8: User's reference manual.* Chicago: Scientific Software.

Kenward, M. G., & Molenberghs, G. (1998). Likelihood based frequentist inference when data are missing at random. *Statistical Science, 13,* 236–247.

Ladouceur, R., Gosselin, P., Laberge, M., & Blaszcynski, A. (2001). Dropouts in clinical research: Do results reported reflect clinical reality? *The Behavioral Therapist, 24,* 44–46.

Lavori, P., Dawson, R., & Shera, D. (1995). A multiple imputation strategy for clinical trials with truncation of patient data. *Statistical Medicine, 14,* 1912–1925.

Little, R. J. A. (1988). A test of missing completely at random for multivariate data with missing values. *Journal of the American Statistical Association, 83,* 1198–1202.

Little, R. J. A., & Rubin, D. B. (1987). *Statistical analysis with missing data.* New York: John Wiley.

Little, R. J. A., & Rubin, D. B. (2002). *Statistical analysis with missing data* (2nd ed.). Hoboken, NJ: John Wiley.

Little, R. J. A., & Yau, L. H. Y. (1996). Intent-to-treat analysis for longitudinal studies with dropouts. *Biometrics, 52,* 1324–1333.

Liu, G., & Gould, A. L. (2002). Comparison of alternative strategies for analysis of longitudinal trials with dropouts. *Journal of Biopharmaceutical Statistics, 12,* 207–226.

Mallinckrodt, C. H., Clark, W. S., Carroll, R. J., & Molenberghs, G. (2003). Assessing response to profiles from incomplete longitudinal clinical trial data under regulatory considerations. *Journal of Biopharmaceutical Statistics, 13,* 179–190.

Mallinckrodt, C. H., Sanger, T. M., Dubé, S., DeBrota, D. J., Molenberghs, G., Carroll, R. J., et al. (2003). Assessing and interpreting treatment effect in longitudinal clinical trials with missing data. *Biological Psychiatry, 53,* 754–760.

Mardia, K. V. (1970). Measures of multivariate skewness and kurtosis with applications. *Biometrika, 57,* 519–530.

Meng, X.-L. (1994). Multiple imputation with uncongenial sources of input. *Statistical Science, 9,* 538–573.

Messick, S. (1995). Validity of psychological assessment: Validation of inferences from persons' responses and performances as scientific inquiry into score meaning. *American Psychologist, 50,* 741–749.

Muthén, B. O., Kaplan, D., & Hollis, M. (1987). On structural equation modeling with data that are not missing completely at random. *Psychometrika, 52,* 431–462.

Muthén, B. O., & Muthén, L. K. (2006). Mplus (Version 4.0) [Computer software]. Los Angeles: Author.

Neale, M. C., Boker, S. M., Xie, G., & Maes, H. H. (1999). Mx: Statistical modeling (Version 5th ed.) [Computer software]. Richmond: Virginia Commonwealth University, Department of Psychiatry.

Peto, R., Pike, M. C., Armitage, P., Breslow, N. E., Cox, D. R., Howard, S. V., et al. (1977). Design and analysis of randomized clinical trials requiring prolonged observation of each patient: II. Analysis and examples. *British Journal of Cancer, 35,* 1–39.

Rabound, J. M., Singer, J. D., Thorne, A., Schechter, M. T., & Shafran, S. D. (1998). Estimating the effect of treatment on quality of life in the presence of missing data due to drop-out and death. *Quality of Life Research, 7,* 487–494.

Radloff, L. S. (1977). The CES-D scale: A self-report depression scale for research in the general population. *Applied Psychological Measurement, 1,* 384–401.

Rubin, D. B. (1976). Inference and missing data. *Biometrika, 63,* 581–592.

Rubin, D. B. (1987). *Multiple imputation for nonresponse in surveys.* New York: John Wiley.

Rubin, D. B. (1996). Multiple imputation after 18+ years. *Journal of the American Statistical Association, 91*(434), 473–489.

Rubin, D. B., & Schenker, N. (1991). Multiple imputation in health-care databases: An overview and some applications. *Statistics in Medicine, 10,* 585–598.

Santor, D. A., Ramsay, J. O., & Zuroff, D. C. (1994). Nonparametric item analysis of the Beck Depression Inventory: Evaluating gender item bias and response option weights. *Psychological Assessment, 6,* 255–270.

Satorra, A., & Bentler, P. M. (1994). Corrections to test statistics and standard errors in covariance structure analysis. In A. von Eye & C. C. Clogg (Eds.), *Latent variables analysis: Applications for developmental research* (pp. 399–419). Thousand Oaks, CA: Sage.

Schafer, J. L. (1997). *Analysis of incomplete multivariate data.* New York: Chapman & Hall.

Schafer, J. L. (2000). NORM (Version 2.03) [Computer software]. University Park, PA: Author.

Schafer, J. L., & Graham, J. W. (2002). Missing data: Our view of the state of the art. *Psychological Methods, 7,* 147–177.

Schafer, J. L., & Olsen, M. (1998). Multiple imputation for multivariate missing data problems: A data analyst's perspective. *Multivariate Behavioral Research, 33,* 545–571.

Sinhary, S., Stern, H. S., & Russell, D. W. (2001). The use of multiple imputation for the analysis of missing data. *Psychological Methods, 6,* 317–329.

Song, X. Y., & Lee, S. Y. (2003). Full maximum likelihood estimation of polychoric and polyserial correlations with missing data. *Multivariate Behavioral Research, 38,* 57–79.

Steiger, J. H. (1990). Structural model evaluation and modification: An interval estimation approach. *Multivariate Behavioral Research, 25,* 173–180.

Tabachnick, B. G., & Fidell, L. S. (2007). *Using multivariate statistics* (5th ed.). New York: Pearson Education.

Tyron, W. W. (2001). Evaluating statistical difference, equivalence, and indeterminacy using inferential confidence intervals: An integrated alternative method of conducting nill hypothesis statistical tests. *Psychological Methods, 6,* 371–386.

Van Burren, S., Boshuizen, H. C., & Knoock, D. L. (1999). Multiple imputation of missing blood pressure covariate in survival analysis. *Statistical Medicine, 18,* 681–694.

Verbeke, G., & Molenberghs, G. (2000). *Linear mixed models for longitudinal data.* New York: Springer-Verlag.

von Hippel, P. T. (2005). How many imputations are needed? A comment on Hershberger and Fisher. *Structural Equation Modeling, 12,* 334–335.

Weinfurt, K. P., Castel, L. D., Li, Y., Sulmasy, D. P., Balshem, A. M., Benson, A. B., III, et al. (2003). The correlation between patient characteristics and expectation of benefits in Phase I clinical trials. *Cancer, 98,* 166–175.

Wothke, W. (1993). Nonpositive definite matrices in structural equation modeling. In K. A. Bollen & J. S. Long (Eds.), *Testing structural equation models* (pp. 256–293). Newbury Park, CA: Sage.

Wothke, W. (2000). Longitudinal and multigroup modeling with missing data. In T. D. Little, K. U. Schnabel, & J. Baumert (Eds.), *Modeling longitudinal and multilevel data* (pp. 219–240). Mahwah, NJ: Lawrence Erlbaum.

Yuan, K.-H., & Bentler, P. M. (2000). Three likelihood-based methods for mean and covariance structure analysis with nonnormal missing data. *Sociological Methodology, 30,* 165–200.

16

IS DISATTENUATION OF
EFFECTS A BEST PRACTICE?

JASON W. OSBORNE

In social science research, many variables we are interested in are also difficult to measure, making measurement error a particular concern. Despite impressive advancements in measurement in recent years (see particularly Chapter 4 on Rasch measurement), simple reliability of measurement is still an issue in much research. Unreliable measurement causes relationships to be *underestimated* (or attenuated), increasing the risk of Type II errors. In the case of multiple regression or partial correlation, effect sizes of other variables can be *overestimated* if another variable in the equation is not reliably measured, as the full effect of that variable might not be removed.

This is a significant concern if the goal of research is to accurately model the "real" relationships evident in the population. Although most authors assume that reliability estimates (Cronbach alphas) of .70 and above are acceptable (e.g., Nunnally, 1978), and Osborne, Christensen, and Gunter (2001) reported that the average alpha reported in top educational psychology journals was .83, measurement of this quality still contains enough measurement

error to make correction worthwhile (as illustrated below).

Correction for low reliability is simple and widely disseminated in most texts on regression but rarely seen in the literature. I argue that authors should correct for low reliability to obtain a more accurate picture of the "true" relationship in the population and, in the case of multiple regression or partial correlation, to avoid overestimating the effect of another variable.

Note that in this age of user-friendly structural equation modeling programs such as Amos and others, modeling and eliminating measurement error is a real and present possibility with almost every analysis. While this topic is discussed in detail elsewhere in this volume (Chapter 32), the discussion below pertains to this sort of analysis as well. Specifically, one can view use of structural equation modeling as another option for reducing the effect of measurement error. Furthermore, readers are encouraged to explore more modern measurement methodologies as another avenue to achieving the same goal—the more accurate modeling of that which we

Author's Note: This chapter is based on a previously published article: Osborne, J. W. (2003). Effect sizes and the disattenuation of correlation and regression coefficients: Lessons from educational psychology. *Practical Assessment, Research, and Evaluation, 8*(11). Available at http://pareonline.net/getvn.asp?v=8&n=11

observe and study. For example, primers in Rasch measurement are presented in Chapters 4 and 5, this volume.

RELIABILITY AND SIMPLE REGRESSION

Since "the presence of measurement errors in behavioral research is the rule rather than the exception" and the "reliabilities of many measures used in the behavioral sciences are, at best, moderate" (Pedhazur, 1997, p. 172), it is important that researchers be aware of accepted methods of dealing with this issue. For simple correlation, Equation 1 provides an estimate of the "true" relationship between the independent variable (IV) and dependent variable (DV) in the population:

$$r_{12}^* = \frac{r_{12}}{\sqrt{r_{11}r_{22}}}. \tag{1}$$

In this equation, r_{12} is the observed correlation, and r_{11} and r_{22} are the reliability estimates of the variables. There are examples of the effects of disattenuation in Table 16.1 and Figure 16.1. For example, even when reliability is .80, correction for attenuation substantially changes the effect size (increasing variance accounted for by about 50% compared with simple attenuated correlations). When reliability drops to .70 or below, this correction yields a substantially different

picture of the "true" nature of the relationship and potentially avoids Type II errors.

RELIABILITY AND PARTIAL CORRELATIONS

With each independent variable added to the regression equation, the effects of less than perfect reliability on the strength of the relationship become more complex and the results of the analysis more questionable. With the addition of one independent variable with less than perfect reliability, each succeeding variable entered has the opportunity to claim part of the error variance left over by the unreliable variable(s). The apportionment of the explained variance among the independent variables will thus be incorrect. The more independent variables added to the equation with low levels of reliability, the greater the likelihood that the variance accounted for is not apportioned correctly. This can lead to erroneous findings and increased potential for Type II errors for the variables with poor reliability and Type I errors for the other variables in the equation. Obviously, this gets increasingly complex as the number of variables in the equation grows.

A simple example, drawing heavily from Pedhazur (1997), is a case where one is attempting to assess the relationship between two variables controlling for a third variable ($r_{12.3}$). When one is correcting for low reliability in all

Table 16.1   Example Disattenuation of Correlation Coefficients

Reliability Estimate	Correlation Coefficient					
	r = 0.10 (.01)	r = 0.20 (.04)	r = 0.30 (.09)	r = 0.40 (.16)	r = 0.50 (.25)	r = 0.60 (.36)
0.95	0.11 (.01)	0.21 (.04)	0.32 (.10)	0.42 (.18)	0.53 (.28)	0.63 (.40)
0.90	0.11 (.01)	0.22 (.05)	0.33 (.11)	0.44 (.19)	0.56 (.31)	0.67 (.45)
0.85	0.12 (.01)	0.24 (.06)	0.35 (.12)	0.47 (.22)	0.59 (.35)	0.71 (.50)
0.80	0.13 (.02)	0.25 (.06)	0.38 (.14)	0.50 (.25)	0.63 (.39)	0.75 (.56)
0.75	0.13 (.02)	0.27 (.07)	0.40 (.16)	0.53 (.28)	0.67 (.45)	0.80 (.64)
0.70	0.14 (.02)	0.29 (.08)	0.43 (.18)	0.57 (.32)	0.71 (.50)	0.86 (.74)
0.65	0.15 (.02)	0.31 (.10)	0.46 (.21)	0.62 (.38)	0.77 (.59)	0.92 (.85)
0.60	0.17 (.03)	0.33 (.11)	0.50 (.25)	0.67 (.45)	0.83 (.69)	—

NOTE: Reliability estimates for this example assume the same reliability for both variables. Percent variance accounted for (shared variance) is in parentheses.

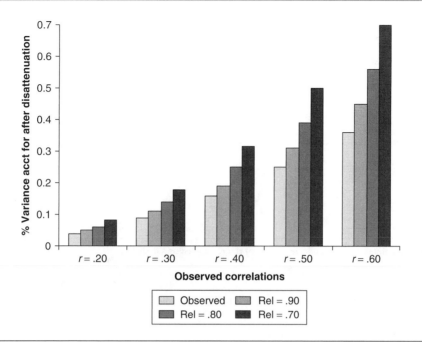

Figure 16.1   Selected effect size of original and disattenuated correlation coefficients.

three variables, Equation 2 is used, where r_{11}, r_{22}, and r_{33} are reliabilities, and r_{12}, r_{23}, and r_{13} are relationships between variables. If one is only correcting for low reliability in the covariate, one could use Equation 3.

$$r_{12.3}^* = \frac{r_{33}r_{12} - r_{13}r_{23}}{\sqrt{r_{11}r_{33} - r_{13}^2}\sqrt{r_{22}r_{33} - r_{23}^2}} \qquad (2)$$

$$r_{12.3}^* = \frac{r_{33}r_{12} - r_{13}r_{23}}{\sqrt{r_{33} - r_{13}^2}\sqrt{r_{33} - r_{23}^2}} \qquad (3)$$

Table 16.2 presents some examples of corrections for low reliability in the covariate (only) and in all three variables. Table 16.2 shows some of the many possible combinations of reliabilities, correlations, and the effects of correcting for only the covariate or all variables. The following points are of interest: (a) As in Table 16.1, even small correlations see substantial effect size (r^2) changes when corrected for low reliability—in this case, often toward reduced effect sizes; (b) in some cases, the corrected correlation is substantially different not only in magnitude but also in the direction of the relationship; and (c) as

expected, the most dramatic changes occur when the covariate has a substantial relationship with the other variables.

Reliability and Multiple Regression

Research by Bohrnstedt (1983) has argued that regression coefficients are primarily affected by reliability in the independent variable (except for the intercept, which is affected by reliability of both variables), while true correlations are affected by reliability in both variables. Thus, researchers wanting to correct multiple regression coefficients for reliability can use Formula 4, taken from Bohrnstedt, which takes this issue into account:

$$\beta_{yx.z}^* = \left(\frac{\sigma_y}{\sigma_x}\right) \frac{r_{zz}r_{xy} - r_{yz}r_{xz}}{r_{xx}r_{zz} - r_{xz}^2}. \qquad (4)$$

Some examples of disattenuating multiple regression coefficients are presented in Table 16.3. In these examples (which are admittedly and necessarily a very narrow subset of the total possibilities), corrections resulting in impossible values were rare, even with strong relationships

Table 16.2   Values of $r_{12.3}$ and $r^2_{12.3}$ After Correction of Low Reliability

Examples				Reliability of Covariate			Reliability of All Variables		
				.80	.70	.60	.80	.70	.60
r_{12}	r_{13}	r_{23}	Observed $r_{12.3}$	$r_{12.3}$	$r_{12.3}$	$r_{12.3}$	$r_{12.3}$	$r_{12.3}$	$r_{12.3}$
.30	.30	.30	.23	.21	.20	.18	.27	.30	.33
.50	.50	.50	.33	.27	.22	.14	.38	.42	.45
.70	.70	.70	.41	.23	.00	−.64	.47	.00	—
.70	.30	.30	.67	.66	.65	.64	.85	.99	—
.30	.50	.50	.07	−.02	−.09	−.20	−.03	−.17	−.64
.50	.10	.70	.61	.66	.74	.90	—	—	—

NOTE: Some examples produce impossible values, which are denoted by a dash.

Table 16.3   Example Disattenuation of Multiple Regression Coefficients

Reliability of All Variables	r_{xz}	Correlations r_{xy} and r_{yz}							
		$r = 0.10$	$r = 0.20$	$r = 0.30$	$r = 0.40$	$r = 0.50$	$r = 0.60$	$r = 0.70$	$r = 0.80$
0.90	0.10	0.10	0.20	0.30	0.40	0.50	0.60	0.70	0.80
0.90	0.40	0.08	0.15	0.23	0.31	0.38	0.46	0.54	0.62
0.90	0.70	0.06	0.13	0.19	0.25	0.31	0.38	0.44	0.50
0.80	0.10	0.11	0.22	0.33	0.44	0.56	0.67	0.78	0.89
0.80	0.40	0.08	0.17	0.25	0.33	0.42	0.50	0.58	0.67
0.80	0.70	0.07	0.13	0.20	0.27	0.33	0.40	0.47	0.53
0.70	0.10	0.13	0.25	0.38	0.50	0.63	0.75	0.88	—
0.70	0.40	0.09	0.18	0.27	0.36	0.45	0.55	0.64	0.73
0.70	0.70	0.07	0.14	0.21	0.29	0.36	0.43	0.50	0.57
0.60	0.10	0.14	0.29	0.43	0.57	0.71	0.86	—	—
0.60	0.40	0.10	0.20	0.30	0.40	0.50	0.60	0.70	0.80
0.60	0.70	0.08	0.15	0.23	0.31	0.38	0.46	0.54	0.62

NOTE: Calculations in this table used Formula 4, assumed all independent variables (IVs) had the same reliability estimate, assumed each IV had the same relationship to the dependent variable (DV), and assumed each IV had the same variance in order to simplify the example. Numbers reported represent corrected r_{xz}.

between the variables, and even when reliability is relatively weak.

Reliability and Interactions in Multiple Regression

To this point, the discussion has been confined to the relatively simple issue of the effects of low reliability, and correcting for low reliability, on simple correlations and higher-order main effects (partial correlations, multiple regression coefficients). However, many interesting hypotheses in the social sciences involve curvilinear or interaction effects. Of course, poor reliability in main effects is compounded dramatically when those effects are used in cross-products, such as squared or cubed terms, or interaction terms. Aiken and West (1996) present a good discussion on the issue. An illustration of this effect is presented in Table 16.4.

Table 16.4   The Effects of Reliability on the Reliability of Cross-Products in Multiple Regression

Reliability of X and Z	Correlation Between X and Z			
	r = 0	r = 0.20	r = 0.40	r = 0.60
0.90	0.81	0.82	0.86	0.96
0.80	0.64	0.66	0.71	0.83
0.70	0.49	0.51	0.58	0.72
0.60	0.36	0.39	0.47	0.62

NOTE: These calculations assume both variables are centered at 0 and assume that both X and Z have equal reliabilities. Numbers reported are cross-product reliabilities.

As Table 16.4 shows, even at relatively high reliabilities, the reliability of cross-products is relatively weak. This, of course, has deleterious effects on power and inference. According to Aiken and West (1996), there are two avenues for dealing with this: correcting the correlation or covariance matrix for low reliability and then using the corrected matrix for the subsequent regression analyses, which of course is subject to the same issues discussed above, or using structural equation modeling (SEM) to model the relationships in an error-free fashion.

Protecting Against Overcorrecting During Disattenuation

The goal of disattenuation is to be simultaneously accurate (in estimating the "true" relationships) and conservative in preventing overcorrecting. Overcorrection serves to further our understanding no more than leaving relationships attenuated.

There are several scenarios that might lead to inappropriate inflation of estimates, even to the point of impossible values. A substantial underestimation of the reliability of a variable would lead to substantial overcorrection and potentially impossible values. This can happen when reliability estimates are biased downward by heterogeneous scales, for example. Researchers need to seek precision in reliability estimation in order to avoid this problem.

Given accurate reliability estimates, however, it is possible that sampling error, well-placed outliers, or even suppressor variables could inflate relationships artificially and thus, when combined with correction for low reliability, produce inappropriately high or impossible corrected values. In light of this, I would suggest that researchers make sure they have checked for these issues prior to attempting a correction of this nature (researchers should check for these issues regularly anyway).[1]

Other Solutions to the Issue of Measurement Error

Fortunately, as the field of measurement and statistics advances, other options to these difficult issues emerge. One obvious solution to the problem posed by measurement error is to use SEM to estimate the relationship between constructs (which can be theoretically error free given the right conditions), rather than using our traditional methods of assessing the relationship between measures. This eliminates the issue of over- or undercorrection, which estimate of reliability to use, and so on. Given the easy access to SEM software and a proliferation of SEM manuals and texts, it is more accessible to researchers now than ever before. Having said that, SEM is still a complex process and should not be undertaken without proper training and mentoring (of course, that is true of all statistical procedures).[2]

Another emerging technology that can potentially address this issue is the use of Rasch modeling. Rasch measurement uses a fundamentally different approach to measurement than classical test theory, which many of us were trained in. Use of Rasch measurement provides not only more sophisticated and probably accurate measurement of constructs but also more sophisticated information on the reliability of items and individual scores. Even an introductory treatise on Rasch measurement is outside the limits of this chapter, but individuals interested in exploring more sophisticated measurement models are encouraged to refer to Bond and Fox (2001) or Chapter 4 (this volume) for an excellent primer on Rasch measurement.

An Example From Educational Psychology

To give a concrete example of how important this process might be as it applies to our fields of inquiry, I will draw from a survey I and a couple of graduate students completed of the educational psychology literature from 1998 to 1999 (Osborne, in press). This survey consisted of recording all effects from all quantitative studies published in the *Journal of Educational Psychology* during the years 1998–1999, as well as ancillary information such as reported reliabilities.

Studies from these years indicate a mean effect size (d) of 0.68, with a standard deviation of 0.37. When these effect sizes are converted into simple correlation coefficients via direct algebraic manipulation, $d = 0.68$ is equivalent to $r = .32$. Effect sizes one standard deviation below and above the mean equate to rs of .16 and .46, respectively.

From the same review of the literature, where reliabilities (Cronbach's α) are reported, the average reliability is $\alpha = .80$, with a standard deviation of .10.

Table 16.5 contains the results of what would be the result for the field of educational psychology in general if all studies in educational psychology disattenuated their effects for low reliability (and if we assume reported reliabilities are accurate). These results are presented graphically in Figure 16.2 as well. For example, while the average reported effect equates to a correlation coefficient of $r = .32$ (accounting for 10% shared variance), if corrected for average reliability in the field ($\alpha = .80$), the better estimate of that effect is $r = .40$ (16% shared variance, a 60% increase in variance accounted for). These simple numbers indicate that when reliability is low but still considered acceptable by many ($\alpha = .70$, one standard deviation below the average reported alpha and a level decidedly *not* considered acceptable to this author), the increase in variance accounted for can top 100%—in this case, our average effect of $r = .32$ is disattenuated to $r = .46$ (shared variance of 21%). At minimum, when reliabilities are good, one standard deviation above average ($\alpha = .90$), the gains in shared variance range around 30%—still a substantial increase.

SUMMARY, CAVEATS, AND CONCLUSIONS

Many of the same concerns people have about dealing with missing data (see Chapter 15, this volume, on dealing with missing data) are reflected in discussions of disattenuation. However, if the goal of research is to be able to provide the best estimate of the true effect within a population, and we know that many of our statistical procedures assume perfectly reliable measurement, then we must assume that we are consistently underestimating population effect sizes, usually by a dramatic amount. Using the field of educational psychology as an example, and using averages across 2 years of studies published in top-tier empirical journals, we can estimate that while the average reported effect size is equivalent to $r = .32$ (10% variance accounted for), once corrected for average reliability, the average effect is equivalent to $r = .40$ (16% variance accounted for). If you take these numbers seriously, this means that many studies in the social sciences *underestimate* the population effects by about one third.

However, there are some significant caveats to this argument. In order to disattenuate relationships without risking overcorrection, you must have a good estimate of reliability, preferably Cronbach's alpha from a homogeneous scale. Second, when disattenuating relationships, authors should report both original and disattenuated estimates and should explicitly explain what procedures were used in the process of disattenuation. Third, when reliability estimates drop below .70, authors should consider using different measures or alternative

Table 16.5   An Example of Disattenuation of Effects From Educational Psychology Literature

	Small Effect ($r = .16$, $r^2 = .025$, $d = 0.32$)	Average Effect ($r = .32$, $r^2 = .10$, $d = 0.68$)	Large Effect ($r = .46$, $r^2 = .21$, $d = 1.04$)
Poor reliability	$r = .23$	$r = .46$	$r = .66$
($\alpha = .70$)	$r^2 = .052$	$r^2 = .21$	$r^2 = .43$
	$d = 0.47$	$d = 1.04$	$d = 1.76$
Average reliability	$r = .20$	$r = .40$	$r = .58$
($\alpha = .80$)	$r^2 = .040$	$r^2 = .16$	$r^2 = .33$
	$d = 0.41$	$d = 0.87$	$d = 1.42$
Above-average reliability	$r = .18$	$r = .36$	$r = .51$
($\alpha = .90$)	$r^2 = .032$	$r^2 = .13$	$r^2 = .26$
	$d = 0.37$	$d = 0.77$	$d = 1.19$

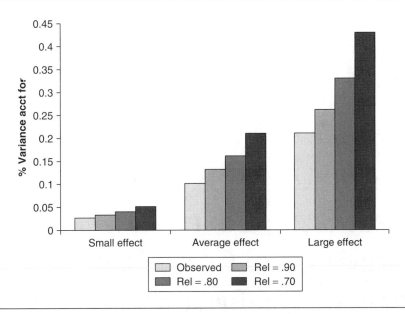

Figure 16.2   What does educational psychology look like disattenuated?

analytic techniques that do not carry the risk of overcorrection, such as latent variable modeling, or better measurement strategies such as Rasch modeling.

NOTES

1. Interested readers can refer to Chapter 14 (this volume) on detecting and dealing with outliers.

2. Interested readers can refer to Chapter 32 (this volume) for an introduction to best practices in SEM.

REFERENCES

Aiken, L. S., & West, S. G. (1996). *Multiple regression: Testing and interpreting interactions.* Thousand Oaks, CA: Sage.

Bohrnstedt, G. W. (1983). *Measurement.* In P. H. Rossi, J. D. Wright, & A. B. Anderson (Eds.), *Handbook of survey research* (pp. 70–114). San Diego: Academic Press.

Bond, T. G., & Fox, C. M. (2001). *Applying the Rasch model: Fundamental measurement in the human sciences.* Mahwah, NJ: Lawrence Erlbaum.

Nunnally, J. C. (1978). *Psychometric theory* (2nd ed.). New York: McGraw-Hill.

Osborne, J. W. (in press). Sweating the small stuff in educational psychology: How trends in effect size and power reporting failed to change from 1969 to 1999, and what that means for the future of changing practices. *Educational Psychology.*

Osborne, J. W., Christensen, W. R., & Gunter, J. (2001, April). *Educational psychology from a statistician's perspective: A review of the power and goodness of educational psychology research.* Paper presented at the national meeting of the American Education Research Association (AERA), Seattle, WA.

Pedhazur, E. J. (1997). *Multiple regression in behavioral research* (3rd ed.). Orlando, FL: Harcourt Brace.

17

COMPUTING AND INTERPRETING EFFECT SIZES, CONFIDENCE INTERVALS, AND CONFIDENCE INTERVALS FOR EFFECT SIZES

BRUCE THOMPSON

The uptake of null hypothesis statistical significance tests (NHSST) as a vehicle to evaluate social science results did not occur until the 1950s (Hubbard & Ryan, 2000), even though many of these tests were first formulated in the early 1900s (Huberty, 1999). However, the publication of criticisms of over-reliance on NHSST occurred even as many of the tests first appeared. For example, early in the 20th century, Boring (1919) published an article titled, "Mathematical vs. Scientific Importance," in which he argued that $p_{\text{CALCULATED}}$ values should *not* be the primary focus in scholarship.

The $p_{\text{CALCULATED}}$ values in NHSST are mathematical probability statements about the likelihood of the sample statistics, assuming samples came from populations exactly described by the null hypothesis, and given the sample size (Thompson, 2006a). Because NHSST evaluates the probability of sample results, and *not* of populations values, NHSST results do *not* evaluate whether the sample results are replicable (Carver, 1978; Cohen, 1994).

NHSST $p_{\text{CALCULATED}}$ values also cannot inform judgment about the scientific importance of results, because NHSST invokes a deductive logic, starting with the premise that the null exactly describes the population. A valid deductive logic *cannot* contain in conclusions any information not present in the deductive premises. Because NHSST does not invoke premises involving human values, NHSST's mathematical probability statements contain *no* information about the scientific import of the sample results. As Thompson (1993) explained, "If the computer package did not ask you your values prior to its analysis, it could not have considered your value system in calculating p's, and so p's cannot be blithely used to infer the value of research results" (p. 365).

The limitations of NHSST have been argued with increasing frequency, across both decades and a wide array of disciplines, as illustrated in the graphic offered by Anderson, Burnham, and Thompson (2000). Included are disciplines such as biology (e.g., Suter, 1996; Yoccuz, 1991), economics (Ziliak & McCloskey, 2004), education

(Carver, 1978; Thompson, 1996), psychology (Cohen, 1994; Schmidt, 1996), and the wildlife sciences (Johnson, 1999).

The tenor of the commentary can be represented in Schmidt and Hunter's (1997) argument that "Statistical significance testing retards the growth of scientific knowledge; it never makes a positive contribution" (p. 37). Rozeboom (1997) was equally direct:

> Null-hypothesis significance testing is surely the most bone-headedly misguided procedure ever institutionalized in the rote training of science students. . . . [I]t is a sociology-of-science wonderment that this statistical practice has remained so unresponsive to criticism. (p. 335)

Of course, proponents of NHSST have been equally forceful in their advocacy for the continued use of NHSST, and some thoughtful views have been offered (cf. Abelson, 1997; Robinson & Wainer, 2002). The book by Harlow, Mulaik, and Steiger (1997) provided a thorough and balanced treatment of the various related perspectives (e.g., statistical, philosophical) on these controversies. However, the most comprehensive and penetrating treatment is Fidler's (2005) 70,000-word doctoral dissertation, *From Statistical Significance to Effect Estimation: Statistical Reform in Psychology, Medicine, and Ecology.*

In any case, social scientists today place an increasing emphasis on the scientific or the practical importance of their results, rather than on the mathematical probability of their results, as suggested in the title of one of Roger Kirk's (1996) important articles, "Practical Significance: A Concept Whose Time Has Come." Effect sizes can be used to inform judgment regarding the practical significance of results. Although effect sizes also have a long and storied history (Huberty, 2002), advocacy for reporting and interpreting effect sizes has only reached a crescendo within the past dozen years. For example, two of the journals to first require effect size reporting were *Measurement and Evaluation in Counseling and Development* in 1988, and later *Educational and Psychological Measurement* (Thompson, 1994).

In 1996, the American Psychological Association (APA) Board of Scientific Affairs appointed the APA Task Force on Statistical Inference. In 1999, the Task Force issued its recommendations,

and emphasized that effect sizes (e.g., Cohen's d, Glass's Δ, η^2, adjusted r^2 or adjusted R^2, Hays's ω^2) should "*always*" be reported along with p values, and that "reporting and interpreting effect sizes in the context of previously reported effects is *essential* to good research" (Wilkinson & the APA Task Force, 1999, p. 599, emphasis added).

In response, the fifth edition of the APA (2001) *Publication Manual,* used by more than 1,000 journals, included a new declaration that "For the reader to fully understand the importance of your findings, it is *almost always necessary* [emphasis added] to include some index of effect size or strength of relationship in your results section" (pp. 25–26), and labeled the "failure to report effect sizes" a "defect in the design and reporting of research" (APA, 2001, p. 5).

However, given the limitations of the *Manual* (Fidler, 2002), two dozen journals have gone further and now explicitly *require* effect size reporting. Two of these journals have subscriptions greater than 50,000, and are the organizational "flagship" journals of the Council for Exceptional Children and the American Counseling Association.

In 2002, Fidler noted that, "Of the major American associations, only all the journals of the American Educational Research Association [AERA] have remained silent on all these issues" (p. 754). Happily, in 2006, the AERA finally did speak, publishing standards noting that

> . . . Statisticians have long warned against overreliance on significance testing to the exclusion of other methods of interpreting statistical analyses. Statistical significance tests combine both magnitude of relations (or estimates) and their uncertainty into the same quantity. Interpretation of statistical analyses is enhanced by reporting magnitude of relations (e.g., effect sizes) and their uncertainty separately. . . . It is important to report the results of analyses that are critical for interpretation of findings in ways that capture the magnitude as well as the statistical significance of those results. (AERA Task Force on Reporting of Research Methods in AERA Publications, 2006, p. 37)

Thus, the milestones in the recent movement toward effect size reporting include as benchmarks:

1988 First social science journal requires effect size reporting

1994 Second social science journal requires effect size reporting; APA *Publication Manual,* used by more than 1,000 journals, first mentions effect sizes, and "encourages" their reporting

1996 APA appoints Task Force on Statistical Inference to make recommendations on whether statistical significance tests should be banned from APA journals

1999 Wilkinson and APA Task Force on Statistical Inference publish their recommendations in the *American Psychologist,* the APA flagship journal

2005 > 24 journals include explicit effect size reporting expectations within their author guidelines

2006 AERA publishes its standards on reporting empirical research

Purpose of the Chapter

The purpose of the present chapter is to explain how to compute and interpret (a) selected effect sizes, (b) confidence intervals, and (c) confidence intervals for effect sizes. The focus here is on practical explanations and applications of these important tools.

EFFECT SIZES

As Grissom and Kim (2005) emphasized in their excellent book on effect sizes, NHSST

> does not sufficiently indicate how much better the superior treatment is or how strongly the variables are related. . . . If two treatments are not equally effective, the better of the two can be anywhere from slightly better to very much better than the other. (p. 2)

Grissom and Kim (2005) also noted that readers "have a right to see estimates of effect sizes. Some might even argue that not reporting such estimates in an understandable manner . . . may be like withholding evidence" (p. 5).

Effect sizes can be defined at three different levels of generality. First, some authors equate effect size with a single, specific effect size (e.g., Cohen's *d*) from among the 40 or more effect sizes catalogued by Kirk (1996). Second, some authors somewhat more broadly equate effect

sizes with a particular category of effect sizes (e.g., standardized mean differences, variance-accounted-for statistics). Third, some authors broadly define effect sizes as *any statistics that quantify the degree to which sample results diverge from the expectations specified within the null hypothesis* (Kline, 2004).

In this chapter, this last, broadest definition of effect size is invoked. One crucial implication of the fact that there are dozens and dozens of effect sizes is that authors *must* tell readers what effect size they are reporting, and *not* ambiguously state merely that "The effect size was . . ." Because different effect sizes have different ranges, and different properties, readers cannot intelligently interpret effect sizes unless they know exactly which effect size is being reported.

Furthermore, effect sizes can be mathematically converted into each other's metrics (e.g., Aaron, Kromrey, & Ferron, 1998; Thompson, 2002a). But conversions of effect sizes into a common metric across prior reports are possible only if authors clearly identify which effect sizes are being reported.

Here, some of the more commonly used effect sizes are discussed. Not covered are some of the elegant, but less commonly seen effects, such as the "probability of success" effect (Grissom, 1994) or Huberty's group overlap index (*I;* Hess, Olejnik, & Huberty, 2001; Huberty & Holmes, 1983; Natesan & Thompson, 2007). Alternative treatments of effect size choices are provided in the book by Grissom and Kim (2005), or the shorter pieces by Snyder and Lawson (1993), Rosenthal (1994), Kirk (2003), Vacha-Haase and Thompson (2004), or Thompson (2006a).

FRAMEWORK FOR DISCUSSION

Heuristic Data

The data presented in Table 17.1 are used to make the discussion concrete and to facilitate the replication by interested readers of the examples reported here. The table reports a random sample of real data provided by roughly 1,000,000 library users at more than 1,000 libraries from around the world with respect to the perceived quality of academic library services (cf. Thompson, Cook, & Kyrillidou, 2005, 2006).

Included in the data are scores on the LibQUAL+™ total scale, and three subscales: Affect of Service, involving how librarians are perceived

Table 17.1   Random Sample of LibQUAL+™ Data

				SPSS Variable Names				
ID	ROLE	SEX	LIBQ_TOT	SERVAFFE	INFOCONT	LIBPLACE	OUTCOME	SATISFAC
01	1	0	6.36	6.11	6.88	6.00	6.80	6.33
02	1	0	5.41	7.33	5.25	2.20	4.60	7.00
03	1	0	8.52	8.50	9.00	7.80	7.40	8.00
04	1	0	6.00	5.75	6.43	5.80	6.80	8.33
05	1	0	1.68	1.78	1.50	1.80	2.40	2.33
06	1	0	7.38	6.75	7.88	7.60	8.80	8.67
07	1	0	8.00	7.44	8.50	8.20	6.80	8.00
08	1	0	5.77	5.78	5.63	6.00	4.80	4.33
09	1	0	4.20	3.25	5.00	4.60	4.60	4.00
10	1	0	7.36	7.22	7.38	7.60	6.60	7.00
11	1	0	7.41	6.89	7.50	8.20	6.20	8.67
12	2	0	7.14	7.67	6.88	6.60	7.60	8.00
13	2	0	7.05	7.00	8.25	5.20	6.60	8.00
14	2	0	8.05	7.44	8.50	8.40	6.80	8.00
15	2	0	6.90	6.56	8.13	5.25	6.00	7.00
16	2	0	6.77	7.44	6.63	5.80	6.20	7.00
17	2	0	6.14	5.22	6.63	7.00	6.80	6.00
18	2	0	8.36	9.00	9.00	6.20	8.60	9.00
19	2	0	7.59	7.33	7.88	7.60	5.80	7.67
20	2	0	7.05	6.67	7.63	6.80	6.40	8.00
21	2	0	7.14	6.67	7.13	8.00	4.80	7.33
22	2	0	5.41	5.44	5.38	5.40	5.60	4.33
23	3	0	5.14	5.00	6.13	3.80	3.00	5.00
24	3	0	6.16	6.33	6.13	5.50	4.80	5.33
25	3	0	7.09	8.11	6.63	6.00	4.20	6.33
26	3	0	8.76	9.00	8.43	9.00	7.60	9.00
27	3	0	6.23	6.00	6.75	5.80	5.80	6.33
28	3	0	7.20	7.56	5.71	9.00	5.60	6.00
29	3	0	7.14	7.88	6.13	7.60	7.60	8.67
30	3	0	8.14	8.78	8.63	6.20	8.60	8.00
31	3	0	8.30	8.56	7.88	8.67	8.40	8.00
32	3	0	8.64	8.78	8.88	8.00	8.60	9.00
33	3	0	9.00	9.00	9.00	9.00	9.00	9.00
34	1	1	7.00	7.11	6.13	8.20	5.60	8.33
35	1	1	8.59	8.44	8.63	8.80	6.60	9.00
36	1	1	6.24	5.00	5.25	9.00	5.20	5.00

(Continued)

Table 17.1 (Continued)

				SPSS Variable Names				
ID	ROLE	SEX	LIBQ_TOT	SERVAFFE	INFOCONT	LIBPLACE	OUTCOME	SATISFAC
37	1	1	7.36	7.78	7.38	6.60	6.00	7.33
38	1	1	7.68	7.56	7.88	7.60	7.80	8.00
39	1	1	6.86	7.00	6.50	7.20	7.40	7.33
40	1	1	7.23	8.22	6.88	6.00	4.80	8.33
41	1	1	6.64	7.33	6.63	5.40	5.20	5.00
42	1	1	8.76	8.50	9.00	8.80	8.00	8.67
43	1	1	7.58	7.00	7.67	8.40	8.00	6.67
44	1	1	7.41	7.22	7.75	7.20	8.20	9.00
45	2	1	8.00	7.89	8.17	4.00	7.00	8.00
46	2	1	7.88	8.33	8.14	6.75	7.00	8.33
47	2	1	6.73	7.67	6.00	6.20	6.20	8.00
48	2	1	7.32	7.11	7.50	7.40	7.00	7.00
49	2	1	8.77	9.00	8.38	9.00	8.00	8.33
50	2	1	6.81	7.25	6.00	8.00	7.20	7.67
51	2	1	7.00	7.33	6.88	6.60	7.80	7.33
52	2	1	4.00	2.44	5.50	4.40	4.40	5.00
53	2	1	6.33	6.00	7.57	5.20	7.00	7.33
54	2	1	3.00	3.00	3.00	3.00	5.00	5.00
55	2	1	5.95	6.44	6.75	3.80	6.00	6.33
56	3	1	7.11	7.86	7.43	5.25	4.20	7.67
57	3	1	7.10	7.11	6.67	7.60	7.60	8.33
58	3	1	7.31	7.29	7.63	5.00	7.40	7.33
59	3	1	6.93	8.14	6.29	3.00	8.20	7.00
60	3	1	7.64	8.44	7.38	6.60	4.60	7.67
61	3	1	7.64	7.44	7.25	8.60	8.40	8.00
62	3	1	3.63	3.11	4.43	3.33	3.60	3.33
63	3	1	6.00	7.11	6.00	4.00	2.00	5.00
64	3	1	7.33	7.86	7.29	6.50	6.00	7.33
65	3	1	8.36	8.89	8.00	8.00	7.00	8.67
66	3	1	8.00	8.67	7.75	7.20	6.60	7.67

as interacting with users; Information Control, involving users' perceptions of whether users can find information how they want it, when they want it; and Library as Place, which involves the physical library facility and the role of the physical library as a symbol. Also included are scores on perceived outcome impacts of library use, and generic user-reported satisfaction with library service quality. Finally, user group (1 = undergraduate student, 2 = graduate student, 3 = faculty) and gender (0 = female, 1 = male) are reported.

General Linear Model

Perhaps the most important conceptual framework for understanding statistical analyses is the General Linear Model (GLM; Thompson, 2000, 2006a). The General Linear Model was popularized within the social sciences primarily in an important series of papers written by Cohen (1968), Knapp (1978), and Bagozzi, Fornell, and Larcker (1981), respectively. The basic concepts of the General Linear Model are that *all* analyses (a) are correlational, (b) yield variance-accounted-for effect sizes analogous to the bivariate r^2, and (c) apply weights to measured variables to estimate scores on composite or latent variables (Thompson, 2006a).

The GLM is a fundamentally important concept in statistics. However, the statistical concept, the General Linear Model, does *not* refer to computer programs presented as menu choices within some statistics software, even though some software packages may describe a choice as "GLM." The take-home message is, do not confuse a software choice with a statistics concept, even though the software choice might have been somewhat inspired by the statistics concept.

Statisticians have long recognized that sample estimates of parameters made within the General Linear Model using ordinary least squares (OLS) statistical theory tend to overestimate population effect sizes. This is because samples, like people, each have their own unique features, colloquially called "flukiness," or more formally labeled "sampling error variance." Three factors impact sampling error, and thus the positive bias of effect sizes computed using sample data with OLS estimation theory (Thompson, 2002a, 2006a).

First, studies with smaller sample sizes have more sampling error, and thus, on average, for a given small n, more positive bias in effect size estimation, than studies with larger sample sizes. This is because it is easier to draw unrepresentative or fluky samples when sample size is small.

Second, studies involving more measured variables have more sampling error, and thus yield more biased effect estimates, than studies involving fewer measured variables. This is because outliers are people who have anomalous scores on some variables on some statistics, and probably everybody is "weird" or an outlier on at least a few variables (Thompson, 2006a). Thus, the more variables we include in a study, the greater is the likelihood that the "outlyingness" of the particular participants in the sample will be manifested.

Third, samples drawn from populations with smaller population effect sizes have more sampling error, and thus more positively biased effect sizes. This dynamic is not as obvious as the first two influences. But as Thompson (2002a) explained,

> As an extreme heuristic example, pretend that one was conducting a bivariate r^2 study in a situation in which the population r^2 value was 1.0. In this population scattergram, every person's asterisk is exactly on a single regression line. In this instance, even if the researcher draws ridiculously small samples, such as $n = 2$ or $n = 3$, and no matter which participants are drawn, the researcher simply cannot incorrectly estimate the variance-accounted-for effect size. That is, *any* two or three or four people will always define a straight line in the sample scattergram, and thus r^2 will always be 1.0. (p. 68)

Of course, the researcher attempting to correct for this third influence confronts the dilemma that if the population effect size was known, research with sample data would not be conducted. In practice, researchers resolve this dilemma by using the sample effect size estimate to correct itself, or use as part of the correction a mean or median estimate from prior related studies.

Three Major Kinds of Effect Sizes

The most commonly used of the dozens of effect sizes can be organized into three categories, although some effect sizes not considered in detail here (e.g., the Huberty *I* indices, and the "probability of superiority") do not readily fit within this conceptualization.

Standardized Differences. Standardized differences can be computed easily in experimental studies in two steps. First, the mean difference is computed between the mean of the experimental group and the mean of the control group (i.e., $M_E - M_C$). In some disciplines (e.g., medicine), this *unstandardized* mean difference is readily understood and universally used (e.g., deaths per thousand in two groups receiving two different drug treatments). When unstandardized differences have a recognized meaning, these effect sizes are strongly recommended (Wilkinson & the APA Task Force, 1999).

However, in the social sciences, (a) many of our measures (e.g., self-concept, intelligence, academic achievement) have no intrinsically natural metric, and (b) different measures have different metrics (i.e., *SD*s). So, in such cases, second, we create *standardized* differences by removing the metric (i.e., the *SD*) of the effect via division, so that effect sizes can be compared for a given outcome across measurements with different scaling.

One common choice is Glass's (1967) Δ, which uses the standard deviation of the control group as the estimated population *SD*. Glass reasoned that an intervention not only might impact the central tendency of the intervention, but also might affect the dispersion of that group's outcome scores. Under this line of reasoning, because SD_C has not been influenced by intervention, SD_C is the best estimate of population σ. So, this effect estimate is computed as:

$$\Delta = (M_E - M_C)/SD_C. \qquad (1)$$

Of course, medians could also be used in this estimate, because for some data, medians are better estimates of central tendency than means (Grissom & Kim, 2005; Thompson, 2006a).

Cohen's (1969, 1988) *d* is another standardized difference effect size. Cohen reasoned that some interventions may not affect the dispersion of outcome scores, and that in such cases, better estimates of the population σ would be realized by creating a weighted average of the *SD*s in both groups, because the estimate would be based on a larger sample size (i.e., both n_E and n_C, rather than only n_C). This alternative effect can be computed for equal-sized groups as:

$$d = (M_E - M_C) / [(SD_E^2 + SD_C^2)/2]^{0.5}. \qquad (2)$$

The fact that these (and other) standardized differences exist makes explicit that using effect sizes is *not* about the business of using a single effect choice in every research situation. The researcher must be guided by theory about various intervention effects and the sample sizes resulting from using a single or a pooled estimate of σ. Cohen's *d* will be preferred if (a) n_C is small and (b) theory or research suggests that the intervention does not affect outcome variable dispersion. In the words of Huberty and Morris (1988), "As in all statistical inference, subjective judgment cannot be avoided. Neither can reasonableness!" (p. 573).

Variance-Accounted-for Statistics. Because all analyses are correlational, an r^2 analog can be computed in all parametric analyses, and even in some nonparametric situations (Cohen, 1968; Thompson, 2006a). For example, in the bivariate case, the Pearson r^2 can be computed as:

$$r^2 = SOS_{EXPLAINED}/SOS_{TOTAL}, \qquad (3)$$

where *SOS* is the sum of squares, and $SOS_{EXPLAINED}$, $SOS_{REGRESSION}$, SOS_{MODEL}, and $SOS_{BETWEEN}$ are all synonymous terms.

In analysis of variance, the related effect size, η^2, can be computed as:

$$\eta^2 = SOS_{EXPLAINED}/SOS_{TOTAL}. \qquad (4)$$

Indeed, recent versions of SPSS provide this computation as an effect size output under the OPTIONS menu for a wide range of different analyses.

In multiple regression, the R^2 can be computed as:

$$R^2 = SOS_{EXPLAINED}/SOS_{TOTAL}. \qquad (5)$$

The similarity of Equations 3, 4, and 5 is, of course, an artifact of the reality that these analyses are part of a single General Linear Model.

"Corrected" (or "Adjusted") Effect Sizes. A "corrected" *d*, *d** (Hedges, 1981, 1982), can be computed as:

$$d^* = d\,[1 - \{3/((4\,(n_E + n_C - 2)) - 1)\}]. \qquad (6)$$

The Pearson r^2, the multiple R^2, and the canonical R_C^2 can all be corrected (cf. Thompson, 1990; Wang & Thompson, 2007) using a formula proposed by Ezekiel (1930):

$$r^{2*} \text{ or } R^{2*} \text{ or } R_C^2 = 1 - ((n-1)/ \\ (n-v-1))\,(1-R^2), \qquad (7)$$

where the R^2 in the rightmost portion of the formula is the relevant variance-accounted-for estimate, *n* is the sample size, and *v* is the number of predictor variables. The formula can be equivalently expressed as:

$$r^{2*} \text{ or } R^{2*} \text{ or } R_C^2 = R^2 - ((1 - R^2) \\ (v/(n-v-1))). \qquad (8)$$

In analysis of variance (ANOVA), the corrected estimate, Hays's (1981) ω^2, can be computed as:

$$\omega^2 = [SOS_{\text{BETWEEN}} - (k-1)MS_{\text{WITHIN}}]/$$
$$[SOS_Y + MS_{\text{WITHIN}}], \qquad (9)$$

where k is the number of levels in the ANOVA way, and MS is the mean square.

Uncorrected and corrected estimates will more strongly diverge as sample sizes are smaller, the number of measured variables is greater, and the population effect size is smaller. Corrected effect sizes are theoretically more accurate estimates of population values, but should be especially preferred when in the researcher's judgment the two types of estimates diverge substantially.

ILLUSTRATIVE EFFECT SIZE CALCULATIONS

The Table 17.1 data will now be used to illustrate various effect size calculations. This discussion is organized by the various analyses most frequently seen within the social sciences (cf. Edgington, 1974; Elmore & Woehlke, 1988; Kieffer, Reese, & Thompson, 2001; Willson, 1980).

t test/One-Way ANOVA

In the presence of an outcome variable that is at least intervally scaled and a nominal grouping variable, researchers interested in testing mean differences can conduct either a *t* test or a one-way ANOVA and will obtain identical $p_{\text{CALCULATED}}$ values and effect sizes from either choice (Thompson, 2006a). A number of effect size choices are possible. Here, from Table 17.1, LIBQ_TOT is used as the outcome variable, and SEX is used as the grouping variable.

Standardized Differences (Δ and d*).* To make this example concrete, and so that we can talk about a control group, let's pretend that the Table 17.1 gender variable is instead experimental group assignment, with "0" indicating assignment to the control group. Using Equation 1 for our data, we have:

$$(6.98 - 6.89)/1.47$$
$$0.09/1.47$$
$$\Delta = 0.061$$

The related *d* effect size computed using Equation 2 is:

$$(6.98 - 6.89)/[(1.32^2 + 1.47^2)/2]^{0.5}$$
$$0.09/[(1.32^2 + 1.47^2)/2]^{0.5}$$
$$0.09/[(1.74 + 2.16)/2]^{0.5}$$
$$0.09/[3.90/2]^{0.5}$$
$$0.09/1.95^{0.5}$$
$$0.09/1.40$$
$$d = 0.064$$

Variance-Accounted-for (η^2). If we compute the independent samples *t* test for these variables, we obtain $t_{\text{CALCULATED}} = -.238$, $p_{\text{CALCULATED}} = 0.813$. If we instead conduct a one-way ANOVA, we obtain $F_{\text{CALCULATED}} = 0.057$, $p_{\text{CALCULATED}} = 0.813$. Of course, for this design, $t^2_{\text{CALCULATED}} = -.238^2 = F_{\text{CALCULATED}} = 0.057$. The uncorrected variance-accounted-for effect size is computed using Equation 4 as:

$$0.11/124.77$$
$$\eta^2 = 0.00088 = 0.088\%$$

"Corrected" Estimates (d* and ω^2). For these data, the *d** is computed using Equation 6 to be:

$$0.064\,[1 - \{3/((4(33+33-2))-1)\}]$$
$$0.064\,[1 - \{3/((4(66-2))-1)\}]$$
$$0.064\,[1 - \{3/((4(64))-1)\}]$$
$$0.064\,[1 - \{3/(256-1)\}]$$
$$0.064\,[1 - \{3/255\}]$$
$$0.064\,[1 - 0.012]$$
$$0.064\,[0.988]$$
$$d^* = 0.063$$

The Hays's ω^2 is computed using Equation 9 as:

$$[0.11 - (2-1)1.95]/[124.77 + 1.95]$$
$$[0.11 - (2-1)1.95]/126.72$$
$$[0.11 - (1)1.95]/126.72$$
$$[0.11 - 1.95]/126.72$$
$$-1.8373/126.72$$
$$\omega^2 = -0.014 = 1.4\%$$

Note that corrected variance-accounted-for effect sizes can be negative, just as reliability coefficients can be negative, even though both these statistics are in a squared metric (Thompson, 2003). However, negative variance-accounted-for effect sizes suggest that the study may have involved considerably too few participants, given the loss of all the initial effect size after correction, and then some.

Multiway/Multifactorial ANOVA

Table 17.2 presents the analysis for a 3×2 ANOVA (Role × Sex) using library-related outcomes (SPSS variable OUTCOME) as the dependent variable. The reader is encouraged to reproduce the η^2 values reported in the table using either SPSS, or Excel, or both.

Multiple R^2

Here we illustrate the computation of R^2 and $R^{2\star}$ values for the Table 17.1 data using LIBQ_TOT scores as the dependent variable and OUTCOME and SATISFAC scores as the predictor variables. When the REGRESSION procedure is invoked, SPSS automatically reports that for these data, $R^2 = 72.7\%$. We can confirm this computation using Equation 5 to determine that:

$$90.70/124.76$$

$$R^2 = 72.7\%$$

SPSS also always reports "adjusted" R^2 (here 71.8%) when the REGRESSION procedure

is used. We can use Equation 8 to confirm the computation:

$$0.727 - ((1 - 0.727) \, (2/(66 - 2 - 1)))$$

$$0.727 - ((1 - 0.727) \, (2/(64 - 1)))$$

$$0.727 - ((1 - 0.727) \, (2/63))$$

$$0.727 - ((1 - 0.727) \, (0.032))$$

$$0.727 - ((0.273) \, (0.032))$$

$$0.727 - 0.009$$

$$R^{2\star} = 0.718 = 71.8\%$$

MANOVA/Descriptive Discriminant Analysis (DDA)

For this design, we use OUTCOME and SAT-ISFAC as the dependent variables, and ROLE as the factor for a one-way multivariate analysis of variance (MANOVA) design. This design can also be called a descriptive discriminant analysis (DDA; Huberty, 1994). However, conceptualizing the problem as a DDA (a) yields the standardized weights, the structure coefficients, and the centroids necessary for a correct post hoc interpretation of results, and (b) avoids what may well be *the most common analytic error within the published literature (i.e., the use of ANOVA as a method post hoc to MANOVA).*

As Borgen and Seling (1978) argued:

> When data truly are multivariate, as implied by the application of MANOVA,

Table 17.2   Two-Way Factorial ANOVA Example With the OUTCOME Scores as the Dependent Variable

Source	SOS	df	MS	$F_{CALCULATED}$	$p_{CALCULATED}$	η^2	Partial η^2
Role	0.79	2	0.39	0.16	0.860	0.488%[a]	0.505%[b]
Sex	0.01	1	0.01	0.00	0.952	0.006%[c]	0.006%[d]
Role × Sex	4.93	2	2.47	0.95	0.393	3.045%[e]	3.108%[f]
Within	156.17	60	2.60				
Total	161.90	65	2.49				

a. 0.79/161.90 = 0.488%.

b. 0.79/(0.79 + 156.17) = 0.79/156.56 = 0.505%.

c. 0.01/161.90 = 0.006%.

d. 0.01/(0.01 + 156.17) = 0.01/156.18 = 0.006%.

e. 4.93/161.90 = 3.045%.

f. 4.93/(4.93 + 156.17) = 4.93/158.64 = 3.108%.

a multivariate follow-up technique seems necessary to "discover" the complexity of the data. Discriminant analysis is multivariate; univariate ANOVA is not. (p. 696)

It simply makes no sense whatsoever to first declare interest in a multivariate omnibus system of outcome variables, and then to explore detected effects in this multivariate world by conducting non-multivariate tests!

SPSS reports that Wilks's lambda is 0.990. A multivariate η^2 value can be computed as $1 - \lambda = 0.010 = 1.0\%$. SPSS upon request when executing the procedure named GLM reports the multivariate partial η^2 value for these data to be $0.005 = 0.5\%$.

Canonical Correlation Analysis

The canonical problem requires at least two variable sets each consisting of at least two measured variables (Thompson, 1984). For this example we use OUTCOME and SATISFAC as one variable set, and the LibQUAL+™ subscale scores (i.e., SERVAFFE, INFOCONT, and LIBPLACE) as the second variable set.

The SPSS syntax with which to conduct a canonical correlation analysis is:

```
MANOVA
outcome satisfac WITH
ServAffe InfoCont LibPlace /
PRINT SIGNIF(MULTIV EIGEN DIMENR) /
DISCRIM=STAN COR ALPHA(.99) /
DESIGN .
```

For our data, SPSS then outputs the two squared canonical correlation coefficients, $R_C^2 = 0.732 = 73.2\%$ and $R_C^2 = 0.067 = 6.7\%$. We can apply the Ezekiel (1930) correction to these values, if we wish to compute "adjusted R_C^2" (Thompson, 1990).

CONFIDENCE INTERVALS

The most recent *Publication Manual* of the American Psychological Association (2001) suggested that confidence intervals (CIs) represent, "in general, *the best* reporting strategy. The use of confidence intervals is therefore *strongly recommended*" (p. 22, emphasis added). However,

empirical studies show that confidence intervals are reported very infrequently in published research (Finch, Cumming, & Thomason, 2001; Kieffer et al., 2001). And as Thompson (2002b) suggested, "It is conceivable that some researchers may not fully understand statistical methods that they (a) rarely read in the literature and (b) infrequently use in their own work" (p. 26). Indeed, recent research (Belia, Fidler, Williams, & Cumming, 2005) confirms that many (perhaps most) researchers do not understand confidence intervals.

The Exploratory Software for Confidence Intervals (ESCI) developed by Geoff Cumming, and available at **www.latrobe.edu.au/psy/esci**, is used here to produce the graphics that make this discussion accessible. Related explanations have been offered by Cumming and Finch (2001, 2005) and Cumming, Williams, and Fidler (2004).

The top portion of Figure 17.1 presents a hypothetical population in which $\mu = 50$ and $\sigma = 15$. Here, 150 random samples of size $n = 12$ have been drawn from this population, and results related to the samples and the sample means are presented in the bottom portion of Figure 17.1. For example, the last sample of $n = 12$ scores in the most recent sample are presented as circles drawn along the top margin of the bottom portion of the figure. Note that the last (i.e., 150th) sample somewhat undersampled the left half of the population distribution, and the mean for this sample was 54.7 ($SD = 10.5$).

The bottom of Figure 17.1 presents the distribution of the 150 mean statistics of the randomly drawn samples. If an infinite number of these sample means had been drawn and plotted, the resulting distribution technically would be labeled the *sampling distribution of the mean for n = 12*. In order to confuse people, who would otherwise understand the related critical foundational concepts, the standard deviation of the sampling distribution is *not* called "the standard deviation of the sampling distribution," and instead is called "the standard error of the mean" (Thompson, 2006a).

The standard error is very important for either or both of two purposes: (a) inferentially conducting NHSST, or (b) descriptively characterizing the presumed stability of our point estimate (e.g., here the mean). In *inferential* applications, all test statistics and $p_{\text{CALCULATED}}$ values are derived by dividing parameter estimates by their estimated standard errors (Thompson, 2006a). In *descriptive* applications, when we

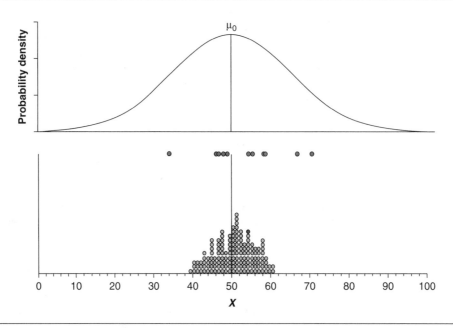

Figure 17.1   Population for $\mu = 50$ and $\sigma = 15$ and sampling distribution of the mean for 150 samples at $n = 12$.

NOTE: The last (i.e., 150th) sample somewhat undersampled the left half of the population distribution, and the mean for this sample was 54.7 ($SD = 10.5$).

focus on the stability of the point estimate, we place greater faith in the precision of our point estimates (e.g., the mean, SD, r, Cohen's d) when the standard error of the estimate is smaller. Indeed, we can add to and subtract from our point estimate (e.g., here the mean) some function of the standard error, to describe the precision of our point estimate. We call the resulting range of values a "confidence interval."

Figure 17.2 presents twenty-five 95% confidence intervals drawn from our population. Note that some intervals are wider (e.g., the bottom, 1st interval) and some intervals are narrower (e.g., the most recent, 25th interval at the top of the 25 intervals). More important, note that 3 of the 25 intervals (i.e., the top 2 and the 3rd interval) do *not* capture what in this case is the known population parameter, $\mu = 50$.

The figure makes clear what the "95% confidence" statement is about when dealing with 95% confidence intervals. This confidence statement says that if we drew *infinitely many* 95% intervals from our population, exactly 95% would capture our true population parameter, and exactly 5% of the intervals would not capture the parameter.

A common misconception about 95% confidence intervals is the belief that a single interval from a single sample is 95% likely to capture the population parameter. That is *not* what confidence intervals do! We can see the fallacy of confusing (a) a statement about infinitely many intervals with (b) a statement about a single interval. As Thompson (2006b) proved in his penetrating proof of his Equation 29.3,

$$1 \neq \infty \text{ (Thompson, 2006b, \#29.3)}.$$

CONFIDENCE INTERVALS FOR EFFECT SIZES

Formulas can be used to compute (a) statistics, (b) confidence intervals for statistics, and (c) effect sizes. With respect to CIs about a mean, the widths (W) of the intervals for a given n and a given SD do not vary (i.e., are what statisticians call "pivotal").

For example, for $n = 10$ and $SD = 15$, for $M = 100$, the 95% CI about the mean can be computed as $M \pm (.5)W$. The required t_{CRITICAL} value for $df = n - 1 = 9$ can be found using the Excel function:

$$= \text{tinv}(.05, (10\text{-}1)),$$

which returns the value of 2.26. We compute the half-width ($W_{1/2}$) of the 95% CI for M_X (both

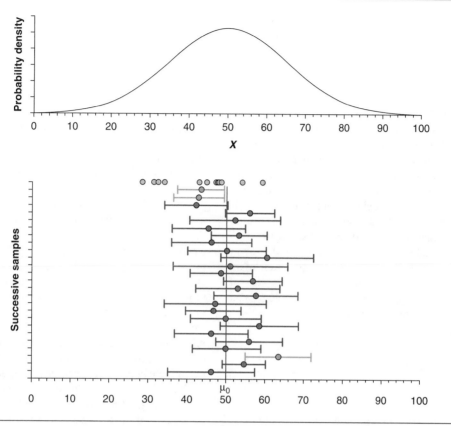

Figure 17.2   95% confidence intervals for the mean of 25 random samples ($n = 12$) from a population with $\mu = 50$ and $\sigma = 15$.

subtracted and added to the mean to obtain the final interval with width W) as:

$$W_{1/2} = t_{CRITICAL} \, (SE_M)$$
$$t_{CRITICAL} \, [SD_X \, (n^{0.5})]$$
$$2.26 \, [15.0 \, (10^{0.5})]$$
$$2.26 \, [15 \, (3.16)]$$
$$2.26 \, [4.74]$$
$$W_{1/2} = 10.72$$

(10)

So our 95% CI about $M = 100$ is $M - W_{1/2} = 100.0 - 10.72 = 89.28$, and $M + W_{1/2} = 100.0 + 10.72 = 110.72$. The full width is $W = 10.72 + 10.72 = 21.44$ (or $110.72 - 89.28 = 21.44$).

If we keep $n = 10$ and $SD = 15$, but change M to be 50, for the 95% CI about the mean, the half-width is nevertheless *still computed* as:

$$W_{1/2} = t_{CRITICAL} \, (SE_M)$$
$$t_{CRITICAL} \, [SD_X \, (n^{0.5})]$$

$$2.26 \, [15.0 \, (10^{0.5})]$$
$$2.26 \, [15 \, (3.16)]$$
$$2.26 \, [4.74]$$
$$W_{1/2} = 10.72$$

And our 95% CI about $M = 50$ is $50.0 - 10.72 = 39.28$, and $50.0 + 10.72 = 60.72$. The full width is $W = 10.72 + 10.72 = 21.44$ (or *still* $60.72 - 39.28 = 21.44$).

But formulas *cannot* be used to compute confidence intervals for effect sizes, because the widths of CIs about effect sizes are *not* pivotal (see Cumming & Finch, 2001). Instead, computer-intensive estimation invoking statistical iteration (i.e., an initial estimate successively tweaked until a given statistical criterion is approximated) must be used to estimate confidence intervals for effect sizes.

To illustrate that the widths of CIs for effect sizes are *not* pivotal, let's consider the data set {5.0, 5.5, 5.5, 6.0, 6.0, 6.0, 6.0, 6.5, 6.5, 7.0}. For these data, $n = 10$, $SD = 0.577$, $M = 6.0$. If we use the null hypothesis that M is not different from a presumed parameter $\mu = 5.0$, using the ESCI software, Cohen's d is computed to be 1.73, and the 95% CI is [0.72, 2.71]. The width of this CI is 1.99 (i.e., 2.71 − 0.72).

However, if we change the data to {6.0, 6.5, 6.5, 7.0, 7.0, 7.0, 7.0, 7.5, 7.5, 8.0}, n remains 10, SD remains 0.577, but now M is 7.0, and d is 3.46. The 95% CI about d is [1.77, 5.13]. The W of the interval, even though n and SD remain fixed, is now 3.36 (i.e., 5.13 − 1.77), and *not* 1.99!

The software required to estimate CIs for various effect sizes is widely available. The software is available to run stand-alone on a microcomputer (e.g., Steiger & Fouladi, 1992), in Excel (Cumming & Finch, 2001), in SPSS (Smithson, 2001), or in SAS (Algina & Keselman, 2003; Algina, Keselman, & Penfield, 2005a, 2005b). This is an area of quickly developing theory and methodology (e.g., Keselman, Algina, & Fradette, in press).

Best Practices

Effect Sizes

A common, but extremely unfortunate practice in interpreting effect sizes is to use the benchmarks for "small," "medium," and "large" effects that Cohen first offered decades ago. However, the view taken here is that these benchmarks are *not* generally useful. Cohen (1988) himself intended these only as general guidelines, mainly useful when working in unexplored territory, and he emphasized that

> these proposed conventions were set forth throughout with much diffidence, qualifications, *and invitations not to employ them if possible* [italics added]. . . . They were offered as conventions because they were needed in a research climate characterized by a neglect of attention to issues of [effect size] magnitude. (p. 532)

As noted elsewhere, "if people interpreted effect sizes [using fixed benchmarks] with the same rigidity that $\alpha=.05$ has been used in statistical testing, we would merely be being stupid in another metric" (Thompson, 2001, pp. 82–83). In relatively established areas of research, "there is no wisdom whatsoever in attempting to associate regions of the effect-size metric with descriptive

adjectives such as 'small,' 'moderate,' 'large,' and the like" (Glass, McGaw, & Smith, 1981, p. 104).

The correct interpretation of effect sizes instead focuses on "the retrospective interpretation of new results, once they are in hand, via *explicit, direct* comparison with the prior effect sizes in the related literature" (Thompson, 2002b, p. 28, emphasis added). Such a focus facilitates the realization of two coequally important benefits from using effect sizes.

First, the use of effect sizes to inform judgments about practical significance via these direct comparisons with prior literature forces the researcher to evaluate effects *within a given research context.* Very small effects may still be extremely important when (a) outcomes are especially valued (e.g., human longevity), (b) outcomes are highly resistant to change, or (c) small effects cumulate over time (Abelson, 1985; Prentice & Miller, 1992). For example, the variance-accounted-for effect sizes of smoking on lung cancer incidence (Gage, 1978, p. 21) and aspirin taking on heart attack incidence (Rosenthal, 1994) are both only about 1%, yet we deem these both effects remarkably important!

Second, the benefits of using effect sizes to inform judgments about result replicability are *only* realized if we make these comparisons across studies. Unfortunately, p values are *completely useless* as a mechanism for evaluating result replicability (cf. Carver, 1978; Cohen, 1994; Thompson, 1996), regardless of how we use $p_{CALCULATED}$ results.

Confidence Intervals

Some researchers erroneously see no comparative benefits of using confidence intervals as against NHSST (e.g., Knapp & Sawilowsky, 2001). Certainly, it is true that "if we mindlessly interpret a confidence interval with reference to whether the interval subsumes zero, we are doing little more than nil hypothesis statistical testing" (Thompson, 1998, pp. 799–800). But the correct use of confidence does *not* employ CIs to conduct NHSST!

Instead, the correct use of CIs is direct and explicit comparison of CIs across studies. As Thompson (2006a) emphasized,

> The beauty of such integrative comparisons is that by comparing CIs across studies (*not* by evaluating CIs by whether they subsume an hypothesized expectation) we will eventually

discover the true parameter, even if our initial expectations are wildly wrong (Schmidt, 1996)! (p. 206)

The integrative use of CIs across studies facilitates the "meta-analytic thinking" advocated by contemporary scholars (e.g., Thompson, 2002b). This application also forces us to understand that the *p* values from a single study do *not* evaluate either result import or result replicability and that, indeed, single studies have limited value, and even that limited value derives primarily from the single study's contribution to a larger corpus of literature. As Schmidt (1996) noted,

> Meta-analysis . . . has revealed how little information there typically is in any single study. It has shown that, contrary to widespread belief, a single primary study can rarely resolve an issue or answer a question. (p. 127)

The graphic portrayal of CIs is particularly powerful, because a pictorial representation can "convey at a quick glance an overall pattern of results" (APA, 2001, p. 176) across either a study or a literature. For this reason, the APA Task Force on Statistical Inference recommended, "In all figures, include graphical representations of interval estimates whenever possible" (Wilkinson & the APA Task Force, 1999, p. 601).

Happily, the Excel software makes the creation of CI graphs quite easy, and once created, these can be readily cut and pasted into other documents, such as manuscripts. Simply click on the icon for the CHART WIZARD, select STOCK, and then input respectively the HIGH, the LOW values of the CIs, and then the point estimates as CLOSE.

Discussion

Researchers use effect sizes for two purposes, which are of *coequal* importance. First, researchers use effect sizes to inform judgments about the *practical significance of results* (Kirk, 1996), given the substantive context of a given study and the researcher's personal valuing of the dependent variable(s). As Eden (2002) noted in a recent editorial in the *Academy of Management Journal,* "the importance of any particular effect size depends upon the nature of the outcome studied" (p. 845).

Second, researchers use effect sizes to evaluate the *replicability of results*. Researchers judge results to be replicable when the direct and explicit comparison of their effect sizes with those in related prior studies suggests that effects are stable over time, or even generalize over some variations in design or analysis. Finding relationships that replicate over stated conditions is, after all, the very business of scientific inquiry.

Ironically, this "righteous obsession with result replicability" (Thompson, 2006b, p. 594) is *exactly* the same concern that has motivated *both* the critics (e.g., Carver, 1978; Cohen, 1994; Thompson, 1996) and the defenders (e.g., Abelson, 1997; Robinson & Wainer, 2002) of statistical significance testing. Confidence intervals for point estimates, and confidence intervals for effect sizes, both focus our attention on the "reflective examination of the replicability of results across related studies" (Thompson, 2006b, p. 600).

References

Aaron, B., Kromrey, J. D., & Ferron, J. M. (1998, November). *Equating r-based and d-based effect size indices: Problems with a commonly recommended formula.* Paper presented at the annual meeting of the Florida Educational Research Association, Orlando, FL. (ERIC Document Reproduction Service No. ED433353)

Abelson, R. P. (1985). A variance explanation paradox: When a little is a lot. *Psychological Bulletin, 97,* 129–133.

Abelson, R. P. (1997). A retrospective on the significance test ban of 1999 (If there were no significance tests, they would be invented). In L. L. Harlow, S. A. Mulaik, & J. H. Steiger (Eds.), *What if there were no significance tests?* (pp. 117–141). Mahwah, NJ: Lawrence Erlbaum.

AERA Task Force on Reporting of Research Methods in AERA Publications. (2006). Standards for reporting on empirical social science research in AERA publications. *Educational Researcher, 35*(6), 33–40.

Algina, J., & Keselman, H. J. (2003). Approximate confidence intervals for effect sizes. *Educational and Psychological Measurement, 63,* 537–553.

Algina, J., Keselman, H. J., & Penfield, R. D. (2005a). An alternative to Cohen's standardized mean difference effect size: A robust parameter and confidence interval in the two independent group case. *Psychological Methods, 10,* 317–328.

Algina, J., Keselman, H. J., & Penfield, R. D. (2005b). Effect sizes and their intervals: The two-level repeated measures case. *Educational and Psychological Measurement, 65,* 241–258.

American Psychological Association. (2001). *Publication manual of the American Psychological Association* (5th ed.). Washington, DC: Author.

Anderson, D. R., Burnham, K. P., & Thompson, W. (2000). Null hypothesis testing: Problems, prevalence, and an alternative. *Journal of Wildlife Management, 64,* 912–923.

Bagozzi, R. P., Fornell, C., & Larcker, D. F. (1981). Canonical correlation analysis as a special case of a structural relations model. *Multivariate Behavioral Research, 16,* 437–454.

Belia, S., Fidler, F., Williams, J., & Cumming, G. (2005). Researchers misunderstand confidence intervals and standard error bars. *Psychological Methods, 10,* 389–396.

Borgen, F. H., & Seling, M. J. (1978). Uses of discriminant analysis following MANOVA: Multivariate statistics for multivariate purposes. *Journal of Applied Psychology, 63,* 689–697.

Boring, E. G. (1919). Mathematical vs. scientific importance. *Psychological Bulletin, 16,* 335–338.

Carver, R. (1978). The case against statistical significance testing. *Harvard Educational Review, 48,* 378–399.

Cohen, J. (1968). Multiple regression as a general data-analytic system. *Psychological Bulletin, 70,* 426–443.

Cohen, J. (1969). *Statistical power analysis for the behavioral sciences.* New York: Academic Press.

Cohen, J. (1988). *Statistical power analysis for the behavioral sciences* (2nd ed.). Hillsdale, NJ: Lawrence Erlbaum.

Cohen, J. (1994). The earth is round ($p < .05$). *American Psychologist, 49,* 997–1003.

Cumming, G., & Finch, S. (2001). A primer on the understanding, use and calculation of confidence intervals that are based on central and noncentral distributions. *Educational and Psychological Measurement, 61,* 532–575.

Cumming, G., & Finch, S. (2005). Inference by eye: Confidence intervals and how to read pictures of data. *American Psychologist, 60,* 170–180.

Cumming, G., Williams, J., & Fidler, F. (2004). Replication, and researchers' understanding of confidence intervals and standard error bars. *Understanding Statistics, 3,* 299–311.

Eden, D. (2002). Replication, meta-analysis, scientific progress, and *AMJ*'s publication policy. *Academy of Management Journal, 45,* 841–846.

Edgington, E. S. (1974). A new tabulation of statistical procedures used in APA journals. *American Psychologist, 29,* 25–26.

Elmore, P. B., & Woehlke, P. L. (1988). Statistical methods employed in *American Educational Research Journal, Educational Researcher,* and

Review of Educational Research from 1978 to 1987. *Educational Researcher, 17*(9), 19–20.

Ezekiel, M. (1930). *Methods of correlational analysis.* New York: John Wiley.

Fidler, F. (2002). The fifth edition of the APA *Publication Manual:* Why its statistics recommendations are so controversial. *Educational and Psychological Measurement, 62,* 749–770.

Fidler, F. (2005). *From statistical significance to effect estimation: Statistical reform in psychology, medicine, and ecology.* Unpublished doctoral dissertation, University of Melbourne. Available at http://www.botany.unimelb.edu.au/envisci/fiona/fidlerphd_aug06.pdf

Finch, S., Cumming, G., & Thomason, N. (2001). Reporting of statistical inference in the *Journal of Applied Psychology:* Little evidence of reform. *Educational and Psychological Measurement, 61,* 181–210.

Gage, N. L. (1978). *The scientific basis of the art of teaching.* New York: Teachers College Press.

Glass, G. V (1976). Primary, secondary, and meta-analysis of research. *Educational Researcher, 5*(10), 3–8.

Glass, G. V McGaw, B., & Smith, M. L. (1981). *Meta-analysis in social research.* Beverly Hills, CA: Sage.

Grissom, R. J. (1994). Probability of the superior outcome of one treatment over another. *Journal of Applied Psychology, 79,* 314–316.

Grissom, R. J., & Kim, J. J. (2005). *Effect sizes for research: A broad practical approach.* Mahwah, NJ: Lawrence Erlbaum.

Harlow, L. L., Mulaik, S. A., & Steiger, J. H. (Eds.). (1997). *What if there were no significance tests?* Mahwah, NJ: Lawrence Erlbaum.

Hays, W. L. (1981). *Statistics* (3rd ed.). New York: Holt, Rinehart & Winston.

Hedges, L. V. (1981). Distribution theory for Glass's estimator of effect size and related estimators. *Journal of Educational Statistics, 6,* 107–128.

Hedges, L. V. (1982). Estimation of effect size from a series of independent experiments. *Psychological Bulletin, 92,* 490–499.

Hess, B., Olejnik, S., & Huberty, C. J. (2001). The efficacy of two improvement-over-chance effect sizes for two-group univariate comparisons under variance heterogeneity and nonnormality. *Educational and Psychological Measurement, 61,* 909–936.

Hubbard, R., & Ryan, P. A. (2000). The historical growth of statistical significance testing in psychology—and its future prospects. *Educational and Psychological Measurement, 60,* 661–681.

Huberty, C. J (1994). *Applied discriminant analysis.* New York: John Wiley.

Huberty, C. J. (1999). On some history regarding statistical testing. In B. Thompson (Ed.), *Advances in social science methodology* (Vol. 5, pp. 1–23). Stamford, CT: JAI Press.

Huberty, C. J. (2002). A history of effect size indices. *Educational and Psychological Measurement, 62,* 227–240.

Huberty, C. J. & Holmes, S. E. (1983). Two-group comparisons and univariate classification. *Educational and Psychological Measurement, 43,* 15–26.

Huberty, C. J. & Morris, J. D. (1988). A single contrast test procedure. *Educational and Psychological Measurement, 48,* 567–578.

Johnson, D. H. (1999). The insignificance of statistical significance testing. *Journal of Wildlife Management, 63,* 763–772.

Keselman, H. J., Algina, J., & Fradette, K. (in press). Robust confidence intervals for effect size in the two-group case. *Journal of Modern Applied Statistical Methods.*

Kieffer, K. M., Reese, R. J., & Thompson, B. (2001). Statistical techniques employed in *AERJ* and *JCP* articles from 1988 to 1997: A methodological review. *Journal of Experimental Education, 69,* 280–309.

Kirk, R. E. (1996). Practical significance: A concept whose time has come. *Educational and Psychological Measurement, 56,* 746–759.

Kirk, R. E. (2003). The importance of effect magnitude. In S. F. Davis (Ed.), *Handbook of research methods in experimental psychology* (pp. 83–105). Oxford, UK: Blackwell.

Kline, R. (2004). *Beyond significance testing: Reforming data analysis methods in behavioral research.* Washington, DC: American Psychological Association.

Knapp, T. R. (1978). Canonical correlation analysis: A general parametric significance testing system. *Psychological Bulletin, 85,* 410–416.

Knapp, T., & Sawilowsky, S. (2001). Constructive criticisms of methodological and editorial practices. *Journal of Experimental Education, 70,* 65–79.

Natesan, P., & Thompson, B. (2007). Extending improvement-over-chance *I*-index effect size simulation studies to cover some small-sample cases. *Educational and Psychological Measurement, 67,* 59–72.

Prentice, D. A., & Miller, D. T. (1992). When small effects are impressive. *Psychological Bulletin, 112,* 160–164.

Robinson, D. H., & Wainer, H. (2002). On the past and future of null hypothesis significance testing. *Journal of Wildlife Management, 66,* 263–271.

Rosenthal, R. (1994). Parametric measures of effect size. In H. Cooper & L. V. Hedges (Eds.), *The handbook of research synthesis* (pp. 231–244). New York: Russell Sage Foundation.

Rozeboom, W. W. (1997). Good science is abductive, not hypothetico-deductive. In L. L. Harlow, S. A. Mulaik, & J. H. Steiger (Eds.), *What if there were no significance tests?* (pp. 335–392). Mahwah, NJ: Lawrence Erlbaum.

Schmidt, F. L. (1996). Statistical significance testing and cumulative knowledge in psychology: Implications for the training of researchers. *Psychological Methods, 1,* 115–129.

Schmidt, F. L., & Hunter, J. E. (1997). Eight common but false objections to the discontinuation of significance testing in the analysis of research data. In L. L. Harlow, S. A. Mulaik, & J. H. Steiger (Eds.), *What if there were no significance tests?* (pp. 37–64). Mahwah, NJ: Lawrence Erlbaum.

Smithson, M. (2001). Correct confidence intervals for various regression effect sizes and parameters: The importance of noncentral distributions in computing intervals. *Educational and Psychological Measurement, 61,* 605–632.

Snyder, P., & Lawson, S. (1993). Evaluating results using corrected and uncorrected effect size estimates. *Journal of Experimental Education, 61,* 334–349.

Steiger, J. H., & Fouladi, R. T. (1992). R^2: A computer program for interval estimation, power calculation, and hypothesis testing for the squared multiple correlation. *Behavior Research Methods, Instruments, and Computers, 4,* 581–582.

Suter, G. W. I. (1996). Abuse of hypothesis testing statistics in ecological risk assessment. *Human Ecological Risk Assessment, 2,* 331–347.

Thompson, B. (1984). *Canonical correlation analysis: Uses and interpretation.* Thousand Oaks, CA: Sage.

Thompson, B. (1990). Finding a correction for the sampling error in multivariate measures of relationship: A Monte Carlo study. *Educational and Psychological Measurement, 50,* 15–31.

Thompson, B. (1993). The use of statistical significance tests in research: Bootstrap and other alternatives. *Journal of Experimental Education, 61*(4), 361–377.

Thompson, B. (1994). Guidelines for authors. *Educational and Psychological Measurement, 54,* 837–847.

Thompson, B. (1996). AERA editorial policies regarding statistical significance testing: Three suggested reforms. *Educational Researcher, 25*(2), 26–30.

Thompson, B. (1998). In praise of brilliance: Where that praise really belongs. *American Psychologist, 53,* 799–800.

Thompson, B. (2000). Canonical correlation analysis. In L. Grimm & P. Yarnold (Eds.), *Reading and understanding more multivariate statistics* (pp. 285–316). Washington, DC: American Psychological Association.

Thompson, B. (2001). Significance, effect sizes, stepwise methods, and other issues: Strong arguments move the field. *Journal of Experimental Education, 70,* 80–93.

Thompson, B. (2002a). "Statistical," "practical," and "clinical": How many kinds of significance do counselors need to consider? *Journal of Counseling and Development, 80,* 64–71.

Thompson, B. (2002b). What future quantitative social science research could look like: Confidence intervals for effect sizes. *Educational Researcher, 31*(3), 24–31.

Thompson, B. (Ed.). (2003). *Score reliability: Contemporary thinking on reliability issues.* Thousand Oaks, CA: Sage.

Thompson, B. (2006a). *Foundations of behavioral statistics: An insight-based approach.* New York: Guilford.

Thompson, B. (2006b). Research synthesis: Effect sizes. In J. Green, G. Camilli, & P. B. Elmore (Eds.), *Handbook of complementary methods in education research* (pp. 583–603). Washington, DC: American Educational Research Association.

Thompson, B., Cook, C., & Kyrillidou, M. (2005). Concurrent validity of LibQUAL+™ scores: What do LibQUAL+™ scores measure? *Journal of Academic Librarianship, 31,* 517–522.

Thompson, B., Cook, C., & Kyrillidou, M. (2006). Using localized survey items to augment standardized benchmarking measures: A LibQUAL+™ study. *portal: Libraries and the Academy, 6,* 219–230.

Vacha-Haase, T., & Thompson, B. (2004). How to estimate and interpret various effect sizes. *Journal of Counseling Psychology, 51,* 473–481.

Wang, Z., & Thompson, B. (2007). Is the Pearson r^2 biased, and if so, what is the best correction formula? *Journal of Experimental Education, 75,* 109–125.

Wilkinson, L., & the APA Task Force on Statistical Inference. (1999). Statistical methods in psychology journals: Guidelines and explanations. *American Psychologist, 54,* 594–604.

Willson, V. L. (1980). Research techniques in *AERJ* articles: 1969 to 1978. *Educational Researcher, 9*(6), 5–10.

Yoccuz, N. G. (1991). Use, overuse, and misuse of significance tests in evolutionary biology. *Bulletin of the Ecology Society of America, 72,* 106–111.

Ziliak, S. T., & McCloskey, D. N. (2004). Size matters: The standard error of regressions in the *American Economic Review. Journal of Socio-Economics, 33,* 527–546.

18

ROBUST METHODS FOR DETECTING AND DESCRIBING ASSOCIATIONS

RAND R. WILCOX

Two of the best-known methods for detecting and describing an association between two or more variables are Pearson's correlation and least squares regression. As is well-known, there are conditions where these methods can provide a satisfactory summary of data and where the associated inferential techniques, which are typically used, provide an adequate indication of whether there is an association among variables. However, there are several fundamental ways in which these methods can be highly unsatisfactory. Briefly, nonnormality, heteroscedasticity, and outliers can mask true associations; they can wreak havoc on Type I errors and confidence intervals; and they can result in a distorted sense of how the bulk of the points are related. One immediate goal of this chapter is to provide a more detailed sense of when and why practical problems can occur. Then more modern methods, aimed at correcting known problems, are described, and practical reasons for using these methods are illustrated. (Comments on easy-to-use software are given near the end of this chapter.) First, however, some general remarks about power and the meaning of robustness are provided.

POWER AND NOTIONS OF ROBUSTNESS

At one time, robustness generally referred to the ability of a method to control the probability of a Type I error. But today, it has a more general meaning (Hampel, Ronchetti, Rousseeuw, & Stahel, 1986; Huber, 1981; Staudte & Sheather, 1990). Roughly, a parameter, such as the population mean, μ, or Pearson's correlation, ρ, is said to be robust if its value does not change much with small changes in the underlying distributions. Estimators, such as the usual sample mean, $\bar{X}$, or r, are said to be robust if small changes in the observed data have little or no effect on their values. A classic illustration that the population variance, σ^2, is not robust is based on a contaminated normal distribution where sampling is from a standard normal distribution with probability .9; otherwise, sampling is from a normal distribution with mean 0 and standard deviation 10. Figure 18.1 shows a standard normal and the contaminated normal just described. As is evident, the two distributions appear to be nearly identical. Although the standard normal has variance 1, the contaminated normal has variance 10.9. That is, a small departure from normality can greatly inflate the variance.

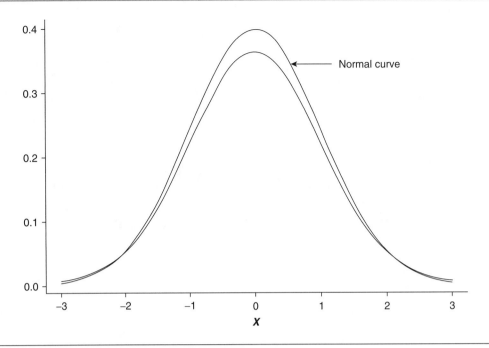

Figure 18.1   Normal and contaminated normal distributions.

At first glance, the illustration just given might appear to be in error. From basic training, when one normal distribution has a standard deviation that is 50% larger than another normal distribution, there is a very noticeable difference between the two distributions, even when they have the same mean. But when dealing with symmetric, bell-shaped distributions that are not normal, this property does not necessarily hold, as was just illustrated.

A criticism of this illustration might be that in practice, perhaps we never encounter a contaminated normal distribution. But robustness concerns do not hinge on whether data follow a contaminated normal distribution. Rather, the contaminated normal illustrates a basic principle: Regardless of which distribution we consider, small changes in the tails of the distribution can drastically alter the population variance, σ^2. In particular, if we assume normality, but our assumption is off just by a little bit, σ^2 can become relatively large, which can affect power substantially. The same is true for the population mean μ (e.g., Staudte & Sheather, 1990) as well as ρ. The left panel of Figure 18.2 shows a bivariate normal distribution with correlation $\rho = .8$, and in the right panel, the correlation is $\rho = .2$. Figure 18.3 shows a bivariate distribution that has an obvious similarity to the left panel of

Figure 18.2, where $\rho = .8$, but $\rho = .2$. In Figure 18.3, X has a normal distribution, but the distribution of Y is contaminated normal.

In terms of observed data, quantities such as the sample mean, the sample variance, and the usual estimate of ρ, r, are not robust in the sense that even a single outlier can drastically alter their values. This is of considerable practical importance because modern outlier detection techniques suggest that outliers are common, consistent with a prediction made by Tukey (1960) before good outlier detection techniques were available.

Consider the data shown in Figure 18.4, which were taken from a study dealing with predictors of reading ability. Pearson's correlation is $r = -.03$, and Student's t has a p value of .76. Also shown is the least squares regression line. It is evident, however, that the six largest X values are outliers. If we eliminate the six points for which $X > 120$, now $r = -.39$, and Student's t has a p value less than .001. So a very simple process—namely, eliminating obvious outliers—leads to a decidedly different conclusion.[1] Sometimes this simple process is satisfactory, but under general conditions, it can be unsatisfactory and even disastrous.

There are at least two central issues to keep in mind. The first is that outliers or influential points are not always obvious when simply looking at a scatterplot. The second is that eliminating

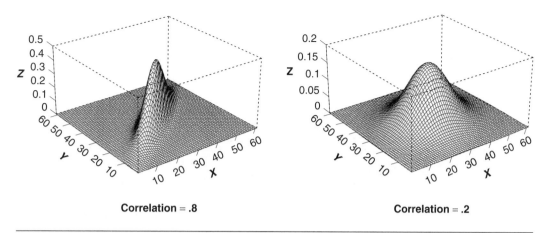

Figure 18.2   Two bivariate normal distributions.

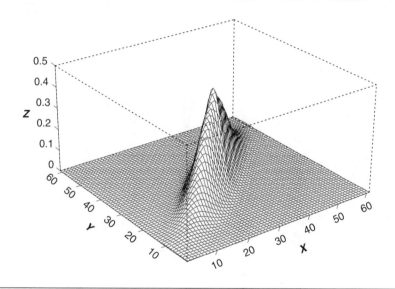

Figure 18.3   A bivariate distribution with correlation $\rho = .2$.

outliers can invalidate Student's t as an appropriate test of $H_0 : \rho = 0$. If a data point is simply erroneous, it can and should be removed, and Student's t remains valid if erroneous values occur at random. However, if points are valid but unusual, eliminating them creates technical difficulties that can cause serious practical problems.[2]

If we simply restrict the range of X values, without regard to the Y values, Student's t remains valid. And if we restrict the range of Y values, ignoring X, again Student's t can be used. But if we remove outliers among both the X and Y values, Student's t is no longer valid because it is based on an inappropriate estimate of the standard error. More generally, when eliminating points flagged as outliers by some appropriate outlier detection method, special techniques are required to control the probability of a Type I error in a reasonably satisfactory manner. Moreover, the adjustment made depends on the particular outlier detection technique that is used (e.g., Wilcox, 2004).

Figure 18.5 shows the same data as in Figure 18.4, only now, points declared outliers, using a so-called projection-type outlier detection method (Wilcox, 2005a, section 6.4.9), are marked by an o.[3] Note the two points flagged as outliers in the left portion of the plot. With the outliers

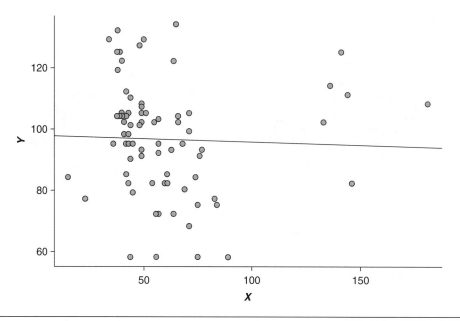

Figure 18.4   Plot of the reading data plus the least squares regression line.

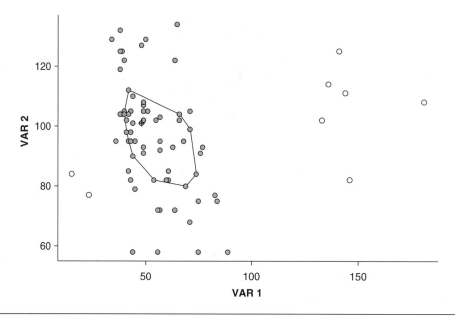

Figure 18.5   Plot of the reading data with outliers marked by an *o*.

indicated by an o removed, $r = -.49$, in contrast to $-.39$ when only the six obvious outliers are removed. And using a method in Wilcox (2003, 2005a) specifically designed to be used with a projection-type outlier detection method, we reject $H_0 : \rho = 0$ at the .05 level.[4]

To provide another perspective on power and robustness, consider the simple ordinary least squares model $Y = \beta_0 + \beta_1 X + \varepsilon$, where X and ε are independent, and ε has mean zero and variance σ^2. The lack of robustness associated with σ^2 has practical implications about power when using the conventional method for testing

$$H_0: \beta_1 = 0.$$

Let b_1 and b_0 be the usual least squares estimates of β_1 and β_0, respectively, based on the random sample $(X_1, Y_1), \ldots, (X_n, Y_n)$. From basic principles, assuming the model is correct, the squared standard error of b_1 is

$$\frac{\sigma^2}{\sum (X_i - \overline{X})^2},$$

where $\overline{X} = \sum X_i / n$. So, because small departures from normality can greatly inflate σ^2, small departures from normality can result in relatively low power. A related concern is that even a single outlier can greatly inflate the usual estimate of σ^2,

$$\hat{\sigma}^2 = \frac{1}{n-1} \sum r_i^2,$$

where $r_i = Y_i - b_0 - b_1 X_i$ are the residuals. This is a practical concern because modern outlier detection methods suggest that outliers are commonly encountered (e.g., Wilcox, 2005a).

Yet another feature of data that can substantially inflate the standard error of b_1 is heteroscedasticity. Even under normality, if the (conditional) variance of Y, given X, varies with X, various alternative regression estimators can have a substantially smaller standard error (e.g., Wilcox, 2003, p. 493). Nonnormality exacerbates practical problems.

AN OVERVIEW OF PRACTICAL CONCERNS WITH STANDARD TECHNIQUES

The usual regression model assumes that for some outcome variable Y and p predictors, $X_1, \ldots, X_p$,

$$Y = \beta_0 + \beta_1 X_1 + \ldots + \beta_p X_p + \varepsilon,$$

where the error term, ε, has a normal distribution with mean zero and unknown variance σ^2, and where ε is independent of $X_1, \ldots, X_p$. Of particular importance here is the fact that standard inferential techniques not only assume normality but also assume homoscedasticity. But as pointed out in numerous journal articles, and for reasons summarized by Wilcox (2003, 2005a), when either of these assumptions is violated, the result can be poor power, poor control over the probability of a Type I error, and inaccurate confidence intervals. Indeed, even under normality, heteroscedasticity can result in poor power. A positive feature of standard inferential techniques is that under independence, all indications are that they provide reasonably good control over the probability of a Type I error. That is, when a significant result is reported, it is reasonable to conclude that the variables under study are indeed dependent.

A concern, however, is that there are many features of the data that can account for a significant result, meaning that the nature of the association is unclear unless very restrictive assumptions are made. Another general concern is that true associations can be missed for various reasons to be reviewed.

Pearson's Correlation

To elaborate a bit, let ρ represent Pearson's correlation between the variables X and Y. The usual Student's t test of

$$H_0: \rho = 0$$

assumes that either X or Y has a normal distribution. The test statistic is

$$t = r\sqrt{\frac{n-2}{1-r^2}},$$

which is derived under the assumption that X and Y are independent, which in turn implies homoscedasticity. If there is heteroscedasticity, the wrong standard error is being used, which invalidates t as an appropriate test of $H_0: \rho = 0$. For example, Wilcox (2003) describes a situation where H_0 is true, yet the probability of rejecting increases as the sample size gets large due to heteroscedasticity. That is, t is sensitive to more than just situations where $\rho \neq 0$; it is sensitive to heteroscedasticity. So when rejecting with Student's t, it is reasonable to conclude that there is dependence, but the main reason for rejecting could be heteroscedasticity.

To complicate matters, there are at least five features of data that affect the magnitude of r:

1. The slope of the regression line (e.g., Barrett, 1974; Loh, 1987)

2. The magnitude of the residuals

3. Restriction of range

4. Curvature

5. Outliers

All of these features can affect power when testing $H_0 : \rho = 0$ with Student's t. Of course, if H_0 is rejected, and if $r > 0$, for example, a reasonable conclusion is that the least squares regression line is positive, but the least squares regression line is itself affected by outliers, curvature, and a restriction in range. And standard inferential techniques are well-known to be adversely affected by heteroscedasticity. In practical terms, when Pearson's correlation, or least squares regression, indicates an association, there is doubt about the nature of the association. Although $r > 0$ indicates that the least squares line has a positive slope, for the bulk of the points, a negative association might exist, which was missed due to outliers. Another result that is often encountered is that a positive (or negative) association is detected, but modern methods indicate this positive (or negative) association has a limited range. In particular, it is common to encounter a range of X values where an association is linear, but outside this range, no association exists at all. This represents a type of curvature that modern methods seem to suggest is common. Also, when Student's t test fails to reject $H_0 :$ $\rho = 0$, this might be because power is being affected by heteroscedasticity or one of the five features of data just listed that affect the magnitude of r. That is, when Pearson's correlation or least squares regression fails to detect an association, we cannot assume that no association exists.

Curvature

Another general concern when dealing with regression problems is curvature. Of course, a simple strategy is to consider a model where X is raised to some power—say, a. So in the one predictor case, a simple model would be

$$Y = \beta_0 + \beta_1 X^a,$$

where a is to be determined. And of course, more complex models, such as $Y = \beta_0 + \beta_1 X + \beta_2 X^a + \varepsilon$, could be used, where now a is some constant other than 1 or 0. But with multiple predictors,

it can be difficult determining which powers of the X values should be considered, and even in the single predictor case, this more general model might not be flexible enough.

As a simple illustration, consider the scatterplot in Figure 18.6, which is based on data taken from Hastie and Tibshirani (1990) and stems from a study involving diabetes in children. The goal is to predict log C-peptide levels at age of diagnosis. The line in Figure 18.6 is an example of what is called a smooth and was created with the R function lplot. Roughly, smooths are an attempt to approximate a regression line (or surface) without specifying a particular parametric form for the regression line. In more formal terms, assume that

$$Y = m(X) + \lambda(X)\varepsilon, \tag{1}$$

where $m(X)$ is some conditional measure of location, given X, such as the median or mean, and λ is some unknown function used to model heteroscedasticity. Smoothers are attempts at estimating $m(X)$. There are many variations, some of which are outlined later in this chapter. Note that in Figure 18.6, there appears to be a positive association for X (age) small, but the association appears to disappear for older children. This illustrates a situation that smoothers seem to suggest is common: There are regions of X values where there is an association with Y, but there are regions where no association appears to exist.

As another example, Denson and Earleywine (2006) conducted an investigation dealing generally with the amount of marijuana and alcohol consumed as well as a measure reflecting how often the participants engaged in acts of aggression (e.g., slapping, pushing, arguing, throwing things). Figure 18.7 shows an approximation of the regression surface based on a particular smooth.[5] As is evident, the regression surface does not appear to be a plane but rather a somewhat complex function of the two predictors (alcohol and marijuana use). The hypothesis that the regression surface is a plane can be tested using the method in Wilcox (2003, section 14.4.2; Wilcox, 2005a, section 11.5.1), which is rejected for the data used here when testing at the .05 level.[6]

Establishing Dependence

One possible way of beginning a regression study is simply to see whether there is evidence suggesting dependence among the variables

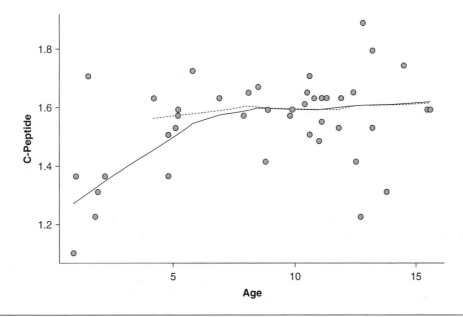

Figure 18.6   Two smooths of the diabetes data.

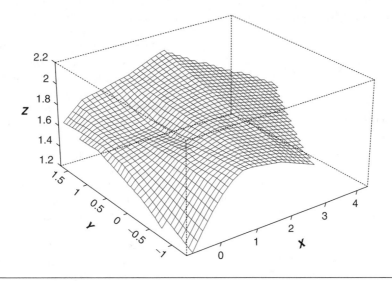

Figure 18.7   A smooth where the two predictors are marijuana and alcohol consumption, and the dependent variable is a measure of aggression.

under study. Based on the general model given by Equation 1, there are several ways this might be done. One broad approach is to consider methods that test

$$H_0: m(X) = \mu_y, \tag{2}$$

where μ_y is the population mean of Y. So the hypothesis is that the mean of Y, given X, does not vary with X. That is, the regression line is both straight and horizontal. The alternative hypothesis is that $m(X)$ varies with X, but just how it varies is not specified. Another general approach is to test the hypothesis of independence using some type of correlation coefficient. The three best-known correlations are Pearson's, Kendall's tau, and Spearman's rho. But there are some additional correlations that will be described.

Note that independence implies homoscedasticity. That is, in Equation 1, $\lambda \equiv 1$. So yet another way of trying to establish dependence is to test

$$H_0 : \lambda \equiv 1. \qquad (3)$$

An outline of several methods is provided that might be used to test Equation 3, but it is stressed that these methods are not recommended for justifying homoscedastic techniques. The reason is that it is unknown when these methods have enough power to justify the conclusion that homoscedasticity is approximately true. Rather, these methods are useful for establishing that a particular type of dependence exists.

Testing Equation 2

The hypothesis given by Equation 2 can be tested for the general case where there are $p \geq 1$ predictors, but for simplicity, the method is described only when $p = 1$. (For $p > 1$, see Wilcox, 2005a.) Based on a random sample of n points, the test statistic is computed as follows. Fix j and let

$$R_j = \frac{1}{\sqrt{n}} \sum I_i (Y_i - \overline{Y}),$$

where $\overline{Y}$ is the usual sample mean of the Y values. Then the test statistic is

$$D = \max |R_j|,$$

the maximum of all n of the $|R_j|$ values. The null hypothesis is rejected if $D \geq d_c$, where the critical value d_c is determined using what is called a wild bootstrap method.[7] By design, this wild bootstrap method is not sensitive to heteroscedasticity. For the data in Figure 18.4, testing Equation 2 with D, the p value is .016 versus .76 using Student's t test of $H_0 : \rho = 0$.

Robust Correlations

Yet another way of detecting dependence is to test the hypothesis that some robust correlation coefficient is equal to zero. There are two types of robust correlations. The first are M-type correlations that guard against outliers among the marginal distributions. Examples are Spearman's rho, Kendall's tau, and a Winsorized correlation.

(Details about this latter correlation can be found in Wilcox, 2003, 2005a. The R function wincor performs the calculations.) However, a criticism of these correlations is that they do not take into account the overall structure of the data when dealing with outliers. For example, it is possible to find no outliers among the X values (ignoring Y) and no outliers among the Y values (ignoring X), yet there are outliers that greatly influence not only Pearson's correlation but also Spearman's rho, Kendall's tau, and the Winsorized correlation.

Figure 18.8 provides an example. Twenty points were generated where $Y = X + \varepsilon$ and where X and ε are independent, standard normal random variables. Then two points were added at $(X, Y) = (2.1, -2.4)$. Clearly, these two points are unusual based on how the first 20 points were generated, and they are declared outliers by methods that take into account the overall structure of the data (such as the projection method previously mentioned). Yet, applying a boxplot rule to the X values, the value 2.1 is not flagged as an outlier, and similarly, for the Y values, -2.4 is not declared an outlier. Ignoring the two points at $(X, Y) = (2.1, -2.4)$, $r = .68$, and Student's t has a p value less than .001. But with the two outliers included, $r = .21$, and the p value is now .34. Kendall's tau has a p value of .40, and for Spearman's rho, the p value is .48. There are many correlation coefficients that take into account points flagged by outliers, where the outlier detection method takes into account the overall structure of the data. But in terms of testing the hypothesis of a zero correlation, currently only one of these correlations can be used—namely, the skipped correlation coefficient in Wilcox (2003, section 9.4.3). For the data in Figure 18.8, the test statistic is 2.2, and the .05 critical value is 2.6,[8] so the method does not quite reject at the .05 level.

Detecting Heteroscedasticity

Another possible approach to detecting dependence is to test the hypothesis of homoscedasticity, as given by Equation 3. In some cases, tests of the hypothesis of homoscedasticity can detect dependence when other methods find no association. Many methods have been proposed, but currently only three appear to perform well in simulations. One is a method derived by Koenker (1981). The second is based on a

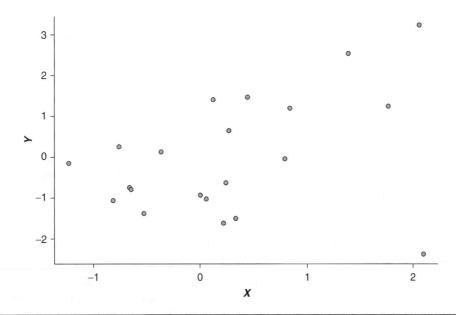

Figure 18.8   A scatterplot of points where there are no outliers among the X values (ignoring Y) or among the Y values (ignoring X), yet there are outliers that influence various correlation and regression methods.

quantile regression estimator. Using a method in Koenker and Bassett (1978), it is possible to estimate the γ quantile of Y, say Y_γ, given X, assuming that $Y_\gamma = \beta_{0\gamma} + \beta_{1\gamma}X$.[9] If, for example, $\beta_{1.2} \neq \beta_{1.8}$, there is heteroscedasticity and, in particular, a type of dependence. A method for testing $H_0 : \beta_{1.2} = \beta_{1.8}$ that performs well in simulations is described in Wilcox and Keselman (2006). Another approach is to estimate $m(X)$ using a smoother (described in the next section of this chapter), compute the resulting residuals, and then test the hypothesis that the absolute values of the residuals do not change with X (Wilcox, 2006).[10]

Smoothers

Another important tool, particularly in the preliminary stages of analysis, is a so-called smooth aimed at approximating $m(X)$. There are many variations (e.g., Efromovich, 1999; Eubank, 1999; Fan & Gijbels, 1996; Fox, 2001; Green & Silverman, 1993; Gyorfi, Kohler, Krzyzk, Walk, & Gyorfi, 2002; Hardle, 1990; Hastie & Tibshirani, 1990; Wilcox, 2005a). It is impossible to give complete details here, but it might help to at least describe the basic strategy behind these methods. Roughly, given X, the strategy is to use the X_i values close to X in an attempt to estimate Y. One of the earliest strategies (Cleveland, 1979) searches for the k closest points to X, k fixed, and then Y is estimated using weighted least squares, with the weights depending on how close each point is to X. A closely related approach is to use all points "close" to X. There are several ways in which closeness can be measured, but the many details go beyond the scope of this chapter.

Smoothers can be useful in at least three general ways. First, when $p = 1$ or 2, they provide a graphical check on the nature of the association. In particular, these graphs provide an informal check on whether a linear model provides an adequate summary of the data.[11] Second, they provide a flexible approach when the main goal is to estimate Y. Results comparing several methods, in terms of mean squared error and bias, can be found in Wilcox (2005a).[12]

A third appeal of smoothers is that they provide a flexible approach to certain inferential problems. For example, a well-known strategy for investigating regression interactions is to fit the model

$$Y = \beta_0 + \beta_1 X_1 + \beta_2 X_2 + \beta_3 X_1 X_2 + \varepsilon$$

and test the hypothesis $H_0: \beta_3 = 0$. An alternative approach, set in a broader context, is to fit the model

$$Y = \beta_0 + m_1(X_1) + m_2(X_2) + m_3(X_1 X_2) + \varepsilon$$

and then test the hypothesis

$$H_0: m_3(X_1 X_2) \equiv 0,$$

that is, the null hypothesis is that some function of the product $X_1 X_2$ is not needed to model the data.[13]

As an illustration, consider again the data in Figure 18.7. Using least squares regression and the standard Student's t test of $H_0: \beta_3 = 0$, the p value is .58. But the function adtest has a p value equal to .01.

A plot of how the regression line between Y and X_1 changes as a function of X_2 helps add perspective, and the R function kercon can be used to create such a plot. By default, it uses three values for X_2: the estimated quartiles. Figure 18.9 shows the output from kercon using the data in Figure 18.7. The line with the largest slope is the estimated regression line between Y and X_1, given that X_2 is equal to its (estimated) .25 quantile. The other line shows the regression when X_2 is equal to its median and .75 quantile. (These latter two regression lines are virtually identical.)

The method for studying interactions, just described, is a special case of a general approach to regression based on what are called generalized additive models. When there are p predictors, these methods fit the model

$$Y = m_1(X_1) + \ldots + m_p(X_p).$$

This is done by the R function adrun.[14] Explicit expressions for the functions $m_1 \ldots, m_p$ are not provided. The R function adtest can be used to test

$$H_0: m_k(X_k) = 0$$

for any k $(1 \leq k \leq p)$.

Robust Regression Estimators

In some cases, it might suffice to fit the model

$$Y = \beta_0 + \beta_1 X_1 + \ldots + \beta_p X_p + \varepsilon. \qquad (4)$$

What is needed now are estimators that avoid misleading results or poor power due to outliers

or heteroscedasticity. Numerous alternatives to the ordinary least squares estimator have been proposed, many of which can have a considerable practical advantage. Even under normality, several estimators can have substantially smaller standard errors than the least squares estimator when there is heteroscedasticity. Space limitations make it impossible to describe all of these estimators in great detail. A fairly comprehensive summary can be found in Wilcox (2005b), but even now, not all estimators are covered. The goal here is to outline a few estimators and comment on their relative merits.

Minimizing Functions of the Residuals

A general approach, which contains many estimators as a special case, is to estimate $\beta_0, \ldots,$ β_p with the values $b_0, \ldots, b_p$ that minimize some function of the residuals. More formally, let

$$r_i = Y_i - b_0 - b_1 X_1 - \ldots - b_p X_p$$

be the residuals corresponding to any choice for $b_0, \ldots, b_p$. Then determine the values $b_0, \ldots, b_p$ that minimize

$$\Sigma \psi(r_i)$$

for some function ψ to be determined. Least squares corresponds to $\psi(r_i) = r_i^2$. The choice $\psi(r_i) = |r_i|$ is called least absolute value (LAV) regression and predates least squares by about a half century. In contrast to least squares, LAV regression is aimed at estimating the median of Y, given X, as opposed to the mean. LAV regression provides protection from outliers among the Y values, but outliers among the X values can cause practical problems. Moreover, in terms of achieving a small standard error under heteroscedasticity, other estimators provide a distinct advantage.

Although the LAV regression estimator has some practical concerns, relative to other methods that might be used, an extension of this method, derived by Koenker and Bassett (1978), has practical value. In particular, they proposed a generalization of the LAV estimator aimed at estimating any quantile of Y, given X, as opposed to the median only. To estimate the qth quantile of Y given X, let

$$\rho_q(u) = u(q - I_{u < 0}),$$

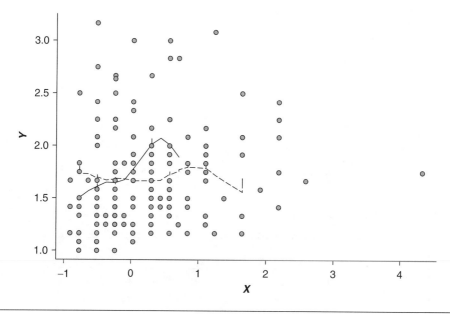

Figure 18.9   A plot used to summarize regression interaction.

where I is the indicator function. Then the regression line is determined by minimizing

$$\Sigma \rho_q(r).$$

So $q = .5$ corresponds to the least absolute value estimator and yields an estimate of the median of Y, given X.[15]

Williams et al. (2005) conducted a study dealing generally with the Porteus Maze Test (PMT), which is used to evaluate intelligence and executive functioning and screen for intellectual deficiency. A portion of the study dealt with the association between the so-called Q score resulting from the PMT and a measure of maladjustment for the participants in this study. The sample size was $n = 940$. Figure 18.10 shows a plot of the data. The three straight lines, starting from the bottom, are the .5, .8, and .9 quantile regression lines. So it appears that as we move from the median value of Y toward the higher quantiles, an association appears.

$H_0 : \beta_{1,9} = 0$ is rejected at the .05 level. (The slope of the least squares regression line is approximately the same as the slope for the .8 quantile.)

Theil-Sen Estimator

Momentarily focus on $p = 1$. The Theil (1950) regression estimator is based on the strategy of finding a value for the slope that makes Kendall's

correlation tau, between $Y_i - b_1 X_i$ and X_i, (approximately) equal to zero. Sen (1968) showed that this is tantamount to the following method. For any $i < i'$, for which $X_i \neq X_{i'}$, let

$$s_{ii'} = \frac{Y_i - Y_{i'}}{X_i - X_{i'}}.$$

The estimate of the slope is b_{1ts}, the median of all the slopes is represented by $S_{ii'}$. The intercept is estimated with

$$M_y - b_{1ts} M_x,$$

where M_y and M_x are the usual sample medians of the Y and X values, respectively.

There are at least three general ways the Theil-Sen estimator might be extended to two or more predictors (Wilcox, 2005b), but only one is described here. The strategy is to determine $b_1, \dots, b_p$ so that $\Sigma \hat{\tau}_j$ is approximately equal to zero, where $\hat{\tau}_j$ is the estimate of Kendall's tau between X_j and $Y - b_1 X_1 - \dots - b_p X_p$. Note that this approach can be used to generalize the Theil-Sen estimator by replacing Kendall's tau with any reasonable correlation coefficient.

A positive feature of the Theil-Sen estimator is that when there is heteroscedasticity, it can have a substantially smaller standard error than the ordinary least squares estimator. With $p = 1$, it can

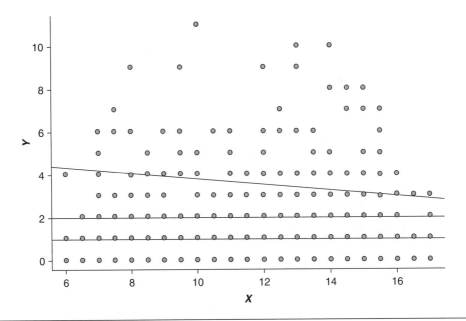

Figure 18.10   Quantile regression lines for the Porteus Maze data.

handle a fairly large proportion of outliers, but as p gets large, the number of outliers it can handle decreases. One way of possibly reducing this problem is to check for outliers, remove any that are found, and then apply the Theil-Sen estimator to the remaining data. One multivariate outlier detection method that seems to be relatively effective is called a projection method, which is described in Chapter 6 of Wilcox (2005b). But several other outlier detection methods probably have practical value. When using the projection method, followed by the Theil-Sen estimator, this will be called method OP.

M-Estimators

Yet another approach is based on what are called M-estimators. Roughly, rather than use the squared residuals, or the absolute value of the residuals, some other function of the residuals is used with the goal of being relatively insensitive to outliers and simultaneously performing well when in fact the usual error term is normal and homoscedastic. There are many variations. One version, which is called a generalized M-estimator, is computed as follows:

1. Set $k = 1$ and compute the residuals, $r_{i,k}$, based on some initial, such as least squares. Let M_k be equal to the median of the largest $n - p$ of the $| r_{i,k} |$, $\hat{\tau}_k = 1.48 M_k$, and let $e_{i,k} = r_{i,k} / \hat{\tau}_k$.

2. Form weights,

$$w_{i,k} = \frac{\sqrt{1 - h_{ii}}}{e_{i,k}} \psi \left(\frac{e_{i,k}}{\sqrt{1 - h_{ii}}} \right),$$

where $\psi(x) = \max(-K, \min(K, x))$ is Huber's ψ with

$$K = 2\sqrt{(p+1)/n}.$$

3. Use these weights to obtain a weighted least squares estimate and increase k by 1.

4. Repeat Steps 1 to 3 until convergence. That is, iterate until the change in the estimated parameters is small.[16]

This estimator can have a substantially smaller standard error than the ordinary least squares estimator under heteroscedasticity, but a criticism is that it provides relatively poor protection against outliers. Yet another M-estimator with excellent theoretical properties, which provides relatively good protection against outliers, was derived by Coakley and Hettmansperger (1993), but no details are given here.[17]

Inferential Methods

When testing the hypothesis

$$H_0 : \beta_1 = \ldots = \beta_p = 0, \tag{5}$$

or when testing hypotheses about the individual parameters, it currently seems that the most accurate inferential methods are based on a percentile bootstrap method. When computing a confidence interval for the individual parameters, the method is applied as follows.

1. Randomly sample with replacement n vectors of observations from $(X_{11}, \ldots, X_{1p}, Y_1), \ldots,$ $(X_{n1}, \ldots, X_{np}, Y_n)$.

   The result is called a bootstrap sample.

2. Estimate the slope parameters based on the bootstrap sample.

3. Repeat Steps 1 and 2 B times; $B = 600$ seems to suffice in terms of controlling the probability of a Type I error. For the jth parameter, label the results $b_{j1}^*, \ldots, b_{jB}^*$.

4. Put the $b_{j1}^*, \ldots, b_{jB}^*$ in ascending order and label the results $b_{j(1)}^* \leq \ldots \leq b_{j(B)}^*$.

5. The $1 - \alpha$ confidence interval for β_j is given by the middle 95% of these bootstrap estimates:

$$b_{j\,(l+1)}^*, b_{j\,(u)}^*,$$

where $l = \alpha B/2$, rounded to the nearest integer, and $u = B - 1$.

To compute a p value, let $\hat{p}^*$ be the proportion of bootstrap estimates greater than zero. The p value (for a two-sided test) is $2\min(\hat{p}^*, 1 - \hat{p}^*)$.[18]

No attempt is made to explain the complete computational details when testing Equation 5. Roughly, the strategy is to determine how deeply the zero vector is nested within the bootstrap cloud of estimated slopes. Interested readers can refer to Wilcox (2003, section 14.5.1) or Wilcox (2005a, section 11.1.1).[19]

More Illustrations

A practical issue is whether the choice of regression estimator ever matters, and if the answer is yes, which method should be used? In fairness, situations are encountered where using some alternative to least squares regression makes little difference. But the reality is that the choice of method can make a substantial difference. To complicate matters, the optimal method for detecting and describing an association is a complex function of several features of the data, including curvature, heteroscedasticity, skewness, and outliers. Moreover, the location of the outliers can be crucial as well.

As a simple illustration, consider again the data in Figure 18.4, but to demonstrate a point, suppose the goal is to estimate digit-naming speed based on a measure of word accuracy. Now the data appear in Figure 18.11. Also shown is a smooth, suggesting that the regression line is reasonably straight. The p value when using the usual least squares test of $H_0 : \beta_1 = 0$ is .76. It is evident that the top six points are outliers, and outliers among the outcome variable can result in low power. But simply removing them and applying the usual Student's t test to the remaining data is invalid from a technical point of view. Although we can restrict the range of the X values, restricting the range of the Y values and applying the usual t test results in using the wrong standard error. If instead we use the Theil-Sen estimator, the p value is .035. Using the Coakley-Hettmansperger estimator, the p value is .063.

As another illustration, consider the data in Table 6.3 of Wilcox (2003, p. 179). The outcome variable is a recall test score, and the predictor is a measure of marital aggression. Figure 18.12 shows a scatterplot, and the ragged line is a smooth based on the goal of estimating the mean of Y given X. As is evident, there appears to be curvature in the sense that there is a negative association for low measures of marital aggression, but the association appears to become negligible as marital aggression increases. The test of the hypothesis that the regression line is straight, which is based in part on the Theil-Sen estimator, has a p value of .008 (using the R function lintest). So in particular, this provides empirical evidence that an association exists. If we fit a least squares regression line with a quadratic term—namely, $Y = \beta_0 + \beta_1 X + \beta_2 X^2$—the hypothesis $H_0 : \beta_2 = 0$ is rejected at the .05 level, but when testing $H_0 : \beta_1 = 0$, the p value is .061 using the usual t test. The smooth line in Figure 18.12 is the resulting regression line. If, however, we test $H_0 : \beta_1 = 0$ using a method that allows heteroscedasticity (the S-PLUS function lsfitci was used), the p value is .013.

Prediction error refers to the ability to predict future Y values given X. Using the R or S-PLUS function regpre, which belongs to the library of R and S-PLUS functions to be described, estimates of prediction error indicate that the model $Y = \beta_0 + \beta_1 X$ performs better than the model $Y = \beta_0 + \beta_1 X + \beta_2 X^2$. (The so-called .632 estimator was used, details of which can be found in Wilcox, 2005a.) Note that the

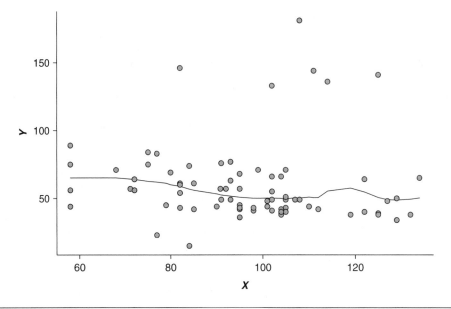

Figure 18.11   A plot of the reading data used to illustrate the effects of outliers among the dependent variable.

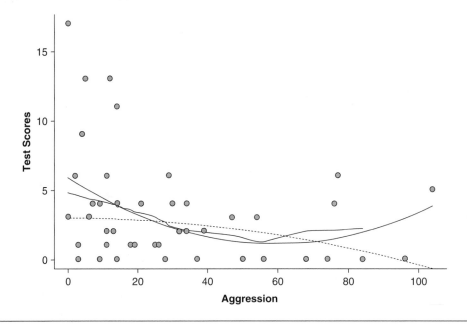

Figure 18.12   A scatterplot of the marital aggression data. Shown is a smooth and two regression lines.

quadratic model, used in conjunction with the least squares estimator, indicates that β_2 is positive, suggesting that as marital aggression increases, eventually recall test scores will increase as well, on average. But if we fit a quadratic model using the Theil-Sen estimator or the Coakley-Hettmansperger estimator, the estimate of β_2 is now negative. The dashed line in Figure 18.12 is the regression line based on the Theil-Sen estimator. Yet another possible description of the data is that there is heteroscedasticity. Tests of the assumption that there is homoscedasticity failed to reject, but this might be due to low power. So in summary, there is evidence of a negative association when the aggression measure is relatively low. But for relatively high aggression, there is doubt whether an association even exists. The main point here is that multiple techniques seem to be needed to get a good summary and understanding of the data.

Although the Theil-Sen estimator is designed to be robust to outliers, using something like a projection outlier detection method followed by the Theil-Sen estimator (method OP) can make a practical difference, but special methods are needed to test hypotheses (Wilcox, 2005b, p. 480). For the data in Figure 18.12, using the R (or S-PLUS) function opregpb, which is based in part on the Theil-Sen estimator, now the test of $H_0 : \beta_1 = 0$ has a p value of .008.

Software

A practical issue is being able to apply the modern methods, summarized here, with easy-to-use software. All of the methods that were described are readily applied using functions written in R or S-PLUS. These software packages are nearly identical and provide a powerful and flexible approach to data analysis that, in general, makes modern methods readily accessible. R is free and can be downloaded from cran.r-project.org. The R functions for applying the methods covered here are available in two files: Rallfunv1-v6 and Rallfunv2-v6.

These files can be downloaded from www-rcf.usc.edu/~rwilcox/. With Version 2.2.0 of R, store these files in C:\Program Files\R\R-2.2.0\. (So as new versions come out, 2.2.0 will be replaced by the new version number.) Once R is started, the command source ("Rallfunv1.v6") will incorporate all of the functions in the file Rallfunv1.v6 into your version of R. (The packages listed on the R Web site are another excellent source of functions aimed at applying recently developed methods.) When using S-PLUS, download the files allfunv1-v6 and allfunv2-v6 instead and again use the source command. Some of the functions relevant to the methods covered here are described in Wilcox (2003) and in Wilcox (2005a). But some of the newer functions are not covered in any book, so for convenience, the names of these functions are given here.

Concluding Remarks

There are many issues and methods beyond those covered in this chapter. For example, there is a well-known connection between regression and analysis of variance (ANOVA), it is known that standard ANOVA techniques suffer from practical problems illustrated here, and many modern methods are now available aimed at correcting known problems. The main message here is that many new tools are available for better detecting and understanding associations. Some of the more promising methods have been outlined here, but this is not to suggest that methods not described have no practical value. Moreover, advances continue to appear on a fairly regular basis. There is no agreed-on list of methods to try, let alone an order in which these methods should be used. A suggestion, in the early stages of an analysis, is to consider flexible methods for establishing an association, such as the wild bootstrap method, and to take advantage of modern graphical techniques, particularly smoothers. In the event a linear model seems appropriate, various robust estimators can be invaluable. Theil-Sen and robust M-estimators seem like good candidates, but certainly other estimators can offer distinct advantages in some situations.

Notes

1. For a more thorough discussion of outliers, see Chapter 14, this volume.
2. Generally, eliminating valid values that happen to be extreme induces dependence among the remaining observations. The result is that special methods are required to get valid estimates of standard errors. A relatively nontechnical explanation can be found in Wilcox (2003, section 4.9).
3. The R or S-PLUS function outpro applies this method. The polygon contains the central half of the data. For details on obtaining the library of R and S-PLUS functions used here, see "Software."
4. The R function scor can be used.
5. The R function lplot was used.
6. The R function is lintest.
7. The computations are simple, tedious, but readily performed with the R (or S-PLUS) function indt.
8. Computed with the R function scor.
9. The R or S-PLUS function qreg performs the calculations. When using R, you must first issue the command install.packages ("quantreg"), assuming

you are connected to the Web. This command makes the quantreg package permanently available. When using S-PLUS, this command is not needed.

10. The R functions that apply these methods are khomreg (using Koenker's method), qhomt (using the quantile regression approach), and rhom.

11. When creating plots with R, and when $p = 2$, it is necessary to activate the package akima with the command install.packages ("akima").

12. Two performed especially well. One is based on a simple extension of a method derived by Fan (1993), which is applied by the R function kerreg, and the other is a method given in Wilcox (2005a) and is applied by the R function runpd.

13. The method can be applied with the R function adtest.

14. Another option is to use a function built into R and S-PLUS called gam. To make this a bit easier, a function called gamplot has been supplied in the library of functions described at the end of this chapter. (When using R, you must also activate the packages akima and mgcv.)

15. When using R, access to an appropriate function is provided by the command install.packages ("quantreg"), assuming you are connected to the Web. Once this package is installed, the function rqfit can be used; it estimates the parameters and returns $1 - \alpha$ confidence intervals. By default, $\alpha = .05$ is used, but rqfit contains an argument alpha allowing the user to reset α. (The function rqfitpv will report p values, but it has a somewhat higher execution time than the function rqfit.) Setting the argument xout=T will eliminate outliers among the X values.

16. This estimation method can be applied with the R function bmreg.

17. Use the R function chreg.

18. The computations are performed by the R function regci and can be used with any regression estimator.

19. The R (or S-PLUS) function regtest performs the calculations.

References

Barrett, J. P. (1974). The coefficient of determination: Some limitations. *Annals of Statistics, 28,* 19–20.

Cleveland, W. S. (1979). Robust locally weighted regression and smoothing scatterplots. *Journal of the American Statistical Association, 74,* 829–836.

Coakley, C. W., & Hettmansperger, T. P. (1993). A bounded influence, high breakdown, efficient regression estimator. *Journal of the American Statistical Association, 88,* 872–880.

Denson, T. F., & Earleywine, M. (2006). *Alcohol, marijuana, hard drugs and aggression: A structural equation modeling analysis.* Manuscript submitted for publication.

Efromovich, S. (1999). *Nonparametric curve estimation: Methods, theory and applications.* New York: Springer-Verlag.

Eubank, R. L. (1999). *Nonparametric regression and spline smoothing.* New York: Marcel Dekker.

Fan, J. (1993). Local linear smoothers and their minimax efficiencies. *Journal of Statistics, 21,* 196–216.

Fan, J., & Gijbels, I. (1996). *Local polynomial modeling and its applications.* Boca Raton, FL: CRC Press.

Fox, J. (1997). *Applied regression analysis, linear models, and related methods.* Thousand Oaks, CA: Sage.

Fox, J. (2001). *Multiple and general nonparametric regression.* Thousand Oaks, CA: Sage.

Green, P. J., & Silverman, B. W. (1993). *Nonparametric regression and generalized linear models: A Rughness penalty approach.* Boca Raton, FL: CRC Press.

Gyorfi, L., Kohler, M., Krzyzk, A., Walk, H., & Gyorfi, L. (2002). *A distribution-free theory of nonparametric regression.* New York: Springer-Verlag.

Hampel, F. R., Ronchetti, E. M., Rousseeuw, P. J., & Stahel, W. A. (1986). *Robust statistics.* New York: John Wiley.

Hardle, W. (1990). *Applied nonparametric regression* (Econometric Society Monographs No. 19). Cambridge, UK: Cambridge University Press.

Hastie, T. J., & Tibshirani, R. J. (1990). *Generalized additive models.* New York: Chapman & Hall.

Huber, P. J. (1981). *Robust statistics.* New York: John Wiley.

Koenker, R. (1981). A note on studentizing a test for heteroscedasticity. *Journal of Econometrics, 17,* 107–112.

Koenker, R., & Bassett, G. (1978). Regression quantiles. *Econometrika, 46,* 33–50.

Loh, W.-Y. (1987). Does the correlation coefficient really measure the degree of clustering around a line? *Journal of Educational Statistics, 12,* 235–239.

Sen, P. K. (1968). Estimate of the regression coefficient based on Kendall's tau. *Journal of the American Statistical Association, 63,* 1379–1389.

Staudte, R. G., & Sheather, S. J. (1990). *Robust estimation and testing.* New York: John Wiley.

Theil, H. (1950). A rank-invariant method of linear and polynomial regression analysis. *Indagationes Mathematicae, 12,* 85–91.

Tukey, J. W. (1960). A survey of sampling from contaminated normal distributions. In I. Olkin, S. Ghurye, W. Hoeffding, W. Madow, & H. Mann (Eds.), *Contributions to probability* and statistics (pp. 448–485). Stanford, CA: Stanford University Press.

Wilcox, R. R. (2003). *Applying contemporary statistical techniques*. San Diego: Academic Press.

Wilcox, R. R. (2004). Inferences based on a skipped correlation coefficient. *Journal of Applied Statistics, 31*, 131–144.

Wilcox, R. R. (2005a). Estimating the conditional variance of Y, given X, in a simple regression model. *Journal of Applied Statistics, 32*, 495–502.

Wilcox, R. R. (2005b). *Introduction to robust estimation and hypothesis testing* (2nd ed.). San Diego: Academic Press.

Wilcox, R. R. (2006). Testing the hypothesis of a homoscedastic error term in simple, nonparametric regression. *Educational and Psychological Measurement, 66*, 85–92.

Wilcox, R. R., & Keselman, H. J. (2006). Detecting heteroscedasticity in a simple regression model via quantile regression slopes. *Journal of Statistical Computation and Simulation, 76*, 705–712.

Williams, N., Stanchina, J., Bezdjian, S., Skrok, E., Raine, A., & Baker, L. (2005). *Porteus' mazes and executive function in children: Standardize administration and scoring, and relationships to childhood aggression and delinquency.* Unpublished manuscript, Department of Psychology, University of Southern California.

PART IV

BEST PRACTICES IN QUANTITATIVE METHODS

19

RESAMPLING

A Conceptual and Procedural Introduction

CHONG HO YU

WHAT IS RESAMPLING?

Resampling is a controversial methodology because its inference is based on repeated sampling within the same *finite* sample instead of an *infinite* theoretical distribution, which is why this methodology is called resampling. Sometimes, resampling techniques are categorized as nonparametric procedures (e.g., Cytel Corp., 2004; SPSS, 2006) because they were originally developed as distribution-free procedures that did not require parametric assumptions. Thus, in some texts, the status of resampling is defined as a reactionary force against parametric procedures. It is unfortunate that many texts introduce resampling in opposition to parametric methods, and the merits of resampling are usually defined by its immunity to violations of parametric assumptions, such as departure from normality and unequal variances. The following statement made by Fisher (1925) is commonly cited as an indication of the inadequacy of conventional procedures and as the rationale for replacing legacy statistics with resampling:

The traditional machinery of statistical processes is wholly unsuited to the needs of practical research. Not only does it take a cannon to shoot a sparrow, but it misses the sparrow! The elaborate mechanism built on the theory of infinitely large samples is not accurate enough for simple laboratory data. Only by systematically tackling small problems on their merits does it seem possible to apply accurate tests to practical data. (p. vii)

Although in his later years, Fisher reinterpreted some components of significance testing, there is no evidence that he had any intention of abandoning the theory of infinitely large samples altogether. The above statement was made in the context of biological sciences. Therefore, at most, Fisher's statement expressed the limitations of the theory of infinitely large samples in certain applications.

It is my conviction that the confrontation between parametric methods and resampling is unnecessary. Actually, violations of certain parametric assumptions do not automatically

Author's Note: Special thanks to Dr. Sandra Andrews, Dr. Zeynep Kilic, Dr. Jason Osborne, and Mr. Charles Kaprolet for reviewing this manuscript and providing me with valuable input.

invalidate use of any parametric tests. There are many remedies to address the issue of assumption violations, such as robust procedures (as presented in Chapter 18), but there is no convincing evidence to show that resampling is the best way to go. Hence, resampling should be treated as one of many options in quantitative methodologies, and researchers are encouraged to employ multiple ways to triangulate the data.

Second, as with any research methodology, resampling has both merits and limitations. Contrary to popular belief, some resampling techniques are also affected by parametric assumptions. The permutation test, in which observations are shuffled across groups, assumes that observations in different groups are exchangeable under the null hypothesis. Thus, the assumptions of equal variance and independence of observations are also applicable to the permutation t test. In this sense, the permutation t test has the same weakness as the classical Student's t test. Taking the above two points into consideration, this chapter by no means attempts to declare the superiority of resampling over parametric procedures. Last, resampling should not be equated with nonparametric methods because today parametric bootstrap methods are broadly available (Chernick, 1999).

Resampling is in fact a collection of statistical techniques. On some occasions, it is considered an extension of existing procedures, while at other times, it is not, depending on the software used.[1]

Regardless of how different software developers implement resampling, this methodology is a way of looking at data analysis that can be applied to virtually *all* procedures. Let us take exploratory data analysis (EDA) as a metaphor. Some researchers still maintain that there is a sharp distinction between exploratory and classical confirmatory analyses, but this demarcation will become blurred if EDA is akin to a detective mentality that is applicable to all scenarios. Specifically, results yielded from confirmatory procedures can also be taken as tentative conclusions leading to further inquiry, and there is no reason that data visualization, a common tool in EDA, cannot be employed in classical analysis. In a similar vein, resampling should be treated as a *reasoning mode that augments classical probabilistic inferences.* For example, at first glance, factor analysis, a conventional multivariate procedure, is unrelated to resampling, but parallel analysis, a method of estimating eigenvalues based on repeated sampling, can be used to determine the proper number of factors to be retained (Horn, 1965).

TYPES OF RESAMPLING

There are at least four major types of resampling. Although today they are unified under a common theme, it is important to note that these four techniques were developed by different people at different periods of time for different purposes.

1. Permutation test: Also known as the randomization exact test, the permutation test is a type of statistical significance test basing its inference on an empirical distribution obtained by permuting all possible values of the test statistic. This test was developed by R. A. Fisher (1960), the founder of classical statistical testing. Later, this test was refined by Freeman and Halton (1951) and promoted by Pitman (1937, 1938), Dwass (1957), and Chung and Fraser (1958). However, Fisher eventually lost interest in the permutation method because there were no computers back then to automate such a laborious method. The original goal of developing the randomization exact test was to explore an alternative to theoretical distributions as the foundation for probabilistic inferences. Fisher recognized the usefulness of an empirically generated sampling distribution, but he was forced to rely on the theoretical sampling due to limited computational resources at that time. Hence, the exact test was conceptualized as a forward-looking methodology (Box, 1978).

2. Cross-validation: In cross-validation, a sample is randomly divided into two or more subsets, and test results are validated by comparing across subsamples. Simple cross-validation was proposed by Kurtz (1948) as a remedy for the Rorschach test, a form of personality test that was criticized by psychometricians for its lack of data normality. Based on Kurtz's simple cross-validation, Mosier (1951) developed double cross-validation. Later, Stone (1974) and Geisser (1975) promoted the idea of cross-validation as a tool to verify statistical predictions. Finally, double cross-validation was extended to multicross validation by Krus and Fuller (1982). The major goal of cross-validation is to avoid overfitting, which is a common problem when modelers try to account for every structure in one data set. As a remedy, cross-validation double-checks whether the alleged fitness is too good to be true (Larose, 2005). In short, the objective of cross-validation is to verify replicability and stability of results.

3. *Jackknife:* Jackknife is a step beyond cross-validation, in which the same test is performed repeatedly removing one subject each time. In this technique, the deleted subject is added back into the sample, and then another one is chosen for removal. This is also known as the Quenouille-Tukey jackknife because this tool was invented by Maurice Quenouille (1949) and later developed by John W. Tukey (1958). As the father of EDA, John Tukey attempted to use jackknife to explore how a model is influenced by subsets of observations when outliers are present. Mosteller and Tukey (1977) stated that jackknife is an all-purpose statistical tool, used as a substitute for specialized tools that may not be available, just as the Boy Scout's trusty tool serves so variedly. Jackknife was developed to assess stability and bias of estimates rather than performing hypothesis testing, though the variance estimate obtained through this method can be easily used to define confidence intervals or to do standard hypothesis testing (Rodgers, 1999).

4. *Bootstrap:* "Bootstrap" means that one available sample gives rise to many others by repeated sampling (a concept reminiscent of pulling yourself up by your own bootstraps). This technique was invented by Efron (1979, 1981, 1982, 1983) and further developed by Efron and Tibshirani (1993). The bootstrap procedure was originally developed as a means of estimating "statistical accuracy." However, the objective of "statistical accuracy" is usually misunderstood as obtaining precision in parameter estimation or the true parameters (how right it is); rather, the goal is more about examining bias and variability (how wrong it could be).

Simon (2001) argued that cross-validation and jackknife do not fit the definition of resampling. According to Simon, resampling, as the name implies, must involve reuse of samples. However, cross-validation is simply a one-time sample splitting, and thus no data are reused. Similarly, jackknife reduces the sample size in each recomputation and never uses the data

in their totality for each calculation. Since systematic reuse of the available data is the central theme of resampling, cross-validation and jackknife are not qualified to be classified into the resampling arena. Hence, this chapter will concentrate on permutation tests and bootstrapping only. Nevertheless, this does not imply that cross-validation and jackknife have no merits. As a matter of fact, cross-validation is still a common practice in factor analysis. To be specific, usually a factor modeler divides the data set into two subsets. Exploratory factor analysis is conducted with the first subsample for proposing a factor structure, whereas confirmatory factor analysis is employed to verify whether the factor pattern holds in the second subsample (Mulaik, 1987). By the same token, cross-validation is still popular in the context of model building, including the time-series models, regression models, and discrimination models (Chernick, 1999). Also, it is a common practice for data miners to split the data into a training set, in which a provisional model is proposed, and a validation set, in which the fitness is evaluated (Han & Kamber, 2006; Larose, 2005). In some applications, jackknife and bootstrapping are fused together. For example, in the resample library of Splus (Insightful, Inc., 2005), there is a function named "Jack after boot." As the name implies, jackknife is used first to subset the data, and then bootstrapping is employed to resample from the subset. In the following sections, permutation tests and bootstrapping will be illustrated with concrete examples. The beauty of resampling comes from its conceptual clarity and procedural simplicity. Henceforth, readers will not encounter equation-dense pages in this chapter.

Permutation Test

The permutation test is also known as the randomization exact test, exact nonparametric inference, or permutational inference (Cytel Corp., 2004). The best-known type of permutation test is Fisher's exact test or Fisher's randomization test. Edgington (1995) maintained that there is a subtle difference between permutation tests and randomization tests. For randomization tests, data permutation generates hypothetical outcomes or counterfactual scenarios for the same subjects under alternative random assignments. Swapping observations between two groups in a randomized, two-independent-sample *t* test is an example. For permutation tests, data permutation does not create hypothetical outcomes for the same subjects but outcomes for other subjects randomly drawn from identical infinite populations. An example is testing the value of the location parameter of a distribution using a series of observations from that distribution. However, in many situations, the two terms are used interchangeably.

As the name implies, Fisher's randomization test was invented by R. A. Fisher, and the subsequent development of all other variants of the permutation test is based on Fisher's idea. The origin of Fisher's exact test is a very interesting story, and it is worthwhile to illustrate the concept of permutation tests through the telling of this story.

Lady Tasting Tea

In 1920, R. A. Fisher shared a story with his colleagues about how he resolved a statistical question in an innovative way. Once, Fisher met a lady who insisted that her tongue was sensitive enough to detect a subtle difference between a cup of tea with the milk being poured first and a cup of tea with the milk being added later. Fisher was skeptical, and he presented eight cups of tea to this lady. Four of these eight cups were "milk first," and four others were "tea first." All cups were arranged in a random order, yet the lady correctly identified six out of the eight cups (Salsburg, 2001). The test results are summarized in Table 19.1.

Did the woman really have a super-sensitive tongue? This question can be reformulated as a statistical problem with the following two hypotheses:

- Null hypothesis: The order in which milk or tea is poured into a cup and the lady's detection of the order are independent.
- Alternate hypothesis: The lady can correctly tell the order in which milk or tea is poured into a cup.

In this case, the alternative hypothesis is one-sided. Although it is possible that either the woman's detection is better than guessing by chance alone or that her detection is worse than random guessing, Fisher was only interested in knowing whether her detection was better than guessing by luck. One way to approach this problem is to employ Pearson's chi-square test of goodness of fit, in which a *p* value of .0786 can be obtained. However, in order to legitimately use the chi-square test, the minimum expected cell count for all cells should be at least 5 (Cochran, 1954), and obviously, this small data set does not satisfy the minimum requirement. The Pearsonian research tradition, which will be discussed in a later section, insists on inferences using the data at hand and confines scientific inquiry to mere description of the observable events. In this sense, the insufficient data from the "lady tasting tea" experiment would urge the researcher to stop right here.

The story did not end here, of course. As a *counterfactual* thinker, Fisher attempted to make this seemingly untestable problem testable by proposing that for eight cups of tea, one could enumerate all possible random guesses and then calculate how many of those guesses would yield six or more correct responses. It is important to emphasize that the following illustration is presented with Microsoft Excel, which was not available at Fisher's time. For an alternative way of conceptualizing the "lady tasting tea" problem, please consult the chapter entitled "Introduction to the Fisher Tradition" in Maxwell and Delaney (2004).

The strategy of solving this problem is as simple as follows:

1. Use the factorial formula to calculate the number of all possibilities.

2. Permute the order of all cups *n*! times and sum the number of matched pairs to construct an empirical distribution.

Table 19.1   Test Results of Lady Tasting Tea

Guess/Actual	Pour Milk First	Pour Tea First	Row Total
Guess milk first	3	1	4
Guess tea first	1	3	4
Column total	4	4	8

3. Compute the exact probability by comparing the observed data to the empirical distribution.

Fisher did not have a computer, and thus this tedious permutation was done by hand. Today we have software to walk through thousands of permutations in a few seconds. Readers are encouraged to download "Resampling Stat for Excel" (RSE; Resampling Stat, 2004) from www.resample.com and follow the instructions below. By the end of the tutorial, you will know exactly what the exact test means.

1. RSE requires the *Analysis ToolPak* and *Analysis ToolPak—VBA* Extensions to run. Please make sure to check both items in *Tools/Ad-ins,* close Excel, and then reopen Excel. In addition, the macro feature in Excel must be enabled. After installing and configuring RSE, open a new Excel spreadsheet. The add-in functions for resampling will appear. For this tutorial, we need only three add-in functions: *Shuffle,* which is symbolized by the icon "S"; *Repeat and Score,* signified by "RS"; and *Histogram,* depicted by a histogram icon.

2. In column A of the Excel spreadsheet, enter "Actual" as the header. It denotes that there are actually four cups of tea with the milk being poured first and four with the tea being poured first. Next, enter the string "Milk" from A2 to A5 and the string "Tea" from A6 to A9. You can randomize the cup order, as Fisher did, but this is not required because the software package can randomize it in the "guessing" column (see Figure 19.1).

3. Enter "Guess" in B1 as the header. This denotes all the possibilities of random guessing. Select A2 to A9 and then select the function "Shuffle." A2 to A9 will appear in the input range. For the top cell of output range, enter

or select B2. For the number of cells in output range, enter 8. Then click OK. The Shuffle function will randomly select values from A2 to A9 without replacement and put them into B2 to B9. This simulates random guessing by the lady tasting tea. Please keep in mind that shuffling is *resampling without replacement.* In other words, after a value from column A is drawn, that particular value will not be put back into column A. In this way, you will obtain exactly four occurrences of "Milk" and four occurrences of "Tea" in column B; otherwise, every value can be drawn more than one time, and column B could be populated by eight counts of "Milk" or eight counts of "Tea."

4. Enter the formula "=IF(A2=B2,1,0)" into C1. Select C1 and then drag the mouse downward until C9 is reached. Formulas from C2 to C9 will compare whether the value of each cell in column A is the same as that in column B. In C10, use the "Summation" function in Excel to sum the values from C2 to C9. In this simulation, there are six matches between the actual and the random guess (see Figure 19.2).

5. Select C10 and invoke the function "Repeat and Score." You can simulate 1,000 trials (see Figure 19.3). If you have a fast computer, you can simulate more trials. But please keep in mind that by permuting a different number of possibilities, you may obtain a slightly different result.

6. By repeating the simulations, sometimes we obtain more than six matches, but sometimes we have fewer. A distribution can be constructed using the function called *Histogram.* This distribution is called the *empirical distribution* because it is data driven. It is also known as the *reference set* or the *reference class* because the probability of obtaining the observed data can be computed with reference to this distribution.

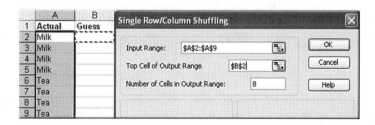

Figure 19.1   Simulation of random guess of the milk-tea order.

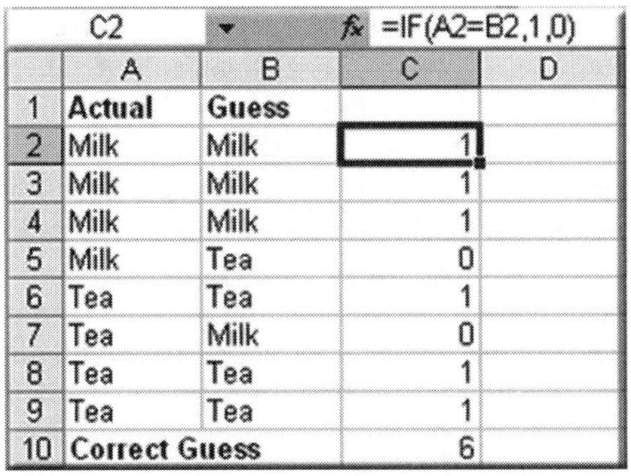

C2	fx =IF(A2=B2,1,0)		
	A	B	C
1	Actual	Guess	
2	Milk	Milk	1
3	Milk	Milk	1
4	Milk	Milk	1
5	Milk	Tea	0
6	Tea	Tea	1
7	Tea	Milk	0
8	Tea	Tea	1
9	Tea	Tea	1
10	Correct Guess		6

Figure 19.2 Matching between the actual and the random guess resulting from one shuffle.

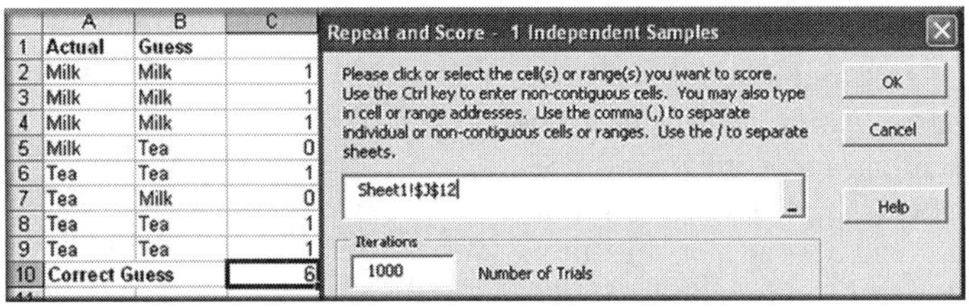

Figure 19.3 Repeat the same type of shuffling and score the results.

Click on column A and then click on the histogram icon. All 1,000 numbers in column A will be put into the data input range. Alternatively, you can enter "A1:A1000" into the data input range. Select C1 as your output area for the frequency table and accept the default value for other options. Then click *Draw.*

7. The frequency table shows that there are 218 cases in which six out of eight pairs are matched, and there are 25 cases in which all pairs are matched (you may not get the same number). In other words, by chance alone, 243 (218 + 25) out of 1,000 cases result in six or more correct answers. This results in a *p* value of .243 (243/1,000), which is quite different from the one-sided chi-square test result of .0786 (see Figure 19.4). The *p* value obtained from the exact test is called the *exact* p *value* or the *permutational* p *value.*

As demonstrated above, the original exact test invented by Fisher is used with a 2 × 2 contingency table. Obviously, its application is too limited, and thus Fisher's exact test was extended to unordered R × C tables by Freeman and Halton (1951). Hence, the exact test is also known as the Fisher-Freeman-Halton test. Many other permutation tests are built upon the same simple counterfactual inference proposed by Fisher.

Example of Verifying Survey Findings Using Permutation Testing

It is a good learning experience to walk through the entire permutation process as demonstrated in the preceding example. In order to obtain quick results, many software packages today perform permutations behind the scenes, and usually all the user needs to do is simply select a test procedure. A similar example to the "lady tasting tea" is demonstrated with the use of StatXact (Cytel Corp., 2004). In 2005, in order for Arizona State University (ASU) to redesign the physical infrastructure of its downtown campus and evaluate the strategy of using instructional technology, a survey was distributed to collect information relevant to its readiness for implementing a one-to-one computing model. A one-to-one computing model is an instructional technology application that enables all users to have their own mobile multimedia digital

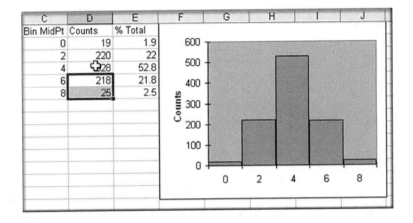

Bin MidPt	Counts	% Total
0	19	1.9
2	220	22
4	528	52.8
6	218	21.8
8	25	2.5

Figure 19.4   Frequency counts and histogram of the number of correct guesses.

devices, such as iPods used for downloading Podcast lectures. Despite sending follow-up letters, the overall response rate of this survey was just 15%, with a total sample of 463 participants (Table 19.2).

One of the survey questions was concerned with the number of students who owned an iPod. The results are indicated in Table 19.3.

The chi-square test was conducted on the ownership frequency of iPods to examine whether there was a significant difference between ownership of iPods across colleges. The p value yielded from the chi-square test is .12, and thus the difference is considered to be nonsignificant. However, since the response rate is low relative to the population (see Table 19.2), the ASU team was highly skeptical of the conclusion. As a countermeasure, Fisher's exact test

was also conducted for verification. In StatXact, after the frequency was entered into a 2 × 2 table, it was found that Fisher's exact test yields the exact p value as .14, and thus the ASU team stood by the finding (DiGangi et al., in press).

Do We Need Tests on the Entire Population?

The preceding examples are illustrated with small data sets. Indeed, the capability of testing untestable problems, such as small n scenarios, is one of the merits of permutation tests. However, it is a mistake to assume that resampling cannot be used when the sample size is large. Sometimes, large data sets result from the situation that one has accessibility to an entire population. It is a common perception that no statistical analyses

Table 19.2   Sample Pool, Number of Respondents, and Response Rate

College	Total Students	Percentage Responded	Number of Respondents	Response Rate (%)
NU (nursing)	1,561	50.63	184	12
PP (public programs)	1,522	49.37	279	18
Total	3,083	100	463	15

Table 19.3   Ownership of iPods by College Students

College	Own iPod	Do Not Own iPod	Total
NU (nursing)	59	125	184
PP (public programs)	71	208	279
Total	130	333	463

are needed when the full population data are available. First, when the "true" parameters are *certainly* known, it does not seem to make any sense to estimate the confidence interval, which is an expression of *uncertainty*. Second, the aim of hypothesis testing is to make inferences from the sample to the population. However, the knowledge of the population is *direct* rather than inferential.

Whether the population parameter is an invariant constant is highly debatable because even *within* the same subject, there is a variability of the same construct if repeated measures are conducted. Frick (1998) used an example of the "Planet of Forty" to illustrate why inferences to a finite population are still necessary. Imagine that on the Planet of Forty, there are only 40 residents, and they live forever but cannot reproduce offspring. Imagine that their memory can be erased so that a treatment effect will not carry over to the next study. When they are split into two groups and are exposed to two different treatments, are the two mean scores considered fixed parameters? The answer is no. A month later, when the researcher wipes out what they have learned in the first experiment and asks them to start the experiment over, the scores may vary. This is one of the reasons why statistical tests are still useful even if the researcher has full accessibility to the population.

Another perspective on this issue is the concept of an *infinite population*. The Planet of Forty is fictitious; in reality, there is no finite population. When a policy maker at a university conducts a campuswide survey of all university students, the researcher should be aware that the data are nothing more than a snapshot of an ever-changing population, in which freshmen keep coming in and graduates keep leaving. Another example can be found in the debate of university faculty salary equity studies. Haignere, Lin, Eisenberg, and McCarthy (1996) suggested that use of statistical significance is improper when the complete population of faculty members is studied. To counter this argument, Dizinno (1999) stated that the current faculty group is only a sample that reflects an ongoing reconfiguration of the population. In other words, they are a sample of the population, not the complete population. Hence, salary-setting policies must be based on inferential statistics rather than on "true" parameters.

Conducting a statistical test on the entire population is trickier than one might expect. When a researcher obtains a sample from a population whose properties are unknown to us, the researcher may justify using classical procedures by saying that the sample distribution does not significantly depart from normality and other parametric assumptions, given that the sample is large. But, when the researcher has access to the entire population, obvious violations of assumptions can occur. Permutation tests are a convenient way to perform tests on populations (Hesterberg, Monaghan, Moore, Clipson, & Epstein, 2003), for in resampling, it does not matter whether the data are a sample or the entire population. The resampling simulates, by chance alone, what the distribution would look like regardless of whether the source of variation comes from within-subject variability or between-group variability. If the population data set is too large, the researcher can employ Monte Carlo–based inferences instead of exact inferences.

BOOTSTRAPPING

In classical procedures, parameter estimation requires certain parametric assumptions, but bootstrapping replaces the unknown population distribution with known empirical distributions, which are also called bootstrap distributions. The bootstrap methods began to attract more and more attention after Diaconis and Efron (1983) published an essay explaining bootstrapping using layman's terms in *Scientific American*. As discussed in this chapter's introduction, the beauty of resampling is its conceptual clarity. Resampling is highly accessible to many researchers whose primary concern is the content area of psychology or biology rather than mathematics. More important, as many permutation tests are built on Fisher's counterfactual reasoning, basic bootstrapping principles also pave the way to advanced bootstrapping.

In the following example, let us revisit the simple yet intellectually powerful example depicted by Diaconis and Efron (1983) in *Scientific American*. Please notice that in the following, the bootstrap method will be illustrated with the use of Splus (Insightful, Inc., 2005), which was not available at the time of Diaconis and Efron's writing. Henceforth, the demonstration below is slightly different from that in the *Scientific American* essay.

In their article, Diaconis and Efron (1983) asked readers to consider a group of 15 law schools, for which the academic achievements of each freshman are measured in terms of the average undergraduate grade point average (GPA) and the average score on the Law School Admission Test (LSAT) (Table 19.4). This small data set indicates that the correlation between GPA and LSAT scores is .776.[2]

Given Table 19.4, how confidently can the researcher assert that there is a positive correlation between GPA and LSAT in the law student population? Diaconis and Efron (1983) proposed the following strategy:

1. The original sample is duplicated 1 billion times. As a result, we have 15 billion observations instead of 15. This expanded sample is treated as a *virtual population* or a *proxy population.*

2. Samples are drawn from this virtual population to verify the estimators. Unlike permutation methods in which observations are *resampled without replacement,* the bootstrap employs *resampling with replacement.*

Table 19.4   Law School Data Used by Diaconis and Efron (1983)

LSAT	GPA
576	3.39
635	3.30
558	2.81
578	3.03
666	3.44
580	3.07
555	3.00
661	3.43
651	3.36
605	3.13
653	3.12
575	2.74
545	2.76
572	2.88
594	2.96

3. *Bias* is checked by comparing the statistic of the original sample against that of the empirical distribution. The bias estimated by the bootstrap method is the mean of the empirical distribution minus the statistic for the original sample.

It is highly advisable for readers to walk through the process using the full version or the trial version of Splus, as explained below:

1. Like RSE to Excel, the Resample Library is an external add-in module to Splus. After downloading the Resample Library and opening Splus, select *Load Library* from *File* and choose "resample."

2. Enter the law school data into a data set.

3. Select *Correlation/Resample* from *Statistics/Data Summary.*

4. Go to the tab *Bootstrap.* Check the boxes *Perform Bootstrap, Both Distribution and QQ, Percentiles, BCa Confidence Interval.* Set *Number of Resamples* to 1,000. Then click OK.

During the bootstrapping process, the computer randomly selects 15 pairs of scores 1,000 times. At the end, these 1,000 resamplings generate an empirical distribution as shown in Figure 19.5. As you would expect, sometimes the resample yields a low correlation coefficient. In some extreme cases, the correlation is close to zero, but most of the time, it returns a high correlation. The mean of these correlation coefficients is depicted as a dotted line, which almost overlaps the original observed correlation coefficient, 0.776, shown as a solid line.

Besides the graphical output, the bootstrap procedure also returns numeric output (Table 19.5). In this example, there are three sets of numbers. The first is the summary statistics based on the observed sample. The correlation coefficient based on the original 15 pairs of scores is .776, while the mean of the correlation coefficients that resulted from 1,000 resamples is .77. The bias (observed − mean) is just −0.005869. The second set informs us about the percentiles of the empirical distribution. The interval between the 2.5th and 97.5th percentiles of the empirical distribution is called the *bootstrap percentile confidence interval* (BPCI). According to the BPCI, the correlation coefficient

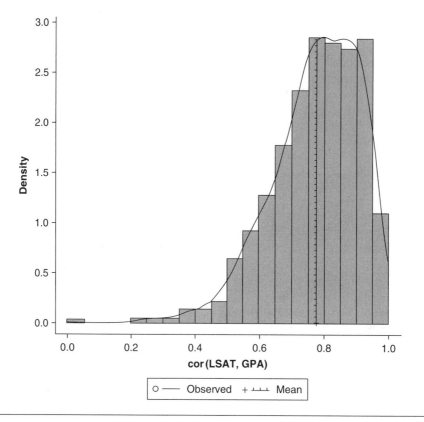

Figure 19.5   Empirical distribution of correlation coefficients.

Table 19.5   Bootstrap Confidence Intervals

Number of Replications: 1000				
Summary Statistics: Observed Mean Bias SE				
cor(LSAT,GPA)	0.7764	0.7705	−0.005869	0.1339
Percentiles:	2.5%	5%	95%	97.5%
cor(LSAT,GPA)	0.4521574	0.5160707	0.9469423	0.9593821
BCa Confidence Intervals:	2.5%	5%	95%	97.5%
cor(LSAT,GPA)	0.3221232	0.4134285	0.9249759	0.9419221

between LSAT and GPA for the law student population could range from .452 to .959.

The graphical output indicates that the empirical distribution is skewed, and thus we need the third numeric output, the *bootstrap bias-corrected accelerated* (BCa) *confidence interval*. The BCa confidence interval's endpoints are percentiles of the empirical distribution that are adjusted to correct for bias and skewness. If the statistic is skewed in either direction, the BCa bias correction adjusts the endpoints of the interval. According to the BCa confidence interval, in this example, the population correlation coefficient spreads from .32 to .94. It is important to note that 1,000 resamples are insufficient for the BCa confidence interval to achieve high accuracy. This number of resamples is chosen here merely for a faster computation. Five thousand or more would yield a better result (Hesterberg et al., 2003).

Advantages of Bootstrapping in One-Sample Problem and Assumptions

Permutation methods require at least two samples or one sample with two or more measures:

for example, permuting observations in two groups for conducting randomized two-sample exact *t* test and shuffling orders for testing independence between "actual" and "guess" in Fisher's tea example. If there is only one sample or one measure, it is virtually impossible to perform permutations. The only exception is to permute observations from one sample to test for a location parameter.

But bootstrap can still be employed in a one-sample problem. Take the law school data as an example again. Before computing correlation coefficients, researchers who like to scrutinize data sets through data visualization and EDA may want to look at the attributes of the distribution of each variable, such as the five-point summary and the trimmed mean, which is less affected by extreme scores. For this purpose, the Splus user can select *Summary Statistics/Resample* from *Statistics/Data Summary*. Not surprisingly, only bootstrap is available for this resampling because shuffling scores within the same variable will not generate any variability.

Let us examine the LSAT scores. After drawing 1,000 resamples, you can see six empirical distributions: the first quartile, the mean, the trimmed mean, the median, the third quartile, and the standard deviation. To save space, these graphics are omitted here, but the numeric output is depicted in Table 19.6. As with the law school example that estimates the confidence interval for correlation, these various bootstrap results inform us about the confidence intervals of the preceding six descriptive statistics.

Following Diaconis and Efron (1983), this chapter uses examples for computing descriptive statistics, such as correlation coefficient and summary statistics. Nevertheless, the bootstrap methods can also be used in inferential statistics. It is crucial to mention that while permutation tests exhaust all possibilities and obtain the exact *p* value, bootstrapping constructs the empirical distribution by many, but not all, combinations. Thus, the *p* value yielded from the bootstrap method is not exact. Put another way, the reference set for permutation tests is a closed set if the researcher exhausts all possibilities. But this is not the case in bootstrapping. The reference set, or the empirical distribution, will change if the researcher increases the number of resamples from 1,000 to 5,000.

Last but not least, permutations test hypotheses concerning distributions, whereas bootstrap methods test hypotheses concerning parameters. Thus, bootstrapping entails less stringent assumptions. To be specific, when a test is conducted in a permutation fashion, it is assumed that all observations come from the same distribution, but this assumption is not needed for the bootstrap method (Good, 2000).

Limitations in Small Data Sets

Criticisms against bootstrapping to some extent are understandable because overly simplistic illustrations using small data sets may give users a false sense of security. Westfall and Young (1993) called the bootstrap procedure "a small sample asymptotic procedure" (p. 18). In actuality, using bootstrapping with a small sample can lead to a test that has low statistical power. Simulation studies showed that with low-dimensional data sets (e.g., $k = 1$), the bootstrap procedure does not inflate the Type I error, even though the sample size is as small as 10. However, with the larger number of variables and small sample sizes, the Type I error rate resulting from the employment of bootstrapping is greater than .05 (Troendle, Korn, & McShane, 2004). Although Hesterberg et al. (2003) are vocal advocates for bootstrapping, they warn that bootstrapping does not overcome the weakness of small samples as a basis for inference, and thus one must use it with caution in any inference.

Two Methodological Traditions: Empiricism and Counterfactual Reasoning

The preceding discussion mentions just one of many potential pitfalls of bootstrapping. Whether resampling is a viable methodology has been an ongoing debate for some time, but readers may not necessarily benefit from revisiting all arguments and counterarguments. Readers who are interested in the debate can consult Yu (2003). In this short chapter, only one common objection to resampling will be examined through a historical and philosophical analysis, namely, "One cannot make something out of nothing." At first glance, resampling "invents" data, and thus the widespread protest against this approach is understandable. Actually, making statistical inferences based on real data and making inferences using cases that do not exist represent two different research traditions in statistics—namely, the Pearsonian and the Fisherian schools.[3]

Table 19.6   Bootstrap Confidence Interval of Six Descriptive Statistics for LSAT

*** Bootstrap Results ***

Label: bootstrap : law : Summary Statistics

Number of Replications: 1000

Summary Statistics:	Observed	Mean	Bias	SE
1stQ..LSAT	573.50	570.56	−2.9440	8.470
Mean:.LSAT	600.27	599.93	−0.3409	10.655
TrmM:.LSAT	596.22	595.88	−0.3389	14.465
Medn:.LSAT	580.00	589.36	9.3560	19.046
3rdQ:.LSAT	643.00	631.46	−11.5385	23.856
StDv:.LSAT	41.79	39.99	−1.8076	5.113
Percentiles:	2.5%	5%	95%	97.5%
1stQ..LSAT	555.00000	556.50000	579.00000	586.00000
Mean:.LSAT	580.53500	583.00333	618.66667	621.60000
TrmM:.LSAT	571.89444	574.33333	622.87778	626.66667
Medn:.LSAT	572.00000	575.00000	635.00000	651.00000
3rdQ:.LSAT	579.00000	587.00000	657.00000	661.00000
StDv:.LSAT	27.76194	31.16255	47.11576	48.20961
BCa Confidence Intervals:	2.5%	5%	95%	97.5%
1stQ..LSAT	555.0000	556.50000	579.00000	585.00000
Mean:.LSAT	581.9718	585.10199	620.69853	626.16577
TrmM:.LSAT	574.3333	577.46683	626.66667	634.41974
Medn:.LSAT	575.0000	575.00000	635.00000	651.00000
3rdQ:.LSAT	586.0000	592.50000	661.00000	662.79796
StDv:.LSAT	32.9816	34.94513	49.40236	50.55608

Karl Pearson was strongly influenced by Ernst Mach, a scientist who zealously subscribed to the pro-observation and anti-counterfactual positivist view. Mach initially rejected the existence of shock waves caused by bullets going faster than the speed of sound because this could not be directly observed by scientists (as cited in Shipley, 2000). Based on the same reasoning, Mach was opposed to untestable "absolute space" in Newtonian physics (as cited in Greene, 2004). In addition, Mach (1941) said,

> The universe is not twice given, with an earth at rest and an earth in motion; but only once, with its relative motions, alone determinate. It is, accordingly, not permitted us to say how things would be if the earth did not rotate. (p. 284)

Influenced by Mach, Pearson asserted that the goal of scientific methods is to obtain a mere description of observable phenomena based on the data *at hand* (Yu, 2006).

Fisher asserted that Pearson's pro-observation and anti-counterfactual approach was a hindrance to science because in Fisher's view, scientists must contemplate a wider domain than solely the actual observations. For instance, biologists would take the existing two sexes for granted; no biologist would be interested in modeling what organisms might experience if there were three or more sexes. However, for Fisher, it is logical to consider this question with reference to a system of possibilities wider than the actual cases (Box, 1978). Although Fisher did not develop counterfactual-based methodologies such as modal logic in philosophy or path-searching algorithms in structural equation modeling, his design of experiments definitely carries certain counterfactual elements. To be specific, the researcher designing experiments can go beyond the actual world to counterfactual worlds by creating situations (treatment groups) that did not naturally happen (Yu, 2006). Not surprisingly, as a counterfactual thinker, Fisher is the inventor of permutation testing.

No doubt Karl Pearson and R. A. Fisher were the two most prominent statisticians in the first half of the 20th century, and it is not exaggerating to say that today's statisticians still use, on a day-to-day basis, procedures developed by these two giants. Today, many researchers have adopted not only the procedures from both schools but also the implicit assumptions that could affect how a researcher evaluates the efficacy of a methodology. The controversy pertaining to resampling may be an echo of the tension between the research tradition that insists on using empirical data and the tradition that favors counterfactual reasoning. In the section entitled "Lady Tasting Tea," readers saw how the Pearsonian and Fisherian approaches handled the same problem differently.

ANALOGY OF CONVENTIONAL METHODOLOGY

As mentioned in the previous section, one common criticism against resampling is that this technique seems to "make something out of nothing." Nevertheless, the logic of resampling has a strong connection to conventional methodology. Consider estimating sample errors in survey methodology. In probability sampling, the researcher is concerned with two issues: *sampling bias* and *sampling variance*. Both are serious threats to the validity of the survey results. If some elements in the sampling pool have a zero probability of being selected, this problem is called sampling bias. If the sample results yield a wide range of variation and thus precision is low, this problem is called sampling variance (Groves et al., 2004). Estimating sampling bias and sampling errors requires a theoretical ground, which resembles that of resampling. When probability sampling is employed, one single sample is actually selected. However, given that every element in the sampling pool has a nonzero probability to be drawn, there are

many other possible samples composed of different elements. In survey methodology, these alternatives are called *realizations*. In resampling, these cases are termed *permuted* or *bootstrap scenarios*, whereas in philosophy, they are known as *counterfactuals* or *possible worlds*. Each sample design can yield many possible sample realizations. The number of possible realizations is a function of the number of units in the sample, the number in the sampling pool, and the sample design. If those possible realizations were actualized, there would be a distribution showing the variability of all the possible realizations. At this point, readers who are familiar with the central limit theorem can tell that this distribution is just the sampling distribution. Based on the theory of sampling distribution, the researcher can use formulas derived from the theory to compute the variance, the standard error, and the confidence interval when only the actual sample is available and other sample realizations were not realized. The major difference between this methodology and resampling is that the latter actualizes the potential cases.

Not surprisingly, Hesterberg et al. (2003) used the central limit theorem and sampling distributions to illustrate the concept of resampling. According to Hesterberg et al., confidence intervals, hypothesis tests, and standard errors are all based on the distribution of values taken by the statistic in all possible samples of the same size from the same population. In theory, we admit the importance of these realizations, but in practice, we cannot take a large number of random samples in order to construct this sampling distribution. As a shortcut, a model for the distribution of the population and the laws of probability are used to obtain the sampling distribution. In resampling, the statistician takes things a step further by constructing the distribution instead of using the shortcut. Hence, viewing resampling through the lenses of sample realization, sampling distribution, and the central limit theorem enables us to identify the continuity between the traditional and the resampling approaches.

SUMMARY

Although permutation and bootstrapping share a common thread in terms of systematically reusing the available data, they still have quite a few differences, which are summarized in Table 19.7.

Table 19.7   Differences Between Permutation and Bootstrap

	Permutation	Bootstrap
Resampling method	Resample without replacement (Shuffle)	Resample with replacement
Problem type	Requires two or more samples, one sample with two or more measures	Can work with a single sample or a single variable
Sample requirement	Can yield accurate results with as few as 10 subjects in many situations	Cannot yield much variability in the empirical distribution when sample size is too small
Assumption	Testing hypotheses concerning distributions, more stringent assumptions (e.g., exchangeability)	Testing concerning parameters, less stringent assumptions
Inferences	Exact p value based on a close reference set	Nonexact p value based on an open reference set

Before arguing for or against a particular school of thought or adopting or rejecting a specific procedure, it is crucial to understand the philosophical assumptions of different methodologies and their historical contexts. Classical procedures were developed along the tension between two research traditions: the Pearsonian school, which prefers the observable to the unobservable entities, and the Fisherian school, which embraces counterfactual reasoning based on scenarios that never existed but could be actualized. The concepts of sample realization and the central limit theorem can be viewed as a manifestation of counterfactual reasoning. In this sense, the confrontation between parametric and resampling methods may be misguided because the logic of resampling is compatible with that of the classical Fisherian legacy.

Today, resampling features are available in many statistical software applications, such as SAS, SPSS, SyStat, Splus, NCSS, ViSta, StatXact, and Resampling Stat for Excel. Proficient programmers may embrace the freedom of manipulation in the SAS programming environment, while visually oriented users may favor the graphical user interface of other software packages. Instructors may enjoy using Resampling Stats for Excel to illustrate every step of computation, but others may prefer more automated methods. Different statistical software packages, however, have different configurations to which users should pay attention. For example, where StatXact users can enter data in a crosstab tabular form, the SPSS Exact Test does not accept data in this format. Where StatXact users can specify certain options (e.g., sample size) in Monte Carlo tests, options in SPSS's Exact Test are limited. Furthermore, in order to use the resampling features of Splus, users must reload the resample library when the program starts up. In addition, SyStat outputs individual resampling results but does not provide users with a summary of all simulations. By no means, nevertheless, are these comments meant to discourage users from using the preceding software applications. These so-called limitations may be amended in the next release. Also, the merits of these software programs certainly outweigh those minor inconveniences. Users are encouraged to explore them on their own. The best tool is the one that fits what you need.

APPENDIX: DATA SETS

Lady_tasting_tea.xls (Excel spreadsheet for permutation tests)

Lasy_tasting_tea.rxl (Resampling Stats for Excel algorithms)

Law_school.xls (Excel spreadsheet; can be imported into Splus or SyStat for bootstrapping)

NOTES

1. For example, Splus (Insightful, Inc., 2005) developers set aside procedures with resampling capabilities as new modules, such as "Summary statistics/resample" as opposed to "Summary

Statistics" and "Correlation/Resample" as opposed to "Correlations." On the contrary, SyStat Software, Inc. (2004) developers did not create new categories such as "regression with resampling" or "ANOVA with resampling." Rather, resampling in SyStat is embedded into conventional modules (e.g., regression and analysis of variance). Some statistical software companies (e.g., SPSS) treat resampling as a specialized or advanced tool beyond the basic statistical module, whereas others (e.g., SAS; SAS Institute, 2005) regard resampling as both a basic and a specialized tool.

2. One may argue that Diaconis and Efron (1983) used a bad example because the so-called 15 "observations" are actually summarized data; these are average test scores from 15 unknown distributions (law schools), not the full data set from individual law students. Like Fisher's "lady tasting tea" problem, Diaconis and Efron's LSAT problem is also presented here in a historical fashion because Diaconis and Efron's essay stimulated massive attention to the bootstrapping methodology.

3. Editor's note: Readers will note similar arguments against various missing data–handling procedures as discussed in Chapter 15.

REFERENCES

Box, J. F. (1978). *R. A. Fisher: The life of a scientist.* New York: John Wiley.

Chernick, M. R. (1999). *Bootstrap methods: A practitioner's guide.* New York: John Wiley.

Chung, J. H., & Fraser, D. A. S. (1958). Randomization tests for a two-sample problem. *Journal of the American Statistical Association, 53,* 729–735.

Cochran, W. G. (1954). Some methods for strengthening the common χ^2 tests. *Biometrics, 10,* 417–454.

Cytel Corp. (2004). StatXact [Computer software and manual]. Retrieved September 12, 2006, from http://www.cytel.com

Diaconis, P., & Efron, B. (1983). Computer-intensive methods in statistics. *Scientific American, 248,* 116–131.

DiGangi, S., Kilic, Z., Yu, C. H., Jannasch-Pennel, A., Long, L., Kim, C., et al. (in press). 1 to 1 computing in higher education: A survey of technology practices and needs. *AACE Journal.*

Dizinno, G. (1999, March 29). Population vs. sample: Implications for salary equity study. Educational Statistics Discussion List (EDSTAT-L). Available by e-mail: edstat-l@jse.stat.ncsu.edu

Dwass, M. (1957). Modified randomization tests for nonparametric hypothesis. *Annals of Mathematical Statistics, 28,* 181–187.

Edgington, E. S. (1995). *Randomization tests.* New York: Marcel Dekker.

Efron, B. (1979). Bootstrap methods: Another look at the jackknife. *The Annals of Statistics, 7,* 1–26.

Efron, B. (1981). Nonparametric estimates of standard error: The jackknife, the bootstrap and other methods. *Biometrika, 63,* 589–599.

Efron, B. (1982). The jackknife, the bootstrap, and other resampling plans. *Society of Industrial and Applied Mathematics CBMS-NSF Monographs, 38.*

Efron, B. (1983). Estimating the error rate of a prediction rule: Improvement on cross-validation. *Journal of the American Statistical Association, 78,* 316–331.

Efron, B., & Tibshirani, R. J. (1993). *An introduction to the bootstrap.* New York: Chapman & Hall.

Fisher, R. A. (1925). *Statistical methods for research workers.* Edinburgh, UK: Oliver and Boyd.

Fisher, R. A. (1960). *The design of experiments* (7th ed.). New York: Hafner.

Freeman, G. H., & Halton, J. H. (1951). Note on an exact treatment of contingency, goodness of fit and other problems of significance. *Biometrika, 38,* 141–149.

Frick, R. W. (1998). Interpreting statistical testing: Process and propensity, not population and random sampling. *Behavior Research Methods, Instruments, & Computers, 30,* 527–535.

Geisser, S. (1975). The predictive sample reuse method with applications. *Journal of the American Statistical Association, 70,* 320–328.

Good, P. (2000). *Permutation tests: A practical guide to resampling methods for testing hypotheses* (2nd ed.). New York: Springer.

Greene, B. (2004). *The fabric of the cosmos: Space, time, and the texture of reality.* New York: Vintage.

Groves, R. M., Fowler, F. J., Couper, M. P., Lepkowski, J., Singer, E., & Tourangeau, R. (2004). *Survey methodology.* Hoboken, NJ: John Wiley.

Haignere, L., Lin, Y. J., Eisenberg, B., & McCarthy, J. (1996). *Pay checks: A guide to achieving salary equity in higher education.* Albany, NY: United University Professors.

Han, J., & Kamber, M. (2006). *Data mining: Concepts and techniques* (2nd ed.). Boston: Morgan Kauffman.

Hesterberg, T., Monaghan, S., Moore, D. S., Clipson, A., & Epstein, R. (2003). *Bootstrap methods and permutation tests: Companion Chapter 18 to the practice of business statistics.* New York: W. H. Freeman.

Horn, J. L. (1965). A rationale and test for the number of factors in factor analysis. *Psychometrika, 30,* 179–185.

Insightful, Inc. (2005). Splus [Computer software and manual]. Retrieved September 12, 2006, from http://www.insightful.com

Krus, D. J., & Fuller, E. A. (1982). Computer-assisted multicross-validation in regression analysis. *Educational and Psychological Measurement, 42,* 187–193.

Kurtz, A. K. (1948). A research test of Rorschach test. *Personnel Psychology, 1,* 41–53.

Larose, D. T. (2005). *Discovering knowledge in data: An introduction to data mining.* New York: John Wiley.

Mach, E. (1941). *The sciences of mechanics.* La salle, IL: Open Court.

Maxwell, S. E., & Delaney, H. D. (2004). *Designing experiments and analyzing data: A model comparison perspective* (2nd ed.). Mahwah, NJ: Lawrence Erlbaum.

Mosier, C. I. (1951). Problems and designs of cross-validation. *Educational and Psychological Measurement, 11,* 5–11.

Mosteller, F., & Tukey, J. W. (1977). *Data analysis and regression.* Reading, MA: Addison-Wesley.

Mulaik, S. (1987). A brief history of the philosophical foundations of exploratory factor analysis. *Multivariate Behavioral Research, 22,* 267–305.

Pitman, E. J. G. (1937). Significance tests which may be applied to samples from any populations. *Journal of the Royal Statistical Society, Supplements, 4,* 119–130, 225–232.

Pitman, E. J. G. (1938). Significance tests which may be applied to samples from any populations, Part III: The analysis of variance test. *Biometrika, 29,* 322–335.

Quenouille, M. (1949). Approximate tests of correlation in time series. *Journal of the Royal Statistical Society, Series B, 11,* 18–84.

Resampling Stat. (2004). Resampling Stat for Excel [Computer software and manual]. Retrieved October 14, 2005, from http://www.resample.com

Rodgers, J. (1999). The bootstrap, the jackknife, and the randomization test: A sampling taxonomy. *Multivariate Behavioral Research, 34,* 441–456.

Salsburg, D. (2001). *The lady tasting tea: How statistics revolutionized science in the twentieth century.* New York: W. H. Freeman.

SAS Institute. (2005). SAS [Computer software and manual]. Retrieved September 12, 2006, from www.sas.com

Shipley, B. (2000). *Cause and correlation in biology: A user's guide to path analysis, structural equations and causal inference.* Cambridge, UK: Cambridge University Press.

Simon, J. L. (2001). *The resampling method for statistical inference.* Retrieved September 9, 2004, from http://www.resample.com/content/teaching/philosophy/part3/chapIII-1.txt

SPSS, Inc. (2006). SPSS [Computer software and manual]. Retrieved September 12, 2006, from http://www.spss.com

Stone, M. (1974). Crossvalidatory choice and assessment of statistical predictions. *Journal of the Royal Statistical Society, Series B, 26,* 111–147.

SyStat Software, Inc. (2004). SyStat [Computer software and manual]. Retrieved September 12, 2006, from http://www.systat.com

Troendle, J. F., Korn, E. L., & McShane, L. M. (2004). An example of slow convergence of the bootstrap in high dimensions. *The American Statistician, 58,* 25–29.

Tukey, J. W. (1958). Bias and confidence in not quite large samples. *Annals of Mathematical Statistics, 29,* 614.

Westfall, P. H., & Young, S. S. (1993). *Resampling-based multiple testing: Examples and methods for p-value adjustment.* New York: John Wiley.

Yu, C. H. (2003). Resampling methods: Concepts, applications, and justification. *Practical Assessment, Research & Evaluation, 8*(19). Retrieved December 2, 2005, from http://PAREonline.net/getvn.asp?v=8&n=19

Yu, C. H. (2006). *Philosophical foundations of quantitative research methodology.* Lanham, MD: University Press of America.

20

CREATING VALID PREDICTION EQUATIONS IN MULTIPLE REGRESSION

Shrinkage, Double Cross-Validation, and Confidence Intervals Around Predictions

JASON W. OSBORNE

I magine you have developed a great new intervention to help obese people lose weight. Your intervention works well, but it's extremely expensive, and so only those who are most at risk for adverse health outcomes stemming from their obesity can have access to it. How are you going to decide who should get the intervention?

Or imagine you are in charge of admissions for your college or university. You know that certain things predict success in your school, at least partly. How do you decide who gets admitted?

Most research we hear about is *explanatory*, meaning the goal of the research is attempting to understand a phenomenon. Does a particular variable predict success in your college? What things can help ameliorate the negative effects of obesity? How can we help students having

difficulty reading? Part of almost every research study published is a section at the end where the authors tell us why we should care about their particular findings. In essence, these summary statements (e.g., people with height-to-waist ratios of less than 1.5 might benefit most from this intervention, students scoring above the 80th percentile on this particular measure are three times as likely to succeed in our college as are students scoring lower) are predictions of efficacy in the future.

But how do we know that these results will generalize to your patients, your students, your applicants? You can try replicating the results in another sample (see also Chapter 7 on the p_{rep} statistic), and you can keep replicating the results ad nauseam, and that will give you more confidence if you keep getting the same results.

Author's Note: This chapter is based on Osborne, J. W. (2000). Prediction in multiple regression. *Practical Assessment, Research, & Evaluation.* Available at http://pareonline.net/getvn.asp?v=7&n=2

This chapter seeks to present a process of validation, as well as an example of how best to do this, so that scientists are not left attempting to do prediction in an ad hoc manner. Authors have been writing about this process for decades, yet it is rarely covered in depth in statistics textbooks.

OVERVIEW

There are two general applications for multiple regression (MR): prediction and explanation.[1] These roughly correspond to two differing goals in research: being able to make valid projections concerning an outcome for a particular individual (prediction) or attempting to understand a phenomenon by examining a variable's correlates on a group level (explanation). There has been debate as to whether these two applications of MR are grossly different, as authors such as Scriven (1959) and Anderson and Shanteau (1977) assert, or necessarily part and parcel of the same process (e.g., DeGroot, 1969; Kaplan, 1964; for an overview of this discussion, see Pedhazur, 1997, pp. 195–198). As I have asserted above, I believe both are necessarily part of the scientific process. In almost all cases, we seek to take our understanding of phenomena from our research and apply it to people who were not specifically involved in our research (a process called generalization)—otherwise, why bother to do the research? While they are theoretically part of the same goal and process, there are different analytic procedures involved with the two types of analyses. The goal of this chapter is to present (a) the concept of prediction via MR; (b) the assumptions underlying multiple regression analysis; (c) shrinkage, cross-validation, and double cross-validation of prediction equations; and (d) how to calculate confidence intervals around individual predictions.

What Is the Difference Between Using MR for Prediction and Using MR for Explanation?

When one uses MR for explanatory purposes, that person is exploring relationships between multiple variables in a sample to shed light on a phenomenon, with a goal of generalizing this new understanding to a general or specific population. When one uses MR for prediction, one is using a sample to create a regression equation that would optimally predict a particular phenomenon within a particular population. The difference is that because the equations are going to be applied to people not yet studied or measured (i.e., individuals *not in the sample used in the analysis*), we need to have some confidence that what we saw in our particular sample will generalize. Let us imagine researchers creating a regression equation to predict 12th-grade achievement test scores from 8th-grade variables, such as family socioeconomic status, race, sex, educational plans, parental education, grade point average (GPA), and participation in school-based extracurricular activities. The goal is not to understand why students achieve at a certain level, as we already have abundant research on these issues, but to create the best equation so that, for example, guidance counselors can predict future achievement scores for their students, as well as (hopefully) intervene with those students identified as at risk for poor performance, or select students into programs based on their projected scores. And while theory is useful for identifying what variables should be in a prediction equation, the variables do not necessarily need to make conceptual sense. If the single greatest predictor of future achievement scores was how high that student could jump or the number of hamburgers the student could eat, it should be in the prediction equation regardless of whether it makes sense (although researchers paying attention might be interested enough in this type of finding to pursue some explanatory research on the topic, again demonstrating the relatedness of these two processes).

HOW IS A PREDICTION EQUATION CREATED?

The general process for creating a prediction equation involves gathering relevant data from a *large, representative sample* from the population you wish to generalize to. What constitutes "large" is open to debate, and while guidelines for general applications of regression are as small as $50 + 8 \times$ number of predictors (Tabachnick & Fidell, 1996),[2] guidelines for prediction equations are more stringent due to the need to generalize beyond a given sample. While some authors have suggested that 15 subjects per predictor is sufficient (Park & Dudycha, 1974; Pedhazur, 1997), others have suggested a minimum total sample (e.g., 400; see Pedhazur, 1997), and still others have suggested a minimum of 40 subjects per predictor (Cohen & Cohen, 1983; Tabachnick & Fidell, 1996). Similar analyses of exploratory factor analysis (which again seeks to created optimally weighted linear combinations of variables that generalize) that I conducted with Anna Costello (see Chapter 6, this volume) indicated that 40 subjects per predictor may be only marginally sufficient, depending on many factors. We found significant issues of generalizability even at a ratio of 100:1. Of course, as the goal is a stable regression equation that is representative of the population regression equation, more is better, but only to the extent that it increases the representativeness of the sample. The effect of sample size on shrinkage and stability will be explored below.

Let me be excruciatingly clear on this next point: Getting a truly representative sample of the population you wish to generalize to is the key ingredient in this type of research. You can do all the fancy analyses you want, but at the end of the day, if you validate a prediction equation on a sample that does not mirror the intended use, you have wasted your time. True representativeness is one of the holy grails of research, and something that is not talked about quite enough. It's not usually something you can test for, so most assume their sampling strategies are adequate. Yet this is probably not the case. Make sure you clearly define your population of interest, and sample in such a way as to maximize the probability of getting a representative sample(s).[3]

Methods for Entering Variables Into the Equation. There are many ways to enter predictors into the regression equation. Several of these rely on the statistical properties of the variables to determine order of entry (e.g., forward selection, backward elimination, stepwise). Others rely on the experimenter to specify order of entry (hierarchical, blockwise) or have no order of entry (simultaneous). Almost all statisticians today eschew stepwise methods in favor of analyst-controlled entry and discourage entry based on the statistical properties of the variables as it is atheoretical.[4] I agree with this point of view for the majority of research, which is often explanatory. But when one comes to creating prediction equations, the only goal is creating the best prediction equation. If you examine the processes most authors recommend for creating prediction

equations, they essentially involve manual stepwise entry. I see no compelling reason not to use stepwise methods, providing (a) your *only* goal is creating a prediction equation, and (b) you have a good knowledge of stepwise methods and can make educated decisions about how to manage the process.

Regardless of the entry method ultimately chosen by the researcher, it is critical that the researcher examine individual variables to ensure that only variables contributing significantly to the variance accounted for by the regression equation are included. Variables not accounting for significant portions of variance should be deleted from the equation, and the equation should be recalculated (which is essentially what many stepwise procedures do automatically). Furthermore, researchers might want to examine excluded variables to see if their entry would significantly improve prediction (a significant increase in R-squared; again, what some stepwise methods do).

WHAT ASSUMPTIONS MUST BE MET WHEN DOING A REGRESSION ANALYSIS?

It is absolutely critical that researchers assess whether their analyses meet the assumptions of multiple regression. These assumptions are explained in detail in many places such as Pedhazur (1997) and Cohen and Cohen (1983), as well as in detail in Osborne and Waters (2002), and as such will not be addressed further here. Failure to meet necessary assumptions can cause problems with prediction equations, often serving to make them less generalizable than they otherwise would be or causing underprediction (accounting for less variance than they should, such as in the case of curvilinearity or poor measurement; note that there is no reason why curvilinear effects could not be modeled in a prediction equation through the entry of variables raised to powers).

HOW ARE PREDICTION EQUATIONS EVALUATED?

In a prediction analysis, the computer will produce a regression equation that is optimized for the sample at hand. Because this process capitalizes on chance and error in the sample (a phenomenon authors refer to as "overfitting"), the equation produced in one sample will not generally fare as well in another sample (i.e., R-squared in a subsequent sample using the same equation will not be as large as R-squared from the original sample), a phenomenon called shrinkage. The most desirable outcome in this process is for minimal shrinkage, indicating that the prediction equation will generalize well to new samples or individuals from the population examined. While there are equations that can estimate shrinkage, the best way to estimate shrinkage and test the prediction equation is through cross-validation or double cross-validation.

Cross-Validation. To perform cross-validation, a researcher will either gather two large samples or one very large sample, which will be split into two samples via random selection procedures. The prediction equation is created in the first sample. That equation is then used to create predicted scores for the members of the second sample. The predicted scores are then correlated with the observed scores on the dependent variable ($r_{yy'}$). This is called the *cross-validity coefficient.* The difference between the original R-squared and $r_{yy'}^2$ is the shrinkage. The smaller the shrinkage, the more confidence we can have in the generalizability of the equation.

In our example of predicting 12th-grade achievement test scores from 8th-grade variables, a sample of 700 students (a subset of the larger National Education Longitudinal Survey of 1988 from the National Center for Education Statistics) was randomly split into two groups. In the first group, analyses revealed that the following 8th-grade variables were significant predictors of 12th-grade achievement: GPA, parent education level, race (White = 0, non-White = 1), and participation in school-based extracurricular activities (no = 0, yes = 1), producing the following equation:

$$Y' = -2.45 + 1.83(\text{GPA}) - 0.77(\text{Race}) + 1.03(\text{Participation}) + 0.38(\text{Parent Ed}).$$

In the first group, this analysis produced an R-squared of .55. This equation was used in the second group to create predicted scores, and those predicted scores correlated $r_{yy'} = .73$ with observed achievement scores. With an $r_{yy'}^2$ of .53

(cross-validity coefficient), shrinkage was 2%, a good outcome.

Double Cross-Validation. In double cross-validation, prediction equations are created in both samples, and then each is used to create predicted scores and cross-validity coefficients in the other sample. This procedure involves little work beyond cross-validation and produces a more informative and rigorous test of the generalizability of the regression equation(s). In addition, as two equations are produced, one can look at the stability of the actual regression line equations.

The following regression equation emerged from analyses of the second sample:

$$Y' = -4.03 + 2.16(\text{GPA}) - 1.90(\text{Race}) + 1.43(\text{Participation}) + 0.28(\text{Parent Ed}).$$

This analysis produced an R-squared of .60. This equation was used in the first group to create predicted scores in the first group, which correlated .73 with observed scores, for a cross-validity coefficient of .53. Note that (a) the second analysis revealed larger shrinkage than the first, (b) the two cross-validation coefficients were identical (.53), and (c) the two regression equations are markedly different, even though the samples had large subject-to-predictor ratios (over 80:1).

So How Much Shrinkage Is Too Much Shrinkage? There are no clear guidelines concerning how to evaluate shrinkage, except the general agreement that less is always better. But is 3% acceptable? What about 5%? 10%? Or should it be a proportion of the original R-squared (so that 5% shrinkage on an R-squared of .50 would be fine, but 5% shrinkage on an R-squared of .30 would not be)? There are no guidelines in the literature. However, Pedhazur (1997) has suggested that one of the advantages of double cross-validation is that one can compare the two cross-validity coefficients, and if they are similar, one can be fairly confident in the generalizability of the equation.

The Final Step. If you are satisfied with your shrinkage statistics, the final step in this sort of analysis is to combine both samples (assuming shrinkage is minimal) and create a final prediction equation based on the larger sample. In our data set, the combined sample produced the following regression line equation:

$$Y' = -3.23 + 2.00(\text{GPA}) - 1.29(\text{Race}) + 1.24(\text{Participation}) + 0.32(\text{Parent Ed}).$$

How Does Sample Size Affect the Shrinkage and Stability of a Prediction Equation?

As discussed above, there are many different opinions as to the minimum sample size one should use in prediction research. As an illustration of the effects of different subject-to-predictor ratios on shrinkage and stability of a regression equation, data from the National Education Longitudinal Survey of 1988 (NELS 88, from the National Center for Education Statistics) were used to construct prediction equations identical to our running example. This data set contains data on 24,599 eighth-grade students representing 1,052 schools in the United States. Furthermore, the data can be weighted to exactly

represent the population, so an accurate population estimate can be obtained for comparison. Two samples, each representing ratios of 5, 15, 40, 100, and 400 subjects per predictor, were randomly selected from this sample (randomly selecting from the full sample for each new pair of a different size). Following selection of the samples, prediction equations were calculated, and double cross-validation was performed. The results are presented in Table 20.1.

The first observation from the table is that, by comparing regression line equations, the very small samples have wildly fluctuating equations (both intercept and regression coefficients). Even the 40:1 ratio samples have impressive fluctuations in the actual equation. While the fluctuations in the 100:1 sample are fairly small in magnitude, some coefficients reverse direction or are far off of the population regression line. As expected, it is only in the largest ratios presented, the 100:1 and 400:1 ratios, that the equations stabilize and remain close to the population equation.

Table 20.1 Comparison of Double Cross-Validation Results With Differing Subject-to-Predictor Ratios

Sample Ratio (Subjects: Predictors)	Obtained Prediction Equation	R^2	$r^2_{yy'}$	Shrinkage
Population	$Y' = -1.71 + 2.08(\text{GPA}) - 0.73(\text{race}) - 0.60(\text{part}) + 0.32(\text{pared})$	.48		
5:1				
Sample 1	$Y' = -8.47 + 1.87(\text{GPA}) - 0.32(\text{race}) + 5.71(\text{part}) + 0.28(\text{pared})$	.62	.53	.09
Sample 2	$Y' = -6.92 + 3.03(\text{GPA}) + 0.34(\text{race}) + 2.49(\text{part}) - 0.32(\text{pared})$	.81	.67	.14
15:1				
Sample 1	$Y' = -4.46 + 2.62(\text{GPA}) - 0.31(\text{race}) + 0.30(\text{part}) + 0.32(\text{pared})$	.69	.24	.45
Sample 2	$Y' = -1.99 + 1.55(\text{GPA}) + 0.34(\text{race}) + 1.04(\text{part}) - 0.58(\text{pared})$	.53	.49	.04
40:1				
Sample 1	$Y' = -0.49 + 2.34(\text{GPA}) - 0.79(\text{race}) - 1.51(\text{part}) + 0.08(\text{pared})$	.55	.50	.05
Sample 2	$Y' = -2.05 + 2.03(\text{GPA}) - 0.61(\text{race}) - 0.37(\text{part}) + 0.51(\text{pared})$	.58	.53	.05
100:1				
Sample 1	$Y' = -1.89 + 2.05(\text{GPA}) - 0.52(\text{race}) - 0.17(\text{part}) + 0.35(\text{pared})$	.46	.45	.01
Sample 2	$Y' = -2.04 + 1.92(\text{GPA}) - 0.01(\text{race}) + 0.32(\text{part}) + 0.37(\text{pared})$	.46	.45	.01
400:1				
Sample 1	$Y' = -1.26 + 1.95(\text{GPA}) - 0.70(\text{race}) - 0.41(\text{part}) + 0.37(\text{pared})$	.47	.46	.01
Sample 2	$Y' = -1.10 + 1.94(\text{GPA}) - 0.45(\text{race}) - 0.56(\text{part}) + 0.35(\text{pared})$	.42	.41	.01

Comparing variance accounted for, it is over-estimated in the equations with smaller than 100:1 ratios. Cross-validity coefficients vary a great deal across samples until a 40:1 ratio is reached, where they appear to stabilize. Finally, shrinkage appears to minimize as a 40:1 ratio is reached. If one takes Pedhazur's (1997) suggestion to compare cross-validity coefficients to determine if the equation is stable, from these data, one would need a 40:1 ratio or better before that criterion would be reached. If the goal is to get an accurate, stable estimate of the population regression equation (which it should be if that equation is going to be widely used outside the original sample), it appears desirable to have at least 100 subjects per predictor given these data.

Calculating a Predicted Score and Confidence Intervals Around That Score

There are two categories of predicted scores relevant here: scores predicted for the original sample and scores that can be predicted for individuals outside the original sample. Individual predicted scores and confidence intervals for the original sample are available in the output available from most common statistical packages. Thus, the latter will be addressed here.

Once an analysis is completed and the final regression line equation is formed, it is possible to create predictions for individuals who were not part of the original sample that generated the regression line (one of the attractive features of regression). Calculating a new score based on an existing regression line is a simple matter of substitution and algebra. However, no such prediction should be presented without confidence intervals. The only practical way to do this is through the following formula:

$$Y' \pm t_{(\alpha/2,\, df)} (S_{y'}),$$

where $S_{y'}$ is calculated as

$$\sqrt{S_{\mu'}^2 + MS_{\text{residual}}},$$

where $S_{\mu'}^2$ is the squared standard error of mean predicted scores (standard error of the estimate, squared) and the mean square residual, both of which can be obtained from typical regression output.[5]

Summary and Suggestions for Further Study

Multiple regression can be an effective tool for creating prediction equations, provided that adequate measurement, large enough samples, and assumptions of MR are met and that care is taken to evaluate the regression equations for generalizability (shrinkage). Researchers interested in this topic might want to explore the following topics: (a) the use of logistic regression for predicting binomial or discrete outcomes, (b) the use of estimation procedures other than ordinary least squares regression that can produce better prediction (e.g., Bayesian estimation; see, e.g., Raudenbush & Bryk, 2002), and (c) alternatives to MR when assumptions are not met or when sample sizes are inadequate to produce stable estimates, such as ridge regression (for an introduction to these alternative procedures, see, e.g., Cohen & Cohen, 1983, pp. 113–115). Finally, if researchers have nested or multilevel data, they should use multilevel modeling procedures (e.g., HLM; see Raudenbush & Bryk, 2002, or Chapters 29 and 30, this volume) to produce prediction equations.

Notes

1. Some readers may be uncomfortable with the term *explanation* when referring to multiple regression, as these data are often correlational in nature, while the term *explanation* often implies causal inference. However, *explanation* will be used in this chapter because (a) it is the convention in the field, (b) here I am talking of regression with the *goal* of explanation, and (c) one can come to an understanding of phenomena by understanding associations without positing or testing strict causal orderings.

2. Personally, I find rules of thumb less useful than processes such as power calculations or calculations such as Killeen's probability of replication statistic (see Chapter 7, this volume). Please take all such rules of thumb with a large grain of salt and skepticism.

3. If you happen to have a good, scholarly treatise on representativeness, please contact me so that I can explore including it in the next version of this book.

4. A thorough discussion of this issue is beyond the scope of this chapter, so the reader is referred to Cohen and Cohen (1983) and Pedhazur (1997) for overviews of the various techniques, as well as Thompson (1989) and Schafer (1991a, 1991b) for more detailed discussions of the issues.

5. It is often the case that one will want to use standard error of the predicted score when calculating an individual confidence interval. However, as that statistic is only available from statistical program output and only for individuals in the original data set, it is of limited value for this discussion. Here I suggest using the standard error of the mean predicted scores, as it is the best estimate of the standard error of the predicted score, knowing it is not completely ideal but lacking any other alternative.

References

Anderson, N. H., & Shanteau, J. (1977). Weak inference with linear models. *Psychological Bulletin, 84*, 1155–1170.

Cohen, J., & Cohen, P. (1983). *Applied multiple regression/correlation analysis for the behavioral sciences*. Hillsdale, NJ: Lawrence Erlbaum.

DeGroot, A. D. (1969). *Methodology: Foundations of inference and research in the behavioral sciences.* The Hague, The Netherlands: Mouton.

Kaplan, A. (1964). *The conduct of inquiry: Methodology for behavioral science.* San Francisco: Chandler.

Osborne, J. W., & Waters, E. (2002). Four assumptions of multiple regression that researchers should always test. *Practical Assessment, Research, and Evaluation, 8*(2). Available at http://pareonline .net/getvn.asp?v=8&n=2

Park, C., & Dudycha, A. (1974). A cross-validation approach to sample size determination. *Journal of the American Statistical Association, 69*, 214–218.

Pedhazur, E. J. (1997). *Multiple regression in behavioral research.* Orlando, FL: Harcourt Brace.

Raudenbush, S. W., & Bryk, A. S. (2002). *Hierarchical linear models: Applications and data analysis methods* (2nd ed.). Thousand Oaks, CA: Sage.

Schafer, W. D. (1991a). Reporting hierarchical regression results. *Measurement and Evaluation in Counseling and Development, 24*, 98–100.

Schafer, W. D. (1991b). Reporting nonhierarchical regression results. *Measurement and Evaluation in Counseling and Development, 24*, 146–149.

Scriven, M. (1959). Explanation and prediction in evolutionary theory. *Science, 130*, 477–482.

Tabachnick, B. G., & Fidell, L. S. (1996). *Using multivariate statistics.* New York: HarperCollins.

Thompson, B. (1989). Why won't stepwise methods die? *Measurement and Evaluation in Counseling and Development, 21*, 146–148.

21

BEST PRACTICES IN ANALYZING COUNT DATA

Poisson Regression

E. MICHAEL NUSSBAUM

SHERIF ELSADAT

AHMED H. KHAGO

In the social sciences, researchers often use variables that take the form of counts, such as the number of self-explanations generated in a think-aloud protocol, number of teachers leaving the profession in a given year, and number of student absences per semester. Counts are typically treated as interval/ratio variables because the distances between points on these variables are constant and they have a true zero point. These variables are then usually analyzed using traditional methods such as t tests, analysis of variance (ANOVA), or regression by ordinary least squares (OLS).

Unfortunately, count data are often highly skewed, making it more appropriate to use Poisson methods to analyze these variables, specifically measuring degree of fit to a Poisson distribution and using Poisson regression. The Poisson is a skewed, nonnegative distribution that is especially suited for low-frequency count variables when many of the counts are zero and/or when the distribution is positively skewed. Poisson methods are often more statistically powerful than traditional methods with

count variables when the population distribution is skewed and the distribution approximates the Poisson distribution. Unfortunately, use of Poisson methods in social science research has been relatively rare to date, primarily because of a lack of understanding of the underlying theory.[1] This chapter therefore provides an introductory overview of Poisson regression.

THE POISSON DISTRIBUTION

The Poisson distribution is named after the French mathematician and physicist Siméon-Denis Poisson (1790–1840). Mathematicians at the time were concerned with developing the foundations of the field of probability, including various probability formulas, such as the binomial formula.

The Binomial Formula. With the binomial formula, one can theoretically calculate the probability of a certain number of successful trials (k), given the number of trials (n) and the probability of a success (π). The formula is

$$\frac{n!}{k!(n-k)!}\pi^k(1-\pi)^k.\tag{1}$$

So, for example, the probability of 15 successes out of 20, when $\pi = 0.5$, is

$$[20!/(15!*5!)]*.5^{15}*(.5)^5 = .015.$$

Note that in this example, the factorial 5! ($5*4*3*2*1$) = 120, 15! = 1,307,670,000,000, and 20! = 2,432,902,008,176,640,000. These numbers become unmanageably large as n increases, and the binomial formula cannot be easily applied when n is very large even with contemporary computer applications.[2]

Discovery of the Poisson. Poisson addressed this problem by asking what happens to the binomial distribution, in the limit, as n approaches infinity and π approaches zero. The result (derived in the appendix) is the Poisson distribution, a positively skewed, nonnegative distribution (see Figure 21.1, first two distributions).

Poisson suggested that this distribution could be used as an approximation to the binomial distribution when rare events are involved, that is, when π is very low and n is high. (This finding is sometimes called *the law of rare events* or *the law of small numbers.*) For example, the probability of developing a rare disease might be low (one in a thousand) and the population quite large (for example, hundreds of millions of people), so that the number of people who contract the disease per year (or some other period of time or space) might be usefully described by the Poisson distribution. The distribution is skewed because there is a high probability of not contracting the disease (the number of zeros is high), and it is nonnegative because counts cannot be less than zero.

The discovery of the Poisson distribution has been at the same time productive and unfortunate. It has been productive because it allows the probability of rare events to be modeled but unfortunate because the manner in which it was discovered caused a misconception that the distribution applies only to rare events. In fact, many count distributions are Poisson in shape even though events are only semi-rare. For example,

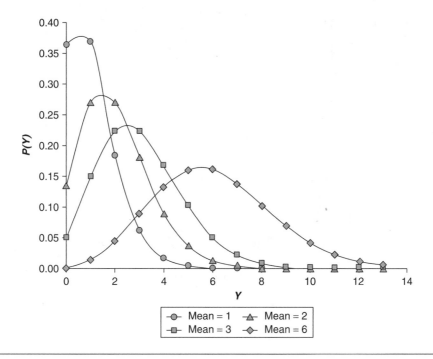

Figure 21.1   Poisson distributions for different values of lambda. Y is a count, and lambda is the average count per unit of time (or space).

Nussbaum and Kardash (2005) encountered a Poisson distribution while conducting research on argumentation in essay writing. In response to various interventions, students were asked to write essays on whether watching television causes children to become more violent. There was a low number of counterarguments and rebuttals, which is typical of student opinion essays (Leitão, 2003; Stapleton, 2001). The distributions of these two variables were Poisson in shape (see Figure 21.2). This was true even though the probabilities that a student would include a counterargument or rebuttal in his or her essay, although low (38% and 34%, respectively), were not extremely rare. Nevertheless, we did not initially consider using the Poisson distribution to analyze these data.

The rarity misconception stems from the original context in which the Poisson distribution was developed and applied, but in recent years, statisticians have adopted a wider view of the Poisson distribution as a distribution generally applicable to counts, a fact recognized within 50 years of Poisson's discovery (Larsen & Marx, 1990) and

applied to such things as the total number of particles detected by a Geiger counter (Rutherford, Chadwick, & Ellis, 1951) or the number of Prussian cavalry soldiers kicked to death by their horses (Bortkiewicz, 1898). Other applications have included such things as the number of customers who arrive at a bank in a given time interval (Padilla, 2003), the number of accidents per year along a given stretch of highway (Antelman, 1997), the frequency with which a computer's CPU fails, or the number of daily transactions of a particular stock. In business, the Poisson distribution has been central to queuing and inventory theory and quality control. According to Padilla (2003), the Poisson distribution has been used in biology and medicine for

analyzing cell and virus counts of a given blood or solution sample; describing the spatial distribution of bacteria colonies in a plate of agar; studying of neural impulses; counting the number of defective teeth per individual; enumerating the number of chromosome interchanges induced by X-ray

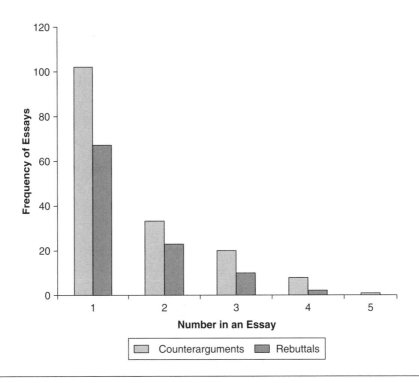

Figure 21.2   Argumentation histogram. Reflects number of counterarguments and rebuttals in opinion essays on TV violence.

SOURCE: Nussbaum and Kardash (2005).

irradiation; and in generalization of epidemic models to count number of victims of specific diseases . . . per year. In terms of agriculture and ecology, the distribution of plants and animals in either space or time is frequently Poisson. (p. 38)

Other applications have included frequency of earthquakes, alpha emissions from radioactive sources, distribution of bones and artifacts in archeological finds, and, in astronomy, the distribution of stars in space or the occurrence of meteors over a specific time period.

The Poisson distribution is generated by a *Poisson process*, which is a process that generates a number of cases (up to a few) per time period. As an example, suppose we have 20 orange trees, all of which look alike (Rosenfeld, 2002). During the harvest season, we put a basket under each tree hoping to catch a few oranges each day. As long as each tree is similar, so that the same processes apply to each tree, and as long as each orange's fall into the basket is a separate and independent event, this situation will represent a Poisson process and can be described by the Poisson distribution. The distribution will tell us how many baskets we can expect to contain 0, 1, 2, 3, 4, or more oranges on a given day.

A Poisson process can often be represented by a straight line that represents time (or space). Each point represents an independent Bernoulli random variable, where the event in question either happens or does not (Antelman, 1997). Of course, the number of points is infinite, reflecting the fact that a binomial distribution (series of Bernoulli trials) approaches the Poisson as N becomes infinite and π approaches zero. But this is an idealized case, and we can make the number of points finite by making the points have a length, in effect creating small bins. The bins must be small enough that the probability that more than one event will occur in the time period represented by the bin is extremely small (Issac, 1995). As a result, the probability of an event occurrence in a bin can still be represented by Bernoulli (yes or no) random variables. Here, π is the Bernoulli probability of an event occurring in the bin (for example, a radioactive particle being omitted, a neuron firing, or, in our previous example, an orange being grown). Although π is small but given a large number of bins, the average number for a given length of time will typically be in the range of 1 to 5.

Ruhla (1989/1992) states that to have a Poisson process that can be modeled statistically, π should be less than .01, N should be greater than 100, and the mean should be under 10. However, while a Poisson process will generate a Poisson distribution, *one can still have a variable that follows the Poisson distribution but that was not necessarily generated through a Poisson process.* These guidelines should therefore not be rigidly applied in determining when to perform a Poisson analysis.

Form and Parameters of the Poisson. The basic functional form of the Poisson distribution is

$$P(Y = y) = \lambda^y e^{-\lambda}/y!, \qquad (2)$$

and for the cumulative probability distribution, it is

$$\Sigma \lambda^y e^{-\lambda}/k!. \qquad (3)$$

The basic parameter of the Poisson distribution is the mean (λ), which is the average number of something (γ) per unit of time or space. For example, one can calculate the number of deaths per year due to thyroid cancer in the United States from 1980 to 2000 for a random sample and then calculate a mean count for your sample. Lambda (λ) represents the mean count for the population and in some sense represents the likelihood of an event occurring. (We shall see later that it is related to π, the probability of a hit.) Figure 21.1 shows Poisson distributions for various values of λ. For low values of $\tilde{\lambda}$ the distributions have the usual skewed shape, but as λ becomes large (e.g., a mean of six occurrences), the distribution converges to the normal distribution.

A special feature of the Poisson distribution is that the variance is equal to the mean, so λ represents the population variance as well. Recall that the Poisson distribution was derived from the binomial distribution in the limit when n approaches infinity and π approaches 0 (with π estimated by the sample proportion p). The estimated variance of the binomial distribution is npq (where q is the probability of a miss, so that $q = 1 - p$). If p approaches 0, q approaches 1, so the estimated variance npq reduces to np. Although p becomes 0, this does not cause the variance to become 0 because simultaneously, n approaches infinity. Rather, np remains a positive number. The term $n\pi$ (estimated by np) is the expected or mean number of hits in the binomial (and Poisson) and is expressed by λ. Thus, λ is the variance, as well as the mean, of the Poisson distribution.

Random N. Another feature of the Poisson distribution is that there is typically another source of random variation in addition to the probability of a success or failure. For example, the number of people who develop thyroid cancer is affected in a given year not only by the chance of being exposed to carcinogens but also by variations in the size of the population (e.g., the number of people living in the United States). This variable is referred to as the *offset*, and data are often reported with the offset included. For example, if one were studying student discourse and presenting the frequency with which students ask critical questions, one might also count the number of speech turns as an offset. Other examples might include number of gang-related crimes per year offset by the number of gangs or number of dropouts per school district offset by the number of students per district.

In these situations, one could just calculate a percentage by dividing the count by the offset; one would then have percentage of speech turns that are critical questions, percentage of students in each district who drop out, or probability that a gang member will be involved in a gang-related crime (since proportions can be used to estimate probabilities). One then becomes involved in estimating a π rather than λ. It might be tempting in these situations to just use the binomial distribution (or the normal approximation to the binomial). But doing so ignores the fact that not only is the count a random variable, but so is the offset.

A basic difference between the binomial and Poisson distribution is that with the binomial distribution, the proportion (p) of hits can vary, but n is a fixed variable. With the Poisson distribution, n is a random variable. Consider the following thought experiment. A person takes 10 coins, throws them up in the air, and counts the number of heads. According to the binomial distribution, the most likely outcome is the mean, which is $n\pi$ (or 5), assuming a fair coin and that the probability of a head is one half. The probability of getting 8 heads, according to the binomial formula, is 0.04. In this case, n is fixed at 10. Now consider another scenario. The person reaches into a huge jar of coins, takes a large handful, and throws them up in the air. The probability of getting 8 heads cannot be predicted by the binomial

formula because we do not know the number of coins that will be tossed in each trial. The number of coins will vary from toss to toss, depending on the number of coins grabbed from the jar.

However, the probability can be calculated from the Poisson distribution, as long as one has an estimate of λ, the mean number of heads per toss. Suppose the person grabs a handful of coins 100 times, the number of heads is calculated, and λ is estimated to be 5. Then the probability of obtaining 8 coins in a toss according to the Poisson distribution is .065. Note that the probability has gone up. It is easier to obtain 8 coins because one can sometimes grab more than 10 coins. Furthermore, the variances have increased. The variance of the binomial distribution is given by $n\pi(1 - \pi)$, or $10 * 0.5 * 0.5 = 2.5$. The variance of the Poisson distribution is given by λ, which is 5.0. The distributions are graphed in Figure 21.3. The Poisson has a higher variance because of the random nature of n. Thus, even though the means might be the same ($\lambda = n\pi$) and can be estimated by np (where p is the sample proportion), because both n and p are random variables, the Poisson will have more variation. Also note that with the binomial, the variance is estimated by npq, whereas with the Poisson, the variance is just np ($= \lambda$). The term q, which is a number less than 1 (estimated probability of a miss), makes the variance of the binomial distribution smaller.

This discussion shows that even with nonrare events (e.g., $\pi = 0.5$), use of the Poisson distribution is applicable. However, the Poisson distribution does become more symmetrical and approaches the normal distribution as λ becomes larger. But count variables are often asymmetrical. It is therefore important to know whether specific count variables follow a Poisson or normal distribution. Although nonnormality is often addressed through the central limit theorem, which shows that in large samples, the sampling distribution (distribution of possible parameter estimates) follows a normal distribution, we shall see later that that does not necessarily maximize statistical power.

Identifying a Poisson Distribution. How can one identify whether the distribution for a particular variable follows a Poisson distribution? Our method is to perform a one-sample Kolmogorov-Smirnov (KS) test. The KS test finds the data point with the greatest difference from the value

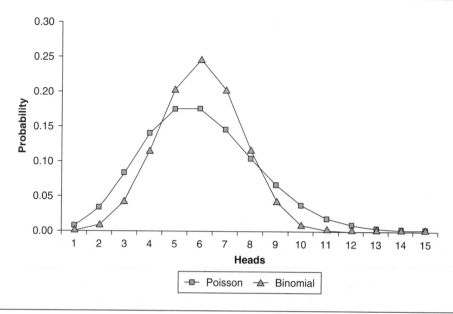

Figure 21.3   Poisson versus binomial distribution, from number of heads in a coin toss. The Poisson distribution shown assumes an average of 5 heads per toss ($\lambda = 5$); the binomial distribution shown assumes 10 coins were tossed, and the probability of a head is 0.5.

expected if the variable had followed a specific distribution and uses this difference as the test statistic (which follows a z distribution). The KS test is easy to perform in such statistical packages as SPSS, which can compare a variable against both the Poisson and normal distributions, as well as exponential and uniform distributions. (The test is contained within the nonparametric analysis menu.) A significant value indicates that one can reject the null hypothesis that the distribution is Poisson, or whatever distribution is being tested. Theoretically, one could also use a chi-square test to evaluate hypotheses about the shape of a distribution, depending on the options afforded in available software.

One disadvantage of the KS test is that if the sample is very large, the test gains a lot of statistical power and therefore is sensitive to small departures from an ideal distribution. Another approach is to construct a Q-Q plot, which compares the quantiles of the actual distribution with those of an ideal distribution, in this case the Poisson. A perfect fit would be reflected by a straight line where $X = Y$.[3] A simple, graphical approach was proposed by Ord (cited in Johnson, Kotz, & Kemp, 1992, p. 167) and can be implemented in simple worksheet programs such as EXCEL. Let X be the values of the variable (e.g.,

0, 1, 2, 3, etc.) and f_x the frequency of each value. Define μ_x as $\mu_x = X^* f_x / f_{(x-1)}$ and plot μ_x against X. For a Poisson distribution, the plot should be a horizontal line with $\mu_x = \lambda$.

POISSON REGRESSION MODEL

Poisson regression is appropriate when the dependent (response) variable approximates a Poisson distribution. Recall that such a distribution may be generated by a "Poisson process." Using our previous example of orange trees, we assumed that each tree generated oranges at the same average rate, with a mean count of λ_1. Suppose, however, that the last row of trees in the orchard receives more sunlight (Rosenfeld, 2002). In that case, the row of trees will generate oranges at a higher rate, with a mean count of λ_2. The mean count (λ) will therefore be affected by an independent variable, the amount of sunlight. In Poisson regression, counts are predicted by one or more independent variables. The variables can be interval/ratio or nominal.

The regression model is a type of general linear model that can be used as an alternative to t tests, ANOVA, and OLS regression. While it is not uncommon for analysts using these approaches to ignore distributional issues, on the grounds that the central limit theorem can make the sampling distributions of the estimates approximately normal, this approach may not be the most statistically powerful one. With traditional methods, skew in the distribution of a variable—and the Poisson is the quintessential skewed variable—can reduce statistical power. Compared with normally distributed variables, skew can increase standard errors, making it harder to achieve statistical significance. Another common approach is to reduce skew by using a Box-Cox transformation (Box & Cox, 1964)—for example, through a logarithmic, square root, or reciprocal transformation. Such transformations, however, produce parameter estimates that are often difficult to interpret and explain to readers. Although Poisson regression also requires some explanation for readers, interpreting the parameter estimates is much more straightforward, as will be explained later.

Exponential Assumption. The Poisson regression model makes two basic assumptions: first, that the response variable is Poisson, and second, that the relationship between the response variables and the predictors is exponential. The second assumption may initially sound counterintuitive; why should one assume that the relationship between two variables is nonlinear just because one of them is Poisson? In fact, exponential growth curves can approximate a linear relationship for a certain range of the independent variable if the amount of curvature (i.e., growth) is initially small. An exponential relationship also has the advantages of affording certain mathematical properties, for example, ensuring that a count will not be negative.[4]

The form of the exponential growth curve is

$$Y = e^{a + bx}, \quad (4)$$

where e is the constant 2.72. The y-intercept is e^a, also written as $\exp(a)$. $\exp(b)$, the exponentiation of the slope, represents the rate of growth. If one takes the natural logarithms of both sides of Equation 4, we find that

$$\ln(Y) = \ln(e^{a + bx}) = a + bx. \quad (5)$$

The right side of the equation is linear; thus, this equation is considered a general linear model using a log link function (the link function

connects the predictor and response variables). Equation 4 forms the starting point of the Poisson regression model, except that we need to also factor in the offset as a source of variation. Let us call the offset s_i. Then the Poisson regression model is

$$E(Y_i) = s_i * (e^{\alpha + \beta x}). \quad (6)$$

Greek letters are used in the model to indicate that these are population parameters; furthermore, the expected value of Y_i is used because no error term is shown. With an error term, we would have

$$Y_i = s_i * (e^{\alpha + \beta x + \varepsilon}). \quad (7)$$

The response variable in Equation 7 is a count, for example, the number of deaths in a given year. The offset (s_i) is also a count, for example, the size of the population in that year. Equation 7 controls for the effect of s_i.

The next step in interpreting the model (in Equation 7) is to take the natural log of both sides:

$$\ln(Y_i) = \ln(s_i) + \alpha + \beta x + \varepsilon. \quad (8)$$

Note that it is not necessary to include an offset term. Mathematically, omitting an offset term is equivalent to setting s_i to 1; because $\ln(1) = 0$, the offset term falls out of the equation. Including or excluding an offset term can be easily done with statistical programs that perform Poisson regression, as will be discussed later in the chapter.

Interpreting the β Parameter. Of interest is whether the independent variable, X, adds anything to the predictions of the counts (i.e., is β significantly different from zero?). Assuming that β is significant, what exactly does it represent? Because the relationship is exponential, $\exp(\beta)$ is akin to the rate of "growth" in the probability that a case will be positive. This can be seen from Equation 7, which—if one moves the offset to the left side of the equation—transforms into

$$Y_i / s_i = e^{\alpha + \beta x + \varepsilon}, \quad (9)$$

where Y_i / s_i is a proportion $(P_i = Y_i/s_i)$. This value reflects the probability that a randomly chosen case will be positive given a certain value of X. β represents the rate of growth of this probability. For example, $\exp(\beta) = 1.15$ would be interpreted as "a one-unit increase in X is associated with a 15% increase in the probability of an event." Without an offset, $s_i = 1$ and $Y_i/s_i = Y_i$, so in this situation, the result could be interpreted as a 15% increase in the expected count given a one-unit increase in X.

Equation 9 is known as a Poisson rate model and is an appropriate alternative to Equation 7. One simply divides the count by the offset to obtain a proportion and then uses that as the dependent variable (Selvin, 2001). This is sometimes necessary if the software being used does not provide an accessible option for an offset. With this model, λ represents an average rate, rather than an average count, for different values of X.

Risk Ratios. When X is binary, β is sometimes referred to as a *relative risk* ratio.[5] Use of the term *risk* reflects the roots of Poisson regression in biostatistics and epidemiology, where Y typically measures number of fatalities or people contracting a disease. The term *risk* can be used more generally to refer to a probability. The relative risk ratio is therefore just a ratio of probabilities. For example, suppose you are calculating the voter turnout rate for a general election in a hypothetical state of several million people. Suppose the voter turnout rate in 2004 (a presidential election year) was 87%, but it was 53% the year before. If one assumes that the percentages presented above are representative of an adult's propensity to vote in presidential versus nonpresidential election years, then the relative risk ratio would be 1.64 (or .87/.53).[6] The ratio can be interpreted as indicating that the probability that a citizen is likely to vote increases by 64% in a presidential election year. However, one cannot necessarily assume that the percentages are representative of the general probabilities. That is where Poisson regression comes in. One can collect data over a period of time—say, 25 years—to estimate the probabilities or, more specifically, the relative risk ratio (given by the $\exp(\beta)$ estimate). Table 21.1 gives hypothetical data, expressed as counts. The response variable (Y) is the number of people who vote; the predictor (X_1) is a binary variable indicating whether a specific year is a presidential election year. X_2 is an interval/ratio variable indicating year (under the hypothesis that the rate of voter turnout may increase over time due to voter education). The offset is the number of eligible voters in the state.

In this example, the number of time periods is 25. As will be explained later, this may not be a sufficient number, but the example is kept small for purposes of exposition. A Poisson regression yielded the following parameter estimates for the predictors:

| Presidential election year | $b_1 = 0.291$ | $\text{Exp}(b_1) = 1.338$ |
| Time | $b_2 = 0.037$ | $\text{Exp}(b_2) = 1.038$ |

The results suggest that, on average, voter turnout is 33.8% higher in a presidential election year. Furthermore, voter turnout is increasing by 3.8% per year. The values 1.338 and 1.038 are relative risk ratios for a one-unit increase in X; because the presidential election year variable (X_1) is nominal, there is only a one-unit increase (from 0 to 1). Note that from Equation 9, the ratio of the probabilities for $(X_1 = 1)/(X_1 = 0)$ (i.e., the relative risk ratio) is simply

$$(e^{\alpha + \beta x + \varepsilon})/(e^{\alpha + \varepsilon}). \qquad (10)$$

Subtracting exponents (because one term is divided by another), Equation 10 reduces to $e^{\beta x}$, which can be estimated by $\exp(b)^* X$. This shows that an estimate of the relative risk ratio is given by $\exp(b)$.

Nevertheless, in social science research, as opposed to biostatistics, it is usually more intuitive to simply present $\exp(b)$ as the percentage change in the probability of a hit. To present the coefficient estimates in this way, it is necessary to subtract 1.0 from the estimates. As seen in the previous example, 1.338 reflects a 33.8% increase in the probabilities. A ratio of 2.442 would reflect a 144.2% increase in probability. When the coefficient estimates are negative, this reflects a decrease in probabilities. For example, $b = -0.223$ reflects a negative relationship. $\text{Exp}(-0.223) = 0.80$, so 0.80 is the relative risk ratio. A risk ratio of less than 1.0 reflects a negative relationship (1.0 reflects a flat relationship, with 0% rate of growth from an increase in X, so 0.80 reflects a declining "rate of growth"). Subtracting 1.0 from the estimate yields -0.20, which indicates a 20% decline in the chance of a "success" from a one-unit increase in X. In preparing research reports, coefficients can be easily interpreted for readers but do require a few sentences of explanation.

We have one note of caution. Risk ratios are sometimes confused with odds ratios, which are

Table 21.1   Voter Turnout Data (Hypothetical State)

Year	Presidential Election Year	Number of Eligible Voters (Offset)	Number Who Vote	Proportion Who Vote (%)
1980	Yes	805,339	292,960	36.4
1981	No	833,917	193,969	23.3
1982	No	858,637	223,452	26.0
1983	No	887,683	190,162	21.4
1984	Yes	913,562	565,573	61.9
1985	No	942,927	467,056	49.5
1986	No	976,405	259,374	26.6
1987	No	1,000,309	314,818	31.4
1988	Yes	1,036,545	281,748	27.2
1989	No	1,064,957	336,404	31.6
1990	No	1,100,046	511,552	46.5
1991	No	1,135,884	268,093	23.6
1992	Yes	1,116,095	588,197	50.5
1993	No	1,194,259	540,254	45.2
1994	No	1,234,805	557,362	45.1
1995	No	1,277,110	782,352	61.3
1996	Yes	1,318,434	896,213	68.0
1997	No	1,357,719	763,420	56.2
1998	No	1,395,730	700,778	50.2
1999	No	1,440,492	538,319	37.4
2000	Yes	1,477,967	1,045,155	70.7
2001	No	1,521,285	1,115,397	73.3
2002	No	1,571,800	987,822	62.8
2003	No	1,619,271	854,665	52.8
2004	Yes	1,671,863	1,462,564	87.5

used in logistic regression. As noted previously, risk ratios are made up of probabilities, which are not the same thing as odds. For example, if the probability that a citizen will vote are 87%, the odds that he or she will vote is 87%/(1 − 87%), or 6.69. Although coefficients in logistic regression reflect the percentage increase in the log-odds, those in Poisson regression reflect the percentage increase in the probabilities (after exponentiating). When probabilities are very high or low, risk ratios become extremely close to odds ratios (Le, 1998), so the terms are sometimes used interchangeably when discussing rare events, but Poisson regression is used in other contexts as well, so it is best to only discuss risk ratios. It is also typically easier for readers to understand explanations couched in terms of probabilities than in terms of odds. Terms such as *risk, chance,* and *likelihood* are all familiar to most readers, whereas the concept of odds is used less extensively in statistics.

Parameter Estimation. It is important to remember that the coefficients in regression are merely estimates of population parameters. Population parameters emerge from the process by which the data are generated in nature. The authors, however, generated the hypothetical data in

Table 21.1 using preselected beta parameters—specifically, 0.2 (exp(β) = 1.22) for the election year variable and 0.02 (exp(β) = 1.02) for time. The Poisson regression estimates (1.34 and 1.04) are somewhat close to the actual parameter values but not identical because of the inclusion of a random error term when generating the data. We extended the number of years of data from 25 to 250 and obtained much more accurate estimates (1.19 and 1.02, respectively).

Poisson regression uses maximum likelihood estimation (MLE), which chooses the parameter estimates that are most likely to produce the observed data. (This requires a large sample.) The estimation is performed by maximizing the likelihood function, $L(Y|\alpha, \beta)$, which is the likelihood of obtaining the observed data (Y) given certain parameters (α, β). The likelihood function combines the two major aspects of Poisson regression: first, that Y (and the associated error term) follows a Poisson distribution, and second, that the relationship between Y and X is exponential. Combining Equation 2, the Poisson distribution, and Equation 6, the exponential function, and noting that $E(Y) = \lambda$, we obtain

$$L(Y_i|\alpha, b) = \frac{[s_i(\alpha + \beta X_i)]^{Y_i} \exp[-s_i(\alpha + \beta X_i)]}{Y_i!}. \quad (11)$$

The likelihood for all the data points (assuming independence among them) is the joint probability, which is given by multiplying all the probabilities together:

$$L(Y|\alpha, b) = \prod_{i=1}^{N} \frac{[s_i(\alpha + \beta X_i)]^{Y_i} \exp[-s_i(\alpha + \beta X_i)]}{Y_i!}. \quad (12)$$

Although this equation is formidable, in practice it can be ignored because software packages automate the MLE process. It is important, though, to recognize the theoretical assumptions. The most important assumption is that the response variable, Y_i, follows a Poisson distribution. In this case, the error term will also have a Poisson distribution. The mean of the error term, for each value of X, will be $\lambda|X$, where $\lambda|X = E(Y_i) = s_i * (e^{\alpha + \beta x(i)})$. The means of the error term, for each value of X, define the regression line.

It is therefore important to check, before conducting a Poisson regression, that the response variable does in fact have a rough Poisson shape. Otherwise, one might not gain much in terms of statistical power from using Poisson regression. Checking the shape of the distribution also helps provide a methodological rationale for using the approach. If one uses traditional methods (e.g., ANOVA, OLS regression) and the response variable has a skewed, Poisson shape, then this will produce higher standard errors and a corresponding loss of statistical power. This is the key point of this chapter; researchers may be missing some important findings because of not taking into account the Poisson shape of many of their count variables. The point is illustrated in Figure 21.4, again using simulated data. The variable, Y, has a skewed, Poisson shape at each level of X (which has seven levels). The means form a regression line (shown by the triangles, which indicate predicted values). The line has a slight curve shape to satisfy the assumption of an exponential relationship between X and Y. (It is only very slightly curved because we wish to focus on the other major assumption, regarding the distribution of Y, for the time being.) We also used OLS to fit a line, and graphically that line was not distinguishable from that fitted with Poisson regression.

The major difference between OLS estimation and Poisson maximum likelihood estimation is in the statistical power afforded by each approach. For the null hypothesis that $\beta = 0$, probability values were calculated by dividing the estimated βs by the standard errors. This statistic follows a t distribution for OLS and a z distribution in MLE (z^2 is known as the Wald statistic). The results are shown in Table 21.2. The Poisson regression yields a lower standard error; however, that comparison is misleading because the variables in the different regressions are on different scales. More notable is that Poisson regression yields the lowest *prob*-values, indicating more statistical power than the other methods in this case. Although all the *prob*-values are low, the difference in statistical power may be critical for results at or near significance. The advantage in statistical power of Poisson regression was large: There was almost a 75% reduction in the deviance (G^2). The reduction was statistically significant ($p < .001$).

What accounts for this difference? OLS assumes that the error term is normally distributed, and Poisson assumes a Poisson distribution. The data here better fit the assumptions of the Poisson approach. The fact that the sample data are skewed creates what, in the normal

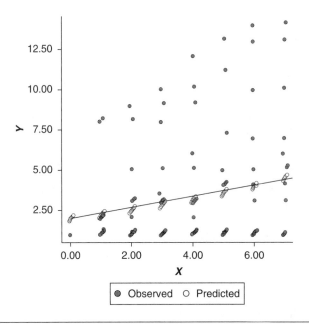

Figure 21.4   Regression with hypothetical data. Y follows a Poisson distribution. The open circles are the predicted values from a Poisson regression and define a regression line. The line from an OLS regression was indistinguishable.

Table 21.2   Poisson Versus Ordinary Least Squares Regression Using Hypothetical Data (N = 148)

Type of Regression	a	b	SE(b)	t or z	p	G²
Poisson	0.62	0.12	0.02	z: 5.30	.000	357.19
OLS (linear)	1.67	0.36	0.12	t: 3.07	.003	1438.73

general linear model, are considered a number of extreme observations, or outliers. OLS "thinks" that there is a lot of variability in the data and that there are many different regression lines—with different slopes—that could be drawn from the population data, which is what it means to have high standard errors. The Poisson model is more robust against having several high counts—in the midst of many low ones—because (a) such high counts are expected, once in a while, and (b) the approach is not trying to fit a symmetrical, normal model to the data and to account for the high counts with high variance estimates. In addition, with a Poisson distribution, there are fewer possible regression lines (i.e., lower standard errors) because the distributions (one for each level of X) are more narrow at the upper ends than with the normal distribution (see Figures 21.1 and 21.2). This constrains the number of possible regression lines that can be estimated from

the population, resulting in lower standard errors. These are the features that give the Poisson model its greater power with positively skewed distributions.

One can also perform a Poisson regression when the relationship between X and Y is linear (a different likelihood function is used). This is considered a Poisson general linear model with an identity link ($Y = a + bX$). No exponentiation is necessary, and the beta estimate is interpreted the same as in OLS; it gives the expected increase in the mean $E(Y_i) = \lambda$, from a one-unit increase in X (Agresti, 2002, p. 128). Remember that the linear assumption only applies to the link between X and Y; one still needs to assume that the Y variable (or the error term) follows a Poisson distribution.

Overdispersion. For the standard error estimates of a Poisson regression to be considered valid, the response variable should follow the

Poisson distribution, at least roughly. This requires that the variance of the response variable be approximately equal to its mean. When the variance is significantly greater than the mean, the variable is considered overdispersed. This often occurs due to uncontrolled variables that increase the heterogeneity among subjects (Agresti, 2002).

There are two ways of correcting for overdispersion. First, one can compute a Pearson chi-square (or deviance) fit statistic, reflecting the deviation of the predicted from the observed values. A dispersion factor, ϕ, can be computed by dividing the chi-square statistic by degrees of freedom (Frome & Checkoway, 1985). If the dispersion factor (ϕ) is much greater than 1.0, this is a sign of overdispersion. The variance-covariance matrix can then be multiplied by ϕ; in this way, the model recognizes, and accounts for, the additional variation (Le, 1998).

A second option is to fit a negative binomial distribution to the response variable. With a series of independent hit-or-miss trials, assume that Y represents the number of successes before the kth failure; the probability of Y follows the negative binomial distribution. With a small k (e.g., $k = 1$), the distribution is roughly shaped like the Poisson; the probability is initially high but declines exponentially as the count (i.e., number of successes) grows. The variance of the negative binomial, however, can exceed the mean, with k^{-1} acting as the dispersion factor (ϕ). (The variance is $\lambda + \lambda^2\phi$.) We can test the null hypothesis that $\phi = 0$ against the alternative hypothesis that $\phi > 0$; if $\phi = 0$, then the variance reduces to λ (and we have a Poisson distribution). We should reject the null hypothesis of no overdispersion and use the negative binomial if the latter fits the data significantly better—for example, if the difference between the likelihood ratio statistics (−2LL) is greater than $\chi^2(1 - 2\alpha, 1\ df)$ (see Cameron & Trivedi, 1998). This provides a formal test and correction for overdispersion.

An Empirical Example: Counterargument Frequency

The following example is based on a study by Nussbaum and Schraw (in press), although only the Poisson estimates are presented there. The purpose of that study was to examine how a training program (on the normative criteria of what constitutes a "good" argument) and a graphic organizer would affect the number of counterarguments generated by students when writing opinion essays. The graphic organizer involved a worksheet where students could brainstorm and evaluate arguments and counterarguments on a controversial question ("Does watching television cause children to become more violent?") and then generate an overall final opinion. Participants were 84 undergraduate college students enrolled in an educational psychology course, randomly assigned to conditions (2×2 factorial). Participants were given 30 minutes to write their essays after administration of the interventions.

It was found that both conditions resulted in more integration of arguments and counterarguments. However, integration was measured on an ordinal scale and was analyzed through ordinal, not Poisson, regression, and so we do not focus on that here. Rather, we examine the number of counterarguments that students included in their essays. (Including counterarguments can increase the persuasiveness of an essay if those counterarguments are rebutted [see O'Keefe, 1999] or used to argue for a creative solution that reduces problems identified in the counterarguments.)

Number of counterarguments was a "count" variable, and inspection of the histogram clearly indicated that its distribution was Poisson. Of the 84 essays, 45% contained no counterarguments, 45% contained one or two, and a handful (10%) contained three or four. According to a one-sample Kolmogorov-Smirnov test, the distribution could be rejected as normal ($z = 2.40$, $p < .001$) but not as Poisson ($z = 0.65$, $p = .79$). The mean number of counterarguments (estimate of λ) was 0.96 ($SD = 1.10$).

Table 21.3 shows the results of regression analyses using both OLS and Poisson regression. Poisson is clearly a more powerful approach, as the probability values for all the variables were cut in half. In addition, the training variable was not quite statistically significant using OLS ($p = .06$) but was significant using the Poisson approach. The example demonstrates the value of using more modern statistical methods. The point of conducting both types of regressions is to demonstrate the increased statistical power of using Poisson regression; of course, in conducting actual empirical research, one should use the approach most justified by the type of data one has. In this case, because the response variable was a count following the Poisson distribution,

Table 21.3   Effects of Training and Graphic Organizer on Number of Counterarguments and Supporting Reasons, Contrasting OLS and Poisson Regression ($N = 84$)

	B		SE		Prob-Value	
Independent Variable	OLS	Poisson	OLS	Poisson	OLS	Poisson
(Constant)	0.52	−0.65	0.23	0.29	.02*	.02*
Training	0.83	0.96	0.35	0.36	.02*	.01**
Graphic organizer	0.61	0.77	0.32	0.35	.06	.03*
Interaction	−1.01	−1.12	0.48	0.46	.04*	.02*

NOTE: Data from Nussbaum and Schraw (in press). Poisson *prob*-values based on chi-square (1 *df*) test, using MLwiN 1.1 statistical software (Rabash et al., 2000).

*$p < .05$. **$p < .01$.

it was methodologically better to use Poisson regression.

The regression coefficients are a bit more complicated to interpret with Poisson regression, but only a bit. In both cases, the constant is the same, because $\exp(-.65) = 0.52$. (This result implies that in the control condition—without either intervention—the average number of counterarguments was 0.52—that is, about every other essay contained a counterargument.) With Poisson regression, the coefficient for the training variable was 0.96. Exponentiating, the coefficient is $\exp(0.96) = 2.36$, which is the relative risk ratio. In other words, training resulted in a 136% increase in the number of counterarguments. (One subtracts 1.00 from the ratio to reach this conclusion; a ratio of 1.00 indicates no effect.) Using the same reasoning, the graphic organizer resulted in an 84% increase in counterarguments ($\exp(0.61) = 1.84$). The two treatments did not combine additively; the authors theorized that the negative interaction was a result of cognitive load.

Although we have found that reporting percentage increases makes it easier for readers to understand the results than if just risk ratios are reported, some critics might argue that percentage increases can be misleading when the base is low. For example, a 136% increase in counterarguments might appear to be a huge effect, but it really implies the mean increased by "only" one unit (i.e., 1.23). The criticism, in our view, is also misleading because a one-unit increase can still be pedagogically significant. For a variety of reasons, many students have difficulty distancing themselves from one side of an issue to consider an opposing side, so movement from "none to

one" may be a significant accomplishment. Furthermore, in writing opinion essays, students are normally expected to develop and support their points, so writing a long paragraph that presents a counterargument can represent a significant investment of time. This is another reason why one would not expect a large increase in the counts and why an increase of just one unit can still be practically significant. The point that we would like to make is that practical significance is a matter of interpretation. Percentage increases can be used to mislead, but when properly contextualized and perhaps presented in conjunction with information on means, this problem can be avoided.

A Simulated Extension

Having considered an empirical example, there is still the question of generalizability: How much more powerful would Poisson regression be over OLS for other data sets? To answer this question, we simulated 20 additional data sets in Excel. Each data set consisted of 100 observations; we did not use a larger N size because we wanted to limit statistical power. We used one independent variable (X); X values were assigned randomly using a uniform distribution. Y error values were assigned randomly, selecting from a Poisson distribution (as we only claim that Poisson regression is more powerful in this situation).[7] Y values were calculated using Equation 7. For all the simulations, we set the intercept at −0.65, which was taken from our previous example on argumentation. We conducted the first half of the simulations with one set of parameter values for the slope and λ (mean of the Poisson error term) and different parameter values for the second set. We set the βs small so as to limit statistical power, as we did not want both regression approaches to yield highly significant results. The specific parameter values and results (estimated slopes and probability values) are shown in Table 21.4.

Table 21.4 illustrates that Poisson regression was consistently more powerful. For the first set

of parameter values, the median OLS *prob*-value was 0.10; the median *prob*-value for Poisson regression was one fifth the size ($p = .02$). For the second group of parameter values, using Poisson regression reduced the median *prob*-value from 0.42 to 0.03.

For both these simulations, we used λ values that were fairly small (0.5 for the first group, 1.0 for the second group), which was in the same

Table 21.4   Simulation Results, Comparing OLS and Poisson Regression

Simulation Trial	Deviances OLS	Deviances Poisson	Slopes OLS	Slopes Poisson	Prob-Values OLS	Prob-Values Poisson
With model parameters 1[a]						
1	133.03	69.49	0.06	0.05	.15	.15
2	527.85	170.82	0.14	0.08	.10	.00
3	308.96	122.79	0.10	0.07	.10	.02
4	777.99	196.04	0.26	0.12	.01	.00
5	247.59	97.37	0.09	0.06	.09	.03
6	253.77	100.95	0.05	0.03	.42	.29
7	705.92	189.22	0.22	0.12	.02	.00
8	633.38	195.31	0.06	0.03	.53	.23
9	584.00	169.31	0.14	0.05	.09	.00
10	27,786.98	1,625.91	0.23	0.03	.70	.03
Mdn	555.93	170.07	0.12	0.06	.10	.02
With model parameters 2[b]						
1	2,310.07	411.82	0.17	0.06	.35	.01
2	2,222.59	401.07	−0.13	−0.04	.43	.03
3	13,278.76	1,002.92	−0.49	−0.11	.22	.00
4	7,748.84	580.57	0.68	0.22	.03	.00
5	1,392.87	297.77	0.06	0.02	.65	.30
6	2,431.02	438.32	0.15	0.05	.42	.02
7	17,890.28	1,230.40	−0.50	−0.11	.28	.00
8	13,270.99	980.72	0.11	0.03	.65	.13
9	9,712.18	889.53	0.04	0.01	.93	.65
10	1,637.27	336.66	0.07	0.03	.62	.22
Mdn	5,089.93	509.45	0.07	0.03	.42	.03

NOTE: Data simulated in Excel with Poisson error term. $N = 100$, and X ranged from 1 to 10 with uniform distribution. Constant term set to −0.65.

a. Model parameters 1: $\beta = 0.05$, $\lambda = 0.5$.

b. Model parameters 2: $\beta = 0.01$, $\lambda = 1.0$.

range as our empirical example. We expect that the advantage of Poisson regression would decrease as λ increases; recall that the Poisson distribution converges to the normal distribution as λ approaches 6.

A Second Empirical Example: Popcorn

We end with one final empirical example pertaining to how various factors affect the number of kernels of popcorn that are inedible (because they haven't yet popped)! The data were reported in Myers, Montgomery, and Vining (2002), and although the number of observations was small, the example is nevertheless illustrative. The independent variables were temperature, amount of oil, and the time (in seconds) that the kernels were cooked. The authors do not report the total number of kernels that were cooked per trial, but we assume that it was held constant. The dependent variable was found to follow a Poisson distribution using the KS test ($z = 1.19$, $p > .05$). Table 21.5 presents the parameter estimates from OLS and Poisson regression. None of the independent variables were significant with OLS. Poisson regression cut many of the probability

values in half and identified time as a significant factor. The coefficient for time was negative (-0.03), indicating that there are fewer inedible kernels with more cooking time, as one would hope. The exponent of the coefficient ($\exp(-0.03) = 0.97$) reflects the risk ratio; subtracting 1.0 gives the percentage increase, which is -0.03. This implies that the number of inedible kernels decreases by 3% with each additional second of cooking. While not necessarily surprising, the point of the example is that OLS did not identify this finding as a statistically significant result.

As a final note, we also applied various Box-Cox transformations to the Y variable, but none of the transformations improved the findings over OLS.

SOFTWARE

One of the best software programs with which to conduct Poisson regression is SAS. Poisson regression can be easily conducted using the "genmod" procedure (Le, 1998), specifically with the code in the box below.

```
data ____;
set ____;
Ln=log(____);
run;
proc genmod data=___;
class ____;
model ___ = ____ /dist=poisson link=log offset=LN PSCALE;
run;
```

Table 21.5   Effects of Temperature, Oil, and Time on Inedible Popcorn Kernels, Contrasting OLS and Poisson Regression ($N = 15$)

	B		SE		Prob-Value	
Independent Variable	OLS	Poisson	OLS	Poisson	OLS	Poisson
(Constant)	201.66	8.24	71.64	1.66	.02*	.00**
Temperature	−12.13	−0.35	7.93	0.19	.15	.07
Oil	−3.13	−0.09	7.93	0.19	.70	.64
Time	−0.93	−0.03	0.53	0.01	.11	.04*

NOTE: Data from Myers, Montgomery, and Vining (2002, p. 154). Poisson estimates account for overdispersion.

*$p < .05$. **$p < .01$.

```
glm.1 <- glm(Y ~ X, family=poisson())
glm.1
anova(glm.1, test="F")
summary(glm.1)
## for Poisson results use
Anova(glm.1, dispersion =1, test="Chisq")
Summary(glm.qD93, dispersion = 1)
```

"Class" represents categorical independent variables (if any). PSCALE indicates that the model is being adjusted for overdispersion using the Pearson chi-square dispersion factor. (To use the deviance, which is an equivalent fit statistic using logarithms, use DSCALE.) Alternatively, one can use the negative binomial (dist = negbin) with either a log or identity link (the latter if the relationship between X and Y is linear). One can also specify an identity link with the Poisson.

Poisson regression can also be implemented by MLwiN multilevel statistical software (Rabash et al., 2000) and by R. R is available free at http://www.r-project.org/. The R code for Poisson regression is shown in the box above.

Finally, the procedure can be implemented—on a limited basis—with nominal variables and several covariates in SPSS using the general log-linear procedure (with cases weighted by the response variable frequencies). We have found the procedure, however, to be less flexible and the output more difficult to interpret in SPSS. So that interested readers can try their hand at Poisson regression, we provide access to several data sets at http://www.unlv.edu/faculty/nussbaum/poisson/poisson.htm.

SUMMARY

In analyzing count data, the Poisson distribution can be used as an approximation to the binomial when rare events are involved. It is also useful as a distribution in its own right when average counts per time period are low (say under 6). Poisson regression proves a more powerful approach than ordinary least squares when the response variable distribution is Poisson in shape. Additional power is important in such areas as argumentation

research, where highly significant results are rare. (This is because of substantial measurement error due to subjectivity in coding.) It is generally good practice to use the most powerful statistical methods available when those methods are appropriate. Poisson regression has been underused in the social and behavioral sciences, however, because of a misconception that the distribution is applicable *only* to extremely rare events. It is hoped that this situation will change as researchers begin to appreciate the underlying theory and the power of this approach.

APPENDIX

Derivation of the Poisson Distribution

The binomial distribution approaches the Poisson distribution as p (probability of a success) approaches 0 and n approaches infinity. The formula for the binomial distribution (with k successes) is

$$\frac{n!}{(n-k)!k!} * p^k (1-p)^{(n-k)}.$$

Because $\lambda = np$, $p = \lambda/n$, so the formula can be rewritten:

$$\frac{n!}{(n-k)!k!} * \left(\frac{\lambda}{n}\right)^k \left[1 - \left(\frac{\lambda}{n}\right)\right]^{(n-k)}.$$

Because

$$\frac{n!}{(n-k)!} = n(n-1)(n-2)\ldots(n-k+1)$$

and because

$$\left(\frac{\lambda}{n}\right)^k = \frac{\lambda^k}{n^k},$$

we have

$$\frac{n(n-1)(n-2)\ldots(n-k+1)}{n^k}$$

$$* \frac{1}{k!}\lambda^k \left[1 - \left(\frac{\lambda}{n}\right)\right]^{(n-k)}.$$

Breaking the last term into two, we have

$$\frac{n(n-1)(n-2)\ldots(n-k+1)}{n^k}$$

$$* \frac{1}{k!}\lambda^k \left[1 - \left(\frac{\lambda}{n}\right)\right]^{n} * \left[1 - \left(\frac{\lambda}{n}\right)\right]^{-k}.$$

The first term approaches 1 as n approaches ∞, since

$$\left(\left(\frac{\infty}{\infty}\right) = 1\right).$$

Because

$$\left(\frac{\lambda}{n}\right)$$

approaches zero, the last term approaches 1 as well, because, from calculus, we have

$$\lim_{n\to} \infty_{xxx} \left(1 - \frac{\lambda}{n}\right)^n = e^{-\lambda},$$

and the equation reduces to

$$\frac{1}{k!}\lambda^k e^{-\lambda},$$

which is the formula for the Poisson distribution.

Notes

1. Poisson methods are used more extensively in engineering, physics, and epidemiology than in the social sciences.

2. For example, Excel returns an error message starting with 171!

3. Padilla (2003) recommends calculating the squared correlation between the two quantile variables to test for linearity and testing the correlation for significance against $R^2 = 1$, but the procedure is moderately complex, involving bootstrapping a sampling distribution of R^2 (for details, see Padilla, 2003, p. 63).

4. As will be explained later, however, one does have the option of specifying a linear relationship with certain software packages.

5. A risk ratio is different from an odds ratio because it is composed of probabilities rather than odds, as discussed in Chapter 25 (this volume), which also discusses odds ratios and risk ratios.

6. The odds ratio, on the other hand, would be $(0.87/0.13)/(0.53/0.47) = 5.94$. Odds are defined as $P/(1 - P)$.

7. The RAND() function was used to calculate two random numbers between 0 and 1 for each observation. The VLOOKUP function was then used to assign values of X and Y error so as to follow a uniform or Poisson distribution. To create the Poisson look-up table, we used the function for the Poisson cumulative probability density function.

References

Agresti, A. (2002). *Categorical data analysis* (2nd ed.). Hoboken, NJ: Wiley Interscience.

Antelman, G. (1997). *Elementary Bayesian statistics.* Lyme, NH: Edward Elgar.

Bortkiewicz, L. (1898). *Das gesetz der kleinen zahlen.* Leipzig: Teubner.

Box, G. E. P., & Cox, D. R. (1964). An analysis of transformations. *Journal of the Royal Statistical Society, B, 26,* 211–234.

Cameron, C., & Trivedi, P. K. (1998). *Regression analysis of count data.* Cambridge, UK: Cambridge University Press.

Frome, E. L., & Checkoway, H. (1985). Use of Poisson regression models in estimating rates and ratios. *American Journal of Epidemiology, 121,* 309–323.

Issac, R. (1995). *The pleasures of probability.* New York: Springer-Verlag.

Johnson, N. L., Kotz, S., & Kemp, A. W. (1992). *Univariate discrete distributions* (2nd ed.). New York: John Wiley.

Larsen, R. J., & Marx, M. L. (1990). *Statistics.* Englewood Cliffs, NJ: Prentice Hall.

Le, C. T. (1998). *Applied categorical data analysis.* New York: John Wiley.

Leitão, S. (2003). Evaluating and selecting counterarguments. *Written Communication, 20,* 269–306.

Myers, R. H., Montgomery, D. C., & Vining, G. G. (2002). *Generalized linear models: With applications to engineering and science.* New York: John Wiley.

Nussbaum, E. M., & Kardash, C. M. (2005). The effects of goal instructions and text on the generation of counterarguments during writing. *Journal of Educational Psychology, 97,* 157–169.

Nussbaum, E. M., & Schraw, G. (in press). Promoting argument/counterargument integration in students' writing. *Journal of Experimental Education.*

O'Keefe, D. J. (1999). How to handle opposing arguments in persuasive messages: A meta-analytic review of the effects of one-sided and two-sided messages. In M. E. Roloff (Ed.), *Communication yearbook* (Vol. 22, pp. 209–249). Thousand Oaks, CA: Sage.

Padilla (2003). *A graphical approach for goodness-of-fit of Poisson model.* Unpublished doctoral dissertation, University of Nevada, Las Vegas.

Rabash, J., Browne, W., Goldstein, H., Yang, M., Plewis, I., Healy, M., et al. (2000). *A user's guide to MLwiN.* London: Centre for Multilevel Modelling, Institute of Education, University of London.

Rosenfeld, M. J. (2002). *Some notes on different families of distributions.* Retrieved from http://www.stanford.edu/~mrosenfe/soc_388_notes/soc_388_2002/pdf%20version%20of%20notes%20on%20diff%20distributions.pdf

Ruhla, C. (1992). *The physics of chance: From Blaise Pascal to Niels Bohr* (G. Barton, Trans.). New York: Oxford University Press. (Original work published in 1989)

Rutherford, E., Chadwick, J., & Ellis, C. D. (1951). *Radiations from radioactive substances.* Cambridge, UK: Cambridge University Press.

Selvin, S. (2001). *Epidemiologic analysis: A case-oriented approach.* New York: Oxford University Press.

Stapleton, P. (2001). Assessing critical thinking in the writing of Japanese university students. *Written Communication, 18,* 506–548.

22

TESTING THE ASSUMPTIONS OF ANALYSIS OF VARIANCE

YANYAN SHENG

ANOVA ASSUMPTIONS

The analysis of variance (ANOVA) F test is commonly employed to test the omnibus null hypothesis regarding the effect of categorical independent variables (or factors) on a continuous dependent variable. It is generally well-known that certain assumptions have to be satisfied in order for the F test to produce valid statistical results. Briefly, the assumptions are independence of observations, normality in population distributions, and homogeneity of population variances (Penfield, 1994; Scheffé, 1959; Stevens, 1996). The first assumption can be handled through research design and sampling frame, whereas the latter two assumptions are concerned with the populations under investigation and therefore are oftentimes beyond the control of the researcher. Statistical methods are called robust if their inferences are not seriously invalidated by the violations of the assumptions (Miller, 1986; Scheffé, 1959). Robustness is often operationalized as the actual Type I error—namely, the probability of erroneously rejecting a true null hypothesis, being near the nominal α level. When the assumptions for the ANOVA F test are violated, the Type I error rate can be seriously inflated, resulting in spurious rejection of the null hypothesis with a reduced statistical power, the probability of correctly rejecting a false null hypothesis. Hence, inferences made about a given set of data may be invalid.

Many applied researchers in the social sciences are often tempted simply to ignore checking the assumptions or ignore the violation of the assumptions (e.g., Breckler, 1990; Keselman et al., 1998; Micceri, 1989). A great number of studies have been conducted to evaluate the ANOVA F test under various degrees of assumption violations in the literature (e.g., Glass, Peckham, & Sanders, 1972; Harwell, Rubinstein, Hayes, & Olds, 1992; Lix, Keselman, & Keselman, 1996; Scheffé, 1959; among others). They concluded that the F test is robust to some but not all of the assumption violation situations. Consequently, checking the necessary ANOVA assumptions and, more importantly, understanding the performance of the ANOVA F test under various degrees of assumption violations are essential for an applied educational and psychological researcher to understand specific data-analytic conditions and caution against false results from invalid F test procedures, for "the relevant question is not whether ANOVA assumptions are met exactly, but rather whether the plausible violations of the assumptions have serious consequences on the validity of probability statements based on the standard assumptions" (Glass et al., 1972, p. 237).

When violation of a particular ANOVA assumption seriously jeopardizes the validity of statistical inferences for a given data set, one may choose to either transform the data (such as a logarithm transformation or a square root transformation) and perform the usual F test or use an alternative procedure that is robust to assumption violations, which can be a parametric alternative such as the Welch (1951) test or a nonparamatric alternative such as the Kruskal-Wallis (Kruskal & Wallis, 1952) test.

However, none of these options are optimal in all situations. Transformation can create difficulties in interpretation, for the results are based on the transformed scores instead of the original scores (e.g., Krutchkoff, 1988). Conclusions that are drawn on transformed data do not always transfer neatly to the original measurements. Furthermore, transformation may not provide a simple solution, for a variety of transformations can be adopted depending on the type and the degree of assumption violation presented in the data (cf. Oshima & Algina, 1992).

Regarding the robust alternatives, studies have shown that they may be superior to the ANOVA F test in the majority of assumption violation situations (e.g., Levy, 1978; Tomarken & Serlin, 1986), but each procedure suffers from its own weakness.[1] For instance, the Kruskal-Wallis procedure has possible substantial statistical power when the data are nonnormal (Blair & Higgins, 1980), but it is sensitive to heterogeneity of variance, especially with unequal group sizes (Tomarken & Serlin, 1986). The Welch test is robust to variance heterogeneity but not to the presence of high skewness (Lix et al., 1996). The effects of assumption violations on ANOVA alternative procedures have not yet been fully investigated. Furthermore, some of the alternative procedures are only applicable in one-way designs. Studies are needed to extend them to a diverse range of design types. Given these considerations and the popularity of the F test, it is becoming more vital and necessary to understand the degrees of violations and the consequences of each violation on the validity of the statistical inference made on a particular set of data.

In this chapter, I describe the assumptions for the ANOVA F test in the order of checking sequence, present procedures for testing them, and discuss the consequences of each assumption violation. For simplicity of illustration, one-way ANOVA is considered. However, examples of factorial designs are provided for assessing the assumptions.

The linear model underlying a simple one-way ANOVA fixed effects design is

$$Y_{ij} = \mu_j + \varepsilon_{ij}, \qquad (1)$$

where Y_{ij} is the dependent variable associated with the ith observation in the jth treatment group for $i = 1, \ldots, n_j$, and $j = 1, \ldots, k$ (where $\sum_{j=1}^{k} n_j = N$ is the total sample size), μ_j is the population mean for the jth group, and ε_{ij} is the random error associated with Y_{ij}. The null hypothesis for the omnibus F test, $H_0 : \mu_1 = \mu_2 = \ldots = \mu_k$, is tested by comparing the computed F statistic to a critical F value at the α level with $k - 1$ and $N - k$ degrees of freedom (df), $F_{1-\alpha}$ $(k-1, N-k)$. It is assumed that the ε_{ij}s are independent and normally distributed with a mean 0 and a common variance, σ^2, within each of the k levels—that is, $\varepsilon_{ij} \sim N(0, \sigma^2)$. The linear model for factorial ANOVA designs can be generalized based on the number of factors in the model.

Independence of Observation

Independence of random errors (i.e., ε_{ij} in Equation 1) means that the value of one observation in the dependent variable, Y_{ij}, provides no information about or is not influenced by the value for any other observation, $Y_{i'j'}$. The independence of the observation assumption is a basic requirement of experimental design. Violation of this assumption leads to dependent or correlated observations. An illustrative example for such a violation can be students taught by a particular instructor in an educational setting. They are not independent as they share the same teaching. We say the students are nested within the instructor. One may also argue that individuals in a corporation are nested and hence nonindependent due to similarity in their background and experiences. With such nonindependent/nested data, one has to adopt techniques such as nested ANOVA designs and/or hierarchical linear modeling (HLM).

The independence assumption can be decided and controlled by the researcher when planning and executing the experiment. In most research situations, the requirement for independence is typically realized by randomization (i.e., using a random sample of separate, unrelated subjects).

Test the Assumption

For a simple one-way ANOVA design, an intraclass correlation (ICC) can be used to assess whether this assumption is tenable (Stevens, 1996). One can compute the ICC using the SPSS RELIABILITY procedure. But the data layout has to be constructed differently from the format in the usual ANOVA analysis—for example, the layout in the DIST data (see Appendix A for a description of the data). For instance, to evaluate the assumption of independence of correct responses (NUMRIGHT) from three treatment conditions (CONDIT), one has to create three continuous variables (c1, c2, c3) out of NUMRIGHT, each representing correct responses in one treatment condition, so the layout of the data is as shown in Table 22.1. The responses are randomly arranged in each group. It has to be noted that the order of the subjects in each group does not affect the extent to which the scores correlate, although the ICC and *p* values could be different with another ordering.

Table 22.2 displays the SPSS syntax and output for computing the ICC with the data shown in Table 22.1. A large *p* value ($p = .920$) suggests low nonsignificant correlations among observations from the three treatment conditions. Hence, the independence of observations can be assumed.

However, this procedure is only applicable in a single-factor design. One may also test this assumption using a run chart of the residual scores (e.g., for the one-way design, $\hat{\varepsilon}_{ij} = Y_{ij} - \overline{Y}_{\bullet j}$, where $\overline{Y}_{\bullet j}$ denotes the sample estimate of the *j*th population mean), particularly if the time order of data collection is available. Unlike the method with ICC, this procedure can be used in factorial ANOVAs as well. To illustrate, suppose one sets up a two-factor ANOVA investigating how correct responses (NUMRIGHT) are affected by the background conditions (CONDIT) and the participant's gender (GENDER) in the DIST data. Because the data do not concern the time order of data collection, one may use the participant's id number (ID) to check the independence assumption. Residuals are obtained by fitting a factorial ANOVA model using the SPSS GLM procedure and are further plotted against ID using the SPSS GRAPH procedure. Figure 22.1 shows the SPSS syntax and the chart, which indicates that with no clear patterns in the residuals, the independence assumption can be assumed.

Table 22.1   Number of Correct Responses in the Three Treatment Conditions

c1	c2	c3
16	15	8
18	18	17
17	19	11
14	15	13
19	19	11
16	16	16
16	18	14
17	14	13
15	16	8
19	19	15
19	18	11
19	9	13
17	14	9
16	15	15
19	19	12
18	20	11
16	19	13
14	18	12
17	16	17
17	20	10
18	20	17
14	18	13
17	17	15
16	17	11
17	19	14

Effects of Violations

In cases of nonindependence, the scores/observations of the subject are influenced by other subjects or previous scores. Failure to satisfy the independence assumption can have serious effects on the validity of probability statements in the ANOVA *F* procedure (Glass et al., 1972; Harwell et al., 1992; Scheffé, 1959; Stevens, 1996), leading to tests with inflated Type I error and reduced power even though the sample size is large (Scariano & Davenport, 1987). The nature of nonindependence (i.e., positive or negative relationship in the observations) has different effects on *F* tests. Specifically, positive

Table 22.2 SPSS Syntax and Output for Evaluating the Independence Assumption With a Single Factor

SPSS syntax:

```
RELIABILITY
/VARIABLES=c1 c2 c3
/FORMAT=NOLABELS
/SCALE(ALPHA)=ALL/MODEL=ALPHA
/ICC=MODEL(ONEWAY) CIN=95 TESTVAL=0.
```

Output:

Intraclass Correlation Coefficient

	Intraclass Correlation	95% Confidence Interval		F Test With True Value 0			
		Lower Bound	Upper Bound	Value	df1	df2	Significance
Single Measures	−.159	−.302	.074	.589	24	50	.920
Average Measures	−.699	−2.281	.194	.589	24	50	.920

NOTE: One-way random effects model where people effects are random.

SPSS syntax:

```
GLM numright BY condit gender
/SAVE = RESID.
GRAPH
/SCATTERPLOT(BIVAR)=id WITH res_1.
```

Run chart of residuals:

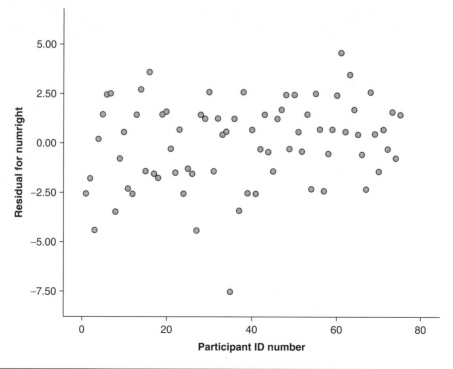

Figure 22.1 SPSS syntax and output for a visual check of the independence assumption.

correlations yield a more liberal test, whereas negative correlations lead to a more conservative test (Cochran, 1947). In addition, the higher the correlations, the more different the actual significance level is from the nominal level.

To further illustrate the effect of violation on Type I and II errors, let's consider two simulated data sets, each containing three treatment groups and six observations per group, as displayed in Table 22.3. The two data sets satisfy two conditions—namely, conditions with and without the independence of observations. In the latter case where the assumption is violated, moderate correlations ($\rho = 0.5$) between treatment groups are assumed. In addition, in both sets, the values in Groups 1, 2, and 3 are random draws from normal distributions with a common variance 1 and means 0, 1, or 2, respectively. The effect size is kept similar in both conditions. This actually specifies that the true population means are different among the three groups, and the omnibus F is supposed to show significance for both data sets. Indeed, with the uncorrelated data (i.e., when the independence assumption is satisfied), the ANOVA F test shows significance at the .05 level ($p = .038$) and a .636 probability of correctly rejecting a false null hypothesis (see "Summary of Analysis" in Table 22.3 for uncorrelated data). However, the correlated data result in a nonsignificant F test with a higher p value ($p = .063$) and a lower power estimate (.542).

Outliers

There are many reasons for an extreme score in ANOVA (discussed in detail in Chapter 14). As with other procedures, outliers can be detected using the standardized residuals so that any values more than 3 standard deviations away from the mean can be considered as outliers. Using the DIST data, for a two-factor ANOVA using the background conditions (CONDIT) and the participant's gender (GENDER) to model correct responses (NUMRIGHT), standardized residuals can be obtained using the GLM procedure shown in Table 22.4. From the saved standardized residuals displayed in the table, it is obvious that ID 35 is an outlier, whose standardized residual

Table 22.3   ANOVA F Tests for the Data Simulated From Uncorrelated and Correlated Distributions

Correlated Data $\rho = .5$			Uncorrelated Data		
Group 1	Group 2	Group 3	Group 1	Group 2	Group 3
1.128	1.660	2.305	−2.231	3.719	7.580
2.093	1.941	2.643	0.652	4.239	3.914
1.472	2.636	1.517	2.476	−1.292	0.097
2.266	3.449	5.257	0.548	1.459	3.815
2.177	2.950	2.897	0.369	2.317	3.566
1.214	2.595	3.550	0.908	0.410	3.699

Summary of Analysis for Correlated Data						
Source	SS	df	MS	F	p	Power	η_p^2
Groups	5.201	2	2.601	3.343	.063	.542	.308
Error	11.668	15	.778				
Total	16.870	17					

Summary of Analysis for Uncorrelated Data						
Source	SS	df	MS	F	p	Power	η_p^2
Groups	33.546	2	16.773	4.115	.038	.636	.354
Error	61.138	15	4.076				
Total	94.683	17					

is −3.37. A sensitivity analysis can subsequently be carried out to check if this outlier seriously affects the F test. Table 22.5 summarizes the ANOVA results using the original data (the upper part of the table) and using the data without the outlier (the lower part of the table). The two tests, resulting in different F statistics, p values, or estimated effect sizes, indicate that the presence of the outlier does affect inferences drawn from the F tests. Actually, the presence of this outlier depresses the estimated effect size, especially for the interaction. Hence, the observation of ID 35 should be examined more carefully to determine whether it should be retained in the data.

Homogeneity of Population Variances

The assumption of homogeneity of variances states that the error variances are the same across the populations under investigation (e.g., $\sigma_1^2 =$ $\sigma_2^2 = \ldots = \sigma_k^2$ for a one-way design). In performing F tests, the common variance, σ^2, estimated by the mean square error (or within-group mean square), is the denominator of the F ratio. Conceptually, the mean square error is considered as the pooled or the weighted average of the sample variances. It estimates the baseline variation that is present in a response variable. When populations differ widely in variances, this average is a poor summary measure.

Test the Assumption

A visual check of the homogeneity assumption can be made by inspecting and comparing the side-by-side boxplots of the residuals (e.g., $\hat{\varepsilon}_{ij}$) from different populations. The relative height of the boxes or the interquartile range (IRQ)—that is, the distance between the upper quartile (75th percentile) and the lower quartile (25th percentile)—indicates the relative variability of the

Table 22.4   SPSS Syntax for Detecting Within-Cell Outliers

SPSS syntax:

```
GLM numright BY condit gender
/SAVE = ZRESID.
```

Standardized residuals by ID

ID	ZRE_1	ID	ZRE_1	ID	ZRE_1	ID	ZRE_1	ID	ZRE_1
S1	−1.15	16	1.6	31	−0.64	46	0.55	61	2.04
2	−0.79	17	−0.7	32	0.55	47	0.75	62	0.26
3	−1.98	18	−0.79	33	0.19	48	1.09	63	1.54
4	0.1	19	0.65	34	0.26	49	−0.14	64	0.75
5	0.65	20	0.7	35	−3.37	50	1.1	65	0.19
6	1.1	21	−0.14	36	0.55	51	0.26	66	−0.26
7	1.12	22	−0.67	37	−1.53	52	−0.19	67	−1.03
8	−1.56	23	0.31	38	1.15	53	0.65	68	1.15
9	−0.35	24	−1.14	39	−1.14	54	−1.03	69	0.2
10	0.26	25	−0.59	40	0.31	55	1.12	70	−0.64
11	−1.03	26	−0.7	41	−1.15	56	0.31	71	0.31
12	−1.15	27	−1.98	42	−0.14	57	−1.09	72	−0.14
13	0.64	28	−0.64	43	0.64	58	−0.24	73	0.7
14	1.2	29	−0.55	44	−0.19	59	0.31	74	−0.35
15	−0.64	30	−1.15	45	−0.64	60	1.09	75	0.64

Table 22.5   Sensitivity Analysis With and Without Case 35

Summary of Analysis on All Data						
Source	SS	df	MS	F	p	η_p^2
Conditions	134.958	2	67.479	13.484	.000	.281
Gender	32.858	1	32.858	6.566	.013	.087
Condition × Gender	2.394	2	1.197	.239	.788	.007
Error	345.292	69	5.004			
Total	676.347	74				

Summary of Analysis Without Case 35						
Source	SS	df	MS	F	p	η_p^2
Conditions	150.488	2	75.224	18.096	.000	.347
Gender	22.565	1	22.565	5.429	.023	.074
Condition × Gender	7.925	2	3.962	.953	.391	.027
Error	282.664	68	4.157			
Total	632.554	73				

residual scores in each treatment condition. Equal variability can be assumed if boxplots have relatively equal spread or IRQ across populations.

Consider the DIST example of the correct responses (NUMRIGHT) obtained from three treatment conditions (CONDIT) for male and female (GENDER) participants, after removing the potential outlying case (ID 35). The boxplots as well as SPSS syntax for obtaining them on the saved residuals are shown in Figure 22.2. It is obvious from the figure that the boxplots are dissimilar in their spread or IRQ. Specifically, the box for the (FEMALE, CONSTANT SOUND) condition is the smallest, whereas that for the (MALE, NO SOUND) condition shows the largest distance. The latter appears to be about twice as wide as the former. However, given the unit of the scale, it is hard to decide whether the difference in the IRQ or population variances is substantial. One has to check the significance of this inequality numerically.

There are a number of tests for the homogeneity of variance assumption, including Bartlett's chi-square test, Hartley's F-max test, Cochran's C test, Levene's test, and Brown-Forsythe's test, and most software packages incorporate at least one. The first three tests are sensitive to even slight departures from normality (Box, 1953), while the latter two tests are shown to be fairly robust even when the underlying distributions deviate significantly from the normal distribution (Olejnik & Algina, 1987) and hence are recommended. They have an added advantage of simplifying the

procedure by allowing normality tests conducted after the homogeneity of variances is tested, which will be explained further in a later section.

The Brown-Forsyth test is a modification of the Levene test (Brown & Forsythe, 1974). The null hypothesis for the two tests is that the variances are homogeneous ($H_0: \sigma_1^2 = \sigma_2^2 \ldots = \sigma_k^2$). In both tests, original values of the dependent variable (Y_{ij}) are transformed to derive a dispersion variable on their absolute deviations from the respective group means ($|Y_{ij} - \bar{Y}_{.j}|$) for the Levene test, or medians ($|Y_{ij} - m_j|$, where m_j denotes the median of the jth group) for the Brown-Forsythe test. ANOVA is subsequently performed on the dispersion variable, and the significance level for the test of homogeneity of variance is then the p value for the ANOVA F test on this variable. Thus, if the F test is significant at a predefined critical level (usually .05), the hypothesis of equal variances should be rejected in conclusion of the violation of the assumption.

Generally, Brown-Forsythe's test is preferred over Levene's test (when available) when there is unequal sample size in the two (or more) groups that are to be compared. In addition, it is reported to be the most robust and best at providing power to detect variance differences while protecting the Type I error (Conover, Johnson, & Johnson, 1981; Olejnik & Algina, 1987).

The previous side-by-side boxplots suggest that the residuals appear to differ much in their spread of variability across groups. Formal statistical tests can be conducted to test the homogeneity of

SPSS syntax:

```
GLM numright BY condit gender
/SAVE = RESID PRED.

EXAMINE
VARIABLES=res_1 BY pre_1
/PLOT BOXPLOT
/STATISTICS=NONE
/NO TOTAL.
```

Boxplots:

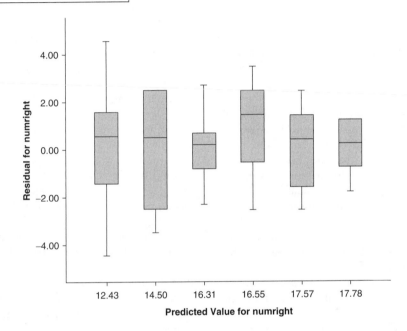

Figure 22.2   SPSS syntax and output for a visual check of the equal variances assumption.

variances in correct responses (NUMRIGHT) at the three treatment conditions (CONDIT) for male and female (GENDER) participants by setting up the null and alternative hypotheses as $H_0: \sigma_1^2 = \sigma_2^2 \ldots = \sigma_6^2$ and H_1: not all σ_i^2 are equal, respectively.

The result (displayed in Table 22.6) shows a nonsignificant Levene's test, $F_{(5, 68)} = 2.175$, $p = .067$, on the dispersion variable. Hence, the null hypothesis is retained, and equal variances can be assumed at the .05 level.

Brown-Forsythe's test is not directly implemented in SPSS (it is, however, implemented in SAS). The procedures can get very complicated if there are many factors or groups (in which case, one can consider using other statistical packages such as SAS). For the above example, the Brown-Forsythe test, for which procedures are detailed in Appendix B, results in a nonsignificant F ratio, $F_{(5, 68)} = 1.587$, $p = .175$ (see

Table 22.6   SPSS Syntax and Output for an Example of Using Levene's Test

SPSS syntax:

```
GLM numright  BY condit gender
/PRINT = HOMOGENEITY.
```

Output:

Levene's Test of Equality of Error Variances[a]

Dependent Variable: Number correct over 20 trials

F	df1	df2	Significance
2.175	5	68	.067

NOTE: Tests the null hypothesis that the error variance of the dependent variable is equal across groups.

a. Design: Intercept + condit + gender + condit × gender.

Table B1 in Appendix B). The test shows no evidence for heterogeneity. Therefore, one can assume homogeneity of variances and proceed with an ANOVA F test for the differences among the population means.

Although Levene's and Brown-Forsythe's tests are robust to nonnormality, some authors (e.g., Glass & Hopkins, 1996) have pointed out that the tests themselves rely on the homogeneity of variances assumption (of the absolute deviations from the means or medians), and hence it is not clear how robust these tests are themselves in the presence of significant variance heterogeneity and unequal sample sizes.

Effects of Violations

The prevailing conclusion drawn from early studies on the effects of variance heterogeneity (see Glass et al., 1972, for a review of this earlier literature) indicated that the F test was quite robust against violations of this assumption, especially when sample sizes were equal. However, the robustness of the test has been somewhat misinterpreted in the literature (Krutchkoff, 1988). Research initiated by Box (1953) has shown that F tests are not robust to all degrees of variance heterogeneity even when the sample sizes are equal (e.g., Rogan & Keselman, 1977; Weerahandi, 1995; among others). It is true that the value of the F statistic does not dramatically change due to small or even moderate departures from this assumption when sample sizes are equal. However, as the degree of heterogeneity increases, the F test is more biased with inflated error rates and reduced power, especially with small sample sizes. The effect of variance heterogeneity may be more serious when sample sizes are not equal. It is also noted that when the variances are positively paired with the sample sizes—that is, when the group with the largest sample size, for example, has the largest variance—the true Type I error will be less than the nominal significant level. On the other hand, when the variances are negatively paired with the sample sizes, the true Type I error will exceed the nominal level (Glass et al., 1972; Harwell et al., 1992).

When variances are heterogeneous, Welch's (1951) test should be used in most one-way designs with balanced or unbalanced data. However, this test is sensitive to large skewness in the data. Lix et al. (1996) pointed out that skewness greater than 2.0 might result in inflated error rates for the Welch test. They further recommended using sample sizes no less than 10. It has to be noted that extension of Welch's test to a variety of univariate and multivariate designs is possible Lix & Keselman, 1995).

To further illustrate effects of the variance heterogeneity, let's consider the DIST data again. One of the variables in the data is HETERVAR, which was simulated from three normal distributions, each corresponding to the CONSTANT SOUND, RANDOM SOUND, and NO SOUND conditions, with population means 3, 10, and 6 and standard deviations 0.1, 10, and 15, respectively. The F test, Welch's test, and Levene's test can be performed simultaneously with the SPSS ONEWAY procedure. The syntax, together with the output, is shown in Table 22.7.

The Levene test is significant with an extremely small p value ($p < .001$), indicating a great degree of variance heterogeneity in HETERVAR among the three treatment conditions. This further results in an F test not significant at the .05 level, $F_{(2, 72)} = 2.878$ ($p = .063$, $= .074$), suggesting that the data do not provide sufficient evidence against the null hypothesis of equal population means. However, the Welch test, not assuming equal variances, reports significant mean differences, $F_{w(2,32)} = 6.875$, $p = .003$, which is consistent with the actual situation. As pointed out earlier, Welch's test is not commonly implemented in statistical packages and is only available for one-way design in SPSS. Hence, one has to adopt other robust tests when variance homogeneity is not attainable.

In this example, we see that the heterogeneity of variance has greatly deteriorated the power of the F test even with equal sample sizes ($n_j = 25$). For the effect with unequal sample sizes, readers can use the simulated variable HETERVAR in the HSB data, evaluate the equal variances assumption of this variable across the three socioeconomic status (SES) levels, and compare the F test result with the Welch test result. The effects of unequal variances on the Type I error rates and power for F tests have been mainly investigated using Monte Carlo studies in the literature. For an excellent review as well as a summary of consequences of the violations, see Harwell et al. (1992).

Normality in Treatment Population

In addition to equal variances, ANOVA fixed-factor models make an additional distributional assumption that the random errors are normally distributed in all treatment conditions.

Table 22.7   SPSS Syntax and Output for the ANOVA *F* Test and the Welch Test When Variances Are Heterogeneous

SPSS syntax:

```
ONEWAY hetervar BY condit
/STATISTICS HOMOGENEITY WELCH.
```

Outputs:

Test of Homogeneity of Variances

A variable with heterogeneity of variance between the three treatment conditions (departure from equal variances)

Levene Statistic	df1	df2	Significance
23.709	2	72	.000

ANOVA

A variable with heterogeneity of variance between the three treatment conditions (departure from equal variances)

	SS	df	MS	F	Significance
Between groups	501.179	2	250.589	2.878	.063
Within groups	6269.073	72	87.070		
Total	6770.252	74			

Robust Tests of Equality of Means

A variable with heterogeneity of variance between the three treatment conditions (departure from equal variances)

	Statistic[a]	df1	df2	Significance
Welch	6.875	2	32.008	.003

a. Asymptotically *F* distributed.

Test the Assumption

The normality assumption can be assessed using graphics, descriptive statistics, and formal statistical tests on the residual scores (e.g., $\hat{\varepsilon}_{ij}$). Graphics provide the simplest and most direct way to examine the shape of a distribution. While histograms can aid in visual inspection of normality, normal probability plots (graphs of the empirical quantiles based on the data against the actual quantiles of the standard normal distribution, also called normal Q-Q plots) are considered to be more informative. The points will fall close to a straight line if the distribution is approximately normal. Points that are above the straight-line pattern suggest that residuals are smaller than expected for normal data. Points that are below the straight-line pattern suggest that residuals are bigger than expected for normal data.

Simple descriptive statistics (i.e., the coefficients for skewness and kurtosis) provide important information relevant to this issue. For example, perfect normal distributions are symmetrical with a zero skewness and moderately spread with a zero kurtosis. If the result of dividing skewness or kurtosis by its corresponding standard errors exceeds 2, the distribution departs significantly from a normal distribution.

More precise information can be obtained by performing one of the statistical tests of normality to determine the probability that the sample came from a normally distributed population (e.g., the Kolmogorov-Smirnov [KS] test or the Shapiro-Wilks test). For both tests, a *p* value smaller than a predefined critical level (usually .05) suggests rejection of the null hypothesis that the data follow a normal distribution. It should be noted that tests of normality do not reflect the magnitude of the departure. That is, these tests only reflect whether the data depart from normality. Small p values indicate that the distribution almost definitely departs from normality. They do not, however, indicate that the distribution departs *substantially* from normality, especially when the sample size is large. In general, the Shapiro-Wilks test is too sensitive to minor deviations from normality, and even the KS test is relatively sensitive, and none of the statistical tests can substitute for a visual examination of the data.

Effects of Violations

The fixed effects model F test is relatively robust to deviations from normality (see Glass et al., 1972; Harwell et al., 1992, for summaries of the effects), except when sample sizes are small and power is being evaluated.

Studies indicate that severe skewness can have a greater impact than kurtosis (e.g., Lumley, Diehr, Emerson, & Chen, 2002; Scheffé, 1959). Its impact on the F test varies. Tiku (1964) concluded that distributions with skewness in different directions had a greater effect on Type I errors than distributions with skewness values in the same direction. Harwell et al. (1992) observed that when sample sizes are unequal, skewed distributions can result in slightly inflated Type I error rates. Skovlund and Fenstad (2001) also reported that the level of significance is sensitive to severely skewed distributions with unequal sample size and unequal variances.

To illustrate the effects of nonnormality due to skewness or kurtosis, let's consider the NORMAL, SKEWED, and UNIFORM variables in the DIST data. Observations for the three variables were randomly simulated from a normal, a positive skewed, and a uniform distribution, respectively, so that the cell means are the same for each distribution. It should be noted that a uniform distribution is an extreme case when the distribution is flatter than a standard normal distribution with a kurtosis around −1.2. Figure 22.3 displays the histograms of the three variables aggregating over the three treatment conditions. The overall distributional shapes suggest that SKEWED and UNIFORM deviate from normal distributions in that the former is right-skewed whereas the latter looks platykurtic.

F tests are then performed to test the overall mean differences between the three conditions (CONDIT) in NORMAL, SKEWED, and UNIFORM. To make sure that nonnormality is not complicated by variance heterogeneity, the homogeneity of variance is checked using the Levene procedure, and the resulting nonsignificant p values suggest that equal variances can be assumed for the three F tests. Table 22.8 summarizes the ANOVA results, which indicate a significant mean difference in SKEWED $(F_{(2,72)} = 3.584, p = .033, \eta_p^2 = .091)$ but not in NORMAL $(F_{(2,72)} = .662, p = .519, \eta_p^2 = .018)$ or UNIFORM $(F_{(2,72)} = .123, p = .884, \eta_p^2 = .003)$.

To evaluate the F results, the Kruskal-Wallis (KW; Kruskal & Wallis, 1952) test, a nonparametric alternative to the F test, is conducted to

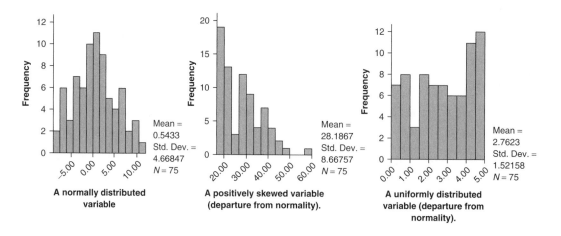

A normally distributed variable

Mean = 0.5433
Std. Dev. = 4.66847
$N = 75$

A positively skewed variable (departure from normality).

Mean = 28.1867
Std. Dev. = 8.66757
$N = 75$

A uniformly distributed variable (departure from normality).

Mean = 2.7623
Std. Dev. = 1.52158
$N = 75$

Figure 22.3   Histograms of aggregated NORMAL, SKEWED, and UNIFORM variables.

Table 22.8   *F* Tests of Mean Differences Between CONDIT in NORMAL, SKEWED, and UNIFORM

			Summary of Analysis for NORMAL			
Source	*SS*	*df*	*MS*	*F*	*p*	η_p^2
Conditions	29.121	2	14.561	.662	.519	.018
Error	1583.679	72	21.996			
Total	1612.800	74				

			Summary of Analysis for SKEWED			
Source	*SS*	*df*	*MS*	*F*	*p*	η_p^2
Conditions	503.387	2	251.693	3.584	.033	.091
Error	5056.000	72	70.222			
Total	5559.387	74				

			Summary of Analysis for UNIFORM			
Source	*SS*	*df*	*MS*	*F*	*p*	η_p^2
Conditions	.586	2	.293	.123	.884	.003
Error	170.741	72	2.371			
Total	171.326	74				

Table 22.9   SPSS Syntax and Output for the Kruskal-Wallis Test

SPSS syntax:

```
NPAR TESTS
/K-W = normal skewed uniform    BY condit(1 3).
```

Output:

Test Statistics [a,b]

	A Normally Distributed Variable	A Positively Skewed Variable (Departure From Normality)	A Uniformly Distributed Variable (Departure From Normality)
Chi-square	1.172	5.686	.201
df	2	2	2
Asymp. Sig.	.556	.058	.905

a. Kruskal-Wallis test.

b. Grouping variable: PRESENTATION CONDITION.

test the respective mean differences between CONDIT in the three variables. This test does not assume normal distributions. However, it can still be affected by some form of nonnormality when variances are unequal (Cribbie & Keselman, 2003; Oshima & Algina, 1992; Tomarken & Serlin, 1986). The KW test results as well as the SPSS syntax are shown in Table 22.9. Different from the significant *F* result obtained with the positive skewed variable (SKEWED), the KW test reports a slightly higher *p* value ($p = .058$), resulting in a nonsignificance test at the .05 level. Actually, the *p* values for the normal and uniform variables are a little larger than the corresponding *p* values from the *F* test as well. However, they do not affect the significance levels tremendously. From this example, we see that skewed distributions can result in spurious rejection of the null hypothesis. For practice, the reader can also conduct the *F* test and the KW test on the simulated variable NONNORMAL across the levels in SES in the HSB data to further understand the effect of the assumption violation.

Summary Remarks

As most applied researchers who employ inferential statistical techniques make extensive use of ANOVA procedures, the importance of testing the *F* test assumptions and understanding the effects of violations cannot be overstated. The notions that dependence among observations, heterogeneity of variance, or nonnormality does not affect inferences based on the ANOVA *F* test have to be dispelled. Dependence of observations can be overcome by carefully designing the research through randomization. However, unequal variances and nonnormal distributions have to be evaluated even though the study is carefully designed. From the previous discussions, we see that *F* tests are relatively robust to nonnormality assuming equal variances but not to variance heterogeneity when normality is assumed, regardless of whether sample sizes are equal. Cramer (1994), among others, examined the effect of simultaneous violations of normality and equality of variance assumptions, reported serious problems, and suggested that the ANOVA *F* test be avoided when simultaneous violations are detected. Consequently, it is essential for a researcher to compare treatment means with an appreciation for the underlying assumptions of the *F* test.

Although several statistical procedures are available for examining a particular ANOVA assumption, no technique is completely adequate. Statistical tests are flawed in two major ways: (a) The assumption tests were not designed to show that the null hypothesis is true, and thus, the usual .05 critical level might not be an appropriate significance level; and (b) the precision of the tests depends on sample sizes. The *F* test is fairly robust with respect to nonnormality, and the degree of robustness is dependent on the number of observations per treatment. As the number of observations increases, normality tests become more sensitive or more likely to declare nonnormality. Likewise, testing the variance homogeneity assumption, one is likely to accept the null hypothesis with small samples even when variances are heterogeneous but reject the null hypothesis with large samples even when the differences between treatment variances are too small to be a problem. Therefore, given the above problems associated with statistical tests, the use of graphics approaches is generally recommended as a key part of any examination of assumptions.

When one is conducting an ANOVA with a between-group factor, it is more appropriate to use the residual scores than the raw scores to check the assumptions. The ANOVA test is based on the *F* ratio, which is the between-groups variance divided by the within-group variance. The latter is the average squared deviation of scores around their group mean (i.e., the average squared residuals). In order to ensure that no observation has a strong influence on the calculation of the within-group variance, we should examine these residuals and look for heterogeneity in variances, outliers, or extremely nonnormal distributions. If the assumptions of normality and variance homogeneity are reasonable, then certain characteristics should be evident for the residuals. Deviations from these characteristics suggest that ANOVA assumptions may not be met. It has to be noted again here that the test of normality on the residuals is not appropriate if there is a heterogeneity of variance problem. Hence, it is recommended that normality be examined after the unequal variances problem has been dealt with.

As a practice, the reader can follow the procedures described in this chapter to evaluate the assumptions for a two-factor ANOVA design using students' sex (SEX) and socioeconomic status (SES) to model their science scores (SCI) in the HSB data.

APPENDIX A: DATA SET

Example Data

Throughout the chapter, a major data set is used to illustrate the procedures for evaluating ANOVA assumptions and setting up contrast coding. The data are based on a study investigating the effect of background sound on learning. It is predicted that students will learn most effectively with a constant background sound, as opposed to an unpredictable sound or no sound at all. In order to test this, participants were asked to study a passage of text for 30 minutes. Then they were given 20 multiple-choice questions to answer based on the material. Each participant was randomly assigned to one of the three studying groups. One group had background sound at a constant volume. A second group studied with noise that changed volume periodically in the background. A third group had no sound at all.

The data are stored in an SPSS data file DIST.SAV. Each variable is described in the table to the right. NUMRIGHT shows the number of correct responses over the 20 items. CONDIT is the grouping variable with the three experimental conditions. Other quantitative variables—NORMAL, SKEWED, UNIFORM, and HETERVAR—are variables simulated from distributions that are normal, positively skewed, uniform, and heterogeneous in variances, respectively. Furthermore, INDEPEND and DEPEND are variables simulated from distributions with and without independent observations.

Practice Data

Another data set is provided for those who want to practice or experiment with the techniques described in this chapter. The data are revised from the High School and Beyond Study (Glass & Hopkins, 1996) and are stored in an SPSS data file HSD.SAV. Achievement (reading, math, and science scores) and demographic (sex, SES) information was recorded for a national representative sample of 600 high school seniors. HETERVAR and NONNORMAL are variables simulated from distributions with unequal variances and nonnormal distributions, respectively. A description of each variable is as follows.

Variable Name	Variable Label/Value Label
ID	Participant ID number
CONDIT	Treatment condition /
	1 = 'CONSTANT SOUND'
	2 = 'RANDOM SOUND'
	3 = 'NO SOUND'
GENDER	Gender of participant / 1 = "Male," 2 = "Female"
NUMRIGHT	The number correct over 20 items
NORMAL	A normally distributed variable
SKEWED	A positively skewed variable (departure from normality)
UNIFORM	A uniformly distributed variable (departure from normality)
HETERVAR	A variable with heterogeneity of variance between the three treatment conditions (departure from equal variances)
DEPEND	A simulated variable with dependent observations and different means across CONDIT
INDEPEND	A simulated variable with independent observations and different means across CONDIT

Variable Name	Variable Label/Value Label
ID	Student ID number
SEX	Gender of student /
	1 = "Male," 2 = "Female"
SES	Socioeconomic status/
	1 = 'Lower'
	2 = 'Middle'
	3 = 'Upper'
RDG	Reading T-score
MATH	Math T-score
SCI	Science T-score
HETERVAR	A simulated variable with variance heterogeneity and different means across SES
NONNORMAL	A simulated variable with nonnormality and different means across SES

APPENDIX B: BROWN-FORSYTHE'S TEST

For the DIST example, within-group medians—that is, medians of correct responses (NUMRIGHT) for male and female participants (GENDER) at three treatment conditions (CONDIT)—are first computed using the MEANS procedure:

MEANS

TABLES = numright BY pre_1

/CELLS MEDIAN.

The medians are reported to be as follows for the six (GENDER*CONDIT) groups.

Median:

	Predicted Value for numright					
	12.43	14.50	16.31	16.55	17.57	17.78
Number correct over 20 trials	13.00	15.00	16.50	18.00	18.00	18.00

Then the NUMRIGHT scores are transformed to derive the dispersion variable on their absolute deviations from the respective group medians ($|Y_{ij} - m_j|$) using the following syntax:

IF (pre_1<13) dispersion = ABS(numright-13) .

IF (pre_1<15 & pre_1>13) dispersion = ABS(numright-15) .

IF (pre_1<16.5 & pre_1>15) dispersion = ABS(numright-16.5) .

IF (pre_1>16.5) dispersion = ABS(numright-18) .

A new variable, DISPERSION, is then created in SPSS. The upper part of Table B1 shows the values for the original NUMRIGHT and the dispersion variables at each treatment condition. ANOVA F test is then performed to test group difference in DISPERSION with the ONEWAY procedure using the fitted values as the factor:

ONEWAY dispersion BY pre_1.

F test results are summarized at the bottom of Table B1, which are the result for the Brown-Forsythe test.

NOTE

1. Readers can refer to Chapter 18 (this volume) on robust methods for more information, although the chapter is more focused on regression-style methodology.

REFERENCES

Blair, R. C., & Higgins, J. J. (1980). A comparison of the power of the Wilcoxon's rank-sum statistic to that of student's t statistic under various non-normal distributions. *Journal of Educational Statistics, 5,* 309–335.

Box, G. E. P. (1953). Non-normality and tests on variances. *Biometrika, 40,* 318–335.

Breckler, S. J. (1990). Application of covariance structure modeling in psychology: Cause for concern? *Psychological Bulletin, 107,* 260–273.

Brown, M. B., & Forsythe, A. B. (1974). Robust tests for the equality of variances. *Journal of the American Statistical Association, 69,* 364–367.

Cochran, W. G. (1947). Some consequences when the assumptions for the analysis of variance are not satisfied. *Biometrics, 3,* 22–38.

Conover, W. J., Johnson, M. E., & Johnson, M. M. (1981). A comparative study of tests for homogeneity of variances, with applications to the outer continental shelf bidding data. *Technometrics, 23,* 351–361.

Cramer, D. (1994). *Introducing statistics for social research: Step-by-step calculations and computer techniques using SPSS.* London: Routledge.

Cribbie, R. A., & Keselman, H. J. (2003). The effects of nonnormality on parametric, nonparametric, and model comparison approaches to pairwise comparisons. *Educational and Psychological Measurement, 63,* 615–635.

Glass, G. V., & Hopkins, K. D. (1996). *Statistical methods in psychology and education* (3rd ed.). Needham Heights, MA: Allyn & Bacon.

Table B1   An Example of Using the Brown-Forsythe Test to Test Homogeneity of Variance

Y_{11j}	$|Y_{11j} - m_{11}|$	Y_{12j}	$|Y_{12j} - m_{12}|$	Y_{13j}	$|Y_{13j}\, m_{13}|$	Y_{21j}	$|Y_{21j} - m_{21}|$	Y_{22j}	$|Y_{22j} - m_{22}|$	Y_{23j}	$|Y_{23j} - m_{23}|$
8	5	17	2	14	2.5	18	0	15	3	8	5
13	0	11	4	19	2.5	19	1	15	3	13	0
11	2	13	2	16	0.5	18	0	19	1	11	2
16	3	17	2	17	0.5	14	4	16	2	16	3
14	1			15	1.5	9	9	16	2	14	1
8	5			17	0.5	14	4	19	1	8	5
15	2			16	0.5	19	1	18	0	15	2
11	2			18	1.5	18	0	15	3	11	2
13	0			16	0.5	16	2	19	1	13	0
9	4			14	2.5	20	2	20	2	9	4
15	2			17	0.5	17	1	20	2	15	2
12	1			17	0.5			18	0	12	1
11	2			18	1.5			17	1	11	2
13	0			14	2.5			19	1	13	0
12	1			17	0.5			16	2	12	1
10	3			16	0.5			18	0	10	3
17	4							17	1	17	4
13	0							16	2	13	0
15	2							19	1	15	2
11	2							19	1	11	2
14	1							19	1	14	1
								19	1		
								17	1		

Summary of Analysis

Source	SS	df	MS	F	p
Between	11.583	5	2.317	1.587	.175
Error	99.255	68	1.460		
Total	110.838	73			

Glass, G. V., Peckham, P. D., & Sanders, J. R. (1972). Consequences of failure to meet assumptions underlying the fixed effects analyses of variance and covariance. *Review of Educational Research, 42,* 237–288.

Harwell, M. R., Rubinstein, E. N., Hayes, W. S., & Olds, C. C. (1992). Summarizing Monte Carlo results in methodological research: The one-and two-factor effects ANOVA cases. *Journal of Educational Statistics, 17,* 315–339.

Keselman, H. J., Huberty, C., Lix, L. M., Olejnik, S., Cribbie, R. A., Donahue, B., et al. (1998). Statistical practices of educational researchers: An analysis of their ANOVA, MANOVA, and ANCOVA analyses. *Review of Educational Research, 68,* 350–386.

Kruskal, W. H., & Wallis, W. A. (1952). Use of ranks in one-criterion variance analysis. *Journal of the American Statistical Association, 47,* 583–621.

Krutchkoff, R. G. (1988). One-way fixed effects analysis of variance when the error variances may be unequal. *Journal of Statistics, Computational Simulation, 30,* 177–183.

Levy, K. J. (1978). An empirical comparison of the ANOVA *F*-test with alternatives which are more robust against heterogeneity of variance. *Journal of Statistical Computation and Simulation, 8,* 49–57.

Lix, L. M., & Keselman, H. J. (1995). Approximate degrees of freedom tests: A unified perspective on testing for mean equality. *Psychological Bulletin, 117,* 547–560.

Lix, L. M., Keselman, J. C., & Keselman, H. J. (1996). Consequences of assumption violations revisited: A quantitative review of alternatives to the one-way analysis of variance F test. *Review of Educational Research, 66,* 579–619.

Lumley, T., Diehr, P., Emerson, S., & Chen, L. (2002). The importance of the normality assumption in large public health data sets. *Annual Review of Public Health, 23,* 151–169.

Micceri, T. (1989). The unicorn, the normal curve, and other improbable creatures. *Psychological Bulletin, 105,* 156–166.

Miller, R. G. (1986). *Beyond ANOVA, basics of applied statistics.* New York: John Wiley.

Olejnik, S. F., & Algina, J. (1987). Type I error rates and power estimates of selected parametric and non-parametric tests of scale. *Journal of Educational Statistics, 12,* 45–61.

Oshima, T. C., & Algina, J. (1992). Type I error rates for James's second-order test and Wilcox's H_m test under heteroscedasticity and non-normality. *British Journal of Mathematical and Statistical Psychology, 42,* 255–263.

Penfield, D. A. (1994). Choosing a two-sample location test. *Journal of Experimental Education, 62,* 343–360.

Rogan, J. C., & Keselman, H. J. (1977). Is the ANOVA F-test robust to variance heterogeneity when sample sizes are equal? An investigation via a coefficient of variation. *American Educational Research Journal, 14,* 493–498.

Scariano, S. M., & Davenport, J. M. (1987). The effects of violations of independence in the one-way ANOVA. *The American Statistician, 41,* 123–129.

Scheffé, N. (1959). *The analysis of variance.* New York: John Wiley.

Skovlund, E., & Fenstad, G. U. (2001). Should we always choose a nonparametric test when comparing two apparently nonnormal distributions? *Journal of Clinical Epidemiology, 54,* 86–92.

Stevens, J. (1996). *Applied multivariate statistics for the social sciences* (3rd ed.). Mahwah, NJ: Lawrence Erlbaum.

Tiku, M. L. (1964). Approximating the general non-normal variance-ratio sampling distributions. *Biometrika, 46,* 114–122.

Tomarken, A. J., & Serlin, R. C. (1986). Comparison of ANOVA alternatives under variance-covariance heterogeneity and specific noncentrality structures. *Psychological Bulletin, 99,* 90–99.

Weerahandi, S. (1995). ANOVA under unequal error variances. *Biometrics, 51,* 589–599.

Welch, B. L. (1951). On the comparison of several mean values: An alternative approach. *Biometrika, 38,* 330–336.

23

BEST PRACTICES IN THE ANALYSIS OF VARIANCE

DAVID HOWELL

The previous chapter addressed the basic questions behind the analysis of variance and presented material that is critical to an understanding of what the analysis of variance is all about. This chapter builds on that material to discuss important measures of power and effect size, to expand on alternative ways of approaching comparisons among individual group means, to discuss the treatment of missing data, and to consider alternative approaches to the treatment of nonnormal data or heterogeneous variances. More than the usual focus is given to individual contrasts and their implications for power and effect size calculations, and less to the omnibus F and associated measures. This idea is certainly not new, but such suggestions in the literature have not always led to changes in practice.

ONE-WAY DESIGNS

A study by Foa, Rothbaum, Riggs, and Murdock (1991) evaluated four different types of therapy for rape victims. The stress inoculation therapy (SIT) group ($n = 28$) received instructions on coping with stress. The prolonged exposure (PE) group ($n = 20$) went over the events in their minds repeatedly. The supportive counseling (SC) ($n = 22$) group was simply taught a general problem-solving technique. Finally, the waiting list (WL) control group ($n = 20$) received no therapy. Data were constructed to have the same means and variances as the original study, although I have doubled the sample sizes for purposes of this example. I will use these data to address a number of issues that are important to a complete analysis of variance. The questions that we will explore in this analysis will lay the groundwork for what follows and will also be the general approach that we will take with other designs.

Predictions

In this example, we basically have two major treatment groups (SIT and PE) and two different control groups (SC and WL). The authors of the study would likely expect differences between the two treatment groups and the two control groups. Depending on the effectiveness of supportive counseling, we might see a difference between the supportive counseling group and the waiting list group, which received no treatment, though that is certainly not the major focus of the study. It would certainly be of some interest to ask whether stress inoculation therapy is a more or less effective treatment than prolonged exposure. Notice that these predictions are quite specific. Predicting that "the four groups will differ" follows from the other predictions, but the overall main effect is really not the question at hand, though it is frequently treated that way. To put this differently, if the analysis found that not all treatments were equally effective, you would be neither particularly surprised nor satisfied. You would demand more specific answers. This point is more important than it might at first appear because it will color our discussion of missing data, power, and effect size.

Sample Sizes

Notice that in this experiment, we have unequal sample sizes. They are not grossly unequal, but they are unequal. In a one-way design, inequality of sample sizes is not particularly important unless we have heterogeneous variances, but it can become a problem when the variances are also unequal. There is no completely satisfactory way of dealing with this problem, although it is mitigated to some extent if we focus on specific contrasts, with error terms based only on the data at issue, rather than on the omnibus F and its error term. Unequal sample sizes assume a much larger role in our discussion of factorial designs.

Power

Researchers have recently been asked to pay attention to the power of their experiments. Important work on power for psychologists has been available since J. Cohen (1969), though it is only fairly recently that psychologists have started to take the issue seriously (see Wilkinson, 1999, for guidelines from the American Psychological Association [APA] panel on statistical methods). For the example we are using, it would be foolish to undertake this study unless we were reasonably confident that the study had

sufficient power to find differences between groups if those differences were as large as we expect. We will look briefly at the power of this design, assuming that the true differences are similar to the difference we obtained.

Effect Size

Finally, we are going to need to say something about the size of the effect we found. We want to be able to tell our readers whether the differences that we do find are important considerations in choosing a treatment or if these are minor differences that might be overridden by other considerations. However, it will be important to decide just what effects should play a role in the determination of effect size.

THE OVERALL ANALYSIS

The results obtained by Foa et al. (1991) follow, where the dependent variable is based on symptoms of stress. (The data for this example are available at www.uvm.edu/~dhowell/Anova Chapter/FoaDoubled.dat.)

Group	n	Mean	SD
SIT	28	11.07	3.88
PE	20	15.40	10.82
SC	22	18.09	6.96
WL	20	19.50	6.92

The following analyses were produced by SPSS ONEWAY, though any standard software will produce similar results. In this situation, SPSS's ONEWAY is more useful than GLM because it allows you greater flexibility in specifying the contrast coefficients for subsequent analyses.

ANOVA

symptoms

	Sum of Squares	df	Mean Square	F	Sig.
Between Groups	1015.680	3	338.560	6.389	.001
Within Groups	4557.475	86	52.994		
Total	5573.156	89			

The results show a significant difference among the groups, as expected, although it is not a particularly meaningful finding. The effect size estimate (eta-squared = 0.18) refers to the omnibus F test, which is of little interest to us, as does the post hoc test of power (which was 0.96).[1]

Unequal Variances

We should note that Levene's test for heterogeneity of variance, which follows the analysis of variance (ANOVA) summary table, shows that the variances are not homogeneous, and this should give us some pause. I would be much more concerned if our sample sizes were more unequal, but we still need to attend to them. Both Welch (1951; see Howell, 2007) and Brown and Forsythe (1974; see B. H. Cohen, 2000, or Field, 2004) have proposed tests that can be used in place of the standard omnibus F when the sample sizes and variances are unequal. Of these, the Welch test tends to be more conservative and more powerful at the same time (Tomarken & Serlin, 1986) and is the test of choice. SPSS calculates the results of both tests, and these are shown below. Again, there is no question that the differences among the groups are significant. But, again, it isn't the overall F that is of central concern to us.

Test of Homogeneity of Variances

symptoms

Levene Statistic	df1	df2	Sig.
13.913	3	86	.000

Robust Tests of Equality of Means

symptoms

	Statistic[a]	df1	df2	Sig.
Welch	11.670	3	40.363	.000
Brown-Forsythe	5.795	3	53.210	.002

a. Asymptotically F distributed.

Individual Contrasts

Before discussing questions of power and effect size, it is important to look at individual comparisons among the groups. Those contrasts are more in line with our interests than is the omnibus F, and our concerns about effect size and power are more appropriately directed at those contrasts.

The traditional approach to testing differences between individual groups relies heavily on standard multiple comparison procedures such as the Tukey or Scheffé tests. These procedures compare each group with every other group and produce a display indicating which group means are heterogeneous and which are homogeneous. A common textbook characterization of post hoc tests is that they allow you to make comparisons of means even if they were not planned before the experiment was conducted. (A priori tests are normally restricted to situations where the contrasts were planned.) We sell ourselves short if we routinely assume that we have not thought through our analysis when we design a study, and post hoc tests generally extract a heavy penalty in terms of power. However, the output from a post hoc test which follows on the next page, to illustrate the approach. In our particular example, which has unequal sample sizes and unequal variances, the most appropriate approach is the Games-Howell procedure because it is designed to handle such conditions. (Tukey's test does not handle heterogeneity of variance well, and contrasts such as those by Helmert rarely address questions of interest.)

From this table, we can see that the SIT group is significantly different from the SC and WL groups, but no other groups are different from each other. There are two things about this answer that are not very satisfying. In the first place, we see that SIT and PE are not different, but although SIT is different from SC and WL, PE is not. This *appears* to fly in the face of common sense because if A is equal to B and A is unequal to C, we expect that B will be unequal to C. The problem is that the structural rules of logic and the probabilistic rules of statistics do not always mesh.[2]

The other difficulty with this approach (which is shared by all multiple comparison procedures such as the Tukey and the Scheffé tests) is that we are asking a number of questions that are not really of interest to us, and doing so detracts from the statistical power to find differences on the things that really do matter. I do care if the major therapies (SIT and PE) are better than the control conditions (SC and WL), and I care if one of the therapies is better

Multiple Comparisons

Dependent Variable: symptoms

Games-Howell

(J) group	(I) group	Mean Difference (I − J)	Std. Error	Sig.	95% Confidence Interval	
					Lower Bound	Upper Bound
SIT	PE	−4.329	2.528	.341	−11.34	2.68
	SC	−7.019*	1.655	.001	−11.51	−2.53
	WL	−8.429*	1.711	.000	−13.11	−3.75
PE	SIT	4.329	2.528	.341	−2.68	11.34
	SC	−2.691	2.839	.779	−10.38	5.00
	WL	−4.100	2.872	.492	−11.88	3.68
SC	SIT	7.019*	1.655	.001	2.53	11.51
	PE	2.691	2.839	.779	−5.00	10.38
	WL	−1.409	2.144	.912	−7.16	4.34
WL	SIT	8.429*	1.711	.000	3.75	13.11
	PE	4.100	2.872	.492	−3.68	11.88
	SC	1.409	2.144	.912	−4.34	7.16

than the other, but that is as far as it goes. I want to ask two questions, but the multiple comparison procedures ask six questions (there are six pairwise comparisons), extracting an unnecessary price in power and sensitivity.

If we want to compare the therapy conditions with the control conditions, as well as the SIT condition with PE, we can do so with a simple set of contrast coefficients rather than using a less powerful multiple comparison procedure. These coefficients (c_j) are shown in the following table.[3]

	SIT	PE	SC	WL
SIT & PE vs. SC & WL	.5	.5	−.5	−.5
SIT vs. PE	1	−1	0	0

These coefficients can be applied to the individual group means to produce a t statistic on the relevant contrast. We simply define

$$\psi = \Sigma c_j \bar{X}_j$$

and

$$t = \sqrt{\frac{\psi^2}{MS_{error}\left(\Sigma \frac{c_j^2}{n_j}\right)}}.$$

Applying these coefficients to the group means, we obtain the set of contrasts shown on the next page for the equal variance case. For the unequal variance case, we replace MS_{error} with more specific error terms and define

$$t = \sqrt{\frac{\psi^2}{\Sigma \frac{c_j^2 s_j^2}{n_j}}}.$$

This gives us a t statistic based only on the variances of the groups involved in the contrasts.

Here you can see that both contrasts are significant if we assume equal variances, but only the contrast between the therapy groups and the control groups is significant if we do not assume

Contrast Tests

		Contrast	Value of Contrast	Std. Error	t	df	Sig. (2-tailed)
symptoms	Assumes equal variances	1	−5.56	1.549	−3.589	86	.001
		2	−4.33	2.131	−2.031	86	.045
	Does not assume equal variances	1	−5.56	1.657	−3.355	51.430	.001
		2	−4.33	2.528	−1.712	22.511	.101

equal variances. The Levene test was significant, in part because the variance in PE is many times larger than the variance for SIT, so I would have to choose the unequal variance test. The equal variance solution would use the common (average) error term (MS_{error}) for each contrast, and when the variances are unequal, that does not make much sense.[4]

Power

The traditional treatment of power would concern the probability of finding a significant omnibus F if the population means are as we think that they should be. Suppose that on the basis of prior studies, Foa et al. (1991) hypothesized that the two control groups would present about 20 symptoms of stress, that the SIT group would present about half that number (i.e., 10 symptoms), and the PE group would be somewhere in between (say about 14 symptoms). This is usually about the best we can do. Assume that Foa et al. also think that the standard deviation of the SIT group will be approximately 4, and those of the other groups will be approximately 8. They plan to have approximately 20 subjects in each group. The "what-if" and "approximate" nature of these predictions is quite deliberate because we rarely have more specific knowledge on which to base comparisons. Using G*Power,[5] we can calculate that the power of this experiment is .99, which is extremely high. But that answer is not directly relevant to my needs. That result tells me that I am almost certain to reject the omnibus null hypothesis, but what I really care about are the two contrasts discussed above. And of these two contrasts, the one least likely to be significant is

the contrast between SIT and PE. What I really want to know is the power to find a significant difference for that contrast. We can answer that question using G*Power for what amounts to a t test between those two groups. With homogeneity of variance, df for error would be based on MS_{error} for all four groups and would be 76. However, with heterogeneous variances, the appropriate t test would consider only the two groups of 20 participants per group. This test would have approximately 28 degrees of freedom using the standard Satterthwaite correction. To be safe, we will assume that we'll have heterogeneous variances. This yields a power of 0.40, which is not very encouraging. Increasing the sample size to approximately 40 subjects in each condition will be necessary to have a good chance of rejecting the null hypothesis for that contrast (although the exact calculation requires an iterative process).

To reiterate the fundamental point being made here, we need to tailor our analysis to the questions we want to answer. There is nothing wrong with having four groups in this experiment—in fact, that is a perfectly reasonable way to design the study. However, when looking at power or, as we will shortly do, effect sizes, we want to tailor those estimates to the important questions we most want to answer.

Effect Size Estimates

As you can guess, an effect size measure that involves all four conditions is not particularly useful. I can find one, however, and it is estimated by either η^2 or ω^2, the latter being somewhat less biased. For this experiment, we have

$$\eta^2 = \frac{SS_{treatment}}{SS_{total}} = \frac{1015.68}{5573.16} = 0.18,$$

$$\omega^2 = \frac{SS_{treatment} - (k-1)MS_{error}}{SS_{total} + MS_{error}}$$

$$= \frac{1015.68 - (3)52.994}{5573.16 + 52.994} = \frac{856.698}{5626.15} = 0.15.$$

Whichever measure we use, we can say that we are explaining under a fifth of the variation in our data on the basis of treatment differences. Rosenthal (1994) referred to measures such as η^2 and ω^2 as *r*-family measures because they are essentially squared correlations between the independent and dependent variables. One problem with *r*-family measures is that most people do not have an intuitive understanding of what it means to say that we can account for *x*% of the variation, and, in fact, that percentage may depend on other variables in our design.

When we look at effect sizes for specific contrasts, which is what we really want to do, we have better measures than those in the *r*-family. Rosenthal (1994) referred to these as *d*-family measures because they focus on the size of the *difference* between two groups or sets of groups. Measures in the *d*-family represent the difference between groups (or sets of groups) in terms of standardized units, allowing us to make statements of the form, "The means of Groups A and B differ by approximately 0.5 standard deviations." There are a number of related measures that we could use, and they differ primarily in what we take as the standard deviation by which we standardize the difference in means. If we let c_j represent the set of coefficients that we used for individual contrasts, then we can define our measure of effect size for contrast j ($\hat{d}_j$) as

$$\hat{d}_j = \frac{\psi}{s_e} = \frac{\Sigma(c_j\overline{X}_j)}{s_e}.$$

The numerator is a simple linear contrast, while the denominator is some unspecified estimate of the within-groups standard deviation.

The preceding formula raises two points. In the first place, the coefficients must form what is sometimes called a "standard set." This simply means that the absolute values of the coefficients must sum to 2. This is why I earlier used fractional values for the coefficients, rather than

simplifying to integers. The resulting F or t for the contrast would be the same whether I used fractional or integer values, but only the standard set would give us a numerical value for the contrast that is the difference between the mean of the first two groups and the mean of the last two groups. This is easily seen when you write

$$\psi = (.5)(\overline{X}_1) + (.5)\overline{X}_2 + (-.5)(\overline{X}_3) + (-.5)\overline{X}_4$$
$$= \frac{\overline{X}_1 + \overline{X}_2}{2} - \frac{\overline{X}_3 + \overline{X}_4}{2}.$$

The second point raised by our equation for $\hat{d}$ is the choice of the denominator. There are at least three possible estimates. If we could conceive of one of the groups as a control group, we could use its standard deviation as our estimate. Alternatively, we could use the square root of MS_{error}, which is the square root of the weighted average of the four within-group variances.[6] Finally, we could use the square root of the average of the variances in those groups being contrasted.[7] That makes sense when the groups you are contrasting (such as SC and WL, though not others) have homogeneous variances. But in a case such as the contrast of SIT with PE, the variances are 15.03 and 117.09, respectively, and it is hard to justify averaging them. But I have to do something, and there can be no hard-and-fast rule to tell me what to do. For this contrast, I will use the square root of the weighted average of the variances of the two control conditions because those conditions form a logical basis for standardizing the mean difference.[8] In describing the results, we should point out that the large variance of the SIT data suggests that stress inoculation therapy may work well for some victims but not for others.

For the contrast of the treatment groups with the control groups, we have

$$\psi = (.5)(\overline{X}_1) + (.5)\overline{X}_2 + (-.5)(\overline{X}_3) + (-.5)\overline{X}_4$$
$$= (.5)11.07 + (.5)15.40 + (-.5)\,18.09 + (-.5)19.50$$
$$= -5.56$$

and

$$s_e = \sqrt{\frac{21(6.96^2) + 19(6.92^2)}{21 + 19}} = \sqrt{48.18} = 6.94.$$

Our effect size is $-5.56/6.94 = -0.80$, which can be interpreted as indicating that those who receive one of the two major forms of therapy have fewer symptoms, by approximately eight tenths of a standard deviation, than do those in the control groups.

Two questions arise over the computation of the effect size for the contrast of the SIT and PE groups. That difference was not significant when we controlled for heterogeneous variances ($p = .101$). So if we have concluded that we do not have a reliable difference, does it make sense to go ahead and report an effect size for it? A solution would be to report an effect size if the difference is "nearly significant" but, at the same time, to remind the reader of the nonsignificance of the statistical test.[9] The second question concerns the denominator for our effect size. As I suggested earlier, one possibility is to use the square root of the weighted average variance of the control conditions, and we just found that to be 6.94, and it seems like a reasonable scalar.

For this contrast, we have

$$\psi = (1)(\bar{X}_1) + (-1)\bar{X}_2 + (0)(\bar{X}_3) + (0)\bar{X}_4$$
$$= 11.07 - 15.40$$
$$= -4.33.$$

Using the standard deviation defined above as the standardizing statistic produces an effect size measure of $-4.33/6.94 = -0.62$, indicating that the participants receiving SIT therapy are a bit less than two thirds of a standard deviation lower on symptoms than are the PE participants.

But we need to keep two things in mind. First, the contrast was not significant, and second, the variances are very heterogeneous. This suggests to me that we might want to examine our data even more closely for outliers and consider alternative transformations of the data. (For these data, neither approach is productive.) The best solution is probably to conduct another study looking more closely at those two treatments, perhaps dropping the control conditions. The present data might suggest that SIT is useful for some victims but not for others, and an effect size comparison of its mean with the mean of PE may not be relevant. A subsequent study looking closely at whether there are important individual differences in the effectiveness of SIT would seem useful in clarifying the clinical implications of the treatment.

NONNORMAL DATA

It is well-known that the traditional analysis of variance assumes that the random errors within each condition are normally distributed in the population. We often say that the analysis of variance is robust to violations of this assumption, although we know that this is not always the case. Especially when we have long-tailed distributions, alternative procedures may better approximate the desired level of α and have more power than a standard analysis of variance. (We might have long-tailed distributions for the example used here because it is easy to imagine a few participants who report many more symptoms of stress than do others in their group and a few that, for whatever reason, are reluctant to report any symptoms.) Wilcox and Keselman (see, e.g., Keselman, Holland, & Cribbie, 2005) have done considerable work on robust measures and strongly favor the use of trimmed means and Winsorized variances[10] in place of the usual least squares estimates of means and variances. It has taken a long time for this approach to take hold, but it slowly seems to be doing so. A different approach to multiple comparison procedures, using bootstrapping and randomization tests, is discussed by Keselman and Wilcox (2006). In addition, for count data of this nature, Poisson analysis (see Chapter 21, this volume) may be more appropriate.

FACTORIAL DESIGNS

Almost all issues in the analysis of variance become somewhat more complex when we move from one-way designs to factorial and, later, repeated-measures analysis of variance. In this section, I will expand on the basic material on factorial designs in ways that are similar to what I said about one-way designs.

I have chosen an example that again involves unequal sample sizes and presents some interesting challenges to interpretation. Much that was said about one-way designs, such as the need to focus on the specific questions of interest and to calculate power and effect sizes accordingly, would apply equally well here. I will not belabor those points in this discussion. Instead, the main focus will be on the treatment of unbalanced designs and some interesting questions that arise concerning effect sizes.

The following example came from Jo Sullivan-Lyons, who was at the time a research psychologist at the University of Greenwich in London. In her dissertation, she was concerned primarily with how men and women differ in their reports of depression on the HADS (Hospital Anxiety and Depression Scale) and whether this difference depends on ethnicity. So we have two independent variables, gender (male/female) and ethnicity (White/Black/other), and one dependent variable, the HADS score.

I have created data that reflect the cell means and standard deviations that Sullivan-Lyons obtained, and these are available at www.uvm.edu/~dhowell/AnovaChapter/JSLdep.sav. The cell means and standard deviations are given in the table below.

Unequal Sample Sizes

One of the first things to notice from this table is that the cell sizes are very unequal. That is not particularly surprising when dealing with ethnicity because very often a sample will be heavily biased in favor of one ethnic group over others. What would at first seem somewhat reassuring is that the imbalance is similar for males and females.

Dr. Sullivan-Lyons was primarily concerned with a difference due to gender, and she noted that a *t* test on males versus females produced a

statistically significant result, with males reporting a mean HADS score that was approximately half of that for females. (Even when we allow for heterogeneity of variance, $t = -5.268$, $p < .000$). However, because ethnicity was also an independent variable, she ran a factorial analysis of variance and found the following results.

Notice that in this analysis, the effect due to gender is not close to statistical significance ($p < .83$). Her question to me was, "What happened?" I think almost anyone would be inclined to ask such a question, and the answer highlights the importance of careful consideration of unbalanced factorial designs, especially in the presence of a significant interaction effect, which we have for these data.

A standard *t* test or a one-way analysis of variance on gender is heavily influenced by the difference in sample sizes. The predominance of White participants means that their mean difference between genders dominates the overall gender effect. The most common form of a factorial analysis of variance, however, treats the means differently.

Before discussing the alternative models for dealing with unbalanced factorial designs, it would be helpful to go back to a technique that was particularly common before desktop computing was widely available. Notice that the table of means shows that White males report fewer symptoms than White females, but the direction of that difference is reversed for the other

Descriptive Statistics

Dependent Variable: HADS

Gender		White	Black	Other	Total
Male	Mean	1.4800	6.6000	12.5600	2.4729
	Std. Deviation	1.63000	1.78000	2.74000	3.31211
	N	133	10	9	152
Female	Mean	2.7100	6.2600	11.9300	4.7324
	Std. Deviation	1.96000	1.24000	4.11000	4.24192
	N	114	19	28	161
Total	Mean	2.0477	6.3772	12.0832	3.6351
	Std. Deviation	1.88886	1.42616	3.79638	3.97697
	N	247	29	37	313

Tests of Between-Subjects Effects

Dependent Variable: HADS

Source	Type III Sum of Squares	df	Mean Square	F	Sig.	Partial Eta Squared	Observed Power[a]
Corrected Model	3577.528[b]	5	715.51	161.854	.000	.725	1.000
Intercept	5465.033	1	5465.0	1236.2	.000	.801	1.000
Gender	.214	1	.214	.048	.826	.000	.056
Ethnicity	2790.110	2	1395.1	315.574	.000	.673	1.000
Gender * Ethnicity	32.663	2	16.331	3.694	.026	.024	.676
Error	1357.152	307	4.421				
Total	9070.746	313					
Corrected Total	4934.680	312					

a. Computed using alpha = .05.

b. R-squared = .725 (adjusted R-squared = .720).

two ethnic categories. In what used to be called an "unweighted means solution," the analysis would weight all means equally rather than allowing dominance by the large cells. For example, the male mean would be

$$\overline{X}_{Male} = \frac{\overline{X}_{WhiteMale} + \overline{X}_{BlackMale} + \overline{X}_{OtherMale}}{3}$$
$$= \frac{1.48 + 6.60 + 12.56}{3} = 6.88.$$

Similarly, for females:

$$\overline{X}_{Female} = \frac{\overline{X}_{WhiteFemale} + \overline{X}_{BlackFemale} + \overline{X}_{OtherFemale}}{3}$$
$$= \frac{2.71 + 6.26 + 11.93}{3} = 6.96.$$

Notice that the two unweighted means are almost equal.

Current practice in the treatment of unequal sample sizes with factorial designs produces results that are very similar to the old practice of comparing unweighted means. So it is not surprising that the analysis of variance gave us a nonsignificant result for gender. Once we control for ethnicity and the Gender × Ethnicity interaction, there really is no effect due to gender. The interaction and the unequal sample sizes work in concert here. If we hold the interaction

constant but balance the sample sizes, our overall significant t will disappear, and the analysis of variance and t will be consonant.

The default for SPSS, SAS, and many other statistical programs is to compute what are called Type III sums of squares, which adjust each effect for all other effects in the model. In other words, we look at gender adjusted for ethnicity and the Gender × Ethnicity interaction, at ethnicity adjusted for gender and the Gender × Ethnicity interaction, and at the Gender × Ethnicity interaction adjusted for gender and ethnicity.

There are other ways to compute this analysis of variance. We could use Type II sums of squares, which adjust the gender effect for ethnicity but not for the interaction (and similarly for ethnicity) but adjust the interaction for the two main effects. If we used a Type II analysis here, we would find an F for gender of 14.402, $p < .000$. Alternatively, we could use Type I sums of squares, which would apply no adjustment to the first-named main effect, adjust the second-named main effect for the first, and adjust the interaction for both main effects. If we ran that analysis, specifying gender before ethnicity and therefore not adjusting gender for ethnicity or the interaction, we would obtain an F for gender of 90.296, which is huge.[11]

You might very well ask why you would choose one of these analyses over the other. If you have a balanced design, all approaches produce identical results. The Type III analysis generally makes the most sense when we think in terms of an analysis of variance, which is why it is usually the default. Someone looking at a Type I analysis might wonder why anyone would ever entertain such an approach. However, the Type I analysis bears a strong relationship to what you might do in a study where the main analysis was multiple regression instead of the analysis of variance. There, for example, you might wish to look at the relationship between stress and internal factors and then ask what effect external factors have on stress *after* adjusting for internal factors.

That is exactly what the Type I analysis is doing. To put this in terms that are more common in regression studies than in the analysis of variance, an analysis with Type I sums of squares allows gender to assume priority over other variables, then lets ethnicity assume priority over variables other than gender, and so on. Type III analyses do not give priority to any variable.

Dealing With the Interaction

So what was Dr. Sullivan-Lyons to conclude from her data? To answer that, we need to look a bit further into the results of the analysis of variance. There we will see that the interaction of gender and ethnicity was significant. That tells us that unless we have strong reasons to the contrary, it would be appropriate to look at the simple effects of gender at each level of ethnicity or ethnicity at each level of gender. In her study, she was concerned primarily with difference due to gender, with only subsidiary interest in ethnicity.

Therefore, it would make the most sense for her to look at gender at each level of ethnicity. We can best accomplish that by splitting the file by ethnicity and then comparing gender at each level of ethnicity using a one-way analysis. The results are shown in the table below.

Here you can see that there are gender differences for White participants, $F(1, 245) = 28.991$, but not for either of the other two ethnic groups. Although examining an interaction by looking at simple effects is the standard approach, it does increase the probability of a Type I error by increasing the number of significance tests. One way around this problem is to set the required significance level more stringently (for example, from .05 to .01). Doing so in this case would still leave the gender difference for Whites but not for the other ethnic groups. It is entirely possible that the lack of significance for the other two ethnic groups was due, in part, to the small sample sizes and lack of power. But it appears likely that even if there actually are differences in the populations, they are small compared with those for Whites and perhaps even in the opposite direction.

For the simple effects, you could have computed the *F*s somewhat differently, basing each *F* on MS_{error} from the overall analysis. That was the approach that nearly all textbooks once advocated. However, with such disparate sample sizes and with such clear differences due to ethnicity, it would make more sense, as well as avoid possible problems with heterogeneity of variance, to run separate analyses. This will be particularly

ANOVA

HADS

Ethnicity		Sum of Squares	df	Mean Square	F	Sig.
White	Between Groups	92.869	1	92.869	28.991	.000
	Within Groups	784.812	245	3.203		
	Total	877.680	246			
Black	Between Groups	.757	1	.757	.364	.551
	Within Groups	56.192	27	2.081		
	Total	56.950	28			
Other	Between Groups	2.703	1	2.703	.183	.671
	Within Groups	516.148	35	14.747		
	Total	518.851	36			

true when we look at repeated-measures designs.

COMPARING MEANS ON ETHNICITY

It is quite apparent in this study that Whites report far fewer symptoms of depression than do participants from the other two groups. We could follow up this difference using post hoc multiple comparison procedures, or we could run simple contrasts. In this case, it probably does not matter which we use because there are only three possible pairwise comparisons, resulting in only modest adjustment to the Type I error rate. Using Tukey's test or the slightly more powerful Ryan-Einot-Gabriel-Welsch-Q test shows that all three groups are different from each other. You might legitimately argue that because there was a significant interaction, these tests should be done on the simple effects, but the same results would hold in that analysis. Clearly, the degree to which people report symptoms of depression depends on their ethnicity.

Effect Sizes

Now that we have shown that there are differences between gender (for White respondents) and differences due to ethnicity (either collapsing across gender or analyzing data for each gender separately), it is important to tell our readers something about the size of these effects. This is where things get interesting.

When discussing the one-way design, we defined our effect size measure as

$$\hat{d} = \frac{\psi}{s_e} = \frac{\Sigma(c_j \overline{X}_j)}{s_e}$$

and discussed possible choices for s_e. In discussing factorial designs, we will take our independent variables one at a time. When we look at the effect size for gender, we are faced with two questions. The first concerns how we calculate the numerator. In our analysis, the only real gender effect was for White participants, who were by far the most numerous ethnic group, and it would seem reasonable to calculate the numerator only using the data from Whites. We would have $c_1 = 1$ and $c_2 = -1$, and the numerator is simply the difference between the means of

White males and White females. So $\psi = 1.48 - 2.71 = -1.23$. For the denominator, we would most likely use the square root of MS_{error}, but which MS_{error}? We could use the one from the overall factorial analysis, but that is based on data that include responses from ethnic groups not represented in the calculation of the numerator. Instead, we will take the square root of MS_{error} from the simple effect of gender for White participants, which is $\sqrt{3.203} = 1.79$. Then,

$$\hat{d} = \frac{\psi}{s_e} = \frac{-1.23}{1.79} = 0.69.$$

We can conclude that the mean number of symptoms reported by White females is about $\frac{2}{3}$ of a standard deviation higher than the mean number of symptoms reported by White males, a notable difference.[12]

Now let's look the effect size of ethnicity. Although there was a statistically significant interaction, we will not do very much injustice to the effect size by basing it on the main effect. Doing so will allow me to introduce one of the complicating factors in effect sizes with factorial designs.

Again, the first problem that we have in calculating an effect size is in deciding what we want for the numerator. Remember that the numerator (ψ) is a contrast between two means or sets of means. We do not ask how all three means differ from each other, but how one mean differs from another mean. If it is important to look at the mean difference between Whites and the average of the other two groups, we will use $c_j = [1, -.5, -.5]$. This gives us

$$\psi = (1)2.0477 + (-.5)6.3772 + (-.5)12.0832 = -7.08.$$

There are several different denominators that we could use in a factorial design, and the choice hinges on the nature of the independent variables (Kline, 2004). Kline distinguishes between the *factor of interest* (in this case, ethnicity) and *off-factors* (in this case, gender). If the off-factor varies naturally in the population, then its variability should contribute to the denominator—the standardizing term. If the off-factor does not vary naturally in the population (which often means that it is a manipulated variable), then it should not contribute to the denominator. In this particular study, there is a good deal of variability that is "natural" to the setting. There is random noise (MS_{error}), there is variability due to differences in gender, and there is variability due to the Gender × Ethnicity interaction. All of those logically form a background against which to compare the mean difference between Whites and non-Whites. Thus, our denominator would not be the square root of MS_{error}, which has these effects partialed out, but

$$s_e = \sqrt{\frac{SS_{Gender} + SS_{G*S} + SS_{error}}{df_{Gender} + df_{G*S} + df_{error}}}$$

$$= \sqrt{\frac{0.214 + 32.663 + 1357.152}{1 + 2 + 307}}$$

$$= \sqrt{\frac{1390.029}{310}} = 2.12.$$

If, instead of gender, our off-factor for this effect had been treatment (e.g., therapy vs. control), we would have a different situation. Here our manipulation has introduced differences into the experiment by way of the treatment variable, leading to an artificial increase in variability. In this case, it would make sense to remove the treatment and T × G interaction effects from the denominator by using MS_{error} from the overall analysis.

Returning to our contrast on White versus non-White with gender as the off-factor, we would have

$$\hat{d} = \frac{\hat{\psi}}{s_e} = \frac{-7.08}{2.12} = -3.34.$$

The mean symptom level of Whites is about $3\frac{1}{3}$ standard deviations below the mean of non-Whites. This suggests that ethnicity plays a major role in depression. (This is a common finding in the literature; see Plant & Sachs-Ericsson, 2004.)

Power

There is not much that needs to be said about power for factorial designs beyond what was discussed for the one-way design. When we have two factors, such as gender and ethnicity, we have two main effects and an interaction. When we calculate the power of such a design, we need to ask, "Power for what?" There is the level of power to detect a gender effect, a different level

of power to detect an ethnicity effect, and yet a third level of power for the interaction. I recommend that you determine which effect(s) are most important to you and calculate power accordingly. This way, you can be sure that the effects you care most about have at least a minimally acceptable degree of power. Alternatively, if you think that all effects are important, you should try to maximize power for the smallest of the effects.

REPEATED-MEASURES DESIGNS

There are many different kinds of repeated-measures designs, and I certainly cannot cover them all. This section will include observations about the treatment of missing data, the role of trend analyses, some interesting findings on power by Bradley and Russell (1998), and a discussion of effect sizes.

We will take as an example a modification of a study by Evans, Bullinger, and Hygge (1998). Evans et al. were interested in the effects of noise exposure on the physiological responses of children. It comes down to the public policy issue of whether loud noise from airports is a serious stressor to those who live nearby. The city of Munich recently built a new airport, and the authors were able to test children before the airport was built, 6 months after it was opened, and 18 months after it was opened. I have extended the study by adding fictitious data for 24 months after it was opened to allow me to better discuss the analysis of trends in the data. The authors used the same children at each of the four times and had a control group of children from the same city who lived outside the noise impact zone. One of their dependent variables was the epinephrine level in these children. This is a variable that would be expected to increase with increases in stress.

The data can be found at www.uvm.edu/~dhowell/AnovaChapter/AirportModified.dat, and the results follow, where higher scores represent greater stress. It is apparent from these data that children living near the airport show an increase in stress over time, whereas those living away from the airport show little, if any, change.

The analysis of variance follows and confirms the previous statement.

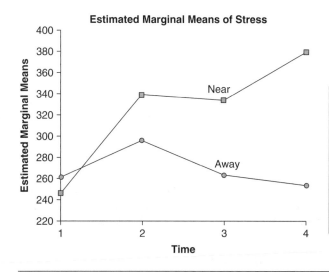

Estimated Marginal Means of Stress

Location * time

Measure: MEASURE_1

Location	time	Mean	Std. Error
Near airport	1	246.378	21.402
	2	340.237	21.979
	3	334.464	25.327
	4	380.691	25.763
Away from airport	1	260.859	21.402
	2	297.118	21.979
	3	263.566	25.327
	4	253.737	25.763

Source	df	SS	MS	F	p	Partial Eta Squared
Between subjects	199	24,702,189.55				
Groups	1	641,233.11	641,233.1	5.28	.038	.026
Subjects within groups	198	24,060,955.44	121,520.0			
Within subjects	600	21,488,017.10				
Time	3	552,898.46	184,299.5	5.36	.001	.026
T × G	3	519,425.04	173,141.7	5.04	.002	.025
T × Subjects within groups	594	20,415,693.60	34,369.86			
Total	799	46,190,206.65				

Although there is a significant group effect and a significant effect due to time, neither of those deserves much attention in this analysis. It is clear that the groups were very similar at baseline and only differed later in the study, making the overall group effect ambiguous. Similarly, it is clear that stress increased in one group but not in the other. Since main effects are averaged over the levels of the other variable, whether the resulting average is significant or not is unimportant. What is important is the significant interaction, which results from the characteristics just described. From the table, we can see that the "Partial Eta Squared" for the interaction is .025. This statistic is referred to as "partial" because group effects and error associated with between-subject differences have not been included in the calculation. The partial eta

squared is defined here as $SS_{TXG}/SS_{within\ subjects} =$ 519,425.04/21,488,017.10 = .025. This can be interpreted to mean that the interaction accounts for 2.5% of the within-subject variability. It is difficult to know whether we should consider .025 to be large. This is a problem with most r-family measures of effect size.

Comparing Means With a Trend Analysis

The interaction suggests that we should look closely at the simple effects of time for each group, and the ordered spacing of the time intervals suggests that we look at polynomial contrasts on the means. Instead of comparing the means at two different times, as we would with standard contrasts, it makes more sense to

Location	Trend	SS	F	p
Near	Linear	568,412.361	8.67	.004
	Quadratic	114,353.424	2.95	.089
	Cubic	86,635.725	1.42	.236
Away	Linear	15,080.359	1.43	.235
	Quadratic	53,102.690	3.82	.054
	Cubic	43,743.800	2.66	.106

try to understand what is happening across the four times taken together. On the basis of past experience, we might expect that for the near group, stress levels will increase over time but would probably level off eventually. This would suggest both a linear and a quadratic trend. We would expect no trend in the away group because there is nothing to cause a change in stress levels. The results of the trend analysis are shown in the table above.[13]

As expected, there is a linear trend for children near the airport. The expected quadratic trend was not significant ($p = .089$), suggesting that stress levels have not begun to level off after 24 months—although visual inspection of the data and the relatively small associated p value suggest that they may be starting to. What looks like a nearly significant quadratic trend for the away children probably simply reflects the unexpected bump in scores at Time 2, and there seems no theoretical reason to make much of this effect.[14]

Effect Size

While it would be theoretically possible to calculate an overall d-family measure of effect size for the linear trend in the near group, I am not sure what it would mean. What would standardized units in a linear trend represent? We could calculate an r-family measure of effect size with polynomials, but it is also difficult to give the reader an intuitive understanding of what that would mean. Perhaps a better way of calculating an effect size is to set aside the two intermediate measures and express the gain (from baseline to 24 months) in terms of the standard deviation at baseline. This would be

$$\hat{d} = \frac{\hat{\psi}}{s_e} = \frac{380.69 - 246.38}{282.39} = \frac{134.31}{282.39} = 0.48$$

and shows that epinephrine levels have increased to nearly half of a standard deviation over a 24-month period. This is a substantial increase.

Missing Data

Missing data are not usually a problem for repeated-measures designs in experimental psychology, but they can be a problem in clinical settings. In an experimental study, participants often either have no (or very little) data, in which case they are discarded from the analysis, or they have complete data, in which case there is no problem. In long-running clinical studies, we frequently have participants who are missing one or more pieces of data, and it is often feasible to replace those observations by imputation (see Howell, 2008).[15]

Power

We often think of repeated-measures designs as providing improved statistical power by removing subject differences from the analysis. While this is generally true, Bradley and Russell (1998) have pointed out an anomaly that is worth mentioning. It is logical to think that if we simply collect more data from each participant, we will increase the power of our design. Similarly, it seems intuitively clear that the higher the correlation between trials, the less the random error and the more powerful the analysis. While these conclusions might seem correct, they are in fact wrong in many cases.

Bradley and Russell (1998) investigated the question of increasing the number of repeated measures and came to some unexpected conclusions (see also Overall, 1996). If we think for a moment about a standard factorial design (such as a 2×5) with both variables representing between-subject differences, the expected mean square for the error term is

$$E(MS_{w/cell}) = \sigma_e^2.$$

Now suppose that we compare those same two treatments across five trials, where *trials* is a within-subject variable. Then there are two error terms, the first testing between-subjects effects and the second testing within-subject effects. The expected mean squares for error are now those shown below, where the subscripts *b* and *w* stand for between- and within-subject terms.

$$E(MS_{error_b}) = \sigma_e^2 = \sigma^2[1+(t-1)\rho],$$
$$E(MS_{error_w}) = \sigma_e^2 = \sigma^2[1-\rho].$$

Note that the error term for the within-subject effect will shrink as ρ increases, giving us greater power to detect a within-subject difference. However, the error term for the between effects will increase as ρ increases. It will also increase as *t*, the number of trials, increases. Thus, for tests on the between-subjects effects, power will *decrease* as we increase the number of trials—all other things being equal. If our interest were primarily in our repeated-measures variable, there would not be a problem. However, the repeated measure, such as trials, is often not of primary concern, or the effects are so strong that power is not an issue. Generally, it is the between-subjects measures that we care most about, and there we often do not have power to spare.

This is not to suggest that repeated-measures designs are not a good choice—they are often a very good choice. But we need to be judicious in how we set up our studies and not add additional trials just to be thorough. McClelland (1997) has made similar suggestions dealing with the design of between-subjects studies.

Hierarchical Linear Models

Repeated-measures analysis of variance requires several assumptions to be valid, and these are discussed in detail in any standard work on the analysis of variance (e.g., Howell, 2007). The assumption of sphericity assumes a specific pattern for the variance/covariance matrix, and violations of this assumption can radically alter the power of the design.[16] The analysis also requires complete data on all trials from all participants or at least estimation of missing observations by a procedure such as multiple imputation. Finally, repeated-measures analysis of variance can only handle certain types of nested designs. In recent years, there has been considerable work on hierarchical or multilevel linear modeling (HLM), and these approaches circumvent the limitations of repeated-measures analysis by allowing missing data, giving the data analyst the option of specifying an unstructured covariance matrix, and easily handling multiple levels of nesting. There is, however, a considerable increase in the complexity of the analysis. Discussion of these models does not fall within the range of this chapter, but the interested reader is referred to Bryk and Raudenbush (1992), Maxwell and Delaney (2004), and Chapter 30 in this volume.

Conclusions

The analysis of variance is a powerful tool that has served behavioral scientists well over the years. We know how to calculate power for various designs, we can derive effect size measures to provide meaningful interpretation of our results, and we have developed ways to work with missing observations and heterogeneous variances. However, most discussions of the analysis of variance focus on the omnibus *F* test, which considers all means simultaneously, or on traditional or innovative multiple comparison procedures focusing on all pairwise comparisons. One purpose of this chapter was to point out that we will do well to attend clearly and directly to those effects that we consider most important. That means that we need to derive our power estimates based on those contrasts rather than on the omnibus *F*; that we need to direct our attention to very specific and, it is hoped, few contrasts; and that we will do well to present effect size measures that speak to those contrasts.

Notes

1. Hoenig and Heisey (2001) have criticized post hoc power as not a particularly useful statistic. Editor's note: Others have pointed out that post hoc power is important when interpreting null results.

2.   The nonsignificant difference might be attributable to the unusually large variance in the PE condition, but the point about logical and probabilistic rules still holds.

3.   Many readers will be more familiar with using integers than with using fractional values for the coefficients (e.g., 1, 1, −1, −1 instead of .5, .5, −.5, −.5). I use fractional values because they fit nicely with the following discussion on effect sizes. The results for significance tests are the same whichever coefficients we use.

4.   Both logarithmic and square root transformations fail to reduce the heterogeneity of variance, in part because the PE group does not contain any unusual outliers. Readers can refer to Chapter 13 on transformations for more information.

5.   A freely available program available at http://www.psycho.uni-duesseldorf.de/abteilungen/app/gpower3.

6.   This is often known as Hedge's g and is what you obtain from standard formulas for converting t or F directly to an effect size measure.

7.   This approach is closely related to a measure often known as Glass's Δ.

8.   This approach is in line with the suggestion by Kline (2004) that it is appropriate for cases of heterogeneity of variance.

9.   Editor's note: The reader should refer to Chapter 7 (this volume) on p_{rep} as it seems to eliminate some of these thorny issues when p values are close to .05.

10.   An h% trimmed mean has h% of the observations at each end of the distribution removed from the data. A Winsorized mean or variance is calculated on data for which we have replaced the trimmed values with the largest or smallest of the remaining values, adjusting the degrees of freedom for the removed or replaced values.

11.   This F is not equal to the squared value of t that we computed earlier ($5.268^2 = 27.75$) because, although we have not adjusted the means, variability due to ethnicity and the interaction have been partialed from MS_{error}. This was not the case with our t test.

12.   There are no important differences found for the other ethnic groups, and we would not calculate effect size measures for them—their differences were so far from statistically significant that the effect sizes would not have any meaning.

13.   For this analysis, I have split the data by group. The standard Greenhouse-Geisser or Huyhn-Feldt adjustments for violations of the sphericity assumption are very effective for the overall analysis but do not necessarily apply if we use overall error terms for simple effects or contrasts (see Howell, 2007).

14.   I could easily be faulted for essentially suggesting that a p value of .089 is "borderline significant" but that a p of .054 is not worth

worrying about. My only defense is that there appears to be something meaningful going on in the near group but not in the away group.

15.   Readers can refer to Chapter 15 on missing data for a more thorough discussion of this issue.

16.   There are corrections for violations of sphericity, but these are not always applicable for the problem at hand.

REFERENCES

Bradley, D. R., & Russell, R. L. (1998). Some cautions regarding statistical power in split-plot designs. *Behavior Research Methods, Instruments, and Computers, 30,* 462–477.

Brown, M. B., & Forsythe, A. B. (1974). The ANOVA and multiple comparisons for data with heterogeneous variances. *Biometrics, 30,* 719–724.

Bryk, A. S., & Raudenbusch, S. W. (1992). *Hierarchical linear models: Applications and data analysis methods.* Newbury Park, CA: Sage.

Cohen, B. H. (2000). *Explaining psychological statistics* (2nd ed.). New York: John Wiley.

Cohen, J. (1969). *Statistical power analysis for the behavioral sciences.* Hillsdale, NJ: Lawrence Erlbaum.

Evans, G. W., Bullinger, M., & Hygge, S. (1998). Chronic noise exposure and physiological response: A prospective study of children living under environmental stress. *Psychological Science, 9,* 75–77.

Field, A. (2004). *Discovering statistics using SPSS for Windows* (2nd ed.). London: Sage.

Foa, E. B., Rothbaum, B. O., Riggs, D. S., & Murdock, T. B. (1991). Treatment of posttraumatic stress disorder in rape victims: A comparison between cognitive-behavioral procedures and counseling. *Journal of Consulting and Clinical Psychology, 59,* 715–723.

Hoenig, J. M., & Heisey, D. M. (2001). The abuse of power: The pervasive fallacy of power calculations for data analysis. *The American Statistician, 55,* 12–24.

Howell, D. C. (2007). *Statistical methods for psychology* (6th ed.). Belmont, CA: Wadsworth.

Howell, D. C. (2008). The treatment of missing data. In W. Outhwaite & S. Turner (Eds.), *Handbook of social science methodology.* London: Sage.

Keselman, H. J., Holland, B., & Cribbie, R. A. (2005). Multiple comparison procedures. In B. S. Everitt & D. C. Howell (Eds.), *Encyclopedia of statistics in behavioral science* (pp. 1309–1325). Chichester, England: John Wiley.

Keselman, H. J., & Wilcox, R. R. (2006). Multiple comparison tests: Nonparametric and resampling approaches. In B. S. Everitt & D. C. Howell (Eds.), *Encyclopedia of statistics in behavioral science* (pp. 1325–1331). Chichester, England: John Wiley.

Kline, R. B. (2004). *Beyond significance testing: Reforming data analysis methods in behavioral research.* Washington, DC: American Psychological Association.

Maxwell, S. E., & Delaney, H. D. (2004). *Designing experiments and analyzing data: A model comparison perspective* (2nd ed.). Mahwah, NJ: Lawrence Erlbaum.

McClelland, G. H. (1997). Optimal design in psychological research. *Psychological Methods, 2,* 3–19.

Overall, J. E. (1996). How many repeated measurements are useful? *Journal of Clinical Psychology, 52,* 243–252.

Plant, E. A., & Sachs-Ericsson, N. (2004). Racial and ethnic differences in depression: The roles of social support and meeting basic needs. *Journal of Consulting and Clinical Psychology, 72,* 41–52.

Rosenthal, R. (1994). Parametric measures of effect size. In H. Cooper & L. V. Hedges (Eds.), *The handbook of research synthesis* (pp. 231–244). New York: Russell Sage Foundation.

Tomarken, A. J., & Serlin, R. C. (1986). Comparison of ANOVA alternatives under variance heterogeneity and specific noncentrality structures. *Psychological Bulletin, 99,* 90–99.

Welch, B. L. (1951). On the comparison of several mean values: An alternative approach. *Biometrika, 38,* 330–336.

Wilkinson, L. (1999). Statistical methods in psychology journals: Guidelines and explanations. *American Psychologist, 54,* 594–604.

24

BINARY LOGISTIC REGRESSION

JASON E. KING

Regression procedures aid in understanding and testing complex relationships among variables and in forming predictive equations. Linear modeling techniques, such as ordinary least squares (OLS) regression, are appropriate when the predictor (independent) variables are continuously or categorically scaled and the criterion (response, dependent) variable is continuously scaled. Discriminant analysis allows prediction of a categorical criterion when all predictors are continuous and strong assumptions are met. However, a more intuitively appealing approach is to directly model the nonlinear relationship using a nonlinear methodology. In fact, discriminant analysis "is in the process of being replaced in most modern practice by logistic regression" (Darlington, 1990, p. 458). Logistic regression allows categorically and continuously scaled variables to predict any categorically scaled criterion. Applications include predicting or explaining pass/fail in education, survival/ nonsurvival in medicine, or presence/absence of a clinical disorder in psychology.

Though logistic regression was slow to catch on initially (White, Long, & Tansey, 1997), the past two decades have seen tremendous growth in its use within the social sciences. Nevertheless, many social scientists remain unfamiliar with its workings. One reason is the complexity of the procedure. Textbooks such as those by Hosmer and Lemeshow (2000) and Kleinbaum and Klein (2002) are valuable resources but are written at an intermediate level of difficulty. There is also a general lack of agreement on terminology.

The aim of this chapter is to describe binary logistic regression at an introductory level with the realization that some important complexities and nuances will be neglected. Significant attention is given to odds ratios, effect size measures, and variable selection procedures. Best practices are emphasized. The chapter by Drs. Anderson and Rutkowski (Chapter 26, this volume) offers a more advanced treatment of logistic regression, including prediction to a polytomous criterion.

HEURISTIC DATA SET

Illustrations are made using the *Employee* data set, which comes bundled with recent versions of the Statistical Package for the Social Sciences (SPSS) and can also be freely downloaded at http://support.spss.com. The database includes measures of employee education level (in years), sex (recoded as 0 = male, 1 = female), minority status (0 = no, 1 = yes), current salary, previous experience (in months), case ID, and job category (custodial, clerical, managerial). The custodial and clerical job categories were combined to form a dichotomous criterion and recoded as custodial/clerical = 0 and managerial = 1. Deleting 24 cases with missing values on the experience variable left 450 usable observations, which were the basis of all analyses.

Why Not Use Linear Regression?

A brief review of the workings of OLS linear regression will lay the groundwork for explaining logistic regression. In linear regression, one derives an estimation equation composed of predictors (X variables) that maximally explain the variation of scores on the criterion (Y variable). The equation is composed of an intercept/additive constant (a weight) and one or more slopes/multiplicative constants (b weights), also called unstandardized regression coefficients. When an error term (e) is included, the equation perfectly defines the criterion variable:

$$Y = a + b_1X_1 + b_2X_2 + \ldots + b_kX_k + e, \quad (1)$$

where k = the number of predictor variables. If the error term is excluded, scores resulting from the equation produce a synthetic variable composed of *predicted scores* or *fitted values*:

$$\hat{Y} = \hat{a} + \hat{b}_1X_1 + \hat{b}_2X_2 + \ldots + \hat{b}_kX_k, \quad (2)$$

where the hat ($\wedge$) indicates an estimated or predicted value. The estimated intercept ($\hat{a}$) is the criterion score when all predictors are set to 0. The estimated b weight ($\hat{b}$) is the change in the mean of the criterion probability distribution for a unit increase on the predictor while holding all other predictors constant.

The b weights are derived such that the sum of the squared deviations of the criterion (Y) scores from the predicted ($\hat{Y}$) scores are minimized. This is equivalent to saying that the (squared) errors are minimized, and hence the mathematical method of obtaining such a solution is denoted *ordinary least squares* estimation. No other solution will produce smaller (squared) errors if the assumptions of linear regression are met. A standardized weight (beta; β) quantifies the amount that a standardized criterion will change when a standardized predictor is increased by one unit and all other predictors are held constant. Larger coefficients indicate stronger predictors in the equation. Yet because collinearity may exist, one should also interpret structure coefficients in determining variable importance (Courville & Thompson, 2001; Thompson & Borrello, 1985). If the criterion variable is a dichotomy, a predicted value is equal to the *predicted probability* of a criterion

value of 1. In this special case, the OLS regression model is called the *linear probability model*.

Among the assumptions required for linear regression, several are of interest here: (a) The relation between the criterion and each predictor is linear in the parameters, (b) error variance is constant across levels of each predictor (i.e., homoscedasticity), (c) errors are normally distributed, and (d) the criterion is a random variable. Assumption (a) does not require a linear relationship between the criterion and each predictor but only linearity *in the parameters*. Nonlinear relations can be modeled by transforming (e.g., raising to powers, multiplying, taking the square root of) the predictors and/or criterion, yet the parameters themselves (i.e., the a and b weights) cannot be transformed.

Unweighted OLS regression applied to a categorical criterion will invalidate these assumptions. For example, (d) suggests that Y has a range of possible values each having an associated probability. If a criterion is dichotomous, then its relationship with each predictor cannot be made linear without transforming parameters. Second, a dichotomous criterion will not yield normally distributed error terms, which can affect statistical significance tests and confidence intervals. Furthermore, linear regression assumes that a change in one of the predictors has a constant marginal effect on the probability of the event occurring. This assumption may be invalidated because criterion values near the extremes will be weakly related to the predictor, yet predicted probabilities will not reflect the curvilinear relationship. To understand this dynamic, consider the relationship between income level and home ownership. For persons in the top and bottom income brackets, an increase of $10,000 will have little effect on the probability of owning a home (i.e., the probabilities will approach 1 and 0, respectively). The strongest effect will be in the middle of the distribution, such as moving from the $50,000 to $60,000 income level. A sample drawn from the middle of the salary distribution will consequently produce a different prediction equation than one drawn from the tails.

Model A predicts job category (custodial/clerical, managerial) using sex, minority status, education, and experience (see Appendix A for a list of illustrative models used in this chapter). The linear regression estimates in Table 24.1

point to sex, minority status, and education as the most important predictors in the equation.

Figure 24.1 demonstrates how the qualitative criterion caused failure to meet the error distributional assumptions.

As another example, in Model B, salary predicts job category and yields these linear regression estimates: $\hat{a} = -0.45$, $\hat{b}_{Salary} = 0.000018$. The *observed probabilities* (equivalently, observed proportions or observed conditional means) are calculated by taking the mean proportion of cases in which job category = 1 (managerial) for each salary level represented in the data set. From Figure 24.2, it is evident that there is a nonlinear relationship between salary and the observed conditional probabilities.

A well-fitting model should yield predicted probabilities that are similar to the observed

Table 24.1   Linear Regression Predicting Job Category—Model A

Variable	$\hat{b}$	$SE\ \hat{b}$	$\hat{\beta}$	t	Probability	r_s
(Constant)	−0.80	0.09	—	−8.77	0.000[a]	—
Sex	−0.08	0.03	−0.10	−2.55	0.011	−0.47
Minority	−0.13	0.04	−0.14	−3.76	0.000[a]	−0.33
Education	0.08	0.01	0.57	13.47	0.000[a]	0.96
Experience	0.00[a]	0.00[a]	0.06	1.59	0.113	−0.17

NOTE: r_s = structure coefficient. Multiple R^2 = 0.40.

a. Value less than 0.005.

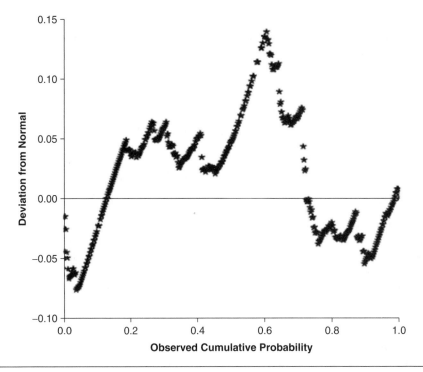

Figure 24.1   Detrended probability plot of residuals from a linear regression of Model A. Points should cluster above and below the reference line with no discernible pattern if errors are normally distributed.

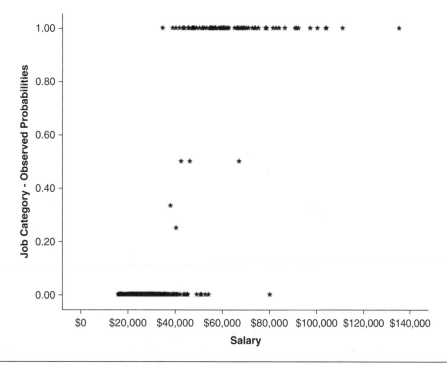

Figure 24.2   Observed probabilities for Model B demonstrating a nonlinear relationship.

probabilities. Yet the relationship between salary and predicted probabilities is linear (see Figure 24.3), unlike the nonlinear relationship reflected in the observed probabilities. Clearly, the linear probability model does not accurately model the observed relationship. In addition, probabilities exceeding the permissible range of 0 to 1 are uninterpretable.

Why Not Use Discriminant Analysis?

Discriminant analysis attempts to estimate a linear function that best discriminates between scores on the criterion (Huberty & Barton, 1989). One or more canonical discriminant functions are created by linearly combining the discriminating (predictor) variables to maximally divide the groups (i.e., scores on the criterion). As in linear regression, discriminant analysis employs OLS estimation and makes use of additive and multiplicative weights in deriving the equation. Yet unlike regression, predicted probabilities of group membership will always fall within acceptable bounds (0 to 1).

Among the assumptions required by discriminant analysis are the following: (a) Each group must be drawn from a population that is multivariate normal, and (b) population covariance matrices must be equal for each group (Klecka, 1980). Table 24.2 presents results from a discriminant analysis applied to Model A. Again, sex, minority status, and education are the strongest discriminators in the equation, as evidenced by their relatively large structure coefficients and standardized discriminant function coefficients. Predicted probabilities for membership in Group 1 vary from 0.0004 to 0.9973, all within the desirable range.

Assumption (a) may be assessed via scatterplots and more complex methods. The assumption cannot hold for minority status and sex because these qualitative variables are not normally distributed and will not yield bivariate normal distributions. Thus, a significant limitation of discriminant analysis is inability to include categorical predictor variables. Though perhaps overly conservative, Box's test of equality of covariance matrices may be used to evaluate assumption (b). Here, the test fails,

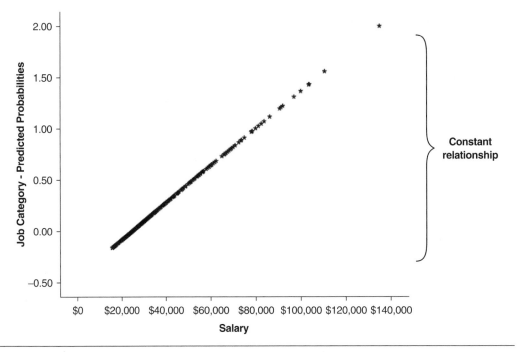

Figure 24.3   Predicted probabilities from a linear regression of Model B.

Table 24.2   Discriminant Analysis Predicting Job Category—Model A

Variable	Function	Standardized Function	r_s
(Constant)	−5.19	—	—
Sex	−0.43	−0.20	−0.38
Minority	−0.69	−0.28	−0.26
Education	0.40	0.93	0.94
Experience	0.00[a]	0.13	−0.13

NOTE: r_s = structure coefficient. Canonical R^2 = 0.40 (Wilks's λ = 0.60).

a. Value less than 0.005.

$F_{(10,100696.7)} = 11.389$, $p < .001$. These data appear to invalidate at least two assumptions required of discriminant analysis.

LOGISTIC REGRESSION

The procedures examined above are subsumed under the *general linear model*, which posits that

errors are normally distributed and the model is linear in the parameters. Logistic regression frees up these expectations and is more robust across varied conditions (for a comparative simulation study, see Pohar, Blas, & Turk, 2004). Logistic regression falls within the family of *generalized linear models* in which "some nonlinear function of the conditional mean [predicted probability] can be written as a linear function of the parameters" (Dunteman & Ho, 2006, p. 4). The underlying relationship between criterion and each predictor is assumed to be nonlinear and represented by an S-shaped function called a sigmoid. A sigmoid is linear in the middle and nonlinear at the ends so that the strength of relationship differs across values of the predictor. Logistic regression does not assume normally distributed errors but rather a binomial distribution, a more reasonable expectation given a dichotomous criterion. Of particular benefit is the ability to easily model both categorical and continuous predictors in the logistic equation.[1] Table 24.3 lists variable scaling requirements for several widely used statistical procedures.[2]

There are three approaches from which logistic regression results may be viewed. These can

Table 24.3   Selecting a Statistical Procedure Based on Variable Scaling

	Scale of Criterion	
Scale of Predictor	*Categorical*	*Continuous*
Categorical	Logistic regression or log-linear analysis	ANOVA
Continuous	Logistic regression or discriminant analysis	OLS regression
Categorical or continuous	Logistic regression	OLS regression with dummy coding

be thought of as three "worlds," each having unique terminology and unique variable transformations applied in defining the logistic regression equation. In the *log-odds world*, only the criterion is transformed; in the *odds world*, both the criterion and predictors are transformed; and in the *probability world*, only the predictors are transformed. It is important to keep in mind, however, that all three approaches are equivalent ways of modeling the relationship between predictors and criterion, varying only in the perspective from which the variable relationships are viewed.

The Probability World

The *probability world* employs this logistic regression equation,

$$Y = \frac{\exp(\alpha + \beta_1 X_1 + \beta_2 X_2 + \ldots + \beta_k X_k)}{1 + \exp(\alpha + \beta_1 X_1 + \beta_2 X_2 + \ldots + \beta_k X_k)} + e, \quad (3)$$

and this estimated prediction equation,

$$\hat{Y} = \hat{\pi} = \frac{\exp(\hat{a} + \hat{b}_1 X_1 + \hat{b}_2 X_2 + \ldots + \hat{b}_k X_k)}{1 + \exp(\hat{a} + \hat{b}_1 X_1 + \hat{b}_2 X_2 + \ldots + \hat{b}_k X_k)}. \quad (4)$$

Equation 4 is called the *logistic probability model* and is analogous to the *linear probability model*. A predicted score (here, $\hat{\pi}$ rather than $\hat{Y}$) is equivalent to the probability that group membership equals 1. The left side of Equation 4 is identical to the linear regression model, but the exponentiated weights cause the model to be nonlinear in the parameters (for a review of exponents, see Appendix B). This transformation hinders interpretation because the strength of the predictive relationship becomes dependent on which values of the predictor variable are under consideration.

Illustration

To illustrate how logistic regression models the non-constant relationship, recall that in linear regression, a *b* weight indicates how much the dependent variable will change given a one-unit increase on a predictor. The linear model is *additive* in the sense that change is constant across the entire range of scores (Figure 24.3). Using the linear regression estimates for Model B ($\hat{a} = -0.45$, $\hat{b}_{\text{Salary}} = 0.000018$), suppose that George is earning \$35,000 and wants to know the probability of someone with his salary being in management. Equation 2 yields a predicted probability for that salary level of $\hat{Y} = 0.185936$, a relatively low probability.[3] Kramer's salary is one dollar higher and yields a $\hat{Y}$ of 0.185954. The change in predicted probabilities is 0.000018, which exactly matches the *b* weight. Similarly, Jerry and Elaine earn \$50,000 and \$50,001, respectively, and also have a difference in predicted probabilities of 0.000018. Therefore, the linear regression model produces an additive, constant rate of change across values of the predictor (see Table 24.4).[4]

Yet under the logistic probability model, because the slope parameters form a ratio of exponentiated terms, the amount that *Y* increases for a unit increase in *X will vary* depending on where the *X* value falls along the function. The expected increase is neither additive nor multiplicative but *interactive* depending on the values of the predictor. Consequently, *b* cannot be interpreted as a constant change expected of the criterion. Instead, the functional relationship must be evaluated across a range of values to understand the impact of the predictors on the criterion.

A logistic regression applied to Model B yields the following *logistic coefficients: $\hat{a} = -11.26$,*

Table 24.4   Additive Change in Predicted Probabilities for the Linear Probability Model—Model B

Increment	Salary	Linear Predicted Probability ($\hat{Y}$)	Δ in Probability
$1	$35,000	0.185936	—
	$35,001	0.185954	+0.000018
	$50,000	0.458007	—
	$50,001	0.458025	+0.000018
$1,000	$35,000	0.185936	—
	$36,000	0.204074	+0.018138
	$37,000	0.222212	+0.018138
	$38,000	0.240350	+0.018138
	$39,000	0.258488	+0.018138

$\hat{b}_{\text{Salary}} = 0.00024$. The predicted probability for a person at George's salary level is calculated from Equation 4 as $\hat{\pi} = \exp(-11.26 + (0.000239 \times 35,000))/(1 + \exp(-11.26 + (0.000239 \times 35,000))) = 0.052334$. The $\hat{\pi}$ for Kramer's salary is 0.052346. The one-unit difference between their salaries is associated with an increased predicted probability of 0.000012. On the other hand, a one-unit change between Jerry and Elaine's salary levels yields an increase of 0.000053. Neither matches the b weight of

0.00024. Table 24.5 lists changes in predictive probabilities across several salary levels.

Figure 24.4 plots the logistic predicted probabilities with the predictor. All probabilities now fall within the permissible range of 0 to 1. The changes in predictive probabilities in the tail of the function are smaller than those near the middle because a weaker relationship is modeled for that portion of the curve.

To summarize, logistic regression models a nonlinear relationship between the predictors

Table 24.5   Interactive Change in Predicted Probabilities for the Logistic Probability Model—Model B

Increment	Salary	Logistic Predicted Probability ($\hat{\pi}$)	Δ in Probability
$1	$35,000	0.052334	—
	$35,001	0.052346	+0.000012
	$50,000	0.665061	—
	$50,001	0.665114	+0.000053
$1,000	$35,000	0.052334	—
	$36,000	0.065526	+0.013192
	$37,000	0.081757	+0.016231
	$38,000	0.101571	+0.019814
	$39,000	0.125530	+0.023959
	$45,000	0.375625	—
	$46,000	0.433068	+0.057444
	$47,000	0.492370	+0.059301
	$48,000	0.551886	+0.059517
	$49,000	0.609953	+0.058066

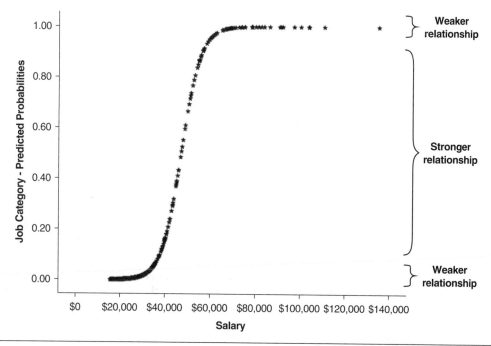

Figure 24.4   Predicted probabilities from a logistic regression of Model B.

and the dichotomous criterion. Even if linear regression produces similar parameter estimates, inaccurate standard errors may affect results. In the logistic probability model, changes in predicted probability are conditioned on the values of the predictors, with a weaker predictive relationship modeled for the tails of the distribution.

The Odds World

A second interpretive framework is the *odds world*. Instead of transforming only the predictors, here the criterion is modified as well. This is needed because assigning a conceptual meaning to the logistic regression coefficients in the *probability world* is all but impossible due to the ratio of exponentiated terms in Equation 4. The equation is rearranged such that the right side becomes only a single exponentiated term, thereby causing the left side of the equation to form a ratio of two probabilities, otherwise known as an odds:

$$\text{odds}(Y=1) = \frac{\hat{\pi}(Y=1)}{1 - \hat{\pi}(Y=1)} \tag{5}$$

$$= \exp(\hat{a} + \hat{b}_1 X_1 + \hat{b}_2 X_2 + \ldots + \hat{b}_k X_k).$$

This is termed the *logistic odds model.* We will come back to interpreting the equation after a brief discussion of odds.

Odds

Many social scientists are initially uncomfortable in this world due to limited experience with *odds*. A probability is the *chance* or *likelihood* that something has occurred or will occur, while the odds are equivalent to the ratio of two probabilities, namely, the probability that something occurs divided by the probability that it does not occur.[5] The following equalities allow conversion between odds and probabilities: prob = odds/(1 + odds); odds = prob/(1 − prob). Unlike probabilities, odds can range from 0 to infinity. When odds are greater than 1, the event is more likely to occur than not. When odds are between 0 and 0.9̄9̄, the event is less likely to occur. When the probability of occurrence equals the probability of nonoccurrence, the condition is termed *even odds*.

Suppose it is known that the probability of a filmmaker releasing another *Harry Potter* movie is 0.80. We could say that there is an 80% likelihood (i.e., probability) of the event, and the

Table 24.6   Calculation and Interpretation of Odds

Probability of Occurrence	Interpretation	Probability of Nonoccurrence	Odds of Occurrence	Relation	Interpretation
0.25	1 in 4 probability of occurrence	0.75	0.25/0.75 = 0.33	"1 to 3"	3 times less likely to occur than not
0.50	1 in 2 probability of occurrence	0.50	0.50/0.50 = 1.0	"1 to 1"	Even odds of occurrence
0.80	4 in 5 probability of occurrence	0.20	0.80/0.20 = 4.0	"4 to 1"	4 times more likely to occur than not
0.999	999 in 1,000 probability of occurrence	0.001	0.999/0.001 = 999.0	"999 to 1"	999 times more likely to occur than not

probability of the occurrence is four times greater than the probability of nonoccurrence. The odds of the event are equivalently 4 parts (80%) to 1 part (20%) = "4 to 1" = 0.80/0.20 = 4/1 = 4. The reverse condition can also be predicted. The probability of NOT making the movie is 1 − 0.80 = 0.20, with odds calculated as 0.20/0.80 = "1 to 4" = 1/4 = 0.25. See Table 24.6 for additional examples.

Odds Ratio

Although odds are calculated by dividing two probabilities, an odds can be divided by another odds to form an *odds ratio* (OR). This descriptive statistic is especially useful for comparing groups. When the odds for Group 1 is divided by the odds for Group 2, an odds ratio greater than 1 indicates a larger odds associated with Group 1, and conversely. A simple formula that expresses the OR as a percentage change in odds aids in interpretation:

$$\% \text{ change} = 100(OR - 1). \quad (6)$$

An OR of 1.5 is interpreted as follows: The odds for the event or group in the numerator are $100(1.5 - 1) = 50\%$ larger than the odds for the event or group in the denominator. Odds ratios of 2, 0.5, and 1 indicate, respectively, that the odds of the group in the numerator are 100% larger (doubled), 50% smaller (halved), and neither larger nor smaller than the odds of the group in the denominator.

Say we wish to compare the odds of two movie sequels being produced. Using the scenario described earlier in which the odds of

another *Harry Potter* production are 4, assume it is also known that there is only a 0.33 probability of production of another *Rocky* movie, yielding an odds for this occurrence of 0.5. Dividing the odds of 4 by the odds of 0.5 yields an OR of 8 having this interpretation: The odds of a *Harry Potter* sequel are eight times as large as the odds of a *Rocky* sequel (see Table 24.7).

The odds ratio has several desirable properties as a measure of association. First, whether an odds ratio is greater than or less than 1 can be thought of as its "sign" because this value separates increasing from decreasing odds. Second, shifts in sample size do not affect its value. Morgan and Teachman (1988) list additional properties.

It is important to understand that the OR does not quantify the increase in the *probability* associated with an event or group (Zhang & Yu, 1998). Odds ratios are often misinterpreted such that an OR of 10 is treated as a 10-point increase in likelihood or probability. Yet the odds ratio says very little about the probabilities underlying the odds estimates. Various probabilities can be combined into odds to yield equivalent odds ratios. If the probabilities associated with the *Harry Potter* and *Rocky* movies were reduced to 0.40 and 0.08, respectively, the OR would still equal 8.

Nor does an odds ratio indicate absolute strength or weakness. Suppose that we wished to compare the odds of boys eating Play-Doh to the odds of girls eating Play-Doh. Assume that an odds ratio of 3 is found. The result sounds impressive in that the odds of boys eating Play-Doh are three times as high as those of girls, yet less so if it is discovered that the odds for each group were very low to begin with, only 0.09 and

Table 24.7   Calculation and Interpretation of Odds Ratio

Event	Probability	Odds	Odds Ratio	Interpretation
Making of another *Harry Potter* movie	0.80	0.80/0.20 = 4.0	4.0/0.5 = 8.0	Odds of another *Harry Potter* movie are 8 times as large as the odds of a *Rocky* movie.
Making of another *Rocky* movie	0.33	0.33/0.66 = 0.5	0.5/4.0 = 0.13	Odds of another *Rocky* movie are 0.13 times as large as the odds of a *Harry Potter* movie.

0.03, respectively. In absolute terms, the odds do not differ much between the groups.

Interpreting Change in Odds

Coming back to the logistic odds model, it is instructive to rewrite Equation 5 as

$$\text{odds}(Y = 1) = \frac{\hat{\pi}(Y = 1)}{1 - \hat{\pi}(Y = 1)}$$
$$= \exp(\hat{a}) \times \exp(\hat{b}_1 X_1) \times \tag{7}$$
$$\exp(\hat{b}_2 X_2) \times \ldots \times \exp(\hat{b}_k X_k).$$

A property of this model is that a one-unit change in X, while holding all other predictors constant, multiplies the odds (i.e., the criterion) by $\exp(\hat{b})$. Thus,

$$\text{odds}_2 = \exp(\hat{b}) \times \text{odds}_1. \tag{8a}$$

Equation 8a can then be expressed as a ratio of two odds:

$$\widehat{OR} = \frac{\text{odds}_2}{\text{odds}_1} = \exp(\hat{b}). \tag{8b}$$

It is now clear that $\exp(\hat{b})$ can be interpreted as an odds ratio estimating the multiplicative change required to move from odds$_1$ to odds$_2$, given a one-unit increase on X.[6] Consequently, the logistic odds model is said to be "multiplicative in the odds." Like the logistic probability model, there is a nonlinear relationship between the criterion (i.e., the odds) and the predictor, yet the rate of change is multiplicative and constant. This steady rate of change allows for easier interpretation of parameters.

Illustration With a Continuous Predictor

To illustrate the multiplicative relationship, assume that a single predictor model yields $\hat{b}_x = 0.6932$. This number is easy to work with because $\exp(0.6932) = 2$. Assume also that X and Y are standardized so that the a weight can be safely ignored in Equation 7 because $\exp(0) = 1$. If $X = 0$, the odds will be $\exp(0.6932 \times 0) = 1$, meaning that there is an "even" chance of the criterion taking the value of 1. The predictive probability is calculated as $\exp(0)/(1 + \exp(0)) = 0.5$ and is congruent with that interpretation. Now if X is increased to 1, the odds double to become $\exp(0.6932 \times 1) = 2$, yet the probability increases only to 0.67. So the odds increase multiplicatively per unit increase in X but not the predicted probabilities.

Taking a slightly more complex example, recall that Model B yielded the following logistic regression coefficients: $\hat{a} = -11.255$, $\hat{b}_{\text{Salary}} = 0.00024$. The estimated odds ratio is $\widehat{OR} = \exp(0.00024) = 1.00024$.[7] From Equation 6, this value is associated with a percentage increase of $100(1.00024 - 1) = 0.024$. So we expect that the predicted odds of being a manager will increase by a multiplicative constant of 0.024% with each one-dollar increase in salary. To verify, we will first determine the predicted odds of holding a management position for a person at George's salary level of \$35,000. Applying Equation 7, we obtain an odds of $\exp(-11.26) \times \exp(0.000239 \times 35,000) = 0.055224$. Kramer's one-dollar higher salary yields an odds of 0.055238. We can now use Equation 8a to demonstrate that a one-dollar increase in salary raises the odds by $\exp(b)$. Multiplying George's estimated odds of 0.055224 by the exponentiated b value of 1.00024 yields Kramer's odds of 0.055238.

The formula exp(cb) is useful in computing change in odds in increments other than a single unit for continuous predictors. For example, a $1,000 change in salary would be associated with a 27% increase in odds: $\widehat{OR}$ = exp(1000 × 0.00024) = 1.2697 (see Table 24.8). Figure 24.5 plots predicted odds against a subset of salary levels to further illustrate the multiplicative relationship.

Illustration With a Dichotomous Predictor

The odds model is particularly useful for interpreting a dichotomous predictor.[8] Model C predicts job category = 1 using sex and produces the following logistic regression results: $\hat{a}$ = −0.91, $\hat{b}_{Sex}$ = −1.99, $\widehat{OR}$ = 0.14, $p < .001$. Applying Equation 6 leads to the conclusion that a one-unit change on the predictor from male (0) to female

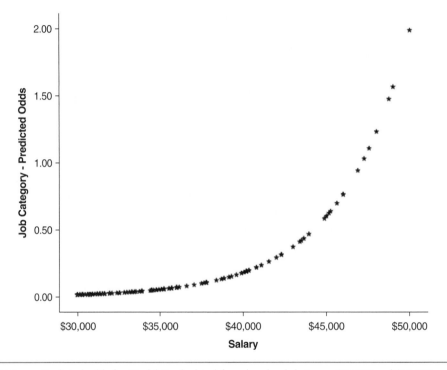

Figure 24.5   Predicted odds for Model B calculated for salary levels between $30,000 and $50,000.

Table 24.8   Change in Logistic Regression Predicted Probabilities, Odds, and Logits

| Salary | *Probabilities* | | *Odds* | | | *Logits = Ln(Odds)* | |
	$\hat{\pi}$	*Change[a]*	*Odds*	*Change[b]*	*% Increase*	*Logit*	*Change[c]*
$35,000	0.052	—	0.0552	—	—	−2.896	—
$36,000	0.066	+0.013	0.0701	+0.015	27.0	−2.658	+0.239
$37,000	0.082	+0.016	0.0890	+0.019	27.0	−2.419	+0.239
$38,000	0.102	+0.020	0.1131	+0.024	27.0	−2.180	+0.239
$39,000	0.126	+0.024	0.1435	+0.030	27.0	−1.941	+0.239

NOTE: Values were rounded before calculating change.

a. Nonlinear (interactive) increase.

b. Multiplicative increase.

c. Additive increase.

(1) reflects an 86% decrease in the odds of holding a management position. Had our statistical software predicted a criterion score of 0, the estimated odds ratio would have been 7.32 and interpreted as follows: The odds of a male holding a management position are 632% as large as the odds of a female doing so. These are two equivalent ways of describing the same relationship. In interpreting odds ratios, a researcher must be aware of the scale of the predictor as well as the value of the criterion modeled in the software.

Illustration With Multiple Predictors

Table 24.9 presents logistic regression results for Model A. When modeling multiple predictors, neither unstandardized logistic coefficients nor odds ratios should be used to directly compare the importance of variables in the equation unless the units of measurement are comparable. Only standardized coefficients and statistical significance tests should be used for this purpose (see discussion below). Furthermore, the odds ratios of greatest magnitude will not necessarily be associated with the smallest *p* values (e.g., in Table 24.9 the reciprocal of the odds ratio for minority status [11.49] is larger than the odds ratio for education [5.88]).

Nevertheless, in comparison to unstandardized coefficients, odds ratios offer a more intuitive and practical understanding of the marginal effect of each predictor on the criterion. Consider the odds ratio interpretations for sex, minority, and experience:

(a) In the previous section, we noticed a large and statistically significant effect for sex on

the odds of holding a management position in Model C. But with the addition of other predictors in Model A, the odds ratio for sex drops to 0.45 and is no longer statistically significant. This indicates that sex is not strongly related to the odds of holding a management position after controlling for the other variables. The odds ratio is interpreted as follows: The odds of females holding management positions are about half as large (−45%) as the odds of males doing so.

(b) Minority is a categorical variable that produced a statistically significant coefficient in the equation. Its odds ratio is interpreted as follows: The odds of minorities holding management positions are 93% lower than the odds of nonminorities doing so.

(c) Previous experience is a continuously scaled variable. We can interpret its odds ratio of 1.002 to mean the following: While holding all other variables constant, every 1-month increase in experience is associated with a trivial 0.2% increase in the odds of holding a management position.

Although one cannot strictly compare odds ratios across variables, it is possible to roughly gauge relative magnitude by making comparisons in terms of the values needed to see equivalent effects on the criterion variable. For example, we know that the odds of males being in management is 124% greater than those of females and that a 0.2% increase in predicted odds is associated with every 1 month gained in experience. Dividing 124 by 0.2 allows us to determine that an increase of approximately 620 months (52 years) of experience is needed to equal the difference in predicted odds observed for males over females. Such a comparison sheds

Table 24.9   Logistic Regression Predicting Job Category—Model A

Variable	$\hat{b}$	$SE \, \hat{b}$	Wald t	Probability	OR
(Constant)	−28.30	4.30	43.24	0.000[a]	0.00
Sex	−0.81	0.45	3.17	0.075	0.45
Minority	−2.44	0.82	8.89	0.003	0.09
Education	1.77	0.28	41.40	0.000[a]	5.88
Experience	0.00[a]	0.00[a]	0.41	0.524	1.002

NOTE: OR = odds ratio. $D_0 = -2LL_{Intercept} = 433.22$; $D_M = -2LL_{Model} = 165.89$; $G_{(4)} = 267.33$, $p < .001$.

a. Value less than 0.005.

light on the relative magnitude of each variable's effect. Similar comparisons could be applied to the other predictors.

The Log-Odds World

In the *log-odds* or *logit world*, the predictive relationship involving the X variables is linear:

$$logits = \ln \left(\frac{\hat{\pi}(Y = 1)}{1 - \hat{\pi}(Y = 1)} \right) \qquad (9)$$
$$= \hat{a} + \hat{b}_1 X_1 + \hat{b}_2 X_2 + \ldots + \hat{b}_k X_k.$$

Although the right side of the equation is linear with constant, additive effects, the criterion values are no longer probabilities or odds but the natural log of odds. Log-odds are equivalently termed *logits*. Though not technically identical, logistic regression is often referred to as "logit modeling." Odds and odds ratios can range from 0 to positive infinity and are asymmetric around 1. By taking the log of the odds, the floor restriction is removed so that logits can vary from negative to positive infinity. Because all three "worlds" are interrelated, it is useful to remember that a logit of 0, an odds of 1, and a probability of 0.05 are equivalent quantities.

Illustration

Returning to Model B with salary as the predictor, the logistic parameter estimates ($\hat{a} = -11.26$, $\hat{b}_{Salary} = 0.00024$) can now be interpreted as in linear regression, with logits serving as the criterion variable; b is the amount the logit changes for a one-unit increase on the predictor. In this case, a one-dollar increase in salary produces a 0.00024 increase in the log-odds of job category.

Equation 9 gives the predicted logit for George's salary level as $-11.26 + 0.00024(35,000) = -2.896348$. The logit for Kramer's salary level is -2.896109. The difference between their logits (i.e., 0.00024) exactly matches the value of b, as in OLS regression. It is evident from Figure 24.6 and Table 24.8 that changes in logits are linear, unlike changes in probabilities and odds.

Yet the transformed criterion is difficult to interpret. What does it mean to say that the log-odds of George being a manager is -2.896? What interpretation can be given to the 0.00024 change in log-odds? Due to unfamiliarity with the log-odds metric, researchers typically prefer to interpret the probability and odds models.

STATISTICAL COMPUTING SOFTWARE

Most of the popular software packages now contain at least one logistic regression routine. Both SPSS 13.0 and SAS 9.1 allow "point-and-click" access to most options. Keep in mind the following issues when using these packages. SAS code models a criterion value of 0 by default, whereas SPSS models the largest criterion value. This will occasion some estimates to diverge. One should always run descriptive statistics to verify the direction of relationships indicated by the sign of the b weights and to ensure proper interpretation of the odds ratio estimates. Second, when using a categorical predictor, the SAS CLASS subcommand applies design coding (i.e., values of 1 and -1) in transforming the variable, which will generate different coefficients, standard errors, and Wald statistics than will dummy coding. The SPSS CATEGORICAL subcommand assigns 0 to the largest value on the predictor by default (i.e., the "Last" category is set as the referent in defining contrasts). So a 0/1 dichotomy is essentially transformed into a 1/0 dichotomy. This transformation will affect the coefficient for the constant term and can affect main effects in an interaction model. The interaction effect will be correctly estimated, but the sign of the coefficient will depend on which value of the predictor is modeled. To avoid confusion, the safest course is always to set the contrast reference category to "First." If one does not have access to SAS or SPSS, a free online calculator for computing logistic regression estimates is available at http://statpages.org/logistic.html (last accessed June 16, 2007).

MODEL BUILDING

Data modeling is a complex process that entails assessing the fit of sample data to a theoretically derived model or evaluating multiple competing models. Modeling may aim to identify predictors that best *explain* the criterion or that most accurately *predict* the criterion, with the ultimate goal of finding a parsimonious model that fits the data well and makes substantive sense. After establishing a candidate model, it is often

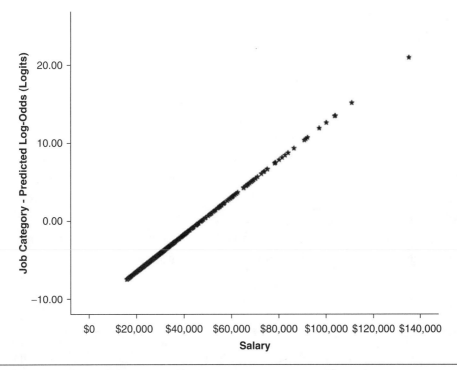

Figure 24.6   Predicted log-odds for Model B.

informative to add back in excluded variables one by one and reassess model fit. This process aids in identifying variables that act only in combination with other variables (e.g., suppressors). Hosmer and Lemeshow (2000) present a logistic modeling approach that is both systematic and relatively comprehensive.

The software packages deluge the researcher with tests and indices for comparing logistic models. We will notice only a few of the more useful measures, including the likelihood ratio test, the Wald test, Hosmer and Lemeshow's goodness-of-fit test, and various measures of association, keeping in mind that one should never base decisions entirely on statistical significance tests (Thompson, 2006a; Ziliak & McCloskey, 2004).

Assessing the Full Model

Maximum Likelihood Estimation

Researchers typically use a *maximum likelihood* algorithm to estimate logistic parameters (for details, see Neter, Kutner, Nachtsheim, & Wasserman, 1996). Contrary to linear regression, in which predicted scores ($\hat{Y}$) and observed scores (Y) are compared in a squared metric (i.e., sum of squares), logistic regression compares predicted scores ($\hat{\pi}$) and observed probabilities (Y) using a log-likelihood (LL) function:

$$\text{LL} = \sum_{i=1}^{N} [(Y_i)] \ln(\hat{\pi}_i) + (1 - Y_i) \ln(1 - \hat{\pi}_i). (10)$$

Maximum likelihood procedures are iterative in that various *a* and *b* weights are tried until a best-fitting solution is found, one that maximizes the log-likelihood function. A disadvantage of iterative procedures, and thereby of logistic regression, is the possibility that the solution will not converge on a best estimate. For statistical significance testing, it is necessary to multiply the log likelihood by –2, denoted –2LL. Table 24.10 illustrates calculation of a log likelihood for Model B using the final 13 observations in the *Employee* data set (i.e., ID numbers 462–474).

Likelihood Ratio Test

The first step in modeling is to determine whether a relationship exists between the criterion and predictor variables. In linear regression,

Table 24.10 Calculation of Log Likelihood Using the Final 13 Observations in the *Employee* Data Set—Model B

Salary	Y_i	$1 - Y_i$	$\hat{\pi}$	$ln(\hat{\pi})$	$ln(1 - \hat{\pi})$	$(Y_i)ln(\hat{\pi}_i) + (1 - Y_i)ln(1 - \hat{\pi}_i)$
$34,410	1	0	0.187	−1.679	−0.206	−1.679
$20,700	0	1	0.004	−5.612	−0.004	−0.004
$47,550	1	0	0.924	−0.080	−2.571	−0.080
$33,900	0	1	0.164	−1.806	−0.180	−0.180
$23,400	0	1	0.008	−4.802	−0.008	−0.008
$32,850	0	1	0.125	−2.077	−0.134	−0.134
$55,750	1	0	0.993	−0.007	−4.972	−0.007
$25,200	0	1	0.014	−4.265	−0.014	−0.014
$26,250	0	1	0.019	−3.954	−0.019	−0.019
$26,400	0	1	0.020	−3.909	−0.020	−0.020
$39,150	0	1	0.489	−0.715	−0.672	−0.672
$21,450	0	1	0.005	−5.387	−0.005	−0.005
$29,400	0	1	0.048	−3.033	−0.049	−0.049

Sum = LL = −2.871
−2LL = 5.741

three sum of squares (*SS*) estimates are used in making model comparisons. SS_{Total} quantifies the total variability in the data set, $SS_{Regression}$ the variability attributable to the model, and SS_{Error} the variability not explained by the model. Each component has an analogous log likelihood in logistic regression (see Table 24.11).

Analogous to SS_{Total}, D_0 is computed as −2 times the log likelihood of an intercept-only model ($LL_{Intercept}$). The zero subscript indicates that no predictors are included in this null/baseline model. Model A produces a D_0 of 433.22 (see Table 24.9).

Analogous to SS_{Error}, D_M is computed as −2 times the log likelihood of the full model. Though some computing packages treat D_M as having a known distribution and report an associated *p* value, D_M is not necessarily chi-square distributed and generally should not be tested for significance (Katsaragakis, Koukouvinos, Stylianou, & Theodoraki, 2005; Menard, 2002; Simonoff, 1998).[9] The D_M for Model A is 165.89.

To quantify the extent to which inclusion of the set of predictors improves model fit, D_M is subtracted from D_0 and multiplied by −2. This holds similarities to $SS_{Regression}$. Essentially, we are asking how much the predictors reduce unexplained

variability in the criterion, with a better fitting model yielding a greater reduction in D_0. The resulting difference is variously referred to as model chi-square, improvement chi-square, *G*, deviance difference, and likelihood ratio statistic.[10] *G* follows a chi-square distribution with *p* degrees of freedom, where *p* = the number of predictors in the model, and can be tested for significance. This *likelihood ratio test* is equivalent to the overall model *F* test in linear regression in which the null hypothesis states that $b_1 = b_2 = \ldots = b_p$, where *p* equals the number of predictors in the full model. Applying the likelihood ratio test to Model A produces the following results: $G_{(4)} = 433.22 − 165.89 = 267.33, p < .001$. We conclude that the full model containing all predictors improves on the intercept-only model.

More broadly, the likelihood ratio test allows comparisons between any two log likelihoods if the models are *nested*. Nesting implies that all parameters in the smaller model are found in the larger model. For example, an intercept-only model is nested within a larger model containing the intercept, variable *X*, and variable *Z*. A model containing *X* and *Z* is nested within a model containing *X*, *Z*, and the $X \times Z$ interaction. In this case, the *G* statistic would be calculated as

Table 24.11   Analogous Quantities in Linear Regression and Logistic Regression

Linear Regression	Logistic Regression		
Quantity	Quantity	SAS Label	SPSS Label
SS_{Total}	$D_0 = -2 \times LL_{Intercept}$	−2 log likelihood (under "Intercept Only")	Initial −2 log likelihood
SS_{Error}	$D_M = -2 \times LL_{Model}$	−2 log likelihood (under "Intercept and Covariates")	−2 log likelihood
$SS_{Regression}$	$G = D_0 - D_M$	Likelihood ratio (under "Chi-Square")	Model (under "Chi-Square")

NOTE: $LL_{Intercept}$ = log likelihood of the intercept model. LL_{Model} = log likelihood of the full model.

$(-2LL_{Larger\ model}) - (-2LL_{Smaller\ model})$ and tested with degrees of freedom equal to the difference in degrees of freedom between the two models.

Goodness of Fit

Another set of measures that should inform modeling decisions are *goodness-of-fit* tests. These tests appraise the difference between pairs of observed and predicted values in an absolute sense, not in comparison to predicted values from another model as with the likelihood ratio test. A well-fitting model is suggested when the contribution from each pair of differences is small and not systematically related to the error variance. Goodness-of-fit tests assess overall model fit, while diagnostics (discussed later) are analogous measures at the individual case level.

One of the most available and widely reported indices is a test proposed by Hosmer and Lemeshow (1980) that entails rank ordering the observations by predicted probability and then splitting them into g groups based on the percentiles associated with the ordered values. The observed probabilities are then compared with the predicted probabilities falling into each group via the Hosmer-Lemeshow goodness-of-fit statistic, $\hat{C}$. $\hat{C}$ is obtained by calculating the Pearson chi-square statistic on the frequencies of observed and predicted values in each of the g groups. The statistic is approximately chi-square distributed with $g - 2$ degrees of freedom. A small p value indicates that the model is inadequate. Because 10 groups are typically formed, it is sometimes denoted the "deciles of risk" test. The authors of the test suggest a minimum sample size of $n = 400$ to achieve acceptable probability values.

The Hosmer-Lemeshow test is based on the asymptotic assumption that the expected cell frequencies are large. If some of the cells contain small frequencies, one may combine adjacent cells and reduce the number of groups. Fewer groups means fewer degrees of freedom and less statistical power. This should be considered before endorsing a model that passes the test based on a limited number of groups (e.g., fewer than 6; Hosmer & Lemeshow, 2000). Applying the test to Model A yields the following results: $\hat{C}_{(8)} = 74.88$, $p < .001$. The significant p value suggests lack of fit. In examining the contingency table used to calculate $\hat{C}$ (see Figure 24.7), it is observed that several cells have expected frequencies less than 1. Combining the first five rows to form a total of five groups yields the following results: $\hat{C}_{(3)} = 10.83$, $p = .013$. Even with lessened power, the test suggests unacceptable fit.

The Hosmer-Lemeshow test is appropriate for models in which one or more predictors are continuously scaled. The test is not valid for *saturated* models in which there are no degrees of freedom available for testing. Due to lack of power and dependence on arbitrarily defined groupings of predicted probabilities, newly developed alternatives to this index may be preferred (Hosmer, Hosmer, le Cessie, & Lemeshow, 1997; Lin, Wei, & Ying, 2002; Verdes & Rudas, 2002). Tang (2001) has proposed an exact goodness-of-fit test to minimize reliance on asymptotic dynamics (cf. Mehta & Patel, 1995). These newer measures are currently unavailable in most computing packages, though other overall model tests such as the Wald test and the score test are available. Indices such as the Akaike information criterion (AIC) are useful when

| | Job Category = Custodial/Clerical | | Job Cagegory = Managerial | | |
	Observed	Expected	Observed	Expected	Total
Step 1	45	45.000	0	.000	45
2	45	44.998	0	.002	45
3	46	46.984	1	.016	47
4	45	44.979	0	.021	45
5	45	44.920	0	.080	45
6	45	43.127	0	1.873	45
7	43	38.577	2	6.423	45
8	37	35.756	9	10.244	46
9	13	20.817	32	24.183	45
10	2	.842	40	41.158	42

Figure 24.7   Contingency table for the Hosmer-Lemeshow goodness-of-fit test applied to Model A.

comparing nonnested models (e.g., comparing Model X with Model Z).

Strength of Association

Effect sizes should always be reported when possible (Thompson, 2006b; Vacha-Haase, Nilsson, Reetz, Lance, & Thompson, 2000). There exist a large number of logistic regression R^2-type measures, with two accessible through SAS and SPSS. The maximum likelihood R^2 (R^2_{ML}; aka Cox & Snell R^2, generalized R^2, Maddala R^2), which SAS labels "R-Square," can be interpreted as a measure of information gained due to inclusion of the predictors in comparison to an intercept-only model. The Nagelkerke adjusted R^2 (R^2_{ML-Adj}; aka Craig & Uhler's R^2, Max-rescaled R^2) corrects R^2_L to equal 1 under perfect prediction. Both are limited by their "lack of a reasonable interpretation" (Shtatland, Kleinman, & Cain, 2002, p. 2).

Of greater benefit would be an index analogous to the linear regression R^2. One option is to apply the ordinary linear regression R^2 to predicted probabilities saved from a logistic regression. The squared correlation between the criterion scores and predicted probabilities reflects the reduction in sum of squares (R^2; aka Efron's R^2, sum of squares R^2). Though the measure can only be used with a dichotomous criterion, R^2 is intuitively appealing because it is

bounded between 0 and 1, allows comparisons between logistic regression models and linear models, and has a familiar interpretation (Menard, 2002).

The McFadden or likelihood ratio R^2 (R^2_L; aka deviance R^2, entropy R^2) is closely related to the linear regression R^2 when calculated using this formula: $1 - SS_{Error}/SS_{Total}$. In view of the analogies between sums of squares quantities and log likelihoods, the parallel is evident:

$$R^2_L = 1 - \frac{LL_{Model}}{LL_{Intercept}} = 1 - \frac{-2LL_{Model}}{-2LL_{Intercept}}$$
$$= 1 - \frac{D_M}{D_0}. \tag{11}$$

Regrettably, neither the SPSS BINARY routine nor SAS calculates the McFadden measure. Macros are available (e.g., Mittlböck & Schemper, 1999), but R^2_L is easily calculated from the values of D_M and D_0 from the logistic output. This index measures the reduction in maximized log likelihood, or the percentage that the fitted model increases the log likelihood in comparison to the intercept model. Simulations indicate that R^2_L typically runs lower than R^2 (Mittlböck & Schemper, 1996). Parsimony-adjusted R^2 measures are available (Liao & McGee, 2003), with Shtatland, Moore, and Barton (2000) offering a corrective to R^2_L:

$$R_{L-Adj}^2 = 1 - \frac{LL_{Model} - \dfrac{(k+1)(n-1)}{n-k-1}}{LL_{Intercept} - 1}, \quad (12)$$

where k equals the number of predictors in the full model. (Note that the equation requires dividing the outputted $-2LL$ values by -2.) Strengths of R_{L-Adj}^2 include the following: (a) a correction for sample size bias, (b) a range between 0 and 1 (usually), (c) an interpretation analogous to the linear regression-corrected R^2, and (d) application to both nested and nonnested models.

No consensus has emerged as to an optimal R^2 measure, and some discourage reporting any value (Hosmer & Lemeshow, 2000). The two McFadden measures are attractive due to their straightforward interpretation and relationship to linear regression measures of association. Model A yields the following effect sizes: $R_L^2 = 1 - (165.89 / 433.22) = 0.62$, $R_{L-Adj}^2 = 0.60$ (with $k = 4$ and $n = 450$). Thus, the four predictors explain about 60% of the total variance. For comparison, squaring the correlation between $\hat{\pi}$ and Y values yields $R^2 = 0.67$, while the R_{ML}^2 and R_{ML-Adj}^2 values obtained from the computer output are 0.45 and 0.73, respectively.

Classification of Cases

Another approach to appraising model fit is to measure the accuracy of classifying each case into one of two groups based on predicted criterion scores. The process is simple: (a) Select a criterion cutoff value, (b) place cases with predicted probabilities above the cutoff value into one group and those below in another group, and (c) report the percentage of cases correctly classified in comparison to observed scores on the criterion variable. The accuracy of classification is dependent on the cutoff value. Typically, 0.5 is the default cut point, but other values may be selected if the costs of mistakenly predicting a case are not equivalent for both categories (e.g., in predicting pass/fail, it may be more detrimental to incorrectly classify individuals as having failed when they really passed).

Predicted probabilities obtained from Model A result in 94.0% of cases correctly classified (see Figure 24.8). Comparatively, we could correctly predict 81.3% of the cases by merely assuming that every case falls into the custodial/clerical category. The question then arises as to the extent to which the model has improved classification. There are a number of tests and measures of association that assist in answering this question (see Hosmer & Lemeshow, 2000; Menard, 2002).

A weakness of classification procedures is the discarding of reliable score variance as a result of dichotomizing the predictor (Taylor, West, & Aiken, 2006). It is possible for a strong relationship to exist between predictors and criterion yet produce predicted values that do not fall cleanly into two groups. In sum, unless the stated goal of the study is classification, these indices generally should not be reported.

Classification Table[a]

			Predicted		
			Job Category		
Observed			Custodial/ Clerical	Managerial	Percentage Correct
Step 1	Job Category	Custodial/ Clerical	356	10	97.3
		Managerial	17	67	79.8
	Overall Percentage				94.0

Figure 24.8   Classification table for Model A.

a. The cut value is .500.

Assessing the Contribution of Individual Predictors

Wald Test

The full-model likelihood ratio test allows us to determine whether one or more b weights in the equation differ significantly from zero. A logical next step is to examine each coefficient individually. Both the Wald and score tests have univariable analogs. A Wald statistic for testing the statistical significance of a b weight is found by dividing the coefficient by its standard error and then squaring the result. The variate will follow a chi-square distribution with 1 df. This statistic is analogous to the t test in linear regression. A Wald test is calculated for each predictor in the model.

To illustrate, consider Model D predicting job category by experience and yielding the following parameter estimates: $\hat{a} = -1.19$, $\hat{b}_{Exper} = -0.00309$; $\hat{SE}_{Exper} = 0.001384$; $\widehat{OR} = 0.997$. The Wald statistic for $\hat{b}_{Exper}$ is calculated as $(-0.00309/0.001384)^2 = -4.98$, with an associated p value of .026. We reject the null hypothesis of $\hat{b}_{Exper} = 0$ and conclude that the log likelihood of being a manager is reduced with increased experience. This seems plausible because those individuals having higher levels of education are likely to have spent more time in school and less time acquiring work experience.

Likelihood Ratio Test

Because the Wald test loses power under some conditions, a preferred approach is to compute a likelihood ratio test for each parameter of interest. This entails calculating logistic regression results for models with and without the predictor of interest and then testing the difference in chi-square values. An alternative to this time-intensive process is to use Wald tests in preliminary model building and then move to likelihood ratio tests when refining models.

Applying a likelihood ratio test to Model D yields chi-square values of $\chi^2_{null} = 433.22$ and $\chi^2_{exper} = 427.53$. The resultant difference of 5.69, tested with 1 df because a single predictor is under consideration, yields a p value of .017. Here, both the Wald test and likelihood ratio test yield significant results, but that will not always be the case. The likelihood ratio test is versatile and can be used to test various effects within nested models, including variable transformations and interaction effects.

Confidence Intervals

The formula for calculating a confidence interval (CI) around a logistic coefficient is

$$\hat{b}_1 \pm z_{1-\alpha/2} \, \widehat{SE}(\hat{b}_1), \qquad (13)$$

where $z_{1-\alpha/2}$ is the upper $100(1 - \alpha/2)\%$ point from the z distribution. If a given interval spans 1, the hypothesis of no relation between predictor and criterion cannot be rejected. We obtain a 95% confidence interval for the education variable in Model A of $1.77 \pm (1.96 \times 0.28)$ and are thus 95% confident that the change in logits for a 1-year increase in education is between 1.23 and 2.31. Upon request, SAS and SPSS will calculate confidence intervals around odds ratio estimates as well.

Standardized Coefficients

Though some researchers discourage the use of standardized coefficients (Darlington, 1990) or warn against interpreting them as indicators of variable importance (Neter et al., 1996; Pedhazur, 1997), the most recent publication manual of the American Psychological Association (2001) encourages their routine use and reporting. They are especially useful when variables are measured on an arbitrary scale (e.g., Likert-type ratings). Although things become appreciably more complex, it is possible to obtain standardized coefficients in logistic regression (Long, 1997). SAS prints a partial or semi-standardized coefficient that is not without limitations (Kaufman, 1996). I have elsewhere (King, 2007) described standardized coefficients in detail and provided computer capabilities for a useful coefficient developed by Kaufman (1996).

Assessing the Contribution of Individual Cases

Upon request, both SPSS and SAS output casewise diagnostic criteria such as standardized residuals, leverage, Cook's distance, and dfbeta. These indices aid the researcher in identifying observations that act as outliers or strongly influence the prediction equation. Most of the indices function in a manner analogous to their application within linear regression.

Additional Issues in Modeling

Model Selection Procedures

Theory and application should guide variable selection. Yet in some exploratory studies, a strong theoretical base is lacking. In other studies, prediction is of sole concern irrespective of theoretical underpinnings. In these cases, statistical algorithms that assist in reducing a large number of predictors to one or more sets of "best" predictors may prove useful.

Stepwise Logistic Regression. A family of computer-automated statistical algorithms known as stepwise logistic regression procedures ostensibly selects for the user an optimal set of predictors. There are several variations on the algorithm. Forward-variable selection enters the predictors one by one into an empty regression equation based on an entry criterion (e.g., $p < .05$). Backward selection begins with a full or saturated model that includes all predictors and then eliminates them one at a time based on an exclusion criterion. Stepwise selection combines forward and backward procedures by entering or excluding variables according to specified criteria. SAS and SPSS contain forward and backward selection algorithms, with SAS additionally permitting a stepwise procedure.

Though perhaps useful in rare instances, stepwise methods are not recommended for several reasons (Huberty, 1989; Thompson, 2001). Most important, stepwise methods ignore the cumulative effect of variable combinations. Adding the "best" predictor followed by the "second best" and the "third best" is not equivalent to adding all three variables simultaneously to determine their joint effects. As with adolescents, variables often behave differently when acting in concert!

Best Subsets Logistic Regression. A preferable approach is to use a best subsets or all possible regressions routine to obtain comparative indices for every combination of predictor variables. Unlike stepwise methods, best subsets allows the researcher to thoughtfully appraise cost and benefit attendant to various models. For example, a researcher comparing four- and five-variable models may decide that a modest increase in predictive power is not worth the trouble of attaining scores on a difficult-to-measure fifth variable.

Best-subsets procedures are currently unavailable in SPSS. SAS includes a best-subsets routine within PROC LOGISTIC that outputs two comparative indices: the maximum likelihood R^2 and the relatively unfamiliar *score* statistic. A more useful and familiar index for evaluating models of differing size is Mallows's C_p (Mallows, 1973). This measure of predictive squared error penalizes less parsimonious models. Smaller values of C_p are preferred, with adequate models expected to produce a C_p roughly equal to $p + 1$, where p = the number of predictors in the fitted model. Although C_p is unavailable in PROC LOGISTIC, the SAS linear regression routine (PROC REG) permits the calculation. Hosmer, Jovanovic, and Lemeshow (1989) demonstrated how logistic estimates can be obtained from a linear regression routine through transformations and case weights. Appendix C presents the relevant SAS code (for a fuller description, see King, 2003). A second option is to transform the score statistic estimated for each model into Mallows's C_p (see Hosmer & Lemeshow, 2000, p. 134).

Illustration. For Model A, the forward-selection procedures in SPSS and SAS both settled on an "optimal" model consisting of minority and education. The SAS backward and stepwise procedures chose the same model, while SPSS backward elimination chose minority, education, and sex. The latter discrepancy is due to varying default p values used for variable removal (i.e., 0.05 in SAS, 0.10 in SPSS). This illustrates another problem with stepwise methods: Results vary based on the probability settings selected.

Table 24.12 depicts results from a best-subsets logistic regression. In addition to C_p, SAS outputs R^2 values in the modified PROC REG procedure. These R^2 values are invalid and for heuristic purposes have been replaced in the table with the adjusted McFadden index and the ordinary R^2 (i.e., the squared correlation between the criterion and the logistic-predicted probabilities). To obtain these two indices, it was necessary to test and run all possible models separately. Of course, one would ordinarily select candidate models based on the C_p values.

According to model fit and parsimony, the model consisting of education is optimal

Table 24.12   Summary Statistics for a Best Subsets Logistic Regression—Model A

Predictor Variable (s) in Model	R^2_{L-Adj}	R^2	C_p
Educ	0.59	0.61	−0.34
Exper	0.02	0.01	10.90
Minor	0.06	0.04	11.17
Sex	0.11	0.09	11.63
Minor Educ	0.61	0.65	1.14
Educ Exper	0.59	0.61	1.65
Sex Educ	0.14	0.62	1.66
Minor Exper	0.07	0.05	12.68
Sex Exper	0.14	0.62	12.88
Sex Minor	0.18	0.15	13.17
Minor Educ Exper	0.62	0.65	3.03
Sex Minor Educ	0.63	0.67	3.12
Sex Educ Exper	0.60	0.62	3.65
Sex Minor Exper	0.20	0.17	14.67
Sex Minor Educ Exper	0.63	0.67	5.00

NOTE: R^2_{L-Adj} = Adjusted McFadden R^2. R^2 = ordinary R^2. C_p = Mallows's C.

($C_p = -0.34$). Here, one variable strongly predicts the criterion with weaker contributions from the remaining variables. Based on theoretical or predictive reasons, however, the researcher may see value in a model having more parameters (i.e., predictors) that still produces an acceptable C_p. Several models in Table 24.12 fit those criteria. The point is that in using a best-subsets procedure, the researcher is not forced to blindly accept a single model determined by a stepwise algorithm; she or he may allow theory to inform decision making.

Because there are $2 \wedge p - 1$ (where p = number of predictors) possible variable combinations, it may not be practical to examine every model given a very large number of predictors. An alternative offered by Shtatland, Cain, and Barton (2001) combines stepwise and best-subsets procedures in conjunction with the AIC in selecting a range of viable models

(Shtatland, Kleinman, & Cain, 2003, extend this approach to R^2_{L-Adj}).

Confounding and Interaction Effects

Confounding and interaction effects can greatly complicate model interpretation and are often present whether realized or not (for a full discussion, see Kleinbaum & Klein, 2002; Rice, 1994). When the relationship between X and Y is interpreted differently due to inclusion of Z in the model, Z is said to be a *confounder*. A confounder must be controlled for before assessing other predictive relationships. Some suggest that this be done by inclusion of every imaginable confounder, but such an approach can lead to increased standard errors and biased estimates of effect (Sonis, 1998). Identification of confounding in logistic regression should proceed by selecting a potential confounder based on theory and then comparing the odds ratios estimated for the other predictors when modeled with and without the variable in question. Large changes in odds ratios indicate strong confounding. Commonly used rules of thumb are based on the percentage change between the two odds ratios (e.g., a 5% or 10% change may point to confounding).

For Model C in which sex predicts job category, recall that sex was statistically significant ($p < .001$) and yielded an odds ratio of 0.14, meaning that the odds of males being managers are 7.3 times as large as the odds for females. Once education is added to the equation, sex is no longer significant ($p = .125$), and the odds ratio drops to 0.52. The odds for males are now only about two times as large as the odds for females after controlling for education. Inclusion of education decreased the odds ratio of sex by 277%, which identifies it as a strong confounder. Descriptive statistics reveal the cause: Only 29% of females in the sample had completed postsecondary education in comparison to 67% of males. Variation in education levels should be controlled for by comparing the sex groups at a common level of education or through matching or stratification.

An *interaction* occurs when the relationship between X and Y depends in some way on Z (commonly denoted a *moderating variable* or an *effect modifier*). In the example above, an interaction would be present if the relationship between sex and job category differed in strength or form (e.g., linear/nonlinear) at various levels of education. A variable may function as a confounder, a moderator, or both. Interaction effects take precedence over confounding and should always be assessed initially.

Addition of an education × sex interaction term to the model produces nonsignificant results ($\chi^2_{(1)} = 2.14$, $p = .143$). Had an interaction been present, odds ratios for females and males would need to be computed separately for various levels of education. Another option would be to graph the relationship between logits and education separately for females and males. The nonparallel lines would reveal the form of the interaction. Variables are often centered prior to computing interaction effects.

Confounding and interaction can also occur with two ordinal/continuous predictors. In the *Employee* data set, education interacts with experience. Specifically, a strong relationship is found between experience and the log-odds of being a manager for those with an eighth-grade education, while a weaker relationship is seen for high school graduates and no relationship for college graduates. The reader is encouraged to independently verify these findings.

Nonlinear Predictors

Nonlinear predictors may be modeled in logistic regression by taking the usual approach followed in linear regression. Nonlinear predictors may also be modeled by necessity if an important logistic regression assumption fails. Unlike linear procedures described earlier, logistic regression does not assume homoscedasticity, normality of errors, equality of covariance matrices, or multivariate normality, though meeting these conditions will usually produce more stable parameter estimates. Nevertheless, logistic regression is not without model assumptions, including independence of observations, predictors measured without error, inclusion of all relevant predictors in the equation, and errors distributed as a logistic function. In assessing goodness-of-fit indices, all pairs of *categorical* predictors should meet the usual chi-square requirement of no expected frequencies less than 1 and no more than 20% of cells with observed frequencies greater than 5. Categories may be collapsed to meet this assumption. Some researchers mistakenly assume that because

logistic regression does not require the criterion to be linearly related to a function of the predictors, there is no linearity assumption. In fact, the logistic model assumes linearity between the transformed criterion (i.e., the log-odds) and a function of the *continuous* predictors in the model. The Box-Tidwell procedure aids in assessing linearity of the logit (see Tang & Hirji, 2002, for newer tests). The method proceeds by multiplying each continuous predictor by its natural logarithm (i.e., $X \times \ln(X)$) and adding the resulting cross-product to the full model. If the term is statistically significant, then nonlinearity in the logit exists. The procedure does not identify the precise form of nonlinearity, so follow-up assessment is needed, at which point the predictors can be transformed as needed.

Model E consists of the following predictors: sex, minority, education, experience, and salary. The latter three variables are approximately continuously scaled and require assessment of linearity in the logit. After multiplying each predictor by its natural log, the three transformed variables were added as a block to Model E. The statistically significant block change in chi-square indicates nonlinearity: $\chi^2_{(3)} = 11.97$, $p = .007$. The only significant Wald test within the block is the transformed salary variable ($p < .001$). One approach to identifying the shape of a suspected nonlinear relationship is to group values of the predictor into categories, take the log-odds of the mean of the criterion for each category, and then graph the categories against the log-odds (see Figure 24.9). Adding a term for the square of salary to Model E results in a significant change in chi-square, $\chi^2_{(1)} = 8.69$, $p = .003$, though an even better fit is achieved by taking the natural log of salary, $\chi^2_{(1)} = 13.47$, $p = .001$. Interpretation becomes appreciably more complex with inclusion of nonlinear predictors in an already nonlinear model.

Collinearity

Collinearity (or multicollinearity) indicates a linear relationship among the predictors due to high intercorrelations. Outlying cases can also strongly influence collinearity (Sengupta & Bhimasankaram, 1997). Collinearity does not affect the ability of the equation to predict the criterion but can produce unreliable *b* weights and inflated standard errors, which affects how

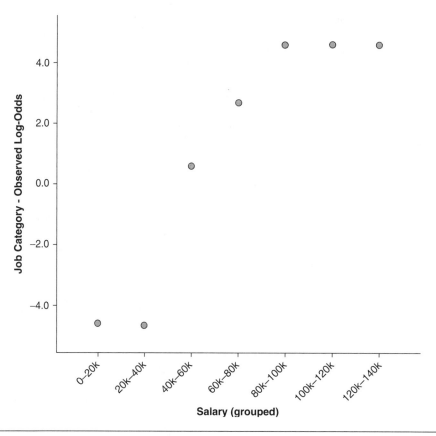

Figure 24.9   Observed log-odds plotted against salary for Model E.

one interprets the contribution of individual predictors.

Essentially, the same dynamics are in play in logistic regression as in linear regression. As explained by Menard (2002), "Because the concern is with the relationship among the *independent* variables, the functional form of the model for the dependent variable is irrelevant to the estimation of collinearity" (p. 76). This allows use of familiar linear regression indices for detecting collinearity (e.g., variance inflation factor, tolerance, condition index, variance proportions).

Contrary to popular opinion, centering is not recommended for reducing collinearity (Gatignon & Vosgerau, 2005; Katrichis, 1992; Kromrey & Foster-Johnson, 1998). One solution is removal of one of the offending variables. Perhaps a better alternative is to combine the correlated variables into a latent factor or component, which should be measured with less error than each variable taken individually.

The trade-off is the complexity of interpreting a structural model. Commonality analysis (Beaton, 1973) is a particularly effective tool for decomposing the variances unique to each predictor and common across all predictors or sets of predictors.

Nonconvergence

Logistic regression employs maximum likelihood estimation, a procedure that sometimes fails to converge on permissible estimates. Unusually large coefficients or standard errors are red flags that suggest estimation problems. Nonconvergence occurs in the *Employee* data set when modeling sex, minority, and sex × minority as predictors. The cause is likely a cell with zero frequency counts—namely, there were no minority females holding managerial positions in the sample. Discussion of alternative solutions is beyond the scope of this chapter, with the interested reader referred to Hosmer and Lemeshow (2000, pp. 135–141).

Alternatives to "Nil" Null Hypotheses

The discussion so far has assumed a null hypothesis of no relationship between criterion and predictors, which is certainly improbable. There is no requirement that one make comparisons to such a "nil null" hypothesis (Cohen, 1994). The nested and nonnested model comparison procedures and R^2 statistics available in logistic regression easily allow a researcher to compare any number of reasonable alternative models. Such an approach more faithfully represents the goal of scientists to develop and refine theories consistent with previous studies rather than assuming a theoretical "tabula rasa."

Assessing Result Replicability

The generalizability of sample results is strengthened through replication. Though cost may prohibit the drawing of multiple, independent samples for the purpose of assessing replicability, a practical alternative is to hold out a portion of the sample to confirm or disconfirm initial findings (i.e., cross-validation). Another approach is to resample cases with replacement to determine whether various configurations of the data yield similar results (i.e., bootstrapping). These can be implemented in logistic regression (e.g., Lunneborg, 2000). In the past, bootstrap and cross-validation were viewed as separate procedures, each with its own limitations. With the recent development of hybrid approaches, distinctions between the two may blur in future developments (Shtatland, Kleinman, & Cain, 2004).

CONCLUDING REMARKS

This brief treatment necessarily neglects a number of topics that are important for valid interpretation of logistic regression results (e.g., detailed assessment of assumption testing). It is hoped that this introduction prompts the reader into further study of this sophisticated modeling technique. As logistic regression grows in popularity and usage, social scientists should occupy the forefront in applying the most current and effective methodological practices, which will in turn lead to stronger scientific research.

APPENDIX A: ILLUSTRATIVE MODELS

Model	Predictor Variable(s)
A	Sex, minority, education, experience
B	Salary
C	Sex
D	Experience
E	Sex, minority, education, experience, salary

APPENDIX B: AN OVERVIEW OF EXPONENTS AND LOGARITHMS

The exponent of a number is equal to the constant e raised to that number, where e equals approximately 2.718. The exponent of 3 is equivalently written as $\exp(3) = e^3 = 2.718^3 = 2.718 \times 2.718 \times 2.718 = 20.09$. A related mathematical function is the natural logarithm, or just natural log, written as ln or $\log_e$. As subtraction negates addition, the natural log negates an exponent, and vice versa. The natural log of 20.09 is written as $\ln(20.09) = \log_e(20.09) = 3$. On most calculators, the exponent and natural log functions are on the same button, with one function accessed by first pressing the inverse ("inv") button. The abbreviations "ln" and "$\log_e$" both refer to the natural log, whereas "log" typically refers to a different calculation.

APPENDIX C: SAS SYNTAX FOR OBTAINING A BEST SUBSETS LOGISTIC REGRESSION WITH MALLOWS'S C_p

* Run logistic regression for full model, saving predicted probabilities (pred);

```
PROC LOGISTIC;
    MODEL jobcat = educ exper sex minority;
    OUTPUT out = output1
                p = pred;
```

* Define two new variables: z and u;

$$z = \log(\text{pred} / (1 - \text{pred})) + ((\text{jobcat} - \text{pred}) / (\text{pred} * (1 - \text{pred})));$$
$$u = \text{pred} * (1 - \text{pred});$$

* Run linear regression with case weights;

```
PROC REG;
    MODEL z = educ exper sex minority
        / SELECTION = RSQUARE CP;
    WEIGHT u;
```

NOTES

1. The similar, but not identical, *logit* model is appropriate if all predictors are categorical (Demaris, 1990).

2. The table is not meant to be exhaustive. When faced with all categorical variables, for example, a chi-square test of independence could be applied. However, log-linear analysis is preferable due, in part, to its ability to include interaction terms in the model.

3. Note that we are calculating an expected probability for a given salary level, not for a specific individual. George is either a manager or he is not.

4. It is possible to calculate change in predicted probabilities in increments other than a single unit, which is useful with a continuous predictor variable. The difference in probabilities associated with a change in *c* units is given by the expression *cb*. For example, changes in salary levels in 1,000-unit increments correspond to changes in predicted probabilities of $1,000 \times 0.000018 = 0.018$.

5. Odds may also be calculated using frequency counts in a contingency table.

6. For this reason, SPSS labels odds ratio estimates as "Exp(B)."

7. The estimated beta and odds ratio here do not share identical values to the right of the decimal but only appear so due to rounding.

8. Dummy coding can be used to compare odds ratios for values on a polytomous predictor.

9. Some writers refer to this quantity as the deviance and use the notation G^2.

10. The reader is warned that researchers are not agreed on equivalent usage for all of these terms.

REFERENCES

American Psychological Association. (2001). *Publication manual of the American Psychological Association* (5th ed.). Washington, DC: Author.

Beaton, A. E. (1973). *Commonality*. Princeton, NJ: Educational Testing Service.

Cohen, J. (1994). The world is round ($p < .05$). *American Psychologist, 49,* 997–1003.

Courville, T., & Thompson, B. (2001). Use of structure coefficients in published multiple regression articles: Beta is not enough. *Educational and Psychological Measurement, 61,* 229–248.

Darlington, R. B. (1990). *Regression and linear models.* New York: McGraw-Hill.

Demaris, A. (1990). Interpreting logistic regression results: A critical commentary. *Journal of Marriage and the Family, 52,* 271–276.

Dunteman, G. H., & Ho, M.-H. R. (2006). *An introduction to generalized linear models* (Sage University Paper Series on Quantitative Applications in the Social Sciences, 07-145). Thousand Oaks, CA: Sage.

Gatignon, H., & Vosgerau, J. (2005, May). *Moderating effects: The myth of centering.* Paper presented at the annual meeting of the European Marketing Academy, Milan, Italy.

Hosmer, D. W., Hosmer, T., le Cessie, S., & Lemeshow, S. (1997). A comparison of goodness-of-fit tests for the logistic regression model. *Statistics in Medicine, 16,* 965–980.

Hosmer, D. W., Jovanovic, B., & Lemeshow, S. (1989). Best subsets logistic regression. *Biometrics, 45,* 1265–1270.

Hosmer, D. W., & Lemeshow, S. (1980). A goodness-of-fit test for the multiple logistic regression model. *Communications in Statistics, A10,* 1043–1069.

Hosmer, D. W., & Lemeshow, S. (2000). *Applied logistic regression* (2nd ed.). New York: John Wiley.

Huberty, C. J. (1989). Problems with stepwise methods—better alternatives. *Advances in Social Science Methodology, 1,* 43–70.

Huberty, C. J., & Barton, R. M. (1989). An introduction to discriminant analysis. *Measurement and Evaluation in Counseling and Development, 22,* 158–168.

Katrichis, J. (1992). The conceptual implications of data centering in interactive regression models. *Journal of Market Research Society, 35,* 183–192.

Katsaragakis, S., Koukouvinos, C., Stylianou, S., & Theodoraki, E.-M. (2005). Comparison of statistical tests in logistic regression: The case of hypernatreamia. *Journal of Modern Applied Statistical Methods, 4,* 514–521.

Kaufman, R. L. (1996). Comparing effects in dichotomous logistic regression: A variety of standardized coefficients. *Social Science Quarterly, 77,* 90–109.

King, J. E. (2003). Running a best subsets logistic regression: An alternative to stepwise methods.

Educational and Psychological Measurement, 63, 392–403.

King, J. E. (2007, February). *Standardized coefficients in logistic regression.* Paper presented at the annual meeting of the Southwest Educational Research Association, San Antonio, TX.

Klecka, W. R. (1980). *Discriminant analysis* (Sage University Paper Series on Quantitative Applications in the Social Sciences, 07-019). Beverly Hills, CA: Sage.

Kleinbaum, D. G., & Klein, M. (2002). *Logistic regression: A self-learning text* (2nd ed.). New York: Springer-Verlag.

Kromrey, J. D., & Foster-Johnson, L. (1998). Mean centering in moderated multiple regression: Much ado about nothing. *Educational and Psychological Measurement, 58,* 42–68.

Liao, J. G., & McGee, D. (2003). Adjusted coefficients of determination for logistic regression. *The American Statistician, 57*(3), 161–165.

Lin, D. Y., Wei, L. J., & Ying, Z. (2002). Model-checking techniques based on cumulative residuals. *Biometrics, 58,* 1–12.

Long, S. (1997). *Regression models for categorical and limited dependent variables.* Thousand Oaks, CA: Sage.

Lunneborg, C. E. (2000). *Data analysis by resampling: Concepts and applications.* Pacific Grove, CA: Duxbury.

Mallows, C. L. (1973). Some comments on C_p. *Technometrics, 15,* 661–675.

Mehta, C. R., & Patel, N. R. (1995). Exact logistic regression: Theory and examples. *Statistics in Medicine, 14,* 2143–2160.

Menard, S. (2002). *Applied logistic regression analysis* (2nd ed., Sage University Paper Series on Quantitative Applications in the Social Sciences, 07-106). Thousand Oaks, CA: Sage.

Mittlböck, M., & Schemper, M. (1996). Explained variation for logistic regression. *Statistics in Medicine, 15,* 1987–1997.

Mittlböck, M., & Schemper, M. (1999). Computing measures of explained variation for logistic regression models. *Computer Methods and Programs in Biomedicine, 58,* 17–24.

Morgan, S. P., & Teachman, J. D. (1988). Logistic regression: Description, examples, and comparisons. *Journal of Marriage and the Family, 50,* 929–936.

Neter, J., Kutner, M. H., Nachtsheim, C. J., & Wasserman, W. (1996). *Applied linear statistical models* (3rd ed.). Chicago: Irwin.

Pedhazur, E. J. (1997). *Multiple regression in behavioral research* (3rd ed.). Fort Worth, TX: Harcourt Brace College.

Pohar, M., Blas, M., & Turk, S. (2004). Comparison of logistic regression and linear discriminant analysis: A simulation study. *Metodološki Zvezki, 1*(1), 143–161.

Rice, J. (1994). Logistic regression: An introduction. In B. Thompson (Ed.), *Advances in social science methodology* (Vol. 3, pp. 191–245). Greenwich, CT: JAI.

Sengupta, D., & Bhimasankaram, P. (1997). On the roles of observations in collinearity in the linear model. *Journal of the American Statistical Association, 92,* 1024–1032.

Shtatland, E. S., Cain, E. M., & Barton, M. B. (2001, April). *The perils of stepwise logistic regression and how to escape them using information criteria and the Output Delivery System.* Paper presented at the annual meeting of the SAS Users Group International, Long Beach, CA.

Shtatland, E. S., Kleinman, K., & Cain, E. M. (2002, September). *One more time about R^2 measures of fit in logistic regression.* Paper presented at the annual meeting of the NorthEast SAS Users Group, Buffalo, NY.

Shtatland, E. S., Kleinman, K., & Cain, E. M. (2003, April). *Stepwise methods in using SAS PROC LOGISTIC and SAS ENTERPRISE MINER for prediction.* Paper presented at the annual meeting of the SAS Users Group International, Seattle, WA.

Shtatland, E. S., Kleinman, K., & Cain, E. M. (2004, April). *A new strategy of model building in PROC LOGISTIC with automatic variable selection, validation, shrinkage, and model averaging.* Paper presented at the annual meeting of the SAS Users Group International, Montréal, Canada.

Shtatland, E. S., Moore, S., & Barton, M. B. (2000, April). *Why we need an R^2 measure of fit (and not only one) in PROC LOGISTIC and PROC GENMOD.* Paper presented at the annual meeting of the SAS Users Group International, Indianapolis, IN.

Simonoff, J. S. (1998). Logistic regression, categorical predictors, and goodness-of-fit: It depends on who you ask. *The American Statistician, 52,* 10–14.

Sonis, J. (1998). A closer look at confounding. *Family Medicine, 30,* 584–588.

Tang, M.-L. (2001). Exact goodness-of-fit test for binary logistic model. *Statistica Sinica, 11,* 199–211.

Tang, M.-L., & Hirji, K. F. (2002). Simple polynomial multiplication algorithms for exact conditional tests of linearity in a logistic model. *Computer Methods and Programs in Biomedicine, 69,* 13–23.

Taylor, A. B., West, S. G., & Aiken, L. S. (2006). Loss of power in logistic, ordinal logistic, and probit regression when an outcome variable is coarsely categorized. *Educational and Psychological Measurement, 66,* 228–239.

Thompson, B. (2001). Significance, effect sizes, stepwise methods, and other issues: Strong arguments move the field. *Journal of Experimental Education, 70,* 80–93.

Thompson, B. (2006a). *Foundations of behavioral statistics: An insight-based approach.* New York: Guilford.

Thompson, B. (2006b). Research synthesis: Effect sizes. In J. Green, G. Camilli, & P. B. Elmore (Eds.), *Complementary methods for research in education* (pp. 583–603). Washington, DC: American Educational Research Association.

Thompson, B., & Borello, G. M. (1985). The importance of structure coefficients in regression research. *Educational and Psychological Measurement, 45,* 203–209.

Vacha-Haase, T., Nilsson, J. E., Reetz, D. R., Lance, T. S., & Thompson, B. (2000). Reporting practices and APA editorial policies regarding statistical significance and effect size. *Theory & Psychology, 10,* 413–425.

Verdes, E., & Rudas, T. (2002). The π^* index as a new alternative for assessing goodness of fit of logistic regression. In Y. Haitovsky, H. R. Lerche, & Y. Ritov (Eds.), *Foundations of statistical inference* (pp. 167–177). Berlin: Springer-Verlag.

White, M. C., Long, R. G., & Tansey, R. (1997). Logistic regression: The generalized linear model in the social sciences. *Perceptual and Motor Skills, 85,* 66.

Zhang, J., & Yu, K. F. (1998). What's the relative risk? A method of correcting the odds ratio in cohort studies of common outcomes. *Journal of the American Medical Association, 280,* 1690–1691.

Ziliak, S. T., & McCloskey, D. N. (2004). Size matters: The standard error of regressions in the *American Economic Review. Journal of Socio-Economics, 33,* 527–547.

25

BRINGING BALANCE AND TECHNICAL ACCURACY TO REPORTING ODDS RATIOS AND THE RESULTS OF LOGISTIC REGRESSION ANALYSES

JASON W. OSBORNE

L ogistic regression is becoming more widely used in the social sciences as more texts (e.g., Pedhazur, 1997) include chapters on the technique and more articles aimed at the social science researcher introduce the concept (e.g., Davis & Offord, 1997; Peng, Lee, & Ingersoll, 2002). However, with more widespread adoption of the technique comes more opportunity for researchers to incorrectly interpret the results of this analysis. As Pedhazur (1997) and others (e.g., Davies, Crombie, & Tavakoli, 1998; Holcomb, Chaiworapongsa, Luke, & Burgdorf, 2001) have pointed out, correctly interpreting odds ratios for either a scientific or practitioner audience is particularly challenging and usually done incorrectly. For example, Holcomb et al. (2001) reported that in a survey of high-quality medical journals, more than one quarter of the articles explicitly misinterpreted odds ratios. As the technique is newer

to the social sciences, it is more likely that misinterpretation is happening in these literatures.

The goal of this chapter is to briefly review the challenges to successfully and (more important) correctly interpreting the odds ratio (as compared to the more intuitive probability ratio or relative risk estimate), to highlight a simple way for transforming odds ratios to the more easily interpreted relative risk estimate, and to highlight a method of dealing with odds ratios (ORs) and relative risk (RR) that are less than 1.0 to bring them into perceptual balance with those mathematically identical (but perceptually different) ratios over 1.0.

WHAT IS AN ODDS RATIO?

The odds ratio has a long tradition in epidemiological and medical research where one is

Author's Note: This chapter is based on Osborne, J. W. (2006). Bringing balance and technical accuracy to reporting odds ratios and the results of logistic regression analyses. *Practical Assessment Research & Evaluation, 11*(7). Available at http://pareonline.net/getvn.asp?v=11&n=7

examining whether different factors contribute to disease (morbidity) or mortality. There are several ways to produce odds ratios, some of which are directly computed by hand from 2×2 contingency tables but most commonly are produced from logistic regression and similar analyses. Logistic regression brings the general processes of ordinary least squares regression (including multiple regression) to bear on dependent variables that are either categorical (yes/no outcomes, such as whether students have dropped out or individuals have become pregnant, voted, purchased a specific product, etc.) or discrete and categorical (e.g., choice of major, purchase of one of several products, and many behavioral outcomes such as educational attainment).

Yet with the advantages of logistic regression comes a challenge: interpreting the standardized coefficients, which are not betas but rather often odds ratios (exp(b)). To more concretely understand these odds ratio (and also relative risk, as well as the computational and conceptual differences between the two), refer to Table 25.1, which uses some sample data we will use for illustrative purposes.

In order to understand the difference between relative risk (probability ratios) and odds ratios, one can simply examine the (completely fabricated) data above. The *probability* that a student would be recommended to remedial reading is computed as the number recommended divided by the total possible, which equals 45/200 or 0.225. However the probability (or risk) of being recommended to remedial reading varies as a function of student sex. Specifically, the probability that a boy would be recommended is 35/100 (0.35) while the probability that a girl would be recommended is 10/100 (0.10). These are straightforward to interpret.

While probability uses group total as the denominator, the odds are a different animal. The odds of a student being recommended is the number recommended divided by *the number*

not recommended. Note that this is a very different denominator, especially when researching an outcome that is relatively common such as in these data. The odds of a student being recommended are 45/155 (0.29), but again that varies by student sex. The odds of a boy being recommended are 35/65 (0.54) while the odds of a girl being recommended are 10/90 (0.11).

Note that the difference between probability (risk) and odds is the denominator, which then influences their interpretation. Probability (risk) is interpreted in a straightforward manner: Boys will be recommended for remedial reading about 35% of the time, on average, while girls are recommended about 10% of the time. Odds are less well understood by researchers, practitioners, and the lay public (Davies et al., 1998; Holcomb et al., 2001). The odds of a boy being recommended for remedial reading are 0.54:1, while for girls they are 0.11:1. In other words, for each boy *not* recommended for remedial reading, 0.54 boys will be recommended. A similar interpretation would be offered for girls.

This brings up two important points: First, as authors such as Davies et al. (1998) point out and as we have demonstrated empirically, odds tend to inflate the effect size of an analysis (this is particularly true when events being studied are relatively common; see Davies et al., 1998, for more explication). Second, because of the different denominators between probabilities (risk) and odds, probabilities are relatively straightforward to interpret, yet odds can be tricky. This will be discussed more below.

Ratios. Analyses rarely end with the calculations of odds or probabilities. Generally, researchers want to calculate probability ratios (also called relative risk or RR) and/or odds ratios (OR). Using the data in Table 25.1, if one wants to know if boys are at greater risk of being recommended to remedial reading than girls, we can calculate a relative risk by dividing the probability for

Table 25.1   Sample Data for Student Sex and Remedial Reading Classification

	Not Recommended (Coded as 0)	Recommended (Coded as 1)	Total N	Probability of Being Recommended	Odds of Being Recommended
Boys	65	35	100	0.35	0.54
Girls	90	10	100	0.10	0.11
Total	155	45	200	0.23	0.29

boys by the probability for girls (.35/.10), which yields a relative risk of 3.50. In other words, boys are 3.50 times as likely to be recommended for remedial reading than girls. This is intuitive, yet this statistic is *rarely the one reported in research*. Odds ratios are much more common, partly because many popular software packages readily report ORs. The odds ratio for these data is the odds for boys divided by the odds for girls (.54/.11), which yields an odds ratio of 4.91. In this case, the odds for boys are 4.91 that of girls.

However, that does not mean one can say that boys are 4.91 times as likely or 4.91 times more likely to be recommended to remedial reading than girls. Technically, the *odds* of being assigned are 4.91 times greater for boys relative to girls. But since odds are tricky to understand, the meaning of this is less clear. Technically, it means that for every boy *not recommended* to remedial reading, 4.91 times as many boys will be recommended for remediation (0.54) than the number of girls recommended for every girl *not recommended*.

Confused? You should be. Unless you work with odds and probabilities for a living, you should find relative risk (probability ratios) much easier to understand than odds ratios. Odds are not intuitive like probabilities are, and the language needed to technically describe an odds ratio is (as you can see) quite convoluted.

The situation is not helped by authors' tendency to whitewash this important distinction and use probabilistic language when discussing odds ratios. Even highly sophisticated researchers will summarize odds ratios using language similar to "boys are 4.91 times more likely to be recommended to remedial reading than girls" or "boys are 4.91 times as likely to be recommended" when technically the odds ratio should be summarized as "the odds of boys being recommended are 4.91 times greater than the odds of girls being recommended," which does not address exactly what it means for odds to be greater in one group than another. Pedhazur (1997, pp. 760–761) takes great pains to highlight this common error, as do other authors (e.g., Cohen, 2000; Davies et al., 1998; Holcomb et al., 2001). Holcomb et al. (2001) report that 26% of authors in top-tier medical journals explicitly misinterpreted ORs as RRs.

Why is this an issue? First, it is incorrect. While the OR and RR will be in the same direction (both will be either above or below 1.0 if they are significant), ORs can illegitimately inflate the effect size substantially, as Davies et al. (1998)

demonstrate. This effect is particularly egregious when the outcome being examined is not rare (e.g., occurs in more than 5% of the population) and becomes magnified as the RR moves away from 1.0—commonly inflating the apparent effects 80% to 90% or more.

Fixing This Issue

One can report odds ratios as long as an accurate interpretation of the OR is provided. However, as noted above, odds are nonintuitive and not easily understood by nontechnical audiences. It is probably more effective to calculate relative risk directly or, if that is not possible, calculate it from the following formula (presented in Davies et al., 1998; Holcomb et al., 2001; original work presented by Zhang & Yu, 1998).

$$RR = OR/[(1 - P_0) + (P_0 \times OR)], \qquad (1)$$

where RR = relative risk, OR = calculated odds ratio, and P_0 = the proportion of nonexposed individuals (e.g., those lacking the independent variable or the reference group) that experience the outcome in question. In the case of our example, P_0 would be .10, the probability that girls would be referred to remedial reading, and the OR is 4.91. Completing the calculations, we end up with an estimated RR of 3.53, a very close approximation to the actual RR of 3.50. While this might seem like a trivial issue, as both effects are large, alert readers will note that the effect size estimate is inflated 39.1%. I doubt we would accept that in other effect size estimates.

How Should We Interpret Odds Ratios or Relative Risks Less Than 1.0?

One significant problem with RRs and ORs is that they are asymmetrical. They can theoretically range from 0.00 to ∞. A value of 1.0 means there is no difference in risk or odds (i.e., there is no effect of the independent variable). Ratios less than 1.0 indicate that being in the exposed/selected group *decreases* the odds/risk of experiencing the outcome, whereas ratios greater than 1.0 indicate that being in the exposed/selected group *increases* the odds/risk of experiencing the outcome.[1] The imbalance comes with the fact that increasing ratios are unbounded. They can vary from 1.0 to infinity, yet decreasing odds ratios are bounded by 0. They can range from 1.0 to 0 only, yet they encompass, technically, the same infinite range.[2]

Two issues arise here. First, use of directional language such as "individuals in Group 1 are X times *more likely* to experience a specific outcome than in Group 2" or "individuals in Group 2 are X times *less likely*." Leaving for a moment the difficulty with cogently describing an odds ratio, the difficulty here comes in the common mistake people make in describing decreasing ratios. If you have an RR of 3.50, as we did, it is straightforward to say, "Boys are 3.50 times more likely (or "as likely" as I prefer) to be referred than girls." But what if we had coded the variables differently, so we were comparing girls to boys? With the same numbers, we would have gotten an RR of 0.29, meaning exactly the same thing—that girls are much less likely than boys to be referred. Yet the careless author (and many of my former students) might be tempted to say, "Girls are 0.29 times less likely than boys" when in fact that is not the case. And furthermore, to say that girls are .71 times less likely fails to convey the same magnitude as an RR = 3.50, although mathematically they are identical.

My advice has always been to use *as likely* rather than *less* or *more likely*. Saying "girls are 0.29 times as likely as boys" is more accurate and foolproof (providing you are discussing an RR rather than OR) and carries some more of the psychological gravity as saying "3.50 times as likely" . . . but not quite. Which brings us to the second issue: the psychological impact of ratios and accurately conveying effect sizes when the effect sizes themselves vary depending on whether they are increasing or decreasing odds.

Taking a more extreme example, imagine a drug that made the risk of experiencing a cancer relapse RR = 0.001 compared to people who do not take the drug. Mathematically, that is identical to saying that taking the drug makes you 1,000 times less likely to experience relapse, or not taking the drug makes you 1,000 times more likely to have a relapse. But are they perceptually identical? No. Further elaborating, let us say you have two drugs. One produces an RR = 0.001 and one an RR = 0.01. Even the most technically proficient of us will view these as pretty close (i.e., really small). However, if the direction of the independent variable were arbitrarily reversed, the RRs would

be 1,000 and 100, respectively. Most people will interpret those both as "pretty large," but in the latter case, it is much more apparent that the magnitude of the effect is 10 times different.

Thus, the final recommendation for those of you engaged in logistic regression and similar analyses using odds or probability ratios—When possible, refrain from reporting RRs or ORs less than 1.0. It would make sense to standardize the reporting of this effect size so that all ratios be reported as > 1.0. Analyses that result in ratios less than 1.0 would take the inverse of the RR/OR and reverse the categories or the description of the results to keep the conclusion consistent.[3]

Not only do ratios less than 1.0 have a different psychological impact (despite being mathematically identical), but as Figure 25.1 shows, the relationship between ratios > 1.0 and their mathematically equivalent < 1.0 counterpoints is nonlinear. This is suboptimal for an effect size, which RR and OR are de facto, and a situation easily remedied in most cases.

Summary

In sum, procedures such as logistic regression are powerful and useful tools to scientists. However, the commonly reported odds ratio is difficult to understand conceptually, quite often misinterpreted, and particularly difficult to disseminate to a lay/practitioner audience. Relative risk (probability ratios) is more intuitive and much easier to disseminate, so when possible, researchers should report and interpret RRs rather than ORs. Second, ORs/RRs are relatively unique in the effect size world in that they are asymmetrical. Ratios below 1.0 behave very differently than ratios above 1.0 because they asymptote toward 0.0, whereas ratios above 1.0 are unbounded. More important, this creates asymmetry in the perception of effect size, which is also undesirable. The second recommendation, therefore, is to convert all ratios < 1.0 to their corresponding ratio counterpart above 1.0 by taking the inverse of the RR/OR and adjusting the narrative accordingly.

These simple steps should increase the technical quality of reporting these analyses and standardize the metric of the effect size being used.

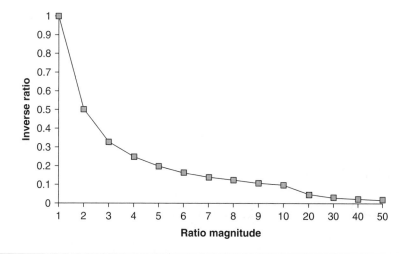

Figure 25.1   The nonlinear relationship between increasing and decreasing ratios.

NOTES

1. Be sure to examine confidence intervals and significance values for ORs and RRs. If either includes 1.0, then the effect is *not significant and should not be interpreted*. There are many examples of published studies with nonsignificant results (i.e., ORs that incorporate 1.0 in the confidence interval) that are interpreted substantively by the authors.

2. Which brings us to the confusing mathematical world of "smaller" and "larger" infinities, which tends to give me a headache. Those of you interested in understanding how infinities can be smaller or larger are referred to the works of Georg Cantor and his followers.

3. Pedhazur (1997) suggests an alternative solution to this issue—taking the natural log (ln) of all RRs/ORs. This has the effect of moving the "null effect" point from 1.0 to 0.0 and removing the lower bound so that effect size distribution is symmetrical. The drawback to this elegant solution is that it changes the effect from substantively interpretable (relative risk) or interpretable with some difficulty (odds ratio) to something much more complex to interpret—the natural log of a relative risk or an odds ratio. Thus, I would not recommend this solution.

REFERENCES

Cohen, M. P. (2000). Note on the odds ratio and the probability ratio. *Journal of Educational and Behavioral Statistics, 25*(2), 249–252.

Davies, H. T. O., Crombie, I. K., & Tavakoli, M. (1998). When can odds ratios mislead? *British Medical Journal, 316,* 989–991.

Davis, L. J., & Offord, K. P. (1997). Logistic regression. *Journal of Personality Assessment, 68*(3), 497–507.

Holcomb, W. L., Jr., Chaiworapongsa, T., Luke, D. A., & Burgdorf, K. D. (2001). An odd measure of risk: Use and misuse of the odds ratio. *Obstetrics and Gynecology, 84*(4), 685–688.

Pedhazur, E. (1997). *Multiple regression in behavioral research.* New York: Harcourt Brace.

Peng, C. J., Lee, K. L., & Ingersoll, G. M. (2002). An introduction to logistic regression analysis and reporting. *Journal of Educational Research, 96*(1), 3–14.

Zhang, J., & Yu, K. (1998). What's the relative risk? A method of correcting the odds ratio in cohort studies of common outcomes. *Journal of the American Medical Association, 280,* 1690–1691.

26

MULTINOMIAL LOGISTIC REGRESSION

CAROLYN J. ANDERSON

LESLIE RUTKOWSKI

C hapter 24 presented logistic regression models for dichotomous response variables; however, many discrete response variables have three or more categories (e.g., political view, candidate voted for in an election, preferred mode of transportation, or response options on survey items). Multicategory response variables are found in a wide range of experiments and studies in a variety of different fields. A detailed example presented in this chapter uses data from 600 students from the High School and Beyond study (Tatsuoka & Lohnes, 1988) to look at the differences among high school students who attended academic, general, or vocational programs. The students' socioeconomic status (ordinal), achievement test scores (numerical), and type of school (nominal) are all examined as possible explanatory variables. An example left to the interested reader using the same data set is to model the students' intended career where the possibilities consist of 17 general job types (e.g., school, manager, clerical, sales, military, service, etc.). Possible explanatory variables include gender, achievement test scores, and other variables in the data set.

Many of the concepts used in binary logistic regression, such as the interpretation of parameters in terms of odds ratios and modeling probabilities, carry over to multicategory logistic regression models; however, two major modifications are needed to deal with multiple categories of the response variable. One difference is that with three or more levels of the response variable, there are multiple ways to dichotomize the response variable. If J equals the number of categories of the response variable, then $J(J-1)/2$ different ways exist to dichotomize the categories. In the High School and Beyond study, the three program types can be dichotomized into pairs of programs (i.e., academic and general, vocational and general, and academic and vocational).

How the response variable is dichotomized depends, in part, on the nature of the variable. If there is a baseline or control category, then the analysis could focus on comparing each of the other categories to the baseline. With three or more categories, whether the response variable is nominal or ordinal is an important consideration. Since models for nominal responses can be applied to both nominal and ordinal response variables, the emphasis in this chapter is on extensions of binary logistic regression to models designed for nominal response variables. Furthermore, a solid understanding of the models for nominal responses facilitates mastering models for ordinal data. A brief overview of models for ordinal variables is given toward the end of the chapter.

A second modification to extend binary logistic regression to the polytomous case is the need for a more complex distribution for the response variable. In the binary case, the distribution of the response is assumed to be binomial; however, with multicategory responses, the natural choice is the multinomial distribution, a special case of which is the binomial distribution. The parameters of the multinomial distribution are the probabilities of the categories of the response variable.

The *baseline logit model*, which is sometimes also called the *generalized logit model*, is the starting point for this chapter because it is a well-known model, it is a direct extension of binary logistic regression, it can be used with ordinal response variables, and it includes explanatory variables that are attributes of individuals, which is common in the social sciences. The baseline model is a special case of the *conditional multinomial logit model*, which can include explanatory variables that are characteristics of the response categories, as well as attributes of individuals.

A word of caution is warranted here. In the literature, the term *multinomial logit model* sometimes refers to the baseline model, and sometimes it refers to the conditional multinomial logit model. An additional potential source of confusion lies in the fact that the baseline model is a special case of the conditional model, which in turn is a special case of Poisson (log-linear) regression.[1] These connections enable researchers to tailor models in useful ways and test interesting hypotheses that could not otherwise be tested.

MULTINOMIAL REGRESSION MODELS

One Explanatory Variable Model

The most natural interpretation of logistic regression models is in terms of odds and odds ratios; therefore, the baseline model is first presented as a model for odds and then presented as a model for probabilities.

ODDS

The baseline model can be viewed as the set of binary logistic regression models fit simultaneously to all pairs of response categories. With three or more categories, a binary logistic regression model is needed for each (nonredundant) dichotomy of the categories of the response variable. As an example, consider high school program types from the High School and Beyond data set (Tatsuoka & Lohnes, 1988). There are three possible program types: academic, general, and vocational. Let $P(Y_i = $ academic$)$, $P(Y_i = $ general$)$, and $P(Y_i = $ vocational$)$ be the probabilities of each of the program types for individual i. Recall from Chapters 24 and 25 that odds equal ratios of probabilities. In our example, only two of the three possible pairs of program types are needed because the third can be found by taking the product of the other two. Choosing the general program as the reference, the odds of academic versus general and the odds of vocational versus general equal

$$\frac{P(Y_i = \text{academic})}{P(Y_i = \text{general})} \tag{1a}$$

$$\frac{P(Y_i = \text{vocational})}{P(Y_i = \text{general})}. \tag{1b}$$

The third odds, academic versus vocational, equals the product of the two odds in (1a) and (1b)—namely,

$$\frac{P(Y_i = \text{academic})}{P(Y_i = \text{vocational})}$$
$$= \frac{P(Y_i = \text{academic})/P(Y_i = \text{general})}{P(Y_i = \text{vocational})/P(Y_i = \text{general})}. \tag{2}$$

More generally, let J equal the number of categories or levels of the response variable. Of the $J(J-1)/2$ possible pairs of categories, only $(J-1)$ of them are needed. If the same category is used in the denominator of the $(J-1)$ odds, then the set of odds will be nonredundant, and all other possible odds can be formed from this set. In the baseline model, one response category is chosen as the *baseline* against which all other response categories are compared. When a natural baseline exists, that category is the best choice in terms of convenience of interpretation. If there is not a natural baseline, then the choice is arbitrary.

As a Model for Odds

Continuing our example from the High School and Beyond data, where the general program is chosen as the baseline category, the first model contains a single explanatory variable, the mean of five achievement test scores for each student (i.e., math, science, reading, writing, and civics). The baseline model is simply two binary logistic regression models applied to each pair of program types; that is,

$$\frac{P(Y_i = \text{academic}|x_i)}{P(Y_i = \text{general}|x_i)} = \exp[\alpha_1 + \beta_1 x_i] \quad (3)$$

and

$$\frac{P(Y_i = \text{vocational}|x_i)}{P(Y_i = \text{general}|x_i)} = \exp[\alpha_2 + \beta_2 x_i], \quad (4)$$

where $P(Y_i = \text{academic}|x_i)$, $P(Y_i = \text{general}|x_i)$, and $P(Y_i = \text{vocational}|x_i)$ are the probabilities for each program type given mean achievement test score x_i for student i, the α_is are intercepts, and the β_is are regression coefficients. The odds of academic versus vocational are found by taking the ratio of (3) and (4),

$$\begin{aligned} \frac{P(Y_j = \text{academic}|x_i)}{P(Y_j = \text{vocational}|x_i)} &= \frac{\exp[\alpha_1 + \beta_1 x_i]}{\exp[\alpha_2 + \beta_2 x_i]} \\ &= \exp[(\alpha_1 - \alpha_2) + \\ & \quad (\beta_1 - \beta_2)x_i] \\ &= \exp[\alpha_3 + \beta_3 x_i], \end{aligned} \quad (5)$$

where $\alpha_3 = (\alpha_1 - \alpha_2)$ and $\beta_3 = (\beta_1 - \beta_2)$.

For generality, let $j = 1, \ldots, J$ represent categories of the response variable. The numerical values of j are just labels for the categories of the response variable. The probability that individual i is in category j given a value of x_i on the explanatory variable is represented by $P(Y_i = j|x_i)$. Taking the Jth category as the baseline, the model is

$$\frac{P(Y_i = j|x_i)}{P(Y_i = J|x_i)} = \exp[\alpha_j + \beta_j x_i] \quad (6)$$

$$\text{for } j = 1, \ldots, (J - 1).$$

When fitting the baseline model to data, the binary logistic regressions for the $(J - 1)$ odds must be estimated simultaneously to ensure that intercepts and coefficients for all other odds equal the differences of the corresponding intercepts and coefficients (e.g., $\alpha_3 = (\alpha_1 - \alpha_2)$ and $\beta_3 = (\beta_1 - \beta_2)$ in Equation 5). To demonstrate this, three separate binary logistic regression models were fit to the High School and Beyond data, as well as the baseline regression model, which simultaneously estimates the models for all the odds. The estimated parameters and their standard errors are reported in Table 26.1. Although the parameters for the separate and simultaneous cases are quite similar, the logical relationships between the parameters when the models are fit separately are not met (e.g., $\hat{\beta}_1 - \hat{\beta}_2 = 0.1133 + 0.0163 = 0.1746 \neq 0.1618$); however, the relationships hold for simultaneous estimation (e.g., $\hat{\beta}_1 - \hat{\beta}_2 = 0.1099 + 0.0599 = 0.1698$).

Besides ensuring that the logical relationships between parameters are met, a second advantage of simultaneous estimation is that it is a more efficient use of the data, which in turn leads to more powerful statistical hypothesis tests and more precise estimates of parameters. Notice that the parameter estimates in Table 26.1 from the baseline model have smaller standard errors than those in the estimation of separate regressions. When the model is fit simultaneously, all 600 observations go into the estimation of the parameters; however, in the separately fit models, only a subset of the observations is used to estimate the parameters (e.g., 453 for academic and general, 455 for academic and vocational, and only 292 for vocational and general).

A third advantage of the simultaneous estimation, which is illustrated later in this chapter, is the ability to place equality restrictions on parameters across odds. For example, if two βs are very similar, they could be forced to be equal. The complexity of the baseline model increases as the number of response options increases, and any means of reducing the number of parameters that must be interpreted can be a great savings in terms of interpreting and summarizing the results. For example, if we modeled career choice with 17 possible choices, there would be 16 nonredundant odds and 16 different βs to interpret for

Table 26.1   Estimated Parameters (and Standard Errors) From Separate Binary Logistic Regressions and From the Simultaneously Estimated Baseline Model

Odds	Parameter	Separate Models		Baseline Model	
		Estimate	SE	Estimate	SE
$\dfrac{P(Y_i = \text{academic}\|x_i)}{P(Y_i = \text{general}\|x_i)}$	α_1	−5.2159	0.8139	−5.0391	0.7835
	β_1	0.1133	0.0156	0.1099	0.0150
$\dfrac{P(Y_i = \text{vocational}\|x_i)}{P(Y_i = \text{general}\|x_i)}$	α_2	2.9651	0.8342	2.8996	0.8156
	β_2	−0.0613	0.0172	−0.0599	0.0168
$\dfrac{P(Y_i = \text{academic}\|x_i)}{P(Y_i = \text{vocational}\|x_i)}$	α_3	−7.5331	0.8572	−7.9387	0.8439
	β_3	0.1618	0.0170	0.1698	0.0168

each (numerical) explanatory variable in the model.

Turning to interpretation, the regression coefficients provide estimates of odds ratios. Using the parameter estimates of the baseline model (column 5 of Table 26.1), the estimated odds that a student is from an academic program versus a general program given achievement score x equals

$$\frac{\hat{P}(Y_i = \text{academic}|x)}{\hat{P}(Y_i = \text{general}|x)} = \exp[-5.0391 + \quad (7)$$
$$0.1099x],$$

and the estimated odds of an academic versus a general program for a student with achievement score $x + 1$ equals

$$\frac{\hat{P}(Y_i = \text{academic}|x + 1)}{\hat{P}(Y_i = \text{general}|x + 1)} = \exp[-5.0391 + \quad (8)$$
$$0.1099(x + 1)].$$

The ratio of the two odds in Equations 8 and 7 is an odds ratio, which equals

$$\frac{\hat{P}(Y_i = \text{academic}|x + 1)\,\hat{P}(Y_i = \text{general}|x)}{\hat{P}(Y_i = \text{general}|x + 1)\,\hat{P}(Y_i = \text{academic}|x)}$$

$$= \frac{\exp[-5.0391 + 0.1099(x + 1)]}{\exp[-5.0391 + 0.1099x]}$$

$$= \exp(0.1099) = 1.12.$$

This odds ratio is interpreted as follows: For a one-unit increase in achievement, the odds of a student attending an academic versus a general program are 1.12 times larger. For example, the odds of a student with $x = 50$ attending an academic program versus a general one is 1.12 times the odds for a student with $x = 49$. Given the scale of the achievement variable (i.e., $\bar{x} = 51.99$, $s = 8.09$, min = 32.94, and max = 70.00), it may be advantageous to report the odds ratio for an increase of one standard deviation of the explanatory variable rather than a one-unit increase. Generally speaking, $\exp(\beta c)$, where c is a constant, equals the odds ratio for an increase of c units. For example, for an increase of one standard deviation in mean achievement, the odds ratio for academic versus general equals $\exp(0.1099(8.09)) = 2.42$. Likewise, for a one standard deviation increase in achievement, the odds of an academic versus a vocational program are $\exp(0.1698(8.09)) = 3.95$ times larger, but the odds of a vocational program versus a general program are only $\exp(-0.0599(8.09)) = 0.62$ times as large.

Odds ratios convey the multiple one odds is relative to another odds. The parameters also provide information about the probabilities; however, the effects of explanatory variables on probabilities are not necessarily straightforward, as illustrated in the "Multiple Explanatory Variables" section.

As a Model of Probabilities

Probabilities are generally a more intuitively understood concept than odds and odds ratios. The baseline model can also be written as a model for probabilities. There is a one-to-one relationship between odds and probabilities. Using Equation 6, the model for probabilities is

$$P(Y_i = j|x_i) = \frac{\exp[\alpha_j + \beta_j x_i]}{\sum_{h=1}^{J} \exp[\alpha_h + \beta_h x_i]}, \quad (9)$$

where $j = 1, \ldots, J$. The sum in the numerator ensures that the sum of the probabilities over the response categories equals 1.

When estimating the model, identification constraints are required on the parameters. These constraints do not influence the goodness of model fit, odds ratios, estimated probabilities, interpretations, or conclusions. Identification constraints do affect the specific values of parameter estimates. The typical constraints are to set the parameter values of the baseline category equal to zero (e.g., $a_j = \beta_j = 0$) or to set the sum of the parameters equal to zero (e.g., $\sum_j a_j = \sum_j \beta_j = 0$). In practice, it is very important to know what constraints a computer program uses when writing the model as a model for probabilities. In our example, the software program (by default) set $a_j = \beta_j = 0$. Since $\exp(0) = 1$ for the general program, the estimated models for probabilities equal that shown in equation 10.

The estimated probabilities are plotted in Figure 26.1. The baseline model will always have one curve that monotonically decreases (e.g., $P(Y_i = \text{vocational}|x_i)$) and one that monotonically increases (e.g., $P(Y_i = \text{academic}|x_i)$). All others will increase and at some point start to decrease (e.g., $P(Y_i = \text{general}|x_i)$). At any point along the horizontal axis, the sum of the three probabilities equals 1.

Multiple Explanatory Variables

Multiple explanatory variables are typically available in most studies. Models with multiple explanatory variables are illustrated here by adding to our model a nominal (i.e., whether the school a student attends is public or private) and an ordinal variable (i.e., socioeconomic status reported as low, middle, or high).

Discrete variables are added using either dummy or effect coding. For example, school type could be coded either as a dummy variable (Equation 11a) or as an effect code (Equation 11b):

or

$$p_i = \begin{cases} 1 & \text{if public} \\ 0 & \text{if private} \end{cases} \quad (11a)$$

$$p_i = \begin{cases} 1 & \text{if public} \\ -1 & \text{if private} \end{cases} \quad (11b)$$

Most computer programs will automatically create the codes for discrete variables; however, proper interpretation requires that the user know how variables are coded.

The model presented and developed here has main effects for achievement, school type, and socioeconomic status (SES). Effect codes for school type, which are given in Equation 11b, are used to add school type to the model. The effects codes used to add SES, which has three levels, to the model are as follows:

$$\hat{P}(Y_i = \text{academic}) = \frac{\exp[-5.0391 + 0.1099x_i]}{1 + \exp[-5.0391 + 0.1099x_i] + \exp[2.8996 - 0.0599x_i]}$$

$$\hat{P}(Y_i = \text{vocational}) = \frac{\exp[2.8996 - 0.0599x_i]}{1 + \exp[-5.0391 + 0.1099x_i] + \exp[2.8996 - 0.0599x_i]} \quad (10)$$

$$\hat{P}(Y_i = \text{general}) = \frac{1}{1 + \exp[-5.0391 + 0.1099x_i] + \exp[2.8996 - 0.0599x_i]}$$

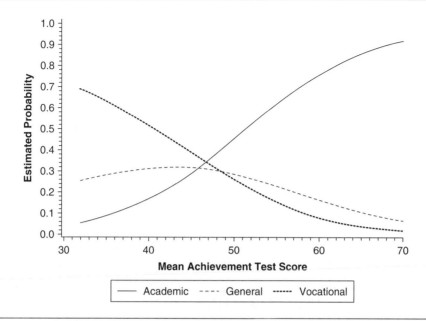

Figure 26.1   Estimated probabilities of attending different high school programs as a function of mean achievement.

$$
s_{1i} = \begin{cases} 1 & \text{for low SES} \\ 0 & \text{for middle SES} \\ -1 & \text{for high SES} \end{cases} \quad (12a)
$$

and

$$
s_{2i} = \begin{cases} 0 & \text{for low SES} \\ 1 & \text{for middle SES} \\ -1 & \text{for high SES} \end{cases} \quad (12b)
$$

Defining $j = 1$ for academic, $j = 2$ for vocational, and $j = 3 = J$ for general program, the first model with multiple explanatory variables examined here is

$$
\frac{P(Y_i = j | x_i, p_i, s_{1i}, s_{2i})}{P(Y_i = J | x_i, p_i, s_{1i}, s_{2i})} = \quad (13)
$$

$$
\exp[\alpha_j + \beta_{j1} x_i + \beta_{j2} p_i + \beta_{j3} s_{1i} + \beta_{j4} s_{2i}]
$$

for $j = 1, \ldots, J - 1$. Additional regression coefficients (i.e., β_js) are estimated, one for each explanatory variable or code in the model. The same model expressed in terms of probabilities is

$$
P(Y_i = j | x_i, p_i, s_{1i}, s_{2i}) =
$$

$$
\frac{\begin{aligned}\exp[\alpha_j + \beta_{j1} x_i + \beta_{j2} p_i \\ + \beta_{j3} s_{1i} + \beta_{j4} s_{2i}]\end{aligned}}{\begin{aligned}\sum_{h=1}^{J} \exp[\alpha_h + \beta_{h1} x_i + \beta_{h2} p_i \\ + \beta_{h3} s_{1i} + \beta_{h4} s_{2i}]\end{aligned}}. \quad (13)
$$

The model has main effects of each of the variables. The estimated parameters and their standard errors are reported in Table 26.2.

The parameter estimates and statistics given in Table 26.2 have been rounded to two decimal places, which reflects a reasonable level of precision and is in line with American Psychological Association (APA) guidelines for reporting results. It should be noted that more decimal places were used in computations. For simplicity, in Table 26.2 and the remainder of the chapter, the explanatory variables are dropped from the symbols for the modeled probabilities; that is, $P(Y_i = j)$ will be used instead of $P(Y_i = j | x_i, p_i, s_{1i}, s_{2i})$. The values of the parameter estimates for high SES and private schools are included explicitly in the table to aid in the proper interpretation of the model.

The interpretation in terms of odds ratios is the same as binary logistic regression; however, the number of parameters to interpret is much larger than in binary logistic regression. Using the parameters reported in Table 26.2, for a one-unit increase in mean achievement, the odds of an academic versus a general program are 1.10 times larger, and for a one standard deviation increase, the odds are $\exp(0.10(0.809)) = 2.25$ times larger. The odds of academic versus general programs are larger for higher levels of

Table 26.2   Estimated Parameters, Standard Errors, and Wald Test Statistics for All Main Effects Model

Odds	Effect	Parameter	Estimate	SE	$exp(\beta)$	Wald	p Value
$P(Y_i = \text{academic})$	Intercept	α_1	−3.92	0.83		22.06	< .01
$\overline{P(Y_i = \text{general})}$	Achievement	β_{11}	0.10	0.02	1.10	37.80	< .01
	School type (public)	β_{12}	−0.61	0.18	0.54	12.01	< .01
	School type (private)	$-\beta_{12}$	0.61		1.84		
	SES (low)	β_{13}	−0.46	0.18	0.63	6.83	.01
	SES (middle)	β_{14}	−0.07	0.15	0.94	0.19	.66
	SES (high)	$-(\beta_{13} + \beta_{14})$	0.53		1.70		
$P(Y_i = \text{vocational})$	Intercept	α_2	2.88	0.88		10.61	< .01
$\overline{P(Y_i = \text{general})}$	Achievement	β_{13}	−0.06	0.02	0.94	13.28	< .01
	School type (public)	β_{22}	0.13	0.24	1.94	0.27	.60
	School type (private)	$-\beta_{22}$	−0.13		0.88		
	SES (low)	β_{23}	−0.23	0.19	0.80	1.45	.23
	SES (middle)	β_{24}	0.24	0.17	1.28	2.16	.14
	SES (high)	$-(\beta_{23} + \beta_{24})$	−0.02		0.98		

NOTE: SES is treated as a nominal variable.

achievement, private schools, and higher SES levels. It appears that the odds of vocational versus general programs are larger for public schools and lower SES levels; however, this conclusion is not warranted. These parameters are not significantly different from zero (see the last two columns of Table 26.2). Statistical inference and nonsignificant parameters are issues that are returned to later in this chapter.

To illustrate the effect of the extra variables on probabilities, the estimated probabilities of attending an academic program are plotted against mean achievement scores in Figure 26.2 with a separate curve for each combination of SES. The figure on the left is for students at public schools, and the figure on the right is for private schools. The discrete variables shift the curves horizontally. In particular, the horizontal distance between the curves for high and middle SES for either public or private schools is the same regardless of the mean achievement value.

When there is no interaction, the curves for the estimated probabilities of the response category that is monotonically increasing (e.g., academic programs) will be parallel; that is, they will have the same shape and are just shifted horizontally. The curves for the response category where the probabilities monotonically decrease (e.g., vocational programs)

will also be parallel; however, this is not true for the other categories. In fact, the curves for responses whose probabilities increase and then decrease are not parallel and may even cross within the range for which there are data. To illustrate this, the probabilities of students attending a general program for private schools are plotted against mean achievement scores with a separate curve for each SES level at the top of Figure 26.3. The curves for different SES levels cross. In normal linear regression, this would indicate an interaction between achievement and SES; however, this is not the case in logistic regression. Crossing curves can occur in the baseline model with only main effects because the relative size of the numerator and denominator changes as values of the explanatory variables change. If there are no interactions in the model, then curves of odds ratios and logarithms of odds ratios will not cross. This is illustrated at the bottom of Figure 26.3, where the logarithms of the odds are plotted against mean achievement. The logarithms of the odds are linear, and the lines are parallel. Although probabilities are more intuitively understandable, figures of estimated probabilities may be misleading to researchers unfamiliar with multicategory logistic regression models. Care must be taken when presenting results such as these.

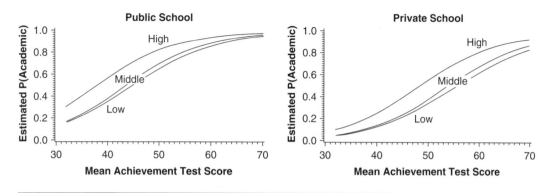

Figure 26.2   Estimated probabilities of attending an academic high school program as a function of mean achievement with a separate curve for each SES level.

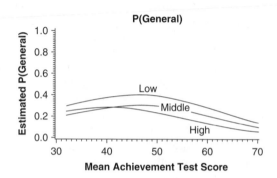

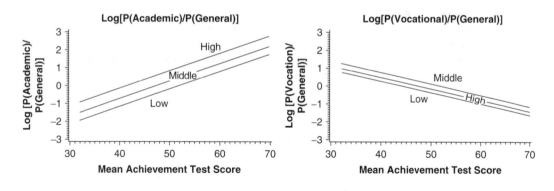

Figure 26.3   At the top is a plot of estimated probabilities of attending a general high school program for private schools as a function of mean achievement with a separate curve for each SES level from the model with only main effects. The two lower figures are plots of the estimated logarithm of odds ratios using parameters from the same model.

With ordinal explanatory variables such as SES, one way to use the ordinal information is by assigning scores or numbers to the categories and treating the variables as numerical variables in the model (e.g., like mean achievement). Often, equally spaced integers are used, which amounts to putting equality restrictions on the

βs for the variable. In our example, suppose we assign 1 to low SES, 2 to middle SES, and 3 to high SES and refit the model. In this model, only one β parameter is estimated for SES rather than two for each of the $(J - 1)$ odds. Using SES as a numerical variable with equally spaced scores in the model imposes restrictions on the βs. In our example, $\beta_{j3} = \beta_{j4}$ for the odds for $j = 1$ and 2 (i.e., academic and vocational, respectively). The parameter estimates for the model where SES is treated numerically are reported in Table 26.3.

Placing the restrictions on the βs for ordinal variables is often a good way to reduce the complexity of a model. For example, the estimated odds ratio of academic versus general for middle versus low SES equals $\exp(\hat{\beta}_{13}(2-1)) = \exp(\hat{\beta}_{13}) = 1.70$, which is the same as the odds ratio of high versus middle SES, $\exp(\hat{\beta}_{13}(3-2)) = 1.70$.

In our example, putting in equally spaced scores for SES is not warranted and is misleading. When no restrictions were imposed on the parameters (see Figure 26.3 and Table 26.2), the order of the SES levels for the odds of academic (versus general) schools is in the expected order (i.e., the odds of an academic program are larger the higher the student's SES level), and the parameter estimates are approximately equally spaced. On the other hand, the parameter estimates of SES for odds of vocational schools do not follow the natural ordering of low to high, are relatively close together, and are not significantly different from zero. The numerical scores could be used for the SES effect on the odds of academic programs but the scores are inappropriate for the odds of vocational programs. There may not even be a difference between vocational and general programs in terms of SES. Furthermore, there may not be a difference between students who attended vocational and general programs with respect to school type (Wald $= 0.27$, $df = 1$, $p = .60$). In the following section, these conjectures are incorporated into the model, which permits statistical testing of these hypotheses.

Conditional Multinomial Logistic Regression

The conjectures described above regarding possible equalities, nonsignificant effects, and restrictions on parameters can be imposed (and tested) by reexpressing the baseline model as a conditional multinomial logistic regression model, which is a more general model. The conditional multinomial logistic regression model is also known as the "discrete choice model," "McFadden's model," and "Luce's choice model." Some sources for more complete introductions to this model include Long (1997), Agresti (2002), and Powers and Xie (2000). Unlike the baseline model, the conditional model permits explanatory variables that are attributes of response categories.

The general form of the conditional multinomial logistic model is

$$P(Y_i = j | \mathbf{x}_{ij}^*) = \frac{\exp(\boldsymbol{\beta}^{*'}\mathbf{x}_{ij}^*)}{\sum_h \exp(\boldsymbol{\beta}^{*'}\mathbf{x}_{ih}^*)}, \quad (15)$$

where $\boldsymbol{\beta}^*$ is a vector of coefficients and $\mathbf{x}_{ij}^*$ is a vector of explanatory variables. The explanatory variables $\mathbf{x}_{ij}^*$ may depend on the attributes of an individual (i), the response category (j), or both, but the coefficients $\boldsymbol{\beta}^*$ do not depend on the response categories. To reexpress the baseline

Table 26.3   Estimated Parameters, Standard Errors, and Wald Statistics for All Main Effects Model

Odds	Effect	Parameter	Estimate	SE	$\exp(\beta)$	Wald	p Value
$P(Y_i = \text{academic})$	Intercept	α_1	−4.97	0.83	—	35.73	< .01
$P(Y_i = \text{general})$	Achievement	β_{11}	0.10	0.02	1.10	37.48	< .01
	School type	β_{12}	−0.61	0.18	0.55	11.80	< .01
	SES	β_{13}	0.53	0.18	1.70	11.80	< .01
$P(Y_i = \text{vocational})$	Intercept	α_2	2.57	0.87	—	8.78	< .01
$P(Y_i = \text{general})$	Achievement	β_{13}	−0.06	0.02	0.95	12.96	< .01
	School type	β_{22}	0.12	0.24	1.13	0.26	.61
	SES	β_{23}	0.17	0.19	1.19	0.92	.34

NOTE: SES is treated as a numerical variable with scores of 1 = low, 2 = middle, and 3 = high.

model in the general form of the conditional logistic model given in Equation 15, data need to be reformatted from having one line in the data file for each individual to multiple lines of data for each individual. When fitting conditional multinomial models, the data must have one line of data for each response category for each individual to incorporate explanatory variables that are characteristics of the response categories.

The format of the data file for the baseline model where mean achievement is the only explanatory variable in the model is given in Table 26.4. In the data, Y is the response variable that indicates a student's high school program. The indicators, d_{ij}, are the key to putting the baseline model into the form of the conditional multinomial model, as well as to specifying different models for the different program types (i.e., levels of the response variable). In our example, the two indicator variables, d_{i1} and d_{i2}, indicate the category of the response variable corresponding to particular line in the data file. They are defined as

$$d_{i1} = \begin{cases} 1 & \text{when program type is academic} \\ 0 & \text{otherwise} \end{cases}$$

$$d_{i2} = \begin{cases} 1 & \text{when program type is vocational} \\ 0 & \text{otherwise} \end{cases}$$

For general programs, $d_{i1} = d_{i2} = 0$.

For our simple baseline model with only achievement test scores in the model, $\beta^{*'} = (\alpha_1, \alpha_2, \beta_{11}, \beta_{21})$ and $x_{ij}^{*'} = (d_{i1}, d_{i2}, d_{i1}x_i, d_{i2}x_i)$. Using the definitions of d_{ij}, β^*, and x_{ij}^*, we obtain our familiar form of the baseline model,

$$P(Y_i = j) = \frac{\exp[\alpha_j + \beta_{j1}x_i]}{\begin{array}{c}(1 + \exp[\alpha_1 + \beta_{11}x_i] \\ + \exp[\alpha_2 + \beta_{21}x_i])\end{array}}, \quad (16)$$

which, for our example, corresponds to

$$P(Y_i = \text{academic}) = \frac{\exp[\alpha_1 + \beta_{11}x_i]}{\begin{array}{c}(1 + \exp[\alpha_1 + \beta_{11}x_i] \\ + \exp[\alpha_2 + \beta_{21}x_i])\end{array}}, \quad (17)$$

$$P(Y_i = \text{vocational}) = \frac{\exp[\alpha_2 + \beta_{21}x_i]}{\begin{array}{c}(1 + \exp[\alpha_1 + \beta_{11}x_i] \\ + \exp[\alpha_2 + \beta_{21}x_i])\end{array}}, \quad \text{and} \quad (18)$$

Table 26.4   The Format of the Data File Needed to Fit the Baseline Multinomial Model as Conditional Multinomial Model With Mean Achievement as the Explanatory Variable

Student ID	Achievement x_i	Program Type	Y	d_{i1}	d_{i2}	$d_{i1}x_i$	$d_{i2}x_i$
1	32.94	General	0	0	0	0	0
1	32.94	Academic	0	1	0	32.94	0
1	32.94	Vocational	1	0	1	0	32.94
⋮	⋮	⋮	⋮	⋮	⋮	⋮	⋮
102	43.74	General	1	0	0	0	0
102	43.74	Academic	0	1	0	43.74	0
102	43.74	Vocational	0	0	1	0	43.74
⋮	⋮	⋮	⋮	⋮	⋮	⋮	⋮
600	70.00	General	0	0	0	0	0
600	70.00	Academic	1	1	0	70.00	0
600	70.00	Vocational	0	0	1	0	70.00

$$P(Y_i = \text{general}) =$$

$$\frac{1}{\begin{array}{l}(1 + \exp[\alpha_1 + \beta_{11}x_i]\\ \quad + \exp[\alpha_2 + \beta_{21}x_i])\end{array}} . \qquad (19)$$

Note that the parameters for the last category, which in this case is general programs, were set equal to zero for identification (i.e., $\alpha_{31} = 0$ for the intercept, and $\beta_{31} = 0$ for achievement test scores).

The conditional model was introduced here as a means to refine and reduce the number of parameters of the baseline model. First, the complex model will be represented as a conditional multinomial model, and then, by appropriately defining x^*_{ij}, restrictions will be imposed on the parameters. To express the complex baseline model as a conditional multinomial logistic model, we define β^* and x^*_{ij} as

$$\beta^{*\prime} = (\alpha_1, \alpha_2, \beta_{11}, \beta_{21}, \beta_{12}, \beta_{22}, \beta_{13}, \beta_{23}, \beta_{14}, \beta_{24})$$

and

$$\begin{aligned}\mathbf{x}^{*\prime}_{ij} = (&d_{i1}, d_{i2}, d_{i1}x_i, d_{i2}x_i, d_{i1}p_i,\\ &d_{i2}p_i, d_{i1}s_{1i}, d_{i2}s_{1i}, d_{i1}s_{2i}, d_{i2}s_{2i}).\end{aligned}$$

Using these β^* and x^*_{ij} in Equation 15, the complex baseline model with main effects for achievement (x_i), school type (p_i), and SES (s_{1i}, s_{2i}) expressed as a conditional multinomial model is

$$\begin{aligned}P(Y_i = j) = \exp[&\alpha_j d_{ij} + \beta_{j1}d_{ij}x_i\\ &+ \beta_{j2}d_{ij}p_i + \beta_{j3}d_{ij}s_{1i}\\ &+ \beta_{j4}d_{ij}s_{2i}]\kappa_i, \end{aligned} \qquad (20)$$

where $\kappa_i = \sum_h \exp[\alpha_h d_{ih} + \beta_{h1}d_{ih}x_i$
$\qquad + \beta_{j2}d_{ih}p_i + \beta_{h3}d_{ih}s_{1i} + \beta_{h4}d_{ih}s_{2i}]$.

When reexpressing the baseline model as a conditional multinomial model, a good practice is to refit the baseline models that have already been fit to the data as conditional models. If the data matrix and conditional models have been correctly specified, then the results obtained from the baseline and conditional models will be the same (i.e., parameters estimates, standard errors, etc.).

One simplification of Equation 20 is to treat SES numerically for academic programs (i.e., use

$s_i = 1, 2, 3$ instead of s_{1i} and s_{2i}). The parameters for SES and school type for vocational and general programs can be set to zero by deleting the terms $d_{i2}p_i$, $d_{i2}s_{1i}$, and $d_{i2}s_{2i}$ from the data matrix, which implicitly sets $\beta_{22} = \beta_{23} = \beta_{24} = 0$. Making these changes, the models for the probabilities for each high school program type become

$$P(Y_i = \text{academic}) =$$

$$\frac{\exp[\alpha_1 + \beta_{11}x_i + \beta_{12}p_i + \beta_{13}s_i]}{\begin{array}{l}1 + \exp[\alpha_1 + \beta_{11}x_i + \beta_{12}p_i + \beta_{13}s_i]\\ \quad + \exp[\alpha_2 + \beta_{21}x_i]\end{array}}, \text{ and}$$

$$P(Y_i = \text{vocational}) =$$

$$\frac{\exp[\alpha_2 + \beta_{21}x_i]}{\begin{array}{l}1 + \exp[\alpha_1 + \beta_{11}x_i + \beta_{12}p_i + \beta_{13}s_i]\\ \quad + \exp[\alpha_2 + \beta_{21}x_i]\end{array}},$$

$$P(Y_i = \text{general}) =$$

$$\frac{1}{\begin{array}{l}1 + \exp[\alpha_1 + \beta_{11}x_i + \beta_{12}p_i + \beta_{13}s_i]\\ \quad + \exp[\alpha_2 + \beta_{21}x_i]\end{array}} .$$

The parameter estimates for this final model are given in Table 26.5 and are similar to those in the baseline model with no restrictions on the parameters (i.e., Table 26.2). The model with restrictions fit as a conditional multinomial model is more parsimonious than the baseline model (i.e., 6 vs. 10 nonredundant parameters). The models for the probabilities of different high school programs do not have the same effects. As stated earlier, by fitting all of the odds simultaneously, the logical restrictions on the parameters are maintained, and the standard errors of the parameters are smaller (i.e., there is greater precision).

Switching to the conditional multinomial model emphasizes that users of multinomial logistic regression are not restricted to the standard models that computer programs fit by default, which often fail to address specific research questions. By creating new variables, using indicator variables, and using a slightly more general model, researchers can tailor their models to best match their research questions. Imposing restrictions on parameters when they are warranted can greatly simplify a complex model. This was illustrated in our example. Compare Tables 26.2 and 26.5. In the model reported in Table 26.2, there were 10

Table 26.5   Estimated Parameters From the Conditional Multinomial Logistic Regression Model

Odds	Effect	Parameter	Estimate	SE	exp(β)	Wald	p Value
$\dfrac{P(Y_i = \text{academic})}{P(Y_i = \text{general})}$	Intercept	β_{11}	−4.87	0.82		35.31	< .01
	Achievement	β_{12}	0.10	0.02	1.10	39.81	< .01
	School type (public)	β_{13}	−0.66	0.15	0.52	20.61	< .01
	School type (private)	$-\beta_{13}$	0.66		1.93		
	SES (low)	β_{14}	0.46	0.14	1.58	10.22	< .01
$\dfrac{P(Y_i = \text{vocational})}{P(Y_i = \text{general})}$	Intercept	β_{21}	2.83	0.81		12.33	< .01
	Achievement	β_{22}	−0.06	0.02	0.94	1.42	< .01

nonredundant parameters, some of which are not significant and others that are. An additional reason for going the extra step of using the conditional model is that novice users often succumb to the temptation of interpreting nonsignificant parameters such as those in Table 26.2. The better approach is to avoid the temptation. Alternatively, researchers may simply not report the nonsignificant effects even though they were in the model. This also is a poor (and misleading) practice. Table 26.5 contains only 6 nonredundant parameters, all of which are significant. What is statistically important stands out, and the interpretation is much simpler. In our example, it is readily apparent that students in general and vocational programs only differ with respect to achievement test scores, whereas students in academic programs and those in one of the other programs differ with respect to achievement test scores, SES, and school type.

STATISTICAL INFERENCE

Simple statistical tests were used informally in the previous section to examine the significance of effects in the models discussed. The topic of statistical inference is explicitly taken up in detail in this section. There are two basic types of statistical inference that are of interest: the effect of explanatory variables and whether response categories are indistinguishable with respect to the explanatory variables.

Tests of Effects

If $\beta = 0$, then an effect is unrelated to the response variable, given all the other effects in the model. The two test statistics discussed here

for assessing whether $\beta = 0$ are the Wald statistic and the likelihood ratio statistic.

Maximum likelihood estimates of the model parameters are asymptotically normal with mean equal to the value of the parameter in the population—that is, the sampling distribution of $\hat{\beta} \sim N(\beta, \sigma_\beta^2)$. This fact can be used to test the hypothesis $\beta = 0$ and to form confidence intervals for β and odds ratios.

If the null hypothesis $H_0 : \beta = 0$ is true, then the statistic

$$z = \frac{\hat{\beta}}{SE},$$

where SE is the estimate of σ_β^2, has an approximate standard normal distribution. This statistic can be used for directional or nondirectional tests. Often, the statistic is squared, $X^2 = z^2$, and is known as a Wald statistic, which has a sampling distribution that is approximately chi-square with 1 degree of freedom.

When reporting results in papers, many journals require confidence intervals for effects. Although many statistical software packages automatically provide confidence intervals, we show where these intervals come from, which points to the relationship between the confidence intervals and the Wald tests. A $(1 - \alpha)\%$ Wald confidence interval for β is

$$\hat{\beta} \pm z_{(1 - \alpha)/2}(SE),$$

where $z_{(1 - \alpha)/2}$ is the $(1 - \alpha)/2$th percentile of the standard normal distribution. A $(1 - \alpha)\%$ confidence interval for the odds ratio is found by exponentiating the end points of the interval for β.

As an example, consider the parameter estimates given in Table 26.5 of our final model from the previous section. The Wald statistics and corresponding p values are reported in the seventh and eighth columns. For example, the Wald statistic for achievement for academic programs equals

$$X^2 = \left(\frac{0.0978}{0.0155}\right)^2 = 39.81.$$

The 95% confidence interval of β for achievement equals

$$0.0987 \pm 1.96(0.0155) \rightarrow (0.06742, 0.12818),$$

and the 95% confidence interval for the odds ratio equals

$$(\exp(0.06742), \exp(0.12818)) \rightarrow (1.07, 1.14).$$

The ratio of a parameter estimate to its standard errors provides a test for single parameters; however, Wald statistics can be used for testing whether any and multiple linear combinations of the βs equal zero (Agresti, 2002; Long, 1997). Such Wald statistics can be used to test simultaneously whether an explanatory variable or variables have an effect on any of the models for the odds. Rather than present the general formula for Wald tests (Agresti, 2002; Long, 1997), the likelihood ratio statistic provides a more powerful alternative to test more complex hypotheses.

The likelihood ratio test statistic compares the maximum of the likelihood functions of two models, a complex and a simpler one. The simpler model must be a special case of the complex model where restrictions have been placed on the parameters of the more complex model. Let $\ln(L(M_0))$ and $\ln(L(M_1))$ equal the natural logarithms of the maximum of the likelihood functions for the simple and the complex models, respectively. The likelihood ratio test statistic equals

$$G^2 = -2(\ln(L(M_0)) - \ln(L(M_1))).$$

Computer programs typically provide either the value of the maximum of the likelihood function, the logarithm of the maximum, or −2 times the logarithm of the maximum. If the null hypothesis is true, then G^2 has an approximate chi-square distribution with degrees of freedom equal to the difference in the number of parameters between the two models.

The most common type of restriction on parameters is setting them equal to zero. For example, in the baseline model with all main effects (nominal SES), we could set all of the parameters for SES and school type equal to zero; that is, $\beta_{j2} = \beta_{j3} = \beta_{j4} = 0$ for $j = 1$ and 2. The complex model is

$$\frac{P(Y_i = j)}{P(Y_i = J)} = \exp[\alpha_j + \beta_{j1}x_i + \beta_{j2}p_i + \beta_{j3}s_{1i} + \beta_{j4}s_{2i}],$$

and the simpler model is

$$\frac{P(Y_i = j)}{P(Y_i = J)} = \exp[\alpha_j + \beta_{j1}x_i].$$

The maximum of the likelihoods of all the models estimated for this chapter are reported in Table 26.6. The difference between the likelihood for these two models equals

$$G^2 = -2(-541.8917 + 520.26080) = 43.26.$$

The degrees of freedom for this test equal 6, because 6 parameters have been set equal to zero. Comparing 43.26 to the chi-square distribution with 6 degrees of freedom, the hypothesis that SES and/or school type have significant effects is supported.

Equality restrictions on parameters can also be tested using the likelihood ratio test. Such tests include determining whether an ordinal explanatory variable can be treated numerically. For example, when SES was treated as a nominal variable in the baseline model, SES was represented in the model by $\beta_{j3}s_{1i} + \beta_{j4}s_{2i}$, where s_{1i} and s_{2i} were effect codes. When SES was treated as a numeric variable (i.e., $s_i = 1, 2, 3$ for low, middle, high), implicitly the restriction that $\beta_{j3} = \beta_{j4}$ was imposed, and SES was represented in the model by $\beta_{j3}s_i$. The likelihood ratio test statistic equals 3.99, with $df = 2$ and $p = .14$ (see Table 26.6). Even though SES should not be treated numerically for vocational and general programs, the test indicates otherwise. It is best to treat categorical explanatory variables nominally, examine the results, and, if warranted, test whether they can be used as numerical variables.

Tests Over Regressions

A second type of test that is of interest in multinomial logistic regression modeling is whether two or more of the response categories are indistinguishable in the sense that they have

Table 26.6   Summary of All Models Fit to the High School and Beyond Data Where Mean Achievement, School Type, and SES Are Explanatory Variables

			Likelihood Ratio Tests				
Model	Number of Parameters	Ln(Likelihood)	Models Compared	G^2	df	p	AIC
M_1: All main (nominal SES)	10	−520.2608	—				1061
M_2: Achievement only	4	−541.8917	M_2 & M_1	43.26	6	< .01	1092
M_3: All main (ordinal SES)	8	−522.2579	M_3 & M_1	3.99	2	.14	1061
M_4: General and vocational indistinguishable?	6	−528.3721	M_4 & M_1	16.22	4	< .01	1069
M_5: Restrictions on parameters	6	−522.8114	M_5 & M_1	5.10	4	.28	1058

the same parameter values. If there is no difference between two responses—say, j and j^*—then

$$(\beta_{j1} - \beta_{j^*1}) = \ldots = (\beta_{jK} - \beta_{j^*K}) = 0, \quad (21)$$

where K equals the number of explanatory variables. If two response levels are indistinguishable, they can be combined (Long, 1997). In our example, the parameter estimates for the two main effect models have nonsignificant odds for vocational versus general (see Tables 26.2 and 26.3). This suggests that vocational and general programs may be indistinguishable.

The indistinguishability hypothesis represented in Equation 21 can be tested in two ways. The simple method is to create a data set that only includes the two response variables, fit a binary logistic regression model to the data, and use a likelihood ratio test to assess whether the explanatory variables are significant (Long, 1997). In our example, the model in Equation 13 was fit to the subset of data that only includes students from general and vocational programs. According to the likelihood ratio test, the explanatory variables are significant ($G^2 = 17.53$, $df = 4$, $p < .01$).

The second and preferable way to test the indistinguishability hypothesis makes use of the fact that the baseline model is a special case of the conditional model. Besides using all of the data, this second method has the advantage that it can be used to simultaneously test whether three or more of the responses are indistinguishable or to place restrictions on subsets of parameters. To test the indistinguishability hypotheses for vocational and general programs relative to the baseline model with all

main effects, we fit the conditional multinomial model with $\beta^{*\prime} = (\alpha_1, \alpha_2, \beta_{11}, \beta_{12}, \beta_{13}, \beta_{14})$ and $x_{ij}^{*\prime} = (d_{i1}, d_{i2}, d_{i1}x_i, d_{i1}p_i, d_{i1}s_{1i}, d_{i1}s_{2i})$; that is, the terms with d_{i2} indicators were all dropped from the model except for the intercept α_2. The reduced model is M_4 in Table 26.6, and $G^2 = 16.22$, $df = 4$, and $p < .01$. The null hypothesis is again rejected, and the general and vocational programs are distinguishable on at least one of the three explanatory variables.

MODEL ASSESSMENT

Before drawing conclusions, the adequacy of the model or subset of models must be assessed. Goodness of fit, model comparisons, and regression diagnostics are discussed below.

Goodness of Fit

Two typical tests of goodness of fit are Pearson's chi-square statistic and the likelihood ratio chi-square statistic; however, for tests of goodness of fit to be valid, these statistics should have approximate chi-square distributions. For the sampling distribution of the goodness-of-fit statistics to be chi-square requires two conditions (Agresti, 2002, 2007). First, most fitted values of "cells" of the cross-classification of the response variable by all of the explanatory variables should be greater than 5. Second, as more observations are added to the data set, the size of the cross-classification does not increase. In other words, as observations are added, the number of observations per cell gets larger.

The High School and Beyond data set, even with 600 students, fails both of the requirements. Consider the model with only achievement. The cross-classification of students by high school program type and achievement is given on the right side of Table 26.7. There are 545 unique values of the mean achievement scores, so most cells equal 0. If a new student is added to the data set, it is possible that his or her mean achievement level will be different from the 545 levels already in the data set, and adding a new student would add another row to Table 26.7. Even if only school type and SES are included in the model, the closeness of the approximation of the sampling distribution of goodness-of-fit statistics is uncertain. The cross-classification of programs by SES by school type is given on the left side of Table 26.7, and 5 of the 18 (28%) of the cells are less than 5. The sampling distributions of Pearson's chi-square and the likelihood ratio statistics may not be close to chi-square. The solution is not to throw away information by collapsing data. Alternatives exist.

In the case of binary logistic regression, the Hosmer-Lemeshow statistic is often used to assess model goodness of fit (Hosmer & Lemeshow, 2000); however, no such statistic is readily computed for the multinomial case. Goodness-of-fit statistics for large, sparse contingency tables, including multinomial logistic models, is an active area of research (e.g., Maydeu-Olivares & Joe, 2005). Until more suitable procedures become available in standard statistical packages, one suggestion is to perform dichotomous logistic regressions and compute the Hosmer-Lemeshow statistic for each of them (Hosmer & Lemeshow, 2000).

The Hosmer-Lemeshow statistic is basically Pearson's chi-square statistic,

$$X^2 = \sum_{\text{cells}} \frac{(\text{observed} - \text{expected})^2}{\text{expected}}.$$

The observed and expected values are frequencies found by ordering the predicted values from a binary logistic regression model from smallest to largest and then partitioning the cases into approximately equal groups. Both the data and the expected values from the regression are cross-classified into tables of group by response category. Even though the sampling distribution of the Hosmer-Lemeshow statistic is not chi-square, comparing the Hosmer-Lemeshow statistic to a chi-square distribution performs reasonably well.

A dichotomous logistic regression model for academic versus general was fit with achievement, school type, and SES as an ordinal variable and yielded a Hosmer-Lemeshow statistic = 8.84, $df = 8$, and $p = .36$. For the binary logistic regression model of vocational and general programs with only achievement as an explanatory variable, the model had a Hosmer-Lemeshow statistic = 9.00, $df = 8$, and $p = .34$. In both cases, the models appear adequate.

Model Comparisons

When a subset of models is available and a user wishes to select the "best" one to report and interpret, various measures and statistics are

Table 26.7   Cross-Classifications of the 600 Students in the High School and Beyond Data Set by School Type, SES, and High School Program (Left) and by Mean Achievement and High School Program Type (Right)

School Type	SES	High School Program			Achievement	High School Program		
		General	Academic	Vocational		General	Academic	Vocational
Public	Low	40	40	44	32.94	0	0	1
	Middle	63	111	75	33.74	0	0	1
	High	24	82	20	⋮	⋮	⋮	⋮
Private	Low	3	4	1	43.74	2	0	0
	Middle	7	36	7	⋮	⋮	⋮	⋮
	High	1	35	0	70.00	0	1	0

available for model comparisons. If the models are nested, then the conditional likelihood ratio tests discussed in the "Statistical Inference" section are possible. Although the goodness-of-fit statistics may not have good approximations by chi-square distributions, the conditional likelihood ratio tests often are well approximated by chi-square distributions. One strategy is to start with an overly complex model that gives an adequate representation of the data. Various effects could be considered for removal by performing conditional likelihood ratio tests following the procedure described earlier for testing effects in the model.

When the subset of models is not nested, information criteria can help to choose the "best" model in the set. Information criteria weight goodness of model fit and complexity. A common choice is Akaike's information criterion (AIC), which equals

$$-2(\text{maximum log likelihood} - \text{number of parameters})$$

(Agresti, 2002). The model with the smallest value of AIC is the best. The AIC values for all the models fit in this chapter are reported in Table 26.6. The best model among those fit to the High School and Beyond data is model M_5, which is the conditional multinomial model with different explanatory variables for the program types.

When AIC statistics are very close (e.g., M_1 and M_3), then the choice between models must be based on other considerations such as interpretation, parsimony, and expectations. An additional consideration is whether statistically significant effects are significant in a practical sense (Agresti, 2007). Although many statistics can be reported, which make model selection appear to be an objective decision, model selection is in the end a subjective decision.

Regression Diagnostics

Before any model is reported, regression diagnostics should be performed. Lesaffre and Albert (1989) extended diagnostic procedures for dichotomous responses to the multicategory case of multinomial logistic regression. Unfortunately, these have not been implemented in standard statistical packages. One recommendation is to dichotomize the categories of the response,

fit binary logistic regression models, and use the regression diagnostics that are available for binary logistic regression (Hosmer & Lemeshow, 2000).

Observations may have too much influence on the parameter estimates and the goodness of fit of the model to data. Influential observations tend to be those that are extreme in terms of their values on the explanatory variables. Most diagnostics for logistic regression are generalizations of those for normal linear regression (Pregibon, 1981; see also Agresti, 2002, 2007; Hosmer & Lemeshow, 2000), but there are some exceptions (Fahrmeir & Tutz, 2001; Fay, 2002). One exception is "range-of-influence" statistics. Rather than focusing on whether observations are outliers in the design or exert great influence on results, range-of-influence statistics are designed to check for possible misclassifications of a binary response (Fay, 2002). They are particularly useful if the correctness of classifications into the response categories is either very costly or impossible to check.

Problems With Multinomial Regression Models

Two common problems encountered in multinomial regression models when there are multiple explanatory variables are multicollinearity and "quasi" or "complete separation." As in normal multiple linear regression, multicollinearity occurs when explanatory variables are highly correlated. In such cases, the results can change drastically when an explanatory variable that is correlated with other explanatory variables is added to the model. Effects that were statistically significant may no longer be significant.

To illustrate multicollinearity, two-way interactions between all three main effects in our model were added (i.e., between mean achievement, SES as a numerical variable [1, 2, and 3], and school type). Table 26.8 contains the Wald chi-square test statistics for testing whether the βs for each effect equal zero, the degrees of freedom, and p value for each test. The third and fourth columns contain the results for the model with only main effects and show that the three effects are statistically significant. When all two-way interactions are added to the model, nothing is significant (i.e., the fifth and sixth columns). To reveal the culprit, correlations between

Table 26.8   Statistical Test for Effects When There Are Only Main Effects in the Model, All
Two-Way Interactions (Highly Correlated Effects) and All Two-Way Interactions
Where Mean Achievement and SES Are Standardized

Effect	df	Main Effects		Unstandardized		Standardized	
		Wald	p Value	Wald	p Value	Wald	p Value
Achieve	2	87.62	< .01	5.42	.07	18.06	< .01
SES	2	11.08	< .01	1.10	.58	11.44	< .01
School type	2	20.72	< .01	0.96	.62	16.72	< .01
Achieve × SES	2			0.29	.87	0.29	.87
Achieve × School type	2			0.93	.63	0.93	.63
SES × School type	2			4.07	.13	4.07	.13

achievement, SES, school type, and interactions containing them are reported in Table 26.9. Four of the nine correlations are greater than 0.70, and two of these are greater than 0.90.

Dealing with multicollinearity is the same as that for normal multiple linear regression. If correlations between main effects and interactions lead to multicollinearity, then the variables can be standardized. Table 26.9 also contains the correlations between the standardized explanatory variables, and these are all quite small. In our example, standardization solved the multicollinearity problem. As can be seen in the right side of Table 26.8, the main effects are significant when the explanatory variables are standardized.

A problem more unique to multinomial logistic regression modeling is "quasi-complete separation" or "complete separation of data points." Separation means that the pattern in the data is such that there is no overlap between two or more response categories for some pattern(s) of the values on the explanatory variables (Albert & Anderson, 1984). In other words,

using the model to classify individuals into response levels performs perfectly for one or more of the response categories. In a very simple case, if only men attend vocational programs, then including gender in the model would lead to separation. Typically, the situation is not quite so simple when specific combinations among the explanatory variables occur such that one or more categories of the response variable can be predicted perfectly. When data exhibit quasi-complete or complete separation, maximum likelihood estimates of the parameters may not exist. Some computer programs will issue a warning message that quasi-complete separation has occurred, and others may not. The estimated standard errors for the parameter estimates get very large or "blow up." For example, separation is a problem in the High School and Beyond data set if the variable race is added to the model that includes all two-way interactions for achievement, SES, and school type. Most of the standard errors are less than 1; however, there are many that are between 10 and 64. Separation occurs when the model is too

Table 26.9   Correlations Between Unstandardized Explanatory Variables and Standardized
Explanatory Variables

	Unstandardized			Standardized		
	SES	Achieve	School Type	SES	Achieve	School Type
SES × School type	0.74	0.28	0.76	−0.05	−0.04	−0.05
Achieve × School type	0.27	0.49	0.92	−0.04	−0.18	−0.04
SES × Achieve	0.93	0.64	0.17	−0.05	0.01	−0.06

complex for the data. The solution is to get more data or simplify the model.

Software

An incomplete list of programs that can fit the models reported in this chapter is given here. The models were fit to data for this chapter using SAS Version 9.1 (SAS Institute, Inc., 2003). The baseline models were fit using PROC LOGISTIC under the STAT package, and the conditional multinomial models were fit using PROC MDC in the econometrics package, ETS. Input files for all analyses reported in this chapter as well as how to compute regression diagnostics are available from the author's Web site at http://faculty.ed.uiuc.edu/cja/Best Practices/index.html. Also available from this Web site is a SAS MACRO that will compute range-of-influence statistics. Another commercial package that can fit both kinds of models is STATA (StataCorp LP, 2007; see Long, 1997). In the program R (R Development Core Team, 2007), which is an open-source version of SPLUS (Insightful Corp., 2007), the baseline model can be fit to data using the *glm* function, and the conditional multinomial models can be fit using the *coxph* function in the *survival* package. Finally, SPSS (SPSS, 2006) can fit the baseline model via the multinomial logistic regression function, and the conditional multinomial model can be fit using COXREG.

Models for Ordinal Responses

Ordinal response variables are often found in survey questions with response options such as *strongly agree, agree, disagree,* and *strongly disagree* (or *never, sometimes, often, all the time*). A number of extensions of the binary logistic regression model exist for ordinal variables, the most common being the proportional odds model (also known as the cumulative logit model), the continuation ratios model, and the adjacent categories model. Each of these is a bit different in terms of how the response categories are dichotomized as well as other specifics. Descriptions of these models can be found in Agresti (2002, 2007), Fahrmeir and Tutz (2001), Hosmer and Lemeshow (2000), Long (1997), Powers and Xie (2000), and elsewhere.

MANOVA, Discriminant Analysis, and Logistic Regression

Before concluding this chapter, a discussion of the relationship between multinomial logistic regression models, multivariate analysis of variance (MANOVA), and linear discriminant analysis is warranted. As an alternative to multinomial logistic regression with multiple explanatory variables, a researcher may choose MANOVA to test for group differences or linear discriminant analysis for either classification into groups or description of group differences. The relationship between MANOVA and linear discriminant analysis is well documented (e.g., Dillon & Goldstein, 1984; Johnson & Wichern, 1998); however, these models are in fact very closely related to logistic regression models.

MANOVA, discriminant analysis, and multinomial logistic regression all are applicable to the situation where there is a single discrete variable Y with J categories (e.g., high school program type) and a set of K random continuous variables denoted by $X = (X_1, X_2, \ldots, X_K)'$ (e.g., achievement test scores on different subjects). Before performing discriminant analysis, it is the recommended practice to first perform a MANOVA to test whether differences over the J categories or groups exist (i.e., $H_0 : \mu_1 = \mu_2 = \ldots = \mu_J$, where μ_j is a vector of means on the K variables). The assumptions for MANOVA are that vectors of random variables from each group follow a multivariate normal distribution with mean equal to μ_j for group j, the covariance matrices for the groups are all equal, and observations over groups are independent (i.e., $X_j \sim N_K(\mu_j, \Sigma)$ and independent).

If the assumptions for MANOVA are met, then a multinomial logistic regression model *must necessarily* fit the data. This result is based on statistical graphical models for discrete and continuous variables (Laurizten, 1996; Laurizten & Wermuth, 1989). Logistic regression is just the "flip side of the same coin." If the assumptions for MANOVA are not met, then the statistical tests performed in MANOVA and/or discriminant analysis are not valid; however, statistical tests in logistic regression will likely still be valid. In the example in this chapter, SES and school type are discrete and clearly are not normal. This poses no problem for logistic regression.

A slight advantage of discriminant analysis and MANOVA over multinomial logistic regression may be a greater familiarity with these methods by both researchers and readers and the ease of implementation of these methods. However, when the goal is classification or description, these advantages may come at the expense of classification accuracy, invalid statistical tests, and difficulty describing differences between groups. As an illustration of classification using the High School and Beyond data, discriminant analysis with achievement as the only feature was used to classify students, as well as a discriminant analysis with all main effects. Frequencies of students in each program type and the predicted frequencies under discriminant analysis and multinomial logistic regression are located in Table 26.10. In this example, logistic regression performed better than discriminant analysis in terms of overall classification accuracy. The correct classification rates from the multinomial logistic regression models were .58 (achievement only) and .60 (main effects of achievement, SES, and school type), and those for linear discriminant analysis were .52 in both cases.

If a researcher's interest is in describing differences between groups, multinomial logistic regression is superior for a number of reasons. The flexibility of logistic regression allows for a number of different models. In our example, we were able to test whether SES should be treated as an ordinal or nominal variable. Furthermore, we were also able to discern that students who attended general and vocational programs were indistinguishable in terms of SES and school type, but students who attended academic programs versus one of the other programs were distinguishable with respect to achievement test scores, SES, and school type. We were also able to describe the nature and amount of differences between students who attended general and vocational programs in a relatively simple way.

The differences between students in academic programs and either a general or vocational program were slightly more complex but still straightforward to describe.

Exercises

1. Use the High School and Beyond data set (Tatsuoka & Lohnes, 1988) to model students' career choice as the response variable. Consider gender, achievement test scores, and self-concept as possible explanatory variables. Do any of the careers have the same regression parameters? Note that some careers have very low numbers of observations; these may have to be deleted from the analysis.

2. The English as a second language (ESL) data come from a study that investigated the validity and generalizability of an ESL placement test (Lee & Anderson, in press). The test is administered to international students at a large midwestern university, and the results are used to place students in an appropriate ESL course sequence. The data set contains the test results (scores of 2, 3, 4), self-reported Test of English as a Foreign Language (TOEFL) scores, field of study (business, humanities, technology, life science), and topic used in the placement exam (language acquisition, ethics, trade barriers) for 1,125 international students. Controlling for general English-language ability as measured by the TOEFL, use this data set to investigate whether the topic of the placement test influences the test results. In particular, do students who receive a topic in their major field of study have an advantage over others? Majors in business were thought to have an advantage when

Table 26.10   Predicted Frequencies of Program Types for Linear Discriminant Analysis (DA) and Multinomial Logistic Regression (LR)

		Predicted Frequency			
Program Type	Observed Frequency	DA—Achieve	DA—All Main	LR—Achieve	LR—All Main
General	145	99	132	0	40
Academic	308	292	284	429	398
Vocational	147	209	184	171	162
Correction classification rate:		.52	.52	.58	.60

the topic was trade, and those in humanities might have had an advantage when the topic was language acquisition or ethics. Create a variable that tests this specific hypothesis.

NOTE

1. See Chapter 21 (this volume) for details on Poisson regression.

REFERENCES

Agresti, A. (2002). *Categorical data analysis* (2nd ed.). New York: John Wiley.

Agresti, A. (2007). *An introduction to categorical data analysis* (2nd ed.). New York: John Wiley.

Albert, A., & Anderson, J. A. (1984). On the existence of maximum likelihood estimates in logistic regression models. *Biometrika, 71,* 1–10.

Dillon, W. R., & Goldstein, M. (1984). *Multivariate analysis: Methods and applications.* New York: John Wiley.

Fahrmeir, L., & Tutz, G. (2001). *Multivariate statistical modeling based on generalized linear models.* New York: Springer.

Fay, M. P. (2002). Measuring a binary response's range of influence in logistic regression. *The American Statistician, 56,* 5–9.

Hosmer, D. W., & Lemeshow, S. (2000). *Applied logistic regression* (2nd ed.). New York: John Wiley.

Insightful Corp. (2007). S-Plus, Version 8 [Computer software]. Seattle, WA: Author. Available from http://www.insightful.com

Johnson, R. A., & Wichern, D. W. (1998). *Applied multivariate statistical analysis* (4th ed.). Englewood Cliffs, NJ: Prentice Hall.

Lauritzen, S. L. (1996). *Graphical models.* New York: Oxford University Press.

Lauritzen, S. L., & Wermuth, N. (1989). Graphical models for associations between variables, some of which are qualitative and some of which are quantitative. *Annals of Statistics, 17,* 31–57.

Lee, H. K., & Anderson, C. J. (in press). Validity and topic generality of a writing performance test. *Language Testing.*

Lesaffre, E., & Albert, A. (1989). Multiple-group logistic regression diagnostics. *Applied Statistics, 38,* 425–440.

Long, J. S. (1997). *Regression models for categorical and limited dependent variables.* Thousand Oaks, CA: Sage.

Maydeu-Olivares, A., & Joe, J. (2005). Limited and full-information estimation and goodness-of-fit testing in 2^n contingency tables: A unified framework. *Journal of the American Statistical Association, 100,* 1009–1020.

Powers, D. A., & Xie, Y. (2000). *Statistical methods for categorical data analysis.* San Diego: Academic Press.

Pregibon, D. (1981). Logistic regression diagnostics. *Annals of Statistics, 9,* 705–724.

R Development Core Team. (2007). R: A language and environment for statistical computing [Computer software]. Vienna, Austria: Author. Available from http://www.R-project.org

SAS Institute, Inc. (2003). SAS/STAT software, Version 9.1 [Computer software]. Cary, NC: Author. Available from http://www.sas.com

SPSS. (2006). SPSS for Windows, Release 15 [Computer software]. Chicago: Author. Available from http://www.spss.com

StataCorp LP. (2007). Stata Version 10 [Computer software]. College Station, TX: Author. Available from http://www.stata.com/products

Tatsuoka, M. M., & Lohnes, P. R. (1988). *Multivariate analysis: Techniques for educational and psychological research* (2nd ed.). New York: Macmillan.

27

ENHANCING ACCURACY IN RESEARCH USING REGRESSION MIXTURE ANALYSIS

CODY S. DING

Conventional regression analysis is typically used in social science research. Usually, such an analysis implicitly assumes that a common set of regression parameter estimates captures the population characteristics represented in the sample. In some situations, however, this implicit assumption may not be realistic, and the sample may contain several subpopulations such as high math achievers and low math achievers. In these cases, conventional regression models may provide biased estimates since the parameter estimates are constrained to be the same across subpopulations. This chapter advocates the applications of regression mixture models, also known as latent class regression analysis, in educational and social sciences research. Regression mixture analysis is more flexible than conventional regression analysis in that latent classes in the data can be identified and regression parameter estimates can vary within each latent class, which enhances prediction accuracy. An illustration of regression mixture analysis is provided based on an authentic data. The strengths and limitations of the regression mixture models are discussed in the context of educational research.

Typical ordinary least squares (OLS) regression analyses are common in educational and social science research. Typically, regression analysis is used to investigate the relationships between a dependent variable (either continuous or categorical if using logistic regression) and a set of independent variables based on a sample from a particular population. Often, the particular interest is placed on assessing the effect of each independent variable on the dependent variable, and such an effect is considered as the average effect value across all subjects in the sample. For example, if math achievement scores of 500 students are regressed on a measure of their motivation, the value for the slope or the regression coefficient quantifies the average change in math achievement across all 500 students for one unit change in motivation. The problem is that these 500 students are treated as one homogeneous group regarding motivation influences on math achievement, and the implicit assumption is that these students are from the same population with similar characteristics. What if the relationship between these two variables is different between different groups of students in some way that is not explicitly modeled?

410

These (often interesting) differences would be masked.

This chapter describes the use of the regression mixture model as a tool to study the relationship between a dependent variable and a set of independent variables by taking into consideration unobserved population heterogeneity, which can enhance the prediction accuracy.

BACKGROUND

In any standard statistical textbook, a general regression model can be written as

$$y_i = \beta_0 + \beta_1 x_1 + \beta_2 x_2 + \ldots + \beta_k x_k + \varepsilon_i, \quad (1)$$

where β_0 is the intercept, β_k is the regression slope or coefficient for a given independent variable k, and ε_i is the error term for individual i. Equation 1 has one key feature. It assumes that all individuals are drawn from a single population with common population parameters.

However, when a sample consists of various groups of individuals, such as males and females, or different intervention groups, regression analysis can be performed to examine whether the effects of independent variables on a dependent variable differ across groups, in terms of either intercept or slope. These groups can be considered from different populations (e.g., male population or female population), and the population is considered heterogeneous in that these subpopulations may require different population parameters to adequately capture their characteristics. Since this source of population heterogeneity is based on observed group memberships such as gender, the data can be analyzed using regression models by taking into consideration multiple groups. In the methodology literature, subpopulations that can be identified beforehand are called groups (e.g., Lubke & Muthén, 2005; Muthén, 2001).

In this chapter, nevertheless, special attention is devoted to the situations in which population heterogeneity is unobserved. In other words, group membership of individuals in the population is latent (McCutcheon, 1987; Waller & Meehl, 1998). For example, students may differ with respect to socioemotional development, and they may belong to either of two

qualitatively different types, such as children with high math self-efficacy and children with low math self-efficacy. If we were to study the effect of socioemotional development on student math achievement using a regression model as represented in Equation 1, we would evaluate the average values of intercept and slope (or rate of change) across these two types of students; that is, there is one regression line that describes the relationships between student socioemotional development and math achievement. In this typical regression analysis, the investigator assumes that the sample is from a homogeneous population and that the common parameter estimates are adequate to depict the population characteristics represented in the sample. In other words, the conventional regression model assumes that all individuals belong to a single population, and *independent variables have the same influence on the dependent variable for all individuals* (often not a tenable assumption). The variance that cannot be explained by this common model is treated simply as random error. For example, Figure 27.1 shows the association between the teacher's rating on the child's math proficiency level and his or her math test score based on a large data set (the data will be discussed below). It seems likely that there may be some distinct subgroups in these data, especially when national representative data are involved. If we ignore such heterogeneity in the data, the regression model in Equation 1 may provide biased estimates for the data at hand. For instance, it is possible that children with a larger math gain may be more influenced by math self-efficacy with respect to their proficiency level than by school environment, while children with low math gain may be more influenced by both math self-efficacy and school environment. Thus, the assumption of population homogeneity may not be realistic. As another example, the variation in reading development among poor readers may be affected more by family environment, whereas the variation in reading development for good readers may be more influenced by teaching methods or vice versa. Moreover, the variances of the residuals may also differ for these two groups of students, and such group differences in variance may contribute to the unequal variance across combinations of the levels of the independent variables.

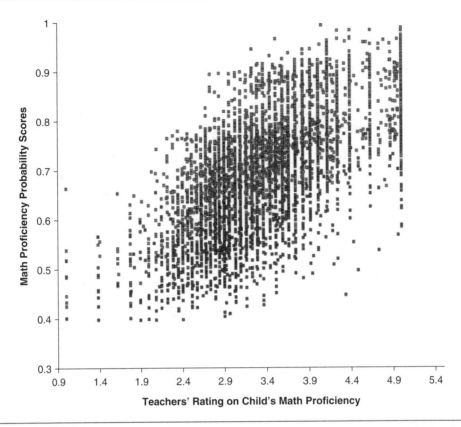

Figure 27.1   Scatterplot between children's math proficiency probability scores and the teacher's rating of the child's math self-concept of proficiency. Different shapes may suggest the possible existence of different subpopulations or latent classes of children in the sample.

LINEAR REGRESSION MIXTURE MODEL

This chapter focuses on applications of the linear regression mixture model in situations where population heterogeneity is unobserved (i.e., latent class) and observed group variables such as gender are incorporated in the analysis as covariates. Regression mixture models,[1] also known as latent class regression analysis (Andersen, 2004; Bouwmeester, Sijtsma, & Vermunt, 2004; Vermunt & Magidson, 2005), are a part of a general framework of finite mixture models (Lubke & Muthén, 2005; Muthén, 2001; Muthén & Muthén, 2000; Nagin & Tremblay, 2001; Vermunt & Magidson, 2002) and can be viewed as a combination of the conventional regression model and the classic latent class model (Lazarsfeld & Henry, 1968; McCutcheon, 1987). These models are used to identify the relationships between the dependent variable and a set of independent variables

along with the number of latent classes that best fit the data and to test potential predictors for a given latent class. Unlike conventional regression analysis, which assumes that the regression function in the sample arises from a single multivariate normal distribution, the linear regression mixture model allows for heterogeneous regression functions by modeling a mixture of distinct multivariate normal distributions, each corresponding to a latent class. Individuals within each latent class share the same regression function.

Thus, regression mixture analysis relaxes the single population assumption to allow for parameter differences across unobserved subpopulations. This is accomplished by using latent classes, which implies that individuals vary around different regression functions. For example, in a study of the factors that may influence student math achievement, a researcher may include student self-efficacy, motivation, teaching methods, and classroom size as independent variables. The starting point of performing regression mixture analysis is first to identify the number of latent classes that best fit the data. Then the influences of independent variables on the dependent variable can be examined within each latent class. It may be possible that for a given latent class, only self-efficacy has any effect on math achievement, while for a second latent class, math achievement may be influenced by teaching methods and classroom size. Combined use of latent classes with regression models results in a very flexible analysis framework. On the other hand, certain unique issues of regression mixture analysis deserve some special attention:

1. *Deciding the number of latent classes.* Since the linear regression mixture model is a part of finite mixture models (B. O. Muthén, 2001), multiple criteria are available to evaluate the number of latent classes for regression analysis because different indices provide information about different aspects of model fit. Comparisons between competing models assess relative fit to the data. For instance, the likelihood ratio test (Lo, Mendell, & Rubin, 2001) can be used to compare regression mixture models with differing numbers of latent classes; a significant chi-square value (e.g., $p < .05$) indicates that the specified model is unlikely to be generated by a model with one less class. Also, selection of a final model can be based on information criteria, such as the Akaike information criterion (AIC; Akaike, 1973) or the Bayesian information criterion (Schwarz, 1978). Lower observed criterion values are indicative of improved fit. Another index is Entropy (Ramaswamy, DeSarbo, Reibstein, & Robinson, 1993), which assesses the classification accuracy of placing people into classes based on their model-based probabilities. It ranges from 0.00 to 1.00, with higher values indicating better classification. Also, proportion of classification errors, which is the opposite of Entropy, is used as well (Bouwmeester et al., 2004). It should be pointed out that although a number of model fit statistics can be used to evaluate a plausible model, the choice of a final model also depends on considerations of substantive issues, previous research results, model parsimony, consistency with theory, and so on. One should note that it is difficult to identify the exact number of latent classes that represent true population heterogeneity (Bouwmeester

et al., 2004). Model selection is a complex issue (Burnham & Anderson, 2002), and so far there is no consensus regarding the best criteria for determining the number of classes in the mixture modeling literature.

2. *Interaction between categorical and continuous variables.* In a conventional regression analysis, one often examines whether the intercept or slope of a regression model is common among different groups (e.g., gender or ethnic groups) when such grouping variables are included in the model. This is usually specified in terms of interaction between categorical variables and continuous variables in an analysis.[2] In regression mixture analysis, however, the observed group membership variables are specified as covariates rather than as predictors, and they are used to predict the latent class membership. In other words, the formation of the latent classes is expected to be influenced by the covariates. Thus, the power of regression mixture analysis is that the specific behavior patterns as measured by the dependent variable can be distinguished by a particular class, and comparison of regression models across various classes can be examined with respect to the influence of covariates.

3. *Curvilinear effects.* As in conventional regression analysis, curvilinear effects can be modeled by adding powered terms of a certain predictor.[3] For example, if a curvilinear relationship (e.g., quadratic shape) between reading achievement and hours spent on reading is hypothesized based on previous results, a quadratic term for hours spent on reading can be added to the regression mixture model. Then one can examine whether such a quadratic shape holds across different latent classes of individuals.

4. *Outliers and equal variance.* Two key assumptions of conventional regression analysis are equal variance and being free from outliers.[4] When outliers occur, one simple strategy can be to delete them, provided that these "outliers" are from a different population. With regression mixture analysis, these outliers may be considered as members of some latent classes. This is one of the advantages of regression mixture analysis when the population is heterogeneous. For example, there may be some slower learners in a sample under study who may have a much

lower math score than the rest of the "normal" students. Parameter estimates from regular regression analysis may be biased when a common set of parameters is estimated for all students. But these slower learners can be identified as a distinct latent class in regression mixture analysis, thus leading to a more accurate prediction of math achievement for this class of students as well as that of other classes. Moreover, since individuals in each latent class are more likely to be homogeneous with respect to certain personal characteristics, the likelihood of equal variance across different values of predictors is also increased within each class. This possibility of violating these two assumptions, which is sometimes difficult to deal with, can be alleviated.

Through the above brief discussion of those four issues, one can see some advantages of regression mixture models as well as unsolved problems. But the regression mixture model is a very general and flexible model that can be applied to a wide range of behavioral phenomena. A basic linear regression mixture model can be conceptualized as follows:[5]

$$y_{i(c)} = \beta_{0(c)} + \beta_{1(c)}x_1 + \beta_{2(c)}x_2 + \quad (2)$$
$$\dots + \beta_{k(c)}x_k + \varepsilon_{i(c)}.$$

Equation 2 has the appearance of a conventional regression model except for the subscript c ($c = 1, 2, \dots, C$), which indicates that the parameters may vary around different latent classes. In other words, individuals within each latent class c have the same parameter estimates, which, however, differ across latent classes. Equation 2 says that a dependent variable can be predicted as a function of predictor variables, and a C category latent class variable c is included, with each category representing a homogeneous subpopulation having identical regression coefficients. In essence, this represents another way of modeling Group × Predictor interactions that many of us attempt to model in conventional regression.[6]

Although a few software programs can perform regression mixture analysis, the major computer programs for such an analysis are Mplus (Muthén & Muthén, 2001), GLLAMM (Skrondal & Rabe-Hesketh, 2004), and LatentGold (Vermunt & Magidson, 2005). In the following section, the LatentGold 4.0 program was used to demonstrate the linear regression mixture analysis based on a real data set.

ILLUSTRATION OF REGRESSION MIXTURE ANALYSIS

To illustrate these points, I present an example of how relationships between independent variables and a dependent variable in the potential presence of population heterogeneity may be investigated with the linear regression mixture model. The latent class variable c is used to model unknown heterogeneity, whereas observed group membership variables that are known to introduce heterogeneity are treated as covariates. In linear regression mixture analysis, one first needs to specify the number of latent classes. In the model estimation process, the parameters of the model are estimated, and the posterior probabilities with which each individual belongs to each of the classes are computed. The results include the model parameters such as within-class regression coefficients, within-class and an overall R^2, within-class error variance, and so on, as well as the posterior class probabilities for each individual.

Research Questions. To illustrate linear regression mixture analysis in comparison to conventional regression analysis, this example is framed around the following research questions:

1. What is the relationship between children's fifth-grade math achievement, children's math self-concept, and teachers' rating of children's math proficiency, approaches to learning, and self-control? This research question addressed the issues of (a) whether self-reported math self-concept is predictive of children's math achievement, (b) how predictive teacher judgments of students' academic performance are, and (c) whether teachers' assessment of children's adaptive behaviors and approach to learning predicts children's math achievement.

Marsh, Relich, and Smith (1983) found that math self-concept was most highly correlated with math achievement ($r = .55$). In addition, it has been found that teacher judgment of children's academic competence has concurrent or predictive validity. For example, Hoge and

Butcher (1984) found a correlation coefficient of .71 between the teacher's judgment and the student's actual scores on standardized tests. In the studies they reviewed, Hoge and Coladarci (1989) indicated that judgment accuracy ranged from .28 to .92, with a median correlation of .66. Thus, it would be interesting to replicate such a finding using a national representative sample of actual children.

Regarding teachers' rating of children's social competence, extensive research has taken place regarding the importance of social competence and the skills that contribute to that competence. Social competence has been found to be a significant predictor of academic achievement from kindergarten through sixth grade (Clark, Gresham, & Elliot, 1985). On a study of fifth graders, Walker, Stieber, and Eisert (1991) have found teachers' ratings of social skills to be the best predictor of future academic achievement, school adjustment, and delinquency in the next 3-year period. Therefore, teachers' ratings on the approach to learning and self-control were used to see whether some of the findings could be replicated.

2. Do children in different latent classes vary in terms of children's gender and race? In this research question, we attempted to examine whether children's gender and racial background were associated with latent classes in the data.

It is important to note that many of the variables may be related to children's math achievement, and they are not explored in this investigation. The variables examined here were just a few of the variables that can or should be examined in the data and were selected to demonstrate the range of information that may be obtained from the linear regression mixture analysis and may help shape the design for future studies. Readers, however, are cautioned not to draw definitive causal inferences based on the results presented in this example but rather to focus on the proposed analysis paradigm.

Data. The data used in this illustrative analysis were from the Early Childhood Longitudinal Study (ECLS), an ongoing study by the U.S. Department of Education, National Center for Education Statistics, that focuses on children's early school experiences beginning with kindergarten (Tourangeau, Nord, Lê, Pollack, & Atkins-Burnett, 2006). The study follows a nationally representative sample of children from kindergarten through fifth grade. The sample reflected all children from various racial and language backgrounds. Sampling for the ECLS was based on a dual-frame, multistage sampling design, with 100 primary sampling units (PSUs). For simplicity, only the data collected during 2004 from the fifth graders were in this study. The sample size in the current analysis was 1,342 children, which included 650 males and 692 females. Among the total analysis sample of children, 797 were White, 126 were Black, 230 were Hispanic, 141 were Asian, and 48 were multiracial.

Measures. In the present analysis, four measures were used as independent variables. They were the following:

Self-Description Questionnaire—Math Self-Concept (Marsh, 1990). This measure assesses how children think and feel about themselves in terms of math competence. This scale includes eight items on math grades, the difficulty of math work, and interest in and enjoyment of math, with the score scale ranging from 1 to 4. The analysis used the average score of each participant.

Academic Rating Scale—Math. This is the teachers' ratings of children's academic performance in math. Teachers were asked to rate each child's proficiency in the following areas: number concepts, measurement, operation, geometry, math strategies, and beginning algebraic thinking, with the score scale ranging from 1 to 5. The analysis used the average score of each participant.

Social Rating Scale—Approach to Learning. This is the teachers' judgment of children's social competence. The approach to learning scale measures behaviors that affect the ease with which children can benefit from the learning environment. It includes six items that rate the child's attentiveness, task persistence, eagerness to learn, learning independence, flexibility, organization, and following of classroom rules, with the score scale ranging from 1 to 4. The analysis used the average score of each participant.

Social Rating Scale—Self-Control. This measure has four items that rate the child's ability to control behavior by respecting the property rights of others, controlling temper, accepting peer ideas for group activities, and responding appropriately to peer pressure, with the score scale ranging from 1 to 4. The analysis used the average score of each participant.

In all above measures, the scores were coded positively, with high scores indicating higher self-concept and higher teacher rating on academic and social competence. The reported reliability for these independent variables ranged from .79 to .92 (Tourangeau et al., 2006).

The dependent variable used was a composite math proficiency probability score that was computed as an average across nine math skill levels: count/number, relative size, ordinality/sequence, add/subtract, multiply/divide, place value, rate and measurement, fractions, and area/volume. The probability scores were from 0.00 to 1.00, with a larger probability score indicating an overall higher achievement across these math skill levels.

In addition, children's gender and race were included as covariates. They were used to increase the classification accuracy of individuals into each latent class. In this chapter, children's race was represented in five categories: White, Black, Hispanic, Asian (which includes Pacific Islanders and American Indians), and multiracial.

Fitting the Linear Regression Mixture Model. Since the scores of the dependent variable used were continuous, the appropriate regression mixture model was a linear analysis. The analysis was exploratory with respect to the sources of latent population heterogeneity. Commonly, a key interest in an exploration of population heterogeneity is to determine the number of latent classes that best fit the data.

Regression mixture models ranging from a one-class latent model to a four-class mixture model were tested using LatentGold 4.0. In all of these models, the dependent variable was math proficiency probability scores, and the same set of independent variables was used, with child's gender and race as covariates. Among these four models, we sought a model with the smallest AIC value and a large overall R^2.

Table 27.1 shows the evaluation statistics that were used to choose a final model. Although a four-class model had the smallest AIC value, the difference from the AIC value of a three-class regression model was less than 10 points, indicating that a three-class regression model was also plausible (Burnham & Anderson, 2002). In addition, overall R^2 for the three-class regression model was only 3% less than that of the four-class regression model, and the proportion of classification errors increased again after the three-class regression model. It was interesting to notice that the model with one class had the largest AIC in comparison with other models, which suggested that population homogeneity was not likely to be a realistic assumption in the sample. On the basis of the evaluation of fit statistics, the three-class linear regression model was selected as optimal. In this three-class model, regression coefficients and error variance were class dependent; that is, they were freely estimated without any equality constraints.

Results. Table 27.2 provides the regression coefficients for each of the three latent classes, along with the estimated class proportions and the mean math probability scores. Table 27.3 shows the classification profile information. It can be seen that for Class 1, which consisted of 57% of the sample, math achievement was significantly associated with only the teacher's rating on math competence. This variable only accounted for about 49% of the variance in math achievement. What this implied was that for individuals within this class, teacher judgment of these children's math competence was statistically accurate in predicting their actual achievement. Other information provided in the analysis, as shown under "Covariates" in Table 27.2, was that male children

Table 27.1   Model Fit Statistics for Four Latent Class Models

Number of Classes	AIC Value	R^2	% of Classification Errors
1	11,278.37	.44	0.00
2	10,972.97	.77	0.15
3	10,951.36	.85	0.25
4	10,947.42	.88	0.30

NOTE: AIC = Akaike information criterion.

were more likely to be members of Class 1 than were female children, and White children were also more likely to be members of Class 1 than were children of other ethnic backgrounds. The class proportion size for Class 1 suggested (as shown in Table 27.3) that 57% were male children and 43% were female children. White children constituted 82% of Class 1 individuals.

For individuals in latent Class 2, their math achievement was significantly associated with teacher rating on math competence and on approach to learning. These two variables accounted for about 63% of variances in math achievement. Thus, it seemed that children with higher math achievement had a higher teacher rating on math competence and approach to learning. This class consisted of 39% of the total sample, of which 61% were female children and 39% were male children. Class 2 also had 33% White children, 18% Black children, 29% Hispanic children, 16% Asian children, and 4% multiracial children (see Table 27.3).

Table 27.2   Parameter Estimates and Model-Based Class Size

	Class 1	Class 2	Class 3	β[a]
Class proportion size (%)	57	39	4	
Mean math probability scores	.75	.63	.66	
	Regression Coefficients			
Math self-concept	0.006	0.005	0.034*	0.006*
	(0.005)	(0.005)	(0.008)	(0.003)
Academic Rating Scale—Math	0.084**	0.097**	0.065*	0.089**
	(0.006)	(0.005)	(0.017)	(0.004)
Social Rating Scale—Learning	0.015	0.026*	0.028	0.023**
	(0.008)	(0.006)	(0.078)	(0.006)
Social Rating Scale—Self-Control	0.005	−0.016	0.22**	−0.0003
	(0.007)	(0.015)	(0.033)	(0.006)
Error variance	0.005**	0.003**	0.001	0.065
R^2	.49	.63	.94	.44
Covariates				
Gender				
Male	0.519[a]	−0.044	−0.475	
Female	−0.519	0.044	0.475	
Race				
White	2.320[b]	0.409	−2.730[b]	
Black	−0.525	0.401	0.123	
Hispanic	−0.196	0.168	0.027	
Asian	−1.234	−0.351	1.586	
Multiracial	−0.363	−0.628	0.992	

NOTE: Standard errors are in parentheses.

a. Indicates regression coefficients are from conventional regression analysis.

b. Indicates regression coefficients significantly differ from zero at $p < .05$.

$*p < .05. **p < .01.$

Table 27.3   Covariates Associated With Latent Class Membership (in Percentages)

	Class 1	Class 2	Class 3
Covariates			
Gender			
Male	56.63	38.81	25.36
Female	43.37	61.19	74.64
Race			
White	82.21	32.62	0.81
Black	3.43	18.47	7.96
Hispanic	8.99	28.87	14.84
Asian	3.05	15.63	62.32
Multiracial	2.32	4.40	14.07

For Class 3, children's math achievement was significantly associated with children's math self-concept, teacher rating of math competence, and self-control. Children with high math scores thus tended to report a higher math self-concept and had a higher teacher rating for math competence and self-control. There was some information about children in Class 3 that was interesting to note: (a) About 95% of the variance in math achievement was accounted for by these three variables; (b) this class consisted of about 4% of the total sample, of which 75% were female children; (c) among these 4% of the children, 62% were Asian, 15% were Hispanic, 14% were multiracial, 8% were Black, and about 1% were White (see Table 27.3); and (d) White children were less likely to be members of this class ($\beta = -2.73$, $p < .05$).

To contrast the linear regression mixture model with the conventional regression analysis, a conventional regression analysis was performed with the same dependent variable and independent variables while controlling for gender and race. The results are shown in the last column of Table 27.2. It can be seen that children's math achievement was significantly related to their math self-concept, teacher rating on math competence, and teacher rating of approach to learning. Teacher rating of children's self-control was not significantly related to math achievement. On the surface, the conclusion could be that, on average, children who had high math scores tended to report high self-concept in math and had higher teacher ratings of math competence and approach to

learning. However, it was important to point out that although it almost looked to the readers that the conventional regression model provided a "superior" analysis since three predictors were statistically significant, the key issue was that each class had its own unique predictor pattern rather than a number of statistically significant predictors. Thus, the results from conventional regression analysis were biased since it failed to consider population heterogeneity in the data. It was inappropriate to compare what type of analyses (i.e., regression vs. regression mixture) would be better on the basis of the number of statistically significant predictors.

Conclusion. To address the research question regarding relationship between children's math achievement with math self-concept and teacher judgment of math competence and of social competence, the findings indicated that teacher judgment of math competence was statistically accurate in predicting children's math performance across all three latent classes. This was a quite robust finding and replicated the previous findings about accuracy of the teacher judgment (e.g., Hoge & Butcher, 1984). However, children's math self-concept and teacher ratings of their approach to learning and self-control were statistically significantly associated with math achievement only for distinct subgroups of children. That is, this relationship depended on types of children in the population. Thus, the previous findings concerning this association were replicated only for some children, particularly children of specific ethnic groups. For instance, teacher rating of self-control was found to be statistically significantly related to math performance for children who consisted of only 4% of the sample, of whom 62% were Asian children and 75% were female children. It was interesting to note that if the conclusions were based on the results from conventional regression analysis, then the previous findings would be replicated, in that the children's math self-concept would be a strong predicator of actual math performance (Marsh et al., 1983), social competence, and approach to learning; however, self-control would not be predicative of math performance (e.g., Clark et al., 1985) for "average" children. Population heterogeneity in the sample, therefore, would be completely overlooked, and valuable information regarding differential subgroup performance would be lost in explaining mathematics achievement.

DISCUSSION

Regression mixture models are a tool to investigate population heterogeneity. As anticipated, this application of regression mixture modeling to an actual data set indicated that multiple latent classes might be embedded with the single regression functional form. Compared with conventional regression analysis, which assumes one equation would fit all individuals, a regression mixture analysis can provide a detailed description of subpopulations of individuals within a sample. In the illustration, the conventional regression analysis revealed only average results across all children, the error variance was quite large, and R^2 was quite small in comparison to the results of linear regression mixture analysis. For instance, the error variance was close to zero, and R^2 was .94 for Class 3, indicating a good fit between the model and the data from these individuals. In contrast, the conventional regression model had an inferior model-data fit. Thus, regression mixture models may improve predictability because the individual differences are systematically classified to form homogeneous groups. The regression mixture analysis resulted in subpopulations with specific patterns of regression function and with differing proportions of female and ethnic children.

It should be pointed out that regression mixture modeling is a different analytical technique for studying population heterogeneity than multiple group modeling. The purpose of regression mixture analysis is to identify differing regression functions across latent classes, and such an approach is appropriate if the interest is in detecting and characterizing the relationships among variables according to subpopulations of individuals. The observed grouping variables such as gender may be used as covariates to help predict the latent class membership. For instance, in the illustration, Class 1 is predicted by gender and race, while Class 2 is not predicted by either grouping variables. Thus, the latent class has a different interpretation, and it is used to describe a different kind of heterogeneity in the sample. But one should realize that classification of individuals into latent classes is model dependent, and it is not intrinsic to the individuals in the sample (Lubke & Muthén, 2005). On the other hand, the purpose of multiple-group regression analysis is to compare these groups with respect to their regression functions, and the observed group membership is an intrinsic characteristic of the individual (e.g., individuals are either male or female).

Regression mixture analysis is not without its limitations. First is the determination of the proper number of latent classes in the data. As Bauer and Curran (2003) suggested, mixture modeling can detect population heterogeneity as well as distribution skewness. If there exists nonnormality within class, nonnormality of observed variables, or nonlinearity, the latent class may simply describe the skewness and may not reflect latent classes of individuals in the sample. Thus, in addition to ensuring the normality and linearity assumptions, one should also consider at a conceptual level whether an additional class is providing meaningful information about the heterogeneity.

Second, a model identification index such as AIC may not provide sufficient evidence for models of heterogeneity (Bauer & Curran, 2004). There is no consensus, as discussed previously, regarding which model identification index can be used to select "best" models. Therefore, ambiguity in model selection will continue. In this chapter, linear regression mixture analysis is used as one possible way of exploring the data; such an approach is similar to conventional exploratory regression analysis, and results should be regarded as preliminary. Independent replication of the study would be essential for generalizing the results.

Readers should keep these limitations in mind when applying regression mixture models. But it seems that regression mixture models are a useful tool and can be used to model heterogeneity in regression function, thus leading to improved regression solutions. In a sense, conventional regression models are a special case of regression mixture models where only one class is assumed and aggregate regression function is concerned. However, it would be necessary to investigate this constraint that a set of common parameter estimates is sufficient to capture the population characteristics. Regression mixture models, on the other hand, place the regression structure in a much more flexible way.

NOTES

1. It should be noted that there are various types of regression mixture models (e.g., Vermunt & Dijk,

2001), but this chapter will only focus on the linear regression mixture model. There are also different terms used for what I will refer to as the regression mixture model, including *latent regression analysis* (e.g., Andersen, 2004), the *mixture regression model* (e.g., Zhu & Zhang, 2004), or the *finite mixture regression model* (e.g., Grun & Leisch, 2004).

2. Editor's note: For more information on testing interactions in multiple regression, the interested reader may refer to Aiken and West (1996).

3. Editor's note: For more information on testing curvilinear relationships in multiple regression formats, the interested reader may refer to Aiken and West (1996).

4. Readers interested in outliers should refer to Chapter 14 (this volume) on the benefits of outlier removal, as well as Chapter 18 (this volume) on robust methods.

5. Technically speaking, formulation of the regression mixture model is mathematically much more complicated than that in Equation 2. For the purpose of simplicity, Equation 2 shows that the conceptual idea of a multiple regression function is estimated for a number of classes, including influence of covariates.

6. As mentioned earlier, different types of regression mixture models exist. Depending on the scale type of the dependent variable, various regression mixture models can be estimated. For instance, if a dependent variable is continuous, the linear regression mixture model can be performed, as shown in Equation 2. On the other hand, if the dependent variable is dichotomous or nominal, binary or multinomial logistic regression mixture analysis can be formulated and performed, which would require a substantially different model. Moreover, for models containing $C > 1$ latent classes, covariates such as gender can be included in the model to improve classification of each case into the most likely class; that is, covariates can be used to predict the latent class membership.

REFERENCES

Aiken, L. S., & West, S. G. (1996). *Multiple regression: Testing and interpreting interactions.* Thousand Oaks, CA: Sage.

Akaike, H. (1973). Information theory as an extension of the maximum likelihood principle. In B. N. Petrov & F. Csaki (Eds.), *Second International Symposium on Information Theory* (pp. 267–281). Budapest: Akademiai Kiado.

Andersen, E. B. (2004). Latent regression analysis based on the rating scale model. *Psychology Science, 46*(2), 209–226.

Bauer, D. J., & Curran, P. J. (2003). Distributional assumptions of growth mixture models: Implications for overextraction of latent trajectory classes. *Psychological Methods, 8,* 338–363.

Bauer, D. J., & Curran, P. J. (2004). The integration of continuous and discrete latent variable models: Potential problems and promising opportunities. *Psychological Methods, 9,* 3–29.

Bouwmeester, S., Sijtsma, K., & Vermunt, J. K. (2004). Latent class regression analysis for describing cognitive developmental phenomena: An application to transitive reasoning. *European Journal of Developmental Psychology, 1*(1), 67–86.

Burnham, K. P., & Anderson, D. R. (2002). *Model selection and multimodel inference: A practical information-theoretic approach* (2nd ed.). New York: Springer.

Clark, L., Gresham, F. M., & Elliot, S. N. (1985). Development and validation of a social skills assessment measure: The RROSS-C. *Journal of Psychoeducational Assessment, 4,* 347–356.

Grun, B., & Leisch, F. (2004, August). *Bootstrapping finite mixture models.* Paper presented at the COMPSTAT 2004 Symposium, Prague.

Hoge, R. D., & Butcher, R. (1984). Analysis of teacher judgments of pupil achievement level. *Journal of Educational Psychology, 76,* 777–781.

Hoge, R. D., & Coladarci, T. (1989). Teacher-based judgments of academic achievement: A review of the literature. *Review of Educational Research, 59,* 297–313.

Lazarsfeld, P. F., & Henry, N. W. (1968). *Latent structure analysis.* Boston: Houghton Mifflin.

Lo, Y., Mendell, N., & Rubin, D. B. (2001). Testing the number of components in a normal mixture. *Biometrika, 88,* 767–778.

Lubke, G. H., & Muthén, B. (2005). Investigating population heterogeneity with factor mixture models. *Psychological Methods, 10*(1), 21–39.

Marsh, H. W. (1990). *Self-description questionnaire manual.* Campbelltown N.S.W., Australia: University of Western Sydney, Macarthur.

Marsh, H. W., Relich, J., & Smith, I. D. (1983). Self-concept: The construct validity of interpretations based upon the SDQ. *Journal of Personality and Social Psychology, 45,* 173–187.

McCutcheon, A. L. (1987). *Latent class analysis.* Thousand Oaks, CA: Sage.

Muthén, B. O. (2001). Second-generation structural equation modeling with a combination of categorical and continuous latent variables: New opportunities for latent class/latent growth modeling. In L. M. Collins & A. Sayer (Eds.), *New methods for the analysis of change* (pp. 291–322). Washington, DC: American Psychological Association.

Muthén, B. O., & Muthén, L. K. (2000). Integrating person-centered and variable-centered analyses: Growth mixture modeling with latent trajectory classes. *Alcoholism: Clinical and Experimental Research, 24,* 882–891.

Muthén, L. K., & Muthén, B. O. (2001). *Mplus user's guide.* Los Angeles: Author.

Nagin, D., & Tremblay, R. E. (2001). Analyzing developmental trajectories of distinct but related behaviors: A group-based method. *Psychological Methods, 6,* 18–34.

Ramaswamy, V., DeSarbo, W., Reibstein, D., & Robinson, W. (1993). An empirical pooling approach for estimating marketing mix elasticities with PIMS data. *Marketing Science, 12,* 103–124.

Schwarz, G. (1978). Estimating the dimension of a model. *Annals of Statistics, 6,* 461–464.

Skrondal, A., & Rabe-Hesketh, S. (2004). *Generalized latent variable modeling: Multilevel, longitudinal, and structural equation models.* Boca Raton, FL: Chapman & Hall/CRC.

Tourangeau, K., Nord, C., Lê, T., Pollack, J. M., & Atkins-Burnett, S. (2006). *Early Childhood Longitudinal Study, Kindergarten Class of 1998–99 (ECLS-K), combined user's manual for the ECLS-K fifth-grade data files and electronic codebooks (NCES 2006-032).* Washington, DC: U.S. Department of Education, National Center for Education Statistics.

Vermunt, J. K., & Dijk, L. V. (2001). A nonparametric random-coefficients approach: The latent class regression model. *Multilevel Modeling Newsletter, 13,* 6–13.

Vermunt, J. K., & Magidson, J. (2002). Latent class cluster analysis. In J. A. Hagenaars & L. M. Allan (Eds.), *Applied latent class analysis* (pp. 89–106). Cambridge, UK: Cambridge University Press.

Vermunt, J. K., & Magidson, J. (2005). *Latent Gold 4.0 user's guide.* Belmont, MA: Statistical Innovations, Inc.

Walker, H. M., Stieber, S., & Eisert, D. (1991). Teacher ratings of adolescent social skills: Psychometric characteristics and factorial replicability across age-grade ranges. *School Psychology Reivew, 20*(2), 301–314.

Waller, N., & Meehl, P. E. (1998). *Multivariate taxometric procedures: Distinguishing types from continua.* Thousand Oaks, CA: Sage.

Zhu, H. T., & Zhang, H. P. (2004). Hypothesis testing in mixture regression models. *JRSS-B, 66,* 3–16.

28

MEDIATION, MODERATION, AND THE STUDY OF INDIVIDUAL DIFFERENCES

A. ALEXANDER BEAUJEAN

A century ago, psychology was a young field, greatly influenced by the physiological tradition of Hemholtz and Weber, that looked at psychological phenomena in an experimental fashion, and "only that which could be directly observed and studied under controlled laboratory conditions was deemed worthy of study" (Minton & Schneider, 1980, p. 7). Any individual variation in these experiments was just considered error.

Galton, with his precocious nature and Darwinian influence, sought to apply "the principles of variation, selection, and adaptation to the study of human individuals" through his study of quantitative genetics, mental chronometry, and statistics (Anastasi & Foley, 1949, p. 9). Likewise, Cattell (1890) sought to assess individual differences in his "mental tests," which he administered to a generation of freshmen at Columbia College. It was the work of Binet and Henri (1896) and Stern (1900) that focused psychologists on major concerns such as (a) the nature and extent of differences in individuals and groups, (b) the factors that determine these differences, and (c) how the differences are manifested.

Paramount to this study of individual variation was the study of psychometrics and statistics, as "an intelligent interpretation of almost any study in differential psychology requires an understanding of certain fundamental statistical concepts" (Anastasi, 1958, p. 9). Yet few texts on individual differences include sections on the appropriate statistical methods for studying these issues, such as statistical moderation, mediation, and moderated mediation (but see Reyonds & Willson, 1985). In fact, it was not until Baron and Kenny (1986) published their paper on testing these ideas systematically that the issue was brought to the fore. In the 20 years since, the importance of individual differences has continued to grow, yet many researchers fail to use best practices in properly testing for these phenomena. Consequently, this chapter will focus on the concepts of moderation, mediation, and moderated mediation within the framework of ordinary least squares (OLS) multiple regression. Although more advanced modeling techniques are available—for example, covariance structure analysis (Jaccard & Turrisi, 2003) and multilevel models (Davison, Kwak, Seo, & Choi,

Author's Note: I thank Kristopher Preacher for his feedback on an earlier draft of this manuscript and Andrew J. Knoop and Lindsay Shockley for their help in editing the chapter.

2002; Raudenbush & Bryk, 2002)[1]—the ubiquitous use of multiple regression within the field of individual differences suggests that determining and delineating best practices are both necessary and advantageous. Moreover, alternative techniques can be overly complex and require a more refined statistical background for their interpretation, and currently, there is no consensus as to what non regression procedure is "the best" for a given analysis. Third, and probably most important, the best practice concepts involved in mediation, moderation, and moderated mediation are not strictly dependent on a specific method per se. Thus, gaining an understanding of best practices within a multiple regression framework can help determine the same in more complex models.

DEFINING THE CONCEPTS

Moderation

Statistical moderation is the specification of a variable (or variables) whose variation determines the conditions upon which a given magnitude of an effect occurs. Put another way, a moderator variable affects the relationship between two other variables, so that the nature of the impact of the predictor on the criterion varies according to the level or value of the moderator (Holmbeck, 1997).[2] While Baron and Kenny (1986) write that moderator variables are typically introduced when there is an unexpectedly weak or inconsistent relation between an independent and an outcome variable, moderation is also of specific concern to many studies in the social sciences because results indicate "when" or "for whom" a variable most strongly predicts or causes an outcome variable (Frazier, Tix, & Barron, 2004).

Some examples of studies ripe for moderation analysis include the following:

Is the relationship between Spearman's (1904) g and academic achievement the same for males and females?

Does reaction time predict psychometric test performance the same across the entire spectrum of cognitive abilities?

Do race and level of extroversion interact in the prediction of sexual orientation from serotonin reuptake ability?

Mediation

Mediation is the specification of a variable (or set of variables) that provides a link (often causal in nature) between an independent variable and a dependent variable that have an already determined effect.[3] It is "the generative mechanism through which the focal independent variable is able to influence the dependent variable of interest" (Baron & Kenny, 1986, p. 1173). In other words, mediating variables offer an explanation as to why or how certain effects occur.

Historically, mediation hypotheses, per se, have not held as much interest in the field of individual differences as moderation studies, although they can be of value to the field, as they can help identify variables that might be plausible moderators for a given relationship (Baron & Kenny, 1986). Moreover, they can help give a stronger theoretical justification for the presence of moderation. For example, if sex moderates a given relationship, further inquiry may find that estrogen level is the causal mechanism behind that relationship.

Moderated Mediation

Moderated mediation is the specification of a variable (or variables) whose variation determines the conditions upon which a mediation effect occurs. In other words, "if the moderator is an individual differences variable, then it would mean that the mediating process that intervenes between the treatment and the outcome is different for people who differ on that individual difference" (Muller, Judd, & Yzerbyt, 2005, p. 854).

An example may help clarify the concept. It is known that socioeconomic status (SES) and longevity are positively related, as people who have more money tend to live longer (Adler et al., 1994; Adler & Ostove, 1999). Gottfredson (2004; Gottfredson & Deary, 2004) hypothesized that the relationship is due to cognitive ability (i.e., cognitive ability is the underlying variable that explains why SES and longevity are related). Thus, cognitive ability is hypothesized to mediate the SES-longevity relationship. One could take Gottfredson's hypothesis a step further and hypothesize that cognitive ability mediates the SES-longevity relationship for Caucasians but not for people of color. If the second hypothesis holds, then race is said to moderate the ability of cognitive ability to mediate the SES-longevity relationship.

Formulaic Structures and Related Issues

Moderation

Before going into the statistical details, it is wise to heed the advice of Frazier et al. (2004), who write that any study involving moderation needs to be well based in theory. This is important for any branch of systematic scientific inquiry, but especially when related to moderation. First, in order to apply the findings to some new set of conditions, one must understand the underlying mechanisms of the initial moderation. Second, to develop an appropriate design (i.e., adequate power, appropriate levels of the moderating and outcome variables), one has to have a grasp of the underlying reasons why a moderation effect might be found (B. Smith & Sechrest, 1991). Third, for a study to be set up properly (e.g., testing a specific hypothesis), there has to be an overarching theory on which to base the design (i.e., do not commit a Type III error; Mitroff & Featheringham, 1974). For example, if one of the moderating variables is categorical, theory should, a priori, give an indication of what specific categories should be assessed and how the effect(s) will differ across them.

Conceptually, Figure 28.1 represents multiple regression with a moderating variable: X is related to Y of the magnitude B_1. Now, if a third variable was added, Z, that affects the X-Y relationship at different levels of Z (e.g., Z_1, Z_2, . . . , Z_m), then Z is a moderator.

Formulaically, a simple moderation model looks as follows:

$$Y = B_0 + B_1X + B_2Z + B_3XZ, \qquad (1)$$

where the moderation effect is quantified by B_3, the unstandardized regression coefficient associated with the interaction.[4]

When there is an interaction term in the equation, the magnitude of the regression of the dependent variable on the predictor(s) depends specifically on the particular value of the moderator at which the regression of the outcome variable on the predictor is taken (Cohen, Cohen, West, & Aiken, 2003), which means the Bs are conditional and require special interpretation. This is dealt with in depth later in the chapter.

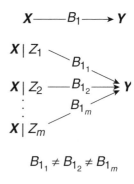

Figure 28.1   Models of moderation effects.

Types of Moderators

In ordinary multiple regression, predictor variables can be either categorical (qualitative) or continuous (quantitative), but the outcome variable is expected to be quantitative (Cohen et al., 2003; Kutner, Nachtsheim, Neter, & Li, 2004; Pedhazur, 1997).[5] Likewise, moderating variables can be either qualitative or quantitative.

Qualitative Moderator

When using a qualitative variable (e.g., race, sex, current school attending), one must code the data appropriately, and the appropriateness is dependent on the questions being asked (Aguinis, 2004; Cohen et al., 2003). Briefly, *dummy coding* compares the means of all groups with the mean of one specified comparison group, *effect coding* compares each group's mean with the overall mean (either weighted or unweighted), and *contrast coding* makes a specific set of planned comparisons. For more detailed overviews of data coding, see Chapter 8 of Cohen et al. (2003) or Chapters 11 and 12 of Pedhazur (1997).

Multiple Levels for the Qualitative Variable

It is not uncommon for the qualitative variable to have more than two levels. The only major difference is that the statistical test for the presence of an interaction does not rely on a single B coefficient; rather the omnibus hierarchical F test needs to be used. Moreover, when making the model's interaction terms, terms need to be made between the independent variable(s) *and each variable representing an aspect of the qualitative variable.* That being said, the *B* coefficients for the multiplicative terms have the same interpretation—namely, they represent slope differences between the two groups coded by the qualitative variable. Likewise, the *B* coefficients for the simple effects (i.e., the terms without an interaction) carry similar meanings, although the exact interpretation is dependent on the coding scheme used (for more information on this and other topics, such as homogeneity of error variance, see, e.g., Aguinis, 2004; Cohen et al., 2003).[6]

Quantitative Moderator

Structurally, the formula for a regression with a quantitative moderator is the same as that for a qualitative one (i.e., Formula 1). The difference is in the interpretation, as the moderation effect is not just between a finite number of groups but (in theory) across the infinite spectrum of values the quantitative variable can take.

The major assumption in using Formula 1 to assess a quantitative moderator is that the interaction between the predictor and moderator is linear at every value of the moderator (i.e., the *B* associated with the independent variable changes at a constant rate as a function of changes in the moderator; Cohen et al., 2003). If this is not the case, it can be accounted for in the model, but that is beyond the scope of this chapter.

Testing Moderation Effects

The method for testing moderation is dependent on the nature of the independent and moderating variables. More specifically, testing of moderation effects depends on the dimensionality of the regression equation. With two continuous variables, one continuous variable and one categorical variable with only two levels, or two categorical variables each with only two levels, a *t* test of the interaction (i.e., the *B* associated with the multiplicative term) will provide a test of the significance of the interaction. When there are more than two variables and/or a categorical variable has more than two levels, the moderator effect needs to be tested with a multiple *df F* test that represents the change in the regression model by adding the interaction(s). If this omnibus test is significant, then the single *df t* tests related to the specific interaction terms are assessed to determine what interactions are

important. Failure to find a moderation effect could mean that (a) there is no interaction, (b) an interaction exists but is of a different functional form (i.e., a quadratic moderation effect), or (c) the study does not have enough power to detect an extant effect. Even if a given interaction is not significant, though, one may still choose to keep it in the model if there are very strong theoretical reasons for expecting the interaction. This is a rather tenuous issue, though, and interested readers should see Aiken and West (1991) for a more elaborate discussion.

If an *F* test is going to be used to test significance, Frazier et al. (2004) recommend that the first step in testing the moderation model is to enter all the predictor and moderator variables and then, as a second step, enter the interaction terms, noting that in the case where two or more interaction terms were created because the qualitative variables had more than two levels, *all the product terms associated with a given predictor and moderating variable should be entered in the same step.* Once the *B* coefficients for the two models are estimated, compare the R^2 values across models. If an interaction is present, then the difference between the two R^2 values will be significant, using the hierarchical *F* test.[7]

Interpreting the Moderation Study

One needs to interpret the *unstandardized regression coefficients* (i.e., *B*s) instead of the standardized ones (i.e., beta weights, or βs) for models that have a multiplicative term.[8] In a "regular," additive (only) multiple regression, regression coefficients (i.e., *B*s) describe the effects of each independent variable on the dependent variable as constant (i.e., overall values of the other independent variables); in a moderation model, though, the regression coefficients are interpreted as conditional effects. More specifically, without an interaction (from Equation 1), B_1 is the effect of *X* on *Y*, taking into account each level of *Z* (i.e., it is a general relationship, averaging across all levels of *Z*). With an interaction, though, B_1 then becomes the measure of influence of *X* on *Y* when *Z* equals 0 (i.e., the relationship is conditioned on a specific value of *Z*). This then raises a problem in most research in individual differences. Namely, the measures do not usually contain a valid zero point. For example, if IQ was a moderating variable, academic achievement was the predictor variable, and annual income was the outcome variable, then B_1 would be the influence of academic achievement on annual income, for people whose IQ is 0. But IQ instruments do not have 0 as a valid, obtainable value, making the interpretation of B_1 nonsense. This issue is addressed in the following section, on centering variables.

Assuming the moderator has a valid zero value, the B_3 coefficient for a two-variable moderation analysis indicates the number of units that the slope of Y on X changes given a one-unit increase in Z. In other words, for every one-unit change in Z, the slope of Y on X is predicted to change by B_3 units. Using the rules of algebra, it is possible to calculate the estimated effect of X on Y, for any given value of Z. If Z assumes a specific numerical value, Z_0, the value of Y, as a function of X, at Z_0, is

$$Y = B_0 + B_1 X + B_2 Z_0 + B_3 X Z_0, \quad (2a)$$

$$Y = B_0 + B_2 Z_0 + X(B_1 + B_3 Z_0), \quad (2b)$$

$$Y = \underbrace{B_0 + B_2 Z_0}_{B_0^*} + X \underbrace{(B_1 + B_3 Z_0)}_{B_1^*}, \quad (2c)$$

$$Y = B_0^* + B_1^* X. \quad (2d)$$

The standard error for B_1^* in (2d), s_{B_1}, is

$$\sqrt{s_{B_1}^2 + 2 Z_0 s_{B_1 B_3} + Z_0^2 s_{B_3}^2}, \quad (3)$$

where s_B^2 is the variance of a B coefficient, and $s_{B_1 B_2}$ is the covariance of B_1 and B_3. Formula 3 indicates that, like the slope, the standard errors of the conditional coefficients vary according to the level of the Z.

Centering Variables

Only rarely in the social sciences do scales exist such that zero has meaning (Blanton & Jaccard, 2006; Jensen, 2005). Consequently, because moderation model Bs are interpreted as conditional effects—*at the value of 0* for the other variables in the model—it makes sense to center quantitative variables that do not have natural, meaningful 0 points (Cohen et al., 2003; Frazier et al., 2004). Using centered independent variables, the Bs represent the first-order

relationship at the new center point on both predictors. In addition, not only does centering help with interpretation, but it reduces problems associated with multicollinearity.

While centering a variable will, in general, affect the magnitude of the B coefficient associated with the variable, it has no effect on the B associated with the highest order term in the equation.[9] Likewise, centering a variable has no effect on the statistical significance associated with its Bs or multiple R (Cohen, 1978). Consequently, "any additive transformation of the original variables has no effect on the overall interaction or on any aspect of the interaction we might choose to examine" (Aiken & West, 1991, p. 32).

When choosing to center a variable, the obvious choice is to use the variable's mean as the center point. One need not necessarily use the mean, though, as any specific, valid, obtainable value of the variable will suffice. For example, if using IQ, again, as a moderating variable, one may wish to center the variable on an IQ of 70, thus making B_1 the influence of variable X on variable Y for those individuals at the threshold of mental retardation.

If the predictor and moderator variables are centered, their interaction term does not need to be centered. Likewise, as most qualitative coding schemes use 0 as a real value, there is usually no need to center the qualitative variables, nor is there a need to center the outcome variable, as leaving it in its original metric allows predicted scores to be on the same scale as the outcome variable (Aiken & West, 1991).

Graphing

If the moderation effect is significant (or if it is not, but for theoretical reasons, the interaction term is kept in the model), it is beneficial to create a graphical depiction or a table summarizing the form of the moderator effect, as it can help in understanding moderation effects. A pictorial representation of the data, even if incomplete, can offer key insights into both the data's structure and the exact nature of the interaction. This is tantamount to specifying the various regression equations for the different groups (if the moderator is qualitative) or selecting points on the moderator's continuum to form the regression equation (if the moderator is quantitative).

Following Cohen et al. (2003) and Aiken and West (1991), the regression of the outcome variable on the predictor variable, at a finite point of the moderator, is a *simple regression line or a simple slope*. If these simple regression lines are not parallel to each other, then they interact at some point—with one of the questions to determine in an analysis being if the interaction occurs within the range of the moderator's valid data points.

If the moderating variable is qualitative, the number of simple slopes to plot is the number of levels of the moderating variable. If the moderating variable is quantitative, this can become a bit trickier, as there are an infinite number of points on the moderator's continuum at which to compare the regression lines. Ideally, the theory behind the analysis will have specified points on the continuum at which to test for differences. As a rule of thumb, though, plotting the lines at the mean value of the moderator as well as ±1 or ±2 standard deviations will give a general impression of how the moderating variable is influencing the predictor-outcome relationship. If the moderating variable also has finite bounds (e.g., if a Likert-type scale is used as the moderator), then plotting at the maximum and minimum might also be informative. As a third option, the Johnson-Neyman technique (Johnson & Neyman, 1936) can be used to find the limiting points for the "region(s) of significance," which are viable candidates on the moderating variable of where to plot the simple slopes (discussed below).

Of interest in some analysis is the point where two given simple regression lines cross. If the moderator has finite bounds, it can be very informative to determine if the simple slopes derived from conditioning on the extreme moderating values cross within the data range or outside it. To find the value of the predictor where the simple slopes cross, simply set the two regression lines equal to each other and solve for X; this will yield the following formula for a two-variable model:

$$X_{\text{cross}} = \frac{-B_2}{B_3}. \tag{4}$$

Johnson-Neyman (J-N) Procedure

Johnson and Neyman (1936) first developed a procedure to find two points (if they exist) that define ranges for which the slopes of the regression lines are (or are not) significantly different at a given α value. The purpose of the J-N technique, at least in moderation studies, is simply to identify the values of the moderator that are associated with significant group differences on the outcome variable, that is, to be able to make a statement about regions of significance and nonsignificance (Huitema, 1980; Rogosa, 1980, 1981). The reasoning behind needing such a procedure is as follows. The test to see if a simple slope differs from zero, conditional on a specific value of the moderator (Z_0), is distributed as a t statistic, with $(n - k - 1)$ *df*, that is,

$$\frac{B_1 + B_3 Z_0}{\sqrt{s_{B_1}^2 + 2Z_0 s_{B_1 B_3} + Z_0^2 s_{B_3}^2}} \sim t_{(n-k-1)}, \tag{5}$$

where $s_{B_1}^2$, $s_{B_3}^2$, and $s_{B_1 B_3}^2$ are defined as in Equation 3, and k is the number of predictor variables in the model. Note that the denominator in Equation 5 varies as Z varies, and thus the slope may be significant at one value of Z, say Z_0, but not at another, say $Z_{0'}$. Unless the moderator is qualitative or theory specifies differently, the value chosen for Z_0 is ultimately arbitrary. Thus, an alternative procedure is to determine the values of Z for which the simple slope (i.e., the regression of Y onto X) is statistically significant, which is what the J-N procedure does.

For the J-N procedure, first an α is chosen based on the level of significance desired, α_0. Then, the associated t value is found, given α_0, n, and k: t_0; Equation 5 (with uncentered variables) is then reversed to solve for Z. As Equation 5 is quadratic, there will be two solutions, although one or more may be nonapplicable. The reversed equation for a two-variable moderation model is shown in Equation 6.

Again, the obtained values answer the question: For what values of Z is the simple regression equation (i.e., $Y = a + bX$) significant? For a simple walk-though on how to use the J-N procedure with two variables, see the walk-through section of this chapter as well as Bauer and Curran (2005). For details of how to implement the J-N procedure under other conditions, see Chapter 13 of Huitema (1980).

$$Z = \frac{-2(t_0^2 s_{13} - B_1 B_3) \pm \sqrt{[2(t_0^2 s_{13} - B_1 B_3)]^2 - 4(t_0^2 s_3^2 - B_3^2)(t_0^2 s_1^2 - B_1^2)}}{2(t_0^2 s_3^2 - B_3^2)}. \tag{6}$$

Specific Type of Single-Moderator, Single-Predictor Relationships

If there is only one moderator and one predictor variable, then there are four different types of moderation relationships, depending on the nature of the variables (e.g., qualitative or quantitative). This section gives brief overviews of each, with the idea that if there are more than two independent variables, the examples are easy to extend.

Moderation 1: Independent: Qualitative; Moderator: Qualitative

This is perhaps the easiest case to assess, as it is done via a two-factor analysis of variance (ANOVA).[10] When one qualitative variable moderates another, there is an interaction between the two factors. In ANOVA terminology, moderation (interaction) exists when two (or more) factors account for variance in the outcome variable if, *above and beyond* any additive combination of the separate (main) effects, they have a joint effect. The major issues of concern here are to match the coding method with the hypotheses of the analysis and, if a variable has more than two levels, to make sure all the interaction terms are specified (Kutner et al., 2004).

Moderations 2 and 3: Independent: Quantitative; Moderator: Qualitative OR Independent: Qualitative; Moderator: Quantitative

The analysis here is simply looking to see if regression equations are the same across groups. In some contexts, this type of moderation is called an aptitude-treatment interaction (Cronbach & Snow, 1977; Pedhazur, 1997), and in others it is called an analysis of covariance (Kutner et al., 2004). While the mathematics behind these models does not necessitate the delineation of whether the predictor or moderator variable is qualitative or quantitative, it significantly aids in interpretation to delineate them before performing any type of analysis.

When the moderator variable is qualitative and the predictor is quantitative, then the analysis is simply looking to see if the slopes across the various levels of the qualitative variable are the same. If reversed, the analysis looks to see if group differences are the same across the levels of the quantitative moderator.

A major caveat in this type of moderation analysis is that the amount of measurement error in the quantitative variable across levels of the qualitative variable needs to be approximately the same (Baron & Kenny, 1986). If this is not the case, bias results and reliabilities need to be estimated separately for the quantitative variable across the levels of the qualitative variable, and the slopes disattenuated accordingly. This can be implemented in most structural equation modeling programs via a multiple-group analysis, but this is beyond the scope of this particular chapter (for more information, see Jaccard & Wan, 1996).

Moderation 4: Independent: Quantitative; Moderator: Quantitative

Here, the analysis seeks to find out if a regression equation holds across the spectrum of values available for the moderating variable. For example, if IQ predicts salary well after someone has been out of school for at least 10 years, does the magnitude of the IQ-salary relationship hold across all levels of perceived job satisfaction, or does it shrink as job satisfaction increases (i.e., Are people willing to sacrifice a high salary for high job satisfaction?)?

A major assumption when there are two quantitative variables is that the effects of the independent variables (predictor and moderator, alike) are linear in form. This means that the predictor variable's relationship to the outcome variable is linear (i.e., Y is a linear function of X) and that, if an effect exists, it is an orderly, monotonic linear relationship between changes in the slope and changes in the moderator variables. Moderation need not necessarily be constrained to a bilinear model, but nonlinear models (either for the independent variables or the moderation variables) are more complex and require more detail.[11]

Measurement error in either the independent or moderating variables can have a detrimental effect on this moderation analysis (Baron & Kenny, 1986). If much error exists in the instruments, structural equation modeling would be a better approach than multiple regression.

More Than One Moderator

Moderation models are not limited to one moderating variable. In fact, as interaction models are merely extensions of "regular" multiple regression models, in theory, the models can have an unlimited number of independent and moderating variables (although as the number increases, interpretation and obtaining a suitable N become much more difficult).

As a starting place, the formula for a model with three independent variables, two of which are significant moderators, is as follows:

$$Y = B_0 + B_1X + B_2Z + B_3W + B_4XZ + \quad (7)$$
$$B_5XW + B_6WZ + B_7XZW,$$

where X, Y, and Z are the same as in Equation 1, and W is the second moderating variable.

Before starting the analysis, one needs to first specify the independent and moderator variables and to map out the logic for the underlying, complex interactions (Jaccard & Turrisi, 2003). As there are two different moderators, one must also decide which moderator is going to be the first-order moderating variable (i.e., moderate the relationship between X and Y) and the second-order moderating variable (i.e., moderate the relationship between Z and its relationship with X and Y). Moreover, one must make all the multiplicative variables, including pairwise products (e.g., XZ) and the three-way interaction (i.e., XZW).

Once the models are specified (i.e., the full and reduced models), the variables should be centered (if needed), and the test for a three-way interaction is simply the test of the B associated with the three-way multiplicative term (assuming the variables are quantitative or have only two levels if qualitative). The tricky part is in interpreting the B coefficients. B_1 is still the measure of influence of X on Y when $Z = W = 0$, but the B associated with the two-way interactions (e.g., XZ) reflects the effect of the interaction between the two variables on Y, when the third variable (in this case, W) is equal to 0.

The B associated with the three-way multiplicative term, if significant, is interpreted as the predicted change in the two-way interaction of B associated with XZ given a one-unit change in W.

MEDIATION

Picking a Mediating Variable

When picking the mediating variable, theory is of great importance in determining the proposed relationships (Frazier et al., 2004). There should be a clear reason, based in the literature within a given field, for the hypothesis that the predictor is related to or causes the mediator.

Another factor to consider when picking a mediating variable is the size of the relationship between the mediator and the outcome variables, in comparison to the size of the relation between the predictor and mediator variables, as this has a direct influence on power to detect mediation (more detail is given in the section on power).

Error

As discussed in Chapter 16 (this volume), measurement error generally works to attenuate the size of association measures (cf. Ree & Carretta, 2006). Baron and Kenny (1986) write that the presence of error in the mediator tends to produce an underestimate of the mediator and an overestimate of the effect of the independent variable on the dependent variable (assuming coefficients are positive). The common approach to unreliability is to have multiple operations or indicators of the construct, such as is readily done in structural equation modeling (Bollen, 1987).

A second source of bias in mediation models is feedback. In multiple regression analysis of mediation, there is the assumption that the mediator is not caused by the dependent variable. If the model is misspecified in such a manner (i.e., a confusion of mediating and dependent variables), this is feedback bias (Baron & Kenny, 1986). A solution to this was provided by E. R. Smith (1982) that involves two-stage least squares estimation. A second solution is to use structural equation modeling and incorporate feedback directly into the model. Neither method is within the scope of this chapter.

Analyzing Mediation Data

Baron and Kenny (1986) contend that mediation analysis is a procedural process. More specifically, three conditions must be met for a variable to be considered a mediator. Assuming the mediating variable is significantly related to the outcome variable, (a) the independent variable must be significantly related to the mediating variable, (b) the independent variable must be significantly related to the outcome variable, and (c) the magnitude of relationship between the independent variable and the outcome variable must (significantly) decrease after controlling for the mediating variable.[12]

If the predictor-outcome relationship goes to 0, this evinces a single-variable mediation process. If the relation significantly decreases

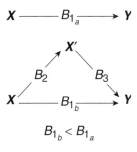

Figure 28.2   Models of mediation effects.

but does not go to zero, it indicates that other mediating processes are involved.[13] Frazier et al. (2004) emphasize that it is not enough to show that the predictor-outcome relationship is smaller when the mediator variable is added to the model, but rather a test for the significance of the change is critical. MacKinnon, Lockwood, Hoffman, West, and Sheets (2002) reviewed 14 different ways to test for a mediation effect, and while they did not explicitly state the best way to assess for mediation, they wrote that the aforementioned causal steps "have very low power, unless the effect or sample size is large. . . . Studies that use the causal steps methods described by Kenny and colleagues are the most likely to miss real effects but are very unlikely to commit a Type I error" (p. 96).

One way to assess for the significance of a mediation effect was developed by Sobel (1982). Using the labels from Figure 28.2, the difference between the total effect of the predictor on the outcome (B_{1_a}) and the direct effect of the predictor on the outcome (B_{1_b}) is equal to the product of the paths from the predictor to the moderator (B_2) and from the mediator to the outcome (B_3). Thus, the significance of the difference between (B_{1_a}) and (B_{1_b}) can be assessed by testing the significance of the products of paths B_2 and B_3. More specifically, B_2B_3 is divided by its standard error, which yields a test in the z score metric. The error term derived by Sobel (1982) is

$$\sqrt{B_3^2 s_{B_2}^2 + B_2^2 s_{B_3}^2}, \qquad (8)$$

where B_2 and B_3 are unstandardized regression coefficients, and s_{B_2} and s_{B_3} are their standard errors.

A problem with using a normal z distribution to assess the significance of

$$\frac{B_2 B_3}{\sqrt{B_3^2 s_{B_2}^2 + B_2^2 s_{B_3}^2}} \qquad (9)$$

is that the statistic is not normally distributed (Shrout & Bolger, 2002); so, using a standard z table will give biased results, usually resulting in underpowered tests of mediation. MacKinnon, Lockwood, and Hoffman (1998) developed empirical sampling distributions for B_2B_3 via extensive simulations for various values of B_2 and B_3. Thus, using the standard error Sobel (1982) developed (see Formula 8) and the table of critical values (MacKinnon et al., 1998), one can test if a mediation effect exists.[14]

An alternative method to using MacKinnon et al.'s (1998) distribution, and one that is likely a better alternative given typical sample sizes in the behavioral sciences, is to use bootstrap methods to derive the test of significance (and confidence intervals) for the numerator in Equation 9. Based on the work of Bollen and Stine (1992) and Shrout and Bolger (2002), Preacher and Hayes (2004) developed macros for SPSS and SAS to compute bootstrap estimates for the significance test (more detail below).

Interpreting Mediation Analysis

At its core, mediation hypotheses are causal hypotheses (Cole & Maxwell, 2003; Kenny, Kashy, & Bolger, 1998; MacKinnon & Dwyer, 1993; but see Kraemer, Wilson, Fairburn, & Agras, 2002), but assuming the analysis shows a significant mediation affect, the conclusions are only correct if the causal assumptions are valid. In addition to the normal regression assumptions, Kenny et al. (1998) delineate three specification assumptions.

First, it is assumed that the mediating variable causes the outcome variable. If this is not the case (i.e., the outcome variable causes the mediator), this is a reverse causal effect. As the mediating and outcome variable are not manipulated variables, if they are interchanged in the regression model and the outcome appears to "cause" the mediator, then this is an indication to be wary of the initial model. While the model may fit well, an alternative specification would be equally viable in this case. If, theoretically, the reverse effects are implausible, then this particular misspecification issue becomes less of an issue. Likewise, if the study's design has the mediating variable being measured temporally before the outcome, then the reverse causal hypothesis becomes less viable.

Even if the mediation study shows complete mediation (which they seldom do), there are likely to be other models (i.e., other mediating variables) that are consistent with the data, indicating that there is likely to be more than one "correct" mediation model (Frazier et al., 2004; MacCallum, Wegener, Uchino, & Fabrigar, 1993). Unfortunately, for nonexperiential or cross-sectional studies, the number of alternative models is much greater than for experimental studies (MacCallum et al., 1993).

A second assumption is that all the variables involved in the causal chain are specified in the mediation model. If, for instance, there is a fourth variable in the mediation model (Figure 28.2) that causes both X' and Y, yet the regression model does not include it, then this is an omission error, and the regression coefficients are likely to be biased (Frazier et al., 2004; Judd & Kenny, 1981). Unfortunately, the only real solution to the problem is to measure and specify such variables and control for their effects in the regression model. One artificial source of the mediator-outcome covariance can be controlled by design, though. That is, if the mediator and outcome variables are measured the same way (e.g., by the same instrument completed by the same person), then this common method effect is likely to be a common cause of the mediator and outcome. Thus, the mediation design should avoid this situation by using different variables, different instruments, or different respondents.

The third assumption is that the mediating variable is measured without error. If there is significant error in measuring the mediator, B_{1_b} is likely to be overestimated and B_3 is likely underestimated, assuming B_2B_3 is positive (which it often is). The solution, obviously, is to measure the mediator with an instrument that is highly reliable. If this is not possible, then use a latent variable approach (e.g., Holbert & Stephenson, 2001).

In sum, causation is hard to establish in the social sciences, much less if the studies are nonexperimental in design. Thus, it has been a source for much discussion not only in the mediation literature (Frazier et al., 2004; James & Brett, 1984; MacKinnon et al., 2002) but in the sciences in general (Humphreys, 1989). This chapter will simply state that causation is difficult to establish and that much care must be taken before absolute causal language

should permeate a given mediation analysis (Rubin, 1974; Spirtes, Glymour, & Scheines, 1993).

Multiple Mediators

Complete mediation is rare in the social sciences, especially in nonexperimental studies. Preacher and Hayes (2006) write that multiple mediation models are advantageous for multiple reasons, with the foremost being that the omitted variable problem is less likely to occur, and including more than one mediator in the same allows research to pit competing theories against each other in a single model. Nonetheless, these models are seldom used or presented (but see MacKinnon, 2000; West & Aiken, 1997).

As with simple mediation models, there are multiple approaches to assess the effects, including causal steps, product of coefficients, and bootstrapping.[15]

MODERATION AND MEDIATION

Although moderation and mediation are distinct concepts, with different types of hypotheses and different tests of effects (Frazier et al., 2004; Holmbeck, 1997; Rose, Holmbeck, Coakley, & Franks, 2004), it does not mean they cannot be used together. For example, Baron and Kenny (1986) write that one may begin with a moderator but end up finding a mediation process. More explicitly, they write that finding a moderating variable could help suggest a possible mediation variable. Thus, when predicting moderating variables, one should select them to do more than improve predictive power: "One should choose the [moderating] variable that more readily lends itself to specification of a mediational mechanism" (p. 1178). Likewise, mediators can help to find moderating variables. If one can understand the mediational process behind a relationship, one can choose an appropriate intervention and then test whether the intervention has a moderating effect on the variables' relationships. In other analyses, mediators and moderators can work together to help better understand the predictor-outcome relationship (Kraemer, Stice, Kazdin, Offord, & Kupfer, 2001). Of particular note, a variable, in and of itself, does not necessarily lend itself to either mediation or moderation analysis; the same variable can serve as either (or both), depending on the underlying theory and research question at hand.

Moderated Mediation: Combining Mediation and Moderation

One way of using both moderating and mediating variables is to explicitly combine them in a single model, such as with moderated mediation. James and Brett (1984) first used the term *moderated mediation,* defining it as a mediation model that requires the addition of a moderator to the predictor-mediator relationship, the mediator-outcome relationship, or both.[16] Similarly, Muller et al. (2005) write that moderated mediation happens when the mediating process that is responsible for producing the effect of the predictor on the outcome depends on the value of a moderator (cf. Rose et al., 2004). Their definition implies that the mediating variable mediates the predictor-outcome relationship for some particular group of people, but *it does not imply any overall moderation of the treatment effect.* Thus, what varies as a result of the moderator is not the magnitude of the predictor's overall effect on the outcome but the mediating process that produces it.

Perhaps the most generic, and hence most encompassing, definition comes from Preacher, Rucker, and Hayes (2006), who define moderated mediation as when "the strength of an indirect effect depends on the level of some variable . . . when mediation relations are contingent on the level of the moderator" (p. 12). For the purposes of this chapter, we will assume there is a moderating variable (Z) that affects the predictor-mediator relationship, the mediator-outcome relationship, or both. More specifically, looking at Figure 28.3A, there is an overall treatment effect (B_{1_a}) that is not moderated. Figure 28.3B posits that the mediator, X', explains at least part of the predictor-outcome relationship, as $B_{1_b} < B_{1_a}$ or, to put it in terms of a significance test, $B_{1_a} - B_{1_b} > 0$. Figure 28.3C takes the mediation a step further and posits that the mediating process is moderated; either the effect of the predictor on the mediator depends on the moderator ($B_{2_b} \neq 0$), the effect of the mediator on the outcome is moderated ($B_{3_b} \neq 0$), or both.

Testing Moderated Mediation Models

In one of the first articles to discuss moderated mediation, Baron and Kenny (1986)

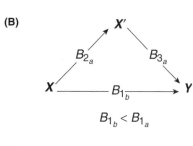

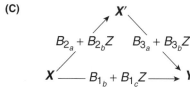

Figure 28.3   Models of moderated mediation effects.

extended their causal steps approach, writing that analyzing a moderated mediation model is a three-step process. Muller et al. (2005) extended Baron and Kenny's (1986) conceptualization, noting that, parallel to the case of simple mediation, there exists the following fundamental equality among the parameters:

$$-B_{1_c} = B_{3_a}B_{2_b} + B_{3_b}B_{2_a}. \tag{10}$$

Thus, if moderated mediation exists, first, $B_{1_a} \neq 0$. Then, using (10), if the predictor's effect on the mediator depends on the moderator ($B_{2_b} \neq 0$), there must be an effect of the mediator on the outcome ($B_{3_a} \neq 0$), or likewise, if the effect of the mediator on the outcome depends on the moderator ($B_{3_b} \neq 0$), then the predictor should have an overall effect on the mediator ($B_{2_a} \neq 0$). Stated another way, if moderated mediation exists, one of the terms on the right-hand side of Equation 10 must not be 0, which then implies that B_{1_c} also departs from 0. This, in turn, means that the residual direct effect of the predictor on the outcome, controlling for the mediator, is moderated.

Muller et al.'s (2005) procedure for testing moderated mediation is as follows:

1. Run the simple moderation model (i.e., Equation 1), expecting B_3 to equal 0 but B_1 to be different from 0.

2. Test the models in Figure 28.3C:

A. $X' = B_0 + B_{2_a}X + B_{2_c}Z + B_{2_b}XZ$

B. $Y = B'_0 + B_{1_b}X + B_{1_d}Z + B_{1_c}XZ + B_{3_a}X' + B_{3_b}X'Z$

Either B_{2_b} and B_{3_a} are both significant, or B_{2_a} and B_{3_b} are both significant (or both).

3. B_{1_c} is likely to be significant now, although Muller et al. (2005) do not see this as a necessary step.

Like Baron and Kenny's (1986) approach, Muller et al.'s (2005) approach is rather piecemeal. Preacher, Rucker, and Hayes (2006) have developed an alternative method for testing the whole moderated mediation model. Drawing on the fact that in simple mediation models, the strength of the mediator is assessed by examining the B_{2_a} and B_{3_a} terms in Figure 28.3B, a variable that moderates this quantity means that the indirect effect is conditional on this other variable. Consequently, they extended their bootstrap mediation approach (Preacher & Hayes, 2004) to include moderated mediation. While they specify five different types of moderated mediation, this chapter will focus on the three that match the aforementioned definition: (a) The predictor-mediator relationship and the mediator-outcome variable are moderated by the same fourth variable, Z; (b) only the predictor-mediator relationship is moderated; or (c) only the mediator-outcome relationship is moderated. More information about the bootstrap procedure is found in the walk-through section.

Predictor-Mediator Relationship and the Mediator-Outcome Are Moderated by the Same Variable

Using Figure 28.3C, if the path from the predictor to the mediator and the path from the mediator to the outcome are both moderated by the same variable, Z, then the indirect effect of X on Y is $f_1(X, Z) = (B_{2_a} + B_{2_b}Z)(B_{3_a} + B_{3_b}Z)$, and this term's (approximate) variance is as follows (Preacher, Rucker, & Hayes, 2006, p. 21):

$$VAR_1(X, Z) \approx (B_{3_a} + B_{3_b}Z)^2(s^2_{B2_a} + 2s_{B2_aB2_b}Z + s^2_{B2_b}Z^2) + (B_{2_a} + B_{2_b}Z)^2 \quad (11)$$
$$(s^2_{B3_a} + 2s_{B3_aB3_b}Z + s^2_{B3_b}Z^2) + (s^2_{B2_a} + 2s_{B2_aB2_b}Z + s^2_{B2_b}Z^2)$$
$$(s^2_{B3_a} + 2s_{B3_aB3_b}Z + s^2_{B3_b}Z^2).$$

Thus, given a specific value of the moderator, Z_0, one can assess whether there is a significant

mediation effect using a standard normal table, that is,

$$\frac{(B_{2_a} + B_{2_b}Z_0)(B_{3_a} + B_{3_b}Z_0)}{\sqrt{VAR_1(X, Z_0)}} \sim N(0,1). \quad (12)$$

As with simple moderation, it is possible, using the J-N technique, to find the bound(s) on Z that define a region of significance.

Path From Predictor to Mediator Is Moderated

This is just a simplification of the previous case. Specifically, using Figure 28.3C, only the path from the predictor to the mediator is moderated, so the indirect effect of X on Y simplifies to $f_2(X, Z) = (B_{2_a} + B_{2_b}Z)B_{3_a}$, and this term's (approximate) variance is then as follows (Preacher, Rucker, & Hayes, 2006, p. 18):

$$VAR_2(X, Z) \approx (B_{2_a} + B_{2_b}Z)^2 s^2_{B3_a} + (B^2_{3_a} + s^2_{B3_a})$$
$$(s^2_{B2_a} + 2s_{B2_aB2_b}Z + s^2_{B2_b}Z^2). \quad (13)$$

As with the previous example, given a specific value of the moderator, Z_0, one can assess whether there is significant mediation using a standard normal table; likewise, it is possible to find the bound(s) on Z that define a region of significance.

Path From Mediator to the Outcome Is Moderated

This situation is directly analogous to the previous one, except that the variables whose relationship is moderated differ. Thus, using Figure 28.3C, if the path from the moderator to the outcome is the only moderated relationship, then the indirect effect of X on Y is $f_3(X,Y) = (B_{3_a} + B_{3_b}z)B_{2_a}$, and this term's (approximate) variance follows directly from (11) and (13). Likewise, it is possible to find the bound(s) on Z that define a region of significance.

POWER, N, AND EFFECT SIZES

Both the moderation and mediation literature are replete with the finding that both effects are difficult to find and thus require relatively large sample sizes to find them (Aguinis, 2004; Hoyle & Kenny, 1999; MacKinnon et al., 2002; McClelland & Judd, 1993). This is largely due to the fact that mediation and moderation effects tend to be small, at least when compared with other effects, such as those in a single-factor ANOVA. While design and analysis features can be implemented in both types of analyses to increase power, the fact will still remain that before any undertaking of mediation or moderation studies, the N will necessarily need to be large and likely larger than most any other type of "regular" regression studies.

Power and Moderation

Authors have frequently expressed concerns about the low power to detect an interaction effect in regression models (Aguinis, 1995; Aguinis & Stone-Romero, 1997), arguing that their detection is unlikely even when the moderator test is the focal issue in a research study. One of the most influential factors in this is that the effect size for most interaction work is small (Chaplin, 1991; Frazier et al., 2004).

For moderation studies, the strength of the interaction can be measured in multiple ways. One of the most common unstandardized ways is to look at the B coefficient associated with the interaction term(s), for as the farther away it is from 0, the stronger the interaction, *ceteris paribus*. Regarding standardized metrics, the most common is to compare the squared multiple correlations for the models both with and without the interaction terms. For small sample sizes, this index is biased, but for larger samples and higher values of R^2, the bias is negligible. Aiken and West (1991; cf. Cohen, 1978) define a different moderation effect size, f^2, as

$$f^2 = \frac{r^2_{Y.MI} - r^2_{Y.M}}{1 - r^2_{Y.M}}, \qquad (14)$$

where M are the main effects, I is the interaction term, $r_{Y.MI}$ is the multiple correlation for all variables, and $r_{Y.M}$ is the multiple correlation for the "main effects" only. For additional effect sizes under different conditions, as well as "measures of improved condition," see Chapter 9 of Aguinis (2004).

In addition to the interaction's effect size, though, the regression's total effect (i.e., the R^2 of the full model) should be estimated before collecting data, as moderator effects have the most

power when the overall relationship between the predictors and outcome variables is large (Chaplin, 1991; Jaccard, Turrisi, & Wan, 1990). Consequently, one way to increase power is to increase the overall R^2 by adding additional (significant) predictors in the model as covariates (Jaccard & Wan, 1996).

A second factor affecting power is the decision of which variable(s) to use as moderator(s). If the moderator is categorical, one needs to pay attention to the differences in n across groups as well as differences in error variances (Aguinis, 2004; Aguinis & Pierce, 1998). If the moderator is continuous, one needs to consider the reliability of the moderator (as well as the independent variable[s]), as unreliability dramatically reduces power, especially in the interaction term, which, in turn, increases the standard error and decreases the power of the significance test. One also needs to be cognizant of range restriction (i.e., the sample does not adequately represent a random selection of individuals from a population), as it can have a significant effect on power (Aguinis & Stone-Romero, 1997). Last, the outcome variable should be reliable and have enough variability (i.e., have a wide range of response options). At a minimum, the outcome should have a number of responses that are equal to the product of the number of predictor and moderator responses; otherwise, the scale may be too coarse to detect a moderation effect (Russell & Bobko, 1992).

Aguinis (2004) and Frazier et al. (2004) both describe multiple methods to increase power in moderated multiple regression: (a) Rely on theory when planning a moderator analysis; (b) use an experimental design when appropriate; (c) determine and obtain a sample size needed to achieve adequate power based on estimated effect sizes; (d) if an independent variable is qualitative, attempt to collect equal numbers of participants for different levels; (e) test the homogeneity of error variance assumption and use appropriate tests if violated; (f) find instruments that are highly reliable for your population; (g) use an outcome variable that approximates a continuous variable as much as possible (i.e., do not use a Likert-type scale with seven response options as the sole outcome variable);[17] (h) do not di- or polychotomize a truly continuous variable; (i) if possible, choose outcome and predictor variables that are strongly related to each other; and (j) weigh the pros and cons of increasing the α from the traditional .05.

Determining Power

For a model with a single qualitative moderator, Aguinis, Boik, and Pierce (2001) have developed a free program called MMRPOWER.[18] Using this program, one can plug in various values for the subgroup ns, α, and predictor-outcome correlations (as well as other factors, such as range restriction and reliability estimates) and obtain power estimates. For a single continuous moderator, Jaccard et al. (1990) provide tables for power estimation in moderation (some of which are reproduced in Aiken & West, 1991) that require the R^2 estimates before and after the addition of the multiplicative term.

Alternatively, from Maxwell (2000) and Aiken and West (1991), a rough rule of thumb for an appropriate N, assuming one predictor, one moderator, and setting power to .80, is

$$N \approx \frac{7.85(1 - r_{Y.M}^2)}{r_{Y.MI}^2 - r_{Y.M}^2}, \qquad (15)$$

where M, I, r_{YMP} and $r_{Y.M}$ are the same as in Equation 14.

POWER AND MEDIATION

Power in mediation studies is essentially a function of collinearity—specifically, the relationship between the predictor and the mediator. While the pattern somewhat varies depending on the effect size, the N, and the mediator's reliability, in general, Hoyle and Kenny (1999) found that mediation studies maximize their power (using the Sobel test in Equation 8) when the effect of the mediator on the outcomes exceeds the effect of the predictor on the mediator. "Thus, from a statistical power perspective, the ideal spacing between observations of the [predictor] and the mediator and the mediator and the outcome would ensure that path $[B_3]$ equals or exceeds path $[B_2]$ in magnitude" (p. 218).

As was emphasized with moderators, mediation analysis is affected by the reliability of the variables, specifically the mediating variable. As the reliability of the mediating variable decreases, the effect of the mediator on the outcome variable is underestimated, and the effect of the predictor variable on the outcome variable is overestimated (Frazier et al., 2004). Hoyle and Robinson (2003) recommend that the reliability be at least .90 and, if it is not, then use methods of analysis that can account for unreliability (e.g., covariance structure analysis). In their Monte Carlo study on statistical power in mediation, Hoyle and Kenny (1999) concluded that even for studies with highly reliable measurement, the sample needed was usually close to 200.

WALK-THROUGH

Data for the following analyses were simulated specifically for this chapter (see Table 28.1) and can be found on the book's accompanying data CD. The variables and their descriptions are given in Table 28.1.

Moderation

This moderation walk-through will use continuous variables for the outcome, predictor, and mediator. For a similar walk-through using a qualitative moderator, see Chapter 3 of Aguinis (2004). For the moderation study, we want to see if achievement motivation (*motiv*) moderates the relationship between years in school (*school*) and annual income (*salary*). The usual first steps are to mean-center the predictor and the potential moderator, and then create the interaction term between the predictor and potential moderator. These steps were already completed, and the interaction term is labeled *schmot* in the data set.

Now, the first step is to run a regression model with just years of school and achievement motivation predicting salary. This yields the following regression equation:

$$\hat{salary} = 79.015 + 3.567(school) - .487(motiv),$$

with an R^2 value of .167. The next step is to run the same model but add the interaction term, *schmot*. This yields the following equation:

$$\hat{salary} = 74.360 + 3.400(school) - .488(motiv) + 3.032(schmot),$$

with an R^2 value of .205. Using the hierarchical F test,

Table 28.1   Description of Variables

partic	Participant's number
salary	Participants annual salary in $10 increments.
school	Number of years (and months) the participant attended school
	The mean was 14.28, and it has already been mean centered.
iq	Participant's Intelligence Quotient measured during this study
sex	Participant's sex. As the data are simulated, labeled nondescriptively as Sex 1 and Sex 2
motiv	Participant's average score on a set of instruments designed to measure achievement motivation
schmot	motiv × school

$$F = \frac{(.205 - .167)/(3 - 2)}{(1 - .205)(300 - 3 - 1)}$$

$$= 14.148 > F_{(\alpha=.025, 1, 296)} = 5.075,$$

indicating that achievement motivation modifies the years in the school–annual salary relationship. Note that if the bilinear nature of the moderating relationship is assessed, there is some evidence, however slight, that the moderating relationship is curvilinear (in the X^2Z^2 term), but probing that is beyond the scope of this text.

To find the region(s) of significance using $\alpha/2 = .025$ and a two-sided test, we simply plug in the numbers required from (6). Of note, though, the J-N formula requires uncentered values, so 25.1347 was added to each value of *motiv* and 14.28 was added to each value of *school*, and the interaction term was recalculated:

$$Z_{1\&2} = \frac{-274.66 \pm 13.90}{-11.76} \begin{cases} 22.17 \\ 24.53 \end{cases}$$

To test to see where the region of significance lies, the significance of B_1 was calculated at $Z = 23$ by fitting an equation with *school* (mean centered), *motiv* (using 23 as the centering value instead of the mean score of 25.13), and an interaction of both of these variables.

This yielded a B_1 value of −3.07 with a standard error of 1.83 and a *t* value of 1.682, which is not significant at $\alpha = .05$. Thus, for all values of $Z > 24.53$ and $Z < 22.17$, years of education significantly predicts annual salary.

Next, a graphical representation of the data will be useful to better understand the moderation

effect. Three different values of the moderator to use will be 13.39, 23.50, and 36.88. The first and last values represent values at two standard deviations away from the moderator's mean, while the third is in the region of nonsignificance. Because *motiv* is already mean centered, we need to use the Z values of −3.91, −1.63, and 3.91. The corresponding three regression equations are

$$Y_{Z = 36.88} = 76.26 - 8.46(school),$$

$$Y_{Z = 23.5} = 75.16 - 1.54(school), \text{ and}$$

$$Y_{Z = 13.39} = 72.45 + 15.26(school).$$

The equations are plotted in Figure 28.4. The figure also makes the notion of a region of significance more explicit, as at ±2 standard deviations of *motiv*, the regression of salary on school has relatively steep slopes, whereas when *motiv* equals 23.50, the regression line is almost completely horizontal.

For this particular study, it appears that years of education does predict annual salary, but this effect is moderated by the individual's achievement motivation. More specifically, around the "average" achievement motivation (i.e., 22.17 < Z < 24.53), years in school does not predict annual salary; around the high end of achievement motivation ($Z = 36.88$), there is a negative relationship between years in school and annual salary, while around the low end of achievement motivation ($Z = 13.39$), there is a positive relationship between years in school and annual salary.[19] For a more explicit example of graphing moderation in regression models, see Preacher, Curran, and Bauer (2006).

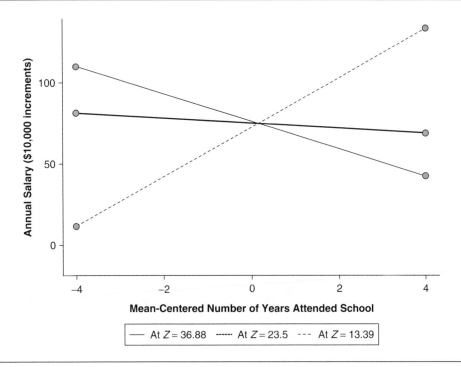

Figure 28.4   Graph of moderation analysis.

Mediation and Moderated Mediation

For the mediation and moderated mediation walk-through, we will use the same data set used in the moderation example, although this time, instead of hypothesizing that the years in school–annual salary relationship is moderated, we will test to see if the relationship is mediated by IQ (*iq* in the data set). Then we will take the analysis one step further and check to see whether the mediational relationship (or lack thereof) is then moderated by sex (*sex* in the data set).

As discussed above, mediation relationships are best analyzed by testing to see if the $B_2 B_3$ relationship is significant (MacKinnon et al., 2002). Of course, this assumes that the statistic's distribution is normal, which does not appear to be the case (MacKinnon et al., 1998; Preacher & Hayes, 2004). Thus, a bootstrap approach is likely the best way to assess the relationship. While the concepts involved in bootstrapping analysis are not necessarily complex (Effron & Tibshirani, 1993) and good introductions can be found in many mathematically oriented and nonparametric statistics

texts (e.g., Wilcox, 2003), the process can be tedious because it involves computer programming. Preacher and Hayes (2004) developed SAS and SPSS macros that provide bootstrap analysis of a mediation study, so it will be used for this walk-through.[20]

First, the indirect effect is as follows: $B_2 B_3 = (2.961)(.325) = .962$, which, using (8), is significant at $\alpha = .05$. Second, bootstrapping $B_2 B_3$ 5,000 times produces a distribution similar to Figure 28.5, although the distribution will slightly differ for each bootstrap analysis due to random sampling. The sample's 2.5th and 97.5th percentiles are .302 and 1.609, respectively. Since the percentiles do not contain 0, this is an indication that there is a significant mediation effect.

The next question that arises is whether the mediation effect is moderated. That is, does IQ explain the same amount of the schooling-salary effect for males as it does for females? To assess this, one has to assess a moderated mediation model. There are multiple moderated mediation models to assess (Muller et al., 2005; Preacher, Rucker, & Hayes, 2006), and for this

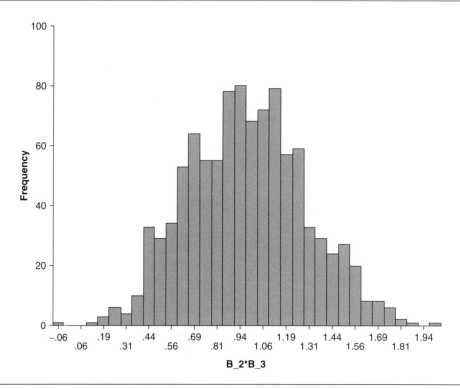

Figure 28.5   Bootstrap distribution of B_2B_3.

particular analysis, we are going to assess whether the relationship between the mediator and outcome variable is moderated.[21] To do that, we are going to use the macro written by Preacher, Rucker, and Hayes (2006) that not only assesses for the various moderated mediation models but provides bootstrap estimates of the effect.[22]

The results from the macro indicate that for Sex 1, the indirect effect (B_2B_3) is .512, but for Sex 2, the indirect effect is 1.338, with the former being insignificant and the latter being significant at $\alpha = .05$. When the statistics were bootstrapped, Sex 1's average effect was .489, while Sex 2's average effect was 1.303, with the former not being significant and the latter being significant. Because bootstrapping techniques do not rely on the normality assumption, taking values at the 2.5th and 97.5th percentiles will give a 95% confidence interval around the statistic instead of assessing for significance. The (bias-corrected) 95% confidence interval of the effect for Sex 1 is [−.311, 1.449], while for Sex 2, it is [.545, 2.334], giving evidence that the former could be 0, while the latter likely is not 0. Thus, it appears that sex does moderate the mediated relationship.

NOTES

1. Editor's note: Interested readers can refer to Chapter 29 (this volume) for more information on multilevel models. Although mediation and moderation and mediated moderation are not specifically addressed in the chapter, they can be assessed via structural equation modeling (SEM), and therefore readers may want to refer to Chapter 32 on best practices in SEM.

2. In other words, it represents an interaction between two variables.

3. If there is not an already determined effect, then the analysis could be a suppression study (MacKinnon, Krull, & Lockwood, 2000), which is a similar analysis but beyond the scope of this chapter.

4. *Moderation* and *interaction* are used somewhat synonymously in the psychological and educational literature. For this text, *interaction* will refer to the multiplicative term in the regression equation, while *moderation* will refer to the overall principle.

5. The principles discussed in this chapter can equally apply to logistic regression frameworks. For an explicit introduction to the topic, see Jaccard (2001). For a more general introduction to logistic regression, see Chapters 24–26 in the current volume.

6. Editor's note: In the case of a categorical moderator variable, it may be easier to use SEM to model parallel models and test the interaction by

testing whether corresponding relationships are constant across groups. This topic needs its own chapter, hopefully in a future version of this book!

7. The hierarchical F test is as follows:

$$ F = \frac{(R_s^2 - R_i^2)/(k_s - k_i)}{(1 - R_s^2)(N - k_s - 1)} $$

where R_i^2 is the squared multiple R value of the initial model, R_s^2 is the squared multiple R value of the supplemental model, k is the number of predictors in the respective models, and N is the total sample size. F is then distributed with $k_s - k_i$ and $N - k_s - 1$ degrees of freedom.

8. Because variables and their multiplicative terms are highly colinear, estimations of the βs are not substantially interpretable (Frazier et al., 2004). Unstandardized regression coefficients are not affected by differences in the variances of the moderator or differences in measurement error in the dependent variable (Baron & Kenny, 1986). If one is interested in standardized regression coefficients, though, one need only standardize the initial variables and read the B coefficients (for more information, see Aiken & West, 1991).

9. This is the multiplicative term in simple moderated regression, but in other models, it can be the B associated, for example, with a quadratic, cubic, quadric, and so on, term.

10. For an overview of best practices in ANOVA, see Kutner et al. (2004) and Chapter 23 in the current volume.

11. The interested reader can find a good introduction to the topic in Chapter 5 of Aiken and West (1991).

12. Kenny et al. (1998) write that the demonstration of a significant effect between the predictor and outcome variables is not necessary if, for example, one is looking at a suppression study (MacKinnon et al., 2000) or a multiple mediator study (for more examples, see Frazier et al., 2004), or if the predictor-outcome relation is temporally distal (Shrout & Bolger, 2002).

13. Editor's note: Other options exist, such as poor measurement of the construct, incomplete measurement of the proposed mediator, and so on.

14. The MacKinnon et al. (1998) values are available freely at http://www.public.asu.edu/davidpm/ripl/methods.htm.

15. Bootstrapping (see Chapter 19, this volume) is an attractive alternative because it does not impose a theoretical sampling distribution. For a particularly informative walk-through of the bootstrapping approach using multiple mediators, as well as comparing indirect effects from the same model, see Preacher and Hayes (2006).

16. Moderated mediation and mediated moderation rely on the same analytic models (and the same fundamental equality; see Equation 10) (Muller et al., 2005; Preacher, Rucker, & Hayes, 2006). The difference in emphasis depends on the theoretical rationale behind the analysis. This chapter will examine the phenomenon from the moderated mediation perspective.

17. Editor's note: The obvious exception to this would be for logistic regression-style analyses.

18. MMRPOWER is freely available on the Internet at http://carbon.cudenver.edu/~haguinis/mmr/and http://www.math.montana.edu/~rjboik/power.html.

19. The graph was generated in *S-Plus*, but a similar graph can be computed using Rweb at http://www.quantpsy.org.

20. Andrew Hayes has developed a more complete macro entitled INDIRECT.SPS, which is freely available at his Web site: http://www.quantpsy.org/.

21. Some examples of an alternative moderated mediation are having one variable affect the predictor-mediator relationship, while another affects the mediator-outcome relationship; likewise, the independent variable could also moderate one (or both) of those paths.

22. The macro is entitled MODMED.SPS and is freely available at http://www.quantpsy.org/.

REFERENCES

Adler, N. E., Boyce, T., Chesney, M., Cohen, S., Folkman, S., Kahn, R., et al. (1994). Socioeconomic status and health: The challenge of the gradient. *American Psychologist, 49,* 15–24.

Adler, N. E., & Ostove, J. M. (1999). Socioeconomic status and health: What we know and what we don't. *Annals of the New York Academy of Sciences, 896,* 3–15.

Aguinis, H. (1995). Statistical power problems with moderated multiple regression in management research. *Journal of Management Research, 21,* 1141–1158.

Aguinis, H. (2004). *Regression analysis for categorical moderators.* New York: Guilford.

Aguinis, H., Boik, R. J., & Pierce, C. A. (2001). A generalized solution for approximating the power to detect effects of categorical moderator variables using multiple regression. *Organizational Research Methods, 4,* 291–323.

Aguinis, H., & Pierce, C. A. (1998). Heterogeneity of error variance and the assessment of moderating effects of categorical variables: A conceptual review. *Organizational Research Methods, 1,* 296–314.

Aguinis, H., & Stone-Romero, E. F. (1997). Methodological artifacts in moderated multiple regression and their effects on statistical power. *Journal of Applied Psychology, 82,* 192–206.

Aiken, L. S., & West, S. G. (1991). *Multiple regression: Testing and interpreting interactions.* Newbury Park, CA: Sage.

Anastasi, A. (1958). *Differential psychology: Individual and group differences in behavior* (3rd ed.). New York: Macmillan.

Anastasi, A., & Foley, J. P., Jr. (1949). *Differential psychology: Individual and group differences in behavior.* New York: Macmillan.

Baron, R. M., & Kenny, D. A. (1986). The moderator-mediator variable distinction in social psychological research: Conceptual, strategic, and statistical considerations. *Journal of Personality and Social Psychology, 51,* 1173–1182.

Bauer, D. J., & Curran, P. J. (2005). Probing interactions in fixed and multilevel regression: Inferential and graphical techniques. *Multivariate Behavioral Research, 40,* 373–400.

Binet, A., & Henri, V. (1896). La psychologie individuelle [Individual psychology]. *Année Psychologique, 2,* 411–465.

Blanton, H., & Jaccard, J. (2006). Arbitrary metrics in psychology. *American Psychologist, 61,* 27–41.

Bollen, K. A. (1987). Total, direct, and indirect effects in structural equation models. In C. C. Clogg (Ed.), *Sociological methodology* (Vol. 17, pp. 37–69). Washington, DC: American Sociological Association.

Bollen, K. A., & Stine, R. A. (1992). Bootstrapping goodness-of-fit measures in structural equation models. *Sociological Methods & Research, 21,* 205–229.

Cattell, J. M. (1890). Mental tests and measurements. *Mind, 15,* 373–380.

Chaplin, W. F. (1991). The next generation in moderation research in personality psychology. *Journal of Personality, 59,* 143–178.

Cohen, J. (1978). Partialed products are interactions; partialed powers are curve components. *Psychological Bulletin, 85,* 858–866.

Cohen, J., Cohen, P., West, S. G., & Aiken, L. S. (2003). *Applied multiple regression/correlation analysis for the behavioral sciences* (3rd ed.). Mahwah, NJ: Lawrence Erlbaum.

Cole, D. A., & Maxwell, S. E. (2003). Testing mediational models with longitudinal data: Questions and tips in the use of structural equation modeling. *Journal of Abnormal Psychology, 112,* 558–577.

Cronbach, L., & Snow, R. E. (1977). *Aptitudes and instructional methods: A handbook for research on interactions.* Oxford, England: Irvington.

Davison, M. L., Kwak, N., Seo, Y. S., & Choi, J. (2002). Using hierarchical linear models to examine moderator effects: Person-by-organization interactions. *Organizational Research Methods, 5,* 231–254.

Effron, B., & Tibshirani, R. J. (1993). *An introduction to the bootstrap.* New York: Chapman & Hall.

Frazier, P. A., Tix, A. P., & Barron, K. E. (2004). Testing moderator and mediator effects in counseling psychology research. *Journal of Counseling Psychology, 51,* 115–134.

Gottfredson, L. S. (2004). Intelligence: Is it the epidemiologists' elusive "fundamental cause" of social class inequalities in health? *Journal of Personality and Social Psychology, 86,* 174–199.

Gottfredson, L. S., & Deary, I. J. (2004). Intelligence predicts health and longevity, but why? *Current Directions in Psychological Science, 13,* 1–4.

Holbert, R. L., & Stephenson, M. T. (2001). The importance of indirect effects in media effects research: Testing for mediation in structural equation modeling. *Journal of Broadcasting and Electronic Media, 47,* 556–572.

Holmbeck, G. N. (1997). Toward terminological, conceptual, and statistical clarity in the study of mediators and moderators: Examples from the child-clinical and pediatric psychology literatures. *Journal of Consulting and Clinical Psychology, 65,* 599–610.

Hoyle, R. H., & Kenny, D. A. (1999). Sample size, reliability, and tests of statistical mediation. In R. H. Hoyle (Ed.), *Statistical strategies for small sample research* (pp. 195–222). Thousand Oaks, CA: Sage.

Hoyle, R. H., & Robinson, J. I. (2003). Mediated and moderated effects in social psychological research: Measurement, design, and analysis issues. In C. Sansone, C. Morf, & A. T. Panter (Eds.), *Handbook of methods in social psychology* (pp. 213–233). Thousand Oaks, CA: Sage.

Huitema, B. E. (1980). *The analysis of covariance and alternatives.* New York: John Wiley.

Humphreys, P. (1989). *The chances of explanation: Causal explanations in the social, medical, and physical sciences.* Princeton, NJ: Princeton University Press.

Jaccard, J. (2001). *Interaction effects in logistic regression.* Thousand Oaks, CA: Sage.

Jaccard, J., & Turrisi, R. (2003). *Interaction effects in multiple regression* (2nd ed.). Thousand Oaks, CA: Sage.

Jaccard, J., Turrisi, R., & Wan, C. K. (1990). *Interaction effects in multiple regression.* Newbury Park, CA: Sage.

Jaccard, J., & Wan, C. K. (1996). *LISREL approaches to interaction effects in multiple regression.* Newbury Park, CA: Sage.

James, L. R., & Brett, J. M. (1984). Mediators, moderators, and tests for mediation. *Journal of Applied Psychology, 69,* 307–321.

Jensen, A. R. (2005). Mental chronometry and the unification of differential psychology. In R. Sternberg & J. E. Pretz (Eds.), *Cognition and intelligence: Identifying the mechanisms of the mind* (pp. 26–50). New York: Cambridge University Press.

Johnson, P. O., & Neyman, J. (1936). Tests of certain linear hypotheses and their application to some educational problems. *Statistical Research Memoirs, 1,* 57–93.

Judd, C. M., & Kenny, D. A. (1981). Process analysis: Estimating mediation in treatment evaluations. *Evaluation Review, 5,* 602–619.

Kenny, D. A., Kashy, D. A., & Bolger, N. (1998). Data analysis in social psychology. In D. T. Gilbert, S. T. Fiske, & G. Lindzey (Eds.), *The handbook of social psychology* (4th ed., pp. 233–265). New York: Oxford University Press.

Kraemer, H. C., Stice, E., Kazdin, A., Offord, D., & Kupfer, D. (2001). How do risk factors work together? Mediators, moderators, and independent, overlapping, and proxy risk factors. *American Journal of Psychiatry, 58,* 848–856.

Kraemer, H. C., Wilson, G. T., Fairburn, C. G., & Agras, W. S. (2002). Mediators and moderators of treatment effects in randomized clinical trials. *Archives of General Psychiatry, 59,* 877–883.

Kutner, M. H., Nachtsheim, C. J., Neter, J., & Li, W. (2004). *Applied linear statistical models* (5th ed.). Boston: McGraw-Hill.

MacCallum, R. C., Wegener, D. T., Uchino, B. N., & Fabrigar, L. R. (1993). The problem of equivalent models in applications of covariance structure analysis. *Psychological Bulletin, 11,* 185–199.

MacKinnon, D. P. (2000). Contrasts in multiple mediator models. In J. Rose, L. Chassin, C. C. Presson, & S. J. Sherman (Eds.), *Multivariate applications in substance use research: New methods for new questions* (pp. 141–160). Mahwah, NJ: Lawrence Erlbaum.

MacKinnon, D. P., & Dwyer, J. H. (1993). Estimating mediated effects in prevention studies. *Evaluation Review, 17,* 144–158.

MacKinnon, D. P., Krull, J. L., & Lockwood, C. M. (2000). Equivalence of the mediation, confounding, and suppression effect. *Prevention Science, 4,* 173–181.

MacKinnon, D. P., Lockwood, C., & Hoffman, J. (1998, June). *A new method to test for mediation.* Paper presented at the annual meeting of the Society for Prevention Research, Park City, UT.

MacKinnon, D. P., Lockwood, C. M., Hoffman, J. M., West, S. G., & Sheets, V. (2002). A comparison of methods to test mediation and other intervening variable effects. *Psychological Methods, 7,* 83–104.

Maxwell, S. E. (2000). Sample size and multiple regression analysis. *Psychological Methods, 5,* 434–458.

McClelland, G. H., & Judd, C. M. (1993). Statistical difficulties of detecting interactions and moderator effects. *Psychological Bulletin, 114,* 376–390.

Minton, H. L., & Schneider, F. W. (1980). *Differential psychology.* Monterey, CA: Brooks/Cole.

Mitroff, I. A., & Featheringham, T. R. (1974). On systemic problem solving and the error of the third kind. *Behavioral Science, 19,* 383–393.

Muller, D., Judd, C. M., & Yzerbyt, V. Y. (2005). When moderation is mediated and mediation is moderated. *Journal of Personality and Social Psychology, 89,* 852–863.

Pedhazur, E. J. (1997). *Multiple regression in behavioral research: Explanation and prediction* (3rd ed.). Fort Worth, TX: Harcourt Brace.

Preacher, K. J., Curran, P. J., & Bauer, D. J. (2006). Computational tools for probing interactions in multiple linear regression, multilevel modeling, and latent curve analysis. *Journal of Educational and Behavioral Statistics, 31,* 437–448.

Preacher, K. J., & Hayes, A. F. (2004). SPSS and SAS procedures for estimating indirect effects in simple mediation models. *Behavior Research Methods, Instruments, & Computers, 36,* 717–731.

Preacher, K. J., & Hayes, A. F. (2006). *Asymptotic and resampling strategies for assessing and comparing indirect effects in simple and mediator models.* Manuscript submitted for publication.

Preacher, K. J., Rucker, D. D., & Hayes, A. F. (2006). *Suggested procedures for addressing moderated mediation hypotheses.* Manuscript submitted for publication.

Raudenbush, S. W., & Bryk, A. S. (2002). *Hierarchical linear models: Applications and data analysis methods* (2nd ed.). Thousand Oaks, CA: Sage.

Ree, M. J., & Carretta, T. R. (2006). The role of measurement error in familiar statistics. *Organizational Research Methods, 9,* 99–112.

Reyonds, C. R., & Willson, V. L. (Eds.). (1985). *Methodological and statistical advances in the study of individual differences.* New York: Plenum.

Rogosa, D. R. (1980). Comparing nonparallel regression lines. *Psychological Bulletin, 88,* 307–321.

Rogosa, D. R. (1981). On the relationship between the Johnson-Neyman region of significance and statistical tests of parallel within-group regressions. *Educational and Psychological Measurement, 41,* 127–134.

Rose, B. M., Holmbeck, G. N., Coakley, R. M., & Franks, E. A. (2004). Mediator and moderator effects in developmental and behavioral pediatric research. *Developmental and Behavioral Pediatrics, 25,* 58–67.

Rubin, D. (1974). Estimating causal effects of treatments in randomized and nonrandomized studies. *Journal of Educational Psychology, 66,* 688–701.

Russell, C. J., & Bobko, P. (1992). Moderated regression analysis and Likert scales: Too coarse for comfort. *Journal of Applied Psychology, 77,* 336–342.

Shrout, P. E., & Bolger, N. (2002). Mediation in experimental and nonexperimental studies: New procedures and recommendations. *Psychological Methods, 7,* 422–445.

Smith, B., & Sechrest, L. (1991). Treatment of Aptitude × Treatment interactions. *Journal of Consulting and Clinical Psychology, 59,* 233–244.

Smith, E. R. (1982). Beliefs, attributions, and evaluations: Nonhierarchical models of mediation in social cognition. *Journal of Personality and Social Psychology, 43,* 248–259.

Sobel, M. E. (1982). Asymptotic confidence intervals for indirect effects in structural equation models. In S. Leinherdt (Ed.), *Sociological methodology 1982* (pp. 290–312). Washington, DC: American Sociological Association.

Spearman, C. (1904). "General intelligence": Objectively defined and measured. *American Journal of Psychology, 15,* 201–292.

Spirtes, P., Glymour, P., & Scheines, R. (1993). *Causation, prediction, and search.* New York: Springer-Verlag.

Stern, W. (1900). *Uber psychologie der individuellen differenzen* [The psychology of individual differences]. Leipzig: Barth.

West, S. G., & Aiken, L. S. (1997). Toward understanding individual effects in multicomponent prevention programs: Design and analysis strategies. In K. J. Bryant, M. Windle, & S. G. West (Eds.), *The science of prevention: Methodological advances from alcohol and substance abuse research* (pp. 167–209). Washington, DC: American Psychological Association.

Wilcox, R. R. (2003). *Applying contemporary statistical techniques.* San Diego: Academic Press.

PART V

BEST ADVANCED PRACTICES IN QUANTITATIVE METHODS

29

A BRIEF INTRODUCTION TO
HIERARCHICAL LINEAR MODELING

JASON W. OSBORNE

Hierarchical, or nested, data structures are common throughout many areas of research. However, until recently, there has not been any appropriate technique for analyzing these types of data. Now, with several user-friendly software programs available[1] and some more readable texts and treatments on the topic, researchers need to be aware of the issue and how it should be dealt with. The goal of this chapter is to introduce the problem and how it is dealt with appropriately, as well as to provide examples of the pitfalls of not doing appropriate analyses.

WHAT IS A HIERARCHICAL DATA STRUCTURE?

People (and most living creatures, for that matter) tend to exist within organizational structures, such as families, schools, business organizations, churches, towns, states, and countries. In education, students exist within a hierarchical social structure that can include family, peer group, classroom, grade level, school, school district, state, and country. Workers exist within production or skill units, businesses, and sectors of the economy, as well as geographic regions. Health care workers and patients exist within households and families, medical practices and facilities (e.g., a doctor's practice or hospital), counties, states, and countries. Many other communities exhibit hierarchical data structures as well.

Raudenbush and Bryk (2002) also discuss two other types of data hierarchies that are less obvious: repeated-measures data and meta-analytic data.[2] Once one begins looking for hierarchies in data, it becomes obvious that data repeatedly gathered on an individual are hierarchical, as all the observations are nested within individuals. While there are other adequate procedures for dealing with this sort of data, the assumptions relating to them are rigorous, whereas procedures relating to hierarchical modeling require fewer assumptions. Also, when researchers are engaged in the task of meta-analysis, or analysis of a large number of existing studies, it should become clear that subjects, results, procedures, and experimenters are nested within experiment.

Author's Note: This chapter was originally published as Osborne, J. W. (2000). Advantages of hierarchical linear modeling. *Practical Assessment, Research & Evaluation, 7*(1). Available at http://pareonline.net/getvn.asp?v=7&n=1. Thanks to Bob Croninger for catching a technical issue discussed in Note 6.

Why Is a Hierarchical Data Structure an Issue?

Hierarchical, or nested, data present several problems for analysis. First, people that exist within hierarchies tend to be more similar to each other than people randomly sampled from the entire population. For example, students in a particular third-grade classroom are more similar to each other (especially after several months of class) than to students randomly sampled from the school district as a whole or from the national population of third graders. This is because students are not randomly assigned to classrooms from the population but rather are assigned to schools based on geographic factors. Thus, students within a particular classroom tend to come from a community or community segment that is more homogeneous in terms of morals and values, family background, socioeconomic status, race or ethnicity, religion, and even educational preparation than the population as a whole. Furthermore, students within a particular classroom share the experience of being in the same environment—having the same teacher, being in the same physical environment, and having similar experiences—which may lead to increased homogeneity over time.

The Problem of Independence of Observations. This discussion could be applied to any level of nesting, such as the family, school district, county, state, or even country. Based on this discussion, we can assert that individuals who are drawn from an institution, such as a classroom, school, business, or health care unit, will be more homogeneous than if they had been randomly sampled from a larger population. Herein lies the first issue for analysis of this sort of data. Because these individuals tend to share certain characteristics (environmental, background, experiential, demographic, or otherwise), observations based on these individuals are not fully independent. However, most analytic techniques require independence of observations as a primary assumption for the analysis. Because this assumption is violated in the presence of hierarchical data, ordinary least squares regression produces standard errors that are too small (unless these so-called design effects are incorporated into the analysis). In turn, this leads to an inappropriately greater probability of rejection of a null hypothesis than if (a) an appropriate statistical analysis were performed or (b) the data included truly independent observations.

The Problem of How to Deal With Cross-Level Data. Going back to the example of our third-grade classroom, it is often the case that a researcher is interested in understanding how environmental variables (e.g., teaching style, teacher behaviors, class size, class composition, district policies or funding, or even state or national variables, etc.) affect individual outcomes (e.g., achievement, attitudes, retention, etc.). But given that outcomes are gathered at the individual level and other variables at the classroom, school, district, state, or nation level, the question arises as to what the unit of analysis should be and how to deal with the cross-level nature of the data.

One strategy would be to assign classroom or teacher (or school, district, or other) characteristics to all students (i.e., to bring the higher-level variables down to the student level). The problem with this approach, again, is nonindependence of observations, as all students within a particular classroom assume identical scores on a variable.

Another way to deal with this issue would be to aggregate up to the level of the classroom, school, district, and so on. Thus, we could talk about the effect of teacher or classroom characteristics on average classroom achievement. However, there are several issues with this approach, including (a) the fact that much (up to 80%–90%) of the individual variability on the outcome variable is lost, which can lead to dramatic under- or overestimation of observed relationships between variables (Raudenbush & Bryk, 2002), and (b) the fact that the outcome variable changes significantly and substantively from individual achievement to average classroom achievement.

Neither of these strategies constitutes a best practice, although they are commonly performed. Neither of these strategies allows the researcher to ask truly important questions, such as, What is the effect of a particular teacher variable on student learning? A third approach, that of hierarchical modeling, becomes necessary in this age of educational accountability and more sophisticated hypotheses.

HOW DO HIERARCHICAL MODELS WORK? A BRIEF PRIMER

The goal of this chapter is to introduce the concept of hierarchical modeling and explicate the need for the procedure. It cannot fully communicate the nuances and procedures needed to actually perform a hierarchical analysis. The reader is encouraged to refer to Raudenbush and Bryk (2002; see also, e.g., Draper, 1995; Nezlek & Zyzniewski, 1998; Pedhazur, 1997) for a full explanation of the conceptual and methodological details of hierarchical modeling.

The basic concept behind hierarchical modeling is similar to that of ordinary least squares (OLS) regression. On the base level (usually the individual level, referred to here as Level 1, the lowest level of your data), the analysis is similar to that of OLS regression: An outcome variable is predicted as a function of a linear combination of one or more Level 1 variables, plus an intercept, so

$$Y_{ij} = \beta_{0j} + \beta_{1j}X_1 + \ldots + \beta_{kj}X_k + r_{ij},$$

where β_{0j} represents the intercept[3] of group j, β_{1j} represents the slope of variable X_1 of group j, and r_{ij} represents the residual for individual i within group j. On subsequent levels, the Level 1 slope(s) and intercept become dependent variables being predicted from Level 2 variables:

$$\beta_{0j} = \gamma_{00} + \gamma_{01}W_1 + \ldots + \gamma_{0k}W_k + u_{0j},$$

$$\beta_{1j} = \gamma_{10} + \gamma_{11}W_1 + \ldots + \gamma_{1k}W_k + u_{1j},$$

and so forth, where γ_{00} and γ_{10} are intercepts, and γ_{01} and γ_{11} represent slopes predicting β_{0j} and β_{1j}, respectively, from variable W_1. Through this process, we accurately model the effects of Level 1 variables on the outcome, as well as the effects of Level 2 variables on the outcome. In addition, as we are predicting slopes as well as intercepts (means), we can model cross-level interactions, whereby we can attempt to understand what explains differences in the relationship between Level 1 variables and the outcome. This will be discussed a bit more below.

AN EMPIRICAL COMPARISON OF THE THREE APPROACHES TO ANALYZING HIERARCHICAL DATA

To illustrate the outcomes achieved by each of the three possible analytic strategies for dealing with hierarchical data, disaggregation (bringing Level 2 data down to Level 1), aggregation (bringing Level 1 data up to Level 2 in the form of averages), and multilevel modeling, data were

drawn from the National Education Longitudinal Survey of 1988 from the National Center for Education Statistics. This data set contains data on a representative sample of approximately 25,000 eighth graders in the United States at a variety of levels, including individual, family, teacher, and school. The analysis we performed predicted composite achievement test scores (math, reading combined) from student socioeconomic status (family SES), student locus of control (LOCUS), the percentage of students in the school who are members of racial or ethnic minority groups (%MINORITY), and the percentage of students in the school who receive free lunch (%LUNCH). Achievement is our outcome, SES and LOCUS are Level 1 predictors, and %MINORITY and %LUNCH are Level 2 indicators of school environment. In general, SES and LOCUS are expected to be positively related to achievement, and %MINORITY and %LUNCH are expected to be negatively related to achievement. In these analyses, 995 of a possible 1,004 schools were represented (the remaining 9 were removed due to insufficient data).[4]

Disaggregated Analysis. In order to perform the disaggregated analysis, the Level 2 values were assigned to all individual students within a particular school. A standard OLS multiple regression was performed via SPSS, entering all predictor variables simultaneously. The resulting model was significant, with $R = .56$, $R^2 = .32$, $F_{(4, 22899)} = 2648.54$, $p < .0001$. The individual regression weights and significance tests are presented in Table 29.1.

All four variables were significant predictors of student achievement. As expected, SES and LOCUS were positively related to achievement, while %MINORITY and %LUNCH were negatively related.

Aggregated Analysis. In order to perform the aggregated analysis, all Level 1 variables achievement, LOCUS, SES) were aggregated up to the school level (Level 2) by averaging. A standard OLS multiple regression was performed via SPSS, entering all predictor variables simultaneously. The resulting model was significant, with $R = .87$, $R^2 = .75$, $F_{(4, 999)} = 746.41$, $p < .0001$. As seen in Table 29.1, both average SES and average LOCUS were significantly positively related to achievement, and %MINORITY was negatively related. In this analysis, %LUNCH was not a significant predictor of average achievement.

Table 29.1   Comparison of Three Analytic Strategies for Dealing With Nested Data

	Disaggregated			Aggregated			Hierarchical		
Variable	B	SE	t	B	SE	t	B	SE	t
SES	4.97 a	.08	62.11***	7.28 b	.26	27.91***	4.07 c	.10	41.29***
LOCUS	2.96 a	.08	37.71***	4.97 b	.49	10.22***	2.82 a	.08	35.74***
%MINORITY	−0.45 a	.03	−15.53***	−0.40 a	.06	−8.76***	−0.59 b	.07	−8.73***
%LUNCH	−0.43 a	.03	−13.50***	0.03 b	.05	0.59	−1.32 c	.07	−19.17***

NOTE: *B* refers to an unstandardized regression coefficient, and is used for the hierarchical linear modeling analysis to represent the unstandardized regression coefficients produced therein, even though these are commonly labeled as betas and gammas. *SE* refers to standard error. *B*s with different subscripts were found to be significantly different from other *B*s within the row at *p* < .05.

***p < .0001.

Multilevel Analysis. In order to perform the multilevel analysis, a true multilevel analysis was performed via hierarchical linear modeling (HLM), in which the respective Level 1 and Level 2 variables were specified appropriately. Note also that all Level 1 predictors were centered at the group mean, and all Level 2 predictors were centered at the grand mean.[5] The resulting model demonstrated goodness of fit ($\chi^2_{(5)}$ for change in model fit = 4231.39, *p* < .0001). This analysis reveals significant positive relationships between achievement and the Level 1 predictors (SES and LOCUS) and strong negative relationships between achievement and the Level 2 predictors (%MINORITY and %LUNCH). Furthermore, the analysis revealed significant interactions between SES and both Level 2 predictors, indicating that the slope for SES gets weaker as %LUNCH and %MINORITY increase. Also, there was an interaction between LOCUS and %MINORITY, indicating that as %MINORITY increases, the slope for LOCUS weakens. Although there are effect size estimates in HLM, there is no clear preference in the literature as to which one is superior at this time.

Comparison of the Three Analytic Strategies

For the purposes of this discussion, we will assume that the third analysis represents the best estimate of what the "true" relationships are between the predictors and the outcome. Unstandardized regression coefficients (*B*s in OLS, betas and gammas in HLM) were compared statistically via procedures outlined in Cohen and Cohen (1983).

In examining what is probably the most common analytic strategy for dealing with data such as these, the disaggregated analysis provided the best estimates of the Level 1 effects in an OLS analysis. However, it significantly overestimated the effect of SES and significantly and substantially underestimated the effects of the Level 2 effects. The standard errors in this analysis are generally lower than they should be, particularly for the Level 2 variables.

In comparison, the aggregated analysis overestimated the multiple correlation by more than 100%, overestimated the regression slope for SES by 79% and for LOCUS by 76%, and underestimated the slopes for %MINORITY by 32% and for %LUNCH by 98%.[6]

These analyses reveal multilevel modeling as a best practice for anyone with nested or multilevel data. Neither OLS analysis accurately modeled the true relationships between the outcome and the predictors. In addition, HLM analyses provide other benefits, such as easy modeling of cross-level interactions, which allows for more interesting questions to be asked of the data. With nested and hierarchical data common in the social and other sciences, and with recent developments making HLM software packages more user-friendly and accessible, it is important for researchers in all fields to become acquainted with these procedures.

ADVANCED TOPICS IN HLM

As many authors have discovered in the years since HLM became available, there are many applications for these analyses. Generalizations to three- and four-level models are available, as are logistic regression analogs (e.g., HLM with binary or polytomous outcomes), applications for meta-analysis, powerful advantages for longitudinal analysis (as compared with other methods such as repeated-measures analysis of variance [ANOVA]), and many of the fun aspects of OLS regression (such as modeling curvilinear effects) possible in HLM as well.

There is little downside to HLM, aside from the learning curve. If one were to use HLM on data where no nesting, dependence, or other issues were present, one would get virtually identical results to OLS regression from statistical software packages such as SPSS or SAS or R.

Two particular topics merit brief discussion. Chapter 30 discusses applications of multilevel modeling to longitudinal data. There are significant issues with longitudinal data, including the fact that the assumptions of repeated-measures ANOVA (RMANOVA) are rarely met in practice and that missing data and unequal time periods between measures can severely cripple a RMANOVA analysis. However, HLM has none of these drawbacks. So long as any individual has one data point, it can be included in a repeated-measures HLM analysis. Furthermore, unequal time intervals between measurements can be explicitly modeled to remove as much potential for error variance as possible. Growth curves are easily modeled, and the estimation procedures in HLM tend to produce smaller standard errors, all of which make HLM a best practice for longitudinal data analysis.

Another less common but equally interesting application is that of meta-analysis, which is discussed in Chapters 12 and 31. In particular, any meta-analysis is automatically a nested data situation, as subjects are nested within experiments or studies. Many meta-analytic strategies involve summary statistics, which amount to the aggregation strategy presented above. This represents a significant loss of information over using HLM, where one can use all subjects as Level 1 data and study characteristics as Level 2 (or higher) data. Meta-analysis in itself represents a best practice, as it leverages the efforts of many researchers to produce higher-quality conclusions, and meta-analysis using multilevel modeling is the best practice for performing this important and useful analysis.

NOTES

1. My personal favorite is HLM, most likely because I have been using it since the mid-1990s.

There are many high-quality packages out there for this type of analysis, and readers are encouraged to explore them.

2. Readers interested in these applications can refer to Chapters 30 and 31 in this volume or Raudenbush and Bryk (2002).

3. This can be left uncentered or moved to represent the mean, as one can do in OLS regression (see, e.g., Hoffman & Gavin, 1998).

4. This highlights one of the restrictions of multilevel modeling—in general, you need complete data on all subjects at the *highest* level of analysis, in this case, Level 2. Of course, missing data procedures can ameliorate this problem, as outlined in Chapter 15. Furthermore, one of the strengths of this over other procedures is that you do *not* need complete data at the lower level(s), a significant advantage over repeated-measures ANOVA. Refer to Chapter 30 for applications of HLM to repeated-measures data.

5. Centering variables in HLM changes the intercept's meaning from the value of Y when $X = 0$ (traditional interpretation) to the value of Y when $X =$ the average score. For more on the technical interpretations of intercepts when various centering strategies are used, see Hoffman and Gavin (1998) and Raudenbush and Bryk (2002).

6. Because I group-mean centered the Level 1 variables in HLM (as is often desirable), the comparisons of the school-level variables across methods (disaggregated, aggregated, HLM) are not truly equivalent. In the disaggregated and aggregated versions, the student-level variables act as controls so that the school variables are adjusted effects (adjusted for either SES and locus at Level 1 or average SES and average locus at Level 2); when group-mean centering is used, however, the levels are orthogonal. The large discrepancy in the effect for %LUNCH between HLM and the other methods may be due to the absence of SES effects at Level 2. Grand-mean centering can handle this issue and may make the Level 2 coefficients look more similar to the coefficients with the aggregated method, but when discussing random effects for the Level 1 measures in your model, grand-mean centering makes less sense when the Level 1 coefficients vary between groups. This model (with group-mean centering) provides more accurate estimates for the respective Level 1 and Level 2 coefficients because these effects are not confounded across levels (i.e., the models are orthogonal). If the researcher wanted to know what these effects might be controlling for average SES or average locus, he or she could include them at the appropriate level in the model. While HLM can disentangle effects across levels of a hierarchy (actually, regardless of centering), the other methods cannot.

REFERENCES

Cohen, J., & Cohen, P. (1983). *Applied multiple regression/correlation analysis for the behavioral sciences.* Hillsdale, NJ: Lawrence Erlbaum.

Draper, D. (1995). Inference and hierarchical modeling in the social sciences. *Journal of Educational and Behavioral Statistics, 20*(2), 115–147.

Hoffman, D. A., & Gavin, M. B. (1998). Centering decisions in hierarchical linear models:

Implications for research in organizations. *Journal of Management, 24*(5), 623–641.

Nezlek, J. B., & Zyzniewski, L. E. (1998). Using hierarchical linear modeling to analyze grouped data. *Group Dynamics, 2,* 313–320.

Pedhazur, E. J. (1997). *Multiple regression in behavioral research.* Orlando, FL: Harcourt Brace.

Raudenbush, S. W., & Bryk, A. S. (2002). *Hierarchical linear models: Applications and data analysis methods.* Thousand Oaks, CA: Sage.

30

BEST PRACTICES IN ANALYSIS OF LONGITUDINAL DATA

A Multilevel Approach

FRANS E. S. TAN

Analyzing longitudinal data has important advantages over cross-sectional data because it can distinguish between changes that occur within subjects and differences between subjects. In cross-sectional data, subjects are measured at a particular moment in time. The differences in characteristics of the subjects are the only source of variation that can be used to explain the outcome of scientific interest. The standard ordinary least squares (OLS) linear regression technique is often sufficient to describe and to make inferences about the relationship between variables in cross-sectional data. There are a number of excellent standard textbooks about this topic at a basic (e.g., Kleinbaum, Kupper, Muller, & Nizam, 1998) and advanced level (e.g., Weisberg, 1985).

Statistical analysis methods for longitudinal data should be able to distinguish between the two sources of variation—that is, the within-subjects variation that accounts for changes within each subject through repeated measurements in time and the between-subjects variation accounting for differences between the subject's performances. The OLS linear regression technique is in general not suitable to analyze longitudinal data because it incorrectly treats all observations as if they were uncorrelated.

Longitudinal data are correlated because of the hierarchical structure of data sampling (i.e., repeated measurements are nested within subjects). Another type of correlation between repeated measurements could arise when, for example, each subject is measured by an observer (possibly self-reporting) whose measurement is influenced by the previous measurement on the same subject. This type of correlation is known as serial correlation, which is different from the former type. One common and appropriate method of analyzing this type of data is repeated-measures analysis of variance (ANOVA) or multivariate ANOVA (MANOVA; see, e.g., Hand & Taylor, 1987, for an introduction to this topic). However, multilevel modeling (often referred to as hierarchical linear modeling or mixed-effects regression) has significant fundamental advantages over repeated-measures ANOVA (RMANOVA) and therefore constitutes a best practice.[1]

EXAMPLES OF LONGITUDINAL DATA

Anti-Alcohol Campaign

The first example is a hypothetical study about the effects of an anti-alcohol campaign, which is performed in different European countries. The objective is a cross-country comparison of the relationship between alcohol consumption and violent behavior. In some countries, there was a large-scale anti-alcohol campaign. Seven of these countries were compared with eight other countries without anti-alcohol campaigns. Within each country, a random sample of about 3,000 subjects was collected. The countries were also subdivided into northern and southern parts. Each subject was measured three times.

This example is structured according to a multilevel design. In general, the number of levels in a multilevel design is determined by the number of random factors. Whether a factor is fixed or random depends primarily on whether the sampling is a random sample from some well-defined population of subjects (within each country) and whether the results will be generalized to a larger population or not. The results of an analysis, based on the subjects in the sample, will be generalized to the population; therefore, subjects will be treated as a random factor. However, if in some (rare) situation, the interest is only to draw conclusions with respect to the subjects in the sample, then the results of the statistical analysis will not be generalized to a larger group, and the subjects as a factor will be considered to be fixed. Variables such as geographic position, treatment status, socioeconomic status, gender, and marital status are usually considered to be fixed factors because interest is only restricted with respect to the observed levels of the variable.

The design of the anti-alcohol campaign study can be considered as an example of a three-level design. The repeated measurements nested within each subject are denoted as first-level observations. The subjects are denoted as second-level observations, while the countries can be denoted as third-level observations. It should be noted that although the countries were nested within the intervention status, the anti-alcohol campaign is not considered to be a level. The same applies for the geographic position. These variables are denoted as third-level factors.

If there is only one country in the sample, then all subjects can be assumed to be uncorrelated. In the present situation, however, the subjects are nested within the presumed independently sampled countries. Alcohol behavior of the subjects within countries is more alike than that of respondents between countries. For example, the amount of alcohol consumption in the Netherlands is, on average, much lower than in France. Consequently, given an observation of a French person, one can almost predict whether an observation of another person is French or Dutch. This induces an arbitrary country correlation between observations at the (second) subject level. We will see later that the amount of correlation is determined by the amount of between-country variability. The same reasoning can also be applied regarding the repeated measurements within each subject. The differences between countries and subjects induce correlation between first-level observations. Apparently, observations at the lower levels tend to be correlated due to the multilevel structure.

Growth Study

The second example is a study of orthodontic growth of 11 girls and 16 boys that was first analyzed by Potthoff and Roy (1964). In this study, the distance (in millimeters) between the pituitary and the maxillary fissure was recorded at four different ages: 8, 10, 12, and 14. These two locations can easily be identified on an X-ray.

This is an example of a two-level longitudinal design. The first-level observations are the (four) repeated measurements, nested within subjects. The second-level observations are the subjects that are considered to be an independent random sample. Since measurements within subjects are more alike than measurements between subjects, there is correlation induced by the multilevel structure. On top of this, there might be serial correlation due to, for example, memory effects. The variable *sex* is a second-level time-independent factor. We will see later in what way the linear mixed-effects regression model can distinguish between serial correlation and correlation induced by the multilevel structure.

Interpersonal Proximity Study

The third and last example is a study concerning the evaluation of teachers' interpersonal behavior in the classroom. The teachers were evaluated on their interpersonal behavior in the classroom each year for a period of 4 years, starting with a baseline measurement at time zero. The degree of closeness between a teacher and the students was measured by means of a "proximity" score. A total of 51 teachers were evaluated. The number of observations for the four time points decreased from 46 at $t = 0$ to 32 at $t = 3$. Hence, we are dealing with an unbalanced design in regard to time. Nonresponse at various time points may be considered to be missing at random.[2] Another Level 2 (person) variable is gender (0 = male; 1 = female). Gender could possibly be a predictor of the proximity score of the teacher. It is also possible that gender has an influence on the relationship between the measurement occasion and the proximity score (i.e., an interaction between gender and occasion may be considered).

It is likely that respondents remember their proximity scores of the preceding years, leading to serial correlations between repeated measurements in addition to the correlation induced by the multilevel structure. Note that serial correlation due to memory effects or other factors that cause a time lag can also be present in the previous two examples. However, in this chapter, we will exclusively approach the problem of serial correlation for the proximity study.

WHY NOT STANDARD REGRESSION TECHNIQUES?

Analyzing Longitudinal Data With OLS

Aggregation

A possible way to deal with correlated data is to aggregate the data. For example, the growth data can be aggregated by first calculating the average head circumference per subject and then using these for further analysis. Standard OLS regression techniques would then be suitable to analyze global sex differences in head circumference. Another possibility is to first calculate the average head circumference for each time point. As Osborne (Chapter 29) discussed, neither of these approaches is desirable.

Disaggregation

Another way to deal with correlated data is to neglect the multilevel structure and serial correlation. By disaggregating the data, all observations are treated as if they were uncorrelated. The standard OLS method would then be applicable. We will discuss the consequences of disaggregating the data with respect to point estimation and corresponding standard errors of the regression parameters. The growth data serve as an example. For ease of presentation, we suppose that there is no missing observation and no serial correlation.

It can be seen from the profiles of all subjects in Figure 30.1a that there is more or less a linear growth of the head circumference (distance). The consequence of disaggregating the data is that all observations are treated equally without distinguishing within- and between-subjects measurements. Figure 30.1b shows the average growth of the head circumference of boys and girls. This suggests that there is an age-by-sex interaction effect because the head circumference for boys grows more rapidly than that for girls. Therefore, it makes sense to specify the underlying regression model as

$$\text{Distance}_{ij} = \beta_0 + \beta_1 \text{sex}_i + \beta_2 \text{age}_{ij} + \beta_3 \text{sex} * \text{age}_{ij} + V_{ij}, \tag{1}$$

where β_k, $k = 1, 2, 3$ are the regression parameters and V_{ij} is the error term for subject i at time point j, $i = 1, \ldots, n$, $j = 1, \ldots, m$, which is supposed to be uncorrelated and normally distributed with mean zero and constant variance σ_v^2. Note that σ_v^2 indicates the deviations of the observations around the sex-specific regression lines. The variable Distance$_{ij}$ is the head circumference. The variable Sex$_i$ is coded as boys = 0 and girls = 1. The time-dependent variable age$_{ij}$ is measured in years.

Consequence of Using OLS

From Tables 30.1 and 30.2, a comparison can be made regarding the point estimates and the corresponding standard errors. Table 30.1 shows the results when treating the data as if they were uncorrelated (i.e., neglecting the multilevel structure).

Table 30.2 shows the results of an appropriate analysis, which accounts for the multilevel structure and hence the correlation structure of the data. We will see later that the random intercept regression model appears to be a better model to describe these data.

First, note that the point estimates of the OLS method are the same as in the appropriate

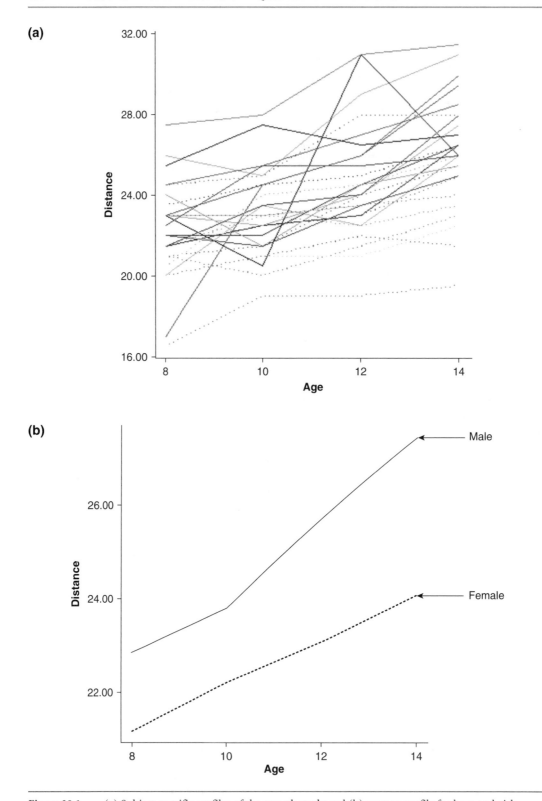

Figure 30.1   (a) Subject-specific profiles of the growth study and (b) average profile for boys and girls.

Table 30.1   OLS (Restricted Maximum Likelihood): Growth Data

Parameter	Estimate	Standard Error	df	t	Significance	95% Confidence Interval	
						Lower Bound	Upper Bound
Intercept	16.34	1.42	104	11.54	.00	13.53	19.15
Age	0.78	0.13	104	6.22	.00	0.53	1.03
Sex	1.03	2.22	104	0.47	.64	−3.37	5.43
Age × Sex	−0.30	0.20	104	−1.54	.13	−0.70	0.09

Table 30.2   Appropriate Analysis (Random Intercept Model [Restricted Maximum Likelihood]): Growth Data

Parameter	Estimate	Standard Error	df	t	Significance	95% Confidence Interval	
						Lower Bound	Upper Bound
Intercept	16.34	0.98	103.99	16.65	.00	14.39	18.29
Age	0.78	0.08	79	10.12	.00	0.63	0.94
Sex	1.03	1.54	103.99	0.67	.50	−2.02	4.08
Age × Sex	−0.30	0.12	79	−2.51	.01	−0.55	−0.06

method. Pleasurable as it may seem, this situation only occurs when all subjects are measured at the same time points (balanced in time) and when there are no missing observations. The parameter estimates of the OLS method are biased for unbalanced data and/or when missing observations occur. Second, as can be seen from Tables 30.1 and 30.2, the standard errors of the estimates are not the same. To explain the discrepancy, let us take a closer look at the sex-specific age effect and the age-specific sex effect.

Age-Specific Sex Effect

An age-specific sex effect reflects the difference between boys and girls for each age-group separately. In terms of the regression parameters, this difference is equal to

$$\text{average distance (male)} - \text{average distance (female)} = -\hat{\beta}_1 - \hat{\beta}_3 \ age. \quad (2)$$

The corresponding standard errors are shown in Table 30.3. The OLS estimates of the

standard errors are biased downward. This can be understood as follows. The amount of information of an additional correlated (repeated) measurement is less than that of an additional independent subject. Therefore, treating correlated observations (over time) as independent observations leads to an exaggeration of the sample size (or, more precisely, exaggeration of the degrees of freedom). Consequently, the standard error of the estimated sex effect for each age level will be too low.

Sex-Specific Age Effect

A sex-specific age effect reflects the amount of growth for boys and girls separately. In terms of the regression parameters, this effect can be determined by substituting the codes of the variables into the regression model (1):

average distance $(t + 1)$ − average distance (t)

$$= \begin{cases} \hat{\beta}_2 & \text{if Sex} = \text{male} \\ \hat{\beta}_2 + \hat{\beta}_3 & \text{if Sex} = \text{female} \end{cases} \quad (3)$$

Table 30.3   Estimated Age-Specific Sex Effects and Their Standard Errors (Restricted Maximum Likelihood)

		Appropriate Analysis (Random Intercept)	Ordinary Least Squares
Age = 8	Sex effect	−1.41	−1.41
	SE sex effect	0.84	0.74
Age = 10	Sex effect	−2.02	−2.02
	SE sex effect	0.77	0.48
Age = 12	Sex effect	−2.63	−2.63
	SE sex effect	0.77	0.48
Age = 14	Sex effect	−3.24	−3.24
	SE sex effect	0.84	0.74

The corresponding standard errors are shown in Table 30.4. As can be seen from Table 30.4, the OLS estimates of the standard errors are biased upward. This can be understood as follows. Using OLS, the standard error of the estimated age effect is calculated based on the combined variability between and within subjects for boys and girls separately. For the estimation of the amount of change over time, however, one should only account for the within-subjects variability. Differences between subjects should not affect the precision of this estimate. Hence, the sex-specific standard errors of the estimated age effects will be too large when using OLS.

The interaction term in model (1) can be interpreted as the difference in growth velocity between boys and girls and should be estimated accounting for only the within-subjects variability.

Table 30.4   Estimated Sex-Specific Age Effects and Their Standard Errors (Restricted Maximum Likelihood)

		Appropriate Analysis (Random Intercept)	Ordinary Least Squares
Sex = 0	Age effect	0.78	0.78
	SE age effect	0.08	0.13
Sex = 1	Age effect	0.48	0.48
	SE age effect	0.09	0.15

This situation is comparable with that of the sex-specific age effect. Consequently, the standard error of the interaction term and the corresponding p values will be too large when using OLS.

In this example, the OLS method leads to a nonsignificant contribution of the interaction term ($p = .13$), whereas the appropriate analysis method leads to a highly significant contribution ($p = .01$). Consequently, the analysis of the growth study with the incorrect OLS method leads to the wrong conclusion that the growth velocity of the boys is equal to that of the girls.

ACCOUNTING FOR THE MULTILEVEL STRUCTURE

There are several ways to deal with correlated data: Treat subjects as either a fixed or a random factor in the model. Each alternative has its own pros and cons.

Treat Subjects as a Fixed Factor in the Model

An obvious way to deal with longitudinal data is to fit separate regression lines for each subject. This can be accomplished by treating the subjects as a fixed factor and including the regression model using dummy variables. For the growth study, the model can be specified as

$$\text{Distance}_{ij} = \beta_0 + \beta_1 \text{sex}_i + \beta_2 \text{age}_{ij} + \beta_3 \text{sex} * \text{age}_{ij} + \beta_4 D_1 \ldots \beta_{13} + D_{10} + \beta_{14} + D_{12} \ldots + \beta_{28} D_{26} + V_{ij}, \quad (4)$$

where the error terms V_{ij} are normally distributed with mean zero and variance σ_v^2, $i = 1, \ldots, 27$ and $j = 1, \ldots, 4$. The variables $D_1, \ldots, D_{10}$ are dummy variables for the female subjects, and $D_{12}, \ldots, D_{26}$ are the dummy variables for the male subjects, respectively. One of the boys (and girls) is chosen to be the reference subject. Each of the regression parameters $\beta_4, \ldots, \beta_{13}$ can be interpreted as the subject-specific deviation from the reference female subject, and $\beta_{14}, \ldots, \beta_{28}$ are the subject-specific deviations from the reference male subject. We will denote this as the analysis of covariance (ANCOVA) approach.

Table 30.5 shows some results. Note that the significance of the interaction term in Table 30.5 is equal to that in Table 30.2. In fact, the

ANCOVA approach also leads to unbiased results. It enables one to estimate the separate regression lines even when the subjects are not measured at the same time points (unbalanced) and when missing observations (missing at random) occur. Some of the subjects are allowed to have only one measurement. The average profile is determined using all available information contained in the data (also from the subject with only one measurement). Time-independent covariates can also be included in the model.

Two major drawbacks of this approach are worthwhile to mention. First, since the subjects are treated as a fixed factor, no generalizations can be made to a larger group. Second, the ANCOVA approach should not be used if there are serial correlations because the within-subjects observations will then be correlated.

Table 30.5   ANCOVA Approach of the Growth Study

Parameter	Estimate	Standard Error	df	t	Significance
Intercept	14.37	1.10	79.00	13.08	.00
Sex	6.73	1.66	79.00	4.06	.00
Age	0.78	0.08	79.00	10.12	.00
Sex × Age	−0.30	0.12	79.00	−2.51	.01
Female: $[D_1$:subj $= 1]$	−5.000	0.98	79.00	−5.10	.00
$[D_2$:subj $= 2]$	−3.38	0.98	79.00	−3.44	.00
$[D_3$:subj $= 3]$	−2.63	0.98	79.00	−2.68	.01
$[D_4$:subj $= 4]$	−1.50	0.98	79.00	−1.53	.130
$[D_5$:subj $= 5]$	−3.75	0.98	79.00	−3.83	.00
$[D_6$:subj $= 6]$	−5.25	0.98	79.00	−5.36	.00
$[D_7$:subj $= 7]$	−3.38	0.98	79.00	−3.44	.00
$[D_8$:subj $= 8]$	−3.00	0.98	79.00	−3.06	.00
$[D_9$:subj $= 9]$	−5.25	0.98	79.00	−5.36	.00
$[D_{10}$:subj $= 10]$	−7.88	0.98	79.00	−8.03	.00
Male: $[D_{12}$:subj $= 12]$	4.75	0.98	79.00	4.85	.00
$[D_{13}$:subj $= 13]$	0.38	0.98	79.00	0.38	.70
$[D_{14}$:subj $= 14]$	1.25	0.98	79.00	1.28	.21
$[D_{15}$:subj $= 15]$	3.63	0.98	79.00	3.70	.00
$[D_{16}$:subj $= 16]$	1.00	0.98	79.00	0.00	1.00
$[D_{17}$:subj $= 17]$	3.38	0.98	79.00	3.44	.00
$[D_{18}$:subj $= 18]$	0.75	0.98	79.00	0.77	.45
$[D_{19}$:subj $= 19]$	0.88	0.98	79.00	0.89	.38
$[D_{20}$:subj $= 20]$	2.13	0.98	79.00	2.17	.03
$[D_{21}$:subj $= 21]$	6.50	0.98	79.00	6.63	.00
$[D_{22}$:subj $= 22]$	0.63	0.98	79.00	0.64	.53
$[D_{23}$:subj $= 23]$	1.25	0.98	79.00	1.28	.21
$[D_{24}$:subj $= 24]$	1.25	0.98	79.00	1.28	.21
$[D_{25}$:subj $= 25]$	1.88	0.98	79.00	1.91	.06
$[D_{26}$:subj $= 26]$	2.88	0.98	79.00	2.93	.00

Treat Subjects as
a Random Factor in the Model

Usually, the purpose of a study is to generalize the findings to a larger group (population) of subjects than indicated by the sample. This problem can be solved by assuming the subjects in the study form a random sample from a certain known distribution. The subjects are then treated as a random factor. This approach also allows the modeling of subject-specific intercepts. In most software programs, these intercepts are assumed to be realizations from a normal distribution. To be more specific, consider the following simplified model for the growth data.

$$\text{Distance}_{ij} = \beta_{0i} + \beta_1 \text{age}_{ij} + R_{ij}, \quad (5)$$

given the following:

$\beta_{0i} = \beta_0 + G_{0i}$

$G_{0i} \sim N(0, \tau_0^2)$ – the random intercept (second level variance component)

$R_{ij} \sim N(0, \sigma^2)$ – the error terms (first level variance component)

G_{0i} and R_{ij} are uncorrelated

Model (5) can be schematically visualized according to Figure 30.2. For ease of presentation, we do not distinguish between boys and girls at this moment. In this example, we assume that the subject-specific regression lines only differ in intercept, which is similar to the ANCOVA approach. That is why the lines in the figure are parallel, with the slope equal to β_1, which can be interpreted as the average growth velocity of the children. Furthermore, the regression intercepts are supposed to be a random sample of a normal distribution. The different intercepts are specified in model (5) as β_{0i}, $i = 1, \ldots, n$, which is denoted as a random intercept, normally distributed with mean value β_0 and variance τ_0^2. The second-level variance τ_0^2 indicates how far the separate regression lines are from the average regression line. The first-level variance σ^2 indicates for each subject how far the observations are from its corresponding regression line, which is assumed to be equal for all subjects.

Comparable to the ANCOVA approach, the random intercept model specifies each subject-specific regression line separately. All regression lines are connected to each other through the underlying assumption of the random intercept and the functional relationship as specified in the model. The maximum likelihood method

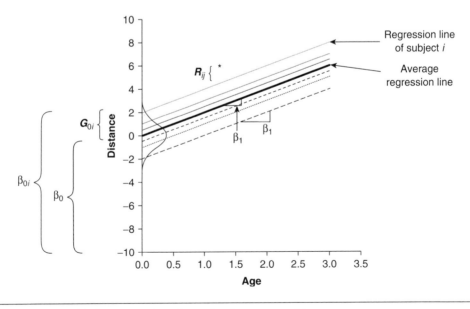

Figure 30.2   Graphical representation of a random intercept model.

(e.g., Diggle, Liang, & Zeger, 1994) is used to estimate all model parameters. The average profile is determined using all available information contained in the data.

Usually, inferences are only made about the average growth. Information about individual regression lines is often not of main interest. Model (5) can be rewritten in a form that is similar to the standard (fixed) regression specification, decomposing the responses into a fixed part of averages and a random part as follows:

$$\text{Distance}_{ij} = \beta_{0i} + \beta_1 \text{age}_{ij} + R_{ij}$$

$$\text{Distance}_{ij} = \beta_0 + \beta_1 \text{age}_{ij} + (G_{0i} + R_{ij})$$

$$\text{Distance}_{ij} = \beta_0 + \beta_1 \text{age}_{ij} + V_{ij}$$

$$V_{ij} = G_{0i} + R_{ij} \tag{6}$$

$$\text{var}(V_{ij}) = \sigma^2 + \tau_0^2$$

$$r(V_{ij}, V_{ij'}) = \text{ICC} = \frac{\tau_0^2}{\sigma^2 + \tau_0^2}$$

ICC is the intraclass correlation. Just like in the fixed effect situation, the responses Distance_{ij} can be decomposed into a fixed systematic part $\beta_0 + \beta_1 \text{age}_{ij}$ (average regression line) and into a random part V_{ij} with overall variance σ_v^2. This variance is a combination of the first-level within-subjects (σ^2) and second-level between-subjects (τ_0^2) variances.

In general, the specification of the systematic part is completely similar as in the fixed regression case, involving quantitative as well as qualitative independent variables. However, the error terms V_{ij} are correlated. It can be shown that these are correlated with correlation equal to

$$\text{ICC} = \frac{\tau_0^2}{\sigma^2 + \tau_0^2}$$

It reflects the proportion of the total amount of variance explained by the differences between subjects. If the between-subjects variance τ_0^2 is large relative to the within-subjects variance (σ^2), then the numerator of the ICC (τ_0^2) will be approximately equal to the denominator of the ICC ($\sigma^2 + \tau_0^2$). The value of the ICC will be close to 1, which corresponds to highly correlated error terms between the time points.

Usually, these variances and correlations are summarized in a table that consists of m rows and m columns. The m rows and columns represent the m different time points. The element in the jth row and j'th column is equal to $\text{corr}(V_{ij}, V_{ij'})$. In particular, the correlation between the responses at the same time point j is equal to $\text{corr}(V_{ij}, V_{ij'}) = 1$. It is assumed that the correlations between time points are equal for all subjects, so that we can drop the subscript i.

In the literature, such a table is denoted as a correlation matrix V_{corr}, leaving out the rows and columns specification. If the number of time points is equal to $m = 4$, the matrix V_{corr} can be written as

$$V_{\text{corr}} = \begin{pmatrix} 1 & \frac{\tau_0^2}{\sigma^2 + \tau_0^2} & \frac{\tau_0^2}{\sigma^2 + \tau_0^2} & \frac{\tau_0^2}{\sigma^2 + \tau_0^2} \\ \frac{\tau_0^2}{\sigma^2 + \tau_0^2} & 1 & \frac{\tau_0^2}{\sigma^2 + \tau_0^2} & \frac{\tau_0^2}{\sigma^2 + \tau_0^2} \\ \frac{\tau_0^2}{\sigma^2 + \tau_0^2} & \frac{\tau_0^2}{\sigma^2 + \tau_0^2} & 1 & \frac{\tau_0^2}{\sigma^2 + \tau_0^2} \\ \frac{\tau_0^2}{\sigma^2 + \tau_0^2} & \frac{\tau_0^2}{\sigma^2 + \tau_0^2} & \frac{\tau_0^2}{\sigma^2 + \tau_0^2} & 1 \end{pmatrix} \tag{7}$$

or in terms of the corresponding matrix of variances and covariances

$$V_{\text{cov}} = \begin{pmatrix} \sigma^2 + \tau_0^2 & \tau_0^2 & \tau_0^2 & \tau_0^2 \\ \tau_0^2 & \sigma^2 + \tau_0^2 & \tau_0^2 & \tau_0^2 \\ \tau_0^2 & \tau_0^2 & \sigma^2 + \tau_0^2 & \tau_0^2 \\ \tau_0^2 & \tau_0^2 & \tau_0^2 & \sigma^2 + \tau_0^2 \end{pmatrix} \cdot \tag{8}$$

This type of correlation (covariance) matrix is called compound symmetry or exchangeable. The covariation between time points is fully determined by the between-subjects variance τ_0^2 (i.e., induced by the two-level design). Note that the covariance can be obtained from the correlation by using the following formula:

$$\text{cov}(V_{ij}, V_{ij'}) = \text{corr}(V_{ij}, V_{ij'}) * \\ sd(V_{ij}) * sd(V_{ij'}), \tag{9}$$

where $sd(V_{ij})$ is the standard deviation of the response of subject i at time point j.

It should be noted that SPSS presents the results of the covariance matrix in a table format (see Tables 30.7, 30.9, and 30.10).

In general, V_{cov} is a matrix that consists of overall variances and covariances of the responses. These variances and covariances are combinations of the between-subjects (Level 2) variances and covariances of the random effects and those of the within-subjects (Level 1) measurement errors. The variances and covariances of the random effects are summarized in a so-called G_{cov} matrix, whereas those of the measurement errors are summarized in a so-called R_{cov} matrix.

Table 30.6 summarizes the notations of the various variance and covariance components for a random intercept (RI) model. For this RI model (Table 30.6, column 3), the subjects only differ with respect to the intercepts. Hence, the Level 2 G_{cov} matrix only consists of the random intercept variance $G_{cov} = (\tau_0^2)$. The Level 1 observations are supposed to be uncorrelated with equal variances over time (i.e., no serial correlations are imposed). The corresponding R_{cov} matrix for the random intercept model has covariances equal to zero and constant variance equal to σ^2. Note that all elements of the R_{cov} matrix should be added by τ_0^2 to obtain the V_{cov} matrix (see Equation 8).

In summary, can be stated the following:

- The elements of R_{cov} are the Level 1 within-subjects variances and covariances indicating the discrepancy between the observations and the subject-specific regression lines. Usually, the same amount of discrepancy is assumed for all subjects.
- The elements of G_{cov} are the Level 2 between-subjects variances and covariances indicating the discrepancy between the subject-specific regression lines and the average regression line.
- The elements of V_{cov} are the overall variances and covariances of the responses indicating the discrepancy between the observations and the average regression line.

Random Intercept Model for the Growth Study

The MIXED→ LINEAR option of SPSS 13[3] has been used to estimate the model parameters (see Landau & Everitt, 2004, appendix). The systematic part of the model is given in Equation 1. The restricted maximum likelihood (REML) approach was performed to obtain unbiased estimates of all model parameters. A random intercept model seems plausible because the subject-specific profiles (see Figure 30.1a) were more or less parallel with considerable between-subjects variability. Part of the SPSS output is depicted in Table 30.7. Note that covariance matrices are presented here in table format.

The random intercept variance in Table 30.7 is estimated as $\hat{\tau}_0^2 = 3.30$, which is the only element of G_{cov}. The R_{cov} matrix has equal residual variances estimated by $\hat{\sigma}^2 = 1.92$. Note that all covariances are equal to zero because no serial correlations were assumed. The corresponding overall correlation matrix V_{corr} is equal to

Table 30.6   Variance-Covariance Components of the Random Intercept Model for m = 4 Time Points

Variances and Covariances	Matrix	Random Intercept
Level 1:		
Measurement error and serial correlations	R_{cov}	$\begin{pmatrix} \sigma^2 & 0 & 0 & 0 \\ 0 & \sigma^2 & 0 & 0 \\ 0 & 0 & \sigma^2 & 0 \\ 0 & 0 & 0 & \sigma^2 \end{pmatrix}$
Level 2:		
Random effects variances and covariances	G_{cov}	$[\tau_0^2]$
Overall	V_{cov}	$\begin{pmatrix} \sigma^2+\tau_0^2 & \tau_0^2 & \tau_0^2 & \tau_0^2 \\ \tau_0^2 & \sigma^2+\tau_0^2 & \tau_0^2 & \tau_0^2 \\ \tau_0^2 & \tau_0^2 & \sigma^2+\tau_0^2 & \tau_0^2 \\ \tau_0^2 & \tau_0^2 & \tau_0^2 & \sigma^2+\tau_0^2 \end{pmatrix}$

Table 30.7   SPSS Output Regarding G_{cov} and R_{cov} Matrix

	G_{cov} Matrix	R_{cov} Matrix			
	Intercept | subj	[age = 8]	[age = 10]	[age = 12]	[age = 14]
Intercept | subj	3.30	[age = 8] 1.92	0	0	0
		[age = 10] 0	1.92	0	0
		[age = 12] 0	0	1.92	0
		[age = 14] 0	0	0	1.92

$$V_{corr} = \begin{pmatrix} 1 & 0.63 & 0.63 & 0.63 \\ 0.63 & 1 & 0.63 & 0.63 \\ 0.63 & 0.63 & 1 & 0.63 \\ 0.63 & 0.63 & 0.63 & 1 \end{pmatrix}. \quad (10)$$

The estimated correlation $(\hat{V}_{ij}, \hat{V}_{ij'})$ between time point j and j' is calculated as

$$\frac{\hat{\tau}_0^2}{\hat{\sigma}^2 + \hat{\tau}_0^2} = 0.63.$$

Apparently, the observations are fairly highly correlated $(r = .63)$ solely due to the two-level structure. The within-subjects residual variance $(\hat{\sigma}^2 = 1.92)$ is smaller than the between-subjects variance $(\hat{\tau}_0^2 = 3.30)$, as expected from Figure 30.1a. The estimates of the fixed parameters are shown in Table 30.2.

Random Slope Model

In many cases, individual regression lines may reveal different regression slopes. To model different regression slopes, a random slope can be added to the random intercept model. An example of a random effects model with a random intercept and slope is

$$Y_{ij} = \beta_{0i} + \beta_{1i}t_{ij} + R_{ij}, \quad (11)$$

where

$\beta_{0i} = \beta_0 + G_{0i}$,

$\beta_{1i} = \beta_1 + G_{1i}$,

$G_{0i} \sim N(0, \tau_0^2)$ is the random intercept,

$G_{1i} \sim N(0, \tau_1^2)$ is the random slope,

$R_{ij} \sim N(0, \sigma^2)$ are the residual components,

G_{0i}, G_{1j} are uncorrelated with R_{ij}, and

τ_{01} is the covariance between the random intercept and random slope.

We assume that the subject-specific regression lines differ in intercept and slope. The regression intercepts and slopes are supposed to be samples of normal distributions. The random intercept is specified in model (11) as β_{0i}, $i = 1, \ldots, n$, with mean value β_0 and variance τ_0^2. The different slopes are specified as β_{1i}, $i = 1, \ldots, n$, which is denoted as random slope, normally distributed with mean value β_1 and variance τ_1^2. Moreover, the random intercept (RI) and the random slope (RS) are supposed to be correlated with covariance equal to τ_{01}. The second-level variances and covariances matrix G_{cov} of the random effects and the first-level matrix R_{cov} of measurement errors for $m = 4$ time points are shown in Table 30.8.

It appears that the variances and covariances of the responses (the V_{cov} components of Table 30.8, column 3) are determined according to the following formula:

$$var(Y_{it}) = \tau_0^2 + 2\tau_{01}t + \tau_1^2 t^2 + \sigma^2,$$
$$cov(Y_{it}, Y_{it_k}) = \tau_0^2 + \tau_{01}(t_j + t_k) + \tau_1^2 t_j \bullet t_k, \quad (12)$$

with $j, k = 1, \ldots, m$. No serial correlations are imposed in this example. All covariances between the responses (see Equation 12) are due to the multilevel design.

Another type of correlation is not due to the multilevel structure but due to the fact that the error of a measurement at a particular point in time on a subject somehow influences the error

Table 30.8   Variances and Covariances of the Random Intercept/Slope Model for $m = 4$ Time Points

Variances and Covariances	Matrix	Random Intercept/ Random Slope	AR (1) Heterogeneous for Balanced Data
Level 1:			
Measurement error and serial correlations	R_{cov}	$\begin{pmatrix} \sigma^2 & 0 & 0 & 0 \\ 0 & \sigma^2 & 0 & 0 \\ 0 & 0 & \sigma^2 & 0 \\ 0 & 0 & 0 & \sigma^2 \end{pmatrix}$	$\begin{pmatrix} \sigma_1^2 & \rho\sigma_1\sigma_2 & \rho^2\sigma_1\sigma_3 & \rho^3\sigma_1\sigma_4 \\ \rho\sigma_1\sigma_2 & \sigma_2^2 & \rho\sigma_2\sigma_3 & \rho^2\sigma_2\sigma_4 \\ \rho^2\sigma_1\sigma_3 & \rho\sigma_2\sigma_3 & \sigma_3^2 & \rho\sigma_3\sigma_4 \\ \rho^3\sigma_1\sigma_4 & \rho^2\sigma_2\sigma_4 & \rho\sigma_3\sigma_4 & \sigma_4^2 \end{pmatrix}$
Level 2:			
Random effects variances and covariances	G_{cov}	$\begin{pmatrix} \tau_0^2 & \tau_{01} \\ \tau_{01} & \tau_1^2 \end{pmatrix}$	Unspecified
Overall	V_{cov}	Combination of elements of R_{cov} and G_{cov} according to Equation 12	$V_{cov} = R_{cov}$

of measurement at another (possibly adjacent) point in time. This may be due to memory effect or due to other reasons that cause a carryover in time within a subject.

SERIAL CORRELATION

Differences between subject characteristics induce correlation between time points. The difference in intercept, for example, may cause correlation that is proportional with it (see Equations 7 and 8). In the random effects model mentioned previously, it is assumed that the R_{cov} matrix contains zero covariances. However, serial correlation affects the structure of the R_{cov} matrix because it affects the first-level within-subjects dependency of observation errors between time points. The AR (1) (first-order autoregressive) correlations are very common in practice. They assumes that the amount of correlation between two time points t_1 and t_2 only depends on the length of the interval between the two time points—that is, the correlation $R_{jk} = \rho^{|t_j - t_k|}$, with $-1 < \rho < 1$ and $j, k = 1, \ldots, m$. Consequently, the AR (1) serial correlations decrease as the interval length between two time points increases. In the growth study, for example, one could argue whether memory effects may influence measurements at consecutive time points. If they do, then it is plausible to assume that the influence weakens as the time

interval length increases. Hence, an AR (1) correlation structure would be a candidate to describe the dependency between the four repeated measurements.

Random Slope Model With Serial Correlation for the Proximity Study

To model the systematic (fixed) part of the model of the proximity data, consider Figure 30.3a. From this, it can be seen that one of the average profiles (female teachers) shows a nonlinear relationship. After a considerable increase in average score from the start of the study to the evaluation after 1 year, the average proximity scores drop again in the second and third years. The profile of the male teachers shows a linear relationship. In this study, however, we are only interested in the comparison of average proximity scores between the different observed occasions. As the regression analog of the ANOVA modeling for group comparisons, the occasions can be considered as four different (time) groups, and this time variable as a factor (discrete variable with four categories) should be included in the regression model. Because an interaction could be expected between occasion and gender, the following regression model is specified.

$$Prox_{ij} = \beta_0 + \beta_1 occ_{1ij} + \beta_2 occ_{2ij} + \beta_3 occ_{3ij} + \beta_4 gender_i + \beta_5 int_{1ij} + \beta_6 int_{2ij} + \beta_7 int_{3ij} + V_{ij}. \quad (13)$$

The dependent variable $Prox_{ij}$ is the proximity score of subject i at occasion $j = 0, \ldots, 3$. The systematic part consists of

- the variables occ_{kij}, $k = 1, 2, 3$, which are dummy variables for occasion k;
- the variable $gender_i$, which is coded 0 for males and 1 for females; and
- the interaction terms int_{kij}, $k = 1, 2, 3$, which are the gender-by-occasion interaction.

The random terms V_{ij} indicate the deviations of the observed values around the lines through the male and female average scores.

The structure of the overall variance and covariances (V_{cov} matrix) should be established first before estimating the regression parameters. As mentioned before, the estimated standard errors of the regression parameters could be biased if an incorrect covariance structure is imposed. A number of covariance structures can be specified by statistical packages such as SPSS. Instead of trying all available covariance structures, we could also try to make an educated guess by first looking at the scatterplot of the observed profiles of all subjects as shown in Figure 30.3b. From this figure, it can be seen that there is a considerable amount of variability between subjects, suggesting the presence of a second-level intercept variance τ_0^2. Moreover, the amount of variability seems to decrease with time, suggesting that a random intercept model is not sufficient to describe the data properly. A model with a random intercept as well as a random slope might be a better choice, suggesting the presence of a second-level slope variance τ_1^2. Covariation between the random intercept and random slope is also possible.

On the other hand, serial correlations are expected because the performances of the teachers were evaluated by the students on a yearly basis. The scores on the proximity scale at a particular time point might be influenced by the scores at preceding time points, leading to correlated errors. Furthermore, there is also a considerable number of missing observations. About 30% of the subjects drop out from the study. By means of an example, two competing covariance structures will be modeled:

1. A random-effects regression model with AR (1) serial correlations for balanced data with heterogeneous variances

2. A random-effects regression model with random intercept and random slope and with no serial correlations

Tables 30.9 and 30.10 show part of the SPSS output of an AR (1) and a random intercept/slope model without serial correlation model, respectively. In Table 30.9, the variances and covariances of the responses (V_{cov} matrix) are presented. This SPSS output can be obtained by specifying the R_{cov} matrix (within-subject variances and covariances) to be AR (1) heterogeneous and leaving the random components (G_{cov} matrix) unspecified. As a result, the V_{cov} matrix equals the R_{cov} matrix (see Table 30.8, column 4). Looking at the elements of the V_{cov} matrix in Table 30.9, it can be seen that the variances decrease with time, which is also observed from the plot in Figure 30.4b. Moreover, the covariances also decrease as the interval width between two time points increases. This is a direct consequence of the AR (1) structure.

Note that in the model specification (13), the variable *occasion* is treated as a discrete variable. To specify a random slope, we assume that the deviation of the subject-specific slope around the line through the averages is changing linearly. This can be accomplished by adding a continuous variable Z with the same values as the discrete variable *occasion* and with random parameter β_{8i}, normally distributed with mean zero and variance τ_1^2, indicating the subject-specific slope.

When a random intercept/slope model is analyzed, SPSS does not calculate the elements of the V_{cov} matrix. This matrix can be calculated from the G_{cov} and the R_{cov} matrix by using the formula in Equation 12. It turns out that the V_{cov} matrix is estimated as

$$V_{cov} = \begin{pmatrix} .28 & .19 & .13 & .08 \\ .19 & .20 & .12 & .08 \\ .13 & .12 & .14 & .08 \\ .08 & .08 & .08 & .12 \end{pmatrix}. \quad (14)$$

From Equation 14, it can be seen that the variances of the responses decrease with time, and the covariances also decrease as the interval width between two time points increases.

It should be noted that the form of the V_{cov} matrix in Equation 14, which shows decreasing variances and covariances, is not typical for a

(a)

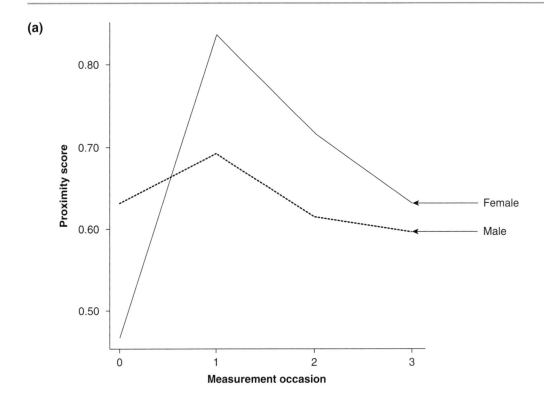

(b)

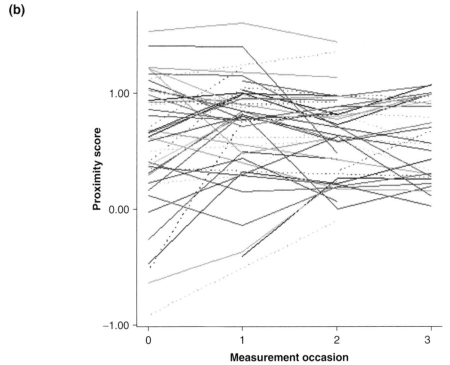

Figure 30.3   (a) Average profile of the proximity study and (b) subject-specific profile of the proximity study.

Table 30.9   SPSS Output of the AR (1) Serial Correlations Model With Heterogeneous Variances of the Proximity Study

Estimates of Covariance Parameters

Parameter		Estimate	Standard Error	Wald Z	Significance
Repeated measures	Var: [occ = 0]	.32	.07	4.77	.00
	Var: [occ = 1]	.22	.05	4.37	.00
	Var: [occ = 2]	.12	.03	4.72	.00
	Var: [occ = 3]	.13	.03	4.08	.00
	ARH1 rho	.75	.05	14.74	.00

V_{cov} *Matrix*

	[occ = 0]	[occ = 1]	[occ = 2]	[occ = 3]
[occ = 0]	.32	.20	.11	.08
[occ = 1]	.20	.22	.12	.09
[occ = 2]	.11	.12	.12	.09
[occ = 3]	.08	.09	.09	.13

Table 30.10   SPSS Output of the Random Intercept/Slope Model (No Serial Correlations) of the Proximity Study

Estimates of Covariance Parameters

Parameter		Estimate	Standard Error	Wald Z	Significance
Repeated measures	Variance	.05	.01	5.00	.00
Intercept + Z [subject = teacher]	UN (1.1)	.24	.06	4.00	.00
	UN (2.1)	−.05	.02	−2.76	.01
	UN (2.2)	.02	.01	2.14	.03

G_{cov} *Matrix*			R_{cov} *Matrix*			
	Intercept | Teacher	Occ | Teacher		[occ = 0]	[occ = 1]	[occ = 2]	[occ = 3]
Intercept | teacher	.24	−.05	[occ = 0]	.048	0	0	0
Z | teacher	−.05	.02	[occ = 1]	0	.048	0	0
			[occ = 2]	0	0	.048	0
			[occ = 3]	0	0	0	.048

random intercept/slope model. If the same study were performed in a different period, say starting between Occasion 1 and Occasion 4, then the V_{cov} matrix could be different. Consequently, the scatterplot of the dependent variable against time can have different shapes depending on the period in which the study is performed. Figure 30.4 shows the three different possibilities:

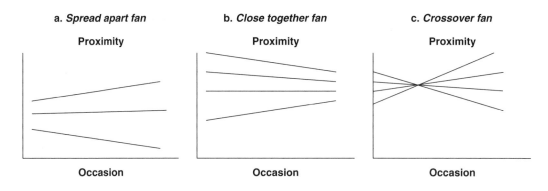

Figure 30.4   Three different fan shapes of the random slope model.

a. The observations spread as time passes.

b. The observations close together as time passes.

c. The observations cross as time passes.

There are no other possibilities due to the quadratic nature and the positive values of the variances of the random effects. For the sake of comparison, suppose that this proximity study was performed between Occasion 1 and Occasion 4. The V_{cov} components would still show decreasing covariances, but the variances are not decreasing and resemble a crossover fan situation, as shown in Figure 30.4c. The corresponding V_{cov} matrix would be

$$V_{cov} = \begin{pmatrix} .20 & .12 & .08 & .04 \\ .12 & .14 & .08 & .06 \\ .08 & .08 & .12 & .07 \\ .04 & .06 & .07 & .13 \end{pmatrix}. \quad (15)$$

In Equation 15, the variances first decrease and increase again at the last occasion.

If the study was performed between Occasion 3 and Occasion 6, the variances (Equation 16) would increase in agreement with a spreading fan, as shown in Figure 30.4a. Note that in this case, the covariances do not decrease.

$$V_{cov} = \begin{pmatrix} .12 & .07 & .07 & .07 \\ .07 & .13 & .10 & .11 \\ .07 & .10 & .17 & .16 \\ .07 & .11 & .16 & .25 \end{pmatrix} \quad (16)$$

Let us go back to the results of the analysis of the observed occasions (0–3). For both the AR (1) heterogeneous model and the random

intercept/slope model, all the estimates of the variances and the covariances are significant at the .05 significance level. This can be seen from the Wald test depicted in Tables 30.9 and 30.10. Both models are competing alternatives to describe the variance-covariance structure of the responses. These tests, however, do not provide any evidence favoring one model over another. Some selection criteria on how to choose the most suitable model will be discussed briefly in the next paragraph.

LIKELIHOOD-BASED TEST STATISTICS FOR MODEL SELECTION

A number of test statistics are used to compare alternative models. For hierarchical (nested) models, the well-known "restricted −2LL" (log-likelihood) test statistic can be used for comparing alternative models that only differ in covariance structures. The term *restricted* (based on the REML) *estimates* is added to distinguish this test from the commonly used −2LL (based on the maximum likelihood [ML] principle). The ML estimates of the variances and covariances lead to an underestimation of the standard errors of the estimates of the variances and covariances and are therefore not recommended in this phase of the analysis (see Verbeke & Molenberghs, 2000, for a thorough discussion).

Roughly speaking, the restricted −2LL is a distance measure between the fitted model and the observed data. The smaller the restricted −2LL, the better the model will be considered. When comparing two hierarchical (or nested) models that only differ in covariance structures, the difference in the distance from model to data will be calculated. This difference is called the log-likelihood ratio and refers to the difference in –2LL between the two random effects models. According to the statistical theory, this difference has an asymptotically known chi-square distribution with known degrees of freedom. The calculation of the degrees of freedom is not straightforward in all situations. For a thorough discussion, refer to Verbeke and Molenberghs (2000) and Snijders and Bosker (1999). For ease of presentation, we propose to follow basically the ideas mentioned by Snijders and Bosker:

1. The two competing hierarchical models should have the same fixed effects part.

2. Estimate all parameters with REML.

3. Calculate the difference in –2LL between the two models (log-likelihood ratio test).

4. If the test concerns the significance of covariances, then the log-likelihood ratio test should be used as a two-sided chi-square test with degrees of freedom equal to the difference in the number of model parameters.

5. If the test concerns the significance of variances, then the log-likelihood ratio test should be used as a one-sided chi-square test with degrees of freedom equal to the difference in the number of model parameters.

Suppose, for example, that the random intercept/slope model is to be compared with the random intercept model. The random intercept model is nested within the random intercept/slope model because the first model can be obtained from the second one by imposing a zero restriction to the random slope variance τ_1^2 and the covariance parameter τ_{01}. Table 30.11 shows the results of this comparison. The random intercept model is depicted in Table 30.11 as Model 2. The –2LL value is 137.66. Ten parameters were estimated. Eight parameters were needed for the fixed part (Equation 13). One parameter was for the random intercept variance τ_0^2, and one was for the residual variance σ^2. Model 3 is the random intercept/slope model with the same fixed part as given in Equation 13. The –2LL value of this model is 122.82. Comparing these two models leads to a log-likelihood ratio value of 14.84 with 2 degrees of freedom. These test statistics can be used to test the null hypothesis

$$H_0 : \tau_1^2 = 0, \text{ against the alternative}$$

$$H_a : \tau_1^2 > 0 \text{ and } \tau_{01} \neq 0.$$

To test this hypothesis, consider it a one-sided test because the variance τ_1^2 cannot be negative. The corresponding one-sided p value is equal to .00, which is highly significant. As expected from the plot (Figure 30.4b), the random intercept/slope model performs better than

Table 30.11   Comparison Between Hierarchical Models With the Same Fixed Part in the Proximity Study

	Model	Number of Estimated Parameters	–2LL (Restricted Maximum Likelihood)	Ref	Log-Likelihood (Chi-Square)	df	p
1	Unstructured	18	112.88	1			
2	Random intercept	10	137.66	1	24.78	8	.00
3	Random intercept + slope	12	122.82	1	9.95	6	.13
4	First-order auto regressive	10	137.54	1	24.66	8	.00
5	Scaled identity	9	193.70	1	80.83	9	.00
6	Random intercept + first-order auto regressive	11	134.68	1	21.81	7	.00
7	Random intercept + first-order autoregressive, heterogeneous variances	14	117.62	1	4.75	4	.31
8	AR (1) heterogeneous variances	13	120.23	1	7.35	5	.20

the random intercept model. On the other hand, The AR (1) heterogeneous model (Model 8 in Table 30.11) has a −2LL value of 120.23. Unfortunately, this model cannot be compared with the random intercept/slope model because these competing models are not hierarchically related.

A popular criterion for model selection is the Bayesian information criterion (BIC). The BIC is a measure of evidence favoring one model over another, and these models are not hierarchically related to each other. It is also a likelihood-based measure with a penalty for the sample size and degrees of freedom. In the proximity study, the

BIC favors the random intercept/slope model slightly. The BIC for the random intercept/slope model is equal to 142.70, whereas the BIC for the AR (1) heterogeneous model is equal to 145.10.

A major drawback of this information criterion is the fact that it tends to favor simple models in practice.[4] Nevertheless, this information criterion seems to be a good alternative to compare nonnested models. It should be noted that subject matter reasoning should prevail over statistical testing, which (not in the least) also applies when the statistical theory does not give a clear-cut rule. Table 30.11 also displays a few other covariance structures. The reader may

Table 30.12   Maximum Likelihood Estimates of the Regression Parameters for the AR (1) Heterogeneous Model

Estimates of Fixed Effects					
Parameter	*Estimate*	*Standard Error*	*df*	*t*	*Significance*
Intercept	.62	.10	47.38	6.52	.00
[occ = 3]	.02	.09	84.37	0.16	.87
[occ = 2]	0.00	.08	67.16	−0.05	.96
[occ = 1]	.10	.07	63.05	1.42	.16
[occ = 0]	0	0			
gender	−.18	.18	47.03	−1.00	.32
[occ = 3] * gender	.21	.18	86.80	1.15	.25
[occ = 2] * gender	.32	.16	69.50	2.00	.05
[occ = 1] * gender	.18	.14	67.77	1.32	.19
[occ = 0] * gender	0	0			

Estimates of Fixed Effects						
Sex of the Teacher	*Parameter*	*Estimate*	*Standard Error*	*df*	*t*	*Significance*
male	Intercept	.62	.09	34.50	6.78	.00
	[occ = 3]	.02	.09	65.66	0.17	.87
	[occ = 2]	0.00	.08	51.78	−0.05	.96
	[occ = 1]	.10	.07	49.27	1.44	.16
	[occ = 0]	0	0			
female	Intercept	.44	.17	12.66	2.60	.02
	[occ = 3]	.22	.16	18.67	1.39	.18
	[occ = 2]	.32	.15	16.05	2.19	.04
	[occ = 1]	.29	.12	14.29	2.39	.03
	[occ = 0]	0	0			

check that there are only two possible covariance structures left if the −2LL test statistic is used to compare different covariance structures (Model 3 and Model 8 in Table 30.11).

Once a choice has been made about the covariance structure, the fixed part of the model can be evaluated for significance. The analysis of the proximity study starts with the specification of the fixed part of the model according to Equation 13. Suppose that we choose for the AR (1) a heterogeneous option.

The top portion of Table 30.12 shows that none of the estimates of the regression parameters are significant at the .05 level. A closer look at the results reveals that the profile of the male teachers does not show any significant trend, whereas the average scores among the female teachers show a significant growth after the first 2 years and then a drop to the reference level in the third year. The same results also apply if the random intercept/slope model is analyzed. Hence, if the covariance structure of the responses is considered to be nuisance, then it does not matter which one we choose because the same results will be found.

To evaluate the fixed regression parameter estimates, it is recommended to use the maximum likelihood estimates and the corresponding −2LL based on these maximum likelihood estimates (cf. Verbeke & Molenberghs, 2000). For large samples, both likelihood methods give unbiased estimates of the fixed parameters, but testing the significance of the fixed parameters estimates cannot be done by means of the restricted −2LL.

EPILOGUE

The past decade has seen a growing number of longitudinal data analyses in the social and behavioral sciences. Random effects modeling offers a very flexible way of analyzing such longitudinal data. Analysis with linear random effects models uses maximum likelihood methods and produces unbiased estimates even when the data are unbalanced in time and contain missing observations. Further advantages include fewer assumptions, particularly some of the often-untenable assumptions of RMANOVA. These types of analyses are commonly available in statistical software packages and specialty packages, leaving few reasons for researchers not to use these powerful tools.

APPENDIX

The following are general guidelines to perform a multilevel and longitudinal data analysis with SPSS 13 and higher option "Mixed→ Linear."

Plotting longitudinal data
Subject-specific profiles
Open your data set.
Go to **Graphs** → **Interactive** → **Line** . . .
Drag the dependent variable to the box for the *y*-variable.
Drag the independent variable to the box for the *x*-variable.
Drag the identification variable to the "Color" box.
Drag the grouping variable to the "Style" box. Select Convert.
Right-click on the identification variable and select Categorical.
Mean profiles
Go to **Graphs** → **Interactive** → **Line** . . .
Click on Reset.
Drag the dependent variable to the box for the *y*-variable.
Drag the (time-dependent) independent variable to the box for the *x*-variable.
Drag the grouping variable to the "Color" box.
Right-click on the grouping variable and select Categorical.
Performing an OLS regression model
Click on the reset button.
Click Continue.
Click the dependent variable into the "Dependent variable" box.
Click the quantitative (or dichotomous) independent variables into the "Covariate(s)" box.
Click the qualitative independent variables into the "Factor(s)" box.
Click the fixed button.
Select the independent variables.
Click the add button.
Click Continue.
Click the statistics button and select the following checkboxes: parameter estimates and covariances of residuals.
Click Continue.
Performing a random effects model
Go to **Analyze** → **Mixed models** → **Linear** . . .
Click on the reset button.
Click the identification variable into the "Subjects" box.
Click Continue.

Click the dependent variable into the "Dependent variable" box.

Click the quantitative independent variables into the "Covariate(s)" box.

Click the qualitative independent variables into the "Factor(s)" box.

Click the fixed button. Select the independent variables.

Click the add button.

Click Continue.

Click the random button.

Select the "Include Intercept" checkbox if a random intercept is required. If random slope is required, then select the relevant independent variable and put it in the Model box. Choose unstructured as Covariance type.

Click the identification variable from the "Subjects" into the "Combinations" box.

Click Continue.

Click the statistics button and select the following checkboxes: parameter estimates, covariances of random effects, and covariances of residuals.

Click Continue.

Specifying a serial correlation
Go to **Analyze → Mixed models → Linear . . .**
Click on the reset button.

Click the identification variable into the "Subjects" box and age into the "Repeated" box. Choose a covariance structure option as the Repeated Covariance type.

Click Continue.

Click the dependent variable into the "Dependent variable" box and age and sex into the "Covariate(s)" box.

Click the statistics button and select the following checkboxes: parameter estimates, covariance of random effects, and covariances of residuals.

Click Continue.

Click the fixed button.

Select the required independent variables and click the add button.

Click Continue.

Notes

1. The computer program SPSS Version 13 is used for all mixed regression calculations. Further reading on this topic can be found in, for example, Hox (2002), Twisk (2003), and Tabachnick and Fidell (2007) at introductory and intermediate levels, as

well as in Diggle, Liang, and Zeger (1994) and Verbeke and Molenberghs (2000) at an advanced level. For an introduction to hierarchical linear modeling, see Chapter 29 (this volume).

2. Readers interested in dealing with missing data can refer to Chapter 15, although multilevel modeling does not require complete data at all time points, a significant strength over RMANOVA. A thorough discussion about missing observations and mixed effects regression analysis can be found in, for example, Verbeke and Molenberghs (2000).

3. Editor's note: Many software packages allow estimation of multilevel models, including SAS, HLM, MLM, R, and many more. Readers should explore different options to best meet their needs (see, e.g., Tabachnick & Fidell, 2007, for an overview).

4. The reader is referred to Weakliem (1999), who criticized the use of the BIC.

References

Diggle, P. J., Liang, K. Y., & Zeger, S. L. (1994). *Analysis of longitudinal data.* Oxford, UK: Oxford University Press.

Hand, D. J., & Taylor, C. C. (1987). *Multivariate analysis of variance and repeated measures.* London: Chapman & Hall.

Hox, J. (2002). *Multilevel analysis: Techniques and applications.* London: Lawrence Erlbaum.

Kleinbaum, D. G., Kupper, L. L., Muller, K. E., & Nizam, A. (1998). *Applied regression analysis and multivariable methods.* London: Duxbury.

Landau, S., & Everitt, B. S. (2004). *A handbook of statistical analysis using SPSS.* London: Chapman & Hall.

Potthoff, R. F., & Roy, S. N. (1964). A generalized multivariate analysis of variance model useful especially for growth curve problems. *Biometrika, 51,* 313–326.

Snijders, T., & Bosker, R. (1999). *Multilevel analysis: An introduction to basic and advanced multilevel modeling.* London: Sage.

Tabachnick, B. G., & Fidell, L. S. (2007). *Using multivariate statistics.* Boston: Pearson.

Twisk, J. W. R. (2003). *Applied longitudinal data analysis for epidemiology.* Cambridge, UK: Cambridge University Press.

Verbeke, G., & Molenberghs, G. (2000). *Linear mixed models for longitudinal data.* New York: Springer.

Weakliem, D. (1999). A critique of the Bayesian information criterion for model selection. *Sociological Methods & Research, 27*(3), 359–397.

Weisberg, S. (1985). *Applied linear regression.* New York: John Wiley.

31

ANALYSIS OF MODERATOR EFFECTS IN META-ANALYSIS

WOLFGANG VIECHTBAUER

As discussed in Chapter 12 (this volume), meta-analysis is a quantitative method for leveraging the proliferation of published research to more scientifically and comprehensively synthesize bodies of research (e.g., Chalmers, Hedges, & Cooper, 2002). Social policy decisions and best practices in various fields are increasingly influenced not by the results from single isolated studies but by the findings from meta-analyses (Cook et al., 1992).

A meta-analysis not only helps to determine whether a particular treatment is actually effective or whether there is indeed an association between variables but also allows the reviewer to examine whether the treatment effectiveness or relationship strength is influenced by the characteristics of the studies. For example, it is conceivable that the effectiveness of a treatment observed in a particular study depends on the treatment duration or intensity (e.g., the length of the psychotherapy or the medication dosage), the characteristics of the sample, the study setting, or the type of outcome measure used. Examining these hypotheses is difficult when conducting a traditional narrative literature review, but such *moderator analyses* constitute an integral and important aspect of a meta-analysis (Lau, Ioannidis, & Schmid, 1998; Thompson, 1994).

SCOPE OF THIS CHAPTER

One can roughly break the process of a meta-analysis down into five stages (Cooper, 1998): (a) problem formulation, (b) data collection, (c) data evaluation, (d) analysis and interpretation, and (e) presentation of results. The majority of the time and effort will typically be spent on the first three stages, which are briefly outlined in Chapter 12 and elsewhere.[1] For the purposes this chapter, we will assume that these steps have already been completed. Instead, the present chapter is meant to provide some guidelines on how to conduct the statistical analysis, once the first three steps have been completed. Again, several books deal extensively with this topic (e.g., Cooper & Hedges, 1994; Hedges & Olkin, 1985), and a single chapter cannot replace these references. However, the statistical methods that should be used for a meta-analysis are constantly being improved and extended. The goal is then to highlight those methods that currently represent best practices.

A Sample Data Set

An example will be used throughout this chapter to make the discussion more concrete and to allow the reader to experiment with the techniques discussed. Consider Table 31.1, which provides the results from $k = 16$ studies examining the effectiveness of massage therapy for reducing state anxiety. In each study, the amount of anxiety was measured among subjects randomly assigned to either a massage therapy or a control/standard treatment group. For each study (i being the index for the studies), the table lists the sample size of the control/comparison and the treatment group (n_i^C and n_i^E, respectively), the effect size estimate (Y_i) in the form of a standardized mean difference (to be discussed in more detail below), the estimated sampling variance ($\hat{v}_i$) of the effect size estimate, the minutes per session of massage therapy provided, whether a fully trained massage therapist or layperson provided the therapy (coded as 1 and 0, respectively), the mean age of the sample, and whether the study was conducted by the Touch Research Institute (TRI) or not (coded as 1 and 0, respectively). The last four variables are examples of *moderator*

variables that may influence the effectiveness of massage therapy for reducing state anxiety.[2]

Standardized Mean Difference

The standardized mean difference (SMD) is usually the effect size measure of choice when we are interested in the difference between a treatment/experimental and a control/comparison group and the outcome variable is quantitative. Let μ_i^C and μ_i^E denote the true (population) means of the control and treatment groups in the ith study, and let σ_i denote the common standard deviation of these groups. Then the effect size in the ith study is defined as

$$\theta_i = \frac{\mu_i^C - \mu_i^E}{\sigma_i},$$

so that θ_i indicates, in standard deviation units, by how much the mean in the control group differs

Table 31.1   Results From 16 Studies on the Effectiveness of Massage Therapy for Reducing State Anxiety

Study	Sample Size n_i^C	n_i^E	Effect Size Estimate (Y_i)	Sampling Variance ($\hat{v}_i$)	Minutes per Session	Trained Therapist	Mean Age	TRI Study
1	30	30	0.444	0.068	30	0	28	0
2	39	46	−0.495	0.049	10	0	42	0
3	15	15	0.195	0.134	20	1	31	0
4	10	10	0.546	0.207	40	1	39	1
5	12	12	0.840	0.181	20	1	17	1
6	10	10	0.105	0.200	30	1	51	1
7	24	26	0.472	0.082	15	1	26	1
8	14	18	−0.205	0.128	10	0	64	0
9	12	12	1.284	0.201	45	1	48	1
10	12	12	0.068	0.167	30	1	40	1
11	15	15	0.234	0.134	30	1	52	1
12	12	12	0.811	0.180	30	1	33	1
13	15	15	0.204	0.134	30	1	20	1
14	18	18	1.271	0.134	60	1	27	0
15	15	15	1.090	0.153	45	1	52	0
16	35	43	−0.059	0.052	10	1	61	0

NOTE: Adapted from Moyer, Rounds, and Hannum (2004), leaving out three studies with missing data and two studies where the duration of massage therapy provided was less than 10 minutes. Minutes per session = minutes of therapy provided per session; trained therapist = 0 for a layperson providing the therapy and 1 for a trained therapist; mean age = mean age of the sample; TRI study = 1 when the study was conducted by the Touch Research Institute (TRI) and 0 otherwise.

from that of the experimental group after the treatment. For the massage therapy meta-analysis, θ_i can be interpreted as a measure of the effectiveness of massage therapy for reducing state anxiety. Specifically, positive values of θ_i indicate lower amounts of anxiety in the treatment group, values around zero indicate no difference between the two groups, and negative values indicate lower anxiety in the control group. Expressing the effect size in standard deviation units makes the results from studies using different outcome measures (i.e., studies using anxiety scales with different raw units) comparable.

Hedges (1981) showed that an approximately unbiased and normally distributed estimate of θ_i is given by

$$Y_i = \left(1 - \frac{3}{4(n_i^C + n_i^E) - 9}\right)\left(\frac{\bar{x}_i^C - \bar{x}_i^E}{s_i}\right), \quad (1)$$

where $\bar{x}_i^C$ and $\bar{x}_i^E$ are the observed means of the treatment and control group in the ith study, and s_i is the pooled standard deviation of the two groups. The sampling variance of Y_i can be estimated with

$$\hat{v}_i = \frac{n_i^C + n_i^E}{n_i^C n_i^E} + \frac{Y_i^2}{2(n_i^C + n_i^E)}. \quad (2)$$

Therefore, Y_i is an estimate of θ_i, and $\hat{v}_i$ is an estimate of the amount of variability in Y_i we would expect due to subject-level sampling variability. In other words, even if the θ_i values (i.e., the true SMDs) are identical in two studies, we would not expect the corresponding Y_i values (i.e., the observed SMDs) to coincide due to sampling differences among the samples. However, should the sample sizes be very large in the two studies, then $\hat{v}_i$ is small (which should be evident from Equation 2); hence, sampling variability decreases, and the two Y_i values would tend to be very close to each other.

META-ANALYTIC DATA IN GENERAL

The SMD is not the only effect size measure used in meta-analyses. Others include correlation coefficients and odds ratios (as discussed in Chapter 17).[3]

However, regardless of the specific effect size measure used in a meta-analysis, assume that k

independent effect size estimates have been collected along with information about one or more moderator variables. As discussed earlier, each effect size estimate Y_i is an estimate of a corresponding parameter θ_i, which indicates the true effect size in the ith study. In general, we can express this idea by writing

$$Y_i = \theta_i + \varepsilon_i, \quad (3)$$

where ε_i is the sampling error for the ith study. The sampling errors are assumed to be normally distributed with mean zero and variance $\hat{v}_i$.

Meta-Analytic Models

Once a collection of effect size estimates (like the one in Table 31.1) has been obtained, several questions arise:

1. Is massage therapy an effective treatment for reducing state anxiety (i.e., how large is the overall effect of massage therapy on state anxiety?)?

2. Does the treatment effectiveness vary across studies and, if yes, by how much (i.e., is the effect size the same in all studies, and if not, how much variability is there among the effect sizes?)?

3. If there is variability in the treatment effectiveness across studies, is this variability, at least in part, systematic and explainable (i.e., do the effect sizes depend on one or more moderators—in particular, the treatment duration, the level of training of the therapist, the mean age of the sample, or whether the study was conducted by the TRI or not?)?

To answer these questions, we must identify the model that most closely approximates the true structure underlying the collection of effect size estimates.

Fixed Effects Model

The simplest case we may consider is the fixed effects model. According to this model, the effect sizes are homogeneous (i.e., $\theta_1 = \ldots = \theta_k$), so the model is given by

$$Y_i = \theta + \varepsilon_i, \quad (4)$$

where θ denotes the (homogeneous) effect size for all k studies. In the context of the massage therapy meta-analysis, this would imply that the treatment effectiveness is the same in all studies, regardless of treatment duration, level of training of the therapist, mean age of the sample, whether the study was conducted by the TRI or not, or any other moderator variable that we did not collect any information on (i.e., the studies may differ in other aspects unknown to us). Therefore, differences among the observed standardized mean differences (i.e., the effect size estimates) are assumed to be a result of sampling variability alone.

Fixed Effects With Moderators Model

On the other hand, when the effect sizes are not all equal to each other, they are said to be heterogeneous. Heterogeneity among the effect sizes may be a result of moderators and therefore entirely systematic. For example, when the effectiveness of massage therapy increases with the minutes of treatment provided and/or the training level of the therapist, then θ_i will be systematically higher in studies where the duration of the therapy was longer and/or the therapy was provided by a trained massage therapist as opposed to a layperson. Differences between the effect size estimates are then not only a result of sampling variability but also a result of the influence of moderators on the effect sizes. This case can be described by a fixed effects with moderators model, which is given by

$$Y_i = \beta_0 + \beta_1 X_{i1} + \ldots + \beta_p X_{ip} + \varepsilon_i, \qquad (5)$$

where X_{ij} denotes the value of the jth moderator variable for the ith effect size. The fixed effects with moderators model therefore assumes that the effect sizes are a linear function of one or more moderator variables. For example, in the massage therapy meta-analysis, the true effectiveness of the treatment may be a linear function of the $p = 4$ moderator variables described earlier.

Random Effects Model

Alternatively, the heterogeneity among the effect sizes may be completely random (unsystematic). In that case, the θ_i values will differ from each other randomly, and it will not be possible to account for differences among the effect sizes based on moderator variables such as treatment duration or the training level of the therapist. In this case, the random effects model applies, which is given by

$$Y_i = \mu + u_i + \varepsilon_i, \qquad (6)$$

where μ denotes the average effect size, and u_i is assumed to follow a normal distribution with mean zero and variance τ^2_{RE}. Therefore, τ^2_{RE} denotes the total amount of heterogeneity among the effect sizes. Differences between the effect size estimates are now assumed to be a result of sampling variability and random differences among the effect sizes.

Mixed Effects Model

Finally, it is possible that the heterogeneity among the effect sizes is, in part, a result of moderators and, in part, random. In that case, the mixed effects model applies, which is given by

$$Y_i = \beta_0 + \beta_1 X_{i1} + \ldots + \beta_p X_{ip} + u_i + \varepsilon_i. \qquad (7)$$

The variance of u_i, now denoted by τ^2_{ME}, represents the amount of *residual heterogeneity*, that is, the amount of excess or unexplainable variability in the effect sizes (i.e., heterogeneity that cannot be accounted for by the moderator variables included in the model). Therefore, the mixed effects model assumes that the effect sizes are a linear function of one or more moderator variables but also allows for the possibility that residual heterogeneity may exist in the effect sizes. It is therefore the most general of the four meta-analytic models and should be the starting point in most meta-analyses (this point will be elaborated on below). In fact, it is easy to see that the fixed effects, fixed effects with moderators, and random effects models are just special cases of the mixed effects model.[4] The nested hierarchy among the four models is illustrated in Figure 31.1. For further discussion of these models, see, for example, Hedges (1994), Hedges and Olkin (1985), and Raudenbush (1994).

Note that the mixed effects and fixed effects with moderators models can accommodate quantitative and categorical moderator variables. For categorical moderator variables, one has to employ an appropriate coding scheme as used in regression analysis when including categorical independent variables in the model (e.g., Neter, Kutner, Nachtsheim, & Wasserman, 1996).

Why Start With the Mixed Effects Model?

The mixed effects model was earlier suggested as the starting point for meta-analyses that are focusing on moderators. This recommendation actually goes contrary to typical practice, as meta-analysts usually first report an overall effect size estimate from a fixed or random effects model before considering the influence moderators. However, several reasons speak against this practice. First of all, heterogeneity is typically present among the effect sizes. Empirical evidence strongly suggests that the effect sizes are influenced considerably, for example, by the methods and procedures used in the studies, the characteristics of the samples, the study settings, or the types of outcome measures used (e.g., Wilson & Lipsey, 2001). Exploring the source of the heterogeneity by examining the influence of moderators on the effect sizes is often one of the most important and useful aspects of a meta-analysis (Lau et al., 1998; Thompson, 1994).

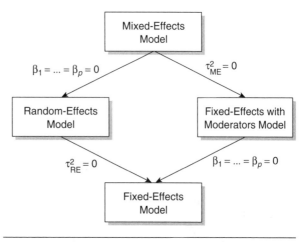

Figure 31.1   The nested hierarchical structure between the meta-analytic models.

In fact, an estimate of the overall effect size is meaningless at best and can even be misleading when moderators are present. Consider, for example, the admittedly extreme but illustrative case where (a) the effectiveness of massage therapy depends only on whether the treatment is given by a trained therapist or by a layperson, (b) the true SMD is equal to 0.5 in studies using a trained therapist and equal to –0.5 in studies using a layperson (i.e., massage therapy given by a trained therapist results in decreased anxiety levels, while a layperson does more harm than good and actually causes an increase in anxiety levels), and (c) the treatment was given by a trained therapist in about half of the studies, while the other half used a layperson. Then an estimate of the overall effect size would fall around zero, suggesting the total absence of an effect.

Moreover, it is unclear what such an overall effect size estimate represents. For the dichotomous moderator that distinguishes between a layperson and a trained therapist, an overall estimate may, with some imagination, represent the effect size for a semi-trained therapist. However, for the dichotomous moderator that distinguishes between studies conducted by the TRI and other laboratories, it is difficult to imagine what such an estimate would describe. Therefore, in those cases where moderators influence the effect sizes, one should resist the temptation to oversimplify matters by reporting a single overall effect size estimate. This implies that we should actually start out with a model that

examines the influence of moderators on the effect sizes. If the influence of the moderators is large (either practically speaking or in terms of statistical significance), then one can provide estimated or predicted effect sizes for some sensible values of the moderator variables based on the fitted model (to be illustrated later on).

Another issue to consider in this context is the use of models that acknowledge the possible presence of (residual) heterogeneity. Although the issue continues to be debated in the literature, a general consensus is beginning to emerge that one should employ random/mixed instead of fixed effects procedures, at least as a starting point in the analysis (e.g., Field, 2003; Hedges & Vevea, 1998; Hunter & Schmidt, 2000; National Research Council, 1992; Overton, 1998). Given the hierarchical nature of the models (cf. Figure 31.1), the mixed or random effects models may ultimately reduce to a simpler model. Specifically, when residual heterogeneity is absent (i.e., $\tau^2_{ME} = 0$), the mixed effects model automatically simplifies to a fixed effects with moderators model, while the random effects model automatically simplifies to a fixed effects model when there is no heterogeneity at all (i.e., $\tau^2_{RE} = 0$). Therefore, instead of adopting a simpler (and possibly incorrect) model a priori, we should examine what model is actually supported by the data.

Fitting the Mixed Effects Model

Fitting the mixed effects model is done in two steps. First, we estimate τ^2_{ME}, the amount of residual heterogeneity in the effect sizes. We then estimate β_0 through β_p, the parameters specifying the relationship between the effect sizes and the moderators.

Estimating the Amount of Residual Heterogeneity

Numerous methods for estimating τ^2_{ME} have been discussed in the literature (e.g., Raudenbush, 1994; Raudenbush & Bryk, 1985; Sidik & Jonkman, 2005; Thompson & Sharp, 1999), but a description of the various methods is beyond the scope of the present chapter. Here, we will simply focus on a commonly used method of moments estimator (e.g., Raudenbush, 1994).

Let the $(k \times (p + 1))$ matrix X contain the values of the p moderator variables to be included in the model, where the first column consists of a vector of 1s, corresponding to the intercept parameter β_0. Also, collect the effect size estimates into the $(k \times 1)$ vector y. Next, let $w_i = 1/\hat{v}_i$, and define W as the diagonal matrix using those weights. Now calculate

$$P = W - WX \, (X'WX)^{-1} \, X'W$$

and finally

$$\hat{\tau}^2_{ME} = \frac{y'Py - (k - p - 1)}{tr[P]}, \qquad (8)$$

where X' denotes the transpose of X and y' the transpose of y, $(X'WX)^{-1}$ denotes the inverse of $(X'WX)$, and $tr[P]$ denotes the trace of the P matrix. Should the estimate be negative, then this indicates the absence of residual heterogeneity, and we set $\hat{\tau}^2_{ME} = 0$.

Illustrative Example

Four moderators will be included in the model for the massage therapy meta-analysis—namely, the minutes of therapy provided, whether a layperson or a fully trained massage therapist provided the therapy, the mean age of the sample, and whether the study was conducted

by the TRI or some other laboratory. Therefore, X, y, and W are given by

$$X = \begin{bmatrix} 1 & 30 & 0 & 28 & 0 \\ 1 & 10 & 0 & 42 & 0 \\ 1 & 20 & 1 & 31 & 0 \\ 1 & 40 & 1 & 39 & 1 \\ & & \vdots & & \\ 1 & 10 & 1 & 61 & 0 \end{bmatrix},$$

$$y = \begin{bmatrix} 0.444 \\ -0.495 \\ 0.195 \\ 0.546 \\ \vdots \\ -0.059 \end{bmatrix}, \text{ and}$$

$$W = \begin{bmatrix} \dfrac{1}{0.068} & 0 & 0 & 0 \\ 0 & \dfrac{1}{0.049} & 0 & 0 \\ 0 & 0 & \ddots & 0 \\ 0 & 0 & 0 & \dfrac{1}{0.052} \end{bmatrix}.$$

Applying Equation 8 then yields $\hat{\tau}^2_{ME} = -0.023$. Since the estimate is negative, we set $\hat{\tau}^2_{ME} = 0$ and conclude that no residual heterogeneity is present, or, in other words, the moderators included in the model account for all of the heterogeneity in the effect sizes.

Estimating the Moderator Parameters

Having obtained an estimate of τ^2_{ME} (with this or any other method), we can then estimate β_0 through β_p with

$$b = (X'WX)^{-1} \, X' \, Wy, \qquad (9)$$

where the elements of the diagonal W matrix are now set to $w_i = 1/(\hat{\tau}^2_{ME} + \hat{v}_i)$. The variance-covariance matrix of the parameter estimates in b is then obtained with

$$\hat{\Sigma} = (X'WX)^{-1}. \qquad (10)$$

Taking the square root of the diagonal elements of $\hat{\Sigma}$ yields the standard errors of the estimates, which will be denoted by $SE[b_j]$.

Illustrative Example

Since the estimate of the amount of residual heterogeneity happened to be zero in our example, $w_i = 1/(\hat{\tau}^2_{ME} + \hat{v}_i)$ actually simplifies to $w_i = 1/\hat{v}_i$, and the **W** matrix remains unchanged. The parameter estimates and variance-covariance matrix obtained by applying Equations 9 and 10 are equal to

$$
b = \begin{bmatrix} -0.263 \\ 0.025 \\ 0.338 \\ -0.007 \\ -0.061 \end{bmatrix} \text{ and } \hat{\Sigma} =
$$

$$
\begin{bmatrix}
.13555 & -.00139 & .00457 & -.00215 & -.02604 \\
-.00139 & .00005 & -.00055 & .00002 & .00013 \\
.00457 & -.00055 & .05620 & -.00045 & -.02970 \\
-.00215 & .00002 & -.00045 & .00005 & .00058 \\
-.02604 & .00013 & -.02970 & .00058 & .04885
\end{bmatrix}.
$$

Therefore, for a 1-minute increase in session duration, the effectiveness of massage therapy is estimated to increase by $b_1 = 0.025$ points in SMD units ($SE[b_1] = \sqrt{.00005} = .007$). For example, an increase in 12 minutes should result in a 0.3 increase in the effect size. Lacking further information about the domain being studied, 0.2, 0.5, and 0.8 are conventionally thought of as small, medium, and large SMDs (Cohen, 1988). Therefore, 12 minutes can mean the difference between a small and a medium or a medium and a large effect. Moreover, the effect size is estimated to be $b_2 = 0.338$ points higher for a trained massage therapist when compared with a layperson providing the treatment ($SE[b_2] = \sqrt{.05620} = .237$). Furthermore, for a 1-year increase in the average age of the sample, the effect size is estimated to change by $b_3 = -0.007$ points ($SE[b_3] = \sqrt{.00005} = .007$).

Finally, studies conducted by the TRI are estimated to yield an effect size that differs by $b_4 = -0.061$ SMD units from that of other laboratories ($SE[b_4] = \sqrt{.04885} = .221$). The b_0 value should not be interpreted here, as it estimates the effectiveness of zero minutes of therapy provided by a layperson to a sample with an average age of zero in a study that was conducted in a laboratory other than the TRI.[5]

Returning to the point made earlier about avoiding a single overall effect size in the presence of moderators, we may now report the estimated effect size for some sensible and representative moderator values. For example, the estimated effect size for 10 minutes of massage therapy provided by a layperson in a non-TRI study to a group with an average age of 40 is −0.293 (i.e., −0.263 + 0.025(10) + 0.338(0) − 0.007(40) − 0.061(0) = −0.293). On the other hand, 30 minutes of therapy provided by a trained therapist to the same group in a non-TRI study is estimated to yield an effect size of 0.545 (i.e., −0.263 + 0.025(30) + 0.338(1) − 0.007(40) − 0.061(0) = 0.545). The estimated effect is actually negative in the first and positive in the second case, and the difference between the two amounts to more than 0.8 SMD units. A simple average would not be able to properly represent such differences.

MODERATOR ANALYSIS

Although we have already seen that the estimated effect changes drastically as a function of the moderators, we may want to test whether the moderators included in the model exert a statistically significant influence on the effect sizes in general. Also, when several moderators are included in the model, we may want to examine the statistical significance of each moderator variable individually. Refined procedures for carrying out such tests, which have been developed in recent years (e.g., Knapp & Hartung, 2003; Sidik & Jonkman, 2003, 2005), will be discussed in the present section.

We start by calculating an adjusted variance-covariance matrix with

$$
\hat{\Sigma}^* = s_{\hat{w}}^2 (\mathbf{X}'\mathbf{W}\mathbf{X})^{-1}, \tag{11}
$$

where either

$$
s_{\hat{w}}^2 = \frac{(\mathbf{y} - \mathbf{X}b)' \, \mathbf{W}(\mathbf{y} - \mathbf{X}b)}{k - p - 1} \tag{12}
$$

or it is set equal to 1 if the value calculated with Equation 12 falls below 1.

Omnibus Test of all Moderators

When multiple moderators are included in the model, we can test the null hypothesis H_0: $\beta_1 = \ldots = \beta_p = 0$ (i.e., whether *any* of the moderator variables are related to the effect sizes) by computing

$$Q_R = b'_{[2]} \, (\hat{\Sigma}^*_{[2]})^{-1} \, b_{[2]}, \qquad (13)$$

where $b_{[2]}$ is the $(p \times 1)$ vector of parameter estimates excluding the first element (which corresponds to the intercept estimate, which we do not want to include in the test), and $\hat{\Sigma}^*_{[2]}$ is the lower right $(p \times p)$ matrix obtained from $\hat{\Sigma}^*$ after deleting the first column and first row. We compare the Q_R value against $p \times F(\alpha; p, k-p-1)$, where $F(\alpha; df_1, df_2)$ denotes the critical value of an F distribution with df_1 and df_2 degrees of freedom at the desired α–level. If $Q_R > p \times F(\alpha; p, k-p-1)$, we reject the null hypothesis and conclude that at least one of the moderators is related to the effect sizes. Otherwise, we conclude that the effect sizes are not influenced by any of the moderators included in the set that was tested.

Illustrative Example

Applying Equation 12 after we have fitted the mixed effects model yields a value of $s_{\hat{w}}^2 = 0.822$. Therefore, $s_{\hat{w}}^2$ is set equal to 1, so that the adjusted variance-covariance matrix, obtained with Equation 11, is identical to the one given earlier. Finally, to test whether at least one moderator is related to the effect sizes, we apply the Q_R test (Equation 13), with

$$b_{[2]} = \begin{bmatrix} 0.025 \\ 0.338 \\ -0.007 \\ -0.061 \end{bmatrix} \text{ and } \hat{\Sigma}^*_{[2]} =$$

$$\begin{bmatrix} .00005 & -.00055 & .00002 & .00013 \\ -.00055 & .05620 & -.00045 & -.02970 \\ .00002 & -.00045 & .00005 & .00058 \\ .00013 & -.02970 & .00058 & .04885 \end{bmatrix}.$$

The value of Q_R is 28.91, which we compare against $4 \times F(.05; 4, 11) = 13.43$. We therefore conclude that at least one of the moderator variables influences the effectiveness of massage therapy.

Individual Moderator Tests

We can also test the statistical significance of each moderator variable individually with

$$t_{b_j} = \frac{b_j}{s_{\hat{w}} SE[b_j]}, \qquad (14)$$

which we compare against the critical values of a t distribution with $k-p-1$ degrees of freedom. Alternatively,

$$b_j \pm t_{(k-p-1; \, 1-\alpha/2)} \, s_{\hat{w}} \, SE[b_j] \qquad (15)$$

provides a $(1-\alpha) \times 100\%$ confidence interval for β_j.

Illustrative Example

Since $s_{\hat{w}}^2$ was set equal to 1, the t_{b_j} values (Equation 14) are obtained by dividing the parameter estimates by the standard errors given earlier. We compare these values against ± 2.20, the critical bounds of a t-distributed random variable with $16 - 4 - 1 = 11$ degrees of freedom (using $\alpha = .05$, two-tailed). Alternatively, 95% confidence intervals can be computed with Equation 15. These results are summarized in Table 31.2, which indicates that only the minutes per session moderator is statistically significant.

The effect size estimates are shown in Figure 31.2 after ordering the studies by the minutes per session moderator variable. The approximate bounds of individual 95% confidence intervals are also shown, which are given by

$$Y_i \pm 1.96\sqrt{\hat{\tau}_{ME}^2 + \hat{v}_i}$$

(note that τ_{ME}^2 happens to be zero in this particular case). As Figure 31.2 clearly demonstrates, the effect size estimates tend to increase systematically with treatment duration. Such a pattern

Table 31.2   Results From Fitting the Mixed Effects Model to the Data in Table 31.1 When Entering All Moderators Simultaneously in the Model

Moderator	b_j	$s_{\tilde{w}}\ SE\ [b_j]$	t_{b_j}	95% CI for β_j
Intercept	−0.263	0.368	−0.71	(−1.07, 0.55)
Minutes per session	0.025	0.007	3.68	(0.01, 0.04)
Trained therapist	0.338	0.237	1.43	(−0.18, 0.86)
Mean age	−0.007	0.007	−0.99	(−0.02, 0.01)
TRI study	−0.061	0.221	−0.28	(−0.55, 0.42)

NOTE: b_j = parameter estimate; $s_{\tilde{w}}\ SE[b_j]$ = adjusted standard error of the parameter estimate; $t_{b_j} = b_j / (s_{\tilde{w}}\ SE\ [b_j])$ (critical values = ± 2.20); estimate of residual heterogeneity: $\hat{\tau}^2_{ME} = 0$; test whether at least one moderator is significant: $Q_R = 28.91$ (critical value = 13.43); test for residual heterogeneity: $Q_E = 9.05$ (critical value = 19.68).

of results could occur by chance, but a more likely explanation is that the effectiveness of massage therapy depends on (or is moderated by) the duration of the treatment. So-called *forest plots,* such as the one shown in Figure 31.2, can be useful devices for concisely displaying the results from a meta-analysis and revealing interesting trends.

The influence of treatment duration is also apparent after plotting the effect size estimates against minutes of therapy provided, as shown in Figure 31.3. Circles represent effect size estimates from studies where a trained therapist provided the treatment, while squares represent effect size estimates from studies with a layperson. Moreover, larger points correspond to effect size estimates with smaller sampling variances. The lines indicate the estimated effect sizes as a function of minutes of therapy provided to a sample with an average age of 40 in a non-TRI study, once for a layperson and once for a trained therapist. The lines were plotted separately just for illustration purposes since the moderator distinguishing between a layperson and a trained therapist providing the treatment was not statistically significant.

Other Models as Special Cases of the Mixed Effects Model

As discussed earlier, the fixed effects with moderators, the random effects, and the fixed effects models are all special cases of the mixed effects model. Therefore, these models are applicable depending on the fit of the mixed effects model and the results from a moderator analysis.

Fixed Effects With Moderators Model

The mixed effects model reduces to the fixed effects with moderators model when $\tau^2_{ME} = 0$ (cf. Equations 5 and 7). Therefore, when the estimate of τ^2_{ME} is zero, this indicates that no residual heterogeneity is present, and the fixed effects with moderators model applies. This is exactly what happened in the illustrative example since $\hat{\tau}^2_{ME} = 0$. Therefore, the mixed effects model we fitted earlier actually corresponds to a fixed effects with moderators model. In general, then, to fit a fixed effects with moderators model, we simply need to apply all of the equations given earlier, except that w_i is always set equal to $1/\hat{v}_i$.

Random Effects Model

When none of the moderators included in the model influence the effect sizes (i.e., we conclude that $\beta_1 = \ldots = \beta_p = 0$), but heterogeneity is present (i.e., $\hat{\tau}^2_{ME} > 0$), then this suggests either that the heterogeneity in the effect sizes is entirely random (and could not be accounted for, no matter which set of moderators is included in the model) or that the heterogeneity is (at least in part) a result of moderators, but we lack the necessary information about the relevant moderators to account for it. In either case, the best we can usually do is to adopt the

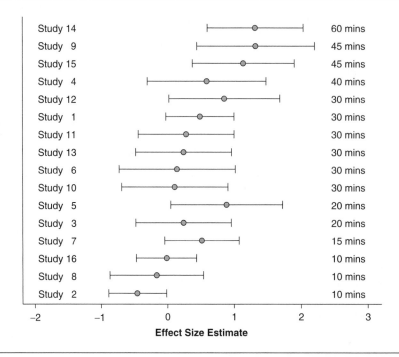

Figure 31.2   Individual effect size estimates (ordered by minutes of therapy provided per session) with corresponding 95% confidence intervals.

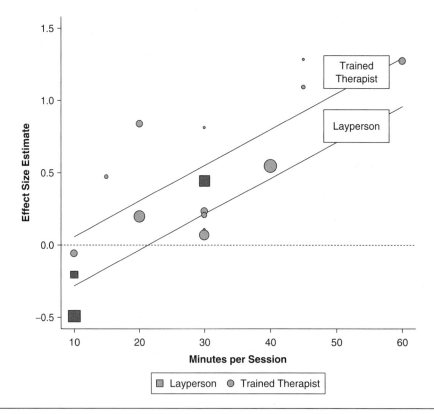

Figure 31.3   Effect size estimates and estimated effect sizes as a function of minutes of therapy provided to a sample with an average age of 40 in a non-TRI study, once for a layperson and once for a trained therapist.

random effects model (Equation 6) and treat the heterogeneity as purely random.

Fitting the random effects model requires that we estimate μ, the average effect size, and τ^2_{RE}, the amount of heterogeneity in the effect sizes. First, we estimate τ^2_{RE} with

$$\hat{\tau}^2_{RE} = \frac{Q - (k - 1)}{\sum w_i - \frac{\sum w_i^2}{\sum w_i}}, \qquad (16)$$

where $w_i = 1/\hat{v}_i$,

$$Q = \sum w_i (Y_i - \hat{\theta})^2, \qquad (17)$$

and

$$\hat{\theta} = \frac{\sum w_i Y_i}{\sum w_i}. \qquad (18)$$

After obtaining $\hat{\tau}^2_{RE}$ we can estimate μ with

$$\hat{\mu} = \frac{\sum w_i Y_i}{\sum w_i}, \qquad (19)$$

where $w_i = 1/(\hat{\tau}^2_{RE} + \hat{v}_i)$. The standard error of $\hat{\mu}$ is approximately equal to

$$SE[\hat{\mu}] = \sqrt{\frac{1}{\sum w_i}}. \qquad (20)$$

Finally, we can test if the average effect size differs significantly from zero (i.e., $H_0 : \mu = 0$) by comparing

$$t = \frac{\hat{\mu}}{s_{\hat{w}} SE[\hat{\mu}]} \qquad (21)$$

against the critical values of a t distribution with $k - 1$ degrees of freedom, where $s^2_{\hat{w}}$ is the larger of

$$s^2_{\hat{w}} = \frac{\sum w_i (Y_i - \hat{\mu})^2}{k - 1} \qquad (22)$$

and 1. Alternatively, a confidence interval for μ can be constructed with

$$\hat{\mu} \pm t_{(k-1; 1-\alpha/2)} s_{\hat{w}} SE[\hat{\mu}]. \qquad (23)$$

Illustrative Example

Although the data strongly suggest that the heterogeneity in the effect sizes is not random, we now fit the random effects model to the data for illustration purposes. First, we calculate the value of $\hat{\theta}$ (Equation 18), which is equal to 0.280. We then apply Equation 17, which yields $Q = 37.959$. From this, we can obtain the estimate of τ^2_{RE} (Equation 16), which is equal to 0.175. This value is now an estimate of the total amount of heterogeneity in the effect sizes (as opposed to the estimate of the residual amount of heterogeneity we obtained earlier when fitting the mixed effects model). The average effect size μ, estimated with Equation 19, is equal to $\hat{\mu} = 0.379$ ($SE[\hat{\mu}] = 0.138$). Equation 22 then yields a value of 0.912 for $s^2_{\hat{w}}$, which is below 1 and therefore set to 1. The value of t (Equation 21) is equal to 2.75, and a 95% confidence interval for μ is given by (0.09, 0.67). This interval excludes zero, which indicates that, on average, massage therapy is effective for reducing state anxiety.

Fixed Effects Model

Should we find that $\hat{\tau}^2_{RE} = 0$, this would provide evidence that the effect sizes are homogeneous. In other words, $\hat{\tau}^2_{RE} = 0$ suggests that neither moderators nor an additional source of random variability are influencing the effect sizes. Equation 18 then yields the estimate of θ, the homogeneous effect size for all studies. The standard error of the estimate, the statistic for testing whether $H_0 : \theta = 0$, and a confidence interval for θ can then be obtained with Equations 20 through 23, replacing $\hat{\mu}$ with $\hat{\theta}$ and setting $w_i = 1/\hat{v}_i$ in all of the equations. The application of the fixed effects model will not be illustrated with the example since the data clearly indicate that the effect sizes are not homogeneous.

Testing for the Presence of Residual Heterogeneity

A common practice in meta-analysis is to test whether the estimated amount of residual heterogeneity in a mixed effects model (i.e., $\hat{\tau}^2_{ME}$) is significantly greater than zero. To test the null hypothesis $H_0 : \tau^2_{ME} = 0$, we fit the fixed effects with moderators model (i.e., we set $w_i = 1/\hat{v}_i$ and use Equations 9 and 10 to obtain $\mathbf{b}$ and $\hat{\Sigma}$) and then calculate

$$Q_E = \sum w_i Y_i^2 - \mathbf{b}' \hat{\Sigma}^{-1} \mathbf{b}. \qquad (24)$$

If Q_E exceeds the critical value of a chi-square random variable with $k - p - 1$ degrees of freedom, we conclude that there is additional heterogeneity in the effect sizes that is not accounted for by the moderators included in the model. This might indicate the presence of other moderators that we have missed, additional random heterogeneity, or both.

Illustrative Example

Since we found $\tau^2_{ME} = 0$ in the example given earlier, we have already fitted the fixed effects with moderators model to our data. Therefore, the Q_E statistic can be directly computed with **b** and $\hat{\Sigma}$ as given above and is equal to 9.05. Compared against 19.68, the critical value of a chi-square random variable with $16 - 4 - 1 = 11$ degrees of freedom, we conclude that no residual heterogeneity is present. This is not a surprising finding since the estimate of residual heterogeneity was zero.

Confidence Interval for the Amount of Residual Heterogeneity

Instead of (or in addition to) testing whether the amount of residual heterogeneity is equal to zero, one can also report a confidence interval for τ^2_{ME}. The most accurate method to obtain such a confidence interval works as follows (Viechtbauer, 2007a). Let $Q_E (\tilde{\tau}^2_{ME})$ denote the value of Equation 24 when setting $w_i = 1/(\tilde{\tau}^2_{ME} + \hat{v}_i)$ (note that **b** and $\hat{\Sigma}$ also need to be recalculated to obtain this value). Moreover, let $\chi^2_{k-p-1; 0.025}$ and $\chi^2_{k-p-1; 0.975}$ denote the 2.5th and 97.5th percentiles of a chi-square distribution with $k - p - 1$ degrees of freedom. Then the lower and upper bounds of a 95% confidence interval for τ^2_{ME} are given by those two $\tilde{\tau}^2_{ME}$ values, where $Q_E (\tilde{\tau}^2_{ME}) = \chi^2_{k-p-1; 0.975}$ and $Q_E (\tilde{\tau}^2_{ME}) = \chi^2_{k-p-1; 0.025}$. These values must be obtained iteratively. The simplest approach is to start with $\tilde{\tau}^2_{ME} = 0$ and to compute $Q_E (\tilde{\tau}^2_{ME})$ repeatedly for increasing $\tilde{\tau}^2_{ME}$ values until $Q_E (\tilde{\tau}^2_{ME})$ is equal to $\chi^2_{k-p-1; 0.975}$ and then equal to $\chi^2_{k-p-1; 0.025}$. If $Q_E (\tilde{\tau}^2_{ME})$ falls below $\chi^2_{k-p-1; 0.975}$ for $\tilde{\tau}^2_{ME} = 0$, then the lower bound is set to zero. Moreover, if $Q_E (\tilde{\tau}^2_{ME})$ even falls below $\chi^2_{k-p-1; 0.975}$ for $\tilde{\tau}^2_{ME} = 0$, then the lower and upper bounds are both below zero, and the confidence interval is equal to the null set.

Illustrative Example

With 11 degrees of freedom, $\chi^2_{11; 0.975} = 21.92$ and $\chi^2_{11; 0.025} = 3.82$. We have seen earlier that $Q_E = 9.05$, which is actually the value of $Q_E (\tilde{\tau}^2_{ME})$ for $\tilde{\tau}^2_{ME} = 0$. Therefore, the lower bound of a 95% confidence interval for $\tilde{\tau}^2_{ME}$ is 0. To obtain the upper bound, we increase $\tilde{\tau}^2_{ME}$ in small steps, each time recalculating $Q_E (\tilde{\tau}^2_{ME})$. For $\tilde{\tau}^2_{ME} = 0.185$, $Q_E (\tilde{\tau}^2_{ME}) = 3.82$. Therefore, a 95% confidence interval for τ^2_{ME} is given by $(0, 0.185)$.

Testing for the Presence of Heterogeneity

We can also test whether the amount of heterogeneity in the random effects model is significantly greater than zero. If the amount of heterogeneity is zero, then this implies that the effect sizes are homogeneous. The null hypothesis is therefore given by H_0: $\theta_1 = \ldots = \theta_k$ (or, equivalently, $H_0 : \tau^2_{RE} = 0$). The statistic needed for this test is actually the one given in Equation 17. The null hypothesis is rejected when Q exceeds the critical value of a chi-square random variable with $k - 1$ degrees of freedom. In that case, we conclude that the effect sizes are heterogeneous, which might indicate the presence of moderators, random heterogeneity, or both.

Illustrative Example

We found earlier a value of $Q = 37.96$. The critical value of a chi-square random variable with $16 - 1 = 15$ degrees of freedom is 25.00; therefore, we reject H_0 and conclude that the effect sizes are heterogeneous.

Confidence Interval for the Total Amount of Heterogeneity

Using the method described earlier, one can also obtain a confidence interval for τ^2_{RE} in the random effects model. Letting $\chi^2_{k-1; 0.025}$ and $\chi^2_{k-1; 0.975}$ denote the 2.5th and 97.5th percentiles of a chi-square distribution with $k - 1$ degrees of freedom and

$$Q(\tilde{\tau}^2_{RE}) = \sum w_i (Y_i - \hat{\mu})^2, \qquad (25)$$

where $w_i = 1/(\tilde{\tau}^2_{RE} + \hat{v}_i)$ and $\hat{\mu}$ is calculated with Equation 19 after setting $w_i = 1/(\tilde{\tau}^2_{RE} + \hat{v}_i)$, we start with $\tilde{\tau}^2_{RE} = 0$ and iteratively increase $\tilde{\tau}^2_{RE}$ until we find those two $\tilde{\tau}^2_{RE}$ values, such that $Q(\tilde{\tau}^2_{RE}) = \chi^2_{k-1; 0.975}$ and $Q(\tilde{\tau}^2_{RE}) = \chi^2_{k-1; 0.025}$.

Illustrative Example

With 15 degrees of freedom, $\chi^2_{15;\,0.975} = 27.49$ and $\chi^2_{15;\,0.025} = 6.26$. We found that $Q = 37.96$, which is the value of $Q\,(\tilde{\tau}^2_{RE})$ for $\tilde{\tau}^2_{RE} = 0$. Increasing $\tilde{\tau}^2_{RE}$ slowly and recalculating $Q\,(\tilde{\tau}^2_{RE})$ each time reveals that $Q\,(\tilde{\tau}^2_{RE}) = 27.49$ when $\tilde{\tau}^2_{RE} = 0.034$ and $Q\,(\tilde{\tau}^2_{RE}) = 6.26$ when $\tilde{\tau}^2_{RE} = 0.524$. Therefore, a 95% confidence interval for τ^2_{RE} is given by $(0.034, 0.524)$.

A Note About the Heterogeneity Tests

When we fail to reject the null hypothesis $H_0 : \tau^2_{RE} = 0$ with the Q test, one should not automatically conclude that the effect sizes are truly homogeneous. The test lacks power to detect heterogeneity when k, the within-study sample sizes, or the amount of heterogeneity are small (Hunter & Schmidt, 2000; Sánchez-Meca & Marín-Martínez, 1997; Viechtbauer, 2007b). This, in turn, might lead researchers to adopt a fixed effects model too often, to miss the presence of moderators, or to attribute unwarranted precision to their results (National Research Council, 1992). Moreover, the Type I error rate of the Q test is only nominal when the within-study sample sizes are sufficiently large. In other words, when analyzing studies with small sample sizes, the test may be very inaccurate (Viechtbauer, 2007b). Therefore, a better approach would be to always adopt a random effects model. When the amount of heterogeneity is estimated to be zero (i.e., $\hat{\tau}^2_{RE} = 0$), then the random effects model simplifies to the fixed effects model anyway.

The same concerns apply to the Q_E test. In other words, one should not assume that residual heterogeneity is completely absent when we fail to reject $H_0 : \tau^2_{ME} = 0$ with the Q_E test. Again, the better approach would be to always start with a mixed effects model, which will automatically reduce to a fixed effects with moderators model when $\hat{\tau}^2_{ME} = 0$ (as demonstrated with the example given earlier).

Quantifying the Amount of (Residual) Heterogeneity

Raw estimates of τ^2_{ME} and τ^2_{RE} are difficult to interpret. For example, in our example, we found that $\hat{\tau}^2_{RE} = 0.175$. Does this value indicate a small or large amount of heterogeneity among

the effect sizes? To answer this question, it may be useful to express the amount of heterogeneity in terms of a value that is easier to interpret.

First note that the amount of variability among the effect size estimates can be decomposed into two parts: heterogeneity among the effect sizes (i.e., variability among the θ_i values) and sampling variability. The amount of sampling variability can be estimated by the $\hat{v}_i$ values, while the amount of heterogeneity among the effect sizes is estimated with $\hat{\tau}^2_{RE}$. Therefore, $\sum (\hat{\tau}^2_{RE} + \hat{v}_i)$ estimates the total amount of variability across the k effect size estimates. Consequently,

$$\hat{V}^2_T = \frac{k\hat{\tau}^2_{RE}}{\sum (\hat{\tau}^2_{RE} + \hat{v}_i)} \qquad (26)$$

denotes the proportion of total variability in the effect size estimates that is due to heterogeneity (i.e., the proportion of variability in the effect size estimates that is not accounted for by sampling variability). An alternative method for estimating this quantity is discussed in Higgins, Thompson, Deeks, and Altman (2003).

Turning now to the amount of residual heterogeneity, first note that $\hat{\tau}^2_{ME}$ will tend to be smaller than $\hat{\tau}^2_{RE}$ if the moderator(s) included in the mixed effects model account for (at least some of) the heterogeneity among the effect sizes. Consequently,

$$\hat{V}^2_R = \frac{k\hat{\tau}^2_{ME}}{\sum (\hat{\tau}^2_{RE} + \hat{v}_i)} \qquad (27)$$

denotes the proportion of total variability among the effect size estimates that is due to residual heterogeneity (i.e., not accounted for by sampling variability and the moderator[s] in the model). A value of $\hat{V}^2_R$ larger than 1 should be truncated to 1. Finally, we can also compute

$$\hat{R}^2 = \frac{\hat{\tau}^2_{RE} - \hat{\tau}^2_{ME}}{\hat{\tau}^2_{RE}} \qquad (28)$$

as an estimate of the proportion of heterogeneity that is explained by the moderator(s) included in the model (Raudenbush, 1994). In rare cases, $\hat{R}^2$ may become negative, in which case it should be set to zero.

Illustrative Example

In the random effects model, we found that $\hat{\tau}^2_{RE} = 0.175$. Based on Equation 26, we then find that $\hat{V}^2_T = 0.56$, indicating that 56% of the total variability in the effect size estimates is due to heterogeneity (and therefore unaccounted for). On the other hand, $\hat{\tau}^2_{ME} = 0$ in the mixed effects model. It requires no further computation to see that $\hat{V}^2_R = 0$ and $\hat{R}^2 = 1$, indicating that the proportion of total variability unaccounted for is zero and that the proportion of heterogeneity accounted for by the moderators is 1.

Testing One Moderator at a Time Is Not Generally a Best Practice

While many authors choose to fit a separate model for each moderator variable of interest (instead of fitting a single mixed effects model that includes all moderators simultaneously), when moderators are correlated, this can cause drastic overestimation of moderator effects.[6] Taking the current example, Table 31.3 summarizes the effects when each moderator is analyzed individually as compared with simultaneously.

In terms of the statistical significance of the moderators, the conclusions from this approach are identical to the ones we obtained earlier (cf. Table 31.2). However, some of the parameter estimates have changed substantially. In particular, massage therapy from a fully trained therapist is now estimated to be 0.6 SMD units higher than when a layperson provides the treatment, almost double compared to what we found when fitting the mixed effects model

with all moderators entered simultaneously (cf. Table 31.2).

The reason why this moderator now appears to have a stronger impact on the effect sizes can be explained based on the correlation among the moderators. Specifically, a layperson provided the therapy in Studies 1, 2, and 8, two of which (Studies 2 and 8) also happen to be studies where only 10 minutes of therapy were provided (see Figures 31.2 and 31.3). Since the effectiveness of therapy increases with treatment duration, the difference in the effectiveness between a layperson and a trained therapist is exacerbated when this moderator is examined by itself.

Note also that the sign of the TRI study moderator has changed. When this moderator is examined by itself, the data suggest that TRI studies yield SMDs that are 0.232 units larger than those in non-TRI studies. On the other hand, with all moderators entered simultaneously into the model, TRI studies are estimated to yield SMDs that are 0.061 units below those of non-TRI studies. In general, one may draw completely different conclusions from the analysis depending on the approach chosen.

MODEL SELECTION STRATEGY

To summarize and complete the recommendations given throughout this chapter, the following model selection strategy is suggested. First, an estimate of the total amount of heterogeneity (i.e., τ^2_{RE}) should be calculated when starting with the meta-analysis. This estimate can be supplemented with the results from the Q test

Table 31.3   Results From Fitting the Mixed Effects Model to the Data in Table 31.1 When Examining One Moderator at a Time

Moderator	b_j	$s_{\tilde{w}}SE[b_j]$	t_{b_j}	95% CI for β_j	$\hat{\tau}^2_{ME}$	95% CI for τ^2	Q_E	$\hat{V}^2_R$	$\hat{R}^2$
Minutes per session	0.030	0.006	5.08	(0.02, 0.04)	0	(0, 0.133)	12.18	0	1
Trained therapist	0.600	0.293	2.04	(−0.03, 1.23)	0.121	(0.007, 0.422)	28.12	.39	.31
Mean age	−0.013	0.009	−1.35	(−0.03, 0.01)	0.153	(0.022, 0.516)	32.25	.49	.13
TRI study	0.232	0.271	0.86	(−0.35, 0.81)	0.166	(0.030, 0.568)	34.05	.53	.05

NOTE: b_j = parameter estimate; $s_{\tilde{w}}SE[b_j]$ = adjusted standard error of parameter estimate; $t_{b_j} = b_j/s_{\tilde{w}}SE[b_j]$ (critical values = ± 2.14); τ^2_{ME} = estimate of residual heterogeneity; Q_E = test for residual heterogeneity (critical value = 23.68); $\hat{V}^2_R$ = proportion of total variability in the effect size estimates due to residual heterogeneity; $\hat{R}^2$ = proportion of heterogeneity that is explained by the moderator.

and, for easier interpretation, given as a proportion relative to the total amount of variability (Equation 26). When τ^2_{RE} is estimated to be zero and the Q test is not significant, one has support for the hypothesis that the fixed effects model holds. However, when in doubt (such as when $\tau^2_{RE} > 0$, regardless of the results from the Q test), one should not adopt the fixed effects model.

When heterogeneity appears to be present, one can try to account for the heterogeneity by fitting a mixed effects model to the data. However, the number of potential moderator variables is usually quite large, especially when compared with the number of effect size estimates. This may lead to overfitting and increases the risk of finding significant moderators by chance alone. Prespecification of moderator variables based on expert knowledge and theoretical considerations is therefore a necessary prerequisite in most meta-analyses (Thompson & Higgins, 2002).

After fitting the mixed effects model, one can proceed with the moderator analysis as demonstrated earlier. A significant Q_R test (Equation 13) can be followed by individual moderator tests with the t_{b_j} statistic (Equation 14) and/or corresponding confidence intervals (Equation 15). Moreover, liberal use of plots and figures such as the ones shown in Figures 31.2 and 31.3 can greatly improve the interpretability of the results.

Due to missing data, it is often not possible to include multiple moderators in the mixed effects model simultaneously. Each study with missing data on any one of the moderator variables would have to be excluded from the model. In this case, one can fit the mixed effects model to each moderator variable separately. The Bonferroni correction may be used then to account for the fact that multiple hypothesis tests are being conducted. However, as demonstrated earlier, this approach is less than ideal, especially when the moderator variables are strongly correlated.[7]

In the unlikely event that none of the moderators appear to be related to the effect sizes, the best we can usually do is to treat the heterogeneity as completely unsystematic and adopt the random effects model. On the other hand, if a model is found that can account for all of the heterogeneity (i.e., the estimate of residual heterogeneity is zero), one automatically adopts the fixed effects with moderators model (as shown in the example given earlier). However, if the estimate of residual heterogeneity is greater than zero (regardless of the results from the Q_E test), the results from the mixed effects model should be reported.

Other Issues

There are many issues one may encounter while conducting a meta-analysis that are beyond the scope of the present chapter. For example, publication bias is a salient issue in meta-analysis and is discussed in Chapter 12 (see also Rothstein, Sutton, & Borenstein, 2005).

Dependent Effect Size Estimates

It was assumed throughout this chapter that the effect size estimates are independent. This assumption may be violated if multiple effect size estimates are obtained from the same sample of subjects. Methods for dealing with dependent effect size estimates can be found in Gleser and Olkin (1994), Kalaian and Raudenbush (1996), and Raudenbush, Becker, and Kalaian (1988).

Conclusions

Over the past three decades, meta-analysis has established itself as a viable approach for dealing with the ever increasing body of primary research. A quick search of the PsychINFO database revealed 17 citations involving the search term *meta-analysis* up to 1979, 918 citations between 1980 and 1989, 2,412 citations between 1990 and 1999, and already 2,418 citations between 2000 and 2005. The same search within the MEDLINE database revealed 1, 497, 5,851, and 9,622 citations involving that search term in the same intervals.

However, meta-analytic techniques currently employed in practice often lag behind recent methodological developments. Too much emphasis is still put on simple overall effects that do not take into account the heterogeneity typically present in the data (Lau et al., 1998). Models that allow for (residual) heterogeneity remain underused (Field, 2003; Hunter & Schmidt, 2000; National Research Council, 1992). Refined techniques for moderator analysis have been developed but appear to be largely unknown among practitioners.

Some of the current meta-analytic methods were introduced in the present chapter, with particular emphasis on model fitting, model selection, and moderator analysis. While this chapter can only scratch the surface of the entire array of techniques available, it is hoped that it will help to make some of these techniques more accessible to the practitioner.

Notes

1. Several books have already been written that describe in detail the entire process from beginning to end (e.g., Cooper, 1998; Cooper & Hedges, 1994; Hunter & Schmidt, 2004; Lipsey & Wilson, 2001; Rosenthal, 1991), and those planning to conduct a meta-analysis would be well advised to consult these sources.

2. Note that we could have considered other moderator variables as well, such as the instrument used in each study to measure anxiety levels (some studies used the State-Trait Anxiety Inventory, others used a visual analog scale, and yet others used measures constructed by the investigator), type of control group (in some studies, subjects in the control group received no treatment at all, while some form of alternative or placebo treatment was used in others), or the gender distribution of the subjects (the percentage of females in the studies ranged from 24% to 100%). However, for this example, we will concentrate on the four moderator variables given in Table 31.1.

3. A more complete discussion of these and other effect size measures is beyond the scope of the present chapter. The interested reader could consult, for example, Fleiss (1994), Lipsey and Wilson (2001), and Rosenthal (1994) for further information.

4. The mixed effects model is, in turn, a special case of a two-stage hierarchical linear model (e.g., Raudenbush & Bryk, 1985). Specifically, the Level 2 structure (for the effect sizes) is given by $\theta_i = \beta_0 + \beta_1 X_{i1} + \ldots + \beta_p X_{ip} + u_i$, while the Level 1 structure (for the effect size estimates) is given by Equation 3. For more information on hierarchical linear modeling, see Chapters 29–31.

5. By centering the moderator variables (in particular, the minutes of treatment and the mean age variables), one can make the intercept more interpretable. For example, subtracting 30 from the minutes of treatment variable and 40 from the mean age variable leaves all of the parameter estimates unchanged, except for the intercept, which is now equal to .214 and indicates the estimated effect for 30 minutes of treatment by a layperson to a sample with a mean age of 40 in a non-TRI study.

6. Editor's note: This issue is similar to running multiple simple regressions to assess the effect of multiple predictors or performing a single multiple regression. Few would argue that multiple simple regressions are superior to one multiple regression.

7. See Pigott (1994, 2001) for information on dealing with this issue. The more general issue of missing data is addressed in Chapter 15.

References

Chalmers, I., Hedges, L. V., & Cooper, H. (2002). A brief history of research synthesis. *Evaluation and the Health Professions, 25,* 12–37.

Cohen, J. (1988). *Statistical power analysis for the behavioral sciences* (2nd ed.). Hillsdale, NJ: Lawrence Erlbaum.

Cook, T. D., Cooper, H., Cordray, D. S., Hartmann, H., Hedges, L. V., Light, R. J., et al. (1992). *Meta-analysis for explanation: A casebook.* New York: Russell Sage Foundation.

Cooper, H. (1998). *Synthesizing research: A guide for literature reviews* (3rd ed.). Thousand Oaks, CA: Sage.

Cooper, H. M., & Hedges, L. V. (Eds.). (1994). *The handbook of research synthesis.* New York: Russell Sage Foundation.

Field, A. P. (2003). The problem in using fixed-effects models of meta-analysis on real world data. *Understanding Statistics, 2,* 105–124.

Fleiss, J. L. (1994). Measures of effect size for categorical data. In H. M. Cooper & L. V. Hedges (Eds.), *The handbook of research synthesis* (pp. 245–260). New York: Russell Sage Foundation.

Gleser, L. J., & Olkin, I. (1994). Stochastically dependent effect sizes. In H. M. Cooper & L. V. Hedges (Eds.), *The handbook of research synthesis* (pp. 339–355). New York: Russell Sage Foundation.

Hedges, L. V. (1981). Distribution theory for Glass's estimator of effect size and related estimators. *Journal of Educational Statistics, 6,* 107–128.

Hedges, L. V. (1994). Fixed effects models. In H. M. Cooper & L. V. Hedges (Eds.), *The handbook of research synthesis* (pp. 285–299). New York: Russell Sage Foundation.

Hedges, L. V., & Olkin, I. (1985). *Statistical methods for meta-analysis.* San Diego: Academic Press.

Hedges, L. V., & Vevea, J. L. (1998). Fixed- and random-effects models in meta analysis. *Psychological Methods, 3,* 486–504.

Higgins, J. P. T., Thompson, S. G., Deeks, J. J., & Altman, D. G. (2003). Measuring inconsistency in meta-analyses. *British Medical Journal, 327,* 557–560.

Hunter, J. E., & Schmidt, F. L. (2000). Fixed effects vs. random effects meta-analysis models: Implications for cumulative research knowledge. *International Journal of Selection and Assessment, 8,* 275–292.

Hunter, J. E., & Schmidt, F. L. (2004). *Methods of meta-analysis: Correcting error and bias in research findings* (2nd ed.). Newbury Park, CA: Sage.

Kalaian, H. A., & Raudenbush, S. W. (1996). A multivariate mixed linear model for meta-analysis. *Psychological Methods, 1,* 227–235.

Knapp, G., & Hartung, J. (2003). Improved tests for a random effects meta-regression with a single covariate. *Statistics in Medicine, 22,* 2693–2710.

Lau, J., Ioannidis, J. P. A., & Schmid, C. H. (1998). Summing up evidence: One answer is not always enough. *Lancet, 351,* 123–127.

Lipsey, M. W., & Wilson, D. B. (2001). *Practical meta-analysis.* Thousand Oaks, CA: Sage.

Moyer, C. A., Rounds, J., & Hannum, J. W. (2004). A meta-analysis of massage therapy research. *Psychological Bulletin, 130,* 3–18.

National Research Council. (1992). *Combining information: Statistical issues and opportunities.* Washington, DC: National Academic Press.

Neter, J., Kutner, M. H., Nachtsheim, C. J., & Wasserman, W. (1996). *Applied linear statistical models* (4th ed.). Chicago: Irwin.

Overton, R. C. (1998). A comparison of fixed-effects and mixed (random-effects) models for meta-analysis tests of moderator variable effects. *Psychological Methods, 3,* 354–379.

Pigott, T. D. (1994). Methods for handling missing data in research synthesis. In H. M. Cooper & L. V. Hedges (Eds.), *The handbook of research synthesis* (pp. 163–175). New York: Russell Sage Foundation.

Pigott, T. D. (2001). Missing predictors in models of effect size. *Evaluation and the Health Professions, 24,* 277–307.

Raudenbush, S. W. (1994). Random effects models. In H. M. Cooper & L. V. Hedges (Eds.), *The handbook of research synthesis* (pp. 301–321). New York: Russell Sage Foundation.

Raudenbush, S. W., Becker, B. J., & Kalaian, H. (1988). Modeling multivariate effect sizes. *Psychological Bulletin, 103,* 111–120.

Raudenbush, S. W., & Bryk, A. S. (1985). Empirical Bayes meta-analysis. *Journal of Educational Statistics, 10,* 75–98.

Rosenthal, R. (1991). *Meta-analytic procedures for social research.* Newbury Park, CA: Sage.

Rosenthal, R. (1994). Parametric measures of effect size. In H. M. Cooper & L. V. Hedges (Eds.), *The handbook of research synthesis* (pp. 231–244). New York: Russell Sage Foundation.

Rothstein, H. R., Sutton, A. J., & Borenstein, M. (Eds.). (2005). *Publication bias in meta-analysis: Prevention, assessment, and adjustments.* Chichester, England: John Wiley.

Sánchez-Meca, J., & Marín-Martínez, F. (1997). Homogeneity tests in meta-analysis: A Monte Carlo comparison of statistical power and Type I error. *Quality & Quantity, 31,* 385–399.

Sidik, K., & Jonkman, J. N. (2003). On constructing confidence intervals for a standardized mean difference in meta-analysis. *Communications in Statistics, Simulation and Computation, 32,* 1191–1203.

Sidik, K., & Jonkman, J. N. (2005). A note on variance estimation in random effects meta-regression. *Journal of Biopharmaceutical Statistics, 15,* 823–838.

Thompson, S. G. (1994). Why sources of heterogeneity in meta-analysis should be investigated. *British Medical Journal, 309,* 1351–1355.

Thompson, S. G., & Higgins, J. P. T. (2002). How should meta-regression analyses be undertaken and interpreted? *Statistics in Medicine, 21,* 1559–1537.

Thompson, S. G., & Sharp, S. J. (1999). Explaining heterogeneity in meta-analysis: A comparison of methods. *Statistics in Medicine, 18,* 2693–2708.

Viechtbauer, W. (2007a). Confidence intervals for the amount of heterogeneity in meta-analysis. *Statistics in Medicine, 26,* 37–52.

Viechtbauer, W. (2007b). Hypothesis tests for population heterogeneity in meta-analysis. *British Journal of Mathematical and Statistical Psychology, 32,* 39–60.

Wilson, D. B., & Lipsey, M. W. (2001). The role of method in treatment effectiveness research: Evidence from meta-analysis. *Psychological Methods, 6,* 413–429.

32

BEST PRACTICES IN STRUCTURAL EQUATION MODELING

RALPH O. MUELLER

GREGORY R. HANCOCK

Structural equation modeling (SEM) has evolved into a mature and popular methodology to investigate theory-derived structural/causal hypotheses. Indeed, with the continued development of SEM software packages such as AMOS (Arbuckle, 2007), EQS (Bentler, 2006), LISREL (Jöreskog & Sörbom, 2006), and Mplus (Muthén & Muthén, 2006), SEM "has become the preeminent multivariate method of data analysis" (Hershberger, 2003, pp. 43–44). Yet, we believe that many practitioners still have little, if any, formal SEM background, potentially leading to misapplications and publications of questionable utility. Drawing on our own experiences as authors and reviewers of SEM studies, as well as on existing guides for reporting SEM results (e.g., Boomsma, 2000; Hoyle & Panter, 1995; McDonald & Ho, 2002), we offer a collection of best practices guidelines to those analysts and authors who contemplate using SEM to help answer their substantive research questions. Throughout, we assume that readers have at least some familiarity with the goals and language of SEM as covered in any introductory textbook (e.g., Byrne, 1998, 2001, 2006; Kline, 2005; Loehlin, 2004; Mueller, 1996; Schumacker & Lomax, 2004). For those desiring even more in-depth or advanced knowledge, we recommend Bollen (1989), Kaplan (2000), or Hancock and Mueller (2006).

SETTING THE STAGE

The foundations of SEM are rooted in classical measured variable path analysis (e.g., Wright, 1918) and confirmatory factor analysis (e.g., Jöreskog, 1966, 1967). From a purely statistical perspective, traditional data analytical techniques such as the analysis of variance, the analysis of

Authors' Note: During the writing of this chapter, the first author was on sabbatical leave from The George Washington University and was partially supported by its Center for the Study of Language and Education and the Institute for Education Studies, both in the Graduate School of Education and Human Development. While on leave, he was visiting professor in the Department of Measurement, Statistics and Evaluation (EDMS) at the University of Maryland, College Park, and visiting scholar in its Center for Integrated Latent Variable Research (CILVR). He thanks the EDMS and CILVR faculty and staff for their hospitality, generosity, and collegiality. Portions of this chapter were adapted from a presentation by the authors at the 2004 meeting of the American Educational Research Association in San Diego.

covariance, multiple linear regression, canonical correlation, and exploratory factor analysis—as well as measured variable path and confirmatory factor analysis—can be regarded as special cases of SEM. However, classical path- and factor-analytic techniques have historically emphasized an explicit link to a theoretically conceptualized underlying causal model and hence are most strongly identified with the more general SEM framework. Simply put, SEM defines a set of data analysis tools that allows for the testing of theoretically derived and a priori specified causal hypotheses.

Many contemporary treatments introduce SEM not just as a statistical technique but as a *process* involving several stages: (a) initial model conceptualization, (b) parameter identification and estimation, (c) data-model fit assessment, and (d) potential model modification. As any study using SEM should address these four stages (e.g., Mueller, 1997), we provide brief descriptions here and subsequently use them as a framework for our best practices analysis illustrations and publication guidelines.

Initial Model Conceptualization

The first stage of any SEM analysis should consist of developing a thorough understanding of, and justification for, the underlying theory or theories that gave rise to the particular model(s) being investigated. In most of the traditional and typical SEM applications, the operationalized theories assume one of three forms:

- A *measured variable path analysis* (MVPA) model: hypothesized structural/causal relations among directly measured variables; the four-stage SEM process applied to MVPA models was illustrated in, for example, Hancock & Mueller, 2004.
- A *confirmatory factor analysis* (CFA) model: structural/causal relations between unobserved latent factors and their measured indicators; the four-stage SEM process applied to CFA models was illustrated in, for example, Mueller & Hancock, 2001.
- A *latent variable path analysis* (LVPA) model: structural/causal relations among latent factors. This type of SEM model is the focus in this chapter and constitutes a combination of the previous two. A distinction is made between the structural and the measurement

portions of the model: While the former is concerned with causal relations among latent constructs and typically is the focus in LVPA studies, the latter specifies how these constructs are modeled using measured indicator variables (i.e., a CFA model).

More complex models (e.g., multisample, latent means, latent growth, multilevel, or mixture models) with their own specific recommendations certainly exist but are beyond the present scope. Regardless of model type, however, a lack of consonance between model and underlying theory will have negative repercussions for the entire SEM process. Hence, meticulous attention to theoretical detail cannot be overemphasized.

Parameter Identification and Estimation

A model's hypothesized structural and nonstructural relations can be expressed as population parameters that convey both magnitude and sign of those relations. Before sample estimates of these parameters can be obtained, each parameter—and hence the whole model—must be shown to be *identified*; that is, it must be possible to express each parameter as a function of the variances and covariances of the measured variables. Even though this is difficult and cumbersome to demonstrate, fortunately, the identification status of a model can often be assessed by comparing the total number of parameters to be estimated, t, with the number of unique (co)variances of measured variables,

$$u = p(p+1)/2,$$

where p is the total number of measured variables in the model. When $t > u$ (i.e., when attempting to estimate more parameters than there are unique variances and covariances), the model is *underidentified*, and estimation of some (if not all) parameters is impossible. On the other hand, $t \leq u$ is a necessary but not sufficient condition for identification, and usually parameter estimation can commence: $t = u$ implies that the model is *justidentified*, while $t < u$ implies that it is *overidentified* (provided that indeed all parameters are identified and any latent variables in the system have been assigned an appropriate metric; see Note 4).

SEM software packages offer a variety of parameter estimation techniques for models whose identification can be established. The most popular estimation method (and the default in most SEM software packages) is *maximum likelihood* (ML), an iterative large-sample technique that assumes underlying multivariate normality. Alternative techniques exist (e.g., generalized least squares [GLS], asymptotically distribution free [ADF; Browne, 1984], and robust estimators [Satorra & Bentler, 1994]), some of which do not depend on a particular underlying distribution of the data, but still, the vast majority of substantive studies use ML.

Data-Model Fit Assessment

A central issue addressed by SEM is how to assess the fit between observed data and the hypothesized model, ideally operationalized as an evaluation of the degree of discrepancy between the true population covariance matrix and that implied by the model's structural and nonstructural parameters. As the population parameter values are seldom known, the difference between an *observed*, sample-based covariance matrix and that *implied* by parameter estimates must serve to approximate the population discrepancy. For a justidentified model, the observed data will fit the model perfectly: The system of equations expressing each model parameter as a function of the observed (co)variances is uniquely solvable; thus, the sample estimate of the model-implied covariance matrix will, by default, equal the sample estimate of the population covariance matrix. However, if a model is overidentified, it is unlikely that these two matrices are equal as the system of equations (expressing model parameters as functions of observed variances and covariances) is solvable in more than a single way.

Abiding by a general desire for parsimony, overidentified models tend to be of more substantive interest than justidentified ones because they represent simpler potential explanations of the observed associations. While data-model fit for such models was initially conceived as a formal statistical test of the discrepancy between the true and model-implied covariance matrices (a chi-square test with $df = u–t$; Jöreskog, 1966, 1967), such a test now is often viewed as overly strict given its power to detect even trivial deviations of a proposed model from reality. Hence, many alternative assessment strategies have emerged (for a now classic review, see Tanaka, 1993) and continue to be developed. Data-model fit indices for such assessments can be categorized roughly into three broad classes (with recommended indices in italics):

- *Absolute indices* evaluate the overall discrepancy between observed and implied covariance matrices; fit improves as more parameters are added to the model and degrees of freedom decrease: for example, the *standardized root mean square residual (SRMR)*, the *chi-square test* (recommended to be reported mostly for its historical significance), and the goodness-of-fit index (GFI).

- *Parsimonious indices* evaluate the overall discrepancy between observed and implied covariance matrices while taking into account a model's complexity; fit improves as more parameters are added to the model, as long as those parameters are making a useful contribution: for example, the *root mean square error of approximation (RMSEA)* with its associated confidence interval, the *Akaike information criterion (AIC)* for fit comparisons across nonnested models, and the adjusted goodness-of-fit index (AGFI).

- *Incremental indices* assess absolute or parsimonious fit relative to a baseline model, usually the null model (a model that specifies no relations among measured variables): for example, the *comparative fit index (CFI)*, the normed fit index (NFI), and the nonnormed fit index (NNFI).

If, after considering several indices, data-model fit is deemed acceptable (and judged best compared to competing models, if applicable), the model is retained as tenable, and individual parameters may be interpreted. If, however, evidence suggests unacceptable data-model fit, the next and often final stage in the SEM process is considered: modifying the model to improve fit in hopes of also improving the model's correspondence to reality.

Potential Model Modification

In a strict sense, *any* hypothesized model is, at best, only an approximation to reality; the remaining question is one of degree of that misspecification. With regard to external specification errors—when irrelevant variables were included in the model or substantively important ones were left out—remediation can only occur by respecifying the model based on more relevant theory. On the other hand, internal specification errors—when unimportant paths among variables were included or when important paths were omitted—can potentially be diagnosed and remedied using *Wald statistics* (predicted increase in chi-square if a previously estimated parameter were fixed to some known value, e.g., zero) and *Lagrange multiplier statistics* (also referred to as *modification indices;* estimated decrease in chi-square if a previously fixed parameter were to be estimated). As these tests' recommendations are directly motivated by the data and not by theoretical considerations, any resulting respecifications must be viewed as exploratory in nature and might not lead to a model that resembles reality any more closely than the one(s) initially conceptualized.

BEST PRACTICES IN SEM DATA ANALYSIS: A SET OF ILLUSTRATIONS

Using the four-stage SEM process as a framework, we turn to an illustration of best practices in the most common type of SEM analyses. We chose to focus on a set of hypothesized models involving structural/causal relations among latent factors (i.e., LVPA models) to demonstrate our preference for using a two-phase approach (i.e., a measurement phase followed by a structural phase) over a single-phase, all-in-one analysis. We conclude this section by illustrating the statistical comparison of hierarchically related or *nested* models (occurring, for example, when one model's parameters are a proper subset of another model's parameters) and addressing the disattenuation (i.e., purification and strengthening) of structural parameter estimates obtained from an LVPA when compared with those obtained from an analysis of the same overall structure but one that uses measured variables only.

Suppose an educational researcher is interested in investigating the structural effects of girls' reading and mathematics self-concept (Read-SC and Math-SC, respectively) on mathematics proficiency (Math-Prof), as potentially mediated by task-goal orientation (Task-Goal). More specifically, the investigator might have strong theoretical reasons to believe that at least one of three scenarios is tenable: In Model 1 (Figure 32.1a), it is hypothesized that the effects of Read-SC and Math-SC on Math-Prof are

both completely mediated by Task-Goal. In Model 2 (Figure 32.1b), only the effect of Read-SC on Math-Prof is completely mediated by Task-Goal, while Math-SC affects Math-Prof not only indirectly via Task-Goal but also directly without other intervening variables. Finally, in Model 3 (Figure 32.1c), Read-SC and Math-SC are thought to affect Math-Prof directly as well as indirectly via Task-Goal. To illustrate the testing of the tenability of these three competing models, multivariate normal data on three indicator variables for each of the four constructs were simulated for a sample of $n = 1,000$ ninth-grade girls. Table 32.1 describes the 12 indicator variables in more detail, while Table 32.2 contains relevant summary statistics.[1]

At this point, it is possible and might seem entirely appropriate to address the research questions implied by the hypothesized models through a series of multiple linear regression (MLR) analyses. For example, for Model 2 in Figure 32.1b, two separate regressions could be conducted: (1) An appropriate surrogate measure of Math-Prof could be regressed on proxy variables for Math-SC and Task-Goal, and (2) a suitable indicator of Task-Goal could be regressed on proxies for Read-SC and Math-SC. If the researcher would choose items ReadSC3, MathSC3, TG1, and Proc from Table 32.1 as surrogates for their respective constructs, MLR results would indicate that even though all hypothesized effects are statistically significantly different from zero, only small amounts of variance in the dependent variables TG1 and Proc are explained by their respective predictor variables ($R^2_{TG1} = 0.034$, $R^2_{Proc} = 0.26$; see Table 32.6 for the unstandardized and standardized regression coefficients obtained from the two MLR analyses[2]). As we will show through the course of the illustrations below, an appropriately conducted LVPA of the models in Figure 32.1 and the data in Table 32.2 will greatly enhance the utility of the data to extract more meaningful results that address the researcher's key questions.

SEM Notation

As the three alternative structural models depicted in Figure 32.1 are at the theoretical/latent construct level, we followed common practice and enclosed the four factors of Read-SC, Math-SC, Task-Goal, and Math-Prof in ellipses/circles. On the other hand, a glance ahead at the operationalized model in Figure 32.2 reveals that the now included measured variables

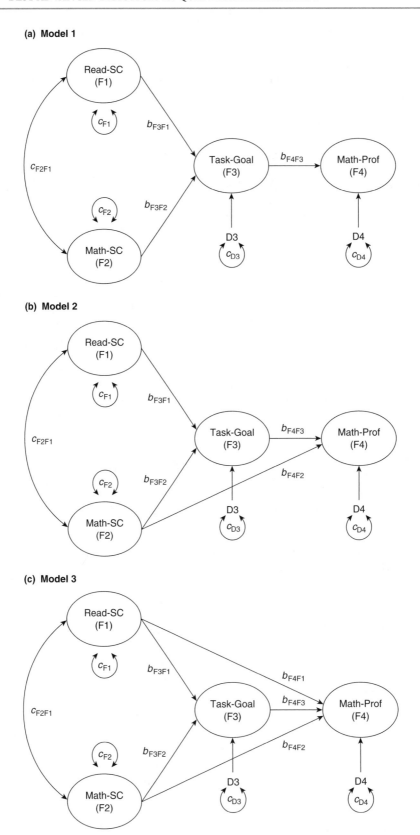

Figure 32.1   The theoretical models.

Table 32.1   Indicator Variable/Item Description

Construct	Variable Label	Item	Scores
Read-SC (F1)			
	RSC1 (V1)	"Compared to others my age, I am good at reading."	1 (*false*) to 6 (*true*)
	RSC2 (V2)	"I get good grades in reading."	
	RSC3 (V3)	"Work in reading class is easy for me."	
Math-SC (F2)			
	MSC1 (V4)	"Compared to others my age, I am good at math."	1 (*false*) to 6 (*true*)
	MSC2 (V5)	"I get good grades in math."	
	MSC3 (V6)	"Work in math class is easy for me."	
Task-Goal (F3)			
	TG1 (V7)	"I like school work that I'll learn from, even if I make a lot of mistakes."	1 (*false*) to 6 (*true*)
	TG2 (V8)	"An important reason why I do my school work is because I like to learn new things."	
	TG3 (V9)	"I like school work best when it really makes me think."	
Math-Prof (F4)			
	Math (V10)		Mathematics subtest scores of the Stanford Achievement Test 9
	Prob (V11)		Problem Solving subtest scores of the Stanford Achievement Test 9
	Proc (V12)		Procedure subtest scores of the Stanford Achievement Test 9

(items RSC1 to RSC3, MSC1 to MSC3, TG1 to TG3, Math, Prob, and Proc) are enclosed in rectangles/squares. Using the Bentler-Weeks "VFED" labeling convention (V for measured Variable/item, F for latent Factor/construct, E for Error/measured variable residual, D for Disturbance/latent factor residual), the latent and measured variables in the current models are labeled F1 through F4 and V1 through V12, respectively. The hypothesized presence or absence of relations between variables in the model is indicated by the presence or absence of arrows in the corresponding path diagram: One-headed arrows signify direct structural or causal effects hypothesized from one variable to another, while two-headed arrows denote hypothesized covariation and variation without structural specificity. For example, for Model 1 in Figure 32.1a, note (a) the hypothesized covariance between Read-SC and Math-SC and the constructs' depicted variances (two-headed arrows connect the factors to each other and to themselves, given that a variable's variance can be thought of as a covariance of the variable with itself), (b) the hypothesized structural effects of these two factors on Task-Goal (one-headed arrows lead from both to Task-Goal), but (c) the absence of such hypothesized direct effects on Math-Prof (there are no one-headed arrows directly leading from Read-SC and Math-SC to Math-Prof; the former two constructs are hypothesized to affect the latter only

Table 32.2   Correlations and Standard Deviations of Simulated Data

	RSC1 (V1)	RSC2 (V2)	RSC3 (V3)	MSC1 (V4)	MSC2 (V5)	MSC3 (V6)
RSC1	1.000					
RSC2	0.499	1.000				
RSC3	0.398	0.483	1.000			
MSC1	0.206	−0.148	−0.123	1.000		
MSC2	−0.150	0.244	−0.095	0.668	1.000	
MSC3	−0.121	−0.091	0.308	0.633	0.641	1.000
TG1	0.141	0.150	0.123	0.140	0.143	0.167
TG2	0.123	0.151	0.134	0.163	0.180	0.145
TG3	0.161	0.199	0.160	0.147	0.151	0.158
MATH	−0.049	−0.007	0.003	0.556	0.539	0.521
PROB	−0.031	−0.009	0.023	0.544	0.505	0.472
PROC	−0.025	−0.029	0.006	0.513	0.483	0.480
SD	1.273	1.353	1.285	1.396	1.308	1.300
	TG1 (V7)	TG2 (V8)	TG3 (V9)	MATH (V10)	PROB (V11)	PROC (V12)
RSC1						
RSC2						
RSC3						
MSC1						
MSC2						
MSC3						
TG1	1.000					
TG2	0.499	1.000				
TG3	0.433	0.514	1.000			
MATH	0.345	0.385	0.337	1.000		
PROB	0.304	0.359	0.281	0.738	1.000	
PROC	0.259	0.330	0.279	0.714	0.645	1.000
SD	1.334	1.277	1.265	37.087	37.325	45.098

indirectly, mediated by Task-Goal). Finally, because variation in dependent variables usually is not fully explainable by the amount of variation or covariation in their specified causes, each dependent variable has an associated residual term. For example, in the operationalized model in Figure 32.2, D3 and D4 denote the prediction errors associated with the latent factors F3 (Task-Goal) and F4 (Math-Prof), while E1 through E3 indicate the residuals associated with the measured indicator variables (V1 to V3) of the latent construct Read-SC.

For purposes of labeling structural and non-structural parameters associated with the connections between measured and/or latent variables in a path diagram, we used the *abc* system[3] (Hancock & Mueller, 2006, pp. 4–6). Structural effects from one variable (measured or latent) to another are labeled $b_{\text{to, from}}$, with the subscripts indicating the *to* and *from* variables (e.g., in Figure 32.2, b_{F3F1} indicates the path

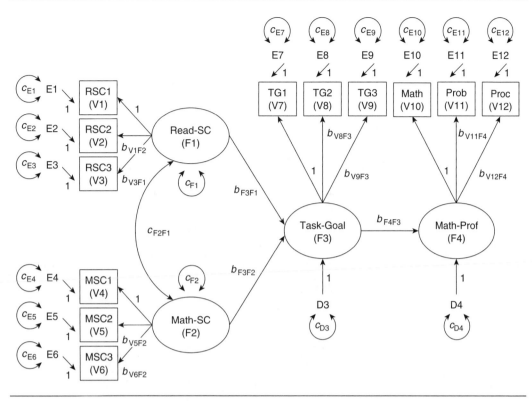

Figure 32.2   Initially operationalized Model 1.

to F3 from F1, and b_{V2F1} denotes the path/factor loading to item V2 from factor F1). On the other hand, variances and covariances are labeled by the letter c (e.g., in Figure 32.2, c_{F1} denotes the variance of the latent construct F1, while c_{F2F1} represents the covariance between the factors F2 and F1).

All-in-One SEM Analysis— Generally Not Recommended

Although we generally do not recommend the analytic strategy outlined in this section, it nevertheless will prove pedagogically instructive and will motivate arguments in later sections. With a hypothesized structure among latent constructs in place and associated measured indicators selected, Model 1 in Figure 32.1a can be operationalized as illustrated in Figure 32.2. This path diagram implies a set of 14 structural equations, one for each dependent variable: two equations from the *structural portion* of the model (i.e., the part that specifies the causal structure among latent constructs) and 12 equations from the *measurement portion* of

the model (i.e., the part that links each of the indicator variables with the designated latent constructs). Table 32.3 lists all 14 structural equations and their associated *endogenous* (dependent) and *exogenous* (independent) variables that together specify the model in Figure 32.2 (variables are assumed to be mean-centered, thus eliminating the need for intercept terms; items V1, V4, V7, and V10 are used as reference variables for their respective factors, and thus their factor loadings are not *free* to be estimated but *fixed* to 1.0; also see Note 4).

Though it might seem that the statistical estimation of the unknown coefficients in the structural equations (the b and c parameters) should be the focus at this stage of the analysis, a prior assessment of the data-model fit is more essential as it allows for an overall judgment about whether the data fit the structure as hypothesized (indeed, should evidence materialize that the data do not fit the model, interpretations of individual parameter estimates might be useless). As can be verified from the path diagram in Figure 32.2 by counting one- and

Table 32.3   Structural Equations Implied by the Path Diagram in Figure 32.2

Endogenous Variable	Structural Equations	Exogenous Variables[a]
Structural Portion		
Task-Goal (F3)	$F3 = b_{F3F1}\, F1 + b_{F3F2}\, F2 + D3$	Read-SC (F1)
		Math-SC (F2)
Math-Prof (F4)	$F4 = b_{F4F3}\, F3 + D4$	Task-Goal (F3)

Endogenous Variable	Structural Equations	Exogenous Variables[b]
Measurement Portion		
RSC1 (V1)	$V1 = (1)F1 + E1$	Read-SC (F1)
RSC2 (V2)	$V2 = b_{V2F1}\, F1 + E2$	
RSC3 (V3)	$V3 = b_{V3F1}\, F1 + E3$	
MSC1 (V4)	$V4 = (1)F2 + E4$	Math-SC (F2)
MSC2 (V5)	$V5 = b_{V5F2}\, F2 + E5$	
MSC3 (V6)	$V6 = b_{V6F2}\, F2 + E6$	
TG1 (V7)	$V7 = (1)F3 + E7$	Task-Goal (F3)
TG2 (V8)	$V8 = b_{V8F3}\, F3 + E8$	
TG3 (V9)	$V9 = b_{V9F3}\, F3 + E9$	
Math (V10)	$V10 = (1)F4 + E10$	Math-Prof (F4)
Prob (V11)	$V11 = b_{V11F4}\, F4 + E11$	
Proc (V12)	$V12 = b_{V12F4}\, F4 + E12$	

a. Residuals D, though technically exogenous, are not listed.

b. Residuals E, though technically exogenous, are not listed.

two-headed arrows labeled with *b* or *c* symbols, the model contains $t = 28$ parameters to be estimated:[4] two variances of the independent latent constructs and one covariance between them, two variances of residuals associated with the two dependent latent constructs, three path coefficients relating the latent constructs, eight factor loadings, and 12 variances of residuals associated with the measured variables. Furthermore, the 12 measured variables in the model produce $u = 12\,(12 + 1)/2 = 78$ unique variances and covariances; the model is overidentified ($t = 28 < u = 78$), and it is likely that some degree of data-model misfit exists (i.e., the observed covariance matrix will likely differ, to some degree, from that implied by the model). To assess the degree of data-model misfit, various fit indices can be obtained and then should be compared against established cutoff criteria (e.g., those empirically derived by Hu & Bentler, 1999, and listed here in Table 32.4). Though here LISREL 8.8 (Jöreskog & Sörbom, 2006)

was employed, running any of the available SEM software packages will verify the following data-model fit results for the data in Table 32.2 and the model in Figure 32.2 (because the data are assumed multivariate normal, the maximum likelihood estimation method was used): $\chi^2 = 3624.59$ ($df = u - t = 50, p < .001$), SRMR = 0.13, RMSEA = 0.20 with CI_{90}: (0.19, 0.20), and CFI = 0.55.

As is evident from comparing these results with the desired values in Table 32.4, the current data do not fit the proposed model; thus, it is not appropriate to interpret any individual parameter estimates as, on the whole, the model in Figure 32.2 should be rejected based on the current data. Now the researcher is faced with the question of what went wrong: (a) Is the source of the data-model misfit indeed primarily a flaw in the underlying structural theory (Figure 32.1a), (b) can the misfit be attributed to misspecifications in the measurement portion of the model with the hypothesized structure among latent

Table 32.4 Target Values for Selected Fit Indices to Retain a Model by Class

Index Class		
Incremental	*Absolute*	*Parsimonious*
NFI ≥ 0.90		
NNFI ≥ 0.95	GFI ≥ 0.90	AGFI ≥ 0.90
CFI ≥ 0.95	SRMR ≤ 0.08	RMSEA ≤ 0.06
Joint Criteria		
NNFI, CFI ≥ 0.96 and SRMR ≤ 0.09		
SRMR ≤ 0.09 and RMSEA ≤ 0.06		

SOURCE: Partially taken from Hu and Bentler (1999).

NOTE: CFI = comparative fit index; NFI = normed fit index; NNFI = nonnormed fit index; GFI = goodness-of-fit index; AGFI = adjusted goodness-of-fit index; RMSEA = root mean square error of approximation; SRMR = standardized root mean square residual.

constructs actually having been specified correctly, or (c) do misspecifications exist in both the measurement and structural portions of the model? To help address these questions and prevent potential confusion about the source of observed data-model misfit, we do *not* recommend that researchers conduct SEM analyses by initially analyzing the structural and measurement portions of their model simultaneously, as was done here. Instead, analysts are urged to follow a two-phase analysis process, as described next.

Two-Phase SEM Analysis—Recommended

Usually, the primary reason for conceptualizing LVPA models is to investigate the tenability of theoretical causal structures among latent variables. The main motivation for recommending a two-phase process over an all-in-one approach is to initially separate a model into its measurement and structural portions so that misspecifications in the former, if present, can be realized and addressed first, before the structure among latent constructs is assessed.[5] This approach will simplify the identification of sources of data-model misfit and might also aid in the prevention of nonconvergence problems with SEM software (i.e., when the iterative estimation algorithm cannot converge upon a viable solution for parameter estimates).

Consider the path diagram in Figure 32.3a. It is similar to the one depicted in Figure 32.2 as it involves the same measured and latent variables but differs in two important ways: Not only are Read-SC and Math-SC now explicitly connected to Math-Prof, but all structural links among latent variables have been changed to nonstructural relations (note in Figure 32.3a the two-headed arrows between all latent constructs that are now labeled with *c* symbols). That is, latent constructs are allowed to freely covary without an explicit causal structure among them. In short, Figure 32.3a represents a CFA model of the latent factors Read-SC, Math-SC, Task-Goal, and Math-Prof, using the measured variables in Table 32.1 as their respective effect indicators.[6]

Measurement Phase. An analysis of the CFA model in Figure 32.3a constitutes the beginning of the *measurement phase* of the proposed two-phase analysis process and produced the following data-model fit results: $\chi^2 = 3137.16$ ($df = 48$, $p < .001$), SRMR = 0.062, RMSEA = 0.18 with CI_{90}: (0.17, 0.18), and CFI = 0.61. These values signify a slight improvement over fit results for the model in Figure 32.2. To the experienced modeler, this improvement was predictable given that the model in Figure 32.2 is more restrictive than, and a special case of, the CFA model in Figure 32.3a (with the paths from Read-SC and Math-SC to Math-Prof fixed to zero); that is, the former model is *nested* within the latter, a topic more fully discussed in the next section. Irrespective of this minor improvement, however, why did the data-model fit remain unsatisfactory (as judged by the criteria listed in Table 32.4)? Beginning to analyze and address this misfit constitutes a move toward the fourth and final phase in the general SEM process, potential post hoc model modification.

First, reconsider the list of items in Table 32.1. While all variables certainly seem to "belong" to the latent factors they were selected to indicate, note that for the reading and mathematics self-concept factors, corresponding items are identical except for one word: The word *reading* in items RSC1 through RSC3 was replaced by the word *math* to obtain items MSC1 through MSC3. Thus, it seems plausible that individuals' responses to corresponding reading and mathematics self-concept items are influenced by some of the same or related causes. In fact, the model in Figure 32.3a explicitly posits that two such related causes are the latent constructs Read-SC and Math-SC. However, as the specification of residual terms (E) indicates, responses to items are influenced by causes other than the hypothesized latent constructs. Those other, unspecified causes could also be associated. Thus, for example, the residual terms E1 and E4 might covary to some degree, particularly since both are associated with items that differ by just one word. Based on similar theoretical reasoning, a nonzero covariance might exist between E2 and E5 and also between E3 and E6. In sum, it seems theoretically justifiable to modify the CFA model in Figure 32.3a to allow residual terms of corresponding reading and mathematics self-concept items to freely covary, as shown in Figure 32.3b. In fact, with enough foresight, these covariances probably should have been included in the initially hypothesized model.

Second, as part of the analysis of the initial CFA model in Figure 32.3a, Lagrange multiplier (LM) statistics may be consulted for empirically based model modification suggestions. These statistics estimate the potential improvement in data-model fit (as measured by the estimated decrease in chi-square) if a previously fixed parameter were to be estimated. Here, the three largest LM statistics were 652.0, 567.8, and 541.7, associated with the fixed parameters c_{E5E2}, c_{E4E1}, and c_{E6E3}, respectively. Compared with the overall chi-square value of 3137.16, these estimated chi-square decreases seem substantial,[7] foreshadowing a statistically significant improvement in data-model fit. Indeed, after respecifying the model accordingly (i.e., freeing c_{E5E2}, c_{E4E1}, and c_{E6E3}; see Figure 32.3b) and reanalyzing the data, fit results for the modified CFA model improved dramatically: $\chi^2 = 108.04$ ($df = 45$, $p < .001$), SRMR = 0.018, RMSEA = 0.037 with CI_{90}: (0.028, 0.046), and CFI = 0.99.

Though the degree of improvement might have been a pleasant surprise, *some* improvement was again to be expected: When compared with the initial CFA model, the modified model places fewer restrictions on parameter values (hence, better data-model fit) by allowing three error covariances to be freely estimated. Once again, the two CFA models are nested, and their fit could be statistically compared with a chi-square difference test, as discussed in the next section. For now, suffice it to say that an informal, descriptive comparison of the fit results for the initial and modified CFA models (e.g., a decrease from $\chi^2_{initial} = 3137.16$ to $\chi^2_{mod} = 108.04$, a drop from $SRMR_{initial} = 0.062$ to $SRMR_{mod} = 0.018$, and a reduction from

$RMSEA_{initial} = 0.18$ to $RMSEA_{mod} = 0.037$) seems to indicate that the data fit the modified model much better. In more absolute terms, comparing the fit results from the modified model to the target values in Table 32.4 suggests that the data fit the model very well (due to the large sample size of $n = 1,000$, relatively little weight should be placed on the still significant $\chi^2_{(45)} = 108.04$). An examination of the remaining modification indices indicated that, even though further modifications would continue to slightly improve fit, none of the suggested modifications were theoretically justifiable (e.g., the largest estimated drop in chi-square, 23.0, could be obtained by freeing c_{E8E2}, the error covariance associated with the items TG2 and RSC2). Thus, no further modifications to the measurement model seem warranted. Figure 32.4 lists partial results for this final CFA model: Standardized factor loadings were statistically significant and sizable, estimated correlations among error terms and among latent factors were significant and of moderate size (except for the nonsignificant correlation between the latent factors Read-SC and Math-Prof), item reliabilities (the squared standardized factor loadings, ℓ^2) ranged from $\ell^2 = .36$ for RSC3 to $\ell^2 = .81$ for Math, and construct reliabilities[8] for the latent factors ranged from $H = .74$ for Read-SC to $H = .89$ for Math-Prof. Thus, with solid evidence of a quality measurement model, we now are ready to proceed to the second phase of the analysis.

Structural Phase. With a final measurement model in place, the *structural phase* consists of replacing the nonstructural covariances among latent factors with the hypothesized structure that is of main interest (currently, Model 1 in Figure 32.1a) and reanalyzing the data. When comparing these new data-model fit results ($\chi^2 = 601.85$ with $df = 47$, $p < .001$, SRMR = 0.12, RMSEA = 0.10 with CI_{90}: [0.096, 0.11], and CFI = 0.93) to those from the final CFA model, we learn that the introduction of two key restrictions—namely, the a priori specified zero paths from Read-SC and Math-SC to Math-Prof—significantly eroded data-model fit.[9] Consulting cutoff criteria in Table 32.4, we may conclude that the data do not fit the conceptual model in Figure 32.1a. Having conducted a two-phase analysis, however, we now know something we could not glean from the all-in-one analysis: The observed data-model misfit must largely be due to misspecifications in the structural portion

(a) Initial CFA Model

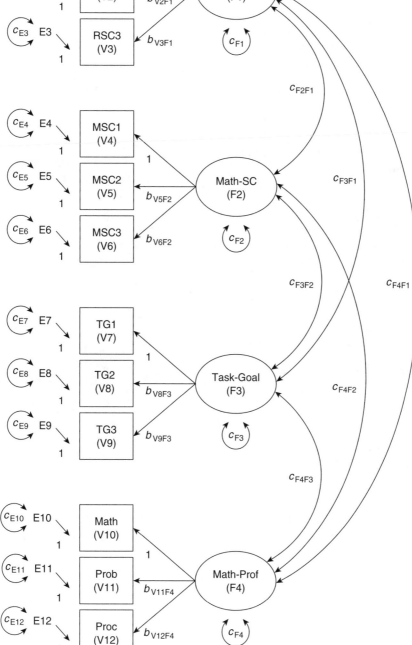

Figure 32.3   The measurement (CFA) models.   *(Continued)*

(b) Modified CFA Model

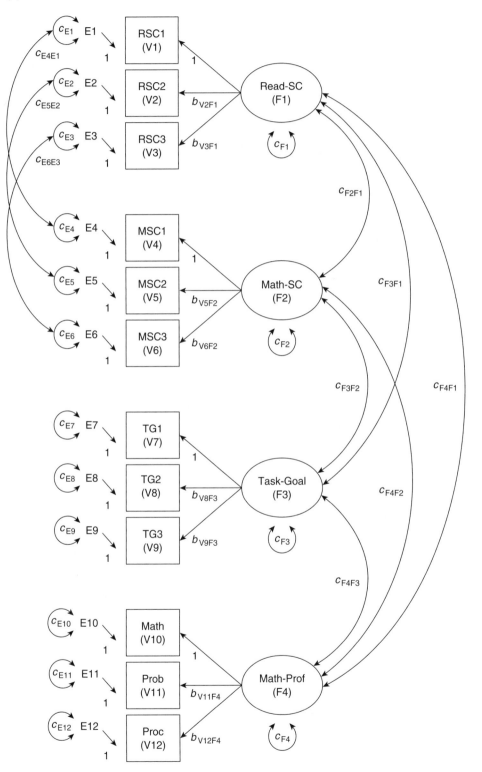

Figure 32.3 (Continued)

of the model since modifications to the measurement portion of the model (freeing error covariances for corresponding reading and mathematics self-concept items) led to a CFA model with no evidence of substantial data-model misfit. Having not yet reached a state where the data fit the hypothesized structure to an acceptable degree, we forego an interpretation of individual parameter estimates for a while longer in favor of illustrating how to compare and choose among the current model (Model 1) and the two remaining a priori hypothesized structures (Models 2 and 3) in Figure 32.1.

Choosing From Among Nested Models

Thus far in the illustrations, the comparison of models with respect to data-model fit could be accomplished only by descriptively weighing various fit index values across models. However, in the special case when two models, say Model 1 and Model 2, are nested (such as when the estimated parameters in the former are a proper subset of those associated with the latter), fit comparisons can be accomplished with a formal chi-square difference test. That is, if Model 1 (with df_1) is nested within Model 2 (with df_2), their chi-square fit statistics may be statistically compared by $\Delta\chi^2_{(df_1 - df_2)} = \chi^2_{(df_1)} - \chi^2_{(df_2)}$, which is distributed as a chi-square distribution with $df = df_1 - df_2$ (under conditions of multivariate normality).

Now reconsider the three theoretical models in Figure 32.1, all now incorporating the final measurement model in Figure 32.3b. As the fit information in Table 32.5 shows, Models 2 and 3 seem to fit well,[10] while Model 1 does not, as previously discussed. Furthermore, note that Model 1, the most parsimonious and restrictive model, is nested within both Models 2 and 3 (letting $b_{F4F2} \neq 0$ in Model 1 leads to Model 2; allowing both $b_{F4F2} \neq 0$ and $b_{F4F1} \neq 0$ in Model 1 leads to Model 3) and that Model 2 is nested in Model 3 (permitting $b_{F4F1} \neq 0$ in Model 2 leads to Model 3). Thus, the chi-square fit statistics for the three competing models can easily be compared by chi-square difference tests. Based on the three possible chi-square comparisons shown in Table 32.5, we glean that out of the three alternatives, Model 2 is the preferred structure (when weighing chi-square fit and parsimony):

1. Both Models 2 and 3 are chosen over Model 1 (they both exhibit significantly

better fit, $\Delta\chi^2_{(1)} = 492.56$, $p < .001$; $\Delta\chi^2_{(2)} = 493.81$, $p < .001$; respectively), and

2. Model 2 is favored over Model 3 (even though it is more restrictive—but hence more parsimonious—the erosion in fit is nonsignificant, $\Delta\chi^2_{(1)} = 1.25$, $p = .264$).

Having chosen Model 2 from among the three alternative models and judging its data-model fit as acceptable (Table 32.5), what remains is an examination and interpretation of the structural parameter estimates that link the latent constructs (see Table 32.6; interpretations of results from the measurement phase are listed in Figure 32.4 and were examined earlier). Note that the latent factors Read-SC and Math-SC explained 20% of the variance in Task-Goal ($R^2 = 0.20$) and that the Math-SC and Task-Goal factors explained more than 70% of the variance in latent mathematics proficiency ($R^2 = 0.71$). All structural estimates were statistically significant and can be interpreted in a manner similar to regression coefficients, but now with a focus on structural direction, given the specific causal nature of the underlying hypothesized theory. For example, considering the standardized path coefficients,[11] one might expect from within the context of Model 2 that a one standard deviation increase in ninth-grade girls' latent reading self-concept causes, on average, a bit more than a third (0.36) of a standard deviation increase in their latent task-goal orientation; similarly, a one standard deviation increase in girls' task-goal orientation leads, on average, to a 0.38 standard deviation increase in latent mathematics proficiency. Given the hypothesized structure, the effect of reading self-concept on mathematics proficiency is completely mediated by Task-Goal, with an estimated standardized indirect effect of $0.36 \times 0.38 = 0.14$ ($p < .05$, as indicated by SEM software).

Finally, recall from the beginning of this section the two separate multiple linear regression analyses for a somewhat crude initial attempt at addressing coefficient estimation for the structure in Model 2. In addition to LVPA results, Table 32.6 also lists R^2 values and the unstandardized and standardized regression coefficients associated with the two implied structural equations (using the proxy variables ReadSC3 for latent reading self-concept, MathSC3 for latent mathematics self-concept, TG1 for latent task-goal orientation, and Proc for latent mathematics proficiency). First, compare the two regression

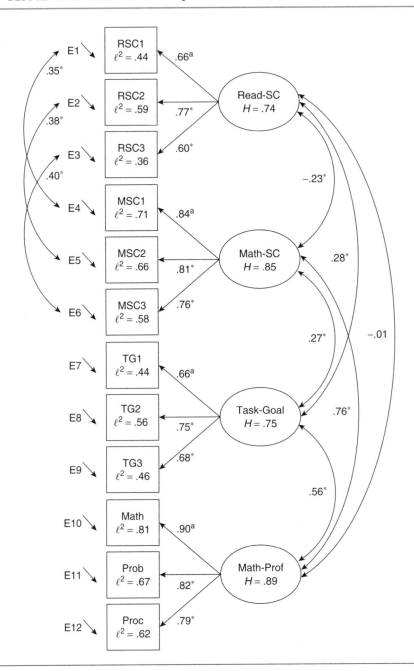

Figure 32.4   Standardized results for final CFA model.

NOTE: ℓ^2 is indicator reliability computed as the squared standardized loading. H is Hancock and Mueller's (2001) measure of construct reliability.

a. Unstandardized loading fixed to 1.0; thus, no standard error computed.

$^*p < .05$.

R^2 values with those obtained from the SEM analysis and appreciate the huge increases observed with the LVPA approach: Explained variability in task-goal orientation jumped from 3.4% to 20%; in mathematics proficiency, it improved from 26% to 71%. Second, compare the MLR to the LVPA coefficients and note how in each case, the standardized LVPA estimates are higher/stronger

Table 32.5   Data-Model Fit and Chi-Square Difference Tests for Nested Models

	Model 2				Model 3			
	$\chi^2(df, p)$	SRMR	RMSEA CI_{90}	CFI	$\chi^2(df, p)$	SRMR	RMSEA CI_{90}	CFI
	109.29 (46, < 0.001)	0.017	0.036 (0.027, 0.045)	0.99	108.04 (45, < 0.001)	0.018	0.037 (0.028, 0.046)	0.99

Model 1

	$\chi^2(df, p)$	SRMR	RMSEA CI_{90}	CFI
	601.85 (47, < 0.001)	0.12	0.10 (0.096, 0.11)	0.93

$$\Delta\chi^2_{(1)} = \chi^2_{M1} - \chi^2_{M2} = 601.85 - 109.29 = 492.56 \; (df = 1, p < .001)$$

$$\Delta\chi^2_{(2)} = \chi^2_{M1} - \chi^2_{M3} = 601.85 - 108.04 = 493.81 \; (df = 2, p < .001)$$

Model 2

$$\Delta\chi^2_{(1)} = \chi^2_{M2} - \chi^2_{M3} = 109.29 - 108.04 = 1.25 \; (df = 1, p = .264)$$

NOTE: Models in the left column are nested within models in the top row.

CFI = comparative fit index; RMSEA = root mean square error of approximation; SRMR = standardized root mean square residual.

than their MLR counterparts. This disattenuation of relations among variables is due to LVPA's ability to "cleanse" estimates of the "noise" in the system that was introduced by the indicator variables' inevitable measurement error. Herein, then, lies one of the strengths of latent variable SEM approaches: Structural parameter estimates become purer, untangled from errors that originated in the measurement portion of the system, thus generating a higher portion of explained variability in dependent constructs.

Best Practices in SEM: Sharing the Study With Others

The four-stage SEM process and pointers gleaned from the above analysis illustrations map nicely onto the broadly accepted manuscript sections of introduction, methods, results, and discussion. What follows are some brief and general best practices guidelines on communicating research that uses SEM.

Introduction Section

Early in a manuscript—in the introduction and background to the problem under study—

Table 32.6   Regression/Structural Coefficients for Model 2

Effect From/To		Analysis Method	
		MLRs	LVPA
Read-SC		0.08*	0.37*
	Task-Goal	0.08	0.36
Math-SC		0.15*	0.25*
		0.14	0.35
Math-SC		15.59*	18.41*
	Math-Prof	0.45	0.65
Task-Goal		6.22*	14.64*
		0.18	0.38
R^2		$R^2_{TG1} = 0.034$ $R^2_{proc} = 0.26$	$R^2_{Task\text{-}Goal} = 0.20$ $R^2_{Math\text{-}Prof} = 0.71$

NOTE: Top coefficient is unstandardized; bottom coefficient is standardized.

*$p < .05$.

authors should convey a firm, overall sense of what led to the initial model conceptualization and of the specific model(s) investigated. The existence of latent constructs, as well as the hypothesized causal relations among them, must be justified clearly and convincingly based on theoretical grounds. Often, the articulation of competing, alternative models strengthens a study as it provides for a more complete picture of the current thinking in a particular field. The justification of measured and/or latent variables and models is accomplished by analyzing and synthesizing relevant literature by authors who proposed particular theories or empirically researched the same or similar models as the one(s) under current investigation. Path diagrams often are helpful in expressing the hypothesized structural links relating the measured and/or latent variables. Especially in complex models involving many variables, the hypothesized causal structure among latent variables can be easily illustrated in a diagram, while the psychometric details of how each latent variable was modeled may be left for the method section.

Method Section

In addition to specific information on participants, instruments, and procedures, this section should include a reference to the specific version of the SEM software package used since results can vary not only across programs but also across versions of a single package (mainly due to differences and continual refinements in estimation algorithms). Given the complexities of demonstrating each parameter's identification—and its necessity for parameter estimation—it is generally accepted to omit detailed discussions of identification issues from a manuscript, unless some unique circumstances warrant their inclusion. However, since the accuracy of parameter estimates, associated standard errors, and the overall chi-square value all depend on various characteristics of the indicators chosen and the data collected, authors should address issues such as multivariate distributions, sample size, missing data, outliers, and potential multilevel data structures, if applicable.

In most applied studies, ML estimates are presented that assume underlying multivariate normality and continuity of the data. Studies have shown that if sample size is sufficiently large, ML parameter estimates are quite robust against violations of these assumptions, though their associated standard errors and the overall chi-square might not be (e.g., West, Finch, & Curran, 1995). Some have suggested, as a rough guideline, a 5:1 ratio of sample size to number of parameters estimated in order to trust ML parameter estimates (but associated standard errors and the model chi-square statistic might still be compromised; e.g., Bentler & Chou, 1987). We hesitate to endorse such a "one-size-fits-all" suggestion for three reasons. First, if data are not approximately normal, then alternate strategies such as the Satorra-Bentler rescaled statistics should be employed that have larger sample size requirements. Second, even under normality, methodological studies have illustrated that for models with highly reliable factors, quite satisfactory solutions can be obtained with relatively small samples, while models with less reliable factors might require larger samples (e.g., Gagné & Hancock, 2006; Marsh, Hau, Balla, & Grayson, 1998). Third, such general sample size recommendations ignore issues of statistical power to evaluate models as a whole or to test parameters within those models (see, e.g., Hancock, 2006).

If the model posits latent constructs, the choice of indicators usually is justified in an instrumentation subsection. First, for each construct modeled, the reader should be able to determine if effect or cause indicators were chosen: Only the former operationalize the commonly modeled latent factors; the latter determine latent composites (see Note 6). In some SEM analyses, emergent constructs are erroneously treated as latent, implying a mismatch between the modeled and the actual nature of the construct, hence leading to the potential for incorrect inferences regarding the relations the construct might have with other portions of the model. Second, each latent construct should be defined by a sufficient number of psychometrically sound indicators: "Two *might* be fine, three is better, four is best, and anything more is gravy" (Kenny, 1979, p. 143). Doing so can prevent various identification and estimation problems as well as ensure satisfactory construct reliability (since latent constructs are theoretically perfectly reliable but are measured by imperfect indicators, numerical estimates of construct reliability are likely to be less than 1.0 but can be brought to satisfactory levels with the inclusion of quality indicator variables; see, e.g., Hancock & Mueller, 2001). Finally, the scale of the indicator variables should be accommodated by the estimation method, where variables clearly yielding ordinal data might warrant the use of estimation strategies other than ML (see Finney & DiStefano, 2006).

Results Section

How authors structure the results section obviously is dictated by the particular model(s) and research questions under study. Notwithstanding, it is the researcher's responsibility to provide access to data in order to facilitate verification of the obtained results: If moment-level data were analyzed, a covariance matrix (or correlation matrix with standard deviations) should be presented in a table or appendix; if raw data were used, information on how to obtain access should be provided.

When analyzing LVPA models, results from both the measurement and structural phases should be presented. For overidentified models, judging the overall quality of a hypothesized model usually is presented early in the results section. Given that available data-model fit indices can lead to inconsistent conclusions, researchers should consider fit results from different classes so readers can arrive at a more complete picture regarding a model's acceptability (Table 32.4). Also, a comparison of fit across multiple, a priori specified alternative models can assist in weighing the relative merits of favoring one model over others. As illustrated, when competing models are nested, a formal chi-square difference test is available to judge if a more restrictive—but also more parsimonious—model can explain the observed data equally well, without a significant loss in data-model fit (alternative models that are not nested have traditionally been compared only descriptively—relative evaluations of AIC values are recommended, with smaller values indicating better fit—but recent methodological developments suggest statistical approaches as well; see Levy & Hancock, 2007).

If post hoc model modifications are performed following unacceptable data-model fit from either the measurement or structural phase of the analysis, authors owe their audience a detailed account of the nature and reasons (both statistical and theoretical) for the respecification(s), including summary results from Lagrange multiplier tests and revised final fit results. If data-model fit has been assessed and deemed satisfactory, with or without respecification, more detailed results are presented, usually in the form of individual unstandardized and standardized parameter estimates for each structural equation of interest, together with associated standard errors and/or test statistics and coefficients of determination (R^2). When latent variables are part of a model, estimates of their construct reliability should be presented, with values ideally falling above .70 or .80 (see Hancock & Mueller, 2001).

Discussion Section

In the final section of a manuscript, authors should provide a sense of what implications the results from the SEM analysis have on the theory or theories that gave rise to the initial model(s). Claims that a well-fitting model was "confirmed" or that a particular theory was proven to be "true," especially after post hoc respecifications, should be avoided. Such statements are grossly misleading given that alternative, structurally different, yet mathematically equivalent models always exist that would produce identical data-model fit results and thus would explain the data equally well (see Hershberger, 2006). At most, a model with acceptable fit may be interpreted as *one* tenable explanation for the associations observed in the data. From this perspective, a SEM analysis should be evaluated from a *dis*confirmatory, rather than a confirmatory, perspective: Based on unacceptable data-model fit results, theories can be shown to be false but not proven to be true by acceptable data-model fit (see also Mueller, 1997).

If evidence of data-model misfit was presented and a model was modified based on statistical results from Lagrange multiplier tests, readers must be made aware of potential model overfitting and the capitalization on chance. Statistically rather than theoretically based respecifications are purely exploratory and might say little about the true model underlying the data. While some model modifications seem appropriate and theoretically justifiable (usually, minor respecifications of the measurement portion are more easily defensible than those in the structural portion of a model), they only address internal specification errors and should be cross-validated with data from new and independent samples.[12]

Finally, the interpretation of individual parameter estimates can involve explicit causal language, *as long as this is done from within the context of the particular causal theory proposed* and the possibility/probability of alternative explanations is raised unequivocally. Though some might disagree, we think that explicit causal statements are more honest than implicit ones and are more useful in articulating a study's practical implications; after all, is not causality the ultimate aim of science (see Shaffer, 1992, p. x)? In the end, SEM is a powerful disconfirmatory tool at the researcher's disposal for testing and interpreting theoretically derived causal hypotheses from within an a priori specified causal system

of observed and/or latent variables. However, we urge authors to resist the apparently still popular belief that the main goal of SEM is to achieve satisfactory data-model fit results; rather, it is to get one step closer to the "truth." If it is true that a proposed model does not reflect reality, then reaching a conclusion of *mis*fit between data and model should be a desirable goal, not one to be avoided by careless respecifications until satisfactory levels of fit are achieved.

CONCLUSION

Throughout the sections of this chapter, we have attempted to provide an overview of what we believe should be considered best practices in typical SEM applications. As is probably true for the other quantitative methods covered in this volume, a little SEM knowledge is sometimes a dangerous thing, especially with user-friendly software making the mechanics of SEM increasingly opaque to the applied user. Before embracing SEM as a potential analysis tool and reporting SEM-based studies, investigators should gain fundamental knowledge from any of the introductory textbooks referenced at the beginning of this chapter. In an effort to aid in the conduct and publication of appropriate, if not exemplary, SEM utilizations, we offered some best practices guidelines, except one, saving it for last. While SEM offers a general and flexible methodological framework, investigators should not hesitate to consider other analytical techniques—many covered in the present volume—that potentially address research questions much more clearly and directly. As it was explained to the second author several years ago, "Just because all your friends are doing this 'structural equation modeling' thing doesn't mean *you* have to. If all your friends jumped off a cliff. . . ." (Marta Foldi,[13] personal communication, 1992).

NOTES

1. Several indicator variables are rating scales that could be argued to provide ordinal-level rather than interval-level data. Given the relatively high number of scale points, however, we analyzed these data as if they were interval (see Finney & DiStefano, 2006).

2. Using different proxy variables, or even composites of indicators, would still yield attenuated

results as none of the options filter the inherent measurement error.

3. Only *b* and *c* coefficients are used here; the letter *a* denotes intercept and mean terms in the analysis of mean structures.

4. To help ensure identification and to provide a metric for each latent factor, *reference variables* were specified (i.e., one factor loading for each latent construct was fixed to 1.0 as indicated in Figure 32.2).

5. Here it is assumed that measured variables of "high quality" were chosen to serve as indicator variables of the latent constructs (i.e., measured variables with relatively high factor loadings). Somewhat paradoxically, the use of low-quality indicators in the measurement portion of the model can erroneously lead to an inference of acceptable data-model fit regarding the structural portion (see Hancock & Mueller, 2007).

6. *Effect* indicators are measured variables that are specified to be the structural effects of the latent constructs that are hypothesized to underlie them (e.g., Bollen & Lennox, 1991). The analysis of models involving *cause* indicators—items that contribute to composite scores to form *emergent* factors, or latent composites—is theoretically different but also possible, albeit more difficult (see Kline, 2006).

7. Typically, LM statistics are not additive; that is, the chi-square statistic is *not* expected to drop by 1761.5 (= 652.0 + 567.8 + 541.7). When a fixed parameter is estimated in a subsequent reanalysis, LM statistics for the remaining fixed parameters usually change. Hence, theoretically justifiable model modifications motivated by LM results should usually occur one parameter at a time unless there is a clear theoretical reason for freeing multiple parameters at once, as is the case here.

8. One way to assess construct reliability is through Hancock and Mueller's (2001, p. 202) coefficient *H*. *H* is a function of item reliabilities, ℓ_i^2, and is computed by the equation

$$H = 1 \Big/ \left[1 + \left(1 \Big/ \sum_{i=1}^{k} \ell_i^2 / \left(1 - \ell_i^2 \right) \right) \right],$$

where *k* is the number of measured variables associated with a given latent factor.

9. Such a statistical comparison is possible with a chi-square difference test since the current model is nested within the final measurement model, as explained next.

10. Perceptive readers will have noticed that fit results for Model 3 equal those previously discussed for the final measurement model. Indeed, this is no coincidence but an illustration of two *equivalent* models, that is, models that differ in structure but exhibit identical data-model fit for any data set (see Hershberger, 2006).

11. For a given sample, only the interpretation of standardized coefficients is meaningful as the latent factor metrics are arbitrary (different choices for reference variables could lead to different latent metrics); unstandardized coefficients can be useful in effect comparisons across multiple samples or studies.

12. If this is impractical or impossible, a cross-validation index could be computed (see Browne & Cudeck, 1993).

13. Mrs. Foldi is the second author's mother; she has no formal training in SEM or in any other statistical technique.

References

Arbuckle, J. L. (2007). AMOS (Version 7) [Computer software]. Chicago: SPSS.

Bentler, P. M. (2006). EQS (Version 6.1) [Computer software]. Encino, CA: Multivariate Software.

Bentler, P. M., & Chou, C.-P. (1987). Practical issues in structural equation modeling. *Sociological Methods & Research, 16*, 78–117.

Bollen, K. A. (1989). *Structural equations with latent variables.* New York: John Wiley.

Bollen, K. A., & Lennox, R. (1991). Conventional wisdom on measurement: A structural equation perspective. *Psychological Bulletin, 110*, 305–314.

Boomsma, A. (2000). Reporting analyses of covariance structures. *Structural Equation Modeling: A Multidisciplinary Journal, 7*, 461–483.

Browne, M. W. (1984). Asymptotically distribution-free methods for the analysis of covariance structures. *British Journal of Mathematical and Statistical Psychology, 37*, 62–83.

Browne, M. W., & Cudeck, R. (1993). Alternative ways of assessing model fit. In K. A. Bollen & J. S. Long (Eds.), *Testing structural equation models* (pp. 136–162). Newbury Park, CA: Sage.

Byrne, B. M. (1998). *Structural equation modeling with LISREL, PRELIS, and SIMPLIS.* Mahwah, NJ: Lawrence Erlbaum.

Byrne, B. M. (2001). *Structural equation modeling with AMOS.* Mahwah, NJ: Lawrence Erlbaum.

Byrne, B. M. (2006). *Structural equation modeling with EQS: Basic concepts, applications, and programming.* Mahwah, NJ: Lawrence Erlbaum.

Finney, S. J., & DiStefano, C. (2006). Nonnormal and categorical data in structural equation modeling. In G. R. Hancock & R. O. Mueller (Eds.), *Structural equation modeling: A second course* (pp. 269–314). Greenwich, CT: Information Age Publishing.

Gagné, P. E., & Hancock, G. R. (2006). Measurement model quality, sample size, and solution propriety in confirmatory factor models. *Multivariate Behavioral Research, 41*, 65–83.

Hancock, G. R. (2006). Power analysis in covariance structure modeling. In G. R. Hancock &

R. O. Mueller (Eds.), *Structural equation modeling: A second course* (pp. 69–115). Greenwich, CT: Information Age Publishing.

Hancock, G. R., & Mueller, R. O. (2001). Rethinking construct reliability within latent variable systems. In R. Cudeck, S. du Toit, & D. Sörbom (Eds.), *Structural equation modeling: Present and future—A Festschrift in honor of Karl Jöreskog* (pp. 195–216). Lincolnwood, IL: Scientific Software International, Inc.

Hancock, G. R., & Mueller, R. O. (2004). Path analysis. In M. Lewis-Beck, A. Brymann, & T. F. Liao (Eds.), *Sage encyclopedia of social science research methods* (pp. 802–806). Thousand Oaks, CA: Sage.

Hancock, G. R., & Mueller, R. O. (Eds.). (2006). *Structural equation modeling: A second course.* Greenwich, CT: Information Age Publishing.

Hancock, G. R., & Mueller, R. O. (2007, April). *The reliability paradox in structural equation modeling fit indices.* Paper presented at the annual meeting of the American Educational Research Association, Chicago.

Hershberger, S. L. (2003). The growth of structural equation modeling: 1994–2001. *Structural Equation Modeling: A Multidisciplinary Journal, 10,* 35–46.

Hershberger, S. L. (2006). The problem of equivalent structural models. In G. R. Hancock & R. O. Mueller (Eds.), *Structural equation modeling: A second course* (pp. 13–41). Greenwich, CT: Information Age Publishing.

Hoyle, R. H., & Panter, A. T. (1995). Writing about structural equation models. In R. H. Hoyle (Ed.), *Structural equation modeling: Concepts, issues, and applications* (pp. 158–176). Thousand Oaks, CA: Sage.

Hu, L., & Bentler, P. M. (1999). Cutoff criteria for fit indexes in covariance structure analysis: Conventional criteria versus new alternatives. *Structural Equation Modeling: A Multidisciplinary Journal, 6,* 1–55.

Jöreskog, K. G. (1966). Testing a simple structure hypothesis in factor analysis. *Psychometrika, 31,* 165–178.

Jöreskog, K. G. (1967). Some contributions to maximum likelihood factor analysis. *Psychometrika, 32,* 443–482.

Jöreskog, K. G., & Sörbom, D. (2006). LISREL (Version 8.80) [Computer software]. Lincolnwood, IL: Scientific Software International.

Kaplan, D. (2000). *Structural equation modeling: Foundations and extensions.* Thousand Oaks, CA: Sage.

Kenny, D. A. (1979). *Correlation and causation.* New York: John Wiley.

Kline, R. B. (2005). *Principles and practice of structural equation modeling* (2nd ed.). New York: Guilford.

Kline, R. B. (2006). Formative measurement and feedback loops. In G. R. Hancock & R. O. Mueller (Eds.), *Structural equation modeling: A second course* (pp. 43–68). Greenwich, CT: Information Age Publishing.

Levy, R., & Hancock, G. R. (2007). A framework of statistical tests for comparing mean and covariance structure models. *Multivariate Behavioral Research, 42,* 33–66.

Loehlin, J. C. (2004). *Latent variable models* (4th ed.). Hillsdale, NJ: Lawrence Erlbaum.

Marsh, H. W., Hau, K.-T., Balla, J. R., & Grayson, D. (1998). Is more ever too much? The number of indicators per factor in confirmatory factor analysis. *Multivariate Behavioral Research, 33,* 181–220.

McDonald, R. P., & Ho, M. R. (2002). Principles and practice in reporting structural equation analyses. *Psychological Methods, 7,* 64–82.

Mueller, R. O. (1996). *Basic principles of structural equation modeling: An introduction to LISREL and EQS.* New York: Springer-Verlag.

Mueller, R. O. (1997). Structural equation modeling: Back to basics. *Structural Equation Modeling: A Multidisciplinary Journal, 4,* 353–369.

Mueller, R. O., & Hancock, G. R. (2001). Factor analysis and latent structure, confirmatory. In N. J. Smelser & P. B. Baltes (Eds.), *International encyclopedia of the social & behavioral sciences* (pp. 5239–5244). Oxford, UK: Elsevier.

Muthén, B. O., & Muthén, L. K. (2006). Mplus (Version 4.1) [Computer software]. Los Angeles: Author.

Satorra, A., & Bentler, P. M. (1994). Corrections to test statistics and standard errors in covariance structure analysis. In A. von Eye & C. C. Clogg (Eds.), *Latent variables analysis: Applications for developmental research* (pp. 285–305). Thousand Oaks, CA: Sage.

Schumacker, R. E., & Lomax, R. G. (2004). *A beginner's guide to structural equation modeling* (2nd ed.). Mahwah, NJ: Lawrence Erlbaum.

Shaffer, J. P. (Ed.). (1992). *The role of models in nonexperimental social science: Two debates.* Washington, DC: American Educational Research Association.

Tanaka, J. S. (1993). Multifaceted conceptions of fit in structural equation models. In K. A. Bollen & J. S. Long (Eds.), *Testing structural equation models* (pp. 10–39). Newbury Park, CA: Sage.

West, S. G., Finch, J. F., & Curran, P. J. (1995). Structural equation models with nonnormal variables. In R. H. Hoyle (Ed.), *Structural equation modeling: Concepts, issues, and applications* (pp. 56–75). Thousand Oaks, CA: Sage.

Wright, S. (1918). On the nature of size factors. *Genetics, 3,* 367–374.

33

INTRODUCTION TO BAYESIAN MODELING FOR THE SOCIAL SCIENCES

GIANLUCA BAIO

MARTA BLANGIARDO

In the context of statistical problems, the *frequentist* interpretation of probability has historically played a predominant role in modern statistics. In this approach, probability is defined as the limiting frequency of occurrence in an infinitely repeated experiment. The underlying assumption is that of a "fixed" concept of probability, which is unknown but can be theoretically disclosed by means of repeated trials, under the same experimental conditions.

However, although the frequentist approach still plays the role of the standard in various applied areas, many other possible conceptualizations of probability characterize different philosophies behind the problem of statistical inference. Among these, an increasingly popular one is the *Bayesian* (also referred to as *subjectivist*), originated by the posthumous work of Reverend Thomas Bayes (1763)—see Howie (2002), Senn (2003), or Fienberg (2006) for a historical account of Bayesian theory.

The main feature of this approach is that probability is interpreted as a subjective degree of belief in the occurrence of an event, representing the individual level of uncertainty in its actual realization (cf. de Finetti, 1974, probably the most comprehensive account of subjective probability). One of the main implications of subjectivism is that there is no requirement that one should be able to specify, or even conceive of, some relevant sequence of repetitions of the event in question, as happens in the frequentist framework, with the advantage that events of the "one-off" type can be assessed consistently.

In the Bayesian philosophy, the probability assigned to any event depends also on the individual whose uncertainty is being taken into account and on the state of background information underlying this assessment. Varying any of these factors might change the probability. Consequently, under the subjectivist view, there is no assumption of a unique, correct (or "true") value for the probability of any uncertain event (Dawid, 2005). Rather, each individual is entitled to his or her own subjective probability, and according to the evidence that becomes sequentially available, individuals tend to update their beliefs.[1]

Bayesian methods are not new to the social sciences—from Phillips (1973) to Iversen (1984), Efron (1986), Raftery (1995), Berger (2000), and Gill (2002)—but they are also not systematically integrated into most research in the social sciences. This may be due to the common perception among practitioners that Bayesian methods are "more complex."

In fact, in our opinion, the apparent higher degree of complexity is more than compensated by at least the two following consequences. First, Bayesian methods allow taking into account, through a formal model, all the available information, such as the results of previous studies. Moreover, the inferential process is straightforward, as it is possible to make probabilistic statements directly on the quantities of interest (i.e., some unobservable feature of the process under study, typically represented by a set of parameters).

Despite their subjectivist nature, Bayesian methods allow the practitioner to make the most of the evidence: In just the situation of "repeated trials," after observing the outcomes (successes and failures) of many past trials (assuming no other source of information), the individuals will be drawn to an assessment of the probability of success on the next event that is extremely close to the observed proportion of successes so far. However, if past data are not sufficiently extensive, it may be reasonably argued that there should indeed be scope for interpersonal disagreement as to the implications of the evidence. Therefore, the Bayesian approach provides a more general framework for the problem of statistical inference.[2]

In order to facilitate comprehension, we shall present two worked examples and switch between theory and practice in every section. In the first part of the chapter, we consider data about nonattendance at school for a set of Australian children, with additional information about their race (Aboriginal, White) and age band also included. We use this data set to present the main feature of Bayesian reasoning and to follow the development of the simplest form of models (conjugated analysis). In the last section of the chapter, we describe a more realistic representation for the analysis of SAT score data. The main objective of this analysis is to develop a more complex model combining information for a number of related variables, using the simulation techniques of Markov chain Monte Carlo methods.

CONDITIONAL PROBABILITIES AND BAYES THEOREM

A fundamental concept in statistics, particularly within the Bayesian approach, is that of *conditional probability* (for a technical review, see Dawid, 1979). Given two events A and B, we can define A | B (read "A given B") as the occurrence of the event A under the circumstance that the event B has already occurred.

In other words, by considering the conditional probability, we are in fact changing the reference population; the probability of the event A, Pr(A), is generally defined over the space Ω, which contains all the possible events under study, including A. Conversely, when considering the conditional probability Pr(A | B), we are restricting our attention to the subspace of Ω where both the events A and B can occur. Such a subspace is indicated as (A & B). Moreover, the basis of our comparison will not be Ω but just its subspace where B is possible. Consequently, the probability of the occurrence of the event A conditional on the event B is formally defined as

$$Pr(A \mid B) = \frac{Pr(A \& B)}{Pr(B)}. \qquad (1)$$

Example: Nonattendance at School in Australia

Paul and Banerjee (1998) studied Australian educational data on the days of nonattendance at school for 146 children by race (Aboriginal, White) and age band (primary, first form, second form, third form). The observed average value of nonattendance days is 16, which will be used as a cutoff threshold for our analysis.

Suppose we are interested in the probability that a student accumulates more than the average number of nonattendance days, conditional on his or her race. We can define the events of interest as follows:

$$H = \{>16 \text{ nonattendance days}\}$$

$$W = \{\text{White race}\}$$

(where H stands for *high* nonattendance) and their complement as

$\bar{H}$ {≤16 nonattendance days}

$\bar{W}$= {Aboriginal race}

Table 33.1 reports the observed frequency for each combination of the four events.

In this simple example, we can interpret the concept of probability in its "statistical" sense (i.e., in terms of the proportion of relevant cases in a suitable population). Therefore, applying (1), we can calculate

Pr(> 16 days of absence|Aboriginal)

$$= \frac{\text{Pr(Aboriginal \& > 16 days of absence)}}{\text{Pr(Aboriginal)}},$$

that is,

$$\text{Pr}(H|\bar{W}) = \frac{\text{Pr}(H\&\bar{W})}{\text{Pr}(\bar{W})} = \frac{32/146}{69/146} = 0.46.$$

Similarly,

Pr(> 16 days of absence|White)

$$= \frac{\text{Pr(White \& > 16 days of absence)}}{\text{Pr(White)}},$$

that is, in symbols,

$$\text{Pr}(H|W) = \frac{\text{Pr}(H\&W)}{\text{Pr}(W)} = \frac{19/146}{77/146} = 0.25.$$

From this analysis, we can conclude that it is more likely for an Aboriginal child to experience more than the average number of nonattendance days than for a White child (0.46 vs. 0.25).

Table 33.1   The Original Data on Nonattendance in Australian Schools by Race

Race Group	Nonattendance Days		Total
	$H > 16$	$\bar{H} \leq 16$	
W: White	19	58	77
$\bar{W}$: Aboriginal	32	37	69
Total	51	95	146

Bayes Theorem

Conditional probability is the basic concept of Bayes theorem. The intuition is that, rearranging (1), we can write the joint probability of events A and B (i.e., the probability that the pair occurs at the same time) as

$$\text{Pr}(A \& B) = \text{Pr}(A \mid B) \times \text{Pr}(B). \quad (2)$$

Suppose now that we are interested in the probability of the event B, conditional on the occurrence of the event A. Applying again definition (1), we have

$$\text{Pr}(B \mid A) = \frac{\text{Pr}(A\&B)}{\text{Pr}(A)}. \quad (3)$$

Finally, substituting (2) into (3), we have Bayes theorem:

$$\text{Pr}(B \mid A) = \frac{\text{Pr}(A \mid B) \times \text{Pr}(B)}{\text{Pr}(A)}. \quad (4)$$

As suggested before, the qualitative interpretation of (4) is quite interesting. In other words, we take into account the prior knowledge of the occurrence of the event B, expressed by $\text{Pr}(B)$, and combine it with a new finding (i.e., the occurrence of the event A) to update our knowledge into the posterior probability $\text{Pr}(B \mid A)$.

This process is relevant in many practical situations: Back to the example, suppose now that, instead of the whole data of Table 33.1, we only have available partial information. For instance, suppose we just know that (a) the probability that a student chosen at random experiences high nonattendance (H) is 34.93% (0.3493), (b) the probability that a student chosen at random is Aborigine ($\bar{W}$) is 47.26% (0.4726), and (c) given that a student experiences high nonattendance, the probability that he or she is Aborigine ($\bar{W} \mid H$) is 62.75% (0.6275). These figures can actually be derived from Table 33.1, but again, suppose that this is all you know.

Using Bayes theorem, we can now calculate the probability that, given that a student is Aborigine, he or she experiences high nonattendance at school ($H \mid \bar{W}$):

$$\Pr(H|\overline{W}) = \frac{\Pr(\overline{W}|H) \times \Pr(H)}{\Pr(\overline{W})}$$

$$= \frac{0.6275 \times 0.3493}{0.4726} = 0.4638.$$

The first piece of information that we analyze is the original probability of high nonattendance (34.93%). Then we process the fact that an Aborigine child is observed, and we use it to update the probability of high nonattendance, conditional on this new piece of information. Since the Aboriginal race is associated with higher probabilities of nonattendance (see also Table 33.1), this observation increases the initial chance of H, which is updated to 46.38%.

BAYESIAN MODELING

The implications of (4) can be extended to more complex statistical models, where we deal with *random variables* (i.e., mathematical functions that map events into numbers) instead of simple events.

Suppose, for instance, that we observe a random variable Y. Typically, even within the classical framework, the uncertainty about this variable is modeled by means of a probability distribution, indexed by a (set of) parameter(s) θ, which is normally the object of the inference we want to draw. For example, Y could represent the observed rate of passing a certain exam, and we might be interested in the average rate of "success" for the whole student population, θ.

Let us indicate this probability distribution[3] by $p(y|\theta)$, to stress the dependence of the variable Y and its possible realization y on the parameters θ. Within the Bayesian framework, unlike the classical approach, the parameters are considered to be random variables (instead of fixed and unknown quantities) and therefore are associated with a suitable probability function, in order to describe the experimenter's uncertainty on their actual value. This distribution is indicated by $p(\theta)$.

Notice that, for the observed data, the variability depends essentially on the sampling selection. Typically, we assume that the data $\mathbf{y} = \{y_1, \ldots, y_n\}$ are a random sample of observations from a reference population, made by $N > n$ units. The uncertainty on the observed variable is given by the fact that we observe a single

sample that is just n out of the possible N units (sampling variability).

Conversely, the uncertainty about parameters is generated by our limited knowledge. Usually, we are not able to observe parameters, which represent latent features of the process under study; the only information that we have on the parameters is that provided by the observed evidence. Consequently, we are usually not able to describe θ with certainty; we only have limited information about it, maybe solely our subjective beliefs, and we can use whatever knowledge we have on θ to define the *prior* distribution, $p(\theta)$.

Also notice that in general, it will be possible to describe this prior knowledge by means of (a set of) *hyperparameters*, ψ. For this reason, it would be more appropriate to write the prior distribution as a function $p(\theta|\psi) = f(\psi)$, to emphasize this relationship. However, for the sake of simplicity, unless strictly necessary, we shall use the notation $p(\theta)$ instead of $p(\theta|\psi)$, considering only implicitly the background information provided by ψ.

The inferential problem is solved within the Bayesian framework, applying (4) to compute

$$p(\theta|y) = \frac{p(y|\theta) \times p(\theta)}{p(y)}. \qquad (5)$$

The quantity $p(y|\theta)$ represents the *likelihood* of the observed data under the assumed parametric model (defined by θ). This should not be too controversial, as it is used also in the frequentist approach, a classic example being the well-known Normal model, where the parameters are $\theta = (\mu, \sigma^2)$, representing the population mean and variance, respectively.

The quantity $p(y)$ is the *marginal* distribution of Y and can be considered a normalization constant (we shall discuss it in more detail later).

Finally, $p(\theta|y)$ is the object of the inference, the *posterior* distribution, which is defined conditionally on the observed random variable Y. With the denominator of (5) being a constant (i.e., not depending explicitly on θ), Bayes theorem is often reported as

$$p(\theta|y) \propto p(y|\theta) \times p(\theta)$$

(read "the posterior is proportional to the product of the prior and the likelihood").

The relations between the observable variable Y and the parameter θ (and possibly the hyperparameter ψ) might be better appreciated using the graphical representation of directed acyclic graphs (DAGs; see Whittaker, 1990, and Gilks, Richardson, & Spiegelhalter, 1996, or Edwards, 2000, for a less technical introduction). In a DAG, the nodes (represented as circles) denote random quantities, while the arrows between the nodes represent stochastic dependencies.

Figure 33.1a shows the alleged *data-generating process:* The arrow leaving the node θ toward the node y means that the distribution of the observable variable depends (i.e., is conditional) on the parameter θ. Conversely, the *inferential process* is depicted in Figure 33.1b. The variable Y is actually observed (i.e., it becomes evidence, whence it is represented by means of a square instead of by a circle); it should be clear that at this point, there is no uncertainty left on Y. The evidence provided by this observation travels "against the arrows" of the DAG (the dashed line). This information is used to update the probability of θ, in light of the observation of Y, by applying Bayes theorem, yielding the posterior distribution $p(\theta \mid y)$.

"Integrating Out" Uncertainty

Let us consider again the situation described in Table 33.1 and suppose that we are interested in the probability of high attendance for a random student, regardless on his or her race group—that is, $\Pr(H)$. This condition can happen when (a) the random student has a high nonattendance at school *and* is White, or (b) the random student has a high nonattendance at school *and* is Aborigine, which can be expressed in formula as

$$\Pr(H) = \Pr(H \,\&\, W) + \Pr(H \,\&\, \overline{W}).$$

since the two events (H & W) and (H & $\overline{W}$) are mutually exclusive.

We refer to this probability as *marginal;* the process whereby we obtain it is called *marginalization,* and it is crucial in the Bayesian framework. In particular, using (1), we can reexpress the marginal probability as a function of the conditional rather than the joint probabilities, that is,

$$\Pr(H) = \Pr(H \mid W)\,\Pr(W) + \\ \Pr(H \mid \overline{W})\,\Pr(\overline{W}).$$

Now, suppose we consider more generally a bidimensional probability distribution $p(x, y)$, which describes the joint variation of a pair of variables (X, Y). For the sake of simplicity, suppose further that X is a discrete variable, taking on the set of values $\{0, 1, \ldots, k\}$. We can apply the same process used for the simpler case of events to probability distributions and obtain the marginal probability of the variable Y as

$$p(y) = p(y \mid X = 0)\,\Pr(X = 0) + \\ p(y \mid X = 1)\,\Pr(X = 1) + \ldots \\ + p(y \mid X = k)\,\Pr(X = k) = \\ \sum_{x=0}^{k} p(y \mid X = x)\,\Pr(X = x),$$

just extending the above reasoning.

Sometimes, we refer to this operation as *integrating out* or *averaging out* the variable X, and this procedure is particularly important when we know or assume that X and Y have a joint probability structure, and although we cannot observe X (for example, when it represents a latent parameter), we still need to compute a probability distribution for Y.

In this case, we first consider the probability of Y for a fixed level of X, which is expressed by $p(y \mid X = x)$. Then, in the absence of the knowledge of which exact value of X obtains, we average over the possible values that it can take on. The marginal distribution of Y can then be regarded as a weighted average of the conditional distributions $p(y \mid X = x)$, the weight being represented by the probability $\Pr(X = x)$ for all the possible values x, a condition that may be expressed as[4] $p(y) = E_{p(x)}[p(y \mid x)]$.

When the role of X is played by a continuous variable, marginalization is performed solving an integral calculation, instead of the simpler sum that is required in the discrete case. For instance, if we consider again the denominator of (5) assuming that the parameter θ is associated with a continuous distribution, the

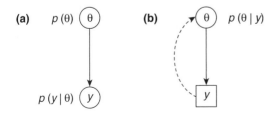

(a) $p(\theta)$ (θ)   **(b)**   (θ) $p(\theta \mid y)$

$p(y \mid \theta)$ (y)   [y]

Figure 33.1   The DAG representation of (a) the data-generating process and (b) the probability updating process.

marginal distribution of the observable variable Y is calculated as

$$p(y) = \int p(y \mid \theta)\, p(\theta)\, d\theta.$$

In this case, the process of marginalization has the effect of integrating out the uncertainty about the parameter.

EXCHANGEABILITY AND PREDICTIVE INFERENCE

One of the most common assumptions underlying statistical models (particularly in the frequentist approach) is that the observed data $y = \{y_1, \ldots, y_n\}$ form a random sample of *independent and identically distributed* (*iid*) observations. This amounts to assuming that if we were able to know the exact value of the parameter θ, considered as a fixed quantity, then the observations y_i (for $i = 1, \ldots, n$) would be conditionally independent on one another, a condition that can be expressed in formula as

$$p(y_1, \ldots, y_n \mid \theta) = p(y_1 \mid \theta) \times \ldots \times p(y_n \mid \theta)$$
$$= \prod_{i=1}^{n} p(y_i \mid \theta). \qquad (6)$$

Recall from probability calculus that if A and B are conditionally independent given C, then $\Pr(A \,\&\, B \mid C) = \Pr(A \mid C) \times \Pr(B \mid C)$, that is, the joint distribution is the product of the marginal probabilities.

A more general concept, which proves to be more realistic in many practical applications, is that the probabilistic structures of the units are just *similar* (rather than *identical*), with respect to a common random generating process. This idea is generally referred to as *exchangeability*, and it has strong connections with the Bayesian framework, thanks to the work of Bruno de Finetti (1974).

In a nutshell, under exchangeability, we regard the data $y = \{y_1, \ldots, y_n\}$ as a random sample of *iid* observations conditionally on the parameter θ, but we also assume that the parameter is a random quantity, represented by a probability distribution $p(\theta)$—exactly how it happens in a Bayesian analysis.

If we consider the simple case with two observations $y = \{y_1, y_2\}$, then the assumption of exchangeability implies that $p(y_1 \mid \theta)$ is not identical with $p(y_2 \mid \theta)$, as would happen if (6) held. This is because they both depend on a parameter that is not fixed but, on the contrary, is generated by the random process described by $p(\theta)$.

For this reason, we consider the two observations as only similar, in the sense that there is a common process that generates the value of the parameter, which in turn determines their probabilistic structure.

The result proved by de Finetti is that exchangeability can be expressed formally as

$$p(y_1, \ldots, y_n) = \int \prod_{i=1}^{n} p(y_i \mid \theta) p(\theta)\, d\theta, \qquad (7)$$

where θ is a continuous random parameter (whence the use of the integral). Notice that (7) is an application of the concept of marginalization described above and a generalization of (6).

Figure 33.2 shows the differences between *iid* and exchangeable samples in terms of DAGs. As one can appreciate, in the former situation, the parameter generates the probability distribution of the observations, and it is considered as fixed, whereby it is represented by a square in the DAG of Figure 33.2a. Conversely, in the case of exchangeable observations, the parameter is a random quantity (i.e., represented by a circle), associated with its own probability distribution. In either case, the observations are conditionally independent given (i.e., *if we could observe*) the value of θ. However, the nature of the unobservable parameter is intrinsically different in the two circumstances.

Apart from relaxing the assumption of identical distribution, exchangeability is also important because from (7) we can derive a predictive result on the observable variable. Suppose that y^* represents a future occurrence (or a value not yet observed in the current experiment) of the random phenomenon described by the information gathered by means of the sample y. In our running example, we might think of y^* as a new student joining the class for whom we assume the information on absence of days from school is not yet available.

If we assume exchangeability for the augmented data set $y^* = (y^*, y)$—that is, the new student has individual characteristics that are similar to those of the other children—we then see that

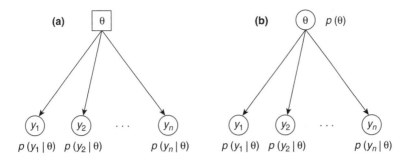

Figure 33.2 The DAG representation of (a) a sample of *iid* observations and (b) a sample of exchangeable observations. In either case, the observed variables depend on a parameter θ, which in case (a) is a fixed quantity (i.e., represented as a square), whereas in case (b), it is a random variable, associated with the distribution $p(\theta)$.

$$p(y^*|\mathbf{y}) = \frac{p(y^*, \mathbf{y})}{p(\mathbf{y})} \quad \text{(from the definition of conditional probability)}$$

$$= \frac{\int p(y^*|\theta)p(\mathbf{y}|\theta)p(\theta)\,d\theta}{p(\mathbf{y})} \quad \text{(by exchangeability)} \tag{8}$$

$$= \frac{\int p(y^*|\theta)p(\theta|\mathbf{y})p(\mathbf{y})\,d\theta}{p(\mathbf{y})} \quad \text{(applying Bayes Theorem)}$$

$$= \int p(y^*|\theta)p(\theta|\mathbf{y})\,d\theta,$$

assuming throughout that θ is a continuous variable.

Equation (8) is meaningful under the assumptions that the variables in y^* are exchangeable (i.e., that the new realization y^* is similar to the ones that have already been observed, **y**). The quantity $p(y^* \mid \mathbf{y})$ is known as *predictive distribution*. Figure 33.3 shows the concepts of exchangeability and predictive distribution in terms of a DAG. The variables y and y^* are generated by the same random process, which is governed by the parameter θ, associated

with a suitable prior distribution, $p(\theta)$. Once Y is observed to the value y, the uncertainty about the parameter is updated into the posterior distribution $p(\theta \mid y)$, which in turn is used to infer the future realization y^*.

Again referring to the new student in the class, using (8) we can predict his or her probability of nonattendance, using the updated (posterior) information gathered from the rest of the class. A practical example is provided in a later section.

CHOOSING THE PRIOR DISTRIBUTION

According to the Bayesian approach, besides the definition of a probability model for the observed data, we also need to choose a suitable distribution for the parameters of interest. In other words, we need to specify a mathematical model, which could well represent the nature of the parameters and our uncertainty about their values. As suggested above, the definition of the prior distribution should be informed by whatever

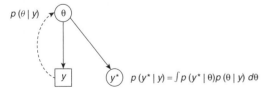

Figure 33.3 A DAG representation of the concept of predictive distribution.

Table 33.2   Some Standard Prior Distributions

Parameter Nature	Support	Typical Distribution
Probability of occurrence of an observable event	$[0;1]$	Beta, Uniform(0,1)
Rate of occurrence of an observable event	$(0;\infty)$	Gamma, Exponential
Unknown continuous symmetric value	$(-\infty;\infty)$	Normal, Student-t
Unknown continuous asymmetric value	$(0;\infty)$	Lognormal, Gamma

knowledge is available on the parameters. For instance, we can derive the prior distribution from the results of previous experiments on the same topic or from elicitation of experts' opinions (Ayyub, 2001; O'Hagan et al., 2006; see also Raiffa, 1968, pp. 161–165, for a nontechnical description of a process of formalization of expert opinions).

Sometimes it is assumed that the prior information is too poor: In this circumstance, it is possible to use a "minimally informative" prior, which basically does not favor any of the possible values that θ can take. For this reason, this is often referred to as "flat" (or "dispersed") prior distribution (see Bernardo & Smith, 1999, for a critical discussion).

Although generally the choice of the prior distribution depends on the specific problem at hand, there are some circumstances in which the nature of the parameters is such that at least one natural candidate exists (some of these classic examples are reported in Table 33.2).

For example, suppose we have conducted a survey to find out which of the two candidates in a political election is most likely to win. One parameter of interest would be the probability of occurrence of the event "Candidate A wins," and for such a situation involving a parameter defined as a continuous variable in the interval $[0;1]$, two standard possibilities for the prior are then represented by the Beta or the Uniform(0,1) distributions.

Obviously, it is not always possible to concentrate on standard models—for example, particularly complex prior information can be encoded in the form of *mixture prior* (Robert, 2001), that is, a combination of different distributions. However, in many practical situations, the options for the prior are restricted to a reasonably small number of possibilities.

Example (Continued)

Back to the example, starting from the total number of days of absence, for each child we can recode our data into a new variable Y that takes the value 1 if a child experienced "high nonattendance" (>16 days of absence) and 0 otherwise (Table 33.3).

For each child, race, and age-group, the variable Y can be suitably represented by a Bernoulli[5] distribution:

$$Y_{ijk} \mid \theta_{jk} \sim \text{Bernoulli}\,(\theta_{jk}),$$

where the symbol "~" is read "is distributed as."

In this case, we suppose that this distribution is governed by a parameter θ_{jk} for each combination of race ($j = 1$ is Aborigine and $j = 2$ is White) and age band group ($k = 1$ is primary school, $k = 2$ is first grade, $k = 3$ is second grade, and $k = 4$ is third grade). The index $i = 1, \ldots, n_{jk}$ represents the number of children in each subgroup, and the parameters θ_{jk} represent the average probability of high nonattendance for each combination of race and age-group of students surveyed. This construction

Table 33.3   The Original Data on Nonattendance and the Recoded Series (Y)

ID	Days of Absence	Race	Age	Y
1	2	Aborigine	Primary school	0
2	11	Aborigine	Primary school	0
...	...	...	...	...
146	37	White	Third grade	1

amounts to assuming that the Y_{ijk}s are exchangeable. In other words, we assume that all the children in the same subgroup (j, k) are similar in terms of their outcome (number of absence days).

The next step in the analysis is the definition of the prior distribution for the parameters θ_{jk} to describe our state of information about them. Each of these represents a proportion—that is, a continuous number in the interval $[0;1]$ that specifies the level of nonattendance rate for each subgroup. Under these modeling assumptions, a good candidate for the prior is the Beta distribution (see Table 33.2).

This is a continuous distribution defined in the set $[0;1]$, and it is characterized by two hyperparameters (usually indicated as α and β). Changing the value for α and β affects the shape and the scale of the distribution. This circumstance renders the Beta distribution quite flexible and applicable to a number of similar situations.

As a first approximation, we suppose that the eight parameters θ_{jk} all come from the same Beta distribution specified by a pair of α and β hyperparameters: $\theta_{jk} \mid \alpha, \beta \sim \text{Beta}(\alpha, \beta)$—notice that in this case, the distribution of θ_{jk} is explicitly written as a function of the hyperparameters $\psi = (\alpha, \beta)$, as opposed to the simpler formulation used earlier.

Once a suitable functional form is identified for the prior, we further need to define the value of the hyperparameters. For the sake of simplicity, we assume for now that the α and β are fixed quantities (for this reason, in Figure 33.4, which depicts the DAG for this model, they are represented in a square).

Suppose that from a survey conducted the year before the current data collection, it emerged that the overall average probability of high nonattendance at school was $\mu = 0.4$, with an estimated variance of $\sigma^2 = 0.03$. We can use this information to define the parameters of the prior. In fact, by the properties of the Beta distribution, we get that

$$\mu = \frac{\alpha}{\alpha + \beta} \quad \text{and}$$

$$\sigma^2 = \frac{\alpha\beta}{(\alpha + \beta)^2(\alpha + \beta + 1)}, \tag{9}$$

or equivalently,

$$\alpha = \mu \left[\frac{\mu(1 - \mu)}{\sigma^2} - 1 \right] \quad \text{and}$$

$$\beta = (1 - \mu) \left[\frac{\mu(1 - \mu)}{\sigma^2} - 1 \right]. \tag{10}$$

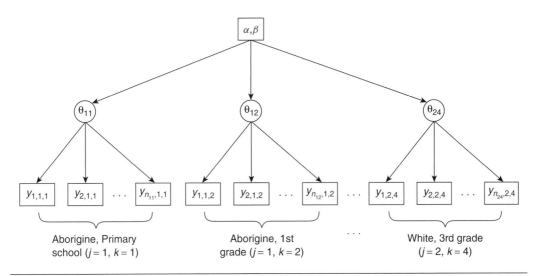

Figure 33.4   DAG of the model: Within each group, the individuals are exchangeable, as they depend on a common random parameter. The parameters are a sample of *iid* realizations from a common distribution that depend on fixed hyperparameters.

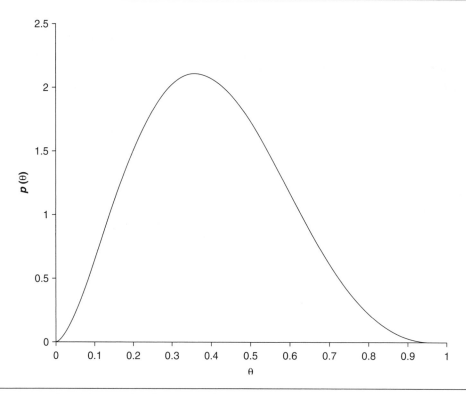

Figure 33.5   Plot of the prior distribution $\theta \mid \alpha,\beta \sim \text{Beta}(2.8, 4.2)$.

Assuming that the parameters θ_{jk} all come from a common distribution with the same mean and variance, we can substitute the values of μ and σ^2 into (10), which yields $\alpha = 2.8$ and $\beta = 4.2$. These values are used as hyperparameters of the Beta prior distribution $\theta \mid \alpha,\beta \sim (2.8, 4.2)$.

Figure 33.5 depicts the prior distribution that we have just derived. As it is possible to see, the experimenter is assigning a positive "belief" to all the values in the admissible interval for the parameter (i.e., $[0;1]$). However, the prior assumption is that the values around 0.4 are the most likely, whereas the extremes (such as $\theta > 0.9$ or $\theta < 0.1$) are considered as very unlikely and therefore associated with a low (almost null) probability mass.

INFERENCE ON THE POSTERIOR DISTRIBUTION

One of the advantages of the Bayesian approach is that, unlike the classical methods, the final inference is performed directly on the whole posterior distribution for the variable of interest θ.

On the one hand, the standard frequentist approach considers the parameter (that is, the objective of inference) as a fixed but unknown quantity and uses the random observed data to perform the inferential process (i.e., to estimate the value of the parameter), using a function of the data, conditionally on the parameter, usually in the form $\hat{\theta} = t(\mathbf{Y} \mid \theta)$. As a typical example, the maximum likelihood estimator (MLE) of a Normal population mean is defined as

$$\hat{\theta} = \sum_{i=1}^{n} \frac{Y_i}{n}.$$

The true value of the parameter is considered as fixed, and it does not enter in the estimator, which is built using the n data points.

On the other hand, the Bayesian procedure is based on a completely reversed philosophy. In fact, it considers the data as a fixed quantity; this is because we have actually observed the value of the sample of interest, and therefore there is no uncertainty left on the value of Y. Conversely, the parameter (still the objective of inference) is not known, and therefore it is considered as a random quantity, associated with a probability distribution. The inferential process is performed by means of a function of the parameter, conditionally on the observed data—that is, the posterior distribution $p(\theta \mid y)$. This distinction is fundamental from both the philosophical and the pragmatic point of view, as it is the feature that allows Bayesian inference to be performed directly on the parameters of interest.

Traditionally, the main practical (but not theoretical!) drawback of the Bayesian approach has been the computational difficulties associated with the calculation of the posterior distribution. In particular, it is in general complicated to derive the normalization constant, which usually involves complex integrations during the process of marginalization. However, a special case in which this problem does not occur is that of *conjugated* models.

A prior distribution $p(\theta \mid \psi) = f(\psi)$, as a function of the (set of) hyperparameters ψ, is said to be conjugated for the data model $p(y \mid \theta)$ if the posterior distribution $p(\theta \mid \psi) = f(\psi^*)$ belongs to the same family of probability distributions f. In this case, the update from the prior to the posterior only involves the hyperparameters, which are modified from ψ to ψ^* (cf. Table 33.4 and see Bernardo & Smith, 1999, for a taxonomic account of conjugate families).

The first column of Table 33.4 presents some of the most used statistical models. Probably the most famous is the Normal model, which we might use to describe a continuous and symmetrical phenomenon, such as the height of a given population. Throughout the table, the relevant parameter (for which we want to make

inference) is indicated by θ (other parameters might be included but not investigated, as in the case of the variance σ^2 in the Normal model).

The second column depicts the conjugate prior distribution for each data model. Again, in the case where we can use a Normal distribution for the observed data, the parameter of interest could be the population average height, θ, assuming that the variance σ^2 is known. As suggested in the table, a suitable conjugate distribution for the mean is again Normal, with hyperparameters (μ_0, τ_0^2).

In the third column, we present the functional form of the posterior distribution. In the example of the population height, we see that, after observing a sample y, the mean height is associated again with a Normal distribution with updated parameters (μ_1, τ_1^2), whose exact formulation is given in the fourth column of the table.

As one can appreciate, with this model being conjugated, the functional form of the distribution for the parameter is unchanged after observing the sample, and the information is included by means of an update of the hyperparameters. Similar reasoning applies for the other standard models described in Table 33.4.

Obviously, given all of the information provided by the posterior distribution, it is possible and useful to summarize it through some suitable synthetic indicators.

Point Estimates

Although Bayesian analysis is mainly concerned with the entire posterior distribution, it is generally useful to determine some point estimators to summarize it. Similarly to what happens

Table 33.4   Some Relevant Conjugated Models

Data Model (Sample of n Units)	Prior Distribution $p(\theta)$	Posterior Distribution $p(\theta \mid y)$	Notes
$y \mid \theta, \sigma^2 \sim \text{Normal}(\theta, \sigma^2)$	$\text{Normal}(\mu_0, \tau_0^2)$	$\text{Normal}(\mu_1, \tau_1^2)$	$\mu_1 = \dfrac{\frac{\mu_0}{\tau_0^2} + \frac{\bar{y}}{\sigma^2}}{\frac{1}{\tau_0^2} + \frac{1}{\sigma^2}}, \tau_1^2 = \frac{1}{\tau_0^2} + \frac{1}{\sigma^2}$
$y \mid \theta \sim \text{Poisson}(\theta)$	$\text{Gamma}(\alpha, \beta)$	$\text{Gamma}(\alpha_1, \beta_1)$	$\alpha_1 = \alpha + s, \beta_1 = \beta + n, s = \sum_{i=1}^{n} y_i$
$y \mid \nu, \theta \sim \text{Gamma}(\nu, \theta)$	$\text{Gamma}(\alpha, \beta)$	$\text{Gamma}(\alpha_1, \beta_1)$	$\alpha_1 = \alpha + \nu, \beta_1 = \beta + s, s = \sum_{i=1}^{n} y_i$
$y \mid \theta \sim \text{Bernoulli}(n, \theta)$	$\text{Beta}(\alpha, \beta)$	$\text{Beta}(\alpha_1, \beta_1)$	$\alpha_1 = \alpha + s, \beta_1 = \beta + n - s, s = \sum_{i=1}^{n} y_i$
$y \mid \theta \sim \text{Exponential}(\theta)$	$\text{Gamma}(\alpha, \beta)$	$\text{Gamma}(\alpha_1, \beta_1)$	$\alpha_1 = \alpha + n, \beta_1 = \beta + s, s = \sum_{i=1}^{n} y_i$

in classical statistics, typical point estimators of location parameters are the mean, the median, and the mode of the posterior distribution. These estimators are calculated according to the usual definitions provided in statistical literature (see, e.g., Mood, Graybill, & Boes, 1993).

For instance, the posterior mean is calculated as[6] $E(\theta \mid y) = \sum_{\theta \in \Theta} \theta p(\theta \mid y)$, where Θ represents the set of possible values for the variable θ (as we have seen earlier, the sum is replaced by the integral when the variable is continuous). Similarly, we can calculate the posterior median as the value that separates the highest half of the posterior distribution from the lowest half: θ_{med}, such that $\Pr(\theta < \theta_{med} \mid y) = 0.5$, or the posterior mode as the value(s) associated with the maximum frequency (or with the maximum density in case of a continuous variable): $\theta^* = \max_\Theta p(\theta \mid y)$—this kind of estimator is often referred to as *maximum a posteriori* (MAP).

Credibility Intervals

The parallel with the classical approach extends to interval estimation. However, the philosophy underlying Bayesian methods is obviously completely different. Actually, in the frequentist framework, a $100 \times (1 - \alpha)\%$ confidence interval (CI) suggests that if we could repeat the same experiment, under the same conditions, for a large number M of times, then the real value of θ would fall outside of that interval only $(100 \times \alpha)\%$ of the times (usually $\alpha = 0.05$). This convoluted statement is *not* equivalent to asserting that the probability that θ lies in the CI is $100 \times (1 - \alpha)\%$ since the parameter is considered as a fixed, unknown value, not as a random variable. Moreover, the definition of the frequentist CI does not help clarify what we can say about the *current* experiment (cf. Table 33.5).

Conversely, within the Bayesian approach, CI will be explicitly related to this probability, that is, in the form $\Pr(\theta \in CI \mid y)$. This is made possible by the fact that the parameter of interest is associated with a probability distribution, which allows us to make probabilistic statements and to take the underlying uncertainty into account. Moreover, no particular reference is made to long-run frequency properties of this estimate. To highlight this difference, we talk about *credibility* (as opposed to *confidence*) intervals. Without the need of approximations or convoluted statements, it is straightforward (at least

theoretically) to calculate a size $100 \times (1 - \alpha)\%$ posterior credibility interval, in general, simply solving for any level α of interest the following probabilistic inequality:

$$p(\theta \in CI \mid y) \geq 1 - \alpha. \qquad (11)$$

Consequently, credibility intervals do not rely on replications of the same experiment or on the reliability of the observed result with respect to the "long run." They are a measure of uncertainty in a particular event of interest, as measured at this occurrence, on the basis of all the pieces of information available to the analysts.

Example (Continued)

Besides representing an appropriate way of describing the natural uncertainty associated with the parameter θ, the Beta distribution has also the good property of being conjugated for the Bernoulli model that we have previously established for the observed data. Consequently, it is possible to show that in this case, the posterior distribution is also a Beta:

$$p(\theta_{jk} \mid y) \sim \text{Beta}\,(\alpha^*_{jk}, \beta^*_{jk}),$$

where $\alpha^*_{jk} = (\alpha + s_{jk})$, $\beta^*_{jk} = (n_{jk} + \beta - s_{jk})$, and $s_{jk} = \sum_{i=1}^{n_{jk}} y_{ijk}$ is the observed number of successes over all the children belonging to the race j and of age k; each of these subgroups is formed by n_{jk} units (cf. Table 33.4).

Notice that, although a priori, each θ_{jk} is associated with the same $\text{Beta}(\alpha, \beta)$ distribution, a posteriori, we obtain eight different distributions since the update of the hyperparameters involves the observed values s_{jk}, which are obviously specific to each subgroup. For this reason, the posterior distribution is indexed by group-specific hyperparameters. Table 33.6 shows the values for α^*_{jk} and β^*_{jk} for the eight groups, the expected value and the variance calculated using (9), and the credibility intervals at the 95% CI for the parameters θ_{jk}.

The posterior for α^*_{jk} and β^*_{jk} show a very different behavior reflecting the number of successes (a success being defined as "high nonattendance at school") in each group: The range varies from 6.8 to 14.8 for α^*_{jk} and from 11.2 to 20.2 for β^*_{jk}. Bearing in mind that $\alpha^*_{jk} = (\alpha + s_{jk})$, where s_{jk} is the number of successes in the group, it is clear

Table 33.5   The Basic Differences Between the Frequentist and the Bayesian Approach

Frequentist	Bayesian
Nature of probability	
The limiting long-run frequency on a large number of identical replications of the experiment at hand	The personal degree of belief on the realization of the specific outcome under study in the experiment at hand
Nature of parameters	
Unknown, unrepeatable quantities	Nonobservable quantities, subject to their own variability, given the knowledge of the experimenter
Nature of inference	
Does not (although it appears to) make probabilistic statements about the parameters of interest	Makes direct probability statements about parameters with respect to the current experiment
Example	
We reject this hypothesis at the 5% level of significance: If the experimental condition were held constant and we could observe an infinite number of equivalent samples, in 5% of the cases, the hypothesis would be rejected (but what happens to the observed sample?).	The probability that this hypothesis is true is 0.05: In the actually available sample, the data suggest a weak evidence to the hypothesis: $Pr(H_0 \mid data) = 0.05$.

SOURCE: Adapted from Luce and O'Hagan (2003).

that a larger α^*_{jk} is associated with a higher success rate. On the other hand, $\beta^*_{jk} = (n_{jk} + \beta - s_{jk})$, so that this hyperparameter takes into account the number of successes and the size of the group (n_{jk}): Given the same number of successes, larger groups tend to have larger β^*_{jk} than smaller ones.

The posterior mean $E(\theta_{jk} \mid y)$ reflects the size of the parameter α^*_{jk}, as larger values of α^*_{jk} are associated with larger values for the posterior mean. On the other hand, the variance determines the width of the 95% CI: The parameter associated with the smallest variance (θ_{22}) is associated with the narrowest credibility interval (width = 0.223), while those that present the highest variability (θ_{11} and θ_{21}) are associated with the largest credibility interval (width = 0.4).

Comparing these values to those observed during the previous year (which were used to define the hyperparameters of the prior distribution of θ), it is possible to notice a large variability within the groups. For some of them, the mean is almost halved, from 0.4 to around 0.2, which is probably an indication of an improvement in the attendance at school, while for

others it remains around the prior value, and for two of them, it increases up to 0.5. On the other hand, the variability is generally reduced: The variance, which was 0.03 the previous year, decreases to values from 0.004 to 0.011.

It is also interesting to compare the results from the Bayesian analysis with the MLEs: In general, there are only minor differences in the values. This is mainly due to the fact that the prior distribution is not particularly restrictive, so that "we are open to revision" of our belief, in light of the observations. The only important exception is for θ_{22}: The MLE is very close to 0, as the observed number of successes is very low, as compared with the total number of cases considered: $\theta^{ML}_{22} = s_{22} / n_{22} = 2/26 = 0.077$.

This is very different from the Bayesian estimation, which gives a value of 0.145. The reason for this difference is that the Bayesian procedure takes into account also the background information that sets the value of the parameters around 0.4. The observation of a very low number of successes for the group (White, first grade) does decrease the value of the posterior mean. However, the extreme result is mitigated by the

Table 33.6 The Posterior Values of the Hyperparameters α^*_{jk} and β^*_{jk} and the Expected Value and the Variance for $\theta_{jk} \mid y$

Groups (parameters)	α^*_{jk}	β^*_{jk}	$E(\theta_{jk} \mid y)$	$Var(\theta_{jk} \mid y)$	95% CI	n_{jk}	s_{jk}	θ_{jk}^{ML}
Aborigine, Primary School (θ_{11})	6.8	13.2	0.340	0.011	[0.155; 0.555]	13	4	0.308
Aborigine, Grade 1 (θ_{12})	9.8	17.2	0.363	0.008	[0.196; 0.549]	20	7	0.350
Aborigine, Grade 2 (θ_{13})	14.8	12.2	0.548	0.008	[0.362; 0.728]	20	12	0.600
Aborigine, Grade 3 (θ_{14})	11.8	11.2	0.513	0.010	[0.314; 0.710]	16	9	0.563
White, Primary school (θ_{21})	7.8	13.2	0.371	0.011	[0.184; 0.582]	14	5	0.357
White, Grade 1 (θ_{22})	4.8	28.2	0.145	0.004	[0.049; 0.282]	26	2	0.077
White, Grade 2 (θ_{23})	6.8	20.2	0.252	0.007	[0.110; 0.428]	20	4	0.200
White, Grade 3 (θ_{24})	10.8	13.2	0.450	0.010	[0.261; 0.647]	17	8	0.471

NOTE: θ_{jk}^{ML} = maximum likelihood estimator.

effect of the prior, providing a more reliable estimation.

These results can be appreciated also by inspecting the entire distributions by means of the density plots. In particular, we can see how the posterior distribution is shifted with respect to the prior in the plots in Figure 33.6.

Again, a differentiation between the groups is evident: The distributions for θ_{22} and θ_{23} show a large shift to the left for the posterior; this happens since the prior supposes a rather large probability of high nonattendance at school (the mean is 0.4), whereas in those groups, the observed rate of high nonattendance is rather low (0.145 and 0.252, respectively). On the other hand, the posterior distributions for θ_{13}, θ_{14}, and θ_{24} are shifted toward the right, as the number of successes is greater than that assumed under the prior distribution (respectively 0.548, 0.513, and 0.450 vs. the prior value of 0.4).

The remaining groups show a high nonattendance probability similar to the one assumed for the prior; this results in an overlap of the prior and the posterior distributions, which is clear in the corresponding plots for θ_{11}, θ_{12}, and θ_{21}.

HYPOTHESIS TESTING

The natural extension of the inference using the posterior distribution is hypothesis testing.[7] Generally, the hypotheses of interest—usually indicated by H_0 (referred to as the *null hypothesis*) and H_1 (*alternative hypothesis*)—are defined in terms of a statement about some properties of the relevant parameters, such as $H_0: \theta \in \Theta_0$ vs. $H_1: \theta \in \Theta_1$. A typical example considers $H_0: \theta = 0$ vs. $H_1: \theta \neq 0$, where θ is the population mean of a Normal population with unknown variance (i.e., the well-known two-sided t test).

Within the Bayesian approach, each hypothesis can be naturally associated with its own prior distribution, representing the experimenter's uncertainty about its truthfulness, which can be updated by the data y using the posterior distribution $Pr(H_0 \mid y)$.

The framework for Bayesian testing can be schematically described as follows:

1. Define the hypotheses of interest. Typically, we shall be concerned with two different "explanations" of the phenomenon under study. In either case, the probability model chosen to represent the problem will be different (be it because of different values for the parameters of interest or of a completely different probabilistic model). For instance, we might be interested in assessing the theory under which the population average effect of a treatment for a certain disease is 0, as opposed to an alternative theory whereby the treatment is actually efficacious. We can express these hypotheses as $H_0: \theta = 0$ vs. $H_1: \theta > 0$.

2. Define a probabilistic model for the observed data y, as a function of the parameter θ. As an example, we might model the observations

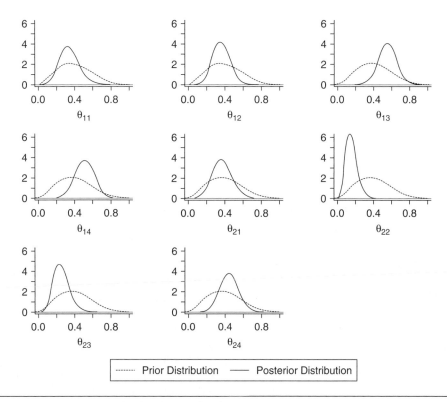

Figure 33.6   Prior posterior plot for each group: The posterior distribution is shifted and the variability is lower, as compared with the prior.

of responses for a set of relevant patients as a random sample from a Normal population—that is, $y \sim \text{Normal}(\theta, \sigma^2)$, possibly assuming that the variance is known.

3. Define the probabilistic structure associated with the parameters of interest within each hypothesis. In other words, this step amounts to reexpressing the conditions defining H_0 and H_1 in terms of a prior probability distribution for the parameter, such as $H_0 : \theta \sim p_0$ and $H_1 : \theta \sim p_1$, where p_0 and p_1 are two probability distributions that suitably represent the behavior of the parameter under the circumstances originally specified by H_0 and H_1. In the example used above, with the null hypothesis being that the parameter θ can assume only one value (namely 0), the associated probability structure is $p_0(\theta = 0) = 1$. On the other hand, under the alternative hypothesis H_1, θ can assume every positive value, so that an associated probability structure can be a distribution characterized by a positive support, such as the lognormal distribution (see Table 33.2) defined as a function of some (possibly known) hyperparameters (λ, τ^2): $H_1 : \theta \sim$ lognormal(λ, τ^2).

4. Define a prior probability for the two hypotheses being tested (which might be supported by previous data or subjective opinions). A typical choice might be to assume minimal information and consider H_0 and H_1 as equally likely—that is, $\text{Pr}(H_0) = \text{Pr}(H_1) = 0.5$. Obviously, there is no reason why we should use this specification in every experiment; in fact, this is just a convenient choice (as we shall show in the following), but this prior distribution, as should all prior distributions, should be based on the available knowledge of the problem at hand.

5. Compute the posterior distributions under the two competing hypotheses. The observed data y will support H_0 if $\text{Pr}(H_0 \mid y) > \text{Pr}(H_1 \mid y)$.

Therefore, Bayesian procedures will not require the definition of a prespecified level of significance, as happens in the classical framework, which can be seen as a major advantage of this approach.

On the other hand, the choice of the prior distribution for θ and for the hypotheses of interest can obviously influence the result. Nevertheless, all the assumptions that lead to the final results are clearly and explicitly stated in this approach and therefore are open to criticism and revision. In the classical framework, the choice of the standard 1% or 5% significance thresholds is almost dogmatic, and sometimes the underlying procedures are just obscure, not allowing for a clear understanding of the testing methodology.

For practical purposes, it is often convenient to report the comparison between the two alternative theories by means of the "odds" form of Bayes theorem:

$$\frac{\Pr(H_0 \mid y)}{\Pr(H_1 \mid y)} = \frac{p(y \mid H_0)}{p(y \mid H_1)} \times \frac{\Pr(H_0)}{\Pr(H_1)}.$$

which is easily derived from (4). The quantity

$$
\begin{aligned}
BF &= \frac{p(y \mid H_0)}{p(y \mid H_1)} \\
&= \frac{\sum\limits_{\theta \in \Theta_0} p(y \mid \theta) p(\theta \mid H_0)}{\sum\limits_{\theta \in \Theta_1} p(y \mid \theta) p(\theta \mid H_1)} \\
&= \frac{\sum\limits_{\theta \in \Theta_0} p(y \mid \theta) p_0(\theta)}{\sum\limits_{\theta \in \Theta_1} p(y \mid \theta) p_1(\theta)} = \frac{E_{p_0(\theta)}[p(y \mid \theta)]}{E_{p_1(\theta)}[p(y \mid \theta)]}
\end{aligned}
\tag{12}
$$

is usually referred to as the Bayes factor (BF) and represents the *weight of the evidence*—that is, an indication of how strongly the observed data y support each of the two hypotheses, regardless of the prior distributions (see Mortera & Dawid, 2006, for an application of Bayesian statistical analysis to forensic problems using the BF).

In (12), $p(y \mid \theta)$ represents the probabilistic model for the observed data as a function of the relevant parameter, whereas $p(\theta \mid H_0)$ is the probabilistic structure associated with θ under

the null hypothesis—which can be equivalently written as $p_0(\theta)$ (a similar reasoning applies for the alternative hypothesis).

By the usual argument of marginalization, we can integrate out the uncertainty about the parameter under the two competing models. Therefore, the Bayes factor is essentially the weighted average of the likelihood functions with respect to the distributions p_0 and p_1 (cf. Equation 12).

Jeffreys (1961) provided a calibration of the Bayes factor that can be used as a rough guide in interpreting the evidence (see Table 33.7).

Example (Continued)

Suppose that we want to test the hypothesis that the general average attendance probability θ is in fact equal to the value previously observed, that is, $H_0 : \theta = 0.4$. The alternative hypothesis could be $H_1 : \theta \neq 0.4$—that is, we do not favor any other possible value for the parameter of interest.

In order to formulate the Bayesian hypothesis testing, we need to translate H_0 and H_1 in terms of suitable probability distributions. The null hypothesis is simple and just assigns probability 1 to the event $\{\theta = 0.4\}$. Therefore, we can define

$$p_0(\theta) = \begin{cases} 1 & \theta = 0.4 \\ 0 & otherwise. \end{cases}$$

On the contrary, the alternative hypothesis is just telling that any other value in support of θ—that is, the interval $[0;1]$—is possible and equally likely, so that we can translate this into the assumption that $p_1(\theta) = \text{Uniform}(0,1)$.[8]

Leaving aside for the moment any discussion of subgroups, we model $Y_h \sim \text{Bernoulli}(\theta)$

Table 33.7   Calibration of the Bayes Factor

Bayes Factor Range $\log_{10}$ Scale	Natural Scale	Strength of the Evidence in Favor of the Hypothesis H_0
> 2	> 100	Decisive evidence
1.5 to 2	32 to 100	Very strong evidence
1 to 1.5	10 to 32	Strong evidence
0.5 to 1	3.2 to 10	Substantial evidence
0 to 0.5	1 to 3.2	"Not worth more than a bare mention" evidence

SOURCE: Jeffreys (1961).

for each child. Consequently, from standard probability theory, we know that the total number of children with a high nonattendance (regardless on their race or age) is associated with a Binomial[9] distribution: $Z \sim$ Binomial(θ, n), with $n = 146$. The observed value of Z in the sample is $z = 51$.

Now, we have to assign a prior probability for the occurrence of each of the two hypotheses of interest. For the sake of simplicity, we assume they are equally likely, that is, $\Pr(H_0) = \Pr(H_1) = 0.5$. In this case, the prior odds are

$$\frac{\Pr(H_0)}{\Pr(H_1)} = 1,$$

and therefore the Bayesian test will be only concerned with the calculation of BF since it will coincide with the posterior odds.

Using the definition of the Binomial distribution, the numerator of BF is

$$\Pr(z = 51 \mid H_0)$$

$$= \sum_{\theta \in \Theta_0} p(z = 51 \mid \theta)p_0(\theta)$$

$$= p(z = 51 \mid \theta = 0.4) \times 1$$

$$+ \sum_{\theta \neq 0.4} p(z = 51 \mid \theta) \times 0$$

$$= \binom{146}{51} 0.4^{51}(1 - 0.4)^{(146-51)} = 0.0312$$

since $p_0(\theta)$ gives positive weight only to the value $\theta = 0.4$.

As for the denominator, since $p_1(\theta)$ specifies a continuous distribution, the sum in (12) is replaced by an integral over the space $\Theta_1 = [0,1]$, which is the support of the Uniform[10] distribution chosen as $p_1(\theta)$:

$$\Pr(z = 51 \mid H_1)$$

$$= \int_0^1 p(z = 51 \mid \theta)p_1(\theta)d\theta$$

$$= \int_0^1 \left[\binom{146}{51}\theta^{51}(1 - \theta)^{146-51} \times 1\right] d\theta = 0.0068.$$

From these probabilities, we can derive

$$\mathrm{BF} = \frac{0.0312}{0.0068} = 4.5924,$$

which in this case also equals the posterior odds. Comparing this result with Table 33.7, we can conclude that the data provide "substantial evidence" in favor of the null hypothesis H_0. In other words, H_0 is 4.6 times more likely than H_1, and therefore we have not enough evidence to reject the theory under which the overall probability of high nonattendance is 0.4, as measured the previous year.

Notice that if we chose a different null hypothesis—for instance, $H_0^* : \theta = 0.35$—then using the same procedure shown above, we would compute the BF as

$$\mathrm{BF} = \frac{0.0691}{0.0068} = 10.1630,$$

so that in this case, the null hypothesis would be more than 10 times more likely than the generic alternative, leading to a more refined estimation.

Finally, it is also possible to perform a sensitivity analysis to the choice of the prior distribution for the null hypothesis. Figure 33.7 shows the values of the (log) posterior odds upon varying the value of $\Pr(H_0)$—we plot the graph on the log scale just for better visualization.

As one can appreciate, when a priori we are not too confident about the null hypothesis (for instance, for values lower than 0.2), the weight of evidence is such that a posteriori, we do not favor it. In the range [0.2, 0.4] for the prior, we then obtain updated posterior odds so that the evidence is poor but still favors H_0. When the prior is in [0.4, 0.65], the evidence becomes substantial, whereas in the range [0.65, 0.85], it is strong. Finally, in [0.85, 0.95], the evidence can be considered as very strong, and if we are willing to assign to the null hypothesis a prior probability of at least 0.95, then the evidence in its favor is decisive.

A Comparison With Significance Tests

In this section, we show a brief comparison with the frequentist alternative to the Bayesian

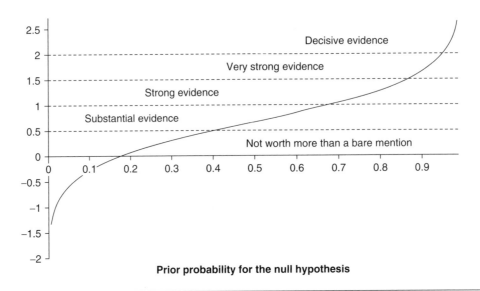

Figure 33.7   Posterior odds in favor of the hypothesis H_0 as a function of $Pr(H_0)$.

testing procedure, the *significance test* (see also Goodman, 1999, for a discussion of the different approaches to hypothesis testing). Suppose we still want to test $H_0 : \theta = 0.4$; the procedure based on the Fisherian significance test aims at calculating the probability that the observed data are "extreme" under the null hypothesis. Intuitively, if this is the case, then either a very unlikely observation obtains, or the null hypothesis is not supported, with the comparison being made with respect to the usual probability yardstick of 0.05.

Practically, given again the assumptions that $Z \sim$ Binomial(θ, n), with $n = 146$ and the observed value of $z = 51$, the significance test is based on the calculation of

$$Pr(Z \leq 51 \mid H_0 \text{ is true}) = \\ Pr(Z \leq 51 \mid \theta = 0.4) = 0.1214. \qquad (13)$$

Generically, in a significance test, we use a "two-sided" alternative hypothesis $H_1 : \theta \neq 0.4$; therefore, we obtain the so-called p value, simply multiplying this probability by 2 (i.e., $p = 0.2428 > 0.05$). Consequently, the typical interpretation of the significance test is that "there is no evidence to claim that the true proportion θ is different from the postulated value 0.4" or that "the data are consistent with the null

hypothesis"—a conclusion similar to the one we reached in the previous section using the Bayesian methodology.

However, care is needed in this interpretation, in order to avoid confusion: By means of Equation 13, we just compute a probability *under the assumption that the null hypothesis is true* (the conditioning event), which we use to support (or disprove) H_0. We cannot interpret (13) as the probability that the null hypothesis is true, simply because under (13), *the null hypothesis is assumed to be true*. Such probability $Pr(H_0 \mid y)$ is only meaningful in the Bayesian approach, where it is indeed calculated as the basis of the test procedure. Moreover, contrary to what happens in (12), Equation 13 does not take into account by any means how likely the observed data are under the alternative hypothesis, which should be used to provide a comparative result.

Model Selection

Another interesting issue related to the Bayes factor is that of *model selection*. With this terminology, we refer to the sensitivity analysis of the prior specification (i.e., not only in the context of hypothesis testing but in the general Bayesian framework).

In fact, whenever we specify a prior distribution (say a model M_0), it is always possible to think of an alternative model, M_1, under which the prior is different. The analysis of the Bayes factor can help identify which of the two models (i.e., which of the two prior specifications) is the most supported by the observed data (notice, though, that this is not the only method that can be applied for model selection—see, for instance, Spiegelhalter, Best, Carlin, & van der Linde, 2002).

A deeper discussion of the problems related to model selection is far from the objective of this chapter, and therefore we avoid it, referring the reader to other pieces of literature such as Raftery (1995).

Monte Carlo Integration

Bayesian inference is centered on the posterior distribution, and the calculation of some relevant syntheses becomes of great interest, as shown in the example above. The distribution might be known in closed form (as, for instance, in the case of conjugated models), but it is often not tractable, meaning that it is extremely difficult to find an analytical result.

The basic idea behind Monte Carlo (MC) integration is that instead of performing calculations analytically, we can compute an approximate result based on a large number of simulations from the model being investigated. The underlying assumption is that the probability distributions involved in the model are all known.

Suppose, for instance, that we know the functional form of the posterior distribution for the parameter of interest θ. We can draw samples from this distribution $\theta^{(1)}, \theta^{(2)}, \ldots, \theta^{(S)}$, and then any summary statistic can be obtained using Monte Carlo integration instead of analytical calculations (possibly involving complex integrals). For example, the posterior mean can be simply obtained as

$$E^{MC}(\theta|\mathbf{y}) = \frac{1}{S} \sum_{i=1}^{S} \theta^{(i)},$$

which represents the MC estimation.

Example (Continued)

Since the Beta distribution is conjugated for the Bernoulli likelihood, we were able to write down the posterior distribution analytically, and therefore we could calculate point and interval estimators through (9) and (11). However, a more convenient, alternative approach is to use MC sampling.

We already found out that the posterior distributions for the θ_{jk}s are Beta with parameters α^*_{jk} and β^*_{jk} depicted in Table 33.6. Using one of the many available statistical packages, we can sample a large number of values, say $S = 10,000$, from these distributions using a random-number generator. For instance, considering just the first group of students ($j = 1$ and $k = 1$), in the language of the software R,[11] this can be done by means of the following commands:

```
alphastar = 6.8
betastar = 13.2
S = 10000
thetaMC = rbeta(S,alphastar,betastar)
```

This produces a vector of S simulations from the posterior distributions ($\alpha^*_{jk}, \beta^*_{jk}$) for the given values alphastar and betastar. In other words, first we assign the values for the hyperparameters and the number of simulations, and then we can draw a MC sample from the posterior (obviously, this operation can be looped over j and k to obtain a MC sample for all the subgroups).

Using these vectors, we can calculate all the estimators of interest. For instance, still using the syntax of R, the MC estimations of the mean and the variance will be as follows:

```
meantheta = (1/S) * sum(thetaMC)
vartheta = (1/(S - 1)) * sum(thetaMC -
  meantheta)^2
```

Table 33.8 presents the MC estimates for $E(\theta_{jk} | \mathbf{y})$ and $Var(\theta_{jk} | \mathbf{y})$, upon varying the number of replications used; as one can see, the approximation level increases with S.

The comparison with the analytical values shows that the MC estimates are close to the real values already using just 1,000 iterations. They become closer to the true values with $S = 100,000$ iterations, and they even equalize the analytical results for some θ.

Table 33.8   Analytical and MC Results for Expected Value and Variances of $\theta_{jk} \mid y$

Groups (Parameters)	Analytical Values		S = 1,000		S = 100,000	
	$E(\theta_{jk} \mid y)$	$Var(\theta_{jk} \mid y)$	$E(\theta_{jk} \mid y)$	$Var(\theta_{jk} \mid y)$	$E(\theta_{jk} \mid y)$	$Var(\theta_{jk} \mid y)$
Aborigine, Primary School (θ_{11})	0.340	0.011	0.338	0.011	0.340	0.011
Aborigine, Grade 1 (θ_{12})	0.363	0.008	0.361	0.009	0.363	0.008
Aborigine, Grade 2 (θ_{13})	0.548	0.009	0.551	0.009	0.548	0.009
Aborigine, Grade 3 (θ_{14})	0.513	0.010	0.514	0.011	0.513	0.010
White, primary school (θ_{21})	0.371	0.011	0.370	0.010	0.372	0.011
White, Grade 1 (θ_{22})	0.145	0.004	0.145	0.004	0.145	0.004
White, Grade 2 (θ_{23})	0.252	0.007	0.252	0.007	0.252	0.007
White, Grade 3 (θ_{24})	0.450	0.010	0.449	0.010	0.450	0.010

NOTE: S = number of values from the posterior distribution.

If we imagine that a new student joins the class, we would be interested in predicting his or her probability distribution for absence from school, knowing which race and age-group he or she belongs to. Recalling the concepts presented earlier and assuming exchangeability between the new students and the ones that we already observed, we can derive the predictive distribution using the following algorithm.

1. Sample a value from the posterior distribution $\theta_{jk} \mid y \sim \text{Beta}(\alpha_{jk}^{\star}, \beta_{jk}^{\star})$.

2. Sample a value for the variable $Y^{\star}$—that is, the indicator variable for the new child that takes on 1 if he or she will experience high nonattendance at school and 0 otherwise, using the sample from the appropriate posterior distribution (upon varying race and age-group), $p(\theta_{jk} \mid y)$.

3. Repeat N times to obtain a sample from the predictive distribution $p(y^{\star} \mid y)$.

Again using the syntax of R, we could use the sample from the posterior distribution for the race and age-group ($j = 1$, $k = 1$) to obtain a sample from the predictive, simply by means of the following command:

```
ystar = rbern(thetaMC)
```

Table 33.9 reports the predictive mean and variance for each group. The expected values generally reflect what we already pointed out for the posterior distribution of the parameters (see Table 33.6). On the other hand, the variability for the predictive distribution is larger than the one observed for the posterior in Table 33.6. This is due to the fact that trying to predict what a future observation will be always includes more variability because, apart from that on the parameters, we have a further layer of uncertainty as the observation of the value for $y^{\star}$ has not been made available yet. This is reflected in the credibility interval as well.

NONCONJUGATED MODELS

Although clearly useful for computational reasons, the property of conjugacy is often too restrictive in practical modeling. When it does not hold, the computation of the posterior distribution is more complicated.

Furthermore, it happens often that *nuisance* parameters are involved in the data model. A typical example is to consider $y \sim \text{Normal}(\mu, \tau)$; in this case, the parameters are the population mean μ and the population variance τ, which will be typically correlated, thus implying a prior joint distribution $p(\mu, \tau)$. Suppose also that, although we are uncertain about the actual value of τ, we are really interested only in the assessment of the mean μ. In this case, through the Bayesian approach, we obtain a joint posterior

Table 33.9 Expected Value and Variance for the Predictive Distribution of the Indicator Variable for Nonattendance at School, for Each Student Group

	Predictive Distribution $p(y^*\mid y)$	
Groups	Mean	Variance
Aborigine, primary school	0.336	0.223
Aborigine, Grade 1	0.365	0.232
Aborigine, Grade 2	0.548	0.248
Aborigine, Grade 3	0.504	0.250
White, primary school	0.365	0.232
White, Grade 1	0.151	0.128
White, Grade 2	0.255	0.190
White, Grade 3	0.449	0.247

distribution $p(\mu, \tau \mid y)$, and we can integrate out the nuisance parameter to obtain the marginal distribution of the parameter of interest:

$$p(\mu|y) = \int_T p(\mu, \tau|y)d\tau,$$

where T is the domain of the variable τ, that is, the interval $[0;\infty]$.

Unfortunately, this marginalization is not usually easy to perform in a standard form, as conjugacy is typically violated by the correlation among the parameters of the model; therefore, approximation by simulations is the solution of choice, and for this reason, computational resources become vital. In fact, the reason for the limited development of Bayesian applications before the 1990s is essentially the lack of powerful calculators able to perform the required integrations.

After the great improvements in computer power, it became relatively easy to perform Bayesian analysis with the advantage that more complex problems could be treated. Among the simulation techniques, the most important are Markov chain Monte Carlo methods.

Markov Chain Monte Carlo Methods

Markov chain Monte Carlo (MCMC) methods are a class of algorithms for sampling from generic probability distributions (again, we do not deal here with technicalities but refer the reader to Robert & Casella, 2004).

A basic concept of MCMC methods is that of the *Markov chain*—that is, a sequence of random variables $Y_0, Y_1, Y_2, \ldots$, for which the distribution of the future state of the process, given the current and past values, depends only on its current state and not on the past:

$$p(Y_{t+1} \mid Y_0, Y_1, \ldots, Y_t) = p(Y_{t+1} \mid Y_t).$$

In a nutshell, MCMC methods are based on the construction of a Markov chain that converges to the desired target distribution p (i.e., the one from which we want to simulate, for instance, the unknown posterior distribution of some parameter of interest). More formally, we say that p is the *stationary* distribution of the Markov chain.

Under regularity conditions (that are usually met by most practical problems), after a sufficiently large number of iterations, referred to as *burn-in,* the chain will forget the initial state and will converge to a unique stationary distribution, which does not depend on t or Y_0. Once convergence is reached, it is possible to calculate any required statistic using MC integration.

Figure 33.8 shows an intuitive representation of the process of convergence for a Markov chain. Initially, the values sampled for the two chains are dependent on the two different starting points. However, after the burn-in period, they tend to converge to the same distribution (this process is also known as *mixing up*). We can then discard the first set of simulated values and use the ones after convergence as a sample from the target distribution.

One of the most popular MCMC methods is the *Gibbs sampling* (Geman & Geman, 1984). The steps needed to perform an MCMC simulation via Gibbs sampling are schematically described in the following.

1. Define an initial value to be arbitrarily assigned to the parameter of interest. The sampling procedure starts from that value.

2. Perform a set of simulations during which the Markov chain converges to the stationary distribution (i.e., the required posterior). It is usually convenient to define more than one chain (two are generally sufficient), starting from distant initial values, in order to assess the convergence more efficiently (see Figure 33.8).

3. Once convergence is reached (this process can be monitored by suitable statistics, such as that proposed by Gelman & Rubin, 1996), draw a sample of values from the estimated target distribution. Using this sample, all the inference of interest can be performed; for instance, the whole distribution might be analyzed (i.e., by means of graphical methods, such as histograms or kernel density estimations), or point estimations such as the posterior mean or median can be computed.

A more detailed description of simulation methods can be found in Gilks et al. (1996) and Gamerman (1997). Jackman (2000) provides an introduction to MCMC methods for social scientists and several applications of Bayesian methodology to political science problems (Jackman 2004a, 2004b).

Example: Analysis of the SAT Score

The SAT score is derived from a 3-hour examination that measures verbal and mathematical reasoning, and it is widely used in the United States. Many colleges and universities use SAT results as part of the data on which they base admissions decisions.

Guber (1999) used the data from the 1997 *Digest of Education Statistics* to evaluate how the average performance of the students in the different U.S. states varies according to variations in some relevant covariates, such as expenditure per student and the percentage of students taking the SAT test.[12] More formally, the variables used in this analysis are the following:

- X_1 = average annual expenditure per student
- X_2 = percentage of students taking the SAT
- Y = total SAT score

The analysis is performed by means of a linear regression model. This is probably the most common statistical analysis and is generally used to predict a response variable using the observed values of a set of covariates.

Since the response Y can be considered as a continuous and symmetric variable, we can describe its variability by means of a Normal distribution (see Table 33.2). For each U.S. state, we can specify a Normal model: $y_i \sim \text{Normal}(\mu_i, \sigma_i^2)$, where μ_i represents the population average. For each $i = 1, \ldots, 50$, the regression model is expressed as follows:[13]

$$\mu_i = \alpha + \beta_1(x_{1i} - \bar{x}_1) + \beta_2(x_{2i} - \bar{x}_2),$$

where α represents the intercept, β_1 is the effect of the variable X_1, and β_2 is the effect of the variable X_2. Each regression coefficient can be interpreted as the variation in Y associated with a unit variation in the relative covariates, *all other things being equal*.

In the Bayesian framework, the coefficients are assumed as random quantities, and therefore we need to define a plausible prior structure. A standard minimally informative prior can then be specified for each of the effects—that is, $\alpha \sim \text{Normal}(0, 0.001)$, $\beta_1 \sim \text{Normal}(0, 0.001)$, $\beta_2 \sim \text{Normal}(0, 0.001)$—notice that in this case, according to WinBUGS syntax, we model the Normal distribution in terms of the precision, rather than the variance, i.e. $0.001 = 1/\sigma_i^2$. This is a simplistic assumption, as we could have different prior knowledge on each of those effects; however, for the sake of simplicity, we use it in this example.

Modeling the regression coefficients implies a probability distribution on the population mean μ_i. As for the population variance, we can further assume that all the observed data y_i share the same value. Hence, we can specify a disperse Gamma prior on the precision $\tau = 1/\sigma^2$ (see Table 33.2): $\tau = 1/\sigma^2 \sim \text{Gamma}(0.001, 0.001)$.

Figure 33.9 shows the DAG representation of the model. The variables y_i and the covariates are observed and therefore are represented in squares. On the other hand, the uncertainty about the parameter μ_i is accounted for by the model for the parameters in the regression

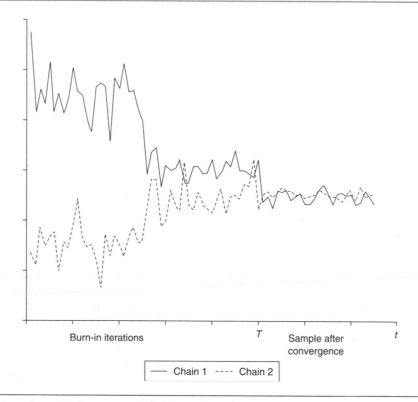

(Burn-in iterations / T / Sample after convergence / t / Chain 1 / Chain 2 labels are part of the figure)

Figure 33.8   A graphical representation of the process of convergence of a Markov chain: The two chains start from very different points, but after the burn-in, they converge to the stationary distribution.

(α, β_1, β_2). Moreover, all the regression parameters are assumed to be independent (therefore they are not linked in the DAG), and finally, the link between the node τ and the variance σ^2 is represented as a dashed arrow to stress the fact that this relationship is essentially deterministic (as are the links connecting the covariates and the regression coefficients to the mean).

We have performed the MCMC simulations[14] using WinBUGS (Bayesian Analysis Using Gibbs Sampling; Spiegelhalter, Thomas, & Best, 2002; see also Congdon, 2001, 2003, for numerous worked examples using WinBUGS and Woodworth (2004) for a tutorial on the use of the software), a freely available software created specifically to analyze Bayesian models through Gibbs sampling.[15] Table 33.10 reports the results from the MCMC simulation based on a sample of 1,000 iterations obtained after a burn-in of 5,000 iterations, to ensure convergence.

The posterior mean of α and β_1 is positive and quite large; in particular, the coefficient α shows a very large standard deviation (*SD*) and hence a wide credibility interval.

From the analysis of β_1, we can conclude that the variable X_1 (the average expenditure for each student in 1 year) is directly associated with the SAT score, so that the higher the expenditure, the larger the observed value of the SAT score. On the other hand, β_2 is negative and smaller than the other parameters; therefore, we can conclude that the covariate X_2 (percentage of students taking the SAT) is negatively associated with the SAT score, meaning that the larger the

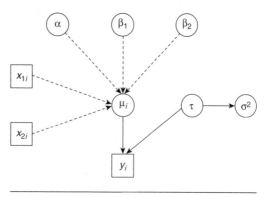

Figure 33.9   DAG of the regression model.

Table 33.10   Synthesis of the MCMC Simulation, Based on a Sample of 1,000 Replicates From the Posterior Distributions

Parameters	Mean	SD	MC Error	2.5%	Median	97.5%	Sample
α	78.56	33.05	1.19	16.52	78.17	146.20	1,000
β_1	163.70	10.29	0.39	142.50	163.80	183.90	1,000
β_2	−4.09	1.28	0.05	−6.41	−4.11	−1.59	1,000

proportion of students taking the SAT, the smaller the score, on average.

If the first relation is relatively easy to understand, as the more money invested in each student means more resources that can potentially help reach better results, it is more difficult to understand the second relation. Guber (1999) proposes a plausible explanation as related to a self-selection of students taking the SAT (as those more interested in attending college) and to the presence of other systems of evaluation (for instance, the ACT is an alternative to the SAT that is popular among many college admission the offices).

CONCLUSIONS

Why should social scientists bother to learn yet another statistical methodology, which involves a more profound knowledge of probability theory and the acquisition of intensive computational skills? In our opinion, there are at least two orders of reasons why this should happen: First, from the philosophical point of view, many logically unsound characteristics of the classical methodology have been pointed out in the literature (see, e.g., Lindley, 2006)—and some of them have been highlighted in this chapter. It has been suggested that scientific methods should not rely on procedures that are potentially dangerous by virtue of some intrinsic logical failures. Bayesian analysis provides a framework that is consistent and more straightforward (as we pointed out earlier) in the interpretation of the findings, therefore representing a more reliable alternative for the problem of statistical inference.

Second, from a more pragmatic point of view, in social sciences, practitioners are confronted with two typical features:

1. Prior knowledge of the phenomenon under study is usually available in the form of previous studies, personal opinions (think, for instance, of election polls), or historical data. The Bayesian approach can include all these pieces of information to provide a coherent estimation procedure.

2. Unlike some natural sciences (such as chemistry or physics), social sciences are characterized by a layer of variability related to the individuals observed in a particular study. Even if the general properties of a system can be postulated and a theory constructed accordingly, in social sciences, we will always observe individual variations. Bayesian methods and the strictly connected principle of exchangeability (which is particularly helpful in such circumstances) can provide a more suitable framework for the problem of inference.

For these reasons, we reckon that the understanding of a problem can be greatly improved when the overall modelization is made in Bayesian terms.

It is true that this involves more complex computations, and generally there is no standard computer software that can be used, simply pressing a button to obtain the results. However, as statisticians, we regard this as a great advantage instead, as it forces every user, even those trained in statistics, to think of the following: (a) What are the questions that we can or cannot answer with the data at hand, (b) what is the information that we have about the problem and how can we use it, and (c) what is the probabilistic structure that can best model the uncertainty related to the problem?

NOTES

1. Several studies in psychology and cognitive science suggest that human reasoning is in fact based on these principles—see, for instance, Dayan, Kakade, and Montague (2000) or Gold and Shadlen (2001).

2. The account of Bayesian statistics that is presented in this chapter is far from exhaustive—more

comprehensive references are Lee (1998), Robert (2001), and the less technical, but quite specific, Spiegelhalter, Abrams, and Myles (2004). Lindley (2006) provides an overview of Bayesian reasoning as applied to different situations dealing with uncertainty.

3. We use the symbol $\Pr(\cdot)$ to indicate the probability of a single event, whereas we use the symbol $p(y)$ to describe the probability distribution associated with a random variable Y.

4. The operator E represents the *expected value* (i.e., the average). Therefore, the notation used here, $p(y) = E_{p(x)}[p(y \mid x)]$, can be read as the average value (with respect to the distribution of X, which we generally refer to as $p(x)$ here) of the conditional distribution of Y given X.

5. A Bernoulli model is used to describe the variability associated with dichotomous quantities—that is, random phenomena that only take on two possible different values (typically 0 or 1). In general, we assume that a variable X has a Bernoulli distribution if it takes on the value 0 in case of a "failure" (i.e., absence of a particular characteristic) or 1 in case of a "success" (i.e., when that characteristic is present).

6. The notation $E(\theta \mid y)$ is used interchangeably with $E_{p(\theta \mid y)}(\theta)$. In either case, the expected value is calculated with respect to the posterior distribution $p(\theta \mid y)$.

7. In this section, we provide just a flavor of Bayesian methods for hypothesis testing: More advanced references include O'Hagan (1994), Lee (1998), Robert (2001), and the less technical Lindley (2006).

8. For the nonmathematical reader: For any continuous probability distribution associated with a variable X, a property holds by which the probability that X is exactly equal to a point is effectively 0 (intuitively, that is why the distribution is continuous: It does not concentrate on any point, but it is spread over an entire interval). Therefore, we can calculate the integral over the whole segment $[0;1]$, including the point 0.4 because $p_1(\theta = 0.4) = 0$.

9. Since the possible value of Y for each child is either 1 or 0 (by the definition of the Bernoulli distribution), the sum of the Y_h will be equal to the total number of "successes" out of the total number of individuals. This situation is naturally described by a Binomial distribution.

10. For the nonmathematical reader: If $X \sim$ Uniform(a, b), then its probability function is defined as

$$p(x) = \frac{1}{b - a}.$$

Therefore, in this case, $(b - a)$ is simply 1, and $p_1(\theta) = 1$. This integral can be solved analytically or by using the extremely precise numerical approximations provided by the most common statistical packages.

11. The software R can be freely downloaded from the R project Web site: www.r-project.org.

12. The data and the paper are publicly available from the American Statistical Association Web site: www.amstat.org/publications/jse/secure/v7n2/datasets.guber.cfm.

13. Although not strictly necessary, centering the variables around their mean improves the convergence of the MCMC chains.

14. Technically, the Bayesian analysis of this model does not require the use of MCMC simulations, as the prior established for the population average is actually conjugate; therefore, in theory, it is possible to work out analytically all the posterior distributions for the parameters of interest (i.e., using a Monte Carlo estimation). Nevertheless, the calculations are computationally intensive, and consequently, the use of MCMC simulations is of great help in estimating the posterior distributions of interest.

15. BUGS and the Windows version (WinBUGS) are freely available from http://www.mrc-bsu.cam.ac.uk/bugs/, where also several worked examples can be found. The idea behind the software is that the user can write his or her own model, specifying the distribution for the data and the prior for the parameters of interest; then, through Gibbs sampling, he or she can obtain a sample from the posterior distribution of the parameters. There are several tools to check the convergence and to visualize the results.

References

Ayyub, B. (2001). *Elicitation of expert opinions for uncertainty and risks*. Boca Raton, FL: Chapman & Hall/CRC.

Bayes, T. (1763). Essay towards solving a problem in the doctrine of chances. *Philosophical Transactions of the Royal Society of London, 53*, 370–418.

Berger, J. (2000). Bayesian analysis: A look at today and thoughts of tomorrow. *Journal of the American Statistical Association, 95*, 1269–1276.

Bernardo, J., & Smith, A. (1999). *Bayesian theory*. New York: John Wiley.

Congdon, P. (2001). *Bayesian statistical modelling*. Chichester, UK: John Wiley.

Congdon, P. (2003). *Applied Bayesian modelling*. Chichester, UK: John Wiley.

Dawid, A. P. (1979). Conditional independence in statistical theory. *Journal of the Royal Statistical Society, Series B, 41*, 1–31.

Dawid, A. P. (2005). Probability and proof. Online appendix to *Analysis of evidence* (2nd ed.), by T. J. Anderson, D. A. Schum, & W. L. Twining. Cambridge, UK: Cambridge University Press.

Dayan, P., Kakade, S., & Montague, P. (2000). Learning and selective attention. *Nature Neuroscience Supplement, 3,* 1218–1223.

de Finetti, B. (1974). *Theory of probability* (Vol. 1). New York: John Wiley.

Edwards, D. (2000). *Introduction to graphical modelling* (2nd ed.). New York: Springer-Verlag.

Efron, B. (1986). Why isn't everyone a Bayesian? *American Statistician, 40,* 1–11.

Fienberg, S. (2006). When did Bayesian inference become Bayesian? *Bayesian Analysis, 1,* 1–40.

Gamerman, D. (1997). *Markov chain Monte Carlo.* London: Chapman & Hall.

Gelman, A., & Rubin, D. (1996). Markov chain Monte Carlo methods in biostatistics. *Statistical Methods in Medical Research, 5,* 339–355.

Geman, S., & Geman, D. (1984). Stochastic relaxation, Gibbs distributions, and the Bayesian restoration of images. *IEEE Transactions on Pattern Analysis and Machine Intelligence, 6,* 721–741.

Gilks, W., Richardson, S., & Spiegelhalter, D. (1996). *Markov chain Monte Carlo in practice.* London: Chapman & Hall.

Gill, J. (2002). *Bayesian methods: A social and behavioral sciences approach.* Boca Raton, FL: Chapman & Hall/CRC.

Gold, J., & Shadlen, M. (2001). Neural computations that underlie decisions about sensory stimuli. *Trends in Cognitive Science, 5,* 10–16.

Goodman, S. (1999). Toward evidence-based medical statistics: 1. The *p* value fallacy. *Annals of Internal Medicine, 130,* 995–1004.

Guber, D. (1999). Getting what you pay for: The debate over equity in public school expenditures. *Journal of Statistical Education, 7*(2), 1–8.

Howie, D. (2002). *Interpreting probability.* Cambridge, UK: Cambridge University Press.

Iversen, G. (1984). *Bayesian statistical inference.* Thousand Oaks, CA: Sage.

Jackman, S. (2000). Estimation and inference via Bayesian simulation: An introduction to Markov chain Monte Carlo. *American Journal of Political Science, 44,* 375–404.

Jackman, S. (2004a). Bayesian analysis for political research. *Annual Review of Political Science, 7,* 483–505.

Jackman, S. (2004b). What do we learn from graduate admissions committees? A multiple rater, latent variable model, with incomplete discrete and continuous indicators. *Political Analysis, 12,* 400–424.

Jeffreys, H. (1961). *Theory of probability* (3rd ed.). Oxford, UK: Oxford University Press.

Lee, P. (1998). *Bayesian statistics.* London: Arnold.

Lindley, D. (2006). *Understanding uncertainty.* Hoboken, NJ: John Wiley.

Luce, B., & O'Hagan, A. (2003). *A primer on Bayesian statistics in health economics and outcome research.* Bethesda, MD: Bayesian Initiative in Health Economics and Outcome Research.

Mood, A., Graybill, F., & Boes, D. (1993). *Introduction to the theory of statistics.* New York: McGraw-Hill.

Mortera, J., & Dawid, A. P. (2006). *Probability and the law* (Research Report 264/2006). London: Department of Statistical Science, University College London.

O'Hagan, A. (1994). *Bayesian inference: Vol. 2B. Kendall's advanced theory of statistics.* London: Arnold.

O'Hagan, A., Buck, C., Daneshkhah, A., Eiser, J., Garthwaite, P., Jenkinson, D., et al. (2006). *Uncertain judgements: Eliciting expert probabilities.* New York: John Wiley.

Paul, S., & Banerjee, M. (1998). Analysis of two-way layout of count data involving multiple counts in each cell. *Journal of the American Statistical Association, 99,* 1419–1429.

Phillips, L. (1973). *Bayesian statistics for social scientists.* London: Thomas Nelson.

Raftery, A. (1995). Bayesian model selection in social research (with discussion). *Sociological Methodology, 25,* 111–196.

Raiffa, H. (1968). *Decision analysis: Introductory lectures on choices under uncertainty.* Reading, MA: Addison Wesley.

Robert, C. (2001). *The Bayesian choice* (2nd ed.). New York: Springer-Verlag.

Robert, C., & Casella, G. (2004). *Monte Carlo statistical methods* (2nd ed.). New York: Springer-Verlag.

Senn, S. (2003). *Dicing with death.* Cambridge, UK: Cambridge University Press.

Spiegelhalter, D., Abrams, K., & Myles, J. (2004). *Bayesian approaches to clinical trials and health-care evaluation.* Chichester, UK: John Wiley.

Spiegelhalter, D., Best, N., Carlin, B., & van der Linde, A. (2002). Bayesian measures of model complexity and fit. *Journal of the Royal Statistical Society, Series B, 64,* 583–639.

Spiegelhalter, D., Thomas, A., & Best, N. (2002). WinBUGS version 1.4 [Computer software]. Cambridge, UK: MRC Biostatistics Unit.

Whittaker, J. (1990). Graphical models in applied multivariate statistics. New York: John Wiley.

Woodworth, G. (2004). *Biostatistics: A Bayesian Introduction.* New York: John Wiley.

34

USING R FOR DATA ANALYSIS

A Best Practice for Research

KEN KELLEY, KEKE LAI, AND PO-JU WU

R is an extremely flexible statistics programming language and environment that is Open Source and freely available for all mainstream operating systems. R has recently experienced an "explosive growth in use and in user contributed software" (Tierney, 2005, p. 7). The "user-contributed software" is one of the most unique and beneficial aspects of R, as a large number of users have contributed code for implementing some of the most up-to-date statistical methods, in addition to R implementing essentially all standard statistical analyses. Because of R's Open Source structure and a community of users dedicated to making R of the highest quality, the computer code on which the methods are based is openly critiqued and improved.[1] The flexibility of R is arguably unmatched by any other statistics program, as its object-oriented programming language allows for the creation of functions that perform customized procedures and/or the automation of tasks that are commonly performed. This flexibility, however, has also kept some researchers away from R. There seems to be a misperception that learning to use R is a daunting challenge. The goals of this chapter include the following: (a) convey that the time spent learning R, which in many situations is a relatively small amount, is a worthwhile investment; (b) illustrate that many commonly performed analyses are straightforward to implement; and (c) show that important methods not available elsewhere can be implemented in R (easily in many cases). In addition to these goals, we will show that an often unrealized benefit of R is that it helps to create "reproducible research," in the sense that a record will exist of the exact analyses performed (e.g., algorithm used, options specified, subsample selected, etc.) so that the results of analyses can be recovered at a later date by the original researcher or by others if necessary (and thus "How was this result obtained?" is never an issue).

Currently, R is maintained by the R Core Development Team. R consists of a base system with optional add-on packages for a wide variety of techniques that are contributed by users from around the world (currently, there are more than 1,100 packages available on the Comprehensive R Archival Network, http://cran.r-project.org/). An R package is a collection of functions and corresponding documentation that work seamlessly with R. R has been called the lingua franca of statistics by the editor of the *Journal of Statistical Software* (de Leeuw, 2005, p. 2).[2]

One of R's most significant advantages over other statistical software is its philosophy. In R, statistical analyses are normally done as a series of steps, with intermediate results being stored in objects, where the objects are later "interrogated" for the information of interest (R Development Core Team, 2007b). This is in contrast to other widely used programs (e.g., SAS and SPSS), which print a large amount of output to the screen. Storing the results in objects so that information can be retrieved at later times allows for easily using the results of one analysis as input for another analysis. Furthermore, because the objects contain all pertinent model information, model modification can be easily performed by manipulation of the objects, a valuable benefit in many cases. R packages for new innovations in statistical computing also tend to become available more quickly than do such developments in other statistical software packages.

As Wilcox (Chapter 18, this volume) notes, a practical problem with modern methods is their implementation. Without accessible tools (i.e., software) to implement new methods, the odds of them being implemented is slim. Because R is cutting edge, many modern methods are available in R.

The need for implementing methods has led to much interest in R over the past few years in the behavioral, educational, and social sciences (BESS), and this trend will likely continue. For example, Doran and Lockwood (2006) provide a tutorial on using R to fit value-added longitudinal models for behavioral and educational data using the *nonlinear mixed effects* (nlme) package (Pinheiro, Bates, DebRoy, & Sarkar, 2007). There is also a special issue in the *Journal of Statistical Software,* with 10 articles on psychometrics in R, and statistical texts used in the applied BESS are beginning to incorporate R (e.g., Fox, 2002; Everitt, 2005). Further evidence comes from Wilcox (Chapter 18, this volume), who provides R functions that implement the methods he has developed for robust methods in R (and S-Plus, a related program).[3] Methods for the Behavioral, Educational, and Social Sciences (MBESS; Kelley, 2007a, 2007b, in press) is an R package that implements methods that are especially helpful for the idiosyncratic needs of the BESS researchers. For example, a set of functions within MBESS is for confidence interval formation for noncentral parameters from t, F, and chi-square distributions, which lead to functions for confidence interval formation for various effect sizes that require noncentral distributions (as discussed in Thompson, Chapter 17, this volume). In addition to confidence interval formation,

MBESS contains functions for sample size planning from the power-analytic and accuracy in parameter estimation approaches for a variety of effects commonly of interest in the BESS.

Perhaps R's biggest hindrance is also its biggest asset, and that is its general and flexible approach to statistical inference. With R, if you know what you want, you can almost always get it . . . but you have to ask for it. Using R requires a more thoughtful approach to data analysis than does using some other programs, but that dates back to the idea of the S language being one where the user interacts with the data, as opposed to a "shotgun" approach, where the computer program provides everything thought to be relevant to the particular problem (Becker, 1994, p. 1). For those who want to stay on the cutting edge of statistical developments, using R is a must. This chapter begins with arithmetic operations and illustration of simple functions. Commonly used methods (e.g., multiple regression, t tests, analysis of variance, longitudinal methods) and advanced techniques within these methods (e.g., confidence intervals for standardized effect sizes, visualization techniques, sample size planning) are then illustrated. We hope this chapter will convey that using R is indeed a *best practice* and can be a valuable tool in research.

Basic R Commands

As mentioned, R is an object-oriented language and environment where objects, whether they be a single number, data set, or model output, are stored within an R session/workspace. These objects can then be used within functions, used to create other objects, or removed as appropriate. In fact, a function itself is an object. The expression <– is the assignment operator (assign what is on the right to the object on the left), as is –> (assign what is on the left to the object on the right). Expressions are entered directly into an R session at the prompt, which is generally denoted >. In this chapter, we use R> as the prompt to emphasize that the R code that follows is directly executable.

Suppose a data set, my.data, exists within an R session (we discuss loading data files in the next section). Typing my.data and then pressing enter/return will display the values contained in the my.data data set:

```
R> my.data
R>    x      y
1     1      2
2     3      4
3     3      8
4     4      9
5     5      10
```

As can be seen, my.data is a 5-by-2 matrix with the first column labeled x and the second labeled y.

The square brackets, "[ ]," can be used to extract information from a data set (or matrix), by specifying the specific values to extract. For example, consider the following commands:

```
R> x <- my.data[,1]
R> y <- ma.data[,2]
R> x
[1] 1 3 3 4 5
R> y
[1] 2 4 8 9 10
```

The first command extracts the first column of my.data, the vector x, and the second command extracts the second column, the vector y. Notice the comma that separates rows and columns. Since no rows were specified, all were selected. We can obtain various pieces of information from the objects by using functions. For example, applying the following functions returns the sum, length, mean, and the variance of the vector x, respectively:

```
R> sum(x) #the summation of x
[1] 16
R> length(x) #the number of components of x
[1] 5
R> mean(x) #the mean of x
[1] 3.2
R> var(x) #the variance of x
[1] 2.2
```

Notice the use of the number sign (#) for comments; anything that follows a number sign on a line is ignored. R uses vectorized arithmetic, which implies that most equations are implemented in R as they are written, both for scalar and matrix algebra (in general). Many computing languages have their own idiosyncratic language for scalar and especially matrix algebra.

To obtain the summary statistics for a matrix instead of a vector, functions can be used in a similar fashion. Using the data set my.data, consider the following commands, which are analogous to the commands applied to the vector:

```
R> sum(my.data)
[1] 49
R> length(my.data)
[1] 2
R> mean(my.data)
x     y
3.2   6.6
R> var(my.data)
       x      y
x      2.2    4.6
y      4.6    11.8
```

In fact, the same functions were used, but R is intelligent enough to apply them differently depending on the type of data specified (e.g., a vector, matrix, data frame, etc.). Notice that the use of length() with x returned 5, the number of elements in the vector, whereas the use of length() with my.data returned 2, indicating there are two variables (i.e., columns), x and y, in the matrix. To obtain the dimensions of matrix or data frame, the dim() function can be used.

```
R> dim(my.data)
[1] 5 2
```

Thus, my.data is a 5 (number of rows) by 2 (number of columns) matrix.

Help files for R functions are available with the help() function. For example, if one were interested in the additional arguments that can be used in the mean, help(mean) could be used. Sometimes one might be interested in a function but not know the name of the function. One possibility is to use the search function, where the term(s) to search are given as a text string in quotes. For example, suppose one were interested in a function to obtain the median but unsure of the function name. The `help.search()` function could be used as

```
R> help.search("median")
```

which returns information on functions that have "median" in their documentation. Another resource is the R Web site, where search facilities allow for searching across help files and mailing list archives: http://r-project.org.

LOADING DATA

R can be used in conjunction with other commonly used statistical (and mathematical) programs, such as Excel, SPSS, and SAS.

Files in the Format of .txt and .dat

The function to load a data set in the form of .txt or .dat file is `read.table()`. This function has a rich array of arguments, but the most common specification is of the form

```
read.table(file, header=FALSE, sep=" ")
```

where `file` is the argument that identifies the file to be loaded into R, `header` is a logical argument of whether the file's first line contains the names of the variables, and `sep` denotes the character used to separate the fields (e.g., "*", ",", "&", etc.).

For example, consider the following command:

```
R> data1 <- read.table(file="data1.dat",
header=TRUE, sep=" ").
```

This command loads the data file "data1.dat" from the current working directory into R (since a specific file location is not specified) and stores the data into the R object `data1`. R's working directory is the folder where R reads and stores files; the default position is where R is installed. If the data file to be loaded is not in the current directory, the user also needs to define the file's position, such as

```
R> data2 <- read.table(file="c:/My
Documents/data2.txt", header=FALSE, sep=",").
```

Notice in the first example that the `sep` argument used a space, whereas a comma was used in the second. This is the case because `data1.dat` and `data2.txt` have fields separated with spaces and commas, respectively. Furthermore, R requires the use of "/" or "\\" to signal directory changes, whereas the notation commonly used for folder separation in Microsoft Windows (i.e., "\") is not appropriate in R; this is the case because R has its origins in Unix, which uses the forward slash. Note that the extension name (e.g., .dat, .txt, .R, etc.) of the file should always be specified. Using `setwd()`, one can set the current working directory to a desired folder, so that one does not need to specify the file's position in the future. To load "data2.txt" in the previous example, instead of defining the file's position, one can use the following commands.

```
R> setwd("C:/My Documents")
R> data2 <- read.table(file="data2.txt",
   header=FALSE, sep=",")
```

It is important to note if the working directory is modified, R, however, sets the default working directory back to where the program is installed whenever R is closed. Because most mainstream statistical and mathematical programs are able to convert data files of their own format into either .dat or .txt format ASCII files, such a conversion and use of the procedures described is always one approach to load data files into R.

Loading Excel Files

We will use the data set in file `salary.xls` to illustrate the methods in this section. This data set, which contains the salaries and other information of 62 professors, comes from Cohen, Cohen, West, and Aiken (2003, pp. 81–82). In future sections, we will also use this data set to illustrate graphical techniques and regression analysis in R. To import Excel files into R requires the RODBC (Lapsley & Ripley, 2007) package. RODBC stands for R Open DataBase Connectivity; ODBC is a standard database access method for connecting database applications. By default, this package is not loaded into an R session. To see which packages are currently loaded, the `search()` function is used, which shows the basic packages that are loaded by default when R is opened:

```
R> search()
```

[1]	".GlobalEnv"	"package:stats"	"package:graphics"
[4]	"package:grDevices"	"package:utils"	"package:datasets"
[7]	"package:methods"	"Autoloads"	"package:base"

When using R in Microsoft Windows, loading a package can be done by selecting the "Packages" tab on the tool bar and then selecting "Load package." A window opens that lists the packages that are installed on the system, which can be selected and loaded. If RODBC is not on the list, it will need to be installed. In Microsoft Windows, select the "Packages" tab on the toolbar and then "Install package(s)," select a server/mirror (generally the closest location), and then choose RODBC. An alternative way to load installed packages is with the library() function, which is illustrated with the RODBC package:

```
R> library(RODBC) .
```

Note that running the library() function without any arguments in the parentheses lists all available packages.

After RODBC is loaded, use odbcConnect Excel() to open an ODBC connection to the Excel database:

```
R>connect <- odbcConnectExcel
("salary.xls").
```

Then function sqlTables() lists the sheets in the Excel file:

```
R> sqlTables(connect)
  TABLE_CAT TABLE_SCHEM TABLE_ NAME
TABLE_TYPE
  1 G:\\Program Files\\R\\R-2.4.1\\salary
<NA> salary$ SYSTEM TABLE
```

Notice that the first sheet, whose name is "salary" (in the column TABLE_NAME), is the sheet that contains the data of interest. Therefore, we use sqlFetch() to obtain the data of interest as follows:

```
R> prof.salary <- sqlFetch(connect, "salary")
```

The data set is then loaded into R and stored in the object called prof.salary.

Loading SPSS Files

The function read.spss(), which is in the *foreign* package (R Development Core Team, 2007a), is used to load an SPSS file into R. For example, after loading the *foreign* package, the following command:

```
R> prof.salary2 <- read.spss(file="salary
.sav")
```

loads salary.sav into R and stores the data set in the object prof.salary2. The file salary.sav contains the same data set as the one in "salary.xls."

Creating and Loading .R Files

After data are created in R, or data of other formats are imported into R, many times it is desirable to save the data in R format, denoted with a .R file extension, so that loading data can be easily done in a future session. This can be achieved by using the dump() function:

```
R> dump("prof.salary", file="prof.salary.R")
```

which creates a file called "prof.salary.R" that contains the object prof.salary in the current working directory. Alternatively, as before when the data were loaded into R, a particular file location can be specified where the data should be "dumped" (i.e., exported/stored).

Loading data from a .R data file can be done in several ways, the easiest of which is to source the data set into R with the source() command, which runs a selected file. When a file consists of a .R data set, that file is then loaded into R and made available for use. For example, to load the data in file "prof.salary.R," consider the following command:

```
R> source("prof.salary.R")
```

GRAPHICAL PROCEDURES

We will use the professor salary data from Cohen et al. (2003), prof.salary, to illustrate some of R's graphical functions.[4] After loading the data, use names() to determine the names of the variables.

```
R> names(prof.salary)
[1] "id" "time" "pub" "sex" "citation" "salary"
```

Here, (a) id represents the identification number; (b) time refers to the time since getting the Ph.D. degree, (c) pub refers to the number of publications, (d) sex represents gender (1 for female and 0 for male), (e) citation represents the citation count, and (f) salary is the professor's current salary. To reference a column of the data set (e.g., pub), one needs to use the dollar sign "$":

```
R> prof.salary$pub
18 3 2 17 11 6 38 48 9 22 30 21 10 27 37 8
13 6 12 29 29 7 6 69 11
. . .
```

A more convenient way is to attach the data set to R's search path. Then the user can reference pub in prof.salary simply with pub.

```
R> attach(prof.salary)
R> pub
18 3 2 17 11 6 38 48 9 22 30 21 10 27 37 8
13 6 12 29 29 7 6 69 11
. . .
```

An attached data set is one where the column names have been "attached," which implies the columns can be directly called upon. At any time, only one data set can be attached. To attach a new data set, one must detach the data set that is currently attached to R. R automatically detaches the data set whenever the user exits the program:

```
R> detach(prof.salary)
R> attach(newdata).
```

Scatterplot

The function plot() can be used to plot data. Although it has a diverse array of arguments, the most common specifications is of the form

```
plot(x, y, type, col, xlim, ylim, xlab, ylab, main),
```

where x is the data to be represented on the abscissa (x-axis) of the plot; y is the data to be represented on the ordinate (y-axis; note that the ordering of the values in x and y must be consistent, meaning that the first element in y is linked to the first element in x, etc.); type is the type of plot (e.g., p for points, l for lines, n for no plotting but setting up the structure of the plot so that points and/or lines are added later); col is the color of the points and lines; xlim and ylim are the ranges of x-axis and y-axis, respectively; xlab and ylab are the labels of x-axis and y-axis, respectively; and main is the title of the plot. All of the above arguments, except x and y, are optional, as R automatically chooses the appropriate settings (usually). For example, to plot the relationship between salary and pub (without the regression line), the following can be used:

```
R> plot(x=pub, y=salary, xlim=c(0, 80),
xlab="Number of Publications",
ylab="Professor's Salary")
```

Note in the application of the plot() function that the range of the x-axis is defined by c(), which is a function to generate vectors by combining the terms (usually numbers). A regression line or a smoothed regression line can be added to the scatterplot if desired. The smoothed regression line fits a regression model to a set of points in a certain "neighborhood," or locally. Such a technique is called *lowess* (or *loess*; see Cleveland, 1979, 1981, for a detailed discussion of smoothed locally weighted regression lines). Adding such a smoothed regression line to a plot can be done as follows using the lines() function combined with the lowess() function:

```
R> lines(lowess(x=pub, y=salary, f=.8)).
```

The lines() function is used to draw lines or line segments, whose basic specification is of the form lines(x, y), where the arguments are the same as

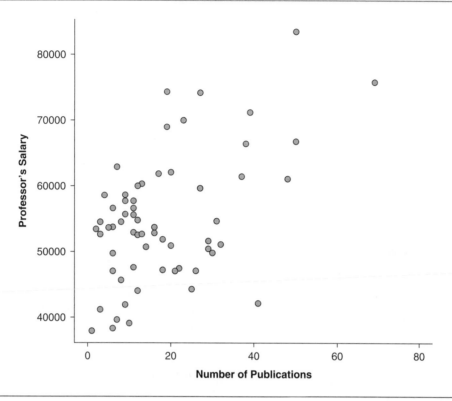

Figure 34.1   Scatterplot for professor's salary as a function of the number of publications.

those in plot(). The lowess() function has f as a smoothing span that defines the width of the neighborhood in which points are treated locally, with a larger f representing a larger "neighborhood," which then gives more smoothness.

The function locator() helps to determine which point in a plot corresponds with which individual in the data. It can be used, for example, to identify outliers and miscoded data. After a scatterplot has been plotted,

```
R> locator()
```

turns the mouse pointer into a cross for point identification by selecting a specific point.

Matrix Plot

The function pairs(), whose arguments are all the same as those of plot(), can be used to produce scatterplot matrices. For example,

```
R> pairs(prof.salary[−1])
```

plots all the variables except the first one (i.e., id) in prof.salary. When the user is interested in only a few variables in a data set, one possibility is to create a new object with only those variables. For example, suppose one is interested in only pub, citation, and salary and does not want all five variables in the matrix plot.

```
R> pub.cit.sal <− data.frame(pub, citation,
   salary)
R> pairs(pub.cit.sal)
```

Histogram

The function to plot histograms is hist(). The basic specification is of the form

```
hist(x, breaks, freq)
```

where x is the data to be plotted, breaks defines the way to determine the location and/or quantity of bins, and freq is a logical statement of whether the histogram represents frequencies

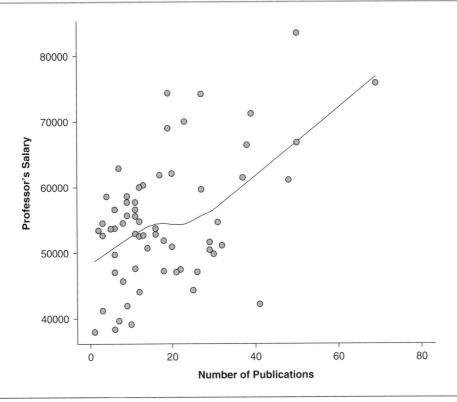

Figure 34.2   A smoothed regression line is added on the scatterplot for professor's salary as a function of the number of publications.

(freq=TRUE) or probability densities (freq=FALSE). For example, to plot histograms of pub, consider the following commands:

```
R> par(mfrow=c(2,2))
R> hist(pub, main="1st")
R> hist(pub, freq=FALSE, main="2nd")
R> hist(pub, freq=FALSE, breaks=10,
    main= "3rd")
R> hist(pub, freq=FALSE, breaks=seq
    (from=0, to=75, by=6), main="4th")
R> lines(density(pub, bw=3))
```

The function par() is used to modify graphical parameters, and it has a rich array of arguments to control line styles, colors, figure arrangement, titles and legends, and much more. With the function par(), the user can customize nearly every aspect of the graphical display. Moreover, all of the arguments in par() can be included in, and thus control, other graphical functions, such as hist() and lines(); put another way, a uniform set of parameters controls all graphical functions and all aspects of figure presentation. The argument mfrow in par() is used to arrange multiple figures on the same page. If mfrow is defined as mfrow=c(m,n), then figures will be arranged into an m-row-by-n-column array.

If breaks in hist() is defined by a single number, then the number is considered by R as the number of bins. In order to define the range of a single bin, the user needs to use a vector giving the breakpoints between the cells. The function to generate such vectors is seq(), whose basic specification is of the form

```
seq(from, to, by)
```

where from and to are the starting and end values of the sequence, respectively, and by is the increment of the sequence. Thus, the fourth histogram bins the data every 6 units. When included as an argument in lines(), the function density() can be used to add a smoothed density line to the histogram. In density(), bw is the smoothing bandwidth to be used, analogous to the span in lowess()—the larger the bw, the smoother the density line. Only when the vertical axis represents the probability can the probability density curve be drawn on the histogram.

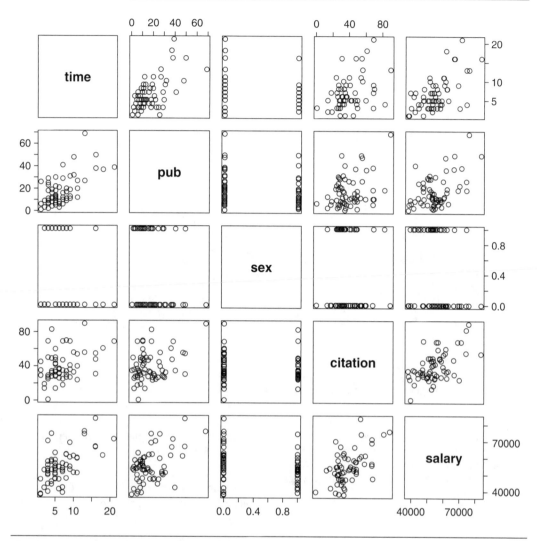

Figure 34.3   Scatterplot matrix for the time since getting the Ph.D. degree, the number of publications, gender, the number of citations, and the current salary.

QQ Plot

The graphical functions to visually inspect for normality are qqnorm(), qqplot(), and qqline(). The function qqnorm() plots the sample quantiles against the theoretical quantiles from a normal distribution. The function qqline() adds a line to the current QQ plot, indicating where the observed values are expected given a normal distribution. The function qqplot() is used to examine the relationship between two variables. Their basic specifications are

```
qqnorm(y)
qqline(y)
qqplot(x, y)
```

where x and y are data to be represented on the x-axis and y-axis, respectively. Suppose we want to examine the normality of pub and the relationship between pub and salary. Because standardized scores are generally preferred in QQ plots, we first standardize pub and salary. The function mean() calculates the mean of a set of data and sd() the standard deviation.

```
R> std.pub <- (pub – mean(pub)) / sd(pub)
R> std.salary <- (salary - mean(salary)) /
      sd(salary)
R> qqnorm(std.pub)
R> qqline(std.pub)
R> qqplot(std.pub, std.salary,
      xlab="Standardized Publications",
```

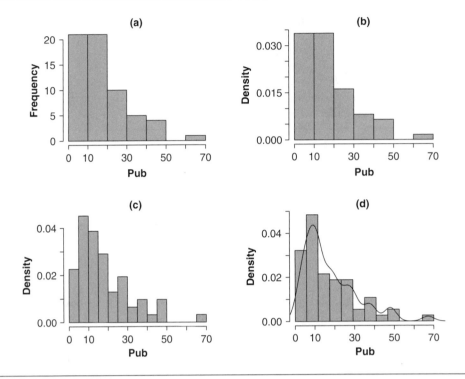

Figure 34.4   Histograms with different specifications for the number of publications.

ylab="Standardized Salary")

Another way to standardize, which is much simpler, is to use scale(), whose common specification is of the form

```
scale(x)
```

where x is the data to be standardized. Therefore, instead of using mean() and sd(), the following commands produce the same QQ plot as Figure 34.5.

```
R> scale.pub <- scale(pub)
R> qqnorm(scale.pub)
R> qqline(scale.pub)
```

MULTIPLE REGRESSION

In this section, we will continue to use the professor salary data set from Cohen et al. (2003), prof.salary, to illustrate how to conduct multiple regression analysis with R.

Fitting Regression Models

R uses ~, +, and −, along with a response variable(s) and K predictor variables, to define a particular model's equation. The generic formula is of the form

```
response variable ~ predictor₁ + (or −)
predictor₂ . . . + (or −) predictorₖ
```

where + signals inclusion of the predictor, and − signals exclusions of the predictor. The minus sign may seem meaningless when defining a new formula, but it is useful in removing predictors from a currently existing model in the context of model modifications.

The function for fitting a linear model is the linear model function, lm(), whose basic specification is in the form of

```
lm(formula, data)
```

where formula is a symbolic description of the model to be fitted (just discussed), and data identifies the particular data set of interest. For example, to study the regression of professors' salaries (Y) conditional on publications (X_1) and citations (X_2), we use the following syntax to fit the model and obtain the model summary:

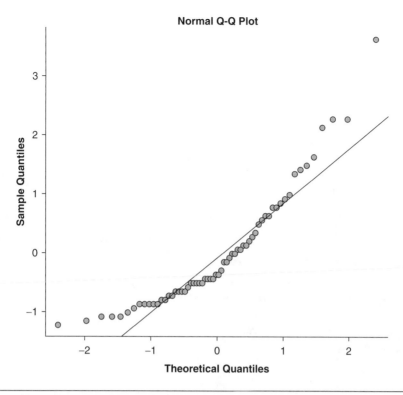

Figure 34.5   QQ plot for the number of publications with the equiangular line indicating the expected publications given the normal distribution as a reference.

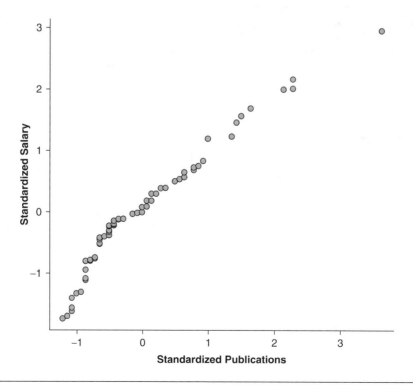

Figure 34.6   QQ plot for standardized professor's current salary and standardized number of publications.

```
R> model1 <— lm(salary ~ pub + citation, data=prof.salary)
R> summary(model1)
Call:
lm(formula=salary ~ pub + citation, data=prof.salary)
Residuals:
```

Min	1Q	Median	3Q	Max
-17133.1	-5218.3	-341.3	5324.1	17670.3

Coefficients:

	Estimate	Std. Error	t value	Pr(>|t|)
(Intercept)	40492.97	2505.39	16.162	< 2e-16 ***
pub	251.75	72.92	3.452	0.001034 **
citation	242.30	59.47	4.074	0.000140 ***

```
—
Signif. codes: 0'***' 0.001'**' 0.01'*' 0.05'.' 0.1' ' 1
Residual standard error: 7519 on 59 degrees of freedom
Multiple R-Squared: 0.4195, Adjusted R-squared: 0.3998
F-statistic: 21.32 on 2 and 59 DF, p-value: 1.076e-07
```

The fitted regression model is thus

$$\hat{Y} = 40493 + 251.8X_1 + 242.3X_2, \quad (1)$$

with the model's squared multiple correlation coefficient being 0.4195. In later sections, we will discuss forming confidence intervals for the population regression coefficients and for the population squared multiple correlation coefficient.

After fitting the model, the residuals can be plotted for visual inspection of the quality of fit:

```
R> par(mfcol=c(2,2))
R> plot(model1)
```

The anova() function can be used to obtain a table of the sums of squares (i.e., an ANOVA table) for the fitted model:

```
R> anova(model1)
Analysis of Variance Table
Response: salary
```

	Df	Sum Sq	Mean Sq	F value	Pr(>F)
pub	1	1472195326	1472195326	26.038	3.743e-06 ***
citation	1	938602110	938602110	16.601	0.0001396 ***
Residuals	59	3335822387	56539362		

```
—
Signif. codes: 0'***' 0.001'**' 0.01'*' 0.05'.' 0.1' ' 1
```

The object model1 contains rich information about the fitted regression model. To see the available objects, the function names() can be used:

```
R> names(model1)
```

[1]	"coefficients"	"residuals"	"effects"	"rank"
[5]	"fitted.values"	"assign"	"qr"	"df.residual"
[9]	"xlevels"	"call"	"terms"	"model"

For example, suppose one wants to check whether there is systematic relationship between the residuals and the predictors. The following commands should be considered (recall how we extracted pub from prof.salary with the sign "$"):

```
R>   par(mfrow=c(2,2))
R>   plot(pub, model1$residuals,
     main="Residuals vs Predictor 1")
```

```
R>   plot(citation, model1$residuals,
     main="Residuals vs Predictor 2")
```

Model Comparison

The function update() is a convenient function for situations where the user needs to fit a model that only differs from a previously fitted model in a nested form. Its basic form is

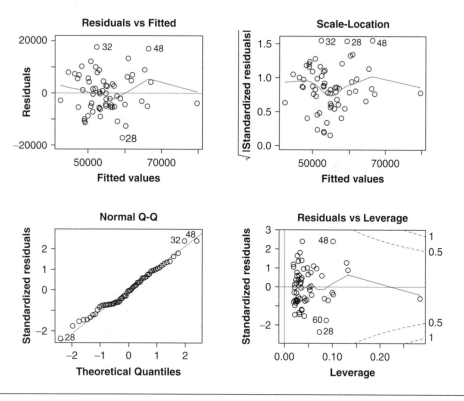

Figure 34.7   Scatterplot for residuals as a function of fitted values with a smoothed regression line (top left), scatterplot for standardized residuals as a function of fitted values (top right), QQ plot for standardized residuals (bottom left), and scatterplot for standardized residuals as a function of leverage (bottom right), all of which are produced by plotting the fitted linear regression model object.

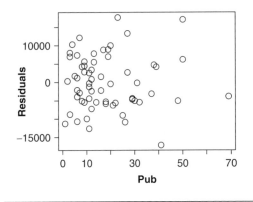
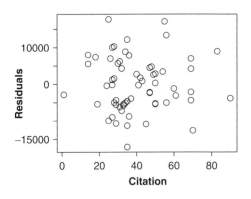

Figure 34.8   Scatterplots for residuals as a function of the number of publications (on the left) and for residuals as a function of the number of citations (on the right).

---

update(object, formula)

---

where object is the originally fitted model, and formula is the new model to be calculated. Also, in defining the new formula, the period (i.e., ".") denotes the corresponding part of the old model formula.

For example, suppose there was interest in adding the predictor time (X_3) and sex (X_4) to the previous model:

```
R> model2 <— update(model1, . ~ . + time + sex)
R> summary(model2)
Call:
lm(formula=salary ~ pub + citation + time + sex, data=prof.salary)
Residuals:
```

Min	1Q	Median	3Q	Max
-13376.8	-4482.5	-989.7	4316.2	20671.2

Coefficients:

	Estimate	Std. Error	t value	Pr(>|t|)
(Intercept)	39587.35	2717.48	14.568	< 2e-16 ***
pub	92.75	85.93	1.079	0.28498
citation	201.93	57.51	3.511	0.00088 ***
time	857.01	287.95	2.976	0.00428 **
sex	-917.77	1859.94	-0.493	0.62360

Signif. codes: 0 '***' 0.001 '**' 0.01 '*' 0.05 '.' 0.1 ' ' 1
Residual standard error: 7077 on 57 degrees of freedom
Multiple R-Squared: 0.5032, Adjusted R-squared: 0.4684
F-statistic: 14.44 on 4 and 57 DF, p-value: 3.357e-08

Given the specifications above, the new model obtained is

$$\hat{Y} = 39587.35 + 92.75X_1 + 201.93X_2 + \\ 857.01X_3 - 917.77X_4, \qquad (2)$$

with the squared multiple correlation coefficient increasing from 0.4195 in the previous model to 0.5032 in the present model.

To compare the full model (i.e., the one with four predictors) with the reduced one (i.e., the one with two predictors), anova() can be used, which evaluates if the sum of squares accounted for by the additional two predictors in the full model leads to a significant decrease in the proportion of variance in Y that was previously unaccounted for in the reduced model. Interested readers may refer to Cohen et al. (2003) or Maxwell and Delaney (2004) for a discussion of model comparisons:

```
R> anova(model1, model2)
Analysis of Variance Table
Model 1: salary ~ pub + citation
Model 2: salary ~ pub + citation + time + sex
```

	Res.Df	RSS	Df	Sum of Sq	F	Pr(>F)
1	59	3335822387				
2	57	2854659884	2	481162503	4.8038	0.01180 *

Signif. codes: 0 '***' 0.001 '**' 0.01 '*' 0.05 '.' 0.1 ' ' 1

Notice that with the additional two variables, a significant reduction ($p < .05$) in the unaccounted for variance was achieved.

Interaction Plots

A general expression for a regression equation containing a two-way interaction is

$$\hat{Y} = \beta_0 + \beta_1 X + \beta_2 Z + \beta_3 X Z, \qquad (3)$$

where β_0 is the intercept; β_1 and β_2 are the regression coefficients of the main effects of X and Z, respectively; and β_3 is the regression coefficient for the interaction between X and Z. Many theories in the social sciences hypothesize that variables interact (there are moderators), and thus the idea of testing interactions is fundamental in many areas of the BESS (Cohen et al., 2003; Aiken & West, 1991). The MBESS R package contains functions to plot two- and three-dimensional interaction plots.

The function intr.plot() in MBESS plots a three-dimensional representation of a multiple regression surface containing one two-way interaction. The most common specification of this function is in the form

```
intr.plot(b.0, b.x, b.z, b.xz, x.min, x.max,
z.min, z.max, hor.angle, vert.angle)
```

where b.0, b.x, b.z, b.xz are the estimates of β_0, β_1, β_2, β_3 in Equation 3, respectively; x.min, x.max, z.min, and z.max define the minimum and maximum values of X and Z of interest, respectively; hor.angle is the horizontal viewing angle; and vert.angle is the vertical viewing angle.

Cohen et al. (2003, pp. 257–263) provide an example for a regression containing one two-way interaction, whose model equation is

$$\hat{Y} = 2 + 0.2X + 0.6Z + 0.4XZ, \qquad (4)$$

with X being [0, 2, 4, 6, 8, 10] and Z being [0, 2, 4, 6, 8, 10]. To replicate this example, intr.plot() can be defined as follows:

```
R>  par(mfrow=c(2,2))
R>  intr.plot(b.0=2, b.x=.2, b.z=.6, b.xz=.4, x.min=0, x.max=10, z.min=0, z.max=10)
R>  intr.plot(b.0=2, b.x=.2, b.z=.6, b.xz=.4, x.min=0, x.max=10, z.min=0, z.max=10, hor.angle=-65,
    vert.angle=15)
R>  intr.plot(b.0=2, b.x=.2, b.z=.6, b.xz=.4, x.min=0, x.max=10, z.min=0, z.max=10, hor.angle=-65,
    vert.angle=5)
R>  intr.plot(b.0=2, b.x=.2, b.z=.6, b.xz=.4, x.min=0, x.max=10, z.min=0, z.max=10, hor.angle=45)
```

The function intr.plot.2d() in MBESS is used to plot regression lines for one two-way interaction, holding one of the predictors (in this function, Z) at values −2, −1, 0, 1, and 2 standard deviations above the mean. The most common specification of intr.plot.2d() is of the form

```
intr.plot.2d(b.0, b.x, b.z, b.xz, x.min, x.max,
mean.z, sd.z)
```

where b.0, b.x, b.z, b.xz, x.min, x.max have the same meaning as those in intr.plot(), and mean.z and sd.z are the mean and standard deviation of Z, respectively.

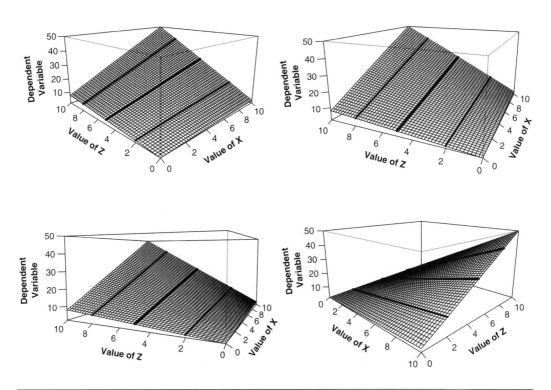

Figure 34.9   Regression surface for $\hat{Y} = 2 + 0.2X + 0.6Z, + 0.4XZ$ displayed from −45° horizontal angle and 15° vertical angle (upper left), −65° horizontal angle and 15° vertical angle (upper right), −65° horizontal angle and 5° vertical angle (lower left), and 45° horizontal angle and 15° vertical angle (lower right). The three bold lines on the regression surface are regression lines holding Z constant at −1, 0, and 1 standard deviations from Z's mean.

Cohen et al. (2003, pp. 263–268) give an example for the regression lines of

$$\hat{Y} = 16 + 2.2X + 2.6Z + 0.4XZ, \qquad (5)$$

holding Z constant at values -1, 0, and 1 standard deviations above the mean, when $X \in [0, 50]$, the mean of Z is 0, and the standard deviation of Z is 1. We can replicate and extend this example by specifying intr.plot.2d() as follows.

R> intr.plot.2d(b.0=16, b.x=2.2, b.z=2.6, b.xz=.4, x.min=0, x.max=50, mean.z=0, sd.z=1)

Confidence Intervals for Regression Parameters

Forming confidence intervals for standardized effect sizes is quite involved because such intervals require the use of noncentral distributions (Kelley, 2007a; Smithson, 2003; Steiger,

2004; Steiger & Fouladi, 1997). Linking the confidence intervals for a statistic of interest and noncentral distributions is achieved with the *confidence interval transformation principle* and the *inversion confidence interval principle,* as discussed in Steiger and Fouladi (1997) and Steiger (2004). Although methods to construct confidence intervals for the population squared multiple correlation coefficient (e.g., Algina & Olejnik, 2000; Smithson, 2003) and for the population standardized regression coefficients (e.g., Kelley, 2007a; Kelley & Maxwell, 2003, in press) have been developed, no mainstream statistical packages besides R with MBESS can perform such tasks without using special programming scripts. Although such confidence intervals are difficult to obtain, they are important nonetheless. The benefits of confidence intervals for standardized effect sizes are the focus of Thompson (Chapter 18, this volume). MBESS has a powerful set of functions that

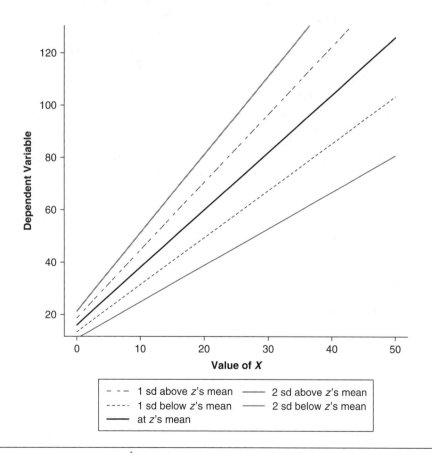

Figure 34.10   Regression lines for $\hat{Y} = 16 + 2.2X + 2.6Z, + 0.4XZ$, holding Z, whose mean is 0 and standard deviation is 1, constant at values -2, -1, 0, 1, and 2 standard deviations from the mean.

implements confidence intervals for noncentral *t*, *F*, and chi-square parameters. These functions (conf.limits.nct(), conf.limts.ncf(), and conf.limits.nc.chi.square()) return the confidence interval for noncentrality parameters, which are then used in other MBESS functions to implement confidence intervals for specific effect sizes that are commonly used in the BESS.

Confidence Intervals for Omnibus Effects

The sample squared multiple correlation coefficient, denoted R^2, often termed the *coefficient of multiple determination,* is defined as

$$R^2 = \frac{SS_{\text{regression}}}{SS_{\text{total}}}. \tag{6}$$

MBESS includes the function ci.R2() to form the exact confidence intervals for the population squared multiple correlation coefficient in the context of fixed (e.g., Smithson, 2003; Steiger, 2004) or random regressors (Algina & Olejnik, 2000; Ding, 1996; Lee, 1971; Steiger & Fouladi, 1992). In almost all applications of multiple regression in the behavioral, educational, and social sciences, regressors are random. When the predictors are random, a basic specification of the function is of the form

```
ci.R2(R2, N, K, conf.level=.95)
```

where R2 is the observed (i.e., sample) squared multiple correlation coefficient, conf.level is the desired confidence interval coverage, N is the sample size, and K is the number of predictors. In the case of fixed regressors, the statement

```
Random.Regressors=FALSE
```

should be included in the ci.R2 function.

For example, to form the 95% exact confidence interval for P^2, the population squared multiple correlation coefficient, of model2, where the predictors are regarded as random, ci.R2() is specified as follows:

```
R> ci.R2(R2=0.5032, N=62, K=4)
$Lower.Conf.Limit.R2
[1] 0.2730107
$Prob.Less.Lower
```

```
[1] 0.025
$Upper.Conf.Limit.R2
[1] 0.6420285
$Prob.Greater.Upper
[1] 0.025
```

Recall that the observed squared multiple correlation coefficient can be obtained from the function summary(). Therefore, the 95% confidence interval for the population squared multiple correlation coefficient of model2, when the predictors are considered random, is

$$CI_{.95} = [0.273 \le P^2 \le 0.642],$$

where $CI_{.95}$ represents a 95% confidence interval.

The function ci.R() is used to obtain the confidence interval for the population multiple correlation coefficient (i.e., P). The most common specification of this function is of the form

```
ci.R(R, N, K, conf.level=.95)
```

where R is the observed multiple correlation coefficient, and other arguments are the same as those in ci.R2(). This function also by default considers the predictors random; when the predictors are fixed, the user can include Random.Regressors=FALSE in the argument.

Because ci.R() and ci.R2() require only the observed multiple correlation coefficient or its square, respectively, and the degrees of freedom, these functions can also be used to form confidence intervals for effects reported in published articles or multiple regression models that were fitted in other programs that do not have the capabilities available in R to implement the confidence intervals.

Confidence Intervals for Targeted Effects

The function confint() is used to construct confidence intervals for unstandardized regression coefficients from a fitted linear model. Its basic specification is of the form

```
confint(object, parm, level=.95)
```

where object is the fitted linear model, parm is the parameter whose confidence intervals are to be formed, and level is the desired confidence level; if parm is not specified, confidence intervals for all regression coefficients will be computed. To obtain a 90% confidence interval for pub in model2, the function confint() is specified as follows:

R> confint(model2, "pub", level=.90)
                  5%   95%
pub   −50.92814   236.4208

Therefore, the 90% confidence interval for the population unstandardized regression coefficient of pub in model2 (i.e., B_1) is $CI_{.90} = [−50.93 \leq B_1 \leq 236.42]$, where $CI_{.90}$ represents a confidence interval at the subscripted level.

However, confint() can only be used to form confidence intervals for unstandardized regression coefficients and always returns a two-tailed confidence interval. Another function to obtain confidence intervals for targeted regression coefficients is ci.rc(), which is contained in the MBESS package. The basic specification of ci.rc() is of the form

---

ci.rc(b.k, s.Y, s.X, N, K, R2.Y_X, R2.k_X.without.k, conf.level=.95)

---

where b.k is the value of the regression coefficient for the kth regressor of interest (i.e., X_k), s.Y is the standard deviation of the response variable Y, s.X is the standard deviation of X_k, N is sample size, K is the total number of regressors, R2.Y_X is the squared multiple correlation coefficient predicting Y from all the predictors, R2.k_X.without.k is the squared multiple correlation coefficient predicting X_k from the remaining $K - 1$ predictors, and conf.level is the desired confidence interval coverage.[5] Unlike confint(), which is based on R's fitted linear model objects, ci.rc() requires only summary statistics, and thus the output from other statistical programs and published articles can be used as input.

For example, to obtain the 90% confidence interval for the population regression coefficient of pub in model2, consider the following steps:

R>model.pub <− update(model2, pub ~ . − pub)
R> summary(model.pub)
Call:
. . .
Residuals:
. . .
Coefficients:
. . .

Multiple R-Squared: 0.433, Adjusted R-squared: 0.4037
. . .
R> ci.rc(b.k=92.75, s.Y=sd(salary), s.X=sd(pub), N=62, K=4, R2.Y_X=0.5032, R2.k_X.without.k=0.433, conf.level=.90)
$Lower.Limit.for.beta.k
[1] −50.92821
$Prob.Less.Lower
[1] 0.05
$Upper.Limit.for.beta.k
[1] 236.4282
$Prob.Greater.Upper
[1] 0.05

Therefore, the 90% confidence interval for the population unstandardized regression coefficient of pub in model2 (i.e., B_1), computed by ci.rc(), is

$$CI_{.90} = [−50.93 \leq B_1 \leq 236.42],$$

which is the same as what confint() returned previously. Moreover, with some additional arguments (namely, alpha.lower and alpha .upper), ci.rc() is also able to form one-tailed confidence intervals or other nonsymmetric confidence intervals, which is not possible with confint(). Note that R2.Y_X is obtained from model2's summary table (the model with all predictors), and R2.k_X.without.k is obtained from model.pub's summary table (the model without the predictor of interest).

The function ci.src() in MBESS is used to form confidence intervals for the population standardized regression coefficient. A basic specification of this function is of the form

---

ci.src(beta.k, SE.beta.k, N, K, conf.level=0.95)

---

where beta.k is the standardized regression coefficient of the kth predictor (i.e., the one of interest), SE.beta.k is the standard error of the kth regression coefficient, and N, K, and conf.level are the same as those in ci.rc().

For example, suppose we want to obtain the 95% confidence interval for the population standardized regression coefficient of pub in model2. Because the data used in model2 are unstandardized and beta.k in ci.src() requires standardized ones, we first need to standardize the fitted model's regression coefficients. When the user inputs standardized data to fit the linear model, the regression coefficients returned are already standardized.

```
R> std.pub <— scale(pub)
R> std.time <— scale(time)
R> std.citation <— scale(citation)
R> std.sex <— scale(sex)
R> std.model2 <— lm(std.salary ~ std.pub + std.time + std.citation + std.sex)
R> summary(std.model2)
Call:

. . .

Residuals:

. . .

Coefficients:
```

	Estimate	Std. Error	t value	Pr(>|t|)
. . .				
std.pub	1.338e-01	1.240e-01	1.079	0.28498

```
. . .

R> ci.src(beta.k=0.1338, SE.beta.k=0.124, N=62, K=4)
$Lower.Limit.for.beta.k
[1] -0.1110479
$Prob.Less.Lower
[1] 0.025
$Upper.Limit.for.beta.k
[1] 0.3774881
$Prob.Greater.Upper
[1] 0.025
```

Thus, the 95% confidence interval for the population standardized regression coefficient of pub in model2 (i.e., β_1) is $CI_{.95} = [-0.111 \le \beta_1 \le 0.377]$.

Sample Size Planning in Multiple Regression

Sample Size Planning for the Omnibus Effect: Power Analysis

Cohen (1988) discussed methods of sample size planning for the test of the null hypothesis that $P^2 = 0$, where P^2 is the population squared multiple correlation coefficient. Cohen provided an extensive set of tables for sample size determination for a large but limited set of conditions. Those methods, and related ones, have been implemented in MBESS so that researchers can plan sample size for a desired power for the omnibus effect in multiple regression.

The function ss.power.R2() in MBESS can be used to plan sample size so that the test of the squared multiple correlation coefficient has sufficient power. Its basic specification is of the form

```
ss.power.R2(Population.R2, alpha.level=0.05,
desired.power=0.85, K)
```

where Population.R2 is the population squared multiple correlation coefficient, alpha.level is the Type I error rate, desired.power is the desired power, and K is the number of predictors.

For example, to obtain the necessary sample size when the population multiple correlation coefficient is believed to be .25, Type I error rate is set to .05, the desired power is .85, and the regression model includes four predictors, ss.power.R2() would be specified as

```
R> ss.power.R2(Population.R2=.25,
alpha.level=0.05, desired.power=0.85, K=4)
   $Necessary.Sample.Size
   [1] 46
   $Actual.Power
   [1] 0.8569869
   $Noncentral.F.Parm
   [1] 15.33333
```

$Effect.Size
[1] 0.3333333

Thus, the necessary sample size is 46.

Sample Size Planning for the Omnibus Effect:
Accuracy in Parameter Estimation (AIPE)

The sample size for multiple regression can be planned in such manner that the confidence interval for the population squared multiple correlation coefficient is sufficiently narrow; "sufficiently narrow" is something defined by researchers depending on the particular situation, much like the desired level of power. This approach to sample size planning is termed *accuracy in parameter estimation* (AIPE; Kelley & Maxwell, 2003; Kelley, Maxwell, & Rausch, 2003; Kelley & Rausch, 2006) because the goal of such an approach is to obtain an accurate parameter estimates. Interested readers may refer to Kelley and Maxwell (2003, in press) and Kelley (2007b, 2007c) for a discussion of AIPE for omnibus effects in multiple regression.

The function ss.aipe.R2() in MBESS can be used to determine necessary sample size for the multiple correlation coefficient so that the confidence interval for the population multiple correlation coefficient is sufficiently narrow. Its basic specification is of the form

ss.aipe.R2(Population.R2, conf.level=.95, width, Random.Regressors, K, verify.ss=FALSE)

where width is the width of the confidence interval, Random.Regressors is a logical statement of whether the predictors are random (TRUE) or fixed (FALSE), conf.level is the confidence interval coverage, Population.R2 and K are the same as those arguments in ss.power.R2(), and verify.ss is a logical statement of whether the user requires the exact sample size (verify.ss=TRUE), which involves a somewhat time-consuming set of intense calculations (specifically an a priori Monte Carlo simulation), or a close approximation (verify.ss=FALSE).

For example, suppose the population squared multiple correlation coefficient is believed to be .5, the confidence level is set to .95, and the regression model includes five random predictors. If one wishes to obtain the exact necessary sample size so that the expected full confidence interval width is .25, ss.aipe.R2() would be specified as

R> ss.aipe.R2(Population.R2=.5, width=.25,
K=5, conf.level=.95, verify.ss=TRUE)
  $Required.Sample.Size
  [1] 125

An additional specification in ss.aipe.R2() allows for a probabilistic component that the confidence interval obtained in a study will be sufficiently narrow with some desired degree of probability (i.e., assurance), which is accomplished with the additional argument assurance. For example, suppose one wishes to have 99% assurance that the 95% confidence interval will be no wider than .25 units. The ss.aipe.R2() function would be specified as

R> ss.aipe.R2(Population.R2=.5, width=.25,
K=5, conf.level=.95, assurance=.99,
verify.ss=TRUE)
  $Required.Sample.Size
  [1] 145

Sample Size Planning for Targeted Effects:
Power for Regression Coefficients

Cohen (1988) and Maxwell (2000) develop methods to plan the necessary sample size so that the hypothesis test of a targeted regressor has a sufficient degree of statistical power to reject the null hypothesis that the regressor is zero in the population. Those methods have been implemented in MBESS with the ss.power.rc() function, which returns the necessary sample size from the power approach for a targeted regression coefficient. Its basic specification is of the form

ss.power.rc(Rho2.Y_X, Rho2.Y_X.without.k,
K, desired.power=0.85, alpha.level=0.05)

where Rho2.Y_X is the population squared multiple correlation coefficient, Rho2.Y_X.without.k is the population squared multiple correlation coefficient predicting the response predictor variable from the remaining $K-1$ predictors, K is the total number of predictors, desired.power is the desired power level, and alpha.level is the Type I error rate. Maxwell (2000) describes an example in which the population squared multiple correlation coefficient is .131 and reduces to .068 when the predictor of interest is removed in a situation where there are five regressors.[6] This example can be implemented with ss.power.rc() as follows:

```
R> ss.power.rc(Rho2.Y_X=0.131,
Rho2.Y_X.without.k= 0.068, K=5,
alpha.level=.05, desired.power=.80)
   $Necessary.Sample.Size
   [1] 111
   $Actual.Power
   [1] 0.8025474
   $Noncentral.t.Parm
   [1] 2.836755
   $Effect.Size.NC.t
   [1] 0.2692529
```

Thus, in the situation described, necessary sample size in order to have a power of .80 is 111.[7]

Sample Size Planning for Targeted Effects: AIPE for a Regression Coefficient

Kelley and Maxwell (2003, in press) develop methods for sample size planning for unstandardized and standardized regression coefficients from the AIPE perspective. These methods have been implemented in functions ss.aipe.rc() and ss.aipe.src() from within MBESS so that the necessary sample size can be obtained. The basic specification of the ss.aipe.rc() function is of the form

```
ss.aipe.rc(Rho2.Y_X, Rho2.k_X.without.k,
K, b.k, width, sigma.Y, sigma.X.k, conf.level=.95)
```

where $Rho2.Y\_X$ is the population squared multiple correlation coefficient, K is the number of predictors, b.k is the regression coefficient for the kth predictor variable (i.e., the predictor of interest), Rho2.k_X.without.k is the population squared multiple correlation coefficient predicting the kth predictor from the remaining $K-1$ predictors, sigma.Y is the population standard deviation of the response variable, sigma.X.k is the population standard deviation of the kth predictor variable, and width and conf.level are the same as those in ss.aipe.R2() function. From the example for the power of an individual regression coefficient, suppose that the standard deviation of the dependent variable is 25 and the standard deviation of the predictor of interest is 100. The regression coefficient of interest in such a situation is 1.18. Supposing a desired confidence interval width of .10, necessary sample size can be planned as follows:

```
R> ss.aipe.rc(Rho2.Y_X=0.131,
Rho2.k_X.without.k=0.068,
```

```
   K=5, b.k=1.18, width=.10,
which.width="Full", sigma.Y=25,
   sigma.X.k=100)
   [1] 99
```

Thus, necessary sample size in the situation described is 99.

The function ss.aipe.src() in MBESS can be used to determine the necessary sample size for the AIPE approach for a standardized regression coefficient of interest. The most common specification of this function is of the same form as given in ss.aipe.src(), except the standardized regression coefficient is specified. Supposing the desired width is .30 for the standardized regression coefficient of .294, necessary sample size can be planned as follows:

```
R> ss.aipe.src(Rho2.Y_X=0.131,
Rho2.k_X.without.k=0.068,
   K=5, beta.k=.294, width=.30,
which.width="Full")
   [1] 173
```

where beta.k is used instead of b.k to emphasize that the regression coefficient is standardized. Thus, the necessary sample size in such situation is 173.

STUDENT'S T TEST IN R

Student's t test is used for testing hypotheses about means when the population variance is unknown. There are three types of t tests: (a) one-sample t test, which compares the sample mean to a specified population mean; (b) paired-samples t test, which compares the means of two paired samples; and (c) the two-group t test, which compares the means of two independent samples. We can use the function t.test() to do all three types of t tests.

One-Sample t Test

When a one-sample t test is desired, the basic specification of t.test() is of the form

```
t.test(x, mu, conf.level=.95)
```

where x is the particular data of interest, mu is the specified population value of the mean, and conf.level is desired confidence interval coverage.

To illustrate the one-sample t test, we employ the data reported in Hand, Daly, Lunn,

McConway, and Ostrowski (1994) on the estimation of room length. Shortly after metric units were officially introduced in Australia, a group of 44 students was asked to estimate in meters the width of the lecture hall in which they were sitting. The true width of the hall was 13.1 meters. To test the hypothesis that students' estimation of the width of the hall in metric units was equal to the true value, the following code is used to load the data and then to test the hypothesis:

```
R> meter <- c(8,9,10,10,10,10,10,10,11,11,
11,11,12,12,13,13,13,14,14,14,15,15,15,15,15,
15,15,15,16,16,16,17,17,17,17,18,18,20,22,25,
27,35,38,40)
    R> t.test(meter, mu=13.1)
    One Sample t-test
    data: meter
    t = 2.7135, df = 43, p-value = 0.009539
    alternative hypothesis: true mean is not
equal to 13.1
    95 percent confidence interval:
    13.85056 18.19490
    sample estimates:
    mean of x
    16.02273
```

The summary table shows that the t statistic, with 43 degrees of freedom, is 2.714 with a corresponding (two-sided) p value less than .01. The 95% confidence interval for the population mean is

$$CI_{.95} = [13.851 \leq \mu \leq 18.195],$$

where μ is the population mean. Thus, the students' estimate of the room length in meters differed significantly from its actual value. Both p value and confidence interval reveal that it is unlikely to observe data such as those in this study if the students were able to make a correct guess in meters.[8]

Paired-Sample t Test

When a paired-sample t test is desired, t.test() is specified as

---

t.test(x, y, mu, paired=TRUE, conf.level=.95)

---

where x and y are the paired groups of data of interest, paired=TRUE signals that the procedure for the paired t test is to be used, and other arguments are the same as those in the one-sample t test context.

We will demonstrate a paired-samples t test using the data from Cushny and Peebles (1905), which was used by Gosset ("Student") to demonstrate the theoretical developments of the t distribution (Student, 1908). The data are the average number of hours of sleep gained by 10 patients on two different drugs, Dextro-hyoscyamine hydrobromide and Laevo-hyoscyamine hydrobromide. Gosset used the paired-sample t test to test the hypothesis that the average sleep gain by two different drugs was the same. We define two vectors, Dextro and Laevo with the scores from Dextro-hyoscyamine hydrobromide and Laevo-hyoscyamine hydrobromide, respectively, and then implement a paired-samples t test:

```
R> Dextro <- c(.7, -1.6, -.2, -1.2, -.1, 3.4,
3.7, .8, 0, 2)
    R> Laevo <- c(1.9, .8, 1.1, .1, -.1, 4.4, 5.5,
1.6, 4.6, 3.4)
    R> t.test(Dextro, Laevo, paired=TRUE)
    Paired t-test
    data: Dextro and Laevo
    t = -4.0621, df = 9, p-value = 0.002833
    alternative hypothesis: true difference in
means is not equal to 0
    95 percent confidence interval:
    -2.4598858 -0.7001142
    sample estimates:
    mean of the differences
    -1.58
```

Thus, the observed t statistic, with 9 degrees of freedom, is -4.0621 with a corresponding (two-sided) p value of .0028. The mean of the differences is -1.58 in the sample, and the 95% confidence interval for the population mean difference is

$$CI_{.95} = [-2.460 \leq \mu_D - \mu_L \leq -0.700],$$

where μ_D and μ_L are the population mean of the hours of sleep for Dextro and Laevo, respectively.

Another way to conduct a paired-sample t test is to calculate the difference between each pair first and then conduct a one-sample t test on the differences. Therefore, an equivalent way to test the hypothesis that the two drugs have equivalent effects on drugs is to calculate the differences and use the t.test() function in the same manner as was done previously in the one-sample context:

```
R> D <- Dextro—Laevo
R> t.test(D, mu=0)
One Sample t-test
data: D
t = −4.0621, df = 9, p−value = 0.002833
alternative hypothesis: true mean is not
equal to 0
95 percent confidence interval:
−2.4598858 −0.7001142
sample estimates:
mean of x
−1.58
```

Notice that the results of the analyses are the same.[9]

Two Independent Group *t* Test

To perform a two independent group *t* test, the most common specification of t.test() is of the form

```
t.test(y ~ x, var.equal=TRUE)
```

where x and y are the particular groups of data of interest, and var.equal is a logical statement of whether the variances of the two groups of data are assumed equal in the population. By default, R assumes that the variances are unequal and uses a degrees-of-freedom correction based on the degree of observed heterogeneity of variance. Because most other statistical programs assume homogeneity of variance, in that they use the standard two-group *t* test, we have specified var.equal=TRUE in our example for comparison purposes.

We use the data reported from Thompson (Chapter 17, this volume), denoted LibQUAL+™, which is a random sample of perceived quality of academic library services from a larger data set (see also Thompson, Cook, & Kyrillidou, 2005, 2006). The data have been added as a data set in the MBESS package and can be loaded with the following data function:

```
R> data(LibQUAL).
```

The grouping variables are (a) Role (undergraduate student, graduate student, and faculty) and (b) Sex. The outcome variables are (a) LIBQ_tot, (b) ServAffe, (c) InfoCont, (d) LibPlace, (e) Outcome, and (f) Satisfac. Thompson (Chapter 17, this volume) uses a *t* test to compare the sex differences on the outcome variable LIBQ_tot and conducts a two-way ANOVA to

compare the effects of role and sex on LIBQ_tot. In the following section, we will demonstrate how to use t.test() and other functions to reproduce the methods discussed in Chapter 17 and related methods with R and MBESS. More specifically, we will discuss how to compute standardized effect sizes, confidence intervals for standardized mean differences, and sample size planning in the *t* test context in R.

After loading the data set LibQUAL, the function class() is used to determine the attribute of the object LibQUAL.

```
R> class(LibQUAL)
[1] "data.frame"
```

Thus, LibQUAL is a data frame, which is a special type of data structure where numeric and categorical variables can be stored. We also need to verify whether Sex has the attribute of a factor because only when a variable is defined as factor can that variable be used as a grouping variable:

```
R> class(LibQUAL$Sex)
[1] "integer"
```

Because the vector Sex is specified as an integer, it needs to be converted to a factor for analysis. Notice that the dollar sign ($) is used to extract a named column from the data frame. We use the function as.factor() to convert the attribute into a factor and then redefine Sex in the data frame as a factor (notice that the dollar sign is used on both sides of the assignment operator) so that we can easily perform the two-group *t* test:

```
R> LibQUAL$Sex <- as.factor(LibQUAL$Sex)
R> class(LibQUAL$Sex)
[1] "factor"
R> t.test(LIBQ_tot ~ Sex, data=LibQUAL,
var.equal=TRUE)
Two Sample t-test
data: LIBQ_tot by Sex
t = −0.2381, df = 64, p−value = 0.8125
alternative hypothesis: true difference in
means is not equal to 0
95 percent confidence interval:
−0.7682029 0.6045665
sample estimates:
mean in group 0 mean in group 1
6.893636 6.975455
```

Notice that the use of the function t.test() on two independent samples is a bit different from the other two kinds of *t* test. A formula much like that discussed in the lm() function is used where the dependent variable, LIBQ_tot, is predicted by the grouping variable, Sex. This implies that the outcome variable LIBQ_tot is modeled by the grouped variable Sex, and the model formula form in t.test()is the general format used in R for model specification.

From the output, the *t* statistic is −.2381 with 64 degrees of freedom with a corresponding (two-sided) *p* value of .8125. The mean of the first group (labeled 0) is 6.894, and the second group (labeled 1) is 6.975 in the sample. The 95% confidence interval for the population mean difference is

$$CI_{.95} = [-0.768 \le \mu_0 - \mu_1 \le 0.605].$$

Alternatively, we can perform the two-group *t* test in a similar fashion as was done with the one-sample *t* test and the paired-samples *t* test. That is, we can specify the form

---

t.test(x, y, mu, var.equal=TRUE, conf.level=.95)

---

where x and y are the two independent groups of data of interest. Notice that compared to paired-samples *t* tests, we exclude the command paired=TRUE but add the command var.equal=TRUE.

Confidence Intervals for Effect Sizes Related to the Group Means and Group Mean Differences

Although the confidence interval from the *t* test output provides helpful information, at times what is of interest is the standardized mean difference and its corresponding confidence interval. A commonly used effect size in the *t* test is the standardized mean difference (e.g., Cohen, 1988), *d*, which is defined as

$$d = \frac{M_1 - M_2}{s} \quad (7)$$

in the sample, where M_1 is the mean of Group 1, M_2 is the mean of Group 2, and *s* is the square root of the pooled variance, assumed equal across groups in the population.

The function smd() in MBESS can be used to calculate the standardized mean difference. It is most commonly specified in the form

---

smd(Group.1, Group.2)

---

where Group.1 and Group.2 are the particular data of interest from Group 1 and Group 2, respectively. Hence, specifying smd() as follows returns the standardized mean difference between the scores on the LibQUAL+™ total scale of the female group (Sex=0) and of the male group (Sex=1):[10]

R> smd(Group.1=LibQUAL[1:33,4], Group.2=LibQUAL[34:66,4])
[1] −0.05862421

To obtain the unbiased estimate of the population standardized mean difference (*d* is slightly biased), the option Unbiased=TRUE can be used:

R> smd(Group.1=LibQUAL[1:33,4], Group.2=LibQUAL[34:66,4], Unbiased=TRUE)
[1] −0.05793406

The correction used in the function smd() yields an exactly unbiased statistic (based in part on the gamma function), whereas that used in Thompson (Chapter 17, this volume) yields an approximately unbiased statistic (see Hedges & Olkin, 1985, for derivations and discussion of the exact and approximately unbiased statistics).

We can obtain the confidence interval for the standardized mean difference with the function ci.smd() in MBESS. Its basic specification is of the form

---

ci.smd(smd, n.1, n.2, conf.level)

---

where smd is the observed standardized mean difference; n.1 and n.2 are sample sizes of Group 1 and Group 2, respectively; and conf.level is the desired confidence interval coverage. Therefore, to construct the 95% confidence interval for the standardized mean difference in the scores on the LibQUAL+™ total scale of the female group and the male group, ci.smd() could be specified as follows:

R> ci.smd(smd=−0.05862421, n.1=33, n.2=33, conf.level=.95)
$Lower.Conf.Limit.smd
[1] −0.541012
$smd
[1] −0.05862421
$Upper.Conf.Limit.smd
[1] 0.4242205

Power Analysis for *t* Test

It is important to consider statistical power when designing a study, as the power of a statistical test is the probability that it will yield statistically significant results (e.g., see Cohen, 1988, for a review). Since power is a function of Type I error rate, standardized effect size, and sample size, after specifying the Type I error rate and standardized effect size, the necessary sample size given a specified power value or power given a specified sample size can be determined. The function power.t.test() in R is used to plan necessary sample size. It is usually specified as

---

power.t.test(power, delta, sd, type)

---

where power is the desired power level, delta is the (unstandardized) mean difference, sd is the population standard deviation, and type is the type of the *t* test ("one.sample" for one sample, "two.sample" for two independent sample, and "paired" for paired sample). Note that when sd=1 (which is the case by default), delta can be regarded as the standardized mean difference. For example, we can get the necessary sample size for each group to achieve a power = 0.8 for a two-sample *t* test when the standardized mean difference is 0.5:

R> power.t.test(power=.8, delta=.5,
type="two.sample"),
    Two-sample t test power calculation
    n = 63.76576
    delta = 0.5
    sd = 1
    sig.level = 0.05
    power = 0.8
    alternative = two.sided
    NOTE: n is number in *each* group

Thus, after rounding to the next larger integer, it can be seen that a per group sample size of 64 is necessary to achieve a power = 0.8 (128 is thus the total sample size). Alternatively, power can be determined when n is specified (instead of power) in the power.t.test() function.

AIPE for Mean Differences and Standardized Mean Differences

The AIPE approach to sample size planning can be used in a similar manner, where what is of interest is the necessary sample size for the expected confidence interval width to be sufficiently narrow, optionally with some assurance that the confidence interval will be sufficiently narrow (Kelley & Rausch, 2006). For example, suppose the population standardized mean difference is .50, and it is desired that the total 95% confidence interval width be .50. The ss.aipe.sm() function in MBESS could be specified as follows:

R> ss.aipe.smd(delta=.5, conf.level=.95,
width=.50)
    [1] 127

Because the standard procedure is for the expected width, which implies that roughly 50% of the time, the confidence interval will be wider than desired, a desired degree of assurance can be incorporated into the sample size procedure to specify the probability that a confidence interval will not be wider than desired. For example, suppose one would like to be 99% assurance that the computed confidence interval will be sufficiently narrow. The ss.aipe.smd() function could be specified as follows:

R> ss.aipe.smd(delta=.5, conf.level=.95,
width=.50, assurance=.99)
    [1] 133

ANALYSIS OF VARIANCE

Analysis of variance (ANOVA) is a method to compare the means of two or more groups. The function for fitting an ANOVA model in R is aov(), whose usage is very similar to that of the lm() function illustrated for the multiple regression examples. The difference between aov() and lm() is that, when summary() is used to present the model summary, aov() objects return an ANOVA table, whereas lm() objects return a regression table. There is a function anova(), not to be confused with aov(), that is used to return the ANOVA table of an existing object or a comparison between nested models.

The basic specification of the function for ANOVA is aov() and is used in the following manner:

---

aov(formula, data)

---

where both arguments are the same as those in lm(). Note that the grouping variable in the formula must have one or more factors (i.e., groups) identified. For example, to perform ANOVA on the LibQUAL+™ data, where the hypothesis is that no mean differences exist in the effects of Role on the outcome variable, LIBQ_tot, consider the following specification of aov():

R> LibQUAL.aov.Role <- aov(LIBQ_tot ~ Role, data=LibQUAL).

The object LibQUAL.aov.Role contains the necessary information to report results, but it does so in only a limited way. The results of interest (i.e., the ANOVA table) are obtained by using either summary() or anova() on the object fitted by aov():

R> summary(LibQUAL.aov.Role)

	Df	Sum Sq	Mean Sq	F value	Pr(>F)
Role	2	2.698	1.349	0.6961	0.5023
Residuals	63	122.072	1.938		

R> anova(LibQUAL.aov.Role)
Analysis of Variance Table
Response: LIBQ_tot

	Df	Sum Sq	Mean Sq	F value	Pr(>F)
Role	2	2.698	1.349	0.6961	0.5023
Residuals	63	122.072	1.938		

We can also use lm() to conduct an ANOVA on the previous example (notice the F-statistic at the end of the output):

R> LibQUAL.lm.Role <- lm(LIBQ_tot ~ Role, data = LibQUAL)

as both ANOVA and regression are special cases of the general linear model. However, the summary() function for an lm object does not return an ANOVA table; instead, it returns a regression table:

R> summary(LibQUAL.lm.Role)
Call:
lm(formula = LIBQ_tot ~ Role, data = LibQUAL)
Residuals:

Min	1Q	Median	3Q	Max
-5.1127	-0.4535	0.2084	0.7965	1.9795

Coefficients:

	Estimate	Std. Error	t value	Pr(>|t|)
(Intercept)	6.792727	0.296775	22.888	<2e-16 ***
Role2	-0.002273	0.419703	-0.005	0.996
Role3	0.427727	0.419703	1.019	0.312

—
Signif. codes: 0 '***' 0.001 '**' 0.01 '*' 0.05 '.' 0.1 ' ' 1
Residual standard error: 1.392 on 63 degrees of freedom
Multiple R-Squared: 0.02162, Adjusted R-squared: -0.009439
F-statistic: 0.6961 on 2 and 63 DF, p-value: 0.5023 . . .

Because the lm() function was used, the sample multiple correlation coefficient, Multiple R-Squared, and the adjusted multiple correlation coefficient, Adjusted R-squared, are made available with the summary() function.

Confidence Intervals for Standardized Effect Sizes for Omnibus Effects

The effect size for the pth factor of the ANOVA model is defined as

$$\eta_p^2 = \frac{\sigma_p^2}{\sigma_T^2} \qquad (8)$$

or

$$\phi_p^2 = \frac{\sigma_p^2}{\sigma_E^2}, \qquad (9)$$

where σ_p^2 is the variance due to factor p, σ_T^2 is the total variance of the dependent variable, and σ_E^2 is the within-group variance of the dependent variable (Fleishman, 1980; Kelley, 2007a; Steiger, 2004).[11] Due to the structure of the effect size, η_p^2 is the proportion of variance in the dependent variable accounted for by the grouping factor, and ϕ_p^2 is the signal-to-noise ratio. The MBESS package contains functions to calculate confidence intervals for these quantities.

The function ci.pvaf() in the MBESS package can be used to calculate the confidence limits for the proportion of variance in the dependent variable accounted for by the grouping variable (i.e., η_p^2). Its basic specification is of the form

---

ci.pvaf(F.value, df.1, df.2, N, conf.level=0.95)

---

where F.value is the observed F value from fixed effects ANOVA for the particular factor, df.1 is the numerator degrees of freedom for the F test, df.2 is the denominator degrees of freedom, N is the sample size (which need not be specified for single-factor designs), and conf.level is the confidence interval coverage. To obtain the 95% confidence interval for η_p^2 in the example we used when discussing the function aov(), ci.pvaf() should be specified as follows.

R> ci.pvaf(F.value=0.6961, df.1=2, df.2=63, N=66)
    $Lower.Limit.Proportion.of.Variance.Accounted.for
    [1] 0
    $Upper.Limit.Proportion.of.Variance.Accounted.for
    [1] 0.1107225

The function ci.snr() in MBESS can be used to obtain the confidence limits for the signal-to-noise ratio (i.e., ϕ_p^2). Its basic specification is of the form

---

ci.snr(F.value, df.1, df.2, N, conf.level=0.95),

---

where all the arguments are the same as those of ci.pvaf(). To obtain the 95% confidence interval for ϕ_p^2 from the example we used when discussing aov(), ci.snr() should be specified as follows:

R> ci.snr(F.value=0.6961, df.1=2, df.2=63, N=66)
    $Lower.Limit.Signal.to.Noise.Ratio
    [1] 0
    $Upper.Limit.Signal.to.Noise.Ratio
    [1] 0.1245084

Confidence Intervals for Targeted Effects

Although the omnibus F test often addresses an important research question, it is many times desirable to perform follow-up comparisons in an effort to examine specific targeted effects. The ci.c() function from MBESS can be used to form confidence intervals for the population contrasts in an ANOVA setting. Its basic specification is of the form

---

ci.c(means, error.variance, c.weights, n, N, conf.level)

---

where means is a vector of the group means, error.variance is the common variance of the error (i.e., the mean square error), c.weights is a vector of contrast weights, n is a vector of sample sizes in each group, N is the total sample size (which need not be specified in a single-group design), and conf.level is the confidence interval coverage. For example, to obtain the 95% confidence interval for the difference between the mean of students (weighted mean of undergraduate and graduate) versus the mean of faculty in the example we used when discussing aov(), ci.c would be specified as follows.

```
R>
ci.c(means=c(6.792727,6.790454,7.220454),
c.weights=c(1/2, 1/2, −1), n=c(22,22,22),
error.variance=1.859, conf.level=.95)
    $Lower.Conf.Limit.Contrast
    [1] −1.140312
    $Contrast
    [1] −0.4288635
    $Upper.Conf.Limit.Contrast
    [1] 0.282585
```

The function ci.sc() in MBESS can be used to form confidence intervals for the population standardized contrast in an ANOVA setting. Its basic specification is of the same form as ci.c(), except that the standardized contrast and confidence limits are returned. For example,

---

```
R>
ci.sc(means=c(6.792727,6.790454,7.220454),
error.variance=1.859, c.weights=c(−1, 1/2,
1/2), n=c(22,22,22), conf.level=.95)
    $Lower.Conf.Limit.Standardized.Contrast
    [1] −0.3570958
    $Standardized.contrast
    [1] 0.1560210
    $Upper.Conf.Limit.Standardized.Contrast
    [1] 0.6679053
```

LONGITUDINAL DATA ANALYSIS WITH R

Longitudinal research has become an important technique in the BESS because of the rich set of research questions that can be addressed with regards to intra- and interindividual change (e.g., Collins & Sayer, 2001; Curran & Bollen, 2001; Singer & Willett, 2003). Multilevel models (also called hierarchical models, mixed-effects models, random coefficient models) are a commonly used method of modeling and understanding change because these models explicitly address the nested structure of the data (e.g., observations nested within individual, individual nested within group, etc.). The *nlme* package (Pinheiro et al., 2007) provides powerful methods for analyzing both linear and nonlinear multilevel models.

We will use the data set Gardner.LD in the MBESS package for illustration purposes. The data set Gardner.LD contains the performance data of 24 individuals, who were presented with 420 presentations of four letters and were asked to identify the next letter that was to be presented. The 420 presentations were (arbitrarily it seems) grouped into 21 trials of 20 presentations. Twelve of the participants were presented the letters S, L, N, and D with probabilities .70, .10, .10, and .10, respectively, and the other 12 were presented the letter L with probability .70 and three other letters, each with a probability of .10. The analysis of longitudinal data in *nlme* requires data to be coded in *person-period* (Singer & Willett, 2003) form (also known as the "the univariate way") so that each person has a row for each of the different measurement occasions. There are four variables in the Gardner.LD data set: ID, Score, Trial, and Group. Because each participant had 21 trials, the dimension of the data matrix is 504 (24 × 21) by 4. As an initial step after loading the *nlme* package and calling into the session the Gardner.LD data, it is desirable to group the data using the groupedData() function, which contains not only the data but also information on the nesting structure of the design:

```
R> data(Gardner.LD)
R> grouped.Gardner.LD <− groupedData
(Score ~ Trial|ID, data=Gardner.LD)
```

The formula Score ~ Trial|ID implies that the response variable, Score, is modeled by the primary covariate, Trial, given the grouping factor, ID. In longitudinal data, the primary covariate that is monotonically related to time (e.g., time itself, grade level, occasion of measurement, etc.) and the grouping factor indicates the variable used to denote the individual. After creating the groupedData object, we can use plot() to plot individual trajectories.

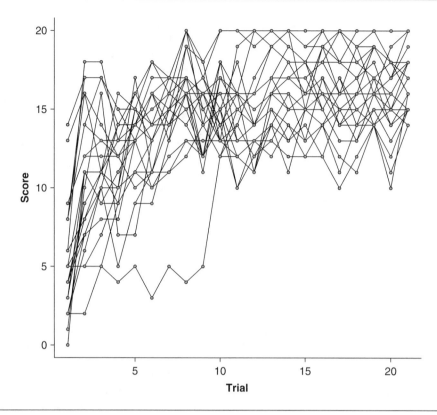

Figure 34.11   The growth trajectories of 24 participants in the Gardner learning data.

```
R> plot(grouped.Gardner.LD)
```

Because information on the nesting structure is contained within groupedData object, the plot() function creates trajectories conditional on each individual in separate plots.

However, it is sometimes desired to plot the trajectories in a single plot to help visualize the amount of interindividual differences in change. The vit() function in MBESS provides the plot with all trajectories in a single figure. Consider the following application of the vit() function:

```
R> vit(id="ID", occasion="Trial",
score="Score", Data=Gardner.LD, xlab="Trial")
```

Similar figures with other options can be obtained with the xyplot() function from the *lattice* package (Sarkar, 2006). Figure 34.12 shows that the change curves for most individuals are

nonlinear, starting at relatively low point and growing toward the upper value of 20.

After plotting the data, it is decided to use a logistic change curve to model the trajectories (a negative exponential model should also be considered). The model selected is defined as

$$y_{ij} = \frac{\phi_{1i}}{1 + \exp[-(t_{ij} - \phi_{2i})/\phi_{3i}]} + \varepsilon_{ij}, \quad (10)$$

where y_{ij} is the score for individual i at time j; t_{ij} is the jth trial for individual i; ϕ_{1i}, ϕ_{2i}, and ϕ_{3i} are parameters for individual i; and ε_{ij} is the error for the ith individual at the jth measurement occasion. The *nlme* package enables the user to use several self-starting functions for commonly used nonlinear regression models. We will use the SSlogis() function within the nlsList() function to obtain parameter estimates for each of the individuals. This can be done with the following commands:

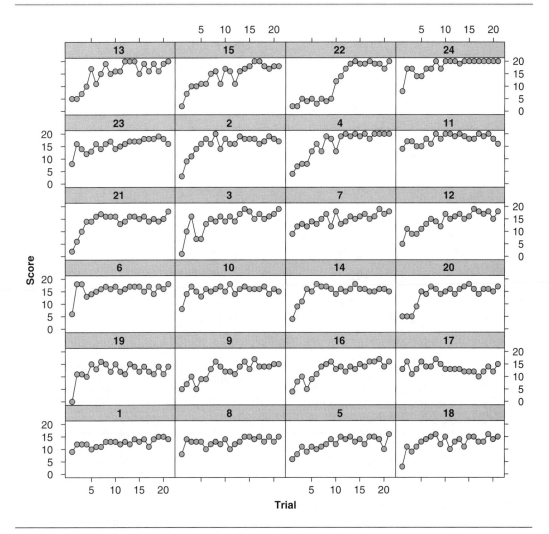

Figure 34.12   The growth trajectory of each participant in the Gardner learning data in a grouped plot.

```
R> NLS.list.GL <— nlsList(SSlogis, grouped.Gardner.LD)
R> NLS.list.GL
Call:
Model: Score ~ SSlogis(Trial, Asym, xmid, scal) | ID
Data: grouped.Gardner.LD
Coefficients:
```

	Asym	xmid	scal
1	20.64888	-0.39425400	25.9868490
8	25.82947	10.77112398	39.0163528
5	14.00626	1.19170594	3.3132692
18	13.76810	1.69643789	1.1114158
19	NA	NA	NA
9	14.67500	2.87314499	3.2330142

16	15.09849	2.95021742	2.7440494
17	43.44157	-69.37127304	-98.5832435
6	NA	NA	NA
10	15.73215	0.99038220	0.4381405
14	15.99992	1.92285958	0.8565851
20	15.93150	3.20708423	1.3398499
21	15.41431	2.42709904	0.7902158
3	16.98242	2.88241004	3.0970538
7	17.70834	-2.30174516	7.1434532
12	17.43223	2.57507721	3.8061267
23	18.17980	-2.16624638	6.0792346
2	17.39742	2.28047778	1.0706019
4	19.60291	3.90543041	2.4649680
11	18.94723	-3.34623016	3.6815169
13	18.11099	3.42193123	1.9878506
15	18.10627	3.84541898	3.4853045
22	19.93583	9.39892560	2.0708870
24	20.12397	-0.05064117	3.4446175

Degrees of freedom: 462 total; 396 residual
Residual standard error: 1.73849

The individuals are fitted using a separate (three-parameter) logistic model to each subject (the ID number is in the first unmarked column). The model from the SSlogic() function in the current example shows the following:

Score ~ SSlogis(Trial, Asym, xmid, scal) | ID

and thus the fitted model becomes

$$\widehat{Score}_{ij} = \frac{Asym_i}{1 + \exp[-(Trial_{ij} - xmid_i)/scal_i]}, \quad (11)$$

where *Asym* represents the asymptote, *xmid* represents the value of trial (or time, more generally) at the inflection point of the curve, and *scal* is the scale parameter. The trajectory of Individual 17 differs considerably from the others individuals and from the logistic model, which is why this individual's parameter estimates differ so considerably from the others. Note that both Individuals 6 and 19 do not

have parameter estimates because the logistic model failed to converge. Examination of the plot reveals that the logistic change model does not adequately describe the trajectories of Individuals 6 and 19 (a negative exponential change model would be more appropriate). Specification of the subset.ids argument in the vit() function allows specific individual IDs to be plotted, which can be helpful for identifying misfits.

The nlsList model is useful when the goal is to model the growth trajectory of a particular fixed set of individuals. However, when interest is in estimating a multilevel model with fixed effects and covariance structure—to examine the variability within and among individuals—the function nlme() can be used.

Since we already have a fitted nlsList() object (NLS.list.GL) for each individual, we can input that object into the function nlme(), where starting values are automatically obtained. To examine the results, consider the following commands:

```
R> nlme.GL <— nlme(NLS.list.GL)
R> summary(nlme.GL)
```
Nonlinear mixed-effects model fit by maximum likelihood
Model: Score ~ SSlogis(Trial, Asym, xmid, scal)
Data: grouped.Gardner.LD

AIC	BIC	logLik
2201.701	2243.926	-1090.850

Random effects:
Formula: list(Asym ~ 1, xmid ~ 1, scal ~ 1)
Level: ID
Structure: General positive-definite, Log-Cholesky parametrization

	StdDev	Corr		
			Asym	xmid
Asym	2.084844	Asym		
xmid	1.988619	0.399		
scal	1.033261	0.522		0.231

Residual 1.750237
Fixed effects: list(Asym ~ 1, xmid ~ 1, scal ~ 1)

	Value	Std.Error	DF	t-value	p-value
Asym	16.062330	0.4400112	478	36.50437	0
xmid	2.092424	0.4277958	478	4.89118	0
scal	1.619961	0.2422403	478	6.68742	0

Correlation:

	Asym	xmid
xmid	0.379	
scal	0.490	0.125

Standardized Within-Group Residuals:

Min	Q1	Med	Q3	Max
-3.25058923	-0.59251518	0.05021871	0.60113672	4.23964442

Number of Observations: 504
Number of Groups: 24

From the output, information about fixed effects, random effects, and the fit of the model is available. Using the object obtained from the nlsList() in nlme() automatically considers each of the fixed effects to be random. This can be modified by specifying fixed and random effects explicitly with the fixed and random options within nlme().

To visually examine the residuals, the following commands can be used:

```
R> plot(nlme.GL)
R> qqnorm(nlme.GL, abline=c(0,1))
```

The residual plot shows that the assumption of equal variances across time seems reasonable. This assumption can be relaxed with additional specification in nlme(). A normal QQ plot for the residual shows that the distribution of residuals seems normal.

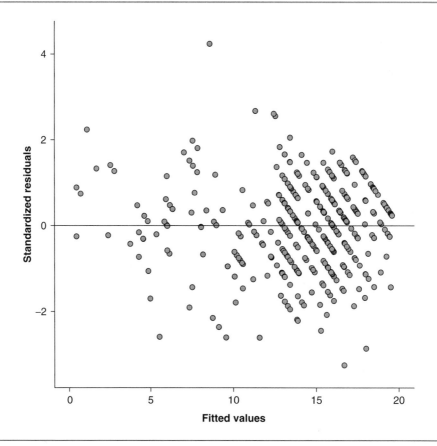

Figure 34.13   Scatterplot for standardized residuals as a function of fitted values for the fitted logistic change model.

We can also plot the fitted trajectories for each individual by applying plot() to certain functions of a fitted nlme() object, which provides important information about potential model misfits:

```
R> plot(augPred(nlme.GL, level=0:1))
```

This section serves as only a brief introduction to the *nlme* package. Readers interested in more comprehensive discussion on analyzing mixed effects models (both linear and nonlinear) with the *nlme* package are referred to *Mixed-Effects Models in S and S-PLUS* (Pinheiro & Bates, 2000). Also helpful is Doran and Lockwood (2006), who recently provided a tutorial on linear multilevel model with the *nlme* package, with special emphasis on educational data.

CONCLUSIONS

We hope that we have successfully illustrated R as a valuable tool for performing a wide variety of statistical analyses. Of course, R can do much more than has been presented. The use of R and the plethora of tools made available with R packages should be considered by researchers who perform statistical analyses. One thing not mentioned is an implicit benefit of R, that many times R code can be slightly modified from analysis to analysis for similar data and research questions, which greatly facilitates future analyses. For researchers who often perform the same type of analysis with different data, such a benefit can save a great deal of time.

We know from experience that many statisticians and quantitative methodologists within the BESS use R for their research. Such research is at times implemented in collaborative efforts with substantive researchers, where R is used to implement the particular method. Having R as a common language would be beneficial in such collaborative relationships. We also know from experience that R is beginning to be used in graduate courses in the BESS at well-known institutions, both in "first-year graduate statistics"

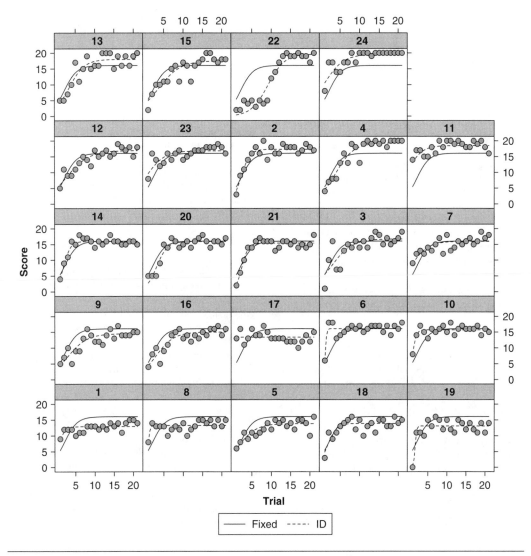

Figure 34.14   Observed values (circles), individuals' fitted values (dashed line), and population estimates of change curve (solid line) for the logistic change model applied to the Gardner learning data.

sequences and (more commonly) for advanced statistics classes. Thus, more and more future researchers will have at least some exposure to statistical analyses implemented in R. Evidence is thus beginning to mount that R will be even more important and widely used in the coming years than it is today. Thus, there is no time like the present to begin incorporating R into one's set of statistical tools.

R cannot do everything, and we do not want to imply that it can. For some techniques, R is quite limited. A large portion of the statistical procedures implemented within R has come from mathematical statisticians and statisticians working outside the BESS. Since such individuals do not use some of the methods that are important to researchers within the BESS, some methods important to BESS researchers have not yet been implemented in R. However, as more packages become available that implement methods especially useful for the BESS, such as MBESS, the "missing methods" will continue to decrease in quantity. We realize that not everyone will immediately download, install, and start using R. However, we do hope that researchers will be open to using the program, realize that it is not as difficult as it might initially seem, and consider making it part of their repertoire of statistical tools.

NOTES

1. The "community of R users," freely available downloadable books, documentation, mailing lists, and software downloads are available at the R Web site: http://r-project.org.

2. He was once editor (1993–1997) of the *Journal of Educational* [now *and Behavioral*] *Statistics.*

3. Like R, S-Plus is a program based on the S language. S-Plus is a proprietary program owned by Insightful Corporation. R and S-Plus share a common history because of the S language, but they are ever growing further apart.

4. This data set has been made available in the MBESS R package. For those who did not create prof.salary.R in the previous sections, after loading MBESS, the following will load the data: data(prof.salary).

5. Note that R2.k_X.without.k is equal to $1 -$ Tolerance$_k$, and R2.k_X.without.k is equivalent to

$$1 - \frac{1}{r_{kk}},$$

where r_{kk} is the kth diagonal element of the inverse of the covariance matrix of the K regressors (Harris, 2001).

6. Actually, Maxwell (2000) describes a specific correlation structure. That correlation structure implicitly defines the values used in the chapter for illustrative purposes via definitional formulas.

7. Note that this result differs slightly from that reported in Maxwell (2000), which is 113. The discrepancy is because of rounding error in the calculations necessary to obtain the squared multiple correlation coefficients and because of the rounding error implicit in Cohen's (1988) tables, which were used to obtain the noncentrality parameter. Given the specified correlation matrix, number of predictors, and desired power, 111 is the exact value of necessary sample size.

8. Interestingly, 69 other students were asked to do the same task, except that the students estimated the length of the room in feet. The results were shown not to be significant, $t = .4624(68)$, $p = .65$ (with 95% confidence limits of 40.69, 46.70; the actual length was 43 feet).

9. Preece (1982) criticized the way Gosset used the Cushny and Peebles (1905) data to illustrate a paired-samples t test. Although we tend to agree with Preece, we used the data because of their historical importance. Also, it should be noted that the data reported in Gosset's work contain a typographical error, in that there was a miscoded datum (but correct summary statistics). We used the correct data as reported in Cushny and Peebles (1905).

10. Note that the result is slightly different from that in Thompson's example (see Chapter 17, this volume), which is –0.064. This discrepancy comes from rounding error. If we use the means and the standard deviations reported in Thompson explicitly in smd(), the result will be the same:

```
R> smd(Mean.1=6.98, Mean.2=6.89, s.1=1.322,
s.2=1.472, n.1=33, n.2=33)
 [1] 0.06433112
```

11. Thompson (Chapter 17, this volume) denotes the effect sizes for one-way ANOVA as η^2 (multiple R-squared) and ω^2 (adjusted R-squared).

REFERENCES

Aiken, L. S., & West, S. G. (1991). *Testing and interpreting interactions.* Newbury Park, CA: Sage.

Algina, J., & Olejnik, S. (2000). Determining sample size for accurate estimation of the squared multiple correlation coefficient. *Multivariate Behavioral Research, 35,* 119–136.

Becker, R. A. (1994). *A brief history of S.* Retrieved from http://cm.bell-labs.com/stat/doc/94.11.ps

Cleveland, W. S. (1979). Robust locally weighted regression and smoothing scatterplots. *Journal of American Statistics Association, 74,* 829–836.

Cleveland, W. S. (1981). LOWESS: A program for smoothing scatterplots by robust locally weighted regression. *The American Statistician, 35,* 54.

Cohen, J. (1988). *Statistical power analysis for the behavioral sciences* (2nd ed.). Hillsdale, NJ: Lawrence Erlbaum.

Cohen, J., Cohen, P., West, S. G., & Aiken, L. S. (2003). *Applied multiple regression/correlation analysis for the behavioral sciences* (3rd ed.). Mahwah, NJ: Lawrence Erlbaum.

Collins, L. M., & Sayer, A. (Eds.). (2001). *New methods for the analysis of change.* Washington, DC: American Psychological Association.

Curran, P. J., & Bollen, K. A. (2001). The best of both worlds: Combining autoregressive and latent curve models. In L. M. Collins & A. G. Sayer (Eds.), *New methods for the analysis of change* (pp. 107–135). Washington, DC: American Psychological Association.

Cushny, A. R., & Peebles, A. R. (1905). The action of optical isomers: II. Hyoscines. *Journal of Physiology, 32,* 501–510.

de Leeuw, J. (2005). On abandoning XLISP-STAT. *Journal of Statistical Software, 13*(7), 1–5.

Ding, C. G. (1996). On the computation of the distribution of the square of the sample multiple correlation coefficient. *Computational Statistics & Data Analysis, 22,* 345–350.

Doran, H. C., & Lockwood, J. R. (2006). Fitting value-added models in R. *Journal of Educational and Behavioral Statistics, 31*(2), 105–230.

Everitt, B. S. (2005). *An R and S-Plus companion to multivariate analysis.* London: Springer.

Fleishman, A. I. (1980). Confidence intervals for correlation ratios. *Educational and Psychological Measurement, 40,* 659–670.

Fox, J. (2002). *An R and S-PLUS companion to applied regression.* Thousand Oaks, CA: Sage.

Hand, D. J., Daly, F., Lunn, A. D., McConway, K., & Ostrowski, E. (Eds.). (1994). *A handbook of small data sets.* London: Chapman & Hall.

Harris, R. J. (2001). *A primer of multivariate statistics* (3rd ed.). Mahwah, NJ: Lawrence Erlbaum.

Hedges, L. V., & Olkin, I. (1985). *Statistical methods for meta-analysis.* Orlando, FL: Academic Press.

Kelley, K. (2007a). Confidence intervals for standardized effect sizes: Theory, application, and implementation. *Journal of Statistical Software, 20*(8), 1–24.

Kelley, K. (2007b). MBESS: Version 0.0.9 [Computer software and manual]. Retrieved from http://www.r-project.org/

Kelley, K. (2007c). Sample size planning for the squared multiple correlation coefficient: Accuracy in parameter estimation via narrow confidence intervals. Revised and submitted to *Multivariate Behavioral Research.*

Kelley, K. (in press). Methods for the behavioral, educational, and educational sciences: An R package. *Behavior Research Methods.*

Kelley, K., & Maxwell, S. E. (2003). Sample size for multiple regression: Obtaining regression coefficients that are accuracy, not simply significant. *Psychological Methods, 8,* 305–321.

Kelley, K., & Maxwell, S. E. (in press). Power and accuracy for omnibus and targeted effects: Issues of sample size planning with applications to Multiple Regression. In J. Brannon, P. Alasuutari, & L. Bickman (Eds.), *Handbook of social research methods.* New York: Russell Sage Foundation.

Kelley, K., Maxwell, S. E., & Rausch, J. R. (2003). Obtaining power or obtaining precision: Delineating methods of sample size planning. *Evaluation and the Health Professions, 26,* 258–287.

Kelley, K., & Rausch, J. R. (2006). Sample size planning for the standardized mean difference: Accuracy in parameter estimation via narrow confidence intervals. *Psychological Methods, 11*(4), 363–385.

Lapsley, M., & Ripley, B. D. (2007). RODBC: ODBC database access [Computer software and manual]. Retrieved from http://cran.r-project.org

Lee, Y. S. (1971). Tables of the upper percentage points of the multiple correlation. *Biometrika, 59,* 175–189.

Maxwell, S. E. (2000). Sample size and multiple regression. *Psychological Methods, 5,* 434–458.

Maxwell, S. E., & Delaney, H. D. (2004). *Designing experiments and analyzing data: A model comparison perspective* (2nd ed.). Mahwah, NJ: Lawrence Erlbaum.

Pinheiro, J. C., & Bates, D. M. (2000). *Mixed-effects models in S and S-PLUS.* New York: Springer.

Pinheiro, J. C., Bates, D., DebRoy, S., & Sarkar, D. (2007). nlme: Linear and nonlinear mixed effects models [Computer software and manual]. Retrieved from http://www.r-project.org

Preece, D. A. (1982). t is for trouble (and textbooks): A critique of some examples of the paired-samples t-test. *The Statistician, 31,* 169–195.

R Development Core Team. (2007a). foreign: Read data stored by Minitab, S, SAS, SPSS, Stata, Systat, dBase [Computer software and manual]. Retrievable from http://www.r-project.org

R Development Core Team. (2007b). R: A language and environment for statistical computing [Computer software and manual]. Vienna, Austria: R Foundation for Statistical Computing. Available from http://www.r-project.org

Sarkar, D. (2006). lattice: Lattice graphics: R package version 0.14-16 [Computer software and manual]. Retrieved from http://cran.r-project.org/

Singer, J. B., & Willett, J. B. (2003). *Applied longitudinal data analysis: Modeling change and event occurrence.* New York: Oxford University Press.

Smithson, M. (2003). *Confidence intervals.* New York: Russell Sage Foundation.

Steiger, J. H. (2004). Beyond the F test: Effect size confidence intervals and tests of close fit in the analysis of variance and contrast analysis. *Psychological Methods, 9*(2), 164–182.

Steiger, J. H., & Fouladi, R. T. (1992). R2: A computer program for interval estimation, power calculation, and hypothesis testing for the squared multiple correlation. *Behavior Research Methods, Instruments, and Computers, 4,* 581–582.

Steiger, J. H., & Fouladi, R. T. (1997). Noncentrality interval estimation and the evaluation of statistical models. In L. L. Harlow, S. A. Mulaik, & J. H. Steiger (Eds.), *What if there were no significance tests?* (pp. 221–257). Mahwah, NJ: Lawrence Erlbaum.

Student. (1908). The probable error of a mean. *Biometrika, 6,* 1–24.

Thompson, B., Cook, C., & Kyrillidou, M. (2005). Concurrent validity of LibQUAL+™ scores: What do LibQUAL+™ scores measure? *Journal of Academic Librarianship, 31,* 517–522.

Thompson, B., Cook, C., & Kyrillidou, M. (2006). Using localized survey items to augment standardized benchmarking measures: A LibQUAL+™ study. *Libraries and the Academy, 6,* 219–230.

Tierney, L. (2005). Some notes on the past and future of Lisp-Stat. *Journal of Statistical Software, 13*(9), 1–15.

INDEX

AAARIS. *See* African American Adolescent Racial
Identity Scale (AAARIS)
Abadie, A., 160, 168
Abraham, W. T., 219, 223
Academy of Management Journal, 133, 259
ACER ConQuest, 75
Acock, A. C., 214, 230
Adjacent percent agreement statistic, 32–33
African American Adolescent Racial Identity Scale
(AAARIS), 126
  data analysis, 131
  methodology, 129–31
  research questions, 128–29
  study purpose, 127
  theoretical framework, 127–28
  validity and trustworthiness, 132
  writing/publishing, 132–33
Aggregated analysis of hierarchical data, 447, *448*
Agodini, R., 171
Agresti, A., 407
Aguinis, H., 434, 435
Aiken, L. S., 242, 243, 425, 426, 434, 435
AIPE for mean differences, 560
Akaike, H., 9
Akaike information criterion (AIC), 9, 120, 373–74
Alban, T., 149
Albert, A., 405
Algina, J., 16, 17, 22
All-in-one structural equation modeling analysis, 495–97
Allison, P. D., 220, 222, 227
American Educational Research Journal, 133
American Journal of Public Health, 7
American Psychological Association, 8, 247, 376
Analysis of covariance. *See* ANCOVA (analysis of
covariance)
Analysis of ratings, 80–83
Analysis of variance. *See* ANOVA (analysis of variance)
ANCOVA (analysis of covariance), 456–57
Anderson, D. R., 246
Anderson, N. H., 300
Angoff procedure
  basic, 17
  versus contrasting-group method, 20
  modified, 17–18
ANOVA (analysis of variance)
  Brown-Forsyth test, 330–31, 337–38, *339*
  checking assumptions in, 324–25, 336

comparing means using, 351–52, 353–54
effect sizes and, 252–55, 342, 345–47, 351–52, 354
factorial designs in, 347–52
hierarchical linear models and, 325, 355
homogenity of population variances, 329–32
independence of observation in, 325–28
individual contrasts in, 343–45
intraclass correlation, 326, *327*, *328*
meta-analysis, 118
missing data and, 354
multiway/multifactorial, 254
nonnormal data and, 347
normality assumption, 332–36
one-way, 253–54, 341–42
outliers and, 209, 210–11, 328–29
power, 345, 352, 354–55
practice data set, 336–37
repeated-measures designs, 352–55
robustness and, 277, 324, 325
R programming language and, 560–63
sample sizes, 342
sensitivity analysis, 328–29, *330*
small sample studies and, 143, 145
true-score theory and, 52
unequal sample sizes and, 348–50
unequal variances in, 343
Anscombe, F. J., 206
Anti-alcohol campaigns, 452
Antliffe, B., 138
Arbuckle, J. L., 222

Bagozzi, R. P., 251
Banerjee, M., 510
Baron, R. M., 422, 423, 429, 432–33
Barry, A., 143
Barton, M. B., 374, 378
Baseline logit model, 391–92
Basic Angoff procedure, 17
Bassett, G., 271
Bauer, D. J., 427
Bayes, Thomas, 509
Bayesian analysis
  Bayes theorem and, 511–12, 524
  choosing prior distribution for, 515–18
  comparison with significance tests, 525–26
  conditional probability and, 510–12
  credibility intervals, 520–22

ABOUT THE EDITOR

Jason W. Osborne, PhD, is Associate Professor of Educational Psychology in the Department of Curriculum and Instruction at North Carolina State University and a Primary Investigator specializing in evaluation in the William and Ida Friday Institute for Educational Innovation. His interest in best practices in quantitative methods began when research methods students started asking questions that seemed direct and simple yet did not have clear, definitive answers in the texts they were using (such as "Why isn't my square root transformation reducing skew?" and "Do I *really* need to remove outliers?").

His current research interests focus on (obviously) best practices in research methods, identification with academics, and stereotype threat. He is active in evaluation, serving as primary investigator on several large-scale evaluations of instructional technology in the public schools and on many projects on health care and nursing practice. He spends his free time systematically dismantling his house in a misguided attempt at interior design and getting kicked in the head by his sons in Tae Kwon Do class (which explains a lot, as his colleagues, friends, and family will tell you).

For more information on Jason, the book, his research, and other minutiae, please visit his Web site at http://jwosborne.com/.

Carolyn J. Anderson is an Associate Professor of Educational Psychology at the University of Illinois, Urbana-Champaign, where she teaches courses in basic statistics, hierarchical linear models, multivariate analysis, and categorical data analysis. Her primary research deals with statistical models for multivariate categorical data, latent variable models for discrete data, and psychometrics. She has also been a statistical consultant on a number of applied projects in education and psychology.

Gianluca Baio graduated with a degree in Statistics and Economics from the University of Florence (Italy), after spending a period studying at the Sheffield Hallam University, Sheffield (UK). Subsequently, he has been a Research Fellow in the University of Siena (Italy), where he started to work on applied Bayesian statistics with particular reference to the economic evaluation of health systems. He completed his PhD in Applied Statistics at the University of Florence, after spending a period at the Program on the Pharmaceutical Industry at the MIT Sloan School of Management, Cambridge, Massachusetts, and currently works as a Research Fellow at University College London (UK). His main interests are in Bayesian statistical modeling, probabilistic expert systems, and applications to decision-making problems, particularly in health care.

A. Alexander Beaujean received concurrent PhDs in School Psychology and Educational Psychology from the University of Missouri–Columbia in 2006, under the direction of Steven Osterlind and Craig Frisby. He spent a predoctoral year doing clinical work and research in Cleveland, Ohio, where he worked with Eric Youngstrom. In 2006, he joined the Educational Psychology faculty at Baylor University, where he currently teaches classes in statistics and psychometrics.

His research interests are in educational and psychological measurement and the influence of individual differences on life outcomes, especially in the area of education. In addition, he studies the history of the London School of Differential Psychology.

Marta Blangiardo graduated with a degree in Statistical, Demographic, and Social Sciences from the University of Milan Bicocca, Italy, in 2001. She obtained her PhD in Applied Statistics from the University of Florence, Italy, in 2005, after spending 6 months as visiting scholar at the Bauer Centre for Genomics Research in Cambridge, Massachusetts. She is a Research Fellow in Biostatistics in the Department of Epidemiology and Public Health of Imperial College, London (UK). Her main interests are in Bayesian modeling with application to gene expression data and demographic data.

Jason C. Cole is the founder and president of Consulting Measurement Group and a senior researcher at QualityMetric. After receiving his PhD in Clinical Psychology, he has engaged in research in cognitive assessment, depression, and creativity. In addition, he publishes and lectures in applied methodology areas, including psychometric, latent modeling, missing data, and power analysis.

Anna B. Costello holds a Master of Science in Industrial and Organizational Psychology from North Carolina State University. She became interested in the methodology of factor analysis while analyzing the data for her thesis and has presented at two international academic conferences. She is currently working in the pharmaceutical industry.

Geoff Cumming has taught research methods and statistics in the School of Psychological Science at La Trobe University for more than

30 years. His main current research is in the area of statistical cognition, as well as the reform of statistical practices in psychology and other disciplines. ESCI (Exploratory Software for Confidence Intervals; www.latrobe.edu.au/psy/esci) is his interactive graphical software that runs under Microsoft Excel and is intended to support better understanding of sampling, confidence intervals, meta-analysis, and other statistical techniques and their use by researchers and students. Further information about his research is available at www.latrobe.edu.au/psy/staff/cumming.html.

Jessica T. DeCuir-Gunby is an Assistant Professor of Educational Psychology in the Department of Curriculum and Instruction at North Carolina State University. She earned her BS degree with a double major in Psychology and Spanish from Louisiana State University. She earned both her MA and PhD degrees in Educational Psychology at the University of Georgia. Her research and theoretical interests include race and racial identity development, Black education, critical race theory, mixed methods research, and emotions.

Cody S. Ding joined the University of Missouri–St. Louis College of Education in 2002 as an Assistant Professor of Educational Psychology. He was trained as a psychologist with emphasis on developmental psychology and methodology at the Pennsylvania State University and the University of Minnesota. His research areas include modeling of growth and development, psychosocial adaptation, perceptual assessment, and educational and psychological measurement. His work has included developing a modeling approach for studying growth heterogeneity in student achievement, employing a latent profile and individual preference modeling for assessing perceptions, and examining how perception influences behaviors. His current teaching interests include educational and psychological assessment, research designs, behavioral analysis, and other methodological-related courses. His teaching is based on the philosophy of active learning and cooperative learning models, with emphasis on students' accountability in their own learning.

Lidia Dobria is an Associate Professor of Mathematics at Wilbur Wright College. She is also a candidate in the Measurement, Evaluation, Statistics, and Assessment (MESA) program at the University of Illinois at Chicago. Her dissertation focuses on modeling rater effects within a hierarchical framework. Her current research interests include multilevel item response theory (IRT) modeling, latent variable modeling, longitudinal investigations of rater effects, and test and rating scale design and analysis.

Sherif Elsadat was a graduate student at the University of Nevada, Las Vegas.

Fiona Fidler is an Australian Postdoctoral Fellow in the School of Psychological Science at La Trobe University, Australia. She has an undergraduate degree in psychology and a PhD in Philosophy of Science. Her postgraduate research explored resistance to statistical and methodological change in the disciplines of psychology, medicine, and ecology. For this research, she interviewed or corresponded with more than 30 prolific advocates of statistical reform, asking about reactions from colleagues, students, and institutions to their work. Her main current research is in the field of statistical cognition (i.e., human cognition of statistical ideas). Further information about her research is available at http://www.botany.unimelb.edu.au/envisci/fiona/fiona.html.

Gregory R. Hancock is Professor in the Department of Measurement, Statistics and Evaluation at the University of Maryland, College Park, and Director of the Center for Integrated Latent Variable Research (CILVR). His research has appeared in such journals as *Psychometrika, Multivariate Behavioral Research, Structural Equation Modeling: A Multidisciplinary Journal, Psychological Bulletin, Journal of Educational and Behavioral Statistics, Educational and Psychological Measurement, Review of Educational Research,* and *Communications in Statistics: Simulation and Computation.* He also coedited the volume *Structural Equation Modeling: A Second Course,* with Ralph O. Mueller. He is past chair of the Structural Equation Modeling special interest group of the American Educational Research Association and serves on the editorial board of a number of applied and methodological journals, including *Structural Equation Modeling: A Multidisciplinary Journal.* He holds a PhD from the University of Washington.

David Howell is Emeritus Professor at the University of Vermont. He gained his PhD from Tulane University in 1967 and has since been associated with the University of Vermont, retiring as Chair of the Department of Psychology in 2002. He also spent 2 separate years as Visiting Professor at the Universities of Durham and Bristol in the United Kingdom. He is the author of several books and many journal papers, and he continues to write even after retiring. His latest project was the *Encyclopedia of Statistics in Behavioral Science,* of which he and Brian Everitt were editors in chief. Professor Howell now lives in Colorado, where he hikes in the summer, skis in the winter, and writes in the two mud seasons.

Cherdsak Iramaneerat is an instructor in the Department of Surgery and an Assistant Dean for Education, Faculty of Medicine Siriraj Hospital, Mahidol University, Thailand. He received his MD in 1997 from the Faculty of Medicine, Siriraj Hospital, Mahidol University. He practiced as a general practitioner for a year before he entered general surgery residency training. He received his Thai Board of General Surgery in 2001. He then worked as an instructor in the Department of Surgery, Faculty of Medicine, Siriraj Hospital. He won the Anandamahidol scholarship from King Bhumibol of Thailand in 2002, which allowed him to pursue graduate study in the United States. He earned the MHPE (Master of Health Professions Education) from the University of Illinois at Chicago in 2004 and PhD in Educational Psychology from the University of Illinois at Chicago in 2007. His research interests include performance assessment, Rasch measurement, health outcomes measurement, and test development.

Ken Kelley is an Assistant Professor in the Inquiry Methodology Program at Indiana University. His research focuses on methodological and statistical issues that arise in the behavioral, educational, and social sciences. More specifically, his research is on the design of research studies, the analysis of change, and statistical computing.

J. Thomas Kellow, PhD, is currently an Assistant Professor of Research and Statistics in the Tift College of Education at Mercer University. He has published numerous articles on applied statistics, program evaluation, and high-stakes testing. He also has published in the areas of sport pedagogy and the social ecology of developmental disabilities.

Ahmed H. Khago was a graduate student at the University of Nevada, Las Vegas.

Peter R. Killeen is Professor of Psychology at Arizona State University. He has recently served as the President of the Society for the Quantitative Analysis of Behavior and as Secretary/Treasurer of the Society of Experimental Psychologist. Killeen's dissertation used Hardy, Littlewood, and Polya's *General Mean Theorem* to infer how animals average the rates of reinforcement in different patches. His subsequent articles sustained that quantitative theme—"Mathematical Principles of Reinforcement and Modeling Games From the 20th Century" are typical titles. Until recently, his modeling has been deterministic, as befits a student of two grand stochastaphobes, B. F. Skinner and S. S. Stevens. Only when teaching Introductory Statistics from a resampling/bootstrap perspective did he confront the foundational problems with our statistico-logical modes of inference. While playing with simulated sampling distributions, Dr. Killeen rediscovered posterior predictive distributions and Fisher's fiducial probabilities. He saw that setting sights lower—to predicting replicability of data rather than truth of hypotheses— simplified inference. With the help of supportive editors, helpful reviewers, and purifying critics, he formulated an alternative to null hypothesis statistical tests. For deciding between well-defined alternative models, many tools—Neyman-Pearson statistics, likelihood ratios, or their Bayesian qualifications—suffice. In most other cases, shifting the focus to replicability permits clearer, simpler, and more useful inferences, as described in his chapter. Dr. Killeen is now generalizing these results to a decision-theoretic framework. At his day job, he studies time perception, conditioning, and ADHD.

Jason E. King, PhD, is Assistant Director of the Office of Continuing Medical Education and Assistant Professor of Allied Health Sciences at Baylor College of Medicine. His research interests include logistic regression, robust statistics, structural modeling, assessing outcomes in continuing medical education. He has published in the *Journal of the American Medical Association* and *Academic Medicine,* and he serves on the editorial boards of the *American Educational Research Journal* and *Educational and Psychological Measurement.* He received his doctorate in Educational Psychology from Texas A&M University, College Station.

Spyros Konstantopoulos is an Assistant Professor of Human Development and Social Policy and Learning Sciences at the School of Education and Social Policy at Northwestern University. His research interests include the extension and application of statistical methods to issues in education, social science, and policy studies. His methodological work involves statistical methods for mixed effects models with nested structure. His current work involves power analysis in nested deigns and meta-analysis regression. His substantive work encompasses research in evaluating educational interventions such as class size, as well as school and teacher effects.

Keke Lai is a doctoral student in the Inquiry Methodology Program at Indiana University. His research interests are on quantitative methods as they apply to the behavioral and educational sciences.

Ralph O. Mueller is Professor of Educational Research and Public Policy and Public Administration and former Chair of the Department of Educational Leadership at The George Washington University, Washington, DC. He is the author of *Basic Principles of Structural Equation Modeling: An Introduction to LISREL and EQS* and recently coedited, with Gregory R. Hancock, *Structural Equation Modeling: A Second Course*. His work deals primarily with the pedagogy and proper application of structural equation modeling (SEM) in the social and behavioral sciences. Dr. Mueller conducts regular professional development seminars on SEM for the American Educational Research Association and is past chair of its special interest group on SEM. He serves on the editorial boards of *Educational and Psychological Measurement* and *Measurement and Evaluation in Counseling and Development* and was a charter board member of *Structural Equation Modeling: A Multidisciplinary Journal*. Currently, Ralph is an American Council on Education (ACE) Fellow and Special Assistant to the Provost at the University of Miami, FL.

E. Michael Nussbaum, PhD, is an Associate Professor of Educational Psychology at the University of Nevada, Las Vegas. He received his doctorate from Stanford University in 1997. His research interests are in problem solving and small group processes, specifically argumentation. He has also published work on science assessment and on conceptual change.

Amy Overbay, PhD, is a Research Assistant Professor with North Carolina State University's College of Education. She holds a BA in English Education from the University of North Carolina–Chapel Hill; an MA in English, North Carolina State University; and a PhD in Curriculum and Instruction, North Carolina State University. Her postdoctoral work includes coordinating a statewide evaluation for the North Carolina Department of Public Instruction (NC DPI) and serving as coprimary investigator of the evaluation of NC DPI's IMPACTing Leadership project. She has published research on evaluation methods and has co-conducted a number of major program evaluations for the Wake County Public School System.

Naomi Jeffery Petersen, Assistant Professor of Education at Central Washington University, developed the Mathematics Teaching Profile, a survey designed to measure an orientation to teaching for mathematical proficiency. Although initial findings are robust, she continues to broaden the psychometric investigation in conjunction with mathematics educators. She is an external evaluator for National Science Foundation and other grants, as well as a consultant to local schools aligning curriculum and assessment. Other projects include exhibit and curriculum development for museums and interpretive centers with a particular focus on the interaction of technology, environment, and society. She teaches foundation courses, including research methods and curriculum theory. Dr. Petersen can be contacted via NJP@cwu.edu.

Donald B. Rubin is the John L. Loeb Professor of Statistics at Harvard University. He is a fellow of the American Statistical Association, the Institute for Mathematical Statistics, the American Association for the Advancement of Sciences, and the American Academy of Arts and Sciences, among others. He has more than 300 publications (including multiple books) on a variety of statistical topics, including Bayesian methods, causal inference, and missing data. He has lectured extensively throughout the United States, Europe, and Asia.

Leslie Rutkowski received her PhD in Educational Psychology from the University of Illinois at Urbana-Champaign in 2007. She is currently a research associate at the International Association for the Evaluation of Educational Achievement (IEA). Her research interests include issues in large scale assessment and using advanced techniques to address applied questions in education and psychology. Leslie regularly consults for researchers from several institutions and her teaching experience includes conducting quantitative methods workshops for researchers in academia and government.

William D. Schafer (EdD, 1969, University of Rochester) is Affiliated Professor (Emeritus), Department of Measurement, Statistics, and Evaluation, University of Maryland, College Park. He was a member of the department faculty for 31 years, specializing in measurement, applied statistics, and research methods. From September 1997 to August 1999, he served as Director of Student Assessment with the Maryland State Department of Education. A former editor of *Measurement and Evaluation in Counseling and Development,* he serves on the editorial boards of *Applied Measurement in Education* and *Educational and Psychological Measurement* and is coeditor of *Practical Assessment, Research, & Evaluation,* an electronic journal available at PAREonline.net. He serves on the technical advisory councils of five states and has recently consulted with the U.S. Department of Education, several state departments of education, and other agencies. A current professional biography and a list of recent publications and presentations may be found at www.education.umd.edu/EDMS/fac/bill/Bill.html.

Yanyan Sheng is an Assistant Professor of Measurement and Statistics at Southern Illinois University–Carbondale. She received her MA and PhD degrees from the University of Missouri–Columbia. Her primary areas of interest are in psychometrics, with an emphasis on Bayesian methodology for item response theory models, dimensionality analysis of test data, and ability estimation in adaptive testing. She has received the APA 2006 Division 5 (*Measurement, Evaluation & Statistics*) Distinguished Dissertation Award.

Everett V. Smith Jr. is an Associate Professor of Educational Psychology at the University of Illinois at Chicago. His specialization is in psychometrics, specifically Rasch measurement with research interests in test and rating scale design and analysis, testing model robustness, and, in general, applications of Rasch measurement to problems found in licensure and certification testing and the social, behavioral, health, rehabilitation, and medical sciences. These applications include studies of dimensionality, DIF, cross-cultural equivalence, equating, item banking, and standard setting. He has co-directed multiple training sessions on Rasch measurement for national and international conferences and research/testing organizations. He is also the co-editor of *Introduction to Rasch Measurement* (2004) and *Rasch Measurement: Advanced and Specialized Applications* (2007) and is currently working on an additional book, *Applications of Rasch Measurement in Criterion-Reference Testing: Practice Analysis to Score Reporting.* He is the Associate Editor of the *Journal of Applied Measurement* and on the editorial board of *Educational and Psychological Measurement* and the *Journal of Nursing Measurement.* Finally, he is responsible for the development of the PhD specialization and MEd program in Measurement Evaluation Statistics and Assessment (MESA) at UIC and currently serves as the Director of the MESA Laboratory.

Richard M. Smith is a Senior Psychometrician at Data Recognition Corporation. He is the founding editor of the *Journal of Applied Measurement.* He is the author of two books on Rasch measurement, *Applications of Rasch Measurement* and *Item and Person Analysis With the Rasch Model,* and the coeditor of *Introduction to Rasch Measurement* and *Rasch Measurement: Advanced and Specialized Applications.* He has published more than 40 articles on Rasch measurement in refereed journals and presented more than 120 papers at regional, national, and international conferences.

Steven E. Stemler is an Assistant Professor of Psychology at Wesleyan University. He received his doctorate in Educational Research, Measurement, and Evaluation from Boston College, where he worked at the Center for the Study of Testing, Evaluation, and Educational Policy as well as the TIMSS International Study Center. He completed his postdoctoral work at Yale University, where he served as the Assistant Director of the Center for the Psychology of Abilities, Competencies, and Expertise. His areas of research interest include measurement and assessment, especially within the domains of intelligence, creativity, intercultural literacy, and social identity.

Elizabeth A. Stuart received her PhD in Statistics from Harvard University in 2004. She is now an Assistant Professor in the Department of Mental Health and the Department of Biostatistics at Johns Hopkins Bloomberg School of Public Health. She was previously a researcher at Mathematica Policy Research, Inc. Her research interests involve methodological developments for prevention and intervention research, particularly regarding causal inference and missing data. Her primary research interests are in the use of matching methods for causal inference, including the use of multiple control groups, diagnostics of matching methods, and sensitivity analyses. Application areas she has been involved in include evaluating schoolwide interventions, examining the effects of adolescent drug use on adult outcomes, and the use of historical patient data to supplement a clinical trial.

Frans E. S. Tan is currently Assistant Professor of Methodology and Statistics at the University of Maastricht, The Netherlands. He teaches statistical methods and research methodology in bachelor's, master's, and PhD courses. He is the author of several chapters of the standard learning textbook about methodology and statistics used at the University of Maastricht. His present research interest is on GLMM, longitudinal models, and optimal designs. He coordinates the project "Optimal and Robust Designs for GLMM Models" and is copromoter of several PhD students.

Bruce Thompson is Distinguished Professor and College Distinguished Research Fellow of Educational Psychology; Distinguished Professor of Library Sciences, Texas A&M University; and Adjunct Professor of Family and Community Medicine, Baylor College of Medicine (Houston). He is coeditor of the teaching, learning, and human development section of the *American Educational Research Journal* (*AERJ:TLHD*), and past editor of *Educational and Psychological Measurement*, the series, *Advances in Social Science Methodology*, and two other journals. He is the author/editor of nearly 200 articles and several books, including the recently published *Foundations of Behavioral Statistics* and *Exploratory and Confirmatory Factor Analysis*. His contributions have been especially influential in moving the field as regards greater emphasis on effect size reporting and interpretation and promoting improved understanding of score reliability.

Jessica Tsai is a graduating senior at Wesleyan University with an undergraduate degree in psychology. Her other research interests include child development, where she has participated in studies involving children's understanding of mathematical concepts.

Wolfgang Viechtbauer was born in Aachen, Germany, but lived in the United States for 11 years, where he received his PhD in Quantitative Psychology from the University of Illinois, Champaign-Urbana. He then returned to Europe and currently works as Assistant Professor in the Department of Methodology and Statistics (Faculty of Health, Medicine, and Life Sciences) at the University of Maastricht, The Netherlands. His research focuses on mixed effects models and their use in the context of meta-analysis, longitudinal data analysis, and multilevel modeling.

Rand R. Wilcox, Professor of Psychology at the University of Southern California, has published seven books and more than 250 articles, most of which deal with statistical issues. His primary research interests deal with robust inferential methods, which cover such topics as ANOVA, regression, rank-based methods, and multivariate techniques, including outlier detection methods. He is an associate editor of *Computational Statistics & Data Analysis, Communications in Statistics,* and *Psychometrika,* and he serves on the editorial board of four other journals. He is an APS fellow and the recipient of the T. L. Saaty Award.

Victor L. Willson is Professor of Educational Psychology and of Teaching, Learning and Culture at Texas A&M University. He teaches courses in statistics and psychometrics and conducts research on children's cognitive, psychological, and academic development; social sciences statistical problems; and longitudinal modeling. He has authored and coauthored more than 150 articles, chapters, and reviews, as well as 4 books.

Edward W. Wolfe is an Associate Professor of Educational Research and Evaluation in the School of Education at Virginia Polytechnic Institute and State University (Virginia Tech). In that position, he advises doctoral students; teaches classes in the areas of statistics, measurement, and research methods; and provides service to the university through membership on program, department, school, and university committees. His research focuses on applications of Rasch models to instrument development and the analysis of ratings, influences of technology in testing on examinee mental states, and differential item functioning evoked by test translation. He received his PhD in Educational Psychology with an emphasis in the areas of Psychometrics and Cognitive Science from the University of California at Berkeley in 1995. He received his MS in Educational Psychology from Purdue University in 1990, and he received his BA in Music Education from Fairmont State College in 1987.

Po-Ju Wu is a doctoral student in the Inquiry Methodology Program at Indiana University. His research interests are quantitative methods in behavioral sciences, where he focuses on methods for longitudinal data analysis, factor analysis, and structural equation modeling.

Chong Ho Yu is currently the Director of Testing, Evaluation, Assessment, and Research in the Applied Learning Technology Institute at Arizona State University (ASU). He holds a doctorate in Educational Psychology, with a concentration in Measurement, Statistics, and Methodological Studies, and another doctorate in Philosophy, specializing in philosophy of science, from ASU. His research interests are diverse, including philosophy of quantitative methods; alternate quantitative procedures, such as resampling, data visualization, and exploratory data analysis; applications of instructional technology; and psychometrics. He has published articles and book chapters on these preceding topics. His Web site is accessible at http://www.creative-wisdom.com.